T0295878

Modern Economic Regulation

Second Edition

Economic regulation affects us all, shaping how we access essential services such as water, energy and transport services, as well as how we communicate with one another in the digital world. *Modern Economic Regulation* describes the core insights of economic theory on which regulatory policies are based and connects this with evidence of how regulation is applied. It focuses on fundamental questions such as: Why are certain industries regulated? What principles can inform regulation? How is regulation implemented? Which regulatory policies have been more, or less, effective in practice? All chapters in this second edition are fully updated to reflect the latest research and evidence, while five new chapters cover behavioural economics and the regulation of rail, aviation, payment systems and digital platforms. Each chapter contains discussion questions and topical case studies, and online materials include over 60 applied exercises that explore real-life regulatory problems from around the world.

Dr Christopher Decker is a research fellow specialising in regulatory and competition economics at the Centre for Socio-Legal Studies in the University of Oxford. He has extensive experience of the application of economic regulation across a range of industries (energy, water, telecommunications, transport, digital markets, payments and financial services) and has advised international bodies (the World Bank, OECD, European Commission, APEC), as well as government departments, regulators and private companies in many parts of the world.

Modern Economic Regulation

An Introduction to Theory and Practice

Second Edition

CHRISTOPHER DECKER
University of Oxford

CAMBRIDGE
UNIVERSITY PRESS

CAMBRIDGE
UNIVERSITY PRESS

Shaftesbury Road, Cambridge CB2 8EA, United Kingdom

One Liberty Plaza, 20th Floor, New York, NY 10006, USA

477 Williamstown Road, Port Melbourne, VIC 3207, Australia

314–321, 3rd Floor, Plot 3, Splendor Forum, Jasola District Centre, New Delhi – 110025, India

103 Penang Road, #05–06/07, Visioncrest Commercial, Singapore 238467

Cambridge University Press is part of Cambridge University Press & Assessment, a department of the University of Cambridge.

We share the University's mission to contribute to society through the pursuit of education, learning and research at the highest international levels of excellence.

www.cambridge.org
Information on this title: www.cambridge.org/highereducation/isbn/9781316514511

DOI: 10.1017/9781009083621

First edition © Christopher Decker 2015

Second edition © Christopher Decker 2023

First published 2015

Second edition 2023

Printed in the United Kingdom by TJ Books Limited, Padstow, Cornwall 2023

A catalogue record for this publication is available from the British Library.

Library of Congress Cataloging-in-Publication Data
Names: Decker, Christopher, 1972–author.
Title: Modern economic regulation : an introduction to theory and practice / Christopher Decker.
Description: Second edition. | New York, NY : Cambridge university Press, [2023] | Revised edition of the author's Modern economic regulation, 2015. | Includes bibliographical references and index.
Identifiers: LCCN 2023011817 | ISBN 9781316514511 (hardback) | ISBN 9781009087735 (paperback) | ISBN 9781009083621 (ebook)
Subjects: LCSH: Public utilities–Government policy. | Public utilities–Economic aspects.
Classification: LCC HD2763 .D36 2023 | DDC 363.6–dc23/eng/20230313
LC record available at https://lccn.loc.gov/2023011817

ISBN 978-1-316-51451-1 Hardback
ISBN 978-1-009-08773-5 Paperback

Additional resources for this publication at www.cambridge.org/decker2

Brief Contents

List of Figures   xii
List of Tables   xiii
List of Boxes   xiv
Preface to the Second Edition   xv
Acknowledgements   xviii
List of Selected Acronyms and Abbreviations   xix

1   Introduction   1

PART I

2   The Perennial Question: Why Regulate?   11
3   Is Economic Regulation Inevitable?   43

PART II

4   Principles of Regulation for Core Network Activities   71
5   Forms of Price Regulation   109
6   Regulation in the Presence of Competition   151
7   Behavioural Economics and Regulation   197

PART III

8   The Institutions of Regulation   233
9   Electricity Regulation   267
10 Gas Regulation   317
11 Telecommunications Regulation   359

12 Payment Systems Regulation   41█

13 Digital Platforms Regulation   45█

14 Rail Regulation   50█

15 Aviation Regulation   54█

16 Water and Wastewater Regulation   59█

17 Conclusions   63█

Cases and Legislation   63█

References   64█

Index   73█

Contents

List of Figures   xii
List of Tables   xiii
List of Boxes   xiv
Preface to the Second Edition   xv
Acknowledgements   xviii
List of Selected Acronyms and Abbreviations   xix

1   Introduction   1
1.1 Why Does Economic Regulation Matter?   1
1.2 What is Economic Regulation?   3
1.3 What is 'Modern' About Economic Regulation?   3
1.4 Structure of the Book   6

PART I

2   The Perennial Question: Why Regulate?   11
2.1 Normative Rationales for Regulation   12
2.2 Alternative Explanations for Regulation   28
2.3 Rationales Based on Fairness and Affordability   35
2.4 Rationales Based on the Characteristics of the Consumer   39
2.5 Implications of the Different Rationales for Regulation   41
     Discussion Questions   42

3   Is Economic Regulation Inevitable?   43
3.1 Competition for the Market   43
3.2 Contestability and the Threat of Entry   46
3.3 State Ownership and Operation   48
3.4 Reliance on Ex Post Competition Law   54

3.5 'Deregulation' Policies and A Reliance on Competition   5

3.6 Reliance on Negotiation as an Alternative to Regulation   6

3.7 Reliance on Private Contracts   6

3.8 Monitoring   6

3.9 Decentralised Provision of Services   6

3.10 Conclusion   6

    Discussion Questions   6

PART II

4 Principles of Regulation for Core Network Activities   7

4.1 Industry Structures   7

4.2 Pricing Principles Under Full Information   7

4.3 Pricing Principles for the Multi-Product Firm   8

4.4 Regulation in the Context of Imperfect Information   9

4.5 Pricing in A Multi-Period Context   9

4.6 Attributes of Desirable Rate Structures   10

4.7 Principles Relating to Quality and Cost Reduction   10

4.8 Conclusion   10

    Discussion Questions   10

5 Forms of Price Regulation   10

5.1 Rate of Return Regulation   10

5.2 Price Cap Regulation   12

5.3 The Relationship Between Rate of Return and Price Cap   13

5.4 Other Approaches to Price Regulation   14

5.5 Price Regulation When Competition is Emerging   14

5.6 Price Regulation When Networks are in Decline   14

5.7 Conclusion   14

    Discussion Questions   15

6 Regulation in the Presence of Competition   15

6.1 Access in Regulated Industries   15

6.2 One-Way Access Pricing   15

6.3 Two-Way Access Pricing   16

6.4 Access Pricing and Investment   17

6.5 Vertical Integration and Separation   18

6.6 Horizontal Integration and Separation   18

6.7   Regulation of Multi-Sided Markets   191
6.8   Regulation of Multiple Competing Suppliers   194
6.9   Conclusion   194
      Discussion Questions   196

7   Behavioural Economics and Regulation   197
7.1   Core Insights of Behavioural Economics   198
7.2   Behavioural Industrial Organisation and Regulation   204
7.3   Application of Behavioural Economics in Practice   218
7.4   Conclusion   226
      Discussion Questions   228

PART III

8   The Institutions of Regulation   233
8.1   The Rationale for Economic Regulatory Agencies   233
8.2   The Evolution of Independent Regulatory Agencies   245
8.3   Design of Regulatory Agencies and the Scope of their Power   252
8.4   Co-Regulation and Industry Codes   259
8.5   Who Regulates the Regulators?   261
8.6   Conclusion   265
      Discussion Questions   265

9   Electricity Regulation   267
9.1   Physical and Economic Characteristics of Electricity   268
9.2   Approach to Electricity Regulation   284
9.3   The Scope and Effects of Restructuring Policies   295
9.4   Regulatory Policy Issues in the Electricity Industry   305
9.5   Conclusion   314
      Discussion Questions   315

10   Gas Regulation   317
10.1   Physical and Economic Characteristics of Gas   318
10.2   Approach to Gas Regulation   330
10.3   The Scope and Effects of Restructuring Policies   340
10.4   Regulatory Policy Issues in the Gas Industry   350
10.5   Conclusion   357
      Discussion Questions   358

11   **Telecommunications Regulation**   359
11.1 Physical and Economic Characteristics of Telecommunications Networks
       and Services   360
11.2 Approach to Telecommunications Regulation   372
11.3 The Scope and Effects of Restructuring Policies   389
11.4 Regulatory Policy Issues in the Telecommunications Industry   401
11.5 Conclusion   412
       Discussion Questions   413

12   **Payment Systems Regulation**   415
12.1 Physical and Economic Characteristics of Payment Systems   416
12.2 Approach to Payment Systems Regulation   429
12.3 The Scope and Effects of Restructuring Policies   440
12.4 Conclusion   449
       Discussion Questions   451

13   **Digital Platforms Regulation**   453
13.1 Physical and Economic Characteristics of Digital Platforms   454
13.2 Should Digital Platforms Be Regulated?   468
13.3 Approach to Regulation of Digital Platforms   488
13.4 Conclusion   500
       Discussion Questions   501

14   **Rail Regulation**   503
14.1 Physical and Economic Characteristics of Railways   504
14.2 Approach to Railways Regulation   514
14.3 The Scope and Effects of Restructuring Policies   524
14.4 Regulatory Policy Issues in the Railways Industry   535
14.5 Conclusion   543
       Discussion Questions   545

15   **Aviation Regulation**   547
15.1 Physical and Economic Characteristics of Aviation   548
15.2 Approach to Aviation Regulation   558
15.3 The Scope and Effects of Restructuring Policies   570
15.4 Regulatory Policy Issues in the Aviation Industry   582
15.5 Conclusion   588
       Discussion Questions   590

16   Water and Wastewater Regulation   591
16.1 Physical and Economic Characteristics of Water and Wastewater   592
16.2 Approach to Water and Wastewater Regulation   602
16.3 The Scope and Effects of Restructuring Policies   610
16.4 Regulatory Policy Issues in the Water and Wastewater Industry   617
16.5 Conclusion   631
       Discussion Questions   632

17   Conclusions   635
17.1 Rationales for, and Alternatives to, Regulation   635
17.2 Linking Regulatory Theory and Practice   636

Cases and Legislation   **639**
Europe   639
UK   642
USA   642
Australia, Canada, Germany and New Zealand   643

References   645
Index   731

Figures

1.1 Average household expenditure on public utilities as a proportion of final household consumption expenditure in selected OECD countries in 2020
2.1 Average cost curve under economies of scale   1
2.2 The sensitivity of natural monopoly to market demand   1
2.3 Subadditivity without economies of scale over the entire relevant range of output   1
2.4 The allocative inefficiency of monopoly   1
2.5 Total surplus maximised: 'first-best' pricing   1
2.6 Losses that can arise from 'first-best' pricing   1
4.1 Vertically integrated monopoly   7
4.2 Vertical separation with competition in upstream and downstream activities   7
4.3 Vertical integration with competition in some activities   7
4.4 'Second-best' pricing and output   7
4.5 Average outlay and marginal outlay under two-part tariff   8
4.6 A self-selecting two-part tariff   8
4.7 The Loeb–Magat incentive arrangement   9
5.1 Earnings sharing mechanism   14
9.1 Centralised electricity system   27
9.2 Decentralised electricity system   27
10.1 Gas system   32
11.1 Fixed line telecommunications network   36
12.1 Interbank payment system   41
12.2 Four-party card payment system   42
14.1 Railway system   50
15.1 Aviation system   55
16.1 Water supply chain   59
16.2 Wastewater supply chain   596

Tables

4.1	Desirable attributes of sound rate structures	101
6.1	Different methods for determining access terms	152
6.2	Different cost concepts	164
9.1	Breakdown of average household electricity bill, 2020	273
10.1	Breakdown of average household gas bill, 2020	322
13.1	Broad typology of digital platforms	456

Boxes

4.1   Industry structures   7.

5.1   Estimating the cost of capital in regulated industries   11

9.1   Adapting rate structures to deal with changing use of networks   29

9.2   Is there a 'missing money' problem in the electricity industry?   30

10.1 Negotiated settlements in the North American gas industry   33

10.2 The 'other gas': the supply and regulation of Liquified Petroleum Gas (LPG)   34

11.1 Competitive bottlenecks and waterbeds in the telecommunications industry   37

11.2 Price–cost tests and contestable markets theory   38

12.1 Competition between real-time interbank and card payment systems   43

14.1 Two tales of rail privatisation: Britain and Japan   52

15.1 Dual-till and single-till approaches to airport charges   56

16.1 The cost of capital and the capital structure of water companies in England and Wales   619

Preface to the Second Edition

Economic regulation is not static in theory or practice. Policy objectives change, new products, technologies and business models emerge, and regulation adapts to reflect changing consumer and societal preferences. Academic research also throws up fresh perspectives from which to examine old questions or address pressing policy concerns. In the eight years since the publication of the first edition of this book, a range of new issues have come to the fore, notably the impacts on economic regulation of digitalisation, decentralisation and decarbonisation policies. Debates have emerged on whether economic regulation should be applied to new industries, and whether it should be withdrawn, or reduced in scope, from activities where competition has developed. There is also increasing focus on how consumers actually make decisions, and on the consumer 'outcomes' (in terms of price and quality of service) associated with different regulatory approaches and restructuring policies.

Accordingly, this second edition has been comprehensively updated to incorporate the latest research, and to focus on the most contemporary issues in economic regulation. The main structural changes include the following.

- **Five new substantive chapters.** These cover topical issues such as: behavioural economics; the need for and approach to regulation of large digital platforms (such as Google, Amazon, Meta); and payment systems (interchange fee) regulation. The book also includes two new chapters on the regulation of railways and of aviation.
- **Discussion questions at the end of each chapter and supplementary online resources.** These are intended to cement the reader's understanding of the most important themes and insights from each chapter. The questions and online resources are also designed to be thought-provoking and to encourage students to offer their opinions on important regulatory debates, or to identify possible challenges in applying theory in practice.
- **New topic boxes that connect theory and practice in the industry chapters.** The discussion in the boxes in Chapters 9 to 16 have been updated to reflect new and topical issues in each industry.
- **New references.** The book contains hundreds of new references to the latest theoretical research and practical evidence on the effects of regulation in practice.

Major thematic, cross-cutting changes to the book include incorporating discussions or

- **behavioural economics research,** including the main insights from behavioural indu
  trial organisation that impact on the rationales for and approach to economic regula
  tion, and also how such insights are being applied by regulators in practice across
  range of regulated industries;
- **affordability and fairness concerns,** which are increasingly prominent in many juris
  dictions, including a discussion of rationales for regulation based on the characte
  istics of the consumer, and the factors that have led to the re-introduction of pric
  regulation in competitive markets in some jurisdictions;
- **the impacts of technological change and digitalisation on regulation,** including th
  implications of new business models and service providers such as overlay servic
  providers in payment systems, over-the-top providers in communications and com
  petitive unmanned aircraft system (drone) traffic management providers in aviation;
- **the impacts of decarbonisation and 'net-zero' policies on regulation,** which is c
  particular relevance in the electricity, gas, water and transport industries;
- **the implications of the shift from centralised networks to decentralised (distribute**
  networks in sectors such as communications, energy and air transport, and the impl
  cations this has for the regulatory architecture;
- **network effects as a rationale for regulation** and how this is influencing the debate
  about the need to regulate digital platforms, payment systems and transport network
- **approaches to the regulation of multi-sided markets,** including payment system
  digital platforms and peer-to-peer platforms in energy and transport;
- **new forms of price regulation,** including the total expenditure approach, which ha
  recently been introduced in the UK, in Australia and in some parts of Europe;
- **how to manage the declining use of some traditional network services,** such as fixe
  line calls and grid-supplied electricity, and the implications of such decline for legac
  costs recovery, price structures and universal access;
- **different governance, ownership and financing models,** including co-regulation an
  principles-based regulation, the use of not-for-profit or community schemes in energ
  and for broadband, and the competitive/merchant investment model in water an
  energy;
- **the factors motivating reverse privatisation or re-municipalisation** in some sector
  and jurisdictions; and
- **new laws, regulations and policy developments in all industry sectors,** for example
  to reflect new Regulations and Directives in the EU, and new regulatory policies i
  North America and elsewhere in the world.

At the same time, this second edition updates the discussions on the most importan
enduring issues in regulation. This includes new research and evidence on: the effects o
introducing competition in essential public utility industries; the pros and cons of vertica
and horizontal separation; whether private or state ownership is more efficient in reduc
ing costs, improving performance and widening access to essential services; the effec
tiveness of different forms of price regulation, including the impacts on the incentive
to invest and innovate; and the merits of various alternative approaches to economi

regulation, such as those based around direct negotiation and agreement between firms and consumer representatives.

Although there have been important changes to this second edition, the overarching aim is the same as the first edition: to provide an accessible textbook that connects the vast, and continually expanding, theoretical literature on economic regulation with the real-world experience of applying such regulation in practice – to bring economic regulation to life.

The scope of the material covered, and the level of accessibility of the book, are intended to appeal to a wide and multi-disciplinary audience with no prior background in economics or regulation. The text is written in such a way that it should appeal to three main audiences: students who want to develop an understanding of the key concepts and foundational principles of economic regulation and understand how such principles are applied in practice; academics and researchers who want to keep abreast of the latest research, or who may be familiar with one area of regulation but want to understand how regulation is applied in other areas; and practitioners and regulators who want to gain insights about how regulation has been applied in other sectors and jurisdictions, or understand the key principles that influence the development of regulatory policy.

Acknowledgements

A book like this is a collaborative effort built on the work of many people, and this second edition has benefited greatly from the insights provided by readers of the first edition. am particularly grateful to the scholars, practitioners and students from around the world who got in touch to provide positive feedback on the first edition and to discuss new ideas, to suggest new papers or to provide examples of regulatory practice in their own countries.

I am also grateful for the constructive suggestions of five anonymous reviewers whose feedback has been immensely valuable in revising the text and in drawing my attention to areas where the exposition could be improved, and on substantive topics that should be addressed.

A final word of thanks to all those who have contributed to the individual research described in these pages. Some authors have continually (and impressively!) generated valuable research and insights throughout the entire 'modern' period of regulation, while others have provided deep and novel insights in specific areas of regulation. While these scholars have provided the raw materials on which this book is based, a separate thanks must go to those who have helped me to fashion those materials into something that resembles a book. Here my enduring thanks must go to the team at Cambridge University Press and to my wife, Felicity, whose tremendous patience and skill has helped me turn technical prose into something accessible to a wide audience.

List of Selected Acronyms and Abbreviations

2G	second generation (of mobile communications technology)
3G	third generation (of mobile communications technology)
4G	fourth generation (of mobile communications technology)
5G	fifth generation (of mobile communications technology)
AATF	Airport and Airway Trust Fund
ACCC	Australian Competition and Consumer Commission
ACER	Agency for the Cooperation of Energy Regulators
ADSL	Asymmetric Digital Subscriber Line
AEMC	Australian Energy Market Commission
AER	Australian Energy Regulator
AIP	Airport Improvement grant Program
AISP	account information service provider
A–J	Averch–Johnson (effect)
ANS	air navigation services
ANSP	air navigation service provider
APA	Administrative Procedures Act 1946
ARCEP	l'Autorité de Régulation des Communications Électroniques et des Postes (telecommunications and post regulator, France)
ARROW	(costs) that are avoided or reduced or recoverable in some other way
ASEAN	Association of Southeast Asian Nations
ATM	air traffic management
AUC	Alberta Utilities Commission
BEREC	Body of European Regulators for Electronic Communications
BOT	build–operate–transfer
BT	British Telecom
BU-LRIC	bottom-up long-run incremental cost
CAB	Civil Aeronautics Board
CAPM	capital asset pricing model

CARD	Credit Card Accountability Responsibility and Disclosure Act (USA)
CAT	Competition Appeal Tribunal (UK)
CATO	Competitively Appointed Transmission Owner
CBDC	central bank digital currency
CCS	carbon capture and storage
CEER	Council of European Energy Regulators
CEGB	Central Electricity Generating Board (England and Wales)
CEGH	Central European Gas Hub
CER	Canadian Energy Regulator
CFC	chlorofluorocarbon
CFPB	Consumer Financial Protection Bureau (USA)
CIS	Capital expenditure Incentive Scheme (water, UK)
CIS	common information service (provider, in aviation)
CLEC	competitive local exchange carrier
CMA	Competition and Markets Authority (UK)
C-MeX	customer measure of experience
CO_2	carbon dioxide
CPI	consumer price index
CPNP	calling party network pays
CPUC	California Public Utilities Commission
CRTC	Canadian Radio-Television Telecommunications Commission
CS	consumer surplus
DCF	discounted cash flow (model)
DEA	data envelopment analysis
DECC	Department of Energy and Climate Change
Defra	Department for Environment, Food and Rural Affairs
D-Mex	developer services measure of experience
DOCSIS	Data Over Cable Service Interface Specification
DoJ	Department of Justice (USA)
DORC	depreciated optimised replacement cost
DSAC	distributed stand-alone cost
DSL	Digital Subscriber Line
DSO	distribution system operator
DWI	Drinking Water Inspectorate (England and Wales)
EC	European Community; European Commission
ECPR	efficient component pricing rule
EEA	European Environment Agency
EEA	European Economic Association
EIA	Energy Information Administration (USA)

ENTSO	European Network of Transmission System Operators for Electricity
ENTSOG	European Network of Transmission System Operators for Gas
EPA	Environmental Protection Authority (USA)
EPEX	European Power Exchange
EPMU	equi-proportionate mark-up
ERCOT	Electric Reliability Council of Texas
ERG	European Regulators Group (for telecommunications)
ERT	economic replicability test
ESP	electricity service provider
ETS	emissions trading scheme
EU	European Union
EV	electric vehicle
EXAA	European Energy Exchange
FAA	Federal Aviation Administration
FAC	fully allocated cost
FCC	Federal Communications Commission (USA)
FCM	financial capital maintenance
FDC	fully distributed costs
FERC	Federal Energy Regulatory Commission (USA)
FIMS	flight information management system
FIR	Flight Information Regions
FIT	feed-in tariff
FORR	final offer rate review
FTC	Federal Trade Commission (USA)
FTM	fixed-to-mobile (access)
FTR	financial transmission right
FTTB	fibre to the basement/building
FTTC	fibre to the cabinet/curb (kerb)
FTTH	fibre to the home
FTTN	fibre to the node
FTTx	fibre to the x (premises)
GAO	Government Accountability Office (USA)
GDP	gross domestic product
GECPR	generalised efficient component pricing rule
GME	Gestore dei Mercati Energetici (Italian Power Exchange)
GOSM	gearing outperformance sharing mechanism
GSM	Global System for Mobile Communications
HDSL	High-bit-rate Digital Subscriber Line
HFC	hybrid fibre coaxial

IATA	International Air Transport Association
ICAO	International Civil Aviation Organization
ICC	Interstate Commerce Commission (USA)
ICT	information and communications technology
IEA	International Energy Agency
IFR	interchange fee regulation
ILEC	Incumbent Local Exchange Carrier
IMF	International Monetary Fund
IP	Internet Protocol
IPEX	Italian Power Exchange
IPP	independent power producer
IPTV	Internet Protocol television
ISO	independent system operator
ISP	Internet Service Provider
ITU	International Telecommunications Union
JKM	Japan Korean Marker
JNR	Japanese National Railways
LCC	low-cost carrier
LMP	locational marginal pricing
LNG	liquefied natural gas
LPG	liquefied petroleum gas
LRIC	long-run incremental costs
LRIC+	long-run incremental costs plus mark-up
LRMC	long-run marginal cost
LSE	load-serving entity
LTE	Long Term Evolution (of mobile communications)
MaaS	mobility as a service
M-ECPR	market-adjusted ECPR
MFJ	Modified Final Judgment (in relation to the AT&T case)
MIBEL	Mercado Ibérico de la Electricidad (Iberian Electricity Market)
MSC	merchant service charge
MTM	mobile-to-mobile (access)
MVNO	mobile virtual network operators
Nacha	National Automated Clearinghouse Association
NAESB	North American Energy Standards Board
NAO	National Audit Office (UK)
NARUC	National Association of Regulatory Utility Commissioners
NBN	National Broadband Network (Australia)
NBP	national balancing point (Britain)

NEB	National Energy Board (Canada)
NEM	National Electricity Market (Australia)
NETA	New Electricity Trading Arrangements (England and Wales)
NGDC	natural gas distribution companies
NGAN	next-generation access network
NGN	next-generation network
NordPool	Nordic electricity trading market
NPA	new payments architecture
NPP	New Payments Platform
NPV	net present value
NRA	National Regulatory Authority/Agency
NRA	National Rivers Authority (now Environment Agency, UK)
NSA	national supervisory authority
NTS	National Transmission System
NYMEX	New York Mercantile Exchange
OCM	operational capital maintenance
OECD	Organisation for Economic Cooperation and Development
OEB	Ontario Energy Board (Canada)
Ofcom	Office of Communications (UK)
Offer	Office of Electricity Regulation (now Ofgem, Britain)
Ofgas	Office of Gas Supply (now Ofgem, Britain)
Ofgem	Office of Gas and Electricity Markets (Britain)
OFT	Office of Fair Trading (UK)
Oftel	Office of Telecommunications (now Ofcom, UK)
Ofwat	Office of Water Services (England and Wales)
ORC	optimised replacement cost
ORR	Office of the Rail Regulator (Britain)
OTC	over-the-counter
OTT	over-the-top
PCR	price cap regulation
PIP	payment interface provider
PISP	payment initiation service provider
PJM	Pennsylvania–New Jersey–Maryland (electricity market, USA)
POLPX	Polish Power Exchange
PPA	power purchase agreement
PPP	public–private partnerships
PSB	Payment Systems Board (Australia)
PSD	Payment Services Directive
PSP	payment service provider

PSR	payment systems regulator
PSTN	Public Switched Telephone Network
PSV	Punto di Scambio Virtuale (Virtual Trading Point, Italy)
PUC	Public Utility Commission
PV	photovoltaic (solar panel)
QoS	quality of service
RAB	regulatory (or regulated) asset base
RAV	regulatory (or regulated) asset value
RBOC	Regional Bell Operating Companies
RCV	regulatory (or regulated) capital value
RGGI	Regional Greenhouse Gas Initiative (USA)
RIIO	revenues = incentives + innovation + outputs
ROR	rate of return
ROSCO	Rolling Stock Leasing Company
RPI-X	retail price index minus X (RPI − X)
RPNP	receiving party network pays
RPP	receiving party pays
RTP	real-time payments
SAC	stand-alone cost
SFA	stochastic frontier analysis
SIM	Subscriber Identity Module
SLA	service level agreement
SMP	significant market power
SMS	strategic market status
SO_2	sulfur dioxide
SRMC	short-run marginal cost
STB	Surface Transportation Board (USA)
SWIFT	Society for Worldwide Interbank Financial Telecommunication
TCP	Transmission Control Protocol
TD-LRIC	top-down long-run incremental cost
TELRIC	total element long-run incremental cost
TGE	Towarowa Giełda Energii (Polish Power Exchange)
TFP	total factor productivity
TKG	Telecommunications Act (Germany)
TNUoS	transmission network use of system
Totex	total expenditure approach
TPP	third-party providers
TSLRIC	total service long-run incremental cost
TTF	title transfer facility

UAS	unmanned aircraft system (drone)
UNECE	United Nations Economic Commission for Europe
USO	universal service obligation
UTM	unmanned aircraft system traffic management
UTMSP	UTM service providers
VDSL	Very-high-bit-rate Digital Subscriber Line
VoIP	Voice-over-Internet Protocol
VPP	virtual power plants
WACC	weighted average cost of capital
WHO	World Health Organization
WiMax	Worldwide Interoperability for Microwave Access
WTO	World Trade Organization
xDSL	x type Digital Subscriber Line (such as VDSL or ADSL)

1

Introduction

This second edition of *Modern Economic Regulation* has two aims. For those new to economic regulation, it aims to provide an accessible entry point to what is a highly technical and specialised area. It focuses on fundamental questions such as the following: Why do we regulate certain industries? What principles should guide economic regulation? Who should regulate? What have been the effects of regulation in practice?

For readers already familiar with regulatory theory or practice, the book aims to help navigate what is a large and ever-expanding body of theoretical research, and to draw on evidence, where available, of the impacts of regulation across a range of industries and countries. In essence, it aims to distil insights on which policies and strategies have 'worked', and which have not. As we will see in the chapters that follow, economic regulation is not a static area, either in theory or in practice. Indeed, despite expectations by some in the 1980s and 1990s that economic regulation would gradually be withdrawn over time in some industries, the size of economic regulators in many jurisdictions has expanded rather than contracted over the past four decades. Moreover, regulatory agencies have now been established in a great many parts of the world: economic regulation is now a global phenomenon.

1.1 WHY DOES ECONOMIC REGULATION MATTER?

All of the services discussed in this book are indispensable to modern life: we could not live as we do without them. One only needs to imagine a widespread failure in one or more of these industries – a prolonged electric power blackout, gas disruption, telephone or internet connection failure, water or sewerage contamination, payment systems failure or shutdown of a rail or aviation network – to appreciate their significance to individuals, societies and economies. Moreover, such services are ubiquitous – each day we consume at least some, if not all, of the services discussed in this book, not only directly as retail customers, but also indirectly through other products and services we consume that have been manufactured using, or enabled by, these services.

For many households around the globe, the proportion of average annual income which is spent on the consumption of services supplied by the industries described in this book – electricity, gas, water, wastewater, transport, payments, digital services and

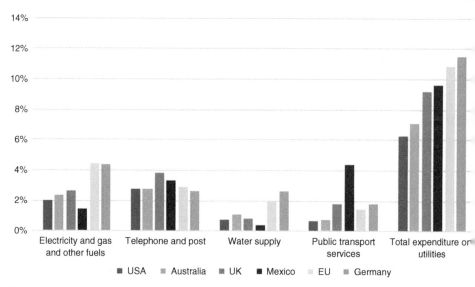

Figure 1.1 Average household expenditure on public utilities as a proportion of final household consumption expenditure in selected OECD countries in 2020. Based on author's own analysis of OECD data

telecommunications services – is significant. As shown in Figure 1.1, the average household in selected OECD (Organisation for Economic Cooperation and Development) countries spent between 6.3 per cent and 11.5 per cent of total household expenditure on utilities in 2020. These proportions are often significantly greater for those on the lowest incomes, while in developing countries a core challenge is to achieve widespread access to these essential services. Beyond the household, the secure, reliable and efficient provision of public utility services – the Internet, electric power, transport systems and clean water – is an extremely important contributor to the economic and social development and growth of countries. In most developed countries the value added of the public utility industries to gross domestic product (GDP) is estimated to be between 4 per cent and 6 per cent.[1]

While all these services are critical to modern life, they are typically provided by firms that occupy strong, and often monopoly, market positions. In some cases this is the natural result of the demand, cost and technological characteristics of the industry (such as economies of scale or scope, or network effects), while in others it reflects public policy decisions. If left unregulated, firms in such positions may exploit their power by charging excessive prices, reducing quality, or failing to invest and innovate. This can be inefficient from a social welfare perspective and harmful to current and future consumers of the services. This potential, coupled with the essential nature of the services they provide, has created longstanding questions for governments, policy makers and academics about how to most effectively guide and control the behaviour of public utility firms: How can we effectively regulate them?

[1] See Guthrie (2006), based on 2001 data from the STAN (structural analysis) database of the OECD.

1.2 WHAT IS ECONOMIC REGULATION?

The term 'regulation' is often used to refer to a range of measures and forms of intervention – introduced by the state or other actors (e.g. industry bodies) – which are intended, in one way or another, to guide or control the behaviour of a firm or individuals.

In this book, the term 'economic regulation' is used to refer to two broad types of interventions and policies. The first type of interventions focus on the *structure* of an industry: for example, by restricting the number of firms that can be involved in the supply of a service, requiring firms to vertically or horizontally separate different activities in a supply chain, or mandating that access to infrastructure facilities be provided to third parties. A second set of interventions attempt to guide or control the *behaviour* of firms in terms of their decisions in respect of pricing, investment, quality and coverage of service, as well as the terms on which access is provided to other firms, including competitors.

Of course, as we will see, many other public policies are directed at controlling or guiding the behaviour of firms, including health and safety policies, environmental policies and social policies. While these policies are sometimes considered to be examples of social regulation rather than economic regulation, such a sharp distinction is not easily made in relation to the industries discussed in this book. For example, it is not possible to talk about the economic regulation of the electricity, transport and water industries without considering environmental policies (where financial subsidies and incentives are frequently used to encourage more environmentally friendly production and consumption decisions), nor is it possible to consider gas or water regulation without considering health and safety considerations (as higher safety standards can impact on the costs associated with operating and maintaining these networks). Affordability and social inclusion policies, such as providing widespread access to certain services at 'fair prices', are also an important part of regulating the industries discussed in this book.

Economic regulation is therefore conceived broadly to capture both 'traditional' interventions – to control prices, entry, quality and other aspects of economic behaviour of firms operating in certain industries – as well as interventions that are intended to guide or compel firms in these industries, through financial incentives or disincentives, towards behaviour consistent with wider social or environmental policy objectives (such as incentives to encourage consumers to conserve water or energy, or to utilise particular forms of transport, or measures that penalise companies for not treating their customers fairly).

1.3 WHAT IS 'MODERN' ABOUT ECONOMIC REGULATION?

Economic regulation is not a new phenomenon. The first regulatory commissions were established in the USA in the late 1880s, and the subsequent expansion of electricity, gas, water, transport and telecommunications services in many other countries led to the introduction of a range of governance arrangements (including state ownership) to establish controls on the prices and quality of these services. Indeed, many of the issues addressed in this book have challenged regulators and policy makers for over a century. There is an equally long history of academic scholarship on the economic regulation of

the public utilities,[2] and many classic and newer texts cover some of the central issues i
regulatory economics.[3]

Against this background, it would seem that there is very little 'new' to be said, and ver
little 'modern' about economic regulation. In part, this is true, and many of the *principl*
of economic regulation discussed in this book remain as relevant today as when they wer
first established. However, the *context* in which economic regulation is applied is constant
changing, and this gives rise to new policy issues and areas of academic inquiry. Four cor
textual changes are particularly relevant to the chapters that follow: digitalisation; environ
mental and sustainability policies; increasing concerns about the affordability of essenti
services; and the influence of behavioural economics on regulatory theory and practice.

The first contextual change involves the significant advances in information and com
munications technology (ICT), sometimes referred to as 'digitalisation'. Digitalisation ha
transformed the supply of telecommunications services, where there is now not only
range of new services and applications offered, but a range of different networks sup
plying these services, such as cable networks, fibre networks and mobile network
Digitalisation has also led to the emergence of whole new industries, such as digit
platforms, and dramatically changed other industries, such as the payments sector. As w
will see, this has raised fundamental questions about whether, and how, these industrie
should be regulated. More generally, all of the industries discussed in this book have bee
affected by digitalisation to some degree. For example: in the energy sector, consumer
can now source or share energy through peer-to-peer platforms or better manage con
sumption in real time; in aviation, the development and use of remotely operated an
controlled unmanned aircraft systems are expected to have significant impacts on a
traffic management; while the movement towards so-called 'smart' networks allow fo
more effective management and control of transport and water systems.

The changed context for regulation also reflects increased community and politica
concern for the environmental impacts of the supply of some services, notably energy
transport and water services. In the electricity sector, this has led to a global policy focu
on decarbonisation, which involves a shift away from heavily polluting forms of elec
tricity generation towards cleaner generation produced from renewable or low-carbo
sources. In the gas industry, policies are focused on a shift towards renewable gases suc
as biomethane (which combines methane, carbon monoxide, hydrogen and other gases
and low-carbon hydrogen. Policies in the water sector have become focused on ensurin
sustainable water extractions, allowing for water trading, and ensuring high levels o
wastewater treatment. Given these developments, some argue that, over the past decade

---

[2] More than one hundred years ago, in May 1914, a special edition of the *Annals of the American Academ*
of Political and Social Science titled 'State Regulation of the Public Utilities' considered many of the
issues that are discussed in the chapters that follow such as: rate setting procedures; regulating quality
of public service utility service; the independence of public utility commissions; and judicial review of
regulatory decisions. See AAPSS (1914).

[3] Bonbright (1961) and Kahn (1971) are classic texts that cover many of the central issues in regulatory
economics. Baumol, Panzar and Willig (1982) and Laffont and Tirole (1993) introduced new analytical
dimensions to different aspects of economic regulation. Vickers and Yarrow (1988), Armstrong, Cowan
and Vickers (1994) and Newbery (1999) examined the early impacts of restructuring and privatisation
in Britain. Florio (2013) provides a spirited critique of restructuring policies, while Auriol, Crampes and
Estache (2021) and Vogelsang (2021) provide recent analyses of regulation in the network industries.

the focus of economic regulators in some industries has shifted away from promoting competitive markets towards managing the transition to more sustainable forms of production and consumption of some essential services.

A third contextual change is increasing social and political concern about the affordability of some essential services. While issues of fairness and affordability have always been relevant to economic regulation, these issues are now at the forefront of debates about the need for, and approach to, economic regulation in many countries. This likely reflects three factors. First, that, as a result of restructuring in some industries since the 1980s, notably electricity and gas, the retail prices paid by consumers now more closely track changes in underlying wholesale prices. While this can be economically efficient, it can give rise to political and social concerns about affordability where sudden and significant increases in wholesale prices lead to major increases in retail prices (as occurred for energy prices in many countries in 2021–2022). Second, price rises are being driven by a need for substantial investments in network infrastructure, whether as a result of decarbonisation policies (such as in the energy sector), or to ensure system resilience in the face of climate change (as in the water sector), or to ensure widespread access to high-speed broadband and digital services. Third, in some countries the focus on affordability reflects a view that the restructuring of the public utility industries has either failed to realise the promised efficiency and performance benefits, or that any efficiency savings that have been realised have not been shared fairly with consumers in the form of lower prices or investments in networks. In essence, it is argued that the major beneficiaries of these policies have not been consumers, but rather the owners and operators of private utility firms. In some jurisdictions, concerns about affordability have encouraged movement towards increased community or citizen involvement in the ownership and operation of certain essential services, while in other jurisdictions 'reverse-privatisation' policies have been introduced, with the purported aim of making essential services more affordable and accessible to citizens.

A final contextual change impacting economic regulation is the increasing influence of behavioural economics research. As we will see in Chapter 7, a growing body of analytical work, as well as practical experience, has called into question some of the foundational assumptions of industrial organisation (theory) and economic regulation. This includes assumptions that all consumers are rational, well informed and 'active', and will take advantage of the choice available to them in competitive markets, and that suppliers in competitive markets will not collectively exploit consumer biases. These insights have significant implications for economic regulatory theory and practice, and regulators in a range of industries are increasingly using behavioural economics research to introduce policies that have the aim of making consumers more informed and active, and limiting the scope for behavioural biases to be exploited.

Modern economic regulation therefore raises a mix of new questions, arising from changes in context, technology and public policies, and older, more enduring questions. These include questions such as: How can a regulator incentivise regulated firms to behave efficiently? How can a regulator overcome problems of asymmetric information between itself and the firms it regulates? Is private or state ownership more efficient in reducing costs, improving performance and widening access to essential services? What are the arguments for or against vertical integration or separation in different industries? What principles can be used to guide the access terms for the 'sharing' of infrastructure? What are the merits of different forms of price regulation, such as rate of return and price cap regulation? What considerations beyond efficiency does a regulator need to consider when setting or approving a rate structure? How can regulation impact on a firm's incentives to invest and innovate? Is it always possible to introduce sustainable and effective competition for all essential service industries? When is it more appropriate to introduce *ex ante* forms of economic regulation (i.e. up-front price controls) or rely on *ex post* competition or antitrust law? What are the pros and cons of alternative approaches to traditional economic regulation, such as those based around direct negotiation and agreement between firms and consumer representatives. Finally, there remain intensely practical questions about how the principles, or *theory*, of economic regulation can best be implemented in *practice* in different institutional settings, and specifically whether it is possible, or even desirable, to transplant the principles and approach to regulation used in developed and industrialised countries to the developing world context.[4]

1.4 STRUCTURE OF THE BOOK

This book comprises three parts. Part I considers the rationale for economic regulation and the alternatives to standard economic regulation that have been proposed and tried in practice. Within Part I, Chapter 2 focuses on why certain industries are subject to economic regulation, and considers both normative explanations (Why *should* we regulate?) as well as alternative, more positivist explanations for the existence of regulation (Why *do* we regulate?). Chapter 3 considers various alternatives to the standard approaches to economic regulation that have been proposed and tried, including control approaches based around franchising or 'competition *for* the market', state ownership, negotiated agreements, as well as reliance on *ex post* competition law or, in relation to activities in which 'deregulatory' policies can feasibly be introduced, on the restraints imposed by competition itself.

Part II of the book considers some of the principles that underlie modern economic regulation, and the five chapters which comprise Part II draw principally upon theoretical work on economic regulation. Chapter 4 begins by outlining some of the commonly accepted general principles developed in theoretical work relevant to the regulation of the core network activities of public utility industries. Chapter 5 builds on this discussion to examine the different forms of price regulation that are typically applied in practice including rate of return regulation, price cap regulation and various adaptations to these approaches, such as earnings and revenue sharing mechanisms and approaches based on yardstick competition or benchmarking. It also considers approaches to price regulation that could be applied in settings where there is some competition, but an incumbent firm still occupies a strong position in the market. Chapter 6 examines the principles for regulating in competitive settings, such as where an entrant in a competitive activity in the production chain (such as retail services) requires access to the services of a core network

---

[4] See the excellent discussion of this issue in Laffont (2005).

operator (such as infrastructure), or where two competing networks need access to each other's services in order to provide an end-to-end service (such as two mobile telecommunications networks). Chapter 7 sets out some of the core insights from behavioural economics that challenge the standard assumptions about consumer decision making and firm behaviour, before considering the possible implications of these results for economic regulation. Chapter 8 considers the institutions involved in the implementation of economic regulation, with a particular focus on the independent economic regulators established in many jurisdictions over the past four decades.

Part III of the book focuses on the *practice* of economic regulation across eight industries – electricity, gas, telecommunications, payment systems, digital platforms, rail, aviation, and water and wastewater. Each industry chapter begins with a description of the economic and technical characteristics of the production and supply structure. Each chapter then discusses the general approach adopted to the regulation of the industry across different jurisdictions, such as what activities in the supply chain are subject to economic regulation, and what approaches to price and quality regulation have been applied in practice. Finally, the focus turns to the available evidence on the effects of regulation and restructuring policies in that industry, and to a discussion of some contemporary issues that are impacting on the regulation of the industry. In each chapter, boxes are used to present examples of specific applications, and adaptations, of some of the principles discussed in Part II in the industry discussed.

Chapter 17 draws out some general conclusions and themes from the book, including a discussion on the relationship between regulatory theory and practice. For all chapters, a list of discussion questions at the end of each chapter draws out the main themes.

Issues of Terminology

Before getting started, some brief remarks about the terminology used in this book are necessary. First, while the focus of the book is on the regulation of a range of industries that provide essential or critical services to modern life (energy, transport, communications, water, payments services and digital platform services), when referring to some regulated industries – namely the electricity, gas, water and wastewater, transport and telecommunications industries – the term 'public utility industries' is sometimes used. Second, while earlier texts used the term 'natural monopoly' to refer to all of the activities in the supply chain of particular public utility services (i.e. gas, electricity, water), this is no longer always appropriate; many jurisdictions have separated, or 'unbundled', activities in the supply chain that have the attributes of a natural monopoly from activities that are potentially competitive. Accordingly, the term 'core network' is used to refer to those activities that have attributes similar to that of a natural monopoly – generally the transportation element of the supply chain (e.g. assets such as pipes, cables, wires, rails and poles). A third terminological issue may arise from references to 'restructuring policies', a phrase used within this book to refer to various policies introduced, generally in the 1980s and 1990s, to change the structure of an industry. Although there is considerable variation across jurisdictions and industries, these policies typically: removed restrictions on entry, and introduced competition, at one or more stages of the supply chain; required that an incumbent operator provide access to core network activities on non-discriminatory terms; and/or required the vertical and horizontal separation of incumbent public utility operators. These policies are sometimes referred to as 'liberalisation' policies or 'deregulation' policies in other texts.[5] Finally, the term 'jurisdiction' is used, rather than 'country', to refer to specifically autonomous geographical areas such as the states or provinces within a federal country. This is important because, as we shall see, different jurisdictions (i.e. states/provinces) within a country such as the USA, Australia or Canada, or different Member States of the European Union, have often adopted different approaches to economic regulation.

---

[5] The term 'liberalisation' is avoided because it can have ideological overtones. The term 'deregulation' is avoided because it is not accurate that regulation has been fully withdrawn and replaced with competition. Rather, policies have generally introduced different forms of regulation and oversight of these industries.

PART I

2

The Perennial Question: Why Regulate?

If I were asked to offer one single piece of advice to would-be regulators, on the basis of my own experience, it is that, as they perform their *every single* regulatory action, they ask themselves: 'Why am I doing this? Is it really necessary.'[1]

Why do we regulate certain industries? There are different responses to this question, each of which, as we shall see, demonstrates both merit and limitations. An important distinction is made in this chapter between normative accounts for regulation (Why *should* we regulate?) and alternative accounts that attempt to explain the existence of regulation (Why *do* we regulate?). Normative accounts typically focus on the public benefit aims of regulation and are based on implicit assumptions about regulators, including that they: operate with good information; can perfectly enforce their decisions; and are generally benevolent and public-spirited in their actions. Alternative accounts of regulation typically eschew any grander purpose for regulation and draw on economic reasoning, as well as the influence of political, distributional and legal considerations, to explain why regulation exists in the form that it does in certain industries.[2]

Appreciating the different perspectives on why we regulate is important for at least two reasons. Firstly, different rationales for regulation imply different regulatory policies and institutions and will guide both the nature of the intervention in economic activities and the form that intervention should take.[3] Secondly, any assessment of the effects of regulation can only proceed by looking at the rationale for why it was introduced. For example, if regulation is introduced on the basis of a policy desire to ensure that regulated firms set efficient prices that reflect underlying costs, any assessment of the regulation effects should measure results against this objective. On the other hand, if regulation is understood as arising from the interaction of different interest groups, then we should not necessarily expect to observe prices that are lower, or that better reflect costs, as a consequence of regulation.

This chapter has five sections. Section 2.1 sets out the traditional normative arguments for regulation, which, in general terms, are based on the close correspondence between the characteristics of some public utility industries and the economic notion of 'natural monopoly'. While this remains a dominant rationale for the regulation of the public utility

---

[1] Alfred Kahn (1981), comment on Joskow and Noll (1981).

[2] As Braeutigam (1989) puts it: 'In any particular case, there may be a host of possible political and economic answers to the question: Why regulate?'

[3] For the importance of distinguishing rationales for regulation more generally, see Breyer (1982).

industries, the chapter also considers several other normative rationales for regulation including the need to control monopoly power or to deal with the presence of externalities (including network externalities). Section 2.2 then discusses alternative accounts for the existence of regulation, including explanations that focus on the influence of different interest groups in regulation (known as the 'economic theories of regulation'). Section 2.3 explores rationales for regulation of some services based on distributional concerns including issues related to fairness, affordability and social inclusion, while Section 2.4 focuses on rationales for regulation based on the characteristics of the consumers who purchase and consume certain products or services. Section 2.5 considers some of the implications of the different rationales for regulation, including how the existence of multiple rationales for why we regulate can potentially explain some of the trade-offs and tensions that exist in regulatory practice.

2.1 NORMATIVE RATIONALES FOR REGULATION

2.1.1 Efficiency Rationales for Regulation

The conventional economic response to the question of 'Why regulate?' often invokes the economic notion of a 'natural monopoly', highlights the potential inefficiencies of such natural monopolies, and then draws a correspondence between an industry and natural monopoly.

What, then, is a 'natural monopoly' industry structure in economics? Put simply, an industry is considered a natural monopoly if it is most cost efficient if a single firm, rather than two or more firms, produces a specific set of outputs.[4] In most cases, this situation arises where production in an industry comprises a large proportion of fixed costs (that is, costs which are incurred regardless of how many outputs are produced). Early concepts of natural monopoly focused on the single-product case where average costs decreased as output increased for all levels of production. In these circumstances, for all levels of market demand, a single firm supplying the market would always have lower average industry costs than two or more rivals supplying different segments of the market.[5] Figure 2.1 shows

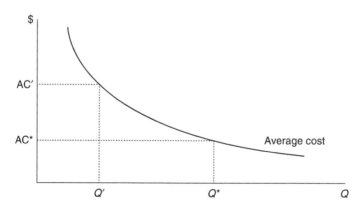

Figure 2.1 Average cost curve under economies of scale

---

[4] Lowry (1973), Sharkey (1982) and Mosca (2008) describe the evolution of the natural monopoly concept.
[5] Assuming that all suppliers have access to a common level of technology and face constant factor input prices.

long-run average costs (AC) declining for all levels of output (Q). In this figure, industry average costs AC* at output level Q* are lower than they are at output level Q', and, indeed, at all output levels before Q* (while long-run average costs continue to fall at all output levels greater than Q*). This conception of natural monopoly focuses on the economies of *scale* in production,[6] including economies of density.[7]

Later research expanded the notion of natural monopoly to account for the fact that firms often supply multiple products rather than a single product. This can give rise to economies of *scope* in production, which, in some circumstances, can also result in it being more cost efficient for a single firm to supply multiple products. For example, it may be more efficient for a single telecommunications company to provide both voice phone calls and broadband services using the same network infrastructure (e.g. wires/cables from a house to an exchange) rather than having two separate providers of wires/cables, one for voice services and one for broadband services. Similarly, in some jurisdictions there is assumed to be substantial economies of scope in railways such that an integrated railroad operator that manages the infrastructure and also provides train services will do so at lower cost than separate providers of rail infrastructure and train services.

Implicit in this notion of natural monopoly, and economies of scale and scope, is an assumption about the nature of technological change in an industry. For example, the economic analysis of natural monopoly implicitly assumes that a constant, or common, type of technology is used in the production process by all firms. In this sense, the definition of natural monopoly corresponds to a given type of production technology – typically equipment that is indivisible (unfeasible to install equipment of a different size), immobile (fixed in a specific location) and durable (expected to operate over a relatively long time scale) – the cost profile being consonant with this. The risks of this assumption are, of course, obvious in industries where technology is changing and, with it, the cost profile of production (for example, see the discussion of telecommunications networks in Chapter 11).

Two further points should be noted about the notion of natural monopoly in economics. Firstly, depending on the shape of the average cost curve, it is possible for economies of scale, or economies of scope, to exist at certain levels of output but not at other levels of output. This means that whether an industry is a natural monopoly is conditioned by the size of the market it serves. For example, in densely populated cities, the size of market demand may mean that industry costs are minimised with more than one firm.

---

[6] The terms 'scale economies' and 'increasing returns to scale' are often used synonymously when discussing natural monopoly. However, although related, the two terms are distinct. Increasing returns to scale refers to a situation where all inputs are increased by a constant amount, and this leads to a greater than proportional increase in output (i.e. if inputs increase by 2 units and output more than doubles). The concept of scale economies is broader and refers to when an expansion of output of a firm or industry results in a reduction in long-run average costs of production.

[7] Economies of density involve reductions in average costs associated with greater usage of a network. Examples include reductions in costs associated with more traffic on an airline or rail network. The implication of economies of density is that it may be efficient for networks not to overlap, and for a single firm to service a particular geographic area (e.g. a single rail operator on a particular route). However, as discussed in later chapters, an implication of this is that smaller high-density networks could result in lower average costs than larger networks with lower density, implying that the efficiencies from having a single operator come from economies of density rather than from economies of scale.

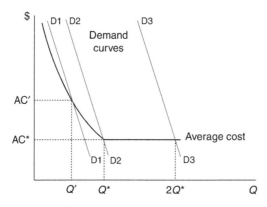

Figure 2.2 The sensitivity of natural monopoly to market demand

This relationship between market demand and natural monopoly is shown in Figure 2.2. In this figure, at output levels less than Q^* – such as Q' – average costs are falling rapidly and industry costs are minimised if there is only a single supplier. The minimum average cost is reached at the output level of Q^*, and the industry remains a natural monopoly in both the region of declining average costs (before Q^*) and where the average cost curve is flat up until $2Q^*$.[8] However, once the level of output reaches $2Q^*$, the industry is no longer a natural monopoly, as two firms can each produce an output level of Q^* at the same average cost as one firm can. It is also possible for economies of scope to exist at some levels of market demand, and not at others. So, for example, total costs might be minimised if only a single producer supplies two products at low levels of demand, but this condition may not hold at higher levels of market demand.

Secondly, whether an industry is defined as a natural monopoly in economics depends on the overall production costs in that industry, having regard to economies of scale and/or economies of scope. Put differently, a natural monopoly need not exhibit scale economies (decreasing average costs) across all its levels of production, nor for all of the products it produces.[9] The critical test is that, accounting for all cost considerations, a single firm is still the most cost-effective method of production. This reasoning is based on the concept of the 'subadditivity' of the cost function. In simple terms, subadditivity is said to exist where, for a given level of one or more outputs, total costs are minimised if only one firm produces these outputs rather than more than one firm, irrespective of how that output is divided among the multiple firms.[10] If we assume that q^1, q^2, ..., q^m are different output vectors which sum to Q such that total output is given by $Q = \Sigma(q^1 + q^2 + \cdots + q^m)$ then, assuming that all firms have an identical cost function, it would be more efficient to have a single supplier produce Q if the following condition is satisfied:

$$C(Q) < C(q^1) + C(q^2) + \cdots + C(q^m). \tag{2.1}$$

---

[8]   At all points between Q^* and $2Q^*$, given the shape of the average cost curve, a single firm still yields the least-cost production. That is, the cost function is subadditive at those levels of output.

[9]   For this reason, it is often stated that economies of scale are a sufficient, but not necessary, condition for a single-product natural monopoly to exist.

[10] Baumol (1977) defines strict subadditivity as where 'the cost of the sum of any m output vectors is less than the sum of the costs of producing them separately'.

In equation (2.1), $C(Q)$ is the total cost associated with jointly producing all of the outputs in combination, while $C(q^1)$ is the cost of producing only output q^1. If this condition is satisfied, then the cost function is subadditive, which implies that it is more cost efficient for a single firm to produce the total output Q than to have the outputs $(q^1, q^2, ..., q^m)$ produced individually by different firms.

To understand subadditivity, consider first the case of a single-product industry where the cost function is such that some portion of average costs decrease as output increases up to a point, after which average costs increase as output increases. That is, the industry cost curve is U-shaped. In these circumstances, given the profile of average costs, the desired level of industry output could potentially be produced by one firm, or by more than one firm whose individual outputs combine to equal the industry output. If a single firm could supply the entire output at a lower average cost than two or more firms, even though some portion of the firm's costs are increasing in production, then this is determined to be the most cost-effective production structure. In Figure 2.3, AC^* is the average cost incurred at the point where demand intersects with the average cost curve at the output level of Q^*. At this point the average cost of production is higher than the minimum average cost of AC', which is attained at the output level Q'. However, although economies of scale only exist up to point Q', and diseconomies exist thereafter, because the cost function is assumed to be subadditive, it is still most efficient for a single firm to produce the output level of Q^*.[11] Figure 2.3 therefore demonstrates the central point that a subadditive cost function does *not* require economies of scale to be present over the entire relevant range of output (in this case, the output up to Q^*).

The same reasoning applies when a production process involves multiple products or services. In these circumstances, it is necessary to consider the cost conditions associated with all of the different outputs provided by the firm (i.e. voice calls, broadband data services, etc.) when considering whether the industry displays the characteristics of a natural

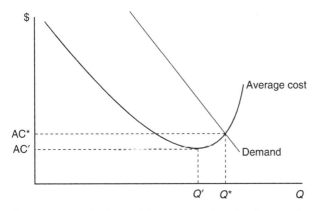

Figure 2.3 Subadditivity without economies of scale over the entire relevant range of output

---

[11] If a second firm entered to produce only $Q^* - Q'$, then, on the basis of the assumption that costs are identical across the industry, this firm would incur a very high level of average costs on that small level of output, which would raise the overall industry costs above that which would exist if a single firm supplied all of the output to Q^*.

monopoly. Again, if the cumulative average costs of one firm producing all products lower than the cumulative costs associated with two or more firms supplying differen combinations of the products, then this satisfies the condition for a natural monopol It follows from these points that the standard definition of a natural monopoly industr used in regulatory discourse today refers to an industry structure where, over the relevan range of market demand, the cost function of a firm is subadditive.

Correspondence with Public Utility Industries

Public utility industries – or, more accurately, some parts of public utility industrie such as the rails, wires and pipes – are often seen as prime examples of natural monop oly activities where it is most cost efficient for a single firm rather than multiple firm to produce a specific set of outputs.[12] The provision of public utility services typicall involves long-term capital investments in durable and immobile assets that are sunk onc incurred (fixed costs), and are followed by relatively low variable or marginal produc tion costs. This gives rise to a cost profile in which average costs decline as productio increases. That is, as production increases, the high level of fixed costs (which by defin ition are largely invariant to levels of output) can be spread across a greater number o output units; it is this ability of a firm to spread such costs over a large level of produc tion that reduces the level of long-run average costs. If the fixed costs associated with th construction of a gas pipeline are $100 million, and there are 100,000 users, the attribute fixed cost per user is $1000, while if there are one million users of the pipeline, the attrib uted fixed cost per user is $100.

However, as discussed in Chapter 1, the perceived 'natural monopoly' activities of th public utility industries have changed in many jurisdictions in recent decades. In jurisdic tions where restructuring and 'unbundling' policies have been implemented, the suppl chain for public utility industries now comprises a mix of natural monopoly-like activ ities (the core network activities, such as owning and operating the electricity wires an poles, copper wire or fibre-optic cables, gas pipelines, rail tracks, or water and wastewate pipes) and potentially competitive activities.

Two types of efficiency arguments are generally posited for regulation in natural mon opoly settings. The first concerns *allocative* efficiency, and here price regulation is used t maximise total surplus and economic welfare. The second argument relates to *productiv* efficiency, and here some form of entry regulation is recommended so as to avoid th wasteful duplication of fixed costs, or to avoid entry by firms who offer no new product or productive technologies and enter the market only to service a select group of the mos profitable customers (so-called 'cream-skimming'). It follows that the standard regula tory prescription, where an industry structure resembles that of a natural monopoly, is t restrict entry to only one firm and, at the same time, to impose price regulation on tha firm to set efficient prices which maximise economic welfare (we consider various alter natives to this standard prescription in Chapter 3).

---

[12] Newbery (1999) describes network utilities as 'the clearest example of natural monopolies'. See also Kahn (1971) and Scherer (1980).

Price Regulation to Achieve Allocative Efficiency

A conventional economic rationale for price regulation in certain industries is to improve allocative efficiency. In general terms, allocative efficiency requires an 'allocation' of products such that the marginal benefit that consumers obtain from consuming an additional unit of the output (as represented by the demand curve) is equal to the marginal cost of producing that additional unit of output. An allocatively efficient price should lead consumers to consume, and producers to supply, an appropriate amount of a good or service.[13] The measure of relative allocative efficiency is typically defined in terms of 'total surplus': the sum of the consumer surplus and producers' profit for a given level of production. Total surplus can be measured as the monetary difference between the benefits of consumption of a service *less* the costs of producing the service or, in more technical terms, the area below the demand curve but above the marginal cost curve for a given level of output.

According to standard microeconomic reasoning, the profit-maximising condition for a monopoly involves producing a level of output at which its marginal revenue is equal to its marginal cost. Assuming that the monopolist faces a downward-sloping linear demand curve, this level of output is lower, and prices higher, than that of a competitive market where prices are, in theory, set at (or close to) marginal costs (and allocative efficiency therefore obtained). This is illustrated in Figure 2.4, where P^* is the price and Q^* is the output associated with perfect competition, and P^{Mon} and Q^{Mon} are the price and output associated with monopoly. The difference between the level of output (prices) in a monopolistic industry and that in a competitive industry is referred to as the allocative inefficiency of monopoly and gives rise to what is known as a 'deadweight loss'. In simple terms, the 'deadweight loss' arises because consumers are paying more than it costs to produce the last unit of output, meaning that there are unrealised gains from trade: if the price was closer to marginal cost, more consumers would purchase the product.

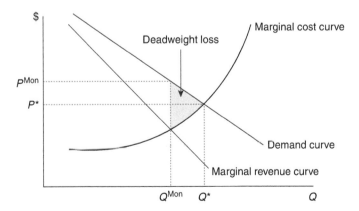

Figure 2.4 The allocative inefficiency of monopoly

---

[13] If the price for a particular service results in a mismatch in demand and supply, then this can have knock-on effects across the economy. This is because it results in either excessive resources being used to produce a good, or too much money being spent on a good relative to its value, and society forgoes the opportunities to use those resources or make those expenditures elsewhere.

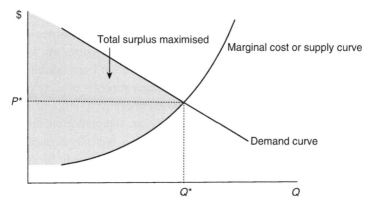

Figure 2.5 Total surplus maximised: 'first-best' pricing

The most allocatively efficient outcome (sometimes referred to as the 'optimal' out come) is where the total surplus is maximised, that is, when the area between the deman curve and the supply/marginal cost curve is greatest for a given level of demand an marginal cost.[14] Standard microeconomic reasoning tells us that total surplus is maxi mised at the level of output where price equals marginal cost, and where firms will us the least-cost inputs in the production process. This is illustrated as the shaded area i Figure 2.5, and is the point at which the area under the demand curve, but above the mar ginal cost curve, is greatest. As this is the maximum total surplus that can be obtaine price regulation that induces such a position is known as 'first-best', as each extra un of output produced is exactly equal to consumers' willingness to pay for it (simply, pric equals marginal cost).

However, as already noted, the public utility industries are generally characterised b high fixed costs, meaning regulatory policy makers can face a dilemma when attemptin to obtain the first-best outcome described above. Specifically, if the firm is compelled b regulation to set a single uniform price for all of its output which equals the marginal cos (in order to maximise allocative efficiency), this will be unsustainable over the long term as the firm will not recover any of its fixed costs of production. Figure 2.6 illustrates th losses that can arise if firms with a high proportion of fixed costs are required to set 'first best' prices (i.e. price equal to marginal cost). In this figure, the shaded area represents th losses incurred by the firm if required to set prices equal to marginal cost (P^0) rather tha at average cost (P'), which would allow it to recover both its fixed and marginal costs fo a given level of output Q^0. In Chapter 4, we consider a number of possible solutions t this dilemma, including the use of a subsidy to cover the fixed costs of production (equa to the shaded area in Figure 2.6), or the use of different (non-linear) pricing policies tha allow the firm to recover its fixed costs from different customers or products.

---

[14] In competitive markets, where all firms are price takers, the supply curve is the sum of the marginal cost curves for the individual firms. The analysis here of total surplus ignores the relative distribution of tota surplus between consumers and producers. As we see in Chapter 4, if an unregulated monopolist engage in price discrimination, this can maximise total surplus, but the producer obtains the entire surplus and there is no consumer surplus.

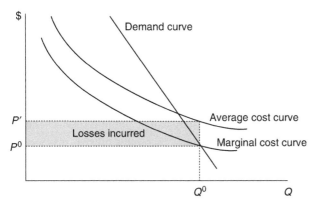

Figure 2.6 Losses that can arise from 'first-best' pricing

While the need for price regulation to address allocative inefficiency is a conventional explanation for regulation (and features in the first pages of almost all textbooks), there is, as discussed below and in Chapter 4, a large body of empirical evidence which suggests that, in practice, regulation has not generally been focused on implementing pricing structures designed to achieve allocative efficiency. For example, as we shall see, the use of demand-reflective prices (so-called Ramsey–Boiteux prices), peak-load prices or other forms of non-linear pricing which can improve allocative efficiency has generally not been adopted by regulators, principally, it appears, because of challenges in gathering the required information and because of distributional concerns.

Entry Regulation to Achieve Productive Efficiency

A different rationale for regulation of industries which have natural monopoly characteristics, but where it is possible for entry to occur, is based on the argument that it is productively efficient for a single supplier to provide relevant services. In other words, such restrictions will result in lower total costs, and consequently lower average prices.

There are a number of dimensions to the argument that regulation should be used to restrict entry into industries with natural monopoly characteristics. The first dimension relates to the potential inefficiencies associated with duplication of fixed costs where rival firms compete. Given the cost profile of natural monopolistic industries, allowing competition in these industries will reduce productive efficiency, as it will necessitate the recovery of two or more sets of fixed costs of production. In these circumstances, entry regulation can improve productive efficiency.[15]

An older, and more controversial, argument for entry regulation is that competition in activities that have natural monopoly characteristics could, in some circumstances, be

---

[15] The New Zealand Commerce Commission (2022) captures this point: 'The fact that there aren't many suppliers in some parts of the supply chain isn't necessarily a problem. In fact, it is potentially a good thing because infrastructure can be very costly to duplicate, and ultimately someone has to pay for it.' More generally, Mankiw and Whinston (1986) show that entry restrictions can be socially desirable where there is a homogeneous product and firms incur fixed set-up costs upon entry. However, they also find that such entry restrictions become unnecessary as the fixed set-up cost becomes small.

'destructive' and lead to price volatility and instability in the industry.[16] 'Destructive com‑
petition', it has been argued, can emerge in settings where the proportion of fixed sun‑
costs is large as a proportion of total costs, where there are substantial periods of exce‑
capacity, and where marginal costs lie below average costs for substantial periods of tim‑
(as in the standard definition of natural monopoly).[17] In these conditions, if demand ‑
relatively inelastic, then, as capacity becomes tight, this may lead to large increases i‑
prices for an extended period before new capacity can be put into service. The prospect c
earning prices significantly in excess of cost may encourage other firms to enter, includ‑
ing by building new capacity, to exploit the conditions of tight supply. However, once a‑
the new capacity enters the system, and the industry is again in a situation of excess cap‑
acity, prices will tend towards marginal cost as a result of intense competition, resultin‑
in bankruptcies. Over time, competition in these conditions is seen to create a situatio‑
of instability in terms of both consumer prices and producer profits. In such context‑
regulation in the form of restrictions on entry is argued to promote stability, and protec
consumers and businesses from the effects of this intense and destructive competition.[1]

Finally, it is argued that, in some circumstances, entry into natural monopolistic indus‑
tries by rival firms who offer no new products or production efficiencies may be sociall‑
inefficient.[19] Where the common costs of production relating to large and indivisibl‑
investments must be recovered across all customers, potential entrants who offer no ne‑
products or productive technologies may be encouraged to selectively enter the market t‑
provide only the most profitable services or to supply only the most profitable customer‑
This potential has given rise to questions about when a natural monopoly is 'sustainable‑
and whether there exists a set of so-called 'sustainable prices' for the service(s) provide‑
by a naturally monopolistic firm such that selective entry does not occur.[20] In the exampl‑
of natural monopoly facing a declining average cost curve for all levels of productio‑
described above, then a firm can always deter entry by rivals by charging a price wher‑
the average cost curve intersects with the demand curve. However, where the averag‑
cost curve is not monotonically decreasing for all levels of production, then, even in th‑
single-product case, it is possible that rival firms may profitably enter and serve only tha‑
section of the market where price is greater than average cost.[21] This practice of selectiv‑
entry at the margin is sometimes referred to as 'cream-skimming', as entrants are seen

---

[16] See Ely (1937) as referenced in Sharkey (1982).

[17] See Kahn (1971).

[18] See Sharkey (1982). Helm and Jenkinson (1997) observe that the monopolistic structure of the utility
industries in the post-war period in the UK was seen to prevent 'the destructive competition which was
widely thought to have pervaded the industries in the 1920s and 1930s'.

[19] See Faulhaber (1975) and Panzar and Willig (1977).

[20] A sustainable price vector is one which offers no profitable opportunities for entry for firms who offer
the same service(s) and face the same cost functions as the natural monopoly, but allows the natural
monopoly to satisfy all demand and to break even across the portfolio of products it supplies (i.e. to earn
a normal profit).

[21] Panzar and Willig (1977) examine the concept of sustainability of a natural monopoly in the context
of the production of multiple products (where rival firms may enter and seek to specialise in the supply
of only one or more of the services provided by the natural monopoly) and conclude that strong
demand substitution effects and product-specific scale economies work against sustainability. Similarly,
Faulhaber (1975) concludes that, where average costs are U-shaped and entry is free and costless, there
may be no stable supply arrangement for a natural monopoly. This is because, for any set of prices for
a particular coalition of customers, there will always be an incentive for a firm to enter the market and
offer lower prices to supply a different subset or coalition of customers.

to capture the 'cream' services, leaving the unprofitable services to the more established firm. However, because this type of selective entry can make it unprofitable for an incumbent natural monopoly firm to supply the rest of the market, regulation is seen as necessary to protect the firm from entry of this type.[22] Despite the various economic rationales for restricting entry described above, this form of regulation is controversial. Many economists advocate caution in restricting entry into the public utility industries.[23] In particular, automatic entry restrictions have been argued to be unnecessary under certain theoretical[24] and real-world[25] conditions. Moreover, restrictions on entry are often argued to impede dynamic efficiency improvements in an industry by insulating the 'protected firm' from market pressures to adopt new technologies or cost-reduction techniques.

2.1.2 Regulation to Control Monopoly Power

A second set of normative arguments for the economic regulation of certain industries arises when – either as a result of restrictions on entry, or because of cost or technological reasons – there is only a single supplier of a service, and therefore this operator may have an incentive, and the ability, to behave in ways that exploit its position of power. A monopoly provider might, for example, set prices considerably above underlying costs, degrade quality, or be insufficiently responsive to cost and other production efficiencies. To address this potential, regulation in the form of price controls and other behavioural regulations (relating to quality, etc.) are seen as necessary.

This rationale for regulation is distinct from the one described in Section 2.1.1, which focused on the fact that firms in a naturally monopolistic position do not have a natural incentive to set efficient prices which maximise economic welfare. The argument for regulation to control monopoly power is not primarily based on a desire to achieve allocatively efficient prices (a specific outcome). Rather, it focuses on controlling the conduct of the firm so it does not exploit or harm consumers, either through charging prices that are substantially higher than the costs of the activity, or by degrading quality or failing to invest, etc.[26] In effect, while traditional arguments for regulation have generally been

---

[22] As described in Chapter 11, the 'duopoly' policy that applied in the telecommunications industry in some jurisdictions in the 1980s is a practical example of such entry restrictions. In the UK the entrant (Mercury) was limited to a market share of voice telephony of 3 per cent of that of BT which, according to Spiller and Vogelsang (1994), 'was meant as a safeguard for BT's envisaged large investment program in expansion and modernisation of its network'.

[23] See Panzar and Willig (1977), Joskow and Noll (1981) and Vickers and Yarrow (1988).

[24] See the discussion of free entry and contestable markets in Sharkey (1982, chapter 7).

[25] Armstrong, Cowan and Vickers (1994) acknowledge the logical possibility of selective entry, but doubt it provides a 'good case for entry restrictions in the utility industries, which are not for the most part remotely contestable and where there is little evidence that cost conditions give rise to non-sustainability'. Similarly, Carlton and Perloff (2000) note that: 'Although it is theoretically possible that natural monopolies are unsustainable, there is little empirical evidence in most regulated industries showing that sustainability problems might justify regulators forbidding entry.'

[26] This reasoning seems consistent with the perceptions of some regulators as to their wider legitimacy. For example, a former Chairman of the Australian Competition and Consumer Commission (ACCC) (which is responsible for economic regulation) has observed that: 'The current rationale given by most economists ... is that we regulate for reasons of allocative efficiency, or to reduce dead weight loss .... Most Australians would, of course, be surprised by this. They think we regulate to make sure that the owners of monopoly infrastructure do not take advantage of their position and "gouge" consumers' (ACCC 2012a).

framed in terms of efficiency concerns, this rationale for regulation also incorporate equity considerations.[27] These relate to concerns associated with 'unjust' or 'exploitative pricing, and to the ability of firms in a monopoly position to exploit their position in market dominance. This rationale for regulation may explain why we sometimes observe activities which do not have natural monopoly attributes being subject to price regulation (such as electricity generation, mobile telephony, retail supply, as well as certain transmission activities where some competition exists, for example, between certain gas pipelines, and some fixed telecommunications networks).

Regulation premised on the need to prevent abuses of power is consistent with perspectives that regulation is a response to the possibility of 'hold-up'. In economics, 'hold-up' arises where either a firm or its customers make sunk investments or incur expenditure on the basis of expectations of the future conduct of the other party, and that other party then acts opportunistically and exploits this fact after the investments have been made. Public utility companies frequently incur large capital costs when making long-term and immobile investments (such as building rail tracks, laying cables or installing transmission or distribution networks) based on the expectation that demand for these services will continue, and that the returns will allow the company to cover its costs. At the same time, users of these services (such as consumers) also make decisions on the basis of expectations regarding the future conduct of the firm – for example, in deciding which type of energy source to use for its activities (gas or electricity).[28] Regulation, in this context, is seen as a method of protecting both parties against opportunistic behaviour by the other party once they have made sunk investments.[29]

Regulation in the face of monopoly power is also premised on cost-efficiency arguments: a firm that does not face the threat of competition will produce at higher levels of cost than those that operate in competitive markets (who are naturally incentivised to cut costs to improve profitability and remain competitive). There are at least three potential causes of this cost inefficiency. The first cause is technical inefficiency: the monopolistic firm may not have the appropriate incentives to ensure that the rate of conversion of inputs to outputs is at its most efficient and, in technical terms, that the firm sits on the efficient frontier of production (which, as discussed in Chapter 5, is a major driver behind certain forms of price control arrangements).

A second potential cause of cost inefficiency is that the management of a monopoly firm will face lower incentives to seek out cost savings, or to take risks, than managers in competitive markets. In the oft-quoted words of John Hicks, 'the best of all monopoly profits is a quiet life'.[30] In this respect, it is assumed that higher levels of managerial activity will generally be associated with lower costs. This cause of inefficiency, sometimes termed 'X-inefficiency', has been distinguished from technical efficiency, and is intended

---

[27] The two rationales are connected insofar as the efficiency rationale regulation focuses on maximising total surplus (or alternatively minimising deadweight losses) while the monopoly power rationale for regulation focuses on the distribution of the producer surplus and consumer surplus.

[28] See Goldberg (1976).

[29] See Williamson (1976) and Biggar (2009). Biggar and Heimler (2021) argue that this reasoning also provides an explanation for competition law.

[30] Hicks (1935). Before that, Adam Smith (1776) described monopoly as 'a great enemy to good management'.

to capture the more general case where 'for a variety of reasons people and organisations normally work neither as hard nor effectively as they could'.[31] X-inefficiency is considered likely to be greater in situations where competitive pressure is severely limited, such as monopoly, and is argued by some to be more detrimental to welfare than allocative inefficiency.[32]

The third potential cause of cost inefficiency, which is of particular relevance in many regulated industries, is how monopoly power affects the incentives of firms to innovate and to seek out and employ new techniques and working practices that could lead to future improvements in economic welfare. This issue is a difficult and controversial one in economics; however, the main arguments can be stated simply here. On one side, firms in most competitive market structures are argued to have a natural incentive to invest some resources to innovate or develop new working practices, as any successful innovations can allow the firm to gain a competitive advantage over its rivals and increase its profits above the competitive level.[33] In contrast, in monopoly structures, these same incentives will not apply and the monopoly firm will only innovate where the expected incremental profit associated with the innovation is greater than the resource costs associated with investing in the innovation. This is because the profits of the monopolist are already potentially above the competitive level.[34] However, an alternative perspective is that the ability to occupy a monopoly position, and to reap monopoly profits, can itself act as an important spur to innovation over the long term, and that this can create an incentive for firms to invest in research and development.[35] Empirically, there is some evidence that the relationship between product market competition and innovation is non-linear, and more specifically that an inverted U-shaped relationship holds, with industries distributed across both the increasing and decreasing sections of the U-shape.[36]

The control of monopoly power as a rationale for regulation has strong explanatory power in terms of understanding both why certain industries are subject to regulation and why, in practice, we do not always observe regulation operating in ways consistent with the natural monopoly rationale outlined above. However, it does leave some questions unanswered. It does not explain, for example, why firms who hold close to monopoly

---

[31] See Leibenstein (1966).

[32] Leibenstein (1966) – contrast with Stigler (1976).

[33] There is an alternative view attributed to Schumpeter (1943) that intense competition can reduce the incentives to innovate, as any profits or rents from the innovation will be reduced if competition results in prices close to marginal cost. Intense competition can also reduce the ability to innovate if it results in lower financial resources to spend on research and development and the firm cannot access capital markets. Griffith and Van Reenan (2021) argue that this can explain the use of patents which grant temporary monopoly rights to innovators.

[34] Arrow (1962) argues that pre-invention monopoly power acts as a strong disincentive to further innovation, because any innovation by the monopolist resulting in lower costs will simply allow it to replace itself, while innovations by firms in a competitive market can allow it to capture a new market. This is sometimes referred to as the 'Arrow replacement effect'. See Shapiro (2011).

[35] The most important reference here is that of Schumpeter (1943). The high levels of innovation in pharmaceutical markets, where firms have exclusive set period monopolies over the supply of new and innovative drugs, are an example often noted.

[36] See Aghion, Bloom, Blundell, et al. (2005). Griffith and Van Reenan (2021) conclude that the inverted U-shaped relationship has 'held up reasonably well over time, although on average the positive effect of competition still seems to dominate empirically'.

positions in some (non-public utility) industries are not subject to the same forms of economic regulation (i.e. regulation over and above normal competition law) as the public utility firms. It also does not explain why the regulation of certain industries, such as public utility industries, generally takes the form of *ex ante* controls (on prices, quality etc.) rather than *ex post* controls (such as competition law prosecutions for suspected abuses of monopoly power). This issue is discussed in Chapter 3.

2.1.3 Externalities as a Rationale for Regulation

A further normative rationale for economic regulation is the need to address the externalities that arise in some industries. Externalities arise where there are wider costs or benefits associated with the supply of a service than those that accrue to the immediate parties to the transaction (i.e. there are uncompensated third-party effects). Externalities take many forms, and there are both positive and negative externalities. The most familiar type of negative externality associated with the electricity and wastewater industries relates to pollution, and harm to the environment, that may be associated with how services are produced and supplied. Examples of positive externalities include the widespread benefits associated with the provision of clean drinking water and adequate sanitation (which reduces the spread and cost of illnesses) or extensive transportation and communications networks (which allow more people to connect with one another). In each of these cases, regulation can be premised on the need to ensure that the wider societal benefits/harms of transactions in certain services are realised/avoided.

The presence of significant externalities as a rationale for regulation of the public utility industries is not a new one.[37] It is, however, increasingly relevant in the context of changes associated with the environment. As we discuss in later chapters, in the energy, water and transport industries (and, to a lesser extent, communications) regulators in some jurisdictions now see an important role for themselves in representing or protecting future consumers/citizens when considering the impacts of current decisions and policies. In effect, such regulators are attempting to identify, and address, the externalities associated with the current practices of firms in these industries on future generations. While a normative rationale for regulation based on the existence of externalities has been around for many years, and is widely accepted,[38] some economists are circumspect about intervention on this basis. In particular, it has been argued that the mere identification of an externality should not automatically justify regulation to subsidise the development of a network.[39] Instead, careful judgement should be applied in determining which externalities require regulatory intervention, and the forms that intervention should take.[40]

---

[37] See Kahn (1971).

[38] Pigou (1932) is often seen as providing a role for government intervention to correct for externalities.

[39] Kahn (1971) argues that a public policy decision to subsidise provision of electricity or telephone services to particular sectors of the populace is, in principle, no different from the decision to provide them with a decent diet, medical care and housing, and that all of these services should be provided by devices other than regulation.

[40] See, generally, Coase (1960).

2.1.4 Network Effects as a Rationale for Regulation

Another argument for regulation arises in contexts where there are network effects or network externalities, which, as we will see, are a particularly important rationale for regulation in sectors such as payments, digital platforms, transport and communications. While the terms 'network externalities' and 'network effects' are sometimes used interchangeably, they are not the same and the arguments for regulation on these bases differ from one another.

Network Effects

Network effects arise where the benefits to one user of a network depend on the number of other users that are connected to, or utilise, the network. Network effects can be positive or negative, and direct or indirect.[41] Direct network effects arise when the number of users of one user group increases (or decreases) the value of the network to other users of that same user group. For example, each owner of a telephone benefits whenever somebody else installs a telephone,[42] and similarly each new user that joins a specific social media or instant messaging platform benefits existing subscribers by increasing the number of users that they can interact with. In short, as a network becomes larger, the value of the network to each and every user of the network increases (i.e. each additional user connected to the network inadvertently creates a positive effect for existing users).[43] Indirect network effects arise when the number of users of one group increases (or decreases) the value of the network to another type of user group.[44] For example, the more hotels are listed on a digital accommodation platform (one group), the greater the options for those who want to choose a hotel (a different group). Similarly, the more cardholders of a specific credit card, the greater the demand for merchants to accept that specific credit card brand (and vice versa).

An important attribute of markets characterised by network effects is that, while there may be intense competition between network operators to attract users to their network, once users have signed up to a network, these effects can naturally lead to high levels of industry concentration. This is because, when network effects are strong, they can create a positive feedback loop (the more people who join a network, the more attractive that network is to others), which can lead to the market 'tipping' in favour of a single, or small number of, network provider(s).[45] For this reason, network effects are characterised as demand-side economies of scale.[46] These economies arise not because expanding output

---

[41] Farrell and Klemperer (2007) present an excellent overview of network effects. Jullien and Sand-Zantman (2021) provide a recent survey of network effects in two-sided markets.

[42] See Rohlfs (1974).

[43] Belleflamme and Peitz (2021) refer to this as the 'attraction loop': 'The higher the activity level of the group, the more attractive it becomes for each group member to increase their activity level, feeding back into the group's overall activity level.'

[44] Belleflamme and Peitz (2021) refer to these as 'attraction spirals' (for positive indirect network effects) and 'attraction/repulsion pendulum' (for negative indirect network effects that generate positive effects for one group but negative effects for another group).

[45] The reverse is also true where there are negative network effects, which could lead to users abandoning a network *en masse* and potentially causing a so-called 'death spiral'. See the discussion of networks in decline in Section 5.6.

[46] See Shapiro and Varian (1999).

decreases average cost (as with supply-side economies of scale) but because expanding the customer base increases the benefit to each consumer of joining the network. In some cases, this can give rise to a demand-side natural monopoly, meaning that consumers may prefer to pay a higher price for a service produced by a single firm rather than multiple firms. In simple terms, this arises if the positive network effects of subscribing to a network are greater than the price effects of the otherwise downward-sloping demand curve.[47]

As discussed in Chapter 13, network effects feature prominently in discussions about the need for the regulation of digital platforms. Belleflamme and Peitz (2021) define a platform as a 'manager of network effects', noting that processes like exchanging information, or even the formation of prices, are no longer decentralised but controlled by the platform.[48] A principal concern is that the existence of strong network effects (coupled with significant economies of scale and scope) can result in users becoming effectively 'locked-in' to some dominant platforms. This arises not because of contractual clauses which lock-in users, but because of the lack of incentives and difficulties of coordinating the migration of contacts and other information and data (such as past purchase history) from an existing platform to a new competing platform. Simply put, a user that migrates to a new platform automatically loses access to all of the users on the platform it is leaving. The challenges of attracting large number of users away from a leading platform can also create substantial barriers to entry which can deter new platforms, including those with superior technology, from entering and challenging an incumbent platform. The result of this, it is argued, is that the market position of some platforms can become entrenched, allowing them to act in ways that exploit their position of market power (e.g. reduce quality, set adverse price terms for specific users, or introduce other non-price terms which are harmful to users). In addition, dominant platforms in one area can benefit from leveraging their user base with its strong network effects into a new platform activity and thus reduce the challenges of having to establish a new user base and exploit network effects for that activity. In effect, the rationale for economic regulation of digital platforms is closely related to the arguments for the control of monopoly power discussed above.

However, as discussed in Chapter 13, a number of factors need to be considered before using network effects as a rationale for *ex ante* economic regulation. Important among these considerations are: the strength of the network effects;[49] the extent to which consumers can 'multi-home' (i.e. join and use multiple digital platforms for similar services); and the scope for potential 'competition for the market' which can capture any rents and discipline the behaviour of the dominant platform.[50] While regulatory remedies to address concerns about network effects of dominant digital platforms vary across jurisdictions,

---

[47] While, as discussed above, a (supply-side) natural monopoly is defined by reference to a cost function which is *subadditive*, in contrast a (demand-side) natural monopoly arises if the demand function is strictly *superadditive*. When this condition holds, net surplus is greater under monopoly than when it is supplied by more than one firm. See Shaffer (1983) and Vogelsang (2021).

[48] They go on to note: 'trade is carried out under the visible hand of intermediary managing the platform'.

[49] Jullien and Sand-Zantman (2021) focus on the estimation of direct and indirect effects.

[50] Farrell and Klemperer (2007) note that optimists argue that competition for the market may perform 'tolerably well' if users benefit in the early stage from intense competition (and gain quasi-rents up-front) which are then 'gouged out of them' at a later date once they sign up to a network.

and are still under consideration in some places, among the options being considered are: the mandated separation of the networks into a series of smaller networks; regulations to require greater interoperability between platforms; and policies that make it easier for users to migrate to new networks such as data portability requirements.[51]

Another important consideration when proposing regulation in multi-sided market settings characterised by network effects is the level of growth or maturity of the industry. While it is generally accepted that network effects can result in intensive competition among different firms initially, as each firm tries to build a critical mass and attract users to its network, and that this may result in price structures where some user groups are subsidised by other user groups, there is a question about whether such price structures are appropriate once a network is mature. As we will see in Chapter 12, this question features prominently in debates about the ongoing need for regulation of card payment systems, and specifically whether interchange fees should be set at levels close to zero given the maturity of the card systems and the view that network effects have been fully captured.[52]

Network Externalities

Network externalities are a specific type of network effect that has not been fully internalised, that is, where there are unexploited gains to be made from greater network participation.[53] Unexploited gains can arise if users are connected to separate networks that are not interoperable with one another, or where, as a result of competition between multiple identical networks, there is excessive fragmentation in a market. As with other forms of externality, a key characteristic of network externalities is that there are wider benefits associated with users' participation in the network than those that accrue to the immediate parties to the transaction. In some industries, particularly where there are economies of scale, regulatory intervention has sometimes been based on a desire to ensure that the benefits of network externalities are harnessed and thus internalised. In other words, just like a single supplier of a service can be most efficient when there are economies of scale and scope in some settings, the argument here is that a supply structure based around a single provider, or a common set of providers using the same technology, can exploit the user benefits associated with a larger or interoperable network.

Broadly speaking, economic regulation has sought to harness network externalities in two ways. Firstly, regulation can restrict entry, either by allowing only a single firm to operate the network (thus fully internalising the externality),[54] or by requiring that

---

[51] More generally, these proposals are consistent with Farrell and Klemperer's (2007) conclusion that, in the presence of a network effect, the 'best policy may be to encourage compatibility and compatible competition. This conclusion is reinforced by the fact that – in large part because of the problems above – the incentives of firms, especially dominant firms, are often biased towards incompatibility.' They also emphasise policies which allow users to coordinate better, such as information policies.

[52] In other words, in a mature system there may be less of a need for one side of the market to subsidise another group of users to encourage participation by that group. For example, in mature payments systems, many people will have a credit or debit card, and many merchants will consider acceptance as a necessary requirement. See the discussion in Vickers (2005) and Productivity Commission (2018).

[53] See Liebowitz and Margolis (1994).

[54] Belleflamme and Peitz (2021) note that one of the purposes of platforms or other intermediaries is to find a way of internalising network effects, and in so doing address the problem that users do not take account of network externalities when making decisions, and as a consequence valuable interactions may fail to occur.

suppliers of network services adopt common technical standards and protocols to ensure network interoperability. The focus of entry regulation here is on improving welfare by ensuring that consumers benefit from a large network using a common technology (compared with smaller competitive networks with different compatibility standards) rather than on the productive efficiency of the single supplier (as in the natural monopoly discussion above). As we will see in later chapters, harnessing network externalities through interoperability requirements is an important aspect of the regulation of communications, payments, rail and aviation industries. A second way in which economic regulation has sought to harness network externalities is through price regulation. Specifically, the prices charged for network use (or to specific categories of user) have sometimes been adjusted from the underlying cost to account for the benefits associated with network growth and a larger network. An example of this approach can be seen in the mobile telephony industry, where regulated prices at the wholesale interconnection level have sometimes been increased (in the form of a network externality surcharge) to encourage mobile phone network operators to reduce retail subscription prices, and thus increase mobile phone penetration.

From a purely static perspective, regulatory interventions which seek to harness network externalities can reduce costs and increase the value to users by reducing network fragmentation. Interoperability requirements in competing networks can also reduce the risk of consumers becoming 'locked in', which can give an operator monopoly power. They can also intensify competition by allowing users of smaller networks to connect with larger dominant networks, thus 'levelling the playing field' and potentially enabling them to challenge these dominant positions. However, such regulations are not appropriate in all circumstances. In industries where there is scope for 'inter-network' competition between different technologies or standards, mandating a single supplier or a common set of interoperable technical standards could result in consumers being collectively locked into an inferior but interoperable technology. In addition, alternative providers using new technologies may be deterred from entry if they assess that they will not be able to attract enough users to be able to operate at the minimum efficient scale. In short, regulation that seeks to harness the benefits of network externalities in the short term might have the effect of harming dynamic competition over the long term.

2.2 ALTERNATIVE EXPLANATIONS FOR REGULATION

The various normative rationales for regulation discussed in Section 2.1 imply that regulation of certain industries is generally premised on a desire to improve economic welfare, either by requiring firms to act efficiently, ensuring an efficient industry structure (through restricting entry), preventing abuses of monopoly power, or addressing specific economic externalities. In effect, each rationale is tied to the aim of generating positive economic welfare improvements.

However, there is considerable empirical evidence suggesting that the practice of regulation is not always consistent with a goal of improving economic welfare.[55] Studies and

---

[55] Joskow and Noll (1981) find that, when considered as positive theory (rather than normative guidance), the public interest theories of regulation are wrong, being generally inconsistent with available evidence.

surveys have suggested, for example, that the application and effects of regulation can differ considerably from what the public interest theories suggest.[56] Moreover, there are a range of activities in the economy that have historically been subject to some form of economic regulation, yet do not appear to be either natural monopolies, or feature characteristics consistent with the other economic rationales for regulation discussed in Section 2.1.[57]

For these reasons, it has been argued that a richer, multi-dimensional account is needed to explain why regulation exists in certain industries and the forms it takes. In the discussion that follows, we consider some of these alternative explanations. One set of explanations, known collectively as 'the economic theories' or 'interest group theories' of regulation, suggests that regulation is best explained by considering the different political and economic actors who interact in society and their incentives, including: politicians or bureaucrats; regulated companies; consumers; and other powerful interest groups affected by regulation, such as workers in a regulated industry. Another explanation conceives of regulation in public utility industries as a response to the need for some form of administrative arrangement to manage the long-term relationship between consumers and producers of public utility services.

2.2.1 Economic or Interest Group 'Theories' of Regulation

An important set of articles published in the 1960s and early 1970s directly challenged the notion that regulation exists solely as a mechanism to address normative concerns about natural monopoly and to improve economic welfare (and, in particular, to compress the gap between price and marginal costs that would otherwise exist in these industries).[58] This work argued that the existence of regulation was more accurately accounted for by a propensity of different groups in society to demand, and then utilise, regulation to achieve private gains and benefits. According to this reasoning, regulation exists not to protect the interests of the *public* at large, but to represent and protect the *private* interests of specific politically effective groups. Collectively, these theories of regulation are sometimes referred to as the 'economic theories of regulation' or 'interest group theories', although there are a number of different strands within this work.

The first strand of these theories builds on the proposition that the existence of regulation might be explained by a desire of firms themselves to be regulated.[59] Evidence of the introduction of state-based regulation of the electric utilities in the USA, and telecommunications regulation, in the early twentieth century appears to support this view,[60] as does

---

[56] See Jarrell (1978), Joskow and Rose (1989), Noll (1989), Knittel (2006) and Biggar (2009).

[57] See Posner (1974) and Stigler (1971).

[58] This work, and particularly George Stigler's (1971) paper, has been described as 'the beginning of the end' of the widely held assumption that regulation was introduced to pursue public interest goals.

[59] Hayek (1944) provides an early exposition of the proposition that aspiring monopolists regularly sought, and frequently obtained, the assistance and power of the state to make their control effective.

[60] Gray (1940) argued that public utility regulation of electric utilities in the USA in the early twentieth century provided a 'haven of refuge for all aspiring monopolists who found it too difficult, too costly, or too precarious to secure and maintain monopoly by private action alone'. Later, Brock (2002) describes the efforts of AT&T chairman Theodore Vail, in the early part of the twentieth century, to 'embrace regulation and use it is as substitute for market forces', noting that 'Vail recognised that regulation could be a way of preserving monopoly power in justifying a system without competition'. Demsetz (1968) argues that regulation provided utilities with 'the comfort of legally protected market areas', and that the force behind the regulatory movement came from the utility companies themselves.

more recent calls for more regulation by some large digital platforms.[61] Regulation, which was viewed primarily as a pro-producer policy, was argued to be in greatest demand b utilities operating in competitive market conditions with low prices and profits.[62] Th potential benefits of regulation to a firm could include: direct subsidies to the industr control over entry by new rivals; and actions to promote complements and restrict su stitute products.[63]

Despite the above, intuitively it might be argued that it would be irrational for firm to seek to be regulated insofar as it may require that prices be set to reflect cos and ensure that regulated firms earn only a normal profit. However, the producer-le explanation is consistent with some empirical studies which suggest that, in prac tice, regulation does not necessarily result in reductions in prices, improvements i efficiency or reductions in industry profits.[64] Nor does regulation necessarily prote consumers from the exploitation of monopoly power.[65] Rather, it can harm consume and workers by restricting entry or growth of new firms and raising barriers to entr in labour markets.[66]

Building on work on collective behaviour and clubs,[67] Stigler sought to explain th supply and demand for regulation by groups in society more fully, developing the ide that policy makers and regulators might act as rational actors when confronted with th political demands of interest groups (particularly producers). Stigler's main conclusion that more highly organised groups (which are typically smaller in size), and who hav large stakes in the outcome, will generally be more successful in acquiring regulatio for an industry. It follows from this reasoning that producers or sellers in a particula industry – who are generally smaller in number than consumers, and have higher pe capita stakes in the outcome of regulation – would be expected to be relatively more suc cessful in bidding for the services of regulation than consumers.[68] Stigler's conclusion often seen to be consistent with the more general 'capture theory' of regulation, whereb

---

[61] Leaders of large digital platforms such as Facebook and Google have also called for more regulation in specific areas such as privacy, data portability and the use of artificial intelligence. See Zuckerberg (2020) and Kharpal (2020).

[62] See Jarrell (1978).

[63] See Stigler (1971). However, these benefits would come at a cost to the industry, which would take the form of votes and resources.

[64] Jarrell (1978) looked at the US electricity industry and concluded that prices and profits increased upon the establishment of state regulation. Stigler and Friedland (1962) find only a very small, and statistically insignificant, effect of regulation on electric utility prices; however, Peltzman (1993) and Joskow and Rose (1989) highlight reasons for exercising care when generalising these results. Cicala (2015) finds that the deregulation of electricity generators in the USA led to substantial price reductions for coal and a shift towards more productive coal mines.

[65] See Jordan (1972). Contrast with Joskow and Rose (1989), who conclude, based on their survey, that price regulation does reduce prices below those of an unconstrained monopolist, but that the structure of prices and distribution of revenues often reflect distributional objectives rather than efficiency objectives.

[66] Gutiérrez and Philippon (2019) find that regulations (especially in industries with high lobby expenditures) have reduced entry and the growth of small firms relative to large ones in the USA. Chambers and O'Reilly (2022) find that regulation can exacerbate inequality by benefiting incumbents through limiting entry of economic participants, such as firms or workers.

[67] Particularly the work of Olson (1965) and Buchanan (1965).

[68] See Peltzman (1989).

regulation is seen to exist to serve, or be applied in ways consistent with, the preferences of the incumbent regulated firm.[69]

However, in work published around the same time, Richard Posner found no single interest group responsible for the capture of regulation. Posner (1971) argued that the prevalence of cross-subsidisation in regulated industries could not be explained by reference to the view that regulation was pro-producer insofar as it would always be better for the regulated firm to stop supplying the below-cost service than subsidising it from other activities.[70] Posner's conclusion was that regulation could perform allocative and distributive functions that were normally associated with taxation by government. The contribution of Posner's analysis is that it broadened the interest group approach view of regulation by showing how certain groups of *customers* may also have a demand for, and an effective influence on, regulation.[71]

Two subsequent papers expanded on this theme that regulation serves a broad constituency.[72] Peltzman (1976) examined how regulation affects the transfer of wealth among different interest groups, where the regulator is subject to some form of regulatory budget constraint. According to this approach, a regulator seeks to make everyone who has political weight 'as happy as possible' and to obtain a politically optimum distribution of wealth, as reflected in profits that producers can earn and the prices charged to consumers.[73] This framework is potentially able to simultaneously explain the existence of both pro-producer-type regulatory outcomes, as well as outcomes that benefit certain consumer groups, such as the existence of cross-subsidisation of some services in regulated industries.[74] In each case, the resulting equilibrium reflects a balance between political considerations, such as the weight and influence of different interest groups, and economic components, such as the demand and cost conditions in the industry.[75]

Adopting a similar framework, Becker (1983) developed the proposition that regulation involves the balancing of considerations of redistribution and efficiency, and concludes that the resulting equilibrium is determined by the size of the deadweight loss which

---

[69] The origins of the proposition that public policies might reflect competition among different interest groups can be found in the work of Bentley (1908). See also Bernstein (1955) on the susceptibility of regulatory agencies over time to capture by the regulated industry.

[70] To Posner, the existence of cross-subsidisation was an 'embarrassment' to those who saw regulation as being imposed to bring about results approximating a competitive market, as it resulted in an outcome 'unthinkable in a competitive market' (i.e. prices for some services below cost).

[71] Posner's analysis is not inconsistent with Stigler's; Stigler's analysis allows for the capture of regulatory processes by other effective political groups, not just regulated firms.

[72] Joskow and Rose (1989) conclude, on the basis of their survey, that labour, in particular, can be an important beneficiary of regulation in certain industries, and even more so than regulated firms. They argue that price and entry regulation is conducive to the development of strong unions.

[73] Peltzman (1989).

[74] Yandle (1983) observes that this can sometimes result in the formation of unusual coalitions between those subject to regulation and other interested groups, such as the alliance between Baptists and Bootleggers in support of alcohol prohibition.

[75] An equilibrium in this framework arises where the marginal benefit (in terms of votes gained by raising profits for the regulated firm) is exactly offset by the marginal loss (in terms of votes lost resulting from an increase in prices for consumers); with the consequence that the resulting price will lie somewhere between the profit-maximising price (suggested by the pro-producer theory) and the perfectly competitive price with zero profits (suggested by the public interest theories).

results from the inefficiency of regulatory policies.[76] An important implication of th
analysis is that regulatory policies directed at efficiency will be introduced in circum
stances where the relative gains to those who favour such policies is much greater tha
the relative losses of those who oppose them.[77] On this reasoning, the regulation of th
public utility industries can be explained by the fact that there are significant marke
failures in those industries, and the potential exists for significant efficiency gains to b
achieved as a result of the introduction of regulation. Becker argues that this analysis uni
fies the normative and interest group views on regulation: that is, regulation can correc
for market failures (such as the inefficiencies associated with natural monopoly), while a
the same time favouring politically powerful groups.

Collectively, these economic theories, or interest group theories, of regulation, are see
to have advanced the understanding of economic regulation, particularly the politica
context in which regulation occurs.[78] However, over time, a number of criticisms an
critiques of these theories have emerged.[79] In particular, it has been argued that the 'eco
nomic' or 'interest group' theories of regulation, like the normative theories of regulatio
they challenge, are effectively 'generalisations' rather than 'theory' and have not bee
systematically confronted with wide-scale empirical testing.[80]

In addition, at the theoretical level, it has been argued that the theories fail to accoun
for various information asymmetries (between regulated firms and regulators, and betwee
regulators and oversight bodies) and to distinguish between political and regulatory insti
tutions, including taking account of the agency relationship between the government
legislator and regulatory agencies.[81] It has also been argued that legislators and regulator
can have ideological concerns which may override any obligations they feel they have t
particular interest groups. More generally, even some leading proponents of the economi
theories of regulation accept that such theories are unable to provide a coherent accoun
of some important questions about regulation, including why it only applies to specifi
industries, why it is introduced when it is, and why deregulation has occurred in som
industries but not others.[82] Nevertheless, the conceptual paradigm, which combines eco
nomics and politics, and highlights the potential susceptibility of regulation to organise

---

[76] Deadweight loss in this context is the difference between the gain to the winner of political influence less the loser's loss from a change in output which can be attributed to regulation.

[77] Becker (1983).

[78] Peltzman (1993) argues that Stigler's (1971) paper is seen to have produced a significant shift in the 'professional center of gravity towards a skepticism [among economists] about the social utility of regulation'. Shughart and Thomas (2019) go further and argue that: 'the public interest theory of regulation largely has been displaced by theories and evidence grounded in a special interest theory'.

[79] Peltzman (1989) presents an excellent survey of these critiques.

[80] There is a recognised difficulty in measuring and causally testing the variables that comprise the theory (such as the relationship between the stakes of a particular group and the gains it receives, or which interest groups will be successful), making the rejection of the null hypothesis virtually impossible; see Posner (1974), Joskow and Noll (1981) and Noll (1989). However, others find empirical support for the interest group theory of regulation; see Ando and Palmer (1998), Knittel (2006) and Bremberger, Cambini, Gugler and Rondi (2016).

[81] See Laffont and Tirole (1991).

[82] See the discussion in Joskow and Noll (1981) and Peltzman (1989). Peltzman (2021) acknowledges that the theory of regulation runs into difficulty in explaining the birth and death of regulation of an industry, but it does help explain how regulation will be implemented once it is established.

interests,[83] has provided an important and enduring framework for considering the role of different influences on the existence and conduct of regulation.[84]

2.2.2 Regulation as a Form of Administration of a Long-Term Contract

A second alternative account for regulation is that it reflects a need for some form of administration of the long-term relationship between consumers and producers of certain services, such as public utility services.[85] On this view, regulation is not principally premised on the need for a regulator to determine efficient prices, but rather on the need for a body to administer, or govern, the terms of trade over a long-term contractual relationship between a firm and its customers in circumstances where there is uncertainty, and the relationship is complex and multi-dimensional. In this context, the need for regulation arises because it is impossible to determine an optimal or complete contract at the outset.[86] This line of reasoning is a variant of a more general problem associated with long-term contracting where parties incur relationship-specific investments (more specifically, where parties make durable and immobile investments).[87]

The claim that economic regulation is designed to address problems associated with long-term contracting has received increased attention in recent years and is seen by some as a useful way of conceiving of economic regulation as it operates in practice.[88] In this respect, the formal regulatory revenue determination and rate-making process might be viewed as a form of 'dispute resolution',[89] of which there are other more informal alternatives. One of these alternatives, discussed in Chapter 3, is the negotiated settlements process used in North America, which involves the settling of rate cases by agreement between the public utility company and its customers and other stakeholders, typically without the involvement of a regulator, although any agreement reached is subsequently submitted to the regulator for approval.[90] Some argue that regulatory economists have 'unduly neglected' alternative processes for settling rate cases in some parts of the world,[91]

---

[83] Yandle (2021) argues that regulation is most durable where there is a 'pairing of private and public interests' such that the private demands of industry for regulation are accompanied by demand from other groups that can provide public interest justification and thus reduce the political cost of supplying regulation. Peltzman (2021) considers this logic in the context of the regulation of non-conventional gas ('fracking'), noting that any regulation could combine conventional gas producer interests with the interests of environmental interests.

[84] Peltzman (2021) argues that the enduring impact of Stigler's (1971) article on the economic theory of regulation is that he asked 'the right questions: why do we (really) have regulation? What can we (realistically) expect it to do?', rather than providing a specific answer. Mayo (2011) submits that this 'view of regulation has provided a powerful general model for understanding regulatory outcomes and has led to a fundamental shift in the research agenda directed toward regulation'.

[85] See, in particular, Goldberg (1976).

[86] Williamson (1976) describes rate of return regulation as 'a highly incomplete form of contracting in which the prospects for windfall gains and losses are strictly limited and, in principle, and sometimes in fact, adaptations to changing circumstances are introduced in a low-cost, nonacrimonious way'.

[87] See Goldberg (1976), Williamson (1976) and Gómez-Ibáñez (2003). See also older conceptions of contract management by Chadwick (1859), as discussed in Crain and Ekelund (1976).

[88] See Gómez-Ibáñez (2003) and Biggar (2009).

[89] Littlechild (2012b).

[90] See Wang (2004) and Doucet and Littlechild (2006).

[91] Doucet and Littlechild (2009) argue that the traditional model for rate setting set out in legal and economics textbooks is no longer the norm, but rather a fallback position.

and that, in fact, 'settlements between utility and consumer representatives are a majo[r] part of modern regulation'.[92]

As discussed in Chapter 3, this alternative characterisation of regulation has importan[t] implications for the role of a regulator, which changes from one in which it is taske[d] with representing the consumer interest and making the final decision on price and reve[-] nue determinations, to one in which it facilitates and enables well-informed participan[ts] (firms and consumers) to reach agreements that are mutually beneficial.[93] In effect, th[e] regulator's focus is the process by which negotiations are conducted, rather than the out[-] comes of that negotiation process.[94]

2.2.3 Other Potential Explanations for the Existence of Regulation

A more general explanation for the regulation of certain industries relates to the import[-] ance of those industries both to an economy and to society. In this context, economic regu[-] lation is argued to reflect societal and political recognition that the pricing and allocatio[n] of some essential services are 'too important' to be left to market processes. As Kahn (197[1?]) observed, the public utility industries have a 'public character' that is uniquely connecte[d] to the process of economic growth, and the efficient provision of public utility services [is] likely to benefit a number of firms in other sectors in an economy. While this argumen[t] alone arguably cannot explain regulation of the public utilities – a range of non-utilit[y] activities also have economic and social significance – it usefully highlights how regula[-] tion can be a response to wider social, economic and political considerations, a point that [is] highly relevant to new areas of regulation such as payment systems and digital platform[s.]

A separate argument is that regulation reflects the institutional interests of regulator[y] agencies themselves.[95] According to this reasoning, the ongoing regulation of specifi[c] industries can, in part, be explained as 'self-interest' on behalf of the regulatory agency to 'stay in business' and maintain or expand its powers and jurisdiction. While th[is] explanation cannot account for why regulation occurs in the first place, it does poten[-] tially have some explanatory power when it comes to considering why regulation is no[t] always withdrawn from activities where competition has developed, as well as the for[m] that regulation has historically taken in some industries. In particular, it may explain wh[y] the scope of activities pursued by many regulatory agencies has tended to increase, rathe[r] than contract, over the past four decades.[96]

---

[92] Littlechild (2009a).
[93] Doucet and Littlechild (2009) describe the use of negotiated settlements by the (then) Canadian Nationa[l] Energy Board as one where: 'The prime role of the Board is no longer to impose its own view of the public interest. It is to enable well-informed market participants with a demonstrable interest to negotiate satisfactorily on something like equal terms with the oil and gas pipelines.'
[94] See Doucet and Littlechild (2009).
[95] Generally, on this topic see Niskanen (1971).
[96] Williamson (1976) discusses this tendency more generally. See also the discussion in Bernstein (1955) on the 'natural tendency' of the first federal regulator in the USA (the Interstate Commerce Commission, ICC) to seek to extend its powers. See also UK House of Lords (2007), which noted that it had received a lot of evidence highlighting that regulators' roles had kept expanding, and that this was taking them away from their eventual demise. Shleifer (2011) argues more generally that the ubiquity of regulation i[n] American and European societies may be explained by the failure of courts to resolve disputes cheaply, predictably and impartially.

2.3 RATIONALES BASED ON FAIRNESS AND AFFORDABILITY

Another explanation for why economic regulation exists, and takes the form that it does, is that it is intended to address various distributional concerns, including issues relating to fairness, affordability and social inclusion. This rationale for regulation has both normative dimensions (regulation *should* be directed at issues of fairness and affordability) and practical dimensions (regulation *does* take account of fairness and affordability).

2.3.1 What Are the Arguments for Regulation on the Basis of Fairness and Affordability?

On the normative level, one aspect relates to the nature of the products that should be regulated. In essence, the argument for regulation is that certain services are 'essential' and should be provided to all citizens of a society and on a broadly equivalent basis.[97] On this line of reasoning, a function of regulation is to ensure wide coverage and fair and affordable access to such services.[98] Public utility services (energy, transport, water and communications services) are often classified as essential in nature insofar as they are argued to be of such importance to either economic or social welfare that consumers require additional protections over and above those provided by the market or general competition laws.[99]

While the phrase 'essential service' is commonly used in policy and regulatory discourse, there is no fixed definition of the phrase, nor standard methodology, for determining what products are essential and therefore should be subject to economic regulation. Notions of 'essentiality' differ across societies and groups within society, and what services are essential can also change over time.[100] In many industrialised countries, the ability to access broadband at a minimum speed is now considered essential to the ability of individuals to participate in society and to social and economic welfare. In contrast, as we will see in later chapters, in many developing economies, access to basic essential services such as water and sanitation services, and energy and transport services, is still often severely limited.

There are different ways to approach the question of whether a particular service, or activity contributing to a service, is essential to a community. Among the approaches that are used explicitly (or implicitly) to determine this are: the degree to which the service is taken up or consumed by members of the public (i.e. ubiquity can be a proxy

---

[97] See the discussion in Helm and Yarrow (1988).

[98] Boyd (2018) argues that: 'relations of reciprocity and fairness in exchange are at the very core of the public utility idea' and that 'prices are more than signals; that they are also relationships and that price relationships can be coercive'.

[99] Energy services, for example, are described by the European Union in Directive 2019/944 as being: 'essential services to guarantee a decent standard of living and citizens' health'. Similarly, the UK Parliament (House of Commons, 2018) describes energy as 'a special and essential service ... an unavoidable necessity of life, which amounts to a significant portion of household budgets'.

[100] Perceptions of essentiality can differ across generations. Van de Walle (2009) found that, in the UK, older people did not see water as a service which should be guaranteed to everyone, presumably on the basis that they are more familiar with shortages from their youth, while younger, less educated males tended to see access to TV channels as an essential service.

for essentiality); whether interruption to, or absence of, the service would endanger life health or personal safety for the whole or part of a population; whether a service has a special 'general interest dimension', such that these services cannot be entirely left to market forces (i.e. without regulation) because of a need to protect certain values or deliver outcomes in the overall public good;[101] whether the cost of the product/service constitutes a relatively large proportion of an average consumer's or household's budget and public opinion about the importance or essentiality of the service.[102]

Access to certain services is also seen as important to ensure social inclusion and stability. For instance, regulators in Europe have spoken of the risk of consumers who are unduly denied access to energy services becoming 'economically, socially and culturally isolated'.[103] This is consistent with the view that there is a 'social licence to operate' between consumers and providers of essential services, and that public utility firms should explicitly recognise the 'public value' of the services they provide.[104] In broad terms, this refers to the idea that providers of essential services need to act in ways which go beyond compliance with the requirements of formal regulation in order to maintain legitimacy and the trust of a community. For example, in order to maintain their social licence, providers must act in ways consistent with societal expectations about the environment and sustainability (particularly important in the energy and water sectors) and fairness, which is sometimes captured in the idea that they should ensure that 'no consumer is left behind'.[105] Although the idea of a social licence has recently gained prominence in regulatory discourse, the underlying concept has long been recognised. For example, in the USA, private providers of utility services have been described as 'public servants', which brings with it the responsibility to ensure that charges are reasonable.[106]

The practical implication of this rationale for regulation is that matters of fairness and affordability are unavoidable and regulators must consider them in applying regulatory

---

[101] In the EU, for example, Services of General Economic Interest (SGEI) are economic activities which deliver outcomes in the overall public good that would not be supplied (or would be supplied under different conditions in terms of quality, safety, affordability, equal treatment or universal access) by the market without public intervention (EC, 2011a).

[102] Using 1997 data, Van de Walle (2009) found that, in Europe, water was considered an essential service by around 88 per cent of respondents, followed by electricity (80 per cent), gas supply (56 per cent), telephone services (24 per cent) and rail transport services (10 per cent). Postal services did not feature as an essential service.

[103] ACER/CEER (2014). Similarly, the EU Directive 2019/944 notes that access to energy services can 'enhance social inclusion', while the California Public Utilities Commission (CPUC) (2018) states that 'energy access is critical to economic and social stability and well-being'. The UK telecommunications regulator (Oftel, 1997) has previously described telecommunications services as so fundamental 'that all people, whoever or wherever they are, must have access to a certain basic level of telecommunications facilities and services if they are to participate fully in modern society'.

[104] Cave and Wright (2021) focus on the wider concept of the public value in the utilities sector, which includes considerations of distributional, innovation and other impacts of customer/citizen welfare. Using the water industry in England and Wales as an example, they suggest that the task of discovery and delivery of the public value could be delegated to the regulated firm.

[105] See Roberts (2018) and Sustainability First (2020). In Britain, energy providers are required to ensure that they 'treat customers fairly' under the regulatory framework.

[106] Justice Brandeis in the opinion in *State ex rel. Southwestern Bell Telephone Co. v. Public Service Commission*, 645 S.W.2d 44 (1982) famously observed that: 'The investor agrees, by embarking capital in a utility, that its charges to the public shall be reasonable. His company is the substitute for the state in the performance of the public service, thus becoming a public servant.'

policy.[107] In some jurisdictions, this requirement may be explicit – such as in the USA, where there are legal requirements to ensure that rates are 'fair' or 'just and reasonable'.[108] In developing countries, while there may be no formal requirement to take account of affordability, there is often an implicit reality of the tension between allowing firms to set full cost recovery tariffs and the ability of a large proportion of the population to access the services on an affordable basis. In all jurisdictions, the need to take account of matters of affordability reflects the reality that the prices of essential services form a substantial part of most household budgets and for this reason are never far from the top of the politician's agenda, or from the front page of the newspapers. Politicians can face intense pressure to 'do something' if prices for these services are not affordable,[109] and increases in prices for essential services can often lead to public protests or feature prominently in election campaigns.[110]

2.3.2 Multiple Interpretations of 'Fairness'

Perceptions of fairness are particularly important in setting price structures, which involves determining how costs should be allocated across different users. While it has long been recognised that the principle of fairness should influence regulated price structures,[111] what is less clear is how this outcome can be achieved in practice. This reflects the multiple interpretations of fairness. For example, a fair price might refer to: a price which is the same for all consumers who trade under the same conditions; a price calibrated to a consumer's ability to pay; a price that is not exploitative and reflects the underlying value of the service (as in competition law in some jurisdictions); a price that allows the provider to recover the full costs of supplying the service (including sunk investments) or, alternatively, only the incremental costs that a consumer imposes on a provider; or a price which is predictable and limits consumer exposure to frequent, unexpected or arbitrary price shocks.

One approach to assessing whether prices are fair is to focus on the extent to which prices faced by one group of users are being subsidised by another group of users. While some argue that the only 'fair' prices are those which are free from cross-subsidy, others set bounds on what is a fair price based on the principle that the prices paid by each customer

---

[107] A concern for 'fairness' is widely acknowledged by regulators in many parts of the world. For example, the England and Wales water regulator (Ofwat, 2011) has noted: 'Water customers ... need to know that the bills they pay are fair and legitimate.' Similarly, State Public Utility Commissions in the USA often refer to their remit as involving ensuring that 'regulated utilities offer their services to the public at a fair price' (Alabama Public Utilities Commission, 2013) and that citizens receive 'adequate, safe, and reliable public utility services at a fair price' (Public Utilities Commission of Ohio, 2013).

[108] Boyd (2018) provides a useful historical account of how the idea of the just price influenced public utility regulation in the USA during the late nineteenth and early twentieth centuries, and was fundamental to battles over rate regulation.

[109] As Braeutigam (1989) observed: '[F]rom a political point of view, perhaps the most significant feature of regulation is that it redistributes income, creating winners and losers, thereby shaping interest groups and coalitions'. Stern (2017) argues that affordability and fairness have affected governments and regulatory agencies since the introduction of railway regulation in the UK and USA after 1850.

[110] Increases in prices for essential services such as transport, communications and energy have triggered protests in recent years in countries such as Brazil, Chile, Greece, Indonesia, Malawi, South Africa, Spain, Turkey and the UK. Similarly, in Australia, Germany and the UK, energy prices and the cost of broadband infrastructure have featured prominently in recent election campaigns.

[111] In his classic analysis, Bonbright (1961) emphasised a need for specific rates to be 'fair' in how they apportion the total costs of service among different consumers. Berg and Tschirhart (1988) and Baumol (1986) also discuss issues of fairness in rate structures.

group should at least cover the incremental costs of supplying the service to that group, b[ ]
no one group should pay a price which is higher than the stand-alone costs of supplyi[ ]
the service.[112] Others suggest that a fair price structure is one where the allocation of cos[ ]
reflects the extent and nature of system use by different types of customers.

A different approach to assessing the fairness of prices is suggested by work in beha[ ]
ioural economics. Specifically, it is proposed that the fairness of a particular price or stru[ ]
ture can be assessed by comparing it to a relevant precedent or reference transaction. Th[ ]
builds on the idea, discussed in Chapter 7, that people often assess gains or losses relati[ ]
to a reference point. In this context, a reference point might refer to a price and level [ ]
profit that both parties (the firm and consumers) consider legitimate and which have bee[ ]
determined before each party made any sunk investments. The fairness of a specific price [ ]
then assessed by how much it deviates from a customer's reference price and a firm's re[ ]
erence profit.[113] If a firm raises a price arbitrarily (say, to exploit market power arising fro[ ]
excess demand) and this increases its profits above the reference level of profit, this will [ ]
considered unfair.[114] However, if the firm faces an increase in its costs and has to raise i[ ]
price in order to maintain its reference level of profit, this will be considered a fair increa[ ]
in the price. Put differently, whether an action is considered to be 'fair' or not is assessed [ ]
changes relative to the reference state rather than changes in absolute terms.

Implications for Regulation

While distributive equity, fairness or affordability considerations can help to explai[ ]
why regulatory practice can sometimes deviate from some of the principles of regula[ ]
tion described in later chapters of this book, this rationale for economic regulation raise[ ]
a number of questions and practical challenges. First, it raises a fundamental questio[ ]
about whether economists have the right tools or a clear set of 'distributive weights' t[ ]
allow for fairness and equity considerations to be dealt with in a systematic and non-a[ ]
bitrary way in regulatory decision making.[115] Put differently, is an economist best place[ ]
to determine what is a 'fair', 'just' or 'reasonable' price, or is that task potentially mo[ ]
suited to the tools and techniques of political science, law (where matters of fairness an[ ]
justice feature prominently), or moral philosophy?[116]

---

[112] See Baumol (1986), who framed the issue of fairness using the concept of compensatory pricing.

[113] See Kahneman, Knetsch and Thaler (1986), who note, for example, that it might be considered fair to allow a firm to raise prices as necessary to maintain its profits at the reference level. However, it would be unfair for the firm to use its market power to raise prices and thereby alter the terms of reference transaction to the direct expense of consumers.

[114] Frey and Pommerehne (1993) find that 80 per cent of respondents to a random survey considered a pric[ ] rise to cope with excess demand to be unfair.

[115] See Schmalensee (1979). Contrast with Baumol (1986), who suggests that fairness is tractable to economic analysis, including in areas such as monopoly pricing and peak or congestion pricing. More generally, Berg and Tschirhart (1995) submit that 'most regulators do not view the world as economists view it' and that the justification that it is too difficult to balance efficiency concerns against other objectives 'does not seem to dissuade regulators from a strong focus on equity or fairness'.

[116] Stigler (1980) once remarked that, despite the fact that 'economists have no special, professional knowledge of that which is virtuous or just', they are often asked to 'deliver confident and distinctive advice to a society that is already well equipped with that commodity'. Indeed, the question of what constitutes a 'just price' dates back to Aristotle (who condemned monopoly on the basis that it resulted in prices that were 'unjust') and also featured prominently in the work of the social and moral philosopher Saint Thomas More in the sixteenth century (who established the concept of oligopoly). Se[ ] Schumpeter (1954) and Boyd (2018).

Second, it is not obvious how considerations of fairness are, or should be, balanced against tenets of economic efficiency in practice. For example, as discussed in Chapter 4, efficient forms of price discrimination to recover fixed costs typically involve applying higher mark-ups to customers with relatively low price elasticities. In some cases, this may result in a disproportionate burden on those sectors of society whose demand is inelastic precisely because they have no real alternatives (i.e. working people who would pay higher transport fares).[117] This presents a very real trade-off for a regulator between economic efficiency and equity considerations in approving or disallowing particular pricing structures.[118] For these reasons, some argue that economic regulation should focus principally on matters of efficiency, and that considerations of inequality or distributive justice are best dealt with through the taxation system or other redistributive policies.[119] While some argue that this focus on efficiency has led modern regulatory theory to ignore wider equity and affordability considerations, this potentially overlooks the fact that much of the analytical work in recent decades has actively sought to identify the trade-offs that confront policy makers, and to assess the potential impacts of different regulatory policies (in terms of who might gain, and lose, from specific policies).[120] Indeed, as we will see in Part II, many important theoretical contributions openly acknowledge the social and political aspects of different regulatory policies.[121]

2.4 RATIONALES BASED ON THE CHARACTERISTICS OF THE CONSUMER

A final rationale for economic regulation, which has gained prominence in recent years, and is discussed in detail in Chapter 7, relates to the characteristics of the consumers who purchase and consume certain products or services. Within this general rationale, there are three broad sub-rationales that inform the need for regulation of certain services.

First, it is argued that, because consumers may have access to poor or limited information, or suffer from decision-making biases, there is a role for regulation to protect consumers from being exploited, and to otherwise 'correct' for these imperfect aspects of consumer decision making. As described in Chapter 7, research in behavioural economics suggests that effective decision making by all, or by a large proportion of, consumers may be hampered by cognitive limitations associated with processing the information, or by

---

[117] See Baumol (1986) and Helm and Yarrow (1988).

[118] Zajac (1978) usefully describes the 'policy maker's dilemma' in setting efficient pricing structures.

[119] Schmalensee (1979) articulates the position more fully that regulators should not 'have to decide conflicts between efficiency and other goals'. Vickers (1997) argues that regulators should not take distributional considerations into account except where specific duties concerning distributional aspects have been given to them by government or parliament. See also Kahn (1971), while, as noted above, Posner (1971) focused on regulation becoming politicised and what he termed 'taxation by regulation'. In contrast, some argue that the need to use regulation as a means of addressing distributive concerns reflects the challenges in developing and implementing a first-best taxation policy as a means of redistribution.

[120] As Tirole (2017) notes, economics has been important in guiding reforms to encourage natural monopolies to adopt 'socially efficient prices'.

[121] In their comprehensive review, Armstrong and Sappington (2007) acknowledge that 'in practice, retail tariffs often are dictated by historical, political, or social considerations'. Similarly, Laffont and Tirole (2000) consider the merits of the argument that differentiated pricing structures (such as Ramsey-Boiteux prices) should be banned for reasons of 'fairness'. See also Laffont (2005) in the context of developing economies, where affordability is obviously a major consideration.

other behavioural and decision-making biases (such as 'the status quo bias', 'anchoring' 'the over-optimism bias' or 'the endowment effect'). Behavioural economics research has also shown how firms who recognise these cognitive limitations can have incentives to exploit them, including through the way they present information, the timing of offers and other tactics.[122] In these circumstances, it is argued that some form of regulation is justified by the need to address such limitations/biases and prevent such exploitation.[1] However, as we see in Chapter 7, attempts to use regulation to address consumer biases (such as attempts to simplify decision making by limiting the number of tariffs on offer) can sometimes backfire and have an opposite effect to that intended.

In addition to regulatory protections aimed at all consumers, regulation can be targeted at protecting specific groups of consumers who are seen to require additional support and protection. This includes consumers sometimes labelled as 'vulnerable', such as those on low incomes or with special needs. While this rationale reflects fairness or social welfare considerations, there is also an economic dimension to it: if a significant proportion of consumers are, for various reasons, inactive (i.e. they lack access or information, or are otherwise not sufficiently equipped to make choices in their own best interests), the active consumers may need to work harder to ensure that competition is effective.[1] However, in practice, it can be difficult to draw bright line boundaries or quantify the size of different vulnerable groups, which can make it challenging to design policies that target a specific group of consumers as vulnerable along some dimension.[125] There is also a longstanding debate about whether more targeted public policies better address problems of financial hardship and vulnerability than economic regulation.[126] Despite these questions, the protection of vulnerable consumers now forms part of the economic regulatory frameworks for some essential services in Europe, the UK, Australia and other jurisdictions.[127]

A third rationale for regulation based around the characteristics of consumers can arise where markets are changing or evolving and where consumers may find it difficult

---

[122] For example, if suppliers recognise an over-optimism bias in certain categories of consumer, such as in relation to the ability to pay bills on time, or expected levels of future consumption of the service, this can create incentives for exploitation (such as high penalties for late payment of bills, and tariff plans which allow for setting a fixed price for a threshold level of consumption but apply a much higher price for exceeding that threshold).

[123] See Ofgem (2011b).

[124] Specifically, if a significant proportion of consumers are not actively engaging in a market this will reduce the competitive pressure that is placed on suppliers.

[125] Concepts such as vulnerability are multi-faceted, and many consumers can potentially be vulnerable on some measures but not on others. For example, a wealthy, older urban consumer may not be digitally savvy, while, in contrast, a young digitally savvy consumer might have limited financial resources. Ofgem (2019) lists a range of other vulnerable characteristics.

[126] Such as policies which introduce lifeline rates or tariffs that subsidise the costs of services to certain low-income users, and are a feature of energy and telecommunications markets in many jurisdictions.

[127] The energy regulators in Britain and Australia have published 'vulnerability strategies', while the UK communications regulator and the water regulator in England and Wales have both published vulnerability guidelines. In the EU, Member States are required to take appropriate measures to ensure that there are adequate measures in place to protect 'vulnerable consumers' in energy markets, although Member States have discretion to apply this concept according to their own situation.

to assess options and make informed choices. For example, in many countries, various regulations were introduced in retail markets at the time of the initial restructuring of communications and energy markets in the 1990s. These regulations were, in part, introduced in the newly opened markets to help achieve the policy objective of promoting competition, for example, to encourage active searching and switching by consumers and to build trust in the competitive market. Similar arguments are arising in the context of the development of digital platforms, where, as discussed in Chapter 13, some consumers may be unaware or unfamiliar with how digital platforms can potentially influence users to spend more time on the platform, share data, or use techniques that lead consumers to take actions that do not accord with their preferences or expectations. An obvious question in relation to this specific rationale is at what point the regulation will no longer be warranted, which we discuss in the next chapter. A traditional view is that, as markets become more established, and consumers more familiar with new products and with exercising choice in these markets, this rationale for regulation becomes less compelling. However, as we will see in later chapters, even if some consumers become familiar with a new market context over time, a substantial number of other consumers may remain 'disengaged',[128] and the re-introduction of regulation has sometimes been premised on a need to protect these consumers.[129]

2.5 IMPLICATIONS OF THE DIFFERENT RATIONALES FOR REGULATION

This chapter has set out various accounts for why economic regulation might exist in certain industries, ranging from normative rationales based on the need to achieve efficiency or control monopoly power, to accounts that focus on the interaction of different interest groups in society and how each group's interests may give rise to a demand for regulation and influence its form. We have also considered other explanations for regulation based on issues of fairness and distributive equity and the need to protect particular types of consumers. Each of these accounts can potentially explain at least some aspects of regulation as it is applied and observed in practice. Yet, no single account seems to explain fully why regulation exists in the form that it does in practice. No doubt this reflects the fact that regulation of specific industries often reflects a combination of rationales, such as the presence of economies of scale and scope, a concentrated supply structure that affords firms significant market power, affordability concerns and the influence of different interest groups.

While it is not possible to pinpoint a single unified and comprehensive rationale for economic regulation, the recognition of different rationales and purposes is, itself, potentially illuminating. It may, for example, help to explain why it is that we observe multiple objectives in the remits of some economic regulators, rather than a single objective, such

---

[128] A body representing EU regulators noted: 'Nearly 25 years since the earliest residential electricity markets were liberalised in Europe, the default pre-disposition of many electricity consumers, who theoretically have a right of choice, is to do nothing and/or choose the utility that they know'. See CEER (2021).

[129] See, for example, the re-introduction of price controls for retail energy markets in the UK and Australia discussed in Chapters 9 and 10.

as to improve economic efficiency, as the traditional normative theory of natural mon
opoly might suggest. It also helps to explain some of the apparent tensions that exi
between regulatory precepts of efficiency and regulatory practices such as cross-subsi
isation. While a recognition that economic regulation is shaped by a range of economi
political and social concerns may reflect reality, it can give rise to challenges in applyir
regulation in practice. As we will see in later chapters, a lack of clarity about the purpos
of economic regulation can sometimes make it difficult for regulators to understand wha
they should be doing and, to paraphrase Alfred Kahn's quote at the start of this chapte
what action is 'really necessary'.

DISCUSSION QUESTIONS

1. What are the key characteristics of natural monopolistic industries and what assump
    tions underpin the concept of natural monopoly?
2. What are some examples of industries that display natural monopoly characteristic
    and why might economic regulation be introduced in these industries?
3. What are some of the dilemmas that confront regulators when introducing pol
    cies to improve efficiency in industries, such as public utilities, that display natura
    monopoly characteristics?
4. What are some of the arguments for regulation based on concerns about monopol
    power? How does it differ from the efficiency rationale for regulation?
5. What are some of the arguments for regulation in industries that display stron
    network effects, such as large digital platforms? Explain some of the factors that ar
    relevant when considering whether to apply economic regulation in these settings.
6. What is the distinction between normative explanations for why we regulate an
    alternative accounts of regulation?
7. Why might a firm want to be subject to economic regulation, and what factors coul
    determine whether it is successful in acquiring regulation for an industry?
8. Do you agree that private interests rather than public interests better explain wh
    certain industries are subject to regulation, and the form that regulation takes
    Explain your reasons.
9. Why might the economic regulation of certain services need to consider distribu
    tional considerations, such as fairness and affordability? What are some practica
    challenges in regulating to address distributional considerations?
10. Why might the characteristics of the consumers of some services give rise to a nee
    for economic regulation? Can you provide examples?

3

Is Economic Regulation Inevitable?

The last chapter discussed various rationales for economic regulation, including the conventional rationale based on the close correspondence between aspects of the cost profile of certain industries and the economic notion of natural monopoly. Price and conduct regulation follow, on this account, to address the allocative inefficiencies of naturally monopolistic industry structures, while entry regulation aims to address concerns about productive inefficiency. However, are these the only ways to 'control' or 'influence' the conduct of firms? This chapter addresses this question by exploring various alternatives to traditional economic regulation that have been proposed, or implemented, in practice. Eight main 'alternative' approaches are considered, including: competition for the market (also sometimes referred to as franchise competition); contestability and the threat of entry; state ownership and operation; reliance on competition law; industry restructuring with deregulatory policies applied to competitive parts of the production chain; a shift towards distributed networks; and the use of negotiated agreement/settlements between firms and their customers.

3.1 COMPETITION FOR THE MARKET

The 'competition *for* the market' or franchise competition approach involves potential providers of a (monopoly-type) service bidding competitively to provide the service exclusively on pre-specified terms and conditions for a specific period. Potential suppliers make a bid at the price they would charge for supplying the service (including providing a minimum level of quality), and the winning supplier is that which offers to serve the market at lowest price. In these circumstances, the competitive price is seen to be achieved as the outcome of the bidding process,[1] and in principle the need for ongoing regulation is eliminated.[2] The government's role is limited to selecting the winner of the bidding process and managing the rules of the competition.[3]

---

[1] Two important assumptions underlie this reasoning. Firstly, all of the bidders must have access to the necessary inputs at competitive prices; and secondly, bidders must not be able to collude (i.e. the bids submitted are assumed to be competitive).

[2] The modern origins for such an approach can be traced to Demsetz (1968), who challenged the link between conditions of natural monopoly and the need for economic regulation, particularly to the extent to which such regulation is premised on concerns associated with monopoly pricing. This built on the principle of 'competition for the field' established in the nineteenth century by Chadwick (1859).

[3] Crain and Ekelund (1976) compare the views of Demsetz and Chadwick on the need for a contract enforcement body as a necessary accoutrement to this approach. Shleifer (2011) argues that, because courts can be expensive, unpredictable and biased, the public may seek regulation. Marques (2017) also argues for combining concession contracts with a regulator.

The 'competition for the market' approach relies on an important distinction betwee scale economies in production, and the number of potential bidders willing to supply product at an initial bidding stage. While natural monopoly industries may always dis play scale economies in supply (meaning it will be most efficient to have only a singl supplier), this does not mean that there are not a number of possible rival bidders willin to compete to be that single supplier.[4] In situations where a single product is supplied, an there are a sufficient number of bidders to make the bidding process competitive, the win ning bid should reflect the average cost of supply, allowing the winning firm to make normal profit, while avoiding the concerns associated with excessive pricing.[5] In additior the 'competition for the market' approach is seen as offering a number of benefits com pared to traditional economic regulation. First, it can reduce information costs associate with regulation by eliminating the need for a regulator to collect ongoing informatio relating to average costs and demand. Second, it can mitigate issues associated with poc or perverse investment incentives that have plagued some traditional forms of economi regulation, such as over-investment under rate of return regulation. Third, it can provid positive incentives for efficiency and innovation insofar as the franchisor or concession aire benefits from any cost savings while it operates the contract.

While the idea of 'competition for the market' is analytically powerful, there have bee equally powerful critiques of the approach. On the theoretical front, critics observe tha while the approach might limit the scope for monopoly pricing, it does not guarantee tha prices charged will be efficient (i.e. at marginal cost) and will promote public welfare In addition, it is argued that the approach does not easily generalise to multiple produc settings[7] and is based on specific implicit assumptions about the legal regime and prop erty rights.[8] Factors such as the timing of the tenders (staggered or synchronous) and th relative size of the franchise area can also impact the practicality and effectiveness of th approach.[9]

Perhaps the most significant criticism of the approach is that, like many large an complex commercial contracts, it can be difficult to specify precisely all of the terms o a franchise or concession contract at the outset. Contractual incompleteness can be a important source of instability where uncertainty is significant and the contract is of long duration.[10] The approach has also been criticised for paying insufficient attentior to the potential for litigation and other costs in managing the contract. Some argue that once the wider practical aspects of the competition for the market approach are allowe

---

[4] Demsetz (1968) notes that there is often more than one supplier of public utility services in nearby markets.

[5] There is a substantial literature on the design of 'optimal' franchise bidding schemes: Riordan and Sappington (1987) develop a 'menu of contracts' approach to maximize consumer welfare; Laffont and Tirole (1987) look at the characteristics of auctions for government projects; and Harstad and Crew (1999) and Chao (2015) examine the use of auctions to award franchises and for renewals.

[6] See Telser (1969). Although see Demsetz (1971).

[7] See Braeutigam (1989) and Baumol, Panzar and Willig (1982). Although a basket approach – involving bids to supply a combination of services – can be used.

[8] See Priest (1993).

[9] See Iossa, Rey and Waterson (2022) on timing and Chong, Saussier and Silverman (2015) on franchise size.

[10] See Hart (2017).

for (such as potential artificial or obscure initial award criteria; monitoring performance and execution of the contract; difficulties in adapting fixed prices to changes in costs; issues with quality standards; and the potential for *ex post* opportunistic behaviour), similar problems and challenges typically associated with traditional economic regulation can emerge.[11] Empirical studies have identified various common problems that have plagued some franchise and concession contracts in practice, including around: the quality of franchise contract design; the bidding and re-bidding process; implementation, adaptation and renegotiation; and bidder parity at the re-franchising stage.

Such criticisms appear to have influenced perceptions of the potential of 'competition for the market' as a full substitute for ongoing economic regulation.[12] Some argue that franchise bidding is, at best, a useful short-run to medium-run solution to the natural monopoly problem and that, over time, the traditional problems of regulation may emerge. In these circumstances, continuous oversight through a regulatory mechanism may be preferred to the administration of a long-term franchising contract.[13] However, proponents of the competition for the market approach insist that competing bids will generate better estimates of cost and demand than regulatory commissions, noting that the approach is most effective when used in low-complexity settings (i.e. not, for example, for complex utilities such as electricity and telephones), and for reduced durations, both of which are seen as more favourable to the contractual approach.[14]

Despite circumspection by some economists about the use of the competition for the market approach, variants of the approach have been widely used in practice for well over a century. In the nineteenth century, gas supply in Paris was put up for 'competition for the whole field',[15] and municipal franchising for utility services was common in the USA.[16] As we will see in Part III, franchises and concession contracts remain a feature of the rail and water industries in many parts of the world, particularly, but in no way exclusively, in transitional and developing economies.[17] Indeed, the competition for the

---

[11] See Williamson (1976), who looked at cable TV licences, while Goldberg (1976) and Crocker and Masten (1996) examine the difficulties associated with the contracting approach in the public utilities. In contrast, Zupan (1989) concludes that franchise bidding works much better than is commonly believed, while Prager (1990) finds that the scope of *ex post* opportunistic behaviour by franchisors is not terribly severe. Littlechild's (2002) study of the electricity distribution contract for London Underground is described as, in many respects, being the opposite to the case study used by Williamson (1976). Nash (2016) and Prosser and Butler (2018) critically examine rail franchises, Yvrande-Billon (2006) focuses on franchising for urban transport, while Cruz and Marques (2013) focus on the problems of monitoring and supervision.

[12] In an early analysis, Armstrong, Cowan and Vickers (1994) concluded that competitive bidding is not likely to be very useful for the capital-intensive activities in the public utility industries, and that the complexities associated with the administration and management of the contract will require ongoing regulatory involvement.

[13] See Williamson (1976). Priest (1993) argues that the distinction between an approach based on the administration of a franchise contract and traditional forms of regulatory oversight is one of degree rather than kind. Marques (2017) and Ruiz Diaz (2017) consider the need for ongoing regulation for public–private partnership (PPP) contracts.

[14] See Gómez-Ibáñez (2003).

[15] See Chadwick (1859).

[16] See Jarrell (1978).

[17] Gómez-Ibáñez (2003) suggests that a preference for the use of concession contracts in the developing world may reflect a perception that courts are less vulnerable to political influence than the regulatory agencies.

market approach is being introduced for new offshore and onshore electricity infrastructure (see Chapter 9); for new water and wastewater infrastructure (Chapter 16) and for payments systems infrastructure (Chapter 12) in some jurisdictions.[18] Policies are also being introduced with the aim of intensifying competition *for* the market in the area of digital platforms (Chapter 13).

3.2 CONTESTABILITY AND THE THREAT OF ENTRY

Another alternative to traditional economic regulation (typically referred to as 'contestability theory' or 'contestable markets theory') argues that in some settings the threat of *potential* competition, through new entry, could be sufficient to control and influence the behaviour of firms operating in a naturally monopolistic industry. The main conclusion of this work was that, in conditions where 'entry is absolutely free and exit is absolutely costless', a market is 'perfectly contestable', and regulation may be unnecessary. This is because any economic profit, or unnecessary cost, of the monopoly firm will instantly be seized upon as an earnings opportunity for an entrant who can seamlessly enter the industry, seize the above-normal profit opportunity, and, if necessary, rapidly exit without any impediment.[19] Critically, proponents of contestability theory argued that, in markets approximating perfect contestability, 'matters can be left to take care of themselves' and that even a single firm in a natural monopoly setting will perform in a competitive fashion if that market can be readily contested.[20]

While this argument potentially undermines the need for traditional economic regulation, three strong assumptions underlie the theories' conclusions.[21] Firstly, it is assumed that potential entrant firms can, without restriction, serve the same market demand and use the same productive techniques as an incumbent. Secondly, it is assumed that there are no sunk costs (all entry costs can be recovered). Thirdly, it is assumed that an entrant can establish itself in a market *before* the incumbent firm adjusts its price (i.e. strategic entry deterrence is not possible). If these assumptions hold, then the theory suggests that any attempt by an incumbent firm to charge a price in excess of the average costs of supply will be seized on by competitor firms to enter the market, attract business through undercutting on price and make an above-normal profit. Ultimately, this process will drive prices down towards average cost, after which the entrant will exit the market with its profit intact.[22]

---

[18] The UK government is actively encouraging this approach for new infrastructure investments. See BEIS (2022).

[19] Baumol (1982a), one of the proponents of the theory, described the process in the following way: 'every deviation from good behaviour instantly makes them [the monopoly firm] vulnerable to hit-and-run entry'.

[20] See Bailey (1981) and Baumol and Willig (1986).

[21] Stiglitz (1987) observes: 'If the contestability doctrine were correct, it would radically alter our attitudes toward antitrust policy. It would imply that an important class of circumstances – those in which there was a natural monopoly (or oligopoly) because of increasing returns – which previously had been thought to give rise to market failure (Pareto inefficiencies), need not or would not do so. Government intervention, if this view were correct, would not be required, even when there was only one firm or a few firms.'

[22] For this reason, this approach is sometimes referred to as 'hit-and-run' entry and exit, or as 'ultra-free' or 'hyper-free' entry and exit.

Crucially, the mere *threat* of entry by other firms is expected to constrain price to the average cost level in contestable markets, implying that *potential* competition is almost as important a control of monopoly power as *actual* competition in contestable markets. This is because, aware of the potential for entry, an incumbent firm will always set its prices so that *no* profit opportunities exist which could attract entry into the market (sometimes referred to as 'shadow entrants'). On this basis, it is argued that the imposition of entry restrictions may be undesirable where a market is contestable because it will remove the threat of these shadow entrants.[23]

Contestability theory caused considerable excitement and controversy when it was first developed in the early 1980s, and much has been written about it. Perhaps the most potent criticism of contestability reasoning is that its assumptions are unrealistic given that most industries are characterised by some lag in entry or exit and the presence of at least some unrecoverable sunk costs. The assumption that an entrant can establish itself in a market faster than an incumbent can respond is seen as implausible,[24] as is the 'total entry' assumption.[25] Others have questioned why there would be a 'reserve army' of 'phantom entrant' firms sitting idly somewhere with under-utilised factors not receiving their opportunity costs.[26] The theory's conclusions have also been shown to be sensitive to small changes in assumptions. For example, allowing for even a short time lag in entry (which allows the incumbent to respond) coupled with a small amount of sunk costs can change the outcomes of the reasoning dramatically.[27] On these bases, it has been argued that contestability theory is of limited applicability to many real industries, and that claims that policy lessons can be derived from the theory are 'naive and premature'.[28]

Proponents of contestability theory argue that such criticisms are misguided. The notion of perfect contestability, it is argued, is not an approximation to the real world, but rather a normative standard against which market outcomes can be judged, in much the same way as the notion of perfect competition.[29] Moreover, as a benchmark case, contestability is said to have a wider application than perfect competition, and can potentially assist in delineating the appropriate scope of regulation, by highlighting those industries or activities which should be candidates for deregulation or the removal of other forms of government intervention.[30]

What can be said, then, about the contestable markets approach as an alternative to traditional economic regulation? Proponents of the theory argue that it is most applicable

---

[23] See Baumol (1982a).

[24] See Schwartz and Reynolds (1983) and Brock (1983).

[25] That is, the assumption that an entrant can immediately duplicate and replace in entirety the incumbent firm in terms of size, technology, product array, brand loyalty and other advantages. See Shepherd (1984).

[26] Cairns and Mahabir (1988).

[27] See Stiglitz (1987), who finds that 'the presence of arbitrarily small sunk costs can serve as an absolute barrier to entry and make potential competition completely ineffective as a discipline device'.

[28] Shepherd (1984). See also Gilbert (1989) and Schwartz (1986).

[29] See Baumol (1982a). However, as Spence (1983) observes, unlike perfect competition, where it is assumed that efficient prices result from the presence of a large number of price taking firms, contestable markets theory replaces price taking with rapid entry and exit.

[30] See Baumol and Willig (1986) and Berg and Tschirhart (1988). As discussed in Chapter 13, debates about the need for regulation of digital platforms often focus on the extent to which the *threat* of entry is a sufficient constraint on the behaviour of existing large incumbent platforms.

to industries where capital is highly mobile, which increases the threat of entry. Airlin
networks, trucking and bus networks are all seen as being characterised by relatively eas
entry and exit (an ability to transfer planes/buses/trucks onto specific routes),[31] and ar
industries where capital is fixed, but not sunk (so-called 'capital on wheels' or 'capita
on wings').[32] However, as discussed in Chapter 15, empirical studies of the deregulation
of the airline sector in the USA found little support for the predictions of contestabilit
theory, and entry of new competitor airlines on specific routes proved difficult and not a
'ultra-free' as the theory might have predicted.[33] Recent studies on the use of 'hit-and-run
strategies for online price comparison sites (which display ultra-low sunk costs) reach
similar conclusion and find that entry only occurs in a segment of the market.[34] Mor
generally, contestable markets theory is seen to have limited applicability to the publi
utility industries given that the core network activities in these industries are highly
capital intensive and involve specific investments in immobile and durable assets (suc
as electricity wires, gas pipelines, water pipes and telephone cables, etc.).[35] For these cor
network activities, the level of sunk costs is likely to be large, the possibility of rapid entr
and exit limited, and the resultant potential threat of entry relatively weak.

In summary, while the contestable markets approach is not generally seen to offer a ful
substitute for traditional economic regulation, contestability theory itself has been influ
ential on the design of regulatory policies in some industries.[36] As discussed in Chapters
and 11 (particularly Box 11.2), the concepts of 'stand-alone cost' (SAC) and 'incrementa
cost' that were developed as part of contestability theory are used as the basis for determin
ing price ceilings and floors in some industries, such as railroads and telecommunications

3.3 STATE OWNERSHIP AND OPERATION

A third alternative to traditional economic regulation is state ownership and operation o
public utilities.[37] While a range of political and other reasons can motivate state ownership, the basic economic reasoning is that a firm in state control will not be motivated by
private gain, and can be directed to act in a socially desirable way: for example, to promote economic efficiency by setting prices that are not in excess of costs, and by making
efficient and timely investment decisions.[38]

---

[31] See Bailey and Panzar (1981) and Baumol and Willig (1986).

[32] See Brock (1983). Baumol and Willig (1986) reconsider the claim that airlines are 'capital on wings'.

[33] See Gilbert (1989) and Baumol and Willig (1986).

[34] See Haynes and Thompson (2014).

[35] Williamson (1985) observes that '[m]arkets are thoroughly contestable ... if asset specificity is presumed
to be absent', and asset specificity provides a link between contestable markets theory and transaction
cost economics, each approach looking at the phenomena of asset specificity but 'through opposite ends
of the telescope'.

[36] This use is broadly consistent with the views of Baumol and Willig (1986), two of its main proponents,
who suggest that the main contribution of the theory was as a guide for regulation, rather than an
argument for the elimination of regulation.

[37] The term 'state ownership' is used in a general way to capture government ownership of public utilities
at different levels of government such as federal, state/regional or municipal ownership. However, state
ownership can take numerous forms, which has implications for the level of control that a government
can exercise.

[38] Gray (1940) described as a 'delusion' the view that private privilege can be reconciled with public
interest by the 'alchemy of regulation'.

Historically, state ownership was a common method for controlling and influencing the conduct of the public utility industries in many parts of the world during the twentieth century.[39] There was a general movement away from the state provision of public utility services in a number of countries during the 1980s and 1990s (notably in Chile, the UK, Argentina, Australia and parts of North America). However, as we will see in Part III, state ownership, including partial ownership, remains widespread in the water, energy and transport sectors.[40] Indeed, in some jurisdictions where privatisation was introduced, there has been a process of 're-municipalisation' or 're-nationalisation',[41] while in other jurisdictions there is growing political pressure from some quarters for past privatisations to be reversed and for all utilities to be brought back into state ownership.[42] Others argue that, in some sectors, state-owned national and regional 'system operators' should be established to take on various public duties, with the regulator performing merely residual duties.[43] In some jurisdictions, newly developed public utility services – such as the broadband networks in Australia and New Zealand – are being provided via state ownership rather than private means.[44] Finally, some countries – notably China, Russia, Brazil, India and Singapore – have provided significant support to their state-owned enterprises with the aim of expanding their operations globally in key public utility and regulated sectors.[45]

The relative benefits of state ownership *vis-à-vis* private ownership of the public utilities is one where considerable debate exists, and where different political and social views can cause sharp divisions and develop into wider ideological debates about the relative merits of free markets versus collective or socialised forms of ownership. Economic analysis has typically focused on two areas: the incentives that exist under the different forms of ownership, particularly for cost reductions and innovation; and whether state-owned utilities are relatively more efficient than privately owned utilities that are subject to regulation.

3.3.1 Incentives and Performance under Different Ownership Structures

The incentives created under different forms of ownership have been examined at length in the economic literature.[46] As a whole, this literature suggests that ownership structure

---

[39] A notable exception being some utility industries in the USA.

[40] See OECD (2017c). Estache (2020) finds that pure private provision is not common, and provides rough estimates that, globally, electricity generation is private in around 40 per cent of countries, electricity distribution in 7 per cent of countries, airports in 3 per cent of countries, and rail in 5 per cent of countries (with 29 per cent mixed), and water is provided under private–public partnerships in 22 per cent of countries. More generally, Bernier, Florio and Bance (2020) claim that state-owned enterprises make up roughly 10 per cent of the world economy.

[41] Bel (2020) discusses municipalisation in the water industry, while Chapter 14 in the present book discusses re-nationalisation in the British rail industry.

[42] For example, in the 2019 UK general election, the Labour party campaigned for all privatised public utilities to be brought under state ownership, thus reversing the privatisation programme of the 1980s and 1990s. This is consistent with what Parker (2021) describes as the transferring backwards and forwards between the state and private sectors throughout history.

[43] Helm (2017) argues that such system operators could be charged with the delivery of various high-level outputs (relating to the security, maintenance and enhancement of the networks) in a cost-effective way.

[44] Avilés (2020) discusses the more general shift towards government-led network deployments in telecommunications.

[45] This is sometimes referred to as 'state capitalism'. See Megginson (2017).

[46] See Vickers and Yarrow (1988), Bös (1991), Newbery (1999) and Florio (2013).

can affect the incentives of management, and therefore the performance of the publ utilities. One perspective used to assess the impact of incentives – known as the 'princ pal–agent' model – focuses on the incentives created where there is a principal (the sta in the case of public ownership, the shareholders in the case of private ownership) ar an agent (the management of the public utility) who may have different objectives, ar access to information.

Generally speaking, the principal's objectives are different for state-owned utiliti than for regulated private utilities. For privately owned utilities, the principal's prima objective will be profit maximisation, whereas, under state ownership, the principal objective, at least according to the public interest perspective, might be to maximise eco nomic welfare as well as the achievement of other socially desirable objectives (the publ interest).[47] The agents (management) of state-owned and private utilities could also hav different objectives,[48] and face different incentives. While managers of private firms ma be incentivised by profit-related pay or stock options and face the scrutiny of share holders, managers of state-owned utilities may have fixed salaries and not face extern shareholder review.[49]

There are, however, well-known challenges associated with analysing the incentive created under state ownership. Central among these is the difficulty of articulating 'public interest' objective with any precision. The state may have a multiplicity of objec ives, some of which may not relate to economic welfare, and some of which may be i conflict.[50] These objectives can change frequently, from one administration to the nex or because of wider policy changes.[51] State-owned utilities may set prices below thos which would be set by a privately owned utility and below profit-maximising levels.[52] Fo example, the state may require that end-user prices for services such as water and electr city be affordable and kept at low levels (even below cost) to address distributional con cerns rather than efficiency considerations. Or prices charged to one group of custome

[47] Cui and Sappington (2021) model access pricing in a mixed oligopoly where private firms maximise profit while public enterprises maximise the sum of their profit and consumer surplus.

[48] Although managers of public monopolies may be motivated by wider considerations/factors. Vickers an Yarrow (1988) record the view of Herbert Morrison (an influential figure in the post-war nationalisation movement in Britain) that the board and officers of public corporations 'must regard themselves as the high custodians of the public interest'. Similarly, Schmalensee (1979) observes that, in the USA, early discussions of public corporations were based on the expectation that they would be managed by 'hard working, competent idealists'.

[49] See Parker (2021). Although, as Sappington and Stiglitz (1987) observe, the government may have a greater ability to directly intervene to influence the behaviour of management in state-owned firms. Arblaster and Zhang (2021) discuss how the Australian and New Zealand governments seek to influence the strategic direction of the state-owned air navigation service providers in those countries by issuing regular letters, called 'Statements of Shareholder Expectations', to which the providers respond with 'Statements of Intent'.

[50] Indeed, when we speak of 'the state' as the principal, we refer to a number of constituent entities and institutions, including the general public, elected politicians and civil servants in the responsible government departments, each of which can be expected to have their own particular objectives and agendas.

[51] See Megginson and Netter (2001) and IMF (2020).

[52] Newbery (1999) argues that there may be 'less pressure to get prices right in the public sector, and specifically to keep them from going too low'. Peltzman (1971) shows how prices set by government firms would be lower than for private firms, and finds empirical support for this by comparing data on government-owned and privately owned electric utilities in the USA. See also the discussion of water pricing in Chapter 16 in the present book.

(for example, rural customers) may be subsidised by other groups of customers (urban customers) in an effort to win political support.[53]

Questions also arise in relation to the incentives of those responsible for monitoring performance of a state-owned utility. Unlike private ownership, where the principals have a pecuniary interest in monitoring management performance closely, politicians and civil servants may have limited incentives to monitor efficient managerial performance if it is not closely related to their own objectives. To address these concerns, state-owned utilities can be subject to oversight by an economic regulator in some jurisdictions. However, as discussed below, this can give rise to tensions between the economic regulator (pursuing one set of objectives) and a relevant ministerial department (pursuing a wider set of objectives).

3.3.2 Public Utility Ownership Structures: Empirical Investigations of Performance

An extensive empirical literature compares the relative performance of state-owned utilities and regulated privately owned utilities. These studies use different approaches to assess relative performance. One approach involves international comparisons of the relative performance of public utilities in a given industry where some firms are state-owned and some are privately owned. A second approach involves examining the performance of state-owned and privately owned utilities within the same country.[54] A third approach involves examining the performance of public utilities that have shifted from state to private ownership, utilising data from the privatisation wave that began in the 1980s and 1990s in many countries.[55]

It is 'notoriously difficult' to draw a comprehensive conclusion on the effects of privatisation from these studies.[56] Some surveys of the effects of privatisation across all sectors of the economy (not just public utilities) report increases in performance following privatisation.[57] Among the explanations for why the financial and operating performance of firms might have increased after privatisation are the following: performance was improved by the restructuring policies and divestments made prior to privatisation, and greater capital market discipline;[58] privatised firms are less controlled by trade unions, creating more flexibility and improvements in labour productivity;[59] there are greater incentives under private ownership to innovate and adopt new technologies;[60] and private

---

[53] See Shleifer and Vishny (1994).

[54] For example, Meyer (1975) and the studies listed in Newbery (1999).

[55] Prominent early examples include Galal, Jones, Tandon and Vogelsang (1994), Newbery and Pollitt (1997) and Andrés, Guasch, Haven and Foster (2008). Estache (2020) provides an excellent recent survey.

[56] Estache (2020) identifies a range of methodological shortcomings of this research, and also notes that (implicit and explicit) ideological biases can impact assessments.

[57] See Megginson and Netter (2001) and Estrin, Hanousek, Kočenda and Svejnar (2009), who find the effect of privatisation to be mostly positive in Central Europe, but more diverse in the Commonwealth of Independent States (CIS) and China. More recent surveys include Megginson (2017) and Parker (2021), who concludes that 'in many cases privatisation has indeed improved economic performance, providing better services and at lower cost to the consumer. In some but not all cases, economic growth and public welfare have benefited'.

[58] See D'Souza, Megginson and Nash (2001).

[59] See Bishop, Kay and Mayer (1994).

[60] Shleifer (1998) has pointed to the importance of the incentives for innovation created under private ownership where the full rewards of innovation can be directly derived by owners and managers alike.

sector participation can reduce corruption, and its effects, leading to improved econom[ic] performance.[61]

Other studies are less positive about the effects of privatisation and report a mo[re] nuanced picture, particularly in the context of developing countries. An important con[c]lusion of these studies – in both developed and developing economies – is that a shi[ft] from state to private ownership does not automatically improve performance.[62] Rathe[r] differences in the performance of privatised firms can depend on: what was privatise[d,] how it was privatised, and whether the privatisation was total or partial; the characteris[-]tics of the owners (especially if foreign owners); the extent of competition; and the reg[-]ulatory regime under which it was privatised.[63] A recurring finding is that effective stat[e] regulation can be critical to performance and to the achievement of efficiency gains,[64] an[d] that, while there may be initial efficiency improvements, these are not always sustained.[65]

Privatisation can also have important distributional impacts, including in terms o[f] access to services, prices and affordability, quality of service and employment.[66] While th[e] stated aim of some privatisations (such as in Britain) was to widen access to share owner[-]ship of public utilities, in some jurisdictions privatisations have had the opposite effect o[f] concentrating substantial wealth in a small number of individuals.[67] Some privatisation[s] have also been accompanied by substantial price/tariff increases,[68] and 'cream-skim[-]ming', whereby the private operator focuses only on serving the richest areas.[69] Som[e] surveys conclude that private sector participation in the provision of water, electricit[y] and telecommunications in developing countries does not seem to have led to significan[t] improvements in access to these services or quality.[70]

The mixed picture on the efficiency and distributional effects of privatisation is reflecte[d] in the specific industries discussed in Part III. In the electricity sector, while some stud[-]ies report broadly positive efficiency effects of privatisation, the impacts on access an[d] affordability were often smaller than expected, and lack of access to electricity continue[s] to be a problem in many developing countries.[71] In water, some studies reported initia[l]

---

[61] Imam, Jamasb and Llorca (2019). However, Auriol, Crampes and Estache (2021) note that delegating the provision of essential services to private operators can also bring risks of corruption, including in procurement processes.

[62] See Estrin and Pelletier (2018) and Estache (2020).

[63] See Radić, Ravasi and Munir (2021) and Estrin and Pelletier (2018).

[64] See Parker (2021), Balza, Jimenez and Mercado (2013) and Bortolotti, Fantini and Siniscalco (1998).

[65] Estache (2020) notes that the initial period of reforms often led to cost savings from employment cuts. However, in some cases the initial static efficiency cost savings may have been achieved at the expense of dynamic efficiency (i.e. under-investment).

[66] Estrin and Pelletier (2018) and Estache (2020) consider this issue.

[67] Notable examples are telecommunications privatisation in Mexico and the process of privatisations pursued in Russia and some Eastern European countries where assets were substantially undervalued when transferred into private ownership.

[68] Mohamad (2014) notes that, in Mexico, Argentina and South Africa, there were substantial increases in tariffs following telecoms privatisations.

[69] Estache (2020).

[70] Thillairajan, Mahalingam and Deep (2013) and Balza, Jimenez and Mercado (2013). Bagnoli, Bertomeu-Sanchez, Estache and Vagliasindi (2021) find evidence that public operators are more likely than private ones to address social needs.

[71] See Blagrave and Furceri (2021) and Bensch (2019). Jamasb, Nepal and Timilsina (2017) conclude that the welfare gains of privatisation in developing countries have mostly benefited the domestic and foreign-owned producers and that the gains from reforms have not trickled down to consumers. Rossi (2021) finds that privatisation of electricity distribution companies in Latin America has improved efficiency.

improvements in performance from private sector participation but found that these have not always been sustained, and that in some cases efficiency was higher under state operation.[72] There is also some evidence that private water operators have charged higher prices and, in some jurisdictions, managed to extract large dividends,[73] while private participation has shown limited (and often negative) impact on access to water.[74] In rail and telecoms, the experience of privatisations is also mixed, with some studies concluding that privatisation has resulted in higher prices and minimal changes in quality[75].

In summary, empirical surveys of the effects of privatisation indicate that a change in ownership does not, of itself, increase performance or distributional outcomes (such as widening access to essential services or more cost reflective prices). Rather, the key finding of this work is that the context in which privatisation is introduced and the institutional environment in which it takes place (including critically the extent of regulatory or state oversight) are critical to whether privatisation will be more or less effective than state ownership.[76]

3.3.3 The Coexistence of State Ownership and Independent Regulation

In some jurisdictions, state-owned utilities are subject to the same forms of price and conduct regulation as privately owned firms. In this situation, state ownership and regulation are not alternatives or substitutes for one another, but coexist as methods of control. Examples of public utilities that are fully, or partly, state-owned but still subject to independent regulation of their activities include: rail networks in the UK and Europe; water supply in Scotland and Brazil; electricity transmission and distribution networks in Australia, New Zealand and the Republic of Ireland; air navigation services in Australia; and water and wastewater services in many parts of the world (including some states of the USA).

The use of an independent regulator to oversee the activities of a state-owned firm can be a response to the perceived inadequacy of the shareholder (the government) in its oversight of the utilities. Where the state-owned enterprise also operates in some competitive markets (e.g. it is integrated and provides both core network and retail services), an independent regulator can also be a mechanism for signalling that the state-owned enterprise will not benefit from undue advantages or preferential treatment (e.g. by shifting costs from commercial to non-commercial activities); in other words, there is competitive neutrality. The use of an independent regulator can also be motivated by a desire to outsource the technical oversight functions to a specialist body that is familiar with applying particular regulatory methods. One problem that can arise when there is an independent regulator overseeing a state-owned entity is that the firm can receive conflicting signals

---

[72] Bel (2020). Buafua (2015) finds no evidence of improved technical efficiency for private versus public water suppliers in sub-Saharan Africa.

[73] As discussed in Chapter 16, this has been a particular issue with the privatisations in England.

[74] See Estache (2020) and Bel (2020).

[75] Mohamad (2014) discusses telecommunications. See Chapter 14 of the present book for a comparison of the Japanese and British experiences of rail privatisation.

[76] As discussed in Chapter 8, the existence of an independent and separate regulator is seen as particularly important to the effects of privatisation. Bagnoli, Bertomeu-Sanchez, Estache and Vagliasindi (2021) conclude that there is little evidence that ownership matters for low-income households, and that the focus should be on the continued inability of regulators to cause firms to deliver on social goals.

from its owner (the government) and the regulator; in short, the firm may work for two masters.[77] In this respect, effective coexistence arrangements may require a clear separation of roles and responsibilities between the government (in its capacity as owner) and the regulator.[78]

3.4 RELIANCE ON *EX POST* COMPETITION LAW

Another method for controlling and influencing the conduct of public utilities involves no *ex ante* (or up-front) restrictions on price or conduct, but rather a reliance on *ex post* (after the fact) competition law (or antitrust law) that applies across all sectors of the economy. Although the nature of competition law varies across jurisdictions, these laws typically offer two possibilities for controlling the conduct of firms: prohibitions on 'exclusionary' conduct (i.e. refusing access to other parties on reasonable terms) and 'exploitative' conduct (i.e. setting prices too high).

Where a public utility occupies a dominant position and refuses access to its facilities (or engages in practices with similar effect),[80] this may constitute a 'refusal to supply' in contravention of competition law. In these circumstances, the public utility is treated in a similar way to other firms who operate 'essential' or 'bottleneck' facilities in an economy; that is, inputs or facilities which others (including rivals) need to access on reasonable terms in order to be able to operate in an industry.[81] The precise definition of a 'bottleneck' or 'essential' facility is controversial in many jurisdictions, and the notion has, at times, been given a wide interpretation by some courts.[82] In Europe, access to the local loop in telephony, and access to electricity transmission and distribution networks, have at different times been classified as an essential facility under European competition law, and therefore subject to provisions addressing abuses of a dominant position.[83]

---

[77] For example, the government as owner may desire a wide network coverage, low prices and significant forward-looking investments to ensure the security of the network (as in energy), to embrace technological change (in telecoms) or meet environmental targets (water). The regulator, on the other hand, may be focused on eliminating subsidies and on the scrutiny of costs, as well as the necessity of any investments.

[78] Peci, D'Assunção, Holperin and de Souza (2017) describe some of the challenges of 'regulating inside the government', drawing on the example of water regulation in Brazil. Mountain (2014) finds that government ownership undermined the authority and independence of regulation in the Australian electricity sector.

[79] Breyer (1982) discusses the possibility of using the antitrust laws to 'police' unregulated markets. See also Vogelsang (2012, 2017), who compares the main properties of regulation and competition policy in terms of solving 'bottleneck' problems, noting that the choice between sector-specific regulation and general competition policy always involves trade-offs.

[80] Such as imposing unfair trading conditions, or charging prices that are unreasonable insofar as they are not economically viable for the buyer to agree to.

[81] The development of the essential facilities doctrine in the USA followed the 1912 judgment in *United States v. Terminal Road Association* in which interconnection requirements were imposed on railroad operators to provide access on reasonable terms. In Europe, there is a general principle that companies who hold a dominant position must not refuse to supply their goods or services to either competitors or customers if the refusal would have a significant effect on competition which cannot be legitimately justified. The leading decision here is *Commercial Solvents* (1974).

[82] To capture, among other things, a football stadium, the New York Stock Exchange and a multi-day ski-pass scheme.

[83] See Motta (2004).

In some jurisdictions, most notably in Europe, competition law can also be used to prohibit public utility firms that occupy a dominant position from abusing that position by charging excessive prices (e.g. prices which do not reflect the underlying economic value of the service). However, there is considerable controversy as to when a dominant firm's price should be held to be excessive, particularly given the difficulties associated with price–cost comparisons, especially in multi-product contexts, where fixed costs need to be attributed to different products and services supplied by the firm.[84]

In principle, using *ex post* competition law to control and influence the conduct of public utilities appears to have several attractive properties. Firstly, it is unnecessary to establish permanent sector-specific regulators in the different public utility industries. The only requirement is a competent and suitably resourced competition authority. Secondly, there is no need to establish *ex ante* rules relating to pricing and other aspects of conduct, which can arguably minimise the scope for regulatory error. Thirdly, this approach allows for government interventions in an industry to be targeted, occurring only when 'problems' arise. Finally, the approach may reduce so-called regulatory 'game playing' and other strategies developed by public utilities to get around the *ex ante* rules that have been established.

There are, however, several potential limitations to relying solely on competition law to control the conduct of public utilities. Firstly, while an *ex post* approach might encourage firms not to charge excessive prices, and to provide access to firms that require its inputs on reasonable terms, it does nothing to ensure that the resultant prices and access terms will be *efficient* in economic terms (although, as noted in Chapter 2, the relevance of this concern depends on how the task of regulation is conceived). Secondly, while the approach might address concerns about monopoly pricing and refusal of access, it does not necessarily address other concerns associated with monopoly identified in Chapter 2, such as the potential for the utility to degrade quality, or be productively inefficient. These types of criticisms are similar in nature to those levelled at the administered contract view of regulation,[85] and, for this reason, a reliance on competition law is unlikely to be attractive to those who view the rationale for regulation as fully eliminating allocative and productive inefficiencies. Finally, there are practical concerns about regulating public utilities in this way. In many jurisdictions, there are not insignificant difficulties associated with enforcing competition law and prosecuting infringements using these laws. In particular, the time and cost associated with acting under the relevant competition laws can be significant.[86] Moreover, lengthy litigation can result in prolonged periods of adverse harm associated with the conduct of a firm abusing its position.

An approach based largely on using competition law to control the public utility industries was applied in New Zealand in the 1990s. This involved the application of

---

[84] See also Box 11.2 on the difficulties in applying price–cost tests.

[85] Goldberg (1976), for example, notes that the effectiveness of regulatory arrangements should be judged on 'reasonableness' grounds rather than on a pure efficiency basis. However, he recognised that: 'Such a nondefinition of efficiency will not sit well with most economists. Having scaled the dizzying heights of optimality, it is difficult and a bit anticlimactic to have to plumb the murky depths of reasonableness.'

[86] Although these costs have to be weighed against the costs associated with standard *ex ante* regulatory approaches.

economy-wide competition law principles, along with some additional 'light-handed' measures to guide the conduct of the public utility firms. It is generally considered not to have been successful,[87] and has since been replaced by a more standard *ex ante* regulatory approach. The experience in other jurisdictions, such as the UK and Australia, where regulators have both competition law powers and traditional *ex ante* regulatory powers, has shown that, in practice, there has been a clear tendency to address issues in the public utility industries using standard *ex ante* regulatory measures rather than competition law.[88] *Ex ante* regulation and *ex post* competition law are sometimes seen as complements rather than substitutes. In the European telecommunications industry, for example, economic regulation (in the form of setting access prices) and the abuse of dominance provisions can be applied concurrently.[89] This can, however, be contrasted with the position in the USA, where antitrust law will not generally apply where a government agency (such as a regulator) has powers to enforce access to a facility.[90]

As discussed in Chapter 13, the question of whether competition law is sufficient to influence and control the conduct of large digital platforms, or whether more traditional forms of economic regulation are required, is one actively being debated in many countries. There is also continuing discussion about whether competition law should replace sector-specific regulation in the telecommunications sector to enhance product innovation.[91]

Ultimately, as with all the alternatives to standard regulation considered in this chapter, the merits of a reliance on competition law to control and influence the conduct of public utility firms must be considered relative to the costs and benefits associated with traditional *ex ante* economic regulation. The distinction between core network activities and competitive activities is again likely to be important here. It may be inappropriate to rely solely on competition law for the core network activities in public utility industries given that adverse conduct might be expected to occur frequently and the potential damage from such conduct could be substantial (i.e. a large number of users would face excessive prices for an extended period). However, as discussed in Section 3.5, for activities where there is competition, a transition from the *ex ante* regulation of these activities to a reliance on *ex post* competition law will be more appropriate as competitive pressures develop.

3.5 'DEREGULATION' POLICIES AND A RELIANCE ON COMPETITION

A fifth alternative to traditional economic regulation of the public utility industries is to implement policies that change the industry structure by allowing competitive entry in some parts of the production chain, and rely on competition in those parts to operate as a control on the behaviour of firms. These policies are sometimes referred to collectively as

---

[87] See Bertram and Twaddle (2005). Evans, Grimes, Wilkinson and Teece (1996) provide an early assessment.

[88] See, for example, NAO (2010) and Decker and Gray (2012).

[89] The European Courts have upheld decisions relating to access pricing (both too high and too low) in the telecommunications industry even though, in some cases, there was government involvement in setting the terms of access to those facilities. See *Deutsche Telekom v. Commission* (2008) and *France Télécom v. Commission* (2009). See also Vickers (2010) for a discussion.

[90] See *Verizon Communications, Inc. v. Law Offices of Curtis V. Trinko LLP* [2004].

[91] See Vogelsang (2017).

'deregulation' policies[92] and involve the withdrawal of *ex ante* restrictions on entry (such as statutory monopoly or duopoly policies) and on prices (i.e. removal of price controls), as well as the introduction, in some implementations, of a regulatory approach that seeks to actively encourage competitive entry into these activities.[93] Given that such 'deregulation' policies are usually only applied to those non-core network activities in the production chain where competition is feasible, in most public utility industries this approach tends to coexist with traditional forms of regulation for core network activities.[94]

3.5.1 Removing Entry Restrictions and Introducing Competition

The question of when entry restrictions to certain activities should be removed relates directly to the specific rationale for economic regulation of these activities in the first place. As discussed in Chapter 2, a widely accepted rationale for public utility regulation, and entry restrictions in particular, is to reap the potential benefits associated with economies of scale in activities where the demand and cost conditions resemble those of a natural monopoly.[95] Adopting this rationale, the existence of entry restrictions should be unnecessary for activities in the production chain that do not have natural monopoly-like characteristics.

While this might imply that determining which activities should be opened to competition is relatively straightforward, the precise conditions under which competition is preferable to regulated monopoly in the public utility industries can depend significantly on context.[96] Monopoly and 'the competitive process' are sometimes seen as examples of different incentive mechanisms, each of which can be more or less imperfect, and each of which is susceptible to various market and regulatory failures.[97] Moreover, even for activities where competition is considered more efficient than regulation, a separate issue is how these efficiency gains are distributed between firms and consumers.

Notwithstanding these points, it is generally widely accepted that, where competition can be introduced, and is effective, it can improve economic welfare. In particular, competition is seen to create incentives for firms to be more responsive to consumer needs, to reduce costs, and to invest and innovate to produce new products and services.[98] Hayek (1968)

---

[92] As noted in Chapter 1, the term 'restructuring policies' is generally preferred to 'deregulation' because most firms operating in public utility industries typically remain subject to a raft of regulatory requirements, ranging from licensing requirements to complying with specific standards of behaviour.

[93] As Vogel (1996) notes, 'deregulation' policies often result more accurately in 're-regulation', that is, new rules tailored to issues that arise under the new form of industrial structure.

[94] Winston (1993) discusses broader deregulation policies introduced across a number of industries (such as the airline, bus, trucking, and banking and finance industries) in the USA since the 1970s.

[95] This includes, in particular, a desire to restrict 'cream-skimming' by entrants.

[96] Mankiw and Whinston (1986) examine the conditions under which the number of entrants in a free-entry equilibrium is excessive, insufficient or optimal, and note that there can be a bias towards excessive entry in imperfectly competitive homogeneous product markets because of the business stealing effect. Armstrong and Sappington (2006) refer to other factors such as: the information conditions in the industry; the ownership structure; and the institutional capacity of the regulatory agency. As Vickers (1995) observes: 'Competition seems very well in practice, but it is not so clear how it works in theory.'

[97] See Armstrong, Cowan and Vickers (1994).

[98] Laffont and Tirole (2000) argue that entrants often offer a differentiated service not offered by the incumbents, may provide existing services at a lower cost, and may force the incumbent to produce more efficiently.

famously characterised competition as a discovery procedure which generates new fac
and information and new ways of doing things, all of which cannot be predicted *ex ante*.
Over time, this process of discovery, through trial and error, is said to lead to a tendenc
for goods and services to be produced that consumers most value, utilising the best tech
nologies and production methods.[100] An implication of this conception of competition
that, where competition is allowed to develop (for example, in one activity in a productio
process), it can often lead to wider dynamic changes and benefits not anticipated at th
time competition was introduced.[101] Finally, as compared to regulation, there are variou
informational advantages associated with competition; in particular, it avoids the problem
associated with an asymmetry of information between a regulator and a regulated firm.
It is argued that the greatest potential gains from competition can arise where: the indus
try scale economies are limited relative to demand; the regulator has limited resource
would suffer from a severe information asymmetry and has a limited ability to comm
to policies; and cross-subsidisation of the incumbent's supplies is not critical, or can b
achieved through other means.[103] At a more practical level, developments in informatio
and communications technology (ICT) are seen to be a critical factor in allowing policies t
introduce competition to be implemented by allowing, among other things, processes suc
as remote metering, trading and settlement platforms, and customer switching protocols.

As discussed in Part III of this book, policies directed at removing entry barriers an
introducing competition have been introduced in many developed countries over the pas
four decades for various public utility activities (with the notable exception of activi
ties in the water and wastewater industries).[105] In implementing these policies, a chal
lenge for regulators has been delineating precisely the boundary between those activitie
where effective competition may develop, and those where industry-specific regulatio
will remain necessary. In many industries, this task has been complicated by the need t
account for technological change (in particular, developments in ICT) and the associate
changes in the cost structure of, and demand conditions for, services.[106] For example, tech
nological changes may alter cost conditions by reducing the benefits of scale economie

---

[99] Hayek (1968, as cited in Snow 2002, page 9). More generally, this definition is seen as important in
characterising competition as a *procedure* or *process* rather than an end state of affairs.

[100] See Littlechild (2002) for a more general discussion of the 'Austrian approach' to competition.

[101] Kahn (2002) describes such developments in the context of the deregulation of the US airline industry,
where the policy 'took on a life of its own, like the proverbial snowball rolling down a hill – the
mirror image of the tendency of regulation, once undertaken, to become increasingly pervasive and
thoroughgoing'.

[102] Armstrong, Cowan and Vickers (1994) discuss the relationship between competition, incentives,
information and innovation.

[103] See Armstrong and Sappington (2006).

[104] Abel and Clements (2001) observe that the opportunity for competition in US local telecommunications
markets followed the advent of fibre-optic cable and computerised switching technologies.
Similarly, Anderson, Hollander, Monteiro and Stanbury (1998) note that, in Canadian energy and
telecommunications, far-reaching technological changes made competition possible in areas which had
previously been ruled out because of natural monopoly characteristics.

[105] Examples of the activities in the public utilities that have been opened to competition in some
jurisdictions include: electricity generation and electricity retailing; gas extraction, storage and retail
activities, and in some cases gas pipeline competition; most telecommunications services, including
long-distance and local calls; competition between airlines and between different providers of passenge
and freight railway services in some jurisdictions; and a more limited set of activities in the water and
wastewater industry, notably non-household retail activities in Britain.

[106] Although, as Kahn (1971) observes, this challenge has confronted regulators for many years.

in some industries (such as the development of localised or distributed generation in the electricity industry), or may lead to the development of competing networks which utilise a different technology (such as mobile or cable networks in the telecoms industry).

Even for those activities where competition is seen as both feasible and beneficial, various impediments may exist to its development, which may suggest an ongoing role for a regulator. For example, it is common in the public utility industries for there to be a former incumbent monopoly supplier with an established position in the relevant market where competition is being introduced. The incumbent may have certain advantages, including long-term supply contracts (often agreed on favourable terms) for key inputs (such as upstream gas supply or wholesale electricity generation), which limits the amount of input capacity available to entrant firms, or it may enjoy a strong brand image and awareness.[107] This can limit the ability for entrants to build their own brand and reputation, exacerbate the customer inertia that can exist for some public utility services (see Chapter 7), and raise the switching costs associated with changing suppliers (such as the need to install new equipment, etc.). Overall, these factors can impede the effectiveness of market opening policies, creating a potential role for a regulator to mitigate the effects of such barriers and to 'promote competition'.[108]

One approach that has been adopted by regulators is so-called 'asymmetric regulation', which involves firms operating within the same sector or activity being subject to different levels of regulation, or different forms of regulatory restraint.[109] There are various possible forms of asymmetric regulation, including: asymmetric price regulation, including requiring incumbents to adopt particular price structures or limiting their ability to reduce prices in response to entry;[110] allowing entrants to charge asymmetrical mark-ups;[111] different reporting and quality standard requirements for incumbent and entrant firms; restrictions on the ability of incumbent firms to expand and diversify their activities into related competitive activities; as well as placing requirements on incumbents to act as a supplier of last resort. Supporters of asymmetric regulatory policies argue that they can act as a powerful policy instrument, changing the incentives of potential entrants and benefiting consumers.[112] However, others object to asymmetric regulation

---

[107] This may be aided in some jurisdictions by the use of the name of the country or state before the service, which was particularly common in the public utility industries, such as British Telecom, British Gas, Deutsche Telekom, Deutsche Bahn, France Télécom, Électricité de France, Telecom New Zealand, etc.

[108] Armstrong, Cowan and Vickers (1994) critically assess a number of ways in which potential entrants could be given assistance to overcome entry barriers, including through: a direct financial subsidy; an indirect subsidy, by exempting entrants from certain obligations placed on the incumbent; special pricing restrictions and/or obligations on the incumbent; measures to reduce search and switching costs (such as internet comparison sites, and number portability in telecommunications); and introducing restrictions on further entry (such as a duopoly policy). Armstrong and Sappington (2006) also set out policies which could potentially assist in fostering long-term industry competition.

[109] According to Haring (1984), Richard Schmalensee is said to have introduced the term 'asymmetric regulation' in 1984 when referring to the Federal Communications Commission's use of more stringent regulations for AT&T than its rivals. Kahn (1998) discusses this approach as a variant of the more general 'infant industries' argument in economics.

[110] Howell (2011) describes how, in New Zealand, the incumbent telephone operator had been subject to obligations which bound it to particular retail tariff structures and levels.

[111] See Peitz (2005) and Di Pillio, Cricelli, Gastaldi and Levialdi (2010), who discuss the use of asymmetric charges in Europe, while Armstrong and Wright (2008) discuss their use in the UK.

[112] Peitz (2005) argues that, by allowing entrants to charge asymmetrical mark-ups in telecommunications markets, entry is more attractive, and therefore likely, and this can intensify competition over the long term.

on the basis that it can distort price signals and impose asymmetric cost burdens, which can create bias towards particular firms or technologies and lead to productive efficiency losses which can reduce welfare.[113] In addition, it can create competitive distortions among operators, and impact on the incentives on firms to invest and innovate.[114] In particular, is suggested that the incentives for investment by the incumbent or regulated firm can be dampened, while the incentives for entrants to invest can be excessive.[115]

3.5.2 Removing Price Regulation

A separate issue to when regulatory restrictions on entry should be removed, and competition allowed, is at what point that competition is sufficiently effective to allow for the removal of *ex ante* restrictions on prices. Again, the question of when such a transition should occur is linked to the underlying rationale for price regulation. As noted in Chapter 2, price regulation is often introduced on the basis of a need to avoid the harm that arises if firms who occupy a position of monopoly (or substantial market power) charge prices significantly in excess of relevant costs. According to this rationale, the removal of *ex ante* price regulation might be warranted where a firm is assessed as being sufficiently constrained from exploiting its market position by either actual or potential competition.[116]

A difficulty for regulators, however, is determining the point at which competitive pressure is sufficient to remove any restraint on prices: Is it when a certain number of competitors exist? Or when the market share of the incumbent firm falls below a particular threshold (say, 60 per cent)? Or must the regulator be satisfied that there are no significant barriers to entry into a particular activity? The core difficulty faced by regulators is that, while the two end states – full monopoly and effective competition – have relatively well-defined characteristics and imply various clear regulatory responses, the appropriate regulatory response for points in between these two end states depends significantly on context. Further, in reaching a decision, the regulator needs to balance the risks associated with an erroneous assessment of competition in a market in either direction. If the regulator applies price regulation to the incumbent firm longer than necessary, this can inadvertently hinder the development of effective competition.[117] However, if the regulator removes price regulation too rapidly, this can allow the incumbent firm to exploit its market power to the detriment of consumers.

---

[113] See Schankerman (1996).

[114] Armstrong and Wright (2008) argue that if incumbents are regulated while new entrants are not, this can lead to a distorted pattern of supply, and refer to the example of the UK termination rates where the entrant had a weekday termination charge almost double that of its regulated rivals.

[115] Abel and Clements (2001) refer to a 'general consensus' that 'asymmetric regulation induces inefficient entry and investment'. More generally, Armstrong and Sappington (2006) argue that the costs of asymmetric regulation often outweigh its benefit; Laffont and Tirole (2000) warn against the (often poorly understood) dangers of 'asymmetric regulations'; and, finally, Vogelsang (2006) attributes some of the failures of US liberalisation policy to 'heavy handed asymmetric regulation of incumbents with respect to end users'.

[116] This is, of course, subject to qualification, and depends on the relative costs and benefits associated with the *ex ante* and *ex post* approaches to controlling market power, as discussed in the previous section.

[117] As discussed in Chapters 5, retaining price controls in industries where effective competition has developed is argued to be distortionary and to reduce overall welfare. See Littlechild (2002) and Yarrow, Decker and Keyworth (2008).

Regulators and policy makers have employed different methods to assess the extent of competition in markets opened to competition, and whether *ex ante* price regulation can be withdrawn. One approach, set out by regulators in Britain in the early 2000s, has been to categorise at a general, conceptual, level the various stages of the transition from monopoly to effective competition.[118] Four stylised stages exist in this transition. First, there is a 'pre-entry stage' where there is no competition, and the incumbent holds close to a 100 per cent market share. The second stage is known as the 'pre-competitive market stage', where there is some entry, but incumbents enjoy substantial legacy advantages (branding, reputation, etc.) and hold a position of strong market power (i.e. dominant or 'super-dominant' in competition law terms). In the third stage, referred to as 'established competition', the incumbent's market power is significantly reduced (although they may still hold a strong or dominant position in competition law terms), the entrants are typically gaining established reputations, and competition is assessed as sufficiently effective in terms of restricting the ability of the incumbent firm to harm consumers. The final stage in this stylised transition is 'effective competition'. In this state, competition between all firms is intense, and, critically, such competition is able to constrain the conduct of all firms operating in the market, including the incumbent operator. At this stage, the risks associated with a firm charging high prices are no greater than that which exists in other sectors of the economy, where *ex post* competition law is generally regarded as a sufficient safeguard.

The practical question for regulators is to identify when the market has shifted from the pre-competitive stage to the established competition stage, bearing in mind that, as competition develops, the risks of consumer harm associated with exploitation of market power decreases, but the risks to competition (and consumers) associated with keeping *ex ante* price regulation in place tends to increase.[119] One approach adopted by regulators in this respect is to periodically assess the extent of market power (and, by implication, the degree of competition) that a firm holds in the supply of particular public utility services. For example, as discussed in Chapter 11, the regulatory framework that applies to the European telecommunications industry requires periodic assessments of market power to allow for a gradual transition from *ex ante* price control to *ex post* competition law over time.[120] Similarly, as discussed in Chapter 15, the decision whether to apply price regulation to airports in some jurisdictions (notably the UK and Australia) can involve

---

[118] This work has been attributed to work by Michael Beesley for the British Energy Regulator (Ofgem): see Yarrow, Decker and Keyworth (2008).

[119] As discussed in Chapter 5, while price regulation is motivated by a desire to restrict the ability of the incumbent firm to exercise any residual market power, the retention of price controls in markets which are competitive can have distortionary effects, and may even be inimical to the development of competition. For example, where price regulation keeps the incumbent's regulated price above what would otherwise be the market clearing level, this could act as a 'focal point' for tacitly collusive price setting and lead to higher prices. Conversely, where the incumbent's regulated price is kept below what would otherwise be the market clearing price, this can act as a disincentive for entry and investment.

[120] In brief, the approach requires National Regulatory Agencies (NRA) in each European Member State to analyse a set of markets for electronic communications that may need *ex ante* regulation. This process involves three steps: (1) the definition of the relevant geographic and product market; (2) a 'significant market power' (SMP) assessment; and (3) a decision on 'remedies'. Firms assessed as holding a position of SMP in a relevant market may be subject to various 'remedies', including *ex ante* price controls, while those assessed as not holding SMP will only be subject to the provisions of general competition law.

a periodic assessment of market power.[121] Finally, as discussed in Chapters 9 and 1
electricity generators and long-distance gas pipeline operators in the USA are sometim
subject to specific tests to assess the extent of market power they hold; with only tho
operators who can demonstrate they do not hold market power[122] entitled to charge ma
ket-based rates (and not subject to standard regulation).

Even where, based on an assessment of competition in a market, there is a polic
decision to move away from the full application of (up-front) *ex ante* price regulatio
various forms of transitional measures may be introduced, including the use of trans
tional price controls, or requirements that a former incumbent make available a standa
offer or product at a specific price. More generally, there may remain a higher level
regulatory oversight of firms formerly subject to price regulation, and additional regul
tory obligations may apply to those firms over and above generally applicable competitic
law.[123] For example, firms may be subject to additional price monitoring requirements;
be restricted in the number and types of tariffs they can offer;[125] or be required to supp
information to consumers in particular ways.

In sum, the possibility of changing the industry structure to introduce competitio
where feasible, represents another alternative to traditional regulation for some activiti
in the public utility industries. As discussed in Part III of this book, this approach has bee
widely adopted across a number of public utility industries. However, the implementatio
of this approach has, in practice, proven no small exercise in many jurisdictions. Indee
some argue that 'regulating for competition has proved much more difficult than regul
tion of monopoly'.[126] The challenges derive, in part, from the fact that such policies ca
significantly affect the distribution of rents, and the allocation of risks, among differer
parties, including consumers, incumbent providers and new entrants,[127] and also from th

---

[121] In addition, when assessing whether retail price controls should be retained in some energy markets, regulators have sometimes conducted a one-time assessment of the degree of competition in those marke and, on this basis, decided whether *ex ante* price controls should be removed. See AEMC (2008, 2013).

[122] 'Market power' here is defined as the ability to raise price above competitive levels without losing substantial business (see Federal Energy Regulatory Commission Order 697 (FERC, 2007)); or, in the context of gas pipelines, the ability to profitably raise prices above competitive levels for a significant period of time (see FERC (1996b)).

[123] As Joskow and Tirole (2007) note: 'Despite all of the talk about "deregulation" of the electricity sector, there continues to be a large number of non-market mechanisms that have been imposed on the emerging competitive wholesale and retail electricity markets.'

[124] For example, the FERC (2008) in the USA has adopted filing requirements, market manipulation rules and enhanced market oversight for those electricity generators entitled to charge market-based rates.

[125] For example, in Britain, firms operating in retail energy markets, where price controls were removed in 2002, have at some points been required to offer only a limited number of tariffs to consumers. Similarly, in a number of retail energy markets in the USA and Europe, suppliers are sometimes require to offer consumers a standard or default tariff.

[126] See Helm and Jenkinson (1997). Crandall, Sidak and Singer (2002) argue that the application of asymmetric regulation to promote entry in the telecommunications industry in the USA led to 'a system of "enduring managed competition" far more complex to administer than traditional regulation of a monopoly service provider ever was'. More generally, Armstrong and Sappington (2006) describe the roa from monopoly to competition as 'particularly long and winding' which is 'seldom straight and smooth'.

[127] Vogelsang (2006) records that one major lesson of US reforms in the electricity and telecommunication: industries is not to expect Pareto improvements, and to recognise that there will be winners and losers from such a reform process. Kahn (2002) argues that one of the factors leading to the collapse of market reforms in the California electricity market in the early 2000s was that of misguided populism: 'promising consumers the anticipated benefits of competition while sheltering them from its risks.'

fact that it can be difficult for the regulator to determine exactly when a market is sufficiently competitive to allow for the withdrawal of *ex ante* price controls.[128]

3.6 RELIANCE ON NEGOTIATION AS AN ALTERNATIVE TO REGULATION

Another alternative to traditional economic regulation is to rely primarily on negotiations between a firm and its users/customers, with the regulator only becoming involved either to approve a negotiated settlement or to act as an arbitrator in the event that agreement cannot be reached.[129]

3.6.1 Negotiated Settlements

The 'negotiated settlement' approach involves utility customers, represented by user and consumer groups, negotiating with a utility, before putting a 'settlement' to a regulatory authority.[130] The agreement between the parties needs to be approved by the regulator, but this does not typically involve a full regulatory hearing. This approach is used for federal energy regulation in North America, and also in a number of states (such as Florida and California) in the USA. The negotiated settlement approach has been considered, and in some cases applied, in the energy and water sectors in the UK, Australia, Denmark and elsewhere.[131]

Numerous advantages of this approach have been advanced.[132] First, it is argued to have allowed consumers, as well as utilities, to achieve agreement and outcomes on points that may not have occurred through the standard regulatory process.[133] In addition, the approach is argued to better reflect the views of consumers, provide a more flexible regulatory approach (rather than 'one size fits all') and improve relationships in the industries where it has been applied.[134] A negotiated settlement can also allow parties to

---

[128] In this respect, it is sometimes argued that regulators might not face appropriate incentives to manage and foster efficient industry competition. Kahn (2002) refers to a 'demonstrated tendency of regulators to assume responsibility not merely for establishing the necessary conditions for efficient competition but for guaranteeing the desired results'. See also Sappington and Weisman (2012) and Kahn (1998).

[129] This can involve requirements that regulated firms consult or 'constructively engage' with users/consumers (or their representatives), although the regulator continues to play a role in making or approving the determination or acting as an arbitrator. Heims and Lodge (2018) and Hahn, Metcalfe and Rundhammer (2020) discuss the experience of greater negotiation and consumer engagement in UK energy and water industries, while Littlechild (2018a, b) discusses the use of constructive engagement for UK airports. Eskesen (2021a, b) considers the use of negotiation for airports and the energy sector in Denmark. Vogelsang (2017) discusses its potential use in telecommunications.

[130] See Wang (2004) and Littlechild (2006a, b). Krieger (1995) presents an overview of the history of settlements in public utility cases in the USA.

[131] A US-style negotiated settlement approach was considered, but not ultimately adopted, by the British energy regulator and the water regulator in England and Wales; see Littlechild (2020). Decker (2013) considers the reasons why the regulators did not adopt a negotiated settlement approach.

[132] Littlechild (2008a) provides a fuller discussion of these points.

[133] In the context of the USA, Littlechild (2012b) concludes that: '[T]he agreed outcomes have been more flexible, more innovative and more closely tailored to the needs of particular users and customers than the previously litigated outcomes determined by US regulators.'

[134] See Littlechild (2008a). Littlechild (2020) observes that: 'As electricity regulator from 1989–98 I had to set rather a lot of these wretched price controls. I have since come to the view that there is a better process for setting them, based on the concept of negotiated settlement, an approach that was unknown to me at the time.'

make trade-offs *across* price control issues as a package, rather than requiring a separate decision to be made on each issue.[135] Other potential benefits of the approach that have been identified include that it: can generally be significantly faster than traditional regulation,[136] is less burdensome for the regulator and other parties, and does not necessarily involve substantial amounts of technical and economic analysis of issues.[137]

The most significant concern with the approach is that, because the agreements are typically concluded between a firm and consumer representatives, there is a risk that not all views are represented in the negotiation process.[138] There are two aspects to this issue. The first is that the approach might not accurately account for customer heterogeneity.[139] This raises questions about the role played by consumer representatives, such as Offices of Consumer Advocates, in the settlement process, and the extent to which they have incentives to represent all consumers.[140] The second issue around representation is that all parties affected by an agreement may not be present at the negotiating table. In particular, it may not be clear how *future* consumers are represented in the negotiated process. An agreement that reflects an acceptable bargain between *current* users and utilities (notwithstanding the points made above about heterogeneity in current consumer preferences) will not necessarily reflect the best interests of future users (and vice versa). For this reason, some argue that there remains a residual role for a regulator in such processes to ensure intergenerational equity.[141] In the absence of the views of future users, negotiated agreements might involve deferring costs to future periods, and therefore future consumers,[142] or, alternatively, involve one generation of users cross-subsidising another generation of users.[143] More broadly, it has been suggested that regulators themselves may be reluctant to embrace the negotiated approach because it moves the focus away from a largely technical economic approach to regulation to one based on collaboration.[144]

---

[135] See Wang (2004).

[136] However, Chakravorty (2015) finds that time saved is not the primary reason for their popularity.

[137] Littlechild (2012a) observes: '[T]he parties generally focus on the main features of the control, including the "bottom line" .... In particular, the parties typically do not spend undue time on detailed econometric comparisons of costs.'

[138] Littlechild and Cornwall (2009) recognise the fear that such an approach could disadvantage those not at the negotiating table, and may therefore be seen as involving an 'abdication of responsibility of the regulator'.

[139] This is an old concern. Morgan (1978), a supporter of the use of settlements, recognised 'the real problem may be guaranteeing that all significantly affected interests are represented in any settlement negotiation'. Wang (2004) makes a similar point.

[140] Gormley (1981), for example, argues that proxy advocates do not champion the full range of under-represented interests in society but confine their attention to 'safe' issues, such as revenue requirements. Holburn and Spiller (2002) conclude, based on an empirical analysis, that consumers do not benefit uniformly from institutionalised representation and that, all else being equal, consumer advocates, on average, leave residential consumers worse off but industrial consumers better off. Chakravorty (2015) finds that consumer advocates agree to settlements that deliver substantial rate reductions as a way of signalling good job performance.

[141] See Kent Fellows (2012).

[142] Kent Fellows (2011) observes that negotiated agreements involving the deferral of depreciation costs have been a feature of settlements in both Florida and Canada.

[143] Bankes (2019) discusses how the Canadian National Energy Board intervened in one negotiated settlement to address what it considered to be 'unreasonable intergenerational inequity'.

[144] Heims and Lodge (2018) observe that '[s]uch a shift, therefore, would constitute considerable changes for economic regulators as the centrality of economic expertise is being challenged'.

An important difference between the negotiated settlement approach and the private contracting approach described in Section 3.7 below is that, in negotiated settlements, there is still a role for a regulator. In particular, even though the bulk of the negotiations are conducted between the parties privately, the regulator can be important in terms of structuring the terms by which the negotiations take place, or can require the utilities to disclose certain information. In addition, in the event that a settlement cannot be reached between the parties, the regulator typically makes a determination through standard regulatory processes (rather than the matter being dealt with through general commercial law processes, as the private contracting approach implies).

A related negotiation-type mechanism, used in access contexts, involves public utilities and their users engaging in commercial negotiations as to the terms of supply in the first instance, with the possibility that, should the negotiations be unsuccessful, a reference can be made to a regulator for resolution of the matter.[145] In this way, the regulator's role becomes one similar to a dispute resolution function. As described in Part III, this 'negotiate–arbitrate' approach has been used in the telecommunications, rail, aviation and water industries in both the UK and Australia, with differing perceptions of effectiveness.[146] In Australia, the approach has been abandoned in the telecommunications industry and replaced by standardised 'access determinations',[147] while it has been seen as more successful for airports and rail.[148]

In summary, while a reliance on negotiation between firms and their users has been used in North America and Australia for decades, variants of the approach – such as greater user/customer engagement, constructive or enhanced engagement and negotiated settlements – are also being considered, and applied, in other jurisdictions. While all of these approaches involve a more collaborative and less adversarial approach,[149] there is considerable diversity in the status given to any agreement reached between the parties and the role of the regulator.[150] In short, while some implementations view such negotiations (and any agreement reached) as an 'input' to the traditional regulatory process, others see it as largely a substitute for much of the work undertaken by traditional economic regulators.

3.7 RELIANCE ON PRIVATE CONTRACTS

A more radical alternative to standard forms of regulation is to rely on long-term private contracts, under which negotiated prices, quantity and quality would be subject to the general legal framework relating to private contracts. Under a private contracting

---

[145] In Australia, the approach was introduced in 1995 as part of an 'economy-wide access regime' which encourages parties to negotiate their own terms and conditions of access to a declared service, but also provides for the regulator to conduct an arbitration and make a determination that binds the parties in the event that agreement cannot be reached.

[146] See ACCC (2013) and Decker and Gray (2012).

[147] That is, a standard set of terms and conditions upon which all access seekers can rely if they are unable to come to an agreement with an access provider on the supply of a declared service.

[148] Arblaster (2016) and Dimasi (2015).

[149] Littlechild (2018) observes that negotiated settlements, constructive engagement and customer engagement are all forms of a discovery process and provide a challenge to companies on costs and prices.

[150] Decker (2013) discusses the role of the regulator in different forms of negotiation. See also Heims and Lodge (2018).

approach, enforcement occurs through the normal commercial courts and processes which, it has been argued, could provide a potentially clearer and stronger commitment than economic regulators and regulatory processes.[151]

While, in principle, this approach can allow for a closer customisation of arrangements between a firm and its customers than terms and conditions being mandated through the regulatory process, there are obvious limitations. In particular, there is a question of the practicability of private contracts where there are large numbers of small customers purchasing relatively small quantities, and in circumstances where it is difficult to specify the requirements of those customers and the public utilities in advance.[152] In addition, the transaction costs associated with negotiating, monitoring and enforcing voluntary agreements in such circumstances may be significantly greater than the costs associated with a system of economic regulation where the regulator collectively acts on behalf of the buyers.[153]

Nevertheless, it is argued that a private contracting approach may be appropriate in some contexts. Gómez-Ibáñez, in particular, notes the use of private contracts as a substitute for economic regulation in the freight railroad and airline industries, and by large industrial customers of electricity and water utilities in the USA.[154] The argument has also been made that the 'small-customer' problem for private contracts is not insurmountable. Brokers or other intermediaries could be used to aggregate preferences and negotiate on their customers' behalf, or public utilities could offer a menu of standardised contracts for small customers.[155]

3.8 MONITORING

There are other approaches to controlling and influencing the conduct of public utilities that are broadly classified as 'light-handed' in nature. One example is subjecting public utilities to monitoring – in terms of pricing, quality and other behaviour – under threat of the imposition, or re-imposition, of economic regulation if behaviour proves unsatisfactory. The principal benefits of the approach are that it minimises compliance and administrative costs and reduces the extent of regulatory intrusion into decision making. As described in Chapter 15, the approach has been adopted in relation to airports in Australia and New Zealand and to some airports in the UK.[156] Some are optimistic about the ability of such ex post mechanisms to be applied to other public utility industries, such as the energy sector.[157] However, the importance of clear criteria for determining when performance is deemed to be satisfactory (or unsatisfactory) is critical under such an approach.[158]

---

[151] See Gómez-Ibáñez (2003).

[152] Schmalensee (1979) considered the possibility of applying an 'unaided market mechanism' to the natural monopoly problem. He concluded that there was 'the general impossibility of eliminating the natural monopoly problem by negotiation among the parties involved' and that transactional difficulties necessitated the need for some entity to act as the buyer's agent, with specialised skills and a legal right to acquire information, and who made decisions for a group.

[153] However, this will depend on the circumstances. Gómez-Ibáñez (2003) argues that, where transactions costs are likely to be low, then private contracts might be an appropriate response to the problem of natural monopoly. In contrast, where transactions costs are extremely high, private contracts are likely to be impracticable and regulation or public ownership could be justified.

[154] Gómez-Ibáñez (2003).

[155] Gómez-Ibáñez (2003).

[156] Arblaster (2014) discusses the Australian and New Zealand experiences.

[157] See, for example, Littlechild (2009b). Contrast with Black, Harman and Moselle (2009).

[158] See Forsyth (2004). Arblaster (2014) notes that this includes the approach to asset valuation.

3.9 DECENTRALISED PROVISION OF SERVICES

Traditionally, the structure through which many utility services have been provided has been highly centralised, with a single entity responsible for managing and providing the core network services within a specific region. As the centralised operator often held a position of monopoly, it was typically subject to traditional forms of economic regulation. However, as discussed in Part III of this book, this structure has changed, or is changing, in a number of industries – notably transport, communications, energy and payment systems – to a more distributed, or decentralised, structure, where a range of participants supply services among themselves using a series of common data sharing protocols, standardization and automation with no, or very little, central coordination. This raises a question about the need for, and future role of, regulation in such decentralised and distributed systems.

A key question in many sectors is the extent to which any entity will have a position of significant market power or monopoly within a distributed or decentralised architecture. As discussed in Chapter 15, such issues are currently being debated in the context of the provision of Unmanned Aircraft System Traffic Management (UTM) where, unlike for traditional air traffic management (ATM), such services will be provided on a decentralised basis in some jurisdictions. In the USA, for example, UTM services will be provided via a decentralised community-based, cooperative traffic management system, where the operators of unmanned aircraft systems (drones) are primarily responsible for the coordination, execution and management of operations, and the regulator's role is mainly limited to setting the 'rules of the road'.[159] In other sectors, such as energy and to some extent water, the shift towards more distributed architecture has led to calls for the establishment of an independent system operator function to oversee, and in some cases actively coordinate and manage, the provision of services within this setting.

3.10 CONCLUSION

This chapter has considered various alternatives to price, conduct and entry regulation to control the conduct of firms in certain industries. Some of the alternative approaches are actively used in practice. For example, approaches based on 'competition for the market' in the form of franchising or concession agreements, or public–private partnerships, are used in many countries, particularly in the water and transport industries. Similarly, state ownership of utility companies can be observed in many jurisdictions, including the USA (water industry), Europe (rail, water as well as the electricity and gas industries in some countries), and Australia and New Zealand (water and electricity industries), and in many developing countries. As noted, in some jurisdictions, state-owned utilities are increasingly being subject to standard price and conduct regulation by an independent regulatory agency, suggesting that state ownership on its own is not perceived to be an effective alternative method for controlling and influencing the conduct of public utility firms. Finally, many jurisdictions have, over the past three decades, sought to change the structure of their public utility industries by introducing 'deregulatory' policies which

---

[159] FAA (2020a).

involve the withdrawal of *ex ante* entry restrictions, and in some cases the removal of price regulation, for certain activities in the production chain. The implementation of these policies, which seek to rely on competition to control the conduct of firms in these activities, has, in practice, proven a challenging exercise in many jurisdictions.[160]

Some of the other alternative approaches that we discussed have been influential in terms of the design of regulation. For example, while the sole reliance on competition law to control the behaviour of firms providing core network activities in the public utility industries is not common, this approach is being used in some jurisdictions as competition develops for non-core network activities in the supply chain (such as retail telecommunications markets and airline competition). Whether economic regulation or competition law is the best approach to controlling digital platforms is also an active area of discussion in many countries. Similarly, while contestable markets theory is generally not seen as providing a sufficient basis to withdraw regulation from core network activities, the concepts and tests it has introduced has influenced policies relating to acceptable bounds of pricing in some public utility industries, such as the telecommunications and rail sectors.

Looking to the future, approaches based on direct negotiations between public utility firms and their customers, with only indirect or limited input from a regulator, have generated considerable interest in a number of jurisdictions, and appear likely to receive further attention as an alternative to traditional forms of price cap and rate of return regulation. The shift away from centralised to more distributed supply architectures in number of industries will also raise fundamental questions about the need for, and scope of, any measures needed to control and influence the conduct of firms.

DISCUSSION QUESTIONS

1. We have considered various alternatives to traditional regulation. Describe the advantages and disadvantages of each. Which is your preferred alternative?
2. What is the relationship between contestable markets theory and the 'competition for the market' approach?
3. What are the conditions under which contestability might act as an effective substitute for traditional economic regulation?
4. Studies of state ownership present mixed results of performance. What are some of the reasons why that may be the case?
5. What are the arguments for and against relying solely on competition law to control and influence the conduct of firms as an alternative to traditional *ex ante* economic regulation?
6. Do you think negotiated agreements could work as an effective substitute to traditional economic regulation? What are some of the benefits of such an approach? What are some of the challenges that could arise?
7. Is competition always desirable in public utility industries? In what circumstances might monopoly provision be preferred?

---

[160] In some cases, such as for energy in Australia and the UK, retail price regulation has been re-introduced

PART II

Principles of Regulation for Core Network Activities

In this chapter and those that follow in Part II of the book, our examination shifts from exploring *why* we regulate, and the alternatives to regulation, to the economic principles and approaches that might guide and inform economic regulation (the '*how* of regulation'). In this respect, we again make a distinction between principles that might inform the regulation of the *core network activities* of an industry (i.e. those activities which most closely resemble natural monopoly and where the prospects for competition are limited) and principles that might inform the regulation of competitive activities in a production chain. Chapters 4 and 5 focus on the principles relevant to the core network activities, while Chapter 6 sets out the economic principles that might inform regulation in competitive market settings.

4.1 INDUSTRY STRUCTURES

As a starting point, it is necessary to distinguish between three broad types of industry structures typically observed in industries subject to regulation. Understanding the different types of industry structure is relevant because the degree to which an industry approximates each of these structures will inform the tasks of the regulator, and therefore the relevant principles and approaches of regulation within a structure. The three generic industry structures are: vertically integrated monopoly; vertical separation with competition in some activities; and vertical integration with competition in some activities. Box 4.1 describes the key properties of the different industry structures.

In this chapter, we consider the principles that relate only to those activities in the production chain where it is either not possible, or not desirable, to introduce competition; that is, the principles that apply to the natural monopoly-like core network activities. This includes all of the activities in the vertically integrated monopoly setting, as well as the core network activities in the other two industry structures described in Box 4.1. In Chapter 6 we discuss principles relevant for regulating those industry structures where competition exists for some activities and competitors need to gain access to the core network facilities (i.e. vertical separation with competition (Figure 4.2), or vertical integration with competition (Figure 4.3)).

There is an extensive literature on the principles of regulation for natural monopoly, and the purpose of this discussion is not to replicate or summarise this work, but to draw

Box 4.1	Industry structures

VERTICALLY INTEGRATED MONOPOLY

In a vertically integrated monopoly structure, a single firm is the only operator in the industry and undertakes all of the activities in the production chain (see Figure 4.1). This industr structure, which was common for most public utility industries in many countries prior t the 1980s and 1990s, involves a single firm (who typically has a legal monopoly) undertak ing the production, transportation/transmission and retail activities associated with the util ity service. While, as we will see in Part III, there has been a trend away from this structur in some industries (notably communications and energy), vertically integrated monopol remains a feature of some public utility industries, such as the water and wastewater an rail industries, in many jurisdictions. Implicit in a vertically integrated monopoly structur is an assessment that the prospects for competition in each of the various activities tha comprise the production chain are limited, or that there are significant economic efficiencie associated with the vertically integrated structure which need to be protected. In this cas the principles of natural monopoly regulation will be most relevant to a regulator and fina retail prices will be regulated. The regulator will not typically be involved in issues relatin to access pricing,[1] which generally arise only where entry restrictions are withdrawn an some competition is introduced at one level of the production chain.

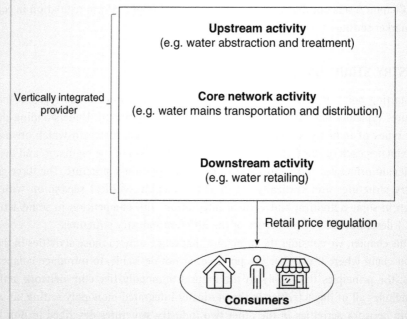

Figure 4.1 Vertically integrated monopoly

VERTICAL SEPARATION WITH COMPETITION IN SOME ACTIVITIES

In a vertically separated structure, the various activities that comprise the vertical production chain are separated into activities that have naturally monopolistic characteristics (cor

---

[1] Except in circumstances where adjacent monopolies need to access each other's network.

network activities) and those which are potentially competitive (see Figure 4.2). Under this structure, the firm operating the core network activity is separate from the firms at other stages of the production chain, and does not operate in those related markets. This type of structure can be observed in the gas and electricity industries in a number of jurisdictions, where the transmission and distribution activities – which have the characteristics of natural monopoly – are separated from generation and retail supply activities. For these structures, the most relevant principles for the regulation of the core network firms are those relating to natural monopoly regulation.[2] However, issues relating to the terms and conditions of one-way access, including access pricing, are also relevant.

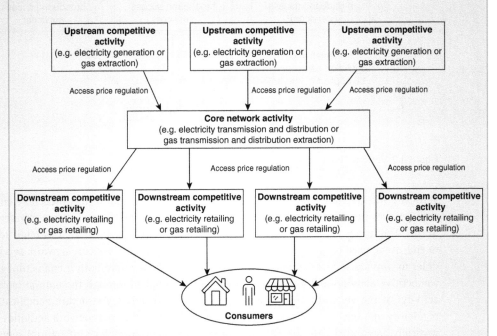

Figure 4.2 Vertical separation with competition in upstream and downstream activities

VERTICAL INTEGRATION WITH COMPETITION IN SOME ACTIVITIES

A third type of industry structure involves the coexistence of a vertically integrated firm (that operates in all of the activities in the production chain), with firms who are only active in some competitive activities in the production chain (see Figure 4.3). The distinguishing feature of this structure is that the firm that operates the core network activity (for example, transportation or transmission) also competes with other firms in markets and activities that have been opened to competition. This type of structure is commonly observed in the fixed line telecommunications industry, where a single firm (typically the former incumbent) owns the local access network (typically the natural monopoly activity in telecommunications),[3] and is also active in competitive segments such as retail services. This structure is also seen in digital platforms, where some digital platform operators are also

---

[2] In addition, some jurisdictions may continue to regulate upstream wholesale and downstream retail prices because of concerns about market power.

[3] Although, as discussed in Chapter 11, there can be facilities-based or infrastructure competition where there are cable or mobile networks.

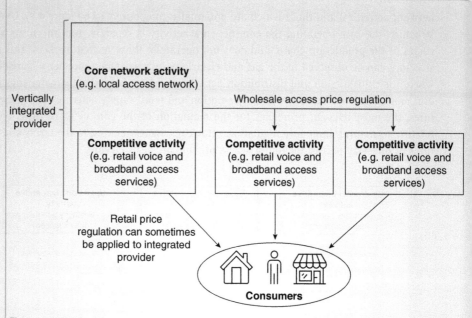

Figure 4.3 Vertical integration with competition in some activities

vertically integrated and provide their own services on the platform, which may compete with services provided by other independent users on the platform. The key characteristic of this structure is that firms operating in the competitive activities, such as retail services to end-users, need to gain access to the vertically integrated firm's core network services in order to provide services to end-users. These firms are therefore both a competitor (in the competitive activity) and a customer (for the input supplied through the natural monopoly activity) of the vertically integrated firm. This type of industry structure complicates the regulatory approach because, in addition to ensuring that the core network activities of the vertically integrated firm are regulated according to the principles of natural monopoly regulation, the regulator must also ensure that the firm does not seek to leverage its market power from the core network activity (where it is a monopoly supplier) into other activities in the production chain where it competes with other firms.

out the most important conclusions for the regulation of core network activities.[4] The principal focus of this chapter is on principles for price regulation, but consideration is also given to principles relevant to incentivising firms to improve quality and engage in cost-reducing activities. Section 4.2 begins by examining the principles developed under the assumption of full information and where the firm only supplies a single product. Section 4.3 maintains the assumption of full information, but looks at principles relevant when a firm supplies multiple products. Section 4.4 then relaxes the assumption of full information, and examines regulatory policies relevant in the context of asymmetric

---

[4] More detailed descriptions are presented in Brown and Sibley (1986), Berg and Tschirhart (1988), Train (1991), Laffont and Tirole (1993), Armstrong, Cowan and Vickers (1994), Armstrong and Sappington (2007) and Joskow (2007a).

information. Section 4.5 looks at principles relevant in the multi-period (or dynamic) context, that is, when the regulator and firm interact over a number of periods. Section 4.6 discusses principles and other factors that influence the design of regulated rate structures in practice. Finally, Section 4.7 looks at principles for incentivising improvements in quality and reductions in costs.

4.2 PRICING PRINCIPLES UNDER FULL INFORMATION

According to the conventional natural monopoly rationale for regulation described in Chapter 2, the essential task for a regulator of core network activities is to implement a pricing arrangement which reaps the maximum efficiency benefits associated with having only one firm supply an output (i.e. a natural monopoly). In this context, the 'efficient price' is the price that maximises total surplus – the sum of consumer surplus and producer profit.

To begin, we abstract from some of the circumstances that confront regulators in practice to focus on what price a regulator would set if: it possessed perfect information about the regulated firm's costs (including its cost-minimising efforts) and demand; the firm produces only a single product; and regulation applies only in a single period (i.e. a static setting). We gradually relax these assumptions as the chapter develops.

A distinction between two different sets of pricing concepts needs to be introduced here, as they are discussed extensively in the next sections. The first distinction is between uniform and discriminatory pricing. A uniform pricing approach is one where the same price is levied for all consumers of one unit of the same product, while a discriminatory pricing approach is one where different types/classes of consumers are charged different prices for the same product depending on their willingness to pay. The second distinction is between linear and non-linear pricing. Linear pricing refers to situations where the price per unit does not vary with the quantity consumed; i.e. the average price per unit is constant regardless of the quantity consumed. In contrast, non-linear pricing refers to situations where the price per unit can vary according to the quantity consumed; i.e. the average price per unit will change as the number of units consumed changes (such that users face lower average per unit prices the more they consume).

4.2.1 The Starting Principle: Marginal Cost Pricing

Marginal cost pricing is frequently considered the *starting* principle for price regulation.[5] This principle has already been introduced in Chapter 2; however, given its central importance, it is worth revisiting the reasoning here. Marginal cost refers to the costs associated with producing one more unit of production (or alternatively the costs saved

---

[5] As Kahn (1971) observes: 'The central policy prescription of microeconomics is the equation of price and marginal cost. If economic theory is to have any relevance to public utility pricing, that is the point at which the inquiry must begin.' The principle of marginal cost pricing is sometimes traced back to the work of the French engineer and economist Jules Dupuit in the mid-1840s. The principle was developed further by, among others, Hotelling (1938), who argued that marginal cost pricing should be applied in decreasing cost industries, and that any deficit caused should be recovered through lump-sum taxation, a proposition that was subject to considerable debate in what has become known as the 'marginal cost controversy'. An overview of some of the important historical contributions is presented in Baumol and Bradford (1970).

or avoided by producing one less unit of production).[6] Setting prices to marginal cost is the most efficient allocation of a firm's production because it is at this point that the total surplus is maximised, meaning that the sum of consumer surplus and profit is at its greatest, and there are no unexploited gains from trade.[7] For this reason, marginal cost pricing is sometimes referred to as 'first-best' pricing, because any deviations of price from marginal cost (in either direction, above or below) can only *reduce* total surplus (see the discussion in Chapter 2).[8]

There are widely acknowledged practical issues associated with marginal cost pricing as an approach to regulating core network activities.[9] In particular, complexities can arise in specifying the relevant time period over which costs should be measured (in particular whether prices should be based on long-run marginal cost or short-run marginal cost) and the relevant 'unit' or increment of production for which the costs should be estimated. Decisions on these matters have direct implications for which costs are considered fixed and which variable (e.g. the longer the time period, the more costs that will be variable). In addition, and as discussed below, where multiple products are produced as a result of the core network activities, there is an issue as to the allocation of any common costs among the different units of production. Such issues have led many to conclude that while the economic ideal would be to set prices based on short-run marginal costs for the smallest possible additional unit of sale (with appropriate adjustments for externalities and second-best effects), in practice it is usually not feasible or desirable to do so.[10]

4.2.2 Accounting for Fixed Costs in Pricing for the Core Network

Perhaps the most significant problem with applying marginal cost pricing is that core network activities are typically characterised by high levels of fixed costs (which do not vary with output) and low levels of variable costs. Accordingly, applying the principle of marginal cost pricing to these activities will result in revenues that do not cover fixed costs and the firm making a loss on production, which will ultimately make supply of the service unsustainable (this was shown in Figure 2.6).[11] As discussed in Chapter 2, this can

---

[6] Critically, it is assumed that the marginal cost will be adjusted to take account of any externalities associated with the product, for example, negative environmental externalities. This is of particular relevance in the water, energy and transport sectors.

[7] Put another way, an 'allocative inefficiency' is said to arise whenever the value placed on an additional unit of a product by consumers deviates from the opportunity cost associated with producing that additional unit.

[8] An important qualification to the 'first-best' nature of marginal cost pricing is that it will not necessarily result in the most efficient allocation where it is only partially applied (i.e. not applied uniformly across a market or industry or economy). If, for example, one product is subject to a regulation to price at marginal cost, but the price of a potential substitute product is not so constrained, this can potentially introduce distortions into the choices of consumers as between the two products. This is known as the theorem of the second-best, first developed in Lipsey and Lancaster (1956).

[9] See, for example, Kahn (1971).

[10] See the discussion in Kahn (1971).

[11] The cost function for core network activities generally comprises both a variable cost c and fixed cost F, such that the total cost function is: $TC(Q) = cQ + F$. Core network activities are usually characterised by economies of scale, meaning that average production costs ($TC(Q)/Q$) decrease with increases in production over a relevant range. In these circumstances, a requirement that the price for a unit of production only equal marginal costs is equivalent to setting price equal to variable costs (c), and will not allow for the recovery of the fixed costs (F).

create a conflict between the achievement of allocative efficiency and ensuring that the regulated firm recovers its fixed costs and remains viable.

Two possible methods for addressing this conflict have been identified. The first method involves transfer subsidies and requires the government or regulator to make a transfer of money to the regulated firm equal to the amount of the shortfall that results from marginal cost pricing.[12] In these circumstances, the firm employs marginal cost pricing to cover its variable costs, while its fixed costs are recovered through the transfer payment/subsidy. While this approach can ensure an efficient allocation of the firm's output and that the firm remains viable, it also has a number of limitations. Firstly, the transfer payment needs to be funded in some way, such as through taxes, and this can involve introducing distortions in the wider economy to generate these funds. In addition, transfers funded through taxation mean that those who do not consume the service will be subsiding those who do. Secondly, in many jurisdictions, regulators are not allowed to provide subsidies or transfer payments to the firms they regulate, for the very good reason that this can potentially make them more susceptible to regulatory capture.[13]

The second method for addressing the conflict between marginal cost pricing and firm sustainability involves the use of pricing approaches that maximise total surplus subject to the constraint that the firm breaks even (i.e. revenues equal total costs).[14] Two main alternative pricing approaches are discussed below. The first approach is to *differentiate* prices according to the preferences of different customer groups, or, in the multi-product context, according to the preferences of customers for the different products supplied by the firm. Ramsey–Boiteux pricing and peak-load pricing are examples of this first approach. A second approach is to allow the firm to charge different per unit prices to consumers, and in particular, where it can do so, offer quantity discounts. The simple two-part tariff and other forms of non-linear pricing are examples of this pricing approach.

4.2.3 Average Cost Pricing: the Second Best

One pricing approach which seeks to maximise total surplus, subject to the constraint that the firm breaks even, involves the firm setting a single uniform price for all units equal to average cost.[15] To see this, consider the following standard welfare function, where V represents total surplus, and comprises a weighted sum of both consumer surplus for a given price, CS(P),[16] *and* producer surplus, which is reflected in the profit of the firm $\pi(P)$:

$$V(P) = CS(P) + \alpha\pi(P) \tag{4.1}$$

---

[12] Hotelling (1938) supports the view that prices should be set at marginal cost and any shortfall relating to fixed costs recovered by general taxation. For a spirited critique, see Coase (1946, 1970).

[13] However, even where a regulator is so restricted, this does not preclude subsidies being provided by a central government or via a treasury, a situation that has arisen in the rail and aviation industries in some jurisdictions.

[14] A number of different alternative principles for efficient pricing have been developed over the last century. Clark (1911) details early examples of non-uniform pricing in the utilities. Steiner (1957) traces work on peak-load pricing to that of Hopkinson's (1892) analysis of electricity tariffs. Baumol and Bradford (1970) discuss early research on 'value of service' and Ramsey–Boiteux pricing.

[15] Prices are linear because the average price is the same irrespective of the amount consumed.

[16] Marginal utility is assumed to be constant across consumers.

where

$$\pi(P) = P(Q(P)) - C(Q(P)).$$

In this equation, P is the price charged by the firm per unit, C is the unit cost, $Q(P)$ is the quantity sold at that price, while α is a constant lying between 0 and 1 which represents the relative weight placed on consumer surplus relative to profit. This allows the regulator to vary the importance given to the firm's profit relative to that of consumer surplus which, as discussed below, is an important assumption in some theoretical models.[17]

Given this welfare function, the regulatory task is to set a price P^* such that welfare $V(P)$ is maximised in equation (4.1), subject to the constraint that profits are non-negative, that is $\pi(P) \geqslant 0$. The most efficient solution to this problem is to set price equal to average cost, i.e. $P^* = C(Q(P^*))/Q(P^*)$, as at this point the firm breaks even (makes zero profit), the uniform price is at its lowest level and consumer surplus is maximised.[18] It follows that, at any point where price is greater than average costs, i.e. $P^* > C(Q(P^*))/Q(P^*)$, consumer surplus can be enlarged, and welfare improved, by reducing prices toward average costs. Conversely, if the price is set below average costs, i.e. $P^* < C(Q(P^*))/Q(P^*)$, then the firm is not recovering all of its costs and will not be able to break even. As shown in Figure 4.4, where there are economies of scale, it is only where price equals average cost ($P^* = AC$) that the distortion to total surplus associated with deviating from marginal cost pricing is minimised, while also allowing the firm to break even. Nevertheless, as shown in Figure 4.4, the requirement that the firm break even, and a single average price be charged, is sub-optimal to the 'first-best' marginal pricing rule from a welfare point of view, as it results in a degree of allocative inefficiency: some consumers who would

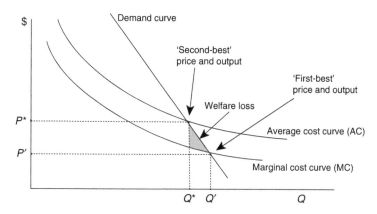

Figure 4.4 'Second-best' pricing and output

[17] Models such as Baron and Myerson's (1982), described below, assume that α is less than 1 on the basis that $1 in the hand of a consumer is more important than $1 of profit to the firm. Armstrong, Cowan and Vickers (1994) suggest one reason why we might make such a weighting: that shareholders tend to be wealthier than consumers. Lim and Yurukoglu (2018), using US data for electricity distribution, find that more conservative political environments place relatively more weight on utility profits than less conservative political environments.

[18] This is irrespective of the value of α.

consume the product if price was set at marginal cost (price set at P' and output level Q') are excluded from the market. For this reason, this approach is often referred to as the 'second-best' approach to pricing.[19]

4.2.4 Optimal Linear Pricing: Allowing for Price Discrimination

The approach described above was based on a single uniform price per unit being charged to all consumers, which, in effect, embodies an equal mark-up to recover fixed costs over all units sold. However, even in the single-product case, it is possible to improve total surplus by introducing some price discrimination, that is, by varying the per unit price paid by different consumers according to their willingness to pay for the product (i.e. to reflect different demand elasticities). For example, residential customers may have less elastic demand than industrial users for a particular utility service, and the per unit price for these customers could reflect this fact.[20] The most prominent example of this approach is Ramsey–Boiteux pricing.[21] In the single-product setting, this approach suggests that a mark-up should be applied above marginal cost for different customer groups, and that the mark-up should be inversely proportional to the elasticity of demand for the product by that particular group of consumers. In principle, the mark-up for different consumers of the product can be chosen in such a way as to allow the service provider to generate sufficient expected revenue across all of its users.[22] The main result of this approach is that per unit prices will *vary* among different groups of consumers: prices will be higher for consumer groups with less elastic demand, and lower for consumer groups with more elastic demand, despite the fact that the marginal cost of production is the same for both groups of consumers.[23] Where feasible, this differential pricing approach represents an improvement on average cost pricing described in Section 4.2.3, as it increases the size of the total surplus. An interesting result is that, where such an approach can be implemented, it resembles that of an unregulated monopolist engaging in third-degree price discrimination, the principal difference in the regulated case being that the price *level* is expected to be lower.[24] We discuss the practicability of employing Ramsey–Boiteux pricing in more detail in Section 4.3.2 below.

---

[19] The magnitude of the difference between the first-best and second-best pricing approaches, or alternatively the extent to which the average pricing rule is considered less optimal than the marginal pricing rule, depends on the size of the difference between marginal costs and average costs (and the extent of any economies of scale) and the elasticity of demand for the product.

[20] For this type of price differentiation to be feasible, the firm must be able to prevent resale of the product between different classes of customer (i.e. residential and industrial customers), and the firm or regulator must be able to identify with some precision the 'willingness to pay' of different types of consumers.

[21] This is sometimes referred to as 'Ramsey pricing'. However, the term 'Ramsey–Boiteux pricing' is preferred, as it reflects the fact that, while the general principle was established by Frank Ramsey on the theory of taxation subject to a given revenue constraint in 1927, it was later applied in the context of pricing for public monopolies by Marcel Boiteux in 1956. See Ramsey (1927), Boiteux (1956) and Baumol and Bradford (1970).

[22] Assuming different groups cannot engage in arbitrage or trade.

[23] Baumol and Bradford (1970) provide a formal derivation of this result, which is sometimes known as the inverse elasticity rule.

[24] See Laffont and Tirole (2000).

4.2.5 Non-Linear Pricing: Uniform Two-Part Tariffs

The above discussion was restricted to settings where the firm can only set linear price
that is, where the price per unit does not vary with quantity, and, although different con
sumers may be charged different prices, the average price per unit for each consume
within a specific group is constant. An alternative pricing approach that can increas
total surplus from that obtained under the simple average pricing approach described i
Section 4.2.3 is non-linear pricing.

The non-linear pricing approach has long been a feature of public utility industrie
where a customer may be levied a fixed or standing charge (levied on a monthly, quar
terly, semi-annual or annual basis) as well as a per unit charge levied on each unit of th
service consumed. For example, electricity customers often pay a flat monthly standin
fee in addition to a charge per kilowatt-hour of electricity that is consumed, and telecom
munications customers may pay a fixed monthly access charge as well as paying for eac
call they make. Different types of non-linear pricing structures can be applied, even in th
single-product setting.[25] One of the most common forms is the simple uniform two-par
tariff, which, as the name implies, involves the firm dividing the total tariff for its produc
tion into two components: a fixed charge and a variable charge.[26] For example, the tari
might be $T = A + p(Q)$, where the fixed access charge A is independent of the amount con
sumed and is only levied on the first unit consumed, while the variable per unit charg
p, is applied to all Q units consumed, and both charges are the same for all consumer
(i.e. they are uniformly applied). The tariff for the first unit consumed is therefore $A + p$
while the tariff for all units consumed thereafter is only p per unit consumed. It follow
that, as shown in Figure 4.5, the average price paid per unit *reduces* as consumption o
the product increases.

In this setting, the regulator faces two constraints. First, it must still ensure that th
firm breaks even (i.e. $\pi(P) \geqslant 0$), and second, it must set the level of the access charg

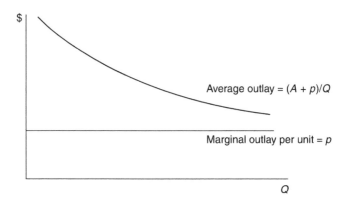

Figure 4.5 Average outlay and marginal outlay under two-part tariff

[25] In addition to the uniform two-part tariff, see also the discussion of declining block tariffs in Berg and
Tschirhart (1988) and Brown and Sibley (1986, chapter 4) and increasing block tariffs in Chapter 16 in
the present book.
[26] Coase (1946) presents an early analysis.

A such that consumers are still willing to consume the product (i.e. CS(P) $\geqslant$ 0), sometimes referred to as the participation constraint. Under the strong assumption that all consumers have identical consumption preferences, the most efficient solution, subject to these two constraints, is for the regulated access charge to be equal to the fixed costs per customer of the firm ($A^* = F$), and for the regulated per unit consumption or usage charge to equal the marginal costs of production ($P^* = c$). This pricing principle therefore combines the benefits of marginal cost pricing in terms of allocative efficiency through the consumption/usage charge (the first-best solution), while at the same time allowing the regulated firm to cover its fixed costs through the access charge, without the need for an external subsidy.

4.2.6 Menus of Two-Part Tariffs and Optimal Non-Linear Pricing

The above discussion suggests that uniform two-part tariffs offer a relatively simple method for setting optimal first-best prices, while, at the same time, allowing the firm to break even.[27] However, this result is based on the strong assumption that consumers have identical, or near-identical, preferences for the service. In reality, this assumption is unrealistic, and consumers are likely to have different willingness to pay for core network services, in large part because of income distribution effects. Accordingly, because consumers are likely to be willing to pay different amounts for the service (e.g. infrequent users may give a lower valuation to a service than heavy users of a service), a uniform two-part tariff may no longer be efficient. For example, some low-usage consumers may not be prepared to pay the fixed access charge, and decide not to consume the product at all.[28] This creates inefficiency because it excludes from the market consumers who may have been willing to pay an amount equal to marginal cost, or even an amount above marginal cost (which would contribute to the recovery of some portion of fixed costs), but lower than the combined two-part tariff, to consume some units of product. The approach also raises the potential that, while welfare may improve in the aggregate as a result of shifting from a system of linear pricing to a two-part tariff system, some consumers may be made worse off by such a shift.[29]

A non-linear tariff design – which allows consumers to choose from a *menu* of two-part tariffs – can potentially address this problem. For example, consumers might be offered two types of two-part tariffs, one with a low access charge but relatively higher per unit charge to attract low-usage consumers, and another tariff with a higher access charge but relatively lower per unit charge which should appeal to high-usage consumers. This approach can be more efficient than offering only a single uniform two-part tariff, as it allows for the inclusion in the market of low-usage consumers. This is illustrated in

---

[27] Berg and Tschirhart (1988) observe that it suggests: 'we can have our cake and eat it too'.

[28] The possibility of this occurring is likely to vary across the different utility sectors. For example, Berg and Tschirhart (1988) suggest that the access fee is unlikely to be viewed as too high by most consumers of electricity, whereas consumers of telephone services may be sensitive to the access price. Brown and Sibley (1986) reach a similar conclusion.

[29] See Berg and Tschirhart (1988). However, as Willig (1978) showed, by making the two-part tariff optional, it is possible that all consumers and producers are better off.

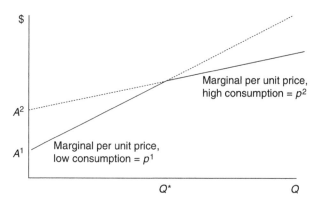

Figure 4.6 A self-selecting two-part tariff

Figure 4.6, where the firm offers two types of two-part tariffs. The first two-part tariff tailored to low-usage consumers and has a low access charge (A^1) but a higher per un usage charge (p^1); while the second two-part tariff is tailored to high-usage consume and has a relatively high access charge (A^2) and a lower per unit charge (p^2). It follow that customers who intend to consume an amount less than Q^* would have a lower tota expenditure if they choose the first two-part tariff (low access charge, high per un usage charge). Conversely, high-usage consumers who expect to consume an amoun greater than Q^* will have a lower total expenditure if they choose the second two-pa tariff (high access charge, low per unit charge). The solid line in Figure 4.6 represents th two-part tariff a rational consumer would choose which minimises expenditure give their expected consumption level. Implementing this menu approach depends criticall on obtaining information about different customer valuations, and on ensuring that th per unit charge for the low-usage consumers is sufficiently high to deter high-usag consumers from switching to choose that tariff (which has a lower access charge). Tha is, consumers of a particular class (low or high usage) must find it optimal to select th two-part tariff tailored to their preferences (represented by the solid line in Figure 4.6).

Two general conclusions can be made about non-linear pricing. The first conclusio is that, under standard assumptions, if a firm offers a schedule of non-linear price consumers will be better off relative to the case of linear average cost pricing (i.e. it is Pareto improvement).[30] Intuitively, by offering a schedule of non-linear prices (or a larg menu of two-part tariffs), a firm can increase participation in the market, and induce th more efficient allocation of the product, as customers self-select among different tari options to match their willingness to pay, while the per unit price of the output (the mar ginal price) moves towards marginal cost as the quantity demanded increases.[31] Howeve while the use of a schedule of non-linear prices can represent a (Pareto) improvement o linear average cost pricing, such a schedule will not necessarily be 'optimal' insofar as i

---

[30] See Willig (1978), Brown and Sibley (1986, chapter 4) and Train (1991, chapter 9).
[31] Willig (1978) shows that, in the standard analysis, Pareto efficiency requires that the marginal price for the largest purchaser is equal to marginal cost. In circumstances where this is not the case, then it is always possible to add an additional non-linear outlay schedule which Pareto dominates this schedule.

may not fully maximise total surplus. The problem of designing optimal non-linear pricing schedules is a highly technical area, but a key conclusion of this work is that optimal non-linear price schedules can involve both quantity discounts or quantity premiums, and that whether or not quantity discounts are optimal depends on the distribution of preferences among consumers.[32]

A second general conclusion is that the optimal non-linear price schedule for a single product can be viewed as a special case of Ramsey–Boiteux pricing, whereby different increments of consumption (for a single product) are effectively treated as separate markets, with the more inelastic increments being subject to higher mark-ups over marginal cost (and contributing most to the total costs of the firm), and the more elastic increments being priced at close to marginal cost. This means that high marginal prices should be established at consumption levels where demand for incremental consumption is relatively inelastic (i.e. not sensitive to price changes), while marginal prices should be set close to marginal cost where the demand for incremental consumption is relatively elastic. It follows that, as the quantity purchased increases along a given optimal non-linear outlay schedule (and assuming that each increment gradually becomes more price elastic), the marginal price will gradually fall and converge towards marginal cost. This implies that quantity discounts, whereby the marginal price paid for the largest quantity purchase is equal to marginal cost, may be efficient. A more general implication is that the inverse elasticity rule, as implied by the Ramsey–Boiteux principle, represents a unifying principle throughout efficient pricing theory, as it unifies optimal linear pricing and optimal non-linear pricing.[33]

4.3 PRICING PRINCIPLES FOR THE MULTI-PRODUCT FIRM

The discussion so far has assumed that a firm produces a single product in only one period, and the regulator has full information. While this assumed setting can highlight some of the general principles of efficient pricing, in the real world, firms supplying core network services almost always produce more than one product, and production occurs over a number of periods. Although the services provided by public utilities can appear similar in physical terms, such as electrons or bits, in economic terms they can be differentiated along a number of dimensions. For example, gas and electricity utilities typically differentiate their services according to the time at which the service is supplied (season and time of day, etc.) and according to the different types of customer (residential or industrial). Similarly, the same assets in a telecommunications utility – local exchanges, switching equipment, fibre-optic or cable loop networks – can be used to supply a range of different products, such as local and long-distance calls, fixed to mobile calls, broadband services and sometimes cable television and other Internet Protocol (IP) services.

As in the single-product case, marginal cost pricing remains the most allocatively efficient pricing approach in the multi-product context. That is, only where the per unit price for each product equals its marginal cost of production will total surplus be maximised

---

[32] Brown and Sibley (1986) present a thorough discussion of this issue.
[33] See Goldman, Leland and Sibley (1984) and Brown and Sibley (1986).

aggregated over all markets. However, as in the single-product case, if marginal pricing is implemented for all products, the firm's revenues may not cover its costs and the regulator is again faced with finding a mechanism that allows the firm to break even. Assuming that transfers or subsidies to the firm are ruled out, the regulator needs to determine which product's prices should deviate from marginal cost pricing, and by how much (recognising that such choices are likely to impact on different types of consumers and may have distributional effects). As in the single-product case, both linear and non-linear pricing approaches can be applied in the multi-product setting to address this problem, and these are discussed below. However, an additional complexity arises in the multi-product setting which relates to the presence of so-called joint and common costs, that is, costs which are common to the production of two or more products, but which are not specifically attributable to any one service.[34] Common costs are ubiquitous in the supply of core network services, and this raises important questions about how such costs can be recovered through prices levied on different products.

4.3.1 Constant Mark-Ups to Recover Fixed and Common Costs

The existence of joint and common costs raises an additional challenge for designing a pricing approach that allows the firm to break even.[35] One approach is to supplement the marginal cost for each product with some constant allocation of fixed and common costs that will allow the firm to break even across all of its products. For example, each product's per unit price might depart from marginal cost by a common percentage mark-up designed in such a way as to allow the firm to break even over all of its products. A common approach is to use some form of cost-based allocation method, such as the fully distributed costs (FDC) method, whereby fixed and common costs are *distributed* to individual products on the basis of their relative share of some measure (such as attributable cost, revenue, output or peak demand).[36] Another method is to allocate costs on the basis of equi-proportionate mark-ups (EPMU), whereby fixed and common costs are allocated to various products in proportion to a product's share of marginal incremental cost.

Cost-based allocation approaches are widely used in practice and allow for the recovery of total costs (i.e. the firm breaks even).[37] However, while these might be desirable from an accounting perspective, they are not useful in the determination of efficient

---

[34] Joint costs are costs that arise where the production of one product results in the joint production of another product in fixed proportions. Consequently, reducing the production of a single output will not reduce joint costs, but reducing the output of all activities will reduce joint costs. In contrast, common costs are costs necessary to produce one or more services, but which cannot be directly assigned to a specific product.

[35] Brown and Sibley (1986) describe the allocation of common costs as 'the source of many of the most muddled, lengthy and unsatisfactory proceedings in regulatory history'.

[36] Brown and Sibley (1986) describe this and other approaches in detail, noting that 'allocations have been done in literally dozens of ways in different regulatory proceedings'.

[37] Regulators tend to favour cost-based approaches to fixed and common cost recovery because they are considered to be 'simple' and 'practical', and because they are also seen as more transparent, which minimises the potential for regulatory gaming, as the necessary information can often be obtained from the firm's regulatory accounting data.

prices and, in economic terms, are arbitrary.[38] The pricing of different services is almost entirely dependent on the way in which allocators are chosen and implemented and, as a consequence, final prices for different products may bear little relationship to the underlying marginal costs for that product.[39] Indeed, cost-based methods can systematically lead to prices that are economically *inefficient*.[40]

4.3.2 Ramsey–Boiteux Pricing in the Multi-Product Setting

Ramsey–Boiteux pricing potentially offers a more efficient pricing approach in the multi-product setting that can minimise the distortion to social surplus from deviating from marginal cost pricing, while allowing the firm to recover its fixed and common costs. In the multi-product setting, where the demands for different products are independent, the per unit price for each product deviates from marginal cost according to the elasticity of demand for that particular product, with elastic products being priced at close to marginal cost and the price for inelastic products deviating from marginal cost by a wider margin, and in such a way so as to allow for the recovery of common costs and for the firm to break even. In effect, the fixed and common costs are spread across different products in such a way that products for which there is a higher willingness to pay (relatively inelastic demand) bear a higher burden of these costs.[41] Once again, the regulator's task therefore is to maximise the welfare function $V(P')$ – which, recall, is the weighted sum of consumer surplus and profit – but where P' now refers not to a single price, but rather to a vector of prices such that $P' = (P_1, P_2, ..., Pn)$. In the context of Ramsey–Boiteux pricing, the regulator would seek to set prices P' such that welfare is maximised:

$$V(P') = CS(P') + \alpha \pi(P')$$

(4.2)

subject to the constraint that profits are non-negative at those prices, that is, $\pi(P') \geqslant 0$. In natural monopoly industries characterised by economies of scale, the regulator's problem can be simplified to choosing a vector of prices (P') that maximise consumer surplus $(CS(P'))$ subject to the firm breaking even (i.e. where revenues are exactly equal to costs, and $\pi(P') = 0$). Where consumer demands for different products are independent (i.e. the

---

[38] See Friedlaender (1969), who argues that the arbitrary elements in all methods of pro-rating common or joint costs make them dangerous to use in prescribing rates. Berg and Tschirhart (1988) conclude that, as the numerous methods for distributing costs over the various outputs are all arbitrary, there is 'no one cost-allocation method that is consistently superior to the others on efficiency grounds'.

[39] Burton, Kaserman and Mayo (2009) argue that a possibly more significant concern is the *mis-estimation* of common costs (not merely the *mis-allocation* of common costs among products), such as the inappropriate characterisation of product-specific costs as being common among multiple products. They argue that the mis-estimation of costs can serve the purposes of both regulated firms (by facilitating entry deterrence) and regulators (by allowing cross-subsidisation to influential interest groups).

[40] See Braeutigam (1980) and Hausman (2000b). Studies in the telecommunications industry have indicated that the welfare costs associated with cost-based allocations may be significant. For example, Crandall and Waverman (1995) estimated the potential welfare gains from a shift to Ramsey–Boiteux pricing in the US telecommunications industry to be around $8 billion at that time.

[41] As Berg and Tschirhart (1988) observe, regulatory practitioners often refer to this approach as 'what the traffic can bear' or 'value of service pricing'. See the discussion of its use in railways in Chapter 14.

cross-elasticities of demand are zero), then the Ramsey–Boiteux pricing rule implies th
the price for each product should be increased in inverse proportion to its elasticity, suc
that the mark-up for each product should be

$$\frac{P_i - C_i}{P_i} = \frac{\lambda}{\eta_i},$$ (4.3)

where

$$\eta_i \equiv -P_i (\partial Q_i \, / \, \partial P_i) \, / \, Q_i.$$

In this Ramsey pricing rule equation (or inverse elasticity rule), P_i is the price of product
C_i is the marginal cost of product i, and η_i is the absolute value of the elasticity of deman
for product i. The value of λ, which is greater than or equal to zero ($\lambda \geqslant 0$), sometime
known as the 'Ramsey number', is proportionally constant and ensures that the resultin
mark-up applied across *all* products is such that the zero profit constraint is satisfied.[42]

It was assumed in the preceding discussion that the demands for the different outpu
produced by the firm are independent from one another. However, if the demand for
particular product is affected by the price of another product (i.e. there are cross-pric
effects) – either because it is a complement or a substitute for that product – then, und
Ramsey–Boiteux pricing, the deviation from marginal cost should incorporate both th
direct and indirect effects associated with a price change. That is, the deviation fro
marginal cost should account for both the own- and cross-price effects of the change i
price for a service.[43] In general, this implies that the mark-up should be smaller for con
plements, and larger for substitutes, reflecting the effects of a price change on comple
mentary or substitute services. This is of particular relevance in the context of the outpu
from core network activities, many of which are intermediate products in the productio
chain (and therefore complements to other services).

The optimality of Ramsey–Boiteux pricing in the multi-product setting is based on
number of important assumptions.[44] The most important of these is that the regulato
has at its disposal reliable information on demand and costs for the different service
provided by the regulated firm, and, more critically, that it can utilise this informatio
to set prices which will maximise total surplus. In addition, for the maximum alloca
tive efficiency gains to be achieved using this pricing approach, it is necessary that th
vector of all relevant prices be adjusted to reflect their elasticities.[45] Put differently,

---

[42] See Brown and Sibley (1986) and Baumol and Bradford (1970) for a fuller exposition of this result.

[43] In this case the elasticities are replaced by 'super-elasticities', which capture cross-price effects as well a
own-price effects. Rohlfs (1979) is generally credited with this development.

[44] One important extension of the Ramsey–Boiteux approach is in settings where the firm is not a monopoli
in all markets. Complex applications of Ramsey–Boiteux pricing might arise, for example, when a service
is supplied by multiple firms operating in an oligopolistic setting, or, alternatively, where a single service
provider offers a range of services, only some of which are regulated. An early analysis of the issues in
the context of inter-modal competition is presented in Braeutigam (1979). Valletti and Houpis (2005) and
Höffler (2006) present an analysis of the welfare effects of Ramsey–Boiteux pricing for mobile terminatio

[45] However, as Armstrong, Cowan and Vickers (1994) note, the Ramsey–Boiteux approach does not requir
that common costs be 'allocated' in any sense to individual products. Accordingly, in the special case
where the demand for one product is very inelastic, the optimum pricing structure may involve setting
the price for the very inelastic product at a level sufficient to cover any shortfall in the firm's profit, and
the prices of all other products should be set at almost close to marginal cost.

the price of only one service is adjusted to reflect its elasticity, while other prices are set on the basis of other factors (such as a uniform mark-up), this is less efficient than if all prices deviate from marginal cost according to their elasticities. Despite the attractive efficiency properties of Ramsey–Boiteux pricing, which have endeared it to many economists,[46] there has been reluctance by regulators and public utility companies to apply the approach in practice.[47] While generally accepting the efficiency properties *in principle*, regulatory agencies have typically avoided using Ramsey–Boiteux-based pricing approaches in practice. Four general reasons are typically given by regulators for this choice. First, that Ramsey–Boiteux pricing is impracticable to implement, as it requires detailed information on demand elasticities.[48] Second, that specific market or structural conditions are not suitable for the implementation of Ramsey–Boiteux pricing. Third, that the fixed and common costs in an activity are *de minimis* and immaterial.[49] Finally, that Ramsey pricing structures, while efficient, may not be equitable – or fair – price structures.[50] This last consideration, sometimes explicitly noted, but more often implicit, highlights the fact that Ramsey–Boiteux pricing can involve distributive issues, and, in particular, concerns that it may result in 'unfair' prices for specific customer groups.[51]

4.3.3 Peak-Load Pricing

A common attribute of most public utility industry services discussed in Part III of this book – such as energy, transport, communications and water services – is that demand can vary significantly across times of the day and seasonally. This has implications for network design and for setting efficient prices. Specifically, it raises the issue of whether the network should be built so as to satisfy demand at all points in time (including peak demand) or whether the network capacity should be conditioned to satisfy lower levels of demand (i.e. average demand), implying that, at times of peak demand, some customers will be rationed and may not access the service at all, or obtain a lower volume of the product than desired.

---

[46] An exception is Kamerschen and Keenan (1983), who describe Ramsey–Boiteux pricing as a 'theoretical curiosity'. Berg and Tschirhart (1988) also discuss some of the more general arguments against Ramsey pricing, including those related to the problems of 'the second best', and note that '[s]ome economists conclude that these limitations invalidate the use of Ramsey principles in practice'.

[47] Laffont and Tirole (1993) observe that even Électricité de France exhibited this reluctance despite the fact that its staff – particularly Marcel Boiteux, who was at one time Chairman – made pioneering contributions to the theory of Ramsey–Boiteux pricing.

[48] For example, the ICC (1985) in the USA stated that: '[T]he amount of data and degree of analysis seemed overwhelming. We concluded that while formal Ramsey pricing is useful as a theoretical guideline, it is too difficult and burdensome for universal application.'

[49] While this may not appear to be relevant to many public utility industries, this reasoning has been used in the context of the setting of mobile termination access services. See ACCC (2005) and Ofcom (2004a).

[50] For example, the UK regulators of postal services and electricity have at times dismissed the use of Ramsey–Boiteux pricing, in part, on this basis. See Postcomm (2006) and Ofgem (2000).

[51] See Zajac (1978) and Berg and Tschirhart (1988) on 'winners and losers' associated with a movement to Ramsey–Boiteux pricing. Tirole (2017) discusses how, notwithstanding the major economic distortions, keeping prices low was a 'relatively painless means of redistribution, as the demand for goods and services such as electricity or telecom connection is inelastic, but an important expenditure for less well-off households'. Vickers (1997) argues that, although Ramsey principles can 'readily be adapted to accommodate distributional concerns', this does not mean that regulators should be permitted to make such adaptations.

In all of the public utility industries, the network is typically built to have sufficient capacity available in periods of peak demand.[52] The essential reason for this is that given the nature of the products, it is difficult, or in some cases impossible, to build up inventories, and therefore the physical capacity of the network must be sufficient to accommodate periods of high demand.[53] This raises a question: who should bear the capital costs associated with building, or expanding, a network to satisfy peak demand? If, for example, a rail network is expanded to satisfy peak-period commuters (the existing capacity being sufficient for off-peak users), should only the peak-period customers face the additional costs? Or should the costs be shared among all users? Moreover, given that the bulk of capital costs in the core network activities tend to be involved in developing assets to be capable of satisfying peak levels of demand – or put differently, peak-demand users are *causing* these costs – how can such (typically large) costs be efficiently recovered through prices?

One method for efficiently recovering peak capacity costs is peak-load pricing.[54] Peak load pricing differentiates between customers in high- and low-demand periods, charging a higher price to 'peak' customers than to 'off-peak' customers, which is intended to reflect the different marginal costs associated with supplying the service at different points in time. In the standard case – where peak demand is always assumed to be higher than off-peak demand – peak-demand prices are set at a high level to reflect the marginal operating costs *and* the marginal capital costs associated with supplying a unit of peak capacity at that time.[55] In low-demand periods, where lower levels of capacity could meet demand, the price is set to recover only the marginal operating costs of producing that unit of off-peak capacity.

Three observations can be made about the peak-load pricing approach. Firstly, in the standard 'firm peak' case described above, *all* of the costs associated with the extra capacity needed to satisfy peak demand are recovered through peak-period prices only.[56] Secondly, in many public utility industries – such as electricity, water and telecommunications – where the level of operating costs per unit are low, applying this approach will result in prices close to zero in off-peak periods. Thirdly, in principle, peak-load pricing can lead to allocative efficiency, as each class of user is paying a price that reflects the

---

[52] This does not mean that there should always be infinite spare capacity available and therefore zero network congestion. In the electricity industry, in particular, there is an important trade-off between the costs of managing congestion and the costs of new capacity. In some cases, it can be efficient to have some network congestion rather than undertake investments in new capacity. The optimal level of congestion depends on the relative costs of congestion *vis-à-vis* investment in new capacity.

[53] For example, the network assets must be able to accommodate the flow of power when it is actually demanded by customers (such as on a hot summer's afternoon), or, in the case of telephone or broadband networks, there must be sufficient capacity available when people actually want to talk to one another or use the Internet. Put differently, having spare network capacity available at 3 a.m. on the telephone, electricity or rail networks is unlikely to be of any use to anyone, as demand is generally low at that time.

[54] Ault and Ekelund (1987), Berg and Tschirhart (1988) and Crew, Fernando and Kleindorfer (1995) present historical accounts of the development of peak-load pricing.

[55] See Boiteux (1949) and Steiner (1957) for expositions of the standard model of peak-load pricing.

[56] In contrast, under the so-called 'shifting peak' case, the marginal cost of capacity is shared between peak and off-peak users, but the peak price reflects a higher proportion than the off-peak price to reflect the differences in the marginal willingness to pay between the two groups of users. See Steiner (1957) and Joskow (2007a).

marginal costs of production, and, at the same time, the firm can recover sufficient revenues to cover total costs by spreading the total costs over different users of the network capacity. In essence, then, this pricing approach assumes units of consumption in peak and off-peak periods are essentially separate products and that efficiency requires their prices reflect their respective marginal supply costs.[57]

However, the standard peak-load pricing result is sensitive to a number of assumptions.[58] One important assumption is that demand at different points in time is largely independent. That is, consumers in peak periods are unlikely to consider consumption in an off-peak period as a substitute, and vice versa. In practice, however, there can be a close degree of substitutability between consumption in different periods, and, depending on the relative price difference, some peak consumers may decide to switch to off-peak consumption.[59] The standard result also assumes that the periods of peak and off-peak demand can be separately defined with some precision. However, in many public utility industries, demand is more continuous and varies at different points during a day and over a year according to a range of factors (weather, etc.). The standard peak-load pricing result also makes specific assumptions about the production technology employed in deriving the results.[60] Finally, peak-load pricing can require considerable amounts of information, including an ability to measure demand at different points in the day and in different seasons with some precision.[61]

4.3.4 Non-Linear Pricing in the Multi-Product Setting

It may be possible to improve allocative efficiency if a multi-product firm is able to implement various forms of non-linear pricing.[62] Here, as in the single-product setting, improvements in efficiency will occur whenever the non-linear pricing structure allows

---

[57] See Joskow (2007a).

[58] Braeutigam (1989) explores these points in relation to technology and demand. Crew, Fernando and Kleindorfer (1995) examine the issue of supply and demand uncertainty.

[59] Joskow (2007a) observes that this situation has occurred in the electricity industry in a number of countries where the off-peak tariff was set so low that some residential consumers installed store-heating equipment that allowed them to utilise electricity in the off-peak period (i.e. overnight).

[60] The standard result is based on an assumed fixed coefficients (Leontief) production technology. However, when other production functions are used (such as a neoclassical production function), different results will follow, implying that care is required in applying the results. See Berg and Tschirhart (1988). Panzar (1976) has shown that, when a neoclassical technology function is assumed, *all* periods – including off-peak – contribute to the cost of capacity, with the largest output making the greatest contribution. Crew, Fernando and Kleindorfer (1995) examine the impact of a 'diverse technology' where more than one type of production technology can meet demand.

[61] This is likely to pose more of a problem in some industries than others. For example, it has historically been more difficult to measure real-time usage in the water and energy industries than in other sectors such as rail and telecommunications. However, the emergence of 'smart meters' and other 'smart grid' innovations can generate greater real-time usage information and allow for the design of real-time pricing in industries such as electricity, where marginal costs vary continuously according to changes in demand and the marginal costs of production. See Joskow and Wolfram (2012). More generally, see the work of William Vickrey, who first proposed a system of congestion pricing for the New York City subway system in 1952. Vickrey (1971) discusses the benefits of introducing responsive pricing for public utility services.

[62] The analysis of the optimal non-linear tariffs for a multi-product firm is technical and complex. The interested reader is referred to Laffont and Tirole (1993,chapter 3), Armstrong, Cowan and Vickers (1994, chapter 3) or Armstrong (1996a).

the marginal prices for the different products to move closer towards their respective marginal costs. More generally, in the multi-product setting, it is possible that allocative efficiency can be improved through the use of tariffs that offer quantity discounts rather than simple two-part tariffs. While this was also the case in the single-product case, in the multi-product case the possibility arises for quantity discounts to be applied across a range of products produced by the firm, such as where a customer purchases both fixed line telephone services and broadband services from the same telecommunications provider.

4.4 REGULATION IN THE CONTEXT OF IMPERFECT INFORMATION

So far we have assumed that the regulator has perfect information about cost levels, consumer preferences, demand and the amount of any cost-reducing effort undertaken by the firm.[63] This assumption is clearly unrealistic and, in almost all settings, there is an information asymmetry between the regulator and the firm: firms know more about their costs, their production technology and the level of effort devoted to reducing costs than the regulator does.[64] Firms will also often have superior information on the sensitivity of demand to changes in price. This information asymmetry can create incentives for a firm to act strategically, for example, by misrepresenting information, such as overstating true costs, which ultimately will result in inefficiency.

The presence of asymmetric information complicates the task of a regulator in setting or approving prices, and requires it to engage in methods to verify the true level of cost of the firm. Looked at in this way, the regulatory task can be seen to embody a form of principal–agent problem, where the regulator (principal) attempts to control the firm (agent) who is in possession of superior information. Accordingly, the regulator's task becomes one of achieving a close to optimal level of efficiency, while minimising the benefit the firm obtains as a result of its information monopoly.[65] In most circumstances, this will require the regulator to trade off allocative efficiency, productive efficiency and distributional concerns.

There are different approaches to analysing the issue of optimal regulatory policies in the context of asymmetric information.[66] In the discussion below, we consider two

---

[63] Baron and Besanko (1984a) observe that, under the full information assumption, '[R]egulation takes a particularly simple form. The regulator determines the optimal policy and the firm implements it faithfully, presumably because the regulator would be able to observe whether the firm deviated from that policy.'

[64] Although, as Weitzman (1978) observed, it should not always be assumed that the managers or engineers of firms will have perfect knowledge about their own production costs.

[65] Caillaud, Guesnerie, Rey and Tirole (1987) describe the firm as having an 'informational monopoly' insofar as it earns rents due to its private information. In essence, the rent arises from the incentives for an efficient (low-cost) firm to hide this fact from the regulator and to present itself as a relatively inefficient (high-cost) firm, in an effort to induce the regulator to set higher prices. Where this occurs, the firm keeps part of the difference between the prices (which were based on the mistaken assumption of it being a high-cost firm) and its true (low level of) costs.

[66] See Laffont (1994) and Armstrong and Sappington (2007). One stream of work, generally associated with Laffont and Tirole (1986), abstracts from the issue of distributional preferences, but assumes that there is a social cost of public funds (i.e. there are costs associated with raising funds from taxpayers). Another stream of work, following from Baron and Myerson (1982), assumes that the regulator has distributional preferences (i.e. prefers consumer surplus to rent) but abstracts from the issue of whether there is a social cost of public funds. Both approaches achieve similar conclusions. Another important difference concerns whether the regulator is assumed to be able to make direct transfer payments to the firm or not.

scenarios: The first is where the firm has better information than the regulator about the cost and demand conditions it faces, but is unable to change these conditions (so-called 'hidden information'). In the second scenario, the firm can influence conditions, such as the level of costs, through its effort, but this information is not known to the regulator (called 'hidden action'). Both of these general cases are examined with a view to high-lighting what they imply about the ability of the regulator to design efficient pricing prin-ciples.[67] For the purposes of the scenarios, it is assumed that the social cost of public funds is zero, but that the regulator has distributional preferences (i.e. the regulator attaches less weight to a firm's profitability than to consumer surplus) and that direct payments are feasible; finally, that the regulator is able to make lump-sum transfers, and the firm produces a single product.[68]

4.4.1 Hidden Information

To begin, it is useful to examine a case where the first-best allocatively efficient outcome (i.e. marginal price equal to marginal cost) can still be achieved *even in* settings charac-terised by asymmetric information, such as where the firm has hidden information about its costs. Loeb and Magat (1979) present a model where both parties have information about consumer demand, but the regulator does not know about the firm's cost function. Loeb and Magat's analysis implies that the optimal outcome can be achieved if the firm chooses its own price, and the regulator subsidises the firm on a per unit basis equal to the consumer surplus at that selected price. Critically for the result, the regulator is assumed to maximise the sum of consumer and producer surplus, but does not apply any weight to reducing the profits of the firm.[69] That is, the regulator is *not* concerned about the distribution of rents between firms and consumers, and the regulated firm is therefore allowed to retain all the revenue from sales *plus* it is entitled to a subsidy equal to the entire consumer surplus.

This result can be explained as follows. Although consumer demand is known by both parties, the regulator does not know about the firm's cost function, which can be expressed as $C(Q,e)$, where Q is the actual costs and e reflects the cost-reducing effort. The regulator's task is, for each price P, to maximise the sum of consumer and producer surplus (but not apply any weight to reduce the profits of the firm) and then make a lump-sum payment to the firm equal to the entire consumer surplus at that price. Accordingly, at price P^* the firm's profit is

$$\pi(P^*) = CS(P^*) + P * (Q(P^*)) - C(Q(P^*), e^*), \tag{4.4}$$

[67] In principal–agent framework terms, the problem of hidden information is essentially an adverse selection problem, while hidden action is a moral hazard problem. See Caillaud, Guesnerie, Rey and Tirole (1987).

[68] Sappington (1983) extends the analysis of information asymmetries to the multi-product setting where the technological capabilities of the firm (i.e. the actual cost function) is unobservable to the regulator. Armstrong, Cowan and Vickers (1994) describe the problem of asymmetric information in a multi-product setting. They conclude that, while the analysis is more complicated, the basic principles of optimal regulation are essentially the same in single-product and multi-product settings.

[69] In other words, the regulator is not concerned about distributional issues, and therefore does not place any lower weight on profit than consumer surplus. That is, $\alpha = 1$ in equation (4.1) above.

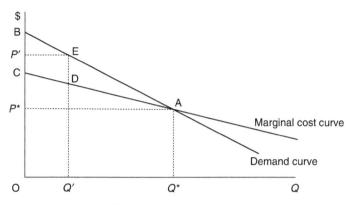

Figure 4.7 The Loeb–Magat incentive arrangement

and the firm will choose P^* and e^* to maximise welfare, which is where the price equal marginal cost, given the level of demand.

This is shown in Figure 4.7, where, at price P^*, the firm will obtain revenue from sale equal to the area OQ^*AP^* and will also receive the entire consumer surplus at that pric as a subsidy from the regulator, the area P^*AB. The variable costs for the firm at tha level of output is equal to the area OQ^*AC, and the overall profit for the firm at price P is therefore the area CAB. Figure 4.7 shows that, if the firm charges any price other tha that where price equals marginal cost P^* for a given level of demand, its profits will b reduced. For example, if the firm charged P' and produced Q', its revenue from sales wi be the area OQ' EP', its transfer subsidy will be the consumer surplus at that price, whic is the area P' EB, and its variable costs will be OQ' DC, making its profits only CDEB. Thi means that, by raising the price above P^*, the firm has reduced its profits by the area DAE Figure 4.7 also illustrates the incentives that the firm has to be productively efficient, a any reductions in marginal costs (a shift downwards in the marginal cost curve) automat ically result in additional profit to the firm.

It follows that, under the Loeb and Magat arrangement, the firm is motivated to se prices at marginal cost, and to engage in cost-reducing effort to the greatest extent pos sible to minimise the total level of costs, as the firm immediately receives the benefit of its cost-reducing efforts through the subsidy payment. In other words, under thes assumptions, full allocative and productive efficiencies are achieved. In addition, becaus price decisions are decentralised, the firm no longer has incentives to overstate its tru costs, and the regulator does not need not to incur expense and effort in verifying th cost data of the firm; thus the problems associated with the cost information asymmetr are avoided. However, while allocative and productive efficiencies can be achieved, thi comes at a cost: producers receive the entire surplus and consumers receive none.[70]

While analytically interesting, Loeb and Magat's analysis sidesteps the important issu of what happens where there is a trade-off between efficiency and distribution, as is ofter

---

[70] Loeb and Magat (1979) recognise this equity issue and note that the arrangement could be combined with the sale of a franchise to operate the firm to reduce or eliminate the net subsidy provided to the regulated firm. Sharkey (1979) critiques the general subsidy approach, noting it 'would be wholly unworkable in practice'.

the case in practice; that is, where the distribution of total surplus between consumers and producers matters. Later work incorporated the trade-off where a regulator is assumed to have both consumer and producer surplus objectives (i.e. the regulator is concerned about the distribution of the total surplus), but where the firm is still assumed to have hidden information about the true level of its costs.

Baron and Myerson (1982) examine a situation where a regulator attempts to maximise a weighted sum of the gains to consumers and the expected profit of the firm (i.e. α, which represents the relative weight given to profits, is assumed to lie in the range $0 \leqslant \alpha \leqslant 1$).[71] As with Loeb and Magat's analysis, the firm's profit function comprises two elements: the profit from sales *and* a transfer payment (either a subsidy or a tax) designed to induce the firm to reveal its costs and allow it to cover its fixed costs. However, unlike the Loeb and Magat arrangement (where the transfer payment was equal to consumer surplus), in this case the transfer payment can vary, and is the mechanism by which the regulator incentivises the firm to honestly reveal its costs; if it is a low-cost firm, it is rewarded by a subsidy when it reports low costs, or, alternatively, punished by a tax if it misreports high costs.

Accordingly, on this reasoning, the regulator uses the transfer payment as an incentive mechanism to get the firm to accurately reveal its costs, which then allows it to set prices at close to marginal cost. However, this gives rise to a trade-off: while better information can allow the regulator to set allocatively efficient prices, this will come at the cost of a higher subsidy and therefore impact on any distributional objectives. An important conclusion of this analysis is that the optimal price may need to be set above marginal cost; this entails a degree of allocative inefficiency, but recognises that the regulator also has distributional objectives.[72] This loss in allocative efficiency relative to what can be achieved under perfect information is the direct result of the firm having private information on costs, and of the need for the regulator to reward the firm for reporting its true level of costs while ensuring some desired distribution of total surplus between consumers and producers. In short, the optimal arrangement involves striking a balance between allocative efficiency and the distributional objectives (minimisation of the transfer rent paid to the firm).[73]

4.4.2 Hidden Action

So far our discussion has focused on settings characterised by hidden information, where costs are assumed to be exogenous and unobservable by the regulator. Laffont and Tirole (1986) examine a situation that involves elements of both hidden information and hidden

---

[71] Baron and Myerson (1982) assume a setting where demand conditions are known by all parties and there is a constant (exogenously set) cost of production, which is a function of output and is known only to the firm, but where the regulator has some prior probability distribution of the likely level of costs.

[72] The degree of allocative inefficiency will be related to the importance attached to distributional concerns. Specifically, the greater the importance, the greater the potential level of allocative inefficiency.

[73] One extension to the Baron and Myerson model is to allow the regulator to audit and monitor costs after production has occurred and to disallow costs, or order refunds to customers, where the firm has misreported its costs at the *ex ante* stage. Baron and Besanko (1984a) analyse this possibility in a one-period model where the regulator has such an ability to audit and make *ex post* adjustments.

action. Specifically, the regulator can observe unit costs and outputs of the firm, but unable to identify the level of cost-reducing effort by the firm, nor the level of efficienc or any potential causes of cost disturbance. In other words, if the regulator observes hig unit costs, it is unable to determine whether this is attributable to the fact that the fir is naturally a high-cost firm, or whether it is the result of the firm not engaging in suff cient cost-reducing actions. In these circumstances, the regulator determines the optim regulatory arrangements on the basis of two observables – prices and costs – and ar transfer is therefore conditioned on both price and cost. This is akin to the regulator offe ing the firm a menu of linear incentive contracts, where the firm is granted a transfer tha decreases with increases in cost; the higher the cost, the lower the transfer payment (an vice versa), such that a high-cost firm will choose a high-cost but low-transfer contrac while a low-cost firm will choose a low-cost but high-transfer contract.[74] Unlike Baro and Myerson's analysis, prices need not deviate from observed marginal costs in this cas but per unit marginal costs (and therefore prices) are higher than in the perfect informa tion scenario. Consequently, while allocative efficiency is achieved, there is still a welfa loss relative to the perfect information benchmark. Once again, this derives from the fir having private information about its own cost-reducing efforts, which can allow it increase marginal cost to a (productively) inefficient level. Assuming that the regulat has distributional objectives, the optimal outcome will therefore involve allowing som degree of productive inefficiency.[75]

A key difference between the Baron and Myerson analysis and that of Laffont an Tirole is that, while *prices* deviate from the optimal level in the former case to limit th firm's rent from its 'information monopoly', in the latter analysis it is *costs* which devia from the optimal level to limit the firm's rent.[76]

4.4.3 Demand Information Asymmetries

To this point we have focused on cases where a firm has private information about i costs; however, the regulated firm may also have better information about demand tha the regulator. Riordan (1984) examines the situation where the regulator has full knowl edge of costs,[77] but the firm has better information about demand than the regulato This analysis concludes that optimal prices involve the use of a subsidy mechanism t

---

[74] Put differently, the most efficient firms would choose a fixed price contract, as this incentivises effort, while less efficient firms would choose a cost-plus-type contract, as this guarantees cost reimbursement

[75] The extent of productive efficiency is again related to the distributional concerns; where the regulator has a high concern for distribution then there will be greater productive inefficiency, and higher marginal prices.

[76] See Armstrong and Sappington (2007). Laffont and Tirole's model has more general implications in terms of the incentives created under different forms of price regulation, as it highlights the trade-off between cost efficiency and information rents, and implies that fixed price regulatory arrangements (such as pure price cap regulation) may improve cost efficiency but this may come at the expense of firms not revealing information about their cost-reducing efforts. Conversely, under pure rate of return regulation, the firm has incentives to reveal its private information about its cost-reducing efforts, but this may come at the expense of potential cost efficiency gains. See Laffont (1999).

[77] Unlike Lewis and Sappington (1988) discussed below, Riordan (1984) assumes that output is produced a a constant marginal cost up to an endogenous capacity level.

incentivise the firm to reveal the true demand conditions (and thus eliminate the information asymmetry) and which establishes a lump-sum subsidy (or tax) for each price.[78] Lewis and Sappington (1988) also examine a setting involving potential transfer payments to the firm in the context of asymmetric demand information. However, under their assumptions, the optimal policy is sensitive to whether marginal costs of production are assumed to increase or decrease with output. Specifically, in the case of increasing marginal costs, the firm obtains no benefit from its private demand information and will therefore implement efficient prices. Conversely, where marginal costs decrease with output, the regulator should not delegate pricing authority to the firm, but rather use its own (imperfect) information to set a single price to be charged across all demand levels (this results in a price above marginal cost for low-demand states, and a price below marginal cost for high-demand states). An important implication of this analysis is that the optimal regulatory policy will differ in qualitative dimensions depending on whether the firm's private information relates to costs or to demand (or both).[79]

4.5 PRICING IN A MULTI-PERIOD CONTEXT

An implicit assumption in the discussion of efficient pricing principles thus far is that production occurs only within a single period. This is an unrealistic assumption for many regulated industries where production typically extends over a long period of time, and where there are multiple interactions between the regulator and the regulated firm. In the multi-period context, the *expectations* of different parties become important, particularly the expectations about how the regulator (or the firm) will behave in the future.

4.5.1 Short-Run and Long-Run Marginal Cost Pricing

One characteristic of core network activities is that they typically involve large capital investments (in pipes, wires or rails) that have a useful life that extends over a number of decades. In these circumstances, the regulator is faced with the question of how these large, and typically indivisible, capital costs should be recovered through prices levied on existing and future consumers. The question of whether efficient prices should be based on long-run marginal costs rather than short-run marginal costs has been extensively analysed,[80] and remains an important issue for regulators in a number of public utility industries.

While short-run marginal cost (SRMC) pricing is the most allocatively efficient in any one period (for the reasons given above), in the multi-period context, prices based on SRMC may have adverse effects on dynamic efficiency. Specifically, they may provide incentives for public utility firms to hold back on investment in additional, or incremental,

---

[78] Specifically, a negative relationship between subsidy and price is established. It is, however, assumed that the regulator knows the short-run marginal cost of output, and the unit cost of capacity. For more on this approach, and how it relates to peak-load pricing, see Train (1991).

[79] See Lewis and Sappington (1988).

[80] Ekelund (1968) observes ambiguity even in Dupuit's (1844) work on marginal cost pricing, and that: 'Dupuit appears to have been intuitively groping toward a long-period concept of marginal costs.'

capacity in circumstances when demand is high, and capacity is close to full utilisation and therefore prices (based on SRMC) are high. In these circumstances, investment in additional capacity may reduce any so-called 'congestion rents'. Similarly, the incentive for innovation may be dampened under SRMC pricing, as such pricing may not allow for any fixed and sunk costs associated with research and development to be recovered through charges.

In practice, long-run marginal cost (LRMC) pricing can address some of these dynamic incentive issues. Prices based on LRMC can create more constant incentives for a firm to invest in incremental capacity by not rewarding firms for failing to alleviate congestion on the network. However, setting prices based on LRMC will, in many circumstances, result in a reduction in short-term allocative efficiency, as prices are likely to deviate, in any period, from those implied by a short-term marginal cost approach. Nevertheless, it is precisely because of the automatic de-linking of prices from short-run costs that the potential for dynamic efficiency gains is seen to arise. Firms, it is argued, will be incentivised to adopt a longer time horizon when considering investments and innovation activities.

4.5.2 Dynamic Regulation with Asymmetric Information and Transfers

Regulation typically involves repeated interactions between a regulator and a regulated firm, and this dynamic relationship can give a different complexion to some of the regulatory principles discussed above. On the one hand, the repeated interaction between the regulator and the firm can alleviate the problem of information asymmetries if the regulator can use information (such as about costs and outputs, etc.) revealed in the first period to improve its implementation of regulatory principles in subsequent periods. On the other hand, the firm may recognise that information revealed in one period – for example, about its actual level of costs – will be used in subsequent regulatory determinations, and this can create incentives for the firm to act strategically, and only take actions in the current period which do not jeopardise future regulatory outcomes.[81]

Incremental Surplus Subsidy Scheme

Where a regulator is able to use transfers to regulated firms (and it should be noted here again that, in practice, most are unable to do so), there are a number of possible mechanisms that could, in principle, result in efficient pricing in the multi-period context. The regulator could, for example, adopt an iterative approach, whereby prices adjust towards marginal costs over time.[82] Sappington and Sibley (1988) draw upon the Loeb and Magat analysis described above (where, recall, the firm receives the entire consumer surplus) to develop a method for returning surplus to consumers over time while still encouraging the firm to set prices at marginal cost. Specifically, they propose an 'incremental surplus subsidy scheme' which involves the regulator paying a transfer to the firm in each period

---

[81] See Baron and Besanko (1984b), and the discussion of the 'ratchet effect' in Chapters 5 and 8.
[82] Finsinger and Vogelsang (1985) present an early exposition of such an approach, where any potential welfare gain is provided to management as income.

equal to the *incremental* change in consumer surplus (not the entire consumer surplus) generated by a price change between the two periods *less* the firm's accounting profit in the previous period. According to this scheme, the firm chooses a price (p^t) in each period t such that it receives: the profit from production in that period (π^t) *plus* a transfer payment in that period (T^t). The transfer payment paid in period t consists of two terms:

$$T^t = (\mathrm{CS}^t - \mathrm{CS}^{t-1}) - \pi^{t-1}. \tag{4.5}$$

The first term in equation (4.5), $(\mathrm{CS}^t - \mathrm{CS}^{t-1})$, represents the incremental change in consumer surplus generated by a change in prices between period $t-1$ and period t. The second term, which is subtracted from the transfer, is the accounting profit in period $t-1$, which is the difference between revenue and expenditure in period $t-1$.[83] In setting prices in any one period, the firm will therefore have regard to: (1) its profit in that period (i.e. $\pi^t(p^t)$); (2) the transfer payment it will generate in this period (i.e. T^t); and (3) its transfer payment in the next period (i.e. T^{t+1}).

The central result is that, at any price set in the first period, the greatest incremental change in consumer surplus will always occur if price is adjusted to marginal cost in the second period, and therefore the firm will be incentivised to set price at marginal cost in the second period and every period but the first. The firm therefore makes a positive rent in only the first period, and in every period thereafter will set price equal to marginal cost while receiving a transfer which allows it to break even. In principle, then, this approach induces the firm to set marginal cost prices and minimise production costs in every period, and eliminates the rents the firm may obtain from its 'information monopoly' in every period but the first.[84]

Regulatory Commitment

An important factor in examining the optimality of different policies in the multi-period context is the ability of the regulator to commit *ex ante* to specific regulatory policies, and, in particular, whether it chooses to use any information revealed in the first period in subsequent periods (we address some of the general issues of regulatory commitment in Chapter 8). A number of studies have focused on the more specific issue of how different levels of regulatory commitment impact on the implementation of optimal regulatory principles in the context of asymmetric information.

In a dynamic extension of the Baron and Myerson (1982) model described above, Baron and Besanko have examined the effect of different levels of regulatory commitment.[85] In the full commitment case – that is, where the regulator can fully commit not to use information revealed in one period in subsequent regulatory reviews – the optimal outcome is the same as in the single-period case; in each period the regulator applies

---

[83] Sappington and Sibley (1988) use expenditure (E^{t-1}) rather than production costs (C^{t-1}) to reflect the fact that a firm can exaggerate costs. Expenditure can also include capital expenditure.

[84] Armstrong and Sappington (2007) provide an exposition of this result. They also identify a number of drawbacks.

[85] See Baron and Besanko (1984b, 1987).

the optimal static arrangement as described in Baron and Myerson (1982) above. This is because, although the regulator could use information obtained in a previous period to adjust prices to marginal cost, it commits to ignore such information for the simple reason that if it did not do so the firm would, anticipating such an adjustment, require a larger transfer payment in the first period.[86] However, where the regulator cannot commit to such a policy, then the situation becomes more complex, and this can create incentives for the firm to act strategically.[87] Specifically, if the regulator adjusts prices in any subsequent period to reflect the marginal costs revealed by the firm in the previous period, then the firm will effectively lose its information monopoly and will obtain no rent transfer in subsequent periods. In anticipation of this possibility, the firm might decide to misreport its costs in the first period, for example, by choosing a slightly higher price than the optimal, which will allow it to earn some profits in the second period when prices are adjusted by the regulator to the inflated level of costs. In short, knowing that the regulator will adjust prices to observed costs in the second period, the firm has an incentive to overstate its level of costs in the first period.

Laffont and Tirole (1988, 1993) also extend their analysis of optimal regulation under asymmetric information (discussed above) to a two-period model. They assume that the regulator is unable to commit itself to not using information about the firm's performance in the second period, and examine the 'ratchet effect' (where, if the firm performs well and produces at low cost in the first period, the regulator tries to extract the firm's rent by being more demanding in a subsequent period). In this context, under different assumptions about the relevant discount factor, they examine the possibility that inefficient firms may decide to mimic an efficient firm in the first period (and obtain a large transfer in the first period) but then 'quit' the relationship in the second period, effectively 'taking the money and running'.[88]

4.5.3 Dynamic Regulation, Imperfect Information and No Transfers

The discussion in Section 4.5.2 has assumed that the regulator is able to use transfers in the multi-period context to induce optimal regulatory outcomes. However, as noted, in practice regulators are generally unable to offer transfers to a regulated firm, and, as a consequence, can only implement optimal regulatory policies through its decisions in relation to pricing.

Accordingly, in this more realistic context, the focus turns to the properties of different forms of price control arrangements, and in particular the incentives that each can create for the firm to set different price structures, which has impacts for efficiency. This is an issue that we address in Chapter 5 in some detail. For current purposes, we briefly introduce an important contribution by Vogelsang and Finsinger (1979) which sought to develop a decentralised incentive mechanism that would motivate a multi-product firm to

---

[86] See Baron and Besanko (1987).

[87] Baron and Besanko (1984b) examine optimal regulatory policies under a number of different assumed information cases, including where marginal costs in different periods are completely independent and where marginal costs are perfectly correlated.

[88] See Laffont and Tirole (1988) and Laffont and Tirole (1993, chapter 9).

set economically efficient prices in a context of asymmetric information.[89] Their analysis suggested that, under certain conditions, a regulator could introduce a pricing mechanism that, over the long term, could result in prices that converge towards Ramsey–Boiteux prices, while at the same time ensuring that the firm does not make a loss. In a nutshell, the mechanism involves the regulator observing the output and cost in one period and then using that information obtained to establish a *constraint* on prices in the following period. Specifically, the constraint is such that the proposed prices in a current period, when applied to the previous period's outputs (i.e. $P^t Q^{t-1}$), does not exceed total observed costs in the previous period (i.e. $C(Q^{t-1})$). In the simple case where the firm only supplies one output, then the mechanism requires that

$$P^t Q^{t-1} \leqslant C(Q^{t-1}). \tag{4.6}$$

In the multiple-product context, such as where the firm supplies two products (*a* and *b*), the constraint becomes

$$P_a^t Q_a^{t-1} + P_b^t Q_b^{t-1} \leqslant C^{t-1}, \tag{4.7}$$

where C^{t-1} represents the total observed costs of the multi-product firm in the previous period. This constraint implies that prices in the current period, when applied to the previous period's output, cannot exceed the observed costs in the previous period (which in the single-product case is equal to average cost in the previous period at that quantity). In this analysis, consumer surplus increases in each period by an amount at least equal to the previous period's profit, while, at the same time, the firm still earns a non-negative (albeit lower) profit in each period.[90] Over time, the firm will progressively lower its price, and increase output, until it reaches a point where the demand curve intersects with the long-run average cost curve (the second-best price and output). Once this point is reached, the regulatory constraint induces the firm to keep charging this price in perpetuity, as the firm has no incentive to charge a lower price, as this will result in a loss.

Although the incentive mechanism appears to provide a relatively simple solution to achieving the optimal outcome in the context of asymmetric information, the mechanism rests on a number of strong assumptions.[91] Vogelsang and Finsinger's analysis has, however, made an important contribution to the development of the principles of incentive regulation, and the properties of different price control arrangements, in at least three respects. Firstly, it focuses on the *incentives* that specific mechanisms can provide for multi-product regulated firms to set efficient prices in a context of asymmetric information, and where the firm is left to make its own decisions as to which price structures to implement subject to the regulatory constraint. Secondly, the mechanism takes advantage

---

[89] Train (1991, chapter 5) examines this mechanism in detail.
[90] This is a function of decreasing ray average costs.
[91] These assumptions include that: the demand and cost functions do not change over time; the firm has decreasing average costs; there are no intertemporal linkages between the cost function; and the firm acts myopically, meaning that it focuses only on its decisions in the current period and ignores the effects of its current decisions on subsequent periods.

of the *regulatory lag* to induce the firm to produce at a cost-minimising point during the lag period, and to potentially alter its price structure having regard to the constraint being set on maximum prices. Thirdly, the analysis makes an important distinction between the *level* of prices and the *structure* of prices, the authors suggesting, that: 'once the rate level has been established the actual freedom of the firms to alter their rate structure on profit-maximising grounds should be increased'.[92]

4.5.4 Yardstick Competition to Overcome the Information Asymmetry

Where there are multiple firms that provide core network services – for example, multiple regional gas, electricity or water distribution companies within a jurisdiction – it might be possible for the regulator to seek to mitigate the information monopoly of individual firms by using comparative performance information on other firms who operate in similar technological and cost conditions. This approach, known as yardstick competition involves the regulator explicitly linking the performance of one firm to that of other comparable firms.[93] Specifically, where the costs of similar regulated core network firms operating in different regions, are highly correlated, it is possible to use the observed information about costs to improve the effectiveness of regulation. In effect, under this mechanism, the price a firm is permitted to charge depends on its own costs and the cost of comparable firms.[94] However, where firms providing similar core network services are not sufficiently comparable, the informational advantages of employing yardstick competition are lost, and indeed the approach introduces the possibility of regulatory error. As discussed in Chapter 5, there are numerous examples of different forms of yardstick competition being adopted in regulatory practice, including benchmarking approaches in the electricity and water industries.[95]

4.6 ATTRIBUTES OF DESIRABLE RATE STRUCTURES

While achieving (some degree) of efficiency in prices/rates is an important principle referred to by many regulators, in practice this objective is often combined with a range of other aims and goals. Some sixty years ago, James Bonbright observed that the criteria for assessing different rate structures in public utility industries is conditioned by what 'desirable results the rate maker hopes to secure, and what undesirable results he hopes to minimise', and that the problem of practical rate design is that they 'do not readily yield to "scientific" principles of optimum pricing'.[96] What, then, are the other principles and factors which are used to inform regulated rate design in practice?

---

[92] Vogelsang and Finsinger (1979).

[93] See the early contribution of Shleifer (1985).

[94] Shleifer (1985) observes that, in the extreme case of 'identical' firms: 'the regulator can expect to be able to reduce costs at the same rate. By relating the utility's prices to the costs of firms identical to it, the regulator can force firms serving different markets effectively to compete'.

[95] See the discussions of the specific applications of benchmarking and yardstick competition in Chapters 9 and 16. Laffont and Tirole (1993) cite early applications in the Spanish electricity industry and in Illinois.

[96] Bonbright (1961) also noted that terms such as 'marginal costs' and 'average costs' must be determined in the light of the purposes served by the public utility rates as instruments of economic policy.

ble 4.1 Desirable attributes of sound rate structures[a]

Revenue-related attributes	It is effective in yielding total revenue requirements, without encouraging undesirable over-investment or discouraging under-provision, or socially undesirable levels of quality and product safety.
	It allows for revenue stability and predictability from year to year, with minimum changes adverse to the company.
	The rates/charges are themselves stable, with a minimum of expected changes which could be seriously adverse to consumers.
Cost-related attributes	It achieves static (allocative) efficiency by discouraging wasteful use of a service while promoting all justified types and amount of use in terms of the total amount of the service supplied, and the relative use of different alternative services by customers (e.g. peak versus off-peak, or higher- versus lower-quality services).
	It reflects all present and future private and social costs and benefits of providing the service (i.e. internalities and externalities).
	The specific rates are 'fair' in how they apportion the total costs of service among different users.
	It avoids undue discrimination so as to avoid subsidising particular customer groups.
	It facilitates dynamic efficiency in promoting innovation and responding economically to changes in demand and supply patterns.
Practical attributes	It has various practical attributes such as simplicity, certainty, convenience of payment, economy in collection, understandability, public acceptability and feasibility of application.
	There is limited controversy as to proper interpretation of the rate structure.

[a] Based on Bonbright, Danielsen and Kamerschen (1988).

Bonbright and co-workers provide a classic exposition of the ten desirable attributes of regulated rate structures.[97] According to Bonbright et al., a 'sound' rate structure is one that displays the desirable revenue, cost and practical attributes as shown in Table 4.1.

Of the ten desirable attributes, Bonbright et al. considered three to be of particular importance: revenue sufficiency, fairness and efficiency. The revenue sufficiency and efficiency objectives are broadly in line with the point made above about the tension in rate design between ensuring an operator covers all of its costs (including fixed costs) and the achievement of allocative efficiency, while the fairness attribute touches on the discussion in Chapter 2 about the purposes and rationales of regulation.

---

[97] Bonbright (1961) set out eight attributes, but two more attributes were added in Bonbright, Danielsen and Kamerschen (1988).

Recent assessments of the desirable attributes of rate structures across different sectors have come up with similar lists of desirable criteria. For example, in the rail sector, nine desirable attributes of track access charges have been identified in some studies, including: no undue discrimination; practicality; cost reflectivity; allows for revenue recovery; optimises network use; promotes network growth; does not adversely affect customers or introduce adverse distributional impacts between different groups; promotes competition; and simplicity.[98] Desirable attributes of electricity tariff structures – particularly in a context of changing household usage – have identified five desirable attributes, including: economic efficiency in consumption and production; equity between consumers and between the utility and customers; revenue adequacy and stability for the utility; bill stability for the customer; and customer satisfaction.[99]

Three general observations can be made about these lists of desirable attributes of rate structures. First, and most obviously, the achievement of allocative efficiency is only one desirable attribute of rate structures introduced in regulated settings. Second, there is a focus on fairness, not only in terms of how total costs are apportioned across different types of consumers, but also in terms of avoidance of a situation where particular groups are subsidised through discriminatory pricing policies.[100] Finally, it is clear that, in practice, regulators often have to balance a range of objectives and aims when setting prices some of which may be difficult to fully reconcile.

4.7 PRINCIPLES RELATING TO QUALITY AND COST REDUCTION

So far we have focused only on principles that may be relevant in relation to efficient pricing of core network services. However, recall from Chapter 2 that among the rationales for regulation of some industries is that firms in such monopoly positions may have incentives to degrade quality or not to engage in cost-reducing efforts. While there is an extensive literature on efficient pricing principles in core network activities, the research on principles related to quality and cost reduction is much less extensive.[101] This may be because the principles are more context-specific and difficult to generalise across firms and industries, but may also reflect the fact that there are difficult issues associated with measurement and verification of quality and cost-reducing effort by firms.

4.7.1 Principles Relating to Quality

In the discussion of pricing principles above, it has been assumed that the product supplied by the firm was of an appropriate and uniform quality. This is an unrealistic assumption, as in practice a firm has a choice about the quality of service it supplies

---

[98] ORR (2010).

[99] See Faruqui, Davis, Duh and Warner (2016). Rábago and Valova (2018) set out other additional attributes for a distributed electricity rate structure.

[100] Gurung and Martínez-Espiñeira (2019) find that Canadian water rates appear to reflect a balancing of efficiency objectives with fairness and political acceptability considerations.

[101] Sappington (2005a) provides an excellent overview of work on quality. See also Laffont and Tirole (1993, chapter 4) on the relationship between different incentive systems and quality, and Berg and Tschirhart (1988).

In this context, 'quality' is broadly defined to capture various dimensions, including the availability and reliability of the product, the safety or environmental attributes of the product, and the responsiveness of the firm to various types of customer requests (new connections, emergencies, complaints, bill paying procedures, etc.). Regulators have a number of instruments at their disposal to address such aspects of quality, including the setting of minimum quality standards, or specifying service quality targets with associated financial penalties and rewards. As described in Part III, ensuring an appropriate level of quality is an important aspect of modern regulatory activity.

At the theoretical level, in examining the incentive of a firm to provide different levels of quality, a comparison is sometimes made with the incentives that an unregulated monopolist has to improve quality. Research in this area suggests that the unregulated monopoly provider can supply either more, or less, than the welfare-maximising amount of quality. The level of quality supplied can depend on factors such as: the extent to which marginal customers value quality more than infra-marginal customers; whether the marginal valuation of quality decreases as output expands; and the ability of consumers to distinguish between high- and low-quality products.[102] Of particular relevance to core network activities are the incentives for quality in settings where networks are interconnected, and there are wider network effects associated with poor quality. This situation can arise where two network operators interconnect with one another, such as different rail networks, telecommunications networks or energy transportation networks. In these circumstances, there may be incentives for an individual firm not to supply the optimal amount of quality, as the full benefits of such efforts will not always be realised, the final level of quality depending also on the quality of any interconnecting networks.[103]

Additional factors can impact on the incentives to supply quality services where firms are subject to regulation. As discussed in Chapter 5, the different forms of price regulation (such as rate of return regulation and price cap regulation) are seen to create different incentives to improve or degrade quality. Generally speaking, it is often argued that, where prices are closely aligned to changes in costs, and firms are reimbursed on this basis, this can provide incentives for firms to incur costs which improve quality. On the other hand, if prices are detached from changes in costs, this may, in some settings, reduce the incentives for firms to incur costs to improve quality, or, alternatively, can create incentives to pursue cost savings that adversely affect service quality.[104] Overall,

---

[102] For a fuller analysis, see Spence (1975), Sheshinski (1976), Berg and Tschirhart (1988) and Sappington (2005a).

[103] There may also be strategic incentives to degrade quality. This includes contexts where the core network provider is vertically integrated and supplies firms in another market where it also competes. In these circumstances, the vertically integrated firm may have incentives to degrade the quality of the core network service it provides to its competitors in the related market. See discussion in Chapter 6.

[104] Laffont and Tirole (1993) examine the relationship between different optimal incentive schemes (such as high-powered and low-powered schemes) and service quality, and observe that the incentives of the unregulated monopolist to provide quality depend on the nature of the product being sold, and that this also affects the choice of the optimal form of incentive scheme (i.e. whether prices are fixed, or costs are fully reimbursed). See also Waddams Price, Brigham and Fitzgerald (2002) and Weisman (2005).

as discussed in the next chapter, the empirical evidence on whether price cap regulation adversely impacts service quality is mixed across sectors.[105]

The regulator's task in maintaining adequate levels of quality is complicated in circumstances where neither the regulator nor the consumer can observe the level of service quality being provided.[106] Accordingly, service quality regulations will vary according to the setting, institutional factors and the amount of information available to relevant parties. Optimal service quality regulation may, therefore, often involve the delegation to the firm of significant discretion, and by incentivising the firm to use its substantial information advantage over the regulator to provide higher levels of service quality.[107] As discussed in Part III, in practice, regulators often use financial rewards (or penalties) for achieving (or not achieving) specific quality targets.[108]

4.7.2 Principles Relating to Cost Efficiency

In much of our earlier discussion of pricing principles, it was implicitly assumed that firm's costs were exogenous, and that the firm, through its actions and choices, could not affect the level of production costs. However, in practice, firms often have an ability to influence the level of costs that need to be recovered through prices. Such influence can arise through choices the firm makes as to the relative share of fixed costs and variable costs, which, in turn, reflects choices made about how much capital to invest in a network. Accordingly, a further regulatory task (additional to the need to ensure prices are efficient and quality standards maintained) is to seek to ensure that costs associated with providing a product are no higher than necessary.

In more formal terms, in the first-best world, with perfect information, a regulator should seek to achieve both allocative efficiency (where the marginal price equals the marginal cost) *and* cost efficiency (where the firm minimises total costs). However, for the reasons described above, the assumption that the regulator will have access to complete information about the level of cost-reducing activity is a heroic one, and, in practice, it is difficult for this first-best world to be attained.[109] Accordingly, much of the work examining optimal incentive structures for both cost efficiency and allocative efficiency situate itself in the realistic setting of the firm having better information about its cost-reducing efforts than the regulator.[110] These approaches are discussed in more detail in Chapter 5.

---

[105] Ter-Martirosyan (2003) finds that the duration of electrical outages increased under incentive (price cap) regulation. Arcos-Vargas, Núñez and Ballesteros (2017) find that price cap, cost plus and revenue cap, in this order, seem to be the most efficient systems to increase quality of service. Banerjee (2003) finds no evidence of a degradation in quality in shifting to incentive regulation for US telecommunications, while Sappington (2003) concludes that the evidence is mixed.

[106] Sappington (2005a) notes, for example, how: 'consumers may only become fully aware of the clarity of telephone calls or the reliability of the electricity supply provided by a particular supplier after experiencing the supplier's service'.

[107] See Sappington (2005a).

[108] However, Weisman (2005) finds that some penalty schemes (such as revenue share penalties) can actually serve to reduce investment in service quality.

[109] There is a further issue associated with the assumed benevolence of the regulator. Laffont and Tirole (1993) examine the potential for collusion between the regulator and the firm in the monitoring of cost-reducing effort.

[110] The incentives for 'cost padding' under different forms of optimal incentive schemes, and the potential role for auditing of costs, are examined in Laffont and Tirole (1993, chapter 12).

when discussing the different forms of price control. The point is nevertheless noted here because, while we have focused so far on principles through which regulation might achieve allocative efficiency, in practice, regulatory policies are often focused on achieving greater cost efficiency (that is, on reducing costs). Indeed, as we will see in Part III of the book, restructuring policies, including policies of privatisation, have often been motivated by a desire to see costs reduced, and firms engage in greater cost-reducing efforts, rather than the achievement of allocative efficiency.

4.8 CONCLUSION

This chapter has presented an overview of economic principles that could inform and guide the economic regulation of core network activities in order to maximise economic welfare. The starting point is that allocative efficiency will be achieved through the application of marginal cost pricing (what is known as the 'first-best' principle), but this is generally infeasible in the context of most regulated industries because of the existence of high fixed costs. Two options for addressing this problem are government payment transfers or subsidies to cover fixed costs, or the implementation of deviations from marginal cost pricing that allow the firm to recover its fixed costs. One pricing approach that allows the firm to cover its total costs, but involves some loss in allocative efficiency, is to set a uniform price based on average cost. However, in principle, it is possible for a firm to recover its fixed costs and improve efficiency (and in some cases obtain the optimal outcome) through the use of other pricing approaches such as Ramsey–Boiteux pricing, peak-load pricing or various forms of non-linear pricing.

For these pricing approaches to be implemented effectively, the regulator requires access to reliable information, including information in relation to consumer demand and the costs associated with the services supplied by the regulated firm. This information is typically not available to a regulator, and once we adopt the realistic assumption that the regulator has imperfect information, the regulator's task becomes considerably more complex. Optimal regulatory policies in the context of asymmetric information – which characterise most real-world regulatory settings – give rise to a trade-off between minimising the rent that the firm obtains from its private information and creating appropriate incentives for efficiency. In this respect, a regulator generally has to trade off allocative efficiency, productive efficiency and distributional considerations. Models of asymmetric information highlight the point that different information conditions can create different incentives, and that this can result in a wide range of potential regulatory solutions to the problem of asymmetric information.[111] Similarly, work on multi-period regulation indicates that, once we allow the regulator and the firm to interact over multiple periods, this can create new issues associated with regulatory commitment, and the incentives for the

---

[111] As Armstrong and Sappington (2007) conclude: '[T]he qualitative properties of optimal regulatory policies can vary substantially according to the nature of the firm's private information and its technology. Optimal regulated prices can be set above, below, or at the level of marginal cost, and the full-information outcome may or may not be feasible, depending on whether the firm is privately informed about the demand function it faces, its variable production costs, or both its variable and fixed costs of production.' Armstrong and Sappington (2004) present a synthesis of models of regulatory design with limited information.

firm to reveal information at different periods in time, which impact on the regulator ability to set efficient prices.

Given the unrealistic assumptions of some of the principles and approaches described this chapter, the question necessarily arises: what is their relevance to a modern econom regulator? Some economists despair at the failure of regulators to follow the prescription of these theoretical models.[112] However, others appear to recognise that, given the stror assumptions and level of abstraction at which these theoretical models operate, such wo can never provide direct prescriptions for a regulator in practice.[113] One reason some of th principles discussed in this chapter have not been applied in practice is the severity of info mation asymmetry faced by regulators in practice.[114] Another obvious reason is the practic need to take account of the distributional consequences of regulatory policies; that is, th need for regulators to consider issues of fairness.[115] As discussed in Chapter 2, issues of di tributive equity and fairness have long been recognised as significant in relation to publ utility services,[116] and may explain why, in practice, some of the approaches described i this chapter which could improve allocative efficiency, such as Ramsey–Boiteux, have ofte been resisted by regulators.[117] More broadly, in practice, regulators often pursue other obje tives and aims, and take account of other considerations, alongside maximising efficienc including practical considerations such as the stability and simplicity of any price system

While specific theoretical prescriptions have not always been transposed directly in practice, they have undoubtedly been influential in shaping regulation. For example, as w shall see in the next chapter, theoretical work on information asymmetries and dynam regulation have clearly influenced the design of incentive regulation, including the deve opment of 'menu regulation' and yardstick competition which take account of the info mation advantage of regulated companies. In short, while many of the principles describe above are not adopted explicitly, they provide a level of conceptual clarity as to the natu of the relevant trade-offs associated with the regulation of core network activities, whic has been important in informing the design and implementation of regulatory policies.

DISCUSSION QUESTIONS

1. Why is marginal cost pricing referred to as the 'first-best' pricing principle, and wha are some of the factors that complicate its practical application in regulated industries

2. What are some of the different ways of addressing a potential conflict between se ting allocatively efficient prices and ensuring a regulated firm remains financiall viable? What are some of the practical limitations of each approach?

[112] Berg and Tschirhart (1988), for example, remonstrate: 'In the war being fought to translate microeconomic theory into public policy, economists have had disappointingly few victories.'
[113] Laffont and Tirole (1993), for example, accept that 'there are three reasons why regulation is not a simple exercise in second-best optimisation theory: asymmetric information, lack of commitment and imperfect regulators'.
[114] See Crew and Kleindorfer (2012).
[115] Feldstein (1972) develops a framework for combining considerations of equity and efficiency in optima pricing using information on price and income elasticity of demand.
[116] As Braeutigam (1989) observes: 'Parties to regulatory hearings as well as commissions themselves have often asked whether a proposed rate is "fair", even in cases in which a party argues that a rate is economically efficient.'
[117] See Decker (2007) and Biggar (2009).

3. In what circumstances could a non-linear pricing, such as a two-part or multi-part tariff schedule, achieve allocative efficiency? What assumptions underpin this result?

4. What are some of the challenges that arise when a regulator has to set prices for multiple products? Discuss some of the benefits and limitations of the different ways in which prices can be set in a multi-product context.

5. What trade-offs can confront regulators in setting prices in the context of imperfect information. Describe some of the different mechanisms that have been proposed to achieve allocative efficiency in the context of asymmetric information. What are the differences between these models, and what important assumptions underpin these mechanisms?

6. What are some of the advantages and disadvantages of short-run and long-run marginal cost pricing? In which circumstances is each approach likely to be more appropriate?

7. What are some of the challenges that regulators confront when setting prices in a multi-period context? Describe one way in which a regulator could incentivise efficient pricing in a multi-period context, including the key assumptions that underpin the approach.

8. Apart from efficiency, what are some of the other aims and objectives that a regulator might need to consider when setting prices and price structures? What are some of the tensions that might arise between these various aims and objectives?

9. What factors might affect the quality of service supplied by an unregulated monopoly firm? Even if a firm is subject to price regulation, how might the form of regulation impact on the incentives to maintain services of sufficient quality?

Forms of Price Regulation

Chapter 4 set out some key principles for the regulation of core network activities, which, in theory, allow a regulator to determine an optimal set of prices that will maximise economic welfare, while allowing the regulated firm to break even. These principles are often derived under a set of strong assumptions, including that the regulator: has full information regarding costs, demand and the behaviour of the regulated firm; has various tools at its disposal to address any revenue shortfall (such as the use of subsidies or multi-part pricing); and, in the multi-period context, is able to credibly commit to its previous decisions. However, in practice, many of these assumptions do not hold, raising difficulties for the direct application of the principles outlined in Chapter 4.

The purpose of this chapter is to explore some of the methods by which price regulation is applied in practice to those activities where competition is limited or non-existent, and as a result the firm is not effectively constrained in what prices it sets for the services its provides. A number of different forms of price regulation are examined, ranging from traditional rate of return regulation to various forms of incentive or performance based regulation, such as price cap regulation and other so-called 'hybrids' involving earnings or revenue sharing mechanisms. This examination, which focuses on the general properties of each type of price regulation, is intended to provide a frame of reference for the discussion in Part III of the more specific techniques and methods that have been adopted to regulate prices in practice across different industries.

5.1 RATE OF RETURN REGULATION

At one extreme of the spectrum of price regulation arrangements is 'traditional' rate of return regulation.[1] This approach has been the most important approach to price regulation historically, and is still widely utilised, notably by state and federal regulatory institutions in the USA. The rate of return approach can be expressed in various ways, but one representation is as follows:

$$R = \text{Opex} + s \cdot (\text{Rate Base}), \tag{5.1}$$

---

[1] Rate of return regulation is also sometimes referred to as 'cost of service' regulation. Laffont and Tirole (1993) argue that the latter term is appropriate on the basis that every regulatory regime determines some rate of return. However, to be consistent with the wider literature, we adopt the term 'rate of return' in this section. Good descriptions of this approach are given in Berg and Tschirhart (1988, chapter 8), Phillips (1993) and Joskow (2007a).

where R is the total revenue the firm needs to obtain from the different service it supplies, Opex are the operating expenses associated with supplying those services (including depreciation expense and taxes), Rate Base is the value of the firm's invested capital (capital stock less accumulated depreciation) and s is the allowed or 'fair' rate of return that is applied to the rate base. The allowed rate of return, s, must be such that the company's revenues equate to its costs so that the overall economic profit is zero. The main idea behind rate of return regulation is that the firm should be able to recover all of the costs associated with supplying a set of regulated services, including an allowable rate of return on a regulated rate base (i.e. a 'fair rate of return'). Critically, the approach does not require that the firm choose prices that are efficient. The only requirement is that prices are set such that the total revenue obtained from supplying the services covers the total costs, which includes a fair return on regulated investments. While the approach appears straightforward in principle, in practice there are a number of distinct tasks that a regulator must undertake and where discretion must be exercised.

In the USA, the process of rate setting is governed by a number of important procedural and judicial rules. The Administrative Procedures Act 1946 sets out the general process for the conduct of rate hearings, while numerous judicial decisions over time have established the substantive principles for rate regulation. Important among these principles are: that the regulated firm is entitled to a *fair return* on the assets it employs for the public convenience;[2] that 'the fixing of "just and reasonable" rates involves a balancing of the investor and the consumer interests';[3] and that a firm must be provided with a reasonable opportunity to recover costs associated with meeting its service obligations, but not more than is necessary to meet such obligations.

5.1.1 The Rate Case Process

An important element of the rate of return approach is the 'rate case', a process whereby regulatory commission considers, through a public process, whether or not a firm's prices or tariffs can be adjusted. In most rate cases, the process starts with a firm applying to the regulator for a rate increase.[4] Generally, the application must be accompanied by supporting reasons for the requested rate change, and proposals as to the classes of different customers (residential, industrial and commercial) to be affected by the rate change. The firm might also provide detailed financial information and expert evidence in support of its application. The consideration of a rate case application then proceeds in two general stages. First, an overall revenue requirement for the firm is determined. Second, a set of tariffs or rates are established, including the prices that will be charged to different types of consumers and for different products.

[2] *Smyth v. Ames* (1898).
[3] The concept of what constitutes a 'just and reasonable' price prohibits the charging of excessive prices/rates, and has been interpreted by the US Supreme Court by reference to the ability that a regulated public utility has to recover prudently incurred costs and a reasonable return on invested capital. See *Duquesne Light Co. v. Barasch* (1989); *FPC v. Hope Natural Gas Co.* (1944); and *Bluefield Water Works and Improvement Co. v. Public Service Commission of West Virginia* (1923).
[4] However, a regulator can also initiate a case on its own initiative, in some cases as a response to complaints from third parties such as customers.

Determination of the Revenue Requirement

In the first stage of a rate case, the regulator determines the firm's allowable costs (costs that it will be able to recover), sometimes referred to as its revenue requirement. This is typically done by reference to estimates of the operating costs (such as labour costs, maintenance, etc.) incurred in a recent 'test' year,[5] and the value of the capital assets, adjusted for depreciation, on which the firm must earn a return (the so-called rate base). The regulator must assess whether the costs proposed by the firm are reasonable and prudent,[6] and this assessment may involve a review of costs by staff of the regulatory authority or by evidence submitted by interveners.[7] The regulator can make various adjustments to these estimates, for example, to disallow imprudent or unjustified expenditure, as well as to account for possible future changes in inflation or any expected and measurable future changes in costs (such as changes in input prices).[8]

Determining the value of the asset 'rate base' on which the firm is entitled to a fair return is of particular importance in the utility industries, being highly capital-intensive.[9] However, this process can be controversial. One recurring issue is the appropriate valuation method, and, in particular, whether the rate base should be valued on an original or historical cost basis (the most common method), or on the basis of replacement or reproduction value. A related issue is the method of depreciation applied to the capital base, which can have important implications for the intertemporal allocation of capital costs.[10] Finally, issues can arise about which assets should be included (or excluded) from the rate base. This has led to the development of a 'used and useful' test for the recovery of capital costs.[11] In some jurisdictions, firms are able to apply for certain forms of 'pre-approval' from the regulator for investment in particular assets to reduce the regulatory uncertainty associated with the future treatment of long-term investments.

Another part of the revenue requirement determination is the regulator's choice as to the allowed rate of return, an important component of which is the cost of capital that will

---

[5] This could be either a historical test year or a forecast test year. However, in most implementations, the assessment is based on a historical annual 'test year' cost of service, which is usually the last accounting year.

[6] In an early Supreme Court judgment, Associate Justice Brandeis defined a 'prudent investment' as 'investments which, under ordinary circumstances, would be deemed reasonable. The term is applied for the purpose of excluding what might be found to be dishonest or obviously wasteful or imprudent expenditures'. See *State of Missouri ex. rel. Southwestern Bell Telephone Co. v. Public Service Commission of Missouri, et al.* (1923).

[7] Joskow (2007a) observes that assessments of the reasonableness of a firm's expenditure was historically rather arbitrary and *ad hoc*, but over time a number of methods have been adopted, including the use of yardstick or benchmarking approaches in relation to certain costs (fuel costs, labour productivity, wages, etc.), and the use of outside experts to provide an opinion on how costs relate to industry norms.

[8] Berg and Tschirhart (1988) note that adjustments may be made where the firm has exaggerated its costs, or incurred costs that are not necessarily in the best interests of consumers (e.g. advertising and charitable expenses).

[9] Phillips (1993, chapter 8) provides an excellent description of the issues involved.

[10] For example, whether a straight-line method, sinking fund method or accelerated depreciation is used.

[11] Joskow (1989) refers to debates about whether investments in nuclear power plants in times of excess capacity should be included in the rate base, or if decommissioned nuclear plants should be included in the rate base.

be applied to the 'rate base' (see Box 5.1).[12] Various approaches can be applied to estimate the cost of capital, but the general idea is that the cost of capital should be consistent with firms that have assets/investments with comparable risks.[13] In many rate case hearings the regulated firm will argue, and present evidence to the effect, that it requires a higher rate of return on the rate base, while the regulator will argue that the required rate of return is too high and not consistent with returns earned by firms with comparable assets and similar levels of risk.[14] An important legal constraint on this process in the USA is the constitutional protection against so-called 'takings'.[15] This has been interpreted as requiring that any rate of return be 'fair'.[16] However, there have been recurring concerns about the ability of regulators to 'scientifically evaluate' rate of return requests.[17]

Box 5.1 **Estimating the cost of capital in regulated industries**

A central aspect of regulation under all forms of price regulation (rate of return and price cap) involves determining the cost of capital that should be applied to a rate base or regulated (or regulatory) asset base (RAB). This is often the most contested part of regulatory proceedings in many parts of the world, as it directly impacts on the revenues that the

---

[12] Phillips (1993) describes the approaches to estimating the cost of capital, including the methods used to estimate the cost of equity capital, such as the capital asset pricing model (CAPM), the discounted cash flow model (DCF), earnings–price ratios and other risk premium approaches. See also Jenkinson (2006).

[13] Berg and Tschirhart (1988) outline some of the practical issues of this exercise. For example, should the cost of capital be based on that for an entire industry or only that of particular firms? Should only regulated or unregulated companies be considered? Should the cost of capital be based on historical data or future estimates? What is the optimal mix of debt and equity, and how does this impact on the calculation? How does regulatory risk feature in the estimation?

[14] Berg and Tschirhart (1988) describe this process as 'essentially a bargaining process with the regulator as an arbitrator between the firm and consumers' where, in some cases, the regulator may seek to set a rate of return slightly higher than the cost of capital so as to provide some economic incentives for the firm. Joskow (1972) describes the role of the regulator as setting a rate of return 'that is not "so low" that the firm cannot perform its service function adequately (or even remain in business) and not "so high" that the firm is being allowed earnings above the amount needed to enable it to maintain the desired level of service quality'.

[15] The 'Takings Clause' of the Fifth Amendment to the United States Constitution reads as follows: 'Nor shall private property be taken for public use, without just compensation.'

[16] Two US Supreme Court decisions are particularly important constraints on this assessment. In its decision in *Bluefield Water Works and Improvement Co. v. Public Service Commission of West Virginia* (1923), the Supreme Court stated: 'A public utility is entitled to such rates as will permit it to earn a return on the value of the property which it employs for the convenience of the public equal to that generally being made at the same time and in the same general part of the country on investments in other business undertakings which are attended by corresponding risks and uncertainties; but it has no constitutional right to profits such as are realised or anticipated in highly profitable enterprises or speculative ventures. The return should be reasonably sufficient to assure confidence in the financial soundness of the utility, and should be adequate, under efficient and economical management, to maintain and support its credit and enable it to raise the money necessary for the proper discharge of its public duties.' In the subsequent Supreme Court decision, *FPC v. Hope Natural Gas Co.* (1944), the principle was established that a 'fair' rate of return involves determining that: '[T]he return to the equity owner should be commensurate with returns on investments in other enterprises having corresponding risks. That return, moreover, should be sufficient to assure confidence in the financial integrity of the enterprise, so as to maintain its credit and to attract capital.'

[17] Joskow (1972) concluded that at that time: 'commissions rely on the general feeling that the return requested by the firm is probably too high on historical relationships between rate of return requests and observable capital costs and on information presented by intervenors'. Over three decades later, Joskow (2007a) observes that, despite advances in theoretical and empirical finance, the methods used to estimate a regulated firm's cost of capital remain 'surprisingly unsophisticated'.

regulated firm is allowed to recover on past investments.[18] Consider the example of the UK's electricity transmission company, which in 2021 had a RAB of £14.5 billion on which it was allowed to earn a return based on a cost of capital of 3.75 per cent. If that cost of capital was to increase (decrease) by just 0.25 percentage points, this would result in a gain (loss) of £36.3 million.[19] Uncertainty about how a regulator will set the future cost of capital that a firm will be allowed to earn can also affect the incentives for investment.

In conceptual terms, the cost of capital can be thought of as the cost incurred by the company in raising funds (capital) to finance their existing operations and to undertake new investments. There are two general sources of finance available to firms: debt financing (where the company borrows money by obtaining a bank loan or issuing corporate bonds) and equity financing (which involves the sale of shares in the company and entitles the holder of that share to some portion of any profits made, in the form of dividend payments). Generally, the costs associated with debt financing are lower than the costs associated with equity financing, for the simple reason that equity investors are exposed to greater risks than are debt financiers (e.g. while interest repayments on debt are guaranteed, there are no such guarantees for dividend payments, which vary depending on performance).

A common approach of regulators to estimating the cost of capital is to employ a weighted average cost of capital (WACC). This represents the weighted average cost of debt and cost of equity, where the weighting is determined by the relative proportions of debt and equity used to finance the firm (i.e.; the gearing or leverage of the firm). The WACC formula is[20]

$$\text{WACC} = r_D \times \frac{D}{D+E} + r_E \times \frac{E}{D+E}. \tag{5.2}$$

As shown in equation (5.2), there are four components to the WACC estimation: an estimate of the cost of debt, r_D; an estimate of the cost of equity, r_E; the proportion of debt in financing the firm, $D/(D+E)$; and the proportion of equity in financing the firm, $E/(D+E)$. As discussed in Box 16.1 in Chapter 16, in some jurisdictions, such as the UK and Australia, regulators apply benchmark or notional gearing ratios when estimating the WACC, rather than use the actual gearing ratios.[21]

Estimating the cost of debt (r_D) is, in principle, relatively straightforward and involves examining the interest rates actually paid on the commercial debt of a company, and by bonds issued by companies with similar ratings and risk profiles.[22] However, there can

[18] For example, between 2001 and 2012, around a quarter of all appeals of regulatory decisions in the energy sector in Australia focused on issues relating to the estimation of the cost of capital. Similarly, recent appeals in the UK energy sector in aviation, energy and water have all had a heavy focus on the regulator's approach to estimating the cost of capital.
[19] The UK Regulator's Network (UKRN, 2020) presents a summary of the current approach to the cost of capital in the UK.
[20] This is sometimes referred to as a 'vanilla' WACC, as it does not take account of taxation in estimating the cost of debt but is based on a post-tax cost of equity. This arises because, in practice, since interest charged on debt is an allowable corporation tax expense (while the distribution of returns on equity is not), this must also be taken into account to determine a post-tax weighted average cost of capital. The post-tax WACC formula is $\text{WACC} = r_D \times \frac{D \times (1-t)}{D+E} + r_E \times \frac{E}{D+E}$.
[21] The cost of capital is sometimes adjusted for inflation to give a real WACC.
[22] However, in a recent price control decision in the English water industry, a major issue of contention was the regulator's approach to the estimation of the cost of embedded (existing) debt allowance. See CMA (2021b).

be debate about the time period over which the estimate of the cost of debt should b estimated (e.g. current cost of debt or estimates of the cost of debt over a longer tim period).

Estimating the cost of equity is, however, typically more difficult and controversia Regulators in many jurisdictions employ various financial models, such as the capital ass pricing model (CAPM), to make assessments as to the cost of equity.[23] In general terms, th CAPM relates a firm's cost of equity to its level of exposure to non-diversifiable or sy tematic risk. Non-diversifiable or systematic risks are those risks that a firm cannot avo by diversifying its portfolio. The CAPM estimates the cost of equity with reference to thre variables: the risk-free rate (r_f), a firm-specific equity beta (β) and a market risk premiu $(r_m - r_f)$. The standard CAPM formula is

$$r_E = r_f + \beta(r_m - r_f). \tag{5.3}$$

The risk-free rate (r_f) is usually an estimate of the tax-free return on government securiti or bonds. The market risk premium $(r_m - r_f)$ is calculated as the difference between the tot expected equity returns on the market (r_m) and the risk-free rate (r_f).[24] Finally, the equi beta (β) measures the non-diversifiable risk of the equity of the regulated firm; that is, th systematic risk of shares of the regulated firm relative to other shares in the market. I simple terms, the CAPM model is based on the idea that the firm should be able to earn return on its equity equal to the risk-free rate *plus* a premium which captures the degre of systematic risk (i.e. non-diversifiable risk) of the firm as a proportion of the total mark return (i.e. determined by β).[25] Perhaps unsurprisingly, given its importance, estimating th value of the equity beta (β) is often the most controversial element of the CAPM approac In practice, regulators often base estimates of the equity beta (β) on similar regulated firm in the same industry or overseas; for example, the equity beta for an electricity distributio company might be benchmarked against other energy companies or overseas electricit distribution companies. The value of an equity beta can change over time as a result changes in regulatory policies (including the introduction of competition or separatio policies), technological change, demand and cost changes, and the regulated firm expand ing its activities into new business lines. All of these changes can increase or decrease th systematic risk of the regulated firm relative to the market.

---

[23] Another model used to estimate the cost of equity (particularly in the USA) is the dividend growth model, which is based on the estimation of the growth of dividends. The formula is $r_E = \dfrac{DIV_0(1+g)}{P_0} + g$ where P_0 is the current share/stock price of the regulated firm, DIV_0 is the current dividend and g is the expected dividend growth rate. The approach is seen as simpler than the CAPM, as it uses the directly observed values for current share price and dividends, while the future growth rate in dividends can be estimated based on comparative data or analyst reports. However, there can be a potential circularity when used to set the forward-looking price controls for regulated firms, as future dividends depend, in part, on the future allowed cost of capital.

[24] The expected equity returns (or stock market returns) are often based on estimates of historical returns, but can also take account of estimates of dividend growth and other conditioning variables.

[25] A value $\beta = 1$ implies that the risk of the firm is equal to that of the market as a whole; a value $\beta = 0.5$ implies that the risk of the firm is half that of the market as a whole; while a value $\beta > 1$ implies that th regulated firm is more risky than the market.

Determination of Rates/Prices

The second stage in the rate case process involves the determination of the rates or prices that should apply for different services and to different classes of customers.[26] In the (unrealistic) situation where the firm only supplies one service, rate of return regulation would imply average cost pricing for that service. However, in practice, public utility firms supply a range of services and there is potentially a range of different price vectors that can satisfy the requirement that total revenues equate to total allowable costs.

In establishing a rate structure, a regulator will identify different types of customers, such as residential, commercial or industrial, and may then further subdivide these types even further (small commercial, large industrial, etc.). As the regulator is then required to approve a set of relative prices, this can give rise to non-trivial issues associated with price discrimination, and the allocation of costs across different services that a firm produces. For example, the ability of the firm to set, and the regulator to approve, relative prices may be constrained by requirements that some groups of consumers are not discriminated against (such as rural users), or that all users of the intermediate product face a common price. For these reasons, where different customers face different rates, this must typically be justified by differences in the costs associated with providing the service to the different categories of customer.

In almost all regulated industries this raises issues around the allocation of joint and common costs. The method of allocation of these costs will determine the 'costs' associated with serving a particular customer group, and therefore the prices that can be charged to that group.[27] As discussed in Chapter 4, the usual method for allocating these costs across different services is by the use of accounting methods such as the fully distributed cost method (which are seen as essentially arbitrary by economists). However, tariff design can also sometimes reflect political, and not economic, motivations, particularly when costs and prices are increasing, and where there may be a desire to avoid passing on these increases to particular types of consumers (who are also voters).[28]

An important question regarding the determination of the rate structure is the extent to which the various principles discussed in Chapter 4 for the setting of efficient price structures are applied. A potential benefit of rate of return regulation is that, in theory, it provides an opportunity for the regulator to establish Ramsey–Boiteux pricing or other efficient non-linear price structures.[29] However, Joskow finds evidence that, in the USA, tariffs have not generally been designed on the basis of the formal application of theoretically efficient pricing principles (such as Ramsey–Boiteux, non-linear pricing and peak-load pricing).[30]

---

[26] See Phillips (1993, chapters 10 and 11). Joskow (1973) argues that this is an important stage as, in reality, regulatory agencies set prices for different services and not rates of return.

[27] Joskow (2007a) argues, however, that: 'In reality, the arbitrariness of allocating joint costs among different groups of customers provides significant flexibility for regulators to take non-cost factors into account.'

[28] See Cicchetti, Dubin and Long (2004). Newbery (2003) notes that the structure of rates can reflect the interests of various interest groups, including rural compared to urban customers, or as between business and domestic customers. Joskow (2007a) observes that, in the USA, many states have had special electricity tariffs for low-income consumers, and for particular types of customers (such as steel mills).

[29] See Liston (1993).

[30] See Joskow (2007a).

An important feature of rate of return regulation, and one that distinguishes it from price cap regulation (discussed below), is that, once prices, and any price adjustment formulas, have been determined through the rate case process, they will generally remain in place until the next rate case.[31] This means that the regulated firm is not able to independently vary its prices to immediately adapt to changes in costs and demand conditions. In addition, unlike under price cap approaches, which typically specify a set period of time between formal price reviews, in theory, prices can be adjusted to costs through a rate hearing at any time.

5.1.2   Advantages and Disadvantages of Rate of Return Regulation

The main advantage of rate of return regulation is that it ensures prices are closely related to, or track, the underlying costs of service, which limits the scope for monopoly pricing. At the same time, as it is essentially a form of 'cost-plus' pricing, it ensures that the firm will remain solvent in times when unavoidable costs are increasing rapidly. In principle then, under this form of regulation, the firm should neither sustain excessive losses nor achieve excess profits.

These benefits were the principal motivation for the historical development of the rate of return approach in the USA, which was to balance the interests of consumers/voters and investors by ensuring that public utility firms were able to recover their costs, but did not exploit their position of monopoly power and earn excessive profits. The fact that the regulated firm is essentially assured to recover all of its legitimate costs can, in principle, have implications for quality under this form of regulation. Specifically, the firm may have incentives to provide higher-quality services, and limited incentives to reduce quality.[32]

Rate of return regulation may also be more effective in attracting capital investment in a regulated sector because investors are effectively guaranteed the recovery of their prudently incurred investment costs.[33] In addition, some legal constraints within the approach (such as the 'used and useful' doctrine in the USA), which at first sight might appear to increase regulatory discretion, can, paradoxically, reduce the possibility of regulatory opportunism and increase a firm's confidence that it will recover the costs associated with long-term investments, lowering the investment risk.[34] This increased certainty can lower the cost of capital for the firm (as compared to price cap regulation), as consumers carry more of the risk of assets being stranded or becoming uneconomic.[35] A final perceived

---

[31] However, some implementations allow for automatic rate adjustment formulas, for example, in relation to fuel cost increases, etc.

[32] See Kahn (1971). However, Laffont and Tirole (1993) find this reasoning incomplete, in part because, under pure rate of return regulation, the firm does not gain by providing higher-quality but costlier services, and so this does not imply a higher incentive to provide quality.

[33] See Sappington and Weisman (2010).

[34] Newbery (1999). However, Lim and Yurukoglu (2018) consider the possibility of regulatory hold-up through the application of the 'used and useful' test, which can exacerbate the time-inconsistency problem and result in under-investment.

[35] This is because, once assets are accepted into the rate base, their costs are generally allowed to be recovered. Cowan (2002) poses the question whether the large infrastructure investments of the nineteenth and twentieth centuries (railways, sewerage and water, natural gas, etc.) would have been made if private firms had not been subject to a form of regulation which guaranteed rates of return.

advantage of the rate of return process is that the regulator will generally hold a public hearing on the rate change, which provides a formal opportunity for interveners – such as those representing consumer groups or non-governmental public interest groups – to present their views about prices and quality of service, and may require the firm to defend its past record on these aspects of performance.[36]

There are also a number of well-recognised limitations of the rate of return approach to price regulation. However, when considering these limitations, it is important to distinguish between what might be termed 'pure' or textbook rate of return regulation, and the different forms of rate of return regulation actually applied in practice. As we will see, many of the criticisms relate to the operation of a pure version of rate of return, and not to its real-life applications. As a result, these critiques fail to appreciate the various adaptations that have been made in practice and can exaggerate the shortcomings of the approach, particularly when it comes to comparing rate of return regulation to other forms of price regulation such as price caps.

The most significant criticism of the rate of return approach is that, because it is, in effect, a form of cost-plus arrangement, the firm has limited incentives to reduce operating costs and operate efficiently. As any efficiency gains associated with cost reductions will automatically be translated into price reductions, the firm has no great incentive to seek out such efficiencies. Moreover, this characteristic of rate of return regulation is argued to create limited incentives to be innovative because any benefits from process improvements are quickly passed on to consumers through the pricing mechanism, minimising the reward for the firm. In practice, however, these risks are tempered by the existence of the 'regulatory lag' in many applications of rate of return regulation, which, as discussed below, can provide some incentive for firms to reduce operating costs and operate efficiently. However, the rate of return approach has also been criticised as asymmetric in terms of the distribution of risks associated with cost changes, placing a substantial risk on consumers. Specifically, while a firm will request a rate hearing in times when costs are rising, it is less likely to do so when costs are falling.[37]

A related criticism of rate of return regulation is that, because of the cost-plus characteristic, and the fact that the regulator generally has limited information about a firm's costs, it may provide an opportunity for the firm to inflate or misrepresent its costs, leading the regulator to set prices that are too high. Again, this criticism is principally directed at a 'pure' version of rate of return regulation and assumes that all of the costs submitted by the firm are automatically passed through into prices. However, as discussed above, it is standard practice for regulators applying the rate of return approach to audit the costs submitted by the firm and to assess whether or not they are reasonable and prudent.

Perhaps the most well-known criticism of rate of return regulation is associated with the work of Averch and Johnson and has become known as the 'A–J effect'.[38] This analysis

---

[36] See Liston (1993). However, as discussed in Chapter 3, the formal regulatory process for rate of return hearings can be inflexible, slow and costly, and this has led to the use of more informal approaches, such as negotiated settlements, whereby the company and its customers agree to the terms of any rate change and avoid the formal administrative process.

[37] See Joskow (1974) and Sappington (2002). According to EIA (2018), of the eighty-nine electric utilities filing rate cases in 2018, ten proposed to decrease rates, one negotiated a rate freeze until 2020, and the other seventy-eight proposed rate increases.

[38] Averch and Johnson (1962).

suggests that, under certain (fairly strong) assumptions,[39] if a firm is subject to a 'fair' rate of return constraint, it may seek to distort the relative use of inputs in production (namely, capital and labour) in order to maximise profits. Specifically, under the critical assumption that the regulator sets the firm's allowed rate of return at a level greater than its true cost of capital, the firm will use too much capital relative to labour for a given level of output (in other words, it will have an inefficient capital/labour ratio for that level of output). The main implication of this result is that the firm's output could be produced more cheaply if more labour and less capital were used.[40] In short, the 'A–J effect' refers to a potential bias under rate of return regulation towards capital relative to other production inputs such as labour. However, the result is sensitive to the assumption that the fair rate of return is above the true of cost of capital. Indeed, if the fair rate of return is set equal to the cost of capital, then the firm becomes indifferent among various input combinations, as in all cases it makes zero economic profit.

A considerable research agenda has focused on extending the Averch–Johnson model of rate of return regulation.[42] One important extension has found that introducing 'regulatory lag' into the analytical framework mitigates the magnitude of the input bias. Specifically, under the standard Averch–Johnson assumptions, allowing for a delay before prices are adjusted can reduce the incentive for a firm to overcapitalise.[43] Another important extension involves introducing uncertainty into the Averch–Johnson framework, in particular to reflect the fact that the firm does not know with certainty the profit it will be able to earn with different combinations of inputs.[44]

While a large number of empirical studies have examined whether overcapitalisation (as predicted by the Averch–Johnson model) can be observed in practice, the overall results of these empirical tests have been described as not 'particularly successful'.[45] One obvious

---

[39] The basic framework is one where a firm produces a single output using two inputs (capital and labour) and where each input is available at a fixed price per unit in unlimited quantities. The regulatory constraint is limited to setting the 'fair' rate of return on the rate base. In all other respects the firm therefore is able to pursue the objective of maximising profit without regulatory interference, that is, the firm can freely choose its level of inputs, production levels and prices provided they are within the regulatory constraint. As Joskow (2007a) notes, the results depend on 'an extreme asymmetry of information between the regulated firm and the regulator. ... In A–J type models, the regulator knows essentially nothing about the firm's cost opportunities, realised costs, or demand. It just sets an allowed rate of return and the firm does its thing.' Critically, there is also no regulatory lag in the A–J analytical framework, and it is assumed that prices are instantaneously adjusted to changes in costs. Finally, the A–J framework is a static one where costs and demand do not vary over time.

[40] The A–J result does not suggest that each of the inputs (labour and capital) will be used inefficiently in the production process; rather, that the firm will chose an inefficient mix of these inputs.

[41] In the case where the fair rate of return is set *below* the true cost of capital, then the firm will lose money and in the long run will choose to utilise no inputs and will not produce any outputs (i.e. it will exit the business). Paradoxically, as the fair rate of return approaches the firm's true cost of capital, the magnitude of the input distortion associated with rate of return increases rather than decreases; that is, the firm will want to increase its use of capital. This result appears counter-intuitive because it implies that the greater the difference between the fair rate of return on capital and the true cost of capital, the smaller will be the use of capital by the firm. See Baumol and Klevorick (1970).

[42] See Train (1991, chapter 1).

[43] See Baumol and Klevorick (1970), Bailey and Coleman (1971), Davis (1973) and Klevorick (1973).

[44] See Peles and Stein (1976) and Klevorick (1973). Train (1991) reviews this literature, and draws the conclusion that: 'The overall picture of ROR [rate of return] regulation under uncertainty is even more distressing than without uncertainty: in addition to utilising an inefficient input mix, the firm probably wastes inputs and could easily produce less output than if it were not regulated.'

[45] See Joskow and Rose (1989) and Joskow (2007a). As described below, numerous empirical studies have concluded that the incentives for investment are higher under price cap regulation than rate of return.

explanation for the lack of empirical support for the A–J effect is the important differences between the Averch–Johnson analytical framework and how rate of return regulation is actually applied in practice.[46] For example, in real-world settings, a regulatory lag is characteristic of the rate of return process, and regulators generally have some (albeit) imperfect information about the firm's costs and demand, and can disallow certain costs and expenditures. Moreover, the fact that firms themselves have imperfect information about the effects of their decisions may also mitigate the effects of the A–J effect in the real world.[47] Ultimately, the principal contribution of this work may be that it highlights the possibility that *regulation* can itself create incentives for firms to produce inefficiently.[48]

While we have considered some criticisms of the *principles* underlying the pure rate of return approach, there are also criticisms of how the approach is applied in practice. One such criticism, already noted, is that the approach has not encouraged the setting of efficient price structures. A related criticism is that, where competition is being introduced into a sector, the lack of flexibility for the firm to unilaterally set its own relative prices (without going through a rate hearing) can limit the ability of the incumbent provider to respond to competition and may encourage 'cream-skimming'. A further criticism sometimes made is that rate of return regulation results in unduly high operating costs because a firm may be slow to replace ageing assets that are in the rate base with more efficient assets.[49] At a practical level, this form of regulation also entails high administrative costs, which can arise from lengthy and complex rate hearings that are litigious in nature and can often involve considerable expert testimony.[50] Moreover, the approach forces the regulator to second-guess the operations of the firm, and evaluate the prudence of its investment decisions and reasonableness of its operating costs, despite the fact that it is at a considerable information asymmetry. This can increase the costs and time associated with the formal regulatory process. It should be noted, however, that each of these practical criticisms is relative, and, as discussed below, one criticism of price cap regulation as it has evolved in some jurisdictions is that it, too, has become administratively complex, costly and intrusive, and also requires the regulator to closely scrutinise and sometimes second-guess the costs and operations of firms.

5.1.3 Developments in Rate of Return Regulation

Despite its long history, and widespread application, the rate of return approach to price regulation has, since the 1980s, developed something of a poor reputation in academic and policy debates as different forms of incentive and performance-based regulatory arrangements have been introduced.[51] However, as discussed in Section 5.3, the distinction

---

[46] This limitation has long been recognised. See, for example, Klevorick (1973) and Joskow (1974).

[47] Baumol and Klevorick (1970) note, for example: '[E]ven if it occurs in practice it does not seem likely to produce effects that are very serious. This seems so, if for no other reason, because, as we have already observed, firms may have neither the extensive information nor the refined decision processes necessary to lead unerringly to the A–J input distortion.'

[48] As Train (1991) observes, the A–J method 'shows that the regulatory procedure does not induce the firm to choose the socially optimal outcome'.

[49] See Sappington (2002).

[50] Lowry, Makos, Deason and Schwartz (2017) note that rate cases are typically held once every three years in the USA. EIA (2018) records that, in 2018, nearly half of all major US electric utilities tried to change electricity rates by filing rate cases with state regulatory commissions.

[51] See Sappington and Weisman (2016a). However, as Joskow (2007a) observes, much of the criticism that deems the 'traditional' approach to be inefficient is based on a poor understanding of how it works in practice.

between rate of return regulation and the various forms of price cap regulation is, i practice, typically one of degree rather than kind. Moreover, in jurisdictions where rate of return regulation is applied, most notably in North America, various adaptations have been made in an attempt to improve the performance of regulated firms.

In practice, then, there is no such thing as 'pure' rate of return regulation, where for example, prices are automatically adjusted to costs, and all costs are automatically approved by the regulator without some form of audit or prudency test. Real-world rate of return regimes have some 'lag' between cost changes and price changes, which allow the firm to 'keep' any deviations between prices and costs during the lag period, which can create important incentives for efficiency.[52] Moreover, as discussed above, most implementations of rate of return regulation have processes in place to ensure that the value of the regulated rate base is determined on the basis of prudent capital costs (through 'used and useful' tests), and can disallow operating costs assessed as not having been efficiently incurred. Whilst these developments have introduced some incentives for efficiency into the rate of return framework, the general incentive properties of the rate of return approach are argued to be inherently weak, and this has led to a focus, in recent decades, on alternative approaches to price regulation with stronger incentive properties. In addition, and separate from efficiency incentives, some US states have introduced decoupling policies, which disassociate revenues from underlying sales, in order to create incentives aligned with specific policy priorities, such as to promote greater conservation of water and electricity.[53]

One development in North America (albeit not necessarily a new one), described in Chapters 3 and 10 (in Box 10.1), is the greater use of negotiated settlements as an alternative to the formal rate of return regulatory process. The use of these agreements is seen as a response to the costs, complexity and time delays associated with the formal rate case process and to related concerns that the process is disproportionately focused on the needs and views of the regulator rather than those of the operators and users of the network. The negotiated settlements approach is seen to allow for settlements that are more innovative and creative than solutions developed and imposed by a regulator, and the approach has been argued to have introduced various aspects of incentive regulation into the traditional rate of return approach.[54]

---

[52] Writing in the 1970s, Joskow (1973) observed that it can take anywhere from six months to a year, and sometimes longer, from the day that a rate increase request is filed until a final decision is reached. During that time, the firm must generally continue to apply the prevailing rates, and is the residual claimant for any cost savings or increases. More generally, because of the regulatory lag and other informal regulatory constraints, 'once a rate increase has been applied for, the possibility of another rate increase is effectively eliminated for 18 to 24 months'. In addition, where deviations between prices and cost extend for a long period of time, this can have an effect on a regulated firm's market value (Joskow, 2007a).

[53] See Eto, Stoft and Belden (1997), Carter (2001) and Michelfelder, Ahern and D'Ascendis (2019). Chu and Sappington (2013) find that a utility will need to receive financial rewards in excess of those provided by revenue decoupling to induce it to undertake energy-efficient efforts. Brennan (2013) argues that decoupling policies can run 'counter to learning in regulatory economics, which has identified various flaws of fixed-profit regulation'.

[54] See Wang (2004), Doucet and Littlechild (2009) and Littlechild (2009a, 2012a).

5.2 PRICE CAP REGULATION

The term 'price cap' regulation has, in practice, come to refer to a range of regulatory arrangements, some of which have quite different characteristics.[55] An essential and distinctive attribute of the general price cap approach is that the prices a firm is able to charge for it services are no longer directly linked to the underlying costs, and prices will, to varying degrees, become detached from costs for a set period of time. This characteristic shifts some of the risk associated with cost variability from consumers to the regulated firm insofar as, if costs increase (or a firm mis-forecasts its future costs), the firm is not automatically able to increase prices to recover those costs during the set period of time in which the price cap is in place. For this reason, such an approach is sometimes seen to 'mimic' a competitive market, where producers cannot influence the market price, and the only way to increase profits is to reduce costs.[56] The approach is now the predominant form of price regulation applied in a number of jurisdictions, including in Europe, Australia and New Zealand.[57]

The origins of the price cap approach can be traced to the influential 1983 report of Stephen Littlechild, which considered the merits of various regulatory schemes for application to British Telecom after privatisation.[58] The report argued in favour of regulating prices not profits, as this was seen to provide greater incentives for efficiency and innovation than rate of return regulation.[59] Littlechild was not the first to identify deficiencies with aspects of the rate of return approach nor to propose that a fixed regulatory lag be introduced. Scholars in the USA had, since the late 1960s, suggested the need for a mechanism to harness the incentives of public utility firms. Writing in 1967, Baumol (1967) suggested that, to address deficiencies in rate of return regulation, rates could be fixed for set periods (say, three years), and during the intervening period the company could have the freedom to adjust its rates as it saw fit and retain all the earnings it makes. At the end of the three-year period, rates could then be reset to provide no more

---

[55] While the term 'price cap regulation' is sometimes used synonymously with the term 'incentive regulation', as is generally well recognised, all regulation (including rate of return regulation) creates incentives (including, in some cases, perverse ones) for economic behaviour. Sappington (1994) defines incentive regulation as 'the implementation of rules that encourage a regulated firm to achieve desired goals by granting some, but not complete, discretion to the firm'.

[56] See Newbery (1999).

[57] Variants of the price cap approach have been used in the following countries: UK (electricity, gas, water and wastewater, post, rail, airports and telecommunications); Australia (electricity, gas, water and wastewater in some states and telecommunications); Ireland (gas); France (gas); New Zealand (gas distribution and telecommunications); Germany (energy); and USA (telecommunications and energy in some states).

[58] The first use of the general price cap approach in the UK was to the dominant firm supplying contraceptive sheaths following a report by the Monopolies and Mergers Commission (1982). The recommendation of that report was that average prices should be restricted to an increase in a cost index less 1.5 per cent. Excellent surveys of the approach are presented in Acton and Vogelsang (1989) and Liston (1993) and in the contributions to the 1989 Symposium on Price Cap Regulation in *RAND Journal of Economics*, vol. 20 (no. 3).

[59] In reaching this conclusion, Littlechild (1983) noted two principal defects with rate of return: firstly, that it was 'burdensome and costly to operate, reduces the incentive to efficiency and innovation, and distorts the pattern of investment'; and secondly, that it covered the whole of the firm and did not focus on the specific services where monopoly power was the greatest. Littlechild's original proposal was to apply such a price control scheme to local telephone services, on the assumption that the other services would be competitive, and was accordingly called 'the local tariff reduction scheme'.

than an *r* per cent rate of return on a firm's historical investments. Subsequent work b
Baumol and Klevorick (1970) concluded that rate of return regulation, applied inflexibl
could eliminate any financial reward for efficiency and innovation.[60] They, and Baile
and Coleman (1971) after them, saw that a 'regulatory lag' could provide incentives fc
efficiency improvements by permitting temporary rewards for efficiency. Another impo
tant development was the Vogelsang and Finsinger (1979) model described in Chapter
which showed that a regulatory constraint could be introduced which might motivate
multi-product firm to set economically efficient prices over time, and is seen by some ;
similar to the tariff basket price cap approach that was first applied to British Telecom.[
   Regardless of its precise origins, the price cap approach (albeit in different specif
forms) has been widely adopted around the world.[62] In the USA, although rate of retu
regulation is still widely adopted, the price cap approach – sometimes referred to ;
performance-based regulation or multi-year rate plans – was first applied in the telecom
munications sector in 1989 and is now used by state public utility commissions in th
industry, and for electricity distribution in some states.

5.2.1 The General Price Cap Approach

Although, as we discuss below, numerous variants of price cap regulation are applied in prac
tice, a common form of price cap regulation is known as 'RPI-X' (Retail Price Index minus
which was the methodology first applied in the UK in the early 1980s) or 'I-X' (I minu
X, where *X* is some expected efficiency improvement and *I* is some measure of inflation
In general terms, under this approach, the regulator sets a maximum, or a ceiling, c
the increase in prices for a set of relevant services for a pre-specified, but significan
period of time, which to some degree is then independent of the actual costs associate
with the provision of those services.[63] Specifically, under the RPI-X approach, the firm
required to ensure that its average increase in prices for a specific basket of services doc
not exceed the increase in the economy-wide rate of inflation (retail price index, RPI),
minus a certain number of percentage points (*X*), sometimes known as an 'offset'. It ca
be represented as follows:

$$P^t = P^{t-1} \cdot (1 + \text{RPI} - X),$$ \hfill (5.4)

---

[60] See also Baumol (1982b).

[61] See Bradley and Price (1988).

[62] In addition to its application in the UK, the USA, Australia and New Zealand, price cap regulation has
    been implemented in many countries including Belgium, France, Honduras, Ireland, Italy, Japan, Mexic
    Panama and the Netherlands: Sappington (2002). Weisman (2002) argues that the pervasive application
    of price cap regulation has profoundly changed the regulatory landscape.

[63] Prices for different services can be controlled individually, but in practice it has been more common
    for different services to be placed into different 'baskets' and for the price control to be applied to a
    representative weighted average basket of services (with the weights determined on the basis of revenue
    or quantity shares of each service in the basket).

[64] RPI is the economy-wide general measure of inflation or change in retail price index. In some
    jurisdictions, such as the USA and Australia, the consumer price index (CPI) may be used, while in
    other cases (such as in Canada) an estimate of industry input inflation has been used. Meitzen, Schoec
    and Weisman (2017) discuss the importance of pairing the inflation measure (*I*) with the corresponding
    X factor.

where P^t is the price for services in the basket in period t, P^{t-1} is the price for services in the basket in the previous period $t-1$, RPI is the economy-wide rate of inflation and X is the offset factor. So, if the price in period $t-1$ was \$10, the economy-wide rate of inflation (RPI) is 4 per cent and the offset (the X factor) is assessed by the regulator as being 5 per cent, then the regulated firm is required to reduce its prices for the services in the basket by 1 per cent on average in the period t, implying a price in period t of \$9.90. The basic idea is that the change in prices for the services should not exceed the change in prices for other goods and services in the economy (i.e. the level of inflation). When X is used to measure changes in productivity (see discussion below), this implies that there is an expectation that productivity improvements in the regulated activity will be greater than elsewhere in the economy and that these will be reflected in lower consumer prices for the services.

In effect, under this approach, allowable changes in prices are indexed to movements in a *non-controllable* (exogenous to the firm) measure, the general rate of inflation, less an amount determined by the regulator (X). While the value of X is frequently the same in each year of the fixed period (e.g. 5 per cent for each year of a five-year price control period), in some cases a different value of X is applied in each year of the price control.

The Duration of the Price Cap

A key aspect of price cap regulation, and one that distinguishes it from pure rate of return regulation, is that changes in average prices are independent of changes in the *controllable* costs of the supplier for a pre-specified fixed period of time.[65] During this fixed time period (which usually ranges between three and five years, but is sometimes longer), the firm has an incentive to improve efficiency and performance, as the firm keeps any gains associated with such improvements. There is a trade-off here. A price cap of a short duration ensures that prices do not deviate too greatly from costs, and consequently that earnings do not remain above target levels for too long a period.[66] However, if the period between regulatory reviews is too short, then it will act in much the same way as rate of return regulation, and may reduce the incentives for the firm to seek out cost efficiencies. In general, shorter price cap periods may be appropriate in circumstances of considerable uncertainty about costs and demand, or where political pressures are such that the regulator would come under intense pressure if profits were either too high or too low.[67]

An important implication of detaching prices from costs is that there may be periods where the firm's earnings are well above (or well below) expected levels. In effect, the price cap approach institutionalises the 'regulatory lag' by restricting the ability of the regulator to reset prices for a fixed period. During this fixed period of time, the regulated

---

[65] In some implementations, various costs that are deemed to be beyond the influence of the firm can be 'passed through' automatically into price changes (such as in RPI-X+Y approaches). Examples of such 'pass-through' costs include energy costs (such as buying gas or purchasing costs) or costs associated with meeting unforeseen government commitments. Sappington and Weisman (2010) refer to 'Z-factor' adjustments in the application of price caps in the USA, which are designed to 'insure the regulated firm against large, unanticipated financial shocks that are beyond its control'. In addition, so-called 'k factors' have sometimes been used in the electricity and water industries to fund additional capital requirements. See Meitzen, Schoech and Weisman (2017).

[66] This issue is of particular importance where the firm is exposed to large exogenous changes in costs, which are not automatically passed through to consumers in the form of +Y factors or Z-factor adjustments.

[67] See Sappington (2002).

firm generally has some freedom to choose relative prices for the different services it sup
plies, subject to remaining within the overall weighted average price constraint.[68]

At the end of this fixed period of time – assuming that the relevant services are sti
subject to price regulation – the regulator may choose to adjust the initial prices for th
next fixed regulatory period to reflect any changes in underlying costs, and to elimin
ate any excess profits being earned by the firm. There is, however, a critical trade-of
to be made by the regulator here between the need to ensure that the incentives on th
regulated firm are constant over multiple regulatory periods, and the need to ensure tha
prices for regulated services do not deviate from costs too greatly and consumers benef
from any efficiency gains made during the previous period. In particular, the regulato
has to be mindful of the so-called 'ratchet effect' whereby cost-reducing efforts of th
firm in one regulatory period are 'rewarded' with tougher cost targets in a subsequen
period (discussed in more detail in Chapter 7).[69] One approach to this trade-off has bee
to make an initial adjustment to prices at the start of the subsequent price control perio
(sometimes called a P_0 adjustment) in order to bring prices into line with costs. Thi
approach allows consumers to immediately benefit from prices that reflect any reduc
tions in costs made in the previous period. However, it can also create incentives for th
firm not to reduce costs in the final stages of the preceding regulatory period, as any cos
reductions will automatically be reflected in lower prices.[70] Another approach has bee
to make more gradual adjustments to the path of prices over the remaining years of th
price control (the 'glide path' approach).[71]

The Scope of Products within the Price Cap and the Number of Baskets

While all of a firm's regulated services can be placed under a single price cap (or withi
a single 'basket') and the RPI-X restriction placed on that basket, in practice, it is com
mon for different services to be divided into various baskets, to which a separate pric
cap restriction is applied. In telecommunications, for example, one basket might includ
business services and another basket might include residential customer services. Th
principal effect of placing services in different baskets is that it limits the ability of th
regulated firm to rebalance prices across the different services it supplies, and still satisf

[68] If individual price caps are applied, then the price constraint for service x is $P_x \leqslant P_{cap}$. However, as is
more commonly the case, if the price cap is applied to a number of services, then the firm may be subjec
to a weighted average price constraint, $\sum_x W_x P_x \leqslant P_{cap}$, where P_{cap} denotes the price cap, P_x is the
price for the individual service x and W_x denotes the weights for each service x subject to the scheme,
such that $\sum_x W_x = 1$.

[69] Without the introduction of measures to address this issue, the regulated firm can have strong incentives
not to engage in cost-reducing effort towards the end of a given regulatory period, since in the later
years of a review period there will be little time to reap financial benefits from lower costs before prices
are 'ratcheted down'.

[70] Where such adjustments are automatic and eliminate any efficiency gains, then it is no different from
lagged rate of return regulation (except that the regulatory lag is fixed).

[71] A 'glide path' provides a mechanism for allowing regulated companies to 'keep' a (decreasing) proportion
of any efficiency gains in one regulatory period in the following regulatory period, and therefore is
intended to encourage the regulated firm to continue to reduce costs over an entire regulatory period.
This approach was common in the UK in the periods immediately following the early privatisations.

an average price constraint. For example, if there are separate baskets for business and residential customers, the firm will not be able to compensate for any increase in the price of residential services with a reduction in prices of business services and still remain within the average price constraint. It follows from these points that the greater the number of price baskets, the lower the flexibility that the firm has to set relative prices across the different services it supplies.

Limiting the flexibility of firms in setting relative prices under price cap regulation is argued to address other concerns: that the firm uses its pricing flexibility to disadvantage rivals where the firm is vertically integrated (by engaging in a price or margin squeeze); or that the prices set by the firm for some services might be inconsistent with particular distributional objectives. Accordingly, where these types of concerns exist, a regulator can apply a sub- or disaggregated price cap on specific services, which is then subject to the RPI-X formula. In setting these individual price caps for specific services, the regulator faces a familiar difficulty: the need to allocate fixed and common costs among the different services in a non-arbitrary way.

Determining the Value of 'X'

A critical task of the regulator applying the price cap approach is determining the value of X. There are, however, some differences of view as to what X represents, which has implications for how it is estimated. On one view, X is intended to reflect changes in productivity, and should be linked directly to some measure of past, future or benchmark productivity performance.[72] Although various methodologies have been adopted, a common approach is to estimate the historical growth in productivity and input costs and to use this as the basis for the estimation of future growth rate. A 'stretch factor' is then sometimes applied to this historical growth rate to reflect the potential for enhanced productivity growth in the future. Some have observed that the notion of X has been interpreted along these lines for price cap regulation in the USA, with X being set on the basis of the expected productivity of the firm.[73]

Another view conceives of X in broader terms, and sees its determination as involving the consideration of factors beyond expected changes in productivity.[74] According to this approach, the basis on which X is reset is within the discretion of the regulator, and a range of factors can influence the regulator's decision as to the value of X for the

---

[72] Sappington (2002) considers that 'the X factor should reflect the extent to which the regulated industry is deemed capable of achieving more rapid productivity growth than is the rest of the economy'. Laffont and Tirole (1993) understand the X factor in similar terms as capturing 'some anticipated rate of technological progress'.

[73] See Sappington and Weisman (2016). Crew and Kleindorfer (1996) note that this approach has been criticised as too mechanistic, but that it has also been seen to potentially address issues associated with commitment by the regulator by limiting the discretion that the regulator has at times of regulatory review.

[74] Beesley and Littlechild (1989), two of the original architects of the UK price cap approach, suggest that: 'The level of X can reflect negotiations with the company, not only about the scope for future productivity agreements, but also about other matters affecting the company's future, including the details of the price constraint formula, the rate at which competition is allowed to develop, the provision of information, and so on. In short, X may be thought of as one of several variables in a political and commercial bargaining process.'

following period.[75] These factors include: past efficiency performance and expected future productivity gains; the need to finance future investments; and expected changes growth and earnings.[76] However, as Littlechild (2021a) argues, this can lead to an undue focus on 'estimating/guessing' how much scope there is to increase efficiency and to g 'X right', which is unrealistic given that five-year forecasts will always be wrong ar the regulator will look foolish or incompetent if the company outperforms the regulator assumptions.

Finally, in some implementations, X is used as a method for ensuring that the allowed revenues of the firm are matched to the expected costs of the firm. According to th approach, the regulator estimates the expected future costs of the firm in the next regulatory period, and then applies a value of X that allows prices to change in such a way as to allow the firm to earn sufficient revenue to cover these costs (see the building block method discussion below).

5.2.2 Determining the *Ex Ante* Revenue Requirement

While in principle there does not need to be a close relationship between the level of the price control and costs under price cap regulation (i.e. prices and costs a detached), in practice, when setting a price cap, many regulators consider the under lying costs of supplying a service to ensure that the prices set are such that the revenue obtained by the firm will cover efficient costs. Two methods are commonly adopted to determine the revenue requirements of the firm: the so-called 'building block approach', and an approach based on estimates of the long-run incremental costs of supplying the relevant services.

Building Block Approaches
In simple terms, under the 'building block approach', the regulator sets the price control to allow the firm to satisfy a forecast revenue requirement.[77] That revenue requirement comprises three main components: (i) an estimate of expected efficient operating cost (ii) the expected depreciation for the period (sometimes referred to as the return *of* capital); and (iii) a rate of return on invested capital (sometimes referred to as the return o capital). This can be represented as follows:

$$R^t = r^t \cdot \mathrm{RAB}^{t-1} + \mathrm{Opex}^t + \mathrm{Dep}^t. \tag{5.5}$$

---

[75] Beesley and Littlechild (1989) argue that an important difference between the British application of RPI-X and US rate of return regulation is that the regulator has greater discretion in setting the value of X, and faces less onerous requirements to reveal the basis on which the value of X has been set. As a consequence of this greater freedom, they argued at that time, there was greater scope for bargaining under RPI-X price controls than under rate of return.

[76] See Beesley and Littlechild (1989). Armstrong, Cowan and Vickers (1994) note that factors such as the value of existing assets, the cost of capital and the progress of competition are relevant when X factors and other licence conditions relating to pricing are reviewed. Makholm (2018a) argues that in the 'UK regulators could effectively invent an X factor value to square current rates with those based on long-term (5- or 10-year) forecasts of costs and volumes in rate re-setting cases'.

[77] For a fuller description, see Biggar (2004).

In equation (5.5), R^t is the revenue requirement in period t, r^t is the allowed cost of capital in period t, RAB^{t-1} is the closing value of the invested capital (known as the regulated asset base, see below) in period $t-1$, $Opex^t$ is operating expenditure in period t and Dep^t is the depreciation expense in period t.

It follows that, in determining the revenue requirement, the regulator must estimate a range of elements such as: the types of services to be provided; the expected output for each service; efficient operating costs; efficient new capital expenditure;[78] the appropriate depreciation charge (having regard to asset lives); and the cost of capital that should be applied to the asset value (see Box 5.1 above). Having estimated the expected efficient costs of the firm over the next regulatory period, the regulator then estimates a value of X that allows real prices to change (given forecast demand) in such a way as to allow the firm to earn sufficient revenue to cover these costs. In effect, X is chosen such that the regulated price results in expected revenues which equate to the estimate of efficient costs, and the firm breaks even at the end of the period. However, as the forward-looking prices are based on an estimate of expected future costs, the firm can improve on its profitability if it beats the regulator's estimates of efficient cost reductions.

As is apparent from this description of the building block approach, in practice, it shares a number of similarities with the rate of return approach, in that prices are determined on the basis of some estimate of efficient costs (including a return on capital). Given this similarity, many of the contentious aspects of rate of return regulation, such as the determination of efficient costs, the value of the asset base and the appropriate cost of capital, have also arisen in implementations of the building block method. The principal difference between the approaches is that, under the building block method, prices/costs are assessed on a forward-looking basis and the price control is fixed for a predetermined period.

An important element of the building block approach is the regulatory asset base (RAB),[79] which represents the value of the firm's assets on which the rate of return is estimated and, in some ways, corresponds to the 'rate base' that is used in rate of return approaches.[80] Two aspects of the RAB deserve further comment: (i) how past capital expenditure is treated; and (ii) how any capital expenditure undertaken within a period is treated.

Two methods for dealing with past investments of the regulated firm are applied under the building block approach. The first approach, referred to as the financial capital maintenance (FCM) method, determines the value of the RAB in such a way that the firm's revenue requirement will be sufficient to earn a fair return on historical capital investments irrespective of changes in the value of those assets.[81] The alternative approach, known

---

[78] A number of considerations often have to be assessed by the regulator such as the necessity of proposed capital additions during the period (i.e. is it needed) and the efficiency of such expenditure (i.e. is it the least-cost way of expanding the network).

[79] This is sometimes referred to as the regulatory asset value (RAV).

[80] However, recall that an important protection afforded firms under rate of return regulation in practice is that, once assets are accepted into the rate base, they can generally be recovered. In principle, no such protection exists under price cap regulation.

[81] The value of the RAB, on which the revenue requirement is based, is set so that the firm can, over time, recover its historical expenditure on capital assets. This approach avoids the risk of assets being stranded, as, once an investment is 'rolled in' or enters the RAB, the value of that asset is fixed at that moment, and it remains in there at that value until it is fully depreciated.

as operational capital maintenance (OCM), determines the value of the RAB so that th
firm earns a fair return on capital investments that are needed to provide the services
supplies. According to this approach, historical investments in capital assets containe
in the RAB can potentially be revalued to reflect changes in technology, asset prices c
obsolescence.[82] The choice between FCM and OCM can have significant impacts on th
incentives of the regulated firm and on the allocation of risk between shareholders of th
firm and consumers.[83]

A second issue related to the treatment of capital expenditure under the buildin
block approach is how any incremental capital expenditure undertaken within a perio
is treated at the end of that period. Here there is a choice as to whether to 'roll in' th
forecast amount of capital expenditure (determined at the start of the regulatory period
or the *actual* amount of capital expenditure (determined at the end of the regulator
period).[84] The choice between the different approaches to rolling new capital investment
into the RAB can also impact on the incentives of the regulated firm.[85]

Long-Run Incremental Cost Approaches

A second approach to estimating the revenue requirement for the firm, which has bee
widely applied in the telecommunications industry, is to base the prices for each servic
on an estimate of the forward-looking long-run incremental costs (LRIC) of supplyin
that service.[86] The general approach is premised on the basis that prices should reflec
the costs that would be incurred by a new efficient operator entering the market, and a
such would replicate the conditions observed in a competitive market. Although there ar
numerous methods for estimating the LRIC, the general approach is based on the idea tha
the regulated price for a service should be sufficient to cover the costs (including capita
and operating costs) that would be incurred by a *hypothetical* network operator who sup
plied an increment of demand for that service.

---

[82] It follows that, depending on changes in asset values, a firm may earn more or less than a fair return on
the investments it undertakes over the lifetime of that asset.

[83] While the FCM approach effectively protects the regulated firm from the risk of assets being stranded
once they are in the RAB, the OCM approach places the risk associated with underlying changes in asset
values with the regulated firm. It is sometimes argued that, because the OCM approach places more
risk on the firm, this will lead to more optimal investments, and will therefore be most appropriate in
markets where there is rapid technological change. On the other hand, to the extent to which there is
volatility in asset prices that deter firms from undertaking new investments under the OCM approach,
the FCM is seen to provide greater assurance that any expenditures will be recovered and may promote
investment in such a context. In practice, the value of the RAB for many core network utilities is
determined according to the FCM principle. However, there are examples where the OCM approach has
been adopted.

[84] In practice, these amounts can differ for various reasons, such as: the firm deferring the start of a
project, resulting in only a proportion of the forecast expenditure being incurred in a period; the
firm making the investment in a more or less efficient way than that which was expected; or the firm
deciding to undertake different projects within the overall capital allowance that was approved.

[85] For example, if the *ex ante* forecast of capital expenditure is automatically rolled into the RAB, this
can create an incentive for a firm to exaggerate its forecasts of capital expenditure, but then to reduce
the amount of its actual capital expenditure. Conversely, if the actual value of the capital expenditure
incurred in the period is rolled into the RAB, this may limit the incentives for a firm to exaggerate
its *ex ante* forecasts of capital expenditure, but also reduce the incentives on the firm to pursue cost
efficiencies when implementing a project.

[86] The first LRIC models in the telecoms sector were developed in the early 1990s. See Mitchell (1989),
Gabel and Kennet (1991) and Arnbak, Mitchell, Neu, *et al.* (1994).

As discussed in Chapter 11, in practice, when estimating the value of LRIC, various choices and assumptions have to be made including: the size of the increment to use; whether the estimates of long-run costs relate to services or elements;[87] the level of optimisation of the network that is assumed;[88] assumptions about the state of technology used;[89] as well as assumptions about the valuation of the assets,[90] and how they are depreciated over time.[91] One important issue is whether the regulated prices based on the estimate of LRIC should be 'marked up' or increased to allow for the recovery of any fixed or common costs associated with supplying the service, and, if so, the method by which these fixed and common costs should be allocated across different services.[92] Where a mark-up on LRIC to recover a proportion of fixed and common costs is permitted, this is generally termed a 'LRIC+' approach to cost recovery.

The main arguments in support of the LRIC approach are: (i) that it can provide the appropriate entry and investment signals in markets that are being opened to competition; and (ii) that, in the presence of rapid technological change, which can significantly alter costs and demand, there is a need to continually reflect the current replacement value of the assets each time a price review is undertaken to encourage efficient investment choices. However, in practice, the approach affords significant discretion to a regulator in estimating the LRIC for a 'hypothetical' competitor on which prices are then based. As discussed in Chapter 11, where there is substantial uncertainty as to how the regulator will exercise this discretion, this may act as a disincentive for new investment and raise the cost of capital.

5.2.3 Forms of Price Cap Regulation

Within the general framework, various forms of price cap regulation are applied in practice. The particular form that the price cap takes can be seen to have differing effects on the incentives of regulated firms to set efficient tariff structures, expand demand and improve the quality of supply. It can also have implications in terms of the risk exposure of regulated firms.[93]

---

[87] As discussed in Chapter 11, in telecommunications, while in Australia and Europe the focus has generally been on *service* costs (total service long-run incremental cost, TSLRIC), in the USA the focus has been on the costs associated with the *elements* providing the services (total element long-run incremental cost, TELRIC). See Brock and Katz (1997) and Gans and King (2004a) on this point.

[88] Two approaches to assess the degree of optimisation in LRIC models are typically used. The first is to adopt a *full* optimisation assumption, also known as a scorched earth assumption, which configures an 'optimal' network taking none of the existing infrastructure and flows as fixed. The alternative *partial* optimisation, or scorched node, assumption takes the infrastructure of the network as fixed, but optimises the flows over that network. In practice, a partial optimisation, or scorched node, approach to estimating costs is often applied, but a scorched earth approach is argued to be appropriate in situations where there is an inefficient network design (for example, where there is an excessive number of local telephone exchange sites).

[89] This sometimes comes down to a choice as to whether the facilities which provide the service are assumed to be 'best-in-use' facilities or 'best-available' facilities.

[90] In telecommunications, the value of assets is often estimated with reference to the 'current' or 'replacement' cost of these assets (i.e. the current value of an asset is determined by the cost of replacing the existing facility with a modern equivalent available asset). This differs from the 'historical' or 'embedded' or 'original' cost approach, where assets are valued at their original (historical) costs. See Tardiff (2015).

[91] In particular, whether an economic approach or accounting approach to depreciation is adopted or not. The decision as to how to allocate capital costs over time (as reflected in the approach to depreciation) can have substantial impacts for users of the different services on the network.

[92] In its purest form, LRIC-based approaches include only the incremental costs of the service *plus* an allocation of product-specific fixed costs associated with the service.

[93] Comnes, Stoft, Greene and Hill (1995) and Sappington (2002) provide fuller descriptions.

Fixed Revenue Cap

A fixed revenue cap limits the amount that the firm can earn to a maximum allowed revenue (R^*), which is set at the start of the period on the basis of forecast demand and operating and capital expenditure requirements.[94] Once set, the maximum allowed revenue (R^*) is constant during the period, and is independent of the volume of services that are supplied. In other words, the regulated firm is not exposed to any volume risk. In subsequent years, the amount of allowable revenue will be reset according to the RPI-X formula, and adjustments can be made to account for any over- or under-recovery of revenue arising in the previous period. This approach is seen as best suited to settings where costs are largely fixed in nature and demand is relatively constant from period to period. A drawback of this approach is that it does not create incentives for the firm to engage in activities that increase demand/output (as this reduces its overall earnings),[95] and indeed can create incentives for the firm to actively minimise the demand for the service (for example, by degrading quality), as this will lower cost and increase the margin between the fixed revenue and total costs. In addition, to induce a reduction in demand, a supplier may have incentives to set inefficient price structures, for example, by setting prices above marginal cost on the most elastic services.

Average Revenue Approach

The average revenue, or revenue yield, approach places a constraint on the average revenue earned by the firm (i.e. the average price). The average yield is set by estimating the total revenue requirements for the firm and dividing it by forecast demand. Once set, the average revenue is only allowed to grow at a rate of RPI minus X over a relevant period. An important aspect of this approach (and one which differs from the weighted average approach described below) is that it does not distinguish between the different services provided by the firm,[96] and therefore the average revenue applies symmetrically to all the firm's services irrespective of differences in costs (i.e. the firm cannot earn lower average revenue for less costly services, or greater average revenue for more costly services). Although the *average* revenue per unit is capped on the basis of forecasts of demand, the amount of revenue that is actually earned on each individual unit of output is not, and as a consequence, the (positive and negative) risks associated with demand volatility fall on the supplier. Accordingly, if demand is *greater* than forecast at the time the price control is set, a supplier will earn higher profits than anticipated. Under this approach, and in contrast to the fixed revenue cap described above, a supplier may therefore have an incentive to expand demand beyond that forecast by the regulator at the time the price cap is set.[98] While this should make the firm more responsive to customer demand, to the

---

[94] In theory, R^* should be set so that economic profit is zero, such that R^* = Fixed costs + Variable costs × (Forecast output).

[95] This can be an advantage in some industries – such as water and energy – where there is a desire for consumers to conserve or limit their consumption of such services for environmental reasons.

[96] This method is seen as most suited to industries where there is a natural unit of 'output': for example, megawatt hours of electricity supplied; per passenger served for airport charges; while in gas it could be based on therms. Bradley and Price (1988) discuss the application of this approach in the UK.

[97] See Sappington (2002).

[98] This incentive may conflict with other objectives such as energy efficiency or water efficiency as discussed in Chapters 9 and 16. In some US states, regulators have introduced policies that 'decouple' revenues or profits from the volume of the commodity delivered such that the utility's profits remain constant despite reductions in demand. Generally, see Brennan (2010) on decoupling.

extent to which a supplier can influence demand it can also result in various inefficient and undesirable outcomes.[99] For example, the supplier may have an incentive to restrict the supply of services that are relatively costly to produce, and to increase the supply of services that are less costly to produce. The supplier might choose to only increase the quality of services offered to high-demand customers (in order to increase demand) or, similarly, may set relative tariffs in such a way as to encourage greater usage by high-demand customers, for example, by setting inefficiently low prices for these customers.

Hybrid Caps

A third price cap approach combines the fixed revenue and average revenue approaches into a 'mixed' or 'hybrid' cap. According to this approach, the firm's revenue is typically a function of a fixed component (like in a fixed revenue cap), and a variable component (as in an average revenue cap). However, unlike the average revenue cap (where revenue earned varies only with output), the revenue earned under the hybrid approach can be determined by additional parameters such as the number of customers connected, peak demand on the network and performance indicators.[100] For example, the total revenue allowed (R^*) may be a function of a fixed component (F), an output measure (q_1) and the number of customer connections (q_2) such that

$$R^* = F + \alpha(q_1) + \beta(q_2),$$

where F, α and β are constant. In setting the hybrid price cap, the regulator is required to estimate the marginal revenue associated with changes in each of the parameters (i.e. a value for the coefficients α and β), which, in principle, should be set such that marginal revenue is close to marginal cost. It follows that the amount of revenue earned under this approach depends on the precise form that the revenue function takes (i.e. which parameters are included in the revenue equation), the sensitivity of revenue to each of these parameters and whether the coefficients attached to each parameter are set so that marginal revenue closely approximates marginal cost. The incentives for the firm to expand demand, increase the quality of services and set efficient tariffs will depend on how the fixed and variable components of the cap are determined, and, in particular, on any difference between the regulator's estimates of marginal revenue and marginal cost for each of the parameters included in the variable component.[101]

Weighted Average Price Cap/Tariff Basket Approach

Finally, the weighted average price cap (or tariff basket approach) involves 'capping' the allowed price increases on the basis of an estimate of a weighted average price for a basket

---

[99] Critiques of this general approach are presented in Bradley and Price (1988) and Crew and Kleindorfer (1996). Sappington and Sibley (1992) examine this in the context of the price cap plan used by the Federal Communications Commission at that time.

[100] Among the factors that have been included in the hybrid revenue caps in electricity include customer numbers, energy demand, length of network lines, energy consumption and system losses.

[101] For example, in the unrealistic situation where the regulator perfectly estimates the marginal parameters in the revenue equation, such that marginal revenue equals true marginal cost for each parameter, then the business will have no incentive to increase or decrease output or the number of connections. However, if marginal revenue is set below marginal cost by the regulator, then the firm will have an incentive to decrease sales and/or to reduce the number of connections.

of services rather than a single service (as in the average revenue approach).[102] Under this approach, the weighted average price changes over time on the basis of the RPI-X formula.[103] The weights attached to each price in the tariff basket are generally estimated on the basis of that service's share of total revenues or output in the previous period.[104] Firms are able to rebalance tariffs for individual services within the basket during the period provided that the overall weighted average price constraint is satisfied.[105] The distinguishing feature of this approach is that it establishes a link between the (disaggregated) marginal revenue for each unit of a particular service sold and the price of that service. On this basis, it is argued that, in principle, a weighted average price cap approach will result in efficient price structures emerging, as suppliers will have incentives to set prices at close to marginal cost for elastic services, and charge higher prices for inelastic services.

5.2.4 Advantages and Disadvantages of Price Caps

There are a number of, in principle, advantages associated with price cap approaches.[106] First, by decoupling average prices from costs for a fixed period of time, price cap approaches are seen to create incentives for firms to minimise costs, invest in cost-reducing technologies and generally improve productive efficiency over time. These incentives are created by the fact that any reductions in costs will translate directly into higher profits being earned until the time that prices are next adjusted. Second, price cap regulation can address some of the information asymmetry problems that can arise between the regulated firm and the regulator, insofar as the firm's behaviour over time will reveal information about its true level of costs. A third perceived advantage is that, by allowing the firm to have pricing flexibility, such an approach should encourage the firm to develop more efficient pricing structures when setting relative prices, which maximise welfare while allowing it to break even.[107] Fourth, price cap approaches are seen as less vulnerable to problems of overcapitalisation, which were perceived to plague rate of return approaches (i.e. the A–J effect). Fifth, the price cap approach is seen to shift some of the risks associated with cost and demand volatility from consumers to the regulated firm, who may be in a better position to manage such risks. Sixth, it is argued that price cap-type approaches are better suited to settings that are undergoing significant change – for example, the

---

[102] This was the approach adopted in relation to British Telecom in 1984, where the average annual increase in prices was limited to RPI less 3 per cent during the period 1984 to 1988.

[103] The rationale for weighting the basket is that, other things being equal, a given price change will have a greater effect on consumers the more they consume of a service. The weights are therefore intended to reflect the relative impact on consumers of changes in prices for different services that they consume, having regard to the amount that they consume of each service. See Sappington (2002).

[104] When quantity levels are used as weights to adjust prices, there is an obvious link between the approach and that proposed by Vogelsang and Finsinger (1979) described in Chapter 4.

[105] In effect, the cap is defined as a price index for a basket of services.

[106] As Sappington and Weisman (2016) observe, price cap regulation 'often is considered to be a superior form of economic regulation quite generally rather than a superior form of regulation only in selected settings.'

[107] Sappington and Weisman (2010) note that such pricing flexibility can be particularly valuable where a firm faces competitive pressure, as it can allow them to respond to 'cream-skimming' by entrants who target only the incumbent's most profitable customers.

electricity and telecommunications industries – as it avoids the need for frequent rate hearings,[108] and reduces the incentives for capital investment when other solutions are more efficient.[109] Seventh, regulators may have stronger incentives to introduce competitive entry under price cap regulation, as, unlike for rate of return regulation, it is no longer responsible for approving any (politically unattractive) increase in rates of the incumbent which may accompany such competitive entry.[110] A final perceived advantage of the price cap approach is that it is 'simpler' for the company and the regulator.[111] However, these are 'in principle' advantages, and when price caps have been applied in practice, some of the potential positive attributes have not materialised to the extent anticipated. For example, the regulatory burden of the price cap approach has not been reduced to the extent anticipated, and is seen by some to have evolved to include similar levels of micro-management as rate of return regulation, and to have led to high levels of confrontation between customers, companies and regulators.[112] There is also inconclusive evidence on whether firms have used the pricing flexibility afforded them under price cap regulation to establish efficient price structures.[113]

Staying at the level of 'in principle', there are also a number of disadvantages or limitations associated with the general price cap approach. First, to the extent to which prices and costs diverge to a significant extent, or cost changes are not quickly reflected in price changes, this can result in allocative inefficiency. In particular, if the divergence between prices and underlying costs results in excessive earnings for the firm, this may create consumer harm and also be inconsistent with a regulator's objectives.[114] Second, price cap regulation can, in principle, create incentives for suppliers to reduce or degrade the quality of service relative to rate of return regulation.[115] This is because, within this framework, suppliers can reduce costs – and increase their profits for a given level of revenue – by offering a lower quality of services to customers.[116] Third, because

---

[108] Lowry, Makos, Deason and Schwartz (2017) and Costello (2019) highlight this benefit in the US context.

[109] Alvarez and Steele (2017) argue that a shift to price cap regulation in the US electricity sector could facilitate the shift from regulated firms focusing on a unilateral supply chain and expanding the grid to accommodate growing demand, to serving as an electricity platform which efficiently manages demand from distributed sources.

[110] However, as Weisman (2019a, b) observes, such policies to propagate competition can be used strategically by a regulator to tighten the effective price cap on a firm, which, in turn, can reduce incentives to engage in cost-reducing activities.

[111] See Beesley and Littlechild (1989).

[112] See Littlechild (2012a, 2021a), who argues that the burden of regulation in the UK is now worse than in the USA and price controls are a full-time activity for regulators. Similarly, Kridel, Sappington and Weisman (1996) found no evidence that incentive regulation in the USA had led to 'streamlined regulatory proceedings' at that time.

[113] Giulietti and Waddams Price (2005) found that the price structures that have evolved in different regulated industries in the UK following the wave of privatisation since the 1980s were less than efficient, and that considerable scope existed to improve overall efficiency by firms rebalancing their tariffs.

[114] Engel and Heine (2017) argue that price caps may not be well suited to dynamic environments, as the regulator may seek to provide over-generous price caps in the face of uncertainty.

[115] Spence (1975) makes the more general observation that, where a monopolist's prices are fixed, the firm will always set quality at too low a level.

[116] However, as discussed above, the effect on quality will depend on the specific form of price cap regulation applied, and, where the firm gets to keep any increases in revenue associated with stimulating demand, they may have an incentive to increase certain dimensions of service quality. As discussed in Chapter 4, the empirical evidence on the relationship between price caps and service quality is inconclusive.

the price cap approach shifts the risks associated with cost volatility from consumer to suppliers, this could raise the cost of capital for the firm. Fourth, price caps may reduce incentives for investment if a supplier is uncertain as to whether or not it will be able to recover efficiently incurred costs, including a return on capital, associated with any investments made when prices are reset.[117] Fifth, in terms of operating costs, the price cap approach might provide inappropriate incentives for firms to delay reducing costs towards the end of a regulatory period for fear that any reduction in costs will be reflected in the new price caps (i.e. the ratchet effect). Sixth, while the pricing flexibility afforded firms under price cap regulation can in principle be used by firms to set more efficient price structures, if such flexibility is not constrained, it might be used by the firm to inefficiently cross-subsidise specific services and behave anti-competitively. Seventh, the principal focus of RPI-X regulation on incentivising cost efficiency argued by some to be inadequate given the challenges confronting network operators in some sectors (such as energy and water) where there is a focus on decarbonisation and adapting the network to different supply configurations (e.g. distributed generation and electric vehicles, etc.).[119] Perhaps the most significant, in principle, disadvantage of price cap approaches compared to rate of return regulation is the so-called 'commitment problem', which has been described as its 'Achilles' heel'.[120] The essential issue here that, unlike rate of return regulation, where a firm has some assurance that prices will be set so as to allow it to recover its prudently incurred costs and remain financially viable, in principle, no such assurance exists under price cap regulation.[121] From the regulated firm's perspective, the concern is that the regulator will use its discretion when resetting the level of X to behave opportunistically (for example, by taking undue heed of political pressure to set a very high value of X with the aim of disproportionately

---

[117] There are two aspects to the reduced incentives for investment relating to the *timing* of when any investment is undertaken, and the incentives to undertake any investment at all. Both aspects depend critically on the credibility and nature of the regulatory regime. For example, if a supplier is concerned about extreme regulatory opportunism, and specifically that any sunk investment undertaken will be disallowed entirely at the time of the next price review, then it will obviously have very limited incentives to undertake investment of any form. Alternatively, in less extreme circumstances, the supplier might simply decide to delay investment until the regulator credibly demonstrates that it will allow for the recovery of past investments undertaken. For a general treatment of these issues, see Guthrie (2006), while Borrmann and Brunekreeft (2020) find that cost-based (rate of return) regulation is more effective in promoting timely investment than price-based regulation. Meitzen, Schoech and Weisman (2017) conclude that while 'inflation-minus' incentive regulation is effective in US telecommunications, it is 'probably not workable' in the US electric distribution industry unless there is some form of supplemental capital funding mechanism (such as a 'K factor') to encourage investment. Martimort, Pommey and Pouyet (2021) develop a model which shows that a price cap regulation alone does not provide enough incentives to invest in airport infrastructure and that a subsidy scheme is needed.

[118] See Beesley and Littlechild (1989). Sappington (2002) notes that such flexibility can also serve to undo any cross-subsidies introduced to address issues associated with fairness or other political objectives.

[119] See Makholm (2018a) and Littlechild (2021a) who describes the problem of inefficiency as 'last century problem'.

[120] See Weisman (2002). Sappington and Weisman (2010) suggest that variation in regulatory commitment powers may explain the different rates of adoption of price cap regulation across the world.

[121] Sappington and Weisman (2016a) suggest that lower levels of adoption of price cap regulation in the US electricity sector may, in part, reflect this risk.

reducing prices).[122] More generally, because the price cap approach detaches revenues from costs for an extended period of time, if a firm earns excessive returns, the regulator may come under political pressure and seek to 're-open' the price control to claw back some of the excessive profits.[123] On the other hand, the significant discretion afforded to the regulator under the approach raises the risk that the regulator is captured by the regulated company, such that the value of X is set so as to allow the firm to retain an excessive amount of profit to the detriment of consumers.

In practice, regulators are generally well aware of these potential drawbacks, and various measures and mechanisms have been adopted to address these issues. In relation to quality issues, prescribed quality standards are included in firms' licences in some jurisdictions, while in other jurisdictions firms are subject to financial rewards or penalties to ensure that quality is not degraded.[124] To address concerns about the process by which X is determined at the time of regulatory review, some regulators publish general guidelines on the process that it will follow or apply known methodologies based on changes in total factor productivity, thus limiting regulatory discretion.[125] To address concerns about commitment, and specifically that the firm will not be permitted to recover its prudently incurred costs, most (although not all) regulators have an obligation to ensure the financeability of the regulated firm, which restricts the ability to set price caps that threaten the viability of the firm. Finally, to incentivise timely investment, some regulators have developed mechanisms that include the approval of forward-looking investment allowances, or the immediate pass-through of investment costs during a regulatory period (but subject to review at the next regulatory reset).[126]

Finally, to address concerns about the 'ratchet effect', some price cap implementations have developed so-called efficiency carry-over mechanisms that allow the firm to retain any efficiency benefits derived in the current period for a specified period of time in a subsequent regulatory period.[127]

[122] In an early analysis, Crew and Kleindorfer (1996) describe the UK approach as making the company a 'hostage to the regulator'. More recently, Weisman (2019a, b) argues that, in the USA, the existing case law (including the standard established in FPC v. Hope Natural Gas, which entitles firms to a 'return ... sufficient to assure confidence in the financial integrity of the enterprise, so as to maintain its credit and attract capital' and to 'enable the company to operate successfully ... and to compensate its investors for the risks assumed ...') potentially gives the regulator broad discretion to 'act with impunity in employing ex post policy changes, including accommodative competitive entry (ACE) policies, to unilaterally reduce the regulated firm's earnings'.
[123] Sawkins (1996) suggests that in 1994 the British electricity regulator bowed to political and consumer pressure that a regulatory settlement was too lenient by re-opening a price control. Similarly, Sappington (2002) suggests that the British telecoms regulator reset prices to better match costs in 1991, by raising the X factor from 4.5 to 6.25 even though the X factor was scheduled to remain at 4.5. See Weisman (1993) for a more general analysis of this issue.
[124] In some cases, the allowable cap on price changes might be increased in circumstances where quality exceeds specific thresholds. Alternatively, when quality standards fall below specific thresholds, then penalties can be imposed. These can take the form of compensation to customers, or reductions in the amount that prices can be increased. In other implementations, there has not been an explicit link between quality and performance and financial incentives, rather, the quality scheme has been limited to the publication of performance data.
[125] See Makholm (2018a).
[126] See Borrmann and Brunekreeft (2020).
[127] An efficiency carry-over mechanism is said to promote an incentive for the firm to constantly pursue efficiency savings, by effectively guaranteeing the firm that it will be able to keep the benefit of the efficiency improvement for a specified period of time, irrespective of when it is earned in the regulatory period. Critically, however, in order to ensure that the incentives on the firm are consistent, the efficiency carry-over mechanism should be applied symmetrically; that is, where the firm does not meet established efficiency benchmarks, then a negative carry-over should be applied across regulatory periods.

5.2.5   Developments in Price Cap Regulation and the 'Totex Approach'

There have been numerous adaptations to price cap frameworks over the almost fort
years in which it has been applied in practice, many of which are discussed in Part III o
the book. Some of these adaptations focus on ensuring that regulated firms remain incen
tivised to operate efficiently, improve quality and invest and innovate where appropriate
Others seek to allocate risks between shareholders of the regulated firm and consumer
appropriately, or to further minimise information asymmetry between the regulator an
the firm.

Some of these adaptations in price cap frameworks (although far from an exhaustiv
list) include: adjustments to the timing of price reviews, and in particular extending th
time of such reviews to enhance the incentives on firms, and to lower the regulator
burden; allowing firms to automatically 'pass through' into prices various costs tha
are deemed to be beyond their influence; the introduction of 'rolling' efficiency incen
tives, which provide constant incentives for efficiency improvements over price contr
periods; greater use of more sophisticated comparative information and benchmarkin
techniques in determining operating expenditure and capital expenditure; the introduc
tion of so-called 'trigger' mechanisms into allowances for specific capital projects; th
introduction of 'menu regulation' approaches to capital expenditure to address the infor
mation asymmetry between the regulator and the regulated firm;[128] and the introductio
of various allowances and incentive schemes to encourage firms to engage in specifi
behaviours, or undertake innovative activity in certain areas.[129]

The 'Total Expenditure' (Totex) Approach

A wider development under price cap-type arrangements in some jurisdictions ha
involved a move away from a so-called 'input-based' price regulation process to a
approach based on 'outputs' or 'outcomes'.[130] This shift has been motivated by a desir
on the part of the regulator to focus on determining the 'high-level' outcomes for th
firm, but to leave the firm to meet these requirements in ways that it sees appropriate. A
applied in Britain, this approach continues to involve the use of an *ex ante* price cap,[13]
but requires regulated firms to consult extensively with stakeholders and consumers t

---

[128] Under this approach, firms are offered a choice among a 'menu' of different regulatory contracts when
the price control is being set, with each contract featuring different combinations of capital expenditure
and with returns on investment linked to whether the supplier meets its target level of capital
expenditure. A supplier can choose a contract that features low levels of capital expenditure but allows
for higher expected return on investment if they beat their expected target investment levels (a high-
powered incentive scheme), or, alternatively, a supplier can choose a contract that provides for high
levels of capital expenditure but with a correspondingly lower share of any difference between actual
and target spend levels (a relatively low-powered scheme). These have at different times been used in
the electricity, gas and water industries in Britain.

[129] For example, allowances to encourage firms to be innovative in respect of the development of demand-
side management mechanisms which will lead to the more efficient use of energy or water.

[130] This was one of the major adaptations to the price cap process for the British energy sector introduced
in 2010 (known as RIIO, or Revenue = Incentives + Innovation + Outputs). A variant of the outcomes
approach is also applied in the water industry in England and Wales.

[131] In the initial implementation in the energy sector, the price control period was extended from five to
eight years. However, it has since reverted back to five years.

identify desirable outcomes which it specifies in a business plan. The business plan is then approved by the regulator.[132]

An important element of this 'outputs' approach is a shift away from setting separate allowances for operating and capital expenditure towards setting a single allowance for the expected efficient *total expenditure* (Totex) for the business.[133] Variations of the Totex approach have been applied in the Netherlands, Germany, Britain and, most recently, Italy.[134] It has also been considered in some US states.[135] In Britain, the shift towards a Totex approach was motivated by concerns that the separate treatment of operating expenditure (opex) and capital expenditure (capex) created incentives for firms to favour capital expenditure (which would form part of the regulated asset base and provide a return on capital) over operating expenditure. In other words, there was a capital bias.[136] There was also a perception that operating expenditure was subject to greater regulatory scrutiny than capital projects (which were often couched in terms of system resilience and reliability).[137]

The main characteristic of the Totex approach is that it allows the regulated firm to decide the best way to spend its total expenditure allowance during a regulated period. However, this flexibility can be affected by the fact that the regulator typically determines the type and proportion of the total expenditure allowance that can be expensed and recovered in the current regulatory period (sometimes known as fast money or a 'pay-as-you-go' rate), and how much of that total expenditure can be capitalised and put into the regulatory asset base (slow money).[138] In addition, a single set of incentives for efficiency in reducing total expenditure is typically applied, rather than separate incentives for capital and operating expenditure. Similarly, any benchmarking assessment is based on total expenditure rather than the separate benchmarking of capital and operating costs.

---

[132] The approval process is based around proportionate treatment, meaning that the degree of regulatory scrutiny and the extent to which a business plan is fast-tracked depends on the quality of the business plan submitted and the company's performance in delivering outputs and value for money in previous periods. Jenkins (2011) provides a fuller description, while Spiegel-Feld and Mandel (2015) consider wider lessons for other jurisdictions.

[133] A Totex approach was first adopted for the energy sector in the 2010 price controls and in the water sector in England and Wales from 2014. Ajodhia, Kristiansen, Petrov and Scarsi (2006) refer to earlier uses of the approach for benchmarking purposes in Norway and the Netherlands.

[134] Cambini, Congiu and Soroush (2020) note that the approach was adopted for energy in Italy in 2020.

[135] The State of New York Public Service Commission considered but rejected such an approach (see NYPSC 2016).

[136] This is sometimes discussed in terms of a bias against focusing on better system management of the existing network ('non-wires solutions') rather than simply more investment in more 'wires'. Brunekreeft and Rammerstorfer (2021) examine the causes of capex bias by extending the Averch and Johnson model.

[137] Hakvoort and Ajodhia (2006) argue that a Totex approach introduces a trade-off between price and quality. Specifically, under a non-Totex approach, quality degradation can be avoided by the regulator, allowing a high level of investment (which can lead to higher quality and prices). However, under the Totex approach, as the regulator no longer controls the firm's investment level, it cannot influence quality, and the firm can have an incentive to reduce costs which could degrade quality.

[138] In the first application in the UK energy sector, certain costs (such as business support costs and non-operational capex) and 15 per cent of all other total expenditure was received as 'fast money', with the rest being capitalised into the regulated asset base (slow money). In the water sector, the 'pay-as-you-go' rate was proposed by the companies. More generally, Brunekreeft and Rammerstorfer (2021) support the idea of a fixed opex–capex share as a method of addressing the capital bias.

To address the uncertainty of technological and demand changes in some industries (such as electricity), it has been suggested that the Totex allowance that can be recovered within the period be subject to an *ex post* adjustment (or delta) mechanism to better reflect the actual evolution of system use and expenditure by the firm and reduce the scope for large forecasting errors.[139]

5.3 THE RELATIONSHIP BETWEEN RATE OF RETURN AND PRICE CAP

While some of the similarities and differences between rate of return regulation and price cap regulation should be apparent from the discussion in the preceding sections, it is useful to briefly summarise the main differences between the two approaches both in theory and in practice.

5.3.1 Differences between Rate of Return and Price Cap in Theory

In analytical terms, the difference between the two approaches has sometimes been approached by highlighting the trade-off between promoting cost reductions and efficiency improvements (which can be achieved via incentives) and extracting any excess rents being earned by the firm for consumers (which can be achieved by ensuring that prices accurately reflect costs). The work of Laffont and Tirole, in particular, examines the conflict between these two goals by comparing the properties of two types of contracts: cost-plus contract and a fixed price contract.[140] A pure fixed price contract is seen to provide high-powered incentives for cost reduction (as the firm is the residual claimant for any cost reductions), but is poor at extracting rent for consumers insofar as any exogenous reduction in costs is kept by the firm. In contrast, a pure cost-plus contract extracts all of the gain associated with any exogenous reduction in costs, but does not provide any incentives for the firm to engage in behaviour which would reduce its own costs. Laffont and Tirole conclude that an incentive scheme is 'high-powered' if the firm is exposed to a high fraction of its realised costs (and receives a higher benefit from any cost efficiencies it can introduce), and 'low-powered' if the firm is exposed to a relatively low fraction of its realised costs (and benefits little from improvements in cost efficiency).

Within this analytical framework, the incentive properties of pure rate of return regulation are 'low-powered', as the firm is not the residual claimant of any cost savings, but as prices generally closely track underlying costs, it is effective in extracting rents from the firm when they arise. In contrast, the incentive properties of pure price cap regulation are 'high-powered', as the firm becomes the residual claimant for any cost savings it introduces. In this way, the two approaches reflect what is sometimes described as the fundamental regulatory trade-off between incentives and rent extraction. A corollary of this trade-off is who bears the risk of, and is exposed to, changes in costs: the owner of the firm or consumers.[141] Pure rate of return regulation limits the exposure of the

---

[139] See Jenkins and Pérez-Arriaga (2017) and Bovera, Delfanti, Fumagalli, *et al.* (2021).
[140] See Laffont and Tirole (1993, 2000).
[141] Weisman (2002) discusses the 'wholesale shift in risk' from consumers to the regulated firm associated with the movement from rate of return regulation to price cap regulation.

owners of the firm to any underlying changes in costs, leaving consumers fully exposed to these changes. However, the ability of the firm's owners to extract excessive rents is limited by the requirement that prices track costs closely. Conversely, under pure price cap regulation, the risks associated with cost changes are fully borne by the owner of the firm during the period of the control rather than consumers. However, if a firm is able to reduce its own costs through efficiency improvements within the price control period, the owners will be the residual claimant for those gains, and consumers will not benefit in the short term.

A number of more specific, in principle, differences between the two approaches can be identified. Firstly, while a regulator applying the rate of return approach approves a specific price that the firm is permitted to charge, under price cap regulation, the 'cap' is a price ceiling; a firm is typically not prevented from setting lower prices.[142] Secondly, prices set under pure rate of return regulation are typically based on *historical* costs (i.e. it is backward-looking), while the price cap set under pure price cap regulation is based on the expected *future* costs and performance of the firm (i.e. it is forward-looking). Finally, under rate of return regulation, the firm and the regulator can request a rate hearing at any time. In contrast, under price cap regulation, the period between regulatory reviews is fixed and the date of the next price review is set in advance. The firm cannot (ordinarily) expect that the price cap set will be 're-opened' during the fixed period that the price cap is in place, and as such it will need to absorb any cost increases it incurs during that fixed period.

5.3.2 Differences between Rate of Return and Price Cap in Practice

Notwithstanding the 'in principle' differences between rate of return regulation and price cap regulation described above, as already noted, in practice, these differences are typically less pronounced. As has already been noted, no regulatory system demonstrates either a pure rate of return or pure price cap approach.[143] Accordingly, although the approaches are often portrayed as polar extremes for the purposes of exposition, in practice, the difference between the two approaches is often one of degree rather than kind.[144]

The extent of difference or similarity between price cap regulation and rate of return regulation depends on the details of each method's implementation.[145] For example, if a specific application of price cap regulation affords a regulated firm limited pricing

---

[142] This is particularly relevant where the cap applies to a basket of services, and the price structure that emerges might involve prices for individual services within the basket that are higher or lower than the average price on which the basket is set.

[143] As Makholm (2016) observes, wider aspects of the political, institutional and legal context in which each approach is applied also need to be considered when comparing the application of the two approaches.

[144] See Sappington (2002), Jamison (2007) and Joskow (2007a).

[145] As Sappington and Weisman (2010) note, 'this fact may help to explain why several studies identify similar industry performance under PCR and ROR'. While, Newbery (2003) notes that '[m]any of the apparent differences between the two forms of regulation disappear at the time of the first regulatory review', where price cap regulators make essentially the same calculation as their rate of return counterparts in relation to the cost of capital. Similarly, Laffont and Tirole (1993) observe that, in assessing future potential productivity gains, price cap approaches, in practice, often assess past performance.

discretion, provides limited incentives for cost reduction and innovation, subjects the firm to frequent regulatory resets (i.e. the duration of the price control is short) and, at the end of each period, transfers all the efficiency gains to consumers, it will operate in a similar way to rate of return regulation.[146] However, if a regulated firm is afforded considerable pricing discretion, the duration of the price cap is relatively long and the firm is able to keep any earnings it generates from efficiency savings, price cap regulation will differ significantly from rate of return regulation.

A number of empirical studies have focused on the impacts of the transition from rate of return regulation to price cap regulation, from which some observations can be made.[147] First, the evidence is mixed on the impact that a transition from rate of return to price cap has on prices. While some studies find that the introduction of price cap regulation is associated with lower prices,[148] other studies find little effect, or that prices are higher under some forms of incentive regulation than rate of return regulation.[149] Second, the empirical evidence on operating costs is also mixed (recall that one of the perceived advantages of the price cap approach is that it creates incentives for cost reductions and efficiency improvements). Some studies reveal a slight increase in operating costs, while others find no evidence of operating cost reductions or that a shift to price caps has reduced costs.[150] A third set of studies examine whether the introduction of price cap regulation is associated with higher levels of growth in a firm's total factor productivity. Here, too, the evidence is once again mixed: some studies find substantial increases in total factor productivity growth associated with price cap regulation (for example, in relation to British Telecom),[151] while others find no evidence of an association.[152] Fourth, recall that a concern associated with price cap regulation is that, in principle, it could result in significant increases in earnings for the regulated firm. On this point there is some evidence that earnings of regulated firms have increased under price cap regulation.[153] Fifth, on the important issue of whether service quality has declined (recall that price cap regulation can in principle create incentives to degrade quality

---

[146] See Sappington and Weisman (2010).

[147] See Kridel, Sappington and Weisman (1996), Abel (2000), Vogelsang (2002) and Sappington and Weisman (2010, 2016a,b). Sappington (2002) concludes, on the basis of his survey, that, while the form of regulation appears to affect industry performance, the impacts are not dramatic. This is, however, qualified by the observation that, in practice, the key differences between the different types of regulation (rate of return, price cap, etc.) might not be as pronounced as they are in principle.

[148] See Mathios and Rogers (1989), Kaestner and Kahn (1990) and Abel (2000). Crowley and Meitzen (2021) find that price caps show a 'slower escalation' in electricity prices.

[149] See Blank, Kaserman and Mayo (1998).

[150] See Sappington (2002) and Lowry, Makos, Deason and Schwartz (2017). Weisman (2019b) argues that one reason for the apparent difference between theory and practice on the incentives to engage in cost-reducing activities which yield efficiencies is because a regulator uses accommodative entry policies to establish a shadow price cap which is lower than the stipulated price cap and which results in the firm no longer being the residual claimant for any efficiency gains.

[151] See Kwoka (1993), although such gains are also associated with other changes such as privatisation.

[152] See Resende (1999).

[153] Hauge and Sappington (2010) find, for example, that British Telecom was able to generate substantial financial returns under the price cap plan for a number of years following its privatisation. More generally, see Sappington (2002). Chennells (1997) discusses the motivation for the imposition of a 'windfall tax' on certain UK utilities in the years following privatisation.

in order to reduce operating costs), the evidence is again inconclusive across different industries.[154] Sixth, in terms of investment incentives, numerous empirical studies have found higher levels of network modernisation and investment in telecommunications and energy networks under incentive regulation than rate of return regulation.[155] Finally, there is the question of the relative burden of the regulatory *process* and the extent to which regulated firms and customers engage with one another. Some have argued that the price cap approach has led to excessive confrontation, and that there is insufficient ability for customers and other interested parties (environmental groups) to participate and 'buy in' to the process.[156]

5.4 OTHER APPROACHES TO PRICE REGULATION

Alongside rate of return and price cap regulation, a number of other approaches to controlling and regulating prices have been considered in theory and adopted in practice. This includes hybrid approaches (which combine rate of return regulation and price cap regulation), yardstick competition and other approaches that involve no formal ongoing regulatory oversight, or alternatively where prices are regulated by contract or set by a government ministry or department.

5.4.1 Hybrid Approaches

A recognition that the detail of the form of price regulation can have important effects on the incentives of the regulated firm, and on the distribution of risk between shareholders of the firm and its customers, has led to various 'hybrid' approaches to regulation. These approaches have sought to combine the incentive effects typically associated with price cap regulation with measures intended principally to address concerns about the firm's earnings deviating from underlying costs for an extended period of time (i.e. the firm earning excessive profits, or making unsustainable losses), and about the information asymmetries between the regulator and regulated firm.

---

[154] In electricity, studies which suggest higher levels of electrical outages (i.e. lower quality) under price caps include: Ter-Martirosyan (2003), Reichl, Kollmann, Tichler and Schneider (2008), Ter-Martirosyan and Kwoka (2010) and Schmidthaler, Cohen, Reichl and Schmidinger (2015). In contrast, Arcos-Vargas, Núñez and Ballesteros (2017) find that price cap, cost-plus and revenue cap, in this order, seem to be the most efficient systems to increase quality of service. In telecommunications, studies which find no evidence of a degradation in quality under price caps include Banerjee (2003) and Roycroft and Garcia-Murrilo (2000). However, other studies that report mixed results on service quality include: Sappington (2003), Façanha and Resende (2004), Ai, Martinez and Sappington (2004) and Ai and Sappington (2005). In the water industry, Bjørner, Hansen and Jakobsen (2021) find that a shift to price cap regulation has not impacted water quality in Denmark, while, in the gas industry, Oliver (2019) finds that price caps can create incentives to invest in gas transmission pipelines and alleviate congestion.

[155] See Ai and Sappington (2002), Cambini and Rondi (2010), Cullmann and Nieswand (2016), Abrardi, Carlo and Laura (2018), Oliver (2019) and Avdasheva and Orlova (2020).

[156] Littlechild (2021a). In contrast, Kaufmann (2019) concludes that, in the US context, his experience is that 'the antagonism inherent in cost of service filings far exceeds that associated with multi-year rate plans (such as Inflation minus X)'.

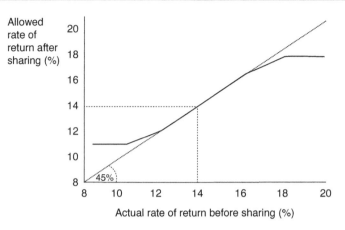

Figure 5.1 Earnings sharing mechanism

Earnings Sharing Mechanisms

One approach sometimes seen as a 'middle ground' between rate of return regulation and price cap regulation is known, variously, as sliding scale regulation or profit sharing earnings sharing regulation.[157] Earnings sharing approaches have been used for telecommunications regulation in the USA in the early to mid-1990s, and also in relation to some energy companies in the USA.[158]

This approach seeks to retain some incentives for the firm to reduce costs, but, at the same time, limit the potential for the firm to make either excessively high profits or unsustainable losses. A typical earnings sharing plan will set out a target rate of return on investment, and will also specify a band around that target rate where the firm will not be required to 'share' its earnings with consumers (see Figure 5.1).[159] Within this band (sometimes called a 'deadband'), the firm can retain all of its actual earnings, and in this way the scheme operates similarly to price cap regulation within this range. However, outside of this band, the regulated firm is able to keep only a portion of the incremental earnings or suffer only a portion of the losses, that sit above or below pre-specified levels. The other portion of earnings or losses must be 'shared' with consumers in the form of either refunds or future reductions in prices (where actual earnings are above the upper threshold of the band), or through higher consumer prices (where the actual earnings are lower than the lower threshold of the earnings band). In effect, where the actual earnings of the firm are either significantly higher or lower than the target rate of return, the earnings sharing mechanism operates in a manner similar to rate of return regulation.

A perceived advantage of the 'sharing' approach is that it provides a flexible combination of price cap regulation and rate of return regulation, and it can balance the

[157] Lyon (1996) and Sappington (2002) present detailed discussions of this approach. Laffont and Tirole (1993) observe that the concept of such sliding scale plans to share profits is an old one, dating back to 1925.
[158] Earnings sharing mechanisms have been used by the state regulators in New Jersey and California, and by the Alberta Utilities Commission. Braeutigam and Panzar (1993) record that twenty-two states had employed 'sliding scale' approaches to telecommunications at that time.
[159] See the discussion in Sappington and Weisman (2010).

competing objectives of providing incentives for the regulated firm to reduce costs while ensuring that prices and costs do not become too misaligned.[160] For this reason, earnings sharing regulation has been seen as attractive to regulators first moving away from rate of return regulation, by providing some degree of protection against excessive earnings.[161]

Sappington (2002) describes the fundamental trade-off associated with earnings sharing mechanisms: while they reduce the incidence of excessive earnings, they can blunt the incentives on the firm to minimise operating costs. It follows that the effectiveness of earnings sharing mechanisms depends on whether the potential benefits from minimising production costs (the impact on incentives) are greater (or less) than the potential benefits from ensuring that prices closely track costs (preventing excessive earnings). In practice, earnings sharing plans can also create various undesirable incentives in firm behaviour. For example, where a firm's earnings are close to the floor of its band, it may have an incentive to invest in riskier projects and activities, as it is only exposed to a proportion of the risk if the project fails. On the same reasoning, if a firm's earnings are close to the ceiling of its threshold, it may have incentives not to invest in projects and activities that would push its earnings above that ceiling. Earnings sharing plans can also create incentives for regulators and firms to 'game' the system, for example, if the regulator disallows certain costs to move returns into the sharing range, while firms can have incentives to shift costs among different years.

Revenue Sharing Mechanisms

An alternative sharing approach is based on the sharing of revenues rather than earnings above a specified threshold. When revenues exceed this predetermined threshold, the firm is required to share a certain proportion of revenues with customers. This approach does not, in principle, reduce the incentives on the firm to reduce costs, nor create incentives for the regulator to disallow certain production costs, and therefore addresses some of the key limitations of the earnings sharing approach.[162] Nevertheless, such revenue sharing approaches can change the incentives of the firm in other ways. For example, the firm may not actively seek out ways of increasing incremental revenue beyond its threshold, including by reducing quality on some services (to reduce demand) or by changing its structure of prices.

Despite being used by numerous regulators in the mid- to late 1990s in the USA, earnings and revenue sharing approaches have been replaced over time by more traditional forms of price cap regulation.[163] However, it appears that earnings sharing mechanisms are still used in some developing and transitional countries.[164]

---

[160] See Lyon (1996).

[161] See Sappington and Weisman (2010).

[162] See Sappington (2002).

[163] Sappington and Weisman (2010) observe that earnings sharing mechanisms are no longer used by state regulators in the USA. They also express surprise at this development and identify a number of reasons why this may be the case.

[164] Hauge and Sappington (2010) note that earnings sharing regulations were used in seven out of forty-eight developing and transitional countries at that time.

5.4.2 Yardstick Competition and Benchmarking

Yardstick competition is an approach to the setting of regulated prices that links the financial rewards of a regulated firm to its performance relative to that of other comparable firms that face similar demand conditions and production opportunities.[165] In simple terms, if the regulated firm performs better than the group to which it is compared, it will be rewarded for its better relative performance (and conversely it will be penalised if its performance is inferior to that of the comparison group). As discussed briefly in Chapter 4, the principal advantage of yardstick competition is that it can reduce the information asymmetries that regulators face when determining the revenue requirement by allowing the regulator to compare the cost-reducing efforts of one firm to other comparable firms. In addition, it is seen as less vulnerable to regulatory gaming, and to create greater dynamic incentive for a firm to reduce costs and converge towards the efficient industry level of production.

'Full yardstick competition' involves a regulated firm's prices being set not on the basis of its own past expenditure, or expected future costs, but rather on the basis of the observed costs of comparable firms (for example, non-competing water companies operating in different states/regions).[166] In effect, each firm is able to charge a price which represents the average industry-wide cost for all firms, and in this way each individual firm's prices are detached from its own individual costs (as in price cap approaches). If a firm's costs are lower than the average (industry-wide) level of costs, then it will make greater profits than those firms whose costs are above the average level (who will make a loss). This provides an incentive for firms to reduce costs towards the average level, and over time for costs to converge to the most efficient cost level. It also mimics the operation of competitive markets, as the performance of any one firm is determined relative to the performance of other firms that undertake the same activities.[167]

While conceptually appealing, there can be a number of challenges in applying the yardstick competition approach. Firstly, there is a need to ensure that the firms who are being compared to one another are not able to collude in such a way as to collectively increase their costs, and in turn the average regulated price. Secondly, there is the problem of ensuring that the firms being compared to one another are sufficiently similar (in terms of both their own operations and the environment in which they supply their services) as to make the cost comparisons meaningful.[168]

[165] Shleifer (1985), Joskow and Schmalensee (1986) and Armstrong and Sappington (2007) present fuller descriptions of this approach.
[166] Sawkins (2001) discusses its use in the water sector in England and Wales in the years following privatisation.
[167] In a seminal paper, Shleifer (1985) argued that, by linking a regulated firm's prices to the costs of comparable firms (rather than its own), there will be incentives for cost efficiency because: 'If a firm reduces costs when its twin firms do not, it profits; if it fails to reduce costs when other firms do, it incurs a loss.'
[168] Joskow and Schmalensee (1986) argue that: 'Utilities differ from one another in so many dimensions, not only because of current market conditions but also because of past investment decisions, that we are not likely to find a large number of truly comparable utilities. ... This implies that comprehensive yardstick approaches to rate setting would impose highly random rewards and punishments; inefficient utilities might prosper while efficient producers might not be viable, and prices would often be out of line with both actual and minimum attainable costs.' In contrast, Shleifer (1985) argued that a system of full yardstick competition can be effective even if firms are heterogeneous, provided that this is accounted for correctly.

In practice, yardstick competition or comparative approaches are most commonly used by regulators not as an alternative system of price regulation, but as part of benchmarking exercises when setting a firm's revenue requirement. A regulator may benchmark a firm's estimates of forward-looking costs to comparable firms, or use benchmarking techniques to determine the expected productivity gains that can be achieved by the firm. Thus, when determining the firm's revenue requirement under a price cap arrangement, the regulator may compare the firm's performance (in terms of indicators such as operating costs, capital costs and quality) relative to other comparable suppliers in the industry, and make an adjustment to the value of X on this basis.[169] Firms that perform close to, or at, the industry average might be assigned a lower level of X than firms that are highly inefficient relative to the rest of the industry and which the regulator may wish to incentivise to improve performance (by having a high value of X). Benchmarking has been used by regulators in Britain, the Netherlands and Austria when setting price caps in the electricity, gas and water industries. In the Netherlands, the X factor for each distribution company in the electricity sector has at times been explicitly linked to the average efficiency improvement in the sector as a whole, with improvements in quality also taken into account.[170] Similarly, in Germany, cost efficiency benchmarking is used to set the revenue caps.[171] A potential downside of benchmarking approaches is that the information requirements can be substantial, and the data required to perform the relevant analysis effectively is not always available.

5.4.3 Other Approaches: Administered Pricing, Negotiation or Prices Regulated by Contract

As described in Part III of the book, there are a range of other ways in which prices are regulated or controlled in practice. In some industries, prices are set through administrative means by either a ministry or a government department, or are set out in law. In Japan, for example, the transport ministry sets a maximum level of prices for private rail operators. In the USA, terms on which private railroads are required to provide access to passenger services operated by the government-owned Amtrak are set out in legislation and based on marginal cost. Similarly, the maximum level of interchange fees for card payments in Europe are set out in law. In other cases, such as for air navigation service charges in the USA, a provider might not recover its costs from user charges directly but be funded through a combination of excise taxes and state subsidy.

In other settings, no formal or ongoing price control or oversight is established and prices can be negotiated between the parties, or unilaterally set by the provider itself subject to certain high-level conditions or principles. For example, airport charges in the USA are negotiated between airports and airport users, or set unilaterally by an airport after consultation with airlines, but must be consistent with five pricing principles (see Chapter 15). In Canada, rail freight charges are determined through negotiation between vertically

---

[169] In some implementations, the performance of a particular supplier is benchmarked against various broader productivity measures of the performance of the general economy, for example, total factor productivity approaches.

[170] See DTe (2002) and Hesseling and Sari (2006).

[171] See Waidelich, Haug and Wieshammer (2022) and WIK (2011).

integrated railways and shippers in the first instance and there is no regulated maximum charge. If agreement cannot be reached, then a shipper can apply for a final offer arbitration. In Europe, rail track access charges are set out in a multi-annual contract by a rail infrastructure manager (which is publicly owned). In determining charges, the infrastructure manager must consult with applicants, and a regulator typically reviews the network statement and can raise objections, including potentially disallowing costs which are not efficient. Finally, in industries where competition for the market exists (e.g. concession or franchise contracts), the level of prices may be set out and agreed in concession contracts and can differ according to region and type of service.

5.5 PRICE REGULATION WHEN COMPETITION IS EMERGING

This chapter has focused on the application of price regulation to core network activities where competition is limited or non-existent. However, a separate set of issues arise when applying price regulation to firms operating in activities where competition imposes some degree of competitive constraint on the regulated firm, but is not fully effective (i.e. when the regulated firm still has a strong position of market power). While the application of price regulation in circumstances of partial competition is not necessarily incompatible with the emergence of competition (as the experience of telecommunications in many jurisdictions indicates), there is a risk that, once the transition to competition reaches a particular point, the standard forms of price control may be inappropriate and may in fact, act to shield the incumbent supplier from the effects of competition, or limit its incentives to reduce its costs.[172] In particular, it is argued that conventional price cap regulation can make entry more difficult, and deter competition, and that removing price controls, where appropriate, can stimulate competition.[173]

As discussed in Section 3.5, in this transitional context, various alternatives to price regulation might be applied, either as complements to the existing price control, or as measures intended to replace formal price regulation. One approach is to remove all formal price regulation but place additional obligations on any firm with significant market power relative to other competitors in recognition of its market position.[174] A second approach entails the substitution of formal price regulation of the firm with a structured oversight or monitoring mechanism, underpinned, in some cases, with the threat of the re-introduction of price regulation. A third approach is for regulators to use shorter price control periods, providing an opportunity for more frequent assessments of whether or not competition has developed to such a point that the formal price regulation can be removed. A related response is the use of a 'precautionary' or 'safeguard' price cap where the price cap is set at a relatively loose level and acts to restrict the ability of the incumbent firm to charge a price well in excess of costs. The rationale for this is that, in

---

[172] Weisman (2019a, b) discusses the disincentives it can create for cost efficiency.

[173] See Littlechild (2008b).

[174] For example, the regulated firm may be required not to discriminate among different customers (non-discrimination obligations), and may be subject to certain rules relating to pricing (such as that prices are cost-oriented) but they may have some flexibility to determine prices within those bounds, or be subject to other information and disclosure requirements.

the presence of effectively developing competition, the incumbent may not seek to price at the maximum level but rather to match the prices being charged by its (unregulated) competitors. A final approach involves the more precise targeting of price controls to cover only those specific services or geographic areas where competition is assessed as limited. The main conclusion that can be drawn is that, in contexts where competition is developing, it is necessary for regulators to continually review the appropriateness of the pricing obligations that are being applied to the incumbent firm.

5.6 PRICE REGULATION WHEN NETWORKS ARE IN DECLINE

While for much of the twentieth century the demand for public utility services was increasing in most jurisdictions, an issue that is increasingly confronting some regulators in practice is how regulation should adapt where demand for a core network service is in decline.[175] Prominent examples of core network services that are in decline include traditional postal network services in most jurisdictions, fixed line telecommunications subscriptions and conventional gas production in some countries.[176] In addition, as discussed in Chapter 9, the growth of distributed generation and storage facilities (including electric cars) in the electricity industry could have significant implications for the future use of centralised transmission and distribution transportation services. Similarly, as discussed in Chapter 10, policies to transition to low-carbon gas or alternative renewable energy sources could, in some scenarios, lead to the decommissioning and gradual phasing out of gas pipelines or the repurposing of those pipelines to transport low-carbon (hydrogen) gases to consumers.[177]

Declining demand can give rise to fundamental questions about the suitability of different forms of price regulation (such as price caps) and more generally the ongoing rationale for regulation. A highly contentious issue is whether a firm should be able to recover all its costs, particularly historical investment costs, given declining network demand.[178] If the level of allowed revenues is not adjusted to reflect new levels of demand, this can give rise to static efficiency losses as 'captive users' (i.e. those who must consume the service and have no other supply options)[179] are required to pay for any historical investments which are redundant given current and (expected) future levels of utilisation. In addition, if revenues and prices are not adjusted to account for changes in demand, this can contribute to the further decline in demand for core network services: this is because a fixed level

---

[175] Decker (2016) defines a 'network in decline' as one experiencing a sustained, non-temporary, reduction in demand, resulting in excess capacity on large parts of the network most of the time.

[176] Weisman (2017) discusses lessons from railroads and telecommunications in the USA.

[177] See New Zealand Government (2021).

[178] Brennan and Boyd (1997) discuss how the introduction of competition in the USA electricity sector in the 1990s changed the regulatory compact. They note that determining whether shareholders or consumers should bear the costs of stranded assets might turn on the question of whether the firm or the regulator was in a better position *ex ante* to know about the (endogenous) chance that the policy might change in the future.

[179] Examples of captive users include those who have no ability to install distributed generation facilities and must rely on grid-supplied electricity, or consumers of fixed line telecommunications services in some jurisdictions who for various reasons rely on voice calls on the fixed line network (and cannot use alternatives such as mobile, cable or VoIP (Voice over Internet Protocol) services).

of costs needs to be recovered from an ever-decreasing demand base, which ultimatel
leads to higher prices, and even lower demand (known colloquially as the 'death spiral').[180]

However, if the level of allowed revenues is adjusted to reflect the lower level o
expected future demand (and the associated network size and configuration needed t
satisfy that demand), this creates stranded assets for the firm and may create dynami
disincentives for investment in other regulated industries. Whether the allowed level o
revenue should be adapted in the face of declining demand can also depend on the specif
ics of the regulatory arrangements. Some argue that price cap regulation is unsuitable fo
industries with declining or sluggish growth in demand because, given scale economies,
firm faces an 'uphill battle' to improve efficiency when demand is declining. In additior
it is argued that the firm could request a rate hearing to take account of the impact o
declining demand on costs under rate of return regulation.[181] In contrast, others argu
that price cap regulation is more suited to declining demand, as it gives the regulated firr
greater flexibility to adjust its rates without a rate hearing.[182]

Different mechanisms have been suggested to achieve a balance between the short-ru
and long-term impacts of declining demand for core network services.[183] One approach i
to decouple or detach the authorised, or allowed, revenues that the network operator ca
earn from the underlying demand for a service. This can stabilise revenues for operator
in the context of decreasing demand, but in so doing effectively shift the revenue ris
associated with declining demand onto consumers. An alternative approach is to 'share
the burden of paying for historical investments in core network assets between the firr
and consumers. This might involve a firm and users agreeing that the rate base, or th
RAB, is subject to a one-off revaluation that involves some assets being written off o
marked down to reflect future levels of demand.[184] While this approach minimises th
harm to allocative efficiency, and can preserve incentives for investment (provided th
circumstances in which such a write down can occur are well recognized and agree
by all parties), it nevertheless exposes the firm to some stranded costs.[185] A differen
approach is to compensate firms above the cost of capital before stranding occurs o
an *ex ante* basis. Although this approach is unlikely to be effective where the core net
work is already in a state of rapid decline, and indeed might accelerate the decline,[186] i

---

[180] In perhaps the first discussion of such a relationship, Hotelling (1938) posited the argument that the
need for some proportion of (fixed) overhead costs to be funded by prices contributed to rising railroad
freight charges during the Great Depression. Borenstein and Bushnell (2015) discuss the 'death spiral'
in electricity, while Brennan and Crew (2016) identify the cost and price elasticity conditions which
contribute to a death spiral.

[181] Brennan and Crew (2016).

[182] See Crowley and Meitzen (2021).

[183] Decker (2016) provides a more detailed discussion.

[184] In the telecoms industry, a distinction is now made between replicable and non-replicable assets in
some jurisdictions. Replicable assets are valued at replacement costs, while non-replicable assets are
valued at the lower of replacement cost and an inflation-adjusted book value (which may be zero in
some cases). See Vogelsang (2014a).

[185] Simshauser and Akimov (2019) suggest a way to address this stranding risk which involves 'parking'
excess capacity and providing temporary finance through government-sponsored loans. 'Parked'
assets can then be re-examined at the end of each five-year regulatory determination, and those which
can then be 'un-parked' are returned to service in line with demand growth that generates sufficient
revenues to contribute again to cost recovery.

[186] For example, where increases in the cost of capital lead to higher prices and further reduce demand.

is potentially a longer-term mechanism for dealing with declining demand in industries where firms make investments in long-term assets and there is some potential for demand to fall in the future.[187] Another approach is to introduce rate structures that allow regulated firms to better recover their fixed costs in the context of declining demand, including the use of a menu of two-part tariffs (as discussed in Chapter 4) to induce 'captive' and 'non-captive' users to 'self-select' a tariff consistent with their use of the service, or the introduction of three-part tariff which incorporates a demand component to recover the costs of a customer being connected to the grid.

5.7 CONCLUSION

The purpose of this chapter has been to describe some of the main, generalised characteristics of the different forms of price regulation applied to core network activities (i.e. activities where competition is limited or non-existent). In general terms, rate of return regulation sets prices that are closely related to, or track, the underlying costs of service, and, in this way, ensures that the firm neither sustains excessive losses nor achieves excess profits. This limits the scope for monopoly pricing, but can reduce the incentives for the firm to minimise costs and improve productive efficiency. The price cap approach decouples average prices from costs for a fixed period of time, and can create incentives for firms to minimise costs and generally improve productive efficiency over time. However, if prices and costs diverge to a significant extent, this can result in excessive earnings, or losses, being sustained by the firm. Significant deviations between costs and prices under the price cap approach can, however, be addressed through the use of pass-through mechanisms (such as 'Z factor adjustments' or an RPI-X+Y formula), which are applied to those costs deemed beyond the influence of the firm. Hybrid earnings or revenue sharing schemes attempt to address the limitations associated with both price cap and rate of return regulation.

A particular point emphasised in this chapter is that, in practice, there are no examples of 'pure' rate of return regulation, or 'pure' price cap regulation. Rather, what can be observed are adaptations to these general approaches to address specific trade-offs, and to reflect the context in which they are applied. This is perhaps unsurprising, as jurisdictions have, over time, sought to develop specific mechanisms that: share efficiency benefits between owners of core network firms and consumers; encourage efficient investment; promote incentives for core network firms to innovate and improve service quality; and address information asymmetries between the regulator and the regulated firm. Standard forms of price regulation have also sometimes been adapted in settings where competition is emerging for a particular activity, or, more recently, to address the issues associated with declining demand for some core network services.

Looking ahead, there are important questions about which forms of price regulation can best accommodate the changes occurring in the different industries discussed in Part III

---

[187] Guthrie (2020) considers the impact of future asset stranding on investment incentives and finds that welfare is maximised by setting 'the allowed rate of return at a higher level than the firm's cost of capital and by depreciating the historical cost of the firm's assets at a faster rate than any plausible measure of actual depreciation'.

of this book. In the energy sector, this includes a need to connect large amounts of distributed electricity resources (including electric cars) and a possible reconfiguration of gas networks towards hydrogen.[188] In telecommunications, the merits of different forms of price regulation are being considered against a policy objective of ensuring widespread access to high-speed broadband services; while in the water sector there is a focus in some jurisdictions on ensuring that water systems are resilient in the context of climate change. As discussed in Chapter 2, there is also an increasing focus on affordability and the perceived fairness of regulatory settlements in many jurisdictions. This in turn raises questions about: the regulatory *process* and the extent to which the process is inclusive and collaborative; the burden and costs of different forms of price regulation; and the extent to which existing approaches are capable of accounting for future uncertainties.

DISCUSSION QUESTIONS

1. What are some of the key attributes of 'pure' rate of return regulation and the two key stages in the process for setting rates under that approach?
2. Assess the principal advantages and disadvantages of pure rate of return regulation and discuss how some of the disadvantages have been addressed in practice.
3. If a regulated company has a cost of debt of 4.18 per cent, a cost of equity of 6.2 per cent and gearing ratio of 60 per cent, what is its nominal weighted average cost of capital (WACC)?
4. What are some of the key attributes of 'pure' price cap regulation, including the key choices about its design?
5. What are the different forms of price cap regulation and how does each approach potentially affect the incentives of firms to set efficient tariffs, expand demand and improve quality of services?
6. Assess the principal advantages and disadvantages of pure price cap regulation, and discuss how some of the limitations of the approach have been addressed in practice.
7. What are some of the other alternative methods and approaches to price regulation? What are their advantages and disadvantages?
8. In many countries there is a need for substantial investments in public utility industries – including energy, water, telecommunications and transport – to encourage widespread access and coverage (telecommunications, rail and water) and as a response to decarbonisation policies (energy). Do you think that price cap regulation, rate of return regulation or another alternative form of regulation is most likely to incentivise the investment needed?
9. What are some of the ways in which regulators might need to adapt regulation in industries where demand for a core network service is in decline? What are the different trade-offs and considerations involved?

---

[188] In the UK the government is also proposing to apply a regulated asset base model to finance the costs associated with the building of new nuclear electricity plants.

6

Regulation in the Presence of Competition

Chapters 4 and 5 focused on principles to guide the regulation of monopoly or core network activities (such as the pipes, cables, wires and rails) where the prospects for competition are limited. In this chapter we focus on the regulatory principles and approaches relevant to regulated industry structures where there is some competition. Examples of where there is competition in some, but not all, activities in a supply chain include: 'downstream' competition between retailers in the telecommunications and energy sectors, or competing rail and aviation services; and 'upstream' competition between generators in electricity or gas extraction and storage, and the trading of bulk water. Examples of direct 'head-to-head' competition in regulated sectors where integrated firms compete with one another include competition between: mobile phone companies; integrated rail freight companies; payment systems operators; and different digital platforms.

This chapter sets out the economic principles that might inform regulation in the presence of competition. We begin by focusing on principles relevant to settings where an 'access provider' is required to 'share' or provide access to a core or indispensable service with 'access users', which can be parties at other stages of a vertical production chain (one-way access) or rivals with whom the access provider competes (two-way access).[1] We consider the price and non-price terms of access and the interaction between access pricing and the incentives for investment, as well as some of the arguments for and against vertical and horizontal separation in certain regulated industries. Finally, we turn to principles relevant to economic regulation in other types of competitive market settings, including in multi-sided markets (such as for payments systems and digital platforms) and in markets with a large number of providers.

6.1 ACCESS IN REGULATED INDUSTRIES

Access issues arise when firms engaged in one market or activity require the service provided by another firm as an essential input. Suppliers at different vertical stages of a supply chain may require 'access' to a core or indispensable product to provide services to end-users (e.g. train companies require access to train infrastructure). Similarly, different

---

[1] For the purposes of the discussion in this chapter, we ignore the question of which activities should be opened to competition, or under what circumstances an incumbent supplier of a network activity should be required to provide access to their facilities.

Table 6.1 Different methods for determining access terms

Commercial negotiation	Parties negotiate the access terms on a purely commercial basis, with protection afforded by general competition law when the access provider holds a dominant position (an *ex post* approach).
Negotiate then arbitrate	Parties negotiate the access terms, but with the additional backstop of regulatory arbitration in the event that negotiations fail.[a]
Regulator establishes access principles	A regulator imposes certain general *ex ante* requirements on specific access providers, such as obligations that access terms are 'just and reasonable' or 'fair, reasonable and non-discriminatory'. Access providers may also have an ability to freely set prices within certain bounds, such as between a price floor and a price ceiling (i.e. constrained market pricing).[b]
Regulator prescribes access terms	A regulator prescribes the specific terms and conditions of access. As discussed below, regulatory prescription of price and non-price access terms and conditions can be particularly important where an access provider is both a supplier of a service and a competitor to other suppliers in a related, competitive market (i.e. it is vertically integrated).

[a] Sometimes referred to as a 'negotiate–arbitrate' approach, it has been used in the telecommunications and water industries in the UK, in Australia and in the USA.
[b] See the discussion of the use of constrained market pricing in rail in Chapter 14.

suppliers of a service operating at the same hierarchical level may need to interconnec with one another to provide an end-to-end service to their customers (e.g. when tw mobile phone networks need to interconnect with one another to facilitate a call).[2] I some cases, parties can negotiate the access terms between themselves. However, in othe circumstances, there may be a need for economic regulation to set out principles an rules about the price and non-price terms of access. Table 6.1 sets out four general way in which access conditions are determined in practice.

6.1.1 The Access Pricing Issue

Questions surrounding access, and access pricing in particular, are some of the most dif ficult policy questions that confront regulators in practice,[3] and considerable resource are spent annually on lawyers and consultants across the globe in disputes relating to th determination of access prices. It might be argued that, in principle, the determinatio

[2] Vogelsang (2003) draws a distinction (in relation to telecommunications, but which is of more general relevance) between interconnection (where two networks are linked to provide particular products to one another, and operate at the same level of the network hierarchy) and access (where networks operate at different hierarchical level and only one network uses the other network to provide services). Noam (2002) distinguishes between horizontal, vertical and parallel interconnection.

[3] According to Armstrong (2002), '[I]t is hard to find a more controversial issue in industrial policy than that concerning the terms on which entrant's gain access to an incumbent firm's network'.

of access prices should pose no particular difficulties. The regulator should simply apply the principles discussed in Chapter 4 to the regulation of the core network activity, which will result in an efficient allocation of resources. However, the issues that can arise when certain activities in a production chain are open to competition go beyond those that arise in rate setting for a vertically integrated monopoly, which focus principally on the interaction between the firm and final consumers. In the new context, consideration has to be given to how different approaches to access pricing impact on firms engaged in intermediate activities in related markets (known as 'access users').[4]

As we shall see, in terms of efficiency, the optimal price of access might sometimes need to be above or below the marginal cost of providing access, depending on factors such as whether: transfers are feasible which allow the access provider to recover fixed costs; the intensity of competition in the final product markets and the extent of any price/cost mark-up; the extent and nature of any network effects; and whether or not the access provider is vertically integrated and also competes in a related competitive market (such as a retail market).

In addition, in this context, both the *level* at which the access price is set and the *structure* of prices resulting from any access pricing framework (such as those between the access price and a retail price) are critical to the effectiveness of regulation, as they directly affect the incentives of the access providers and access users. As we discuss below, different access pricing approaches can have different impacts on the incentives for each of these parties in respect of how the core network is utilised, as well as over the longer term, for investment in core network assets.

6.1.2 The Multiple Objectives Pursued through Access Pricing Policies

Much of the practical difficulty associated with access pricing stems from the fact that a single mechanism – the access price – is being called upon to serve a range of policy objectives. In general terms, a given access price needs to ensure that: (a) the access provider (the firm supplying the core network input) makes a non-negative profit and faces the right incentives to invest and innovate; and (b) the access users, operating in related markets, face the right signals to use the input efficiently and to undertake investments in that market. This is a difficult balancing exercise and can require a regulator to weigh objectives related to allocative efficiency against those of dynamic efficiency. For example, a low access price encourages entry and the development of competition in related competitive markets, leading to dynamic efficiency gains. However, if the access price is set too low, it could result in inefficient entry in the competitive activity and a shortfall in the access provider's revenues, which limits the incentives for the access provider to invest in infrastructure or innovate. Conversely, a high access price provides the access provider with a return that covers costs and creates incentives to invest and innovate, but may limit the development of competition in related markets, frustrating policy objectives

---

[4] Vogelsang (2003) records that the practical relevance of access for competition in the telecommunications sector was made abundantly clear following the expiration of the Bell patents in the USA, where competing networks emerged that were not interconnected to one another; meaning that subscribers on one network could not contact those on another network and vice versa.

relating to competition, and reducing dynamic efficiency gains. Moreover, where the potential for infrastructure competition exists, setting the access price too high might encourage inefficient infrastructure investment and by-pass.

Balancing these multiple objectives is further complicated in practice by the limited number of instruments or tools that the regulator has its disposal to achieve its objectives. While some theoretical work assumes that a regulator has a range of instruments at its disposal (including an ability to set access prices, to set retail prices and to impose a tax on entrants into the competitive activity), other analyses adopt the more realistic assumption that a regulator's instruments are limited to setting the access price, as the retail price is set exogenously and the regulator is not able to impose a tax.[5]

The following two sections examine the pricing principles relevant to one-way and two-way access arrangements. While issues related to 'non-price' access can also be important and affect the incentives of different market participants, such issues are difficult to examine in the abstract and tend to be highly context-specific. Accordingly, the discussion here is limited to access price regulation only.

6.2 ONE-WAY ACCESS PRICING

This section sets out the pricing principles relevant in the context of one-way access where a single firm (the access provider) supplies an essential input to firms operating at different stages in the production chain (the access users), but does not purchase any products from these access users. Examples of one-way access arrangements discussed in Part III of the book include where: generators and retail supply companies need access to electricity transmission and distribution networks; gas shippers need access to gas transportation pipelines; competing providers of retail fixed telephony and broadband services need access to communications network infrastructure (such as the local loop); train operating companies need to access to rail infrastructure (track and stations); airlines need access to airport and air navigation services; or payment service providers (such as banks) need access to interbank payment systems. For the moment it is assumed that the regulator has full information about demand and cost conditions (although this latter assumption is relaxed later).[6]

6.2.1 Access Provider Is Vertically Separated and Does Not Operate in a Related Competitive Market

We start with the case where the core network activity is vertically separated from the competitive activity and therefore the core network firm does not operate in the related market (see figure 4.2 in chapter 4). Perhaps unsurprisingly, the first-best starting principle when considering optimal access prices in this setting is marginal cost pricing.

---

[5] As Laffont and Tirole (1994) argue, 'access pricing rules become more and more complex as well as inefficient as the regulator tries to use access prices, rather than complementary instruments, in order to meet various market structure goals such as inducing proper entry, reducing monopoly power in the competitive segment and achieving distributional objectives'.

[6] Detailed discussions of one-way access pricing are presented in: Laffont and Tirole (1994), Armstrong, Cowan and Vickers (1994, chapter 5), Laffont and Tirole (2000, chapters 3 and 4), Armstrong (2002) and Vogelsang (2003).

situations where the firm can receive a transfer to recover fixed costs, and the downstream activity is competitive (i.e. there is minimal mark-up of retail prices over costs), then the marginal cost pricing of access will be the most efficient. However, this starting principle is sensitive to various assumptions, including the extent of competition in the downstream activity and the ability of the firm to receive transfers to recover any fixed costs.

As noted in Chapter 4, a major difficulty in applying the marginal cost pricing principle in practice is that regulators are typically not able to provide transfers, and setting price equal to marginal cost in industries with decreasing average costs will lead to the access provider not being able to cover its fixed costs. Following the principles developed in Chapter 4, if the firm is unable to receive a transfer to cover fixed costs, then Ramsey–Boiteux pricing can, in principle, offer improvements in efficiency while allowing the firm to break even. This approach was examined in Chapter 4, and the reasoning described there applies equally to settings where a one-way access provider offers multiple products, in fixed proportions, which are used as inputs in a related competitive market. Accordingly, assuming that the downstream market is perfectly competitive, the optimal access prices for the different inputs produced by the firm should be based on the inverse elasticity rule described in Chapter 4.[7]

However, in situations where the downstream competitive activity is *imperfectly* competitive – meaning there is a significant mark-up of retail prices over the cost of access – it may be optimal in some circumstances for the access price to be adjusted in order to compensate for this effect, in particular, by reducing the prices of access *below* marginal cost. The reason is that a lower access price might lead to lower retail prices, which in turn can lead to improvements in allocative efficiency at the final product stage. In effect, the lower-than-cost access price is compensating for the higher-than-cost retail price. Optimal access prices can also be affected by whether or not access users in the retail market are publicly or privately owned.[8] While a public firm might naturally set its price equal to marginal cost (to maximise total surplus), a private firm sets its price above marginal cost (to maximise profit). To correct for this, the optimal access prices for private and public firms differ, with a lower access price being set for the private firm than for the public firm.[9]

While access price adjustments in imperfectly competitive markets may sound sensible in principle, the practical feasibility is questionable, particularly where the access provider is not also active in the downstream activity, raising issues for cost recovery.[10] Moreover, in some circumstances, subsidising access through a low access price may result in excess entry into the retail activity, which may reduce overall productive efficiency to the extent to which it results in the duplication of fixed costs.[11]

---

[7] Recall that, in the multi-product setting, where the demands for different products are independent, the mark-up above marginal cost for each product is inversely proportional to the elasticity of demand for *each product*.

[8] Cui and Sappington (2021). Examples of where private and public providers compete in retail markets include airlines, railroads and energy providers.

[9] The lower access price is to incentivise greater output by the private firm.

[10] Laffont and Tirole (2000) show that a two-part tariff can address the downstream market power of a large user, by charging the large user a (marginal) access price below marginal cost, while allowing the recovery of fixed costs through the payment of a fixed fee.

[11] See Armstrong, Cowan and Vickers (1994).

6.2.2 Access Provider Is Vertically Integrated and Both Supplies an Essential Input to and Competes in, the Competitive Activity

Setting one-way access prices becomes more complicated in situations where the access provider is also active (and typically dominant) in a related competitive market – that is where the access provider is vertically integrated (see figure 4.3 in chapter 4). Although this issue arises across a number of industries (such as the electricity and gas industries in some jurisdictions), it is particularly common in the telecommunications and rail industries where former incumbent operators continue to own and operate the core network activity (the local call access network or the rail network) but are also active in related competitive markets, such as providing retail call and broadband services, or freight or passenger train operating services. In these circumstances, what are efficient pricing principles?

The Impact of Entry on Static Efficiency

When considering different one-way access pricing approaches in competitive settings it is important to appreciate that the analysis of the *static* efficiency effects of opening certain activities in a vertical production chain to competition is typically framed in terms of the effect of such policies on total surplus. In other words, the analysis is indifferent as to whether an entrant or an incumbent provides the product in the competitive segment the focus is on which arrangement will be most productively efficient. Thus, if entrant into the competitive activity produce at higher cost than the vertically integrated incumbent, entry will be assessed as inefficient (in a static sense) and one of the purposes of the access pricing regime will be to control for entry of this type.[12]

Against this background, three access pricing approaches are discussed in this section Ramsey–Boiteux pricing; the efficient component pricing rule (ECPR); and 'cost-based' pricing. As we will see, determining the most efficient access pricing approach is not straightforward and the merits of each approach depend on assumptions about: (1) whether or not the regulator is able to impose a tax/subsidy on entrants; (2) whether or not the prices in the competitive activity are regulated (i.e. whether there is retail price regulation) and (3) whether entrants in the competitive activity are able to 'by-pass' the vertically integrated firm, for example, by investing in the necessary infrastructure to allow it to self-source the desired access product. The difficulty in assessing the different approaches is compounded by the division of economic opinion on the relative merits of each.[13]

6.2.3 Ramsey–Boiteux Pricing

If a regulator can fix both the vertically integrated firm's access price and retail price simultaneously, it is optimal for the regulator to apply Ramsey–Boiteux pricing principles.[1] This approach is the most efficient deviation from marginal cost pricing subject to the firm

---

[12] Laffont and Tirole (2000) frame the question of efficient access pricing as involving the incumbent (voluntarily or involuntarily) subcontracting the provision of the competitive activity to new entrants whenever they gain market share.

[13] See, generally, Armstrong (2002) and Vogelsang (2003).

[14] Armstrong (2002) and Laffont and Tirole (1994) examine the application of Ramsey–Boiteux principles to access and retail prices in detail.

breaking even. Specifically, if all providers in a retail market (access users) can only source the input from the vertically integrated access provider (i.e. where no by-pass opportunities exist), the optimal access price should comprise a mark-up over the marginal cost of access that reflects adjustments for the elasticities of demand for the respective products.[15] In effect, the Ramsey–Boiteux approach treats both the access product and the final retail product (assuming it is regulated) as separate products supplied by the firm and applies mark-ups to marginal cost on this basis.[16]

As discussed in Chapter 4, while the Ramsey–Boiteux approach might be an efficient approach to access pricing in theory, it is often resisted by regulators in practice. There appear to be a number of reasons for this. Firstly, there is a common perception that such an approach is difficult to implement, leading regulators to prefer 'simpler', but not necessarily efficient, approaches.[17] Secondly, because Ramsey–Boiteux prices are differentiated according to demand, they may not be consistent with legal requirements in some jurisdictions that access prices be 'fair and non-discriminatory'. Thirdly, in practice, regulators may not have an opportunity to set access and retail prices simultaneously. In addition, in practice, tariffs for the competitive activity – particularly retail tariffs for essential services – are frequently set according to various political and other non-economic considerations, which limits the ability to apply Ramsey–Boiteux pricing principles.[18]

6.2.4 The Efficient Component Pricing Rule

A second approach to access pricing is the so-called ECPR.[19] There are different representations of the ECPR, but the general approach involves the access price being set equal to the marginal cost of access, *plus* an amount which compensates the access provider for the opportunity cost, or lost profit, associated with not supplying the retail output in

---

[15] Specifically, Laffont and Tirole (1994) express the mark-up over marginal cost of access in terms of super-elasticities, while Armstrong (2002) expresses the access price as a mark-up over the ECPR with the normal elasticity. In circumstances where the firm *can* by-pass the vertically integrated incumbent, and the regulator cannot impose an entrant's tax, Armstrong (2002) shows that the optimal policy is for the access price to be set above marginal cost on the basis of Ramsey–Boiteux principles, and that this entails a degree of productive inefficiency.

[16] This result is based on assumptions about, among other things, demand and cost relationships, technology and the type of competition between the entrant and the incumbent

[17] Laffont and Tirole (2000) find this argument unconvincing when a comparison is made with unregulated businesses, who often engage in sophisticated pricing strategies involving tariff structures which reflect different demand preferences (airlines are perhaps the perfect example). They argue that this suggests pricing decisions should be decentralised to regulated firms. Ivaldi and Pouyet (2018) use estimates of marginal costs and demand elasticities to simulate the impact of policy reforms for French railways.

[18] Armstrong and Sappington (2007) observe that 'in practice, retail tariffs often are dictated by historical, political, or social considerations, and regulators are compelled to set access prices, taking retail prices as given'. Ivaldi and Pouyet (2018) conclude that, in France, the pricing of access to rail infrastructure does not seem to be governed by economic principles, but more by budget considerations.

[19] This approach is also sometimes referred to as the Baumol–Willig rule, after the analysis presented in Willig (1979) and Baumol (1983), or the parity-pricing rule. In regulatory practice, versions of the ECPR have been referred to as 'retail-minus', 'active-minus', the 'margin-rule', 'ARROW pricing' and avoided cost pricing. Detailed descriptions of this approach are presented in: Baumol and Sidak (1994a), Sidak and Spulber (1998, chapter 8), Laffont and Tirole (2000, chapters 3 and 4) and Armstrong (2002).

circumstances where the price in the competitive activity is given (i.e. it is regulated exogenously set). Accordingly, the access price is set according to the following formul

$$a = C_1 + (P - C_2).\qquad(6.1)$$

Here a is the access price, C_1 is the direct marginal cost of providing access to rival dowr stream competitors, P is the final retail price of the incumbent, and C_2 is the incumbent downstream marginal costs of providing the final retail product to consumers. The se ond term on the right-hand side of equation (6.1) (the opportunity cost of access) ha been interpreted in different ways. One view is that it represents the profit contributic foregone by the access provider as a result of having to provide access to a competite who may displace it in the provision of services in the competitive market.[20] In effec this uplift to the direct marginal costs of providing access is intended to compensate th vertically integrated incumbent for changes in policies which opened up certain activitie to competition, and, in particular, where, in the absence of such a contribution, the fir would be unable to fully recover its fixed costs.[21] An alternative interpretation is tha where the retail tariff is fixed by a regulator at a level different from costs (for exampl because of historical or political reasons), the 'opportunity cost' adjustment represents 'second-best' correction for any distortions caused by the retail tariff. That is, it is a mech anism for sending the correct entry signals which allow for only efficient entry.[22]

An implicit assumption in equation (6.1) is that each unit of access supplied to th entrant automatically results in a unit reduction in the demand for the incumbent's reta service. However, if possibilities exist for demand- and supply-side substitutability, a dis placement ratio parameter (σ) is applied to the opportunity cost of access term to captur how the incumbent's retail sales are affected by supplying a unit of access to its rivals. Where there is some product differentiation, or there are opportunities for by-pass c technological substitution, the displacement ratio is less than one (i.e. $\sigma < 1$), and, in th case, the opportunity cost component included in the access price is reduced accordingl Adopting the same notation as in equation (6.1), but where σ represents the displacemer ratio, the ECPR formula becomes

$$a = C_1 + \sigma(P - C_2).\qquad(6.2)$$

An alternative representation of the ECPR, sometimes referred to as the 'margin rule involves setting the access price such that the *difference* between the retail price and th

---

[20] In circumstances where the vertically integrated firm's product in the competitive activity and the product provided by the entrant are sufficiently independent in terms of demand (i.e. they are not substitutes), then the appropriate access price according to the ECPR should be set equal to the marginal cost of providing access with *no allowance* for the opportunity cost of providing access (in these situations, the opportunity cost of access is zero).

[21] See Sidak and Spulber (1998, chapter 8). In this way, retail customers who switch to a new entrant still contribute to the fixed costs of the access provider. If those customers who switched to a new entrant di not contribute to such fixed costs, the customers who remained with the access provider would face eve higher charges to allow for the fixed costs to be recovered.

[22] See Armstrong (2002).

[23] See Armstrong, Doyle and Vickers (1996) and Armstrong (2002).

access price (the entrant's margin) is equal to the incumbent's marginal cost in the competitive activity.

$$P - a = (C_2 - C_1). \tag{6.3}$$

In equation (6.3), a is the access price, P is the regulated final retail price of the incumbent and $(C_2 - C_1)$ is the incumbent's marginal cost in the competitive activity. Rearranging, as in equation (6.4) below, this rule states that the access price is equal to the incumbent's retail price less the incumbent's marginal cost in the competitive activity:

$$a = P - (C_2 - C_1). \tag{6.4}$$

In circumstances where there is a one-for-one displacement of demand for the vertically integrated firm's product in the competitive market, then the two representations (i.e. equations (6.1) and (6.4)) are the same.[24]

A number of perceived benefits are associated with the ECPR approach to access pricing. Firstly, it is argued that the ECPR facilitates productive efficiency, by ensuring that entry will occur in the competitive activity if, and only if, an entrant is at least as efficient as the vertically integrated firm in providing the service in the competitive market.[25] In this way, entrants respond to the 'right' signals. Secondly, as the ECPR does not affect the revenue of the vertically integrated access provider, this reduces the incentives for it to reduce the quality of access services (i.e. to engage in so-called 'sabotage') with the aim of discouraging entry into the competitive activity. Moreover, entry into the competitive activity does not undermine any historical cross-subsidies of the core network activity by the competitive activity, which may make this approach politically attractive.[26]

An important, but commonly misunderstood, aspect of the ECPR approach is that it does *not* seek to address concerns about monopoly pricing in competitive activities, such as in retail markets.[27] Rather, the ECPR operates on the assumption that regulated prices in the competitive activity are constrained by either competition or regulation. Put differently, such a rule is said to only entrench monopoly pricing if it already exists.[28] Accordingly, it is argued that the ECPR should only be introduced where there

---

[24] Armstrong, Doyle and Vickers (1996) show that the two representations will be the same where there is fixed coefficient technology, homogeneous products and no by-pass.

[25] This conclusion holds under certain assumptions, specifically if: (1) the retail products of the vertically integrated incumbent and the entrant are perfect substitutes; (2) no by-pass opportunities exist; and (3) there is fixed input technology (one unit of output requires one unit of input).

[26] See Laffont and Tirole (2000).

[27] See Kahn and Taylor (1994), Economides and White (1995) and the response of Baumol, Ordover and Willig (1997).

[28] See Baumol and Sidak (1994b). Additional concerns arise when the retail prices of a vertically integrated firm are *unregulated*: that is, where the vertically integrated firm is unrestricted in choosing its retail price. In this case, the opportunity cost portion of the access price is determined by deducting the retail costs from the (unregulated) retail price. It is clear that, in this setting, the access provider will have an incentive to set the retail price at, or close to, the monopoly level, as this maximises profits. This was among the issues that featured in the Telecom *Clear* case in New Zealand, where retail price regulation was not in effect during the period of the access dispute. See Baumol and Sidak (1995).

are also complementary rules in place to constrain final prices such as retail pric
regulation.[29]

Much of the controversy about the ECPR approach relates to the fact that the reta
prices are taken as given, while many economists would see the principal benefits c
competition being a reduction in the incumbent's retail prices and a rebalancing of tariff
(i.e. dynamic efficiency gains).[30] Similarly, it is argued that the ECPR approach effectivel
guarantees the pre-entry profits of the incumbent, including preserving any inefficienc
associated with its historical activities.[31] In part, for these reasons, although the ECPI
generally features in every theoretical examination of access pricing, the approach ha
been viewed with some scepticism in practice.[32]

The ECPR and Efficient Access Prices

A separate question, however, is whether the ECPR approach results in efficient acces
prices, and, more specifically, how it compares to the Ramsey–Boiteux approach t
access pricing described above. The answer to this question depends critically on th
conditions that are assumed to prevail in the industry. Laffont and Tirole (2000) shov
that the ECPR access price is equivalent to the efficient access price under condition
which they describe as full symmetry.[33] They conclude that, where there is asymmetr
in at least one of these conditions, the ECPR access price will generally not be equiva
lent to the optimal Ramsey–Boiteux access price, and that in these circumstance
'corrections' to the ECPR must be made which will lead to an access price above o
below the ECPR level. Armstrong (2002) finds that whether or not the two approache
will coincide depends also on the representation of the ECPR that is adopted. If th
'opportunity cost of access' interpretation is adopted (i.e. equation (6.1)), then, accord
ing to Armstrong, the ECPR access price and the Ramsey–Boiteux access price *neve*
coincide.[34]

Three further issues should be raised about the efficiency of the ECPR approach t
access pricing. The first is the relevance of the approach in settings where prices i
the competitive activity are unregulated, and the regulator sets only the access price
In situations where the competitive activity is assumed to be perfectly competitive, th
optimal access price should be set at marginal cost to improve allocative efficiency, an

---

[29] As Baumol and Sidak (1995) note, 'one rule without the other, does not guarantee results that serve the public interest'.

[30] See Vogelsang (2003).

[31] See Economides (2003).

[32] The approach has, in the past, been banned under New Zealand telecommunications legislation. In the USA, while a form of the ECPR (the 'avoided-cost resale' provision) is used for certain wholesale resale services, the Federal Communications Commission (FCC) has apparently made statements that it is not ir favour of the ECPR because it provides no incentives for retail prices to move towards competitive level See discussion in *Albion Water Limited v. Water Services Regulation Authority* (2004).

[33] These full symmetry conditions include: (1) symmetric costs of providing access; (2) no entrant market power; (3) demand symmetry on the competitive segment; and (4) cost symmetry on the competitive segment.

[34] However, if the margin rule interpretation is adopted (equation (6.3)), then it is possible for the approaches to coincide (Armstrong, 2002).

the relevance of the ECPR approach is unclear in this unregulated setting.[35] The second issue relates to the application of the ECPR approach where by-pass opportunities exist (i.e. where an entrant can build their own facilities rather than purchase them from the incumbent). In these circumstances, the ECPR will need to be adjusted. One method proposed for adjusting the ECPR for by-pass is known as the market-adjusted ECPR (M-ECPR), and involves setting the access price by reference to the *entrant's* final retail price rather than that of the vertically integrated firm (as in the standard ECPR).[36] This approach implies that the upper bound for the access price will be the costs of by-pass by an entrant.[37] However, as the access price is based on a market-adjusted retail price (rather than the regulated final price of the incumbent), the revenues obtained from the retail sales and access sales may be insufficient to cover the vertically integrated firm's costs, which may require further adjustments.[38] Finally, the ECPR approach is based on the assumption that a regulator is unable to employ an entrant's tax to correct for distortions to the regulated retail tariff, and the access price is therefore the only instrument that the regulator has at its disposal. If, however, it is possible to introduce an entrant's tax (such as a contribution to a universal service fund to correct for relevant distortions), then access prices could be set at direct costs, thus sending the correct 'make-or-buy' signals to entrants in the competitive activity.[39]

Arguments for and against the ECPR

Much ink has been spilt debating the relative merits and drawbacks of the ECPR approach to access pricing. As noted above, a principal benefit of the ECPR is that it is (relatively) well understood, and, where the conditions are appropriate, could promote efficient entry (in a static sense), while allowing the vertically integrated firm to recover its fixed costs associated with past investments. In other words, the ECPR can ensure that only those entrants with costs *lower* than the incumbent in the competitive activity will be able to profitably enter that market, while at the same time allowing the incumbent firm to recover the direct costs of access and the costs associated with any investments. Moreover, because the incumbent recovers its costs, including the opportunity costs associated with providing access to competitors in a related market, this makes it indifferent as to whether it supplies the service in the retail market or a rival does and thus reduces the incentives to engage in sabotage.

---

[35] See Armstrong (2002). Armstrong and Sappington (2007) identify two other special cases where the price of access should be set equal to cost (where there is no by-pass and demand is linear, and where there are no cross-price effects between the vertically integrated firm and the entrant in the retail market). More generally, they observe: 'when the monopolist has some market power in the retail market the optimal access price will equal marginal cost only in knife edge cases'. Sibley, Doane, Williams and Tsai (2004) propose an adaptation of the ECPR rule – the so-called 'generalised efficient component pricing rule' (GECPR). The GECPR is directed at adapting the ECPR to correct for downstream pricing distortions due to imperfect competition.

[36] That is, $a = C_1 + (P_E - C_2)$, where a is the access price, C_1 are the direct marginal costs of providing access, P_E is the final product price of an *entrant* and C_2 are the marginal costs of providing the final product (i.e. the costs associated with supply in the competitive activity).

[37] See Sidak and Spulber (1998, chapter 9). Economides (2003) presents a critique.

[38] See Vogelsang (2003).

[39] See Armstrong (2002).

Against this benefit there are a number of objections to the ECPR both in theory ar in practice.[40] Firstly, from a practical perspective, in more complex settings (where som by-pass opportunities exist or where there is some product differentiation), the ECPR ca require a large amount of information, including: cost data for both access and retail se vices; demand and supply elasticities; and information about how access prices will affe competition in a related market. In effect, in setting the ECPR, the regulator has to predi how competition will evolve in the market prior to setting access prices.[41] Secondly, a important assumption of the ECPR is that retail prices are constrained at levels close cost, either by regulation or by effective competition in the retail market. However, i practice, there is often a question about the extent to which price regulation, or comp tition, in retail markets sufficiently constrains final retail prices to actual cost. As note if final retail prices are overpriced (inefficiently set above cost), then the ECPR will allo the incumbent firm to be compensated for the loss of this inefficient margin through tl opportunity cost component. Thirdly, the ECPR is sometimes viewed as unduly 'incun bent friendly', a method for shielding incumbents from the effects of competition, ar that this can have adverse effects on dynamic efficiency.[42] Fourthly, as Armstrong (200. emphasises, the ECPR will only represent the preferred approach under certain condition such as where retail prices are fixed in advance and it is not possible to use an 'entrant tax' to correct for any distortions in the retail market (i.e. such as cross-subsidies). Finall although the simple ECPR (margin rule) approach is used in the telecommunication industry (see Chapter 11),[43] and has been considered in the water and wastewater indust (see Chapter 16),[44] the approach remains controversial,[45] and some have suggested that could actually deter entry and the development of competition.[46]

6.2.5 Cost-Based Access Charges

A third general approach to access pricing is to base access prices on the costs of provi ing the access product. This approach typically involves estimating the long-run incre mental or marginal costs incurred by the vertically integrated access provider associate

---

[40] Baumol, Ordover and Willig (1997) examine some of these objections.
[41] For example, how much of the incumbent's services will be displaced by new entry in the competitive activity.
[42] Kahn and Taylor (1994) argue that the dynamic effects of the ECPR are not clear once account is taken of the effect that even (statically) inefficient competitors can have in terms of rectifying inefficient pric structures imposed by regulation, or stimulating improvements in efficiency and service innovation. Similarly, Economides and White (1995) argue that entry by a less efficient rival could yield socially beneficial results.
[43] The retail-minus approach has been applied by telecommunications regulators in Europe and the USA. A variant of the approach – known as 'active-minus' – is applied for access to 'dark' fibre services in the U
[44] A form of the ECPR approach was used for providing access to water infrastructure in England. The approach was also proposed for access to wastewater services in Sydney, Australia.
[45] A 2006 court judgment disallowed its use for access pricing in the England water industry, concluding tha 'We have been provided with no examples or case studies of ECPR being successfully used' (CAT, 2006).
[46] The England and Wales water industry regulator has in the past described a requirement to adopt one form of this approach (a retail-minus approach) as 'one of the biggest obstacles to the development of competition in the water industry' (Ofwat, 2007). Similarly, Weisman (2021) concludes that paradoxicall the retail-minus test might 'not protect against a margin squeeze as much as it preordains one', and in using this approach regulators may unwittingly be adopting wholesale pricing rules that have precisely the opposite effect to promoting welfare-enhancing competition.

with providing access. There are various arguments in support of this approach.[47] Firstly, basing access prices on the direct costs of providing access is seen to send appropriate signals to potential entrants in the competitive activity about the relative costs associated with 'buying' access from the vertically integrated firm versus 'building' or investing in their own core infrastructure. In other words, the entrant will only purchase access if the cost-based access price is *lower* than the costs associated with investing in core network infrastructure and self-supplying the access product. Secondly, because cost-based access prices do not include any compensation to the incumbent for providing access in a retail market (i.e. the opportunity cost), it is perceived to better promote entry and competition in the retail market (as compared to the ECPR).[48] Thirdly, in principle, cost-based access prices should be relatively simple to estimate and implement, as less information is required than for either Ramsey–Boiteux pricing or the ECPR (i.e. no information is required about demand elasticities or entrant characteristics). More generally, cost-based access pricing is appropriate when the access price does not need to correct for distortions in the retail tariff of the incumbent.

However, if the access price is the only instrument available to deal with retail tariff distortions, cost-based access pricing will be sub-optimal.[49] In addition, because cost-based approaches to access do not compensate the incumbent for the opportunity costs (lost revenues) when new entrants gain customers in the retail market, it can create incentives for the access provider to restrict or obstruct access by entrants to its core service (e.g. by degrading quality). There can also be practical challenges in accurately estimating forward-looking costs, especially when the costs of providing access vary significantly across areas (e.g. rural versus urban) or for different types of access user.

Cost Concepts

An important practical question for cost-based access pricing is what measure of costs should be used under the approach. The two broad cost categories that are typically discussed when considering the costs of access are stand-alone costs and incremental/marginal costs, which represent a so-called ceiling and a floor on access prices, respectively.[50] Stand-alone costs reflect the total costs that a (hypothetical) single-product entrant would incur in producing a specific access product (i.e. it is assumed that the entrant does not produce any other service). Stand-alone cost is said to represent an *upper limit* on access prices that can be charged by the vertically integrated operator. Conversely, incremental costs reflect the product-specific costs associated with the increase in the supply of a specific access product

---

[47] See Armstrong (2002).

[48] In *Verizon Communications, Inc. v. FCC* (2002), the US Supreme Court characterised that the cost-based (TELRIC) approach used in the telecoms industry as being 'designed to give aspiring competitors every possible incentive to enter local retail telephone markets, short of confiscating the incumbents' property'. Although, as discussed below, this effect on entry and competition can depend on whether the incumbent seeks to hinder access through entry-deterring strategies.

[49] Armstrong (2002) discusses three settings when cost-based approaches will be appropriate. First, when the retail prices for the vertically integrated firm do reflect underlying costs, and there is therefore no need for the access price to correct for any distortions. Second, when any distortions caused by retail prices that do not reflect underlying costs can be tackled through an output tax on entrants. Third, when the competitive activity is vigorous and the retail tariff is not regulated.

[50] See Baumol and Sidak (1994b).

where the firm produces more than one product.[51] Incremental cost is calculated as the difference in the firm's total costs between producing a specific access product and not producing it. It is therefore said to represent a *lower limit* on the access prices that can be charged by a vertically integrated firm. The difference between the stand-alone and incremental cost categories is that the stand-alone cost will typically include all fixed and common costs associated with the provision of an access service, while the incremental cost includes only a proportion of those fixed costs – those considered specific to the access service. It follows that, on average, stand-alone cost estimates are higher than estimates of incremental cost. Table 6.2 details the different cost concepts, while Box 11.2 in Chapter 11 discusses the practical application of these concepts in the telecommunications and rail industries.

Table 6.2 Different cost concepts[a]

Marginal cost of X	The increase in a firm's total cost as a result of a small increase in the output of X.
Incremental cost of X	The addition to the firm's total cost when the output of X expands by some predetermined increment.
Average incremental cost of an entire service X	The average incremental cost of the entire service, defined as the difference between the firm's total costs with and without service X supplied, divided by the output of X. So, if the firm produces three products, X, Y and Z, the average incremental cost (AIC) of X is $$\text{AIC}_X = \frac{[\text{TC}(X,Y,Z) - \text{TC}(Y,Z)]}{Q_X}$$ where $\text{TC}(X,Y,Z)$ is the total cost of producing the three products (X, Y and Z), $\text{TC}(Y,Z)$ is the total cost of producing the two products (Y and Z) and Q_X is the output of X.
Fully allocated cost (FAC)	The fully allocated cost approach is an accounting method that involves the allocation of the total costs in a company's accounts to the various products it produces. The allocation of these costs is based on sharing factors, which broadly should align with cost causality. This approach tends to be backward-looking and based on the costs already incurred.
Stand-alone cost of X	The stand-alone cost of X is the cost that an efficient entrant would incur if it only produced product X. This estimate of cost includes all the common costs associated with the production of X, such that $\text{SAC}_X = \text{TC}(X)$

[a] Based on Baumol and Sidak (1994a).

---

[51] The definition of the relevant 'increment' is often of critical importance in practice. For small changes in output of, say, a particular component/product (such as the provision of 2 MB call termination services in telecommunications), then the incremental cost will approximate marginal cost. However, when the cost increment is defined to capture a number of components/products (such as all network termination services, or all core network services), then the incremental cost can differ substantially from underlying marginal costs.

Variants of long-run average incremental cost are widely used by regulators in prac-tice.[52] Despite some concerns about this approach in theoretical work,[53] the preference for this approach by regulators appears to reflect a general presumption that (productive) economic efficiency will be improved where prices for intermediate inputs in a pro-duction process, such as telecommunications access services, are cost-based.[54] In some industries – notably the rail sector in the USA – a regulated firm is free to negotiate access prices within the incremental price floor and the stand-alone price ceiling – known as constrained market pricing (see Chapter 14).

Measuring and Estimating Indirect Costs

Access prices are often based on the estimated direct costs of providing access along with some adjustment (or uplift) to the access price to allow for the recovery of any fixed and common production costs (in some jurisdictions this is referred to as the '+', as in LRIC+ pricing). This raises the general issue about the efficiency properties of the different meth-ods for allocating fixed and common costs across different products which we discussed in Chapter 4. In practice, many regulators use cost-based methods (such as the equi-pro-portionate mark-up (EPMU) method) rather than demand-based methods to allocate fixed and common costs across different access products.

A further issue relates to the methods by which costs are measured. In practice, the measurement of costs on which to base access prices typically requires the development of a cost model, which in many regulated sectors is often contested and controversial.[55] In developing such models, important choices need to be made regarding the estimation of costs. In practice, these issues are determined in different ways across industries, reflect-ing the nature of the competitive and regulatory environment and the policy objectives being pursued.[56]

---

[52] Vogelsang (2021) argues that the reason why cost-based pricing has dominated under bottleneck access regulation is because other pricing rules, such as the ECPR or Ramsey-Boiteux pricing, are either inadequate in containing market power or too complicated to apply. A long-run marginal cost methodology has at times been used to determine access prices in water supply, gas and aviation charges in the UK. As discussed in Chapter 11, the dominant approach in the telecommunications industry has been to set access prices on the basis of long-run incremental costs.

[53] Laffont and Tirole (2000) argue that the: 'broad regulatory consensus in favour of LRIC unfortunately is supported by little economic argument. As a matter of fact, an economic analysis reveals several concerns about the whole endeavour.'

[54] Hausman and Tardiff (1995) draw parallels with the work of Diamond and Mirrlees (1971) on optimal taxation. Vogelsang (2003) identifies five other specific reasons for such a preference in the telecommunications industry: (1) a presumption that economies of scope and scale are no longer pronounced in the telecommunications industry; (2) that large network externalities in the industry imply reduced mark-ups of access prices over costs; (3) that mark-ups over cost on intermediate access products can lead to double marginalisation problems where entrants also apply mark-ups; (4) that high access prices can soften the incentives for the vertically integrated firm to compete in the related market; and (5) that high access charges might encourage inefficient by-pass.

[55] Vogelsang (2003) argues that the cost-based approach is hampered by 'tedious and contentious cost determinations that always lag behind cost developments' and that 'common cost markups are unsystematic and not related to allocative efficiency'.

[56] Gómez-Ibáñez (2003) observes that: 'In practice, regulators don't have the time and resources to determine the incremental costs of many different and specialised services. As a consequence, every access price schedule usually involves some simplifications that result in undercharging for some services and overcharging for others.'

6.2.6 Global Price Caps

As we have seen, each of the three access pricing approaches described above, i.
Ramsey–Boiteux pricing, ECPR pricing and cost-based pricing, can raise implementa
tion challenges, in part, because of the substantial and detailed nature of the informa
tion required by the regulator to set prices under each approach. Indeed, in considerin
the merits of each of the three approaches above, an implicit assumption has been mad
throughout that the regulator has perfect information, and is able to implement eac
approach effectively. As discussed in Chapter 4, this assumption does not reflect regula
tory reality, and there is typically a significant information asymmetry between the regu
lator and the regulated firm on key factors such as costs and demand, which can impa
on the regulator's ability to set efficient access prices.

To address the problem of information asymmetry in settings where a vertically inte
grated firm supplies both an access product and a retail product, both of which need t
be regulated, one suggested approach is the use of a so-called global price cap.[57] Th
global price cap approach effectively delegates decisions about access and/or retail pric
to the vertically integrated firm, subject to an overall constraint.[58] Under this approac
the firm does not differentiate between the access product and the retail product – th
products are treated symmetrically – and it is argued that this property will encourag
the firm to use its superior information about demand conditions in both the access an
retail markets to choose an optimal price structure. In certain settings, it is argued tha
the global price cap approach will induce a firm to choose an efficient Ramsey–Boiteu
price structure.[59]

Notwithstanding the attractive theoretical properties, the global price cap approach t
access pricing has not been widely implemented in practice.[60] This could reflect two gen
eral concerns with the approach.[61] First, the approach assumes that the regulator is able t
accurately determine the correct weights in setting the level of the global price cap, whic
requires the regulator to have detailed *ex ante* information about the demand condition
in both the access and retail markets. Second, such an approach allows the verticall
integrated firm significant discretion in pricing, and might lead the firm to engage in
price squeeze (by raising the access price for its competitors in the retail activity while, a
the same time, lowering its own retail price) and still be within the constraints set by th
global price cap. To mitigate this potential, it has been suggested that the global price ca
be used in combination with a margin squeeze or imputation test.[62]

---

[57] Laffont and Tirole (2000).

[58] A global price cap imposes a price ceiling set for a weighted average basket of services provided by the
regulated firm.

[59] Specifically, where the weights applied to different products in the global price cap are exogenously
determined, and are proportionally based on the forecasted quantities of output that will be realised. Se
Laffont and Tirole (2000).

[60] In the telecommunications sector, Briglauer and Vogelsang (2011) attribute the reluctance of regulators
to apply the approach to its dependence on idealised weights, as well as a more general incompatibility
of the global price cap methodology with the approach to deregulation adopted in a number of countrie
(particularly in Europe) which is based on gradual market-by-market deregulation.

[61] For an early critique of global price caps, see Baumol, Ordover and Willig (1997).

[62] See Laffont and Tirole (2000).

6.2.7 Negotiation of Access Prices

In some jurisdictions, access providers and users are encouraged to negotiate directly on access prices and terms in the first instance without the involvement of the regulator. Under this approach, where access terms are successfully determined by such negotiations, the regulator will typically not intervene, even if the prices are inefficient. However, where the parties cannot reach agreement, the regulator can be called upon to determine the terms of access. The approach has been used in the rail and telecommunications industries in North America, although operators may be required to set cost-based rates.[63] This general approach has also been adopted in Australia, where a 'negotiate–arbitrate' model for access regulation was introduced in 1995, on the basis, in part, that it would be less interventionist than regulated outcomes, and facilitate more market-oriented solutions. Similarly, in the telecommunications industry in the UK, and the water and wastewater industry in England and Wales, there are provisions for commercial negotiations relating to network access, after which the regulator can, if required, conduct a dispute resolution process.

'Open', 'Non-Discriminatory' and 'Fair and Reasonable' Access Principles

As discussed in Part III of this book, negotiated access prices and terms are often required to satisfy certain 'access principles', such that access be provided on an 'open', 'non-discriminatory' and 'fair' or 'reasonable' basis.[64]

'Open-access' requirements require that a supplier of a core or indispensable service provides access to that service to anyone that makes a reasonable request. Where an access provider is vertically integrated, it must offer access to the service or facility to third parties on the same terms as any affiliated division of the operator. Open-access requirements are common in the gas, electricity, transport and telecommunication industries, and in some cases thresholds and tests have been established for when a particular asset or service must be provided to third parties on an open-access basis.

'Non-discriminatory access' requirements seek to ensure that an access provider does not, without objective justification, offer different terms and conditions (including charges) to users in the same circumstances, or offer uniform terms or charges to users whose circumstances are different. The broad principle is aligned with that in competition law in some jurisdictions (such as in the EU) which specifies that an abuse of a dominant position might involve applying dissimilar conditions to equivalent transactions with other trading parties, thereby placing them at a competitive disadvantage. Non-discrimination does not mean the supplier must apply a one-size-fits-all approach to users; it can set different terms and conditions for different types of participants, for example, to reflect differences in the cost of supply. In some sectors, differential treatment can be justified on other objective grounds, such as the risk profile of a user, or because of potential impacts on system integrity or stability associated with different types of user.

---

[63] See Gómez-Ibáñez (2003). Brock and Katz (1997) discuss the attempts by the Federal Communication Commission to issue pricing guidelines in relation to the negotiations.

[64] Under current EU communications policy, for example, operators which enter into co-investment agreements for very-high-capacity networks must do so on terms that are fair, reasonable and non-discriminatory. See European Electronics Communications Code (Directive 2018/1972).

'Fair and reasonable access' requirements are more open-textured and interpretation can depend on the setting in which they are applied. One approach is to draw a comparison between what terms are being offered and what would be offered if a market was competitive.[65] Another approach when assessing the fairness/reasonableness of prices in some regulated industries is to apply a cost-based benchmark and to consider whether prices reflect costs which are reasonably, necessarily and efficiently incurred in providing services, including an appropriate return on invested capital.[66]

In summary, while direct negotiation can encourage a commercial orientation and reduce the need for a regulator to gather and analyse vast amounts of information to determine access terms, such negotiations will not necessarily lead to efficient access prices. In addition, the negotiated approach may not be well suited to situations where there are multiple parties seeking access but where negotiations happen on a bilateral basis.[67] This is because the regulator can end up arbitrating essentially the same dispute many times.[68] Much will depend on the relative bargaining strength of the parties, the presence of guidance or pricing principles and the role that the regulator plays in the resolution of any disputes relating to access.[69]

6.2.8 Summary: One-Way Access

This section has described pricing principles and approaches for one-way access. If an access provider is vertically separated from the competitive activity, then marginal cost pricing of access will be most efficient (assuming that the related market is competitive, and the firm can receive a transfer to recover fixed costs). In circumstances where the related market is imperfectly competitive, the access price may need to be adjusted including, in some circumstances, by lowering the access price below marginal cost.

Where the access provider is vertically integrated and competes with entrants in a related market, five approaches to access pricing were discussed. First, if the regulator can control both the access and retail price, then, in principle, the optimal approach is to apply Ramsey–Boiteux principles and adjust the marginal cost of access according to the elasticities of demand for the different access and retail products. An alternative pricing approach is the ECPR, which in simple terms involves access pricing being set equal to the marginal cost of access plus an amount that compensates the access provider for the opportunity cost of providing access. A third approach is to base access prices on the

---

[65] In the area of intellectual property and standards, fair and reasonable has been interpreted as involving charges (royalties) not being disproportionate to what they could have charged under competition conditions that applied *ex ante*, prior to the adoption of the standard.

[66] The UK communications regulator (Ofcom, 2005) has previously noted that a fair and reasonable pricing regime is one in which the costs which a provider is allowed to recover from customers are restricted to those costs which it reasonably, necessarily and efficiently incurs in the provision of those services (including a return that reflects the cost of capital of the investment).

[67] See Gómez-Ibáñez (2003).

[68] This happened in Australia in the telecommunications industry prior to reforms in 2012.

[69] See Brock and Katz (1997), who discuss the links between the economics of bargaining and negotiations. Besanko and Cui (2019) compare regulated access to negotiated access (discriminatory and non-discriminatory) in terms of quality, consumer and total surplus, and find that the bargaining power of the access provider is critical to the assessment.

direct costs associated with providing access, in particular, the long-run incremental cost of access. This approach, which is widely used in practice, typically involves access prices being set on the basis of estimates of forward-looking long-run incremental or marginal costs, often with a mark-up to allow for the recovery of fixed and common costs. A fourth approach is to introduce a global price cap, which effectively delegates decisions regarding access and retail prices to the firm, but subjects the firm to an overall constraint. A final approach involves direct negotiation of access prices between access providers and access users with regulatory intervention only in the event of failed negotiations. This approach has also been adopted by regulators in some jurisdictions.

6.3 TWO-WAY ACCESS PRICING

Two-way access arrangements arise where an access provider supplies some products as inputs to other firms, and, at the same time, purchases products from other access providers as an input into its own production process. In contrast to one-way access, the arrangements are more symmetric because each firm providing an essential input also requires access to essential inputs supplied by other firms in the market. As described in later chapters, two-way access arrangements are a feature of the telecommunications industry (e.g. fixed-to-mobile access, mobile-to-mobile access and internet interconnection), the payments industry, railways and the energy sector. There are different forms of two-way access, including: adjacent monopolies (where firms do not compete for subscribers); one-to-many access arrangements; and two-way access arrangements with competition for subscribers. Each form of access arrangement potentially has different implications for whether firms should be encouraged to collectively set access prices, the need for economic regulation and the form that optimal access pricing should take.

6.3.1 Access Pricing for Adjacent Monopolies

A firm that holds a position of monopoly in relation to a core network service within one jurisdiction may need to connect with firms in adjacent or neighbouring jurisdictions to provide particular end-to-end services. A classic example is if someone living in Oxford makes a fixed line international telephone call to someone in Berlin. This requires the British core network operator (say, BT) to access the German core network operator (say, Deutsche Telekom) and pay a charge for the costs associated with using their network.[70] The charges levied by the access provider in the adjacent jurisdiction are sometimes called settlement charges or termination charges. Examples of adjacent monopolies in other industries include: in electricity markets, where there is a single or national trading market covering a number of states/regions, but separate transmission companies operating in different states who need to interconnect with one another to transfer electricity; or in the rail or aviation industries, where a passenger makes a journey on a train/plane across multiple jurisdictions and in so doing utilises the services of the rail network operator or air navigation service provider in those jurisdictions

---

[70] Carter and Wright (1994) present an early analysis of price setting for international telephone calls.

A key characteristic of two-way access in adjacent monopolies is that the network firms provide *complementary* rather than substitutable services – e.g. BT in the UK does not directly compete for fixed line residential customers with Deutsche Telekom in Germany. In circumstances where settlement prices are set non-cooperatively (i.e. each network firm determines its own access charge), each firm will have an incentive to raise the settlement price, potentially giving rise to a double marginalisation problem. To see this, consider the earlier example. From the German operator's perspective, the choice of termination charge does not impact on the consumer surplus for originating calls, that is callers subscribing to its network *in* Germany will not face the charges levied for terminating calls and are only interested in the originating call price. Instead, it is the callers in Britain (and elsewhere in the world) who are affected by the termination charge levied by the German network. In these circumstances, and where adjacent monopolies choose prices independently, each monopoly can be expected to exploit its monopoly position in termination, and set a termination charge (the access price) at a level above marginal cost.[71] When combined with the retail monopolies of each core network firm in its own jurisdiction, this can give rise to the familiar double marginalisation or double mark-up problem: the firm in each country separately applies a monopoly mark-up to its perceived marginal cost of access, with the result that retail prices in each country are set at levels higher than the industry monopoly price.[72] As in the standard double marginalisation setting, if it is possible for the two adjacent firms to cooperate with one another on the setting of the access charge, the second margin/mark-up is eliminated, and both the firms and consumers can be made better off.[73]

It follows that there are compelling arguments to allow for the cooperative determination of access prices for adjacent (i.e. non-competing) monopolies. Indeed, in situations where the termination charges are reciprocal (i.e. both jurisdictions face the same charge) and the core network firms are symmetric – meaning they have identical costs and levels of call from/to each country – the interests of the companies in each jurisdiction coincide and they will likely agree to set termination charges at marginal cost.[74] However, if these assumptions do not hold – either because a core network provider in one jurisdiction has higher costs, or traffic is unbalanced such that the firm receives a net inflow of calls – there will be a preference by that core network provider to set a higher reciprocal termination charge.

6.3.2 One-to-Many Access Pricing

A particular form of two-way access arrangement – sometimes termed 'one-to-many' access – arises where many firms in the competitive activity are required to purchase access from a single large access provider, and where, at the same time, that single access

---

[71] This is sometimes referred to as the 'chain of monopolies' or 'pancaking problem' in the gas and electricity industries.

[72] Laffont, Rey and Tirole (1998a).

[73] Carter and Wright (1999) observe that international interconnection agreements have historically been determined by bilateral agreement within an international framework.

[74] See Armstrong (2002). This differs from the case discussed below, and in Chapter 11, where network providers compete for subscribers (i.e. provide substitute services), where, under certain circumstances, there may be an incentive for the firms to collude in the setting of cooperative access prices.

provider is required to purchase access inputs from many firms in the competitive activity. This situation is typical of fixed-to-mobile (FTM) interconnections in the telecommunications industry, where a fixed line telephone network operator is required to acquire call termination access inputs from a number of mobile telecommunications operators, and where each mobile operator is required to purchase (termination) access from the fixed network. The principal policy concern with FTM access pricing is that, under certain circumstances, termination charges will be set too high.[75] This is because, no matter how intense competition may be in the mobile market to attract subscribers, each mobile network firm (no matter how small) has a monopoly over calls to its subscribers from the fixed line network and has incentives to exploit this monopoly by setting a high termination price.

The setting of FTM termination charges at levels above cost can have two potential effects. On the one hand, if the higher access charges are passed on to fixed line consumers, it will lead to higher prices and reduce the welfare of consumers of fixed line services. On the other hand, if higher revenues from FTM termination fees are used by mobile operators to lower prices for mobile subscribers (allowing them, for example, to provide free or subsidised devices), this can lead to more intense competition and to overall higher levels of mobile penetration which, as described in Chapter 2, can potentially lead to positive network externalities and enhance the welfare of consumers of mobile services.

This analysis of FTM interconnection characterises fixed services and mobile services as essentially complementary services,[76] and, viewed in this way, the fixed network and mobile networks are a form of adjacent monopolies. However, in many jurisdictions, competition in mobile telephony has intensified to the point that they are now a substitute for fixed line telephony. In such circumstances, the incentives to set high FTM termination charges are mitigated, and the points noted in the next subsection become relevant.[77]

6.3.3 Two-Way Access Pricing where Firms Compete for Subscribers

The discussion of one-way access arrangements in Section 6.2 concluded that, because the access provider had a dominant market position, it had an incentive to set high access prices, which would be economically inefficient. In addition, a vertically integrated access provider might have incentives to foreclose competitors in a related activity where it also operates, thereby distorting competition in that activity.

However, in some settings where access to an essential core input is required, there are a number of *competing* providers of an essential input – for example, between different mobile telephone networks (each of whom provides termination services to one another),

---

[75] In particular, it is typically assumed that: (1) consumers only subscribe to a single mobile network and the mobile network therefore has a monopoly on the setting of the termination rate charged; (2) receivers of calls do not care, or have little incentive to concern themselves, about the price charged by the mobile networks to the fixed network for call termination (i.e. they do not care about the utility of the callers); (3) the calling party pays (i.e. receivers on the mobile network do not pay the termination charge); and (4) there are differences in the prices paid for fixed line termination and mobile termination (i.e. prices are not reciprocal).

[76] This view informed the regulatory arrangements in a number of jurisdictions where, up until the early to mid-2000s, fixed and mobile services were viewed as complements rather than substitutes for one another.

[77] See Genakos and Valletti (2015).

or between a fixed line and cable network for local call telephone services. Two-way access issues can also arise where competing providers of data or information services need to establish terms on which they will share information with one another.[78] For example, competing unmanned traffic management services providers will need to share information about aircraft movements within a local network to ensure shared situational awareness of unmanned aircraft movements (see Chapter 15).

The main difference from the adjacent monopoly example described above is that, for adjacent monopolies, the number of subscribers to each network is determined exogenously (for example, by geography), while, in the settings where networks compete with one another, the number of subscribers to each network is determined *endogenously* through competition. Critically, in circumstances where firms compete for subscribers, there may be intense competition *for* subscribers to a network. However, once a subscriber is signed up to a network, the network firm effectively holds a monopoly position for access *to* that subscriber (assuming consumers cannot or do not multi-home).

This is known as the 'termination monopoly' problem and arises from the fact that in order to supply an end-to-end service to its subscribers, a network operator will typically need to acquire access from other networks (i.e. to allow calls originated on its network to be received on another network). In other words, even though a network operator has its own subscriber base, and may compete with other network firms to build up its subscriber base, in supplying an end-to-end service it typically must acquire access from other network firms, which gives those firms a monopoly in the supply of access services. For example, mobile telephone companies may compete intensively to get you to join their network, but once you are signed up to their network *all* calls that you receive will need to be terminated using their network, for which, in some jurisdictions, they will charge other networks a termination charge.[79] The network operator (such as a mobile phone company) now has to balance two profit streams: the profits they receive from subscribers on their network (including any fixed charges, and per unit prices for calls made), *and* the net profits they receive from levying termination access charges on other networks.[80]

The central policy question is whether these two-way access prices need to be regulated where there are competing network providers, and, if so, what form the regulation should take. As we shall see, the answer to this depends on assumptions about the state of competition in the market, and the types of instruments that a regulator has at its disposal (i.e. whether it has an ability to influence both access and retail prices).

---

[78] The general issues raised here also apply to access pricing for internet services, which also involves interconnection between an originating and terminating network. However, the nature of interconnection between internet providers raises additional issues. As Armstrong (2002) observes, in relation to internet interconnection, there are now two bottlenecks: the Internet Service Provider (ISP) network to which a consumer signs up has a monopoly over access to that consumer (as in the mobile case), but similarly the ISP network that signs up website providers has a monopoly on originating communication from that website.

[79] However, as discussed in Chapter 11 consumers can increasingly multi-home by using certain over-the-top services (such as Skype or WhatsApp calling) as a substitute for phone calls on the mobile network. They can also multi-home by subscribing to various networks or operate various SIM cards or mobile telephones.

[80] See Armstrong and Wright (2009).

Non-Cooperative Access Price Determination

One possibility is for competing network operators to set prices independently from each other, and free of regulatory intervention.[81] This is the situation of non-cooperative access pricing, and, as in the adjacent monopoly case described above, the principal regulatory concern here is that each firm will seek to set termination access prices at inefficiently high levels in order to exploit its monopoly position in termination access.[82] For the reasons given above, the non-cooperative setting of access in these circumstances is inefficient, and both consumers and the firms can be made better off if firms coordinate or cooperate in the negotiation of access prices.[83] However, the possibility of competitors coordinating on the setting of access prices immediately raises standard competition law (antitrust) concerns about collusion.

Cooperative Determination of Access Prices

Where access prices are determined cooperatively in a two-way setting, then, under specific assumed conditions, firms can have collective incentives to effectively 'raise each other's wholesale costs' by agreeing to set access prices above cost in order to facilitate (tacit) collusion at the retail level.[84] For example, for given market shares, a higher reciprocal access price might, under specific assumptions, induce each firm to set a higher retail price and therefore increase joint/industry profits (see Chapter 11). Critically, under these assumptions, even though each firm sets its *retail* price non-cooperatively, there may be little incentive for the firms to compete intensively in the retail market. This is because, although a firm may gain market share by undercutting its competitors in the retail market, this gain will likely involve it making greater net access payments to its rivals if its subscribers take advantage of the lower retail prices by increasing the number of calls they make to competing networks.[85]

However, this collusion result is sensitive to assumptions, and if these assumptions change, so does the likelihood that (tacit) collusion will arise in the retail market if firms cooperatively set access prices.[86] Three points are relevant here. Firstly, collusion of this type may not be sustainable if the services offered by the firms are close substitutes, and thus each network has an incentive to unilaterally lower retail prices in an attempt to

---

[81] In this analysis the firms engage in a two-stage process: first, access charges are set non-cooperatively, and then retail prices are chosen. See Laffont, Rey and Tirole (1998a).

[82] Specifically, if an originating network firm bears all of the costs, and call receivers are indifferent to the welfare of call originators (in terms of the costs they face for originating the call), then each terminating network has the incentive to raise its price above the costs without fear of reducing the number of calls it receives.

[83] Carter and Wright (1999) observe that, if coordination is prohibited under antitrust law, and access prices and retail prices are set non-cooperatively, this is 'the worst possible outcome for firms and consumers'.

[84] Specifically, the assumed conditions are that: the calling party pays; firms offer only linear tariffs (i.e. no two-part tariffs) and cannot price-discriminate among users (i.e. between on-network users and off-network users); demand and cost conditions are symmetrical; and the access charge is reciprocal between firms. Valletti and Cambini (2005) show how tacit collusion can also arise as a result of firms diminishing each other's incentives to invest.

[85] Perhaps on the basis of this analysis, Dessein (2003) observes: 'the idea that high access charges are an instrument of collusion has become widespread among policy makers'.

[86] See Armstrong (2002) and Laffont and Tirole (2000).

corner the market.[87] In contrast, if the services are sufficiently differentiated from one another, a decision by a firm to undercut its competitors' retail price by a small amount will not usually lead to significant switching, and therefore will not necessarily entail significant reduction in net access payments.[88] The key insight is that cooperation to set high access charges to facilitate (tacit) collusion at the retail level is only likely to arise, and be sustainable, where the firms' products are sufficiently differentiated from one another.

Secondly, collusion at the retail level may be unlikely where firms use non-linear prices, such as two-part tariffs that involve a monthly subscription charge and a per-minute calling charge.[90] Unlike the earlier case of linear pricing, where a firm could only build market share by reducing retail prices (which could result in an increase in the volume of calls per customer, and a net outflow of access termination payments),[91] a firm using two-part tariff can offer a low fixed subscription charge to build its market share without having to reduce its retail prices to attract customers, thus avoiding any additional termination payments associated with higher call volumes to rival networks.[92] Under certain assumptions,[93] the access charge may no longer be an instrument of collusion when two part tariffs are used because equilibrium profits become independent of the access charge. In other words, a high access charge will still increase the per call usage prices, leading to higher profits *from calls*, but because of intense competition for subscribers leading to lower fixed subscription charges, this positive effect on profits from calls is 'neutralised' by the lower fees and profits *from subscriptions*. This result is sometimes referred to as the 'profit-neutrality' result.[94] In these circumstances, given that profits are independent of the access charge, it is posited that firms might actually set access prices at the welfare-optimal level of marginal cost.[95]

A third situation under which coordination on access prices may not naturally give rise to high retail prices is where firms continue to use non-linear pricing but also engage in

---

[87] See Laffont, Rey and Tirole (1998a) and Armstrong (1998). Laffont and Tirole (2000) argue that the incentive to undercut at the retail level is likely to be greater where the access price is well in excess of marginal costs.

[88] In these circumstances, because a firm will have to undercut its competitors by a significant amount at the retail level to expand its subscriber base, the collusive retail price is said to be sustainable (i.e. there are no incentives for the firms to deviate).

[89] Carter and Wright (1999) explore the issue of how telephone services, which are typically considered to be homogeneous, are differentiated from one another. They note that one aspect of differentiation may be the complementary services provided by the network operator (such as cable TV as well as local calls) while other aspects might include different retail package bundles and credit and billing practices.

[90] However, Jeon and Hurkens (2008) observe that it is not uncommon in mobile telephone markets for linear prices to be used in terms of prepaid mobile cards and for customers to be offered a linear price contract with no subscription fee, but with a minimum per monthly charge.

[91] Hence, high retail prices are sustained, in part, by a collective reluctance by firms to reduce prices for fear of the increase in call volumes.

[92] It is assumed here that all firms offer the same call charges.

[93] In particular, if it is assumed that customers are homogeneous and there is a balanced calling pattern. See Laffont, Rey and Tirole (1998a) and Armstrong (2002). However, Dessein (2003) shows that collusion may also not arise in situations where customers are heterogeneous. Similarly, Hahn (2004) finds that the profit neutrality, no-collusion result holds even where consumers have different calling patterns (heavy users and light users), and where firms use non-linear tariffs.

[94] See Dessein (2003).

[95] See Dessein (2003). Armstrong and Sappington (2007) explain that '[c]onsequently, firms have no strict preference among access prices, and so are likely to be amenable to setting socially desirable prices for access'.

price discrimination: that is, distinguish between calls made to subscribers that terminate on their own network (on-net calls) and calls made to subscribers that terminate on
a competitor's network (off-net calls).[96] In these circumstances, where a reciprocal access
termination charge is set at a level above cost, off-net calls will be more expensive than
on-net calls (which incur only marginal costs) and, where networks price-discriminate,
this can be expected to lead to a higher retail price for off-net calls than on-net calls.[97]
Using data from the UK, Armstrong and Wright (2009) find this expected outcome borne
out: there was a striking difference in average call charges between on-net and off-net
call charges in 2001 and 2005 (with off-net calls being more expensive), and this led to
a call bias towards on-net calls.

Reciprocal Agreement and 'Bill and Keep'

An important implication of the discriminatory pricing structure just discussed is that it
can generate both positive and negative network externalities. A positive network externality arises whenever on-net prices are cheaper than off-net prices, as subscribers on
larger networks are able to make calls at cheaper prices, and this, in turn, makes larger
networks more attractive to subscribers. Conversely, a negative externality arises if off-
net prices are cheaper than on-net prices, then all else being equal, callers on smaller
networks pay cheaper prices (as they are likely to make more off-net calls), hence making
smaller networks more attractive.

Critically, where access charges are set by reciprocal agreement, firms have a choice
as to whether a positive or negative network effect will arise, and this choice can have
implications for the intensity of competition for subscribers.[98] Firms can use the reciprocal access charge to coordinate on whether to have positive network effects (access
price > marginal cost), no network effects (access price = marginal cost) or negative
network effects (access price < marginal cost). Armstrong (2002) finds that it will be
mutually profitable to choose the third option because of its softening effect on competition.[99] Consequently, the profit neutrality result discussed above – whereby profits are
unaffected by the access price – no longer applies, as firms can increase their profits by
agreeing to reciprocal access charges that are below cost. Gans and King (2001a) discuss the implications of this conclusion for regulatory policies such as 'bill and keep'
(where firms agree not to bill one another for interconnection), or other policies where

---

[96] See Laffont, Rey and Tirole (1998b). Vogelsang (2003) refers to the introduction of 'Friends and Family'
plans in the USA in the 1980s as an early example.

[97] Laffont and Tirole (2000) observe that price discrimination may not facilitate collusion as effectively
as the linear pricing example discussed above because firms are now able to potentially build market
share without incurring the associated increase in net termination payments to competitors, such as by
reducing its prices for on-net calls.

[98] If reciprocal access prices are set above the marginal cost of terminating a call, a positive network effect
arises, and firms will likely seek to build the size of their networks (and therefore reduce the number of
calls terminated on rival networks) by competing for subscribers. In contrast, if reciprocal access prices
are set below the marginal cost of termination, a negative network effect arises and firms will seek to
keep the size of their networks small (and therefore reduce incurring the higher costs associated with
terminating calls on its own network) and firms have little incentive to compete for subscribers.

[99] In other words, because there is a negative network effect, this reduces the incentives for intensive retail
competition.

access prices are set at zero or below cost. Their analysis suggests that, contrary to the conventional view of some regulators, setting access prices at zero or below cost may adversely impact consumers if it softens price competition and results in high subscription charges.[100] However, other studies have suggested that there are advantages of 'bill and keep' arrangements: specifically, that such an approach can create greater incentives for investments in quality prior to the competition stage,[101] can result in the more efficient utilisation of the network by sharing the value of a call between callers and receivers,[102] and can be welfare-improving compared to cost-based arrangements.[103]

Armstrong and Wright (2009) examine why, in practice, regulators have not been concerned about the possibility of access prices being set too low in the context of mobile telephony.[104] They explore each of the explanations presented above as to why firms might want high termination charges – namely to facilitate collusion, or to deter entry – but find the more convincing reason to be that firms want to preserve high *fixed-to-mobile* termination charges (in situations where fixed-to-mobile and mobile-to-mobile charges are uniform). Specifically, where firms determine a uniform termination charge for fixed-to-mobile and mobile-to-mobile independently (i.e. non-cooperatively), then the incentive to extract termination profits through above-cost access pricing dominates the incentive to soften network competition, with the net effect being that access prices are set above cost but at levels lower than the monopoly level. In their view, this tendency to set access prices between the efficient and monopoly levels reduces the welfare gains associated with regulating termination charges.

6.3.4 Efficient Two-Way Access Prices

So far we have focused on the various methods by which access prices might be determined (cooperative, non-cooperative, and bill and keep), and the incentives for collusion and competition that can arise in different settings. However, we have not focused on what is the efficient, or socially optimal, access price. In a simple model of two symmetric firms, where the total number of subscribers is fixed, and where the retail price is regulated at cost (or the market is perfectly competitive) and there are no joint and common costs, the optimal access charge is the marginal cost of termination. However, such assumptions are unrealistic, and determining the optimal access price in real-world settings will depend, among other things, on the extent of competition in the retail market, whether the regulator can set both access and retail prices, the magnitude of joint and common costs, and the degree to which the competing firms have symmetric costs.

Laffont and Tirole (2000) approach the issue of efficient two-way access prices by first looking at an assumed setting where there are no joint and common costs, where retail

---

[100] Gans and King (2001a).
[101] See Cambini and Valletti (2003).
[102] See DeGraba (2003).
[103] See Berger (2005). Hurkens and López (2021) compare the application of the 'bill and keep' approach (and receiving party pays) of the USA to cost-based termination charges (and calling party pays) in the EU, and find the most efficient approach depends on the strength of the call externality.
[104] Armstrong and Wright (2009).

prices are unregulated and only constrained by competition, and the networks enjoy some market power (allowing them to set retail prices above cost). They conclude that the optimal access price should be set *below* the marginal cost of terminating access.[105] The rationale for this *below* marginal cost access pricing is essentially the same as that explored in Chapter 4: that it will offset the retail mark-up. The situation is, however, less straightforward in the presence of joint and common costs because opposite effects arise in this setting, the net results of which are ambiguous. On the one hand, concerns about market power at the retail level (even in the presence of joint and common costs) might be so great as to imply that below marginal cost access pricing may still be optimal. On the other hand, the presence of joint and common costs may require a mark-up on marginal cost of access to allow for the full recovery of costs.

Armstrong (2002) approaches the issue of efficient two-way access pricing by examining the situation where a regulator has an ability to control all tariffs (including fixed subscription charges and retail tariffs). He argues that in situations where the total subscribers are fixed, and firms have the same termination costs (i.e. costs are symmetric), all prices should be set at marginal cost, including the fixed charge. However, where firms have different termination costs, it may be optimal for a regulator to set *retail* charges at marginal cost, but to allow fixed charges to deviate from cost in such a way as to attract subscribers to the network which has the lower termination cost.

An alternative approach to efficient access pricing is based on retail benchmarking, whereby the mark-up on the access termination charge that a network firm pays to a rival firm is linked to its own retail price mark-up.[106] It is argued that this approach provides a unique efficient access pricing rule where networks employ linear prices and, under certain conditions, will result in marginal cost pricing where firms use two-part tariffs. The linking of access prices to retail prices is said to intensify competition because a network can reduce its access payments through reducing its own retail tariff(s).

A range of other issues associated with two-way access pricing that we have not had an opportunity to address have implications for the efficient access price and the development of competition. These include: where competing networks are asymmetric (such as an incumbent against an entrant) in terms of both costs and coverage;[107] where termination charges are non-reciprocal;[108] and where the call receiver either receives a subsidy for receiving the call,[109] or the call receiving party's network is assumed to pay a charge to an originating network (receiving party network pays).[110] There is also the increasingly relevant policy issue of the extent to which other 'over-the-top' substitute services (such

---

[105] Laffont and Tirole (2000).

[106] Jeon and Hurkens (2008) present examples of where access prices have been linked to retail prices. They refer to the 'retail benchmarking approach' adopted in Australia in 2001 whereby the termination access price was required to be reduced at the same amount as the average retail price for the same operator.

[107] Laffont, Rey and Tirole (1998b) observe that, where networks are asymmetric, and an entrant does not have full coverage, then price discrimination can be used as a means by which the incumbent can foreclose entry by insisting on a high access charge which translates into high off-net prices for the entrant. This raises an additional anti-competitive concern. See also discussion of asymmetries in Carter and Wright (1999), Vogelsang (2003) and Hoernig (2014a).

[108] See Armstrong (2002).

[109] See Laffont and Tirole (2000).

[110] See Jeon, Laffont and Tirole (2004) and Laffont and Tirole (2000).

as Voice over Internet Protocol services) can allow consumers to multi-home and the remove the need for regulation of termination charges (see Chapter 11).[111]

6.3.5 Implications for Regulation of Two-Way Access Pricing

It is difficult to draw general conclusions about the regulation of two-way access pricing as the appropriate regulatory response depends on the assumed setting, and the conditions under which network competition takes place.

Nonetheless, the discussion in this section has highlighted a number of insights relevant to regulatory practice. A first insight is that both firms and consumers can in some circumstances be better off if firms are permitted to coordinate on the setting of access prices. For example, in situations of adjacent monopolies, where such monopolies do not compete with one another, coordination may in some settings naturally lead to an efficient outcome (marginal cost pricing). A second insight is that, where networks compete with one another for subscribers, coordination might lead to access prices being set at too high a level and facilitate (tacit) collusion in retail prices. This potential for collusion is, however, subject to a number of important assumptions, and once these are relaxed the result is far less robust. A third insight is that, in settings where firms are able to discriminate between on-net and off-net users, another concern (in theory, if not in practice) is that access prices will be set too low in an attempt to soften competition. Finally, in settings where networks are asymmetric, the potential arises for incumbent firms to use the access price as a method of foreclosing new entrants.

Chapter 11 discusses the different approaches to setting two-way access prices in the telecommunications industry, which includes capping rates based on estimates of cost such as the long-run incremental cost (EU, UK and Australia) and reciprocal arrangements based around a 'bill and keep' approach to setting termination charges (Singapore, Canada, Hong Kong and the USA).[112] We also discuss the evidence on whether reductions in wholesale access prices have led to *increases* in the level of retail prices to compensate for this loss in access revenue (the so-called 'waterbed effect').

6.4 ACCESS PRICING AND INVESTMENT

So far, we have focused on the efficiency properties of different approaches to one-way and two-way access pricing in a largely static context, and not considered how different access pricing approaches might impact on investment, and therefore competition over the longer term. However, it is clearly the case that the *expectations* of access providers and access users as to the level of future access prices can impact on the investment decisions they make now.

---

[111] Vogelsang (2019) notes that, if such substitute over-the-top services exist, then they have the potential to 'kill termination charges' provided they are also not subject to them.

[112] In the USA, termination charges are generally negotiated between mobile operators, although there are requirements that the charges are symmetric. This has led to 'bill and keep' style arrangements frequently being set for interconnection between mobile operators and new entrants. See Hurken and López (2021).

The anticipated regulatory approach to access pricing can influence both the extent and timing of investment.[113] This can create a dilemma for a regulator who must often make a trade-off between optimal access prices in a static sense, and those that are most appropriate in a dynamic context.[114]

6.4.1 The Timing of Infrastructure Investment

In unregulated environments, an access provider will typically only invest in infrastructure projects where an access user commits to a long-term access price that allows for the sharing of any risks associated with the project in both good and bad outcomes, or where access is granted for a shorter period but with a premium on the access price. However, if the investment occurs in a regulated setting (i.e. where the regulator sets prices), it is the *expectations* regarding the commitment of the regulator to various future access pricing policies which impact the timing of investment. In principle, if a regulator can commit *ex ante* to access prices that will apply once an investment is sunk, and which allow for recovery of investment costs, this might facilitate efficient investment in network infrastructure.[115] However, regulators rarely have absolute discretion over future access prices, and, once an investment is made, can be influenced by various legal, economic and political pressures to reduce access prices, all of which can reduce the credibility of any commitment to *ex ante* access prices.[116]

One approach to this commitment problem is for the regulator to commit *ex ante* to forbear from regulating access prices or to allow the firm to have a so-called 'regulatory holiday' or 'access holiday' (see Chapter 11). The access holiday approach involves an *ex ante* commitment by a regulator to an investor in new infrastructure that it will not be subject to access regulation for a specific period of time, and, during that time, the owners of the facility can exploit that investment as they choose, including by charging monopoly prices or by denying access to competitors.[117] The general logic for access holidays builds on the approach to risky innovative activity in patents, whereby, to encourage innovative activity, inventors are granted a temporary monopoly over any innovations.

Another method proposed to encourage timely investment is based on real option theory. Under this approach, the regulatory regime accounts for the option value effects that arise in uncertain environments (e.g. environments characterised by changes in demand, technology or other input prices) by recognising that, in investing early, a firm destroys

---

[113] Guthrie (2006) provides an excellent overview.

[114] Valletti (2003) captures the essence of this trade-off: 'Access regulation based on simple cost recovery rules, while encouraging efficient utilisation of assets, risks discouraging investments. If operators rationally anticipate that, once somebody has invested, the regulator will grant access at cost, everybody will then wait for the investment to be done by somebody else and then seek access.' Gans and King (2003a) refer to this as a 'truncation problem', whereby the risks of a project are asymmetrically shared between the investor and potential entrants.

[115] Gans and Williams (1999) examine the context of investment in non-rivalrous infrastructure.

[116] See Gans and King (2003a).

[117] See Gans and King (2004b). Gans and King (2003a) observe that the appropriate length of the 'holiday' will depend on the risk facing the project and the contestable nature of the project. As discussed in Chapter 11, variants of the approach have been adopted in Europe, Brazil and Turkey. See Ünver (2015).

its option for delaying investment until the uncertainties are resolved.[118] This approach suggests that the firm should be compensated for the opportunity cost associated with destroying the option for delay, in the form of a real option premium to the access price.[119] As discussed in Chapter 5, this type of approach of dealing with future uncertainty has also been considered in industries where demand is declining.[120]

6.4.2 Access Pricing Approaches and the Incentives for Investment

In relation to one-way access arrangements, there is considerable debate about how the different access pricing approaches – such as cost-based pricing or the ECPR – impact on incentives for investment. For example, as discussed in Chapter 11, the application of cost based access pricing in the telecommunications industry has been criticised for resulting in access prices that are too low, and which do not sufficiently compensate access providers for the asymmetric risks they face, which can discourage investment.[121] However, others argue that the margins provided under the ECPR or retail-minus approach provide little incentive for entrants to invest in assets and compete in some markets, as they will need to be 'super-efficient' in order to displace the incumbent provider.[122]

By-Pass and the 'Make-or-Buy' Decision

The forms of competition that exist in the different industries discussed in Part III of this book can be thought of as lying on a continuum. At one end of the continuum, there is so-called service-based competition, where an entrant essentially leases or 'buys' access from an access provider and does not make any investments of their own in physical network assets. Retail activities in many regulated industries are examples of service-based competition. Entrants in these activities seek to differentiate themselves from their competitors largely by the customer service they provide to end-user customers.

At the other end of the continuum, there is facilities-based or infrastructure competition, where an entrant builds and invests in its own network infrastructure and competes directly in end-to-end competition with an incumbent (it does not, in these circumstances, 'buy' access from the access provider). Infrastructure competition allows firms to differentiate themselves not only in terms of the customer service provided to end customers (as in service competition), but also in terms of the specification of the network and technology embodied in the infrastructure assets. An example of infrastructure competition is between cable and fixed line networks providing telecommunications and broadband services. Another example is competition between competing long-distance gas pipelines to serve a particular city.

---

[118] See Dixit and Pindyck (1994) and Dobbs (2004).

[119] See discussion in Guthrie (2006). Dobbs (2004) suggests that allowing for such option value effects in access prices may be quantifiably significant.

[120] See Guthrie (2020) on timing of infrastructure investment in such contexts.

[121] See Hausman (2000a) and Pindyck (2007). Mizuno and Yoshino (2015) describe how low access prices can generate a vicious cycle of under-investment. In contrast, Vogelsang (2014b) argues that the (TS) LRIC approach should, in its classic form, include investment costs. He also argues that the TSLRIC approach can make investment planning more predictable through its ability to deal with technological developments. Genakos and Valletti (2015) find no evidence that cost-based regulation of mobile termination prices has reduced the incentives to invest in mobile networks in the EU.

[122] See, for example, the discussion in the UK Competition Appeal Tribunal on this point: CAT (2006).

The decision of an entrant to engage in service-based competition *vis-à-vis* infrastructure-based competition depends, in part, on the level of the access price charged by an access provider. If the access price is prohibitively high, an entrant may decide to invest in its own infrastructure and 'by-pass' the incumbent's network altogether.[123] On the other hand, if the access price is considered to be low, entrants may have incentives to simply 'buy' access from the access provider rather than make significant investments in network infrastructure. This is sometimes referred to as the 'make-or-buy' effect of the level of access prices,[124] and raises a potential trade-off between the immediate short-run benefits of service competition, and the typically longer-term benefits of infrastructure competition in terms of innovation.[125]

Access Prices and the Incentives to Invest in New Infrastructure

The level and structure of access prices can also affect the incentives of different parties to invest in a new infrastructure network (e.g. a fibre-based next-generation access network in telecommunications, or a new high-speed rail network) and to migrate from an old (legacy) network to the new network.[126] Specifically, incentives will be affected by the differences in the proposed access charges/revenues for the two networks (legacy access charges versus new access charge) relative to their respective costs. Entrants sometimes argue that migration will best be achieved by setting a low access price for the legacy network, which reduces the operator's revenues from the legacy network, and removes any disincentive to cannibalise its own revenues by investing in a new network.[127] In contrast, incumbent providers sometimes argue that a low access price will have the opposite effect of encouraging entrants to stay on the legacy network.[128] Briglauer, Frübing and Vogelsang (2014) survey work on the interaction between access prices and investment, and find that, while these studies generally conclude that higher access charges for a legacy network can encourage investment *by an entrant* in next-generation telecoms networks, for the incumbent the effects of a lower/higher access price on the investment in a new network are ambiguous.[129] In addition, the incumbent's incentives to invest can be

---

[123] There are obviously a number of factors that affect this 'by-pass' ability, including any legal restrictions on by-pass of certain core network activities, as well as the resource constraints faced by the entrant.

[124] Sappington (2005b) challenges the widely held presumption in relation to this effect and argues that an input/access price may have limited impact on an entrant's make-or-buy decision.

[125] Bourreau and Doğan (2004, 2005) argue that service-based competition and infrastructure-based competition are substitute entrance strategies, and that an unregulated incumbent operator may have an incentive to set low access prices to delay the entry of a competitor with superior technology. For this reason, they argue that, if a regulator is concerned about encouraging infrastructure competition, setting a minimum access price (i.e. price floor) may be necessary. In Bourreau and Doğan (2006) they reject the idea that access prices should increase over time, or that 'sunset' clauses be applied to access prices, in order to induce facilities-based competition. Rather, they propose that the regulator should commit to banning unbundled access to the incumbent's facilities once facilities-based entry is feasible and socially desirable.

[126] Bourreau, Cambini and Doğan (2012), Brito, Pereira and Vareda (2012) and Inderst and Peitz (2014) focus on the telecommunications industry, while de Rus and Socorro (2014) examine the incentives to invest in a complementary or rival new infrastructure in the transport sector.

[127] See Hoernig, Jay, Neu, *et al.* (2011).

[128] See Williamson, Black and Wilby (2011).

[129] Bourreau, Cambini and Hoernig (2018) find that low access prices can reduce the incentives for an incumbent and an entrant to 'co-invest', and can reduce welfare. They also conclude that a policy of 'pure' co-investment leads to higher investment and more competition than a regulated access pricing based on the ECPR. Separately, Bourreau, Grzybowski and Hasbi (2019) find that the greater the number of competitors in a local (legacy) network, the lower the incentives to invest in a high-speed network.

reduced if the new network is subject to access regulation, suggesting that, if a regulator wishes to promote investment in new networks, it should adopt less stringent policies for both legacy and new networks.[130]

6.4.3 Dynamic Access Pricing and the 'Ladder of Investment'

The central trade-off, then, is between ensuring that the level of the access price encourages entry into the sector, but is not so low as to preclude cost recovery for the access provider or to discourage entrants from investing in their own infrastructure when it is appropriate to do so. One proposed approach to this trade-off is to employ 'dynamic' access pricing whereby access prices for all network services are initially set at low levels but rise over time according to the degree of replicability of the assets.[131] The approach is based on the idea that it takes time for entrants to develop their competing asset base, to build a reputation and customer loyalty, and otherwise to progressively establish themselves in business.[132] Accordingly, access prices should adjust over time to encourage entrants to move away from pure service-based competition towards higher levels of investment in infrastructure.[133]

This general approach to network investment and access pricing is sometimes referred to as the 'stepping stone' or 'ladder of investment' approach,[134] and has at times been influential in terms of the policy of telecommunications regulators in a number of jurisdictions.[135] One criticism of the approach is a familiar one: that it is heavily dependent on the ability of a regulator to credibly commit to policies which increase access prices over time for certain products.[136] More relevant is whether such policies have, in practice, achieved the anticipated migration from service-based competition to facilities-based or infrastructure competition, an issue we return to in Chapter 11.[137]

---

[130] Briglauer, Cambini and Grajek (2018). This can also level the playing field with other competing networks such as cable networks in the case of telecoms, which do not face such access restrictions.

[131] See Cave and Vogelsang (2003) and Cave (2006a).

[132] This is consistent with the view of Cave and Vogelsang (2003) that it is wrong to expect entrants to emerge as full infrastructure-based competitors, and that, in this context, a policy of high access prices 'may kill the entrant's business model stone dead'. Bourreau and Drouard (2014) focus on how an entrant's progressive accumulation of market experience affects its incentives to invest.

[133] Tardiff and Weisman (2018) argue that wholesale (access) price deregulation could result in temporarily higher retail prices which stimulate investment and thus hasten the 'stepping stone' process.

[134] See Woroch (2002) and Cave (2006a, 2010, 2014). Avenali, Matteucci and Reverberi (2010) present a formal model of the ladder paradigm.

[135] See ERG (2005, 2006) and Hausman and Sidak (2005). However, Vogelsang (2019) records that it is no longer explicitly mentioned in EU policy, while Bouckaert, van Dijk and Verboven (2010) argue that the ladder of investment or stepping stone hypothesis may not provide good guidance for regulatory policy. Serdarević, Hunt, Ovington and Kenny (2016) argue that the applicability of the theory depends on key assumptions about the quality and availability of copper networks, and the cost and risk of investing in alternative infrastructure.

[136] Avenali, Matteucci and Reverberi (2010) refer in passing to examples from the Netherlands and Canada where the regulator has been unable to make such commitments. Hausman and Sidak (2005) attribute the failure of the stepping stone hypothesis, in part, to the failure of regulators to develop transition plans (such as allowing access prices to rise over time), as well as the fact that some of the firms which entered were 'fly by night' firms who were not interested in developing long-term networks.

[137] Cave (2014) finds that bitstream access led to a greater number of local loops. However, Bacache, Bourreau and Gaudin (2014) and Beard, Macher and Vickers (2016) find no support for the next stage of the 'ladder' from local loop unbundling services to investments in new access infrastructures and facilities-based competition. Similarly, Briglauer (2014) finds that wholesale broadband regulation negatively affected investment in next-generation access networks in telecoms.

6.5 VERTICAL INTEGRATION AND SEPARATION

The discussion of access pricing approaches above has highlighted some of the difficult trade-offs that can arise in circumstances where a vertically integrated firm is both an access provider of a core network service (providing access to the pipes, cables, wires and rails) and is also active, and typically has a strong market position, in another complementary competitive market (such as upstream supply or retail activities).[138] The significance of these challenges when setting access prices for vertically integrated firms in some settings has led some to suggest that some form of vertical separation is the only solution.[139] Debates about the relative merits of vertical integration or vertical separation have been fundamental to restructuring policies in certain regulated industries (transport, energy, telecoms), and, as discussed in Chapters 12 and 13, are also relevant to sectors such as payment systems and digital platforms.

6.5.1 The Benefits and Costs of Vertical Integration and Separation

The Potential Benefits of Vertical Integration

While the benefits of vertical integration are dependent on the specific characteristics of the industry, a number of general considerations are relevant to any assessment. First and foremost are considerations relating to the extent of any economies of *scope*. If economies of scope are present, then it will be more productively efficient (i.e. result in lower overall costs) to combine the different activities within a single firm than to have them produced separately by different firms.[140]

A second consideration is whether integration enhances the coordination of investment and operational decisions. In principle, vertically integrated firms can employ a single or integrated decision-making process in relation to its activities at different stages of the production chain, which can be important given the typically interdependent nature of the activities in most regulated industries.[141] Where activities are separated, the

---

[138] For example, as discussed, where an access provider is vertically integrated, it can give rise to a need to compensate it for the opportunity costs that arise when an entrant, rather than that firm, sells the final service.

[139] Laffont and Tirole (1994) make the interesting observation that, in the USA, the historical position of the Department of Justice was that it was impossible to define access rules to the network in telecommunications that would create fair competition in the markets that have been opened to competition.

[140] Armstrong, Cowan and Vickers (1994) observe that, while a link between economies of scope and productive efficiency provides a 'technological answer' to the question of when vertical integration may be more efficient than separation, it does not assist with the more fundamental question of why such economies of scope exist in different organisational forms. Similarly, Baumol, Panzar and Willig (1982) argue that it is important to address the question of *why* such economies of scope may exist in a multi-product firm and note that: 'the traditional view that there are advantages in specialization goes back at least 200 years to Adam's Smith discussion of the division of labour.' More broadly, Pollitt and Steer (2012) note that, in some cases, drawing a precise distinction between those economies which derive from the *scope* of a firm's activities from those which derive from the *scale* of a firm's activities can be challenging. Any observed cost minimisation associated with the joint production of two or more services in a vertically integrated firm could therefore derive from the joint production process or, partially, from cost savings associated with the increased size of the firm.

[141] Newbery (1999) observes in the context of electricity markets that 'efficient service delivery requires an efficient network, and investments in one may reduce the costs of the other'. Similarly, Gómez-Ibáñez (2003) notes that in rail: 'A train operating company cannot offer reliable, high speed passenger service, for example, unless the rail infrastructure company maintains the tracks to a high standard and makes them available when scheduled.' Meyer (2012a, b) provides estimates of the costs of separation (associated with coordination and synergy losses) for the US electricity industry.

coordination of investment and operational decisions is less supported by the structural arrangements and must occur largely through contractual arrangements.[142] In this case although contracting parties may have a common interest in the success of a service they may have conflicting interests regarding who should bear what costs and risks.[143] Related to these points, some argue that the incentives for investments may be stronger under vertical integration in some circumstances.[144] This is because a vertically integrated firm can internalise some of the risks of investments in specific production assets where it also operates in the final supply of the product. Put simply, because it is involved in both production and supply activities, it can generate better predictions about demand and can allow the firm to factor in the expected returns in the supply market to assist in the financing of any infrastructure investment. Risky investments can also potentially be subsidised by the expected returns on other activities under the vertically integrated structure.

Integration can also avoid the 'hold-up' problem that can arise when one firm makes an irreversible relationship-specific investment in an asset that is tailored to the needs of specific user(s), in terms of either function, siting, or to meet an expected level of future demand.[145] Under a non-integrated structure, the concern is that, after one party makes the investment, the other party will behave opportunistically, for example, by renegotiating terms of a contract in the awareness that there are limited alternative uses of that asset.[146] To the extent to which firms feel vulnerable to such *ex post* opportunism, investment may be deterred.[147]

In principle, the benefits of vertical integration could, to varying degrees, be reproduced through the use of contracts, particularly long-term contracts. The question is the extent to which markets can replicate the coordination outcomes of integration. Two factors are relevant here. Firstly, there are the transaction and governance costs associated

---

[142] Howell, Meade and O'Connor (2010) argue that separation in the electricity sector leads to 'mismatches in investment horizons, entry barriers, and risk preference and information asymmetries between generators and retailers leads to thin contract markets, increased hold-up risk, perverse wholesale risk management incentives, and bankruptcies'.

[143] See Gómez-Ibáñez (2003). This is consistent with Williamson's (1971) observation that: 'The advantages of integration thus are not that technological (flow process) economies are unavailable to non-integrated firms, but that integration harmonises interests (or reconciles differences, often by fiat).'

[144] Grossman and Hart (1986) conclude that integration will be optimal when one firm's investment decision is particularly important relative to the other firm's, and separation is desirable whenever investment decisions are only 'somewhat important'. Brown and Sappington (2022a) find that vertical integration in the electricity industry increases industry capacity investment.

[145] See generally Klein, Crawford and Alchian (1978).

[146] Williamson (1983) discusses the 'hostage' problem generally, while Joskow (1985, 1987, 1988) discusses it in the context of the electricity industry. Vogelsang (2021) notes that a classic example of a relation-specific investment is that of coal mines and power plants in areas such as the Appalachian Mountains in the eastern USA. He notes that although, 'ex ante, there are potentially many sites for coal mines and power plants so that there is potential choice and potential competition on both sides. However, after a choice of site has been made, contracts for up to forty to forty-five years have been signed, and investments have been sunk, the situation becomes one of bilateral monopoly.'

[147] The hold-up problem can be mitigated where there are a number of potential users of the assets (which reduces the vulnerability of those making the investment to a specific customer), or if a firm has some assurance from a regulator that it will be able to recover its costs associated with the investment. Klein (2007) presents an interesting non-public utility industry case study of the interaction between the hold-up problem and vertical integration relating to the Fisher Body–General Motors case.

with contracting. In principle, higher levels of transactions costs, and more elaborate governance arrangements, may arise with contracting than when agreements are internalised through integration, particularly where the circumstances are apt to change, requiring regular renegotiation of terms.[148] Secondly, there is a question about the extent to which different types of contractual arrangements – spot contracts, forward markets, long-term contracts – designed to hedge risks have sufficiently developed as a mechanism for spreading risk among different parties.[149] A concern is sometimes expressed that, if long-term contracts which spread risk do not emerge, this will encourage a more short-term perspective on investments, which may lead to a bias in investment decisions (for example, against high capital cost investments).

The Potential Benefits of Vertical Separation

The principal argument in support of vertical separation in certain industries where access problems can arise relates to the positive effect it can have on the development of competition in related markets.[150] In essence, separation removes the incentive and ability that a vertically integrated firm can have to use its market position in supplying a core or indispensable network service to discriminate in favour of its associated business in a competitive activity, either through the prices it charges for access to the core network activity, or through other non-price behaviour (such as reducing quality).

A vertically integrated firm may, for example, seek to exaggerate the level of costs of supplying the core network service, which may increase the price for the core network input, leading to higher operating costs for its rivals in the competitive activity.[151] The vertically integrated firm may also engage in various anti-competitive practices such as a refusal to supply, a price/margin squeeze, or other measures which leverage its market position in the core network activity that are designed to 'raise rivals' costs', or otherwise foreclose the entry and sustainability of rivals in the competitive activity.[152] Where the vertically integrated firm's access prices are regulated at cost, it may have an incentive to engage in various forms of non-price discrimination known as 'sabotage'; particularly, degrading the quality of the input supplied to rivals in the competitive activity.[153] A vertically integrated firm can also use information that it obtains about rivals' business

---

[148] However, this assumption of higher transactions costs does not automatically hold, and internal management and administrative coordination costs may in some cases be greater under integration than separation. See Teece (1980).

[149] As discussed in Chapter 9, in the electricity industry, hybrid institutions and mechanisms for the coordination of market participants have emerged, such as system or market operators and trading pools, which are in effect a formalised spot market for the trading of bulk electricity.

[150] For example, the OECD (2016a) has consistently argued that 'structural separation remains a relevant remedy to advance the process of market liberalization' in regulated industries.

[151] Gilbert (2021) discusses examples from digital platforms (e.g. excessive fees for being listed on an Apple App store).

[152] See Sibley and Weisman (1998) and Weisman (2014). More generally on these issues, see Salop and Scheffman (1983), Hart and Tirole (1990) and Riordan (1998). In digital platforms there have been investigations that Google has biased its search results to promote its proprietary shopping services, while there have also been claims that some platforms seek to raise rivals' costs by charging higher commission fees.

[153] Economides (1998), Beard, Kaserman and Mayo (2001), Sappington (2005a) and Weisman (2014) discuss some of the methods that regulators can use to dissuade such efforts at sabotage or non-price exclusion.

activities or plans to its own advantage.[154] Critically, even if a vertically integrated firm does not actually engage in such price and non-price discrimination practices, the *expectation* that the firm may engage in such behaviour can itself act to deter entry, and the development of competition, in related activities.[155] In contrast, in a separated industry structure, the owner of the core network activity no longer has an incentive to disadvantage firms that operate in related activities (who are, after all, its customers). It is for this reason that some countries have pursued a policy of mandated separation, albeit in different forms (see discussion below), of the core network activity from competitive activities.

Additional benefits are sometimes advanced in support of vertical separation. One perceived potential benefit is that it can allow for a simplified, and cheaper, regulatory structure, as there is no longer the need to monitor the conduct of the vertically integrated firm so closely.[156] It is also sometimes argued that separating the tasks among specialist firms can result in lower costs for the firms themselves, as the coordination and management of a wide range of activities can be complex, and therefore costly. A further perceived benefit of separation is that it may create stronger incentives for new firms to enter the market, who adopt new approaches and techniques. The gains from such new approaches may be particularly important if the internal management and administrative procedures of the vertically integrated firm (which in many public utility industries are often formerly state-owned and -operated incumbents) are inefficiently bureaucratic. A related benefit concerns the potential for innovation under separation. For similar reasons to those discussed above, separation may encourage entrants to adopt beneficial new technologies. Finally, separation may promote the development of new forms of contracting arrangements, with different, and more effective, ways of sharing risks among parties involved at different stages in the production chain.

Each of the potential benefits of separation can, however, be subject to qualification. For example, any reduction in regulatory or administrative costs associated with separation needs to be balanced against the costs associated with industry restructuring (which can be significant), and the costs associated with the design, and monitoring, of contracts between the separate entities.[157] In addition, separation may reduce, rather than increase, the incentives for innovation if the access provider no longer has direct access to final customers and can no longer capture the full value of any innovations it introduces.[158] At a practical level, identifying the 'boundary' between different vertical production activities can be challenging, particularly as such boundaries can change over time (e.g. in

---

[154] As discussed in Chapter 13, there have been claims that some dominant digital platforms have misused information and data they obtain from rivals which use their platform to develop or 'imitate' rival products (e.g. in Europe there were claims that Amazon was using data obtained from its Amazon Marketplace to imitate new products).

[155] Gómez-Ibáñez (2003) notes that '[t]he fact that the monopolists are also in their customers' line of business makes the customers feel much more vulnerable'.

[156] Newbery (1999) observes: 'The evidence from a wider variety of examples suggests that it requires aggressive regulation to prevent abusive entry deterrence by vertically integrated incumbents.'

[157] Gómez-Ibáñez (2003) observes that separation may actually increase the complexity of the regulator's task as 'the regulator must now supervise complex relationships between the monopolistic and competitive segments of the industry, and these relationships are critical to the ultimate quality and cost of service for consumers'. See also Besanko and Cui (2019).

[158] See Sappington (2005a).

response to developments in information technology). For example, some argue that it can be difficult to introduce durable boundaries for telecommunications and digital platforms without interfering with competition and innovation.[159] There are also the familiar concerns about double marginalisation which can arise in a vertical structure where there are two bilateral monopolies, such as an upstream monopoly owner of infrastructure and a downstream monopoly that provides end-user services.[160] Finally, the experience of some past policies of vertical separation – in the Australian and British electricity and US telecoms industries, for example – suggests that, over time, the industry has converged back towards partial or full re-integration.[161]

Drawing all these points together, the only conclusion that can safely be made is that the costs and benefits of vertical integration and separation are highly context-specific and depend, among other things, on the production characteristics of the industry, as well as its governance and other organisational arrangements. In some vertically integrated industries, there is an important trade-off between the losses in coordination associated with separation and the potential benefits of competition that separation may yield. This conclusion is consistent with surveys of the effects of vertical integration more generally across the economy.[162]

The need to design an approach to access pricing is, however, common to both separated and integrated settings but, as discussed, the approach can differ between the two industry structures. In the vertically integrated context, care needs to be exercised to ensure that the access pricing mechanism does not become a means for allowing the integrated firm to exploit its market power in the core network activity through discriminating against rivals in the competitive activity.[163] In the separation context, the general approach to access pricing needs to facilitate some of the benefits associated with coordination, for example, in terms of methods of risk sharing, and the timing and nature of commitments made by access providers and access users.

6.5.3 Forms of Vertical Separation

While the above discussion has made a binary distinction between vertical integration and separation, in practice, separation can take various forms. These include accounting separation, structural/business separation, legal separation and ownership separation. The

---

[159] See Gilbert (2021).

[160] See generally Spengler (1950). As Pittman (2020b) notes: ' Two monopolies, vertically connected, is worse than one vertically integrated monopoly, worse for everyone.'

[161] Brown and Sappington (2022a) provide a theoretical justification for such re-integration and find that vertical integration often reduces retail prices and increases consumer surplus and total welfare.

[162] Joskow (2008c) notes that the overwhelming conclusion of empirical studies on vertical integration is that the specific nature of the investments and other attributes which affect transaction costs are statistically and economically important in the decision to integrate or remain separate. The OECD (2016a) notes that 'the case for structural separation is not an unequivocal or unyielding one' and that 'particular weight needs to be placed on a comprehensive and nuanced balancing exercise of potential advantages and disadvantages of separation'. See also Lafontaine and Slade (2007).

[163] Armstrong and Sappington (2006) identify some inappropriate aspects of access policies in this context, such as where: the access policy is vague and incomplete, affording the vertically integrated firm substantial latitude; there is a failure to establish a timely and functional dispute resolution process; and the access policy is unduly generous to entrants, for example, by establishing access prices below the cost of supply to subsidise entry.

appropriateness of the different forms of separation depends on the strength of the incentive and the ability of the integrated firm to discriminate against rivals. However, even when such incentives are assessed as strong, the benefits associated with separation, in terms of reduced incentives to discriminate against competitors, needs to be balanced against any potential costs associated with the loss of scope efficiencies and increased transactions costs.

Accounting Separation

The least intrusive form of separation involves accounting separation, under which a vertically integrated network firm is required to develop, and submit to the regulator separate accounts for the different activities it undertakes (such as the core network activity and other potentially competitive activities). As the regulator has information about the level of costs of different activities, it can identify whether costs are being allocated shifted between the core network activity and other potentially competitive activities (i.e. it can identify instances of cost padding). Accounting separation can also assist the regulator and (if made public) other parties to identify instances of discriminatory pricing behaviour by the vertically integrated firm, such as a price or margin squeeze.[164]

While accounting separation can assist a regulator to detect certain behaviour, this form of separation does not, of itself, reduce the incentive or ability of a vertically integrated firm to engage in actions that might impede the position of its rivals in related markets.[165] For these reasons, some form of commercial or business separation of the vertically integrated firm may be warranted.

Business Separation

Business separation can take various forms in practice, including operational and functional separation, but the basic idea is that separate business units – which are to different degrees distinct from one another – undertake the different activities of the firm (sometimes referred to as operating with 'Chinese walls'). At a minimum, this involves the creation of a separate core network business division within the vertically integrated firm, which, to different degrees, is separated from the firm's retail activities.[166] The purpose of business separation is to foster equivalence and non-discrimination, meaning that the core network business division should become indifferent in its treatment of internal customers (i.e. the vertically integrated retail division) and external customers.[167] Business

---

[164] See Cave (2006b). However, there is a need for caution in using the information produced as a result of accounting separation as part of any assessment of discriminatory pricing, especially as the information is based on accounting concepts and may not reflect economic considerations (such as how common costs are allocated across different products/services).

[165] Examples of other potential non-pricing-related measures include: placing different restrictions on the terms of access; delaying the processing of orders of rivals; not providing sufficient information regarding a product; or giving preferential treatment of access or quality to the internal division of the vertically integrated firm. In Australia there was a case of 'exchange capping' – where the dominant telecoms incumbent was prosecuted and fined for claiming that it had no room in its exchanges to accommodate entrants.

[166] Cave (2006b) describes the different forms that business separation can take. Different forms of operational separation have at times been introduced in the telecoms sector in the UK, Australia and New Zealand. In addition, business separation was introduced in the Scottish water industry in 2005.

[167] There are two aspects to equivalence in practice: equivalence of inputs (EoI) – Are the inputs used by the regulated firm the same as the inputs used to provide services to the access seeker? – and equivalence of prices (EoP) – Is the price charged to the access user the same as the (imputed) price it charges its own integrated division?

separation can be achieved in various ways, such as: restricting the flow of information between business divisions; having a separate management team for different divisions; or the appointment of an independent board to ensure that external customers are treated equivalently to internal customers. While business separation can affect the ability of an integrated firm to discriminate against rivals, it does not remove the incentive to discriminate. There are also often concerns about the extent to which such 'separation' is effective in practice (i.e. how well the 'Chinese walls' work).

Legal and Ownership Separation

In some circumstances, even business or operational separation may be insufficient to allay concerns that the integrated firm will discriminate against rivals, and two further forms of separation may be considered: legal separation or ownership separation. Under legal separation, the different divisions of the business become separate legal entities with their own boards. However, both entities remain part of the same corporate group and under common ownership,[168] which may raise residual concerns about the wider incentives of the group.[169]

In contrast, full ownership separation involves the integrated firm being broken up, with the result being that separate, unrelated corporate entities undertake the core network activity and the other activities in the production chain (such as upstream production or downstream retail activities). While full ownership separation removes both the ability and incentive to discriminate, it is a major policy intervention which can involve substantial restructuring costs and a potential loss of synergies between different related business activities.

Mandatory and Voluntary Separation

Vertical separation can be introduced voluntarily or by mandate. As discussed in Chapter 11, in the USA, the 1984 break-up of AT&T into a long-distance carrier and seven regional local call providers (Regional Bell Operating Companies) followed a judicial settlement.[170] In Britain, the separation of ownership of certain activities in the electricity and rail industries was mandated at the time of privatisation, but ownership separation (in the gas industry) and business and legal separation (in the telecommunications sector) was undertaken voluntarily by the firms, albeit under considerable pressure from the relevant regulatory authorities.

6.6 HORIZONTAL INTEGRATION AND SEPARATION

While, in principle, there can be efficiency benefits associated with horizontal integration of different substitutable services and activities in terms of economies of scale, scope and network effects, there are several concerns about the potential adverse effects of

---

[168] This is the current situation for telecommunications in the UK.

[169] For example, staff may operate under performance incentive schemes related to the overall performance of the group.

[170] Modified Final Judgment approved by the USA courts in *United States v. AT&T* (1982). This action followed a long history, dating back to 1969, in which AT&T refused to provide local interconnection to long-distance carriers (such as MCI), or placed considerable restrictions on the terms of interconnection.

horizontal integration which are well understood in competition and regulatory econom ics. For this reason, most jurisdictions restrict the ability of rival suppliers of substitu products to enter into horizontal agreements that establish the price and non-price term of supply of those services (i.e. to coordinate or collude). Similarly, when two supplie of substitute services seek to merge with one another, and one or both the suppliers hav market power, then this is typically subject to close scrutiny by competition authoriti because of the potential adverse impacts it can have on competition.

In addition to these policies, which apply across the economy, additional regulato policy measures have sometimes been introduced to address concerns about the hor zontal integration of the industries discussed in Part III of this book. For example, con cerns relating to horizontal integration have arisen about: the common ownership of ga storage facilities; the cross-ownership of large-scale electricity storage facilities by loc distribution utilities; the integration of telecommunications and cable network operator the common ownership of airports in certain areas (e.g. London) or railways (such as Japan); the cross-ownership of payment system infrastructure; and the ability of domin ant digital platforms that operate across several product and service markets to cross-lev erage their position to block entry by more focused or emerging rivals.

6.6.1 Use of Behavioural Obligations

One set of policy alternatives to mitigate the risk of horizontal integration having adver effects on competition involves the imposition of certain 'behavioural' obligations requirements on the horizontally integrated firm. The aim of behavioural obligations is mitigate the ability and incentive of the horizontally integrated firm to take advantage its position in the supply of the substitute services.

Behavioural policies could involve legal commitments on the part of the horizontall integrated entity not to share sensitive operational or financial information across busi ness units, or to ensure the operational autonomy of decision-making bodies and to lim the access that key staff have to certain information. These commitments could be subje to ongoing monitoring by an external body. Behavioural policies might also involve th horizontally integrated entity committing to certain service standards or targets regard ing service quality and network expansion. A principal advantage of such behavioura policy interventions is that they can be tailored to the specific risks/problems identifie and involve minimal restructuring costs. The principal disadvantage of such policies that they can involve high levels of ongoing reporting and monitoring costs, and may b insufficient to change the incentives of the horizontally integrated operator.

6.6.2 Forms of Horizontal Separation

Alternatively, various forms of horizontal separation could be introduced. On approach is to pursue horizontal accounting separation. This can allow the horizon tally integrated operator to continue supplying the substitutable services, but requi that it prepare and submit to the regulator separate accounts detailing the costs asso ciated with supplying each potentially substitutable service (to assist in identifyin areas of cross-subsidy).[171] Another option is to introduce 'line of business' separatio

or 'ring-fencing' policies which again permit the horizontal operator to continue supplying the substitutable services subject to the condition that it establishes legally
separate business and operating units to supply the different services.[172]

A final alternative to mitigate the risk of horizontal integration having adverse effects
on competition involves full horizontal separation. Ownership separation or divestment
requires a horizontally integrated operator to divest of their ownership in the supply of
one or more of the substitutable services.[173] This approach completely removes the incentive and ability of the integrated operator to charge higher prices, or limit its expansion
of services, to maximise profits across the wider business group.[174]

6.7 REGULATION OF MULTI-SIDED MARKETS

Thus far we have focused on how regulation is applied in competitive market settings
either where there is a single access provider of a core or indispensable service that firms
operating in a related market need to access to compete (one-way access), or where there
are multiple competing providers of an access service who need to interconnect with one
another to provide an end-to-end service (two-way access).

Another area where regulation is sometimes applied involves so-called 'two-sided' or
'multi-sided' markets. Examples of multi-sided markets discussed in later chapters include
payment systems, digital platforms, airports and, potentially, in the future, energy markets (such as peer-to-peer energy platforms). In simple terms, a multi-sided market is one
where there is an *interdependence* between different types of user groups and network
effects. User groups are considered *interdependent* in multi-sided markets because the
demand for a service by one user group is conditioned by the demand for the use of the
service by other user groups. For example, the more consumers that use a particular credit
card, the greater the demand will be for merchants to accept that card. Similarly, the
more users of a particular search engine, the greater the demand will be for advertisers to
promote services on that search engine. Multi-sided markets thus give rise to important
network effects which, as discussed in Chapter 2, means that the value of a service to a
user depends on the number of other users that are connected to, or utilise, that service.[175]

A 'two-sided' or 'multi-sided' market provider (what we will refer to as a platform operator) effectively acts as an intermediary between different groups of users (e.g. different

---

[171] EC Directives have in the past required the accounting separation of letter mail postal activities from
other postal services provided in competitive markets (e.g. express mail).

[172] The EC Cable Directive imposed a requirement that telecommunications services and cable television
networks be legally separated. Under relevant EU Gas Directives, in order to ensure the independence
of storage systems, it is required that storage facilities are operated through legally separate entities.
Line of business separation rules are currently being considered in the USA in relation to some digital
platforms that provide services across several product and service markets.

[173] Chapter 14 provides examples of the horizontal separation in railways in Japan and Latin America.
Brown, Eckert and Shaffer (2023) examine the effects of the (virtual) divestiture of generation assets in
Alberta and conclude that 'structural remedies in the form of asset divestitures can serve an important
role in reducing short-run market power in concentrated electricity markets, but that the allocation of
these assets is critically important'.

[174] In the UK electricity sector, generators were split into three companies at the time of restructuring to promote
competition between generators, while more recently British Airports Authority was required to divest of two
London airports to promote competition between airports. In the USA and elsewhere, passenger and freight
railroad operations have been horizontally separated to ensure that activities are not cross-subsidised.

[175] As discussed in Chapter 2, network effects can be direct or indirect, and can be positive or negative.

sides of the market). The main task of platform operators is to match or connect users on 'one side of the market' with users on 'the other side of the market' (e.g. a credit card operator connects card users with merchants). They provide value to users by reducing information and transaction costs and resolving frictions, thus internalising network externalities. Multi-sided markets therefore differ from what are sometimes referred to as 'single-sided' markets where there is no direct interaction between user groups, and the customer relationship is entirely controlled by the single-sided provider.

It follows that multi-sided market platform providers need to incentivise different user groups to join and stay on their platform. In practical terms, this means that they need to think carefully about how they *structure* the prices they set for the different sides of the market: which sides of the market (user groups) should it levy charges on, and how much should each side (user group) contribute to its costs. When setting prices, a platform operator must therefore think about not only how the price it sets for one set of users will affect the demand for that user group, but also how any changes in resultant demand will affect the attractiveness of the platform to other user groups.[176] For example, if a hotel booking digital platform levies a high commission rate on customers who book a hotel on that platform, this will, other things being equal, reduce the demand by customers to use that platform, which in turn will make it a less attractive platform for hotels to list their accommodation. In other words, when setting prices for different user groups, platform operators must take account of the *interdependence* of the demands between user groups and consider the price elasticity of demand of these different groups.[177]

In setting a price structure, platform operators also need to take account of the cost of serving different user groups and whether the costs of one user group should be subsidised by another user group. In some circumstances, a platform operator might adopt a 'tilted' pricing structure which involves charging a negligible or zero price to one group of users (below the costs of serving them) and recover all of its revenues from another set of users.[178] Some platform operators may even choose to reward one group of users through loyalty points or other benefits and to subsidise the costs of such rewards by levying above-cost charges on another group of users. While it may seem irrational to charge one set of users a price *below* the costs they impose on the platform operator, it may be a socially optimal strategy if it achieves the right balance of different types of user groups on the platform.[179] Critically, this means that, given the existence of network effects, it is not socially optimal for the prices set to both sides of the market to reflect marginal cost. Rather, it is generally more efficient to use prices to subsidise the user group that will generate the strongest (positive) indirect network effect on the other side of the market. An implication of this point is that regulations that either (i) require price

---

[176] Belleflamme and Peitz (2021) discuss two strategies: a 'divide-and-conquer strategy' which involves subsidising the user group that exerts the stronger network effects; or to first attract those users that have the highest ratio between the positive network effects they generate for other users, and the cost that needs to be incurred to attract them. This often involve attracting so-called marquee users, which are users that will allow a platform to attract relatively more users from the other side.

[177] Rochet and Tirole (2003).

[178] Evans and Schmalensee (2016) refer to this as a 'subsidy' side and a 'money' side.

[179] Wright (2004) describes how it may also be an efficient price structure because it takes account of the surplus that one side creates for another user.

to be set at marginal cost, (ii) only permit charges on one side of the market or (iii) require that both sides of the market face the same price can be detrimental to the welfare of one group of participants, and in some cases reduce overall welfare.[180]

There is an extensive and growing literature on 'two-sided' and 'multi-sided' markets and the circumstances in which regulation is required, the key insights of which are discussed in detail in Chapters 12 (payment systems) and 13 (digital platforms).[181] The origins of much of this work are analyses of the need for the regulation of credit card interchange fees – a wholesale charge paid by one side of the market (the acquirer/merchant side) to another side of the market (the card issuer/cardholder side) each time a card is used for a transaction.[182] As discussed in Chapter 12, among other things, theoretical work has examined the conditions under which the interchange fee could be 'neutral', meaning that the impacts of the interchange fee on different user groups (e.g. cardholders, merchants) offset one another such that increasing the interchange fee has no real effect and, as such, there is no need for regulation.[183] There has also been a focus on the properties of different fee *structures* in getting 'both sides' (i.e. merchants and cardholders) to participate in the payment system given network effects and various assumptions about underlying market conditions. In other words, what is the relationship between consumer and merchant costs and the benefits of a given interchange fee *structure*?[184]

The need for price regulation of platforms operating in two-sided markets is sometimes based on arguments that the price structures set by a (dominant) platform operator can allow it to over-recover across different sides of the market.[185] Alternatively, price regulation has been introduced to address concerns that the price structure is inefficient insofar as it does not send the right signals to different user groups about the underlying costs and benefits of their use of the platform (e.g. one set of users is cross-subsidising the other side of the market in an inefficient way).[186]

In addition to price regulation, there has been a focus on regulation of the (non-price) 'rules' imposed by (dominant) platform operators on different user groups in multi-sided market settings. For example, as discussed in Chapter 12, certain business rules established

---

[180] For example, if a common regulated price is set for both sides of a platform, this can reduce the welfare of users on one side who would have paid a lower price in the absence of this constraint (because the firm may have subsidised them). However, it also potentially reduces the welfare of the group that faces the lower regulated price if it results in lower participation on the other side of the platform. Belleflamme and Peitz (2021) develop this logic using the example of a heterosexual dating site: a common participation price on both sides might make women worse off (as they are typically subsidised), while at the same time making men worse off as well (because, although they face a lower price, this is outweighed by the smaller number of women on the platform).

[181] See Belleflamme and Peitz (2021) and Jullien, Pavan and Rysman (2021).

[182] See Rochet and Tirole (2002, 2003, 2006), Evans (2003), Armstrong (2006) and Rysman (2009).

[183] For example, where increases in the interchange fee paid by merchants is recovered through surcharges levied on customers at the point of transaction, and these higher prices paid by cardholders completely offset any reductions in cardholder fees (where card issuers use the higher interchange fee revenues to fund the reductions in cardholder fees).

[184] See Rochet and Tirole (2011) and Wright (2012).

[185] That is, the overall revenues (or price levels) earned by the operator are substantially greater than the costs incurred on the different sides (e.g. it is earning monopoly rents across users as a whole).

[186] As discussed in Chapter 12, one of the arguments for the regulation of interchange fees is that merchants (and their customers, some of whom may not use cards) were effectively cross-subsidising credit cardholders who were not exposed directly to the full costs they imposed and benefited from various incentives (e.g. air miles) to encourage greater card use.

by card payment schemes have been banned in some jurisdictions.[187] Similarly, as di
cussed in Chapter 13, there are concerns that (dominant) digital platforms could impo
terms and conditions on users which are exploitative,[188] or act in other ways which a
exclusionary, such as controlling who accesses a platform, and how they access it (e.
which vendor or app can use their platforms).[189]

6.8 REGULATION OF MULTIPLE COMPETING SUPPLIERS

In addition to the settings described above, where regulation has been applied in the pre
ence of competition, regulation is also sometimes applied even where there are competir
providers of a service but only some of these firms are assessed as having substanti
market power. In these circumstances, economic regulation is applied asymmetricall
such that price and quality controls are imposed only on the firm(s) that are assessed a
occupying a position of substantial market power.[190] In other circumstances, all, or a larg
number of, suppliers in a market are assessed as having market power. For example, in th
UK, currently sixty-nine providers of mobile call termination services have been assesse
as holding a position of substantial market power in termination services, and have bee
subject to economic regulation on this basis.[191]

Economic regulation is also sometimes applied to all suppliers of a service in marke
where competition is seen as ineffective or not working well. For example, as discussed
Chapter 9, in the British retail energy market, default energy price caps have been appli
to *all* retail suppliers of gas and electricity since January 2019.[192] While the application
price regulation across multiple suppliers in a competitive market is relatively unusual, it
nevertheless not uncommon in the public utility industries, even where there are multip
competing providers, for firms to be subject to specific licensing or other general cond
tions set by a regulator which cover wider aspects of their operations and performance.[1]

6.9 CONCLUSION

This chapter provides a general overview of the economic principles and approach
for the regulation of industries where there is competition in some activities. We starte
by examining the pricing principles in the context of one-way access, noting that th

[187] These include rules which require merchants to accept all cards of a particular card scheme, or which prohibit merchants from 'steering' customers to a particular payment method.
[188] Such as relating to the use of personal data of individual users, or requiring that merchants of online marketplace platforms agree to certain conditions.
[189] For example, a dominant platform might require an exclusive dealing arrangement (requiring that sellers or advertisers not use rival platforms) or use most favoured nation or parity clauses which restri the ability of sellers to offer lower prices through rival supply channels.
[190] As discussed in Chapter 15, although both London Heathrow and London Gatwick airports have been assessed as holding market power, the form of regulatory oversight differs between the two airports.
[191] Prior to this, only the four largest mobile phone operators were typically subject to *ex ante* regulation on the basis of an assessment of substantial market power.
[192] As discussed in the next chapter, the rationale for the price caps is intended to protect those customers who are not active and do not switch supplier and as a result are on expensive default tariffs.
[193] For example, all providers of electronic communications networks and services in the UK are governed by regulatory requirements as set out in the General Conditions of Entitlement. The general conditions broadly fall into three main categories: network functioning conditions; numbering and other technica conditions; and consumer protection conditions.

principles differ depending on whether the firm providing the core network service is vertically separated from, or vertically integrated with, other activities in the production chain. We considered the merits of various access pricing approaches, including: marginal cost pricing with adjustments to reflect the extent of competition in related markets; Ramsey–Boiteux pricing; the ECPR; cost-based pricing; and, finally, global price caps. Depending on the assumed setting, each of these approaches has potential benefits and drawbacks as a method of access pricing, and, in practice, can require the regulator to make a trade-off between static efficiency and potential dynamic efficiency gains. It was noted that, in practice, many regulators have adopted cost-based approaches to the setting of access prices, in part it seems because of a presumption that economic efficiency will be improved if the prices for intermediate inputs in a production process, such as access, are cost-based.

Our analysis then turned to pricing principles for two-way access. One insight to emerge was that the non-cooperative setting of access prices is likely to be inefficient, and that firms should be permitted to coordinate on the setting of access prices. However, where networks compete with one another for subscribers, such as in mobile telephony, this has naturally given rise to concerns that such coordination on access prices might facilitate collusion. The widely held presumption that coordinated access prices facilitate collusion – which is one rationale for regulation – rests on a number of assumptions, and once these are relaxed, the presumption is less robust. We also considered the range of approaches adopted in practice to setting two-way access prices, including approaches based on estimates of long-run incremental cost (sometimes with mark-ups to allow for joint and common costs) and reciprocal approaches based on bill and keep arrangements.

The chapter then focused on the interaction between access pricing and investment. We noted that expectations as to future access prices are of particular importance in regulated industries, and can impact on both the extent and timing of investment. This can require a regulator to make a trade-off between efficient access prices in a static sense, and those that are most appropriate in a dynamic context. In recognition of the challenges and trade-offs often associated with determining the terms of access where a vertically integrated firm operates the core network activity and also competes with access users in a related market, consideration was given to the merits of arguments for and against vertical integration and separation. The overarching conclusion was that any assessment of the relative benefits of integration *vis-à-vis* separation needs to weigh the benefits of an integrated structure (in terms of efficiency, coordination and lower transactions costs) against the possible harm associated with the integrated firm foreclosing rivals in related competitive markets (such as impeding the entry of new rival firms and forestalling the dynamic benefits of competition).

Finally, we focused on the regulation of 'two-sided' or 'multi-sided' markets, such as card payment systems and digital platforms. We noted that, because multi-sided market platform operators need to incentivise different user groups to join and stay on their platform, this may lead them to adopt a 'tilted' pricing structure involving one group of users facing a price that is below the costs they impose, with the lost revenues recovered from another set of users. A need for price regulation can arise where there are concerns that the price structure set by a (dominant) platform operator allows it to over-recover

across different sides of the market, or to address concerns that the price structure is inef
ficient and does not send the right signals to different user groups about the underlying
costs and benefits of their use of the platform. Regulation can also seek to address certain
'rules' imposed by platform operators on different user groups in multi-sided market set
tings which are considered to be exploitative or are exclusionary (such as controlling who
accesses a platform, and how they access it).

DISCUSSION QUESTIONS

1.   What considerations does a regulator need to balance when setting access prices
     and what are some of the factors which determine whether the 'optimal' access pric
     might be set above or below the marginal cost of providing access?
2.   What is the optimal access price if a one-way access provider is not vertically inte
     grated and does not operate in a related market (e.g. a separate rail infrastructure
     company or electricity transmission company)? What assumptions underpin this
     result, and what happens if these assumptions do not hold?
3.   What are the different ways in which access prices can be set if a one-way access pro
     vider is vertically integrated and competes in a related market? What factors might
     affect the desirability and feasibility of implementing each approach in practice?
4.   What problems can arise when adjacent monopolies who offer complementary ser
     vices need to access each other's networks and independently determine their own
     access price? How can this problem be addressed?
5.   What are the different ways in which access prices can be determined when there are
     multiple firms who compete for subscribers? What are some of the factors that can
     affect the desirability and feasibility of each approach in practice?
6.   How might a regulator's approach to access pricing interact with the incentives for
     investment by an access provider and an access user? What are some of the ways in
     which a regulator can seek to encourage investment?
7.   What are some of the factors which can influence a regulator's decision about the
     merits of vertical integration compared to vertical separation in regulated industries?
8.   What are some of the different ways in which vertical separation can be introduced
     What factors determine which form of vertical separation is most appropriate?
9.   What are some of the characteristics of multi-sided markets and what factors can
     influence how prices are set? Can you give some specific examples of a multi-sided
     market and the different user groups that participate in that market?
10. In what circumstances might regulation of a two-sided market be introduced?

Behavioural Economics and Regulation

Many of the insights discussed in the book to this point are based on industrial organisation models that make certain assumptions about how consumers, and other end-users (for example, small firms), act and respond to market signals. For example, it has been generally assumed that consumers (the 'demand side' of the market) will behave in relatively predictable and stable ways to changes in market signals such as increased choice, high prices or reductions in quality, etc. However, a growing body of theoretical work in behavioural economics, as well as practical experience, has revealed that the assumptions that all consumers respond to market signals in predictable ways, are naturally 'active' in seeking out better deals or will take advantage of any wider choice available to them do not always hold. For example, as we discuss below, in the energy sector, consumers have often been reluctant to switch to competitive retail suppliers even when they can save money. Similarly, in the telecommunications industry, despite the fact that consumers often have a vast array of pricing plans to choose from, many consumers find it difficult to navigate their way through this choice set and assess the suitability of the different options given their usage patterns. Put simply, a growing body of empirical evidence suggests that *real* consumers behave in ways that are inconsistent with the *idealised* concept of the consumer that is used in the industrial organisation models and which has influenced the development of modern economic regulation.[1]

Research has also shown how firms, including new entrants, can exploit consumer decision-making biases.[2] For example, firms can offer 'teaser' rates to attract consumers to switch and then lock them into long-term contracts at a higher rate (so-called 'tease and squeeze' offers). Firms operating in competitive markets can also have incentives to offer an array of tariff plans that confuse and overwhelm the consumer (so-called 'confusopoly'). An important insight of both theoretical work and practical experience is that 'more competition' does not always reduce the incentives for firms to exploit consumer biases.

As we will see in this chapter, these observations have potentially profound implications for regulatory theory and practice. Regulators across a range of industries have

---

[1] Indeed, Stango and Zinman (2020) observe that empirical research shows that the fact that consumers exhibit many biases 'is the rule, not the exception'.

[2] Spiegler (2011) makes the important observation that firms do not necessarily need to be malicious for inefficient outcomes to occur; rather, they may just focus on maximising profits given certain consumer characteristics and competitor behaviour.

drawn directly on behavioural economics research to design policies with the aim of mak
ing consumers more 'active' and 'engaged' in restructured markets, and limiting the scop
for behavioural biases to be exploited. Indeed, while a key element of the restructurin
policies introduced in many regulated industries over the past four decades has focuse
principally on the 'supply side' – such as policies to foster competition by ensuring th
new entrants were not discriminated against, or did not face undue barriers to entry
the past decade has seen many regulators widening their focus to the 'demand side' ar
introducing policies that equip consumers to be more informed and active in markets.[3]

This chapter is organised into four sections. Section 7.1 describes some core insigh
from behavioural economics that challenge the standard assumptions about consum
decision making and behaviour. Section 7.2 presents the results of theoretical resear
in the area known as behavioural industrial organisation, including insights about co
sumer and firm behaviour. It also considers the possible implications of these theoretic
insights for economic regulation. Section 7.3 provides an overview of how econom
regulators have drawn upon the insights of behavioural economics in developing ar
implementing policy. Section 7.4 concludes.

7.1 CORE INSIGHTS OF BEHAVIOURAL ECONOMICS

This section first sets out the assumptions about 'standard' consumer behaviour that unde
pin most of the insights discussed so far in this book. We then describe how these assum
tions have been challenged by theoretical work in the area of behavioural economics ar
behavioural industrial organisation by introducing the notion of 'non-standard' behaviou

7.1.1 Standard Assumptions about Consumer Behaviour

Many of the theories and insights which underpin modern economic regulation are base
on findings from the area of microeconomic research known as industrial organisatio
Within this analytical framework, consumer behaviour is captured through the standar
neoclassical analysis of a demand schedule and related demand curve. In other word
the focus is on examining how a marginal consumer might respond to a change in pric
(movements along a demand curve) or to changes in the prices of other complementary o
substitute goods or other external conditions (movements in the demand curve). A mark
demand curve then aggregates the expected behaviour of individual consumers and
used to quantify the gains associated with trade, such as changes in consumer surplus, a
discussed in Chapter 2.

Three important assumptions about consumer decision making and behaviour are ger
erally made in this standard industrial organisation framework. First, it is assumed tha
a consumer will always seek to maximise (expected) utility subject to a specific budg
constraint. This means that, when faced with a choice, a consumer adopts a valuatio
framework that considers the expected utility (or satisfaction, reward, etc.) attached t

---

[3] As Littlechild (2015) observes: 'Regulators and competition authorities were used to tackling market
failures, and here was another one. They now needed to transform real customers into active and ration
consumers in order to enable competition to deliver its full consumer benefits.'

the different options or choices.[4] As such, the utility a consumer derives from a product is 'revealed' through their actual consumption decisions. In other words, we can infer the level of expected utility a consumer derives from their actual consumption decisions. So, if a consumer purchases one more unit of a product, it can be inferred that the consumer expects that the marginal benefit of consuming that extra unit exceeds the marginal cost given a fixed level of income.[5]

A second important assumption is that consumers will respond in specific and predictable ways to changes in price and other relevant variables. In other words, other things being equal, price decreases will result in a greater level of aggregate consumption of a product as represented by a movement along the demand curve (and vice versa). Consumers in these models are also assumed to have certain computational abilities and behave in certain 'rational' ways in making decisions. In particular, consumers are assumed to: have well-defined, stable and consistent preferences; engage in optimal levels of search activity; select the lowest-price/highest-quality products; have certain abilities when it comes to processing information; seek to maximise their own expected utility, including by switching suppliers when it is optimal to do so; and to be concerned only with their own utility/payoffs and not those of other consumers.[6] Standard industrial organisation models also adopt a notion of equilibrium whereby consumers' beliefs about the future are unbiased and are confirmed in practice (i.e. it is assumed that consumers do not systematically make errors when forming beliefs about the future).[7]

A third assumption is that consumers are not influenced by, or are invariant to, various attributes of the environment in which a product is sold or supplied. In other words, fully rational consumers are assumed to make decisions that maximise (expected) utility given a full understanding and perception of how prices are affected by different possible states of nature.[8] In other words, in weighing up options, consumers engage in what might be described as a Bayesian process that takes account of past outcomes and calibrates choice on the basis of the available alternatives.[9]

---

[4] The link between expected utility theory and individual valuation has its foundation in the work of Bernoulli (1738) and Von Neumann and Morgenstern's (1944) subsequent derivation of expected utility theory using axioms on preference.

[5] Samuelson (1938, 1948) developed the notion of revealed preference, without explicit reference to the notion of utility, but rather on the basis of what choices an idealised consumer (who was not necessarily the rational *Homo economicus*) would make faced with a given set of prices and given income.

[6] As Simon (1955) observed: 'Traditional economic theory postulates an "economic man," who, in the course of being "economic" is also "rational." This man is assumed to have knowledge of the relevant aspects of his environment which, if not absolutely complete, is at least impressively clear and voluminous. He is assumed also to have a well-organized and stable system of preferences, and a skill in computation that enables him to calculate, for the alternative courses of action that are available to him, which of these will permit him to reach the highest attainable point on his preference scale.'

[7] Consumer's beliefs are unbiased insofar as they do not systematically display belief biases such as overconfidence, over-optimism or a failure to account for unforeseen contingencies (i.e. fail to take account of various add-on or additional costs). See Belleflamme and Peitz (2015).

[8] Many attribute this theory of rational decision making under uncertainty to Savage (1954), which involves consumers assigning probabilities to different possible outcomes and then calibrating utilities to value the possible outcomes. The consumer then selects the alternative that offers the highest expected utility.

[9] Bayesian methods provide an inductive framework for revising prior beliefs in response to new, relevant information. As McFadden (1999) explains: 'The standard model in economics is that consumers behave as if information is processed to form perceptions and beliefs using strict Bayesian statistical principles (perception-rationality), preferences are primitive, consistent and immutable (preference-rationality), and the cognitive process is simply preference maximization, given market constraints (process-rationality).'

In sum, within the standard industrial organisation framework, consumers are assumed to be 'rational' insofar as they have a full understanding of the market model, and have the ability to understand and assess the consequences of different choices, and to *fully* respond to any reduction in prices and/or increased quality.[10] Accordingly, in these models, regulatory policies that introduce additional choice, or which intensify price or quality competition, should, other things being equal, result in consumers responding in stable and predictable ways through their consumption decisions.

7.1.2 Behavioural Economics and Consumer Behaviour

An ever-expanding body of behavioural economics research has shed new insights on human decision making, some of which challenge the assumptions about consumer behaviour that underpin standard industrial organisation models.[11] In a nutshell, this research suggests that *real* consumers (as compared to the idealised consumers used in the standard models) are not always perfectly rational and do not always make decisions that maximise utility or are in their long-term interests.[12] This work shows how consumer decision making in the real world is influenced by various psychological factors that challenge the validity of the assumptions of rational choice theory and can affect how consumers make decisions in complex market environments. Rather than being fully rational, consumers can display 'bounded rationality' and take decisions which 'satisfice' rather than optimise.[13] A wide range of deviations from perfectly rational decision making have been identified in behavioural economics research.[14] For current purposes these can be organised under four strands.

A first strand relaxes the assumption that consumers have stable, coherent and consistent preferences.[15] This work shows how consumer preferences can change over time and be affected by context, such as when preferences are formed and how decisions are made.

---

[10] Spiegler (2011) observes that: 'in virtually all [industrial organisation] applications rationality is narrowly practiced: preferences are defined over "simple" consequences, fully specified by the amount of money the consumer pays and the quantity or quality of the product he consumes'.

[11] Mullainathan and Thaler (2000) define behavioural economics as 'a combination of psychology and economics that investigates what happens in market in which some of the agents display human limitations and complications'.

[12] McFadden (1999) refers to consumers that conform to the standard idealised economic model of perception, preference and process rationality as the 'Chicago man'. Consumers in behavioural economic models differ from 'Chicago man' and the more general *Homo economicus* characterisation of consumers as rational, self-interested utility maximisers that have well-defined preferences and are involved in a complex maximisation problem.

[13] See Simon (1955, 1956, 1957, 1979) and Wheeler (2020). Satisficing implies that, rather than seeking out all options to discover 'optimal solutions', consumers may seek search out alternative until an acceptable threshold or satisfactory outcome is achieved.

[14] Sanin, Trillas, Mejdalani, *et al.* (2019) highlight the massive growth in behavioural economics publications, from fewer than 200 in 1990 to over 6000 by 2017. DellaVigna (2009) provides a useful survey of research at that time.

[15] The standard assumption is that preferences are characterised by completeness (all alternatives can be ordered on the basis of a pairwise comparison), transitivity (if A is preferred to be B, and B to C, then A is preferred to C), time consistency, and context independence (preference ordering in one context should be the same in another, such that the presence of other options cannot influence the relative preference between two options). See Tversky and Simonson (1993), Bettman, Luce and Payne (1998) and Dhar and Novemsky (2008).

The models allow consumers to have different degrees of 'sophistication' (or *naïveté*) in the ability to estimate how their preferences will adapt over time in response to changing circumstances.[16] The main insights are that, when making decisions (particularly ones that extend over multiple periods),[17] some consumers can: be unduly loss-averse;[18] over-weight potential losses relative to gains;[19] have issues with commitment;[20] have issues of self-control and discount future preferences in favour of immediate pleasure;[21] be impatient and have a bias towards the present;[22] overestimate the extent to which future preferences and behaviours will resemble current preferences;[23] and construct preferences during the choice process.[24] An important insight from this research is that consumers often lack stable preferences and can be heavily influenced by how choices are presented to them or framed.[25] For example, consumer responses can differ depending on whether prices are labelled as a 'discount' or a 'surcharge'.[26]

A second strand of behavioural economics research relaxes the assumption that consumers are perfectly rational (i.e. that they make a probabilistic assessment of the future expected utility attached to different decisions). Rather, consumers in these models display various 'biases' or 'cognitive anomalies', which are defined as deviations from rationality, which affect their judgement.[27] A large number of 'biases' have been identified in behavioural research.[28] Among the most relevant to consumer behaviour include: bundling bias

---

[16] Strotz (1955) presents an early analysis of sophisticated and naïve consumers. Spiegler (2011) describes models with sophisticated and naïve consumers.

[17] Spiegler (2011) observes that, in an intertemporal context, we can perceive of consumers as a collection of selves with different preferences over time. Similarly, Strotz (1955) refers to the individual over time as an 'infinity of individuals'.

[18] This derives from Kahneman and Tversky's (1979) seminal work on prospect theory. See also Thaler (1980). Gal and Rucker (2018) present a critique noting that loss aversion can be explained by other factors (such as *status quo* bias).

[19] This is related to the 'endowment effect' and the fact that people are more averse to losses than same-sized gains and thus under-weight opportunity costs. Some have questioned the endowment effect, noting that it depends on the design of the experiment in which consumer behaviour is observed and can differ depending on products and context. See Plott and Zeiler (2005) and Isoni, Loomes and Sugden (2011).

[20] See DellaVigna and Malmendier (2004, 2006), Esteban and Miyagawa (2006) and Bryan, Karlan and Nelson (2010).

[21] See Thaler and Shefrin (1981) and Hoch and Loewenstein (1991).

[22] This relates to work on the time inconsistency of preferences and hyperbolic discounting. See Laibson (1997) and Frederick, Loewenstein and O'Donoghue (2002).

[23] Known as projection bias. See Loewenstein, O'Donoghue and Rabin (2003).

[24] Such that preferences are not guided by an internal, stable utility function but are constructed during the choice process. See Griffin, Liu and Khan (2005).

[25] Thus, attacking the assumption that choices are invariant to how they are presented. This follows also from the findings of prospect theory that framing something as a 'gain' or 'loss' relative to a reference point can have differential effects on choices. See Tversky and Kahneman (1981) and Kahneman and Tversky (1984). Rabin (1998) notes that 'frames' may in fact partially determine a consumer's preferences.

[26] Thaler (1980) and Tversky and Kahneman (1986).

[27] The terms 'biases' or 'cognitive illusions' come from the work of Kahneman and Tversky (1996), who use them to refer to a systematic discrepancy, or deviation, between a person's judgement and a norm. Gigerenzer (1991, 2018) is a longstanding critic of this characterisation of decisions being 'biased' and of the distinction between 'correct and erroneous' judgements under uncertainty, noting that such 'biases are not biases' when considered within a wider context of probabilistic reasoning and that what is considered to be a 'bias' may reflect fine-tuned intuitions about chance, frequency and framing.

[28] Wheeler (2020) notes that the number of cognitive biases now numbers into the hundreds.

(valuing items bought in a bundle less than individually);[29] distinction bias (overvaluing differences between options when considered together rather than separately);[30] hindsight bias (a belief that an outcome is more predictable after it becomes known than was before it became known);[31] optimism bias (overestimating the likelihood of positive outcomes);[32] restraint bias (overestimating self-control);[33] salience bias (disproportionately focusing on more visible or prominent information);[34] *status quo* or default bias (attaching undue importance to current choices and commodity bundles and a reluctance to switch to alternative bundles);[35] and overconfidence bias (overestimating the ability to judge the attributes of a service offering or the ability to control future consumption of a service).[36] Consumers have also been shown to use various mental shortcuts or 'rules of thumb' (known as heuristics) when making decisions rather than fully and independently assessing each choice.[37] These include the use of the availability heuristic (basing future decisions on the information that comes to mind quickly and easily),[38] the representativeness heuristic (classifying objects or events into categories based on similarity to other prototypical objects/events)[39] and the anchoring and adjustment bias (a tendency to anchor decisions in current information).[40] Relatedly, decision making can be influenced by the so-called 'sunk cost effect' which is a tendency to continue consuming a product (or consuming more of it) once an investment in money, effort or time has been made rather than making an assessment based on future costs and benefits.[41]

A third strand of research relaxes assumptions about consumers' willingness and ability to search for and compare product offerings. This work shows that consumers may not always choose the best price/product offering because of limited search activity or computational capacities, or confusion when comparing offers. For example, consumers may suffer from choice overload (being overwhelmed by a large number of options),

[29] Soman and Gourville (2001).

[30] Hsee and Zhang (2004).

[31] Fischhoff (1975) and Roese and Vohs (2012).

[32] Weinstein (1980) and Sharot (2011).

[33] Nordgren, van Harreveld and van der Pligt (2009).

[34] Schenk (2011)

[35] See Samuelson and Zeckhauser (1988) (who note that it has implications for the nature of competition in markets), Hartman, Doane and Woo (1991) (who consider this in the context of residential electricity services) and Tversky and Shafir (1992). Spiegler (2011) notes that in some cases a consumer may actually prefer not changing the way things are, and as such choosing another alternative over the *status quo* carries an implicit switching cost.

[36] Grubb (2009, 2015b). The tendency to overconfidence was already recognised by Adam Smith (1776), who noted that 'the chance of gain is by every man more or less over-valued, and the chance of loss is by most men under-valued'.

[37] As Tversky and Kahneman (1973a) observe: 'In making predictions and judgments under uncertainty, people do not appear to follow the calculus of chance or the statistical theory of prediction. Instead, they rely on a limited number of heuristics which sometimes yield reasonable judgments and sometimes lead to severe and systematic errors.'

[38] That is, people over-weight salient, memorable or vivid evidence even when there are better sources of information available. See Tversky and Kahneman (1973b).

[39] Mervis and Rosch (1981) and Tversky and Kahneman (1983). Bordalo, Coffman, Gennaioli and Shleifer (2016) discuss the use of stereotypes based on the representativeness heuristic.

[40] Rather than assessing a new offer objectively, consumers may be biased by an initial starting value and use this as a benchmark. For example, they may consider new tariff offers by reference to their existing tariff plan. See Furnham and Boo (2011).

[41] Arkes and Blumer (1985).

[42] Chernev, Böckenholt and Goodman (2015). More generally, see Iyengar and Lepper (2000), Irons and Hepburn (2007) and Iyengar and Kamenica (2010).

show decision fatigue (where judgement quality is affected by the number of decisions made),[43] have limited or selective attention,[44] rely heavily on anecdotal reasoning,[45] or engage in 'sampling' leading them to exaggerate the degree to which outcomes from a sample resemble the outcomes they could face.[46] Consumer choices can also be affected by how many other people have made a similar choice, the so-called bandwagon effect. More generally, neuroeconomics research suggests that consumer decision making can be affected by cognitive processes and emotional mechanisms that are deeply embedded within human decision making, such as willingness to trust a counterparty.[47]

A fourth research strand relaxes the assumption that consumers are always utility-maximising and allows for other considerations, such as the perceived fairness of a transaction, to affect decision making.[48] For example, the ability of firms with market power to raise prices can, in some settings, be affected by consumer sentiment about the perceived fairness of firms' short-run pricing decisions and in particular the drivers of such price rises (e.g. whether it reflects an increase in demand or a rise in costs).[49] Consumer decision making can also be driven by wider social goals, such as water conservation during a drought or energy reductions for environmental reasons.[50]

Three general points should be emphasised about these insights from behavioural economics research. Firstly, these deviations from rational choice are not considered to be one-off mistakes or aberrations, but *systematic*, meaning that consumers repeatedly act in ways that deviate from the rational choice benchmark.[51] Secondly, research suggests that 'biases' may be the rule rather than the exception and that decisions can be affected by multiple biases simultaneously. Moreover, some studies have found that biases are distinct consumer traits and cannot easily be mapped to underlying characteristics such

---

[43] Sollisch (2016) claims that the average American adult makes 35,000 decisions a day.

[44] See Kahneman (1973) and Schwartzstein (2014).

[45] Spiegler (2011) notes that: 'People tend to reason anecdotally, rather than probabilistically, about random variables. They often find anecdotes more persuasive and informative than they should be according to probabilistic thinking, because anecdotes are concrete stories filled with vivid details that register more powerfully in the decision maker's memory than abstract and general information.'

[46] Tversky and Kahneman (1971) describe this as the belief in the 'law of small numbers'. Spiegler (2011) presents various models of sampling.

[47] Overviews of this research are presented in Camerer, Loewenstein and Prelec (2005), Camerer (2008) and Glimcher, Camerer, Fehr and Poldrack (2009). Decker (2017) discusses some of the implications of these findings for regulation.

[48] Rabin (1993) finds that people want to be nice to those who treat them fairly and want to punish those who hurt them. Thaler (1988) found that notions of fairness can play a significant role in exchange.

[49] See Kahneman, Knetsch and Thaler (1986a, b). Thaler (1985) considers this issue using the concept of 'transactional utility'; this is an ongoing pecuniary relationship between a buyer and a seller, such that the seller considers the short-term gains from charging above a reference price against the long-run loss of goodwill and thus sales. Fehr and Schmidt (1999) find that fairness may be less important in settings where consumers do not have an ability to punish a monopolist.

[50] In an early study Train, McFadden and Goett (1987) found that attitudes about energy conservation can affect choices to switch to different types of electricity tariff.

[51] Tversky observed that his research with Daniel Kahneman (Tversky and Kahneman, 1977) had shown that 'the axioms of rational choice are often violated consistently by sophisticated as well as naïve respondents, and that the violations are often large and highly persistent. In fact, some of the observed biases ... are reminiscent of perceptual illusions'. Similarly, Thaler (1980) observed that: '[I]n certain well-defined situations many consumers act in a manner that is inconsistent with economic theory. In these situations, economic theory will make systematic errors in predicting behavior.' More recently, Spiegler (2011) concludes that 'experimental psychologists have made a powerful case for the claim that decision makers systematically deviate from the model of rational choice as it is typically practiced by economists'.

as income or level of education.[52] Thirdly, many of these insights about human and con
sumer decision making have been generated using psychosocial methods in laborator
(often using students) or field experiments. For some, this raises questions about th
generalisability of some of these insights,[53] and their applicability to real-world context
involving a greater number of heterogeneous consumers.[54]

Having regard to these points, it is clear that insights from the ever-expanding body o
behavioural economics research has potentially significant implications for how we thin
about the consumer in economic regulation. To take some examples. First, it suggests tha
loss-averse consumers may have strong preferences for particular types of pricing struc
tures, such as flat rate pricing.[55] Second, it can explain why some (naïve) consumers may b
attracted to pricing plans that offer 'teaser rates' or 'welcome benefits' without fully takin
account of the fact that these rates may rise once they are locked into a supply agreemen
Third, it suggests that over-optimistic consumers may systematically assign higher probabilit
to certain aspects of their behaviour or to certain outcomes arising, which leads them to mak
decisions like not taking out insurance for an annual rail season ticket on the assumption tha
they do not need to be insured.[56] Similarly, overconfident or overprecise consumers may mak
poor choices among alternative combinations of service offerings, particularly where there ar
threshold charges involved, such as additional data charges for mobile phone use.[57] Fourth
it implies that consumers that rely on sampling-based strategies can potentially fall prey t
obfuscation strategies, which is of particular relevance in the context of digital platforms an
online commerce.[58] Finally, it can provide a range of potential explanations for why consum
ers do not switch providers or always choose the best price offering in restructured markets
including because of: low levels of search activity; confusion when comparing prices an
offers; inertia; or a tendency to make choices based on defaults or rules of thumb.

7.2 BEHAVIOURAL INDUSTRIAL ORGANISATION AND REGULATION

Having described how consumer behaviour can deviate from the standard assumption
used in industrial organisation models, this section presents some of the main insight
from research in the area known as behavioural industrial organisation.[59] This wor

---

[52] See Stango and Zinman (2020).

[53] Becker (2002) notes that: '[T]here is a heck of a difference between demonstrating something in a
laboratory, in experiments, even highly sophisticated experiments, and showing that they are important
in the marketplace. Economists have a theory of behavior in markets, not in labs, and the relevant
theories can be very different.'

[54] These broad methodological objections have long been recognised. Rabin (1998) argues that this position
derives principally from unfamiliarity with the details of the research and an 'aggressive uncuriosity' abou
the findings of behavioural research. Armstrong and Huck (2010) discuss a number of reasons why they
cautiously believe that data from laboratory experiments can be useful in the context of firm behaviour.

[55] See Herweg and Mierendorff (2013).

[56] Alternatively, they may not take account of unforeseen outcomes by assigning a zero probability to
certain events arising, such as a need to purchase 'add-on' products (e.g. the need to 'buy extra minutes'
of a mobile data plan).

[57] See Grubb (2009) and Grubb and Osborne (2015).

[58] Ellison and Ellison (2009) discuss obfuscation in the context of internet price comparison sites and
observe that the 'most popular obfuscation strategy for the products we study is to intentionally create
an inferior quality good that can be offered at a very low price ... if a retailer tries to advertise a decent
quality product with reasonable contractual terms at a fair price, it will be buried behind dozens of lowe
price offers on the search engine's list'.

[59] See Ellison (2006), Spiegler (2011), Grubb (2015b) and Heidhues and Kőszegi (2018).

generally maintains the standard assumptions about firm behaviour (i.e. that they are rational and profit-maximising), but introduces various 'non-standard' assumptions about consumer behaviour. Section 7.2.1 describes the results of studies that have incorporated non-standard consumer behaviour, while Section 7.2.2 relaxes the assumption that firms are perfectly rational and profit-maximising. Section 7.2.3 considers the implications of these results for economic regulation.

7.2.1 Implications for Consumers, Competition and Welfare

Behavioural industrial organisation research focuses on what happens when firms interact with 'non-standard' consumers who, for the various reasons described above, systematically deviate from the 'standard' rational consumer.[60] As we will see, changing assumptions about consumer behaviour has important implications for competition, total surplus (welfare) and the distribution of gains between standard and non-standard consumers.[61]

Integrating Non-Standard Consumers into Standard Industrial Organisation Models

Behavioural industrial organisation models typically focus on how firms can take advantage of non-standard consumer behaviour by charging consumers an 'additional price' which they ignore when they make a purchasing decision (sometimes called a '*naïveté premium*' or penalty fee).[62] In standard benchmark models, while firms may have an incentive to take advantage of non-standard consumers by charging them an additional price, the practical ability for them to do so is limited by competition.[63] In other words, intense competition between firms protects non-standard consumers from being exploited by a high additional price.[64]

However, there are a number of circumstances when, even in competitive markets, this standard outcome may not arise, meaning that non-standard consumers are not fully protected from exploitation by competition. First, there may be limits to the extent to which competition fully dissipates the rents from exploitation, meaning that non-standard consumers still pay some element of the additional price.[65] Second, non-standard consumers may not fully compare available offers, or base their decisions on limited sampling, and thus may not choose the best price or product quality even in competitive markets, with the result that they still pay some part of an additional price. An important insight is that it

---

[60] These consumers are sometimes described as being naïve or unsophisticated because they make systematic errors, such as underestimating their own future preferences and behaviour, overvalue the benefit they derive from a product or are affected by various framing and perception strategies.

[61] This section draws on the excellent analyses in Spiegler (2011) and Heidhues and Kőszegi (2018).

[62] Heidhues and Kőszegi (2018) argue that this additional price can arise because naïve consumers: misunderstand the contractual terms and what they will be paying; misunderstand the price–quality/ value combination; and ignore certain charges (such as add-on or user charges, or they underestimate their ability to control their own demand, leading them to use more than expected). Critically, they also observe that firms do not necessarily have to be malicious in any sense for inefficient outcomes to occur; they are simply providing products that consumers purchase.

[63] Only in the monopoly setting can a supplier fully exploit this naïveté by charging the maximum additional price.

[64] Yariv and Laibson (2004) find that, when consumer have non-standard preferences, competition among agents eliminates rents and protects vulnerable consumers, who could have been exploited by a monopolist.

[65] Heidhues and Kőszegi (2018) describe this in the context of price floors for certain products, such as those imposed by prices in an aftermarket on a primary good market.

is not only firms that can benefit by exploiting non-standard consumers. In some settings standard consumers (i.e. those that fully understand the contracts they enter into and thus avoid the additional price) can also benefit from non-standard consumers paying an additional price.[66] For example, non-standard consumers can inadvertently cross-subsidise the prices paid by standard consumers if they do not fully examine all of the future hidden (or shrouded) costs they will face, or overestimate their levels of future self-control.[67]

Theoretical models which allow for non-standard consumers have shown how it can distort allocations and thus create additional deadweight losses, reducing total surplus (welfare) and efficiency.[68] One source of inefficiency arises because non-standard consumers underestimate the total price of a product (or overvalue the benefit they will obtain), leading to a situation where the marginal benefit is less than marginal cost and the product is overconsumed relative to an efficient benchmark.[69] Alternatively, consumers face high hidden fees, they may decide to curtail their consumption of a service below the efficient level once they discover they are being exploited, so as to avoid incurring the hidden charges.[70] Economic efficiency can also be reduced in circumstances where standard consumers engage in socially inefficient actions to avoid the high hidden charges that non-standard consumers face.[71] Another source of inefficiency arises where it incentivises over-entry into a market to exploit non-standard consumers, or where firms incur costs to innovate to find new ways to 'shroud' or conceal charges from consumers but which bring no actual benefit.[72] The interaction between standard and non-standard consumers can give rise to externalities that can have implications for total surplus (welfare).[73] For example, where standard consumers shop around, and have more elastic demand, they can reduce the equilibrium price for all consumers and increase welfare. Conversely, where non-standard consumers buy add-on services they do not need (i.e. they are 'ripped off'), this can provide a subsidy to the core price that benefits standard consumers who pay only this price, and overall welfare will decrease according to the ability to exploit non-standard consumers.

---

[66] Armstrong and Vickers (2012) refer to the example of the use of high unarranged overdraft fees on bank accounts in the UK. See also Armstrong (2015) for interaction between 'savvy' and 'non-savvy' consumers.

[67] For example, standard consumers who are aware of, and avoid, high hidden charges (such as excess data charges) can be subsidised by non-standard consumers who do not take into account hidden or shrouded charges. See Gabaix and Laibson (2006) and Grubb (2015a). DellaVigna and Malmendier (2004) examine the impacts of overestimating self-control on naïve and sophisticated consumers.

[68] Heidhues and Kőszegi (2018) provide a useful overview. See also Grubb (2015b).

[69] Heidhues and Kőszegi (2015) call this the 'participation distortion' and argue that there should be a redirection away from estimating the welfare losses associated with market power, to quantifying welfare losses associated with firms' reactions to consumer misunderstandings. Grubb (2015b) finds that the magnitude of consumer harm and deadweight loss depends on the elasticity of demand and supply and the pass-through rate. However, de Meza and Reyniers (2012) note that welfare can be increased in circumstances where the increased consumption by non-standard consumers (because they underestimate a hidden or shrouded price) is offset by a lower upfront price which reduces the total price (i.e. a waterbed effect).

[70] Gabaix and Laibson (2006). Heidhues and Kőszegi (2018) refer to this as the 'exploitation distortion' and give the example of consumers reducing their mobile calls once they discover that they face high roaming charges for using their phone abroad.

[71] See Armstrong and Vickers (2012).

[72] Heidhues, Kőszegi and Murooka (2016) refer to this as 'exploitative innovation'.

[73] See Armstrong (2015).

Pricing Decisions with Non-Standard Consumers

In Chapter 4 we saw how it is possible to increase the total surplus from the second-best average cost pricing by allowing firms to price-discriminate, that is, to vary the per unit price paid by different consumers according to their willingness to pay for that product. This analysis assumed that consumers had stable and consistent preferences, and the only reason they faced different prices was because they had different preferences for that product. Behavioural industrial organisation research expands this work to focus on what happens when consumer preferences are no longer assumed to be stable and consistent, and firms price-discriminate on the basis of a consumer's capability to forecast changes in their own future preferences or tastes.[74] In other words, this research examines what happens when firms seek to differentiate prices according to the relative sophistication or *naïveté* of the consumer rather than their preferences.[75] In most models, this *naïveté* manifests as a mismatch between a consumer's *ex ante* beliefs and *ex post* behaviour.[76]

In some settings, discrimination might involve a firm offering contracts which differentiate between consumers based on the consistency of their *ex ante* beliefs about their future preferences/behaviour (i.e. whether they are time-consistent). Standard consumers will always choose contracts which align their *ex ante* beliefs with their future behaviour, while non-standard consumers will choose a sub-optimal contract because of mistaken *ex ante* beliefs about their actual future behaviour. For example, a firm might offer a contract that offers a low price for acting in a way consistent with a consumer's *ex ante* belief but a high price if actual behaviour differs from the *ex ante* belief.[77] Because non-standard consumers mis-predict their future behaviour, they will therefore agree to such a contract, exposing them to higher charges. Such a contract allows the firm to screen for, and charge higher prices to, non-standard consumers who select this contract because of their mistaken belief about their future behaviour. Alternatively, firms might use automatic contract renewals as a means of discriminating between consumers' search behaviour, allowing them to levy higher charges on non-standard consumers that procrastinate and who do not search when a contract comes to an end. The discriminatory strategies that firms can use to exploit non-standard consumers that procrastinate include offering contracts with low initial charges to attract customers (who mistakenly believe they will cancel the auto-renewal) but much higher prices if the contract is automatically renewed (the so-called 'tease and squeeze' strategy).[78]

---

[74] Rubinstein (1993) presents an early analysis of how sellers can profitably discriminate among consumers according to differences in their ability to process information.

[75] As Spiegler (2011) notes, price discrimination arises because of consumer heterogeneity in terms of *cognitive* characteristics rather than *preference* characteristics.

[76] For example, a naïve consumer entering into a mobile phone contract may (mistakenly) believe *ex ante* that they are able to forecast their future usage and will thus not incur additional high charges for data use above a certain threshold. However, in practice, they do not control their data use and thus incur the high charges.

[77] Eliaz and Spiegler (2006) focus on a monopolistic setting where consumers have inconsistent preferences over time, while Eliaz and Spiegler (2008) focus on a monopoly setting where consumers are imperfectly informed about future preferences (i.e. there is uncertainty which can make consumers optimistic about future preferences).

[78] Johnen (2019) finds that competition can lead to greater incentives to engage in such discrimination to exploit consumers that procrastinate relative to monopoly. This is because the more a monopoly tries to attract naïve consumers by offering a low initial price, the greater the incentives to become a sophisticated consumer to take advantage of that price (the tease) and then cancel the contract rather than face the higher auto-renewal price.

Another form of discrimination involves firms using private data or external information about an individual consumer's behaviour to differentiate between standard and non-standard consumers and discriminate accordingly.[79] For example, where a firm and a consumer interact repeatedly (such as online), a firm can use the private information it gathers about how a consumer behaved in one period to discriminate in the offers that are made to that consumer in a subsequent period. In some settings, this ability to discriminate between standard and non-standard consumers makes private data valuable even in highly competitive markets and can reduce rivalry between firms.[80]

Finally, the presence of non-standard consumers can affect firm price structures. For example, a firm facing overconfident consumers (who underestimate the variance of their future demand) may seek to exploit this characteristic by introducing a three-part tariff comprising a fixed fee, a zero marginal price for consumption below a certain threshold (i.e. allowed number of units) and a positive marginal price for consumption above that threshold.[81] Such plans are common in mobile phone and broadband markets.[82] Similarly, firms may introduce a pricing structure that has separate prices for a 'basic service' and for 'add-on' services,[83] and where the latter are charged at a high price but are 'shrouded' from the consumer when they purchase the basic product.[84] Because non-standard consumers do not see and take account of the add-on price, they are exploited, while, in contrast, standard consumers are capable of 'unshrouding' the add-on price and thus can benefit from a cross-subsidy from non-standard consumers.[85]

Framing and the Incentives to Educate or Obfuscate

An important insight described in Section 7.1 is that consumer preferences and decision making can be affected by how an offer is framed and thus perceived by the consumer. One strand of research has examined how different frames affect consumer choice and competition.[86] This work makes an important distinction between firms that use frames to educate consumers (i.e. to assist consumers to choose the best product) and those that use frames to complicate and obscure consumer decision making (i.e. by introducing additional choice complexity and making comparisons harder).[87]

---

[79] See Heidhues and Kőszegi (2017) and Johnen (2020).

[80] Johnen (2020) explains how firms can use private customer data to induce adverse selection by rivals of less profitable customers. Specifically, private data allows the firm to differentiate between the prices it offers to its more profitable (non-standard) customers and its unprofitable standard customers who are more likely to switch. However, because rivals do not have access to this private information and cannot make such a distinction, they do not know whether a customer is standard or non-standard, which creates an adverse selection problem and causes rivals to compete less vigorously.

[81] Grubb (2015c) observes that, even in competitive markets, firms use complicated pricing features to exploit consumer overconfidence. Overconfidence can also be exploited through attention hurdles and barriers to follow-through, such as memory hurdles and self-control traps.

[82] See Grubb (2009).

[83] These are complementary services such as fees, penalties or accessories that the consumer can avoid.

[84] Johnen and Somogyi (2021) consider the use of shrouding by digital platform operators and find that they shroud or unshroud to manipulate cross-group externalities between buyers and sellers. This leads to more shrouding, as digital platform operators have a stronger incentive to 'shroud' seller fees to attract buyers.

[85] Gabaix and Laibson (2006).

[86] Spiegler (2014) distinguishes between utility-relevant aspects of consumer decision making (price, quality) and utility-irrelevant aspects which affect the framing of a decision (such as the measurement units in which prices or quantities are expressed, etc.).

[87] Chioveanu and Zhou (2013) note, for example, that complex tariff structures in utility markets can make it difficult for consumers to understand what type of deal they are on and how to reduce costs.

A longstanding view is that, where consumers have a positive valuation for a product, there is always an incentive for a rival to educate the non-standard consumers of a competitor firm and to capture some of the deadweight loss in the form of higher profits.[88] This leads to a transparent market in equilibrium, as any attempts by firms to obscure or complicate consumer decision making will not be sustainable. However, such a transparent equilibrium may not automatically arise if it removes a cross-subsidy between standard and non-standard consumers. Specifically, if a firm's attempts to educate non-standard consumers results in the market becoming more transparent, this may encourage that firm's standard consumers to switch their custom to competitors that continue to offer a lower cross-subsidised price (rather than face a non-subsidised price), while at the same time the non-standard customers of rivals may simply choose to stay with the rival but act in a more informed way.[89]

Taken as a whole, this work suggests that the incentives for firms to adopt educative frames depends on the product and the market structure.[90] In a monopolistic single-product setting with dynamically inconsistent consumers (i.e. where non-standard consumers mis-evaluate second period preferences), and where a firm can screen for the consumer type and offer standard and non-standard consumers different terms, a firm will have no incentive to educate a non-standard consumer, as this reduces profit.[91] However, even in competitive, multi-product market settings, firms may not have strong incentives to educate consumers. For example, intense competition for a superior product (on which no margin is earned) can reduce the incentive for firms to educate consumers about an inferior product if it results in consumers switching away from the higher-margin inferior product.[92] In principle third-party intermediaries could play an important role in educating consumers, acting as independent information intermediaries. However, the incentives for third parties to do so can depend on the size of the 'additional hidden price' levied by firms, and any commission that a third party receives from firms from not educating consumers about an inferior product.[93]

While the above discussion has focused on firms' incentives to adopt frames that educate consumers which can ultimately lead to a transparent market equilibrium, a different issue concerns the incentives that firms have to use framing strategies that consciously make it harder for consumers to compare products, thus leading to an obscure market equilibrium.[94] For example, where a large number of non-standard consumers rely on

---

[88] Shapiro (1995) describes how, in the context of aftermarkets, firms have a direct incentive to eliminate even the small inefficiency caused by poor consumer information.

[89] Gabaix and Laibson (2006) describe this as the 'curse of debiasing' and discuss this in the context of add-on pricing. Once a naïve consumer understands that they are facing high mark-ups for add-on products, they will continue to buy the basic service but stop consuming the add-on product.

[90] Heidhues and Kőszegi (2018) argue that firms have little incentive to adopt educative frames for 'bad' products which would not survive absent deception.

[91] Spiegler (2011).

[92] Heidhues, Kőszegi and Murooka (2017) find that where there is a superior and inferior product, educating consumers will divert more of them towards the superior product on which no margin is earned. Accordingly, more intense competition for the superior product lowers the incentive for a multi-product firm to educate consumers about the inferiority of an alternative product.

[93] Murooka (2015).

[94] Ellison and Wolitzky (2012) consider obfuscation as an increase in search costs and describe settings where it can be rational for firms to engage in such practices. In an early analysis Ellison and Ellison (2009) show how a group of retailers competing on the Internet have incentives to engage in obfuscation, noting that, rather than reducing frictions, advances in search technology can be accompanied by investments in obfuscation.

'sampling' as a heuristic to evaluate and make inferences about market alternatives, the this can create incentives for firms to obscure decision making and create noisy price di tributions.[95] Importantly, rather than address this tendency, the incentives to obscure ca *increase* with the number of competing firms under some assumptions, as market-wic obscuring can increase industry profits and lower consumer surplus.[96] The intuition that in highly competitive markets the only way for firms to achieve and sustain high margins is to obscure consumer choice, and as such the market as a whole can shi towards obscurity.[97]

Finally, there is a question about the incentives that firms operating in competiti markets face where consumers are inactive insofar as they are inert or display the *statu quo* bias. Non-standard consumers that are inert are less likely to search and switc which gives firms a degree of market power over them. In other words, non-standar consumers effectively lock themselves into a single supplier.[98] While it might be thoug that competition can naturally reduce this market power and encourage consumers t be more active, it may not do so if increasing the number of market choices/alternativ exacerbates rather than reduces consumer inertia. In other words, if inert consume have to compare even more offers, that makes engagement in a market even more cost or overwhelming (see the discussions below on 'confusopoly' in telecommunicatio in Section 7.3.2 and on consumers being 'bamboozled' by offers in energy markets i Section 7.3.1).[99] Once again, how an offer is framed can affect consumer inertia by low ering comparability across different price and quality dimensions, requiring consume to do more to overcome their *status quo* bias.[100] Of particular relevance is the finding some theoretical work that weakening consumer inertia (i.e. making consumers mo active) can actually result in a *less* competitive equilibrium, which has obvious impl cations for regulatory attempts to 'simplify' pricing structures. This is because, in som settings, such measures can actually increase the incentive of firms to adopt comple pricing formats that involve higher prices and profits, and as a result the number of firm that adopt such a frame can go up.[101]

[95] Spiegler (2011) discusses a complementary case where a monopolist can benefit from creating complex temporal price patterns to discriminate between consumers with different abilities to recognise those patterns in the data (what he terms 'coarse reasoning').

[96] Spiegler (2006a) and Chioveanu and Zhou (2013). In an early analysis, Scitovsky (1950) noted that: '[I]n the ignorant market every producer finds it profitable to differentiate his product, not indeed in any objective sense of the word, but by playing on the buyer's ignorance and creating the impression i one way or another that his product is different from competing products. Such differentiation lowers demand elasticities and makes higher profit margins possible.'

[97] Heidhues and Kőszegi (2018) contrast this with the situation in less competitive markets where high margins are sustained by market power.

[98] Miravete and Palacios-Huerta (2014) found that telephone subscribers did not make permanent mistake in estimating expected usage, and that, while inertia existed, it was likely caused by rational inattentio as there was evidence of individuals actively switching to reduce monthly telephone charges.

[99] That is, there is a cost to making a comparison in the market which increases with the number of alternatives. Varian (1980) presents an early analysis of the cost for consumers of being informed.

[100] Armstrong, Vickers and Zhou (2009) examine how the 'prominence' of the presentation of different options affects consumer decision making (such as the first links on a search engine). They find that, where there are no quality differences, then making a firm prominent will typically lead to higher industry profits but lower consumer surplus and welfare.

[101] Spiegler (2011) notes that regulatory interventions which simplify complex pricing formats can be benefici for consumers, while interventions that seek to simplify already simple formats are counterproductive.

Loss- and Risk-Averse Consumers

Biases such as loss aversion or risk aversion can affect non-standard consumer decision making and, in turn, how firms set price structures. Loss-averse consumers can experience a 'loss' (disutility) whenever they purchase a product at a price higher than a reference point.[102] This reference point might be a historical price (such as a sale or discounted price), or what they expect to pay for the product. Loss-averse consumers might consider any departure from the reference price as 'unfair',[103] and be more sensitive to unexpected price increases, or less willing to purchase products when the current price is higher than their expectation, so as to avoid experiencing a disutility from purchasing the product. Loss-averse consumers may also have a greater aversion to products where prices vary frequently, as this gives rise to greater uncertainty about the potential for gains and losses from deviations from an expected price (which has obvious implications for time-of-use pricing in sectors such as electricity). Firms may respond to loss-averse consumers by limiting the frequency at which they change prices (i.e. sticky prices), including in response to demand and cost fluctuations.[104] They may also respond to consumers who are risk- and loss-averse by offering a flat-fee tariff,[105] which can insure such consumers against future uncertain fluctuations in their consumption.[106] In certain settings, a flat-fee structure may be the profit-maximising tariff structure for a firm to adopt.[107]

When consumers consider that they will always be able to obtain a product, then not obtaining it can also give rise to a perceived loss known as the attachment effect.[108] This can incentivise firms to manipulate such consumers through introducing limited availability offers, or temporary price reductions (a bargain), to make the consumer attached to the product, but then withdrawing that offer and replacing it with a higher-priced offer (a rip-off). As the consumer's reference point is raised through the temptation of the bargain, they will still choose to consume the product even at the higher price to reduce their disappointment and the perceived loss.[109]

---

[102] Kőszegi (2010) discusses the concept of a personal equilibrium where an individual gains utility from both physical outcomes and beliefs about physical outcomes (anticipation), while Kőszegi and Rabin (2006) introduce the concept of a 'preferred personal equilibrium', which is a selection of the (typically unique) personal equilibrium with highest expected utility.

[103] This is the so-called comparison effect; see Kőszegi and Rabin (2006). Spiegler (2012) notes that, in order to overcome a consumer's perception that price rises are unfair, firms often try to provide reasons to explain why prices are increasing.

[104] Heidhues and Kőszegi (2004) examine monopoly pricing and note that price stickiness is more likely if: the cost distribution has high density; the price responsiveness of demand is low; or consumers are likely to purchase. Heidhues and Kőszegi (2008) examine the use of focal points in competitive settings in response to loss-averse consumers. Spiegler (2011) notes that the incentive to introduce a rigid pricing structure depends on the number and variance of cost fluctuations.

[105] This is referred to as the 'flat-rate' bias by Train (1991) and has been a particular feature of US telecommunications household pricing.

[106] Herweg and Mierendorff (2013) describe other explanations for why consumer prefer flat-rate prices, including because it decouples payments from consumption and allows consumers to gain pleasure from the service (the so-called taxi-meter effect) or because consumers mis-predict future consumption and thus overvalue consumption for some services.

[107] See Herweg and Mierendorff (2013). These conditions are that marginal costs are low, consumer loss aversion is intense and there are substantial variations in demand.

[108] Kőszegi and Rabin (2006).

[109] See Rosato (2016).

7.2.2 Implications for Firms

While research in behavioural economics has called into question the assumptions under lying standard consumer behaviour in industrial organisation models, it is still ofte[n] assumed that firms (and managers and employees within those firms) behave rationall[y] and seek to maximise profits.[110] While profit is undoubtedly a major driver for busines[s] and there can be strong incentives for suppliers to correct any irrational or biased deci sion making which reduces profit, there are a number of reasons why such an assumptio[n] might not always hold in practice.[111] In other words, there are reasons to believe that som[e] firms may also be 'non-standard' insofar as their behaviour differs from the standar[d] assumptions about firm behaviour used in the industrial organisation models.[112] Afte[r] all, firms often operate in highly complex and uncertain environments which requir[e] quick and complex strategic decisions. As such, firms might rely on heuristics (their gu[t] instincts), copy or imitate another firms' behaviour rather than optimise their own behav iour,[113] or choose to delay or avoid difficult decisions (such as when to exit an activit[y] or product).

The ability to correct for individual biases and decision-making errors could depen[d] on the resources and size of the firm. A sole trader who displays certain non-standar[d] biases as a consumer (loss aversion, *status quo* bias, etc.) will likely also display suc[h] biases when acting as a firm. For example, owners and managers in smaller firms ma[y] display overconfidence about future growth or profitability,[114] or display inattentio[n] to certain information which causes them to overreact.[115] However, such systemati[c] errors are not just limited to small firms. A firm's culture and contractual arrange ments may favour and encourage certain behavioural traits in staff and managemen[t] such as overconfidence.[116] This can increase profits in some circumstances, but coul[d] also lead to a higher propensity for management errors.[117] Management character istics and biases can affect important firm decisions about who to merge with,[118]

---

[110] As Heidhues and Kőszegi (2018) observe, this assumption of profit maximisation is assumed rather than empirically documented, and there are various studies that have identified examples where firms have failed to fully maximise profits.

[111] Armstrong and Huck (2010) observe that, in some settings where firms cannot, or do not aim to, maximise profits, the market can actually be more competitive (e.g. where firms myopically mimic the behaviour of the most profitable rival) or increase the realised profits of a firm (where all firms choose to satisfice rather than optimise profits, this can lead to prices above marginal cost).

[112] Armstrong and Huck (2010) explore this issue but also set out reasons why we might expect firms to be better decision makers than consumers. These include economies of scale in making good decisions (selling to millions of customers), the ability to learn from doing the same thing repeatedly and becaus[e] firms compete with one another and thus can prosper from the poor decision making of rivals.

[113] See Armstrong and Huck (2010).

[114] Manove and Padilla (1999) discuss how entrepreneurs may be unrealistically optimistic and can be overconfident about the future profitability of projects.

[115] Goldfarb and Xiao (2016).

[116] Armstrong and Huck (2010) note that: 'Internal promotion procedures may also have a tendency to favou[r] the over-optimistic, so that CEOs as well as entrepreneurs may be disproportionately over-optimistic.'

[117] See Heidhues and Kőszegi (2018).

[118] Roll (1986) describes how management 'hubris' can lead to firms paying too much in takeover and merger contexts, while Malmendier and Tate (2008) describe how overconfidence can lead managers to overestimate the returns from mergers, leading them to overpay for target companies, and to enter into mergers that are value-destroying.

when to adopt new technologies and when to enter new markets (such as newly opened retail telecommunications markets).[119] Research on whether firms make systematic mistakes when participating in electricity bidding markets has found that the propensity to make mistakes can also depend on firm size and sophistication (including management education).[120]

Certain biases (such as loss aversion) and issues of low trust can also affect the contracting decisions of firms, including the incentives to renegotiate contracts or to enter into long-term supply arrangements. For example, loss-averse parties to a long-term contract may consider the terms of an initial contract as the reference point by which they could experience future losses if the contract is renegotiated. This desire to avoid 'losses' can lead to a general reluctance to renegotiate, or to renegotiate outcomes that are inefficient, as they only seek to adjust from the initial position (a compromise contract) rather than seeking to maximise the surplus of the contracting parties.[121] In some settings, a firm's loss aversion can even create incentives to avoid long-term contracts that establish a reference point from where such losses can arise.[122]

Finally, the decisions of firms and managers may be motivated by factors other than profit maximisation. Some suppliers may be motivated by growth and size (empire building), market status or perception, or geographic coverage even when it is not necessarily the most profitable action.[123] Moreover, some firms may be content to achieve a satisfactory or a fair share of industry profits rather than maximise profits.[124] Non-standard firms might also see a need to recover all costs (including sunk and fixed costs) when setting prices, rather than simply marginal costs as in standard models.[125] Similarly, managers themselves may seek to maximise the terms of their specific employment contract (e.g. bonuses that are linked to output) and thus pursue other goals rather than simply maximising firm profits. Finally, some firms may seek to be good corporate citizens and pursue socially desirable actions which fulfil other goals and objectives which shift the focus away from short-term profit maximisation.[126]

---

[119] Goldfarb and Yang (2009). Goldfarb and Xiao (2011) examine entry into local US telecommunications market after the 1996 Telecommunications Act and find that more experienced and better-educated managers entered markets with fewer competitors.

[120] Hortaçsu, and Puller (2008) and Hortaçsu, Luco, Puller and Zhu (2019) focus on bids made to the Texas electricity spot market.

[121] See Herweg and Schmidt (2015).

[122] Herweg and Schmidt (2015) discuss how it also has implications for the relative suitability of a long-term performance contract *vis-à-vis* asset ownership as a means to protect relationship-specific investments from the hold-up problem discussed in Chapter 6.

[123] For example, Armstrong and Huck (2010) discuss how collusion can in some settings be sustained because there is a social or psychological cost to cheating (e.g. there is a loyalty or personal relationship between conspirators which affects decision making).

[124] As Armstrong and Huck (2010) observe: 'For reasons of complexity, ignorance, or the "easy life", firms might instead engage in satisficing behavior to secure a target level (or "aspiration level") of profit.'

[125] As discussed in Chapter 4, only marginal cost is relevant for profit-maximising pricing decisions in the standard model. See Al-Najjar, Baliga and Besanko (2008).

[126] Goldfarb, Ho, Amaldoss, *et al.* (2012) discuss how social concerns – including fairness – can be particularly important for understanding managerial behaviour.

7.2.3 Implications for Regulation

Having described some of the key insights of behavioural industrial organisation researc
this section considers some of the possible implications of this work for economic regu
lation rationales and policies. Section 7.3 then describes how regulators have drawn o
behavioural economics insights in practice across different sectors.

Implications for the Rationale for Regulation

There are four main implications of the insights just described for the rationale o
regulation.

A first, and perhaps most important, implication is that it challenges the assump
tion that consumer mistakes or biases will be automatically mitigated or 'corrected' i
a competitive market. While such an assumption may hold where a standard consume
makes the occasional 'error' in decision making,[127] many characteristics of non-standar
consumer behaviour are systematic and enduring, which can create incentives for firm
to exploit or manipulate these systematic errors, even in competitive markets.[128] As dis
cussed above, non-standard consumer behaviour can soften price competition, resu
in a proliferation of differentiated products that consumers do not genuinely desire,[1
reduce product quality, and thus ultimately reduce overall welfare.[130] While it is some
times assumed that non-standard consumers are 'protected' by standard consumers i
competitive markets (i.e. there is a positive externality),[131] this protection may only aris
where firms cannot distinguish between consumer types (standard or non-standard) an
where the market alternatives offered to consumers are fixed (i.e. everyone faces the sam
terms).[132] All of these insights have direct implications for restructuring and regulator
policies that have sought to introduce competition into certain retail markets (such a
in energy, telecommunications and transport) that are discussed in Part III of this bool
This is because they directly challenge the conventional assumption that all consume
will benefit from unfettered competition in settings where a majority or large number o
consumers display non-standard behaviour.

---

[127] Muris (2002) succinctly captures the traditional view of how standard consumers influence and
constrain firm behaviour in competitive markets, noting that: 'The consumers' ability to shift
expenditures imposes a rigorous discipline on each seller to satisfy consumer preferences. It often
motivates sellers to provide truthful, useful information about their products and drives them to fulfill
promises concerning price, quality, and other terms of sale. Consumers can punish a seller's deceit or it
reneging on promises made by voting with their feet – and their pocketbooks.'

[128] Spiegler (2011) finds that, even if competition lowers the magnitude of exploitation, it can, in some
settings, increase the ubiquity of exploitative and speculative contracts. See also Akerlof and Shiller
(2015) and Thaler (2018), who describes the incentives for firms (and public authorities) to 'sludge':
using nudges to create frictions that exacerbate behavioural biases. Johnen (2020) observes that in
many markets firms have a better understanding of consumer behaviour than consumers themselves,
which allows them to exploit consumer misunderstandings.

[129] Spiegler (2011) focuses on spurious product differentiation, including proliferation of frames and
multiplicity of price plans. He also examines the use of irrelevant alternatives which are used to screen
consumers and manipulate consumer choice.

[130] Spiegler (2006a) focuses on price competition, while Spiegler (2006b) focuses on product quality. Gamp
and Krähmer (2017) focus on product choice.

[131] In other words, because standard consumers are more responsive to price, they reduce a firm's market
power, which lowers equilibrium prices and benefits all consumers.

[132] See Spiegler (2011) and Armstrong and Vickers (2012).

A second implication relates to prices and price structures. As we discussed, in the presence of non-standard consumers, firms can have incentives to hide or 'shroud' certain charges, introduce complex pricing structures, or otherwise to obfuscate pricing decisions. Firms may also introduce various 'add-on' or 'overage' charges that inattentive or overconfident consumers may not fully factor in to their choices.[133] This can result in highly competitive pricing for a basic product, but monopolistic pricing for contingent add-on services.[134] Alternatively firms could introduce price structures such as three-part tariffs that change with consumption quantity,[135] or offer very low introductory 'teaser' prices to attract consumers which are then increased significantly to the detriment of consumers who are inattentive to the change in price (the 'tease and squeeze' strategy).[136] Where consumers are severely loss-averse, this can lead to flat-pricing structures or affect their willingness to switch to tariffs that create a greater exposure to price fluctuations.[137] As discussed in Section 7.3, some of these general pricing concerns have been identified in energy, air and rail transport and telecommunications markets.

A third implication of work discussed in this chapter thus far concerns the assumptions that regulators make about the willingness, and ability, of consumers to switch between firms in competitive markets. Over the past four decades, regulatory policy has generally been developed around the standard consumer who is assumed to have certain abilities to process complex information, engage in optimal levels of search activity and switch firms when it is optimal to do. However, as described above, non-standard consumers can be affected by inertia, loss aversion, use sampling or heuristics rather than comprehensively searching the market, or be heavily influenced by how a choice is framed. Firms can respond to and exploit this non-standard behaviour by, among other things, introducing auto-renewal contracts (to exploit consumer inertia), obscuring certain aspects of an offer to make it more difficult for consumers to compare suppliers (to take advantage of sampling or limited attention) or frame offers in such a way as to give prominence to certain providers. In short, all of these factors can reduce the level of search and switching from what is assumed in the standard industrial organisation models, which in turn can soften competition among firms in competitive markets and reduce welfare for some consumers.[138] While, in principle, intermediaries or middlemen such as price comparison sites might have an important role to play in helping non-standard consumers to become more active, in practice, this may not always be the case. For example, price comparison websites that are rewarded through commissions may simply choose to exploit non-standard behaviour in a similar way to firms, such as by obscuring comparisons or framing information in specific ways to appeal to certain consumers.[139]

---

[133] See Ellison (2006), Grubb (2009) and Grubb and Osborne (2015).

[134] See Spiegler (2012).

[135] Grubb (2009) and Grubb and Osborne (2015) discuss the use of such structures in mobile pricing plans.

[136] See Johnen (2019). There is some evidence of such a strategy being applied in the British energy market. See the BBC News (BBC, 2016).

[137] Nicolson, Huebner and Shipworth (2017) looked at the UK energy market and found that 93 per cent of bill payers are loss-averse (care more about avoiding financial losses than making savings) and that loss-averse people were substantially less willing to switch to the time-of-use energy tariffs.

[138] Grubb (2015c) notes that, even in homogeneous product markets, insufficient search, confusion and excessive inertia contribute to price dispersion and positive mark-ups, even where there is an increasing number of sellers.

[139] See Armstrong and Zhou (2011).

A final implication relates to distributional issues and specifically the circumstance in which regulation should intervene in markets to address the potential exploitation c non-standard consumers. There is an important difference here between circumstance where regulatory interventions protect non-standard consumers but do not affect the out comes for standard consumers, and settings where a regulatory intervention involves potential gain for non-standard consumers but a loss for standard consumers. For exam ple, where the prices faced by standard consumers are cross-subsidised by non-standar consumers, then regulation which seeks to protect or educate non-standard consumers ca adversely affect standard consumers.[140] Whether or not such a cross-subsidy between stand ard and non-standard consumers necessitates regulation will therefore, in part, depend o the relative welfare weights assigned to different types of consumers in a society.[141]

The Potential Effects of Regulatory Initiatives to Address Non-Standard Behaviour

Alongside challenging some of the rationales for regulation, analytical work has als identified some possible unexpected effects of different regulatory interventions t address or 'correct' non-standard consumer behaviour. To take one example, while regu lators typically assume that measures to encourage consumers to be more active, or whic simplify complex pricing environments, will be beneficial, some studies have shown tha such policies can have the opposite effect in some settings.[142]

At one end of the spectrum, some regulators have been attracted to policies that 'nudge non-standard consumers with the aim of making better choices and decisions.[143] Howeve while nudges can seem like 'light-handed' measures to address non-standard behaviou such policies can 'backfire' if a regulator does not take account of how firms will respond that is, where the regulator does not consider the equilibrium effects of its nudgin policies.[144] For example, using prompts or reminders to nudge non-standard consum ers into thinking about if they will face excess charges or 'bill shock' might ultimatel adversely affect such consumers if they adjust their behaviour to avoid such charges an in response suppliers adjust price structures by raising overall prices.[145]

At the other end of the spectrum, another possible regulatory response to non-standar consumer behaviour is to introduce price regulation with the aim of shielding or protect ing such consumers from exploitation. However, once again, the effects of such interven tions can depend on whether the outcomes for non-standard and standard consumers ar linked, or whether they face contrasting deals. In settings where outcomes are linked, the price regulation can be counterproductive by reducing the incentives for non-standar

---

[140] For a standard consumer, the cross-subsidy might be seen to compensate them for the costs incurred in being active and searching the market.

[141] Armstrong and Vickers (2012) argue that in many settings it may be reasonable to accord a higher welfare weight to non-standard consumers.

[142] Spiegler (2011) concludes that in many cases policies introduced to remedy the exploitative effects of non-standard behaviour often resulted in negative outcomes. Similarly, Grubb (2015c) concludes that theory and evidence show that 'seemingly sensible interventions, such as aiding individual decision making, can be ineffective due to firms' equilibrium responses'.

[143] This builds on the work on the design of 'choice architectures' by Thaler and Sunstein (2008), and emphasises in particular measures which change how choices are presented to consumers.

[144] See Grubb (2015a, c) and Spiegler (2015). More generally, Sunstein (2017) discusses 'nudges that fail'.

[145] Grubb (2009, 2015a, c). Grubb and Osborne (2015) find that bill-shock regulation would not have helpe consumers in the period they examined.

consumers to be informed, reducing price competition and increasing average prices.[146] Indeed, in some settings, firms themselves may favour the introduction of price caps if it limits the incentives for non-standard consumers to become educated and more active.[147] Conversely, where outcomes for standard and non-standard consumers are decoupled, then there is a stronger case for regulation.[148] Another possible regulatory intervention involves the price capping, or banning, of certain additional or 'secondary' prices or tariffs (e.g. hidden add-ons or surcharges) rather than the basic product. While such a disaggregated price cap approach can intensify competition under some assumptions,[149] it could also create incentives for firms to invent new hidden charges or fees to compensate for the lost revenues.[150]

Another common regulatory response to non-standard consumer behaviour is to focus on reducing obscure and complex pricing practices by requiring that firms be more transparent and remove hidden or obscure charges. Such measures can make it easier for some non-standard consumers to compare offers if they increase price transparency, but in so doing could also encourage and assist firms to (tacitly) align their pricing policies. In addition, as discussed above, policies that focus on simplifying consumer choice can, counter-intuitively, have the unintended consequence of incentivising more firms to adopt complex pricing formats involving higher prices.[151] Similarly, policies that limit the ability of firms to exploit non-standard consumers by prohibiting price discrimination can inadvertently lead firms to charge a higher, but uniform, tariff to all consumers.[152]

Overall, analytical work suggests that regulatory measures that seek to educate consumers and make them more equipped to deal with the complexity of the market can be most effective.[153] However, here, too, research across a range of settings suggests that effectiveness depends on how such educative programmes are implemented,[154] and how firms respond to such initiatives. For example, in some settings, firms may respond to mandated education initiatives by further obscuring their offerings.[155] Moreover,

---

[146] See Fershtman and Fishman (1994) and Armstrong and Vickers (2012).

[147] Armstrong (2015) notes that: 'Because profit falls when more consumers are savvy, sellers have an incentive to try to confuse consumers in the way they present their offers, and sellers may welcome regulation which reduces the incentive for consumers to become savvy – i.e. simple price caps.'

[148] See Armstrong and Vickers (2012).

[149] Heidhues, Johnen and Kőszegi (2021) argue that regulation, including in the form of price caps of secondary features of a complex product (such as additional charges or prices), can sometimes intensify competition as it allows consumers with limited attention to do more comparison shopping (browsing) rather than expending time studying or understanding the precise details of the contract and secondary features.

[150] See Heidhues, Kőszegi and Murooka (2016).

[151] Piccione and Spiegler (2012) find that regulatory interventions that enhance comparability may lead to a less competitive market outcome, while Spiegler (2011) argues that regulatory interventions which simplify complex pricing formats can be beneficial for consumers, while interventions that seek to simplify already simple formats are counterproductive.

[152] In the UK, for example, a regulatory measure directed at protecting certain vulnerable and disengaged consumers through banning regional price discrimination was found to have softened competition. See CMA (2016a).

[153] Spiegler (2011) notes that this type of regulatory measure does seem to address some failures associated with consumer's bounded rationality.

[154] Kiss (2014) found that media campaigns can be effective in promoting switching.

[155] Heidhues and Kőszegi (2018) note that some non-standard consumers may only purchase a product in an obscure market setting (i.e. where it is shrouded) and, as such, education efforts can potentially backfire by creating incentives for firms to respond by obscuring the market in different ways so as to maintain the business of those customers.

regulatory requirements that firms provide consumers with more information can poten
tially exacerbate certain biases in some non-standard consumers by making the environ
ment even more complex (e.g. information overload and decision fatigue). The timing of
when consumers receive additional information can also be important to the effectivenes
of policies.[156] Finally, education initiatives can have adverse effects for some consumer
and potentially reduce welfare, where, as a result of such measures, fewer non-stand
ard consumers pay an additional price and a firm responds by raising prices to brea
even. This response can potentially harm both existing standard consumers and thos
non-standard consumers who do not change their behaviour in response to the educatio
initiatives.[157]

7.3 APPLICATION OF BEHAVIOURAL ECONOMICS IN PRACTICE

This section provides a high-level overview of how economic regulators have draw
upon the insights of behavioural economics in developing and implementing policy. Th
discussion focuses on examples of how behavioural economics insights have been used i
the regulated sectors discussed in Part III of this book.[158] However, insights from behav
ioural economics have been used beyond these sectors for a range of purposes, includin
competition law and consumer policies.[159] While the discussion in this section looks a
specific policy measures, behavioural economics insights have also influenced how som
regulators collect and evaluate evidence on policy interventions, most notably throug
the use of randomised controlled trials to test how consumers might respond to certai
policies.

7.3.1 Use of Behavioural Economics in the Energy Sector

Although retail markets in gas and electricity have been open to competition for som
time in countries such as Britain, Australia and EU Member States, energy regulators hav
been concerned about consumer inertia and disengagement in such markets,[160] and tha
this lack of demand-side responsiveness enhances the market power of firms. While som
energy regulators have, at times, adopted a view that behavioural biases do not neces
sarily result in worse consumer outcomes, and can drive consumers to make pruden

---

[156] Johnen (2019) finds that, in the context of auto-renewal contracts, salience policies (such as those
which make auto-renewal clauses more noticeable or prominent at the contracting stage) are more likel
to backfire than reminders that are sent to consumers a short time period before the contract is renewe
automatically. This is because salient policies increase awareness about automatic renewal policies whe
a contract is signed, rather than just before the renewal is about to occur. Murooka and Schwarz (2018)
reach a similar conclusion in the context of mobile phone plans.
[157] See Heidhues and Kőszegi (2018).
[158] Joseph, Ayling, Miquel-Florensa, *et al.* (2022) also provide an overview of the use of behavioural
economics insights in infrastructure sectors.
[159] Wider reviews include Productivity Commission (2007), OFT (2011a) and EC (2016a). Fletcher (2016) review
the effectiveness of behavioural economics inspired remedies in the UK. More general analysis of how
behavioural economics has informed regulatory policy are presented in Lunn (2014) and OECD (2017a).
[160] The body representing EU regulators (CEER, 2021) has noted that 'it is well understood that many
customers are disengaged and are not motivated to interact with the electricity market', and that
twenty-five years in since the creation of residential electricity markets 'the default pre-disposition of
many electricity consumers is to do nothing and/or choose the utility that they know'.

cautious decisions,[161] a number of other energy regulators have drawn on behavioural economics to justify the introduction of new policies. These regulators have sought to address various perceived characteristics of non-standard consumers, including that such consumers: have limited capacity to assess energy products; display the *status quo* bias; are loss-averse; and are time-inconsistent.[162]

One set of policy measures to encourage consumers to be more active in energy markets, and to limit the potential for firms to exploit specific consumer biases, have focused on prices. In Britain, for example, the complexity of energy prices combined with consumer inertia was seen to give firms unilateral market power over their inactive customer base, which was exploited by pricing a default tariff (which is used by households that have not switched) at levels well above that which could be justified by cost differences. A 2016 study estimated that the size of the detriment from the 'excessive prices' levied on inactive domestic customers was, on average, £1.7 billion a year.[163] An early policy response to consumer inertia and confusion involved limiting the number of tariffs that could be offered to consumers to just four, with the aim of reducing consumer confusion, and banning price discrimination, to protect vulnerable consumers. However, these regulatory pricing interventions were later found to have effectively backfired and given rise to an adverse effect on competition, making some consumers worse off.[164] In addition, such measures were seen to harm competition between price comparison websites, by softening their ability to compete with one another. As part of its 2016 review, the UK competition authority drew directly on behavioural economics in developing its remedies.[165] However, as discussed in Chapter 9, in 2019, a price cap was subsequently introduced

---

[161] For example, the Australian Energy Markets Commission (AEMC, 2016a) has noted that: 'Behavioural biases do not necessarily result in worse consumer outcomes. In many cases behavioural biases drive consumers to make prudent, cautious decisions. This is quite important since full deliberation takes effort and is time-consuming; it is simply not possible to do this for every decision. Individuals need to use heuristics for many decisions. In many circumstances decisions made by heuristics may actually be nearly as good or even the same as optimal decisions made by rational agents.' In a similar vein, the UK competition agency (OFT, 2010) has noted in the past that 'markets can be self-correcting and interventions can potentially do more harm than good'. Littlechild (2021c) argues that: 'The implication of all this recent research and evidence is that customers are more economically rational than a simplistic interpretation of the behavioural approach would imply. Customers that do not switch to an apparently lower-cost supplier are not necessarily disengaged or acting irrationally.'

[162] See Ofgem (2011b).

[163] See CMA (2016a). The 'excessive prices' were quantified by comparing the actual prices to costs and the estimate of 'competitive' prices. In effect, this compares what consumers would pay if they were standard consumers (i.e. rational, active consumers who paid the 'competitive price') and not non-standard consumers (i.e. actual consumers who pay the higher default tariff). Littlechild (2021) presents a critique.

[164] The introduction of the four-tariff rule had led to some of the major suppliers changing their tariff structures and removing discounts, which may have made some consumers worse off. CMA (2016a) noted that there were few, if any, signs of consumer engagement improving from these interventions, and that those consumers who disengaged prior to the interventions continued to do so.

[165] See CMA (2016a). In its submission to this inquiry, the UK's Behavioural Insights Team (2015) was critical of some of the proposed remedies, noting that prompting customers to engage may not be sufficient to protect consumers who have never engaged in the market. It also urged caution, when proposing introduction of a regulator-controlled database, in drawing attention to the fact that consumers who are more likely to be on default tariffs may be vulnerable and may be enticed to switch by novel pricing structures which offer short-term discounts but higher prices over the long term. The Behavioural Insights Team also suggested that the default tariff be renamed the 'emergency tariff' in order to highlight the unusual nature of the tariff.

for all customers on the default tariffs.[166] Similar concerns that inactive consumers were being exploited through higher prices in Australia also led to the re-introduction of retail price regulation for customers on default contracts in 2019. In addition, retail suppliers are required to present electricity prices in a standard way by referring to a 'reference price' (a benchmark price for electricity set by the government) so that consumers can compare offers.[167] More radical measures to address consumer inertia were considered in France, where the energy regulator considered a proposal whereby consumers that had not subscribed to a market offer by a particular date would be put on a default 'transitional offer' from their supplier for a maximum period of six months. After that period if the consumer had still not subscribed to a market offer contract, the supply of gas and electricity would no longer be guaranteed.[168]

Alongside these interventions focused on prices, energy regulators have sought to develop policies that provide consumers with more information, or require that information be presented in a specific way with the aim of overcoming consumer inertia and the *status quo* bias. In EU Member States, energy consumers must receive certain pre-contractual information and such information must be clear and understandable and avoid non-contractual barriers (e.g. excessive documentation).[169] Suppliers' bills must be 'user-friendly' and presented in a manner that allows for comparison by consumers.[170] The importance of independent comparison tools, including websites, is also emphasised to reduce search costs and allow smaller customers to assess different offers on the market. Similarly, in US states where there is retail choice, such as Texas, customers must sometimes be provided with an electricity fact sheet so that customers can make an 'apples-to-apples' comparison of the different offers.[171] There are also rules about the presentation and content to be included in customer bills, and the regulator maintains a website which allows consumers to compare offers and choose an electricity provider tailored to their needs.[172] It is notable that Texas is often cited as the state with the most successful retail competition, with some estimates suggesting that up to 92 per cent of customers have exercised their right to choose an electricity supplier.[173] Behavioural economics insights have also been applied to *firms* in some jurisdictions. In the Netherlands the regulator has applied nudging techniques to encourage suppliers to calculate and communicate accurate fee information to consumers during the cooling-off period.[174]

---

[166] When the CMA proposed its remedy package, one panel member offered a dissenting opinion, on the basis that in his view the retail remedy package was unlikely to succeed and that a short-term price cap covering a substantially larger number of customers, was required to reset the market.

[167] See Behavioural Insights Team (2019).

[168] See Commission de régulation de l'énergie (2016).

[169] The CEER (2020), which represent EU Member States energy regulators, has emphasised the importance of simplicity in the information provided to consumers, noting that 'Behavioural science helps to understand consumers and to identify solutions that best suit their needs.'

[170] EC (2015a) found that 'lack of appropriate information on costs and consumption, or limited transparency in offers, makes it difficult for consumers (or reliable intermediaries and energy service companies, such as aggregators, acting on their behalf) to assess the market situation and opportunities'

[171] Consumers must be provided with an electricity fact sheet that provides them with standardised information about an electric plan, including contract terms, pricing, fees and the percentage of renewable energy offered.

[172] Website is powertochoose.org.

[173] See Hartley, Medlock and Jankovska (2019).

[174] OECD (2017a).

Alongside these measures, which focus on making consumers more engaged in competitive retail energy markets, behavioural economics insights have been used to encourage consumers to be more energy-efficient and to be more responsive to changes in demand (by reducing consumption in peak periods).[175] Consumer energy consumption decisions have been found to be affected by the various biases we discussed in Section 7.1, including the *status quo* bias (using the default thermostat temperature), the attitude-behaviour gap (consumer inability to match their beliefs and preferences to behaviour) and framing (lack of salience of energy consumption information).[176] Behavioural economics experiments have informed energy efficiency and conservation policies in Italy, South Africa and Sweden.[177] These interventions have included trying to 'nudge' consumers to conserve energy through social comparison (comparing use to other households), commitment devices and goal setting (such as pledges to conserve energy) and labelling (about the energy consumption of devices).[178]

7.3.2 Use of Behavioural Economics in the Telecommunications Industry

Telecommunications regulators in some jurisdictions have also drawn on behavioural economics insights in developing and implementing policy for broadband, fixed line and mobile services. Among the specific concerns that regulators have sought to address are that some consumers, particularly of fixed line and broadband services, may be inert and subject to the *status quo* bias, while some consumers of mobile telecommunications services are easily confused by the vast array and complexity of tariffs and pricing plans on offer and mis-estimate their future consumption levels.[179] Policy has also been motivated by concerns that telecommunication service providers exploit these biases through specific pricing structures, and by making it difficult for consumers to compare services among providers.

A particular area where insights from behavioural economics have been used is for policies to prevent consumers from facing so-called 'bill shock' – high charges levied for exceeding an agreed usage threshold (such as allowed calls, text messages or data usage) or for using a phone in an area where roaming charges apply.[180] As described above, non-standard consumers who are inattentive, overconfident or have time-inconsistent preferences are particularly susceptible to facing such charges. In the USA, a 2011 voluntary agreement between the Federal Communications Commission and major mobile (wireless) telecoms requires that usage alerts are sent to subscribers on plans

---

[175] Frederiks, Stenner and Hobman (2015) identify the key behavioural biases which affect household energy use. See also Pollitt and Shaorshadze (2013) and Brennan (2016).

[176] OECD (2017b).

[177] OECD (2017a).

[178] Andor and Fels (2018) survey the effects of these nudges in forty-four international studies. See also Sanin, Trillas, Mejdalani, *et al.* (2019).

[179] A study of telecommunications users in Colombia found that they featured the following biases: choice overload; endowment effect; defaults; loss aversion; and hyperbolic discounting. See OECD (2016b).

[180] The FCC (2010a) notes that: '[A]s mobile devices have become more and more complex, consumers have had to navigate more complex plans, choices, and bills. The complexity and confusion put them at increasing risk for "bill shock," a sudden, unexpected increase in their mobile bill from one month to the next.' See also Grubb and Osborne (2015).

with additional charges for exceeding voice, data or text usage limits, and to consume without an international roaming plan/package who may incur charges when travelling abroad. However, there have been persistent concerns about inattentive consumers being exposed to other 'hidden fees', such as so-called 'cramming' (where carriers sometimes permit third parties to add charges to a subscriber's phone bill with minimal levels of notice or consent) or other hidden service charges.[181] Similar policies have been introduced in Europe where, since 2010, regulations have been in place to protect consumers from data roaming bill shock.[182] Mobile providers are also required to send consumers text message when crossing national borders to remind them that they may incur roaming charges. In the Netherlands, the regulator has applied 'nudging' techniques to firms to encourage them to pay the annual fees for the regulation of special service numbers on time.

Behavioural economics insights have also been used to inform the development of information disclosure and contract design policies, and specifically to address the complexity of contracts and price plans. For example, a joint study by the OECD and Colombian Communications Regulator drew extensively on behavioural economics to simplify mobile telephone and internet services contracts.[183] In the UK, the communications regulator has commissioned behavioural and experimental studies on issues such as: the framing of prices;[184] how to best present call price information; how the way information is presented affects consumer switching; and consumer understanding of offers on broadband speed.[185] Behavioural economics research has also informed the UK competition agency's work on the so-called 'loyalty penalty' in broadband and mobile services.[186] This is where existing customers pay more than new customers for the same services, and where firms charge higher prices to existing customers who they think are inert and suffer from *status quo* bias and will not switch.[187] Recommendations include that mobile providers automatically move customers on bundled handset and airtime contracts onto a fairer tariff when their minimum contract period ends, and that consideration be given to pricing interventions in broadband markets, such as targeted safeguard price caps to protect vulnerable consumers.[188]

---

[181] These fees are labelled as a 'service fee', 'service charge', 'other fees', 'voicemail', 'mail server', 'calling plan' or 'membership'.

[182] Operators were originally required to send consumers a warning when they reach 80 per cent of their data roaming bill limit, and could cut off access to the service once the limit was reached, unless the customer has indicated they want to continue data roaming that particular month. In 2017, this was replaced by a ban on EU-based roaming charges. An earlier roaming EU Regulation introduced in 2007 set a cap on roaming charges. McGowan (2018) describes how this regulation was informed by behavioural industrial organisation.

[183] OECD (2016b).

[184] Ofcom (2010) compared the behavioural effects of providing the exact price of a call in a pre-call announcement versus price information on the monthly bill in the form of a list detailing all call charges for all telephone numbers.

[185] See Ofcom (2010) and OECD (2017a)

[186] See Heidhues, Johnen and Rauber (2020).

[187] The size of the loyalty penalty was estimated at £4 billion across the five markets (broadband, mobile, cash savings, home insurance and mortgages), and that vulnerable consumers were more at risk of paying the loyalty penalty.

[188] CMA (2018a).

7.3.3 Use of Behavioural Economics in the Transport Industry

Behavioural economics insights have sometimes been used by regulators in the transport industry. Notably, insights from behavioural economics have been used to address so-called 'partitioned' or 'drip' pricing, and other 'hidden' pricing practices in the airline industry.[189] This is where a headline price is advertised at the start of a booking process to which additional fees and charges (some of which are unavoidable) are 'dripped' and only added to the fare as the booking process continues (such as baggage handling fees, fuel or card surcharges). This effectively shrouds the total cost of the ticket and can be exploited by airlines when dealing with consumers who display the endowment effect or are loss-averse. In Europe, airlines are required to include all applicable taxes, charges and surcharges in the final price, while in the USA carriers and travel agents must advertise the full fare to be paid by the customer including any and all taxes, gasoline surcharges and facility charges. In addition, carriers are required to disclose code-share arrangements in online schedule displays, and carriers and ticket agents are prohibited from engaging in 'undisclosed bias' when displaying fare, schedule or availability information online that includes multiple carriers. In the UK, twelve airlines voluntarily agreed with the regulator that they would include any debit card surcharges in the headline price and present optional credit card fees transparently, while in Australia the regulator has taken legal action against such practices.

In the rail sector, some regulators have drawn on behavioural economics research in considering how to develop performance management systems and effective 'behavioural incentives' where a rail infrastructure company is under public ownership, or when considering the potential benefits of third-party intermediaries assisting customers to make claims for delayed train journeys.[190] Behavioural economics insights have also been brought to bear on the impacts of fare complexity on consumer behaviour in the context of the development of fare simplification policies.[191] Finally, behavioural economics has been used to assess how potential biases and heuristics in judgement within a government agency (the Department for Transport) could be affecting the delivery of rail transport projects.[192]

7.3.4 Use of Behavioural Economics in the Water Sector

Insights from behavioural economics have sometimes been used to develop mechanisms for encouraging consumers to conserve water. Behavioural biases such as the *status quo* bias, the attitude–behaviour gap and framing have all been identified as potentially affecting water consumption decisions.[193] The lack of household water meters in many jurisdictions means that consumers cannot track their consumption, which can make water conservation less salient. Among policies used to encourage consumers to conserve water

---

[189] For an overview of drip pricing, see FTC (2012).
[190] For example, the three studies commissioned by the UK's ORR (2018, 2019, 2020a).
[191] See Anciaes, Metcalfe, Heywood and Sheldon (2019).
[192] UK Department for Transport (2017).
[193] OECD (2017b).

include 'nudges' and social norm policies, such as comparing household water usage t
similar households, and real-time feedback mechanisms (e.g. in-shower smart meters).[19]

7.3.5 Use of Behavioural Economics in Payment Systems

Behavioural economics research has been used by regulators of card and interbank pay
ment systems in some jurisdictions.[195] A particular focus has been on 'hidden' charge
for the use of credit cards. In the USA, the Credit Card Accountability Responsibility an
Disclosure (CARD) Act sought to reduce the ability of credit card companies to explo
various consumer biases through hidden or shrouded charges (so-called 'gotcha' fees
These fees were seen to exploit consumer biases such as: present bias and time inconsist
ency; inattention to specific penalty fees or interest rate charges; over-optimism abou
the likelihood of incurring penalty charges; an inability to appreciate the compounding o
interest; and consumer decision making being anchored in the minimum payment infor
mation.[196] Among other things, the CARD Act required card operators to get consumer
to agree (opt in) to be charged for exceeding their credit limit, and to limit the level o
penalty or late fees to being 'reasonable and proportional'. It also required that custome
bills include information to 'nudge' consumers to repaying early by showing the cost o
repaying balances over thirty-six months versus minimum monthly repayment. Analysi
by the regulator in 2015 estimated that the CARD Act had saved consumers some $16 bil
lion.[197] However, it also identified various outstanding concerns, including: the effect o
deferred interest promotions which 'dangle' the possibility of financing purchases withou
interest; the timing and obscurity of rewards programme information; and the complexit
and length of credit card agreements. The regulator (the Consumer Financial Protectio
Bureau) has also drawn on behavioural research in developing new opt-in provisions fo
debit cards and ATM (automated teller machine; cash machine) overdrafts on checkin
(current) accounts.[198]

   In the UK, the regulator has focused on how various biases (particularly optimism bias
framing effects and anchoring) could lead consumers to sign up to credit card provider
which offer lower introductory rates, to over-borrow on credit cards or to delay repay
ment decisions.[199] It has looked at how nudges can be used to encourage consumers t
pay down credit card debt.[200] The UK payments systems regulator has recently looke

---

[194] OECD (2017b) discusses examples from Costa Rica, Colombia and Switzerland.
[195] More broadly, behavioural economics has been embraced by financial services regulators. A study by
    the UK financial conduct regulator (FCA, 2013) notes that 'behavioural economics enables regulators to
    intervene in markets more effectively, and in new ways, to counter such business models [which result
    in consumer detriment] and secure better outcomes for consumers', while a former Director of the US
    Consumer Financial Protection Bureau has noted that '[w]e must understand what makes consumers
    tick so that we can use our supervision, enforcement, regulation, and education tools to be the best
    consumer protection agency we can be' CFPB (2019).
[196] See Lunn (2014).
[197] CFPB (2015). Agarwal, Chomsisengphet, Mahoney and Stroebel (2015) estimated that, between 2008 an
    2012, consumers saved $11.9 billion per year.
[198] CFPB (2017).
[199] See FCA (2016).
[200] See FCA (2018).

at behavioural economics insights in the context of encouraging smaller merchants to more actively engage in choosing an acquirer to reduce the merchant service charges they face.[201] In Europe, rules prohibit banks, and other payment service providers, from using non-transparent pricing methods to address concerns that it is otherwise extremely difficult for consumers to establish the real price of the payment service.[202] Merchants are also prohibited from levying consumers with hidden surcharges for card-based payments.[203] To address the risks of consumers being caught in 'subscription traps', major credit card companies are required to ensure that all necessary information is presented in the payment window for the consumer when they make a payment online involving recurring subscription fees.[204]

7.3.6 Use of Behavioural Economics for Digital Platforms

Although, as discussed in Chapter 13, the specific regulatory regimes for digital platforms are still being developed in many jurisdictions, studies by competition agencies and other bodies have often drawn on behavioural economics insights when assessing the need for regulation of these platforms.[205] Insights from behavioural economics have been particularly prominent in six areas.[206] First, it has been argued that the 'behavioural limitations' of consumers – particularly towards default options and rankings – may entrench the market power of dominant platforms by creating or reinforcing barriers to entry.[207] Second, behavioural economics research has been used to show how presenting online offers as 'free' to consumers can exacerbate behavioural biases and encourage a narrow way of thinking about more complex decisions (e.g. consumers do not take account of the fact that they are providing the platform with their data).[208] Third, behavioural economics has been used to examine how online information disclosures can be incorporated into policy to address the fact that some consumers consent to transactions without fully informing themselves of the terms and conditions.[209] Fourth, concerns have been expressed that digital platforms with large datasets at their disposal have an ability to develop a granular and highly personal understanding of a consumer's behavioural biases in real time, which can then be exploited through 'framing, nudges and defaults' in ways

---

[201] See PSR (2021a).
[202] See Payment Services Directive PSD 1 (Directive 2007/64/EC).
[203] See Payment Services Directive PSD 2 (Directive 2015/2366).
[204] This is to address situations where hidden or small print about recurring payments is not presented to consumers when entering their credit card details, and only information about a one-off payment amount, not the recurring subscription amount, is shown.
[205] See, for example, Barker (2018), ACCC (2019) and CMA (2020).
[206] Furman, Coyle, Fletcher, *et al.* (2019) discuss how regulators can also be subject to behavioural biases.
[207] See Furman, Coyle, Fletcher, *et al.* (2019). The Stigler Center (2019) notes: 'Consumers do not scroll down to see more search results, they agree to settings chosen by the service, they single-home on one platform, and they generally take actions that favor the status quo and make it difficult for an entrant to attract consumers.' The US House of Representatives (2020) notes that, once a customer is locked in to an online shopping platform, they are less likely to change their behaviour even when pricing is not competitive. See also Crémer, de Montjoye and Schweitzer (2019).
[208] ACCC (2019).
[209] Barker (2018).

that are profitable for the platform.[210] As only one party has access to this personalise
consumer behavioural data, this can also act as a barrier to entry.[211] Fifth, there has bee
a focus on how digital platforms can use advertising, default privacy settings and othe
methods – such as so-called 'dark patterns' – to nudge or manipulate consumers int
making decisions that they would otherwise consciously avoid.[212] Finally, there is focu
on how some digital platforms can promote addictive behaviour by presenting users wit
exploitative or highly sensationalist content, or otherwise feed 'human reward centres'.[2

7.4 CONCLUSION

This chapter has presented an overview of how research in behavioural economics coul
or does, affect the theory and practice of economic regulation. As discussed at the outse
many of the theories and insights that underpin modern economic regulation typicall
assume that consumers are perfectly rational, have a high level of computational skil
and are invariant to how choices are framed or presented to them. However, as we hav
seen, behavioural economics research has identified a number of ways in which rea
consumer behaviour systematically deviates from assumptions about the 'standard con
sumer'. Among other things, this research has shown that consumers do not always hav
stable and consistent preferences, can be affected by various 'biases' which can affec
their judgement, and may not always be willing and able to search and compare produc
offerings. Consumer decision making can also be affected by factors such as the perceive
fairness of the transaction and wider goals.

Analytical work in the area known as behavioural industrial organisation has sought t
incorporate these behavioural economics insights about 'non-standard' consumer behav
iour into industrial organisation models. Among other things, this work reveals that, i
the presence of non-standard consumers, competition may not always automatically pro
tect consumers from being exploited, and can result in distributional outcomes whe
non-standard consumers cross-subsidise standard consumers. Incorporating non-stand
ard consumers into models can also result in distorted allocations, and create additiona
deadweight losses, reducing total surplus. Importantly, these models also show how th

---

[210] As the Stigler Center (2019) notes: 'Platforms that analyze their consumers' behavior can exploit these
biases by framing choices to make certain information salient, designing a status quo that is profitable,
inducing addictive behaviors, generating sales through impulsive consumption, and exploiting
consumers' disinclination to search.'

[211] See Furman, Coyle, Fletcher, et al. (2019).

[212] CMA (2021a) defines a dark pattern as 'user interface designs that trick users into making unintended
and potentially harmful decisions' and notes that: 'Platforms may use other unfair design practices
("dark patterns") to exploit consumers' behavioural biases for commercial gain, including the use of
misleading scarcity messages, which exploit consumers' loss aversion and tendency to be influenced by
the actions of others (social proof).' The Stigler Center (2019) notes: 'Dark patterns are user interfaces
that can confuse users, make it difficult for users to express their actual preferences, or manipulate
users into taking certain actions. ... Behavioral economists have tended to use the term "sludge" (i.e.,
an evil nudge) to describe the same phenomena.' Similarly, Furman, Coyle, Fletcher, et al. (2019) note
that 'online environments provide a variety of new ways in which firms can exploit behavioural biases
and mislead consumers'; while ACCC (2019) discusses how some digital platforms design user interface
to appeal to certain psychological or behavioural biases, leading users to make privacy-intrusive
selections. CMA (2020) considers advertising and privacy issues.

[213] See Stigler Center (2019). Crémer, de Montjoye and Schweitzer (2019) also refer to consumer biases
towards short-term gratification.

presence of non-standard consumers can change firms' incentives and behaviour in various ways.[214] First, it can incentivise them to price-discriminate among consumer types (standard and non-standard) and to structure prices which exploit consumer *naïveté* (e.g. use of hidden or shrouded add-on prices). Second, it can affect how firms 'frame' offers to consumers, and in particular whether they seek to educate consumers or exploit consumer biases through obfuscation. Third, these models have shown how firms can respond to loss- and risk-averse consumers by adopting certain pricing practices (such as flat-fee tariffs), or through manipulating consumers' reference points by making temporary offers to make them attached to the product and then raising the price ('tease and squeeze' strategies). Some models have also focused on how decision-making biases can impact on the behaviour of firms, and in particular on the managers of firms. This work suggests that firms may not always be fully rational and seek to maximise profit. Factors such as a firm's size, culture, degree of trust and management contractual arrangements can all potentially lead to systematic deviations from standard assumptions around a firm's behaviour.

The results of work in behavioural industrial organisation has potential implications for the rationale for certain economic regulatory policies and the possible effects of different regulatory interventions aimed at 'correcting' non-standard consumer behaviour. Of particular relevance is the challenge to the assumption that consumer mistakes or biases will be naturally mitigated or 'corrected' through intense competition.[215] Rather, it shows how, even in competitive market settings, firms can have incentives to exploit consumer biases through using shrouded or hidden prices or making alternatives more obscure and difficult to compare. Similarly, it calls into question assumptions often made by regulators about consumers' willingness and ability to switch between suppliers in competitive markets by highlighting how non-standard consumers can be affected by inertia, loss aversion, sampling and how a choice is framed. Insights from this research also have implications for specific regulatory interventions and policies. For example, studies have shown how policies to simplify prices, introduce price caps or 'nudge' non-standard consumers can backfire in certain settings. While regulatory measures that seek to educate consumers can, in principle, be effective, much depends on how they are implemented.

Behavioural economics research has directly influenced the work of economic regulators in some jurisdictions and sectors. In the energy sector, regulators in some countries have drawn on behavioural economics insights with the aim of making consumers more active and engaged in competitive retail energy markets, and to limit the scope for firms to exploit consumer biases such as inertia. Some of these policies (such as tariff simplification or bans on price discrimination) have met with mixed success in some jurisdictions. In telecommunications, behavioural economics insights have influenced policies requiring firms to assist consumers in avoiding 'bill shock' and which simplify contract design and information disclosures, including the automatic renewal of contracts.

---

[214] More generally, Heidhues and Kőszegi (2018) note that research in behavioural industrial organisation has shown that 'the unrealistically narrow view of consumers and managers in the classical industrial-organization paradigm can lead to a misinterpretation of market phenomena, and thereby to a misguided call for market intervention. Most importantly, a number of puzzling patterns in firm behavior have been attributed to harmful practices such as collusion or predation, when in fact plausible explanations based on richer models of consumer behavior are possible.'

[215] As Spiegler (2011) observes, 'consumers' bounded rationality can generate market failure, but it is far from clear whether it is a failure that can be "fixed".'

In aviation, behavioural economics insights have informed policies relating to transpar ency of prices and to prohibit certain pricing practices (such as 'drip pricing'), while i rail the focus has been on how insights could inform policies to incentivise managemer of rail companies under private ownership and to simplify prices. Behavioural economic has played a role in the development of policies against hidden or 'gotcha' fees in credi card payment systems, and in policies which seek to nudge consumers to paying bac credit card debt early. Finally, behavioural economics is having a major influence on th development of regulatory policies for digital platforms, with many competition agencie and other bodies drawing on insights from behavioural economics to show that consume biases can be exploited and thus justify a need for regulation of this activity.

In summary, behavioural economics has identified many ways in which real consum ers differ from those used in standard models that have informed economic regulatior However, what this means for economic regulation in practice is less clear. In many area there is no clear prescription or set of policies that regulators should apply in practice and there are a number of examples across sectors of policies directed at changing con sumer behaviour or protecting certain consumer groups backfiring or having unintende consequences.[216] Stepping back, perhaps the three most important insights to emerge fror this work are that: (a) consumers are heterogeneous and have different decision-makin; processes, meaning that policies need to be calibrated to actual consumer behaviour (b) suppliers will often react to any attempts to change consumer behaviour or protec consumers, and that such equilibrium effects must be considered in policy making; an (c) regulators should, as far as possible, seek to test policies with real consumers befor implementing them.

DISCUSSION QUESTIONS

1. What are some of the standard assumptions about consumer behaviour that hav informed models of industrial organisation? What do these standard assumption imply about the task of regulation?

2. Describe the different strands of behavioural economics research about consume behaviour, and for each strand provide examples of how this might affect consume decision making and behaviour.

3. Will intensifying competition between firms always protect non-standard consumer from exploitation?

4. Describe some of the ways in which firms can take advantage of consumers that d not have stable and consistent preferences through price discrimination?

5. Discuss how the different ways in which an offer is framed can affect consumer deci sion making. Do firms in competitive markets always have an incentive to educat consumers and make it easier for consumers to compare products?

---

[216] Armstrong and Huck (2010) remind us that regulators and policy makers themselves operate in complex environments and can suffer from biases and may resort to heuristics and satisficing behaviour. They suggest that the absence of competition may result in behavioural biases being more prevalent in policy makers than in the firms they oversee. See also Viscusi and Gayer (2015), Trillas (2016) and OECD (2021d

6. Do you agree with the following statement? 'The findings of behavioural economics research only apply to consumer behaviour and do not apply to firms and managers and employees within those firms.'

7. What are some of the implications of behavioural economics research for the rationale for regulation and the assumptions that regulators typically make when introducing policy interventions?

8. Critically assess some of the different regulatory interventions to address or 'correct' non-standard consumer behaviour that have been applied in practice. What are the potential benefits and limitations of these policy measures?

9. Choose two examples of where a regulator has drawn upon the insights of behavioural economics in developing and implementing policy. Discuss why the policy intervention was introduced (i.e. what problem they are attempting to address) and the form of the specific intervention.

PART III

The Institutions of Regulation

The chapters so far have discussed different rationales for economic regulation, considered possible alternatives, and examined economic principles and approaches for the regulation of certain industries. In this chapter, we turn to the question of *who* regulates: that is, our focus turns to the institutions that influence and apply economic regulation in practice.

With the exception of the USA, there has been a significant shift over the past four decades in how economic regulation is delivered in many jurisdictions, away from regulation by government department towards regulation by independent, or quasi-independent, regulatory authorities.[1] Understanding 'who' implements regulation, and the wider political, legal and social context in which regulation is applied, is critical to any assessment of whether regulation achieves its aims or not. This is because, as discussed below, there is typically a strong link between the 'institutional endowment' of a country,[2] and the ability to constrain opportunistic behaviour on the part of government and regulators, and to influence and control the behaviour of regulated firms.

This chapter first considers the rationale for the establishment of economic regulatory agencies and discusses the historical development of these institutions in three separate time periods. The chapter then focuses on the characteristics of modern economic regulators, and considers the interaction between economic regulators, ministries, competition authorities and different 'levels' of government, such as those which exist in federal jurisdictions such as the USA and Australia as well as the European Union. It then goes on to discuss co-regulatory arrangements that may exist between a regulator and industry. Finally, it examines the question of regulatory oversight and accountability of these agencies.

8.1 THE RATIONALE FOR ECONOMIC REGULATORY AGENCIES

A striking characteristic of modern economic regulation is that the central regulatory institution in many jurisdictions is now a form of independent or quasi-independent regulatory commission or agency. The creation of regulatory agencies has been observed not just in developed countries, but in developing and transitional economies, spurred on,

---

[1] Brown, Stern, Tenenbaum and Gencer (2006) record that almost 200 new infrastructure regulators were established in the period 1996–2006. However, these regulators display varying degrees of independence.

[2] A country's institutional endowment includes the structure and characteristics of the political, judicial and administrative/bureaucratic systems. See Levy and Spiller (1994), Spiller and Vogelsang (1994), Spiller and Tommasi (2008) and Spiller (2013).

in part, by recommendations of international organisations such as the World Bank an
the International Monetary Fund (IMF).

An important characteristic of independent regulatory agencies is that they tend
be (to varying degrees) organisationally and operationally distinct from government:
bureaucracies or ministries. They also tend to be specialised in focus and responsible f
pursuing specific goals and objectives. In other words, the regulator maintains an 'arm
length' relationship with regulated firms, consumers, private interests and politicians
But what is the rationale for creating such agencies?

8.1.1 The Time-Inconsistency Problem and Independent Regulation

A principal perceived benefit of independent economic regulators relates to 'commitmen
Specifically, the establishment of an independent regulator is seen as a commitment by
government to restrict and constrain its future interference in an industry, particularly i
terms of the future expropriation of property rights.

This issue of commitment in the regulated industries is a variant of a more gener:
'time-inconsistency' problem in public policy making.[4] Commitment issues arise where
government commits itself in one period to behaving in certain ways in the future bu
when it comes to a future point in time, reneges on the earlier commitment to reflect i
preferences at that later point in time.[5] In dynamic contexts, this potential time incor
sistency can obviously impact on the actions and decisions of firms, who base the
decisions, in part, on *expectations* of future policy decisions or government actions
Independent regulatory agencies are seen to offer a buffer against such time inconsist
ency and also against fluctuations in the preferences of current and future governments

Time-inconsistency problems frequently arise in the area of monetary policy, wher
a non-independent central bank may be under frequent political pressure to introduc
short-term monetary expansion to boost growth and employment, although this lead
to inflation over the longer term.[8] By establishing an independent central bank, a gov
ernment attempts to 'tie its own hands' by delegating aspects of monetary policy to a
institution which pursues its own objective function and is populated with individua
who are more averse to inflation than average.[9] As an independent central bank

---

[3] In political science, a distinction is sometimes made between formal *de jure* independence (independence
as contained in legal or statutory provisions) and *de facto* independence (effective autonomy in day-to-
day actions).

[4] Harstad (2020) discusses how politicians who fear losing elections will evaluate future investments using
discount factors that increase in relative time, allowing them allocate the budget to 'pet projects'.

[5] These have been described as 'Odysseus-type' situations where *ex ante* resolve is known regularly to
break down in the face of recurrent exigencies/temptations. Williamson (1985) argues that this creates a
need for various institutional developments 'out of awareness that the call of the Sirens would be well-
nigh irresistible'.

[6] See Kydland and Prescott (1977).

[7] See Faure-Grimaud and Martimort (2003).

[8] The first central bank to be given full independence was the German Bundesbank, which, in part,
is attributed to past fears of the effects of hyper-inflation and the recognition of the need for some
institutional restraint on monetary policy. See Goodman (1992).

[9] See Rogoff (1985) and Crowe and Meade (2007).

insulated to some degree from the government of the day, anti-inflation commitments are more credible and can lead to the development of stable expectations by firms and other economic agents.[10]

A broadly analogous rationale to that for the creation of central banks applies to the creation of independent economic regulators. That is, independent economic regulators are seen to reduce the potential for short-term opportunistic behaviour by governments by 'insulating' some aspects of regulatory policy making from the objectives of day-to-day government.[11] There are a number of ways in which the time-inconsistency problem can manifest in regulated industries. These include: the unanticipated introduction of new requirements (such as quality requirements) once an investment is made; unexpected requirements for a regulated firm to use specific inputs in its production process, or to engage in particular employment practices;[12] or unanticipated changes in a policy framework for an industry, such as the introduction of competition in specific activities, which can result in stranded assets and contracts.[13] However, two of the most commonly cited examples of the time-inconsistency problem involve the future expropriation of 'sunk' investments, and the potential for regulators to use the information they obtain over time about the regulated firm to adjust the terms of the regulatory compact (the so-called 'ratchet effect'). These are described below.

8.1.2 Commitment against Future Expropriation of 'Sunk' Investments

One example of the time-inconsistency problem in regulated industries is referred to as 'sunk asset expropriation', which is a specific form of the 'hold-up' problem discussed in Chapter 6.[14] This problem arises where a firm invests in an infrastructure asset based on an expectation, or a commitment, that it will be able to recover all of the costs of its investment through future prices but, after the investment has been made, government policy (or the decision of a regulator reflecting the short-term preferences of government) limits the price that may be charged by the firm to a price below long-run average costs (i.e. that allows only for the recovery of operational costs).[15] In effect, the government renegotiates the terms of the original regulatory compact or commitment in such a way as to provide an insufficient return to the firm.[16] In a static sense, the decision to institute such a policy can be

---

[10] Another example of where the commitment problem arises, and can be dealt with through delegation to an independent authority, is in environmental regulation. Spulber and Besanko (1992) examine the case where the executive appoints the head of an agency whose preferences differ from its own in order to achieve credible commitment to a future plan of action.

[11] Variants of this rationale have been cited by international organisations such as the OECD (2002) and the World Bank (2001).

[12] See Levy and Spiller (1994) and Trillas (2010).

[13] Brennan and Boyd (1997) and Helm and Jenkinson (1997) discuss the stranding of assets and contracts in UK and US energy markets following the introduction of competition. More generally, see Sidak and Spulber (1998).

[14] Williamson (1975) sets out the hold-up problem in the general context of transaction cost economics. Joskow (1991) discusses its relevance in the context of public utilities.

[15] Chambouleyron (2014) and De Meio Reggiani, Vazquez, Hallack and Brignole (2019) discuss the example of government hold-up of natural gas pipelines in Argentina.

[16] A regulatory compact is a broad concept that encompasses both a formal agreement as well as any implicit agreement, bargain, understanding or duty that a regulator and regulated party have with another.

rational for government, as it delivers low prices for current consumers (who are also voters) and, at the same time, the government can be reasonably assured that the firm will continue to supply services as long as it covers its operational costs.[17] In short, such a policy provides the regulated firm with *ex post* incentives to operate, but not to invest in new capital.[18]

The sunk asset expropriation problem is particularly significant in the public utilities industries, where investments often involve large and immobile capital assets and are sunk once made.[19] The problem is also of particular concern in developing countries which require substantial infrastructure investment and where, because of the often weak institutional endowment of such countries,[20] it can be more difficult for governments to commit to allow investors to make a sufficient return.[21] Perceptions of the credibility of commitments will be limited in jurisdictions where political and social institutions are perceived to be unable to restrain the discretion of a regulator or government authority.[22] On the other hand, the incentives for a government to expropriate sunk investments have been argued to be tempered where there is widespread ownership of the regulated firm, raising the political cost of such actions.[23]

While it may be rational in the short term for governments to renegotiate the terms of the regulatory compact, or set prices at low levels, a perception of a lack of commitment by a government to allow the recovery of the full costs associated with an investment once it is sunk may lead firms to adjust their investment behaviour. In particular, such firms may under-invest in infrastructure, or demand a high rate of return to account for the potential risk of future decisions which do not allow it to fully recover costs.[24]

The creation of independent economic regulators, with defined goals and objectives that are different from the short-term objectives of the government of the day, is seen as one method for mitigating the risk of future expropriation, and the time-inconsistency problem, and thus encourage investment.[25] In principle, establishing an independent regulator can send an important *ex ante* signal that a government will not interfere *ex post*

---

[17] This is because the costs for the firm in shutting down and redeploying its assets is likely to be greater than the costs associated with continuing to operate.

[18] Helm (2013) neatly captures this point: 'Current voters have a strong incentive to behave in a time-inconsistent way, and demand marginal cost pricing. Politicians respond, and they have the ability to legislate and hence change property rights. Investors seek legal protection, but governments have multiple ways of impacting on investors ex post.'

[19] Newbery (1999) describes the essential problem in the following terms: 'What would be needed to persuade investors to sink their money into an asset that cannot be moved and that may not pay for itself for many years? The investors would have to be confident that they had secure title to future returns and that the returns would be sufficiently attractive.'

[20] Building on the work of Douglass North (1990), Levy and Spiller (1994) define the 'institutional endowment' of a country as comprising five elements: a country's legislative and executive institutions; judicial institutions; customs and informal but broadly accepted norms; the character and balance of social interests; and administrative capability.

[21] Spiller and Tommasi (2008) find that 'sunk assets expropriation has been more prevalent in the developing world than direct utility takeovers or expropriation without compensation'. See also Estache and Wren-Lewis (2009).

[22] Imam, Jamasb and Llorca (2019) also find that the creation of independent regulators (with private sector participation) in sub-Saharan Africa can mitigate the effects of corruption.

[23] See Armstrong and Sappington (2007).

[24] Newbery (1999) describes the suspension of investment as 'a completely rational act for a utility suddenly faced with uncertainty over its future regulatory regime'.

[25] Cambini and Rondi (2017) find that the presence of independent regulators in Europe has had a positive influence on the investment of regulated firms.

in the pricing of regulated services, particularly in circumstances where one of the objectives of the regulator is to ensure the financial viability of regulated firms. However, in practice, the existence of an independent economic regulator does not always protect against government opportunism in both developed and developing countries.[26]

8.1.3 Commitment to Intertemporal Pricing and the 'Ratchet Effect'

While the establishment of an independent regulator can influence perceptions of 'commitment', it does not necessarily mean that the regulator will act in an appropriate way, or that the wider regulatory process will provide credible commitments. Indeed, the delegation of powers to a regulatory agency can create a 'secondary agency problem', whereby the agency may not face the correct incentives to collect relevant information, or may abuse its power and not use information to benefit the collective.[27]

A critical factor for investment is ensuring that those affected by regulatory decisions are confident that they will not be subject to short-term or opportunistic decision making. One way a regulator might act opportunistically is known as the 'ratchet effect'.[28] As discussed in Chapter 4, this effect arises where there is a multi-period relationship between a regulator and a firm in a context of asymmetric information (that is, the regulated firm has superior information about its costs), and the regulator uses information revealed over time to adjust prices. For example, a firm that reveals itself to be a low-cost firm rather than a high-cost firm might be subject to a more demanding regulatory regime in the future.[29] The adjustment of prices or other regulatory requirements to reflect new information as it is revealed is another manifestation of the time-inconsistency problem, and regulated firms might be expected to anticipate this possibility and adjust their behaviour accordingly. For example, a low-cost firm will have a strong incentive not to reveal information to the regulator that would allow it to be classified as such. As a result, it may not pursue various incentives introduced by the regulator to improve its efficiency, and may be reluctant to reveal cost information that could be used to develop a more demanding incentive scheme by the regulator in the future.[30] Empirical studies indicate that the ratchet effect is not a mere theoretical possibility, but is observed in practice.[31]

---

[26] See De Meio Reggiani, Vazquez, Hallack and Brignole (2019), who discuss the experience of independent regulation in Argentina, while Martimort, Pouyet and Staropoli (2020) discuss how the French government has systematically set electricity retail prices to a different level than that recommended by the independent regulator, which has led to tariff deficits, court rulings and consumer confusion. The UK competition agency (CMA, 2016a) found that two of the most important decisions of the energy regulator (neither of which benefited consumers) were taken against a backdrop of the ministry either taking power or stating its readiness to take powers through legislation, and that this created a perception of a lack of independence on the part of the regulator. Casullo, Durand and Cavassini (2019) record that in OECD countries some independent regulators still receive government guidance on individual cases or regulatory decisions (13 per cent for energy, 16 per cent in communications, 21 per cent in rail, 30 per cent in water and 39 per cent in air transport).

[27] See Laffont and Tirole (2000).

[28] See Baron and Besanko (1984b) and Baron (1989).

[29] See Laffont and Tirole (1988).

[30] See Laffont (2005). More generally, Sappington and Weisman (2021) argue that, to mitigate the ratchet effect, firms 'should be rewarded (penalized) based on their performance relative to external, not internal, benchmarks'.

[31] Spiller and Vogelsang (1994).

The effectiveness of different regulatory commitment mechanisms has been examined in analytical work. Baron (1989) examines three different methods of commitment: firstly where the regulator *can* commit to a policy in respect of how it will use any future information (for example, not to use any future information it obtains, or alternatively to fully use any information it obtains); secondly, where the regulator *cannot* commit to any multi-period mechanism; and finally, an intermediate arrangement, where the regulator agrees to treat the firm 'fairly' once it receives new information and the firm agrees not to leave the regulatory relationship. Baron concludes that any potential for *ex post* opportunistic behaviour by the regulator can be inefficient, and the introduction of restraints on the regulator to improve commitment can improve welfare and efficiency.[32] Armstrong and Sappington (2007) also consider three different commitment scenarios: (i) perfect intertemporal commitment by a regulator (i.e. the optimal multi-period policy simply duplicates the single-period policy in each period); (ii) the regulator has 'moderate' commitment power such that an original agreement can be renegotiated only if both parties agree; and (iii) the regulator can never commit to a policy that it will implement in subsequent periods. The conclusion is that the commitment power of the regulator has important implications for the optimal regulatory policy. For example, if the regulator cannot make binding commitments about how it will use pertinent information, such as realised production costs, then welfare may be higher if the regulator does not have access to such information.

8.1.4 Constraining the Potential for Opportunistic Behaviour by the Regulator

There are a number of potential ways in which opportunistic behaviour by a regulator may be restrained, and commitment enhanced. First, voluntary arrangements might emerge between a regulator and regulated company that sustains a commitment to a regulatory compact. Second, specific regulatory policies may enhance commitment, including the form of price regulation as well as the relative weight that a regulator places on the balance of consumer and producer interests. Finally, the wider legal framework can restrain opportunistic behaviour by regulators.

Voluntary Solutions to the Commitment Problem
One way of approaching the regulatory commitment problem is to model the relationship as involving a long-term strategic interaction between a firm and the regulator within a game-theoretic framework.[33] This approach recognises the strategic nature of the relationship between a regulator and a regulated firm (which is based, in part, on expectations of future behaviour) and the incentives that both parties have to behave opportunistically. For example, a regulated firm may refuse to expand capacity or refurbish its assets to satisfy demand or allow quality to deteriorate, while the regulator may disallow particular investments, require that prices be set at levels below long-run average cost, or introduce other measures which effectively expropriate some of the rents of the regulated firm.[34]

---

[32] Baron (1989).
[33] See Salant and Woroch (1992), Gilbert and Newbery (1994) and Newbery (1999, chapter 2).
[34] See Salant and Woroch (1992).

One conclusion of this work is that a regulatory compact between a regulator and a firm is unlikely to be sustainable when the relationship is short term in nature because the temptation for the parties to 'cheat' is likely to be too great. However, when the regulatory compact involves the regulator and the firm engaging with each other on a long-term basis (i.e. in a multi-period repeated game), the potential exists, under some conditions,[35] for a self-enforcing agreement to be voluntarily sustained that is mutually beneficial to both parties and strikes a balance that allows for continued investment by the firm while removing the temptation of the regulator to expropriate returns on existing investments.[36] An equilibrium is achieved wherever, for both parties, the future gains from cooperation of sticking to the regulatory compact are greater than the short-term benefits of acting opportunistically by deviating from the compact.[37] As in most games of strategic, multi-period interaction, the relationship is sustained by a combination of reputation for honouring commitments (a history of not deviating from the regulatory compact in past periods) and the threat of punishment for breaking the regulatory compact (for the regulator, punishment takes the form of allowing only operational costs, while, for the firm, it will be a decision not to invest again).

The main insight from this work is that the commitment problem could be addressed voluntarily in some circumstances. This is of particular relevance to settings where the ability of the parties to formally commit to one another is fairly limited and is not supported by external institutions and policies. For example, reputation, rather than the rule of law, has been seen as the crucial factor in ensuring that governments honour commitments to provide a promised return on capital in developing countries.[38] However, in many circumstances, voluntary cooperation between the regulator and regulated firm will not be sufficient to address the commitment problem and, under some fairly standard conditions, a regulator can have an incentive to 'cheat' on the regulatory compact to yield a short-term benefit.

The Form of Price Regulation

Different forms of price regulation – such as rate of return regulation and price cap regulation – can affect a regulator's ability to behave opportunistically. Newbery (1999), for example, concludes that rate of return regulation can support adequate levels of investment if it is credible and sustainable, and that it is more likely to be sustainable in the presence of legislative constraints (such as a 'used and useful doctrine') which increase the cost to the regulator of breaking the regulatory compact.[39] In contrast, price

---

[35] In particular, where the depreciation rate is high, the rate of consumer demand is not too small and the discount factor is large (implying that the parties are not too short-sighted).

[36] As Salant and Woroch (1992) observe, this framework uses the logic of the folk theorem applied in oligopoly theory (see Friedman 1971) to the firm–regulator relationship.

[37] However, as in most folk theorem models, a principal limitation is the existence of multiple equilibria and the difficulty in determining which equilibrium will prevail.

[38] See Wren-Lewis (2013).

[39] Armstrong and Sappington (2007) identify problems with this policy, particularly the difficulty in predicting with any precision the merits (and future need) for some investment projects. Moreover, if a regulator has discretion as to which assets are included in the asset base, this again raises the problem of regulatory commitment insofar as the potential for investments to be 'disallowed' might chill a firm's investment decisions.

cap regulation, which results in more variable profits for the firm than under cost-base approaches, can make it more tempting for the regulator to renege on the regulatory compact and expropriate profits when they are high.[40] A price cap approach is argued to be particularly inappropriate in developing countries where governments may care less about preserving the profit levels of the firm (either because share ownership is limited or firms are foreign-owned, or because the government is concerned with equity) and be more willing to expropriate high levels of profits.[41] This implies that a rate of return approach may, in these contexts, be more likely to foster investment.

The Objectives of the Regulator and the Balance between Consumer and Producer Interests

Another factor that can enhance or reduce perceptions of commitment is the regulator's objective function, and in particular the relative weight that a regulator is required to place or in practice places, on the balance of consumer and producer interests. As discussed in Chapter 4, in some theoretical models, the regulator favours consumers' interests over producer interests, on the basis that, while consumers reside within a regulator's jurisdiction the shareholders of the firm may be widely dispersed or reside overseas. These models are supported by anecdotal evidence of the relative weighting given to producer and consumer interests by regulatory commissions in the USA.[42] However, the need to balance producer and consumer interests creates a trade-off.[43] Credibility is enhanced where a regulator is known to place a greater relative weight on producer interests (and profits) than society does, and, in this respect, it is argued that the ratchet effect can be mitigated through delegating power to an independent regulator that is more pro-industry than government.[44] It is perhaps for this reason that, in some jurisdictions, a regulator is required under law to ensure that regulated firms remain financially viable or is able to earn a return that is 'just and reasonable'.

The Use of Contracts

The possibility of using contracts to specify, as completely as possibly, the commitment of different parties is similar to the franchise contract discussion in Chapter 3. In principle, these types of contracts can enhance commitment by specifying legally binding commitments and providing for redress either through the courts or by arbitration. However as noted in Chapter 3, a challenge with the approach is making regulatory contract

---

[40] As Braeutigam and Panzar (1989) put it: 'Can the regulator credibly pre-commit to a system of price cap regulation? Stated differently, can today's regulatory commission bind its successor? A regulatory agency is likely to be subjected to considerable political pressure to change the price cap or price cap formula over time. If a firm regulated by price caps begins to earn large profits, consumers will no doubt petition the regulator to lower the price in the core market.' Armstrong and Sappington (2007) observe that price cap regulation can also encourage expropriation by introducing competition, as, unlike rate of return regulation, the regulator is under no obligation to raise prices in an industry if an incumbent firm's profit falls, and this may encourage the regulator to encourage entry into an industry in order to facilitate even lower prices for consumers. Weisman (2019b) makes a similar point.

[41] See Wren-Lewis (2013, 2014) and Rodríguez Pardina and Schiro (2018).

[42] See Baron (1988, 1989).

[43] Lim and Yurukoglu (2018) explore this trade-off for electricity distribution regulation in the USA. They find that conservative regulators (that place more weight on utility profits and grant higher rates of return) promote more investment and mitigate the time-inconsistency problem. However, because these regulators engage in less auditing, this reduces the managerial effort by the utility and exacerbates the information asymmetry (a moral hazard problem). Overall, they find that the welfare loss from time inconsistency is greater than that from the moral hazard problem.

[44] See Evans, Levine, Rickman and Trillas (2011).

credible over an extended time period. If, as is often the case, firms consider that contracts will be renegotiated in the future, they might be expected to take strategic actions to anticipate that behaviour.[45] In this respect, the ability to rely solely on contracts (such as concession contracts) as a commitment device can been limited, largely because of the prevalence of contract renegotiation, which acts as a serious impediment to private sector involvement.[46] In practice, then, the use of (incomplete) contracts tends to be a complement rather than an alternative to the establishment of regulatory institutions.[47]

The Wider Legal Framework within which the Regulator Operates

A range of other mechanisms can restrict the discretion of regulators and thus reduce the potential for short-term opportunistic behaviour. One mechanism is the wider framework of rules and procedures in a jurisdiction. In the USA, administrative law plays an important role in restraining the actions of regulatory agencies and in specifying how regulators can behave, how they can reach decisions and how regulated firms can challenge those decisions. These established administrative procedures can provide legal protection to firms, enabling them to challenge unreasonable regulatory decisions and enhancing the credibility of the regulatory regime. In addition, an important body of judicial precedent – for example, doctrines establishing that regulated firms are entitled to 'fair' rates of return, and the 'just and reasonable' standard for rates – has developed over the past 100 years, which, in principle, provides additional certainty to regulated firms that assets will not be expropriated by regulatory decisions after the investments are made.[48]

In other jurisdictions, such as the UK, the regulatory framework is typically based on a contractual approach, where the opportunism of the regulator is, in principle, constrained by outlining the rights of regulated firms in utility contract licences.[49] These licences contain specific information, such as the nature of price regulation that applies, and deviations from the terms of these contract licences can be judicially challenged. Pricing and other substantive amendments can only be affected through a licence change procedure, which requires the agreement of the licence holder and, in the absence of agreement, referral to a third party.[50] This means the regulator cannot unilaterally make drastic changes to the regulatory compact.

---

[45] See Baron and Besanko (1984b).

[46] See Guasch, Laffont and Straub (2008) and Estache and Wren-Lewis (2009).

[47] This approach, which combines regulation by contract with a regulatory agency, is sometimes referred to as a 'hybrid' model of economic regulation; see Eberhard (2007) and Marques (2017). Jensen and Wu (2017) discuss the extensive use of this approach in Africa, Latin America and Asia, but also consider its limitations, such as lower coordination and higher risk of corruption and mismatches between the binding contract and the flexibility of agency regulation. Drawing on the example of economic regulation of water services in Manila, they conclude that 'if not well designed the hybrid model may bring out the worst of both regulatory systems'.

[48] Vogelsang (2021) argues that important US Supreme Court decisions have provided substantial commitment power and as a result is part of the reason that the rate of return approach to regulation has survived to this day.

[49] Spiller and Tommasi (2008) argue that the effectiveness of a licence approach in enhancing regulatory credibility depends on a number of factors, such as whether the courts are likely to view the licences as contracts and are willing to uphold these contracts against the administration, and the degree to which the licences are specific and limit what the regulator can and cannot do (i.e. the extent to which regulatory policy is 'hard-wired' in the licence).

[50] As described in Chapter 11, there is a different approach in telecommunications, where specific conditions are applied to firms assessed as holding a position of significant market power.

In Chile, another pioneer of public utility restructuring in the early 1980s, a large rule-based approach has been used, where legislation severely restricts the administrative discretion of regulators, and in some areas provides precise details on how regulation should be applied (including setting out a formula for estimating the rate of return). More recently, New Zealand has adopted an 'input methodologies' approach that set out formal methodologies for the determination of regulatory costs and pricing that are binding on the regulator in successive price control periods.

As Spiller and Vogelsang (1994) note, the appropriate safeguards on the unconstrained exercise of regulatory discretion can be highly context-specific. For example, while judicial restraint of administrative discretion may be an effective way of providing commitment to regulated firms in the USA,[52] contractual arrangements may prove a more effective approach in the UK given its constitutional position and a judicial tradition of upholding contracts. More generally, in countries with weak social and political institutions, a system of inflexible regulatory rules may enhance commitment because they 'fit' the institutional endowment of the country and can provide substantial incentive to invest.[53]

Commitment by the Regulated Firm and the Need for Flexibility

Two additional points should be raised before leaving this discussion on regulatory commitment. Firstly, while we have focused on mechanisms that can ensure commitment by a regulator to any intertemporal regulatory compact, a regulated company can also have incentives to renege on the arrangement. In the developing world, for example, there are numerous examples of dominant public utility firms acting in ways that are either prohibited or unapproved under the regulatory compact.[54] Secondly, while there are benefits associated with restricting a regulator's discretion to renegotiate a regulatory compact, there are obviously risks associated with a regulator not being able to exercise discretion in certain circumstances. For example, in a context of asymmetric information, a regulator with no discretion to alter the terms of an *ex ante* regulatory compact could 'lock-in' consumers to a bad deal, and reduce a firm's incentives to control its costs.[55] Inflexibility in regulatory arrangements is a particular concern in technologically evolving areas such as telecommunications, payment systems or digital platforms. In short, there is a trade-off between providing a degree of regulatory commitment through restrictions on the regulator's discretion, and allowing the regulator the flexibility to adapt arrangements to reflect new information and circumstances. As with all trade-offs, there is unlikely to be a single method for striking the appropriate balance and, in practice, this may involve the discretionary powers of regulators being well specified, and exercised within an accountable and transparent institutional framework.[56]

---

[51] See Levy and Spiller (1994) and Galal (1996).
[52] See discussion in Makholm (2016) on wider aspects of the US regulatory context.
[53] See Levy and Spiller (1994).
[54] See the discussion in Laffont (2005, chapter 4) and Estache and Wren-Lewis (2009).
[55] See Salant and Woroch (1992).
[56] Spiller and Tommasi (2008) emphasise a need to be able to distinguish between arbitrary and useful discretion. More generally, Sidak and Spulber (1998) argue that flexibility needs to be exercised within a framework, and one which allows for 'just' compensation for any changes in the regulatory contract.

8.1.5 Specialisation

A second perceived benefit of independent economic regulators is that they bring a degree of specialisation and expertise that might not be available in a more generalist government department or ministry. In particular, the pooling of expertise within a single regulatory agency is seen to confer informational advantages, and it is also argued that specialist agencies may be more effective at eliciting relevant information from regulated firms and at processing this information.[57] This rationale for regulatory agencies is a feature of some models of regulation discussed in Chapter 4, where the purpose of a regulator is to reduce the asymmetry of information, and learn the value of the different cost parameters over time. In short, the establishment of regulatory agencies is seen as a proactive step by government to address the asymmetric information problem.[58]

8.1.6 Risks Associated with the Creation of Independent Regulators

While establishing an independent regulator operating at 'arm's length' from government can, in principle, improve credibility and address the time-inconsistency problem, as well as provide specialisation and informational advantages, it also carries a number of potential risks. Among these are the risk of a divergence between the government and the regulator,[59] and risks relating to the 'capture' of the regulator by various interest groups.

The delegation of powers by the government to a regulatory agency creates a principal-agent relationship between the two bodies.[60] This can potentially give rise to a divergence in objectives between the government and the regulator. As the principal (government) cannot fully observe the agent's (regulator's) actions, it may seek to monitor the behaviour of the agency through various forms of control and accountability mechanisms, which can be costly.[61]

Another risk associated with delegation is that it might increase the potential for capture of the regulator by different interest groups.[62] Specifically, in a context of information asymmetry between the political principal and the regulated firm, a self-interested regulator and regulated firm might decide to collude against the political principal (and, therefore, typically, in this case, consumers). This might be achieved, for example, by the regulator hiding from the political principal information it receives from the regulated firm in exchange for side payments, or future job opportunities for employees at the regulated company.[63]

---

[57] Laffont and Tirole (2000) describe regulators as 'informational intermediaries'. However, as Trillas (2020) observes, the experts that are needed to correct this information asymmetry may be subject to various behavioural biases known to influence expert decision making in other contexts (such as availability bias or confirmation bias). More generally, Viscusi and Gayer (2015) examine the behavioural biases of regulators.

[58] However, as Estache and Wren-Lewis (2009) note, in countries (such as developing countries) with poor accounting and auditing systems, or where the regulatory agency lacks sufficient expertise, it can be more difficult to address the information asymmetry and this will lead to a lower probability that the regulator will be able to bridge the information gap.

[59] Howell and Sadowski (2018) describe how the regulator's determination of lower prices for the copper telecommunications network in New Zealand in 2012 was seen by the government of the day as undermining policies to promote the migration from copper to fibre broadband networks.

[60] Spiller (1990) and Spiller and Urbiztondo (1994) focus on how multiple principals (including interest groups) influence the behaviour of the regulator.

[61] See, generally, Macey (1992).

[62] See Dal Bó (2006).

[63] See Laffont and Tirole (1993, chapter 11) and Martimort (1999).

However, somewhat counter-intuitively, it has been argued that a degree of capture of the independent regulator by the regulated firm can mitigate the 'commitment problem' by making the regulator more susceptible to industry lobbying, which, in turn, may develop into a pro-industry bias that could help to create stable expectations and foster private investment.[64] It has also been argued that movements of employees between the regulator and the regulated firm can help ensure that decision makers (at both the regulator and the firm) maintain a stake in the firm–regulator relationship, and do not approach decisions in a finite way which might promote short-term opportunistic behaviour.[65] In this respect, policies that prohibit employees or ex-employees of regulators from being employed by a regulated firm for a set period of time after leaving office – which are typically predicated on reducing the potential for regulatory capture – have been argued to exacerbate the commitment problem.[66] However, these points obviously have to be balanced against the potential harm that may arise if a regulator privileges the interests of regulated firms over consumers.

Other potential risks that have been associated with the establishment of an independent regulatory agency include: a reluctance on the part of the independent agency to coordinate with other parts of government; a potential lack of political skills necessary to push through policy reforms; isolation from public opinion; and high costs associated with delegation. It has also been suggested that the creation of an independent regulatory agency may not of itself address the issue of commitment, as it simply relocates the commitment problem, and transforms it into one of the government's commitment to preserve regulatory independence.[67] In addition, as discussed in Chapter 7, regulators can be subject to many of the same behavioural biases which affect consumers and firms (such as overconfidence or 'group think').[68] Issues associated with government commitment to regulatory independence have arisen in both developing and developed countries, leading to a description of the role of independent regulators as 'perilous work'.[69] Perhaps for these reasons, Bertoméu-Sánchez, Camos and Estache (2018) conclude that academics and practitioners have become somewhat cynical of the possibility of achieving independence from inappropriate political interference in regulation.[70]

---

[64] See Estache and Wren-Lewis (2009).

[65] See Salant (1995).

[66] See Che (1995).

[67] See Trillas (2010).

[68] See Trillas (2020).

[69] See Jamison (2005) and Winsor (2010). In the USA, Hauge, Jamison and Prieger (2012) find evidence that the 'ousting' of state regulators in US states with high electricity prices, and that the threat of ousting, acts to discipline their replacements to keeping prices low. Estache and Philippe (2016) argue that regulatory weakness is not just a developing country issue and 'independence is not that common in Europe'. Rodríguez Pardina and Schiro (2018) note that '[i]n practice, many developing countries operate with "advisory regulators" whose main role is to provide technical support to the ultimate political decision makers'.

[70] Estache (2020) notes that: '[P]olitical interference continues to be an issue in all country groups and regulatory institutions have not been able to deliver as expected. ... In many ways, the bargaining power of regulators was often insufficient when compared to the leverage of private actors.' Similarly, Trillas (2020) observes that: '[I]ndependent regulatory agencies are in general relatively vulnerable, especially but not only in developing countries. Many of them experience changes for political reasons when there is government change, even in cases where regulatory independence is prescribed by law.'

Finally, there is a question about whether, in practice, independent regulators are associated with improvements in performance or credibility.[71] On this point, some empirical studies suggest only modest improvements.[72]

8.2 THE EVOLUTION OF INDEPENDENT REGULATORY AGENCIES

Section 8.1 looked at potential rationales for the existence of independent regulators. However, in countries such as the USA, independent public utility regulators have a long history that pre-dates theoretical accounts of their existence. Laffont (2005) attributes the historical design of regulatory institutions in industrialised countries to two main factors: the technical characteristics of particular industries,[73] and the political organisation of the state.[74] In addition, he argues that demand for regulatory agencies can come from different interest groups, including from the firms that will be regulated by these agencies.

The establishment of independent regulatory agencies around the world can be considered to have occurred in three separate time periods. The first regulatory agencies were established in the USA in the late nineteenth and early twentieth centuries. In the 1980s, regulatory agencies were created in the UK. Finally, between the 1990s and the 2000s, regulatory agencies emerged in Europe, Latin America, Australia, New Zealand and many other countries, including in the developing world.[75] A brief overview of some of the contextual factors that led to the establishment of these agencies is presented below.

8.2.1 The First Independent Regulatory Agencies in the USA

The earliest independent regulatory commissions emerged in the Midwest states of the USA in the 1870s and had power over railroad rates.[76] In 1887, the first federal independent regulatory commission – the Interstate Commerce Commission (ICC) – took responsibility for the regulation of inter-state freight railroad rates.[77] Until the 1920s, the regulation of other public utility industries in the USA comprised a mix of municipal- and state-based

---

[71] Stern and Holder (1999) set out six broad criteria for assessing economic regulatory systems and the degree of independence: clarity of roles and objectives; autonomy; accountability; participation by relevant parties in the process; transparency; and predictability. See also OECD (2016c, d).
[72] See Trillas (2010), Evans, Levine, Rickman and Trillas (2011), Trillas and Montoya (2013), Mande Buafua (2015) and Bertoméu-Sánchez, Camos and Estache (2018). This is consistent with some studies of central bank independence that have not found a dramatic effect of central bank independence on inflation.
[73] In particular, economies of scale in regulation, the movement from municipal- to state- or federal-based regulatory agencies reflecting the technical characteristics of the industry and, in particular, that firms operated over a larger geographic scale requiring regional coordination, and the development of specific skills and expertise.
[74] Including the impact of government and political structures, which are linked to the cultural environment. Accordingly, Laffont (2005) argues that independent regulatory agencies appeared early in the USA and not elsewhere in the world, where the answer to the problems associated with the public utility industries was considered to be state ownership.
[75] In China, for example, an independent State Electricity Regulatory Commission was established in 2003. However, it was subsequently merged into the National Energy Administration in 2013. Similarly, autonomous regulatory agencies have been introduced in many African countries.
[76] By the late 1880s it is estimated that twenty-five states had created such commissions.
[77] This responsibility was initially shared with some of the states. The ICC became fully independent in 1889.

regulation, with a gradual transfer of power over time to state-independent regulatory agencies known as state Public Utility Commissions (PUCs). During the New Deal era, two new powerful independent commissions were established at the federal level to regulate the telecommunications and power industries: the Federal Communications Commission (FCC)[78] and the Federal Power Commission (FPC), which later became the Federal Energy Regulatory Commission (FERC).[79] The emergence of independent regulatory institutions in the USA has been attributed more generally to deficiencies in judicial and legislative processes for the purposes of economic regulation – the judicial process being deficient in terms of timing and in its ability to handle complex economic relationships, and the legislature being too inflexible.[80] Independent regulatory commissions gave the promise of 'stability' and 'continuity' to regulatory policy, attributes which relate closely to some of the issues associated with the time-inconsistency and commitment problem described above.[81] In addition, the expert staff of a regulatory agency were seen to be better placed than executive departments in handling regulatory tasks.

Three observations on the evolution of US regulatory agencies merit further comment. The first is that the 'model' of regulatory independence developed in the USA is closely associated with that country's judicial model. The first federal regulator, the ICC, regarded itself as an administrative tribunal to adjudicate disputes among parties, and modelled itself closely on the judiciary in an attempt to acquire the respectability and acceptability of the courts. Consequently, the pattern of ICC operations came to closely resemble those of a court, despite the fact that the new form of administrative regulation was designed to overcome some of the disadvantages of judicial processes.[82] The quasi-judicial character of the ICC provided a precedent for the design of other regulatory agencies in the USA and remains an important characteristic of many regulatory institutions to this day. A second observation is that the design of US regulatory agencies has, in some respects, evolved differently at the state and federal levels. As discussed in Section 8.3.1, while state-based PUCs are typically multi-sectoral agencies, the federal regulators focus on specific industries (communications, energy, transport). Finally, the development of independent regulation in the USA has been influenced by a related development: the emerging role

---

[78] The Federal Communications Act 1934 established the FCC. The Telecommunications Act (1996) expanded the authority of the FCC.

[79] The FPC was established under the Federal Water Power Act 1920, although it failed to secure adequate funds and was only reorganised into an independent commission in 1930. The FPC was replaced by the FERC in 1977.

[80] See Bernstein (1955) and Shleifer (2011).

[81] See Bernstein (1955) who argues: 'The commission system was regarded as a bulwark against unwise changes in policy and a safeguard against partisan influences in administration. ... [F]requent changes in basic policy would undermine the stability and health of regulated enterprises, and to prevent or moderate sharp changes was one of the justifications of the commission. Continuity and stability were considered as positive values to be earnestly sought in regulatory affairs.' Even earlier than this, a 1937 report for the US government stated that: 'It is probable that the independence of these authorities is necessary to give stability to long-range policies and relative freedom from pressure groups.'

[82] Bernstein (1955) attributes this, in part, to the fact that the first chairman of the ICC was a judge, who established a judicial pattern of operation. In addition, Bernstein observes that the quasi-judicial character of the ICC reflects the rivalry that existed at the time with the courts over jurisdiction for rate determination and that '[i]n order to overcome the hostility of the courts, the commission assumed the protective coloration of the judicial environment'. See also Fesler (1940).

of judicial review in restricting the discretion of agencies. The Administrative Procedures Act 1946 (APA), in particular, created a framework for the operations of federal agencies, and established a process for federal courts to review administrative decisions, which plays an important role in structuring the processes and activities of economic regulators to this day.

8.2.2 The Establishment of Independent Regulators in the UK in the 1980s

A second significant episode in the development of independent economic regulators began in the UK in the 1980s.[83] A new regulatory framework followed directly from a programme of privatisation of the formerly state-owned utility suppliers during the 1980s and 1990s. Under this framework, independent regulatory agencies were established in telecommunications, electricity, gas, water and rail.

The first regulatory office – the Office of Telecommunications (Oftel), established in 1984 – was modelled on the UK competition authority (the Office of Fair Trading, OFT) in terms of powers, and degree of independence from government, and was charged with ensuring 'fair competition and fair prices'.[84] In this respect, the UK did not take its model of independent regulation directly from those that existed in the USA,[85] but, rather, utilised the existing institutional arrangements in the UK, including the template of the independent competition authority (OFT), and an existing ability of government to issue licences to firms in the public utility industries. The principal focus at the time was not on any commitment, or protection, that the independent regulatory offices might provide to investors in the newly privatised companies, but more on controlling the dominant market position of the newly regulated entities.[86] As a result of this focus, important issues of regulatory design, and the exercise of regulatory discretion, do not appear to have been explicitly considered in the pre-privatisation material in the public utility industries.[87] Perhaps the most important issue not explicitly considered was how to value the asset base of the companies. As a consequence, this problem was left to the discretion of each regulator at the time of the first price review, a surprising result given that the issue had proved so vexed and contentious in the USA.[88] Nevertheless, in the period since the first independent regulatory authorities were established, the protections that independent regulatory authorities can provide to investors appear to have been clearly recognised.[89]

---

[83] Spiller and Vogelsang (1994) and Ogus (1994) refer to antecedents in Britain from the nineteenth century.

[84] See Department of Industry (1982).

[85] Prosser (1997) observes that '[t]he creation of the utility regulators from 1984 involved a conscious rejection of earlier history and of overseas experience'.

[86] The first National Audit Office report (NAO, 1996) on the work of the Directors General stated that: 'It was to protect customers and potential competitors from abuse of this [monopoly power] that the regulatory system was established.'

[87] See Vickers and Yarrow (1988). Grout and Jenkins (2001) speculate on the possible reason for the government's approach, noting that 'a detailed discussion of the regulatory framework may not be a particularly appealing backdrop for the management of companies or a government trying to emphasise the benefits and freedom of private ownership'.

[88] See Grout and Jenkins (2001).

[89] See McCarthy (2004).

Unlike in the USA, judicial review was not initially perceived to be an important con
straint on regulatory discretion, in part because the Directors General were under n
statutory duty to give reasons for their decisions, or to consult before taking a decision.
Consequently, much was dependent on the individual chosen as Director General an
how they exercised their duties. It follows that the perceptions of regulatory commitmen
was highly dependent on the personality of the Director General, and the appointment o
academics as the first Directors General in telecommunications and electricity has bee
argued to reflect a deliberate choice to reinforce the independence of the position.[91]

Aspects of this initial regulatory framework have changed over time, including th
transformation of Directors General to Regulatory Boards or Authorities (considered mor
fully in Section 8.3) and the characteristics of the individuals appointed to chair regula
tory bodies, who now often have experience of working in government, business or th
civil service. However, fundamental elements of this regulatory framework remain i
place in the UK – including the role of empowering statutes and licences.

8.2.3 The Development of Regulatory Agencies in Other Parts of the World

A third wave in the emergence of economic regulatory agencies occurred during th
1990s and the first decade of the 2000s. In many jurisdictions, this proliferation in regu
latory agencies was part of the general trend of restructuring of the public utility indus
tries, which, as we discuss in Part III of the book, in some cases was associated with th
privatisation of the public utility assets.

The European Union

While regulatory agencies existed in some EU Member States prior to the 1990s, the
were (with the exception of the UK) relatively rare. The principal development of nationa
regulatory authorities (NRAs) in Europe only began in earnest in the mid- to late 1990s
with regulatory agencies in telecommunications typically being the first established i
the mid-1990s, followed by the establishment of agencies in energy in the mid- to lat
1990s. The emergence of these agencies appears to reflect, in part, the requirements o
EU Regulations and Directives, which have been directed towards establishing a singl
common market for many public utility services across Europe.[92] In particular, with th
exception of the water and wastewater industry, these policy Regulations and Directive
have sought to introduce competition in some activities, and to remove barriers whic
restrict the ability of public utility firms operating in one EU Member State to operate i
another. Although, as discussed in Part III of this book, the policy frameworks vary acros
industries, they tend to place obligations or duties on Member States to establish vari
ous principles and procedures for the regulation of incumbent providers.[93] EU Directive

---

[90] See Vickers and Yarrow (1988) and Thatcher (1998).
[91] See Spiller and Vogelsang (1994).
[92] This is said to follow directly from the Single European Act 1987, which focused on the integration of
the national markets into a single European trading area.
[93] Such as in relation to: providing access to the facilities of the incumbent provider; licensing and
authorising market participants; controlling or monitoring the behaviour of firms operating in the
market; and in some cases settling disputes which arise between the parties.

now also contain provisions to ensure the independence of the regulatory authority (e.g. budgeting, staffing and appointment/dismissal of agency head).

An early implementation issue in applying the EU regulatory frameworks was that, in many EU Member States, the incumbent provider was under state ownership.[94] Accordingly, a new form of institutional structure was required and Directives sought to effect a structural separation of the regulatory function from the ownership and control of public utility activities.[95] Partly in consequence of these requirements, many EU Member States introduced independent regulatory agencies in some utility industries. The establishment of independent regulators has also been closely associated with policies aimed at the 'supra-national' integration of the hitherto separate markets in the different EU Member States. Independent national regulatory authorities are seen to remove any potential conflict between the Member State acting in its capacity as regulator and the Member State acting in its capacity as owner or operator of the firm. While this objective is clear, the speed at which separate and independent agencies have been established has varied between industries and Member States, as does the degree of autonomy,[96] an issue we return to in Section 8.3.2.

Australia and New Zealand

In Australia, as in Europe, there had been a history of state ownership and control in the public utility industries; however, by the early to mid-1990s restructuring policies were introduced in some states with the aim of introducing competition into some public utility industries. As the majority of public utility firms in Australia were either owned or controlled by the state, there was a potential conflict in terms of the role of the state as both owner of the firm and regulator of the industry as competition was introduced. An influential report, which preceded these changes, identified this 'dual role' as problematic, and recommended the separation of the regulatory and commercial functions in these industries.[97] This led to an agreement in the mid-1990s between the federal and state governments for the introduction of a national competition policy, and the establishment of the Australian Competition and Consumer Commission (ACCC) as an independent, multi-sectoral regulator to administer and enforce this policy.[98]

---

[94] Edwards and Waverman (2006) note that: 'For a country to benefit from the liberalisation process, its government must convince entrants as new investors that the regulatory environment will provide no special favors to the publicly owned incumbent.'

[95] For example, Article 7 of the Commission Directive on competition in the markets for telecommunications services (Directive 90/388/EEC). In rail, the requirement for independence can be found in the first Railways Directive (Article 30 of Directive 2001/14/EC). The second Internal Electricity and Gas Market Directives required independent regulatory authorities to be mandatory in all Member States (Directive 2003/54/EC and Directive 2003/55/EC). Moreover, in an important 1991 decision of the European Court of Justice (*Régie des télégraphes et des téléphones v. GB-Inno-BM*), it was found that, where markets are open to competition, the combination of regulatory and commercial functions within a single entity breached the competition provisions of the EU Treaty. Geradin (2000) notes that the implication of this decision was that 'once a market is liberalised, the incumbents should be stripped of the regulatory functions they played in the monopoly era'.

[96] See Wassum and De Francesco (2020).

[97] See Hilmer (1993).

[98] The ACCC replaced the existing Prices Surveillance Authority and the Trade Practices Commission.

Around the same time, New Zealand also restructured its public utility industrie
However, as noted in Chapter 3, in contrast to many countries around the world, th
approach initially adopted in New Zealand was not to introduce industry-specific regu
lation in areas such as telecommunications and energy, but rather to rely principally o
general competition law, alongside information disclosure requirements and the threat o
more intrusive regulation (including the imposition of price controls). This approach wa
in part, motivated by the perceived disadvantages of industry-specific regulation an
regulatory offices in other jurisdictions,[99] and has been described as an 'attempt to creat
regulation without regulators'.[100] While attractive in principle, a number of limitation
of this approach quickly emerged. In telecommunications, there was a protracted acces
dispute between the incumbent operator and an entrant;[101] while in the energy secto
firms were seen to have earned profits above what would have occurred under a moi
conventional regulatory framework.[102] Overall, the 'light-touch' regulatory arrangemen
were seen to be an ineffective substitute for the establishment of a regulatory agency. A
a result, the regulatory arrangements have seen changes across the different public utili
industries in recent years, and the competition authority (Commerce Commission) no
has responsibility for the regulation of these industries.

Developing and Transitional Economies

The rationale for the establishment of regulatory agencies in developing and trans
tional economies appears to reflect a rationale distinct from those we have discusse
Since the mid-1980s, many governments of developing and transitional economies hav
sought to encourage the involvement of the private sector in the public utility industrie
most commonly through a process of privatisation of state-owned assets and concessio
agreements (including private–public partnerships). International organisations such a
the World Bank and the IMF have been particularly prominent in encouraging goverr
ments in these countries to allow for greater private sector involvement in public utilit
industries, positing potentially 'substantial' economic benefits, including more efficier
operations and service delivery, reductions in the burden on governments finances an
the encouragement of international investment.[103] The resulting changes in ownershi
have often been accompanied by the creation of a regulatory agency, a move seen a
central to attracting private investment by: providing credible institutional commitmen
against government expropriation; insulating decision making from improper pressur
and developing specialist technical expertise.[104]

---

[99] See Patterson (2011).

[100] Hogan (2002).

[101] *Clear Communications Ltd v. Telecom Corporation of New Zealand Ltd* (1993). A central issue in this
case involved the question of whether the efficient component pricing rule (discussed in Chapter 6) is a
acceptable form of access pricing. Patterson (2011) describes this case as the 'death knell of light-hande
regulation'.

[102] See Bertram and Twaddle (2005).

[103] See World Bank (1995). Bortolotti and Perotti (2007) assert that both the World Bank and the IMF made
their assistance in some developing countries conditional on privatisation.

[104] See Brown, Stern, Tenenbaum and Gencer (2006) and the three notes on different aspects of utility
regulation design in developing countries published in 1997 by the World Bank (Smith 1997a, b, c).

While there has been a rapid growth in regulatory agencies in developing and transitional economies over the past four decades,[105] problems have emerged with many of the new agencies. In particular, regulators have been seen as unable to provide the expected credible commitments to encourage new or additional investment.[106] The possible sources of this inability may include the absence of democracy in some countries, the weakness of the rule of law and an absence of well-functioning institutions, all of which can make it difficult for regulatory institutions to credibly commit to long-term policies.[107] A major weakness has been the regulators' capacity to implement their own regulatory frameworks or enforce their own regulations, and a lack of independence.[108] The African Development Bank (2021) records that, in Africa, governments and stakeholders have influence on regulatory authorities in the electricity sector in 93 per cent of the forty-five countries surveyed. More generally, problems of independent regulation in developing countries have been linked to a mismatch between regulatory design (including the level of regulatory discretion) and the underlying institutional and political context of such developing countries.[109] Finally, the success of independent regulation in encouraging investment has been seen to depend on implementation issues. Wallsten (2002) finds sequencing problems in some Eastern European and former Soviet economies where the incumbents were privatised prior to the creation of a regulatory authority. He finds evidence that, where a regulatory authority was established prior to privatisation, this substantially increased the proceeds from privatisation, which he associates with the greater regulatory certainty and commitment.

8.2.4 Reconciling Factors Motivating the Establishment of Independent Regulators

The historical development of independent regulatory agencies in different jurisdictions just described reflects a number of contextual factors and influences, not all of which are wholly associated with the time-inconsistency problem identified in Section 8.1 above. In the USA, the establishment of independent regulators does, in part, appear to have its roots in a perceived need to provide stability and continuity to regulatory policy, and to pool specialist expertise. However, other contextual factors, such as perceptions of the relative abilities of the legislature and the courts to act as regulators, also appear to have been influential. In the UK the establishment of independent regulators was closely associated with the process of privatisation and, in particular, a perceived need to protect

---

[105] Gassner and Pushak (2014) record that the number of independent regulators in developing countries had increased from nine in 1982 to over 200 by 2014.

[106] Brown, Stern, Tenenbaum and Gencer (2006) record a general dissatisfaction with the performance of regulatory agencies in many developing countries at that time. Wren-Lewis (2014) concludes that for African countries the 'creation of an independent regulatory agency styled on the UK model is unlikely to do much to solve the commitment problems present in infrastructure regulation'. Similarly, Gassner and Pushak (2014) argue that the 'de-politicization' of regulatory institutions can be more challenging to achieve because of the prevalence of below cost recovery tariffs and state ownership. In contrast, Sarr (2015) finds that independent regulation in the electricity industry in developing countries has been effective in improving performance.

[107] See Laffont (2005).

[108] See African Development Bank (2021).

[109] Eberhard (2007) observes that 'developing countries often demonstrate only weak political commitment to independent regulation and face considerable constraints in terms of institutional capacity'.

consumers against the potential exploitation of private monopoly power. Issues of commitment do not appear to have featured prominently in the initial design of the regulatory framework. In the EU, the move towards independent regulation in many Member States appears to be inextricably linked to the policy of market integration, which, in some cases, has required the separation of regulatory functions from commercial functions where firms remain under state ownership. A similar rationale for the development of independent regulatory agencies can be seen in Australia, where, in the face of restructuring policies, it was seen as important to separate the task of regulation from the commercial operation of utilities. Finally, in developing and transitional countries, the establishment of regulatory agencies appears to have followed from a desire to encourage private investment in public utility industries; independent regulators being seen to provide greater credibility and commitment to investors by 'insulating' regulatory decisions from undue political influence. International organisations also appear to have had an important influence on the creation of independent agencies.

8.3 DESIGN OF REGULATORY AGENCIES AND THE SCOPE OF THEIR POWER

There are a number of key design aspects of modern economic regulatory agencies. One is the scope of regulatory responsibility, specifically whether an agency's responsibilities are industry-specific or multi-sectoral. A second is the powers and discretions conferred on the regulatory agency. This involves questions as to how responsibility for the creation, implementation and enforcement of regulatory policy is allocated between an agency and the government (and sometimes multiple levels of government) and between an agency and other regulatory bodies (including competition authorities).

8.3.1 Industry-Specific or Multi-Sectoral Regulators

An important structural issue is whether a regulator has regulatory responsibilities across multiple industries or sectors (multi-sectoral) or is focused on only one industry (industry-specific). Among the factors relevant to this decision are: the extent of industry differentiation across a sector; the availability of regulatory resources and expertise; issues related to coordination and the sharing of experience across regulatory agencies; and the trade-off with regulatory competition and experimentation.[110]

Integrating the regulation of multiple industries within a single agency can bring various benefits such as: avoiding conflicts between agencies and ensuring a coherent and consistent approach to firms, which can increase regulatory certainty; allowing for a smoother transition from regulation and competition in some markets; and allowing for the pooling of specialist technical and regulatory expertise in ways which exploit any economies of scale and scope in common regulatory tasks across different industries (e.g. the need to determine the cost of capital in regulated sectors).[111] A single agency might

---

[110] See Laffont (2005).
[111] Trillas and Xifré (2016) records that in Spain the government estimated that combining the competition authority with sectoral regulators would result in total savings of €28 million.

be particularly attractive in jurisdictions where there are a limited number of specialist regulatory personnel available.[112]

On the other hand, there are potential limitations of the single-agency model. First, the agency may become a 'conglomerate', which can create problems in terms of differences of culture and a loss of specialist industry knowledge. Second, splitting regulatory tasks, and the different dimensions of information obtained through the regulatory process, among several regulators can reduce the discretion of the regulator and therefore reduce the prospects for collusion.[113] Third, combining economic regulation with competition law enforcement may not fully account for differences in the tasks of regulation and competition law enforcement.[114] Finally, there is a risk that poor performance in one area (e.g. problems in regulating a specific regulated sector) can create wider reputational damage across the single agency and reduce its legitimacy.

Looking at the institutional design of regulatory agencies across the world, considerable diversity can be observed. In Argentina, separate industry-specific regulators were created in each of the different public utility industries, a design which at times has received a mixed assessment in terms of its effectiveness.[115] Similarly, in Brazil, separate regulators were established from the late 1990s in energy, telecommunications, water, aviation and transport. In the UK, the initial institutional framework also involved separate regulators for each public utility industry. Today, however, gas and electricity are regulated under a sector-specific energy regulator, and telecommunications, radio broadcasting and post are regulated under a single communications regulator.[116] However, there are separate regulators for aviation, rail, water and payment systems. At the opposite end of the spectrum, Australia's multi-sectoral regulator has responsibility for the regulation of telecommunications, rail and some aspects of water and energy, and is also responsible for the enforcement of competition law and consumer protection law.[117] The decision to create a multi-sectoral regulator and competition authority followed a review of the UK and US experience of independent regulation.[118] New Zealand's regulatory framework has

---

[112] See Estache and Wren-Lewis (2009).

[113] See Laffont and Martimort (1999) and Laffont (2005). However, Macey (1992) notes more generally that: 'Where a regulatory agency represents a single "clientele", the rules it generates are far more likely to reflect the interests of that clientele than the rules of an agency that represents a number of clienteles with competing interests.'

[114] Economic regulation involves the implementation of a specific policy agenda that can pursue various goals and have wide distributional and social consequences (e.g. on the environment), while competition law involves an 'enforcement activity' which is in principle blind to distributional and wider societal consequences (infringe/not infringe).

[115] See Estache (1997).

[116] Other countries that have adopted sector-specific regulators include: France (for energy and communications); Ireland (energy, communications/post and aviation); South Africa (communications/post and energy); and Sweden (energy, communications/post and transport).

[117] State and territory regulators in Australia are responsible for some aspects of economic regulation of energy, water and wastewater, and rail. A 2015 report commissioned by the Australian Government (Harper, Anderson, McCluskey and O'Bryan (2015) proposed that a separate 'Access Pricing Regulator' be established on the basis that the 'culture and analytical approach required to regulate an industry differ from those typically characteristic of a competition law enforcement'. This proposal was not, however, adopted.

[118] In a report preceding the reforms (Hilmer, 1993), concerns about potential 'capture' of a single agency were dismissed as being 'over-simplistic' and inconsistent with the experience of the UK. The report highlighted the potential benefits associated with specialisation and concentration of expertise within a single organisation.

also evolved to be multi-sectoral, with a single agency responsible for economic regula tion and the enforcement of competition law. A similar structure is adopted in Estoni the Netherlands (where a single agency is responsible for economic regulation, comp tition law and consumer protection) and in Spain (where the competition authority ha been combined with six sectoral regulators).[119]

In between these extremes, organisational structures have been adopted which combin aspects of the industry-specific and multi-sectoral approaches. For example, Germany Bundesnetzagentur is a multi-sectoral regulator responsible for regulation in the gas, ele tricity, telecommunications, post and rail industries; however, unlike Australia and Ne Zealand, the responsibility for the enforcement of competition law rests with a separa agency. In the USA, sector-specific regulatory agencies tend to be the norm at the fe eral level, including separate regulatory agencies for energy (Federal Energy Regulato Commission, FERC), communications (Federal Communications Commission, FCC), ra (Surface Transportation Board, STB) and aviation (Federal Aviation Administration, FAA However, at the state level, it is typically the case that regulatory agencies are multi-se toral and have responsibility for regulation across a range of public utility industries. In Canada, regulatory responsibility is divided between the federal government and th provinces. Separate federal bodies are responsible for the regulation of telecommun cations (Canadian Radio-Television Telecommunications Commission, CRTC), and son aspects of the energy (Canadian Energy Regulator, CER) and transport industries. At th provincial level, regulation can occur within a single multi-sectoral organisation,[121] or i sector-specific agencies.[122]

8.3.2 Division of Powers and Responsibilities

Regulatory systems require a number of tasks to be performed. Broadly, these can b categorised under four headings: (1) policy determination, (2) policy implementation, (compliance and enforcement, and (4) the adjudication of disputes. The allocation of th various tasks among different institutions goes to the heart of choices about regulato design. This involves decisions about the extent and scope of powers and discretion tha should be conferred on regulators as well as the extent of oversight or control that is the exercised over such institutions. There is also a decision about how responsibility for eco nomic regulation interacts with competition policy enforcement. In jurisdictions whe power is shared between different levels of government – such as in federal systems there is also a question about how regulatory responsibility is shared between these level

Division of Power between Regulatory Agencies and Government Ministries
It is sometimes argued that the appropriate division of responsibilities between regulator agencies and government ministries should be one where the ministry develops, and se

---

[119] The motivations for combining the agencies in the Netherlands and Spain are discussed in Ottow (2014 and Trillas and Xifré (2016).
[120] The California Public Utilities Commission (CPUC), for example, is responsible for aspects of the regulation of the electricity, gas, telecommunications, water and rail industries in California.
[121] Such as the Alberta Utilities Commission (AUC), which regulates water and energy.
[122] Such as the Ontario Energy Board (OEB).

out, the long-term objectives for a particular industry (including defining the broad strategy for the achievement of those objectives, such as the role of competition, investment incentives or any subsidies, etc.), while the regulator focuses on developing and enforcing relevant industry-specific rules which reflect this wider strategy for the industry. For example, a government might decide what airspace and airport capacity is needed, and where it should be provided, while the economic regulator is responsible for ensuring that such aims are achieved in a cost-effective way. Similarly, investment priorities in water and wastewater systems needed to ensure high quality, wide access and limited environmental impact might be identified by government, with the regulator responsible for ensuring that these investments are cost-effectively delivered.

However, this 'technocratic' view of regulation – that ministers choose policies and regulators simply implement them – is increasingly viewed as simplistic and, in practice, the boundaries between policy choice and policy execution can be a grey area.[123] It is now widely recognised that how a regulator implements policy can, over time, impact on the achievement of particular policy goals and objectives. For example, as described in Chapter 6, the choices a regulator makes about access pricing can impact on the incentives for investment and entry in an industry in ways that might enhance or frustrate the achievement of particular strategic policy goals (see the example of investments in high-speed broadband networks in Chapter 11). In some jurisdictions, governments have sought to provide greater strategic direction to regulators, including requiring that they have regard to the 'vision' for the utility sectors and to other government plans such as a national infrastructure strategy.[124] In other jurisdictions, the government may indicate preferences through the use of advisory councils, media statements, informal contacts or written responses.[125]

The division of responsibilities between ministries and regulators raises the more general issue of the relative degree of independence a regulatory system has from ministerial or political input and influence.[126] A considerable body of work exists which seeks to define, and examine, what 'independence' means in the context of public utility regulation.[127] In this work, independence is typically conceived as the legally assured freedom to make decisions within the regulator's scope of authority without having to obtain prior approval from other officials or agencies of the government (i.e. the regulator being adequately insulated from short-term political pressure).[128] However, 'independence' does not typically mean 'isolated from public policy'. Most regulators work within a framework of ministerial guidance that allows for policy input, although this, it is argued, should

---

[123] See Alesina and Tabellini (2007).
[124] For example, in the UK, see Department for Business, Energy and Industrial Strategy (2022).
[125] OECD (2016c).
[126] OECD (2017d) identifies entry points (pinch points) for undue influence on regulators, as well as five 'dimensions' that can foster a culture of independence (role clarity, transparency and accountability, financial independence, leadership independence, and staff behaviour).
[127] See OECD (2017d), Brown, Stern, Tenenbaum and Gencer (2006) and Smith (1997c).
[128] For example, Article 3 of the European Union Gas Directive (2003/55/EC) states that: 'It is a generally accepted principle that the regulators should enjoy appropriate independence in their day-to-day work from regional or national government. This is to guarantee regulatory stability and to avoid situations in which the decisions of the regulator are constantly modified.'

not undermine independence on crucial matters of pricing and investment. Accordingly, in addition to the legal or formal aspects of independence, it is important to consider the actual independence of the regulatory agency in practice.[129]

Regulators display variable degrees of formal independence across jurisdictions and across regulated industries. In some jurisdictions, regulators operate according to their own legal mandate, and the relevant ministry has no formal ability to influence the day to-day implementation decisions of the regulator. However, the wider framework of the regulatory and political system can affect the practical independence of the regulator and in some countries regulators can receive strategic direction or guidance from government.[130] More generally, as we discuss in Part III of this book, economic regulators in some jurisdictions are increasingly seen as essential to the achievement of wider political, environmental and social goals, such as the transition to a low-carbon economy or the development of important infrastructure that supports economic growth and social inclusion.[131] Some claim that this widens the scope for ministerial involvement and potentially encroaches upon regulatory independence and could result in regulators simply becoming the 'delivery agents' for governments.[132]

Because of the importance of decisions that regulators take, the relationship between an independent regulator and relevant ministers or politicians has sometimes been described as a 'combustible state of affairs', where there will inevitably be tensions.[133] The potential tension between ministerial objectives and the independence of regulators can manifest itself in a number of ways, some of which can be subtle. For example, a regulator may internalise the preferences of the relevant ministry in its decision making, or may become overly responsive to press reports or other commentary in relation to certain areas of its activity (the most common being adverse reports relating to increasing prices).[134]

Division of Powers with Competition Authorities

Another aspect of the division of powers concerns responsibility for antitrust or competition law enforcement in regulated industries.[135] As discussed in Chapter 13, this issue is

---

[129] Joskow (2007a) observes that '[w]hile policymakers frequently refer to "independent" regulatory agencies in the abstract, the reality is that no regulatory agency is completely independent of political influences'. Cambini and Rondi (2017) observe that the mere presence of *de jure* independent agencies (who are not effective in constraining political interference) does not help to reduce uncertainty and regulatory risks and may only generate extra administrative costs.

[130] For example, in the UK, the government provides strategy and policy guidance to economic regulators which sets out strategic priorities and desired policy outcomes for the regulators to act in accordance with.

[131] In the UK, the government has noted that it sees the economic regulation framework as vital to delivering its Net Zero Strategy.

[132] Lodge and Stern (2014).

[133] See Winsor (2010).

[134] Joskow (2010) has argued that political influence on regulatory agencies in the USA typically takes two forms. The first is where the regulators become targets of political competition, while the second is where the staff and commissioners at regulatory agencies become oversensitive to political considerations. He writes: 'In my view, this has become a more serious problem over time as "independent" regulatory agencies once heavily populated by reasonably independent technocratic experts with clear public interest goals have increasingly come to be populated by commissioners and senior staff with narrower political goals whether it is on the less regulation or more regulation extremes of the political spectrum depending on which political faction is in power.'

[135] Useful discussions of this issue, including the merits of combing competition agencies and regulators, are presented in Dunne (2015, chapter 5), Ennis (2019) and Alexiadis and da Silva Pereira Neto (2019).

prominent in debates about whether competition agencies or specialist regulators should be used to oversee digital platforms.[136]

As already noted, in some countries (such as Australia, New Zealand, Spain and the Netherlands), the competence for enforcing the competition laws and for economic regulation are combined within a single organisation. In the UK, each of the sectoral economic regulators has a concurrent ability to enforce UK competition rules in its industry alongside the economy-wide competition authority, and are required to consider whether the use of their competition law powers is more appropriate before using their sectoral powers to promote competition.[137]

In other jurisdictions, the ability of economic regulators to enforce the competition laws appears to differ by industry, or by type of competition law provision. In the USA, the FERC, the STB and the FCC regulators share concurrent jurisdiction with the federal antitrust authorities in respect of the review of certain mergers in their respective sectors. In some cases, the merger criteria applied by the regulatory agencies can differ from those applied by the antitrust authorities and can result in additional conditions being imposed on the merger by the regulator. In other areas, the antitrust authorities retain exclusive competence (such as in relation to the enforcement of the criminal provisions of the Sherman Act).[138] An interesting aspect of the arrangements in the USA is the willingness of the antitrust authorities to make submissions and file comments in regulatory proceedings relating to competition. For example, the federal antitrust agencies – the Department of Justice (DoJ) and Federal Trade Commission (FTC) – both submitted extensive comments in the FERC's consultation on third-party access to transmission lines, while the FTC made a submission to the FCC in relation to proceedings on the issue of net neutrality.

At the EU level, the Competition Directorate of the European Commission is responsible for the enforcement of the relevant provisions of the European Treaty in relation to anti-competitive conduct in the public utility industries, and is responsible for the approval of mergers (over a particular threshold), as well as monitoring State Aid in the utility industries. At times this has created conflicts with the policies of regulatory agencies in some EU Member States.[139]

The Division of Power with Other Levels of Government

A final aspect of the allocation of powers in a regulatory system concerns the division of regulatory powers among multiple levels of government.[140] The sharing of powers and

---

[136] In the UK, for example, a new 'Digital Markets Unit' has been created within the competition authority.

[137] This requirement was introduced to address a perceived problem of insufficient precedent in competition law.

[138] However, in some cases, where a regulator believes that the antitrust rules may have been contravened, it has notified the relevant antitrust authorities. One example is the FCC notification of the DoJ about suspected bid rigging in licence auctions, which led to consent decrees being filed against three firms.

[139] The role of the Competition Directorate in the regulated sectors was highlighted in *Deutsche Telekom AG v. Commission of the European Communities* (2010), where although the German regulator had approved the access tariffs, these tariffs were found by the European Commission to result in a margin squeeze and to be in contravention of the relevant EU competition law provisions.

[140] Tirole (1994) examines this general topic and argues that the control of public enterprises may be best achieved by creating 'multiple principals' within government with dissonant objectives.

responsibilities among different levels of government raises important concerns abou[t] the coordination of regulatory policy, particularly in respect of the development an[d] implementation of regulation. Although there is some theoretical debate about what [is] an appropriate level to regulate,[141] in practice, the division of powers and competenci[es] between different levels of government tends to be heavily influenced by a jurisdiction[s] wider political and legal structure.

In the USA, responsibility for the regulation of the public utility industries is allocate[d] between the federal regulatory authorities and the state PUCs. In very general terms, th[e] responsibility for the regulation of *inter*-state activities typically tends to rest with a fe[d]eral agency, while responsibility for the regulation of *intra*-state activities rests with th[e] state PUCs. In the energy sector, the FERC is responsible for regulating the inter-stat[e] transmission of natural gas and electricity and the wholesale electricity market, while th[e] state PUCs are responsible for the regulation of the retail markets and intra-state elec[t]ricity.[142] A similar division of responsibilities can be observed in telecommunication[s] where the FCC is responsible for regulation of inter-state and international aspects [of] communications, while the state PUCs are responsible for regulating intra-state commu[ni]cations services.[143] A notable aspect of the arrangements in the USA is the ability [of] state PUCs to challenge federal agency regulatory orders before the courts. This potenti[al] was highlighted following the introduction of the Telecommunications Act 1996, whe[n] some state PUCs and local incumbent operators challenged the FCC Order which pre[sc]ribed a pricing approach – based on a form of long-run incremental costs (total eleme[nt] long-run incremental costs, TELRIC) – a matter that went all the way to the Suprem[e] Court.[144] As described in Chapter 16, the division of responsibilities in the US water an[d] wastewater sector is somewhat different from other utility industries, with state PU[Cs] playing the prominent role.

In other federal countries such as Canada and Australia, the division of powers an[d] responsibilities between different levels of government varies by industry. In Canada, th[e] regulation of telecommunications rests with a federal body (CRTC), while the Canadia[n] Energy Board is responsible for the regulation of the inter-provincial aspects of the ga[s] and electricity industries. Most provinces and territories have regulatory bodies respon[ma]sible for regulating public utilities in their jurisdictions, which includes the approval [of]

---

[141] Brock and Katz (1997) list some of the different considerations relevant to the division of responsibiliti[es] between different levels of government, including: economies of scale and scope in the implementatio[n] of policy; jurisdictional externalities; the need to adjust to local conditions; and the value of experimentation. Baldwin, Cave and Lodge (2012) consider the issue of at what level of government it is appropriate to locate the regulatory authority, noting that such an issue turns out to be highly problematic. Auriol, Estache and Wren-Lewis (2018) consider the costs and benefits of supranational regulation, and conclude that it can may reduce or exacerbate the challenges of national institutional weaknesses.

[142] Stalon and Lock (1990) describe tensions in the relationship between federal and state regulators in the energy sector, particularly in the 1980s, where efforts to permit greater competition, and an inability fo[r] the regulatory system to adapt sufficiently to major economic and legal changes, are cited as having le[d] to increasing tension in the relationship.

[143] The Telecommunications Act (1996) altered the regulatory arrangements between the FCC and the state PUCs, including the introduction of a national policy framework for the telecommunications industry under which the FCC established national uniform rules for some regulatory issues.

[144] See Brock and Katz (1997) for background to the matters in dispute.

infrastructure and tariffs for electricity and gas networks. A similar division of responsibilities can be observed in Australia, where the responsibility for telecommunications
regulation rests with a federal body (the ACCC), while responsibility for the regulation of
the energy sector has been allocated between federal and state regulators.[145]

In Europe the division of responsibilities between the European Commission (the
executive arm of the European Union) and Member States reflects a different architecture.
Unlike the arrangements in the USA, Canada and Australia described above, there is no
EU-wide regulator for each of the public utility industries.[146] Rather, at the EU level, the
responsibility for specific different industries (energy, transport, communications, water)
rests with various Directorates within the European Commission, each of which is, in general terms, responsible for the formulation of a regulatory framework in that industry.[147]
Each Member State is then required to transpose the high-level principles of regulation in
each industry. The NRA in each Member State is then responsible for applying and implementing regulatory policies contained in the domestic legislation, and can, within limits,
adopt different regulatory approaches and methods even when they are regulating the
same industries. Although this general division of powers is intended to allow NRAs discretion in applying these principles, there is some evidence that it can lead to a situation
where different NRAs adopt divergent approaches in applying the principles.[148] In light
of these concerns, it is now a requirement in some sectors (such as energy, rail and telecommunications) for there to be cooperation between national regulatory bodies and the
European Commission via a network of regulators, such as the European Union Agency
for the Cooperation of Energy Regulators (ACER) and the Body of European Regulators
for Electronic Communications (BEREC).

8.4 CO-REGULATION AND INDUSTRY CODES

Co-regulation refers to a regulatory arrangement where the regulator and industry cooperate or collaborate, and where governance is made up of both public and private 'governors'. Co-regulation is sometimes described as the 'middle way' between state regulation
and pure industry self-regulation. Co-regulatory arrangements tend to lie on a spectrum
that reflects the extent to which the regulator becomes involved in the development and
enforcement of the rules in an industry. Some co-regulatory frameworks delegate the
responsibility for developing and implementing rules (or a code) to the industry but provide for a backstop 'veto' by a regulator over specific rules in prescribed circumstances.
Other co-regulatory arrangements delegate the full responsibility for rule change requests

---

[145] The federal Australian Energy Regulator (AER) is responsible for regulation of the transmission and
distribution networks, while state regulators are generally responsible for the regulation of the retail
energy markets within their jurisdictions.

[146] One of the proposals made by the European Commission in the 2007 Telecoms package was for the
creation of a single European Communications Market Authority to ensure that communications
markets are regulated more consistently across EU Member States. This proposal was rejected by the
European Council.

[147] The European Commission can take action against Member States for failure to transpose the Directives.

[148] In telecommunications, for example, the Commission has in the past noted considerable divergence
in approaches to setting cost-oriented wholesale access prices across Member States that cannot be
accounted for by variations in underlying costs (EC, 2011b).

to the industry, and the regulator is only empowered to intervene on complaint from participant or consumer (and thus performs more of an arbitrator role).

Among the potential benefits of a co-regulatory approach is that: it can be more flexible and adaptable than traditional regulation (e.g. rules/codes can be updated quickly to respond to changing circumstances); it can involve lower administrative, monitoring and enforcement costs if the industry is effective in policing itself; and it focuses attention away from the command and control approach of traditional regulation towards joint problem solving and the use of controlled discretion by a regulator. Co-regulation can also allow for greater differentiation and experimentation by encouraging the regulator, industry and other stakeholders to work together and apply their own specialist knowledge to test and develop rules to address specific problems and risks as and when they arise. Co-regulation is sometimes seen as best suited to sectors that are changing rapidly and where the information available to regulators about new products and services, and the associated risks, is very limited. In other words, given future uncertainty, it can reduce the risk of a regulator independently developing rules that either over- or under-protect consumers, create an uneven playing field or potentially impede the development of the new products and services. It is perhaps for this reason that a co-regulation approach has been discussed as one way to regulate digital platforms, as discussed in Chapter 13.[149]

While a co-regulatory approach has various benefits in principle, the effectiveness of co-regulation in practice depends critically on two factors: the scope of participation and how it is implemented, monitored and enforced. If participation is voluntary, there is a risk of under-representation of certain firms or stakeholders, which obviously weakens its effectiveness. A second practical issue is that co-regulation operates without adequate regulatory oversight and enforcement. For instance, if there is insufficient regulatory involvement in the design, monitoring and enforcement of a code, then the industry may have too much control over which rules are introduced and how actively they follow the rules (i.e. in effect, they will capture the process and the rules).

As discussed in Chapters 9 and 10, a co-regulatory structure based around the use of industry codes is a feature of energy markets in some jurisdictions. These codes set out many of the rules regarding participation in the electricity and gas markets, including rules about connection to, and use of, the networks. In some jurisdictions, a co-regulatory structure has been developed where the industry, or a not-for-profit entity separate from the regulator, is responsible for managing the code, and for assessing proposed changes to the code.[150] If a party believes that certain aspects of the rules are not working well, it can

---

[149] See OECD (2019a), CERRE (2021) and UK Government (2021). See also Cusumano, Gawer and Yoffie (2021), who argue that self-regulation coupled with the threat of government intervention might yield the best results.

[150] In the USA, in some regions and states (such as the Midwest, California and Texas), not-for-profit independent system operators (ISOs) are responsible for preparing various 'business practice manuals' (BPMs), which detail the operating rules and implementation procedures that govern how market participants in the electricity sector do business with one another and with the ISO under the terms of its tariff. In Europe, the Agency for the Cooperation of Energy Regulators (ACER) has developed common code frameworks in energy and gas with the cooperation of the EU associations of system operators in gas and electricity – the European Network of Transmission System Operators for Electricity (ENTSO) and the European Network of Transmission System Operators for Gas (ENTSOG).

propose a modification to the code, which is sometimes then considered by a panel comprising industry members, other stakeholders (including users such as generators and suppliers) and a representative of the regulator. Code modifications can be proposed by the individual parties, but can sometimes require the approval of the regulator. This provides protection against an industry developing rules/regulations in ways that are favourable to their own interests, and contrary to, say, the interests of users or consumers. Moreover, because they have the power to propose amendments, disaffected parties can ensure that issues are addressed by proactively proposing code modifications without having to wait for the regulator to act. In short, the co-regulatory structure may serve to mitigate market power deriving from any undue influence of particular parties over rule books.

8.5 WHO REGULATES THE REGULATORS?

If the questions 'Why regulate?' and 'Who should regulate?' are among the most enduring in the area of economic regulation, an equally important issue concerns the oversight and accountability of regulatory agencies, or more specifically: 'Who regulates the regulators?' While this question has featured in debates since the creation of the early regulatory agencies in the USA, it has taken on an increasing importance as the scope of the powers, and the discretion, of regulatory authorities has expanded, and as rights of appeal and challenge of regulatory decisions are provided to a greater number of parties. Effective oversight of regulators ensures that investors, firms and consumers can be confident that regulatory decisions are made in line with the legal duties of the regulators, which in turn enhances the legitimacy of those decisions and of the regulatory framework.

When considering the supervision of regulatory agencies, a useful distinction can be made between general oversight of a regulator's conduct and performance, and the oversight or scrutiny of specific decisions or actions. We will consider the issue of the review of specific decisions first, before turning to more general oversight and accountability mechanisms.

8.5.1 Review of Specific Regulatory Decisions

Rights of appeal of regulatory decisions are seen as a critical component of fair and transparent administrative decision-making processes and are an important mechanism by which regulatory agencies are held accountable for their decisions. In many jurisdictions, there is some form of redress or right to some form of legal challenge or appeal of the decisions of regulatory agencies. However, differences can be observed across jurisdictions in terms of: the form in which this challenge can take; the relevant reviewing body; and who is able to challenge a decision ('standing'). There are also important differences in terms of the processes for appealing decisions of regulatory agencies.

Appeals of Process or Substance

The scrutiny to which regulatory decisions are subject depends on the nature of appeal rights and, in particular, whether there is a right to appeal the substance of a regulatory

decision (the merits) or whether any appeal is limited to questions of whether a prop
process was followed (judicial review). Under full merits review, a reviewing court
tribunal is asked to reconsider afresh the evidence and analysis that the regulator relie
on when making its decision.[151] In contrast, the judicial review of a regulatory decisio
involves the court or tribunal assessing whether the process undertaken by the regulato
for the consideration of the evidence was reasonable and lawful (the court does not typ
ically consider the evidence afresh).

Determining an appropriate standard of review for regulatory decisions is often a cor
tentious issue, and one that touches on issues of regulatory discretion, accountabilit
and independence. On the one hand, it is argued that allowing regulatory decisions to b
subject to full merits review involves unnecessary duplication by the courts of a functio
that has, in many cases, been entrusted to an independent expert specialist regulator. Tha
is, asking the courts to 'second-guess' the decisions of the regulator effectively turns th
appeals process into a second regulatory hearing, which can increase the costs associate
with regulation, and potentially encourage a culture where, because of the large sums o
money involved, firms have strong incentives to appeal each case and have 'another ro
of the dice'. On the other hand, because economic regulators often have significant discre
tion, and their decisions can have substantial impacts on consumers and the industry,
may be entirely appropriate for regulatory decisions to be subject to thorough, full righ
of appeal. Full rights of appeal enhance the credibility of a regulatory regime, and provid
greater confidence to investors that they will not be subject to regulatory opportunism. I
addition, there can be normative benefits associated with granting full rights of appea
regulators will, over time, recognise deficiencies in their processes and decision makin
and be incentivised to avoid further appeals by improving performance.

General Courts or Specialist Tribunals

A separate issue in designing mechanisms of regulatory oversight is whether regulator
appeals are reviewed by an expert or specialist tribunal or by a general court. The mai
advantage of specialist tribunals is that they can bring specific relevant expertise to th
review of a regulator's decision.[152] Such tribunals often operate in an informal manne
and are less legalistic in character and process than traditional courts.[153] On the othe
hand, generalist courts are perceived to offer their own advantages. In particular, judge
who already deal with complexity arising in a wide set of contexts, can bring a broade
understanding to regulatory matters, and avoid the risk that members of more narrowl
focused, specialised bodies hold the same preconceptions or world view.[154]

---

[151] The extent to which new evidence (including expert evidence) can be submitted and examined as part
the appeal differs among jurisdictions.

[152] In the UK, the Competition Appeal Tribunal (CAT) refers to itself as a specialist judicial body with
cross-disciplinary expertise in law, economics, business and accountancy. In Australia, the Australian
Competition Tribunal (ACT) comprises a president (who must be a judge) and other 'lay' members who
have knowledge of or experience in industry, commerce, economics, law or public administration.

[153] However, this is not invariably the case, and it is notable that the processes and character of some
tribunals have come to resemble general courts – with the participation of leading lawyers and
substantial amounts of documentary evidence being submitted.

[154] Robson (1951) refers, more generally, to a potential tendency in narrowly specialised tribunals for
'narrow professional instincts and group habits to assert themselves without let or hindrance'.

Permanent specialist tribunals and review bodies have been established to review the decisions of economic regulators in a number of countries including the UK and Australia.[155] Conversely, general courts are used as the forum for appeals of regulatory decisions in New Zealand, Canada and France. In the USA, contested regulatory decisions are generally subject to review internally by an impartial administrative law judge within the regulatory agency as a first step before appeal is made to the courts.

Where a foreign investor seeks to challenge a regulatory decision, it can sometimes make use of international arbitration tribunals as an alternative to national courts under investor–state dispute settlement clauses.[156] This has given rise to concerns that national regulatory preferences and decisions can be replaced by *de facto* supra-national regulation.[157]

Standing to Appeal Decisions

Who is able to challenge, or participate in, appeals of regulatory decisions differs across jurisdictions. In some cases, the right to challenge a decision, or to participate in proceedings, is restricted to the regulated firm and the regulator, while, in other cases, appeal rights are granted to any party that made a submission to a regulator during the regulatory proceedings. In some jurisdictions, third parties have an ability to participate or intervene in the appeals process, if they can show that they have a sufficient interest in the decision made by the regulatory authority, or that they will be adversely affected by the regulatory decision. The question of participation rights in challenges to regulatory decisions obviously presents a trade-off between ensuring that all parties materially affected by a decision have a right of challenge, and avoiding too many opportunities for challenge, such that the appeals process becomes drawn out and frivolous, increasing costs and reducing regulatory certainty.

8.5.2 General Oversight and Accountability

As discussed, while some degree of independence from direct government interference is generally a desirable characteristic of the independent regulatory agency model, it also means that regulatory officers and commissioners, who are unelected officials, have significant delegated decision-making powers. It follows that an important component of any regulation system are mechanisms that allow for general oversight, and the accountability of regulators. There are a number of different forms of oversight of regulatory agencies employed in practice across jurisdictions.

---

[155] Bernstein (1955) notes that the creation of a special administrative court to review regulatory decisions was proposed in the USA as early as the 1930s; however, this ceased to be advocated by the American Bar Association, in part because of a fear that the special court might become sympathetic to the views of regulatory agencies.

[156] Such as the World Bank International Centre for Settlement of Investment Disputes and International Chamber of Commerce.

[157] Auriol, Estache and Wren-Lewis (2018) discuss the limitations of such supra-national regulation, including the risk of capture.

Political or Executive Oversight

Political or executive oversight of the regulator is, in many jurisdictions, a primary method for ensuring regulatory accountability. This may include requirements for a regulator to periodically appear, and answer questions, in political or executive arenas. For example, regulators may be called to present and respond to oral and written questions at various standing and select parliamentary or congressional committees, including general public accounts committees. While requirements to appear before parliamentary or congressional committees can, in principle, be an effective means of regulatory oversight, potential risk is that regulators become unduly concerned with headlines and internalise political perceptions, an outcome that can compromise regulatory independence. Other mechanisms of accountability for regulators can include information obligations, such as requirements to submit annual reports and accounts to Parliament or Congress, and periodic or *ad hoc* reviews of regulatory performance and conduct.[158] Examples of the latter include the reviews of the performance of regulation, and the implementation of specific policies, by the National Audit Office (NAO) in the UK and the US Government Accountability Office (GAO).[159] Specific regulatory agencies can also become the subject of an *ad hoc* review of their performance and conduct.[160]

Finally, in addition to these formal mechanisms of general oversight, there are a number of other mechanisms that can potentially constrain and influence the behaviour of regulatory agencies, and provide a form of informal oversight and accountability. One example of this is the role played by groups, or associations, of regulatory agencies, such as the National Association of Regulatory Utility Commissioners (NARUC) in the USA and the associations of national regulators in the different industries in Europe.[161] These bodies seek to establish best-practice standards within their membership. Regulators can, of course, also be subject to close scrutiny from consumer, user or other representative bodies. Consumer representative bodies, in particular, are often perceived to address a risk that, absent this perspective, a regulator may have undue regard for the (often) more organised and better resourced industry interests.[162]

---

[158] See OECD (2016d) for examples.

[159] These reviews can be on specific issues of implementation, such as GAO's (2008) review of electricity restructuring and the FERC's role in that, or the NAO's (2008) review of the impacts of the removal of retail price controls in energy and telecommunications. The reviews can also examine the performance of regulatory agencies themselves, such as the UK NAO's (2010) review of the UK telecommunications regulator Ofcom, and its earlier review of the utility regulators (NAO, 2002). The Australian Government Productivity Commission has also, at various times, been asked to consider issues relating to specific regulatory policy in the network sectors, which can involve examining how regulation has been implemented in those sectors.

[160] See the reviews of the British energy regulator (DECC, 2011) and water regulator (Gray, 2011).

[161] Such as Council of European Energy Regulators (CEER) or the Independent Regulators Group for Telecoms.

[162] In practice, however, there may be limitations associated with relying on representative bodies to ensure accountability and supervision. Among these are the following: the potential that the representative body is itself politicised (i.e. they see their role as being a consumer champion and 'anti-regulator' or 'anti-industry'); and that such bodies may focus only on influencing regulatory decisions over the short term (e.g. in the case of consumer bodies, securing lower prices in the short term, at the expense of longer-term investment).

8.6 CONCLUSION

To mark the shift in this book towards examining the practice of regulation, this chapter focused on the institutions that apply economic regulation and, in particular, the role of independent regulatory agencies.

An important rationale for the development of independent regulators is associated with time inconsistency in policy making, and the establishment of an independent regulator is seen as a commitment by a government to restrict short-term interference in certain industries. Another rationale for the establishment of independent regulators is that they bring a degree of specialisation and expertise to the task of regulating, which may not exist in a more generalist government department or ministry. Specialist regulators can potentially be more effective in addressing the problem of asymmetric information between regulators and regulated firms.

The creation of an independent regulatory agency does not, however, automatically mean that the regulator and the regulatory process itself will be able to provide credible commitments. Indeed, one problem with independent regulators is that they may use their discretion and autonomy to act opportunistically by using information revealed over time to adjust prices. In this chapter, we considered various possible constraints on regulatory discretion that might limit the potential for opportunistic behaviour, and potentially enhance commitment; however, in practice, the use of such constraints needs to be balanced against the need to allow the regulator sufficient flexibility to adapt to new information and circumstances when necessary.

A review of the development of independent regulatory agencies across the world revealed that the independent regulatory model has a long history in countries such as the USA that pre-dates the various rationales which seek to account for its existence. Regulators have been established: to ensure stability and continuity in a regulated industry; to address concerns that newly privatised firms will exercise monopoly power; to separate the regulatory and commercial functions where utility firms remain state-owned; and, in the context of developing and transitional economies, to attract private investment by providing credible institutional commitments against government expropriation.

In practice, the design and powers of economic regulators differ in terms of: their structural and organisational form; the division of powers and responsibilities with other bodies such as ministries and competition authorities; and issues of regulatory accountability and oversight. Finally, it was noted that the allocation of powers and responsibilities in a modern regulatory system can be complex, involving not only regulators, but ministerial departments, competition agencies, industry through co-regulation arrangements, associations of regulators, courts and tribunals, and parliamentary oversight.

DISCUSSION QUESTIONS

1. What is the 'time-inconsistency' problem and how can it manifest in regulated industries?
2. What are some of the benefits of establishing of a regulator at 'arms length' from the government of the day?

3. Does the establishment of an independent regulator always ensure that a regulated firm will not be subject to opportunistic behaviour? If not, how can this risk be controlled for?

4. Describe some of the factors that have motivated the establishment of independent regulators in different jurisdictions over time. To what extent are they consistent with the theoretical benefits of establishing a regulator you identified in question 2

5. What are some of the arguments for and against creating a single regulator with responsibilities across multiple industries or sectors?

6. What are some of the benefits and risks of co-regulation? In what settings might such an arrangement be most suited?

7. Why is it important to oversee the decisions and activities of economic regulators and what are some of the different ways in which regulators can be held to account in practice?

9

Electricity Regulation

Electricity is fundamental to modern economies and societies. It is an essential energy source for many households and businesses and an important input to many industrial production processes. The safe and reliable supply of electricity is considered critical to both economic performance and consumer welfare.[1] Notwithstanding this, some 840 million people worldwide do not have access to electricity, while billions of others face unreliable supply on a daily basis.[2] Even in developed countries, problems with the reliability of electricity supply can cause significant disruption.[3] From the consumer perspective, large and volatile changes in electricity prices can squeeze household budgets (particularly for those on lower incomes) and prompt calls for regulatory intervention.[4]

For all of these reasons, the design and operation of electricity systems, and how they are regulated, is never far from the news cycle or politicians' agendas, and over the past four decades there has been a push in many parts of the world to 'restructure' the electricity industry, with the aim of reducing costs and improving performance and reliability. While the specifics of restructuring policies have differed across jurisdictions, they have typically involved some common elements, such as introducing competition in generation (and sometimes retail activities), separating core transportation activities from other activities in the supply chain, and introducing a specialised economic regulator. As we will see below, the perceived 'success' of these restructuring policies varies significantly across jurisdictions. This mixed scorecard in part reflects the unique and technically complex characteristics of electricity as a commodity, and the economic, social and political challenges of restructuring the industry.[5]

---

[1] In South Africa it is estimated that periodic blackouts experienced in 2022/23 cost the economy $51 USD million per day. Similarly, in Pakistan it was estimated that in 2013 electricity shortages and inefficiencies had retarded economic growth by at least 2 per cent a year, or 10 per cent over the previous five years. See USAID (2013).

[2] Foster and Rana (2020).

[3] Examples of major blackouts over the last two decades in developed countries include the 2003 blackouts in the northern USA, Canada and Italy, the Europe-wide blackout in 2006, Brazil in 2009, Turkey in 2015, South Australia in 2016 and Texas in 2021.

[4] As is occurring in Europe and many other parts of the world in 2022 as a result of rising wholesale gas prices.

[5] Hogan (2021) observes: 'The physics of power transmission systems make existing electricity markets unlike markets for other commodities. Markets cannot solve the problem of electricity market design and simple analogies to other markets can lead design astray.' Similarly, Wolak (2021) notes: 'It is difficult to conceive of an industry where introducing market mechanisms at the wholesale and retail level is more challenging for a policymaker.'

The experience of regulation of the electricity industry illustrates how some of the more theoretical issues described in Parts I and II of this book have been addressed in practice. Prominent among these are: the effects of vertical separation; the potential for a revenue shortfall to arise if prices are set only on the basis of short-run marginal cost; and the interaction of economic regulation with other policy areas, notably environmental policy. The discussion also shows how retail prices which may be efficient in an economic sense – insofar as they track underlying wholesale costs – may nevertheless face calls to be regulated because of concerns about fairness and affordability. Finally, the experience of restructuring the industry shows how consumers may, for a range of reasons, fail to actively engage in competitive markets.

Looking ahead, it is widely acknowledged that the regulation of the industry will need to adapt to the significant technological, market and behavioural changes which are transforming how consumers buy, manage, share and sell electricity. The decentralisation of electricity supply is providing increasing numbers of consumers with a choice about when and how they source energy, including the option to access energy from sources such as stand-alone or community networks, behind-the-meter generation or battery storage. Digitalisation is also allowing more consumers to participate more actively in electricity markets and to manage their consumption of electricity including through various demand-side response measures. The future operation and regulation of the industry will also be shaped by decarbonisation policies which seek to transform the industry from its current reliance on higher-polluting generation sources towards low-carbon or renewable sources.[6] Regulators are increasingly being charged with managing this change, which raises questions about the role of independent regulators and how objectives relating to efficiency, affordability and the environment are reconciled in practice.

9.1 PHYSICAL AND ECONOMIC CHARACTERISTICS OF ELECTRICITY

9.1.1 Characteristics of the Product

A number of attributes of electricity distinguish it from many other commodities. Firstly, although electricity can be produced from different input sources – such as nuclear power, coal, natural gas, hydropower, solar sources, wind, biomass and geothermal energy – it is a highly standardised product at point of production. Each source produces a certain unit of electricity of a particular quality. Secondly, electricity is generally a non-storable product,[7] which implies that any electricity that is produced needs to be consumed almost immediately, and it is not possible to build up stocks or inventories. Thirdly, to keep an

---

[6] The IEA (2021a) 'net zero roadmap' projects that, to achieve this target by 2050, 88 per cent of electricity will be generated from renewable electricity sources (solar, wind and hydropower), complemented by nuclear (7.7 per cent), hydrogen (2.4 per cent) and a small contribution from fossil fuels with carbon capture and storage (1.9 per cent).

[7] Traditionally, there has been some supply-side storage mechanisms such as ponded hydropower (where water is held behind a dam for use when electricity is most needed) or 'pumped storage' (where water is stored in dams and then pumped uphill and released to control the level of generation within a certain time period). However, as described below, new devices such as flywheels, capacitors and batteries provide new ways to store electricity.

electrical system 'in balance', and to prevent the risk of blackouts or outages, it is necessary that supply and demand of electricity be kept in constant equilibrium at every point during the day, and all over a particular network. A failure to equate demand and supply on one part of the network has the potential to cause wider systemic failure across the network. This means that a shortfall or surplus of electricity on one part of the network does not only affect specific customers, but can also affect the stability of the entire electricity network, and all of the network's customers.[8] The organisation of the supply of electricity is therefore complex, and requires a high level of coordination between the different stages of production in the supply chain.

Electricity production is a large emitter of greenhouse gases (such as carbon dioxide, sulfur dioxide and nitrogen oxides). For this reason a range of public policies and other measures targeted at reducing such emissions (low- and zero-carbon policies) are aimed at changing the way electricity is produced and consumed in many countries. As discussed in Section 9.4.2, these policies have had fundamental effects on all aspects of the electricity supply chain, including production (with a shift from traditional fossil fuel generation sources to low-carbon and renewable sources), transmission and distribution (requiring the development of new transmission lines to accommodate renewable energy sources and changed distribution networks to accommodate distributed energy resources), as well as on consumption (through demand management and efficiency measures).

There are four main types of electricity customer, and these types, and their respective share of demand, can be considered using the USA as an example. Residential customers use electricity for cooking, lighting, heating and cooling, and to power electrical appliances (washers, computers, refrigerators) and in the USA account for an estimated 39 per cent of demand.[9] Commercial customers (such as offices, restaurants, retail stores, commercial businesses) use electricity mainly for heating, cooling and lighting, and account for around 35 per cent of demand in the USA. Industrial customers (such as manufacturing, construction, mining, agriculture) use electricity in production processes and account for around 26 per cent of US demand, while transportation (such as for trains and metros) accounts for around 0.1 per cent of demand in the USA.

The demand for electricity is generally considered to be highly inelastic in the short term. There are a number of reasons for this, including the fact that many consumers, particularly household consumers, are not exposed to real-time changes in wholesale prices, as they tend to be on longer-term retail contracts at a fixed average price. In addition, for many consumers of electricity, including commercial/industrial and residential consumers, the possibilities to reduce consumption, or substitute to an alternative fuel source, are often limited in the short term (e.g. for domestic heating, cooling and cooking).[10]

---

[8] Spulber and Yoo (2005) refer to the 'seemingly innocuous' event of a failure of a handful of transmission lines on 14 August 2003, which resulted in power cuts to over 50 million homes in the USA and Canada.
[9] Estimates for 2020. See EIA (2021d).
[10] While it is possible to substitute away electricity for domestic purposes to other fuels such as gas in the medium term, this often requires changes to appliances.

9.1.2 Electricity Supply System

The supply of electricity to consumers can involve up to four activities: the generation of electricity using different energy inputs; the transmission of electricity over long distance along high-voltage power lines; the distribution of electricity in regional and local area using lower-voltage power lines; and the retail supply of electricity to 'load' customers.[11] While the centralised supply of electricity involves all four of these stages (as shown in Figure 9.1), there are increasingly other ways in which electricity can be supplied which involve only some of these stages. For example, generation can be connected directly to a distribution network to connect to load customers (known as distributed generation), or in some cases customers themselves can produce electricity on-site which they then consume (sometimes referred to as behind-the-meter or micro-generation) or use electricity that has been stored. Figure 9.2 shows some of the alternative ways in which electricity can be supplied in a decentralised or distributed electricity system. It also shows how in a decentralised system, the task of system operation can be divided into transmission system operation and distribution system operation, and there is also a much greater role for demand-side response including by supplying electricity to the distribution network.

Table 9.1 shows relative costs of supply along the centralised supply chain in three jurisdictions. Wholesale generation costs generally represent around one-third of the average household electricity bill in all three jurisdictions, transportation charges account for between 22 and 46 per cent, and supplier costs, taxes and other charges around 20 to 40 per cent. In the USA, approximately 56 per cent of the average electricity price in 2020 was represented by the wholesale charge, while transmission charges accounted for about 13 per cent and distribution charges about 31 per cent.[12]

Generation

A range of energy inputs can be used to produce or generate electricity. These include 'non-renewable' inputs such as coal, natural gas, oil and nuclear fuels, and 'renewable' inputs such as hydroelectric power, solar power, tidal power, wind power, biomass and geothermal energy. Each of these inputs for generating electricity has different characteristics in terms of operational performance and reliability and the ability to respond to peak demand.[13] They also affect the environment in different ways, including through air pollution (burning of fuels which emit harmful substances into the atmosphere such as carbon dioxide, sulfur dioxide, mercury), harmful water discharges (when cooling water is returned to water sources at warm temperatures) and the creation of hazardous waste (such as radioactive waste or coal ash, which contains mercury).

In terms of global electricity generation, in 2019, coal was the dominant generation input worldwide (accounting for 36.7 per cent of all production), followed by natural gas

---

[11] 'Load' is the term used to refer to an end-use device or customer (such as homes, factories, businesses and other consumers of electricity) that receives electricity from an electricity system. A load centre is a location, such as a city or major industrial area, where electricity consumption is concentrated.

[12] See EIA (2021a). These figures do not include supplier charges or taxes.

[13] The environmental impact of different sources of electricity production also depends on the age of the generating plant, how it is operated and the extent of pollution controls employed.

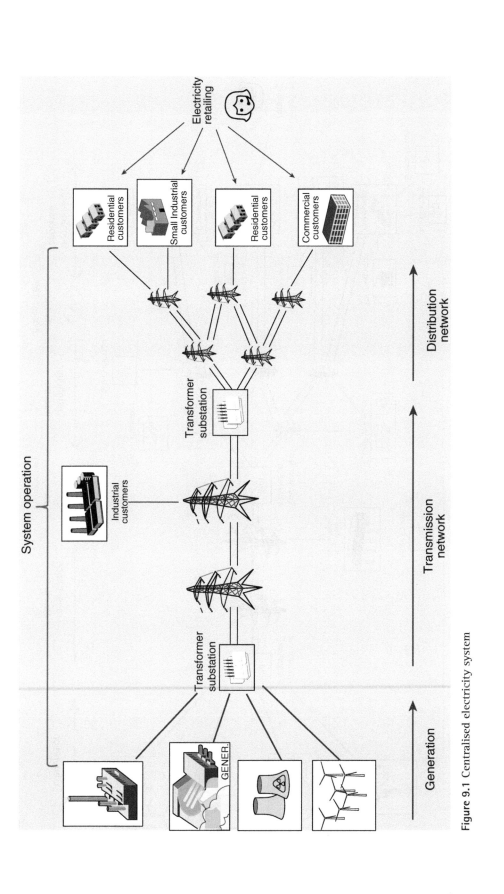

Figure 9.1 Centralised electricity system

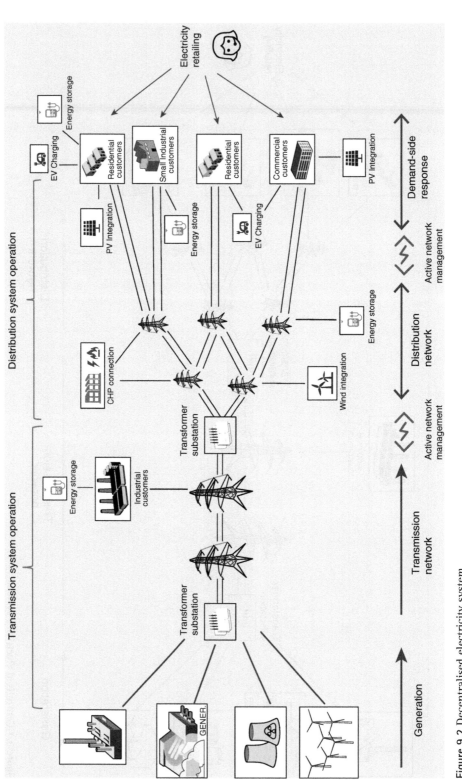

Figure 9.2 Decentralised electricity system

Table 9.1 Breakdown of average household electricity bills, 2020[a]

	Britain	EU Member States (average)	Australia
Wholesale generation	34%	37%	34%
Transportation (transmission and distribution)	22%	29%	46%
Supplier costs and margin	16%	34%	11%
Other levies (environmental costs and social obligations)	23%		9%
VAT	5%		
Total	100%	100%	100%

[a] Based on data from National Grid (2021), ACER/CEER (2021a) and ACCC (2021a).

(23.5 per cent), hydroelectric power (16 per cent), nuclear power (10.3 per cent) and oil (2.8 per cent). Non-hydro renewables accounted for around 10.8 per cent of electricity generation.[14] However, in some countries, renewable electricity in the form of hydroelectric power already accounts for a high proportion of production (e.g. Norway around 98 per cent, and New Zealand 85 per cent). In other countries, such as Germany, which have sought to transition away from high-carbon energy sources, the share of renewables is now over 50 per cent. It is generally argued that an efficient electricity system will have a generation profile that includes a mix of different technologies and plants; some that can operate continuously at low levels of marginal costs, and other more expensive generation technologies and plants which can be used to meet peak demand.

Electricity can be generated in a centralised or distributed way. Centralised electricity generators are often large-scale facilities that are located away from large load centres and supply electricity to a high-voltage transmission network. Centralised electricity generators can be classified into three broad operating patterns, each of which is associated with different variable operating costs: base-load plants (which run many hours of the year, have low variable costs but can be inflexible to changes in output); peaking plants (which may not run for many hours in a year, can start/stop quickly, and typically have higher variable costs); and intermediate plants (which run more often than peaking plant, but less than base-load plants and can be older base-load plants which are less efficient). Different energy sources suit particular operating patterns. For example, nuclear power plants operate most efficiently if they are operated continuously and are often used as a base-load source of generation. Gas-powered generators have lower construction costs than coal or nuclear power plants but the operating costs are sensitive to movements in wholesale gas prices, and in many electrical systems are used to meet peak demand. Many renewable energy sources, such as wind and solar power, are variable or intermittent in terms of their supply of electricity, and the output from these sources cannot be predicted precisely. This can require additional reserves of (conventional) generation to

[14] IEA (2021d).

be installed alongside these renewable generation facilities to ensure that the electricity system remains in equilibrium in times when the generation produced from renewable sources is insufficient. There are also different costs associated with the construction, ongoing operation and decommissioning of each form of centralised generation.[15] For example, nuclear power plants involve significant up-front sunk costs and long-lead development times, but once operational can generate electricity at very low levels of marginal cost. However, there can be high costs of nuclear decommissioning and for the long-term storage and disposal of the spent radioactive waste.

Distributed generation refers to various technologies that produce electricity at locations on-site or close to where it will be used and typically have lower levels of generating capacity than conventional or centralised generation.[16] Distributed generators can be used to service a single user (such as a business or a home) or can be part of a small micro-grid or community energy system. Distributed generation that is connected to distribution network can be used to export electricity to other users connected to the distribution network and thus act as a substitute for centralised generation. Prominent examples of distributed generation used by households include small solar photovoltaic (PV) panels and small wind turbines located 'behind the meter', while in the commercial sector examples include solar PV panels, combined heat and power systems, wind, biomass and solid waste incineration. The use of distributed generation is growing in many countries as a result of cost reductions for some technologies (such as solar PV panels, government policies to promote renewable energy, the development of micro-grids and the emergence of community energy systems. Distributed generation generally has less negative environmental impact than centralised energy generation because it typically uses renewable energy sources (solar and wind) or harnesses waste (such as combined heat and power) or can alleviate the need for excess generation that is needed to compensate for line losses when electricity is transported over long distances.

In addition to centralised and distributed forms of generation, a new form of 'generation' emerging in Australia, Europe and the USA is known as virtual power plants (VPP). This source of generation is described as 'virtual' as the VPP operator does not own conventional plant but uses an internet-based system to aggregate and manage electricity services from a range of distributed energy sources to provide a reliable overall supply. An example is the Tesla Virtual Power Plant project in South Australia, which will involve solar and home batteries installed at 3000 social housing properties. In simple terms, VPP operator gains control over a portfolio of assets both 'in front of' and 'behind the meter' (such as wind and solar PV panels on households), storage devices (such as batteries, electric vehicles (EVs) and/or EV charging stations) as well as other controllable load devices (such as water heaters, air conditioners, pool pumps, water pumps).[17] All of these

---

[15] The estimation of the levelised costs associated with different forms of generation requires various assumptions to be made about factors such as the economic lifetime of the plant, the average load factor and discount rates, etc.

[16] Distributed energy resources is the term used to describe distributed generation, plus other forms of storage or generation, such as electricity storage and electric vehicles.

[17] See Sioshansi (2021).

devices are then connected and remotely monitored, and the operator of the VPP uses artificial intelligence to flexibly control and shift electricity across the assets it owns, and to sell electricity in the wholesale market either as energy into a balancing market or as form of ancillary service to ensure grid stability.

Electric Storage

Electric storage is expected to play a more prominent role in future electricity systems.[18] While historically storage – principally in the form of pumped hydropower – has played only a minor role, technological developments are leading to the wider use of other forms of storage such as batteries and flywheels.[19] Among the benefits of electricity storage are that it can make an electricity system more flexible and reliable, which in turn can reduce the costs of the system. By allowing electricity to be withdrawn from the system and stored at times of low demand (with low prices), and then injected back into the system in periods of peak demand (with high prices), electricity storage can provide a flexible and cost-efficient mechanism to balance supply and demand. Storage can also be used to provide services to maintain grid reliability such as frequency reserve and ancillary services, which as discussed below is particularly important for systems reliant on large amounts of variable renewable energy (such as wind and solar power).[20] Over the longer term, the widespread integration of storage can reduce the capital costs of investments in peak generation capacity, the need to expand and reinforce transmission and distribution networks, and the operating costs associated with system operation.[21]

Storage facilities can be developed at different scales and technologies. Large utility-scale storage facilities (sometimes referred to as 'front-of-the-meter' storage) can be connected to transmission and distribution networks and act as a direct substitute for particular types of generation providing peak power and ancillary services.[22] In the future it is expected that large-scale storage facilities will be co-located alongside renewable energy generation facilities (particularly solar power). Storage facilities can also be developed by community energy systems or VPP operators to create a closed system which allows for excess electricity to be stored (e.g. from solar panels) and then used at a later point. At the household level, 'behind-the-meter' storage is also likely to have a more prominent role in the future. This includes batteries that are connected to, and store excess energy from, on-site solar PV facilities, as well as storage in EVs. Storage facilities can effectively turn consumers who also produce electricity on-site into 'consumer-generators' or 'prosumers' and allow them to be more active participants in electricity markets at any time of the day or night. Policies to promote investment and development of electricity storage have

---

[18] In the USA, it is estimated that 13 per cent of new electricity generating capacity additions in 2022/2023 will be battery storage. See EIA (2021c).

[19] Lithium-ion batteries are the most prevalent type.

[20] Strbac, Aunedi, Konstantelos, *et al.* (2017) conclude that the business case for storage rests on it providing a range of system services such as energy arbitrage, balancing, network management and capacity market adaptability.

[21] See Strbac Aunedi, Konstantelos, *et al.* (2017).

[22] EIA (2021b) records that in 2019 there were 163 large-scale battery storage systems in the USA, which was a 28 per cent increase over the previous year. IRENA (2019c) refers to examples of large-scale battery systems in Australia, Germany, Japan, the UK and the USA.

been introduced in some jurisdictions. For example, some US states have set targets for the amount of storage capacity that utility companies must procure.[23] In other jurisdictions, policies have been directed at promoting the deployment of EVs, which are seen as a potentially important way to store electricity.[24]

Transmission of Electricity

Once generated, electricity needs to be transported from the source of generation to the point of consumption. In centralised electricity systems, this typically involves the transportation of electricity over long distances along a high-voltage transmission network to major load centres of demand, usually for onward carriage via more localised distribution systems to end-consumers, but sometimes to individual large end-users themselves (such as large industrial plants). Transmission networks are highly capital-intensive to construct, involve significant sunk costs and, in many settings, fit the classic definition of natural monopoly, being inefficient to duplicate and involving immobile physical assets.[25]

An important characteristic of electricity supply is that generators of electricity do not sell a specific, identifiable electron to a buyer. Rather, they supply a quantity of (indistinguishable) electrons at one point of the transmission network (known as a node) which enters into the more general system. Buyers of electricity then withdraw their required amount of electricity at the closest node for distribution onto final consumers. Unlike trains on rail networks, or gas molecules in gas pipelines, it is not possible to direct electricity along a specific path in a transmission network towards a designated point of demand (or customer). Instead, the power flows on an electrical network are governed by the rules of physics.[26] For example, the export of electricity from France to Germany can lead to significant electricity flows through Belgium, the Netherlands and Switzerland. The requirement to ensure that the injections of power on an electrical system are matched by the withdrawals of power on the network, and that the system is 'in balance' on a minute-by-minute basis at all times, and at all nodes on the transmission network, is a task known as 'system operation'. System operators are responsible for the short-term management and balancing of the network.[27] In some jurisdictions, such as in the USA, this is undertaken by an independent not-for-profit entity, which is separate from the entity that owns and operates the transmission network.[28] An independent system operation function can mitigate short-term coordination problems by ensuring that generators are dispatched in a non-discriminatory manner, and that the system operates reliably and avoids potential failures. As discussed below, given the changing configuration of electricity systems, the system operator concept is now being extended to the creation of 'distribution system operators' (DSOs).

---

[23] For example, in California, Massachusetts and New York. Strbac Aunedi, Konstantelos, Moreira *et al.* (2017) identify market and regulatory barriers to storage development in the UK at that time.

[24] IRENA (2019a) notes that EVs can create vast electricity storage capacity.

[25] Weiss (1975) referred to electricity transmission as the 'classic natural monopoly' activity. However, as discussed below, in some jurisdictions there is potential for competition for merchant transmission lines

[26] Essentially, electricity follows the path of least resistance. These are known as Kirchhoff's laws.

[27] Interestingly, Joskow and Schmalensee (1983) in their discussion of a 'full restructuring scenario' foresaw the need for the creation of some pooling and coordination entity.

[28] Known as 'independent system operators' (ISOs).

A number of features of an electricity transmission network can impact on the efficiency of an electricity system, and on the costs of electricity for end-consumers. The first is the configuration of the transmission network, in particular the location and distance between the sources of generation and the major load centres of demand. The transmission of electricity involves what is known as 'line losses', which are amounts of electrical energy that are lost in the transmission of electricity, much of which is thermal in nature. For example, if 100 MWh (megawatt-hours) of power is injected into a transmission network from a generator at a particular node, on average only about 93 MWh of electricity will be withdrawn from a node by an end-user, implying transmission and distribution losses of around 7 per cent on average. Generally, the longer the distance that electricity is transmitted, and the lower the voltage, the larger the losses and the higher the level of transmission costs that need to be recovered through charges.[29]

A second factor that impacts on the efficient operation of the electricity system is the amount of transmission capacity available at any point in time. Transmission capacity is constrained whenever a particular line or element reaches its limit and cannot carry any more electricity than it is already carrying. In these circumstances this part of the network is said to become congested, and, in order to keep the system in balance, adjustments are required to generation and consumption at other parts of the network. Transmission constraints can have important implications for the costs associated with purchasing electricity from different geographic areas. Specifically, it can restrict the ability of power purchasers to acquire electricity from low-cost generators who have generation capacity available, but who lie 'on the wrong side' of a transmission constraint. In these circumstances, power purchasers may need to turn to higher-cost generation sources from areas where transmission is not constrained in order to satisfy demand. This results in higher electricity costs for consumers. A third, and related, feature of transmission networks is the potential existence of 'pockets' of short-term market power that can be caused, or exacerbated, by the existence of transmission constraints on the network. As noted above, transmission constraints restrict the amount of electricity that can be imported into a particular region to satisfy demand. As a consequence, generation sources *within* that (import-constrained) region become pivotal to meeting demand in that region and keeping the system in balance (see Section 9.4.1 below). That is, generators – even generators with a relatively small share of production – within an import-constrained region can raise the price for the marginal electricity that it produces, and which is needed to satisfy demand. In short, the existence of transmission constraints can limit the exposure of generators in certain regions to competition from generators in other regions.[30]

---

[29] However, the higher the voltage of a transmission line, the more it costs to build per kilometre, but the greater its capacity and the lower the energy losses.

[30] This is a more acute problem in electricity markets than other markets because inventories or stores of electricity cannot be maintained to limit the ability of suppliers within an import-restricted region from driving up prices. In addition, in many other markets, demand is more elastic in the short term, and there is not a need for instantaneous matching of demand and supply (that is, consumers can adjust their behaviour over time in response to attempts to raise prices in this way). See Borenstein and Bushnell (2000).

Electricity Distribution

Transmission networks transport electricity at high voltage in order to minimise energy losses. However, once the electricity reaches a load centre, or offtake point, the voltage of the electricity must be reduced for its transport by a local or regional distribution network to end-customers.[31] Distribution networks use transformers to reduce the voltage of electricity to levels that can allow it to be safely used by industrial, commercial and domestic customers. Distribution networks comprise substantial physical infrastructure (such as overhead wires and underground lines) that criss-cross specific urban and regional areas to provide electricity to every customer within that distribution region. As is the case with transmission networks, distribution network activities generally involve large sum investments in long-lived and immobile capital assets, and this, along with other factors gives rise to cost conditions similar to that of a natural monopoly.[32] There are important economics of density associated with distribution networks. While there is typically only one, or a small number of, transmission network companies supplying a specific jurisdiction or wide geographic area, there can be many more electricity distribution network companies that service particular regional areas. In countries such as Austria, France Germany, Italy, Poland, Spain, Switzerland and the USA, there are over a hundred (and in some cases several hundred) regulated distribution companies.[33]

As discussed below in Section 9.4.2, technological developments and decarbonisation policies have led to changes in the structure and operation of distribution networks. One change arises from the need to accommodate the various forms of distributed energy resources (such as distributed generation and storage) which are directly connected to the distribution network rather than the transmission network. As described above, some of these distributed energy resources can be used to export power to the distribution network for sale to utilities or other market participants. Distributed generation requires that distribution network operators develop new interconnection standards, and establish the terms of connection and access of distributed generation to a network. Looking ahead, there is likely to be a need to expand and adapt distribution networks to accommodate the expected large increase in EV connections.

In addition, as distribution networks have traditionally been configured to carry electricity in one direction only – from transmission offtake points to specific customer locations – distributed generation connections will lead to changes in the flows around the electricity network as a whole, which may make flows less predictable and require more active management of the distribution systems. This has led to a shift from distribution companies being 'passive' network operators to becoming 'active' DSOs.

---

[31] In practice, the distinction between transmission and distribution systems may not always be that clear. FERC Order 888 (1996) sets out seven distinguishing features of local distribution systems.

[32] A typical distribution network consists of assets such as overhead lines and poles, cables, underground channels that carry the electricity, as well as substations, transformers, switching equipment, and monitoring and signalling equipment such as meters.

[33] See Küfeoglu, Pollitt and Anaya (2018). Analysis by Growitsch, Jamasb and Pollitt (2009) indicates that while distribution networks need not be large to benefit from economies of scale, there are likely to be unexploited scale economies in countries where there are a large number of small distribution networks

[34] Distribution networks have generally been operated as passive systems, but the integration of distributed generation will require the development of more active network management techniques. This, of course depends on the type and location of the new distributed generation and, in some cases, small amounts of distributed generation can, if located suitably, be integrated into existing distribution networks without such adaptations being required. See, generally, Strbac (2008).

DSOs will be tasked with using real-time data to manage the distributed energy resources in their area; this includes managing the two-way flows on the network and procuring flexibility and reliability services from network users (including customer-generators or 'prosumers' and those operating storage facilities).[35] A major advantage of more active distribution system management is that, by better managing available resources at the local level, it can avoid the need for significant transmission network upgrades. In some circumstances, DSOs could also provide flexibility and ancillary services to transmission companies.

Retail Supply

The final stage in the production and supply chain of electricity involves the retail supply of electricity to customers. In countries where retail supply competition has been introduced, the functions of distribution and retail supply are separated, meaning that, while the electricity distribution network operator is responsible for delivering power to specific locations and customers, retail electricity suppliers sell this electricity to domestic and commercial customers.[36] Retail supply companies combine the various charges incurred at the different stages of the electricity production chain – wholesale generation costs, transmission and distribution network charges as well as any retailing and marketing costs – into a single charge or tariff for electricity which is offered to customers. In jurisdictions where retail supply competition, or retail choice, has been introduced, customers can choose from a range of different retail suppliers, each of which can offer different prices and types of tariffs.

Three developments in the retail supply of electricity merit further comment. The first is the development of a range of new tariffs in jurisdictions where retail competition has been introduced.[37] This includes 'dual-fuel' tariffs (where customers are able to source both electricity and gas from a single retail supplier), 'green energy tariffs' which reflect the fact that electricity has been sourced primarily from renewable energy sources, and 'real-time' tariffs that effectively shift some of the risk of wholesale electricity price movements onto consumers. A second development in some jurisdictions is the installation in customer premises of 'smart meters' which allow customers to receive near real-time information on their energy consumption and how much it is costing. A third development is the emergence in many jurisdictions of new ways for customers to source electricity, manage their consumption in real time and actively participate in the market. These changes are raising questions about who 'supplies' electricity and what regulatory obligations should be applied to these new supply arrangements.[38]

---

[35] See IRENA (2019b).

[36] In some jurisdictions, such as the USA, the terms 'electricity service provider' (ESP) or 'load-serving entity' (LSE) are more commonly used to refer to retail providers of electricity.

[37] Generally, Littlechild (2006c, 2009c, 2021b).

[38] These changes mean that some consumers will sometimes have a supply arrangement with a non-traditional electricity supplier (such as an apartment block owner or a community grid operator), which raises important questions about who should be a regulated 'supplier' of electricity, and what regulatory obligations should apply to them. Energy sharing arrangements in particular (such as community energy systems, virtual sharing over the grid, or sharing of local production through community grids) are said to defy the classic supplier–customer relationship. Decker (2021) considers these issues in more depth.

9.1.3 Trading Arrangements for Wholesale Electricity

As described in Section 9.3, up until the 1980s the various activities in the electricity supply chain just described were typically undertaken by a single vertically integrated entity in many parts of the world. In the USA these vertically integrated entities tended to be privately owned but regulated, while in Europe, Latin America and Australia the integrated firms tended to be state-owned.

From the late 1970s, a number of countries began to introduce competition at the wholesale generation level.[39] In the USA this involved the creation of new independent power producers (IPPs) that would sell power to incumbent utilities,[40] while in other countries it involved the restructuring of the industry through horizontal and vertical separation of generators from other entities in the supply chain.[41]

Looking around the world, there are now various ways through which generators supply electricity to load customers. A first way is through self-supply where a generator uses its own plant to meet retail demand. In centralised systems that have not been restructured, this typically involves a vertically integrated entity owning generation facilities, transporting electricity using its transmission and distribution networks and directly supplying consumers. In distributed electricity systems, this can involve self-supply either via on-site generation facilities (such as solar PV) or through sharing in community energy systems.

A second supply arrangement involves the buying and selling of electricity via a centralised and mandatory wholesale spot market – known as an 'electricity pool' – which is a form of auction through which generators sell, and load customers purchase, electricity.[42] In a 'gross pool' it is mandatory for all generators and all load customers of electricity to trade their physical output via the pool. In other words, sellers and buyers of electricity do not directly trade with one another; rather, the trading interface is first between the seller of electricity (the generator) and the pool market operator, and then between the pool market operator and the buyer of electricity (such as local distribution or retail supply companies). Generators make advance bids into the pool for supplying power for a particular interval of time (say, each half-hour of the following day) and these bids are then used to determine the dispatch or merit order to meet expected demand. As part of this process a market-clearing price for the specific time interval is established by the pool market operator (the price at which the bids of offers to sell electricity matches the bids of offer

---

[39] There is an extensive literature that examines the principles and experience of the development of wholesale market trading arrangements. These include Stoft (2002), Griffin and Puller (2005), Green (2008), Sioshansi (2008) and Glachant and Lévqêue (2009). Wolak (2021) and Joskow and Léautier (2021) provide useful contemporary overviews of wholesale market design.

[40] The passing of the Public Utility Regulatory Policies Act 1978 (PURPA) in the USA was perhaps the first step in this process. Steinhurst (2011) records that the passing of this act was prompted by the oil price shocks of the 1970s, and a desire to diversify the types of companies generating electricity and reduce dependence on fossil fuels. Joskow (1989) presents a detailed discussion of the implementation and effects of PURPA.

[41] Reforms in Chile were introduced in 1982, while the Electricity Pool of England and Wales was established in 1990, and the Norwegian spot market pool the year after in 1991. See, generally, Al-Sunaidy and Green (2006). On the Chilean experience, see Pollitt (2004) and Joskow (2008a). Newbery (1999, chapter 6) provides background to the reforms in England and Wales, as well as in other countries.

[42] Joskow and Schmalensee (1983) describe earlier, and different, 'pooling' arrangements in the USA.

to purchase electricity).[43] This market-clearing price, which varies for each time interval (i.e. half-hour in our example), is then used to determine the price paid to all generators in respect of the amount of scheduled electricity supplied. If generators' bids reflect their marginal costs of operating different plants, then the merit order constructed would (with adjustments for losses) reflect an efficient dispatch, and the system marginal price would reflect the operating cost of the marginal plant in the system required to balance demand and supply at that time.[44] In order to manage the volatility of pool prices, generators and load customers of electricity tend to hedge their positions by entering into financial contracts (such as contracts for differences) with agreed prices.[45] Examples of pool arrangements include regional markets operated by independent system operators (ISOs) in the USA (such as Pennsylvania–New Jersey–Maryland (PJM), Texas, New York and California), the Australian National Electricity Market and the Irish Single Electricity Market.

A third type of trading arrangement is where generators enter into bilateral contracts with buyers of electricity (load customers) directly for the wholesale supply of electricity, with the price determined through bilateral negotiations. Bilateral transactions may occur through direct contract negotiations, a tendering process or negotiated over-the-counter (OTC) transactions. Under these arrangements, market participants 'self-dispatch' and are only required to inform the system operator of how much electricity will be injected and withdrawn from the network. Participants can alter their position up to one hour before dispatch, and can also voluntarily participate in close-to-real-time markets (such as a balancing market) which are run by the system operator to ensure that the system remains in balance in real time by contracting for any surplus demand, or clearing any residual electricity on the network.[46] This type of arrangement is common in European markets, including in Britain.[47]

A fourth form of trading arrangement, which has been used in many Asian, African and Eastern European countries, is based around a 'single-buyer' model.[48] This form of trading arrangement involves a nominated company (such as the transmission network operator, or in some cases a vertically integrated incumbent) acting as a single buyer for all electricity produced by IPPs. Competition in these arrangements typically involves the single buyer issuing periodic competitive tenders for new capacity, following which a power purchase agreement (PPA) is signed between the single buyer and successful bidder.[49]

---

[43] In Australia, the market operator receives between six and eight million rebids annually.

[44] However, one of the arguments for the abolition of the England and Wales pool was that generators would exercise market power and try to manipulate the pool price. On the experience of pricing in the England and Wales pool, see Green and Newbery (1992), Wolfram (1999) and Sweeting (2007).

[45] This includes two-way contracts for difference, where a user pays a generator if the spot price is below a pre-specified benchmark price, or one-way contracts for difference, where payments are only made if the spot price exceeds the benchmark price.

[46] Pollitt (2021) observes that both generators and retailers have incentives to minimise participation in balancing markets because generators receive less, and retailers pay more, than they would in day-ahead markets (retailers will likely be buying on short days, and generators likely selling on long days).

[47] These are sometimes referred to as 'net pool' arrangements. The Norwegian market (which became NordPool) and the Chilean market are early examples.

[48] See Kessides (2012).

[49] For a further discussion, see World Bank (2000) and Newbery (2002). A number of risks associated with the single buyer approach have been identified, including that: it can misallocate risk; it creates the potential for *ex post* opportunism by the monopsonist buyer; and the risk of long-term power purchase contracts becoming stranded.

A final way in which wholesale electricity is traded is where the government effectivel guarantees a minimum price for sale of electricity. A prominent example of this approac is the use of feed-in tariffs (FITs) as a way of incentivising investment in renewable an low-carbon energy resources.[50] FITs are sometimes described as a form of PPA whic guarantees a fixed level of compensation for a set period at a rate that allows the investe a guaranteed return on investment. In Germany, FITs (which were used up until 202◆ provided a guaranteed tariff for renewable energy for a period of 20 years. Under th arrangements, grid operators were legally required to purchase all the power produce from renewable energy facilities at the FIT rate, which they then sold into the whol sale market. Any shortfall between the FIT price and the wholesale price was recovere through a compulsory surcharge applied to the bills of consumers (although some indu◆ trial consumers were exempt). It is therefore often said that the substantial investmen in renewable energy in Germany was not funded through public funds, but rather v electricity consumers.[51] Although the use of FITs was effective in terms of achieving hig levels of installation of renewable generation, this result came at a substantial cost, whic was largely borne by retail (particularly household) consumers.[52] In 2017, the FIT syste was replaced by a market-based procurement model whereby a predetermined amount ◆ capacity for different renewable sources (wind, solar, biomass) are periodically auctione◆ with the price for that generation determined through that competitive process. A sim lar system of auctions for low-carbon capacity were introduced in Britain in 2015 base around a contracts for difference approach. Generators participating in this scheme se energy in the market as usual but the government agrees to pay the difference betwee the wholesale electricity price and an agreed strike price: if the market reference price below the agreed strike price, then the generator receives a 'top-up' payment to the agree strike price (and vice versa).

Electricity Markets and Exchanges

Within these general frameworks for selling and buying wholesale electricity, a divers set of markets and exchanges has emerged to facilitate the trade of different electricit 'services', and to manage the risks associated with volatility in electricity prices. Thre common types of markets that can be observed include: energy markets, ancillary mar kets and capacity markets.

Energy markets offer participants the opportunity to buy or sell electricity, or to adju positions, at different points prior to the dispatch of electricity. Such markets migh include a day-ahead market and a real-time market, and are typically operated by th

[50] The first example of a FIT was introduced as part of PURPA in 1978 in the USA which established a class of non-utility generators who could build small generation facilities and co-generation plants (so-called qualifying facilities) and produce power for resale. Incumbent utilities were required to purchase electricity from these qualifying facilities on an avoided cost basis, and this led to the development of long-term contracts between incumbent utilities and entrants (who became known as IPPs). The avoide◆ costs were determined by state regulators and were not therefore market prices. In some states, such as California, Texas, Maine and New York, this led to the establishment of 'standard-offer contracts' at hig levels.
[51] This distinction is important in the context of the European State Aid rules.
[52] German household electricity prices are the highest in the European Union.

system or market operator. Day-ahead markets allows participants to sell and purchase electricity the day before delivery and to hedge their position against price volatility. The operator of the day-ahead market uses the offers and bids received to construct aggregate supply and demand curves at different locations, which are then used to determine the market clearing price at that location. This results in a binding operational and financial schedule for the generation and consumption of electricity on the following day. Intra-day and close-to-real-time balancing markets allow participants to adjust their positions to meet the energy needs within shorter intervals such as each hour or five-minute peri-ods, and prices tend to be more volatile than in day-ahead markets.

In some regional markets in the USA, price risks associated with transmission con-straints and associated congestion on the network are managed through trading in what are known as financial transmission rights (FTRs).[53] FTRs do not involve a physical right to deliver power, but provide the holder with the right to a share of any congestion rev-enues accumulated on a transmission path, and therefore allow a market participant to hedge its position against congestion costs by acquiring sufficient FTRs that are consist-ent with their energy deliveries. FTRs can be acquired through auctions (which includes one-year FTRs and monthly FTRs) or in a secondary market.

Markets have also developed to allow for the trade of ancillary electricity services. Ancillary services maintain key technical characteristics of the system, including stand-ards for frequency, voltage, network loading and system restart processes. These services are procured by a system operator to manage the power system and ensure that it oper-ates securely and reliably.[54] Markets for real-time ancillary services allow the system operator to manage the system in real time, while forward reserve ancillary markets involve generators committing in advance to making capacity available to address system contingencies should they arise.

A third set of markets, particularly prevalent in the USA (with the exception of Texas), are known as capacity markets.[55] As discussed later in Box 9.2, capacity markets require buyers of electricity (load customers) to purchase sufficient generation capacity to cover their expected loads (including reserves) and are intended to compensate generators for investing in capacity in a way which takes into account where capacity is most needed. Many regional system operators in the USA operate capacity markets that allow load-serving entities (LSEs) to purchase capacity for certain periods in advance, such as a month, year or even up to three years. In the UK, a centralised capacity auction market was introduced in 2014 which involves capacity providers (which can include both gen-erators and demand-side response participants) committing to have a certain amount of capacity available for a one-year period. In exchange for these obligations, capacity providers receive a monthly payment from suppliers. The auctions are held four years in advance of the delivery year for existing plant and for fifteen years in advance for new plants. Some European countries, such as France and Italy, have introduced market-wide

---

[53] These are sometimes referred to as transmission congestion contracts (TCCs). See Hogan (1992), Joskow and Tirole (2000) and Kristiansen (2004).

[54] In some jurisdictions, the system operator maintains separate markets for ancillary services, where providers of such services (such as generators) bid in a similar way to how they bid into an energy pool.

[55] See Cramton and Stoft (2005) and Joskow (2008b).

capacity mechanisms which involve capacity payments being made to generators.[56] However, the European Commission is concerned that the use of national capacity mechanisms could distort the development and operation of an integrated European energy market and only allow them to be used for a finite period.[57]

Wholesale electricity markets are sometimes organised on a regional basis, which does not necessarily reflect country or state borders. The four Nordic countries (Denmark, Sweden, Norway and Finland) have operated a single market for trading electricity known as NordPool since the early 2000s, which has now extended operations across sixteen European countries. Similarly, since 1998, Spain and Portugal have gradually been developing a regional electricity market, known as the Iberian Electricity Market (MIBEL). In the USA there are various combined regional wholesale electricity markets that extend over state boundaries, such as the PJM market (which extends over thirteen states including Pennsylvania, New Jersey, Maryland and the District of Columbia), the Midwest ISO (which covers fifteen states and one Canadian province) and the New England market (which covers six states). Other examples of regional markets include the Australian National Electricity Market (which connects six states and territories) and the Southern African Power Pool (which includes twelve countries).

Finally, in many restructured markets, electricity-trading exchanges have developed to facilitate the trading of contracts related to electricity products. Electricity exchanges can allow for the over-the-counter trading of standardised electricity contracts (for example, for day-ahead electricity), as well as offering financial futures and other forward hedging contracts to manage risk.[58] Where such exchanges facilitate trades between physical market traders (that is, generators and load customers), these participants are still required to notify and schedule delivery of electricity with the system or market operator.

9.2 APPROACH TO ELECTRICITY REGULATION

9.2.1 Activities Subject to Regulation in the Production and Supply Chain

Competitive Activities in the Supply Chain

While it is difficult to generalise about the structure of the electricity industry across jurisdictions, where competition exists it typically involves (wholesale) competition between electricity generators and, in some jurisdictions, competition in the retail supply of electricity. In addition, as discussed below, 'competition for the market' for new transmission lines has also been introduced in some places.

---

[56] In France the capacity payments are intended to ensure capacity for winter peak periods. These capacity payments are determined through administrative means and not through a capacity market.

[57] Such distortions could arise where a national energy-only market coexists with markets that include both capacity and energy payments. Under the EU Clean Energy Package, capacity mechanisms should only be introduced to address problems or circumstances that cannot be resolved by market reforms alone and for a finite period of time.

[58] These include the European Energy Exchange (EXAA, based in Leipzig), the Italian Power Exchange (GME), the European Power Exchange (EPEX) for the UK, Belgium and the Netherlands, and the Polish Power Exchange (TGE). In the USA, the Intercontinental Exchange (ICE) is a major venue for over-the-counter trades. Brown and Sappington (2021) examine how the extent of equilibrium forward contracting varies by: the number of generators and buyers, their aversion to varying profits and the structure of retail tariffs. Willems, Pollitt, von der Fehr and Banet (2022) note that the 2022 energy crisis in Europe revealed that many suppliers were not well hedged against a rise in wholesale prices, and that it remains an open question how well the markets for risk hedging actually work.

The basic rationale for introducing competition in generation was that the economies of scale associated with electricity generation were modest. There were also seen to be potential gains associated with allowing the different sources of generation (gas, hydro, coal) to compete with one another given their different production profiles, technologies and costs. Competition between generators was also expected to enhance the incentives for controlling the costs of construction and operation of new and existing generation capacity (investors would now bear the risk of excess capacity), and to encourage innovation in power supply technologies.[59] As described above, competition in wholesale generation markets can take different forms, including: allowing IPPs to compete alongside an incumbent to provide electricity; a single buyer model where competing wholesale generators sell electricity to a single buyer (such as a transmission company); the establishment of wholesale market competition in the form of a pool arrangement; or direct bilateral contracting between generators and retailers (or LSEs). In some jurisdictions, these policies have led to competitive wholesale markets and the subsequent withdrawal of formal price controls on generators, such as in the UK, Europe, Australia and, for those generators assessed as not having market power, in the USA.[60] Consequently, wholesale electricity generation prices are – subject to certain important limits and maximum price caps designed to mitigate the potential exploitation of market power described below – generally unregulated in these jurisdictions.

Retail supply is also considered a potentially competitive activity, in part, because of the limited fixed and sunk costs associated with trading and marketing activities. In addition, the introduction of policies which allow consumers to choose among competing retail suppliers is argued to lead, over time, to a fuller array of retail products being offered which are better tailored to consumer preferences and provide greater opportunities for demand-side management. As discussed in Section 9.4.1, the success of introducing competition for retail supply is a topic of considerable debate, and there are recurring concerns in some jurisdictions that retail competition is not working effectively, and that retail suppliers might be exploiting consumers who are inactive and remain on standard and default tariffs.[61] As described below, in part for this reason, some form of retail price control still exists for competitive markets in some European countries and the USA, and have recently been reintroduced in Britain and Australia.

Another activity in the electricity supply chain where competition has been introduced is for 'merchant investments' in transmission capacity. This involves independent third-party investors developing new transmission links to generators or which interconnect two markets.[62] The investor can either directly negotiate the terms of the investment with the expected users (such as generators or a downstream supplier) or can build the investment in anticipation of capturing the congestion rents associated with trading between

---

[59] See Joskow (2008a).
[60] In the USA, the ability of a generator to charge 'market-based' rates rather than cost-based pricing is based on an assessment of the market power of the generator (that is, the ability to raise price above competitive levels without losing substantial business). See FERC (2007).
[61] See discussion in Chapter 7.
[62] Chao and Wilson (2020) note that: 'Merchant investment in transmission capacity expansion is appealing because it places the financial risks of investment on investors rather than consumers, while bypassing the bureaucratic processes for regulated transmission companies.'

two different locations with different locational prices. To date, there has been onl
limited experience with the use of merchant investments.[63] This may in part reflect per
ceptions of the regulatory challenges associated with such an approach and that the scop
for such merchant investments in transmission may be limited by technology.[64] Howeve
this is changing as a result of the need for networks to accommodate larger amounts c
low-carbon and renewable generation and to facilitate regional or cross-border intercor
nections. In some jurisdictions, a 'competition for the market' approach has been adopte
for some new transmission investments. In 2009, Britain introduced a competitive tende
process to appoint offshore electricity network operators, while in 2016, the regulato
proposed a Competitively Appointed Transmission Owner (CATO) regime for new, sep
arable and high-value onshore electricity transmission assets. Successful bidders will b
paid through a largely fixed annual revenue stream that was bid during the tender proces
over a twenty-five year term.[65] A similar competitive tendering approach for transmissio
investment was used in the state of Victoria in Australia in 2019.[66] Some argue that in th
future a hybrid model may emerge where merchant investments and regulated transmis
sion investments coexist and complement one another.[67]

Activities Subject to Price Control and Other Controls

In almost all parts of the world, transmission and distribution networks are general
subject to some form of price and other regulatory controls. This reflects the cost char
acteristics of these activities (large sunk capital costs, immobile assets, increasing returr
to production) which approximate those of a natural monopoly, and the fact that, abser
regulation, there would in most cases be limited competitive constraints placed on oper
ators, leaving them in a *de facto* monopoly position.[68] In addition, the efficiency of th
competitive segments of the electricity market (such as generation and retail supply
depends on the core network transportation activities. As described below, regulator
policies typically restrict entry to transmission and distribution activities (i.e. implemen
a geographic monopoly), regulate prices and quality, and require transmission and dis
tribution network operators to provide access to their networks on non-discriminator
terms and conditions.[69]

---

[63] Brunekreeft (2005) refers to examples of merchant investments in the USA, Latin America, Europe and Australia. Of the three examples in Australia, two subsequently sought to be subject to regulation.

[64] Joskow and Tirole (2005) conclude that it can lead to inefficient transmission investment decisions. Brunekreeft (2005) and Brunekreeft, Neuhoff and Newbery (2005) also conclude that merchant interconnector investment is not unproblematic and raises new regulatory issues. Hogan, Rosellón and Vogelsang (2010) observe that certain investments in transmission upgrades can have negative network effects and can reduce total network capacity.

[65] Ofgem (2016).

[66] For the Western Victoria Transmission Network Project.

[67] See Chao and Wilson (2020). Hogan, Lindovska, Mann and Pope (2018) argue that there is a need for a hybrid system with a deference to merchant investment, and regulation only being applied for large projects with substantial free-rider problems.

[68] There can be competition around the edges of major networks, including from independent networks at the local level (e.g. new housing estates, interconnectors or offshore electricity networks).

[69] In the USA, this is captured in FERC Order 888 (FERC, 1996a), which requires investor-owned utilities that own transmission assets to make them available to competitors on favourable terms. In the EU, this is captured in the non-discrimination requirement in Articles 7 of the 1996 Electricity Directive.

In addition to the regulation of transmission and distribution network operation, in some jurisdictions, the activities associated with balancing and coordinating demand and supply, and managing constraints on an electricity network – known as system operation activities – are also subject to regulation. In the USA, system operation activities in regional markets are often undertaken by an ISO, which is typically a not-for-profit entity that does not own any transmission infrastructure and is responsible for ensuring non-discriminatory access to the transmission grid as well as operating competitive markets for electricity. The costs of an ISO associated with grid management and system operation are recovered through a grid tariff or management tariff that requires approval by the Federal Energy Regulatory Commission (FERC). In Britain, the same company that owns the transmission network in England (but not Scotland) also performs the system operation function, and separate price controls are applied for each activity. The system operator price control includes incentives designed to improve performance in three areas: control centre operations; market development and transactions; and system development and planning.

The question of whether large-scale storage facilities should be subject to regulation is being debated in some jurisdictions, reflecting the fact that storage services can be both a substitute for existing generation energy services in some circumstances, as well as a complement to generation services when they are used to provide ancillary services to support the safe operation of the network. In some jurisdictions, transmission and distribution operators cannot own and operate storage facilities on the basis of concerns that they might, absent such restrictions, unduly favour their own storage services, and effectively foreclose access to their networks for third parties.[70] In some US states, utilities can own storage systems providing they procure a certain proportion of mandated storage requirements from independent storage providers through a competitive process. Other states prohibit local distribution utilities from owning any generation resources, which has been defined to include storage facilities. At the federal level, the FERC has issued a rule to assist electricity storage resources to participate in the energy, capacity and ancillary service markets.[71] In the EU, transmission and distribution network operators cannot own or operate storage. However, there are various derogations which allow network operators to own and operate certain storage facilities in certain circumstances. Similarly, in Britain, distribution network operators can operate storage facilities only in very specific circumstances, while in Australia distribution network companies are prohibited from supplying contestable services using storage (such as a battery).

Finally, retail electricity supply is subject to price regulation in some jurisdictions, particularly where restructuring has not occurred and consumers are supplied by a vertically integrated monopoly provider.[72] As described below, price regulation is applied in

---

[70] However, allowing transportation companies to own and operate some storage facilities could in some circumstances be efficient. Storage is a valuable source of flexibility that can be used for system and network operations which could be used to reduce system operation costs in the short term and also potentially reduce the need for investments in flexible generation sources, including any costs associated with extending or reinforcing the transportation network.

[71] FERC Order 841 (2018).

[72] IEA (2020a) estimate that around one-third of global retail electricity demand is supplied by regulated monopolies.

some restructured competitive markets with the aim of protecting vulnerable consumer or consumers who remain on default or standard tariffs. In addition to price regulation retail electricity suppliers in most jurisdictions are also subject to various other non-price regulatory requirements that establish minimum service standards, and in competitive retail markets are directed at facilitating competition and promoting switching. This can include specific regulatory requirements relating to: consumer access (obligations to provide connections, restrictions on disconnections and interruptions); competition (disclosure and information requirements, rules on switching); contractual terms (minimum contractual guarantees and mandatory cooling-off periods); service levels and reliability (supply reliability and fault management obligations); as well as protections relating to fairness and the protection of specific consumer groups (vulnerable consumers or those experiencing financial hardship).

9.2.2 Form and Scope of Price Regulation for Transmission and Distribution Network

In almost all jurisdictions where transmission and distribution activities are owned or controlled by private companies (and in some cases where they are under state ownership), some form of price regulation is applied to the transmission and distribution network operators. The two main forms of price regulation described in Chapter 5, price cap regulation (which includes price caps and revenue caps) or rate of return regulation (which includes rate of return and cost plus regulation), are both applied in this industry.

Price Caps

Price cap regulation is applied to electricity transmission and distribution network companies in Australia, Canada, most European countries (including the UK),[73] some Latin American and Caribbean countries,[74] a handful of countries in Asia and Africa,[75] and a small number of US states.[76] As described in Chapter 5, this generally involves the regulator setting a maximum, or a ceiling, on the average increase in prices or revenues related to a set of relevant services for a pre-specified, but significant, period of time (say, five years). The precise type of price cap arrangement applied varies across jurisdictions, and there are examples of total revenue caps, average revenue caps and weighted average price caps being applied to electricity transmission and distribution network companies in different jurisdictions (including different states in the same country).[77] When determining the revenue requirement under the price cap, a common approach adopted is based on some variation of the building block approach which, as described in Chapter 5,

[73] Such as Albania, Austria (distribution), Belgium, Czech Republic, Denmark (distribution), Finland, France, Germany, Greece (transmission), Hungary, Iceland, Ireland, Italy, Latvia, Lithuania, Luxembourg, the Netherlands, Norway, Romania, Slovakia, Slovenia, Spain and Sweden.
[74] Including Colombia, Dominican Republic and Peru.
[75] Including Philippines and Senegal.
[76] See Lowry, Makos, Deason and Schwartz (2017) and Sappington and Weisman (2016a, 2016b) for discussion of the application in the USA.
[77] In Europe, of the twenty-one countries that apply incentive regulation to distribution, fourteen use revenue caps and seven use price caps. For electricity transmission, revenue caps are used in fifteen countries, and price caps in ten countries.

determines a forecast revenue requirement for the firm such that it can recover its efficient costs and earn a return on a regulated asset base. As discussed in that chapter, some jurisdictions have sought to move away from the separate treatment of operating and capital expenditure towards setting a single allowance for the expected efficient *total expenditure* (Totex) for the business.

Price cap arrangements applied to electricity transmission and distribution network companies typically incorporate specific incentive mechanisms for capital expenditure, operational efficiency, service quality, innovation (such as the connection of distributed generation) and demand management. Capital expenditure incentives aim to ensure that transmission and distribution companies respond to signals for additional investment and reinforcement, and that investment projects are cost-efficient. In relation to both capital and operating expenditure, cost benchmarking techniques are often used by regulators to determine the base-year level of operating costs, and to assess the efficiency of the forecast level of costs.[78] These include: total factor productivity (TFP) approaches; partial performance indicators; data envelopment analysis (DEA); and the use of econometric methods.[79]

Various quality and service incentive schemes are also employed to reward or penalise the electricity transportation company according to their performance against certain measures. These can include: a losses incentive; an interruption incentives scheme; stakeholder engagement; and a customer satisfaction reward scheme. In the Netherlands, there has been an explicit link between quality of service and the total revenue that distribution companies can earn.[80] Finally, in some jurisdictions, network operators are further incentivised to address various challenges, such as: the integration of distributed generation, storage systems and EVs; the development of demand-side response and management techniques; and, in terms of investment in their networks, particularly to facilitate interconnection between different jurisdictions and the roll-out of smart grid assets.

Rate of Return

Rate of return regulation is a common approach to the regulation of electricity transmission and distribution network companies in North America, Asia and Africa, and is also applied in a small number of European countries.[81] As described in Chapter 5, this approach allows the electricity transmission or distribution company to recover all of the costs associated with supplying a set of regulated services, including an allowable rate of return on a regulated rate base (a 'fair rate of return'). Rates are determined through an adjudicated rate case process which often begins when a firm makes an application or, in a small number of cases, if the regulator initiates a review. There are generally two stages in this process: the determination of the overall revenue requirement of the firm, and then

---

[78] Benchmarking of distribution network costs is particularly prevalent in European countries, given the large number of distribution companies that operate.

[79] See ACCC (2012b) for a discussion of the use of such techniques by energy regulators. Haney and Pollitt (2009, 2012) survey the different benchmarking approaches used in the electricity industry at that time.

[80] See Hesseling and Sari (2006).

[81] Such as transmission in Austria, Estonia, Latvia and Poland and for distribution in Greece, Estonia and Latvia.

the design of the tariffs or rate structure. At the end of the process, an order is issue which stipulates the new tariffs. It is estimated that around sixty electricity and gas case are filed on average annually in the USA, and that the average time between application being made was two years.[82] As discussed in Chapter 3, while traditionally rate cases i the USA were conducted through formal contested proceedings, in some cases the regu lated firm, consumer representatives and other parties can negotiate and agree rates an other terms in what are known as negotiated (or stipulated) settlements.

As applied in practice, the implementation of the rate of return approach involve various rules, processes and reporting requirements such as: standard rules relating t cost accounting; and templates for the reporting of costs, output, prices and other aspec of firm performance.[83] In addition, the rate of return approach has evolved over time t include mechanisms that incentivise firms to improve performance, including: the us of regulatory lags; ensuring that the value of the regulated rate base is determined o the basis of prudent capital costs ('used and useful' tests); and the disallowance of cos assessed as not having been efficiently incurred.[84] In addition, around sixteen US state have some form of decoupling mechanism in place which diminishes the link betwee revenues and sales.[85]

While some states in the USA moved away from applying the standard rate of retur regulation approach in the early 1980s and began to apply performance-based measure to specific components of electricity utilities' costs or operating performance,[86] compre hensive incentive regulation mechanisms have, it has been argued, been slow to spread i the electricity industry in the USA.[87] Nevertheless, some commentators suggest that alter natives to rate of return regulation – such as 'inflation minus X' multi-year rate plans c other forms of performance-based regulation – may be more attractive to electric utilit companies and regulators as a way of responding to the changes in future electricity net works (such as the need to connect and efficiently manage greater amounts of distribute generation and be responsive to demand-side measures rather than investing in moi capital infrastructure).[88]

---

[82] See Davies and Hevert (2020).
[83] Detailed descriptions of the steps applied using this approach are presented in NARUC (2003).
[84] See Joskow (2007a).
[85] See Cappers, Satchwell, Dupuy and Linvill (2020), who find that the majority of annual adjustments to rates are small. However, once a decoupling surcharge is introduced, there is an 86 per cent chance it will be applied in the following year.
[86] Sappington, Pfeifenberger, Hanser and Basheda (2001) record that, in 2001, twenty-eight electric utilitie in sixteen states operated under some form of performance-based mechanism.
[87] See Joskow (2007b). Sappington and Weisman (2016a, 2016b) set out various reasons for this, including a more limited scope for regulatory bargains (where a regulator agrees to no or little oversight of discretionary services in exchange for stringent caps on basic services), environmental considerations and a desire to reduce demand in electricity, reliability concerns, relatively slow and diminishing productivity growth and limited scope for competition.
[88] Aggarwal (2018) records that thirteen states were considering performance-based regulation (PBR) at that time. See also Alvarez and Steele (2017), McDermott and Hemphill (2017), Kaufmann (2019), Davie and Hevert (2020) and Crowley and Meitzen (2021). Makholm (2016, 2018a) sets out an alternative view Weisman (2019a) argues that the PBR approach needs to adapt so that it does not involve regulatory takings, while Sappington and Weisman (2021) contend that PBR can deliver stronger incentives for performance if a regulator rewards firms based on external benchmarks and where regulators offer firm a choice among carefully designed regulatory options.

Regulation of Rate Structures

While price cap and rate of return regulation determine the overall *level* of allowed revenues that regulated transmission and distribution companies can recover, a separate issue
is how that allowed revenue is recovered across different customers of their networks.
How allowed revenues are recovered and the *structure* of transmission and distribution
network charges is an important regulatory choice that has both distributional and efficiency aspects. As discussed in Box 9.1, the question of who should pay transmission and
distribution network charges, and how such charges are calculated, is increasingly important as the networks adapt to accommodate greater amounts of distributed generation
and battery storage, while at the same time respond to more consumers self-supplying
and using the traditional network services only as a 'back-up' source of supply.[89] There is
also a question about whether those who relieve network congestion – such as demand-
side responses to reduce electricity use at peak times – should be compensated for taking
action which has avoided costs being incurred.

Box 9.1	Adapting rate structures to deal with changing use of networks

As distributed energy sources and storage options become more commercially viable and
widespread, many regulators are considering how rate structures for transmission and distribution networks might need to adapt to better reflect how the transportation networks
are used by different types of user, and to send signals about the efficient use of networks.[90]
However, when considering changes to rate structures, regulators have to consider both the
efficiency and distributional impacts.[91]

In terms of distributional impacts, the core questions are: Who should contribute to the
cost of the transmission and distribution networks? And how much should they contribute? One concern is that technological and market changes could result in their being two
general types of consumer: 'captive' costumers who obtain all of their electricity supply
under a traditional supply arrangement and have limited, or no, substitution possibilities;
and 'non-captive' customers such as residential customers with behind-the-meter generation facilities or storage, who might use traditional electricity networks less frequently and
maintain a connection as a 'back-up' service. Under rate structures where a large proportion
of fixed costs are recovered through usage charges, this could give rise to a situation where,
given their lower usage patterns, non-captive customers contribute to only a proportion of
fixed network cost recovery, with the main burden being levied on captive customers who

---

[89] As Pérez-Arriaga, Jenkins and Batlle (2017) observe: 'Improved, cost reflective prices and charges are
essential to efficiently guide the myriad decisions made by electricity consumers, distributed resource
providers, aggregators, and other businesses.'

[90] Pérez-Arriaga, Jenkins and Batlle (2017) argue that it is 'imperative to proactively improve electricity
rate design to align the distributed decisions made by individuals and businesses with the efficient
operation and planning of the power system and to create a level playing field for competition and
coordination between centralized and distributed resources'. Rábago and Valova (2018) discuss ways
in which Bonbright's principles of rates described in Section 4.6 should be updated for the distributed
energy resource world.

[91] Faruqui (2013) observes that changes in rate structures can raise difficult issues for both regulators and
consumers, because, as a consequence of this shift, the fixed charge for many consumers may have to
increase, and small consumers in particular may see their bills increase as a result of this change.

have limited substitution possibilities (i.e. because they do not have behind-the-meter generation and cannot access storage).[92] As captive customers are typically considered to be on lower incomes (as they cannot afford behind-the-meter generation or do not own their own home), this raises affordability and distributional issues.

In terms of efficiency, it is argued that efficient network charges should combine a number of elements, including data about a user's location, contributions to peak flows or contracted capacity, and profiles of power injection or withdrawal at a particular point.[93] It is also argued that price signals will need to be more granular in terms of both time and location, and some have even spoken about the feasibility of introducing a fully nodal or distributed system, where prices are highly differentiated at every connection point.[94]

Proposed changes to rate structures include introducing new elements based on: time of use; installed capacity; customer peak demand; or network peak demand.[95] Some suggest that a three-part tariff be introduced, where one part of the tariff is a fixed access charge to cover metering and customer care; a second part is a demand charge (based on the maximum kilowatt demand over a specified period), intended to recover the costs of being connected to the grid; and the third part should be a volumetric time-varying usage charge.[96] Another proposal involves increasing the access charges levied on specific forms of retail distributed generation (such as solar PV) in order to recover a more significant share of fixed costs from non-captive customers ('prosumers' or 'customer-generators' who may not use the traditional network much but maintain a connection to it. A third proposal involves developing network charges around a reference network model that identifies key drivers of distribution network costs (i.e. whether the network is developed to guarantee contracted capacity, or alternatively to take account of energy flows (including losses)) and then allocates costs to different users according to their share of the contribution.[97] Over time, some argue that some form of 'platform market pricing' might emerge where distribution companies operate as a platform provider that, like in other multi-sided markets, supply services to a different side of a market, such as conventional generators, final consumers and providers of flexibility services.[98] As in other platforms, charges faced by different groups of participants would be set to maximise the use of the platform (see Chapters 12 and 13).

---

[92] See Decker (2016) and Pollitt (2018).

[93] See Pérez-Arriaga and Bharatkumar (2014) and Pollitt (2021).

[94] As Pérez-Arriaga, Jenkins and Batlle (2017) note: 'The theoretically ideal price signal for electrical energy would be to extend locational marginal prices down through the distribution network to capture the time- and location-varying value of electricity at every connection point to the system, including prices for active and reactive power.' Similarly, Pownall, Soutar and Mitchell (2021) discuss a proposal for new local balancing and coordinating markets in Britain that would be located at each grid supply point (the transmission and distribution interface) through the implementation of a distributed locational marginal pricing structure. However, there are questions about whether these proposals for highly granular markets are computationally possible.

[95] Schittekatte, Mallapragada, Joskow and Schmalensee (2022) find that time-of-use rates can reasonably replicate load shifting incentives and thus can be considerably more socially valuable than previously considered.

[96] Faruqui (2015a, b) and Simshauser (2016).

[97] Pérez-Arriaga and Bharatkumar (2014) argue that, by adapting the allocation of network costs to underlying drivers, this can allow regulators to address objectives such as equity.

[98] See Pollitt (2018).

Charges for Using Transmission Networks

There are two general approaches to transmission network pricing.[99] One approach, widely used in the USA, is known as 'locational marginal pricing' (LMP) or 'nodal pricing'. This approach does not involve the levying of a separate predetermined transmission *usage* charge; rather, the value of transmission services (i.e. the price) is calculated based on the different prices being paid for electricity (the commodity being transported) at different points (nodes)[100] on the network.[101] The two main determinants of any differences in the short-run value of transmission services are network losses and transmission capacity constraints.[102] It follows that, if there is no congestion on the network, the differences between the values at different nodes simply reflect marginal energy losses. To protect themselves against price risk arising from differences in the energy price between two specific locations on the network, market participants can acquire transmission rights in advance of the actual use of the transmission networks.[103] Such rights are typically auctioned by an ISO in annual, monthly or seasonal auctions and entitle the holder to access a proportion of any congestion revenues that arise,[104] thus allowing participants to hedge their exposure to the presence of network congestion.[105] The LMP approach is often seen as 'optimal' insofar as the short-run energy price for each node on the network incorporates the underlying costs associated with supplying transmission to that point on the electricity network (i.e. the cost of congestion).[106] However, while in theory LMP pricing can allow for a transmission

---

[99] For early contributions, see Bohn, Caramanis and Schweppe (1984), Schweppe, Caramanis, Tabors and Bohn (1988), Hogan (1992), Oren, Spiller, Varaiya and Wu (1995), Bushnell and Stoft (1996), Chao and Peck (1996), Hogan (1999) and Oren (2000). Green (1997) and Hsu (1997) usefully set out some of the wider issues surrounding transmission pricing. Bell, Green, Kockar, *et al.* (2011) set out a number of important transmission charging design dimensions.

[100] A node is defined as any point on the electricity system where power is injected into the network by a generator, or withdrawn from the network by an LSE. In the US PJM market there are thousands of nodes.

[101] While participants do not pay a separate fixed predetermined transmission *usage* charge, load customers may pay an *access* charge to allow for the recovery of the transmission revenue requirement. In addition, separate reservation charges can be levied on those who export through the network.

[102] In effect, the cost of using the transmission network is incorporated into the location-specific price or spot price insofar as the location-specific price contains three elements: the energy price (marginal cost of energy at that point), a marginal losses component and a congestion component. See Schweppe, Caramanis, Tabors and Bohn (1988) and Newbery (2011).

[103] An important distinction exists between physical and financial rights. Physical rights are defined as a right to deliver/inject a physical amount of power to the transmission network, and the right to seek compensation in the event that such access is denied. By contrast, financial transmission rights (FTRs) do not involve a physical right to deliver power, but provide for the right of a share of any congestion revenues accumulated on a network (such rights are independent of the actual physical decisions of the holder). Various intermediate forms of rights, some of which combine both physical and financial aspects, also exist. Generally, see Joskow and Tirole (2000).

[104] Congestion revenues arise because of differences between the nodal payments by load to the system operator and the nodal payments made by the system operator to generation. See, generally, Hogan (1992).

[105] In theory, the effect of FTRs is to make the holders of such rights indifferent to the presence of congestion, as the FTR is intended to reimburse to the holder the same amount by which the short-term price of transmission has been increased as a result of network congestion. FTRs can take various forms and can be distinguished on the basis of whether they are 'flowgate rights' or 'point-to-point rights': the former being attached to particular flows or links on a network which are known to be congested, and the latter to specific flows between two nodes on the network (and, therefore, although more accurate, are more difficult to estimate). See Hogan (2000).

[106] See Pérez-Arriaga, Olmos and Rivier (2013). Baldick, Bushnell, Hobbs and Wolak (2011) argue that LMP can provide sufficient information to allow for both short-term operational efficiency and longer-term signals for efficient investment.

network to recover its required transmission revenue allowance (which covers its costs
in practice this approach typically does not achieve this aim and there is often a need fo
some form of complementary charges to make up any such revenue shortfall.[107]

A second transmission pricing approach, used in Britain, Europe and Australia
involves the levying of a set of predetermined transmission *use-of-system* charges o
users of the network. Such use-of-system charges can be levied on either generator
or LSEs (or a combination of both), and are typically estimated on the basis of long
run cost principles. In general terms, charges for the use of the transmission networ
are intended to recover some proportion of an estimate of the long-run incrementa
costs of using a network at a particular location.[108] These transmission usage charge
can be differentiated by zone, such that a given electricity system may have differen
charges depending on where electricity is injected and withdrawn from the network.[109]
This approach is argued to provide generators with longer-term signals as to the effec
of their locational decisions, which may be more accurate and reliable than short-ru
approaches that require the generator to estimate the future evolution of a series c
short-run prices. However, it is recognised that any such advantages of long-term charg
ing approaches may come at the cost of short-term efficiency gains insofar as the 'price
charged for use of the transmission network are unlikely to reflect the short-term valu
of transmission, and therefore congestion, at any one point in time on the network.[110]

Charges for Using Distribution Networks

Distribution network use-of-system charges are intended to recover the costs of networ
operation and maintenance and past investments made in the distribution network. A
with transmission charges, different approaches are used to estimate the costs of th
network, including incremental cost methods (as in the UK) or reference node methoc
(as in Spain). Once estimated, the total costs of operating a distribution network are the
generally allocated to different user classes – such as residential, commercial and indus
trial users – according to some measure of their utilisation of the distribution networ
In Europe, the typical structure of distribution charges comprises a volume componer
based on energy withdrawal, a capacity component based on peak withdrawal over
certain period, and a fixed component to cover metering and administration cost.[111]

9.2.3 Retail Price Controls

While, as described in Section 9.2.1, retail price controls have been withdrawn in som
jurisdictions that have restructured their electricity markets (e.g. some European countrie

---

[107] See Pérez-Arriaga, Rubio, Puerta, *et al.* (1995).
[108] Examples include the 'cost-reflective network pricing' methodology allocation in Australia, which levies
charges on load on a zonal basis, and the investment cost-related pricing methodology (ICPRM) applied
to estimate the locational element of the transmission network use-of-system (TNUoS) charges in Britair
[109] In Britain there are currently fourteen demand zones and twenty-seven generation zones.
[110] In addition, some argue that longer-term charging approaches do not provide useful signals,
including investment signals and incentives, and may result in excessive investment in transmission
and generation assets. There are also concerns about the complexity and volatility of the charging
arrangements. See Ofgem (2021).
[111] Around thirteen out of sixteen countries recovered more than half of the distribution charges through
usage (kilowatt-hour) charges.

such as Germany and some US states such as Texas), in other jurisdictions retail electricity prices remain subject to some form of price control. In the USA, some states fully regulate retail prices using a rate of return approach, while, in states where retail competition exists, price regulation is limited to that of a default or standard tariff. Some European countries apply a price cap approach for consumers on specific regulated tariffs. In Spain, regulated retail prices follow wholesale prices plus a margin, while, in France, regulated retail prices are set to reflect the costs of alternative suppliers.[112] In Britain and Australia, default electricity price caps were re-introduced in 2019 and apply to consumers who are on default energy tariffs.[113]

9.3 THE SCOPE AND EFFECTS OF RESTRUCTURING POLICIES

9.3.1 The Scope of Restructuring Policies in the Electricity Industry

The 'Standard Restructuring Model' for Electricity

While the state-owned vertically integrated supplier model is still common, it is estimated that around 96 per cent of advanced industrial countries, and 70 per cent of developing countries, have restructured the electricity industry to introduce competition in some activity in the supply chain.[114] The 'standard restructuring model' for electricity typically involves four elements: (1) the corporatisation, commercialisation or privatisation of state-owned entities; (2) the establishment of independent regulatory agencies; (3) vertical and horizontal restructuring of the industry;[115] and (4) the introduction of competition at the wholesale (generator) level, and, in some cases, at the retail level.[116] However, many jurisdictions have only partially implemented this standard template, while others have deviated substantially in terms of design.[117]

---

[112] See ACER/CEER (2021a). In addition, some countries (such as Germany) introduced a temporary 'price break' in 2022 to cap electricity prices for households and small consumers in response to high wholesale gas prices following Russia's invasion of Ukraine.

[113] In Britain, the default caps are calculated every six months based on a consumer with medium energy use, and include costs such as wholesale costs, network costs, policy costs, supplier operating costs and taxes. The level of price caps varies by region, tariff type and payment method. Ofgem (2022) notes that these tariffs are expected to end 'by 2023 at the latest'. Several Australian states also re-introduced a default market offer in 2019 which limits the price that can be charged for customers on default tariffs.

[114] Foster, Witte, Banerjee and Moreno (2017). In other words, only 4 per cent of developed countries and 32 per cent of developing countries are served by traditional monopolies.

[115] As described in Chapter 6, the purpose of vertical separation is to separate the potentially competitive activities of electricity supply from the core network natural monopoly-like activities, while the aim of horizontal separation is to create competition among generators or retailers where the conditions are more favourable to competition.

[116] Kessides (2012). See also Jamasb and Pollitt (2005), Joskow (2008a), Foster and Rana (2020) and Glachant, Joskow and Pollitt (2021), who set out other standard restructuring prescriptions.

[117] Writing in 1983, Joskow and Schmalensee (1983, chapter 8) set out four general restructuring scenarios: (1) the elimination of all regulation of price and entry with no structural changes; (2) the deregulation of wholesale electricity and open power pooling but continued regulation of transmission and distribution; (3) the integration of generation and transmission, but the divestment of distribution and continual regulation of distribution; and (4) the complete vertical disintegration of wholesale power sales, regional power pooling and the creation of transmission entities for coordination and planning. Hogan (2002) refers to these scenarios and notes that: 'In the event, their most radical alternative was more conservative than the patterns that emerged in the complicated policy dance as the electricity industry moved towards greater reliance on markets and competition.'

Starting with the first element of the 'standard restructuring model', at the global leve
it is estimated that around 40 per cent of countries have introduced some form of privat
participation for electricity generation, mainly in the form of the introduction of IPPs.[1]
The full privatisation of transmission and distribution activities is less common, and it i
estimated that only 7 per cent of 175 countries have fully privatised distribution compa
nies, with some 30 per cent of countries having a combination of public and private own
ership.[119] In jurisdictions where retail competition has been introduced, private supplier
have been allowed to enter and compete against an incumbent provider. Overall, there ar
only a small number of jurisdictions where privatisation policies have been introduce
for all activities in the electricity supply chain, notable examples being Chile, the UK an
some Australian states.

In terms of the establishment of independent regulatory agencies, as discussed i
Chapter 8, while some countries – notably the USA – have a long history of independen
regulation, in many other countries new regulatory agencies were established as part o
restructuring policies. Almost 200 new infrastructure regulators were established in th
period 1996–2006,[120] and there are now over 250 energy regulators across the world.[121] I
2015, it was estimated that 91 per cent of developed countries and 72 per cent of devel
oping countries had established a regulator responsible for the electricity industry.[12]
However, as discussed in Chapter 8, these regulators display varying degrees of auton
omy and independence from ministerial departments and from the companies that the
regulate.

The third element of the 'standard restructuring model' involves policies that separat
activities where there is some prospect for competition from those core network activi
ties which display natural monopoly characteristics (sometimes called 'unbundling'). Thi
includes policies for the full horizontal and vertical separation of incumbent electricit
providers (such as occurred in Britain and some states in Australia) as well as poli
cies where the incumbent electricity supplier has remained intact but been placed unde
various obligations (for example, to source some of its generation requirements from
independent generators or to provide non-discriminatory access to the transmission an
distribution grids). In 2015 it was estimated that some 43 per cent of developed coun
tries had introduced vertical and horizontal separation policies, while only 18 per cen
of developing countries have introduced such policies.[123] In many jurisdictions, mor
partial forms of separation have been introduced whereby a single operator can provid
transmission or distribution network services as well as generation or retail services bu
must be operationally or structurally separated (see Chapter 6). In the EU, all Membe

---

[118] Estache (2020).
[119] Küfeoglu, Pollitt and Anaya (2018). Countries that have fully privatised their distribution companies
as part of restructuring include Armenia, Barbados, Belgium, Bulgaria, Chile, El Salvador, Georgia,
Hungary, Macedonia, Panama, Turkey and the UK.
[120] Brown, Stern, Tenenbaum and Gencer (2006).
[121] Including forty in Africa, thirty-nine in Europe, twenty-five in Latin America, twelve in the Caribbean,
twelve in the Mediterranean, sixty-seven in North America, forty-eight in South Asia and twenty-one i
Eastern and Southern Africa.
[122] Foster, Witte, Banerjee and Moreno (2017).
[123] Foster, Witte, Banerjee and Moreno (2017).

States are required to establish an ISO or, in certain circumstances, create a legally separate independent transmission system operator within an integrated group. While many jurisdictions (particularly developed countries) have introduced separation policies, it nevertheless remains the case that the fully vertically integrated supply of electricity is commonly observed around the world. Even in the USA it is estimated that around one-third of electricity demand is served through a vertically integrated construct.[124] At the global level, it was estimated that, in 2015, 26 per cent of developed countries and 57 per cent of developing countries are supplied by vertically integrated power companies.

The final element of the 'standard restructuring model' involves the introduction of wholesale and retail competition. As described in Section 9.4.1, a principal area where competition has been introduced is for the wholesale sale of electricity (i.e. competition between generator sources). In 2015, around 80 per cent of developed countries and 20 per cent of developing countries had introduced some form of wholesale power market.[125] The introduction of a wholesale market is even being piloted in China.[126] Competition in the retail supply of electricity was adopted first in Norway, and then in Britain, and since 2007 has been applied to all consumers in the EU. Similar policies have been introduced in some states in the USA as well as in some states of Argentina, Australia, Brazil, Canada, Chile, New Zealand, Peru, Singapore and Switzerland. Some form or retail choice also exists in India and the Philippines, and in 2016 full retail choice was introduced in Japan.[127] At the global level, in 2015 it was estimated that around two-thirds of developed countries had introduced some form of retail competition, while such measures had been introduced in only 15 per cent of developing countries.[128]

Scope of Restructuring in the USA

In the USA, the federal energy regulator (FERC) has, since the mid-1990s, issued a number of orders requiring transmission owners to provide cost-based access to their networks on a non-discriminatory basis, to provide certain information to third parties to enable them to use the networks more effectively, and to establish more detailed planning principles.[129] Notable among these is FERC Order 2000, which encouraged the creation of large regional transmission organisations on the basis that transmission systems and electricity markets are regional in scope.[130] Subsequent FERC orders aimed at improving the operation and competitiveness of wholesale electricity markets by, among other things, improving demand response, encouraging long-term power contracts,

---

[124] These are primarily located in the southeast, southwest and northwest, in states such as South and North Carolina, Alabama, Mississippi and Colorado. See Cleary and Palmer (2020).

[125] Foster Witte, Banerjee and Moreno (2017)

[126] Liu, Jiang and Guo (2022) explain that this will comprise three primary markets: a mid- to long-term energy market (annually to multi-daily), a spot market (day-ahead and real-time market) and an ancillary services market.

[127] Foster, Witte, Banerjee and Moreno (2017).

[128] Foster, Witte, Banerjee and Moreno (2017).

[129] See FERC Orders 888, 889 and 890 (1996, 1996 and 2007). Hogan (2021) refers to the importance of the Energy Policy Act (1992) in broadening the scope of wholesale market competition, which in turn strongly favoured the development of regional power pools.

[130] See FERC Order 2000 (1999).

strengthening the role of market monitoring and establishing rules for participatio
and cost allocation for regional planning.[131] FERC has also issued various orders to he
remove barriers to the development of electricity storage and to improve participatio
by distributed energy resources.[132] Some states, such as Texas, California and state
in the northeast (Massachusetts, Rhode Island, New Jersey, Maine and Pennsylvania
have, at different points, also introduced policies to restructure the electricity suppl
in their states.[133] Retail competition initiatives in the USA began in the mid-1990s i
Massachusetts, Rhode Island and California, spreading to another dozen or so state
by 2000. Similar policies were being considered in several other states at this time.[1]
However, following (in particular) the collapse of the Californian electricity system i
2000–2001, a number of these states reconsidered their policies, and some states (incluc
ing California) sought to delay, cancel or wind back their restructuring and competitio
policies amidst calls for re-regulation.[135]

Scope of Restructuring in Europe

In Europe, high-level reform has been encapsulated in a range of Electricity Regulatior
and Directives issued in 1996, 2003, 2009 and 2019. The first Electricity Directive of 199
(96/92/EC) required independent generators to be given access to electricity networl
on a transparent and non-discriminatory basis, while the second Electricity Directive ι
2003 (2003/54/EC) placed various so-called 'unbundling' or separation requirements o
Member States' electricity utilities which required the legal, managerial and operation.
separation of those utilities' network activities. The third Electricity Directive of 200
(2009/140/EC) required Member States to ensure that transmission activities are suff
ciently separated from production and supply interests either through mandating th
ownership unbundling of the network activities, introducing an ISO or, in certain ci
cumstances, creating a legally separate independent transmission system operator withi
an integrated group. The 2019 Clean Energy Package comprised a range of new rulε
for: electricity market design and governance; the integration of renewable energy; an
energy efficiency.[136] Among the changes were: new rules to allow generation, storage an
demand to participate on an equal footing in the market; the removal of wholesale ma
ket price caps and rules which restrict the use of capacity mechanisms; and institution.
changes to create an EU-wide DSO entity. Other changes focused on consumers being ab
to participate more actively in all markets, either individually or through citizen energ
communities.

---

[131] See FERC Orders 719, 719-A, 719-B, 745 and 1000 (2008, 2009 and 2011).

[132] See FERC Order 841 (2018).

[133] The electricity system in Texas is not interconnected with the rest of the USA and thus operates outside
of the jurisdiction of FERC (it is regulated by the Texas Public Utilities Commission). Baldick, Oren,
Schubert and Anderson (2021) provide a useful overview of the effects of reforms in Texas.

[134] Borenstein and Bushnell (2015) note: 'There was also much hope that electricity retail competition mig
spur innovation in retail services in the way that it had for telecommunications.'

[135] See Hogan (2002) and Joskow (2006). Williams and Ghanadan (2006) note that the collapse of the
Californian arrangements also had wider implications for electricity reform programmes across differeι
countries.

[136] The Clean Energy Package comprises four Directives and four Regulations. The most relevant are the
Electricity Directive (2019/944) and Electricity Regulation (2019/943), both of which relate to electricit
market design.

Scope of Restructuring Policies in Other Jurisdictions

Elsewhere in the world, restructuring policies have sometimes been introduced based on wider views about reducing the role of the government and the state in electricity markets (such as in Chile and Peru), while in many developing countries restructuring policies were encouraged by multilateral institutions such as the World Bank. Recent analysis of these reforms suggests that the momentum of reform has slowed over time, with more limited uptake in the period 2005 to 2015 compared to 1995 to 2015.[137] Restructuring policies have also been prompted by external events. For example, while Japan has allowed competition in generation for many years, new restructuring policies were initiated following the Fukushima accident in 2011 and concerns about security of supply following the closure of nuclear power stations.[138] In China, concerns about low generation efficiency and the resultant high electricity prices for manufacturing customers have recently led to policies being introduced to deregulate the electricity industry, which include creating short- and long-term power markets and introducing retail competition.[139] In Africa, although many countries have sought to introduce some aspects of restructuring policies, and many have established regulatory agencies (albeit with varying degrees of independence), only a few countries have sought to vertically separate their utilities, and the extent of public participation is typically limited to concession agreements or allowing independent power producers to compete against incumbent state-owned companies at the margin.

9.3.2 The Effects of Restructuring Policies in the Electricity Industry

What, then, have been the effects of the restructuring policies introduced over the past four decades? Have they resulted in greater efficiency, more cost-reflective prices and higher levels of quality (including in terms of investment, reliability and security of supply) as was expected when they were introduced?

Effects of Restructuring in the USA

In the USA, starting with wholesale markets, while there have been high-profile examples of the exercise of market power in these markets (e.g. in California), assessments of wholesale markets in other states have found them to be competitive overall.[140] In part, this is attributed to the high levels of forward commitment between generation and retailers (through either contracting or vertical integration). The variable costs of generators have fallen in some restructured states,[141] and competition has generally improved

---

[137] Foster and Rana (2020).

[138] This includes the establishment of an industry regulator in 2015, the introduction of full retail competition in 2016 and the legal separation of transmission and distribution activities in 2020.

[139] See Yang and Faruqui (2019) and Liu, Jiang and Guo (2022). The increased use of market forces can be dated back to 1978 and include notably the introduction of an independent State Electricity Regulatory Commission (SERC) in 2003. However, this was merged with the National Energy Administration (now part of the NDRC) in 2013.

[140] Bushnell, Mansur and Novan (2017).

[141] Bushnell, Mansur and Novan (2017) find that variable operating costs of regulated privately owned plants (but not state-owned municipal plants) decreased in the period since the 1990s in restructured markets. See also Hartley, Medlock and Jankovska (2019). Abito, Han, Houde and van Benthem (2021) find that the divestitures associated with restructuring allowed the new owners to more easily 'break' the existing contracts.

the efficiency of generators and reduced the costs of dispatch.[142] System coordination between generation and transmission is also seen to have improved as a result of the expansion of regional transmission operators, and significant changes in power flow across states (such as PJM) have led to more efficient dispatch.[143]

While these are generally positive impacts of restructuring policies on wholesale and transportation activities, the effects of such policies on retail price *levels* is largely inconclusive.[144] That said, there is evidence that retail prices more closely track underlying wholesale price changes (particularly changes in wholesale gas input prices) in restructured electricity markets.[145] While this may be efficient insofar as retail prices reflect changes in underlying input costs (e.g. wholesale gas prices),[146] it also means that retail prices can be more volatile in restructured markets.[147] In terms of customer switching and participation, some studies have found that, while there has been robust switching for industrial customers, there have generally been lower levels of switching for residential customers, with many customers continuing to source their electricity from a default provider of last resort in their area.[148]

Overall, the effects of restructuring of the US electricity sector appear to be mixed, and some argue that the full expected benefits have not been realised.[149] While some states have implemented full restructuring policies,[150] other states have limited their focus to wholesale markets and have not pursued a fundamental restructuring programme. This partial reform outcome has been attributed to the absence of a comprehensive mandatory federal restructuring programme and competition policy for the electricity industry, such

---

[142] See studies listed in Borenstein and Bushnell (2015) and Ajayi and Weyman-Jones (2021). Cicala (2022) finds that market-based dispatch caused a 16 per cent reduction in out-of-merit costs, which in turn resulted in reduced production costs of between $3 and $5 billion per year.

[143] See Joskow (2009) and Bushnell, Mansur and Novan (2017). Hogan (2021) concludes that the PJM market design is a successful example of achieving coordination and facilitating competition in electricity markets.

[144] Borenstein and Bushnell (2015) conclude that: 'Thus, while the restructuring era dawned with great hope that regulatory innovations, and the incentives provided by competition, would dramatically improve efficiency and greatly lower consumer costs, that hope was largely illusory. In fact, rates rose in both regulated and deregulated states, and more rapidly in the deregulated ones in the early years of reform.' Similarly, Su (2015) finds that: '[O]verall, retail competition does not seem to deliver lower electricity prices to retail customers across the board or over time.' See also Hartley, Medlock and Jankovska (2019) and Leung, Ping and Tsui (2019).

[145] However, as Borenstein and Bushnell (2015) caution, exogenous shocks to the industry such as gas price movements (which is generally the fuel that sets the marginal cost in most systems) and new technologies (such as improved gas turbines and developments in solar power) have often dominated the incremental benefits of regulatory restructuring.

[146] Hartley, Medlock and Jankovska (2019) find evidence that, in non-competitive areas of Texas, there was more evidence of cross-subsidisation and greater political interference than in competitive areas.

[147] See Department of Energy (2017).

[148] Bushnell, Mansur and Novan (2017). A notable exception is Texas, where it has been estimated that 92 per cent of customers have exercised their right to choose a supplier.

[149] Borenstein and Bushnell (2015) conclude that: 'While electricity restructuring has brought significant efficiency improvements in generation, it has generally been viewed as a disappointment because the price-reduction promises made by some advocates were based on politically-unsustainable rent transfers.'

[150] Baldick, Oren, Schubert and Anderson (2021) point to Texas as a successful example of meeting the challenges of creating a self-sustaining electricity market and the public policy goals of restructuring. However, the robustness and resilience of the system to extreme events was called into question following the Texas blackouts in early 2021. See Bushnell (2021), Makholm (2021b) and Bobbio, Brandkamp, Chan, *et al.* (2022).

as exists in other infrastructure sectors in the USA and in other countries.[151] Significant restructuring decisions have been left to the states, which have often opposed reforms, or adopted a 'wait and see' approach.[152] In short, while there are some areas of improvement, a restructuring of the electricity industry and the transition to competitive markets in the USA is generally perceived to be only partly achieved.[153]

Effects of Restructuring in Europe

In Europe, a similar patchwork of reform and restructuring can be observed over the past two decades, with some European countries being pioneers of restructuring in the electricity industry (notably the UK and Norway), and others (such as France and Germany) at times being slower and more resistant to change.[154] A principal objective of restructuring of the industry – at least for the European Commission – has been greater regional interconnections and the development of a pan-European electricity market through the standardisation of market rules and regulatory structures. Progress has generally been slow, although, as described above, a series of regional interconnected markets has emerged.[155] Recent policy efforts at the European level have been directed at harmonising national rules on energy trading and system operation with the aim of enhancing cross-border trade. This has included 'market coupling' policies to connect all EU Member States and to facilitate the allocation of cross-border transmission capacity between different coupled spot markets on day-ahead and intra-day bases.[156] The strengthening of cross-border competition is seen as an important response to the still strong market positions held by the incumbent generators in a number of EU Member States.[157]

While wholesale electricity markets based around bilateral trading are generally assessed as working well, the significant wholesale gas price increases experienced in 2021/22 led to an examination of whether alternative wholesale electricity market designs are more capable of accommodating such extreme price volatility in gas markets.[158] A key

---

[151] See Joskow (2006, 2008a, 2009), who observed at that time that: 'We have a system that is 1/3 reformed and 2/3 stuck in the structural and regulatory paradigm of the 1935s or somewhere in between.'

[152] See Borenstein (2002).

[153] Kellogg and Reguant (2021) refer to the process of restructuring in wholesale electricity markets as 'tumultuous and slow'.

[154] Good overviews of the European reforms are presented in Glachant and Lévêque (2009) and Roques (2021).

[155] The European Commission (EC, 2016b) noted that, while there has been increasing competition and cross-border trade of electricity, the markets are still underperforming, electricity does not always flow to where it is needed and some Member States use national strategies to minimise risks to security of supply, without taking account of the impact on neighbouring countries.

[156] The aim of market coupling is to limit the differences between national electricity markets and thus to create a common European-wide trading platform for electricity. The EC (2021c) estimates that this could yield welfare benefits of €1.5 billion per year and reduce the need for back-up generation. Before the introduction of market coupling, those who traded across borders on electricity exchanges would have to separately purchase electricity and reserve cross-border capacity. Market coupling combines these activities through an implicit auction where participants now only have to bid for electricity on a power exchange.

[157] In 2020, the average market share of the largest generator operating across each Member State was 45 per cent, and in ten Member States the market share of the largest generator exceeded 50 per cent.

[158] As gas-fired generation often sets the marginal price in some EU Member States, some countries, such as France and Spain, sought to decouple electricity prices from movements in wholesale gas and to move away from marginal cost pricing of electricity. However, the view of ACER (2021) is that there was no clear evidence that alternative market frameworks would reduce prices or improve incentives. Nevertheless, in 2023 a temporary wholesale gas price cap was introduced for one year across Europe.

development in many European wholesale energy markets (including the UK) over th
past decade has been greater state involvement to support the transition to low-carbo
forms of generation and provide incentives for new capacity to ensure security of suppl
Some have described this as leading to a hybrid market model that combines 'compet
tion for the market' (such as tenders for long-term contracts for low-carbon or renewab
capacity (as in Britain and Germany)) with 'competition in the market' in the form c
short-term trading on electricity exchanges.[159]

In terms of retail markets, as in restructured states in the USA, wholesale electricit
market prices in many EU Member States now closely track changes in wholesale ga
input prices, which can make retail electricity prices more volatile.[160] As in the USA, th
means that restructuring has not necessarily resulted in lower retail electricity prices.
Recent assessments have identified numerous barriers to retail competition, includin
high levels of market concentration, and that vertically integrated operators have a
advantage in the market.[162] As discussed in Section 9.4.1, a persistent problem in man
European energy markets (including the UK) has been low levels of customer switchin
and participation.[163] Many consumers remain on default contracts or are considered t
be vulnerable, which has led to the continuing use of retail price regulation in many E
Member States.[164] In fact, only twelve EU countries had no price intervention in 2020,
notwithstanding the fact that EU-wide policy seeks the withdrawal of price regulation fc
retail electricity markets.[166]

Given the role of Britain as a pioneer of electricity industry restructuring in Europe, th
outcomes deserve individual mention, as assessments of effectiveness have changed ov
time. Up until the end of the 2000s, various studies reported significant performance improve
ments along a number of dimensions.[167] However, since that time, criticisms have emerge
about different aspects of the operation of wholesale markets and the development of reta

[159] See Roques (2021).
[160] See ACER (2021).
[161] ACER/CEER (2021a) shows that electricity household prices have gradually risen since 2008 in the EU a
levels higher than inflation, while industrial prices have fluctuated, but in 2020 were roughly similar to
those in 2008. For earlier analysis, see Pollitt (2009) and Florio (2013, 2014).
[162] ACER/CEER (2021a) found that, in sixteen out of twenty-five electricity markets, market concentration
remains high, and although there are requirements for legal separation, the continuation of co-
ownership means that vertically integrated companies are still perceived to be able to use their market
power to gain an advantage in terms of information (e.g. by targeting customers based on consumption
profiles or to win back customers during the switching process, or in terms of access to financing).
[163] However, Littlechild (2021c) argues that 'a low switching rate does not mean that competition is not
effective'.
[164] In 2020, the proportion of households with prices set by regulatory intervention was 68 per cent in
France, 53 per cent in Britain, 46 per cent in Italy and 38 per cent in Spain. See ACER/CEER (2021a).
[165] This includes price regulation for all consumers or price regulation for vulnerable consumers; see ACEF
CEER (2021a).
[166] The European Commission (EC, 2016b) sets out the position that targeted price regulation for vulnerab
consumers should only be used for a transition period until their needs can be addressed through energ
efficiency and social policy measures. It also sets out the view that energy price regulation is the main
obstacle to more active consumers.
[167] Joskow (2008a) records these as including: lower generator operating costs and improved availability;
a dramatic reduction in transmission network congestion management and balancing costs;
improvements in labour productivity and service quality for the distribution network; and a reasonably
successful retail competition programme.

competition.[168] As described above, over the last decade the state/regulator has come to play a more prominent role in wholesale markets (through low-carbon and capacity auctions and direct commissioning of new nuclear generation) and in retail markets (re-introduction of price caps for standard tariffs). There are also concerns that the shift towards the Totex approach to regulation in 2013 (see discussion of RIIO (revenues = incentives + innovation + outputs) in Chapter 5) has resulted in higher-than-expected returns for suppliers.[169]

Effects of Restructuring Policies in Other Jurisdictions

Outside of Europe, the USA and Britain, the progress in restructuring of the electricity industry is mixed. Assessments of the effects of electricity restructuring policies in Chile (the first in the world) conclude that it remains an example of a decentralised energy market that works well, and (alongside Argentina) it has sometimes been referred to as a 'successful poster case' for reform.[170] While other Latin American and Caribbean countries are also seen to have 'led the way' with restructuring reforms,[171] problems have sometimes been identified in countries such as Brazil, Bolivia and the Dominican Republic.[172]

A similarly mixed assessment can be made in relation to Australia and New Zealand. Broadly speaking, the Australian national wholesale market arrangements (which integrate six states and territories) and the New Zealand wholesale market have been assessed as working well.[173] However, at times, there have been concerns in some states in Australia that high wholesale prices were the result of high levels of generator concentration and sudden plant closures.[174] In New Zealand, questions have arisen about the effectiveness of the wholesale contract market.[175] There have also been persistent concerns about high retail electricity prices in restructured states in Australia and in New Zealand. In Australia, these high retail prices have been attributed to substantial investments in the transmission and distribution networks (many of which are state-owned) to meet (high) reliability standards.[176] As in Britain, there are also perceived to be problems of low levels of consumer engagement in Australia and a substantial proportion of customers remain on default tariff contracts.[177] This has led to the re-introduction of some form of retail

---

[168] See CMA (2016a), Helm (2017) and Newbery (2021).

[169] This has been attributed to a higher cost of capital and over-inflated costs. On the other hand, there is also evidence that the RIIO framework was successful at driving improved output delivery for customers (specifically, that customer satisfaction scores have generally been improving), and led to some improvements in safety, environmental and social measures. See CEPA (2018), Ofgem (2020), NAO (2020) and Delta-EE (2022).

[170] See Pollitt (2007), Balza, Jimenez and Mercado (2013) and Serra (2022).

[171] See Foster and Rana (2020) and Rossi (2021).

[172] Pollitt (2007). Balza, Jimenez and Mercado (2013) discuss the re-nationalisation of some assets and a return to more active state involvement in some Latin American countries.

[173] See Simshauser (2021) and New Zealand Government (2019).

[174] In two states, the governments consolidated generators against the advice of the regulator, while in one state the sudden closure of coal plants caused a major blackout. See ACCC (2018a).

[175] See New Zealand Government (2019).

[176] See ACCC (2018a). Mountain (2014) argues that government ownership has undermined the authority and independence of economic regulation. Simshauser (2021) estimates that the regulatory asset base of combined transportation networks servicing the national electricity market increased from A$32 billion in 2004 to A$93 billion in 2018.

[177] ACCC (2018a) attributes this to confusing price structures offered by retailers and to the opaque practice of discounting across the market.

price controls in some Australian states. In New Zealand, there are concerns about th
impacts of high levels of vertical integration on competition in the retail market, and spe
cific retail pricing practices which may reduce the incentives for consumers to switch.[178]

Successive surveys of the experience of electricity restructuring in transitional an
developing countries conclude that they have been slow and unstable in Asia and Easter
Europe, and significantly problematic in Africa.[179] Many countries have experienced obsta
cles to reform, and in some countries restructuring policies have been reversed.[180] A 202
World Bank assessment found that only a dozen developing countries have fully restruc
tured their electricity industries, and in many countries the 'standard restructuring mode'
described in Section 9.3.1 did not fit the economic and political conditions.[181] It conclude
that, while regulation was widely adopted, its 'practice often falls well short of theory an
cost recovery remains an elusive goal'.[182] That said, the analysis found that private secto
involvement has contributed to a substantial expansion of generation in the developin
world (estimated at 40 per cent since 1990) and that wholesale markets had improve
efficiency in those countries that could make them viable. Private involvement in trans
mission and distribution was also assessed as delivering good outcomes in favourabl
settings (such as in Latin America).[183] Other surveys have found that, while restructuring i
developing countries has improved the technical efficiency of the sectors, the benefits hav
not 'trickled down' to consumers because of institutional and regulatory weaknesses.[184]

Overall, then, around the world, while some jurisdictions have made significant progres
with restructuring of their electricity industries, in other countries electricity restructur
ing policies have either stalled, are making minimal progress, or in some cases are bein
reversed. Policies directed at introducing competition in wholesale markets appear t
have had the most success, and new regulators have been established in many countrie
to regulate the transportation networks and retail markets. Progress with retail competi
tion is mixed and there are concerns about the extent to which consumers are willing t
actively engage in such markets. These outcomes are not altogether surprising given th
technical characteristics of electricity and the political economy of the industry.[185]

---

[178] Such as 'saves and win-backs', where a customer is offered a discount not to switch from the incumbent
(a save), or to return to the incumbent after switching (a win-back). See New Zealand Government (2019
[179] See Kessides (2012), Nepal and Jamasb (2015) and Foster and Rana (2020). Imam, Jamasb and Llorca
(2019) examine the impact of corruption on reforms in sub-Saharan Africa, and find that the adverse
effects can be reduced through establishing an independent regulator and privatisation. See also Africa
Development Bank (2021).
[180] See Foster, Witte, Banerjee and Moreno (2017).
[181] See Foster and Rana (2020), who note that: 'Restructuring and liberalization have been beneficial in a
handful of larger middle-income nations but have proved too complex for most countries to implement
[182] Similarly, Rodríguez Pardina and Schiro (2018) find that: 'In practice, many developing countries
operate with "advisory regulators" whose main role is to provide technical support to the ultimate
political decision makers.'
[183] See Foster and Rana (2020).
[184] See Jamasb, Nepal and Timilsina (2017) and also Rodríguez Pardina and Schiro (2018).
[185] Nepal and Jamasb (2015) succinctly capture this point: 'The dynamics of the electricity supply industry and
policy objectives imply that reforms evolve continuously and thus remain work in progress, and their succes
or failure is a complex function of micro- and macro-economic as well as institutional factors.' Similarly,
Borenstein and Bushnell (2015) observe that in restructured markets there is a difference between the averag
cost (used to set regulated prices) and the marginal cost of producing electricity (used as the basis for price
setting in competitive markets). When these two costs diverge, then consumer and political sentiment tilts
towards whichever regime (regulation or competitive markets) offers the lower prices at that time.

9.4 REGULATORY POLICY ISSUES IN THE ELECTRICITY INDUSTRY

This section discusses two policy issues in the electricity industry: the experience of introducing competition in restructured electricity markets; and the impacts of decarbonisation policies on electricity regulation.

9.4.1 Can Effective Competition Be Achieved in Restructured Electricity Markets?

As indicated earlier, a major argument for restructuring of the electricity industry is to reap the benefits associated with the development of competition, particularly in generation and retailing activities. Now that restructuring policies have been in place for almost four decades in some jurisdictions, it is worth examining whether the expectations regarding the benefits of competition (in terms of prices, quality and efficiency) have been borne out and what challenges confront policy makers.

Competition in Wholesale Electricity Markets

In wholesale electricity markets, concerns about generator market power have featured prominently in many restructured electricity markets, and have led to questions about whether effective competition can be achieved.[186] Certain attributes of wholesale electricity markets have been seen to make them particularly vulnerable to abuses of positions of market power, including: transmission constraints which can limit competition geographically and create 'pockets' of market power;[187] an inability to store electricity; and high levels of generation concentration.[188] These factors are arguably compounded by the fact that residential demand for electricity is largely unresponsive to changes in wholesale prices (meaning the possibilities for demand-side responses are limited) and there is often limited supply-side substitutability in the short term. This means that even generators with relatively small market shares can be 'pivotal' to system balancing and in a position to exercise market power in certain circumstances and at certain points in time.[189] These characteristics of the electricity market also mean that any exercise of market power can result in enormous transfers of economic rents to producers at the expense of consumers in very short periods of time.[190] Given the need to keep demand and supply in balance at all times, generators can exercise market power in two ways: they can physically withhold capacity from the market so as to raise the marginal system price (physical withholding), or they can ask for a price for their electricity which is well above the marginal cost of production (economic withholding). There are also often important interactions between wholesale energy markets and other financial markets, such that a

---

[186] See Borenstein, Bushnell and Wolak (2000) and Twomey, Green, Neuhoff and Newbery (2005).

[187] With some foresight, Joskow and Schmalensee (1983) identified the impact that transmission capacity constraints might have on the effective extent of the geographic market, and noted that this created uncertainty as to the likelihood of effective competition for bulk power supply in many parts of the USA.

[188] García and Reitzes (2007) summarise these factors more fully. See also Wolak (2021).

[189] See Borenstein and Bushnell (2000) and Borenstein (2002). Wolak (2021) notes: 'One lesson from the experience of US markets (in particular) is that system conditions can arise when virtually any generation unit owner has a substantial ability and incentive to exercise unilateral market power.'

[190] See García and Reitzes (2007).

generator may have incentives to take unprofitable positions in one market (a physica market) if it reaps a benefit in the other market (a financial market).[191]

Concerns about market power have led to controls being introduced in many restruc tured wholesale markets, such as market price caps to limit the scope to exercise marke power,[192] as well as policies directed at preventing market abuse and market manipula tion.[193] As discussed in Box 9.2, while price caps limit the scope for generators to exercis market power, depending on the level at which they are set, they can also reduce th ability of generators to recover their fixed costs in times of scarcity. This can affect th incentives to invest in generation if there is no other mechanism available to recove these investment costs (such as a capacity mechanism).[194]

There have been a number of well-documented instances of suspected market powe abuse in restructured electricity markets, notably in the early days of the England ar Wales pool, the early eastern US capacity markets and later in California in 2000/01. Market power issues have also been identified in restructured electricity markets in Ne Zealand, Chile, Colombia, the USA (PJM, Texas), Alberta, Brazil and parts of Europe. While there have been some high-profile examples of failures of wholesale market con petition (e.g. California), and concerns about market power and high levels of generato concentration in some countries at particular times, the wholesale electricity markets in th USA (PJM, Electric Reliability Council of Texas (ERCOT)), Australia (the National Electricit Market (NEM)), the Nordic countries (NordPool) and Britain are generally considered a reasonably well-functioning examples of restructured competitive electricity markets.[197]

Box 9.2	**Is there a 'missing money' problem in the electricity industry?**

Investment decisions in the electricity industry have long been recognised as comple because demand can be difficult to forecast, and investment in new generating plant ar core-network assets (such as transmission and distribution networks) can have long lea times. However, a recurring question which has arisen in restructured jurisdictions is wheth the net revenues generated in wholesale electricity markets are sufficient to incentivise ar

---

[191] For example, a generator may seek to manipulate spot market prices in order to benefit from positions taken in a futures market or other derivative market. Or, alternatively, a generator could enter into unprofitable transactions in a day-ahead market to move prices and benefit from its position in anothe market (such as financial transmission rights). Decker and Keyworth (2002) present an early analysis o cross-market manipulation risk; see also Lo Prete, Hogan, Liu and Wang (2019) and FERC (2020).

[192] Sirin and Erten (2022) summarise the current level of price caps used in USA and Europe.

[193] In Europe, these are captured in the Regulation on Wholesale Market Integrity and Transparency (REMIT), and in the USA in FERC Order 670 on market manipulation. In Australia, this is captured through a 'prohibition on false and misleading offers' into the electricity pool. Adelowo and Bohland (2022) describe the algorithms used to monitor and mitigate market power abuse in real time in the US/

[194] See Joskow and Léautier (2021). Brown and Sappington (2022b) examine how the level of the wholesa price cap impacts on the incentives of generators to engage in forward contracting.

[195] On the problems with the England and Wales pool, see Green and Newbery (1992), Wolfram (1999) and Sweeting (2007). On USA, see Borenstein, Bushnell and Wolak (2002), Joskow and Kahn (2002) and Wolak (2021).

[196] See Joskow (2008a).

[197] See Baldick, Oren, Schubert and Anderson (2021), Hogan (2021), Le Coq and Schwenen (2021), Newber (2021) and Simshauser (2021).

support investment in new generating capacity at the right time and places, and, if not, whether some form of additional (capacity) payment is needed to address the shortfall.[198]

The specific concern is that, if generators are only paid for the electricity they produce and the market is competitive, then prices will tend towards marginal costs for most of the time and this will limit a generator's ability to recover its fixed costs to only those times when demand is close to capacity and prices are sufficiently high. Generators may therefore be reluctant to invest in capacity if they cannot be certain that the prices from the energy market will generate sufficient revenues to cover the necessary investments.[199] This situation – sometimes referred to as the 'missing money' problem – can arise, in particular, where a regulator places a ceiling on wholesale electricity prices in periods of high demand in order to prevent the exercise of market power.[200] While such price caps ensure that prices do not get so high such that there is a need to ration consumer supply at periods of high peak demand, it also means that generators that supply electricity at those peak times are not able to recover their fixed costs through scarcity pricing.[201]

The question of the financial viability of baseload and conventional generation has also taken on increasing importance as a result of the shift towards a different generation mix (especially variable renewable resources such as wind and solar) and greater demand-side response.[202] One method of addressing this problem is to introduce a capacity market, where load customers are required to purchase sufficient capacity to cover their expected loads (including reserves). As the revenue generated from the capacity market supplements what generators receive from trading in the energy and reserves markets, this can create incentives for the generator to make efficient investment and operating decisions. At the same time, where capacity markets exist, the regulator can cap payments for electricity at lower

---

[198] Joskow and Schmalensee (1983) note early on that: 'Many objections to both deregulation and reorganisation of the structure of electric power firms focus on perceived problems associated with getting an unregulated market to yield the correct quantity, capacity mix and location of generating plant.' See also Joskow and Tirole (2007).

[199] Joskow and Léautier (2021) observe that: 'this was not a concern at the onset of restructuring, since most restructured power systems had excess generation capacity (which partially explains why they were restructured in the first place)'.

[200] See Borenstein (2000), Hogan (2005) and Joskow (2008b). Joskow and Léautier (2021) make the important point that, when a price cap is imposed, then it is not only the peaking technology that is 'missing money' at the long-term equilibrium, but all technologies are also 'missing money' by the same amount.

[201] Joskow and Léautier (2021) explain that policy makers and system operators have two options for dealing with demand in high peak periods. They can either ration customers for a few hours by not capping the price (which may not be politically acceptable) or cap prices, which has the effect of not allowing generators to recover their fixed generation costs from energy market revenues (which can change the incentives for generators to invest in their assets).

[202] Joskow and Léautier (2021) argue that: '[S]carcity pricing – that is, incidents of very high prices necessary to clear the market – must play a more important role in the future to satisfy generators balanced budget constraints. Economists argue that this outcome is perfectly acceptable; in fact, it is optimal. Consumers and their elected representatives have a different opinion. They argue that profiteering from consumers' need is amoral, hence unacceptable. Resolving this tension is essential to the future of the power industry.'

[203] However, Joskow (2006) finds that, even in wholesale markets where capacity obligations and prices generate additional net revenues (such as the PJM market in the USA), these revenues may be insufficient to fill the revenue 'gap' between the net revenues from energy markets and the fixed costs associated with investment in new generation capacity when measured over several years.

levels, as the recovery of some fixed costs will occur through the capacity market.[203] An alternative to capacity markets is a capacity payment mechanism that involves payments to generators that do not tend to relate directly to the balance between demand and capacity but are fixed at certain levels to incentivise investment.[204] Nevertheless, the perceived need for capacity markets and payments to induce investments in generating capacity is controversial both in theory and in practice, and some argue that they are unnecessary or that there are alternative mechanisms for addressing the perceived problems.[205]

Competition in Retail Electricity Supply

What can be said about the effectiveness of competition in retail electricity supply? Proponents for retail competition argue that it can produce a number of benefits.[206] Firstly, it can limit the potential for regulatory, or political, interference in final prices which is important in times when wholesale electricity prices are rising (because of rising input costs) and there is strong political and popular pressure to artificially keep retail prices low which is not sustainable over the long term.[207] Secondly, retail competition can spur innovation, for example, in the types, and terms, of tariffs that are offered to customers (such as 'dual-fuel' tariffs, 'price guarantee tariffs', 'online tariffs' and 'green tariffs', etc.).[208] It can also lead to tariff structures that allow for greater customer responsiveness to changes in underlying wholesale prices. Flexible retail price tariffs that adjust to changes in the wholesale price can also provide timely signals about the actual power demand and supply balance and scarcity of supply. These signals can improve demand management, and lead to downward pressure on prices.[209]

However, even among those who support electricity restructuring, there is ongoing debate about the benefits of extending retail competition to *all* consumers, including small business and residential customers.[210] For some, there are concerns that, in the absence of some form of regulation, retail electricity prices will be more volatile, and this may be politically unacceptable particularly when prices are rising.[211] In particular, it is

---

[204] Capacity payments were a feature of the England and Wales electricity pool up until 2001, and a centralised capacity auction market was re-introduced in 2014. They have also been a feature of the arrangements in Spain and Argentina, and are a feature of the Irish Integrated Single Electricity Market.

[205] Stoft (2002, chapter 2) argues that, in principle, peak prices should be high enough to allow firms to cover fixed costs and provide an optimal level and mix of generation capacity. On the practice of capacity payments, see Wolak, Bushnell and Hobbs (2007) and Adib, Schubert and Oren (2008). In Europe, capacity mechanisms are only allowed on a temporary basis.

[206] Littlechild (2021b) argues that retail competition in electricity was inspired by the developments in the US and UK telecommunications sectors.

[207] The problem of regulated retail prices not adapting to changes in wholesale prices is perhaps best illustrated by the case of California in 2000/01.

[208] See Littlechild (2003, 2006c).

[209] See Boisvert, Cappers and Neenan (2002).

[210] See Salies and Waddams Price (2004), Waddams Price (2005) and Joskow (2008a). Littlechild (2021b) records that, when he explained his idea for retail competition 'to Hogan and Joskow in Boston around 1983. "No", they said, "the big electricity customers already have good deals and the small customers won't be interested".

[211] However, Pollitt (2007) observes that this is based on the view that 'competition is OK in most markets, but somehow not OK in retail energy markets. This is rather odd, as economists (though not politicians) are happy to see volatile gas prices, but not volatile residential electricity (or natural gas?) prices'.

argued that commercial and residential customers are deeply averse to volatile electricity prices and prefer regulated rates that are 'smoothed' over time, and that they do not have the time and resources to monitor and control their usage.[212] Another argument is that, to be effective, full retail competition requires major advances in infrastructure, such as smart networks and metering. Finally, some doubt that final consumers (particularly residential consumers) are interested in engaging in the market or are responsive to real-time changes in wholesale prices.[213]

As described above, full retail competition (i.e. including residential and small commercial customers) has been introduced in several jurisdictions, including the UK, all European countries, New Zealand, some provinces of Canada, four Australian states and a small number of states in the USA.[214] However, it is important to distinguish between settings where no restrictions are placed on retail prices and those where an incumbent provider (or provider of last resort) is required to offer a default or standard tariff. In the latter case, which is a feature of most US states with retail choice (except Texas), the design of the default retail tariff can be seen to have had significant impacts on the incentives for consumers to switch suppliers, and on the viability of new retail entrants to attract customers.[215] Specifically, where default retail tariffs have been set at levels below the cost (as has occurred in some states in the USA and European countries) this has made it difficult for competitor retailers to attract customers, and led to ever greater political interference.[216] Sub-optimal regulated default retail tariffs can also be in conflict with energy conservation policies if they result in inefficiently high levels of electricity consumption.[217]

Has extending competition brought benefits to retail customers? Broadly speaking, large industrial customers appear to have benefited from retail competition. However, the picture for residential and smaller commercial customers is less clear, and empirical studies of whether prices have reduced as a result of retail competition provide contradictory results.[218] Experience in the Nordic countries, which introduced retail competition in the late 1990s, and placed no restrictions or regulatory controls on retail prices, has been described as a relative success.[219] Similarly, in Texas, the one US state that does not have a regulated default

---

[212] See Chao, Oren and Wilson (2005).

[213] See Joskow and Tirole (2006) and the discussion in Chapter 7 in the present book.

[214] As of 2019, thirteen states and the District of Columbia have active, state-wide residential retail choice programmes, which account for 13 per cent of residential customers. Four other states have limited retail choice for non-residential customers. See EIA (2018),

[215] In most US states with a default tariff, the right to be the default supplier (or the provider of last resort) is determined through a competitive auction, which introduces some element of 'competition for the market'.

[216] See Joskow (2008a). Littlechild (2021b) observes that: 'US regulators seem to have under-priced and cross-subsidized the default supply tariffs, thereby distorting the market against competing suppliers. They have also opened themselves up to continuing political pressures and consumer group complaints, leading in turn to further regulatory intervention.' Similarly, ACER/CEER (2014) notes that: 'In some Member States, regulated prices are set below cost levels, which hampers the development of a competitive retail market.'

[217] See Brown, Eckert and Eckert (2017).

[218] See the surveys presented in Morey and Kirsch (2016) and Littlechild (2021b).

[219] See Le Coq and Schwenen (2021). Earlier assessments are presented in Littlechild (2006c) and Olsen, Johnsen and Lewis (2006).

tariff, high levels of switching behaviour have consistently been observed.[220] Howeve in other US states that introduced retail choice, switching patterns have been assessed a generally disappointing, and there has been limited switching and movement away fro incumbent default or standard tariffs where they have been offered.[221] In Europe, whil there is a policy focus on removing all retail price controls by 2025, as described abov only twelve EU countries had no price intervention in 2020.[222] Levels of switching vary sig nificantly across EU countries, notwithstanding the fact that there are a number of supplie operating in many Member States.[223] In Germany, the switching rate in 2020 was 10.9 pe cent, despite the fact that the retail prices are the highest in Europe and it is estimated tha household customers could save up to €519 a year by switching.[224] In Britain, up until 200 retail competition was perceived by the energy regulator to be effective (the proxy bein switching behaviour, which was strong) and consumers were seen to be receiving benefit in terms of innovative tariffs, and improved customer service.[225] However, this view ha since been reassessed, and since 2011 the regulator and government have introduced range of changes to the retail market including the re-introduction of price controls fc those on standard tariffs.[226] A similar policy has been pursued in some Australian state while in New Zealand some pricing practices have been banned.

The mixed experience of retail competition across the world raises a number of genera points. First, it is apparent that, for a range of reasons, many residential consumers choos not to switch supplier and remain 'disengaged' in the market, notwithstanding the fa that they could save money.[227] Second, regulators and policy makers increasingly see pric discrimination in retail markets as problematic, especially when it involves substantia price differentials between a small group of 'active' consumers and a much larger grou of 'inactive' consumers.[228] Third, concern about inactive consumers being exploited ha led to the introduction, or retention, of regulated default tariffs in a number of jurisdic tions (including most US states, many EU Member States, and now the UK and Australia Fourth, notwithstanding the widespread use of regulated default tariffs, it appears tha retail competition has been most successful in jurisdictions which do not have a regulate default tariff.[229] That is, the existence of a regulated default tariff can reduce the incentiv for consumers to be active, which in turn further reduces the benefits of a competitiv

---

[220] See Joskow (2008a), Kang and Zarnikau (2009) and Baldick, Oren, Schubert and Anderson (2021). Som estimates suggest that 92 per cent of Texas households have exercised the right to switch.

[221] See Bushnell, Mansur and Novan (2017) and Littlechild (2021b). Earlier analysis is presented in Rose (2004), Joskow (2006) and Swadley and Yücel (2011).

[222] This includes price regulation for all consumers as well as vulnerable consumers; see ACER/CEER (2021a

[223] In 2020, only three countries (Norway, Belgium and the UK) had switching rates of 20 per cent or more with fourteen countries having switching rates of less than 10 per cent. This is notwithstanding the fac that, on average across the EU, there were more than fifty active nationwide suppliers operating in a Member State, and some states had a high number of suppliers (Spain had 292 and Italy had 175). See ACER/CEER (2021a).

[224] See EC (2021d). In six other markets, it was estimated that there were annual savings of between €200 and €300 (between 25 per cent and 40 per cent of the bill) from switching.

[225] See Ofgem (2007) and NAO (2008).

[226] For a critique of this approach, see Littlechild (2021c).

[227] Chapter 7 identifies some potential reasons for such disengagement in behavioural economics research

[228] This is described by some as having resulted in a two-tier system. Littlechild (2021b) critiques this view

[229] This is consistent with the survey presented by the Brattle Group (2018), which concludes that: 'We are not aware of any clear example where widely-available regulated prices coexist with successful retail competition.'

market.[230] Fifth, one risk of ongoing price interventions in competitive retail markets is that it over-protects consumers and does not provide the incentive for consumers to learn and adapt to the new environment, which in the longer term could may make them ill-equipped to cope with the substantial technical and market changes occurring in energy markets.[231] As described above, it is expected that in the future consumers will be more actively involved in energy markets and consume, share and potentially produce electricity in different ways than they do today. Finally, the feasibility of retail competition in the long term will clearly depend on the extent to which political pressures to intervene at times of very high and rising prices can be kept at bay. Simply put, while from an efficiency perspective retail competition can result in prices that reflect the efficient wholesale cost of supplying electricity, if wholesale price movements are too volatile, or retail prices are perceived to be high (as experienced in many countries in late 2021 and 2022 following the significant increase in wholesale prices), this can create strong consumer and political pressure to 'do something' and intervene on the basis of affordability concerns.[232]

9.4.2 Decarbonisation Policies and Electricity Regulation

The electricity industry is a major contributor to carbon dioxide (CO_2) emissions, which is a major greenhouse gas.[233] Accordingly, efforts to reduce emissions in the electricity production process can have major impacts on the reduction of overall greenhouse gas emission levels. For this reason, over seventy countries (including the USA, China and the EU) have committed to policies which reduce emissions to 'net zero' by 2050.[234] To achieve these targets, there is a need for the electricity generation mix to move away from high-carbon sources of electricity generation (particularly coal) towards low-carbon and renewable sources. Various specific policies have been introduced to facilitate this shift, or 'energy transformation' as it is sometimes called.[235]

---

[230] This is consistent with findings from behavioural economics research discussed in Section 7.2.3 about how price regulation can be counterproductive by reducing the incentives for non-standard consumers to be informed, reducing price competition and increasing average prices.

[231] See also Littlechild (2021b).

[232] The European Commission (EC, 2022) set out various options to address high electricity retail prices, including the possible introduction of a fixed price for generators, a cap on the cost of generation inputs or a retail electricity cap. Brown, Eckert and Eckert (2017) discuss the introduction of a retail price cap in Alberta on the basis of concerns about high and volatile electricity prices. CERRE (2022) consider the responses in France, the Netherlands, Britain and Norway to rising electricity prices. More generally, they note how 'well-intentioned regulatory measures to improve market performance in general, and competition in particular', such as the British price caps, may have undermined the workings of the market by not allowing retail prices to move in line with changes in wholesale costs and reducing the incentives of suppliers to compete for customers.

[233] Globally, electricity and heat production accounts for 43 per cent of all carbon dioxide (CO_2) emissions.

[234] UN (2020). Net-zero policies mean that total emissions are equal to or less than the emissions removed from the environment. See also IEA (2020a).

[235] These policies are complemented by macro-level and economy-wide 'cap and trade' policies in some jurisdictions, whereby a total 'cap' is set for all sources of emissions, and quotas for emission allowances are then allocated to the various sources of emissions. Emitters then trade among themselves – by buying or selling emission allowances – to encourage least-cost compliance within the total cap for emissions, and the price of emission allowances is determined by the market. The European emissions trading scheme (ETS) is the world's largest scheme covering 10,000 installations. Although the USA does not currently have a nationwide trading system for greenhouse gases, there are state initiatives (such as the Regional Greenhouse Gas Initiative (RGGI) in the northeast) and it has, in the past, been a pioneer in 'cap and trade' systems, notably in relation to chlorofluorocarbon (CFC) emissions and sulfur dioxide (SO_2) emissions.

At the generation level, this includes policies that set renewable generation targets or place obligations on electricity suppliers to source a certain proportion of electricity from renewable sources. Many countries have introduced guaranteed renewable feed-in tariffs, while others (such as the UK and Germany) use auctions to commission renewable energy resources. Investment subsidies and tax credits have also been used to incentivise investment in renewable generation. In addition, in some countries, there are proposals for substantial investments in new nuclear power plants (such as in the UK, France and the USA), while in others, there is consideration of alternative approaches to the emissions problem associated with electricity generation such as carbon capture and storage (CCS) projects.[236]

Policy initiatives directed at electricity transmission and distribution include supporting the development of so-called 'smart grids', which, loosely defined, involve 'computerising' the electric grid to enhance efficiency in the transportation and use of electricity and allow for more dynamic demand-side interactions to manage consumption (including through the integration of distributed generation). There has also been a focus on coordinating and expediting the planning approvals process for the new transmission and distribution infrastructure needed to connect renewable energy sources.[237]

Alongside policies focused on generation and transportation, in many jurisdictions policies have also been directed at the consumption of electricity. These policies, collectively known as demand-side management, have tended to focus on three areas: improving energy efficiency; reducing the overall consumption of electricity; and facilitating higher levels of demand responsiveness to changes in wholesale prices, particularly at peak periods. Improved demand-side management can reduce CO_2 emissions in the same way that shifts in the generation profile towards renewable energy do, but have the additional benefit of reducing costs and customer bills relative to supply-side measures.[238]

While decarbonisation policies bring environmental and health benefits (and thus avoid future social costs), they can increase the current cost of electricity for consumers and thus have regressive effects (as lower-income households spend a higher share of their income on electricity).[239] Decarbonisation policies can also directly affect the design and real-time operation of an electricity system.[240] This is because the output from variable renewable energy sources, such as wind and solar power, depend on weather conditions

---

[236] CCS involves the 'capturing' of the CO_2 produced by fossil fuel stations, which is then transported via pipeline to be stored in deep underground structures (such as used gas and oil reservoirs). Some estimates indicate that up to 90 per cent of CO_2 emissions from a fossil fuel power plant can potentially be captured using this technology.

[237] A 'strategic' approach to transmission system planning can be seen in some jurisdictions, such as Germany's Infrastructure Planning Acceleration Law.

[238] This is because many electricity efficiency measures generally cost less on a per kilowatt-hour basis than the costs associated with the generation, transmission and distribution of electricity, and the implementation of such policies can cost considerably less than investments in new renewable generation capacity and in transmission and distribution lines. In addition, unlike policies focused on the supply side, these measures can have the effect of lowering, rather than increasing, electricity bills paid by end-users.

[239] Owen and Barrett (2020) estimate that in the UK low-carbon policies add 13 per cent to household bills.

[240] Green (2021) discusses two problems for system operation: firstly, solar panels and wind have no inertia meaning that frequency can fall fast; and secondly, renewable stations can sometimes produce 'free' electricity at times when demand is low (or output already high), which can force thermal generators to produce at levels below their minimum operating limits, potentially requiring them to shut down (which reduces their life).

which means that there can be seasonal fluctuations, as well as large fluctuations in electricity generated from hour to hour (and for solar panels from minute to minute).[241] This variability in output has obvious impacts on the generation profile of more conventional plants, which are required to hold sufficient reserves to start up quickly and meet demand at times when wind speeds fall or if there is limited generation available from other renewable sources.[242] In the short term, this variability in output can increase the costs associated with balancing the network in real time (particularly where generators submit their plans to the system operator a day in advance), and lead to more volatile prices, particularly in balancing markets, as hour-by-hour prices can move significantly in response to, for example, sudden changes in available renewable capacity. Over the longer term, substantially more conventional generation capacity may be required to be available, particularly peaking plants that can meet demand in circumstances where variable renewable generation is producing no or limited output.[243] However, as discussed in Box 9.2, for it to be economically viable to invest in peak plants, such plants must be able to price to recover their fixed costs in times when the demand/supply balance is tight; that is, to price significantly above marginal cost. Increased variable renewable generation can also make wholesale prices more volatile in non-peak times, because when wind and solar are generating lots of power, the marginal price bid by windfarms and solar panel operators into the balancing market can be zero or even negative.

In principle, the widespread adoption of battery storage – which can respond very quickly – can potentially provide a substitute to conventional back-up generation and reserve capacity to manage intra-day fluctuations and reduce system operation and balancing costs.[244] However, the incentive to supply electricity to smooth intra-day prices will depend on the opportunity cost of selling (stored) energy at different points in time and in different markets.[245]

The impact of decarbonisation policies on the economic regulation of the industry continues to attract significant attention. While most commentators agree that regulation will need to adapt to accommodate decarbonisation policies, some go further and argue that such policies could actually undo some of the benefits achieved by the restructuring

---

[241] See Green (2021). Borenstein and Bushnell (2015) refer to changes in net load (the difference between forecasted load and expected electricity production from variable generation resources) as more solar power is added to the system as the 'duck chart' (or duck curve) because, at certain times of the year, these curves can produce a 'belly' appearance in the mid-afternoon that quickly ramps up to produce an 'arch' similar to the neck of a duck.

[242] See Green (2021).

[243] Bushnell and Novan (2018) analyse the impact of large-scale solar panel capacity in California and find that short-term power markets can sustain flexible conventional generation, but undermine the viability of traditional baseload generation. Simhauser, Nelson and Gilmore (2023) record that 43% of households have a behind-the-meter solar unit in the Australian state of Queensland and that this has 'displaced approximately 1500MW of base and peaking plant, equating to around $3bn investment.' Green (2021) concludes that in the long run there will be a need for more peaking capacity with relatively short and uncertain annual running hours and that to compensate for this there may be a need for a capacity market or mechanism to ensure a sufficient margin.

[244] Green (2021) notes that: 'There is no question that energy storage can help to even out intra-daily variations in electricity supply and demand, and to provide reserve to deal with short-term fluctuations. A truly massive expansion would be needed to cope with inter-seasonal variations, however.'

[245] See Green (2021). Strbac, Aunedi, Konstantelos, et al. (2017) find that using stored energy as a form of arbitrage in day-ahead markets yields the least value, and the most value of storage comes from using it to help balance fluctuations in demand and generation (i.e. in the balancing market) and providing reserve electricity.

of the industry by creating 'a potential vehicle for the return of old-style intervention in electricity generation and in retail competition' and a return of highly expensive centrally imposed investments in the industry.[246] Others argue that, rather than reverting to a pre-restructuring setting, a 'new paradigm' for regulation is emerging based around 'hybrid model' that combines liberalised markets with state interventions.[247]

More generally, the focus on decarbonisation is expected to bring increasing political interest to the electricity industry, raising concerns that this could lead to a re-politicisation of the regulation of the industry, and change the nature of the independent regulation approach. A potential manifestation of this is a change in the remit of independent regulators in some jurisdictions. For example, in Britain, independent regulators were originally established with a specific set of focused and narrow objectives (such as the promotion of competition, protecting consumers and the encouragement of efficient investment). However, such regulators are now being given additional objectives, such as those relating to the environment and sustainability, and in the eyes of some have become delivery agencies for government.[248] In the USA, it has been suggested that 'traditional' rate making approaches, such as rate of return regulation, may need to be replaced by alternative forms of rate making and cost review, such as price-cap regulation (in the form of performance-based regulation or multi-year rate plans), and regulated rates that promote greater demand response or renewable generation.[249]

9.5 CONCLUSION

The distinctive technical, economic and social characteristics of the electricity industry has long shaped the regulation of the industry. While it is not uncommon for electricity to be supplied by a vertically integrated regulated entity, over the past four decades an 'experiment' in restructuring the electricity industry has been undertaken in many jurisdictions.[250] This has typically involved introducing competition into some activities (such as generation and retail supply), the vertical separation of some activities in the electricity supply chain, and the creation of markets and other trading arrangements. While price controls in the form of rate of return regulation or price caps are almost always imposed on the core network activities of transmission and distribution, wholesale generation and retailing activities are not always subject to formal price regulation but can be subject to other forms or regulatory oversight and monitoring. As many have noted, this outcome is not altogether surprising, as restructuring policies were never likely to lead to

---

[246] See Pollitt (2007, 2008), Green (2008) and Lodge and Stern (2014). For example, policies which provide wholesale price guarantees for low-carbon generation investments have been described as an example of the replacement of market-based mechanisms with a more central planning approach.

[247] Roques (2021). See Helm (2007) on the need for a new paradigm.

[248] See Lodge and Stern (2014).

[249] See Steinhurst (2011) and Alvarez and Steele (2017). Jenkins and Pérez-Arriaga (2017) propose a third approach which involves a multi-year price plan (e.g. five years) based around a Totex approach. Contrast with Crew and Kleindorfer (2012). who suggest that 'cost-of-service regulation seems to be making a comeback', partly as a result of the impact of environmental regulation on utilities.

[250] Pollitt (2007) describes electricity liberalisation as 'one of the longest running and most interesting set of multi-country micro-economic experiments'.

complete withdrawal of regulatory oversight of the industry given the social and political importance of electricity and the characteristics of the supply structure (e.g. core network activities with natural monopoly characteristics).[251]

It is difficult to assess the effectiveness of these restructuring policies in the absence of a well-specified counterfactual. It is clear that some jurisdictions have transitioned to an industry structure where competition and regulation coexist with one another, and where there is some evidence that regulation, and other reforms, have been effective in reducing costs and improving the performance of the industry. The success of the transition in other jurisdictions is less clear, and it is increasingly evident that the restructuring of the electricity industry, and the introduction of competition in that industry, has, in many jurisdictions, proved more difficult than anticipated. Substantial future challenges for regulation include how to implement decarbonisation policies in ways consistent with other regulatory objectives (such as efficiency and fair prices),[252] and how to adapt regulation to account for the impacts of technological changes and the decentralisation of the electricity system.

DISCUSSION QUESTIONS

1. What are some of the important distinguishing characteristics of the electricity industry that make it different from other industries?
2. In what ways is the traditional electricity supply structure changing, and how are the different activities in the supply chain being affected by these changes?
3. What are the different ways in which generators supply or sell electricity to load-serving entities/retailers? What are some examples of wholesale electricity markets that have been established in jurisdictions where competition has been introduced?
4. Describe the activities in the electricity supply chain where competition has been introduced, and which activities are subject to regulation. For activities that are subject to regulation, what are the typical form and scope of that regulation?
5. Discuss the four elements of the 'standard electricity restructuring' model? To what extent do you think that the implementation of this standard model could be considered a success?
6. Do you agree with the following statement? 'The effects of restructuring policies introduced in the electricity industry around the world have not lived up to expectations.' Discuss.
7. What are some reasons why introducing competition in wholesale markets and in retail markets has proven so challenging? How might specific regulatory policies potentially affect the development of competition in both of these activities?
8. In what ways are decarbonisation policies impacting on the electricity industry? What are some of the implications of these policies for economic regulators?

---

[251] See Hogan (2002). Indeed, as Pollitt (2007) observes, the fostering of wholesale and retail competition may require *more* costly and complex regulation to ensure its success.

[252] Some argue that concerns about the transition to low-carbon and renewable energy sources along with the technological changes occurring in the sector have overtaken those relating to restructuring that have dominated the industry for the last forty years.

10

Gas Regulation

Natural gas is an important source of energy in many economies. It is used for domestic purposes, such as heating and cooking, and is also used as an input to various industrial and commercial production process, including electricity generation. Gas is capable of being transported across long distances, including across national boundaries and by sea (in the form of liquefied natural gas (LNG)).[1] This has created the potential, in principle, for a global gas market.[2]

Three main issues tend to shape the regulation of the gas sector: competition in wholesale and retail markets; security of gas supply; and long-term sustainability. Like for other industries discussed in this book, many countries have introduced policies to restructure the gas industry over the past four decades, with the general aim of introducing greater competition and improving efficiency. In some countries, this has led to the emergence of flexible and liquid wholesale gas markets which are more responsive to demand and supply factors. However, it has also introduced the potential for greater volatility in gas prices, which can directly impact household and commercial customers, and, as discussed in Chapter 9, can have spillover effects on wholesale and retail electricity prices given the widespread use of gas to generate electricity.[3]

The experience of gas industry regulation illustrates how some of the theoretical principles and considerations described in Parts I and II in this book have been applied in practice. These include the effects of vertical separation of an industry, and the impacts of a shift in trading arrangements from those based on long-term vertical integration or contracts to short-term markets. The experience also shows how market-based mechanisms, such as auctions and wholesale spot markets, have been used in practice. As we will see, such shifts can introduce greater volatility into wholesale and retail prices, which may be efficient from an economic perspective but raise concerns about fairness and affordability. Another important theme explored in this chapter is the efficiency and

---

[1] 'Liquefaction' involves the cooling of gas to very low temperatures (−160°C) to reduce its volume so that it can be transported in specialised LNG tankers to specific destinations. At the destination (known as LNG receiving terminals), the gas is then converted from its liquid form ('regasified') so that it can be injected into a transmission pipeline.

[2] There are several large intercontinental pipelines in the world, including the Nord Stream pipeline (a pipeline under the Baltic Sea connecting Russia and Germany), and the Central Asia–China gas pipeline (which begins in Turkmenistan, and travels through Uzbekistan and Kazakhstan to China).

[3] Natural gas accounts for about a quarter of global electricity generation.

distributional effects of adopting different structures of fixed and variable charges as we
as of alternatives to formal rate regulation, such as negotiated settlements.

Looking ahead, the future regulation of the gas industry will be affected by net-zer
and decarbonisation policies. While gas-fired electricity generation can be useful i
the short to medium term to support a transition away from higher-carbon generatio
sources (such as coal to gas, or oil to gas), over the long term, it is proposed that unabate
natural gas should be gradually phased out in the electricity sector, and that no ne
gas fields should be used for gas production.[4] A number of jurisdictions are introducin
policy proposals to decarbonise gas markets by shifting towards renewable gases suc
as biomethane (which combines methane, carbon monoxide, hydrogen and other gase
and low-carbon hydrogen.[5] As we shall discuss, these developments, and the uncertaint
attached to them, are likely to raise a number of important issues for the regulation of th
natural gas industry in the future.

10.1 PHYSICAL AND ECONOMIC CHARACTERISTICS OF GAS

Natural gas is a finite and non-renewable resource, and a longstanding concern in ju
isdictions without their own gas reserves is security of supply. In the UK and Europ
concerns about import dependence were brought to the fore in early 2022 following th
Russian invasion of Ukraine, and led to short-term regulatory measures and longer-ter
policies designed to phase out a reliance on gas by the middle of the century. Howeve
the outlook for future natural gas supply is more optimistic in some countries since th
discovery of significant potential stores of 'non-conventional gas' (gas trapped betwee
layers of sedimentary shale rock (shale gas), or trapped in sandstone or limestone forma
tions (tight gas)). In the USA, this has transformed the gas industry, and around 90 p
cent of the USA's natural gas supply now comes from tight/shale gas.[6] Non-conventiona
gas stores have been identified in other countries such as China, Australia, Indonesi
Poland and Mexico. However, for environmental and safety reasons, the extraction o
shale gas using a process called 'fracking' is currently banned in a number of Europea
countries (Germany, France and Spain) and some parts of Australia.

10.1.1 Characteristics of the Product

Natural gas consists principally of methane (a molecule made up of one carbon ato
and four hydrogen atoms (CH_4)) and is generally found deep underground in sedimentar
rock formations. In its pure form, it is colourless and odourless, although it is typicall
odorised to ensure easy detection of leaks. It is a highly combustible fuel and has lowe
emissions than coal or oil. Once extracted, gas is transported along a transmission syste

---

[4] This is to achieve the net-zero targets. By 2050, it is estimated that 88 per cent of electricity will be
generated from renewable electricity sources (solar, wind and hydropower). This will be complemented
by nuclear (7.7 per cent), hydrogen (2.4 per cent) and a small contribution from fossil fuels with carbon
capture and storage (1.9 per cent). See IEA (2021a).

[5] See IEA (2020b).

[6] See EIA (2022a). The figure for 2020, as compared to around 31 per cent in 2000.

at relatively slow speeds, meaning that supply is not instantly responsive to changes in demand. As natural gas is combustible, it is also critical that the supply of gas is continuous and at the right pressure. Major safety issues, like gas explosions, can arise in situations where supply is interrupted and gas escapes from the pipelines, or where air enters the pipeline and mixes with the gas, affecting the natural gas-to-air ratio.

The natural gas and electricity industries are often seen as being sufficiently closely related in terms of supply and demand characteristics that the regulatory issues can be treated in a similar way. On the supply side, both forms of energy typically require transportation along a high-pressure (or high-voltage) transmission network and lower-pressure (or lower-voltage) distribution network before reaching end-users. Moreover, because the physical products are relatively homogeneous (electrons and gas molecules), they are capable of being traded in wholesale markets. On the demand side, the two forms of energy are potentially substitutable for certain types of uses such as heating and cooking, but also for certain industrial processes, such as the gas-fired production of electricity (i.e. generators can use gas to produce electricity in situations where the gas price is below that of the prevailing electricity price). The economic regulation of both industries is also combined in a single 'energy' regulator in most jurisdictions. Finally, it is not uncommon for energy firms to operate in both industries and, in a number of jurisdictions, for retailers to supply both gas and electricity 'dual-fuel' offers to consumers.

There are, however, a number of important differences which distinguish the production and supply of gas from the production and supply of electricity. First, conventional electricity generation can, in principle, occur in any location.[7] By comparison, natural gas deposits and fields or basins are geographically specific, and can be unevenly distributed across jurisdictions and regions. This means that some countries are reliant on gas imports to meet a portion, or all, of local demand. Second, unlike electricity, it is possible to send gas from point to point on a network, and therefore to determine the physical path along which gas will flow and make transportation payments accordingly.[8] Third, there is not the same concern about systemic failures in gas networks that arise in electricity networks. Variations in the pressure on a gas network can be better accommodated than fluctuations in voltage on an electricity network, and it is possible to isolate, and shut down, specific gas pipelines, or segments of pipelines, while leaving the remaining part of the network operational. This means that issues of system operation and coordination – while still important for safety and reliability purposes, and to manage short-term fluctuations in demand and supply on specific pipelines – are of a different nature for gas networks than for electricity networks, where flows on the *entire* network need to be continuously managed. Fourth, it is possible to store gas (including in the pipelines), which means that issues of short-term balancing, and associated problems of market power, are of less critical importance in relation to gas than in relation to electricity (which is still largely non-storable). Indeed, the ability to store gas raises issues that

---

[7] As discussed in Chapter 9, this is not true of all generation (e.g. large offshore wind and hydroelectric power).

[8] Cremer and Laffont (2002) observe that 'the transmission grid in the gas sector bears some similarity with electricity networks, except that the relevant laws of physics differ, providing the operator with a better control of flows'.

do not arise in electricity; those associated with the opportunity cost of gas over time
because gas stored today can potentially be sold tomorrow at a different price. Fifth, it
is possible to transport gas over long distances without incurring significant losses. This
includes LNG, which allows international suppliers of gas to access specific markets via
sea. Finally, unlike electricity, and as discussed in more detail below, the pricing of gas
in many parts of the world (with the exception of the USA and Britain) has traditionally
been linked to the price of fuel sources that are seen to be substitutes, such as oil.

Natural gas faces competition from alternative fuels for some of its uses (such as
domestic cooking and heating), including from liquefied petroleum gas (LPG; see Box
10.2 later), oil, electricity and coal. This potentially introduces a degree of inter-fuel
competition between the different energy sources, albeit largely over the medium to long
term before users have made sunk investments in equipment suited to one particular fuel
type. In the USA, 41 per cent of gas volumes delivered in 2021 was used in the electri
city industry, while 30 per cent was used by industrial customers (to produce steel, glass
paper, clothing and brick). Residential customers, who use gas for heating and cooking
accounted for 17 per cent of gas volumes and commercial customers 12 per cent.[9]

As with electricity, in the short term, residential and commercial demand for natural
gas use tends to be inelastic, as most customers are committed to supply contracts which
do not reflect short-term price changes. However, industrial and electricity demand for
gas (particularly gas used for intermediate and peak generation) is more price-responsive
and can fluctuate significantly. Given the widespread use of gas for heating, non-indus
trial demand for gas is highly seasonal in many countries, with demand on cold winter
days being up to five times greater than that of summer in some places.[10] The demand for
gas also tends to fluctuate during a given day (called a diurnal swing), with demand typ
ically being higher in the morning and evenings, and lower during the day and overnight
Although gas demand fluctuates throughout the day, the production fields or basins
export gas at a steady rate, and this gives rise to a need to manage the flow of the gas net
work throughout the day, which is typically achieved through forms of storage. In some
jurisdictions, periods of high demand are also managed through the use of 'interruptible
contracts' (contracts where gas transmission to a customer can temporarily be cut off,
which are typically offered at a lower price than firm contracts.

10.1.2 Natural Gas Supply Chain

The traditional supply chain for natural gas comprises a number of stages: gas explor
ation, extraction and processing; the transmission of gas in high-pressure pipelines over
long distances to major areas of consumption; the distribution of gas using lower-pressure
pipelines to final users; and the retail supply of gas to end-users. In addition, gas can be
stored at various points, including in depleted gas fields, in transmission pipelines or in
gas holders. An illustration of the traditional gas supply chain is presented in Figure 10.1

---

[9] EIA (2022b).
[10] Given the main uses of gas, the most significant variation in gas demand is seasonal, with winter months
involving higher consumption than summer months. However, demand can also vary between different
days (working and non-working days) and during the day (evening and daytime).

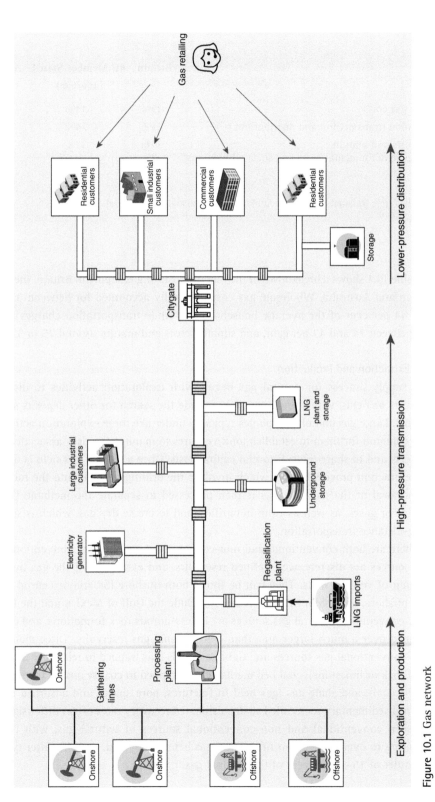

Figure 10.1 Gas network

Table 10.1 Breakdown of average household gas bill, 2020[a]

	Britain	EU Member States (average)	Australia
Wholesale gas costs	39%	44%	33%
Transportation (transmission and distribution)	24%	24%	43%
Supplier costs and margin	30%	32%	25%
Other levies (environmental costs and social obligations)	2%		
VAT	5%		
Total	100%	100%	100%

[a] Based on data from National Grid (2021), ACER/CEER (2021a) and ACCC (2021a).

Table 10.1 shows a breakdown of the relative costs of gas supply in Britain, the European Union and Australia. Wholesale gas costs generally accounted for between 33 per cent and 44 per cent of the average household bill, while transportation charges accounted for between 24 and 43 per cent, and supplier costs and margin around 25 to 32 per cent.

Gas Extraction and Production

The supply process for natural gas begins with exploration activities to discover gas deposits or fields, which often occurs alongside the search for other deposits such as oil or coal. Large gas and oil companies typically undertake these exploration activities, and it is common for them to establish joint ventures to manage the risks associated with the projects and to share the substantial capital costs. Once a natural gas field is discovered, the extraction process begins, which involves the drilling of wells into the rock and the withdrawal of the gas. The gas is then processed to separate the methane from other liquids or gases, as well as from impurities, and to create dry gas, which is suitable for long-distance transportation.

There are both conventional and non-conventional gas sources. Conventional natural gas sources are discrete, well-defined reservoirs, and extraction of the gas involves the drilling of vertical wells. They can be found both onshore (Siberia or central Australia) and offshore, and major offshore reserves include the Gulf of Mexico and the North Sea. Non-conventional natural gas sources are in less-porous rock formations, and can be distributed over a much larger area than conventional gas reservoirs. Three main types of non-conventional gas sources are: tight gas sands (gas trapped in relatively impermeable hard rock or limestone); coal bed methane (gas trapped in coal seams, in the solid matrix of the coal); and shale gas (gas held in fractures, pore spaces and adsorbed onto fine grained sedimentary rock called shale). Estimated recovery rates of gas differ significantly between conventional and non-conventional sources of natural gas, with the former resulting in over 80 per cent of original gas being recovered, and the latter typically in the order of 15–30 per cent of the original gas.[11]

[11] EC report on shale gas (EC, 2012).

Historically, conventional gas sources have dominated worldwide natural gas production. The largest reserves of conventional gas are located in Russia, but there are also large reserves of conventional gas in the Middle East (Qatar, Saudi Arabia, Iran), North America and Africa (Algeria, Nigeria). Many countries have insufficient indigenous gas to meet their demand requirements. In Europe, Germany, Italy, Austria, Poland, France and Hungary are large importers of natural gas, particularly from Russia. Other countries such as Japan and South Korea also have no significant indigenous supplies of natural gas, and rely on imports of LNG to meet virtually all of their natural gas demand. As discussed in Section 10.4.1, the need for imports to satisfy local demand creates political issues around dependence on foreign gas producers, and security of supply issues in relation to the route of importation. For example, long-running disputes between Russia and Ukraine (affecting the flow of Russian gas over Ukrainian territory for export to Europe) have had significant effects on importing countries, such as those in Western Europe.[12]

In recent years, there has been a shift towards non-conventional gas sources in light of the significant discovery of such sources in some countries. Large reserves of technically recoverable non-conventional natural gas (discovered so far) are located in China, Argentina, Algeria, the USA, Canada, Mexico, Australia, South Africa and Russia.[13] According to the IEA, 53 per cent of the world's natural gas resources were non-conventional in 2018, and around 60 per cent of the growth in global gas production to 2030 will come from non-conventional sources, particularly from shale gas in the USA.[14] The extraction process for shale gas and tight gas involves a process known as hydraulic 'fracking', which involves the injection of a mixture of sand, water and chemicals underground into rocks or rock formations to create fractures which allow for the release of the gas. Horizontal drilling is often used to create a maximum surface area in contact with the shale. These extraction methods tend to be more expensive than those of conventional gas extraction and have also raised health and environmental concerns.

Gas Transmission

Once natural gas has been extracted and processed, it is transported from the sites of production to the major areas of consumption, including to cities, towns and large industrial users. Typically, gas fields and processing plants are located far from these major areas of consumption, and the transportation of gas over these long distances occurs by high-pressure transmission pipelines.[15]

These pipelines are large underground steel pipes, and gas travels through these pipelines at around 20 miles per hour. In North America, Australia, Latin America and many parts of Europe, gas crosses over state or national borders in its transportation. In some jurisdictions, all of the transmission pipelines comprise a single gas transmission system

---

[12] For example, the disputes in 2009, 2014 and following the Russian invasion of Ukraine in 2022.

[13] See EIA (2013).

[14] IEA (2019a).

[15] A distinction is sometimes made between 'transit' activities – the transportation of gas across a number of jurisdictions, or via marine transportation in the case of LNG – and 'transmission' – the transportation of gas using high-pressure pipelines within a given market/jurisdiction. However, the distinction is not always a clear one, and for the purposes of this discussion we will use the term 'transmission' to cover both activities.

operated by a single company.[16] In other jurisdictions, transmission pipelines are owned and operated by a number of operators, whose pipelines are located in different regions of the country.[17] A further variation can be seen in Australia and the USA, where there are a number of different owners of specific gas pipelines who are not typically integrated with one another and who interconnect at various geographical hubs. This diversity of ownership structures indicates that economies of scale can be achieved at the individual transmission pipeline level, and gas transmission activities do not have to be integrated under common ownership for such economies to be achieved.

Gas producers and storage providers inject certain nominated quantities of gas into the transmission network each day. The injections are made at certain 'entry' points for transportation to numerous 'exit' points.[18] An important part of managing the flow and volume of gas is the pressure of the pipeline. Pipeline pressure tends to fall as gas is transported over long distances as a result of friction around the pipe, but also as a result of gas being withdrawn at various points. Pipeline operators use compressor stations at various points to increase pressure, and to ensure that the gas flowing remains at a particular pressure level.[19] The use of compressor stations allows the operator to receive gas flows at a constant rate and to transport larger amounts of gas than would otherwise be possible by allowing pressure to build up in some segments of the pipe at times of low demand, and then to be gradually released during periods of high demand. On many larger transmission routes, it is not uncommon for multiple pipelines to be laid parallel to one another (known as 'looping') as a way of increasing capacity within a particular segment of the pipeline system. The use of loops can extend the distance between compressor stations, at which point the multiple pipes can transfer parts of their flow into a single pipeline. Looping can also serve as a storage mechanism, by allowing gas to be effectively stored in separate pipes and released at peak periods.

Users of gas transmission pipelines, such as gas retailers, large industrial customers, electricity generators and market traders (sometimes collectively referred to as 'shippers') procure gas directly from producers, interconnector pipelines, storage or LNG facilities. Some industrial users, such as gas-fired power stations or gas storage facilities, may be directly connected to the transmission network and take gas off at high pressure. Shippers are responsible for scheduling the transportation with the pipeline operator in advance (known as nominations). The nominations include booking the time, pressure and locations at which gas will be injected and withdrawn from the transmission network. This is necessary to allow for gas balancing, which, in simple terms, refers to the requirement

---

[16] In the case of Denmark and Britain, the same company that owns the electricity transmission network.

[17] Such as Austria and France (two operators in each country), Italy (nine operators) and Germany (sixteen operators).

[18] In Britain, for example, gas enters the national transmission system at eight reception points (known as terminals), including six beach terminals and two LNG reception terminals. There are around 180 offtake points from the national transmission network, where local distribution networks and other large users, such as industrial customers and power stations, can receive gas directly from the transmission system. In the USA there are more than 5000 receipt points, 11,000 delivery points and 1400 interconnection points.

[19] In the USA, compressor stations are located at intervals of 50–100 miles along the pipeline, while in Britain they are located every 40–60 miles along the national transmission network.

that the amount of gas a shipper injects into the transmission system in a given time period is matched by the amount of gas withdrawn from the system by its customers. Generally, shippers are responsible for ensuring that their nominated position is 'in balance'; that is, the quantity of gas delivered to the system is approximately the same as the quantity withdrawn. If there is a difference between the quantity injected and withdrawn at the end of a day, shippers can face 'imbalance charges'. As discussed in Section 10.1.3, in many jurisdictions where gas markets have been restructured, shippers can keep their positions in balance by buying and selling gas in different markets, such as on-the-day commodity markets, or through over-the-counter (OTC) trades. In jurisdictions where individual pipelines are separately owned and operated, individual pipeline operators tend to manage their physical operations and ensure that the system is in balance. Where pipeline systems are integrated, such as in Britain, the balancing functions for shippers are typically undertaken centrally by the company that owns all of the pipelines.[20]

Pipeline owners must offer shippers capacity rights or entitlements to transport gas on their pipeline. Capacity allocation refers to how capacity rights are made available to shippers. In the USA, the initial allocation process for long-term capacity rights is based around bilateral contracts signed between pipeline operators and shippers, and there is no formal centralised organised market to facilitate these trades. However, pipeline operators can hold 'open seasons', which are time periods in which the pipeline operator sells capacity to shippers.[21] In open seasons, a pipeline sells parcels of capacity to shippers usually through a sealed-bid auction run on the pipeline operator's website.[22] In addition to the initial allocation of capacity, holders of capacity rights can often resell any unused capacity to other parties in a secondary market, known as a capacity release market. In the USA, such markets are generally hosted on electronic bulletin boards operated by the pipelines. In Australia, shippers usually underwrite capacity in pipelines through long-term contracts, but recent changes have introduced mechanisms (including mandatory day-ahead auctions) for any unused capacity to be acquired by other shippers.[23] In Britain, capacity auctions are used for allocating entry and exit capacity rights to the national transmission network over the long and short term. Since 2015, auctions are also used at points of interconnection across the European gas transmission network.[24] In many jurisdictions with restructured gas markets, capacity rights have specific conditions attached to them – such as so-called 'use it or lose it' provisions – which are intended to prevent hoarding of the rights by large or existing market participants and the potential foreclosure of new entrants.

---

[20] In Britain, system balancing occurs daily, and at a single notional point on the transmission system known as the 'national balancing point' (NBP), and the system operator ensures that the system is in balance by buying/selling gas on the OTC market to meet demand, or by calling upon storage.

[21] FERC Order 636 (1992). See also FERC Order 637 (FERC, 2000). The term 'open season' is also used to refer to a process in relation to new investments where a pipeline operator invites bids from potential shippers for long-term capacity contracts in order to determine whether there is sufficient financial commitment to make the project viable.

[22] During the open season, pipelines are required to sell all available capacity to shippers willing to pay the pipeline's maximum recourse rate.

[23] ACCC (2021a).

[24] See EC Regulation 984/2013 and EC Regulation 2017/459.

Gas Distribution

The local distribution of natural gas involves the transportation of gas from the point of interconnection of the gas transmission pipeline with the local distribution pipeline system (sometimes referred to as the 'citygate') to the final users of gas, such as businesses, industrial customers, households and electricity generators. In physical terms distribution pipelines are of a much smaller diameter than transmission pipelines, and serve a large number of end-users. A typical distribution network can comprise many thousands of kilometres of high-, medium- and low-pressure distribution pipeline which are interconnected with one another, as well as measurement equipment and pressure-regulating stations (which reduce pressure to a suitable level for a customer's requirements).

There is considerable variation in the number of regulated distribution companies operating across jurisdictions. Relatively small numbers of distribution network operators are seen in Australia (thirteen), Britain (five), Latvia (one), Slovakia (one) and Ireland (one). In contrast, in Austria, Germany, Belgium, Czech Republic, France, Italy, Romania and Poland, a large number of small distribution companies serve local areas, and have relatively small number of connections. In Germany, for example, there are some 700 gas distribution companies, and some 95 per cent of these companies have less than 100,000 connected customers.[25] The number of local distribution networks serving commercial and residential customers operating in the USA has been estimated at around 1460.[26]

Gas Storage

An important attribute of the gas supply chain is the potential to store gas. This can assist in smoothing out short-term price volatility by allowing participants (such as producers, shippers and retail companies) to manage the availability of gas during the day, to account for seasonal variations in demand, and to ensure that there is a sufficient store of gas available at times of very high demand (e.g. on very cold winter days). For example, in Europe some 25–30 per cent of gas consumed is drawn from storage in a normal winter. Pipeline operators also use gas storage facilities for system balancing purposes. Gas can be stored in different ways, including underground storage in salt caverns, mines, aquifers, hard rock caverns and depleted oil and gas fields, and above-ground storage in LNG tanks. One method of storage used by gas transmission pipeline operators to manage daily changes in demand is known as linepack storage and involves increasing the pressure in the pipeline during low-demand periods in order to store gas in the pipe which can then be gradually released during the high-demand period. Local distribution networks have also traditionally used various forms of storage, including high-pressure storage in pipes known as bullets (either above or below ground), and the use of gas holders or gasometers, which are large low-pressure containers which fill up with gas overnight and slowly release gas during the day. As discussed below, large gas storage facilities are subject to open-access requirements in some jurisdictions, meaning that the facilities must be offered to third parties on a non-discriminatory basis.

---

[25] See WIK (2011).
[26] See Natural Gas (2012) and EIA (2020). Some 63 per cent of these are municipal companies.

Gas Retailing

The final stage in the natural gas supply chain involves the retailing of gas to end-users, including businesses, large and small industrial customers, and households. As described in Section 10.3, some jurisdictions (including Britain, some states in the USA and Australia) and almost all EU countries have introduced policies which allow all customers (including residential customers) to choose their gas supplier.

0.1.3 Trading Arrangements for Wholesale Gas

Historically, the supply structure for natural gas in many jurisdictions was based around a quasi-vertically integrated structure, where a single firm (state-owned in some jurisdictions, privately owned in others)[27] had a monopoly on some, or all, of the activities described above. A common characteristic of the trading arrangements at that time was a reliance on long-term contracts (up to twenty years in some cases) at fixed prices between various parties in the supply chain.[28] Such long-term contracts were seen as important to underpin the investments in gas production and transmission pipelines, and for sharing risk among different market participants (such as gas producers, pipeline operators and users).

Restructuring policies introduced in many parts of the world in the 1980s and 1990s changed this structure, and the trading arrangements have generally become more short-term and flexible in nature. This trend can be observed in relation to gas procurement transactions, as well as transactions for transmission capacity and storage capacity. The change has been enabled by the development of a number of markets and trading platforms, which allow market participants to buy and sell physical gas, or gas transmission and storage capacity, in OTC transactions at different points in time. A major perceived advantage of more flexible trading arrangements is that market participants can now better manage the risks associated with both short-term and long-term pricing volatility.[29]

Wholesale Gas Spot Markets and Trading 'Hubs'

Wholesale gas spot markets involve short-term trading of natural gas. They are used by retail supply companies and other market participants (such as traders, producers and major industrial users, including electricity generation companies) to manage their physical supplies of gas. Wholesale spot markets cover a range of trading periods, from

---

[27] In many European countries, Australia and New Zealand, important parts of the production and supply chain – such as transportation, distribution and storage – tended to be dominated by a small number of state-owned companies. While in Germany and the USA, the monopolies tended to be largely privately owned.

[28] In the USA, long-term contracts were typically signed between producers and gas transmission pipeline operators, as well as between transmission pipeline operators and local utility companies. Similarly, in Britain, prior to restructuring, the state-owned and vertically integrated British Gas had a series of long-term wholesale contracts, usually for twenty-five years, with North Sea producers (including Norwegian gas producers), and a series of medium- to long-term contracts with customers at the retail level.

[29] The ability to manage short-term risk is seen as particularly important for gas-fired electricity generators, who find it difficult to make long-term commitments to purchase gas because of the volatility associated with electricity pricing and demand. Moreover, in jurisdictions where retail competition or choice has been introduced, the flexibility afforded by the shorter-term trading arrangements is seen to have been helpful for incumbent retailers in dealing with the uncertainty about future prices and their own demand requirements.

intra-day and next-day trading (for balancing purposes), through to month, season, year, or longer trading periods. While spot markets can provide market participants with greater flexibility than long-term contracts, spot prices can be volatile, and fluctuate widely, depending on factors such as short-term demand and supply conditions, changes in production costs, levels of available transmission and storage capacity, weather conditions and other exogenous events.[30] The development of spot markets has led to the emergence of what are known as 'marketers' or 'energy traders' – market participants who are not necessarily involved directly in the production or retailing of gas, but act as intermediaries in the purchase and sale of gas in wholesale and retail markets.

In the USA, wholesale spot markets have developed typically at the point where a number of transmission pipelines interconnect with one another, known as trading 'hubs'. Hubs provide a delivery point for wholesale market transactions and, because they are located at points where various pipelines interconnect, they increase the liquidity and lower the transaction costs associated with wholesale market sales. In addition to allowing market participants to cover any short-term balancing needs, hubs facilitate the trade of other products, such as secondary transmission capacity rights and storage capacity rights, typically through internet-based access to natural gas trading platforms and capacity release programmes. Some hubs provide title transfer services for parties that buy, sell or move their natural gas through the trading hub.[32] Hubs can also act as the pricing and nominated delivery points for various gas hedging and financial contracts (such as futures contracts). In some cases, hubs are physical, meaning that physical delivery of the product takes place at that place, while in other cases, they are virtual.[33]

There are approximately twenty major hubs across the USA, the largest and most liquid being the 'Henry Hub' in Louisiana which has access to major offshore and onshore gas producers.[34] Another important trading hub in North America is the 'AECO Hub' in Alberta, Canada. In Britain, spot market trading occurs at the 'national balancing point' (NBP), which is a 'virtual' trading hub. In continental Europe, the most important gas trading hub is in the Netherlands (the virtual Title Transfer Facility (TTF)), while other important hubs are in Germany (Trading Hub Europe), Italy (Punto di Scambio Virtuale (PSV)) and Austria (the Central European Gas Hub (CEGH), a virtual trading point (VTP)).[35] In Australia, there are three main gas trading hubs, located in Victoria, Queensland (Wallumbilla) and South Australia (Moomba).

[30] Transaction costs can potentially be minimised through the use of standardised contracts suitable for spot market trading, such as the standardised North American Energy Standards Board (NAESB) contracts.

[31] Gas is also traded at major citygates where distribution companies receive gas.

[32] Some hubs also provide the possibility of secondary trading in gas by market participants, such as through the use of 'backhaul' (where gas is notionally transported in the opposite direction and redelivered at a point upstream from the contract's delivery point) and gas swaps (where gas delivered at one location is notionally swapped for the same amount of gas delivered at another location).

[33] A physical hub is one located at the intersection of two or more gas pipelines, and gas traded tends to physically pass through the interchange of pipelines. In contrast, a virtual hub comprise large zones over which gas injections and withdrawals are being balanced, and trade is not limited to any one physical point on the network, but can allow for entry or exit of gas at any point within the zone.

[34] Henry Hub is interconnected with sixteen different inter-state and intra-state pipelines, and is said to offer an interconnect point with all North American producing and consuming areas.

[35] See Heather (2020). There are currently proposals to merge the Italian and Austrian hubs.

Alongside markets for physical trading in gas, a number of physical and financial hedging markets have developed in restructured markets whose purpose is to limit the exposure of market participants to adverse price fluctuations. Examples of physical hedging mechanisms include storage contracts or bilateral physical contracts with prices fixed as hedges. Financial hedging contracts include futures contracts, options and swaps, each of which do not result in any physical delivery of gas, but rather involve financial settlements between parties. Futures market prices are seen to provide important information to all market participants regarding the future expectations of gas prices, and can therefore assist them in making decisions regarding the need for future storage. In the USA, gas futures and OTC delivery markets have grown rapidly since their introduction in the 1990s, and are used by local gas distribution companies and other retail suppliers, among other users, to hedge against physical gas positions. Henry Hub is the delivery point for New York Mercantile Exchange (NYMEX) natural gas futures contracts. Elsewhere in the world, the Japan Korean Marker (JKM) is developing as a focal pricing point for LNG contracts in northeast Asia, while in Britain, futures contracts and other financial hedging products are priced and delivered to the NBP.

Long-Term Contracts for Wholesale Gas Supply

Although there has been a trend towards more flexible and short-term contracting practices, these have not completely replaced other forms of trading arrangements in some jurisdictions, and participants typically use a variety of medium- and long-term contracts alongside trading in wholesale spot markets to manage their risk exposure. Indeed, confidential long-term contracts are still commonly used by market participants in Australia, Asia and continental Europe as a method for procuring and supplying gas. In Australia, most gas production has historically been sold on a long-term basis (sometimes under contracts of up to twenty years); however, there is an increasing trend towards some shorter-duration contracts of five years or less.[36] Similarly, in continental Europe, long-term contracts still account for around half of natural gas procurement, although there are proposals for long-term contracts to be phased out by 2049.[37]

Long-term wholesale gas contracts frequently contain a 'take-or-pay' condition, which requires purchasers to pay for a specified minimum quantity of gas, irrespective of whether or not that gas is taken. While prices can, in some instances, be subject to review during the period of the contract, the prices struck in these contracts generally do not fluctuate on a daily or seasonal basis. However, most wholesale gas contracts contain a provision through which the price is indexed over time. In some countries, wholesale gas contracts are indexed to movements in competing fuels, such as oil prices.[38] Effectively, this means that the gas price paid is contractually linked, typically through a so-called escalation clause, to price movements in one or more competing fuels such as the crude

---

[36] See AEMC (2016b) and Productivity Commission (2015).
[37] See Renou-Maissant (2012), who estimated 70 per cent at that time. Other estimates suggest that spot and short-term contracts now account for around 45–50 per cent of gas sales.
[38] While this was common in Europe, this has since been replaced by a mixture of oil hub-based indexing and oil indexation. See Zhang, Wang, Shi and Liu (2018).

oil price (typical in Asia) or the gas oil and/or fuel oil price.[39] In contrast, in the USA Britain and increasingly in Europe, gas contracts are established on the basis of what known as 'gas-on-gas competition', meaning that they are linked to gas price indices o benchmarks (see Section 10.4.2).

LNG Wholesale Trading

The process for the export and import of LNG begins with natural gas being transporte through a transmission pipeline network to specialised liquefaction facilities which cor dense methane from a gas to a liquid.[40] Once liquefied, the LNG is then transported i cryogenic, or insulated, tanks by specialised ships. At its destination/receiving termina it is then stored as a liquid until it is needed. The process of regasification involves th warming of the LNG to return it to a gaseous state before it is transported to custome using the importing country's transportation network.

There is an increasing amount of international trade in LNG. In 2019, Japan, China an South Korea were major importers of LNG, and the main exporters of LNG were Qata Australia and the USA. It is estimated that some 70 per cent of global LNG trade is dor under long-term contracting arrangements.[41] Major investments in LNG facilities in son jurisdictions, increasing transport capacities and decreasing transportation costs hav connected markets in distant parts of the world (such as Asia and Australia, and Nort America and Europe), and raised the possibility of arbitrage between these regions – suc as between the Pacific Basin and the Atlantic – which could potentially erode price di ferentials, and create a global market for gas. For example, increased capacity in the LN terminals in northwestern Europe has strengthened the link between European and US. gas hub prices.[42]

10.2 APPROACH TO GAS REGULATION

10.2.1 Activities Subject to Regulation in the Supply Chain

Competitive Activities in the Supply Chain

There are typically two main competitive activities in the natural gas supply chain: th production and sale of wholesale gas, and the retail sale of gas to end-users.

Although the activities associated with exploration for, and production from, natura gas fields often involve high capital costs and significant risks, they are not generall considered to be naturally monopolistic activities. This is because the marginal costs o exploration and extraction tend to rise over time, as the most easily accessible field are discovered and exploited, and it is possible for intense competition to exist in suc

---

[39] Typically, the escalation clause entails that, if the price of oil (or another linked fuel) changes, the gas price will be adjusted by some fraction of that change in the price of oil according to some predefined pass-through factor.

[40] Makholm (2020b) observes that the cost of liquefaction can be twice the cost of production.

[41] Rashad (2022).

[42] The USA was the largest source of LNG to the EU in 2021, accounting for 26 per cent; see EIA (2022d). Timera (2020) discusses the influence of Henry Hub on the LNG market and European hub prices over the past decade, noting that the US market is driving European and LNG pricing dynamics.

activities (in anticipation of the large resource rents that are typically attached to the discovery and exploitation of natural gas reserves). For these reasons, gas production activities are not typically subject to ongoing price regulation in jurisdictions where restructuring policies have been introduced.[43] Rather, competition among producers for the discovery and exploitation of gas fields is seen as being sufficient to address concerns about the exploitation of monopoly power. In the USA, where wellhead price controls were abolished in 1978,[44] there are now some 7000 gas producers, and 483,000 active gas wells. In Canada, where gas production prices were deregulated in 1985, it is estimated that there are hundreds of exploration and production firms. In the UK, wellhead prices for natural gas produced in the UK continental shelf are negotiated between gas producers (mainly large oil companies) and large industrial customers and other shippers. In some parts of continental Europe, competition in production comes from imports using international pipelines from Russia, Algeria and Turkey (e.g. the Nord Stream, TurkStream, Maghreb and Medgaz pipelines) and from LNG sales. As the import supply is dominated by a small number of powerful state-supported firms, such as the Russian firm Gazprom, competition law has sometimes been used to address pricing issues that have arisen with these companies.[45]

Retail gas competition has also been introduced in some restructured jurisdictions. This is because there are limited sunk costs associated with entry (although there is a need to secure supplies with producers), and the main operational costs, which are those associated with marketing and sales to retail customers, are generally of a similar scale to those for the retailing of other household services. Retail competition is also considered to provide scope for innovative tariffs and supply contracts to develop, allowing for different exposures to wholesale gas price changes, and for adjustments for different consumption profiles (peak/off-peak, seasonal, etc.). Full gas retail competition (or customer choice) – whereby households and small users can choose to purchase gas from suppliers other than the incumbent in an area – exists in the UK and EU countries, Japan, some states of Australia, and around twenty-four states in the USA (and the District of Columbia).[46] In some jurisdictions, customers can purchase the gas commodity separately from its transportation; for example, in the USA, some local distribution companies offer both a bundled and an unbundled service. A bundled service involves the customer being charged a single price for gas, which is a combination of the wholesale gas cost and transmission

---

[43] However, in some countries, the upstream production of natural gas is regulated under specific laws, concessions agreements and special operating contracts. In other countries, one-off *ex post* 'windfall taxes' have sometimes been proposed or imposed on gas producers, such as following the high gas price spikes in Europe in 2022. In addition, several jurisdictions (including the EU and Australia) introduced temporary gas wholesale price caps in response to the Russian invasion of Ukraine in 2022.

[44] The imposition of wellhead controls followed the US Supreme Court's decision in *Phillips Petroleum Co. v. Wisconsin* (1954), where it ruled that natural gas producers were subject to regulatory oversight by the Federal Power Commission (FPC). The effect of that decision was that wellhead prices (the prices for natural gas in the inter-state market) were regulated in a similar way to those of transportation companies using a rate of return approach.

[45] See Moselle, Black, White and Piffaut (2012), Riley (2012) and Stern and Yafimava (2017). In 2020, the Polish Competition agency levied the world's largest competition fine (€6.5 billion) on Gazprom. In 2022 there were calls for another European Commission investigation into Gazprom following high gas prices.

[46] See EIA (2022c). However, such choice might only be available to customers of particular suppliers in a state.

and distribution charges. An unbundled service involves the levying of charges only fo
the distribution activities performed, allowing customers to purchase the gas commodit
separately from the transportation charges. In the EU, since 2007, all distribution syster
operators have been required to legally unbundle their distribution activities from thei
retail activities.[47]

Activities Subject to Price Regulation and Other Controls

The main activities typically subject to price and other regulatory controls are gas trans
mission, gas distribution and, in some jurisdictions, gas storage and retail supply.

The rationale for price regulation of gas transmission and distribution network oper
ators is essentially that the cost characteristics of these activities can approximate thos
of a natural monopoly.[48] Gas transmission pipelines are highly capital-intensive to con
struct and involve significant sunk costs, and pipeline capacity costs decrease as th
size of the pipeline (in diameter) increases. The operation of a gas distribution networ
generally also involves large sunk investments in long-lived and immobile capital assets
and this gives rises to cost conditions which approximate that of a natural monopoly
As with electricity distribution, there are important economies of density associated wit
gas distribution networks, and it is generally considered to be inefficient to lay multipl
distribution networks in any one area.

In some jurisdictions, there is considered to be scope for competition among trans
mission pipeline operators, and this has affected the regulatory treatment of pipelines
In particular, in jurisdictions (such as Australia and the USA) where gas transmissio
pipelines tend to be 'point-to-point' – i.e. where most of the gas goes from the sam
origin (a large gas field) to the same destination (a citygate) – there is considered t
be scope for so-called pipeline-to-pipeline competition. In Australia, decisions abou
whether or not individual pipelines should be subject to price regulation (so-calle
'coverage decisions') are made having regard to, among other things, the extent of com
petition between pipelines serving the same area and whether it would be uneconomi
for any other party to develop another pipeline to provide the services.[49] Individua
pipelines can thus be subject to 'full regulation' (where the regulator sets prices), 'ligh
regulation' (where pipeline operators and shippers negotiate in the first instance an
the regulator only arbitrates when disputes arise) and 'no regulation' (where pipeline
set their own price and non-price terms, but are required to disclose certain informa
tion to make negotiations easier). In the USA, the pipeline business has been describe

---

[47] Many EU countries have exempted from these provisions distribution companies who serve fewer than a
certain number of customers (such as 100,000 customers).

[48] Moselle, Black, White and Piffaut (2012) conclude that in many, if not most, situations the economies
of scale are sufficiently high that transmission is likely to be a natural monopoly. In contrast, Makholm
(2007) argues that the 'pipeline business is much more complex and difficult to categorise' and that
major pipelines are 'rather lousy natural monopolies'. Similarly, Makholm (2015) observes: 'The wisdom
of the regulatory changes in U.S. gas markets during the 1990s lay in the recognition that FERC-
regulated interstate pipelines were less natural monopolies than competitive rivals.'

[49] This has sometimes been interpreted such that competition will be potentially sufficient in situations
where there are at least three competing providers, or there is some countervailing buyer power. See
Productivity Commission (2004).

as competitive in many regions, with several competing pipelines serving most destinations.[50] Inter-state pipeline operators can apply to the Federal Energy Regulatory Commission (FERC) for permission to charge 'market-based rates' – meaning that they can, with regulatory approval, set their own tariffs. Applicants must satisfy the FERC that they do not have significant market power, and could not therefore profitably raise prices above competitive levels for a significant period of time. The potential for pipeline-to-pipeline competition has also been considered in other countries (e.g. the Netherlands, Germany and China),[51] but to date it has not been seen as sufficient to remove price regulation.

Notwithstanding competition between pipelines in some jurisdictions, in other countries the scope for competition between transmission and distribution gas network operators is limited or non-existent. This is particularly the case where all pipelines are owned and operated by a regional monopoly (such as in Britain or other European countries). This has led to regulatory policies which regulate prices and quality and require third-party access to pipelines. As discussed in Chapter 6, this raises an issue about how parties involved at other stages of the production chain (such as shippers) gain access to the transmission and distribution networks, and has led to policies requiring gas transmission and distribution networks to provide open access to shippers on non-discriminatory terms and conditions.

The development and operation of gas storage facilities is, in principle, also a potentially competitive activity, insofar as different owners and operators can develop facilities at various locations on a transmission network (such as new LNG regasification terminals). In addition, economies of scale are less significant in gas storage than gas transmission and distribution activities. For these reasons, gas storage is not generally seen as possessing the attributes of a natural monopoly.[52] Notwithstanding this point, concerns about market power has led to the regulation of storage operators in many jurisdictions. This is particularly the case for large or strategically located storage facilities (such as underground storage facilities in depleted fields), which can hold a position of *de facto* monopoly power. If storage facilities are owned and operated by integrated transmission pipeline operators, this can create incentives to withhold storage capacities in favour of associated companies. For these reasons, gas storage facilities (including LNG facilities) can be subject to price regulation and to rules that require the storage owner to provide access to the facility to third parties on non-discriminatory terms. In the USA, the FERC regulates storage facilities that serve inter-state commerce, while state Public Utility Commissions (PUCs) regulate some storage facilities of state-based distribution companies. In the EU, Member States retain the ability to choose between a negotiated or

---

[50] See Von Hirschhausen (2006). Littlechild (2012b) notes that some larger distribution companies are hooked up to as many as seven pipelines, and that each pipeline offers access to a number of different gas producers. O'Neill (2005) describes gas transmission pipelines in the USA as oligopolies rather than monopolies. See also Makholm (2015).

[51] Xu, Hallack and Vazquez (2017) note that the Chinese natural gas pipeline network features both regional monopoly and pipeline-to-pipeline competition.

[52] Moselle, Black, White and Piffaut (2012) conclude that 'storage is unlikely to be a natural monopoly activity except in isolated locations where the size of the market or geological factors imply that very few storage facilities are necessary or possible'.

a regulated third-party access regime for storage.[53] There are also additional requiremen
for gas storage operators aimed at preventing discrimination between access seeker
These include a requirement that storage facilities be legally and functionally separate
(where the storage or LNG operators are vertically integrated) from other activities in th
gas supply chain, as well as specific requirements relating to capacity allocation, tradin
in capacity rights and congestion management at storage facilities.

Finally, retail gas supply is subject to price regulation in some jurisdictions. In the USA
state PUCs regulate the rates for distribution services provided by natural gas distributio
companies (NGDCs)/local distribution companies to end-user customers (even in states whe
retail choice has been introduced). In Europe (including the UK), price regulation is applie
in fourteen countries, with the aim of protecting vulnerable consumers or consumers wh
remain on default or standard tariffs.[54] In addition to price regulation, retail gas suppliers i
most jurisdictions are subject to various other non-price regulatory requirements that estab
lish minimum service standards, and in some competitive markets are directed at facilitatin
more active consumer engagement with the aim of promoting switching.

10.2.2   Form and Scope of Price Regulation for Transmission and Distribution Network

The two general types of regulatory mechanisms for controlling prices discussed i
Chapter 5 – price caps and rate of return regulation – are both used to regulate transmis
sion and distribution pipelines in different parts of the world.

Price Caps

The price cap approach is applied to gas transmission and distribution activities in the Uł
Australia and a majority of EU countries.[55] As described in Chapter 5, this approach typic
ally involves the regulator setting a ceiling on the average increase in prices/revenues tha
the firm can earn for a set of relevant services for a pre-specified, but significant, perio
of time (often five years, but sometimes shorter or longer periods). In some jurisdiction
the form of price control applied in the gas industry is a form of revenue cap, such as a
average revenue cap or a hybrid revenue cap (see the discussion in Chapter 5),[56] althoug
weighted average price caps have also been applied in some countries.[57] In setting the rev
enue requirement under the price cap, the approach adopted in many jurisdictions is base
on variants of the building block approach.

---

[53] The First Gas Directive (98/30/EC) required third-party access to gas storage and LNG facilities on eithe
a regulated or a negotiated basis. The Second Gas Directive retained this option for access to gas storag
(unlike access to gas transmission networks, where the option of negotiated access was removed). In
addition, storage facilities and LNG import terminals were given an ability to apply for an exemption
from being required to provide access to third parties on certain grounds. This exemption possibility als
applies to gas interconnectors between EU Member States.

[54] ACER/CEER (2021a). In addition, some countries (such as Germany) introduced a temporary 'price break
in 2022 to cap retail gas prices for households and small consumers in response to high wholesale gas
prices following Russia's invasion of Ukraine.

[55] In Europe, nineteen countries used revenue/price caps for gas transmission and twenty-two countries
used it for gas distribution in 2021.

[56] In Europe, of the nineteen countries that apply incentive regulation to distribution, seventeen use
revenue caps and two use price caps. For electricity transmission, revenue caps are used in seventeen
countries and price caps in five countries.

[57] For example, in relation to gas transmission in Britain and gas distribution in Australia and New Zealan

As in electricity transportation, price cap arrangements for gas transmission and distribution companies can incorporate specific incentive mechanisms within the general price control arrangements. These include: efficiency carry-over mechanisms (which allow the regulated firm to retain a share of any efficiency benefit for a set period of time); error correction mechanisms (which adjust for the under- or over-recovery of revenue on an *ex post* basis); and investment-specific incentives, such as those to encourage investment in interconnector or storage capacity. Other examples of incentives used in some jurisdictions include measures to: encourage the integration of renewable gas/biogas; roll out smart metering; or reward firms for high levels of customer satisfaction or innovation. In many jurisdictions, certain pre-specified cost items can be fully, or partially, 'passed through' to final prices. These can include the costs of shrinkage of gas (i.e. gas lost in transportation), some safety-related costs and licence rates. Regulators are increasingly using efficiency benchmarking studies in applying the price cap approach to inform the determination of future potential efficiency gains.[58] For example, benchmarking studies of the efficiency of gas distribution companies (often based on international comparisons) have been submitted to regulators in Australia, Canada (Ontario), Ireland and New Zealand.[59] In Germany, where there are a large number of transmission and gas distribution companies, cost efficiency benchmarking is used to set the revenue caps and costs that are deemed 'inefficient' and cannot be recovered through tariffs.[60]

Quality of service issues tend to be different in gas than in electricity, in that disruptions to gas service are typically more infrequent, and localised, and there is a far greater concern with safety issues associated with gas leaks. Requirements to provide a high-quality supply service are therefore, in many cases, addressed through relevant health and safety requirements on gas transportation operators. Nevertheless, some jurisdictions have introduced specific financial incentives into their price cap arrangements to reward companies for providing particular service levels to users of the network. In addition, firms can be subject to financial penalties (e.g. requirements to make payments to customers) if certain pre-specified levels of service (in terms of interruptions to supply, etc.) are not met.

Rate of Return

Rate of return regulation is a common approach to the regulation of gas transmission and distribution network companies in North America and in a small number of European countries.[61] As explained in Chapter 5, under this type of approach, the regulated rates for natural gas transportation are those that are 'just and reasonable' and a regulated utility will recover all of the prudent costs associated with supplying the services. These costs include an allowable rate of return on a regulated rate base (a 'fair rate of return'), as well as operating costs, depreciation and taxes. Rate setting begins with a rate case, where the

---

[58] See CEER (2019).

[59] Jamasb, Pollitt and Triebs (2008) argue that international benchmarking of gas transmission companies can have an important role to play in pricing, and companies in the USA in particular can provide an important benchmark by which to assess the efficiency of transmission companies in other countries.

[60] See Waidelich, Haug and Wieshammer (2022) and WIK (2011).

[61] This includes Estonia, Latvia and Poland.

regulator approves the maximum rates that can be charged for transportation service
by gas transmission and distribution companies, as well as other terms and conditions.
Regulated companies (or the regulator) can initiate a rate case when they are concerned
that regulated rates deviate from underlying costs, and that rates are either too high or
too low. As has occurred in the electricity industry, various adaptions to the standard rate
of return approach have been applied in the gas sector in some states in the USA. These
include rate freezes, cost and revenue trackers, multi-year price and revenue caps, formula rate plans and earnings sharing mechanisms.[62] However, as described in Box 10.1,
'negotiated settlements' or stipulations are often used in North America as an alternative
to the traditional rate making approach in the gas industry.

Box 10.1	**Negotiated settlements in the North American gas industry**

In Chapter 3 it was noted that negotiated agreements or settlements offer an alternative to
traditional forms of price regulation. This approach is particularly prevalent for the interstate gas pipeline industry in the USA,[63] with an estimated 90 per cent of the rate cases
being settled by participants rather than being subject to the formal rate hearing process.[64]
Participants in these settlements vary but include customers (mainly large distribution companies), state PUCs (who represent final users) and occasionally other parties such as rival
pipelines and future or potential customers. While the FERC acknowledges that most of
the settlement agreements are 'black box' settlements that do not provide detailed cost-of-
service information, it will approve an uncontested settlement offer upon finding that 'the
settlement appears to be fair and reasonable and in the public interest'.[65]

The process typically begins with the regulated pipeline making an initial filing setting
out its calculations in relation to rates and total revenue (which are made according to the
conventional rate of return approach).[66] FERC trial staff then play an active role in seeking to facilitate agreement, and undertake bilateral and multilateral discussions. They also
prepare an initial analysis of the company's rate proposal, which is sometimes referred to
as the 'first settlement offer'. If, after the process of negotiation, a unanimous agreement
is reached between the parties, a decision will typically state that the agreement must be
accepted as a whole. However, if unanimous agreement cannot be reached, the possibility
exists for consenting parties to the settlement to be bound by the rates and other terms in
the agreement, and non-consenting parties to be excluded from its terms and subject to the
standard full rate-making process.[67]

---

[62] See Costello (2010).

[63] Negotiated settlements are also a feature, to varying degrees, across individual states in the USA.
According to Littlechild (2012b), while settlements may be a more common outcome now than formal
regulatory hearings at the US state level, the proportion of cases settled at the state level is not close to
the number settled by the FERC. Littlechild conjectures that one reason for this is that rate increases at
the state level impact directly on final consumers, and hence are more political.

[64] The framework and process by which negotiated settlements operate at the FERC is described in detail in
Wang (2004) and Littlechild (2012b).

[65] FERC (2018).

[66] See Littlechild (2012b).

[67] Littlechild (2012b) notes, however, that non-unanimous settlements have been abnormal for gas pipeline
cases. In some US states, however, there is no possibility for severing (or dividing) a settlement in this
way, which is seen to give individual parties greater power to 'hold out' in negotiations.

The negotiated agreement approach has also been adopted in Canada since the mid-1980s for major gas pipelines.[68] In many cases, these negotiated agreements are 'full' settlements, but in other cases they are partial settlements, which leave certain issues to be decided by the regulator. Since the mid-1990s almost all major pipelines in Canada have come to settlements with users, and this is seen to have cut regulatory processing times by about one-third.[69] An important design issue has been whether, in reviewing any negotiated agreement, the regulator considers the settlement in its entirety, or whether it considers the various components that make up the package. In Canada, the regulator originally took the approach of determining whether each parameter of a settlement, taken separately, was 'just and reasonable'. However, this was seen to have discouraged settlements, and its approach is now either to accept or to reject a settlement in its entirety.[70] If a settlement is not contested, then the regulator will generally conclude that the rates (tolls) are just and reasonable without a public hearing (however, a public hearing will be held if it raises public interest considerations). The regulator can also approve a settlement in circumstances where the pipeline operator has not been able to gain the agreement of all shippers.

Regulation of Rate Structures

In addition to setting the overall level of allowed revenues, regulators can also play a role in determining the *structure* of gas transportation charges. There are typically two aspects to this: (1) decisions about the basis on which capacity prices are levied (e.g. distance or flat rate); and (2) decisions about the relative split between capacity and commodity charges.

There are two general methods for setting the capacity charge element of gas transportation pipelines: the 'postage stamp' method; and the 'distance-based' method. Under the 'postage stamp' method, the transportation charge is the same at all entry points and all exit points throughout a region/country,[71] and is independent of the distance travelled. The 'postage stamp' approach is sometimes seen as politically favourable, but does not provide any locational signals and results in prices for transportation that are not cost-reflective.[72] An alternative approach is the 'point-to-point' (or distance) charging method where the transportation charge is calculated as a proportion of the distance between the injection and withdrawal points on a network. A shipper effectively purchases a right to inject gas at a specific entry point and to withdraw it at another point. This approach is generally considered most appropriate where transmission pipelines are 'point-to-point'

---

[68] See CER (2022). Negotiated settlements have also been used by some provincial regulatory bodies in Canada, most notably the Alberta Energy and Utilities Board.

[69] See Doucet and Littlechild (2009).

[70] This is subject to the settlement not being illegal or contrary to the public interest; see NEB (2002). A 1994 revision to the settlement guidelines is seen as particularly important in shifting the approach of the regulator from assessing the *outcome* of a settlement towards assessing a settlement based on whether or not the *process* by which it was reached was reasonable. See Doucet and Littlechild (2009).

[71] Although the split of charges between entry and exit points can differ. For example, 100 per cent of costs are allocated to exit points in Sweden, while in Lithuania 73 per cent of costs are allocated to entry points. See ACER (2020).

[72] This approach is used as the reference price methodology in Croatia, Denmark, Estonia, Germany, Hungary, Lithuania, Northern Ireland, the Netherlands, Poland, Romania, Slovakia and Sweden and for some US pipelines, such as Northwest Pipeline, Colorado Interstate Gas and Columbia Gas Transmission. See ACER (2020).

(most of the gas goes from the same origin (a large gas field) to the same destination (a citygate)) rather than closely interconnected or meshed networks (where the movement of gas on a transportation network does not coincide as closely with distance). The capacity arrangements in the USA – which are predominantly based around a point-to-point charging approach – reflect the fact that its numerous merchant pipeline operators build and operate transmission pipelines (compared with a situation where a single firm operates and invests in network capacity).

A separate issue to the setting of the capacity charge is the allocation of costs, as between the capacity (access) charge and the commodity (usage) charge (i.e. the charge for the volumes of gas transported through the system).[73] As discussed above, the majority of costs for gas transportation are fixed in nature (relating to sunk investments in pipeline capacity), while the variable costs associated with the transportation of gas volumes are relatively minor. The relative split between the capacity charge and the commodity charge has implications for how fixed and variable costs are recovered by the pipeline operator, and the relative burden of such cost recovery across different users, which raises distributional issues. For example, charging structures which allocate 100 per cent of fixed costs to capacity charges are seen to benefit high-load users (such as large industrial customers), and to disadvantage more seasonal or intermittent low-load users (such as residential consumers).[74] In the USA, at the federal level, regulation mandates that transmission tariffs be calculated according to a particular formula, such that 100 per cent of fixed costs must be allocated to any capacity charge, and that all variable costs are recovered through a commodity or usage fee.[75] In Europe, several countries allocate 100 per cent of fixed transmission costs to a capacity charge,[76] while in other countries the split between capacity charges and commodity charges ranges from 70/30 per cent to 95/5 per cent.[77]

10.2.3 Price Regulation of Storage

Price regulation is also applied to storage facility operators in many jurisdictions. In the USA, at the federal level, many storage facility operators (particularly those operated by pipeline operators) are required to make capacity available to shippers and other parties. Storage facilities operated by pipelines are typically subject to rate of return regulation

---

[73] Cremer and Laffont (2002) describe a two-part pricing system, where there are separate charges for reserved capacity (and where capacity rights can be traded in a secondary market) and for volumes transported, as potentially being able to achieve 'optimal prices' in a decentralised manner.

[74] Conversely, the allocation of some fixed costs to usage (commodity) charges is seen to allocate a proportionally larger amount of costs to high-load customers, and a lower proportion of network costs to low-load customers.

[75] FERC Order 636 (1992). Known as the 'straight-fixed variable' method. This replaced the 'modified-fixed variable' approach that involved recovering 87 per cent of fixed costs through the capacity charge, and 13 per cent through a volume charge. This shift was, however, not without controversy and was opposed by consumer groups and local distribution companies on the basis that it would increase costs for low-load factor customers.

[76] Such as Austria, Bulgaria, Croatia, Czech Republic, Denmark, Estonia, Finland, France, Germany, Greece, Latvia, Luxembourg, the Netherlands, Poland, Portugal, Slovakia, Slovenia and Sweden.

[77] See ACER (2020).

Non-pipeline operators of storage services can be priced on a traditional rate of return basis or, subject to FERC approval, at market rates.[78]

In Europe, there is a right of third-party access to storage facilities that are technically and/or economically necessary for the supply of customers.[79] However, EU Member States retain the ability to choose between a negotiated or regulated third-party access regime for storage. This decision is informed by, among other things: the extent of competition between storage facilities; barriers to entry into storage; the extent to which storage capacity is booked over the long term; and the number of shippers that have access to the storage facilities (i.e. degree of buyer concentration).[80] Under regulated third-party access, the regulator sets the conditions for access to the storage facility, while under the negotiated access regime, the owner of the storage facility sets access charges and products offered freely in consultation with users, and the regulator does not have the power to review tariffs (although they maintain oversight). EU Member States also have discretion to determine how storage capacity is allocated, and auctions are sometimes used, with any difference between the auction revenues and the allowed revenues (which covers the storage facilities costs) being addressed through a compensation mechanism.[81]

An important policy question is whether LNG storage assets, such as regasification facilities, should be classified as transportation or storage activities (and therefore be required to provide open access to third parties), or as a form of production (and therefore not subject to third-party open-access requirements). Different positions on this debate are adopted in the USA and Europe. In the USA, LNG facilities are now treated as a supply source, rather than as part of the transportation chain, and are no longer subject to open-access provisions. In Europe, LNG facilities used for storage (but not production) can be subject to third-party open-access requirements. However, the possibility exists for LNG import terminals to apply for an exemption from requirements to provide access to third parties.[82]

10.2.4 Retail Price Regulation

While, as described in Section 10.3.1, retail price controls have been withdrawn in some jurisdictions that have restructured their gas markets, in many other jurisdictions, retail gas prices remain subject to some form of price control or oversight. In the USA, retail

---

[78] Under the Energy Policy Act 2005, storage operators no longer need to demonstrate the absence of market power to charge market rates for new storage capacity. However, to make an authorisation, the FERC must determine that market-based rates are in the public interest and are necessary to encourage the construction of the capacity and that customers are adequately protected. The FERC must periodically review the market-based rates authorised to ensure they remain just, reasonable and not unduly discriminatory or preferential.

[79] Although, even for these facilities, access to storage facilities can be refused if there is a lack of capacity, or because of public service obligations. However, a number of conditions must be met if the refusal is based on a lack of capacity, including requirements to establish this in an objective, transparent and non-discriminatory way. Major new gas storage facilities can also request an exemption from third-party access on the grounds that (amongst other requirements) without it the facility is unlikely to be built. CEER (2017) provides additional background.

[80] EC (2010). In the UK, a significant market power test is applied when determining if prices should be regulated.

[81] See ACER (2020).

[82] Article 36 of Third Gas Directive, and Article 22 of the Second Gas Directive.

prices set by local distribution companies are typically regulated by state PUCs using a rate of return approach. In Europe, fourteen countries continue to apply some form of price controls to gas household retail services (four countries also apply it for non-household customers). In Spain, regulated retail gas prices are set on the basis of a rate of return approach, with a cap that includes a profit margin for the supplier.[83] In Britain, retail gas price caps were re-introduced in 2019 and apply to consumers who are on default tariffs.

10.3 THE SCOPE AND EFFECTS OF RESTRUCTURING POLICIES

10.3.1 The Scope of Restructuring Policies in the Gas Industry

Prior to the restructuring policies introduced in the 1980s, the gas supply chain was typically subject to tight regulatory controls from the production stage to the local distribution of gas to consumers. There were also high levels of vertical integration, and in some countries a single state-owned entity was involved in all stages of the supply chain from upstream exploration, to transportation, storage and supply to consumers.

The restructuring policies introduced since the 1980s and 1990s reflect the specifics of the production and supply of gas in each jurisdiction (particularly the extent of indigenous gas reserves) and other objectives (such as the interconnection of markets). However, in broad terms, a 'standard gas restructuring' model has sometimes involved one or more of the following elements: (1) corporatisation, commercialisation or privatisation of state-owned entities; (2) establishment of independent regulatory agencies; (3) vertical restructuring of the industry, particularly the separation of transportation from other 'upstream' and 'downstream' activities; (4) the ability for shippers to gain open and non-discriminatory access to transportation capacity, including through primary and secondary markets; (5) the introduction of competitive gas wholesale spot markets and financial markets to allow participants to better manage price volatility; (6) a shift away from long-term contracts towards more flexible short-term trading arrangements; and (7) in some cases, the introduction of retail competition for both household and non-household customers.[84]

Scope of Restructuring in the USA

In the USA, where the majority of firms involved in the production and supply of natural gas were already under private ownership and subject to independent economic regulation, an important trigger for restructuring was the natural gas shortages of the 1970s which were seen, in part, to emanate from wellhead price regulation.[85] Policies introduced in 1978 to partially deregulate wellhead prices led to further pressures, in the early 1980s from large industrial customers, who started switching to alternative forms of energy in response to subsequent increases in natural gas prices.[86]

---

[83] See ACER/CEER (2021a).
[84] Beato and Fuente (2000) set out other attributes of a competitive model in gas.
[85] See Pierce (1994) and Sickles and Streitwieser (1998).
[86] Sickles and Streitwieser (1998) note that natural gas prices increased by 218 per cent to 1985.

In contrast to the electricity industry, where restructuring policies have often depended on state-level implementation, the principal reforms of the natural gas sector have occurred at the federal level.[87] Federal policies introduced from the mid-1980s allowed customers to purchase gas directly at the wellhead, and to separately pay for transportation on the transmission network. These policies also provided for non-discriminatory access to inter-state gas transmission pipelines on a first-come, first-served basis (so-called open access), and set bounds on minimum and maximum transportation rates that could be levied.[88] In addition, inter-state pipeline companies were required to separate their production and sales activities from their transportation and storage activities.[89] As a consequence, shippers have open access to pipeline facilities and storage facilities on the same terms as any affiliated division of the pipeline company, which is seen as an important step in the development of a competitive gas market in the USA.

The FERC must approve rates charged for use of inter-state pipelines, and also has a role in terms of the approval of siting and abandonment decisions for such pipelines which have been used to interconnect separate markets. This can limit pipeline market power by easing bottlenecks on the transmission network and is seen as having been critical in the transition to a competitive gas market. At the state level, state PUCs regulate *intra*-state gas transmission pipelines and distribution networks. Twenty-four states in the USA (and the District of Columbia) have introduced customer choice programmes, and in some states industrial and residential customers can choose a supplier and purchase the natural gas commodity separately from gas transportation and delivery services.

Scope of Restructuring in Britain and Europe

The process of restructuring in Britain began with the privatisation of British Gas in the mid-1980s.[90] However, British Gas was privatised as a vertically integrated entity; it owned and operated the transmission, distribution, storage and retail supply activities as well as having a series of long-term contracts with North Sea gas producers. Although policies to allow third-party access to the gas transmission network were first introduced in 1982, no access was obtained, and the incumbent operator (British Gas Corporation) was potentially able to use access charges to foreclose competition. As a result of this structure, entry into the gas market was stifled until the vertical separation of British Gas.[91] A network code was introduced to provide a multilateral contractual framework agreement that defined the rules and obligations regarding third-party access to the gas transmission system, and subsequent developments included the introduction of the so-called 'new gas trading arrangements' in the late 1990s.[92]

---

[87] Doane and Spulber (1994), Newbery (1999), O'Neill (2005) and Makholm (2006) present summaries of US regulatory history in the gas industry.

[88] This was instituted by various orders of the FERC, including Order 436 (1985).

[89] FERC Order 636 (1992).

[90] See Newbery (1999, chapter 8) and Stern (2004) for a summary of gas industry development in Britain.

[91] Separate transportation and storage divisions were created in 1994, and tariffs were published for access to the transportation facilities (which also applied to its own trading affiliate). The restructuring of British Gas followed in 1997, which involved the separation of the retail supply activities from the transportation activities, and this led to the de-merger of the retail activities into a separate company from the transmission and storage activities.

[92] See Yarrow (2000) for a description.

In EU Member States, the restructuring process in most countries has largely bee
prompted by a series of EU Gas Directives. The first EU Gas Directive in 1998 laid dow
common rules for the transmission, distribution, supply and storage of natural gas acros
Member States, and among other things required third-party access to transmission pipe
lines and distribution networks and to gas storage and LNG facilities.[93] This Directiv
allowed Member States to choose between two forms of access arrangements: negotiate
third-party access (where customers could negotiate voluntary commercial access agree
ments in 'good faith' within a certain commercial framework), or regulated third-part
access (where gas transportation companies were required to publish tariffs and othe
terms of access). A second EU Gas Directive, effective from 2003, removed the choic
between the two forms of access arrangements, and required third-party access to ga
transmission and distribution networks to be based on regulated access tariffs, approve
by a relevant regulatory authority, and published prior to their entry into force. In add
ition, transmission and distribution activities were required to be legally separated i
circumstances where they were vertically integrated.[94] There was also a requirement t
establish an independent regulatory authority.

Despite these EU Directives requiring legal and functional separation of transmis
sion and distribution activities from other activities in the gas supply chain, subsequen
reviews found that new entrants often lacked effective access to networks and vert
cally integrated incumbents were suspected of favouring their own affiliates.[95] A thir
EU Gas Directive, approved in 2009, required further reforms, including the unbunc
ling of transmission systems and system operator functions, and that Member State
adopt one of three specified forms of separation of transmission network operations fro
other production and supply activities.[96] The Directive also established a body responsibl
for formalising cooperation among transmission operators in different Member State
(European Network of Transmission System Operators for Gas (ENTSOG)), and for deve
oping network codes governing access to, and use of, European gas networks.[97] The ne
work codes were later given the force of law as Regulations.[98] Building on these polic
changes, national gas regulators in the EU set out a vision for a single competitive EU ga
wholesale market (known as the 'Gas Target Model') which included the development c
functioning wholesale markets with liquid trading hubs, the development of cross-bord
interconnections, and measures to improve supply security and encourage investment.

---

[93] See Directive 98/30/EC.
[94] See Directive 2003/55/EC.
[95] See European Commission's 2007 Energy Sector Inquiry (EC, 2007c).
[96] Under the Directive, Member States can choose from three 'separation options' including: that network ownership is unbundled; that an independent system operator be created, responsible for the operation of the transmission network; or that an independent transmission operator be established, which require integrated transmission and supply companies to set and abide by certain rules to ensure that the production and retail supply activities are conducted independently from transmission activities. In its initial proposals the European Commission had required the full structural separation of ownership and operation of the transmission activities from that of production and supply.
[97] This includes codes relating to capacity allocation and congestion management, balancing rules, interoperability, network security and reliability, network connections, transparency rules, etc.
[98] See EU Regulations 312/2014, 2015/703, 2017/459 and 2017/460 dealing, respectively, with: gas balancing on transmission networks; interoperability and data exchange rules; capacity allocation mechanisms; and harmonised transmission tariffs.
[99] See Ascari (2011), CEER (2011) and Yafimava (2013).

Retail choice was introduced for all customers (including household and non-household customers) in EU Member States from July 2007,[100] and national regulatory authorities in each EU Member State are responsible for retail gas regulation.

Looking ahead, it has been claimed that the focus of regulatory policy for natural gas will evolve from 'market integration, competition and security of supply towards sustainability'.[101] In December 2021, the European Commission released a fourth set of proposed changes to the gas market as part of its Hydrogen and Gas Package (see discussion in Section 10.4.3).

Scope of Restructuring Policies in Other Jurisdictions

Elsewhere in the world, policies directed at the restructuring of the gas production and supply structure were introduced in a number of other countries during the 1990s, including Argentina, Australia, Canada, Chile, Colombia, Mexico and New Zealand. While each country has different natural reserves of gas, as well as different institutional and industry structures, a number of common principles of gas regulation can be observed in these countries. These include: privatisation or corporatisation of state-owned entities;[102] allowing non-discriminatory access to transmission pipelines and storage facilities; the separation of transport and storage activities from merchant gas activities; policies to create 'trading hubs'; mechanisms to allow for secondary trading in transport and storage capacity; and measures to improve market transparency in terms of information about supply, demand, capacities and prices.[103] Policies to open retail markets to competition have also been introduced in some countries.

0.3.2 The Effects of Restructuring Policies in the Gas Industry

Although less attention has been paid to the effects of the restructuring of the gas industry than other industries, such as electricity or telecommunications, the overall assessment of the impact of such policies is in some cases generally a positive one, particularly in North America.[104]

Effects of Restructuring in North America

In the USA, while the transition to a competitive market structure has not always been smooth,[105] the general assessment is that the restructuring policies have resulted in a competitive wholesale gas market, where gas prices in the spot market and futures market are determined through the interaction of many buyers and sellers at numerous trading hubs located across the country. Long-term contracts, which were a significant feature of the

---

[100] See Directive 2003/55/EC.
[101] EC (2020a).
[102] As in Argentina and Australia.
[103] See IEA (2000).
[104] See Joskow (2009).
[105] In particular, there were well-documented issues associated with 'take-or-pay' contracts signed in the late 1970s and early 1980s, which were left stranded by the reforms. Pierce (1994) notes that pipelines and producers spent millions of dollars litigating thousands of contract disputes during the 1980s, and that, in retrospect, the FERC underestimated the potential significance of transition costs. See also Doane and Spulber (1994).

trading arrangements up until the 1980s, now play a less prominent role and have been replaced by shorter-term trading at market hubs. This flexibility in wholesale trading arrangements has been argued to facilitate continued supply security even in the face of sudden shocks to demand and supply, such as the California Energy crisis of 2000–2001 and the impact of Hurricanes Katrina and Rita in 2005 (which resulted in Henry Hub shutting down).[106]

The overall result of restructuring is one that has been described as combining 'vigorous gas supply competition' with a tightly regulated pipeline system based on 'transparent, meticulous, and reliable federal gas pipeline tariff and access regulation'.[107] This was not always the case, and early studies on the impacts of restructuring found a significant decline in productivity for the pipeline companies in the first eight years following wellhead price deregulation (which is attributed to the decline in consumption), and that open-access policies achieved only a small reduction in transmission costs and a small increase in firm efficiency.[108] However, the efficiency of pipeline and distribution companies improved from the mid-1980s, particularly via increased labour productivity and reductions in operating and maintenance expenses.[109]

It is difficult to assess the impacts in terms of restructuring on wholesale and retail prices because, unlike electricity, gas trading is based on non-transparent OTC trades and exchange-based standardised contracts and lacks transparency.[110] However, some estimate that the decoupling of gas and oil prices has directly saved consumers in the USA about $1.132 trillion over the decade 2009 to 2019.[111] Given its close connection to the USA, the restructuring of the natural gas market in Canada is also seen to have led to an efficient and competitive market, with a high degree of supply security.[112] However, over the last decade, regulation has had to respond to the effects of greater competition from

---

[106] See Makholm (2007).

[107] Makholm (2021b) describes the US natural gas system as: 'a veritable institutional masterpiece in joining regulation and competition', while Makholm (2007) goes so far as to observe that: '[I]t is not a ridiculous overstatement to call the regulation of American gas pipelines the Stradivarius of inland transport regulation schemes pertaining to pipelines.' He cites the following reasons for this assessment: 'The use of the network is freely competitive with a robust secondary market in capacity rights. New capacity is independent and competitively constructed and relatively easy to license and finance on the basis of long-term capacity contracts with shippers. Those pipeline users in areas served only by one or two pipeline companies are protected from price gouging or denial of availability by traditional cost-based regulation. While those rate cases were once hugely contentious they are now largely perfunctory. Long term gas commodity contracts – once typical – have evaporated on the network, with most gas traded through predictable and reliable physical hubs and established markets.'

[108] See Sickles and Streitwieser (1998) and Granderson (2000). Makholm (2015) notes that 'this competitive yet-regulated setting evolved over decades of trial and error and has come at considerable social cost in terms of shortages, surpluses and "stranded" capital costs'.

[109] See Costello and Duann (1996). Using data on gas transmission companies in the USA from 1996 to 2004 Jamasb, Pollitt and Triebs (2008) find modest improvements in technical efficiency, and some evidence of convergence in terms of the relative performance of firms. More generally, Arano and Blair (2008) conclude that the restructuring of the gas industry in the USA has made the industry more responsive to market conditions, had a positive impact on demand and supply, and resulted in welfare gains.

[110] See Bushnell (2021).

[111] See Makholm (2020b, 2021b). In addition, it is estimated that electricity consumers also indirectly saved some $375 billion during the same period through lower gas prices used for electricity generation.

[112] See IEA (2009).

shale gas in the USA, which has displaced domestic supplies from the west of Canada (Alberta) to the eastern provinces (Ontario and Quebec).[113]

Effects of Restructuring in Britain and Europe

In Britain, although competition did not effectively develop until the late 1990s, a competitive and liquid wholesale gas market has since developed, which now has the second highest level of trading activity in Europe. In addition, diverse gas supplies now serve Britain, including gas from the UK continental shelf, Norway and continental Europe via interconnectors, and LNG from various countries. There has also been considerable merchant investment in capacity, including in interconnector capacity (such as the Langeled pipeline connecting Norwegian natural gas directly to Britain), and in new LNG facilities. Some studies have found that productivity increased following the privatisation of British Gas and, separately, that industrial prices fell across Europe as a result of gas market restructuring.[114] However, these restructuring policies have not necessarily led to lower retail prices for all users; since 2008, gas retail household prices increased (in nominal terms) by 21 per cent.[115] While retail price regulation of gas was removed in 2002, only a few years after the introduction of competition, an energy price cap for consumers on standard gas tariff contracts was re-introduced in 2019 and now covers the highest number of households in Europe.[116] Finally, Britain has relatively high (by international standards) levels of gas switching – estimated at 37 per cent in the early 2000s and 18 per cent in 2020.[117]

The introduction of restructuring policies in EU Member States has generally been more gradual and challenging,[118] particularly up until the introduction of the third energy package in 2012.[119] However, over the past decade, a more competitive wholesale market appears to have emerged, particularly in northwest Europe. Wholesale gas markets are now generally more liquid, and a degree of price convergence has developed across an area covering three-quarters of EU gas consumption.[120] This is in part attributed to: the development of major interconnectors; the establishment of liquid regional gas trading hubs; a lower reliance on oil-linked contracts; and the installation of new LNG capacity in some countries. However, specific regulatory policies have also been important, such as: the use of auctions to allocate capacity, which allows shippers to gain non-discriminatory access to transmission networks in other countries; the introduction of a 'use it or

---

[113] Makholm (2015) discusses how the regulator has responded to these developments by signalling to the main pipeline operator (TransCanada) that it will not be protected from such competition.

[114] Pollitt (2012).

[115] Calculations based on Eurostat, Band D2: 20–200 GJ (household gas consumption). This includes taxes and levies. The increase excluding taxes and levies is 14 per cent.

[116] ACER/CEER (2021a). Chapter 7 discusses the background to this change.

[117] See Ofgem (2002) and ACER/CEER (2021a).

[118] Newbery (1999) details early objections of those resisting reform to continental European gas markets.

[119] Recurring problems included: high levels of market concentration, with incumbent operators able to control gas imports and production; illiquid wholesale markets and low levels of trading at hubs, which meant that entrants in the retail market were often dependent on incumbents for gas supply; and finally that, despite provisions relating to (non-discriminatory) third-party access to networks, pipeline operators had often favoured their own affiliates. See EC's 2007 Sector Inquiry (EC, 2007c).

[120] ACER/CEER (2021b).

lose it rule' to prevent capacity hoarding by incumbents; requirements that pipelines are bidirectional and offer reverse flow capacity, which allows gas to be sent in both direc- tions; and the effects of the harmonised gas network codes on capacity allocation and management and transmission tariffs.[121]

There are, however, four areas where further progress is widely seen as needed. First, there are persistent differences between gas wholesale prices in northwestern Europe and those in central and southeastern European countries, which is, in part, attributed to the lack of liquid and established hubs in those regions.[122] Second, while there has been a gradual movement away from long-term contracts, they still remain common, and this has led to a proposal to ban them from 2049. Third, there are continuing concerns about security of gas supply, which, as discussed below, are shaped by three factors: reduced indigenous conventional gas production from fields in the UK and the Netherlands; decisions by some EU Member States not to explore non-conventional gas reserves; and a heavy reliance on the unstable supply from Russia (which came to the fore with the Russian invasion of Ukraine in 2022). Finally, restructuring has led to greater wholesale price volatility and thus consumer expos- ure to high price spikes. For example, in 2021/22 EU gas hub prices experienced both historical lows (in the spring and summer of 2021) and historical highs (in the winter of 2022).[123] This has led to political calls for intervention to smooth retail prices and make them more stable.

In terms of retail gas market competition, there are now an average of thirty-five active nationwide gas retailers in each EU Member State. However, market concentra- tion, particularly for the household market, is high in most European countries, with only three countries displaying low levels of concentration for household suppliers on standard measures.[124] While there are high to modest levels of retail customer switch- ing in some countries – such as in Belgium (25 per cent) and the Netherlands (19 per cent) – in other countries the level of retail customer switching is low; for example, less than 10 per cent of households switched supplier in twelve EU Member States in 2020.[125] Many consumers remain on default contracts or are considered to be vul- nerable, which has led to the continuing use of retail gas price regulation in many EU Member States.[126] In fact, only eleven EU countries had no price intervention in 2020,[127] despite the fact that EU-wide policy seeks the withdrawal of price regulation for retail gas markets. Restructuring and the emergence of a more competitive whole- sale market emerging in some parts of Europe has not necessarily led to lower retail

---

[121] ACER/CEER (2021b). See also Stern (2018) and Barnes (2018).
[122] ACER/CEER (2021b) estimate that consumers in central and southeastern Europe could save €3 billion if they sourced gas at the hub prices in northwestern Europe.
[123] ACER/CEER (2021b).
[124] Such as the Herfindahl–Hirschman index (HHI). See ACER/CEER (2021a).
[125] ACER/CEER (2021a).
[126] In 2020, the proportion of households with prices set by regulatory intervention was 100 per cent in Poland, Hungary, Bulgaria and Lithuania, 97 per cent in Latvia, 60 per cent in Britain, 39 per cent in Italy and 31 per cent in France.
[127] This includes price regulation for all consumers or price regulation for vulnerable consumers; see ACER/ CEER (2021a).

electricity prices.[128] Over the decade from 2010 to 2020, the average final gas price for household consumers increased by 14.41 per cent (in nominal terms), but decreased by 30.6 per cent for industrial consumers.[129]

Effects of Restructuring Policies in Other Jurisdictions

Much less has been written on the impacts of restructuring of the natural gas industry in countries outside Europe and the USA. Over the past decade, Australia has become a major exporter of LNG to Asia, and around 70 per cent of gas produced in eastern Australia is exported.[130] This has led to domestic gas prices being more closely aligned with international prices, and has also impacted on electricity prices creating 'winners and losers'.[131] Up until the mid-2010s, restructuring was seen as having fostered a secure and competitive gas industry and to have increased the penetration of natural gas in the energy mix.[132] However, a 2016 review found that gas transmission pipelines were using market power to 'engage in monopoly pricing' and that some pipelines were charging high prices for access to secondary capacity and that there was a need to promote competition at gas hubs.[133] Various changes have since been made, including the introduction of capacity trading platforms, and requirements that unused capacity is offered at a mandatory day-ahead auction. While there are still concerns about a divide in spot gas prices between northern states (which predominantly export) and southern states, allowing shippers access to pipeline capacity in day-ahead markets (often at no cost) is seen to narrow the gap by allowing shippers to sell northern gas to southern markets at more competitive prices. Recent years have also seen a shift towards shorter-term contracts (one or two years) with review provisions.[134] In terms of retail competition, gas markets are more concentrated than electricity markets and in some states three suppliers account for around 90 per cent of customers. However, unlike for electricity, retailers set their own standing offer gas prices, which are not regulated.[135] Finally, as in other jurisdictions, there has been significant gas price volatility since 2017, reflecting changes in input costs, and gas prices remain high by historical standards.

Another jurisdiction where substantial restructuring of the gas industry was implemented is Argentina. Despite being an early adopter of policies in the 1990s,[136] since that time policies have at times been described as 'going backwards'. Although Argentina is

---

[128] Herweg, Wurster and Dümig (2018) conclude that, while restructuring was successful in liberalising the sector, it did not affect natural gas prices, which they describe as a '"successful failure" of the European natural gas market reforms'. Other studies have found that end-user prices were not lower as a result of the ownership separation of the industry, and that privatisation had led to higher prices. See Growitsch and Stronzik (2014) and Brandão, Pinho, Resende, *et al.* (2016).

[129] ACER/CEER (2021a). This, of course, does not mean that the market is not competitive, but, rather, it means that it is more responsive to wholesale price changes. It could also reflect various taxes and other costs included in the retail gas bill.

[130] See Productivity Commission (2015) and AER (2021).

[131] ACCC (2016). However, in 2022 a temporary price cap was introduced for gas sold by east coast producers to wholesale customers in Australia. This effectively decoupled the domestic price of gas from the wholesale prices on the international market.

[132] See IEA (2012).

[133] ACCC (2016).

[134] See AER (2021).

[135] AER (2021).

[136] See Delfino and Casarin (2003), Honoré (2004), Makholm (2020a) and Carnicer and Gomes (2021).

the largest gas market in South America (natural gas accounts for around 58 per cent of primary energy supply) and has a comprehensive gas infrastructure network, for the last decade it has largely relied on imports of LNG.[137] Since 2015 incentives have been used to encourage the development of substantial non-conventional gas reserves in Argentina which could make it a large LNG exporter. The experience of Argentina is similar to that of Brazil and Chile, which have also turned to imports of LNG as a more reliable source of imports than overland pipeline imports from other countries. Indeed, a number of intercontinental pipeline projects – such as those connecting Venezuela and Brazil, and Argentina and Chile – have been abandoned in the past.[138]

Unlike in the electricity industry, restructuring policies for the natural gas industry have not been widely adopted in developing and transitional economies. This reflects various factors, including that: access to natural gas infrastructure is less widespread; there is limited inter-regional trade (in Africa there are only two main pipelines); gas accounts for a smaller amount of electricity production; and in some countries (such as Angola and Equatorial Guinea) domestic reserves of gas are used mainly for export.[139] In sub-Saharan Africa, only Nigeria has a developed market for both domestic consumption and exports (by LNG and pipelines). As discussed in Box 10.2, natural gas suppliers are not always under obligations to provide universal access to customers, and many domestic and commercial users rely on alternative sources of fuel such as LPG.

Box 10.2   The 'other gas': the supply and regulation of Liquefied Petroleum Gas (LPG)

While the focus of this chapter has been on the regulation of natural gas supply, in many parts of the world consumers do not have universal access to piped (mains) natural gas and have to rely on other fuels for cooking and heating. Liquefied petroleum gas (LPG)[140] – co-product from the refining of crude oil and extracted from natural gas production – is an important fuel which is used by an estimated three billion people worldwide.[141] LPG is now the dominant household energy source in India, Brazil, Indonesia and Morocco, and is widely used in the Far East, Latin America and North Africa.[142] Since the 1980s, the use of LPG has been actively supported in many developing countries through the use of subsidies, cash transfers and maximum price controls.[143] This is to encourage a shift away from other higher-polluting traditional fuels (such as wood, charcoal, coal, animal waste, kerosene) and to prevent deforestation.[144] LPG is also used by 'off-grid' consumers in other countries

---

[137] See Carnicer and Gomes (2021).

[138] See IEA (2008). In an early analysis, Beato and Fuente (2000) examine some lessons learned from the restructuring policies applied in Argentina, Colombia and Mexico. They describe how, in all three countries, there was separation of some of the different activities in the supply of gas, and policies directed at fostering wholesale market competition. However, they conclude that the large share of production controlled by large private and public companies restricted the development of competition, and that transportation pipeline ownership was concentrated in a few firms only.

[139] See Fulwood (2019).

[140] The two main sources of LPG are propane and butane, and LPG is sometimes referred to as bottled gas or cooking gas.

[141] World Bank (2017a).

[142] Norad (2020).

[143] World Bank (2021) records that many governments have spent billions of dollars over the past several decades subsidising household use of LPG.

[144] World Bank (2017a) records that around 40 per cent of the world's population still use solid fuels and kerosene for cooking.

such as the USA, UK, France, Canada, Portugal, Japan, Korea, Spain and Australia.[145] In many countries, the households that rely on LPG for gas supply are typically poorer and its prices are also highly volatile.

While both LPG and natural gas are either domestically produced or imported, there are important differences in how LPG is supplied to customers, which affects the need for, and type of, regulation applied. The distribution of LPG uses a combination of pipes, trucks and tanks/cylinders, and is typically sold to end-users in three ways: in cylinders of various sizes;[146] in 'bulk', meaning that it is transported by truck to a local storage site where it can then be accessed by customers;[147] or, less commonly, through a dedicated gas pipeline network. Depending on their location, household and commercial users can sometimes choose between multiple LPG sub-distributors or retailers.

The type and extent of regulation in the LPG supply chain is more varied than those applied to natural gas supply. Some jurisdictions treat LPG as an 'alternative fuel' and do not subject it to any additional regulatory oversight or measures beyond those which apply under general competition law. However, in other jurisdictions, regulatory interventions have been motivated by the fact that, from a household perspective, there is a functional equivalence between natural gas and LPG, and that it can be an essential product for some households.[148] In addition, the supply of LPG is often characterised by a small number of vertically integrated providers (which combine the importation/ production, storage and transportation), and regulatory measures have sometimes been introduced to address concerns arising from the concentrated structure of the LPG market.

Some jurisdictions apply ongoing regulatory oversight of LPG prices. For example, LPG prices are regulated in five Canadian provinces, while prices are also regulated in South Africa and Botswana. Fixed price controls for LPG cylinders have been introduced in Portugal since 2020, while in Spain LPG prices are controlled by means of a price cap formula, which is reviewed quarterly for raw materials and transport costs, and yearly for commercialisation costs. In some USA states, LPG (propane) suppliers who use a piping system to at least ten customers are classified as distribution system retailers and can be subject to rate making jurisdiction of the state PUC. Regulatory measures in other jurisdictions have followed investigations into potential anti-competitive pricing by LPG suppliers, including tacit collusion.[149] Finally, concerns about high levels of concentration and vertical integration in the LPG supply structure had led to proposals that negotiated access be provided to some facilities, or that various forms of separation be introduced.[150]

---

[145] Often these customers tend to be in isolated locations or have other specific circumstances which mean that they cannot be supplied with natural gas (e.g. live in a remote village or a caravan park).

[146] One of the benefits of bottled or cylinder LPG is its ability to be transported to the most remote locations.

[147] Bulk supply can be either metered or unmetered; the former involves the customer being charged for actual consumption.

[148] The UK competition authority has noted that 'LPG performs the same household functions as mains gas, but is delivered by road and stored on individual premises'. Similarly, the Portuguese competition agency has noted that LPG has 'an important social role, since they are the only gas based fuel accessible in several regions in the country where natural gas has not arrived, and in sensitive areas of urban districts'. See Autoridade da Concorrência (2009), OFT (2011b) and Casarin (2014).

[149] Examples of countries where LPG pricing issues have been investigated include Korea, Taiwan, Portugal, South Africa, Canada, the UK and Chile.

[150] High levels of concentration and integration have been identified in Portugal (2017), France (2014), the UK (2011), Pakistan (2020), Botswana (2018), South Africa (2017) and Chile (2021).

10.4 REGULATORY POLICY ISSUES IN THE GAS INDUSTRY

This section discusses three important regulatory policy issues in the gas industry: secu[?]ity of future gas supply; the impacts of restructuring on price and investment; an[?] finally, the effects of environmental and decarbonisation objectives, including the shi[?] towards hydrogen gas.

10.4.1 Impacts of Restructuring on Security of Gas Supply

A recurring question in the gas industry is whether a restructured competitive gas indu[?] try is capable of ensuring secure and affordable supplies of gas over the long term. The[?] concerns arise because, unlike other commodities and products discussed in this boo[?] gas is not a manufactured or renewable commodity – rather, it is a finite resource whic[?] is extracted and will ultimately be exhausted. As described above, various factors ca[?] underlie concerns about security of supply, including: diminishing output from dome[?] tic conventional gas resources;[151] an increasing reliance on foreign gas sources fro[?] potentially unstable regions;[152] and the major impact that high gas prices can have o[?] wholesale and retail electricity prices given the increasing use of gas to generate (pea[?] electricity.[153]

Security of gas supply is a particular concern in Europe, where over 80 per cent [?] gas was imported in 2020.[154] Increasing reliance of European countries on gas imports [?] further complicated by regional conflicts (such as those between Russia and Ukraine i[?] 2009, 2014 and 2022), which can rapidly disrupt supply to Europe or lead to very hig[?] wholesale gas prices which flow through to higher retail gas and electricity prices.[155] [?] contrast, while there were predictions up until the mid-2000s that the USA would hav[?] to increasingly rely on LNG imports,[156] the production of non-conventional natural g[?] (such as shale gas) has dramatically changed this picture and the USA is now a major n[?] exporter of gas.

The extent of domestic gas supplies and corresponding reliance on imports is, in pa[?] determined by geography. However, there are different ways in which regulatory polic[?] can promote and facilitate more secure supplies of gas. The first way is through t[?] vertical separation of gas production from transportation, which allows shippers ar[?]

---

[151] Conventional gas reserves in Europe, such as the UK continental shelf and the Netherlands Groningen field, have peaked and are in decline.

[152] Stern (2004) explores the nature of each of these issues. Elkins (2010) notes that security of supply can also refer to other issues such as: 'having enough infrastructure; having enough annual gas; having enough gas to meet demand in extreme weather conditions; but most generally it refers to increased reliance on imported supplies and carries with it the assumption that indigenous supplies are inherentl[?] secure, whereas imports are inherently insecure'.

[153] The European Commission (EC, 2022) records that 'the root cause of the current high electricity prices is the gas market' and that '[i]n the gas spot market, volatility is high and not fully linked to fundamentals'. Similarly, Bushnell (2021) attributes the Texas electricity blackouts in winter 2021 to failures in the gas market. In contrast, see Makholm (2021b). See also Abada and Massol (2011).

[154] See ACER/CEER (2021b). This is for the EU and UK. Imports came from Russia (32.4 per cent), Norway (22.3 per cent) and Algeria (5.3 per cent), with LNG imports accounting for the remaining 20 per cent.

[155] As experienced in the UK and EU countries in 2022 and 2023.

[156] Some estimates suggested that LNG imports would come to account for 17 per cent of gas demand.

end-users to obtain gas from different regions/sources and then separately pay the transportation charges to move that gas.[157] Second, the establishment of liquid trading hubs is seen as promoting security of supply by providing a single forum where large numbers of buyers and sellers can meet to trade for both gas and gas transport capacity.[158] Third, the regulatory treatment of new transmission and storage capacity (particularly LNG facilities) can be important for incentivising investment and reducing reliance on piped gas from one region.[159] Similarly, incentives and policies to promote greater interconnector capacity can connect markets and allow for new sources of supply.[160] This highlights a more general point about the link between predictability and stability of the regulatory environment and security of supply.[161] Fourth, harmonising the rules for access and charging between regions and countries can promote greater interconnection and thus allow gas to flow freely across a wider region. Similarly rules that require bidirectional flows can permit reverse flows on gas pipelines in the event of short-term supply disruptions. Fifth, rules to restrict the hoarding of capacity ('use it or lose it' rules) allow for market-based capacity allocation mechanisms and require non-discriminatory access to transportation networks, which can ensure that any spare capacity is available to all shippers. Finally, although it is beyond the remit of regulators, a jurisdiction's decision about whether to extract non-conventional gas sources also has an impact on future gas security (as seen most clearly in the USA).

Regulators and policy makers in the UK and Europe have responded to security of supply concerns in different ways. The British regulator has conducted a number of investigations into security of supply in the gas sector,[162] while at the EU level, Directives and Regulations have been introduced in an attempt to pre-empt security of gas supply issues.[163] These require EU Member States to cooperate and coordinate to assess common supply risks, to act in solidarity to always guarantee supply to the most vulnerable consumers, and to report on storage capacities and as well as long-term supply arrangements with third countries. In response to the security of supply concerns in 2022, the European Commission has proposed new measures, including: joint EU-wide negotiations with gas

---

[157] As Barnes (2018) observes, countries which rely on imports, such as Germany, now have a choice between sourcing gas from Russia or Norway and using the pipeline connections, or accessing gas from LNG terminals (including terminals located in other countries).

[158] Makholm (2007). However, as discussed in Section 10.4.2 below, some argue that long-term contracts are necessary to bring forward the supplies necessary for the market, and that the shift towards short-term trading that has accompanied restructuring policies will not allow long-term demand requirements to be satisfied.

[159] A shift in regulatory policy in the USA for the treatment of LNG facilities – from treating them as part of the storage/transportation chain, and subject to open access requirements, to treating them as a supply source, and no longer subject to such requirements – is argued to have increased supply security by removing some of the barriers to investment. See Von Hirschhausen (2008).

[160] Over the years the European Commission has directly funded gas infrastructure projects worth billions of euros, principally directed at improving interconnections between Member States, and permitting reverse flows on gas pipelines in the event of short-term supply disruptions.

[161] Makholm (2007) states that: '[T]he FERC regulation of pipelines is a highly predictable affair. Pipeline developers in the US can take that predictability to bank – literally – and the bankable nature of an independent, contractualized network makes supply security a reality.'

[162] See Ofgem (2010, 2012).

[163] See Directive (2004/67/EC), Regulation (994/2010) and Regulation (EU) 2017/1938. De Jong, Glachant, Hafner, *et al.* (2012) discuss the EU gas security of supply policy architecture.

producers; new energy partnerships with the USA, the Middle East and African countries; and a new requirement that all storage facilities are filled to 90 per cent of capacity by the beginning of the winter.[164]

10.4.2 The Impacts of Restructuring on Prices and Investment

As we have discussed above, in many restructured gas industries, there has been a shift in trading arrangements away from longer-term commitments between market participant (where gas commodity and transportation prices were set on the basis of long-term price and adjusted on the basis of some formula) towards shorter-term procurement arrange ments for gas supply, transportation and storage.[165] This has raised questions about the impacts of this shift on prices and affordability (and price volatility) and the incentive for investment.

Impacts on Prices and Affordability

There are two main debates about the impacts of gas restructuring policies on prices. First, whether the shift towards shorter-term trading arrangements, and the resulting price volatility, has benefited or adversely impacted on consumers. Second, whether the rationale for indexing of wholesale gas prices to oil prices used in some jurisdictions is still valid, and the potential impacts of such indexing on consumers.

On the first debate, it is widely recognised that, while long-term contracts can sta bilise prices and reduce price volatility by staggering the pass-through of wholesale price changes into retail prices, they can also be inflexible and lock users (including consumers) into specific trading terms that may not reflect market fundamentals.[166] In contrast, prices set under short-term trading arrangements better reflect actual supply and demand balances but can be volatile.[167] In the USA, for example, restruc turing has at times led to 'wild swings' in gas prices as a result of a tightening supply and demand balance.[168] Similarly, in Europe, recent significant fluctuations in retail gas (and electricity) prices have been directly attributed to wholesale gas price vola tility.[169] The exposure of consumers to such price volatility depends on whether the pass-through of wholesale price changes to retail prices is symmetric or not – i.e.

[164] EC (2022).
[165] The creation of spot and futures markets for gas which supplement, and partly substitute for, the more inflexible system of long-term contracts has also been seen as a decisive regulatory innovation associated with the restructuring of the gas industry. See Newbery (1999).
[166] See Stern (2004) and IEA (2021b).
[167] IEA (2021b) observes that the widespread historical use of long-term contracts in Europe did not allow EU consumers to take advantage of periods of lower-cost supply, such as following the US shale gas revolution.
[168] See Stern (2004). Jenkins-Smith (1987) presents an early discussion of price volatility emerging in the restructured US gas market. Analysis by the EIA (2007) suggests that there is a seasonal pattern to volatility, with colder months being more volatile.
[169] The European Commission (EC, 2022) observes that: 'Today's high electricity price is driven by the high gas price, as gas-based generators are still often the energy providers coming last into the electricity market to close on actual demand. In the gas spot market, volatility is high and not fully linked to fundamentals.'

whether reductions in wholesale prices are passed through to retail prices in the same way as increases in wholesale prices.[170] While price volatility can have significant impacts on gas market participants,[171] and raise concerns about affordability when wholesale prices are high, some argue that the flexibility of such short-term arrangements saves consumers money overall, and that the ability to quickly obtain gas to meet short-term demand will be critical as electricity production shifts towards renewable generation sources.[172]

A separate debate is whether wholesale gas prices should be set on the basis of the fundamentals of the gas market (so-called gas-on-gas competition)[173] or whether the wholesale gas price should be linked to the prices of competing fuels, such as oil. As already noted, while contracts in the USA, the UK and increasingly in Europe[174] are not linked to the price of oil or other competing fuels, this is not the case in other parts of the world such as Asia. This reflects the fact that LNG traded on international markets is typically linked to oil prices.[175] The historical rationale for linking wholesale gas prices to those of competing fuels has been to encourage investment in gas assets, and make gas a substitute fuel for the consumer (the market value principle).[176] It is also seen as a simple approach and one well suited to settings where there is not an established wholesale gas market. While such a rationale may still be relevant for less liquid wholesale markets,[177] or where some customers are prepared to pay for higher oil-indexed prices in exchange for a perception of greater security of supply, its more general relevance is seen as increasingly weak.[178] This is because it divorces gas prices from the fundamentals of the gas market and, potentially, leaves gas market participants – such as electricity generators – at the mercy of an oil cartel, exposing them to oil market volatility and increasing gas prices.[179] In Europe, it is estimated that the gradual transition to gas-on-gas competition over the period 2010 to 2020 reduced import bills by $70 billion.[180]

[170] In an early study of the US transition to competitive markets, Hollas (1994) concluded that there was an asymmetry of pricing as the costs of purchased gas rose and fell. A 2011 study by the British energy regulator found evidence of asymmetric pass-through, such that customer energy bills (for gas and electricity) were more responsive to rising supplier costs than falling supplier costs (Ofgem, 2011a).
[171] Analysis by the EIA (2007) in the USA found that even relatively low levels of volatility in natural gas prices can have large impacts on the market.
[172] IEA (2021b) notes, for example, that: 'The shift towards spot market pricing allowed the EU to benefit from low prices for LNG imports during periods of ample supply.'
[173] Newbery (1999) defines gas-on-gas competition as 'competition between gas producers unconstrained by the prices of other fuels'.
[174] In Europe the majority of wholesale contracts were historically linked; however, over the decade from 2010 to 2020, the share of gas-linked contracts has risen from 30 per cent to 80 per cent. See IEA (2021b).
[175] See ACCC (2016).
[176] See Stern (2007) and Hughes (2011).
[177] One argument for oil-based pricing is that the oil market is too large to manipulate.
[178] See Makholm (2007) and Stern (2007).
[179] See Zhang, Wang, Shi and Liu (2018) and Hughes (2011). The relationship between natural gas prices in the USA and crude oil prices has been examined in a number of studies. See Bachmeier and Griffin (2006) and Brown and Yücel (2008).
[180] IEA (2021b). However, the benefits can vary at particular points in time. For example, it is estimated that EU countries paid around $30 billion more for natural gas in 2021 than if they had stuck with oil indexation.

Impacts of Restructuring on Investment Incentives

An important issue in restructured gas industries is whether they enable the coordination and funding of investments in gas infrastructure, such as transmission, distribution and storage assets.[181] This question did not typically arise prior to industry restructuring, as production was generally secured under long-term contracts, and the transportation, storage and supply of gas were undertaken by an integrated entity which was able to coordinate the planning and funding of the required infrastructure.

Studies suggest that structural separation and restructuring in the US gas industry has not hindered the coordination and funding of infrastructure investment. Rather, the competitive nature of the restructured industry, and strong demand, is said to have led to significant investments in incremental capacity. Various aspects of the regulatory framework are seen as contributing to this outcome, including that: inter-state pipelines are subject to a single regulatory authority; gas pipeline tariff cases follow a specific and predictable administrative procedure; and pipelines are constitutionally protected from expropriation by the regulator.[182] The FERC's approach to regulation of pipeline capacity is also seen to have encouraged investment by removing the price ceiling which applied to the sale of secondary capacity and allowing pipelines to file for peak and off-peak rates and other differentiated rate structures. Other regulatory changes are seen to have made pipeline investment more straightforward, including the shift in policy by the FERC towards incremental pricing for new pipeline capacity.[183] An important element of the US approach to new capacity investment is the open-seasons process, during which a transmission operator will offer firm capacity contracts for new infrastructure and only build the new pipeline if a sufficient number of shippers book capacity to make the project financially viable.[184] This process for new capacity investment is seen to underpin investments in network infrastructure, and to limit the scope for asset stranding. The use of open seasons is now used to underwrite new investments in other restructured gas industries such as in Europe. In particular, longstanding concerns about insufficient interconnector capacity between Member States are partially being addressed by open seasons, which have been used for gas interconnector projects between France and Belgium and between France and Spain.

The issue of the incentives for investment in storage capacity is more complicated than investment in transmission pipelines, as storage capacity confers wider insurance benefits on all market participants (rather than just pipeline owners or users).[185] In the USA

---

[181] Stern (2004) considers the question of whether gas industry investments may be different from similar large investments in other industries, which are often made under competitive market conditions. Von Hirschhausen (2008) considers whether there is a tension between restructured gas markets and investment in gas infrastructure based on the US experience.

[182] See Makholm (2007).

[183] See FERC (1999). In simple terms, incremental pricing places all of the costs of pipeline expansion on the parties causing the expansion. This can be contrasted with 'rolled-in' pricing, which spreads the costs of pipeline expansion over all customers, new and old. Incremental pricing results in a situation where new shippers may be paying a price above or below existing users of the pipeline, while, with rolled-in pricing, each user (including new users) pays the same rate. See also Tye and García (2007).

[184] FERC (2011) has summarised the advantages of the open-seasons process in the following terms: 'An open season is intended to provide transparency to the market concerning potential new capacity and to ensure that new capacity is allocated in a not unduly discriminatory manner. An open season will also provide a project sponsor with valuable information regarding market interest that it can utilise to properly size the project.'

[185] As Newbery (1999) notes, storage provides 'insurance against costly disruptions' and is also 'a public good for consumers who are not on interruptible contracts'.

recognition of the strategic importance of storage led to the introduction of regulatory measures in the mid-2000s to incentivise investment, such as the ability of some storage facilities to charge market-based rates. In Europe, while third-party access to gas storage and LNG facilities is mandated, the possibility exists for storage facilities to apply for an exemption from being required to provide access to third parties for new facilities.[186]

0.4.3 Environmental Policy and the Shift Towards Hydrogen Networks

Although environmental considerations have traditionally been less prominent in the gas industry than in the electricity, water and transport industries, there are three environmental policy issues which could have profound impacts on the future regulation of the gas industry.

Gas-Fired Electricity Production

Natural gas is the fastest-growing fossil fuel source for electricity generation and accounts for about one-quarter of electricity generation worldwide.[187] However, there is an active debate as to the role that gas-fired electricity generation should play in the future generation mix in many countries. For some, gas is seen as part of the 'solution' for mitigating climate change and can act as a 'transition fuel' that allows some countries to move away from high-carbon coal electricity generation and thus achieve a substantial one-off reduction in emissions. It also provides a flexible source of generation to support the development of the more intermittent renewable generation sources (such as wind and solar). Others argue, however, that such a policy is misplaced on the basis that, among other things, gas is a fossil fuel (i.e. it still emits CO_2, albeit at a lower level than coal), and that in some countries (particularly in Europe) an increasing use of gas will mean higher levels of import dependence. In addition, it is argued that too great a reliance on gas-fired electricity as part of the future of electricity generation risks missing a 'golden opportunity' to transform the electricity industry towards one based around renewable sources of generation.

Non-Conventional Gas Extraction

A second active debate concerns the development and expansion of non-conventional sources of gas production, particularly shale gas. As we have already seen, in the USA, the extraction of non-conventional gas has had rapid and far-reaching impacts, including resulting in a significant drop in natural gas prices and allowing it to shift from being a net importer of gas to a net exporter within a decade. However, many other jurisdictions are hesitant about embracing the 'shale gas revolution' on health and environmental grounds.[188] A particular concern is that the process of fracking, used to extract shale gas, could contaminate underground water supplies and also lead to the emission of greenhouse gases. While methane does not stay in the atmosphere as long as carbon dioxide, it is more potent and can trap more heat. Some studies conclude that the release of methane emissions during the hydraulic fracking process could have a 'huge impact on the

---

[186] This exemption possibility also applies to gas interconnectors between EU Member States and LNG terminals.

[187] IEA (2021a).

[188] Specific concerns relate to water pollution, methane leakage and induced seismicity.

greenhouse gas balance',[189] while other studies have drawn a link between a recent spik in global methane levels and oil and gas fracking in the USA.[190] Hydraulic fracking i currently prohibited in many EU countries, the UK, some Australian states and Canadia provinces. While the question of whether or not to allow fracking is a political one, in th USA, the FERC has at times been asked to assess the upstream and downstream green house gas effects of approvals for inter-state gas pipelines involving non-conventiona gas.[191]

Decarbonised and Decentralised Gas Markets

A final environmental issue that could have major impacts on the future operation an regulation of the gas industry are policy proposals to decarbonise gas markets. There ar different aspects to these policies, but broadly speaking they all involve a shift toward renewable gases such as biomethane (which combines methane, carbon monoxide, hydro gen and other gases) and low-carbon hydrogen.[192] Hydrogen is produced through wate electrolysis with electricity, biomass fermentation or from fossil fuels, and does not dir ectly result in any direct greenhouse gas emissions.[193] However, the production of hydro gen can involve carbon emissions being released if the electricity used is not generate from renewable sources, or if carbon capture technologies are not used to capture th emissions from fossil fuels.[194]

Policy proposals foresee hydrogen replacing the use of natural gas (methane) for home and businesses and also for vehicles and transport systems. For this to be achieved, it i necessary for hydrogen to be transported to end-users. Rather than developing new an costly infrastructure to deliver hydrogen, a proposal actively being considered is to 'repur pose' existing natural gas (methane) transport networks and infrastructure to carry hydro gen. This could involve the blending of hydrogen with natural gas and then use of th existing gas infrastructure to deliver it to consumers.[195] Alternatively, it could involve the ful conversion of gas networks and infrastructure to transport pure hydrogen. However, ther are well-recognised physical and technical challenges in fully converting existing gas trans mission pipelines to carry pure hydrogen because of potential embrittlement or degradatio of pipes that can occur when exposed to highly concentrated hydrogen at high pressure ove a long period and a need to control hydrogen permeation and leaks. Regulators in Europ and the UK are funding and promoting research to test if these limitations can be overcom

A related issue is whether there is a need for economic regulation of future hydroge networks, and, if so, whether an entirely new regulatory framework is needed or whethe

---

[189] See European Parliament (2011).

[190] Roberts (2019).

[191] See Makholm (2018b).

[192] See IEA (2020b). IEA (2021c) notes that seventeen governments have hydrogen strategies and twenty more are working to develop strategies.

[193] A distinction is sometimes made between green or no-carbon hydrogen (water electrolysis with renewable electricity), blue or low-carbon hydrogen (produced by fossil fuels with carbon capture and storage) and grey hydrogen (produced from fossil fuels but without carbon capture and storage).

[194] IEA (2020b) records that: 'Almost all hydrogen produced today comes from fossil fuels without carbon capture, resulting in close to 900 million tonnes of CO_2 emissions, equivalent to the combined CO_2 emissions of the United Kingdom and Indonesia.'

[195] See Melaina, Antonia and Penev (2013).

hydrogen systems should be brought within the scope of the existing gas regulatory frameworks.[196] In Europe, proposals for adapting the existing gas regulatory framework to accommodate hydrogen have been brought forward. These include measures which adapt the scope of the existing gas regulations to include renewable gases and hydrogen. It is proposed that the existing rules relating to third-party access, unbundling and independent regulation will also apply to hydrogen networks (although some of these rules will only apply after 2031), and there is the possibility for 'exemptions' or regulatory holidays (see Chapter 6) for major new hydrogen infrastructure in certain conditions.[197] Hydrogen and renewable gases will also receive a discounted tariff for accessing the grid. In the USA, the FERC currently does not have jurisdiction over hydrogen under the Natural Gas Act or the Federal Power Act.[198] However, some US states are actively looking at the decarbonisation of gas distribution networks.[199] In New Zealand and Australia, there has also been a focus on the 'repurposing' of existing gas infrastructure, and how the gas regulatory framework will need to adapt to apply to hydrogen networks.[200]

10.5 CONCLUSION

Over the past four decades, the production and supply structure of natural gas has been transformed in many jurisdictions, beginning with the USA, Britain and Canada, but now including many countries in Europe, Australia, New Zealand and some countries in Latin America. The precise nature of the restructuring of the industry has differed across jurisdictions, but has typically involved the introduction of competition into production activities (through deregulation of the wellhead price), the separation of various activities in the production and supply chain (most notably those of transportation, storage and retail supply) and in some countries the introduction of competition at the retail level. Price regulation generally applies to the transmission and distribution of gas and takes the form of the price cap approach (or a variant of this approach) in jurisdictions such as Britain, Australia and many EU Member States. In North America, a variant of the rate of return approach is typically applied, although direct negotiation of rates is common. Price regulation is also applied to gas storage facilities and retail prices in some jurisdictions.

Broadly speaking, the restructuring of the gas industry has produced competitive wholesale gas markets in the USA, Canada, Britain and increasingly in Europe (particularly in northern Europe). As a range of restructuring policies have been adopted across these jurisdictions, this suggests that more than one approach can support effective competition, and that other non-regulatory factors may also be significant.[201]

---

[196] ACER (2021) provides a succinct overview of the issues.

[197] EC (2021a, b).

[198] Rather, hydrogen currently falls within the remit of the Department of Transportation.

[199] Makholm (2021a) argues that such policies could represent 'the end of independent gas distribution franchises' and would constitute a 'takings of property'.

[200] See AEMC (2022) and New Zealand Government (2021).

[201] Moselle, Black, White and Piffaut (2012) observe that the different experiences of the UK and USA show that, in practice, a range of approaches can support effective competition, but that competition has generally successfully been introduced into jurisdictions that have access to a competitive supply of gas through indigenous production or a diverse range of imports.

While the interactions with other policy areas, particularly environmental policy, hav
historically been less acute in the gas industry than in other industries, this situation
changing and the industry, and its regulation, face a number of possible futures. In som
scenarios, this might involve the gradual phasing out of gas consumption and the decom
missioning of gas pipelines and infrastructure as consumers shift to decarbonised energ
sources. In other scenarios, this involves hydrogen or other low-carbon gases replacin
natural gas (methane) and the existing infrastructure – and regulatory frameworks
being 'repurposed' to deliver these gases to consumers.

DISCUSSION QUESTIONS

1. Describe some of the ways in which the gas and electricity industries are related
    one another.
2. What are the different ways in which shippers (users) can gain access to gas pipelir
    capacity observed around the world?
3. How have trading arrangements for the sale and purchase of wholesale gas change
    in many countries since the 1980s? Give some examples of how gas is now trade
    in jurisdictions where competition has been introduced.
4. Describe the activities in the gas supply chain where competition has been intro
    duced, and which activities are subject to ongoing regulation. For activities that a
    subject to regulation, what is typically the form and scope of that regulation?
5. What are the factors that motivated the restructuring of the gas industry in th
    USA, Britain and the European Union, and what are some of the key elements of th
    restructuring policies introduced?
6. In what jurisdictions have restructuring policies been assessed as being successfu
    What are some of the factors seen as important in enabling the development of com
    petition in these jurisdictions?
7. How can regulatory policy promote and facilitate more secure supplies of gas?
8. What are some potential benefits of restructuring policies which have moved awa
    from long-term contracts and where prices are linked to other fuels (such as oil
    What are some of the risks, or dis-benefits, of this shift?
9. Discuss the different ways in which environmental and decarbonisation policie
    might impact on the gas industry. What are some of the implications of these po
    icies for the long-term viability of the industry, and for economic regulation?

11

Telecommunications Regulation

This chapter focuses on the regulation of the telecommunications industry, which is defined broadly to include fixed (landline or wireline) and mobile (wireless) telecommunications networks as well as cable networks. A vast literature tracks the historical changes in the telecommunications industry, its structure and regulation over the past three decades,[1] and earlier chapters, particularly Chapter 6, have discussed some of the more technical issues related to the regulation of the industry, such as one-way and two-way access pricing approaches. As we will see, the telecommunications industry has transformed from one characterised by monopoly in many countries to one where there is often *intra*-modal competition (between different providers using the same technology, such as fixed line networks) and *inter*-modal competition (between mobile, cable and fixed line networks). How telecommunications networks are used has changed from one based around carrying voice signals to one based around the transmission of data, including data generated from so-called over-the-top (OTT) applications (such as video calls, video streaming and gaming).

The experience of regulation of the telecommunications industry shows how some of the theoretical principles discussed in earlier chapters have been considered or applied in practice. This includes the application of different forms of vertical separation of an incumbent operator, and the controversies around different approaches to access pricing, such as long-run incremental costs (LRIC) and the efficient component pricing rule (ECPR). This chapter also provides insights into what happens when regulatory policy actively seeks to kick-start intra-modal (or facilities-based) competition, by requiring shared, or 'unbundled', access for new entrants to core network facilities. Other themes explored in this chapter concern the appropriate balance between *ex ante* economic regulation and *ex post* competition law and how different regulatory approaches (including forbearing from regulation) can impact on the incentives for investment and innovation.

This chapter also looks ahead to consider the future regulation of the telecommunications industry. Among the issues we consider is how to incentivise the substantial investments in next-generation networks (NGNs) that are needed to ensure widespread access to high-speed broadband services. We also discuss whether the emergence of

---

[1] This includes the early work of Mitchell and Vogelsang (1991), Baumol and Sidak (1994b), Sidak and Spulber (1998) and Laffont and Tirole (2000), and the excellent surveys presented in Cave, Majumdar and Vogelsang (2002), Majumdar, Vogelsang and Cave (2005) and Vogelsang (2021).

intra-modal and inter-modal competition in many countries means that the time is right for *ex ante* regulation to be withdrawn and replaced by a greater reliance on competition law. Separately, we examine the debate around the need for, and the nature of, regulation of the traffic management rules that apply to the Internet (so-called 'net neutrality'). The future regulation of the industry will also be shaped by other factors, such as the potential for the fifth generation of mobile communications technology (5G) to transform connectivity, and the emergence of the Internet of Things (whereby devices within everyday objects, such as smart appliances or wearable fitness devices, share data via the Internet).

11.1 PHYSICAL AND ECONOMIC CHARACTERISTICS OF TELECOMMUNICATIONS NETWORKS AND SERVICES

11.1.1 Characteristics of the Product

The key product supplied by the telecommunications industry is the carriage of signal or data which allows for the two-way interconnection between specific users. This could involve connecting two or more users to a voice telephone call or Short Message Service (SMS; text) message, or multiple users of a particular web or video site. In other words, the 'product' supplied by telecommunication networks is the carriage of voice/data/video signals between two or more users, sometimes across different types of network (e.g. fixed network and a mobile network).[2] In many ways, the telecommunications industry can be thought of as similar to other transport industries – like rail – where the underlying service involves the carriage or movement of something between two or more places and where a range of different services and users share a common infrastructure.[3]

However, while all telecommunications networks involve the carriage of information between different users, the network technologies used to provide those services differ in terms of reliability, capacity, quality and speed of carriage or transmission. For example, transmission technologies used for the traditional fixed line network (known as the Public Switched Telephone Network (PSTN)) provide high-quality and secure voice services, but have limited capacity for data and multimedia services. In contrast, fibre based Internet Protocol (IP) based networks offer considerably more capacity but have historically had problems associated with latency (delays) and reliability for the transmission of certain time-sensitive services. Mobile technology uses spectrum to offer consumers the ability to access voice, data and multimedia services with others from non-fixed locations, while cable technology uses fibre-optic cables to provide voice, data and broadcasting services. In other words, and again like other transport industries, information can be carried using different transmission *modes* and technologies, which

---

[2] Sharkey (2002) defines telecommunications as 'the service of enabling electronic transfers of information from one point to another or from one point to multiple points'.

[3] The transport analogy is a helpful one for conceptualising the modern telecommunications industry. For example, just as freight and passenger trains, of different sizes and configurations, can share the use of a common rail network, so increasingly do data, voice and broadcasting 'packets' share the use of a common telecommunications network infrastructure. Similarly, just as there are often competing rail and road transportation networks, in telecommunications there is, in many cases, increasing competition between different network infrastructure technologies, such as fixed, cable and mobile networks.

as we discuss below, allows for the possibility of inter-modal competition – e.g. between cable, mobile, fixed and satellite. Another feature of telecommunications networks, again shared with other transport industries, is the importance of network externalities.[4] That is, the value to any one user of a telecommunications network increases the greater the number of users connected to that network, or which can be reached through interconnection with other networks.

1.1.2 Fixed Line Telecommunications Network Architecture

As shown in Figure 11.1, fixed line telecommunications networks are based around a 'star topology', where each user is either connected to a street cabinet and then to a local telephone exchange (sometimes called a central office), or directly connected to a local exchange.[5] This is what is known as the 'access network'. To make a call or access the Internet, the end-user requests that the local exchange establish a connection between themselves and the party that they wish to connect with, such as another person for a voice call or text message, or a content provider on the Internet. This process of connecting nodes is known as switching. A second level of switching involves the direct connection of different local telephone exchanges to one another over long distances over what is referred to as a 'core network'. This is sometimes referred to as 'backhaul' and allows end-users to make and receive calls, and send/receive data, from other end-users in distant locations.

Traditionally, circuit switching technology was used to connect different nodes, which meant that a dedicated circuit, or electronic calling path, was established at the time of call set-up and remained dedicated to that specific call until the call was taken down.[6] However, as described below, the switching infrastructure for most fixed line networks is now packet-based. There are also differences in the method by which signals are transmitted across the network. This generally involves what is known as multiplexing, a process where multiple signals are combined onto a single transmission path. There are two main types of multiplexing: frequency-division multiplexing (where each call/packet gets a fraction of that bandwidth for all of the time of the call), which was used for the traditional analogue networks; and time-division multiplexing (where each data packet gets all of the available bandwidth for a fraction of the time), as used by a digital NGN. The two different methods of transmitting calls have implications for the amount of transmission capacity required, and how it is utilised.

---

[4] Network externalities are sometimes also referred to as 'bandwagon effects' in the telecommunications industry, which, according to Rohlfs (2005), can be defined as 'increases in a consumer's utility as others consume the same product or service that she does'.

[5] The star typology reduced the number of transmission paths required between users, and therefore the costs of the network. Hatfield, Mitchell and Srinagesh (2005) explain that a 'full-mesh' topology – where each user is permanently wired to every other telephone – would involve more cost and quickly become impracticable.

[6] Once the calling path was established, the call was not affected by other users on the network. In other words, congestion could only arise when gaining access to a calling path in the first instance (i.e. the failure to get a dial tone). Historically, voice signals were converted to electrical impulses, which were sent over copper wires, but this has been replaced over time, particularly for the long-distance core network, by the use of light signals transmitted along fibre-optic cables.

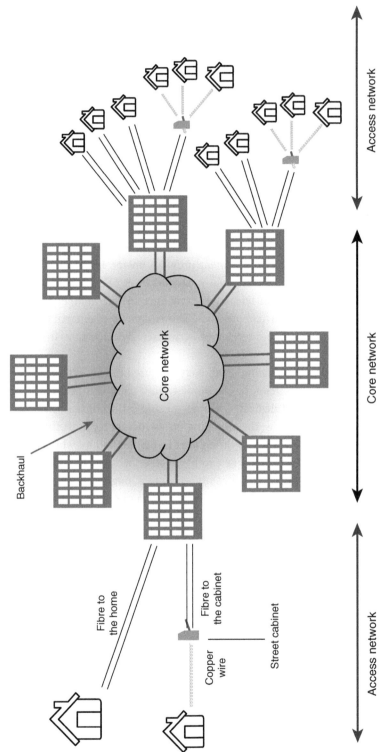

Figure 11.1 Fixed line telecommunications network

Legacy Networks and Next-Generation Networks

The discussion in this chapter will sometimes refer to differences between 'legacy' fixed line telecommunications networks (or the PSTN) and next-generation networks (NGNs).[7] While there are numerous types of NGNs – such as next-generation *access* networks (NGANs) and next-generation *core* networks – a number of key characteristics of the network architecture distinguish them from the traditional PSTN.[8] Firstly, all NGNs are digital, rather than analogue. Secondly, as noted, the switching infrastructure for NGNs is packet-based rather than circuit-based. A third characteristic of NGNs, also described below, is the use of the IP for the switching of packets. In simple terms, the IP contains the addressing information and other control information, which enables packets to be routed from a source to a destination across one or more IP networks. Finally, NGNs generally utilise fibre-optic cables to transmit signals, while legacy networks have traditionally been based around copper networks (particularly for the access network).

A transition from legacy fixed line networks to NGNs, and in particular the ability for networks of different sizes and technologies to interconnect with one another, is now seen as inevitable following the ascendancy of data communications over traditional voice communications.[9] Indeed, the traditional analogue legacy networks have already been 'switched off' in some jurisdictions or are due to be switched off by the middle of the 2020s.[10] This has important implications for regulation, including the continuing applicability of regulatory policies such as 'unbundling' to NGNs (discussed in Section 11.4.2).

1.1.3 The Supply Structure for Telecommunications Services

The supply structure for modern telecommunications networks comprises a number of important elements, including a transmission infrastructure to physically carry signals, and switching technologies that are used to establish connections between different nodes/users. In addition, different service providers offer a range of voice and data services to users. Each of these elements is discussed below.

Transmission Infrastructure

Several transmission infrastructures are used to physically carry electrical, optical and radio signals between users on a telecommunications network. These include twisted copper pairs, fibre-optic cable, hybrid fibre coaxial cable and radio spectrum.[11] Each of these

---

[7] There are various definitions of 'NGN'. The International Telecommunications Union (ITU, 2013) defines NGN as: '[A] packet-based network able to provide services including Telecommunication Services and able to make use of multiple broadband, [quality-of-service] QoS-enabled transport technologies and in which service-related functions are independent from underlying transport-related technologies. It offers unrestricted access by users to different service providers. It supports generalised mobility which will allow consistent and ubiquitous provision of services to users.'

[8] Marcus and Elixmann (2008) note that, in most of the world, network architectures based on the IP are referred to as NGNs; however, in the USA, people speak of convergence rather than of NGNs.

[9] Gillan and Malfara (2012) describe this transformation and the regulatory implications in detail.

[10] Legacy analogue networks have been, or will be, switched off in Germany, Japan, Sweden, Estonia, the Netherlands and the UK.

[11] There are other transmission media that can be used to carry signals between users, including power lines, such as so-called broadband over power lines, and satellite technology.

technologies has different cost structures and innovation potential, which can affect key variables such as price, speed and coverage.

A copper-based network infrastructure traditionally characterised the entire PSTN, and is still a feature of the local loops (i.e. the last-mile connection) of access networks in many jurisdictions. As the twisted copper pairs that comprise the copper-based infrastructure were developed principally to carry voice calls (which require only limited bandwidth for reasonable transmission quality), the traditional bandwidth capability of twisted copper pair networks is limited.[12] However, certain technologies can upgrade the bandwidth capability of traditional twisted copper pairs, such as the Digital Subscriber Line (DSL), which converts ordinary phone lines into high-speed digital lines, capable of accessing services which require higher bandwidth to be viable.[13] The conversion process requires the installation of equipment (such as a modem) at either end of the connection that converts signals into a format which can be sent over a twisted copper wire, and the resulting quality is dependent on how close the user is to the telephone exchange.[14] This ability to upgrade the capability of the traditional copper network has allowed traditional fixed line telephone operators in many countries to be able to offer broadband data services, and to remain competitive against other network operators who can provide such services (such as cable networks, etc.).

A second transmission infrastructure used to carry signals is fibre-optic cable. Unlike traditional copper infrastructure, which sends electrical impulses over the copper wire, fibre-optic cables are made of glass fibre, and use light signals to transmit information across the network links. An advantage of fibre-optic cable infrastructure is significantly greater bandwidth. This allows for much faster internet speeds, and the ability to use bandwidth-heavy services, such as streaming video, music or movie downloads, along with high-quality video calls and other high-demand internet and data applications. A distinction is sometimes made between 'dark fibre' and 'lit fibre' wholesale products. 'Lit fibre' products allow wholesale competitors to access an active optical fibre product that uses the access provider's own equipment at either end of the optic cable. In contrast, 'dark fibre' products allow wholesale competitors to gain access to 'unlit' (hence dark) fibre to which they can attach their own equipment (electronics/optoelectronics) at both ends to provide services to end-users over which they have more control.[15] In many jurisdictions, fibre is replacing copper in the local access network (the last mile) and is being deployed at various points closer to the users' premises. There are various possibilities for how far the cable will be laid, including Fibre to the Node/Cabinet (FTTN/C) or Fibre to

---

[12] The bandwidth capacity required for a voice call is generally considered to be 4 Hz in analogue terms or 64 kbps (kilobits per second) in digital terms.

[13] There are different forms of DSL technology (collectively termed xDSL), including: Asymmetric Digital Subscriber Line (ADSL), HDSL (High-bit-rate Digital Subscriber Line) and VDSL (Very-high-bit-rate Digital Subscriber Line). There is also so-called 'naked DSL', which offers users a stand-alone data connection without traditional telephone capabilities such as a telephone number or an ability to make calls using the PSTN. To make voice calls, customers use the naked DSL combined with Voice over Internet Protocol (VoIP).

[14] DSL can generally only be used over short distances, and it is estimated that ADSL can provide service up to a maximum range of about five kilometres.

[15] For this reason, the FCC (2017a) considers that the ability to access and supply services over dark fibre 'takes on significant aspects of facility-based competition'.

the Premises/Home (FTTP/H). The speeds can vary depending on how close to the user the fibre is deployed.[16] As discussed below, the replacement of copper with fibre for local access networks is a topical issue in many countries, and involves significant costs being incurred, which has led, in some cases, to various forms of government support and subsidies.

A third transmission infrastructure used by cable television operators to provide voice, data and other broadband services (in addition to cable broadcasting services) is hybrid fibre coaxial (HFC) infrastructure. In general terms, HFC networks send signals along fibre-optic cables from a distribution centre (a cable headend) to various individual nodes which are located close to clusters of users' premises within a small geographic area. The optical signals are then converted to electrical signals, and coaxial cable is used to carry the signals from the individual node to each customer's premises.[17] Cable companies are increasingly deploying fibre-optic networks at closer points to the customers' premises to increase the speed and performance of the network.

The fourth transmission infrastructure, used by mobile or wireless network operators, involves the use of radio waves to transmit calls and data between users. Wireless network operators are typically assigned licences to use radio frequency spectrum, which carries the signals between a user's wireless handset (i.e. a mobile phone) and the nearest node or base station. Base stations, which can rise up to several hundred feet in the air, link mobile phone users with other wireless network users and users of the fixed line network. Base stations can be used by different wireless network operators who share the facility, and are connected to a central location, such as a mobile switching centre, either by fibre-optic cables or by higher-frequency radio links.

Switching Technologies

Switching refers to the process of establishing connections between different nodes within a network. Once a connection is made, information can be routed between specific points on the network. There are three main switching technologies used to provide services over the different transmission infrastructures described above: circuit switching; packet switching using a managed IP network; and packet switching using the public Internet.

The dominant technology used to connect calls for fixed telephone networks (PSTN) has traditionally been the circuit switch. This is a device that sets up a call by providing users with a dial tone when they pick up a telephone receiver (if all lines are busy, then no dial tone is given), automatically establishes an electronic calling path through the network and, when the call is complete, 'takes down' the call by breaking the connection and releasing the calling path, allowing the network to be used by other users.[18] Circuit switching has also

---

[16] FTTN involves the use of the existing copper network to transmit signals from the node (such as a cabinet) to the customer.

[17] Although operators control the specifications of their cable networks, the adoption of the general-purpose Data Over Cable Service Interface Specification (DOCSIS) standard makes them flexible, and allows the addition of data transfer on cable networks, allowing cable operators to provide internet services using HFC infrastructure.

[18] Originally, switches involved operators sitting at switchboards in telephone exchanges who would physically make the connection between the caller and the receiving party. Over time, this was replaced by electronic switching.

been used for mobile communications.[19] Circuit switching therefore allows for a continuous calling path across the network for the duration of the call which utilises a specific band width. Historically, switched networks were based around analogue signals, whereby voice frequencies were superimposed on an electrical signal at the switch (hence circuit switching) and carried over the copper wire. As described above, fixed line networks are generally evolving from analogue-based circuit switching to digital-based packet switching.

Packet switching involves the conversion of all signals on the network (including voice calls) into binary digits or bits, which are then assembled into specially formatted units ('groups of bits') called 'packets' and transported using data switching protocols (based on the Transmission Control Protocol (TCP)/IP).[20] In simple terms, the IP contains the addressing information and other control information, which enables packets to be routed from a source to a destination across one or more IP-based networks. The IP is a so-called 'connection-less protocol', and each packet contains all of the addressing and control information necessary for it to be routed from the source to its destination. This allows various packets in a sequence to be separated at one end, follow different routes to a particular destination, and then be reassembled at the receiving end.[21] This transmission process allows for the efficient utilisation of capacity and the more rapid delivery of packets to their destination. Unlike circuit switching, where a single calling path is established for each call and the desired bandwidth is reserved for the duration of the call (and cannot be used to transmit other signals during this time), IP-based packet-switched networks allow users to share the available bandwidth of packet trunks, and other packet processing resources, which increases efficiency. An important aspect of IP-based packet switching is that it can be used on any transmission infrastructure (cable, fibre or DSL), and is not therefore tailored to a specific transmission technology.[22]

While IP-based packet switching allows for the more efficient use of network capacity, it also increases the potential for greater interference among users and, at times of severe congestion (where the number of packets on the network exceeds the available bandwidth capacity), this can lead to certain packets being delayed or even discarded.[23] The potential for delay in delivery, or for packets to be discarded, has obvious implications for some services, such as voice calls and other 'real-time' applications.[24] Managed IP networks

---

[19] Earlier second-generation (2G) and third-generation (3G) networks typically used circuit switching for voice calls and text (SMS) messages and packet switching for data services (such as accessing the Internet).

[20] The 'IP suite' comprises a suite of communication protocols, of which the IP and the TCP are the best known. However, the full IP suite comprises a number of layers, including a link layer, an internet (IP) layer, a transport layer and an application layer.

[21] Bluhm and Lichtenberg (2011) suggest that 'these packets can be thought of as envelopes with address information that allows them to be reassembled at the far end'.

[22] In contrast to the traditional PSTN, which typically used a single technology and single switching technique to carry voice calls, NGNs use a common packet switching technique, based on the IP, to transmit digitised 'bits' (including voice calls) across different network platforms and technologies.

[23] This differs from circuit-switched networks where congestion is managed at the time of trying to gain access to a calling path in the first instance. If a circuit is available, then the call will proceed, otherwise a busy signal is received. Once a calling path is established, then it is allocated a well-defined bandwidth which is constant for the duration of the call.

[24] Other services and applications, such as data packets including email and images, can tolerate some delay and congestion on the network.

address these problems by defining particular classes of service to ensure that the quality of time-sensitive services, such as voice calls and certain data communications, is maintained. Managed IP networks use mechanisms such as prioritisation, and other 'traffic-shaping' techniques, which separate certain voice packets from other traffic to reduce latency (i.e. delay) and ensure greater levels of reliability. In this way, managed IP networks are seen as being able to combine the efficiency and flexibility of packet-based networks with the quality of service associated with circuit switching.

A third type of switching technology is used by certain internet applications, sometimes referred to as 'over-the-top' (OTT) applications (such as Skype, Facetime, Teams, WhatsApp, Zoom or Vonage), to convert voice and video signals into digital packets, which are then transmitted across the public Internet like any other form of data. On the public Internet, information packets are sent from one packet switch to the next just like in the managed IP networks described above. However, there is no router on the public Internet responsible for prioritising time-sensitive services, or for assuring that the packets are delivered in the right sequence, as there are in managed IP networks.[25] Congestion on the public Internet is currently addressed according to a 'best-efforts' standard, where all packets are treated the same way, and queuing is applied at times of congestion, where some packets are delayed at either a router or a source. This process of buffering, or discarding packets, in times of high congestion does not discriminate among packets and can be arbitrary, meaning that packets of all types of information flows can be affected by congestion. This can potentially lead to various quality of service issues, such as latency (delay in delivery of a packet of data from one point to another) or jitter (erratic delivery of packets). However, in times of low congestion, OTT services (such as VoIP) can be provided at a similar level of quality to that provided by managed IP networks.

Services

As noted above, historically, the different transmission infrastructures tended to be closely associated with the services they provided: the PSTN was conditioned to carry fixed (wireline) voice calls, mobile networks were initially designed to carry wireless voice calls, and cable networks were conditioned to broadcast television (TV) signals. However, following the technological developments described above in terms of digitisation, switching technology and the upgrade of capacity of infrastructure, it is now possible for the operators of the different infrastructures (telephone companies, cable companies, wireless companies), as well as new entrants, to offer a range of services. This process is often referred to as 'convergence' in telecommunications. Broadly, the services supplied over telecommunications networks can be categorised as voice services, data services and other multimedia or broadcasting services.

---

[25] Hatfield, Mitchell and Srinagesh (2005) explain this transmission process for the Internet as follows: 'In the Internet, addressed packets of information (IP packets) are sent through the network from one router (packet switch) to the next router in a store-and-forward fashion. The router performs a "dumb" function – it examines the address information and very rapidly forwards the packet to another router topologically "closer" to the intended recipient. Unlike earlier packet switched data networks, Internet routers are not responsible for correcting errors in the information contained in the packets, for lost packets, or for assuring that the packets are delivered in the right sequence. Instead the hosts (e.g. personal computer "clients" and "servers") at the edge of the network take on this responsibility.'

Within the voice category, there are at least three ways in which users can make and receive local calls: intra-state calls, inter-state calls and international calls. First, call can be made using a traditional fixed (or wireline) circuit-based switch service.[26] Second voice and video calls can be transmitted over the Internet.[27] These include managed (or interconnected) VoIP services where the provider of a customer's broadband service also provides the voice service and controls the quality provided,[28] and OTT or unmanaged VoIP applications, such as Skype, Facetime, Zoom, Teams and Vonage, which are accessed using the public Internet. Many OTT or unmanaged VoIP applications do not charge for calls to other subscribers who use that application. Finally, voice calls can be made using wireless or mobile networks.[29] This method for placing and receiving calls has become an increasingly important form of communication over the past two decades, and it is estimated that there are over 8.6 billion mobile subscribers globally.[30] The growth and penetration rates of mobile services in developing countries has also been exponential (increasing by 470 per cent between 2005 and 2021), as they are seen to offer a more effective means of communication than the installation of fixed telephone networks.[31]

A second group of services supplied over telecommunications networks are data services. Different data-related activities require different speeds to be viable. For example low-speed services, such as email, internet audio streaming or web browsing, require relatively low transfer speeds, while other services, such as online gaming applications, can require transfer speeds of over 10 Mbps (megabits per second) to be viable. Various types of access to data services are offered to consumers. While dial-up internet services (sometimes called narrowband services) was the predominant way in which many consumer accessed data services in the past,[32] this has now been replaced by broadband access services in many jurisdictions. Broadband access services are considerably faster and do not require that the customer place a call each time they wish to access the Internet (i.e. they are 'always on'). As described above, different technologies are used to provide broadband access, including various Digital Subscriber Line (xDSL) technologies, cable modem services, and Fibre to the Premises/Cabinet (FTTP/C) services. In 2020, around 33 per cent of fixed broadband subscriptions in OECD (Organisation for Economic Cooperation and Development) countries were cable, 32 per cent were DSL and 32 per cent were fibre.[33]

---

[26] In the USA, in 2020, there were 38 million end-user switched access lines. See FCC (2020a).

[27] From the consumer's perspective, this requires them to connect a landline phone to the back of the broadband router rather than a phone socket in the wall.

[28] In the USA the term 'interconnected VoIP service' is used, while in the UK the term 'managed VoIP' is used. In 2020 there was an estimated 70 million interconnected VoIP subscriptions. See FCC (2020a).

[29] Fourth- and fifth-generation (4G and 5G) networks allow for voice calls using a managed VoIP service or using an OTT application VoIP service.

[30] The reason for the large number of subscribers is that some people have more than one mobile phone. This compares to an estimated 2.2 billion mobile phone users worldwide in 2005. See ITU (2022b).

[31] ITU (2022b). In 2021, there were 6.9 billion subscriptions in the developing world, up from 1.2 billion in 2005.

[32] This service requires that the customer have a modem attached to their computer, which converts analogue signals into digital signals and places a call every time they wish to access the Internet.

[33] The remaining 6 per cent was other. However, there can be significant differences between countries. In the UK, only 20 per cent of fixed broadband connections were cable and 60 per cent were fibre (with the remainder DSL) in 2020; while, in the USA, in 2019, 64 per cent were cable and 16 per cent were fibre (with the remainder DSL). See FCC (2020a), OECD (2021a) and Ofcom (2021a).

The transfer speeds for broadband internet services vary greatly across technologies.[34] Data services can also be acquired by consumers from other media, most notably wireless data access services. Wireless broadband access allows consumers to access data and the Internet via a range of devices and appliances such as mobile phones, tablet computers and other devices. There are different types of wireless broadband access, including via mobile telephone networks as well as through wide-area or local-area networks (such as WiMax and Wi-Fi). New 5G networks will provide high transfer speeds up to 200 times faster than current 4G (Long Term Evolution (LTE)) networks, which will be sufficient to support applications such as smart homes, three-dimensional (3D) videos, remote medical services, and virtual and augmented reality.[35]

A third general type of service supplied on communication networks is multimedia and broadcasting services. Traditionally, broadcasting services were supplied as separate services to end-users on some transmission media, most notably cable networks, where cable TV, data and calls were sold as different products. However, this is changing in many jurisdictions, as multimedia and broadcasting applications (such as Video on Demand, streaming services (such as Netflix) and Internet Protocol television (IPTV) services) allow users to use their broadband data access services to view broadcasting content via the Internet without the need to acquire a separate TV service.

Service Providers

As the range and type of services offered on telecommunications networks have changed, so have the types of providers. In many jurisdictions, the largest fixed line telecommunications providers (such as Verizon and AT&T in the USA, BT in the UK, France Télécom in France, Deutsche Telekom in Germany, Telmex in Mexico and Telstra in Australia) are the successor organisations of those that historically had a monopoly on the supply of fixed line voice services.[36] Alongside these former incumbents, there are now, in many jurisdictions, a number of competing fixed line operators who entered the market following the restructuring policies of the 1980s and 1990s, which lifted statutory restrictions on entry.[37] Another important group of fixed line telecommunications service providers in many jurisdictions are cable companies who, over the years, have emerged as major competitors to the incumbent telecommunications providers for both voice and other services. Today, two of the largest fixed line broadband network providers in the world – Comcast and Charter Communications – began life as cable companies.[38] In the USA, there are now over 1300 providers of fixed line residential services, with the five largest

---

[34] The minimum transfer speed of any broadband access technology is constantly changing, but has been defined as between 2.5 Mbps by the Federal Communications Commission (FCC) and 256 kbps by the International Telecommunications Union (ITU). The transfer speed also varies with the transmission technology. In the USA, the median speeds in 2017 were 20 Mbps for DSL services, 78 Mbps for fibre services and 120 Mbps for cable connections. See FCC (2018).

[35] The OECD (2019b) estimate that 5G download speeds will be up to 20 Gbps (gigabits per second), 10 Gbps upload speeds and latency of one millisecond (1 ms).

[36] In the USA, these are referred to as Incumbent Local Exchange Carriers (ILECs).

[37] In the USA, these are referred to as Competitive Local Exchange Carriers (CLECs).

[38] This conversion of cable companies from supplying only broadcasting services to supplying telecommunications services began in the 1990s when some cable companies installed telephone switching equipment on their networks which could allow for voice calls.

providers (including traditional fixed line providers Verizon and AT&T, and the two cab
companies Comcast and Charter) accounting for 68 per cent of the market.[39] In the UK, th
four main providers of fixed broadband services accounted for 86 per cent of the mark
in 2020, with the former incumbent BT holding a market share of 33 per cent, and th
major cable provider Virgin Media having a share of 20 per cent.[40]

A different set of service providers are mobile communications or wireless carriers, wh
provide wireless voice and data services. The number of mobile network operators vari
across countries and is dependent on the number of spectrum licences issued. Howeve
in many countries, the industry is defined by an oligopolistic structure, with three c
four major mobile network operators.[41] In the USA, there are currently three nationwic
wireless providers (AT&T, T-Mobile and Verizon Wireless), as well as three regional pro
viders, and dozens of smaller wireless providers that supply services in a single, ofte
rural, geographic area.[42] In some countries, retail competition has emerged in the for
of mobile virtual network operators (MVNOs), who do not own licensed mobile spectru
or other physical infrastructure, but purchase wholesale network services and then rese
these services in the retail market.[43]

While the discussion above has categorised providers according to technology, it
important to recall that, as a result of convergence, many providers now offer multip
services. Thus, while cable companies are now major suppliers of telephone and broac
band services, some incumbent telephone companies are now offering digital televisic
services (such as AT&T (DIRECTV Stream) in the USA and BT (BT TV) in the UK). I
addition to these main categories of providers of telecommunications services, there are
range of other providers of specific services that use telecommunications networks, suc
as providers of internet applications (e.g. Skype, Facebook/WhatsApp, Microsoft Team
Snapchat) and providers of streaming and broadcast content services, such as IPTV pro
viders (e.g. BBC iPlayer, Netflix, Disney+ and Hulu).

11.1.4 Allocation of Capacity

In fixed line and cable networks, the transmission capacity needed to use a netwol
is owned and managed by those who make the initial investment. As described belov
while in some jurisdictions a dominant or incumbent fixed line network operator can k
required to 'unbundle' its network and share access to certain network elements, this
typically subject to requirements that capacity be allocated on non-discriminatory term
and that the access provider supplies an equivalent level of service to all access seeke
(including its own internal division if it is vertically integrated).

---

[39] FCC (2020c).
[40] Ofcom (2021a).
[41] Such concentration may not always be harmful to consumers. Using data for thirty-three OECD
countries, Genakos, Valletti and Verboven (2018) found that increasing market concentration in
the mobile sector increased prices, but also increased investment per operator, thus giving rise to a
trade-off.
[42] FCC (2020c).
[43] In the USA, the largest MVNO (TracFone) had 21 million subscribers in 2019.

One area where a market-based capacity-type allocation method is used in the telecommunications industry is for radio spectrum, which is necessary for mobile communications networks, but is also a scarce resource used for other purposes (such as air navigation services, broadcasting, satellite services, military, space research). While non-market/administrative mechanisms, such as so-called 'beauty contests',[44] have been used to allocate mobile (wireless) spectrum licences in the past, the use of auctions to allocate spectrum is now more prominent. Well-designed auctions can be an efficient way to allocate the spectrum licences needed to provide mobile services by requiring bidders to compete with one another to obtain a small number of exclusive licences (typically three or four).[45] Auctions can also provide additional revenues to government. In India, an auction of third-generation (3G) spectrum resulted in an estimated $11 billion revenue for the government,[46] while in the USA it is claimed that spectrum auctions between 1994 and 2019 resulted in collections of $117 billion.[47]

In practice, there can be a trade-off between allocating spectrum licences in a way that maximises consumer and social welfare (particularly by promoting competition in downstream markets) or that maximises the revenues from the proceeds of the auction.[48] This trade-off can arise where an auction allocates spectrum to operators who offer the highest bids (and thus maximise revenues), even if that allocation of spectrum is not one that maximises consumer welfare. For example, incumbent operators might submit high bids for new spectrum in order to keep out new entrants, and thus affect competition in downstream retail markets.[49] Poorly designed auctions can also give rise to strategic behaviour on the part of bidders, allowing them to engage in (tacit and explicit) collusion, which can also be harmful to consumers.[50]

To address these concerns, regulators can implement various measures such as: reserving certain blocks of spectrum for new entrants; limiting or 'capping' the amount of spectrum that any one operator can hold;[51] applying credits or discounts to the bids of certain participants, such as new entrants; and introducing other aspects of auction design to prevent anti-competitive behaviour.[52] Regulators also actively observe the outcomes of auctions in other jurisdictions, and use this information to establish reserve prices. For

---

[44] Gans, King and Wright (2005) define a 'beauty contest' as involving potential users submitting business plans to government, and the winner being chosen from those submitting the plans. This approach was used to award second-generation (2G) spectrum licences in the UK, and for 3G spectrum licences in Sweden, Spain and France.

[45] There is an extensive literature on auction design, including Myerson (1981), Armstrong (2000), Jehiel and Moldovanu (2003), Klemperer (2002a, 2004), Milgrom (2004) and Salant (2014). Indeed, the benefits of using auctions to allocate scarce spectrum for radio stations was first recognised by Coase (1959).

[46] See Cramton, Filiz-Ozbay, Ozbay and Sujarittanonta (2012).

[47] FCC (2020a). In early 2021, it was reported that mobile operators in the USA paid $81 billion for mid-band spectrum to provide 5G services. EU 5G Observatory (2022).

[48] Rey and Salant (2019) explore this trade-off in a setting where an incumbent enjoys a cost advantage over a potential entrant. See also Klemperer (2004) and Cramton, Kwerel, Rosston and Skrzypacz (2011).

[49] In other words, the private valuation of the bidders may not be the same as the social value. See Borenstein (1988) and Kasberger (2020) on post-auction welfare.

[50] See Klemperer (2002b) and Jehiel and Moldovanu (2003).

[51] In the UK, this cap is set at 37 per cent of overall holdings of spectrum by any one provider.

[52] See Cramton, Kwerel, Rosston and Skrzypacz (2011).

example, many countries are currently using auctions to allocate 5G spectrum licences and are closely watching outcomes in other jurisdictions.[53]

In addition to the use of market-based mechanisms for the initial allocation of spectrum, in some jurisdictions annual charges or licence fees are levied which reflect the market value of the spectrum (based on its opportunity cost) and to ensure that spectrum is used efficiently once it is allocated. The possibility of secondary trading in spectrum also exists in some places, whereby existing holders of spectrum rights sell, lease or transfer all or part of their spectrum entitlements.[54] This ability to trade spectrum is seen as important in allowing new entrants to access the mobile market, and therefore increase the prospects of competition in that market. It can also ensure the more effective use of spectrum and introduce greater flexibility. In some countries, spectrum can be reassigned without any regulatory approval, although, in other countries, the regulator needs to approve the assignments and may apply certain conditions to ensure spectrum is not initially acquired with the aim of reselling at a higher price.

11.2 APPROACH TO TELECOMMUNICATIONS REGULATION

11.2.1 Activities Subject to Regulation

Increasing convergence in technologies, and in the services that are offered across different telecommunications networks (fixed line networks, cable networks and mobile networks), means that they now often supply the same, or closely substitutable, services to one another. However, the rationale for and the type of the regulation applied differ for each type of network.

Regulation of the Fixed Line Network
The regulation of fixed line networks has changed over time, reflecting shifting rationales for regulation, particularly as competition has developed and new technological innovations have increased the substitution possibilities. Historically, the fixed line network was considered to be a natural monopoly and regulation took the form of either state ownership or control on entry and retail prices. However, restructuring policies, starting from the 1980s in many countries, introduced competition into all stages or activities in the industry on the basis that the telecommunications network was *no longer* a natural monopoly and all activities were potentially competitive.[55] As described below, an important part of the policies to facilitate competition was a requirement that some essential

---

[53] See EU 5G Observatory (2022). Some jurisdictions (such as Japan, China and Uruguay) are allocating spectrum using direct assignment to incentivise network investment given the high costs of 5G deployment, and to ensure certain roll-out targets are met. See ITU (2022a).

[54] Spectrum trading is allowed in Australia, Brazil, India, New Zealand, the UK and the USA.

[55] See Brock (2002). Robinson and Weisman (2008) note in the US context: 'Exactly when the natural monopoly paradigm shifted to a competitive paradigm is impossible to trace with certainty; but we can say that, more or less Congress declared it officially moribund if not dead with the enactment of the 1996 Telecommunications Act.' Cave, Majumdar and Vogelsang (2002) observe that: 'The earlier view of telecommunication as a natural monopoly has now given way to one in which almost all parts of it are seen as susceptible to some form of competition.'

network elements of the incumbent fixed line operators must be 'unbundled' and shared with competitors.[56]

Three broad forms of competition have since emerged for fixed line networks.[57] A first form is facilities-based competition, or infrastructure competition, where an entrant invests in all the network infrastructure (switches, switching equipment, fibre-optic cables and other transmission equipment) with the aim of competing 'head-to-head' with the incumbent. A second form is 'quasi-facilities'-based competition, where the entrant invests in some equipment, but also purchases some 'unbundled' services/elements from the fixed line incumbent in order to provide end-to-end services to consumers. The final form of competition is resale competition, where an entrant makes minimal investment in network infrastructure and largely acts as a reseller of the incumbent's services (but differentiates itself in terms of customer service, etc.).

The current approach to regulation of fixed line networks in many jurisdictions tends to be calibrated to each of these different types of competition, and can vary according to the level of current or prospective competition in different areas within a jurisdiction.[58] For example, in areas where competition takes the form of quasi-facilities competition, the focus is on ensuring competitive entrants can gain access to unbundled services/elements on reasonable terms. In contrast, in jurisdictions where facilities-based competition has emerged, the focus is on assessing the extent to which such competition is effective in constraining the exercise of market power for certain services or in specific geographical areas.[59] Where it is applied, regulation of fixed line networks tends to focus on three areas. First, incumbent providers (or those assessed as having significant market power/dominance) are obliged to provide access to certain unbundled elements or services at the wholesale level (such as the local loops, ducts, poles) on non-discriminatory terms. Second, the prices and non-price terms for certain wholesale services are required to be cost-based/oriented, or just and reasonable. Third, regulation can also apply to retail prices charged to consumers in some jurisdictions, although increasingly this takes the form of notification requirements. As discussed below, regulation can apply to both 'legacy' copper fixed line networks and services provided on new NGNs.

---

[56] Broadly, the aim of unbundling policies was to allow competitive entrants (sometimes called access seekers) to gain access to technically and commercially important elements or components of the incumbent's network (such as the local loop or the last mile from an exchange to a customer's premises). They could then use these inputs to replicate the offers of the incumbent operator. The overall aim was to create a 'level playing field' where entrants could choose between either 'building' their own infrastructure or 'buying' critical inputs from the incumbent provider (the so-called 'make-or-buy' or 'build-or-buy' decision as discussed in Chapter 6).

[57] Interestingly, Yoo (2017) observes that, in the USA, the 1996 Telecommunications Act envisioned that competition in local telephone service might follow one of three paths: resale competition; full-facilities competition; or, third, an entrant may provide some of the elements needed to offer local telephone service and obtain the rest from the incumbent.

[58] In the UK, for example, three broad areas are identified for regulating residential broadband services: competitive areas (where there is established competition and regulation is not applied); areas with the potential for material competition (where the incumbent fixed line operator is required to provide wholesale access to its network); and remaining areas (where the incumbent fixed line operator is the only provider).

[59] BEREC (2021a) reports that, in Europe, around 50 per cent of national regulatory authorities apply geographical regulation for legacy networks, while around 60 per cent apply it for fibre networks.

In the USA, at the federal level, the FCC is responsible for regulating the charges and practices associated with the provision of 'telecommunications services'. All incumbent fixed line telecommunications service providers (known as incumbent local exchange carriers (ILECs)) must file tariff schedules with the FCC,[60] and the tariffs must be 'just and reasonable and may not be unreasonably discriminatory'.[61] While ILECs were initially subject to extensive rate regulation, as facilities-based competition has developed, there is now a greater reliance on market competition (backed by a complaint mechanism) to ensure that rates are just and reasonable. For some services, such as business data services, the degree of regulation depends on an assessment of whether competition in a specific geographic area reaches certain threshold levels.[62] As described in Section 11.3, the scope of regulation has gradually narrowed over time and fixed line operators are now under limited requirements to provide access to unbundled network elements.[63] The FCC can also forbear from applying regulation where it is in the public interest and the market sector is assessed as competitive, and this approach has, at different times, been applied to broadband internet access services.[64] Since 2017, broadband internet access service providers are subject to a light-touch regulatory framework.[65] State regulators are responsible for overseeing the tariffs for local and intra-state fixed line services and around thirty-eight states have passed legislation which has reduced the scope or eliminated the regulation of traditional fixed line services. In many states, regulators have reduced the scope of regulation in response to increased competition, including by making the filing of tariffs optional, removing oversight of the majority of retail services and exempting these services from regulation for any carrier that faces two unrelated competitors.[66] Notwithstanding the general deregulatory approach to fixed line services, some state regulators have recently sought to impose price regulation by fixing the price that broadband services can be set at for low-income households.[67]

---

[60] Competitive local exchange carriers (CLECs) can also file tariffs with FCC but are not required to do so. Filed tariffs typically include charges for: end-user access; switched access; business data services; and rates for other services such as DSL, packet-switched services and long-distance director assistance.

[61] However, charges for unbundled network elements are based on forward-looking costs, which according to the FCC can differ from the more flexible 'just and reasonable' standard. See FCC (2017a).

[62] Business data services are high-capacity connections used to transmit voice and data traffic over dedicated facilities and are used by businesses, schools, hospitals and a wide range of other institutions. The FCC removed most *ex ante* price regulations on ILECs, but maintained regulation for lower-speed services in areas where competition did not reach certain threshold levels. However, it committed to update its assessment of competition in those areas every three years. See FCC (2017a).

[63] In 2020, the FCC (2020b) eliminated unbundling requirements for a range of services, including voice-grade narrowband services nationwide, and the unbundling requirements for access to 'dark fibre' in circumstances where a competitor fibre network exists within half a mile of a wire centre.

[64] Between 1996 and 2014, broadband internet access services were classified as 'information services' (rather than 'telecommunications services') and as such were subject to light-handed regulatory oversight. However, in 2014, as part of the Net Neutrality regulations (see Section 11.4.3), the FCC reclassified broadband internet access services as a telecommunications service, which led to a more intensive regulation similar to that which applied to traditional fixed voice services. This classification was subsequently reversed in 2017.

[65] See FCC (2018). See also Yoo (2018) for a fuller analysis.

[66] See Lichtenberg (2011, 2015). For example, in New Hampshire, regulated local exchange carriers are no longer required to file a rate schedule or tariff with the PUC but must maintain a publicly accessible website that contains its current rates, terms and conditions.

[67] In April 2021, New York state enacted a law requiring that broadband access service be offered to qualifying low-income households for $15 per month.

In Europe, a common EU-wide process is applied for determining which telecommunications markets should be subject to *ex ante* regulation. As described below, this process involves EU Member States periodically assessing the state of competition in pre-identified markets to identify providers that can exercise significant market power (SMP), and the services which are therefore subject to *ex ante* regulation.[68] The number of recommended pre-identified markets to which *ex ante* regulation might apply has progressively reduced from seventeen markets in 2002 to just two markets in 2020.[69] As competition has developed in many EU jurisdictions, this has led to the removal of *ex ante* retail price regulation, meaning that fixed line regulation principally focuses on wholesale products.[70] Accordingly, under the current EU regulatory framework, national regulatory authorities (NRAs) can impose 'remedies' on fixed line operators within a relevant 'wholesale local access market' or 'wholesale dedicated capacity market' if they have SMP.[71] These remedies can require fixed line operators to provide competitors/entrants with access to specific network facilities (unbundled local loops, sub-loops, and active or virtual network elements and services).[72] NRAs can impose price/charge controls or introduce obligations that access prices be cost-oriented and set out the cost accounting systems that must be used (e.g. current cost or historical cost).[73] In practice, this means that certain wholesale services (such as voice interconnection, wholesale access and wholesale broadband services) are typically subject to access requirements and price regulation where competition is assessed as insufficient. Regulation currently applies to both legacy/copper networks and services and new fibre/NGN networks.[74] However, differences can be seen across EU Member States in the approach to new NGNs. In some countries, unbundling requirements for NGNs have been extended to physical infrastructure such as ducts and pole access,[75] while, in other countries, dark fibre services are also subject to access and price regulation (e.g. in France, Germany and the UK). As discussed below, in Spain and Portugal, a policy of forbearance from requiring access has been adopted to promote investment in ultrafast broadband.

Regulation of Cable Networks

The regulation of cable television networks (used to carry voice and data services, sometimes referred to as cable modem services) has typically been less comprehensive than the regulation of the fixed networks and, in a large number of jurisdictions, there is very

---

[68] The EC (2018) has published guidelines for this process to ensure consistency.
[69] See EC (2020b). These are: the market for wholesale local access provided at a fixed location; and the market for wholesale dedicated capacity.
[70] The 2014 Recommendation on Relevant Markets removed *retail* electronic communications markets as being considered susceptible to *ex ante* regulation.
[71] The products included within a wholesale local access market have progressively expanded from legacy copper network products to fibre-based products, such as fibre and cable networks.
[72] Regulation can apply to both 'passive' wholesale products such as the unbundled local loop (which gives the access seeker greater control) as well as 'active' bitstream products that include electronic components (sometimes called virtual unbundled local access (VULA)).
[73] Cost orientation obligations place the onus on the operator to show that prices are cost-oriented.
[74] BEREC (2021a) records that twenty-four NRAs applied regulation to operators of fibre networks (FTTC and/or FTTH), while only two countries applied regulation only to legacy copper networks.
[75] See WIK (2019).

limited, or no specific, regulatory oversight of cable network operators. In part, this may reflect the different levels of penetration of cable networks across jurisdictions.[76] However, it may also reflect the fact that, to the extent to which cable networks cover the same area (or 'footprint') as the fixed line network, it can offer substitute services to those offered on the fixed line network and is therefore constrained in its actions by *inter*-modal competition.

In the USA, cable modem services have generally avoided being subject to the 'common carrier' requirements that apply to fixed line operators, on the basis of being classified as an 'information service' and not a 'telecommunications service'.[77] This has meant that cable network operators have not been subject to the various unbundling and access requirements that have characterised the regulation of fixed line network.[78]

Policy at the European level in relation to the cable industry began with the 1995 Cable Directive,[79] which sought to remove restrictions on the provision of telecommunications services by cable network operators and to allow cable network operators to provide telephone and internet access under the same conditions as other operators using other infrastructure.[80] Cable network operators are subject to the same EU regulatory framework for electronic communications as fixed line operators, and cable services have at times been included in the assessments of the relevant product markets for wholesale broadband access by NRAs.[81] However, in practice, there have been only a limited number of instances where remedies (i.e. regulatory obligations) have been imposed on cable operators. For example, the European Commission has in the past taken the view that the relevant market for wholesale (physical) network infrastructure access should not be broadened to include wholesale access via a cable network.[82] In relation to wholesale broadband access requirements, NRAs have generally not found cable operators to occupy a position of SMP on any broadband market.[83]

An issue that has arisen in some jurisdictions relates to cross-ownership of cable networks by incumbent fixed line operators. In the USA, cable operators are prohibited from owning more than 10 per cent of local exchange carriers within the cable franchise

---

[76] In the USA, around 89 per cent of households are passed by a cable network. The figure is much lower in Europe, and in 2020 only 45 per cent of EU households had access to high-speed cable broadband services and 27.8 per cent of EU homes were passed by cable networks upgraded to the DOCSIS 3.1 standard. However, in some EU countries, such as the Netherlands, Belgium, Portugal and Romania, cable penetration is above 90 per cent. See EC (2021e).

[77] See FCC Cable Modem Declaratory Ruling (2002).

[78] Hazlett (2005) describes the history of the regulation of the cable industry in the USA.

[79] Directive 95/51 of 18 October 1995 ('Cable Directive') and Directive 96/19 of 13 March 1996.

[80] The overarching purpose of these Directives was, according to the European Commission, 'to stimulate competition in the telecommunications sector by fostering the growth of telecommunications services provided on platforms other than the traditional telephone networks' (EC, 2003).

[81] Between 2014 to 2021, NRAs were required to assess the extent of significant market power for VULA and bitstream access for cable networks. A 2016 review for the European Commission recommended that assessments of competition in wholesale markets should be 'multi-platform' and specifically that cable networks should be integrated into the market definition exercise. See WIK (2016).

[82] This position was adopted in response to the Portuguese regulator's proposal to include wholesale broadband access via cable as part of the relevant market. See EC Portugal (2009).

[83] Although there are exceptions. For example, cable operators were found to have SMP in Belgium and Malta in the past, and the issue of whether a cable operator held a position of joint dominance/SMP has also been looked at in the Netherlands. The Danish regulator has also imposed remedies on a cable operator in the past; however, this reflected the cross-ownership of the DSL network and the cable network.

area.[84] Similarly, in Europe, the 1995 Cable Directive sought to separate the ownership of cable networks and fixed line operators in EU Member States; however, some countries were slow to implement this requirement, and in some cases common ownership of the cable network and the fixed line network existed up until the mid-2000s.[85] In contrast, in Australia, the incumbent fixed line operator Telstra holds a 35 per cent stake in the major nationwide cable operator (Foxtel).

Regulation of Mobile Networks

Mobile or wireless networks present a very different regulatory history to fixed line networks and, perhaps more importantly, jurisdictions have taken varying approaches to the regulation of mobile network operators. While, in the very early days, the expectation was that cost and technical complexity would make mobile/cellular technology a natural monopoly, this position changed such that mobile networks were seen, first, as a complement to the fixed line network, and later as a substitute or competitor to fixed line networks.[86]

Generally speaking, mobile communications have not been subject to direct *retail* price controls; however, price regulation is applied at the wholesale level in some jurisdictions, for the termination of calls (so-called mobile termination charges) and for international roaming (where a customer of a network in one country makes a call while overseas). As discussed in Chapter 6, in jurisdictions where the 'Calling Party Network Pays' (CPNP) principle applies,[87] such as Australia and EU Member States, mobile termination rates have been subject to wholesale regulation to address concerns about the ability of the terminating network operator to exercise market power and charge excessive prices (the 'termination monopoly problem'). This regulation of (wholesale) termination charges has, however, at times given rise to questions about whether regulation that reduces wholesale charges could inadvertently lead to an increase in retail prices – the so-called 'waterbed effect' (see Box 11.1). In other jurisdictions, such as Canada, Singapore, Hong Kong and the USA, there is typically no direct regulation of wholesale mobile termination rates, and interconnection arrangements between mobile providers are based around 'bill and keep' type arrangements, or reciprocity requirements for negotiations between mobile providers.

The Interaction between Regulation and Competition Law

Alongside the *ex ante* regulation of the telecommunications industry, competition policy has historically played an important role in the industry.[88] The prominent role for

---

[84] In 2012, the FCC adapted their approach to forbear from applying this cross-ownership restriction to competitive local exchange carriers. See FCC (2012).

[85] For example, in Germany.

[86] See Yoo (2017).

[87] This is where the calling party's network (the originating network) is levied a charge by other network operators for terminating calls on their network.

[88] In the USA, for example, it was the investigation by the Department of Justice (DoJ) under the antitrust laws which led to the divestiture of AT&T in 1984. Even earlier than this, in 1913 the DoJ filed an action in relation to AT&T's practices under the antitrust laws, which led to the so-called 'Kingsbury Commitment'. Similarly, in New Zealand, the Telecom *Clear Communications* case discussed in Chapter 6, which focused on the ECPR as an access pricing rule, was brought under the competition provisions of the Commerce Act 1986 (albeit in the absence of an industry-specific regulatory framework at that time).

competition law reflects the fact that many of the issues which arise in telecommunica tions are similar to those which arise under the so-called 'essential facilities' doctrine.[89]

In Australia, the telecommunications industry is subject to its own industry-specif competition law provision.[90] In the EU, the regulatory framework has been explicitl modelled on concepts from European competition law and has the stated aim of pro gressively reducing '*ex-ante* sector specific rules as competition in the markets develo and, ultimately, for electronic communications to be governed by competition law only'. Incorporating concepts and methodologies from competition law in the *ex ante* regulator framework is seen as particularly appropriate as the telecommunications industry tran sitions from being an industry characterised by a monopolistic (or oligopolistic) suppl structure to a more competitive market structure. This is because it can capture both th traditional policy concerns associated with monopolies (such as overcharging and ineff cient pricing) as well as concerns that can arise in oligopolistic settings, such as potenti tacit collusion or concerns that vertically integrated operators with SMP might seek t foreclose competitors by engaging in predatory pricing or a margin squeeze.

However, the precise interaction between the *ex ante* price regulation and the appl cation of *ex post* competition law for pricing abuses has at times been unclear. As note in Chapter 8, in Europe, the position is that prices/rates approved by NRAs can still b found as anti-competitive under competition law if they result in a margin squeeze.[92] I contrast, in the USA, the courts have adopted the position that, once rates are subject t regulation, the scope for the application of the antitrust laws is more limited.[93] Question about the appropriate relationship between *ex ante* regulation and *ex post* competitio law also feature prominently in net neutrality debates. As discussed in Section 11.4 below, there are differences of opinion about whether competition law can be used t address the concerns associated with net neutrality, or whether some form of *ex an* regulation is necessary.

Box 11.1	**Competitive bottlenecks and waterbeds in the telecommunications industry**

Seminal papers published in the 1990s by Armstrong (1996b, 1998) and Laffont, Rey an Tirole (1998a,b) explored the question of whether there was a need for regulation of acce charges in competitive bottleneck settings (where network operators compete for subscrib ers but need to purchase access inputs from each other to provide an end-to-end service or whether competing network operators might agree to charges that are socially optima As discussed in Chapter 6, an important insight from this work was that, in certain ci cumstances, freely negotiated access charges could be used as an instrument of collusio

---

[89] See Faulhaber (2005a), Robinson and Weisman (2008) and Renda (2010).
[90] Part XIB of the Competition and Consumer Act 2010.
[91] See European Electronics Communications Code (Directive 2018/1972) and Telecommunications Directive 2009 (2009/140/EC).
[92] See *Deutsche Telekom AG v. Commission of the European Communities* (2010).
[93] See *Verizon Communications, Inc. v. Law Offices of Curtis V. Trinko LLP* (2004).

by network operators, and this could lead to retail prices that are as high as they would be without competition.[94] The practical importance of this work was two-fold. Firstly, it provided a potential explanation for why observed access prices in some telecommunications industries remained high despite the fact there was competition between network operators for subscribers. Secondly, it challenged the idea that head-to-head competition between competing networks would make regulation of the industry obsolete at some future point.[95] In short, the analysis suggested that, even where there is intensive competition between network operators for subscribers, there may be a continuing rationale for regulatory oversight of the wholesale access prices that network operators charge each other.

While this work on competitive bottlenecks provided an early rationale for the regulation of wholesale access prices in two-way access settings, another strand of analytical work focused on how such wholesale regulation might inadvertently lead to an increase in retail prices. Intuitively, this work, which is based on the analysis of two-sided markets (see Chapters 6 and 12), posits that, when the wholesale access price that network operators levy on one another is reduced because of regulation, a network operator may rebalance their tariff structure and *increase* the level of retail prices to compensate for this loss in access revenue.[96] In essence, the argument is that, if regulation reduces wholesale access prices and associated revenues, network operators may in some circumstances be forced to increase some retail prices to fully recover their costs.[97] This rebalancing of retail tariffs in response to the regulation of wholesale access prices is often referred to as the 'waterbed effect'.[98] The important insight is that, in two-way access settings, such as those involving the setting of fixed-to-mobile (FTM) termination rates or mobile-to-mobile (MTM) termination rates, regulatory intervention to reduce wholesale access prices may not automatically lead to lower retail prices, and therefore may not increase consumer welfare overall.

Empirical studies that have examined if the 'waterbed effect' exists in mobile telecommunications have generally concluded that the effect is not complete.[99] Based on a sample of

---

[94] See Armstrong (1998, 2002), Laffont, Rey and Tirole (1998a) and Laffont and Tirole (2000). These circumstances include where the market is symmetric and there is sufficient product differentiation. Later work by the same authors found that the collusion result is sensitive to assumptions. See the discussion in Section 6.3.3.

[95] See Laffont, Rey and Tirole (1998a) and Armstrong (1997).

[96] If a market is one-sided, reducing wholesale prices by regulation would, other things being equal, and assuming that the retail market is competitive, be expected to reduce retail prices. However, where a market is two-sided, 'one side' of the market (e.g. wholesale access revenues) may be cross-subsidising the other side of the market (e.g. retail calls or handset prices to attract new subscribers). See Rochet and Tirole (2003), Armstrong (2006) and Hausman and Wright (2006).

[97] There are various types of retail tariffs which could be increased, including call prices, connection charges, handset subsidies and monthly rentals.

[98] The term 'waterbed effect' was first used in the UK by the Competition Commission (2003) during its 2002 investigation into mobile telephony, defining the effect as the firm's 'rebalancing of the loss of revenue from capping termination charges with its retrieval through raising prices in the retail sector'.

[99] See Growitsch, Marcus and Wernick (2010) and Genakos and Valletti (2007, 2011a, b). As Armstrong and Wright (2009) explain: where there is a 'complete' or 100 per cent 'waterbed effect', the reduced profits from one source are completely clawed back from subscribers, so that the overall profit impact is zero. In these circumstances, and where the market is not expanding, firms should not object to regulatory interventions in termination prices. However, if market expansion is allowed for, the 'waterbed effect' is less than 100 per cent, which implies that mobile networks will prefer a higher termination charge, and will have an incentive to lobby against regulation that reduces termination charges. Hoernig (2014b) argues that the structure of tariffs matters, and that the waterbed effect is stronger under two-part tariffs than linear tariffs.

twenty countries, Genakos and Valletti (2011b) found at that time that, although regulation reduced mobile termination rates by about 10 per cent, this led to a 5 per cent increase in mobile retail prices.[100] This implied that mobile network operators were able, because of their market power, to retain some termination rents which were not fully competed away in the retail market when competing for subscribers. However, in a subsequent analysis using data over a long time period, the same authors found that the waterbed effect 'unwound' and became insignificant.[101] That is, regulation that reduced mobile termination rates no longer resulted in an increase in mobile retail prices. This result was attributed to the bigger role played by MTM traffic in later years as compared to FTM traffic, and implied that capping of mobile termination rates can reduce the price of mobile calls made to other mobile users.[102] These empirical findings may help to explain why regulators in different countries have adopted different positions on the waterbed effect over time. While it has in the past featured prominently in regulatory proceedings in the UK, regulators such as the European Commission and the Australian regulator have questioned the existence of the 'waterbed effect', and have progressively lowered the allowed level of mobile termination rates to levels close to underlying estimates of LRIC.[103] More recently, the 'waterbed effect' has been considered in the context of net neutrality regulation (see Section 11.4.3 below). An important conclusion of this work is that net neutrality regulations which restrict the ability of internet service providers (ISPs) to charge content providers for prioritised access to the Internet could be inefficient, as they do not allow for any surplus generated from one group of users (content providers) to subsidise the prices levied on another group of users (end-users). Put differently, allowing ISPs to levy charges on content providers could – as a result of the waterbed effect – result in a decrease in subscription fees paid by end-users.[104]

11.2.2 Form and Scope of Price Controls

As outlined in the preceding discussion, price controls are typically only applied to wholesale fixed line services and to mobile telecommunications services in jurisdictions that apply the CPNP principle. Retail price controls have generally been withdrawn in many countries, and the extent of retail price oversight now involves price approvals (where the regulator must approve a retail tariff before it is offered) or price notifications (where the regulator receives the tariff for information purposes only). However, as discussed in Chapter 7, regulators in some countries have drawn on behavioural economics research to introduce measures to simplify how different price offers are presented to consumers to reduce potential customer confusion.

[100] See Genakos and Valletti (2011b).
[101] Genakos and Valletti (2015).
[102] They also found that there was no waterbed effect in countries which introduced mobile termination regulation when the mobile traffic was high, and conversely that the waterbed effect arose in countries which introduced mobile termination regulation when there was low mobile traffic.
[103] See, for example, EC (2009) and ACCC (2009a). In contrast, in its 2002 investigation, the UK Competition Commission (2003) concluded that there was a strong and incomplete waterbed effect and that they were 'not persuaded' that setting mobile termination charges at LRIC would reduce mobile retail prices overall.
[104] See Greenstein, Peitz and Valletti (2016). Bourreau and Lestage (2019) examine a setting where one ISP is vertically integrated and provides access to a rival (non-integrated) ISP. They find a waterbed effect also arises between an access price and the 'termination fees' levied on content providers, and that the socially optimal access price may be above the marginal cost of access (as this results in lower termination fees and hence fosters entry of content providers).

Rate of Return and Price Cap Approaches

The two general forms for controlling prices discussed in Chapter 5 – price caps and rate of return regulation – are both used in the telecommunications industry. However, over time, there has been a significant decline in the use of rate of return regulation in many parts of the world, including the USA, where it is estimated that carriers subject to this form of regulation serve less than 5 per cent of access lines.[105] The widespread adoption of the price cap approach in the telecommunications industry is seen to reflect a number of factors, including that such an approach is well suited to an industry where technological change has reduced the cost of key inputs (such as digital switches and optical fibre), and where such cost reductions can be passed on to consumers without the need for frequent formal rate hearings.[106]

The price cap approach, described in Chapter 5, involves the regulator determining a maximum, or ceiling, on the average increase in prices that the firm can earn for a set of relevant services for a pre-specified, but significant, period of time. One important difference in how the price cap approach is applied in the telecommunications industry compared to other industries (such as energy or water) relates to how the revenue requirement is established. Specifically, while price cap regulation in other industries is typically based on some variation of the building block approach, in telecommunications the revenue requirement is often based on an estimation of the LRIC of supplying relevant services. Variants of this general approach applied in the telecommunications industry include: bottom-up long-run incremental cost (BU-LRIC) in Europe; total element long-run incremental cost (TELRIC) in the USA and Japan; and total service long-run incremental cost (TSLRIC) in Australia and New Zealand.[107]

LRIC Pricing

The LRIC approach is premised on the idea that prices should reflect the costs that would be incurred by a new efficient operator entering the market, and thus replicate the conditions observed in a competitive market.[108] The approach tries to achieve two objectives: allowing the regulated provider to recover its efficient costs (including capital and

---

[105] See FCC (2011) and Sappington and Weisman (2016a).

[106] Sappington and Weisman (2010, 2016a) find some support for the conclusion that the use of incentive-based regulation, such as price caps, in the telecommunications industry has increased network modernisation and productivity. Newbery (1999) argues that price caps represent the only viable form of regulation that allows for the transition to competitive and eventually unregulated markets. Mitchell and Vogelsang (1991) suggest that the application of price cap regulation in the USA greatly simplified the tariff review procedures, and lessened the administrative costs of regulation.

[107] In practice, the BU-LRIC is one variant of the TSLRIC approach, and the term TSLRIC is used to cover both approaches in the discussion in this chapter. The principal difference between TSLRIC and TELRIC is that TSLRIC captures the total costs associated with services that use an access facility, while TELRIC captures the total costs associated with the different network elements (such as switches) over which these services flow. The specific treatment under each approach can differ when the costs associated with a specific element (e.g. a switch) are considered to be common to some services and, at the same time, incremental for other services. See Gans and King (2004a).

[108] The FCC document which established the TELRIC approach to setting prices under the Telecommunications Act 1996 states: 'a pricing methodology based on forward-looking, economic costs best replicates, to the extent possible, the conditions of a competitive market' (FCC 1996). Similarly, the European Commission recommendation on interconnection pricing of 1998 states that: 'Interconnection costs should be calculated on the basis of forward-looking long run average incremental costs, since these costs closely approximate those of an efficient operator employing modern technology' (EC 1998).

operating costs), while sending signals to potential entrants to encourage efficient entry to promote competition where it is feasible (the 'make-or-buy' decision).[109]

Although the LRIC approach was described in Chapter 5, it is worth summarising the key elements of the TSLRIC pricing approach as generally applied in the telecommunications industry. Firstly, it is estimated on the 'total' production costs of an entire service (such as unbundled local loop access), including the 'internal' production costs (associated with services used by the access provider), as well as the 'external' production costs (involving sales of the service to third parties). Secondly, the approach focuses on the *long*-run costs of production, and therefore includes capital costs along with operating costs that need to be incurred in order to service the demand of the increment. Thirdly, in estimating the incremental cost, the approach compares the additional costs incurred by the network operator associated with producing a service with the costs if it did not produce that service.[110] Fourthly, some applications allow for some allocation of joint and common costs to be added to the incremental cost (i.e. LRIC+). Finally, to arrive at a per unit estimate of incremental cost, the total incremental cost of providing a total service over a year is divided by the (actual or forecasted) demand for that service. This results in an *average* estimate of the TSLRIC per unit of output (i.e. per loop or minute) and does not measure the marginal cost of providing an extra unit of output. In practice, in implementing the TSLRIC/TELRIC approach, regulators typically adopt two important assumptions. First, the forward-looking estimates of long-run cost are typically based on some estimate of the replacement cost for a hypothetical network operator and not the actual costs of the network operator. Second, it is generally assumed that the network assets should be optimised so that the costs measured are those that would arise if the hypothetical network operator employed the most efficient production methods and available technology. These two aspects of the TSLRIC approach, in particular, have proven highly controversial.[111]

For fixed line networks, the need to determine prices for specific elements or services follows from 'unbundling' policies that require prices to be estimated for different types of access to an incumbent's network. In practice, cost models are used to estimate the LRIC for each particular regulated service/element, and this requires various assumptions

---

[109] However, an open question is why the LRIC approach has also been applied to mobile termination access services in those jurisdictions where that service is regulated. In most jurisdictions, there are limited prospects for entry once spectrum has been allocated, and so the 'make-or-buy' rationale does not apply in this context.

[110] In other words, incremental costs are the avoidable costs of not producing the increment. In practice, there are two general methods for estimating TSLRIC, which are termed the 'bottom-up' (BU-LRIC) and 'top-down' (TD-LRIC) approaches, although hybrids of these approaches are also sometimes used. The 'bottom-up' approach employs engineering data to estimate the costs of network elements associated with particular services. 'Top-down' approaches estimate costs on the basis of assumptions about how costs relate to each specific service using actual accounting or other historical information.

[111] Kahn (2001) expressed disbelief that policy makers would: 'ignore the actual incremental costs of the incumbent suppliers and instead adopt as the basis for policy the costs of a hypothetical, most efficient new entrant, constructing an entire set of facilities as though writing on a blank slate'. For a detailed critique of the approach in telecommunications, see Sidak and Spulber (1998, chapter 12). Other critiques include Harris and Kraft (1997), Hausman (1997), Salinger (1998), Kahn, Tardiff and Weisman (1999), Weisman (2000), Mandy (2002), Tardiff (2002) and Hausman and Sidak (2007, 2014).

to be adopted, and choices to be made as to the values of parameters that are used within that model.[112] A particular, and often contentious, issue associated with the implementation of the LRIC approach is how to allocate the joint and common costs among the different services/elements that comprise the telecommunications network. This is a significant issue because a high proportion of costs are joint or common in nature, reflecting the fact that much of the capital equipment comprising a telecommunications network (such as the switches, exchanges and links) are utilised by many different services.[113] In some countries, such as the UK, this has at times led to the use of price–cost tests which distribute common costs across a wide range of services in order to assess whether the prices for those telecommunications services are 'cost-oriented' or not (see Box 11.2).

As discussed in Chapter 6, in jurisdictions where wholesale mobile termination charges are subject to price regulation, it is common for a LRIC approach to be used to estimate the costs of providing termination services. While historically the price allowed is for the recovery of fixed and common costs (LRIC+),[114] increasingly a 'pure LRIC approach' is used which does not allow for the recovery of common costs in termination rates. Since 2022, all fixed and mobile network operators in EU Member States are subject to a maximum rate for termination of voice services on both fixed and mobile networks. These so-called 'Eurorates' have been calculated using a single (bottom-up) pure LRIC approach based on the costs of an efficient operator with a market share of not less than 20 per cent.[115]

Much has been written in the period since 1996, when the FCC first introduced the concept of TSLRIC/TELRIC,[116] about the relative merits of the approach in telecommunications. One particular criticism of the approach, noted in Chapter 6, is that it may distort entrants' 'make-or-buy' decisions by artificially keeping regulated prices low for unbundled network elements, and thus reduce the incentive for entrants to invest in their own facilities.[117] As the FCC recognised in 2003, to the extent that any such distortion understates forward-looking costs, this can be contrary to the objective of creating incentives for entrants to invest in their own facilities and the promotion of facilities-based competition.[118] Another criticism of the TSLRIC/TELRIC approach is that it can reduce the incentives for incumbents to invest, in part because the asset base is constantly being subject

---

[112] Sharkey (2002) describes the development and features of early cost models.
[113] However, Vogelsang (2021) notes that the issue is less problematic if direct costs are measured correctly, as this will reduce the amount of common costs to be assigned, and will also mean that any common costs that are assigned are fairly proportional to the amount of service produced.
[114] In some jurisdictions, the access price has at times been increased even further above costs – in the form of a so-called 'network externality surcharge' – on the basis that mobile network operators will use the higher termination charges to fund handset and subscription subsidies, which will then increase the penetration of mobile networks.
[115] See EC (2020c). The single mobile and fixed voice termination rates were established in reference to the efficient cost in the highest-cost country.
[116] The FCC First Report and Order (FCC, 1996) prescribed that state utility commissions price access to unbundled elements on this basis. This was challenged through the courts and ultimately settled in a 2002 Supreme Court decision *Verizon Communications, Inc. v. FCC* which upheld the FCC Order. The UK regulator adopted the LRIC approach in 1997, while the European Commission recommended the forward-looking LRIC approach in 1998. In Australia, the TSLRIC approach was adopted in 1997 and in New Zealand in 2001.
[117] See Hausman and Taylor (2012).
[118] FCC (2003a).

to optimisation and revaluation and this can lead to cost under-recovery of past invest
ments if appropriate adjustments are not made.[119] Moreover, as discussed in Chapter 6
over the long term, the uncertainty attached to the TSLRIC/TELRIC approach to pricing
can potentially impede dynamic efficiency by deterring investment.[120]

In some jurisdictions – such as the USA – the debate over the merits of TSLRIC/TELRIC
pricing is becoming one of largely historical interest, as inter-modal and intra-modal
competition develops, and policies relating to the mandatory unbundling of network
are withdrawn and replaced with other policies, such as those based on forbearance.
Similarly, in Australia, the regulation of the new National Broadband Network (NBN
company (which operates a fixed fibre-optic network) has seen a shift away from TSLRIC
pricing to pricing based on the building block approach.[121] However, the TSLRIC approach
remains widely used in Europe, including for new NGN access products.[122]

ECPR, Avoided Costs and Retail-Minus

While the LRIC approach is widely used in practice to set price caps, variants of the
ECPR – such as avoided cost pricing, retail-minus or active-minus – are also used i
some jurisdictions to set specific prices (see Chapter 6 for background to ECPR). I
the USA, while an LRIC approach was used to determine the price of unbundled net
work elements, a different approach (known as the 'avoided-cost resale' provision) wa
adopted for certain wholesale resale services. This required that the resale prices b
calculated from the 'top down' by discounting the full retail prices for any costs tha
the incumbent carriers avoid in providing such a service (such as marketing, billing an
other costs).[123]

In Europe, many NRAs use variants of the ECPR approach (margin squeeze tests whic
subtract downstream costs from the retail price) either as a 'complementary measure
to price controls (based on forward-looking LRIC), or in some cases as a direct form c
'retail-minus' regulation. Three types of margin squeeze tests are applied in practice: a
ex ante margin squeeze test; an economic replicability test (ERT); and an *ex post* retail
margin squeeze test.[124]

---

[119] See Mandy and Sharkey (2003). Evans and Guthrie (2005) argue that the process of optimising assets
out of the regulated firm's asset base, as occurs in the application of TELRIC, exposes the firm to
demand risk, and the firm requires a significant premium for bearing this risk. Davis (2011) notes that
this was acknowledged by the New Zealand Commerce Commission, which has since sought to 'lock-in'
the asset base.

[120] See Hausman (1997), Jorde, Sidak and Teece (2000), Friederiszick, Grajek and Röller (2008) and Taylor
(2010). A survey by Cambini and Jiang (2009) concludes that unbundling policies which apply forward-
looking cost approaches (such as TELRIC/TSLRIC pricing) have tended to discourage investment by
incumbents and competitive entrants alike.

[121] See ACCC (2009b) and NBN (2021).

[122] Twenty-four NRAs used BU-LRIC models for termination rates in 2021. See BEREC (2021a, b).

[123] This now mainly applies mainly to the provision legacy voice services to business and government
customers by CLECs. See FCC (2020b).

[124] See BEREC (2021b). BEREC (2014) discusses the attributes of these different approaches. An economic
replicability test assesses whether the margin between the retail price of the relevant retail products and
the price of the relevant regulated wholesale access inputs covers the incremental downstream costs an
a reasonable percentage of common costs.

| Box 11.2 | **Price–cost tests and contestable markets theory** |

In Chapter 3 we noted that the applicability of contestable markets theory to the public utility industries is generally seen as limited because the level of sunk costs in these industries is typically large, making the threat of rapid entry and exit relatively weak. Nevertheless, as was noted, some of the cost concepts developed as part of contestable markets theory – such as the concepts of stand-alone cost (SAC) and incremental cost – are actively used for determining price ceilings and price floors in some regulated industries.[125] The SAC test benchmark has been used to assess if the prices charged by a dominant access provider for some services are excessive, and proceedings are focused on whether access providers are unlawfully cross-subsidising particular services.[126]

As discussed in Chapter 14, the SAC test has been used by the Interstate Commerce Commission (ICC) – and its successor, the Surface Transportation Board (STB) – for US railroad freight pricing since 1985.[127] The UK telecommunications regulator (Ofcom) has also used a price ceiling test, which it has termed a 'distributed stand-alone cost' (DSAC) test, to determine whether access for specific service components (such as certain trunk access services and a number of other wholesale services) are consistent with regulatory requirements that prices be 'cost-oriented'.[128] However, unlike a SAC test, the DSAC test focuses on the prices for individual service components, and involves two steps. First, it involves the estimation of the SACs of a hypothetical firm that supplies a broad increment of services that share significant common costs. Second, it involves the *distribution* of these common costs among each of the services within that increment on an equi-proportionate (relative to LRIC) basis.[129]

Despite differences in the specific nature of the price–cost tests applied by the STB in the USA and Ofcom in the UK, such tests remain controversial in both theory and practice. First, while the use of such tests is justified by reference to their origins in contestable markets theory,[130] in both jurisdictions questions have been asked about whether the price ceiling tests, as applied, rest on solid economic foundations. Pittman (2010), for example, argues that the STB's application of the SAC test is not well founded in economics, nor is it justified with reference to the original sources relating to contestable markets theory.[131] In the UK, a principal criticism of the DSAC test is that it is even further removed from the SAC test

---

[125] Recall that the SAC of any service (or group of services) is the cost associated with providing that service (or group of services) at existing levels of demand (or specified 'test' levels of demand) without supplying any other services. In contrast, the incremental cost of a service (or group of services) is the additional cost of providing that service (or group of services) over and above the costs associated with the services it already supplies. For example, if a firm supplied three services (X, Y and Z) for a total cost of $C(X,Y,Z)$ and the SAC of supplying only services Y and Z is $C'(Y,Z)$, then the incremental cost of supplying service X is equal to $C(X,Y,Z) - C'(Y,Z)$.
[126] See Faulhaber (2005b).
[127] See Pittman (2010).
[128] See Ofcom (2009, 2012). According to Ofcom (2004b) the price for an individual service would be cost-oriented if it fell between its LRIC and its SAC ceiling.
[129] BT (2020) provides an explanation of how DSAC is calculated.
[130] The ICC (1985) notes: 'The theory behind SAC is best explained by the concept of "contestable markets".' While Ofcom (2013) notes: 'DSAC is derived from the concepts of the underlying contestable market theory.'
[131] See also National Academies of Sciences, Engineering, and Medicine (2015).

as developed in contestable markets theory, insofar as it involves the *distribution* of fixed and common costs to individual services using some accounting-based allocation method which, from an economics point of view, is arbitrary.[132] A second criticism of SAC-based price–cost tests concerns the practical complexities of implementation, which are seen to be highly discretionary, and, given the high amounts at stake, to encourage rent-seeking behaviour.[133]

An important point recognised in the early paper by Faulhaber (1975) is that, in order to properly apply the SAC test, it must be applied not only to each service individually but also to *all* possible groups, or combinations, of services. However, as Faulhaber (2005b) observes, this key insight of his work is 'often missed in regulatory applications'.[134] But, in practice, applying such tests to all possible combinations of services raises the difficulty that a large number of combinations of different groups of services will often have to be assessed; in some cases, this might involve the application of the test to over one billion combinations of services.[135] An additional practical difficulty arises because, properly done, such tests should be based on the costs of a *hypothetical* efficient stand-alone operator and not the *actual* costs of the firm currently supplying the access service. Pittman (2010) observes that, in practice, this has led to highly detailed exercises involving a large number of assumptions about the design of the hypothetical network operator, and, as described in one US court statement, the SAC test has become 'a full employment bill for economists'. In the UK, while it is recognised that the costs should reflect those of an efficient stand-alone telecommunications provider, in practice reliance has been placed on the actual recorded accounting costs of BT in applying the DSAC test.[136] In summary, there appear to be a number of conceptual and practical difficulties associated with applying such tests, and these difficulties suggest against placing too much reliance on the results of such assessments.[137]

'Bill and Keep' and Peering

The terms on which internet traffic is exchanged on IP-based backbone networks are determined by private negotiations between telecommunications operators, without any regulatory intervention. Specifically, traffic is routed along IP-based backbone networks

---

[132] See Chapter 4 on the arbitrariness of such accounting allocation methods and Mautino, Dudley, Prettyman and Heagney (2013).

[133] Pittman (2010) records that one 2009 decision involved a rate reduction and repatriation of $345 million. In these circumstances, he notes: 'both sides in a rate case have strong incentives to add increasing layers of complexity to the inherently uncertain exercise.' Similarly, STB (2019a) suggests that each SAC case can cost a shipper up to $10 million to litigate. In the UK, the regulator Ofcom has recently moved away from applying DSAC tests to Physical Infrastructure Access products and IP interconnection, in part because it can provide too much flexibility to BT, which could be to the detriment of access seekers and consumers. See Ofcom (2020a, 2021c).

[134] Faulhaber (2005b) continues: 'Applying these tests merely to individual services cannot be thought of as an approximation, or "good enough". It is a fatal error.'

[135] In the UK, the burden of showing that prices are cost-oriented rests with the regulated firm (in this case BT) and, in the past, the regulator (Ofcom) has been critical of the company for the incompleteness of the combinatorial tests conducted. However, as the regulator recognises: 'The number of combinatorial tests increases to over a billion if 31 products share a common cost.' See Ofcom (2009).

[136] See Ofcom (2009).

[137] Mautino, Dudley, Prettyman and Heagney (2013) note that, despite the fact that DSAC has no specific economic interpretation, it has 'been used in the sense of absolute rules for regulatory determinations on occasions in the past'. They conclude that it is important to be wary about the use of such tests as universally applicable pricing rules.

through a series of voluntary interconnection agreements between operators (known as peering arrangements) on a 'bill and keep' (unpaid) basis.[138] Traffic is also routed through a series of indirect interconnection agreements (known as transit arrangements) between ISPs operating at different levels of the internet architecture, for which a fee is paid.[139] This approach reflects the fact that no single entity has an ability to connect all of the networks that form part of the Internet. The use of peering arrangements with IP-based routing and switching ensures that if an ISP (such as a telecommunications network operator) attempts to deny carrying the traffic of another ISP, then that content provider can still usually access the end-customer by re-routing its traffic with another ISP using a peering or transit agreement. One consequence of these arrangements is that OTT service providers (such as Netflix, Amazon, Alphabet, Meta and Microsoft) that use the public Internet to supply content to end-users are not directly charged by ISPs for the costs associated with carriage of that traffic over multiple (often global) interconnecting networks. Rather, the costs of maintaining and investing in ISP networks are recovered from the end-users of each ISP via subscription and usage charges.

The substantial growth in data traffic, driven by OTT services such as gaming and video streaming, over the past decade has given rise to questions about this approach to charging and cost recovery. This is because many of these OTT services are data-intensive and require high-quality and high-capacity backbone telecommunications networks to be viable. In addition, the data traffic using the networks is increasingly concentrated in a small number of OTT providers. According to some estimates, in 2021 six companies (Meta, Alphabet, Apple, Amazon, Microsoft and Netflix) accounted for around 56 per cent of all global data traffic on fixed and mobile networks.[140] In Europe, it has been estimated that this OTT traffic imposed costs on fixed and mobile networks in the order of €36 and €40 billion.[141] For this reason, some large ISPs that operate the backbone networks argue that the current approach of only allowing for the recovery of the costs of operating and investing in the network from end-users is asymmetric and no longer fit for purpose.[142]

In principle, ISPs may be able to increase subscription charges to end-users to recover these costs, as the presence of OTT services increases the value of the ISP network to subscribers.[143] However, in practice, there may be two constraints on this ability to recover costs from end-users. First, large ISPs may be constrained by a combination of regulation and intense retail competition if they try to increase retail charges to recover these costs

---

[138] This is used for the exchange of traffic for what is known as Tier 1 ISPs, which have wide international coverage and maintain international connections (such as undersea cables). Examples of Tier 1 ISPs include AT&T, Verizon, T-Mobile, NTT, Orange, Tata and Deutsche Telekom.

[139] This involves a smaller ISP (such as a Tier 2 or Tier 3 ISP) paying a larger Tier 1 ISP a fee for transiting its traffic and allowing it to connect with the wider Internet. For example, a Tier 1 ISP (backbone) connects to other Tier 1 ISPs via peering, while a Tier 2 ISP might peer with other ISP networks but use a transit agreement with a Tier 1 ISP to allow it to connect to all parts of the Internet. Tier 3 ISPs often rely on transit agreements with Tier 2 networks to allow their customers to connect to the Internet.

[140] See Axon (2022) and Financial Times (2022).

[141] Frontier Economics (2022).

[142] In contrast, Analysys Mason (2022) argues that network-related costs for ISPs have remained stable over time even while traffic volumes have grown significantly. Similarly, BEREC (2022) finds that, in general, the costs of IP network infrastructures are not very traffic-sensitive and that there is no evidence of 'free-riding' along the value chain.

[143] See Vogelsang (2021).

from end-users in some jurisdictions.[144] Second, ISPs may be prevented from applying differential charges to end-users that are large OTT providers by net neutrality regulation in some jurisdictions (see Section 11.4.3).

To address this issue, some argue that any remaining wholesale price regulation (such as regulated termination charges) should be removed from telecommunications network operators (that are also ISPs) and be replaced with a 'bill and keep' approach (effectively peering). This would 'level the playing field' between ISPs/telecoms operators and OTTs but may require that ISPs increase their subscription charges to end-users.[145] In contrast some large ISPs argue that they cannot be expected to rely on higher end-user revenue to fully finance the costs of operating and investing in the network, particularly given the expected investments required in high-capacity infrastructure in the future. Rather, they advocate that major OTT providers should be required by regulation to directly contribute funding for the investments in the higher network capacity that they need to provide their high-quality OTT services. Specifically, it has been suggested that direct IP peering or transit agreements be introduced where large OTTs and ISPs negotiate an amount that large OTTs would contribute to the costs of the networks.[146]

Non-Price Regulation

As in the other regulated industries, various types of quality of service obligations are typically applied to firms providing telecommunication services. These obligations are particularly important where a fixed line operator is vertically integrated and both operates the fixed line infrastructure and also provides access services to its competitive rivals in the retail market. In Europe, it is common for regulators to introduce so-called 'equivalence' requirements to ensure that the vertically integrated firm is providing an 'equivalent' service to its competitors in retail markets as it provides to its own downstream retail division (i.e. it is not discriminating in favour of its own retail division).[147]

In the UK, the (vertically integrated) fixed line wholesale network operator (BT Openreach) is subject to minimum quality of service standards set by the regulator and also enters into a service level agreement (SLA) with its customers (i.e. downstream retail telephony providers) to provide service guarantees.[148] At the retail level, all providers of

---

[144] In Europe, operators argue that they are indirectly constrained in raising retail prices by the margin squeeze tests described above. In addition, some argue that the continuing regulation of wholesale access charges in Europe will influence the ability of ISPs to respond.

[145] See Vogelsang (2021).

[146] Axon (2022). Jullien and Bouvard (2022) argue that an inefficiency can arise in settings where the content provider does not properly internalise the traffic cost that its content generates for the network operator. They find that, when a content provider has a high ability to monetise users, cost sharing can lead to lower prices and higher welfare. Another suggestion is that large OTTs be required to contribute to a special fund to finance the network investments.

[147] Broadly, two types of equivalence requirements are used: 'equivalence of input (EoI)', where the services and information provided to internal and third-party access seekers must be on the same terms and conditions, including price and quality of service levels, within the same time scales using the same systems and processes, and with the same degree of reliability and performance; and 'equivalence of output (EoO)', which means the provision to access seekers of wholesale inputs comparable, in terms of functionality and price, to those the SMP operator provides internally to its own downstream businesses, even if using potentially different systems and processes. See BEREC (2021b).

[148] The minimum quality of standards relate to: repairs and installation services; penalties for non-compliance with minimum standards; and requirements to report key performance indicators.

electronic communications services in Europe (including broadband, mobile and landline providers) are required to meet certain standards related to consumers.[149] This includes both quality of service requirements, as well as measures to assist consumers in engaging in the market and switching.[150]

In the USA, state PUCs retain oversight of intra-state access and wholesale services, and many impose quality of service obligations on fixed (wireline) services and require them to periodically report on performance.[151] State PUCs can also impose equivalence requirements where a vertically integrated ILEC provides unbundled services to CLECs. At the retail level, among the quality measures examined by some state PUCs are: speed of installation; time to restore services and make repairs; service availability; and responsiveness to calls for assistance from an operator, or directory assistance, etc.[152] However, there is recognition that, as competition has developed and users of telecommunications services change their demand patterns – for example, by greater use of OTT VoIP applications, and of non-verbal communications such as texting – new quality of service metrics may be needed (such as quality of a voice call for mobile or VoIP users). Some state PUCs are considering the introduction of new minimum quality standards for basic services provided on legacy networks,[153] and are also looking at whether there is a need for a fixed line 'carrier of last resort' in circumstances where significant numbers of customers are using either VoIP or mobile networks.[154]

11.3 THE SCOPE AND EFFECTS OF RESTRUCTURING POLICIES

1.3.1 The Scope of Restructuring Policies in the Telecommunications Industry

The Different Stages of Regulation

Over the past four decades, the regulation of the telecommunications industry has evolved through a number of distinct stages that reflect the shifting rationales for regulation, particularly as competition has developed and technological innovation has increased the substitution possibilities (such as to mobile and cable networks, and more recently VoIP services).

Prior to the restructuring policies of the 1980s and 1990s, the telecommunications industry was typically characterised by a single operator of the fixed line network (PSTN) in a specific area which had a statutory monopoly on the supply of long-distance and local

[149] These measures are contained in the European Electronics Communications Code (2018).
[150] Among other things, these rules include: requirements to supply certain information in contracts; limiting the duration of contracts to 24 months; requiring certain information be sent to consumers at the end of the contract; protections for end-users with disabilities; and rules about switching and porting and bundled offers.
[151] The federal regulator (FCC) is responsible for the regulation of mobile (wireless) services.
[152] In Vermont, for example, quality standards cover five areas: customer-reported troubles; time period for resolving customer troubles; customer service phone answering; service installation performance; and network reliability.
[153] Lichtenberg (2015) refers to studies which suggest that there is a failure of the major ILECs to maintain reliability on the existing copper network as usage declines.
[154] Lichtenberg (2015) records that, in 2015, twenty-nine states had reduced or eliminated the requirement for incumbent carriers to serve as the carrier of last resort (COLR) using copper-based wireline service. Rather, carriers are only required to act as the COLR in areas with limited or no competition.

calls and accepted end-to-end responsibility for these services.[155] In this stage, the industry was generally perceived to have the characteristics of a classic natural monopoly, and was therefore subject to independent regulation (in the case of privately owned networks), o operated as a government department (under state ownership). The main focus of regula tion in this structure was on retail prices for the different services offered, and regulated prices tended to reflect wider issues and political considerations, such as universal servic considerations, and pressures to cross-subsidise particular groups of users.[156] At this stage the only real need for a fixed line network to connect with other networks was to facilitat international or inter-regional calls, which typically involved a dominant monopoly oper ator in one country/region connecting with a dominant monopoly operator in another.

A second stage began with the restructuring policies introduced in the mid-1980s i the USA and the UK, and in other countries in the 1990s. Regulation of the industry i this stage reflected a transition of the industry from monopoly to a more competitiv structure. In the USA, this included the separation of the incumbent national provide (AT&T), and policies to encourage firms to enter and compete with AT&T in the long-di tance market, and to make investments in competing network infrastructure. In oth jurisdictions, restructuring involved the development of a duopolistic market structur intended to allow for the development of an effective competitor to the incumbent pr vider.[157] During this time there also arose a need for the regulator to determine a fram work through which the terms of interconnection between the incumbent and competit firms could be determined.

A third stage started from the mid-1990s and involved the introduction of compet tion into all stages or activities in the industry. To facilitate competition, some essenti network elements of the incumbent fixed line operator were 'unbundled' and shared wit competitors. As discussed below, these policies were based on the implicit assumptio that allowing others to access essential 'elements' or 'services' of the incumbent might a as a 'stepping stone' or 'ladder' to the development of full facilities-based competition. Given the different types of competition emerging – quasi-facilities-based competitio alongside resale competition – the regulation of the industry typically became more com plex and wider in scope. In places where 'unbundling' policies were pursued, like the US/ the UK, Europe, Australia and New Zealand, the regulatory focus shifted towards settin access prices to allow for interconnection between entrants and the incumbent supplie This shift in focus was often controversial, and, as discussed in Chapter 6, raised ne questions about how access prices for the unbundled network elements of the incumbe

---

[155] This monopoly also often extended to a range of other services and products such as, among other things, the supply of equipment (such as phones), installation, maintenance of wiring and sockets, the operation of phone boxes and directory enquiries services.

[156] Cave, Majumdar and Vogelsang (2002) observe that this resulted in a structure where line rentals tende to be low (to encourage high penetration rates and universal service) and local call charges were low (t ensure affordable and geographically uniform tariffs), while long-distance charges were relatively high

[157] Such as in the UK and Australia. The incumbent in each jurisdiction where competition was introduced continued to be regulated, with a particular focus on ensuring that the incumbent firm did not impede entry.

[158] In the USA, this is referred to as the 'stepping stone' approach, while in Europe, it is typically referred to as the 'ladder of investment' approach. The FCC (2020b) notes that the use of unbundled network elements by competitors has long been seen as 'a stepping stone to deployment of their own facilities'.

should be determined. The introduction of unbundling policies also created new regulatory concerns, such as the potential for vertically integrated incumbents to engage in price or margin squeezes.[159] While the regulation of wholesale access became more prominent during this period, in many jurisdictions the incumbent operator still typically occupied a near-dominant position in retail markets, necessitating a continuing need for the regulation of the incumbent's retail prices.

A fourth stage of regulation, since the mid-2000s, emerged in some jurisdictions as competition became more effective for some services, or in some geographical areas (particularly urban or inner-city areas), and as traditional fixed line networks faced increasing *inter*-modal competition from cable networks and mobile telephony. At this point, regulation often focused only on the specific services of the incumbent fixed provider where they did not face sufficient competitive constraints, and was gradually withdrawn for other services where competition had developed (such as for retail prices). In some countries, such as the USA, regulatory requirements relating to unbundling were gradually reduced in scope.[160] During this period, there was also an increasing focus on the regulation of two-way access charges for mobile termination access services in jurisdictions where CPNP applied. Towards the end of this stage, by the 2010s, many countries started to introduce policies to incentivise the development of NGNs. As described below, in some countries (notably the USA) this involved policies based around regulatory forbearance, while in other countries it involved policies to structurally or operationally vertically separate the incumbent provider, or to publicly fund the development of such networks.

Over the last decade, the extent and nature of regulation of the telecommunications industry has become more diverse across the world, reflecting the different degrees to which competition is effective in each market. In many countries, there has been a focus on incentivising the development of broadband networks and managing the transition from the fixed line copper network to NGNs. While sustainable competition has largely led to the abandonment of policies based around unbundling in many parts of the USA,[161] this is not the case in many European countries, where there continue to be policies to facilitate regulated access to unbundled wholesale services, including those provided on NGNs. Mobile networks also continue to be regulated in CPNP jurisdictions, although, as noted above, in Europe a single termination rate has been set for fixed and mobile networks. An important development confronting regulators during the period is the treatment of large OTT service providers which utilise fixed and mobile network infrastructure (see discussion on peering above).

---

[159] A situation where the incumbent firm raises wholesale prices for the network elements, while simultaneously reducing its retail prices, and therefore 'squeezes' out the margins that its competitors could earn.

[160] An early policy shift occurred in 2003 when the FCC (2003b) noted that: '[I]n practice, we have come to recognise more clearly the difficulties and limitations inherent in competition based on the shared use of infrastructure through network unbundling. While unbundling can serve to bring competition to markets faster than it might otherwise develop, we are very aware that excessive network unbundling requirements tend to undermine the incentives of both incumbent LECs and new entrants to invest in new facilities and deploy new technology.'

[161] FCC (2020b) summarises the FCC's current position: 'The Commission has consistently aimed to promote sustainable facilities-based competition, recognizing that permanent unbundling obligations can reduce incentives for both incumbent and competitive LECs to deploy next generation networks.'

Scope of Restructuring in the USA

In the USA, while there had been some earlier developments in the 1950s and 1960s relating to the competitive supply of equipment that attached to the network[162] and long-distance services, a critical event in the restructuring of the industry was the 1984 Modified Final Judgment (MFJ), which required AT&T to separate its activities, created seven Regional Bell Operating Companies (RBOCs) and introduced competition for long-distance calls and in manufacturing and information services.[163] This was followed by the passing of the Telecommunications Act 1996, which, among other things: introduced a federal policy to encourage competition in the local call market;[164] lifted restrictions on the RBOCs from providing inter-state services and manufacturing and information services (subject to approval); and required ILECs to offer new CLECs unbundled network elements and retail telecommunications services for resale, both on a rate-regulated basis. Two aspects of this change were particularly controversial. The first was the decision of the FCC to use a 'necessary' and 'impair' standard, rather than an essential facilities standard, when determining the unbundling requirements for operators.[165] The second controversial element was the decision to require state PUCs to apply TELRIC pricing to the unbundled network elements.

In recent years, various decisions of the FCC have also had important implications for the scope of telecommunications regulation, including, as described in Section 11.2.1, the decisions about whether broadband internet access services and cable modem services should be classified as information services rather than telecommunications services under the relevant legislation (thus exempting them from regulated access requirements). The interconnection arrangements between mobile providers in the USA are based around 'bill and keep'-type arrangements, and since 2020 all inter-state fixed line terminating charges (i.e. the payments that fixed line networks make to each other for the use of each other's networks) are also set on a bill and keep basis (i.e. zero).[166] Another important development is the decision of the FCC to forbear from applying regulation in certain

---

[162] See Brock (2002). In particular, the FCC's so-called 'Computer II decision' of 1980 was important in establishing the separation of customer premises' equipment from the regulated common carrier network, and allowed for competition in equipment which could then connect to the PSTN, such as terminal equipment and modems.

[163] The MFJ required the separation of the industry into the potentially competitive long-distance (or toll) activities and non-competitive activities such as the operation of the local call network. Among other things, the MFJ required AT&T to separate its long-distance and local operations, and to divest its local call operations across the country. Seven local call companies (known as RBOCs, or Baby Bells) were created, which each served roughly 12 per cent of the total population, and AT&T's activities focused on being a long-distance carrier. While AT&T continued to be regulated on its long-distance service following the divestiture, RBOCs were restricted in their ability to provide long-distance service, manufacturing and information services, all of which were considered to be competitive activities.

[164] According to Lichtenberg (2011), prior to the passing of the Telecommunications Act 1996, some states, such as Pennsylvania and Michigan, were already pursuing policies for local call competition.

[165] Section 251(d)(2) of the Telecommunications Act 1996 states that the FCC consider, when determining what network elements should be made available, at a minimum, whether '(A) access to such network elements as are proprietary in nature is *necessary*; and (B) the failure to provide access to such network elements would *impair* the ability of the telecommunications carrier seeking access to provide the service that it seeks to offer' [emphasis added]. On the controversy surrounding this standard, see *AT&T Corp. et al. v. Iowa Utilities Board et al.* (1999), Hausman and Sidak (1999) and Gayle and Weisman (2007).

[166] See FCC (2011). This process began in 2011 and concluded in 2020.

circumstances.[167] The FCC has used this forbearance provision to encourage development of NGNs and to withdraw regulation in circumstances where unbundling and resale obligations had become outdated due to competitive fibre deployment, technological change and inter-modal competition.[168]

Scope of Restructuring in the UK and Europe

Although restructuring policies were also introduced in the UK starting in 1984,[169] the policies were of a different nature from those introduced in the USA. In the UK, the incumbent operator BT was not separated at the time of privatisation in 1984, and instead a 'duopoly policy' was pursued with the intention of creating a full facilities-based competitor to BT. The duopoly policy was subsequently abandoned in 1991, which led to a large number of entrants coming into the market,[170] and, from 1999, BT was required to provide unbundled access to its local loop to other operators. A strategic review of the industry by the regulator in 2005 concluded that competition in the fixed line market was inadequate and not sustainable over the long term. This led to a voluntary undertaking by BT to operationally separate its network activities (to be provided by a new entity known as Openreach) from its other activities, such as retail services. However, concerns about the vertical integration of BT persisted, and in 2017 Openreach was legally separated to become a distinct company with its own staff, management, purpose and strategy within the BT group. The regulation of wholesale residential broadband products and leased line products varies in different parts of the country, reflecting the level of current or prospective competition, and in some areas no regulation is applied.[171] Price caps based on 'pure LRIC' (i.e. with no allowance for common costs) apply to all providers of terminating landline and mobile calls in the UK which are assessed as holding a position of SMP.[172] Regulation is also applied to certain wholesale narrowband services. The current unbundling policy for fixed line networks requires the incumbent wholesale fixed line operator (BT Openreach) to provide physical access to telegraph poles and ducts to allow other networks to lay their own fibre networks. As discussed below, the regulator has committed that any investment in 'gigabit-capable' networks will not be subject to cost-based price controls until at least 2031 (effectively a regulatory holiday),[173] and

---

[167] Three conditions must be satisfied for the FCC to forbear from enforcing the rules. First, when regulation is not necessary to ensure that the charges, practices, classifications or regulations are just and reasonable and are not unjustly or unreasonably discriminatory. Second, when regulation is not necessary for the protection of consumers. Third, when forbearance from applying that requirement is consistent with the public interest.

[168] See FCC (2020b).

[169] This was preceded by the establishment of Mercury Communications in 1981 as a competitor to BT.

[170] According to Newbery (1999) there were over 150 licensed operators competing with BT by 1995, including 125 cable TV companies which offered telephony with cable.

[171] In competitive areas, no regulation is applied, while in areas with the potential for competition, only the entry-level broadband product is regulated. In the remaining areas, where Openreach is the only operator, a cost-based price control is applied. See Ofcom (2021b).

[172] This applies to 188 separate providers of wholesale call termination services and a total of sixty-five separate markets for wholesale mobile call termination services. See Ofcom (2021c).

[173] The regulator notes that, if it does introduce cost-based regulation in the future, it will nevertheless honour the 'fair bet principle': allowing BT to keep the upside (i.e. returns in excess of its cost of capital it has earned up to that point), as well as ensuring it can earn its cost of capital going forwards.

the progressive transfer of regulation from copper to full-fibre services. Finally, broad band and mobile providers are signed up to 'fairness' commitments, which, among other things, require them to commit to offering customers packages that 'fit their needs and have a fair approach to pricing', and are intended to assist customers in making 'well-in formed decisions'.

In Europe, policies directed at the market opening of the telecommunications industry date back to a 1987 Green Paper on the development of a common market for telecom munications services and equipment.[174] Since that time, a number of telecommunication Regulations and Directives have been introduced directed at developing the common market for communications services and restructuring the industry to facilitate inter connection and access.[175] This has included requirements to establish national regulatory authorities (NRAs) in each Member State and a common framework for the application of regulation across Member States. In general terms, the regulatory framework is applied in three steps: firstly, markets susceptible to *ex ante* regulation are defined on the basis of perceived competition problems; secondly, each NRA undertakes a market analysis to assess whether any operators hold a position of SMP in that market; and thirdly, remedies are imposed on those operators who hold SMP. The remedies can include obligations in relation to access, transparency, cost orientation obligations (including price regulation, accounting separation requirements or non-discrimination obligations. To ensure con sistency in the application of the regulatory framework across EU Member States, the Body of European Regulators for Electronic Communications (BEREC) was established in 2009. NRAs in Member States must provide BEREC, and telecoms regulators in other EU countries, with draft policy measures and must take utmost account of any opinion or advice provided by BEREC.

A new set of rules for the telecommunications industry became effective in 2020 which, as noted above, introduced a single maximum EU-wide rate for fixed and mobile termination services ('Eurorates') and reduced the number of predefined markets sus ceptible to *ex ante* regulation to just two.[176] Accordingly, as of 2021, *ex ante* regulation was applied to fixed and mobile termination rates in all but one EU Member State, to wholesale local access in twenty-four Member States, and to wholesale dedicated cap acity in nineteen Member States.[177] The new regulations also enhance the role of BEREC and introduce new rules to protect consumers irrespective of whether they communicate through traditional (call, SMS) or web-based services (Skype, WhatsApp, etc.).[178]

---

[174] EC (1987). For a historical overview, see Oldale and Padilla (2004).

[175] These include the: 1997 Interconnection Directive (97/33/EC); the 1998 Access Notice (98/(C265/02)); the 2000 Regulation on Local Loop Unbundling (EC/2287/2000); the Regulation on BEREC (EU/2018/1971); and the Directives of 2002 (2002/19/EC, 2002/20/EC, 2002/21/EC), 2009 (2009/140/EC and 2018 (2018/1972).

[176] The market for wholesale local access for mass-market broadband services and the market for wholesale access to dedicated connectivity, for business use requiring a higher quality of connectivity; see the European Electronic Communications Code (Directive 2018/1972). Briglauer, Cambini, Fetzer and Hüschelrath (2017) and Vogelsang (2019) assess these changes.

[177] EC (2021f).

[178] Among other things, these rules include: avoiding lock-in effects through disproportionate compensation fees for bundled terminal equipment; facilitating change of provider and strengthening number portability; enhancing comparison tools and consumption control; and promoting tariff transparency and comparison of contractual offers enabling end-users to make informed decisions.

Scope of Restructuring Elsewhere in the World

Restructuring policies have been introduced in most OECD countries and in many transitional and developing countries.[179] The popularity of privatisation and restructuring policies in telecommunications in both developed and developing countries has been argued to reflect concerns that state-owned monopolies would not be able to deal with the rapid technological change that was occurring in the industry.[180] Countries such as the Philippines, Chile, Jamaica, Argentina and Mexico all introduced full privatisation policies in the late 1980s and 1990s, and introduced competition for certain value-added services. A system of price controls (in the form of price caps, rate of return regulation or benchmarking) was also introduced in these countries.

In Australia, a statutory fixed line duopoly initially existed between 1991 and 1997. This was followed by the partial privatisation of the incumbent fixed line operator (Telstra) and the introduction of policies (such as unbundling) to provide access to its facilities. A major change introduced in 2011 involved the structural separation of the vertically integrated incumbent fixed line provider as part of a wider policy to build a new government-owned, wholesale-only national broadband network (NBN). The NBN delivers both telephony and high-speed broadband, and will replace the incumbent's current legacy network. Restructuring policies in New Zealand were introduced in 1989, and the incumbent was privatised in 1990. As discussed in Chapter 3, the initial regulatory regime adopted did not involve industry-specific regulation, but relied primarily on competition law (although this was subsequently amended).

1.3.2 The Effects of Restructuring Policies in the Telecommunications Industry

It is extremely difficult to disentangle the impacts of the restructuring policies outlined above from the impacts of the rapid technological change that has occurred in the telecommunications industry. For example, while there has undoubtedly been a proliferation in the types of services that are offered across different telecommunications platforms over the past four decades, it is difficult to conclude definitively whether these developments have been assisted, or indeed hindered, by particular regulatory actions.[181]

Effects of Restructuring in the USA

The US telecommunications industry looks radically different now from how it did in 1996 when the Telecommunications Act was introduced. The market share of ILECs has reduced from 99.7 per cent in 1996 to around 39 per cent of all fixed line voice services in 2020, and ILECs now have just 9 per cent across all voice technologies (including cable and VoIP). According to the FCC, former monopolist ILECs face fierce competition from CLECs, cable providers and wireless providers, among others.[182]

---

[179] Galal and Nauriyal (1994) estimate that, between 1989 and 1993, twenty-eight developing countries shifted from public to private ownership and introduced some form of restructuring.

[180] See, on this point, Newbery (1999).

[181] According to OECD (2011b), the market opening policies in telecommunications have been a 'success' for business and consumers in OECD countries, noting that at that time data suggested that prices had fallen, new technologies and services had been developed, and penetration had increased

[182] FCC (2020b).

In the broadband market, as at 2019, there were around 105 million connections and over 2000 providers of fixed broadband services to residential consumers using a variety of technologies (cable broadband service, DSL, FTTP, terrestrial fixed wireless service and satellite service). However, many of these providers only cover a small area, and only ten providers cover more than 5 per cent of the US population. Over the period 2015 to 2020 it is estimated that prices for the largest fixed broadband service providers' most popular plans have fallen by over 20 per cent, while average speed increased by 16 per cent. In 2020 it was estimated that 63 per cent of all residential connections could access download speeds of at least 100 Mbps. More generally, it is estimated that broadband providers have invested more than $1.7 trillion in capital expenditure since 1996.[183]

In the mobile market, there were three facilities-based nationwide mobile providers in 2020 which collectively covered 98 per cent of the population. Levels of churn (which indicate switching) were estimated at 19.5 per cent across the mobile industry in 2019. According to some estimates wireless prices have declined significantly since the mid-1990s, and prices fell by 5 per cent between 2017 and 2019.[184] At the same time, it is estimated that mobile service providers have invested over $286 billion in their networks over the decade to 2019.[185]

Numerous studies have examined how restructuring policies have impacted on these outcomes,[186] and the view that regulation has positively contributed to these outcomes is not universally shared.[187] Indeed, some argue that regulation has impeded, rather than facilitated, the competition and technological changes in the industry.[188] Hausman and Taylor (2013) argue that price regulation has, over the years, discouraged the development of facilities-based competition for local call services, and, more generally, that the 'misguided efforts' of regulators, courts and legislators to bring about a particular vision of competition in the telecommunications markets has delayed innovations,[189] misled investors and cost consumers billions of dollars.[190] Yoo (2017) describes the FCC's approach to mobile communications as 'desultory', noting that, although scientists at Bell Labs first conceived of cellular technology in 1947, the FCC's subsequent delays cost consumers tens of billions of dollars in lost welfare.[191]

---

[183] FCC (2020c).

[184] FCC (2020c).

[185] FCC (2020c).

[186] On the break-up of AT&T, see Taylor and Taylor (1993), Noam (1993) and Crandall and Waverman (1995). On the impact of the Telecommunications Act 1996, see Hazlett (2000), Lehman and Weisman (2000), Zolnierek, Eisner and Burton (2001), Crandall (2002), Alexander and Feinberg (2004) and Economides, Seim and Viard (2008).

[187] Yoo (2017) records that the '1996 Act is widely regarded as a failure in the US' and argues that the 'mechanism of change has been more the result of facilities-based competition than government-mandated behavioral requirements'.

[188] Crew and Kleindorfer (2012) argue that 'the role of regulation has been to follow and perhaps slow down the impact of technological change in telecommunications'.

[189] Hausman (1997) presents two examples – voice messaging and cellular phone services – where regulatory delay has hindered innovation and, according to his estimates, cost consumers billions of dollars.

[190] Hausman and Taylor (2012) estimate the costs associated with the restricted ability of the RBOCs to provide long-distance service, manufacturing and information services following the AT&T divestiture to amount to tens of millions of dollars of lost consumer welfare. See also Kahn (1987) on this point.

[191] According to Yoo (2017), the FCC rejected an initial request from AT&T for an experimental licence, and when AT&T formally made a request for a spectrum allocation ten years later, in 1958, it took the FCC another decade to act on it. Although the FCC decided to allocate spectrum to cellular in 1970, it was not until 1981 that the first licences were issued. See also Rohlfs, Jackson, and Kelley (1991).

A large body of work has examined the impact of the mandatory unbundling requirements of the Telecommunications Act 1996, focusing in particular on the incentives it created for short-term entry, as well as for investment in facilities by incumbent operators (ILECs) and by new entrants (CLECs). Hausman and Taylor (2013) argue that, by setting prices for unbundled elements at below-cost levels, the 1996 Act spawned a gold rush of entry into local markets by CLECs in the late 1990s, which was later reversed by consolidation and massive bankruptcies in the early 2000s.[192] Other studies have concluded that mandatory unbundling requirements may have imposed social costs, by distorting the incentives of incumbents to invest, and by reducing the incentives of entrants to invest in their own networks on the basis that it has been cheaper to use the unbundled elements of the incumbent's network.[193] Pindyck (2007), for example, argues that, because entrants could rent unbundled elements in small increments and for short durations, they did not bear any sunk costs, which led to an asymmetric allocation of risk and return between entrants and the incumbent that was not properly accounted for in the prices of unbundled network elements, and therefore acted as a significant disincentive for investment by the incumbent.[194] Others have argued that the FCC's decision to apply the TELRIC price approach for unbundled elements resulted in artificially low prices and led to selective entry, while, in contrast, the decision to apply the avoided cost approach (a variant of the ECPR) for resale services could facilitate efficient and sustainable entry.[195]

For all of these reasons, many commentators are reluctant to attribute the transformation of the telecommunications industry in the USA to a competitive market solely to the restructuring policies introduced in the mid-1990s. Rather, they attribute this development to the asymmetric regulation of cable companies (who have not been required to mandatorily share facilities), the entry of new competitors using different technologies (such as wireless providers), as well as a more general reversal of policies directed at mandatory unbundling, including for next-generation fibre networks.[196]

Effects of Restructuring in the UK and Europe

The telecommunications industry in the UK and Europe has also been radically transformed from a sector characterised by state monopolies in the 1980s and 1990s to one where there is increasing competition, albeit with substantial regional variations.[197]

In the UK, in 2020, there were 27.5 million fixed line broadband market connections, with fibre connections accounting for the majority (around 62 per cent). Four providers accounted for 86 per cent of the market, with the former incumbent BT having a share of 33 per cent of the retail market.[198] The average household spending on fixed and mobile

---

[192] Hausman and Taylor (2013). Similarly Glass, Kolesar, Tardiff and Williamson (2022) argue that the entry and demise of new providers was disruptive and that a major challenge was maintaining affordable rates where there was selective entry, and entrants targeted profitable customers that had been the source of subsidies to keep rates affordable.

[193] See Crandall, Ingraham and Singer (2004), Hausman and Sidak (2005), Hazlett (2005), Sidak (2012), Ford and Spiwak (2016) and Yoo (2017).

[194] Pindyck (2007). See also Cave (2010), who notes that the access price should cover both the entrant's cost of supply and the value of the option that any investment in the network would destroy.

[195] See Kahn (2001) and Glass, Kolesar, Tardiff and Williamson (2022).

[196] See Ford and Spiwak (2016), Yoo (2017) and Glass, Kolesar, Tardiff and Williamson (2022).

[197] See Cave, Genakos and Valletti (2019).

[198] Ofcom (2021a).

voice and data has decreased by 21 per cent between 2007 and 2020, while the speed of broadband services has increased over the same period.[199]

Similar trends can be seen in EU Member States. In 2020, fixed broadband subscriptions covered an estimated 77 per cent of households, with xDSL being the most widely used fixed broadband technology (50 per cent) followed by fibre (26 per cent) and cable (19 per cent). Former incumbent operators remain the market leaders for fixed broadband services in almost all EU Member States, with an EU-wide average market share of 3 per cent of fixed line in 2020 (compared to 55 per cent in 2006). The wholesale rates for both mobile and fixed interconnection rates have fallen significantly across the EU and continue to decrease. In mobile markets, there are at least three mobile operators present in most EU Member States, and there has been a substantial reduction in average mobile termination rates across the EU, having fallen from 14 EUR cents per minute in 2004 to around 0.8 EUR cents per minute in 2020.[200] The capping of mobile roaming surcharges in Europe is estimated to have led to large consumer gains and increases in total welfare.[201]

Once again, there is debate about the extent to which these outcomes can be properly attributed to restructuring policies. A 2016 assessment by the European Commission of the impacts of restructuring policies concluded that 'the regulatory framework has been effective in delivering a competitive sector' and that it had 'generated significant end user benefits, such as widely available (basic) broadband, a significant decrease in price and more choice'.[202] However, the review also noted that 'access regulation has delivered competition more at service than at network level' and that investments in very-high-capacity networks had not taken place at the pace envisaged in all EU Member States. Problems of regulatory consistency (which reduce predictability and affect investment) were also identified, as were problems of spectrum management, which have led to delayed and fragmented roll-out of mobile services.[203] Cave, Genakos and Valletti (2019) also conclude that there has been a transition from monopoly to oligopoly across the EU and that the new competitors are partly infrastructure- and partly access-based. However, they note that this shift has raised new policy issues in terms of the potential for (tacit or explicit) collusion,[204] or the adoption of industry-wide commercial practices which exploit consumer biases (see Chapter 7).

As in the USA, there has been a particular focus on the effects of unbundling requirements on the development of competition and investment in the sector. Policies directed at unbundling were first introduced in the mid-1990s in the UK and some EU Member States and such policies continue to be applied across Europe.[205] This enthusiasm for unbundling and the 'ladder of investment' approach in Europe is argued to reflect the absence of

---

[199] See Ofcom (2021a, 2021c).

[200] BEREC (2021c).

[201] Canzian, Mazzarella, Verzillo, *et al.* (2021). Cave, Genakos and Valletti (2019) observe the irony that roaming policy is perceived as one of the greatest successes, as there was at the time no empirical assessment of it, nor is there a clear economic underpinning for the intervention.

[202] EC (2016c). Similarly, Cave, Genakos and Valletti (2019) conclude that: 'It is fair to say that, overall, telecommunications markets represent one of the success stories of EU policy-making in network industries.'

[203] EC (2016c).

[204] Vogelsang (2019) raises a concern that this shift might be seen as a rationale for expanding the scope for *ex ante* regulation to cover oligopolistic dominance of several firms in a market.

[205] Germany first began local loop unbundling in 1996, followed by Denmark in 1998, the Netherlands and the UK in 1999, and Italy in 2000. See Renda (2012) and de Bijl and Peitz (2005).

facilities-based competition in many EU Member States and, perhaps more critically, the need for a common reference model to achieve convergence in the regulatory approaches across jurisdictions.[206] The evidence on the effects of unbundling policies in Europe is, however, equivocal. A 2005 report of the European Regulators Group (ERG) concluded that there was evidence that new entrants were starting to 'climb the ladder' and move from service-based competition to facilities-based competition.[207] Similarly, a 2007 European Commission report concluded that there has been a 'gradual but steady' development of infrastructure competition.[208] More recent studies conclude that, while local loop unbundling had a positive impact on broadband penetration in the initial stages,[209] the impact decreased as the market reached maturity.[210] That said, studies have found evidence of enduring improvements in quality as entrants continue to differentiate themselves from the incumbent by increasing the variety and differentiation of service offerings.[211]

However, other studies using EU data do not find evidence to support the 'ladder of investment' hypothesis, and rather find that countries with strong unbundling policies experienced lower levels of incumbent network investment,[212] and lower incentives for entrants to invest in infrastructure.[213] This includes investments in high-speed broadband infrastructure.[214] Finally, while competition from cable networks is generally seen to have had a positive impact overall on both penetration and quality, some studies have concluded that local loop unbundling policies may have had the effect of 'crowding out' *inter*-platform competition in areas where alternative networks already have a high share.[215]

---

[206] See Renda (2012). Oldale and Padilla (2004) also examine how the ladder of investment philosophy influenced the EU regulatory framework.

[207] ERG (2005); see also Cave (2010) and Distaso, Lupi and Manenti (2009).

[208] EC (2007a).

[209] This may, in part, reflect reductions in the regulated access price for unbundled local loops (which required the access seeker to make some investment) as compared to the charges for bitstream connections (where the access seeker used the electronics of the incumbent). See Cave, Genakos and Valletti (2019).

[210] See WIK (2016) and Ovington, Smith, Santamaría and Stammati (2017). Nardotto, Valletti and Verboven (2015) look at the UK. Vogelsang (2019), one of the original proponents of the 'ladder of investment', concluded that 'with few exceptions, the ladder of investment was only climbed from resale to ULL [unbundling of the local loop], but not beyond'. Similarly, Cave (2014), another original proponent, observes that '[t]here were no signs of entrants "jumping off the ladder" to build their own local loops', but also cautions that the relevant counterfactual is not network or infrastructure competition between an incumbent and a cable company but monopoly regulation.

[211] See Nardotto, Valletti and Verboven (2015) and Baranes and Savage (2018).

[212] See Crandall and Sidak (2007) and Bacache, Bourreau and Gaudin (2014).

[213] Bacache, Bourreau and Gaudin (2014) 'find no empirical support for this hypothesis, that is, for the transition from local loop unbundling to new access infrastructures, and weak empirical support for the transition from bitstream access lines to local loop unbundling'. Friederiszick, Grajek and Röller (2008) conclude that entrants would have more than doubled their investment in infrastructure if they did not have access to the incumbent's local loops in Europe. See also LECG (2007).

[214] Bourreau, Grzybowski and Hasbi (2019) find, using French data, that the higher number of local loop unbundled competitors in a municipality implied lower incentives to deploy and expand coverage of high-speed broadband with speed of 30 Mbps or more. Briglauer (2014) finds a negative relationship between the adoption of fibre-based broadband services and the effectiveness of access regulation applied to first-generation DSL infrastructure. Briglauer, Cambini and Grajek (2018) also find that stricter access regulations for legacy copper and fibre networks (i.e. a decrease in access price to legacy network and the adoption of fibre regulation) decrease the incumbent operators' fibre investments. Cave, Genakos and Valletti (2019) conclude that, while the European regulatory approach was successful in 'squeezing (static) efficiencies from the existing system', it was less successful in stimulating the (dynamic) transition to next-generation infrastructures.

[215] See Ovington, Smith, Santamaría and Stammati (2017) and Nardotto, Valletti and Verboven (2015).

Effects of Restructuring Elsewhere in the World

In developed (OECD) countries, there has generally been a trend towards greater level of broadband and mobile subscriptions, higher speeds and lower prices over the past tw decades. The average fixed broadband subscriptions have grown from 7 per 100 inhabit ants in 2003 to 34 per 100 inhabitants in 2021,[216] with cable, xDSL and fibre each having on average, around a 30 per cent share of the market.[217] Mobile broadband subscription have also grown dramatically from 31.4 per 100 inhabitants in 2009 to 121.3 per 10 inhabitants in 2021,[218] while the levels of mobile termination rates have generally bee falling in OECD countries.[219]

Again, it is difficult to draw conclusions about how restructuring policies have contrib uted to these outcomes given the differences in policies pursued across countries. Earl assessments of privatisation and restructuring policies in both developed and developin countries concluded that the introduction of competition in fixed line and mobile market improved performance across multiple dimensions.[220] Later analysis of OECD countrie found that pro-entry regulation (including the introduction of unbundling obligations o the incumbent network) and the resulting product market competition did not reduce th incumbents' investment incentives for legacy networks.[221] A 2021 analysis concluded tha the regulatory institutional framework – particularly the existence of a separate, inde pendent regulator – is positively linked to a significant increase in telecommunicatio investment.[222]

The results of studies looking at whether *inter*-platform competition (using the incum bent's network) versus *intra*-platform competition (facilities-based competition) has le to greater broadband penetration are mixed. Some studies find that *intra*-platform com petition has had a considerably lower effect on broadband penetration in OECD countrie (implying that mandatory unbundling requirements on incumbents may not be effec tive),[223] while others conclude the opposite, that *intra*-platform competition can accel erate broadband adoption, and that *inter*-platform competition does not seem to affec broadband adoption.[224]

The effects of restructuring policies in developing countries are more difficult t assess. In 2019, only two African countries, two Latin American countries, five Asia Pacific countries, four Arab countries and three Commonwealth of Independent State (CIS) countries operated under exclusive state monopolies and had not created a separat regulatory authority.[225] In contrast, and at the other end of the spectrum, competitiv

---

[216] OECD (2021b). Note that this is based on individuals, not households, and that household penetration numbers would tend to be at least double these estimates.

[217] OECD (2021a).

[218] OECD (2021b). The fact that it is above 100 per cent suggests that some consumers subscribe to more than one service (multi-home).

[219] OECD (2021c). On average, mobile termination rates decreased from 2.06 USD cents per minute in 2014 to 0.94 USD cents per minute in 2020.

[220] Li and Xu (2004).

[221] Garrone and Zaccagnino (2015).

[222] ITU (2021a).

[223] Bouckaert, van Dijk and Verboven (2010).

[224] Gruber and Koutroumpis (2013).

[225] ITU (2020). Castelnovo, Del Bo and Florio (2019) provide a useful breakdown of private and state-owned/state-invested telecoms companies around the world at that time.

markets based around inter-modal competition exist in countries such as Kenya, Ghana and Malawi (in Africa), Brazil, Mexico and the Dominican Republic (in Latin America), Morocco, Saudi Arabia and Oman (in Arab states) and Armenia in the CIS. Nevertheless, as of 2020, broadband access remains poor in many parts of the developing world, and it is estimated that around 2.9 billion people remain offline, while many hundreds of millions only go online infrequently, via shared devices, or have poor connectivity speeds.[226] Fixed line broadband subscriptions rates were 13 per 100 inhabitants in developing countries and 1.4 per 100 inhabitants in least developed countries in 2021 (compared to 35.7 per 100 inhabitants in developed countries). However, over the past decade, there has been a substantial growth in mobile communication, particularly in sub-Saharan Africa. In 2021, the number of active mobile subscriptions in developing countries was 73 per 100 inhabitants and 38.3 per 100 inhabitants in the least developed countries (compared to 131 per 100 inhabitants in developed countries).[227] This has been important in terms of socio-economic development and allowed new services such as mobile banking services to flourish.

Finally, assessments of the effects of privatisation of telecommunications incumbents in developing countries are mixed. Some studies conclude that privatisation resulted in price increases and reductions in real output, and that the private owners of the firms benefited at the expense of consumers.[228] However, others found that, while privatisation alone brought few benefits, when combined with an independent regulator, sectoral performance was improved.[229]

11.4 REGULATORY POLICY ISSUES IN THE TELECOMMUNICATIONS INDUSTRY

This section considers three issues confronting telecommunications regulators around the world: the continuing rationale for regulation given the emergence of competition in many jurisdictions; how to manage the transition from legacy networks to NGNs, including how different regulatory approaches can affect the incentives for investment in NGNs; and, finally, the various issues associated with 'net neutrality' regulations.

11.4.1 Is Regulation Still Needed to Hold the Fort until Competition Arrives?

In his 1983 seminal report on the regulation of British Telecom, Stephen Littlechild remarked that regulation was needed to 'hold the fort' until competition arrives.[230] Similarly, Vogelsang (2019) observes that achieving sustainable competition and a reliance solely on competition law rather than *ex ante* regulation has been the 'holy-grail' of telecommunications policy since the start of liberalisation in the USA. In the EU, telecommunications regulation has been specifically designed on the expectation that *ex ante* regulation would ultimately be replaced by a reliance on competition law at some point

---

[226] ITU (2021b).
[227] ITU (2021c).
[228] Auriol (2005).
[229] Wallsten (2001).
[230] Littlechild (1983).

in the future. Some four decades from the introduction of the first restructuring policie this raises a question about whether 'competition has arrived', and, if so, what is the con tinuing rationale for economic regulation of telecommunications?

As we have just discussed in Section 11.3, technological and market changes hav radically transformed the types of telecommunications services supplied, the way thos services are supplied and who supplies them in many jurisdictions. The move towar IP-based networks where voice and data are indistinguishable, the emergence of mobi telephony and VoIP as substitutes for traditional fixed line voice services, greater leve of *inter*-modal competition in some jurisdictions (particularly between cable and fib networks, but also mobile networks), and convergence in service offerings are leading fundamental questions being asked about the continuing rationale for *ex ante* regulatio in some jurisdictions.[231]

Various arguments support the view that the time may have come for sector-specific *ante* regulation to be gradually withdrawn. First, as described above, the historical ratior ale for the regulation of fixed line telecoms networks – that the demand and cost charac teristics resemble that of natural monopoly – is arguably no longer valid in jurisdictior where restructuring policies have been introduced.[232] Second, in many jurisdictions, the is now established competition in retail markets between incumbent and competitive fixe line carriers, alternative networks (cable) mobiles and, increasingly, OTT services whic use the public Internet. This has generally led to substantial reductions in wholesale fixe line termination and retail charges, and in some jurisdictions, such as the USA, a shift a 'bill and keep' approach.[233] Third, there is a risk of an asymmetric regulatory approac becoming entrenched if incumbent fixed line operators remain subject to detailed regula tion, while operators using different technologies but providing similar services (such a cable networks and mobile networks) are subject to more limited forms of regulation, no regulation at all. Fourth, as discussed below, there is the important interaction betwee regulation and investment. Some argue that wholesale price deregulation, which resul in upward pricing pressure, can actually speed up the 'stepping stone' effect if temporaril higher retail prices resulting from deregulated wholesale inputs provide stronger incer tives for competitors to invest.[234] In addition, as discussed below, a lack of regulatol predictability about the treatment of new investments could be deterring investments

---

[231] Renda (2012) outlines some of these questions: 'Are we sure that incumbents' networks should be considered as essential facilities today? Are we sure that a player with a substantial share of the fixed-line (sub-)market would be able to exploit any market power and extract any rent from its position?' Vogelsang (2017) considers different deregulation possibilities, including a reliance on competition law symmetric regulation (treating all suppliers the same) and a reliance on negotiation/bargaining.

[232] Kahn (2007) noted that, even at that time: 'The industry is obviously no longer a natural monopoly an wherever there is effective competition – typically and most powerfully, between competing platforms land-line telephony, cable and wireless – regulation of the historical variety is both unnecessary and likely to be anticompetitive. In particular, it is likely to discourage the heavy investment in the development and competitive offering of new platforms, and in increasing the capacity of the Internet to handle the likely astronomical increase in demands on it.'

[233] As Vogelsang (2019) notes: 'substitute OTTs have the potential to kill legacy termination charges, as long as they themselves are not subject to them'. Vogelsang (2021) advocates the removal of wholesale regulated termination charges to allow for greater retail competition between ISPs and to respond to greater OTT traffic.

[234] Tardiff and Weisman (2018).

next-generation infrastructure. Finally, in mobile markets, the main competition issues now typically involve concerns about collusion and coordinated behaviour given the oligopolistic structure, which some argue is better dealt with through competition law than *ex ante* economic regulation.[235] Looking ahead, a shift towards competition law may be prudent given expectations that new players will become more prominent in telecommunications markets (such as large technology companies (Amazon, Google and Microsoft) who are expected to play a greater role in providing mobile networks), and if consumers adopt 'e-SIMs' that allow them to multi-home and switch between mobile providers to use the networks they want.[236]

However, as we have seen in this chapter, new issues are emerging that may justify some form of ongoing *ex ante* regulation or oversight. For example, while competition can be intense in fixed line networks in some geographical areas, it is not universally so, and there may be an ongoing need to protect consumers in areas where competition is weak or non-existent. Similarly, regulators may need to manage the transition from legacy copper networks to next-generation networks; this includes deciding if there is a need for a 'carrier of last resort' to ensure high levels of connectivity. In some jurisdictions, such as Australia, the industry structure for the fixed line network has moved back to a state-owned monopoly for wholesale broadband services, which arguably necessitates some form of ongoing regulatory oversight. Similarly, in other jurisdictions, such as the UK and EU, the regulatory approach to NGNs continues to be based around unbundled access to certain physical assets (ducts, poles) and other access services (dark fibre, bitstream). This, too, can require ongoing regulatory oversight to ensure that the price and non-price access terms are fair, non-discriminatory and cost-oriented. In mobile markets, the main area of regulation is the termination rate in countries where the calling party pays (CPNP), although in the EU the ongoing need for NRAs to assess and set termination rates has been superseded by the setting of a single maximum 'Eurorate'. There may also be a need for regulators not only to manage the allocation of spectrum through initial auctions, but also to ensure it is being put to efficient use once allocated. More generally, in both fixed and mobile markets, new potential regulatory issues may arise from so-called 'virtualisation' and software-defined networking. This is where a physical telecommunications network is configured into separate 'slices', and service providers (such as large technology companies or VoD providers such as Hulu or Netflix) lease a 'slice' of the network in order to provide its own virtual network to end-users.[237] If large OTT providers are required to directly contribute to the funding to telecommunications networks in the future, regulation may also be needed to oversee (and potentially arbitrate) the negotiations between telecommunications companies and large OTT providers. Finally, as discussed in Chapter 7, *ex ante* regulation may be predicated on a need to ensure 'fair outcomes', to prevent consumer

---

[235] Vogelsang (2019).

[236] Ofcom (2020c) discusses some of the potential future changes to mobile networks.

[237] Knieps (2017) considers how alternative network logistics (virtual networks) can deal with heterogeneous quality of service requirements of network traffic in the future. Cave, Genakos and Valletti (2019) note that: '[a] single physical network would then support multiple "sitting tenants," without enjoying a commercial relationship with the universe of end-users', and that this could 'redistribute market power in the value chain: both vertically and horizontally'. Knieps (2022) examines 5G based network slicing based on the concept of virtual networks

exploitation and to assist consumers in actively engaging in the market.[238] This is con
sistent with view of bodies such as the ITU which argue that regulation needs to becom
more 'collaborative' and bring together regulators and all market participants to focus o
behaviours and outcomes, and to place new emphasis on empowering consumers.[239]

11.4.2 The Transition from Legacy Copper Networks to Next-Generation Networks

The transition from legacy copper networks towards IP-based NGNs raises further ques
tions about the appropriate regulatory approach. Two questions are particularly pertinent
first, whether access and 'unbundling' policies should be applied to NGNs; and second
how best to incentivise investments in NGNs.

Shifting the Ladder: Should Unbundling Policies Apply to NGNs?

In Section 11.3.1 we noted that a particular policy pursued in many restructured tele
communications industries has involved 'unbundling' whereby the incumbent networ
operator is required to 'share' access to certain facilities and elements with new entrant
on reasonable terms. As noted, an underlying rationale for unbundling policies is tha
new entrants may not be able, or willing, to make full-scale investments in infrastructur
and that, by granting them different levels of access to specific wholesale access service
this can provide a 'stepping stone' or 'first rung on the ladder' to the building of their ow
networks. Over time, there was an expectation that this would lead to the developmer
of facilities-based competition.[240] However, as discussed in Section 11.3.2, the success c
such unbundling policies in stimulating competition is subject to debate.

An important question for policy makers is whether the logic of the 'stepping stone
or 'ladder of investment' approach also applies to NGNs, and, if so, whether unbundlin
obligations should apply to these networks.[241] There are both engineering and regulator
policy aspects to consider. In engineering terms, an important question is what element
can be physically unbundled in an NGN.[242] On the policy side, it is sometimes argued tha
there is greater prospects for competition in NGNs than for legacy networks,[243] includin
as the result of co-investment initiatives, and, as such, there may not be a need for th
'ladder of investment' approach for NGNs.

Jurisdictions are applying different approaches to the question of whether NGNs shoul
be unbundled.[244] In the USA, the approach has been to forbear from applying mandator

---

[238] This is a particular focus of regulators in the UK and Europe. See BEREC (2020) and Ofcom (2020b).
[239] ITU (2020).
[240] Cave (2010) notes two propositions on which this logic is based: 'that infrastructure competition
should be preferred when it is reasonably attainable, and that the regulator can promote the goal of
infrastructure competition by suitable regulatory policies'. Bourreau, Doğan and Manant (2010) present
critique of the 'ladder of investment' approach.
[241] On whether the ladder of investment approach can be applied to NGNs, see EC (2007a), ERG (2009),
Brito, Pereira and Vareda (2011) and Cave (2010, 2014).
[242] OECD (2007) observes: 'Most of the fibre access solutions are based on a network typology where it is
much harder, technically and/or economically, to unbundle the loop.'
[243] See WIK (2019).
[244] See Briglauer, Cambini, Fetzer and Hüschelrath (2017) for a survey. OECD (2007), Kirsch and Von
Hirschhausen (2008) and Marcus and Elixmann (2008) discuss policy options and approaches.

unbundling requirements to NGNs, in an effort to encourage infrastructure investment. In the EU, there seems to have been a gradual movement away from the ladder of investment approach.[245] NRAs are now required to consider whether access obligations on civil engineering physical products (ducts, poles, wiring) are sufficient before applying other unbundling requirements to specific network elements and facilities, and then only impose access requirements if a denial of access would hinder the development of sustainable competition.[246] Moreover, before imposing unbundling requirements, NRAs are required to take account of: the technical and economic viability of installing competing facilities; the initial investment of the infrastructure owner (including the risk levels of very-high-capacity networks); and the need to safeguard long-term infrastructure-based competition, including from co-investment in networks.[247] However, EU Member States still have discretion in how they apply this framework, and the policy of many EU countries continues to be based around the unbundling of physical access products (such as ducts, poles) as well as other access products (such as dark fibre, sub-loops, bitstream) consistent with the ladder of investment philosophy.[248]

Incentivising Investment in NGNs

Over the past decade, many jurisdictions have been grappling with the question of how to incentivise investments in NGNs (specifically NGANs) that have wide or universal coverage. Investments in NGNs can bring substantial benefits to businesses, citizens and societies. However, the costs and potential risks of deploying NGNs are significant.[249]

The issue raises new challenges because regulation to date has largely focused on legacy networks that were already built, and investments sunk. Now regulation has to be shaped to reflect the impact it can have on the incentives for new large-scale network infrastructure to be developed.[250] As noted above, an obvious consideration is how the incentives to invest in NGNs are affected by the regulatory framework, and in particular the extent to which investors will be subject to future obligations to share, or mandatorily unbundle, their infrastructure.[251] A related interaction is how the level of the regulated

---

[245] Cave (2014) observes that, in Europe, some Member States have shifted away from the goal of moving access-based competitors up the ladder of investment, towards the goal of increasing fibre deployment. Vogelsang (2019) notes that the ladder of investment approach is not mentioned in the 2018 EU Directive.

[246] See European Electronic Communications Code (Directive 2018/1972) and WIK (2019).

[247] European Electronic Communications Code (Directive 2018/1972).

[248] See BEREC (2021b) and WIK (2019).

[249] The cost of the Australian NBN has been estimated at over 51 billion Australian dollars. In the USA, the estimated cost of each FTTH connection is in the vicinity of US$700–800 per passing. In the EU, Bourreau, Cambini, Hoernig and Vogelsang (2021) cite estimates suggesting that it will cost €660 billion to deploy fibre networks, and that it will take twenty-five years to complete the investments.

[250] Abrardi and Cambini (2019) survey studies on regulation and investment incentives for NGNs.

[251] This was recognised in the USA as early as 2003, when the FCC (2003b) noted that: 'The effect of unbundling on investment incentives is particularly critical in the area of broadband deployment, since incumbent LECs are unlikely to make the enormous investment required if their competitors can share in the benefits of these facilities without participating in the risk inherent in such large scale capital investment.' Briglauer, Cambini, Fetzer and Hüschelrath (2017) survey the literature at that time and conclude that 'overall, the empirical literature indicates a negative impact of ex ante access regulations on NGA investment and NGA adoption'.

access price set for legacy networks affects the incentives for access seekers and acce¹ providers to invest in, and migrate to, new NGN infrastructure.[252]

In practice, policy makers and regulators can be confronted with a trade-off between th need to encourage investment in NGNs that provide wide geographic coverage, and ensu ing that consumers benefit from any price reductions and quality improvements whic might flow from allowing access to such facilities once the investments are made. Variou policy proposals have been made to address this trade-off. One is that the regulator com mits to not placing any sharing or access requirements on a network operator for a set, c unspecified, period of time. This approach, which is sometimes referred to as a regulator or access 'holiday', amounts to a time-limited right to refuse the supply of use-of-ne work services to others.[253] An alternative approach, referred to as regulatory forbearanc involves the regulator agreeing not to regulate specific services, but involves no specif time frame, and therefore does not completely rule out the future regulation of the networ

A forbearance approach has been adopted by the FCC in the USA in relation to fib¹ and IP networks since 2003. In Europe, the forbearance approach has been considere but rejected in the past.[254] Current policy is based around the sharing of civil infrastru¹ ture encouraging co-investments. However, as discussed above, the imposition of acce¹ requirements for NGNs is not automatic under the EU regulatory framework, and NR⁴ must take account of factors that include the initial investment of the infrastructu¹ owner and whether it would hinder the development of sustainable competition.[255] A important element of the EU policy is to incentivise investment in NGNs through co-i¹ vestment projects, such as those between electric companies and a telecoms company.² Co-investments can allow for risk sharing and reduce deployment costs faced by an one party, and thus potentially increase investment and broadband roll-out relative ¹ standard access obligations.[257] Under the EU rules, co-investments can be exempt fro¹ wholesale access regulation if the project remains open to new co-investment partners.² However, this exemption is subject to the discretion of NRAs in each Member State, whic

---

[252] Bourreau, Cambini and Doğan (2012) identify three conflicting effects of low access prices for legacy networks on the incentives to invest in NGNs: a replacement effect (low legacy access prices hinder incentives for infrastructure investment by alternative operators); a wholesale revenue effect (low acce¹ prices for legacy networks reduce the opportunity cost from not investing for the incumbent); and a retail margin migration effect (low access prices for legacy networks mean that, in order to encourage migration, the access price for NGNs also must be low).

[253] The concept of a 'regulatory' or 'access' holiday – whereby the regulator commits to not applying *ex ante* access regulation to new investments automatically, and to introducing such regulation only after a lag and after certain conditions are met – was initially suggested by Gans and King (2003a, 2004b) as a mechanism for increasing incentives to invest in innovative infrastructure.

[254] The OECD (2011a) observes that at that time: 'Any suggestion of regulatory forbearance in Europe has been soundly dismissed.' An alternative approach, favoured by the European Commission, was to add ε 'premium' to the cost of capital component of the access price in recognition of the risks associated wi¹ such investments. See EC (2010)

[255] European Electronic Communications Code (Directive 2018/1972).

[256] An example is the co-investment agreement between the electric utility EWE AG and German telecommunications incumbent Deutsche Telekom to expand the fibre network in northeast Germany.

[257] See Briglauer, Cambini, Fetzer and Hüschelrath (2017) and Bourreau, Cambini and Hoernig (2018). Jeanjean (2022) finds that co-investment reduces investment costs and encourages more investment, except if the participating operators are much less efficient than their competitors.Krämer and Vogelsang (2016) identify a need to monitor such agreements for possible tacit collusion.

[258] Briglauer, Cambini, Fetzer and Hüschelrath (2017) and Vogelsang (2019) critically examine this policy.

can increase regulatory uncertainty and reduce the incentives to join a co-investment arrangement.[259] Other measures to incentivise investment in NGNs in the EU include relatively light regulation of wholesale-only firms providing high-capacity connectivity, and giving greater flexibility to the access provider.[260] In addition, some European countries (such as Spain and Portugal) have introduced various forms of 'regulatory holiday'.[261]

Governments in many countries have been actively involved in the development of NGNs through subsidies and direct support for such investments, on the basis that broadband services are a form of public good and that affordable and universal access should be provided to all citizens. Public support for investments in NGNs can take various forms, ranging from fully funded public investments through a separate company (such as has occurred in Australia and India), specific subsidies and other financial incentives to provide investment in specific regions (such as has occurred in Canada, Germany, Greece, Korea, Portugal, Singapore, the UK and the USA), co-investment arrangements such as public–private partnerships (such as has occurred in New Zealand),[262] and public support for municipal initiatives for broadband deployment (such as in Sweden).[263] In China, broadband is listed as 'public strategic infrastructure' and provinces have sought to promote the development of fibre networks, and according to some press reports China now has the world's largest fibre-optic network.[264]

11.4.3 Net Neutrality

One of the most controversial issues in the telecommunications industry over the past decade concerns the question of whether all traffic from all content providers (sometimes called 'edge providers')[265] using the Internet is, or should be, treated equally (i.e. neutrally) by ISPs (which include fixed line, wireless and cable network operators).[266] As described above, historically internet traffic has been managed on a 'best-efforts' basis, meaning that all content is delivered on equal terms. However, as the volume and type of content using the Internet has expanded, concerns have arisen about the traffic rules and practices that ISPs use to manage that traffic.

---

[259] Bourreau, Cambini, Hoernig and Vogelsang (2021) focus on how the incentives of the incumbent to invest are affected by whether potential co-investors adopt a 'wait-and-see' approach and only make an investment decision once demand is realised.

[260] See Vogelsang (2019) and Cave, Genakos and Valletti (2019).

[261] In Europe, the receptiveness to the regulatory holiday concept has varied between regulators and over time. Since 2009, Spain and Portugal have introduced policies of 'initial forbearance' from applying access regulation to new fibre networks. These policies are generally seen as being successful in promoting investment in fibre networks.

[262] Howell and Sadowski (2018).

[263] Using data for thirty-two OECD countries, Briglauer and Grajek (2021) find that state support increases the number of new broadband network connections by 22 per cent in the short term and by 39.2 per cent in the long term. They also find state support to be highly cost-efficient, with programmes breaking even after an average of three years.

[264] Asia Financial (2021).

[265] Edge providers include entities that provide content, applications or services over the Internet or provide devices for accessing the content, applications or services.

[266] The UK regulator defines net neutrality as the 'principle of ensuring that users of the internet can control what they see and do online – not the internet service provider (ISP) that connects them to the internet' (Ofcom, 2021d).

The net neutrality debate centres around two issues. First, whether ISPs should be able to apply certain traffic management practices (such as 'throttling' or slowing down the delivery of some content to relieve congestion) that have the effect of treating some lawful content providers differently from other content providers. Second, whether ISPs should be able to charge different content providers for different transmission services such as premium or specialised services (i.e. differential charges for services).[267] That is whether, in addition to offering access to the 'free' best-efforts Internet, ISPs could also offer so-called 'premium quality' or 'priority' services for access to a 'fast lane' on the Internet. This issue, referred to as 'access tiering', involves payment being made for different levels of quality of service on the Internet.

The Two Sides of the Net Neutrality Debate

ISPs argue that certain 'reasonable' network traffic management practices are essential for the efficient operation of the network, particularly in times of congestion. The need to manage the network, and prioritise traffic, is seen as necessary to ensure that latency-sensitive traffic (such as IPTV, voice and video streaming and conferencing) can be provided at the necessary level of quality to make the service viable.[268] ISPs also argue that allowing them to charge for differentiated services among users is economically efficient and can provide incentives to invest and innovate. As described above, it will also allow ISPs to recover the costs associated with financing the networks from those OTT providers that contribute the most data traffic. However, there is much debate about whether ISPs should be able to engage in wider traffic management practices, such as blocking, slowing down ('throttling', degrading or prioritising certain types of traffic, such as particular content, applications or services, over other services.[269]

Supporters of 'net neutrality' regulations – which include content providers such as Google, Facebook and some civil liberties groups[270] – argue that, without such provisions ISPs have an incentive to discriminate against content providers with whom they compete. For example, access to OTT VoIP services (such as Skype, Telegram, WhatsApp voice or Vonage) could be restricted by an ISP, such as a fixed line operator, in order to promote their own voice products.[271] Similarly, a cable operator could restrict access to movie

---

[267] Wu (2003) provides an early discussion of the issue of net neutrality. He notes that the net neutrality issue is yet another incarnation of issues associated with anti-discrimination and network innovation. Krämer, Wiewiorra and Weinhardt (2013) and Greenstein, Peitz and Valletti (2016) provide useful surveys of academic research and the policy trade-offs. Vogelsang (2019) argues that net neutrality rules are likely to be largely ineffective because market pressures are so strong that they find a way to overcome most of the regulations.

[268] Traffic management is also important to ensure that certain types of illegal content are not distributed.

[269] Wu and Yoo (2007) set out both sides of the debate at that time.

[270] The net neutrality debate also involves wider concerns about the potential for a reduction in rights to freedom of speech, national security and democratic accountability that may be impacted by policies in this area.

[271] In the USA, the first case before the FCC on this issue arose in 2005 when a small telecommunications network operator (Madison River Communications) attempted to block the ability of subscribers to use a VoIP product known as Vonage. This was followed in 2006 by the imposition of net neutrality rules on AT&T as part of the conditions for its merger with Bell South. In Europe, it was estimated that at least 2 per cent of fixed and at least 36 per cent of mobile broadband users have been affected by restrictions on VoIP calls. See EC (2019a).

on demand services, such as Netflix or BitTorrent.[272] More generally, supporters of net neutrality regulations argue that the Internet's non-discriminatory traffic management approach has been critical to its success, and has facilitated the entry of a wide range of content creators by effectively subsidising the production of content and inventions.[273] In addition, it is argued that this approach has avoided the development of a fragmented market whereby content providers who have not concluded agreements with ISPs cannot access all customers, and, similarly, customers on particular ISPs are unable to obtain access to all content on the Internet.[274]

The Economic Trade-Offs Confronting Policy Makers and Regulators

For regulators and policy makers, the net neutrality debate raises familiar questions about static and dynamic efficiency gains of regulatory intervention. In the short term, allowing ISPs to prioritise time-sensitive traffic can, in principle, relieve congestion and lead to efficiency gains in much the same way as congestion pricing works in other regulated sectors (transport, energy).[275] In the absence of market power concerns, it is also argued that the ability for ISPs to levy different charges for different levels of quality of service (i.e. price differentiation) can be welfare-enhancing, and prohibitions on such practices could suppress competition and discourage investment in network infrastructure.[276] Indeed, the prohibition against allowing ISPs to charge their content providers is considered by some to be a form of price regulation where the access price is set at zero.[277]

However, some argue that allowing ISPs to price-differentiate between users reduces welfare by increasing the access price above socially optimal levels, and creating incentives for the foreclosure of independent content/application providers where ISPs are vertically integrated in these activities themselves. It is also argued that the basic 'best-efforts' traffic service will be degraded to coerce content and application suppliers to purchase the prioritised, higher-quality service.[278] That is, access tiering could be a *de facto* way for ISPs to charge internet users, with the 'free' internet service reducing to such a poor quality that content providers are effectively forced to purchase the premium

---

[272] In 2008 the FCC issued a decision against Comcast, who is the largest cable company in the USA, that it had limited the ability of its network subscribers to use the filesharing software BitTorrent.

[273] See Lee and Wu (2009) and Van Schewick (2006).

[274] The Internet is often conceptualised as a two-sided market in which it acts as a platform intermediary that facilitates the interaction of two main groups: content and application providers and users. See Economides and Tåg (2012) and Lee and Wu (2009).

[275] Peitz and Schuett (2016) find that strict net neutrality can lead to a socially inefficient allocation of traffic and traffic inflation. Gans and Katz (2016) also find that strong net neutrality (where ISPs cannot discriminate in charges to content providers or users) can harm efficiency by distorting ISPs' and content providers' service quality and investment decisions.

[276] See Kahn (2007), Weisman and Kulick (2010) and Faulhaber (2015). Brito, Cave, Crandall, *et al.* (2010) is a submission by twenty-one economists which argues that network neutrality regulations should not be adopted, and that the adoption of such regulations would reduce consumer welfare over the short and long terms.

[277] Faulhaber (2015).

[278] The concerns are outlined and critically examined in Sidak and Teece (2010).

[279] See Lee and Wu (2009). Economides (2010) suggests that: 'Paid prioritization could even create an incentive for broadband providers to create congestion to increase the price of prioritized service.' Bourreau, Kourandi and Valletti (2015) also find that a discriminatory regime may bring forth the risk of sabotage by ISPs, and that net neutrality may be a way of addressing this risk if it is too costly or complex to regulate traffic quality. However, as other commentators have noted, should such sabotage occur, then recourse could be had to the relevant competition laws (i.e. this alone does not justify *ex ante* regulation).

service.[279] Overall, the effects of net neutrality rules on static efficiency are ambiguou and can depend on factors such as: whether the content provider passes on charges t end-users; whether ISPs adjust subscription fees on the user side as well as the conten side; and the price structures that ISPs introduce to differentiate between users.[280]

The dynamic aspects of net neutrality regulation are linked to how such policies affec the investment incentives of both ISPs and content providers.[281] Some argue that allowin ISPs to charge for priority access creates incentives for ISPs to under-invest in networ capacity to reap any scarcity rents that arise from the willingness of content provide to pay more to avoid network congestion. Conversely, others argue that allowing ISPs t charge for access increases incentives for ISPs to undertake investments if they are ab to recover these costs by charging differential prices for different types of services.[2] ISPs could also have incentives to invest in network capacity if it expands the mark and encourages more entry by innovative content providers whose additional deman maintains the high value of the priority service.[283]

More generally, it is argued that allowing access tiering can create incentives fc greater innovation and investment by content/application providers and allow for th development of high-value products which are currently non-viable because of th congestion on the Internet associated with high volumes of low-value traffic.[284] Th option of a priority service could also level the playing field if it allows smaller an innovative content providers to gain priority access to help them compete against larg content providers (such as Netflix or Google) that are able to employ innovative tech niques to better address potential congestion.[285] Finally, it is argued that the success c the 'Internet of Things' depends on the provision of heterogeneous quality of servic requirements for network traffic that cannot be provided by the current best-effor Internet.[286]

In addition to these familiar trade-offs between static and dynamic efficiency, there a three other specific policy debates. The first is whether policies that intensify competitio between ISPs could mitigate concerns about harmful traffic management practices an

---

[280] Hermalin and Katz (2007) find that total surplus can rise or fall under net neutrality regulations, but that harm to welfare is likely. Economides and Tåg (2012) also find that total surplus can increase or decrease depending on parameter values. More generally, Greenstein, Peitz and Valletti (2016) conclude that: '[T]here is little support for the bold and simplistic claims of the most vociferous supporters and detractors of net neutrality. The economic consequences of such policies depend crucially on the precis policy choice and how it is implemented.'

[281] Choi and Kim (2010) and Charalampopoulos, Katsianis and Varoutas (2020) consider the interaction between net neutrality policies and the incentives to invest, including in NGNs.

[282] Bourreau, Kourandi and Valletti (2015) find that, where there is competition between ISPs, allowing differential pricing increases the level of content innovation and investments in broadband capacity, and that overall total welfare increases. However, the impact on different parties – ISPs, content providers and end-users – is ambiguous, and that differential pricing may not always be beneficial to ISPs if it intensifies competition for subscribers. In contrast, Choi and Kim (2010) find that a monopolistic ISP's content providers may also have weaker incentives to invest under a differential pricing regime than under net neutrality. See also Cheng, Bandyopadhyay and Guo (2011).

[283] Krämer and Wiewiorra (2012). Choi, Jeon and Kim (2018) also find that prioritisation can facilitate the entry of congestion-sensitive content by high-bandwidth content providers.

[284] See Hausman and Taylor (2013) and Bourreau, Kourandi and Valletti (2015).

[285] Greenstein, Peitz and Valletti (2016).

[286] See Knieps (2017).

thus alleviate the need for net neutrality regulation.[287] A second debate is the treatment of the use of so-called 'data caps' and zero ratings by ISPs. Data caps involve a maximum limit being placed on how much end-users can download in a month, while zero ratings is the practice of exempting certain internet traffic (such as that provided by the ISP itself or affiliates) from counting towards the usage in a data cap. The core question is whether such practices – which effectively involve 'free' services for zero-rated content – is good for consumers overall, or whether such practices have the effect of raising rivals' costs or tipping the competitive landscape.[288] This issue is of increasing relevance in the context of greater vertical integration of ISPs and content providers in some jurisdictions.[289] A final debate is whether the potential harms that net neutrality policies seek to address are best dealt with through *ex ante* regulation or *ex post* competition policy. Some argue that certain conduct – such as where a dominant ISP blocks or throttles the use of the Internet by certain content providers – may be best addressed under general competition law. Similarly, it is argued that, given the potentially ambiguous effects of net neutrality rules on welfare, certain practices such as 'zero rating' may be more effectively addressed by competition law than *ex ante* regulation.[290]

The Regulatory Response

The regulatory response to net neutrality has varied across jurisdictions and over time. In the USA, the FCC first issued an order on this matter in 2010; however, this order was subsequently struck down by the court in 2014.[291] Spurred on by the Obama Administration, the FCC introduced new rules in 2015 known as the 'Open Internet Order', which, among other things, banned fixed and mobile ISPs from blocking (such as blocking access to legal content, application and services), throttling (such as degrading or impairing legal internet traffic on the basis of content, applications or service) and paid prioritisation (i.e. favouring some lawful internet traffic in exchange for payment).[292] However, this order was in effect for only two years, and was repealed in 2017 under the Trump Administration with the FCC's 'Restoring Internet Freedom' rules.[293] The position adopted was that competition/antitrust law, enforced by the Federal Trade Commission, should be used to address any anti-competitive conduct by ISPs. Since that time, various states,

---

[287] Some research supports the view that greater competition can increase welfare and thus reduce the need for net neutrality regulation. However, this arises because of more intense competition among ISPs to attract end-users (who tend to single-home), and not because it affects the incentives for ISPs to price-differentiate to content providers. See Greenstein, Peitz and Valletti (2016) and Bourreau, Kourandi and Valletti (2015).

[288] Greenstein, Peitz and Valletti (2016). Krämer and Peitz (2018) argue that the effects can differ on a case-by-case basis. Similarly, the UK regulator (Ofcom, 2021d) concludes that: '[Z]ero-rated services can be beneficial to consumers and can promote competition. However, in certain contexts they also have the potential to harm competition, innovation and reduce consumer choice.'

[289] Such as the mergers between AT&T and Time Warner in 2016 and Comcast and NBCUniversal in 2009.

[290] Krämer and Peitz (2018).

[291] See FCC (2010b). The 'anti-blocking' and 'anti-discrimination' rules were struck down by the DC Circuit Court of Appeals on the basis that the FCC had imposed *per se* common carriage requirements on providers of internet access services. See FCC (2015).

[292] See FCC (2015).

[293] FCC (2017b). The FCC received over 22 million comments on the Notice of Proposed Rulemaking that preceded this decision.

such as California, have sought to re-introduce net neutrality rules, and President Bide has encouraged the FCC to restore the net neutrality regulations.[294]

In the EU, the Open Internet Regulation became effective in 2016 and requires ISP to treat all traffic equally when providing internet access services.[295] However, there ar three justified exceptions that permit ISPs to use 'reasonable' traffic management meas ures. These exceptions are if the measures: reflect objectively different technical quality o service requirements (and not commercial considerations); are transparent, non-discrim inatory and proportionate; and are not maintained for longer than necessary, and do no monitor specific content. ISPs are not permitted to engage in other forms of traffic man agement (such as blocking, throttling, altering, restricting, interfering with, degrading, o discriminating between content, applications, services or categories of them) except i specific circumstances. However, under the EU rules, ISPs can offer non-internet acces services which are optimised for specific content, applications or services (i.e. 'specialise services') under certain conditions.[296] In addition to these policies in the USA and the EU net neutrality rules have also been introduced in Chile (the first in the world), Argentin Brazil, Canada, India, Israel and the UK.

11.5 CONCLUSION

The telecommunications industry has been radically transformed over the past four dec ades, and this has had major implications for how it is regulated. The development o alternative telecommunications networks (such as cable networks and mobile networks and the separation of network infrastructure from the services provided using that infra structure, has allowed a wide range of new and innovative actors to be involved in th development and provision of services. These include new infrastructure operators (suc as cable and mobile phone companies), as well as those providing specific OTT service content and applications, such as Skype, Telegram, WeChat, Vonage, Apple FaceTim Facebook and Twitter, in addition to gaming and video on demand services, such a Netflix, Amazon Prime, HBO Max, Hulu and Disney+.

A number of technological innovations have driven these changes, but three develop ments in particular have improved the speed of transmission of data and networks' overa transmission capacity.[297] The first is the continual technical improvements in computin ability, which have facilitated digitisation and electronic switching.[298] The second is th

---

[294] White House (2021).

[295] See EU Regulation 2015/2120 on open internet access.

[296] EU Regulation 2015/2120 on open internet access. These include: where optimisation is necessary in order to meet requirements of a specific level of quality; that the network capacity is sufficient to provide these services in addition to any internet access service offered; the services are not offered as a replacement for internet access services; and they are not detrimental to the availability or general quality of internet access services for end-users.

[297] As Noam (2010) describes: 'Whereas the first-generation created networks that operated at kilobit per second transmission capacity, the second-generation reached mass consumer operations in the broadband megabit range, almost a thousand times as fast. And the third-generation will operate at another thousand-fold increase in speed in the gigabit range.'

[298] Improvements in computing capability, for example, in terms of processing speed and memory capacity are said to follow 'Moore's Law', which postulates that the number of electrical components on a microprocessor chip doubles approximately every eighteen months. See Moore (1965).

replacement of copper as the dominant transmission technology for telecommunications networks with fibre-optic cable, including increasingly at the local level (i.e. all the way to – or close to – a customer's premises). A third development has been the gradual transformation of fixed line networks from an analogue network architecture based on circuit switching to an NGN architecture based on digital packet-based switching, which uses the IP. The widespread adoption of the standardised IP suite of protocols by different network technologies has enabled the provision of any service (data, voice, video or other multimedia product) over any physical network infrastructure (fixed networks (copper or fibre) or mobile networks) and facilitated the transformation of the telecommunications industry from a series of independent, vertically distinct, single-service networks into an industry where there are numerous horizontal, multi-service networks all using the IP. In short, services are no longer tied to a particular transmission infrastructure, and voice, video and data can be delivered using cable, fixed line or mobile communications networks (although the quality and price of each delivery infrastructure may differ).

Given all of these changes, there are a number of open questions regarding the future regulation of the telecommunications industry. Some argue that, given the rapidly changing nature of the industry, the emergence of competition, and the substantial implications of inappropriate regulatory policies, the question of the ongoing rationale for regulation should be assessed by comparing the consumer welfare impacts of imperfect competition versus imperfect regulation. Others argue that there continues be a rationale for regulatory oversight of the industry given that concerns about potential market power persist for NGNs, as do concerns about net neutrality. There is also, it is argued, a need for regulation, to oversee wider technological and market changes – such as the substantial potential for 5G mobile connectivity and the emergence of the Internet of Things, and the fact that the use of telecommunications networks is increasingly dominated by data traffic generated by a small number of OTT providers – and to address the potential for consumer biases to be exploited in the changing market context.

DISCUSSION QUESTIONS

1. Describe the different transmission infrastructures that can be used to physically carry voice and data signals. What are the key characteristics of each type of infrastructure?
2. Describe the different types of services that utilise telecommunications networks. How has the provision of these services changed over time?
3. What are some of the trade-offs that can arise when using auctions to allocate spectrum capacity? What other problems can arise if auctions are poorly designed?
4. What are the different forms of competition that have been pursued for fixed line telecommunications networks? What is the 'ladder of investment' or 'stepping stone' approach to competition?
5. Describe differences in the regulation applied to fixed line networks, cable networks and mobile networks. Which activities on each of these networks (if any) are typically subject to regulation?
6. What is the 'waterbed effect', and in what areas of telecommunications does the effect potentially arise?

7. Describe the key elements of the LRIC pricing approach that has been used in th telecommunications industry. Why has it proven to be so controversial?

8. Do you agree with the following statement? 'Restructuring policies have been th main factor that has led to the development of sustainable competition in telecom munications across different jurisdictions.' Please provide reasons.

9. What are the main arguments for and against continuing to apply *ex ante* econom regulation to the telecommunications industry?

10. What are some of the trade-offs that regulators face in deciding whether to regu late NGNs? Describe the different approaches to regulation of NGNs that have bee adopted across jurisdictions.

11. Discuss some of the economic trade-offs and the arguments for and against net neu trality regulations.

12

Payment Systems Regulation

Payment systems which facilitate the transfer of funds between different parties have long been central to the functioning of communities and economies. While systemically important payment systems are subject to oversight by central banks to ensure that they are resilient, the past two decades has seen the emergence of more traditional forms of economic regulation applied to some payment systems in some jurisdictions.[1]

Economic regulation of payment systems has been motivated by various drivers and considerations discussed in Part II of this book. First, it reflects the traditional rationale to improve efficiency, given that some large payment systems are characterised by economies of scale and strong network effects. The regulation of card payment systems, in particular, is motivated by concerns that the price structures set in the two-sided market context may be adversely impacting on consumers and not sending the right signals to consumers about the underlying costs and benefits of using different payment instruments. Second, in some jurisdictions, the introduction of economic regulation reflects concerns about access to, and competition within, payment systems. This includes concerns that the 'rulebooks' governing access and participation in some payment systems are controlled by a small number of large banks, or other unregulated private entities, and that this could be having adverse effects on competition in retail banking or limiting innovation. Third, as in other industries, regulation is sometimes focused on promoting greater infrastructure competition. This includes initiatives to promote 'competition for the market' for infrastructure contracts, and the mandated vertical separation of schemes and processing activities to encourage greater competition in certain activities. Finally, an increasing regulatory focus reflects the importance of payment systems to many citizens,[2] and the substantial innovations occurring with payment interfaces and instruments (such as mobile apps, contactless payments and the ability to initiate payments using wearables, such as watches, or even by parts of the body).

Looking ahead, regulatory oversight of payment systems is likely to become more important as non-cash forms of payments become ubiquitous, particularly post the Covid-19 pandemic. In addition, while traditionally many payment systems were owned

---

[1] Tirole (2011) describes the payment card industry as becoming one of the most heavily regulated industries in some parts of the world.

[2] Some citizen surveys have identified access to payment systems as being an essential service alongside water, electricity, gas, urban transport and telephone services. See Van de Walle (2009).

and operated by associations of banks, large technology companies (many of whom operate the digital platforms described in Chapter 13) are becoming more active in the payments sector.[3] These private platform operators are potentially able to leverage their large customer base and take advantage of network effects to develop new global digital payment systems.[4] Central bank digital currencies (CBDCs) and other forms of privately operated cryptocurrencies are also emerging and offer new ways of making payments using blockchain and distributed ledger technology. While all of these changes have the potential to challenge existing payment systems and bring innovations that yield substantial consumer benefits, they also raise the familiar risks about concentration of market power in a small number of private participants and possible adverse effects on the efficient operation of retail payment systems.

12.1 PHYSICAL AND ECONOMIC CHARACTERISTICS OF PAYMENT SYSTEMS

12.1.1 Characteristics of the Product

A payment involves the transfer of funds (a payment) between a payer (those who make or send the payment) and one or more payees (those who receive the funds). Payment systems facilitate such payments (transfers of funds) and can be thought of as a set of common rules and arrangements for the initiation, acceptance, processing, clearing and settlement of payment transactions.[5] In other words, a payment system is a set of agreed rules and practices that each participant agrees to abide by to facilitate the smooth transfer of funds within the system (e.g. to facilitate a debit card transaction, a cardholder and the card issuing bank, as well as a merchant and its acquiring bank, all have to abide by agreed rules and processes established by the payment scheme to ensure the smooth transfer of funds). These rules are typically also associated with a payments infrastructure comprising a network of interconnections among members of the payment system that provide for transactional information to be processed, for communication among the members, and for a settlement or clearing system. Two important distinctions are between retail and wholesale payment systems, and cash and non-cash payments.

Retail and Wholesale Payment Systems
In most jurisdictions, separate payment systems are used for low-value payments (retail systems) and for high-value payments (wholesale systems). Retail payments involve the transfer of funds between end-users such as individuals, businesses and other entities

---

[3] Including Google (Google Pay), Apple (Apple Pay), Amazon (Amazon Pay), Ant and WeChat.

[4] As CRS (2019) notes: 'Such companies already have large market shares in various technology-related industries and collect huge amounts of consumer data, which could increase as they now seek to expand their scope into the payment industry. Were they to dominate electronic payments, it could pose competition concerns in the payment industry, as well as increase their dominance in their core industries.' See also Usher, Reshidi, Rivadeneyra and Hendry (2021).

[5] The UK competition authority (OFT, 2013) defined a payment system as 'the system of rules, as determined collectively by member organisations, that govern how a particular system of payments is administered, how payments are processed, and the criteria that potential members need to meet to become members'.

(such as charities or government). Individuals use retail payment systems to transfer money to a friend or family member, or to pay for goods and services. Businesses can use retail payment systems to pay wages or salaries to staff or to pay suppliers, while governments use them to make payments for state benefits. Payments made using retail payment systems tend to involve low values compared to wholesale systems, but are much larger in terms of the volume of transactions. For example, in 2019, the four main US retail interbank systems processed some 34.5 billion transactions, with a combined value of $75 trillion and an average payment value of $2170.[6] In the same year, 45 billion transactions were made using the retail interbank systems in the euro area, with a total value of €35 trillion, and an average payment value of €777.[7] As described below, retail payment systems can be operated by private providers (such as large card payment system operators and interbank systems), not-for-profit organisations and public providers.

In contrast, wholesale or clearing payment systems are used for the transfer of very large amounts of funds generally between banks and other financial institutions to facilitate foreign exchange trades, and to settle securities and payments between other central counterparties.[8] As these payments are very large and often time-critical, they need to be settled in a timely manner, often on or at a particular day or time (e.g. payment by a US bank to a British bank of $100 million). While the number of payments made using wholesale payment systems is significantly lower than for retail systems, the value of such payments is substantially larger. For example, in 2019 the two main US wholesale payment systems (US Fedwire Funds Service and CHIPS) processed 286 million transactions with a combined aggregate value of $1113 trillion, and an average value of $3.8 million per transaction.[9] Given the large value of funds being transferred, and the systemic implications of failure, wholesale payment systems are typically operated by central banks.[10] However, there are examples of privately owned and operated wholesale payment systems such as EURO1 (operated by the European Banking Association) and CHIPS in the USA.

Cash and Non-Cash Payments

Another important distinction is between cash and non-cash payments. Historically, cash (e.g. notes and coins) has been an important means by which many end-users – particularly individuals – have paid for goods and services, particularly for low-value transactions.[11] While cash remains an important form of payment for goods and services,[12] it is rapidly being replaced by other forms of non-cash and electronic payments, such as debit

---

[6] Source is BIS Red Book (2021).
[7] EC (2020f).
[8] Individuals can sometimes use wholesale systems to purchase, sell or finance securities transactions or to settle real estate transactions.
[9] Source is BIS Red Book (2021).
[10] Examples include: Fedwire Funds Service in the US, TARGET2 in the European Union, HVPS in China, CHAPS in the UK and the Reserve Bank Information and Transfer System (RITS) in Australia.
[11] Banknotes are also used as a 'store of value' as well as a means of payment.
[12] World Bank (2018) estimates that there are 1.7 billion adults globally who are tied to cash as their only means of payment. In the UK, it is estimated that between 2.2 million and 2.7 million people use cash for all of their day-to-day transactions (approximately 5 per cent of the adult population).

cards, credit cards and other forms of instant interbank transfer or digital currencies. The shift towards a greater reliance on cashless payments has been driven, in part, by the rise of electronic commerce which does not allow the use of cash to pay for goods and services bought online. However, in many emerging economies, the shift has also been facilitated by the greater penetration of mobile phones, which can allow for electronic payments without the need to open or maintain a bank account.[13] In the discussion in this chapter, we focus on non-cash-based retail payment systems – in particular, the card and interbank retail payment systems – as this is the area where economic regulation has typically been applied.

12.1.2 Payment Systems Participants

Five types of participants are typically involved in an interbank payment system: the users of payment systems (end-users and payment service providers, such as banks), and those who set the rules, operate the payment system and process transactions (payment schemes, payment system operators and payment system infrastructure providers), as shown in Figure 12.1.

While the participants are broadly the same, as described in Sections 12.1.4 and 12.1.5 below, there are important distinctions between how interbank and card payment systems operate and process transactions.

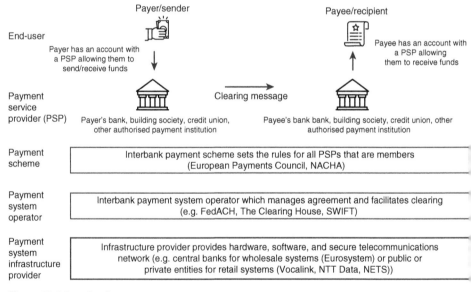

Figure 12.1 Interbank payment system

---

[13] Mobile money allows for funds transfers between mobile phones using the SIM card of the device, and, as such, users do not need to have a bank account or be connected to the Internet (as they do for mobile banking). GSMA (2019) estimate that there were 866 million mobile money accounts in sub-Saharan Africa, with over half the population in some countries using mobile money actively. Mobile money has also been particularly important in Kenya, where the M-PESA platform was launched by the mobile phone operator Safaricom in 2007, and now 96 per cent of households have a mobile money account. See Piper (2020).

End-Users of Payment Systems

The end-users of payment systems include individuals, small and medium-sized enterprises, corporations and large businesses, retailers, charities and not-for-profit organisations and government agencies. Different types of end-user utilise payment systems for various purposes. Individuals tend to use card payment systems (debit or credit) to make payments to businesses (merchants) and government, but not for making payments to another individual (for which they might use a cheque or a real-time interbank payment system). Similarly, businesses might use a bulk interbank payment system to pay salaries to workers, but use a card payment system for one-off payments (such as a commercial card for business expenses).

To initiate a payment within a particular payment system, end-users use a payment instrument, which can be a tool (cheque), device (such as a card) or set of procedures (a direct debit or credit transfer) that a payment service user and a payment service provider (PSP) agree can be used to enable the transfer of funds. The costs of using different payment systems from the end-user perspective are typically small relative to the value of the transaction and to the other charges applied by banks (PSPs) or other participants (such as card acquirers). In the EU, the cost of processing card transactions is capped at between 0.3 and 0.2 per cent of the value of the transaction, while for interbank systems it has been estimated that the median cost of bulk interbank payments is around 0.29 US cents per transaction.[14]

Payment Service Providers

To facilitate a retail payment (the transfer of funds), end-users utilise the services of PSPs with whom they have an account and that are authorised to provide payment services within a particular payment system.[15] PSPs typically include banks and other non-bank providers (such as building societies, credit unions, authorised payment institutions, e-money institutions, Post Offices). PSPs are often privately owned (although some banks can be state-owned), while building societies and credit unions can sometimes operate as not-for-profit entities. Depending on the rules of a payment system, PSPs may have direct access to the payment system (i.e. they are a full participant of the payment system and can directly send and receive payments) or indirect access to the payment system (i.e. the PSP must be 'sponsored' by another PSP with direct access who facilitates the sending and receiving of payments on its behalf).

Payment Schemes

The rules for a specific payment system are set and implemented by a payment scheme. These include the scheme rules relating to who can be admitted as a member/participant of the system and the rules relating to system operation and clearing, etc. Payment schemes are often owned by payment associations (which represent the interests of PSPs) within

---

[14] AFP (2015). Lipis (2015) estimate the costs of low-value bulk transactions in Europe and the US to be broadly comparable with the headline price of 0.15–0.30 pence. In contrast, the median cost of processing a cheque transaction has been estimated at $3.

[15] PSPs can also provide other banking and financial services to users in addition to facilitating payments.

a jurisdiction,[16] although some payment schemes (like the 'card schemes') are privately owned. In some cases, the rules established by a single payments scheme are applied to number of payment systems, including those that are operated by a central bank.[17]

Payment System Operator

A payment system operator is the body which manages the multi-party scheme agreement and facilitates clearing under the rules that govern the transfer of funds between PSP within that system.[18] Payment system operators can be not-for profit entities, privately owned commercial entities or be operated by a central bank. Examples of payment system operators that operate independently of payment schemes include the interbank system for the clearing of debit and credit transfers in the USA (FedACH and The Clearing House (TCH)) and in various European countries (Germany, Belgium, Denmark, Italy, Sweden and in Australia and Brazil.

Payment System Infrastructure Providers

Payment system infrastructure providers include those who provide hardware, software and secure telecommunications network and operating environments that are used to manage and operate payment systems. This infrastructure supports the clearing and/or settlement of a payment, or funds transfer request, once initiated. Infrastructure can be provided by central banks (as is the case with most wholesale systems) or by private entities such as CGI, Vocalink (Mastercard), NTT Data, NETS, Visa, Equens and STET.

The extent to which these three activities (payment scheme management, payment system operation and infrastructure provision) are integrated varies by payment system an jurisdiction. Card systems typically integrate all three activities within a single entity, and some interbank systems are fully integrated.[20] However, in many countries, there i some degree of separation in the activities of scheme management, system operation an infrastructure provision. Some countries integrate the scheme and payment system operation, but outsource infrastructure provision to a separate entity.[21] While, in other countries system operation and infrastructure are fully integrated, but the scheme is separate.[22]

12.1.3 Processing of Payments

While, as discussed below, there are important differences between interbank and card retail payment systems, there are four common elements involved in the transfer of funds across all systems: the establishment of accounts within the payment system; some means

---

[16] For example, Zengin-Net in Japan or the European Payments Council in Europe.
[17] For example, in the USA, the National Automated Clearinghouse Association (Nacha) sets the rules, which apply to both bulk and retail payment systems, including FedACH, which is operated by the Federal Reserve.
[18] Some payment systems integrate the scheme and operation functions. This includes the major card systems (such as Visa and Mastercard) and the interbank systems in the UK, Singapore, New Zealand an Canada.
[19] Although, as discussed below, there are requirements for scheme and processing activities to be structurally separated in Europe.
[20] This includes retail system in Canada and the retail real-time system in Sweden.
[21] Examples include Japan, Singapore, New Zealand and the UK.
[22] Examples include Australia, Brazil, Denmark, Sweden and the USA.

of initiating payments; rules and processes for the clearing of payments; and the final settlement and transfer of funds from one account to another.

To make or receive payments, all end-users (individuals, businesses, governments) need to have a transaction account with a PSP that operates within the payment system, for example, a bank account. This account is used to receive funds from, or transfer funds to, other participants within the payment system. Second, end-users need to have an acceptable means of making payments within the payment system; this includes an access point or service channel (such as a mobile payment application programming interface (API) or internet portal) and an accepted payment instrument or tool (such as a debit card or a credit transfer) that can be used to initiate the payment. Depending on the system rules, payments can be initiated by either a payer (sender) or a payee (receiver). Systems where a payer initiates the payment – such as a direct credit payment – are sometimes known as 'push' payment systems, as the payer 'pushes' the funds from their account to another account.[23] In contrast, systems where the payee initiates the payment are known as 'pull' payment systems, as the payer 'pulls' the funds from the payee's account, and include direct debit payments and credit and debit card payments.[24]

Once a payment has been initiated by an end-user, the payment needs to be *cleared*. Clearing involves the payer's PSP (e.g. the payer's bank) and the payee's PSP (e.g. the payee's bank) exchanging messages to ensure, among other things, that there are adequate funds in the payer's account to make the payment. The need for clearing arises from the fact that a payee and a payer often do not maintain an account with the same PSP (e.g. individuals hold accounts with different banks). Clearing can involve payment messages being sent from one PSP to another individually in real time as the transaction occurs (real-time clearing), or in batches at allocated times within the day (batch clearing). Payment schemes establish the clearing rules for their payment system, while payment system operators facilitate the multilateral clearing of transactions among PSPs within that system.[25]

If a payment has been cleared, the final stage is *settlement*, which involves the release and transfer of funds from the payer's PSP account to the payee's PSP account. Payments can be settled individually in 'real time' or on a 'deferred' basis as a batch. Real-time gross settlement involves each individual payment being settled as soon as it enters the payment system. In contrast, deferred net settlement involves payments between PSPs first being 'netted' off with one another (i.e. outgoing payments to one PSP are offset against incoming payments from that PSP), with the net settlement between PSPs only taking place at particular times (e.g. a specific time each day). The main difference between the two settlement approaches is the amount of liquidity that

---

[23] Examples include: an individual who wants to pay a seller/merchant online and therefore initiates a transaction to settle an invoice; an employer that wants to pay salaries to an employee; or the government initiating transactions to make welfare payments.

[24] Examples include direct debits, where a utility company may request funds be withdrawn from a customer's account on a monthly basis, or debit or credit card payments, where a merchant instructs that funds be withdrawn from the payer's account. Card transactions are considered pull payments because the merchant's PSP requests to 'pull' money out of the customer's account. However, this only occurs once the customer has provided the appropriate authorisation for the funds to be transferred.

[25] An alternative would involve PSPs bilaterally clearing transactions directly. Many payment systems evolved from bilateral agreements among banks about clearing and settlement to the current multilateral agreements.

PSPs need to maintain. PSPs that operate in real-time gross systems need to maintain more funds to ensure they can settle payments as and when they arise, while PSPs that operate in deferred net systems require less liquidity, as they can offset incoming payments against outgoing payments. However, because settlement is not instantaneous in deferred systems, this can give rise to settlement risk; for example, where the payer or payee PSP defaults prior to final settlement (known as credit risk), or has insufficient funds to settle the payment when it is due (known as liquidity risk). Wholesale payment systems typically operate on a real-time gross settlement basis, while retail payment systems can operate on a real-time gross settlement basis (e.g. real-time or instant payment systems) or deferred net settlement basis (electronic debit or credit transfer cheques or card systems).

Some payment systems operate internationally and allow for funds to be transferred between a payer and a payee located in different jurisdictions. Such cross-border payments can arise where an individual travels and purchases something overseas using different currency, or where a payment is made in the same currency but in a different jurisdiction (such as in the euro area). The growth of e-commerce has led to significant growth in cross-border payments. The processing of cross-border payments is broadly similar to that of domestic payments described above (e.g. there must be an account means of initiating a payment, and processes of clearing and settlement). While some payment systems such as the major card systems (Visa, Mastercard) operate internationally, the processing of interbank transfers can require that PSPs use the message standards and infrastructure of a global payment network such as the Society for Worldwide Interbank Financial Telecommunication (SWIFT).

12.1.4 Interbank Payment Systems

Interbank payment systems allow end-users to make and receive payments using the account they have with a PSP, typically a bank account. Interbank payment systems typically evolved from a series of private bilateral agreements between major banks to cover the rules of clearing and settlement between themselves, to ever increasing degrees of multilateral collaboration among a wider group of participants, and where transactions are cleared and settled in a centralised 'clearing house'. As they have evolved, many of the services provided by interbank systems have become increasingly important from a public policy point of view, such that they are now seen to provide something approximating an essential or public-utility-like service. Some retail interbank systems are designated as 'systemically important payment systems' in some jurisdictions, which brings with it certain obligations in terms of governance and access. In many countries, interbank payment systems operate as not-for-profit organisations, often comprising membership which includes the major banks and other PSPs that utilise the system. However, central banks can also operate interbank systems, often with the aim of facilitating access to smaller banks and PSPs.[26]

---

[26] Such as in the USA and Germany.

In many jurisdictions, there are at least two different retail (low-value) interbank payment systems in operation.[27] Each payment system has different participants (e.g. banks) and rules of participation and uses different technical processes and messaging standards.[28] Common examples of interbank systems include: those used for cheque payments; a bulk payment system used for processing direct debits and direct credits; and, in many jurisdictions, a real-time or instant payment system, which can be used for processing of single immediate payments or forward-dated payments.

For end-users, the payment services provided by different interbank payment systems are differentiated across various dimensions including: the speed of the payment (real time or delayed); ways of accessing the system and type of payment instrument use (Internet, telephone, cheque); information that accompanies the payment (type and form of data); security and reliability; cost of the payment; and maximum and minimum payment levels. These differences between interbank payment systems have implications for interoperability between the systems,[29] and the degree to which end-users consider them to be substitutable (and therefore the extent of competition between the systems).

In addition to providing basic payment services, some interbank systems provide the ability for these services to be combined with additional services and functionality known as overlay services.[30] These services can be provided by the payment system operator, or by third parties that use the central infrastructure. As described in Section 12.1.6 and Box 12.1, the development of overlays is central to the design of the new interbank systems in the UK and Australia. Examples of overlay services include: mobile payments (i.e. the ability to send and receive payments using a mobile phone number); current account switching and masking services;[31] and services that allow for the automated management of recurring payments. Overlay products offered to corporate customers include direct debit management services, direct corporate access to the payment systems, and various corporate treasury and account management and reconciliation services.

---

[27] In the UK there are three retail payment systems (one for cheque payments; another bulk payment system used for processing direct debits and direct credits; and a third real-time payment system for processing of single immediate payments, forward-dated payments or standing order payments). In addition, the main wholesale payment system can be used for processing time-critical, lower-value retail payments, like buying or paying a deposit on a property.

[28] Messaging standards are a common set of rules for exchanging relevant payment information in order to enable efficient communication with participants and related infrastructures. Among other things, messaging standards cover such things as: how senders and receivers identify each other; how key properties of a payment message, such as currency, amount and value date, are represented; and what additional information can be included alongside settlement data, and in what format, to enable onward transport and processing of the payment. Common messaging standards for interbank systems include ISO 20022, while the card systems use the standard ISO 8583.

[29] For example, payment systems that use the same messaging standard (such as ISO 20022) offer the potential for some degree of interoperability.

[30] Overlay services sit 'above' the basic infrastructure services that provide a transaction service. Examples could include fraud identification or prevention services, access-related solutions such as payment gateways and software products, reference data distribution services, or services such as request to pay.

[31] Such as the current account switching service in the UK.

12.1.5 Card Payment Systems

Card payment systems allow end-users, such as individuals or business, to make pay
ments to merchants or other service providers (including government agencies) usin
debit cards, credit cards, charge cards or prepaid cards. Card payments can be mad
in-person (including contactless payments or 'chip and pin') or online ('card not pres
ent' transactions). The use of card payment systems to pay for goods and services ha
expanded dramatically in recent years, and, in several jurisdictions, cards are more pop
ular than cash as a means of payment. In the USA, debit cards accounted for around 4
per cent of the value of transactions made in 2018, followed by cash (26 per cent) an
credit cards (22 per cent).[32]

Historically, the major card payment systems such as Visa and Mastercard were estab
lished as not-for-profit entities to set common rules for the processing of card transac
tions and were owned by their members, which were banks. However, in recent year
both Visa and Mastercard have become commercial for-profit entities and are now liste
companies. In some jurisdictions, such as India (RuPay) and China (UnionPay), card pay
ment systems are under the ownership of central banks or the state.

There are two types of card payment system: 'four-party' systems (such as Visa
Mastercard and UnionPay) and 'three-party' (or proprietary) systems (such as America
Express or Diners Club). Figure 12.2 shows the main participants involved in a four
party system, including: cardholders that use a card issued to them to pay for goods an
services; card issuers (often banks, but also other organisations) that are authorised t
issue cards to cardholders; merchants (such as retailers and other businesses) that accep
card payments from that card system; acquirers (banks or other organisations) that pro
cess card payments on behalf of merchants; and card payment schemes (such as Visa
Mastercard or UnionPay) that license issuers and acquirers, manage the scheme rules an
provide the processing services to facilitate the movement of funds between an issuer an
an acquirer. Three-party card systems – such as American Express or Diners Club – dif
fer from four-party systems in that the card payment scheme performs the roles of bot
issuer and acquirer as well as setting the system rules. As such, the three participants ar
the card payment scheme, the cardholder and the merchant.

Figure 12.2 shows the different types of fees and charges that flow between the var
ious participants in a four-party card system. This includes: cardholder fees, which ar
paid by cardholders to issuing banks (such as an annual card fee or interest payments
scheme fees, which are paid by acquirers and issuers to card schemes; and the merchan
service charge (MSC), which is paid by merchants to acquirers for processing payment
and other services.[33] A major component of the MSC is the 'interchange fee', which is a
amount paid by acquirers to issuers each time a card is used for a transaction.[34] Variou
rationales for levying interchange fees have been suggested, including that: it 'balance

---

[32] The remaining 11% was preauthorised payments (4%), prepaid cards (4%), cheques (3%). See Nilson (2019
[33] The MSC is sometimes called a merchant discount fee in some jurisdictions.
[34] The interchange fee is deducted from the amount paid by the issuer to an acquirer. If the interchange
fee is 1 per cent of the value of a transaction, then an issuer that receives $100 from a cardholder for a
transaction will retain $1 for the interchange fee, and transfer the remaining $99 to the acquirer.

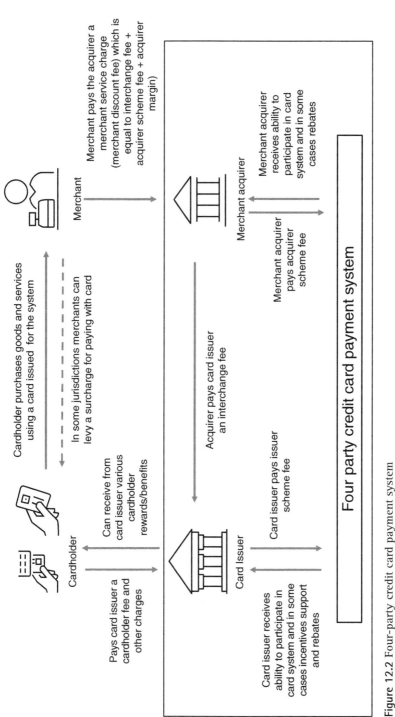

Cardholder purchases goods and services using a card issued for the system

In some jurisdictions merchants can levy a surcharge for paying with card

Can receive from card issuer various cardholder rewards/benefits

Pays card issuer a cardholder fee and other charges

Cardholder

Acquirer pays card issuer an interchange fee

Card issuer pays issuer scheme fee

Card Issuer

Card issuer receives ability to participate in card system and in some cases incentives support and rebates

Merchant pays the acquirer a merchant service charge (merchant discount fee) which is equal to interchange fee + acquirer scheme fee + acquirer margin)

Merchant

Merchant acquirer receives ability to participate in card system and in some cases rebates

Merchant acquirer pays acquirer scheme fee

Merchant acquirer

Four party credit card payment system

Figure 12.2 Four-party credit card payment system

the costs and benefits of processing a transaction for the issuing and acquiring sides;[35] is a way of attracting banks to participate as card issuers in a given card system;[36] it used to compensate issuing banks for their involvement in a transaction;[37] it incentivise cardholders to make payments using a card, and thus expands the size of the system b exploiting network externalities;[38] or in recognition of the fact that cards are a 'must tak' for some merchants.[39]

As described below, interchange fees are now regulated in many jurisdictions to addres concerns that interchange fees have been set at inefficiently high levels. However, reg ulating the structure of interchange fees is complicated by the fact that card paymer systems are characterised as a two-sided market, which, as discussed in Chapter 6, give rise to interdependence between different types of user groups and network effects. I this context, the greater the number of merchants that accept a particular brand of car (Visa, Mastercard, UnionPay), the more willing customers are to hold that brand of car (and vice versa). As discussed below, this has implications for the optimal structure an level of interchange fees.

12.1.6 Emerging Payment Systems and Services

The retail payment landscape is changing rapidly in many parts of the world. Amon the most significant of these changes are: the emergence of new payment systems an services; the expansion of card systems into interbank payments; and new uses and appl cations of existing payment systems.

New Payment Systems Based on Blockchain or Distributed Ledger Technology
An important emerging change to the payments landscape is the potential for entr by new payment systems that utilise distributed ledger technology where a database

---

[35] This is the so-called balancing argument. See ACCC/RBA (2000) and RBA (2004) which note that: 'In some payment systems, interchange fees may be necessary to ensure that all the parties are prepared to participate to provide the service. For instance, in a credit card system, if issuers cannot recover all thei costs from cardholders an interchange fee paid by the merchant's bank might be necessary to make the issuers' participation in the system viable.' Schmalensee (2002) makes a similar point: 'the interchange fee is not an ordinary market price; it is a balancing device for increasing the value of a payment syste by shifting costs between issuers and acquirers and thus shifting charges between consumers and merchants'. The US Supreme Court has also found that: 'To optimize sales, the network must find the balance of pricing that encourages the greatest number of matches between cardholders and merchants (see *Ohio et al. v. American Express Co. et al.* No. 16-1454 (2018)). This general argument follows from Baxter's (1983) analysis on the need for redistributive payments between card issuing banks and merchant banks to cover costs. Frankel (1998) presents a critique noting that costs on the merchant side of the business are actually higher than on the consumer side.

[36] The EC (2013a) argued that high interchange fees act as a barrier to entry for cheaper and more efficien card schemes that offer lower interbank fees but have difficulty convincing issuing banks to switch to national card schemes with lower interchange fees.

[37] The US Federal Reserve characterises debit card interchange fees in this way.

[38] Cardholders can be incentivised to use cards if the revenues from interchange fees are used to 'subsidise cardholders by charging them less than the cost of the payment service they use, or if it is used to fund various rebates or benefits such as loyalty points. See RBA (2002) and Chang and Evans (2000).

[39] This 'must take' attribute allows for positive and high interchange fees to be sustained by payment schemes. See Vickers (2005).

distributed among a network of nodes.[40] This differs from traditional payment systems architecture where transactions involve a single database (centralised ledger) maintained in one place. Among the perceived benefits of distributed ledger systems are: enhanced reliability, availability and resilience by having data stored in nodes at multiple locations; improvements in performance; an ability to access data by using code which is split and executed in several nodes; and that it can be cheaper to increase capacity of a distributed system through the addition of new nodes.[41]

Facebook sought to develop a payment system based around distributed ledger technology known as Diem.[42] Diem described itself as a new financial asset (a crypto-asset or a cryptocurrency) which aspired to be a global currency that will utilise its own global technical infrastructures to enable payments. While the payment system and infrastructure that would underpin Diem transactions was still under development at the time of its sale, in broad terms it was expected that payment information will be stored in a distributed database, where different nodes maintain copies of the database. The network nodes would in turn be maintained by the members of the Diem Association, and only these members would have been able to register and store transactions. To allow the processing of a potentially very large number of payments in a decentralised way, a consensus algorithm would be developed to allow transactions to be approved quickly and efficiently. Facebook was also developing a digital wallet called Novi to help people send and hold Diem, and which could transfer funds using a stand-alone app, but also through WhatsApp and Facebook Messenger.

Central banks in some countries are also exploring the potential for new payments platforms to facilitate the movement of digital currencies, known as central bank digital currency (CBDC).[43] Some CBDC concepts envisage a public–private 'platform' model where the core ledger and payments infrastructure would be operated by a central bank to provide minimum necessary functionality for CDBC payments, and private payment interface providers (PIPs) would use the platform to connect customers on the platform using user-friendly interfaces.[44] PIPs are expected to develop a full range of payment types as overlay services, including push payments (initiated by the payer),

---

[40] The Bank of England (2020) has described distributed ledger technology as comprising four building blocks: *Decentralisation* allows a number of third parties to maintain copies of the ledger and to process updates to the ledger (such as transactions). *Sharing of data* provides access to a wider group of participants to 'read' data on the ledger and/or includes the right to update ('write') data on the ledger. *Use of cryptography* enables different types of functionality, including the use of public key cryptography to verify that someone sending a payment instruction is entitled to do so, or the use of cryptographic proofs to assert facts about the ledger (e.g. that a particular transaction has occurred). *Programmability* allows the creation of so-called 'smart contracts' which can be used to automatically execute the terms of an agreement, and initiate related transactions, without human intervention.

[41] Segendorf, Eklööf, Gustafsson, *et al.* (2019).

[42] Facebook (Meta) withdrew its involvement in Diem in February 2022 and Diem's intellectual property and other assets were sold to a third-party organisation. This was because of regulatory opposition to the project. However, it is expected that other 'big tech' companies will seek to enter this space in the future, including through the development of cryptocurrencies. See Kotovskaia and Meier (2022).

[43] The People's Bank of China is the first central bank to issue a CBDC (the digital yuan, eRMB, or e-CNY). For a more general overview of CBDCs, see Auer, Frost, Gambacorta, *et al.* (2022), Bank of Canada (2022) and ECB (2022).

[44] See, for example, the proposal by the Bank of England (2020).

pull payments (initiated by the payee) and recurring payments. PIPs could also provid value-added 'overlay services' to users, such as smart contracts, micropayments an programmable money.[45] More broadly, it is argued that, by providing an alternativ low-cost payment instrument, particularly for online transactions, a CBDC could offe a 'simpler competition policy tool' than regulating card payment networks, and in th future exert competitive discipline on the expansion of digital platforms into paymen activities.[46]

Expansion by Card and Interbank Payment Systems

Alongside the potential for new entry, another way in which the payment landscape i changing is the expansion of existing card schemes into interbank payments, and vic versa. Card system operators, such as Visa and Mastercard, are expanding into new 'push payment products which involve using the existing card payment infrastructure in th reverse direction; the debit card network is used to 'push' a payment to a debit cardhold er's account almost instantly. This can facilitate almost instant fund transfers betwee individual cardholders, and facilitate person-to-person payments, payments to merchant as well as business-to-business and government-to-consumer payments.[47] New uses o existing interbank systems are also emerging which can allow for credit transfers in rea time and could thus be a substitute for card systems for some uses.[48] As discussed belov it is expected that, as real-time or instant payment systems expand around the world, thi will foster the development of new overlay services that could be a direct competitor t the card systems and potentially erode the market position of card systems, particular for online payments.[49]

Digital Wallets

Another important area of innovation in payment systems has been the rapid develop ment of digital wallets, which provide end-users with a single interface allowing them t choose to make payments using different payment systems. A digital wallet user migh choose to use a debit card stored in the wallet to make a particular payment, or alterna tively directly transfer funds from their bank account to the payer using the interban system. There are different forms and providers of digital wallets, including PayPal (whic owns Venmo), Apple, Google, Amazon and Samsung. Mastercard and Visa have als launched digital wallets (MasterPass and Visa Checkout).

---

[45] Micropayments enable payments for very small amounts which some see as important for the development of Internet of Things (IoT) applications by connecting networks of physical devices, and could also support a shift away from subscription or ad-supported models for digital media. Programmable money involves payments occurring according to specified conditions, rules or events. This programmability could be implemented via the use of smart contracts. See Bank of England (2020).

[46] Usher, Reshidi, Rivadeneyra and Hendry (2021).

[47] Visa Direct allows for the real-time transfer of funds between accounts through transactions on Visa's existing payment network infrastructure to an eligible debit or prepaid card. Mastercard Send allows banks and businesses to use the existing Mastercard payments infrastructure to 'push' money to a recipient in real time with only their debit card number.

[48] This includes iDEAL in the Netherlands, Swish in Sweden and MobilePay in Denmark.

[49] Ovum (2017) forecast that in Europe e-commerce transactions which use instant real-time payment systems will overtake card payments around 2024.

Where both a payer and payee utilise the same digital wallet, the transaction might be internalised and settled as an 'on-us' transaction. This gives rise to the potential that some digital wallet platforms could exploit network effects and evolve into large closed systems that challenge existing payment systems.[50] Some argue that there is considerable scope for non-traditional providers of banking services – such as large technology or social network companies or online retailers and merchants – to leverage their positions (including large customer bases, proprietary data, financial resources, technological capabilities and established reputation) to become major providers of digital wallet or other aggregator services.[51] Examples of this trend can be seen in the substantial growth in China of Alipay, which was created to facilitate payments for an online shopping channel and is now the world's largest mobile platform, and WeChat, which is the largest social media app and also operates WeChat Pay.

12.2 APPROACH TO PAYMENT SYSTEMS REGULATION

12.2.1 Activities Subject to Regulation in Payment Systems

There is considerable diversity in how payment systems are regulated around the world. As described above, in many jurisdictions, payment systems have evolved from a series of bilateral agreements among major banks to facilitate the acceptance, clearing and settlement of payments, to multilateral agreements managed and administered by payment schemes and operators that are increasingly distinct from banks, or, in the case of card schemes, by large listed corporations.

Competitive Activities

The principal users of payment systems are payment service providers (PSPs) – such as banks and other authorised organisations – which, as described above, facilitate the transfer of funds on behalf of end-users. In most jurisdictions, PSPs compete with one another to attract end-users to open payment accounts with them, and therefore no formal economic regulation is applied equivalent to that seen in other industries discussed in this book. However, PSPs are often licensed and subject to prudential, consumer protection and conduct regulations. The number and type of PSPs that are able to participate in a specific payment system can also sometimes be restricted by the rules established by a payment scheme. For example, only certain types of PSPs can become a direct participant of payment systems in some jurisdictions.[52]

There are two potential forms of competition *between* payment systems: *inter*-payment system competition (such as between card systems and interbank systems) and *intra*-payment system competition (such as between different card systems).

---

[50] According to Bech, Shimizu and Wong (2017): 'Closed systems provide payment services to only their customers, and credits and debits occur on their own books.'

[51] See EC (2020d) and Chiu and Koeppl (2022).

[52] In some jurisdictions, this can be limited to PSPs that maintain a settlement account with the central bank and can demonstrate that they meet certain technical, operational and commercial risk management standards.

The extent of *inter*-system competitive pressure that card systems and interbank systems exert on one another has historically been assessed as low in many jurisdictions. This reflects the limited overlap, and hence substitution possibilities, in the payment services that are provided by the card and interbank payment systems.[54] However, as discussed in Box 12.1, this may be changing as a result of the emergence of real-time interbank systems and open banking policies that allow for entry by new third-party providers (TPPs) providing services such as request to pay. Depending on the nature of the payment, proprietary payment networks can also be substitutes for payments made using the card and interbank systems in some circumstances.[55]

The extent of *intra*-payment system competition between different interbank payment systems is conditioned both by the purpose of payments and by the functionality and technical characteristics of the systems. As described, there are important differences between interbank systems (wholesale and retail, 'push' and 'pull', 'real time' and 'bulk') which have historically limited the extent of substitutability between these systems. The extent of competition between interbank systems has also been shaped by the fact that, in most jurisdictions, they operate as not-for-profit entities, and that in some cases a common payment scheme operator (often a national banking association) sets the rules for all of the interbank systems in a jurisdiction. These ownership and governance factors can dull the incentives to promote competition between different interbank systems. That said, there could be areas of overlap for certain payments. For example, individuals or businesses making relatively high-value real-time credit payments (e.g. a house deposit) can choose between a retail real-time payment system and a wholesale payment system in some jurisdictions.[56] Similarly, there can be overlap between bulk and real-time payment system for some recurring payments (e.g. salary payments could over time be made in real time rather than in bulk). In some jurisdictions, users can choose between multiple interbank payment systems for the same transaction. For example, in the USA there are two main automated clearing houses, one operated by the Federal Reserve, known as the FedACH and another, operated by a privately owned operator, known as the Electronic Payment Network (EPN).[57] Finally, within a given interbank payment system there can be competition for certain activities or services, such as the provision of gateway or access services.

In contrast, *intra*-system competition for cards is more intense, as many card schemes are privately owned, commercial for-profit organisations including Visa, Mastercard

---

[53] The UK regulator, for example, has assessed that the interbank system currently provides limited substitution for merchants who use the card system; see PSR (2021a). Card systems have traditionally been seen as closer substitutes for cash.

[54] Card payment systems principally allow individuals to make payments in real time to merchants (businesses) for goods and services, or facilitate business-to-business payments for goods and services. In contrast, interbank systems can facilitate individual-to-individual payments, bulk salary payments by businesses, or transfers from and to government. The main area of overlap is for consumer payments to merchants and government, and business-to-business payments.

[55] For example, fuel cards or store cards, etc. In the USA, there are dozens of proprietary payment networks, many of which are 'limited participation' systems, meaning that the payer and the payee must join that network to make a payment.

[56] In the UK, the wholesale payment system (CHAPS) and the retail real-time system (Faster Payments) can be used to make a large transaction up to an amount of £250,000.

[57] There are also two large-value funds transfer systems – the CHIPS system (which is owned and operated by financial institutions and banks) and the Fedwire system (which is operated by the Federal Reserve).

American Express and JCB (formerly Japan Credit Bureau), and the national or domestic schemes in certain countries.[58] The extent of competition between card systems varies by jurisdiction and card type (credit or debit). Globally, three card payment systems – Visa, Mastercard and UnionPay – collectively accounted for 96 per cent of all purchase transactions in 2020.[59] In the USA, Europe and Latin America, Visa and Mastercard both sustain extremely strong market positions,[60] while in the Asia-Pacific region, UnionPay has an estimated market share of 72 per cent, while RuPay has a share of around 34 per cent in India.[61] There are also differences in the intensity of competition for credit card transactions, debit card transactions and charge card transactions. In the USA and Europe, Visa has a stronger position in debit card transactions than other transactions compared to its closest rival, Mastercard. In addition to competition between different card systems, there is also competition *within* (four-party) card payment systems.[62] Card issuers (including banks but also other organisations that are authorised or licensed to issue cards) compete with one another to attract end-users as cardholders. This includes price competition (in terms of annual cardholder fees and interest rates) but also non-price competition such as benefits (air miles) to encourage greater use of cards. Acquirers, which can include banks as well as other financial technology processing companies and independent sales organisations,[63] compete to attract merchants to participate in a payment system.[64]

The extent of competition for payments infrastructure has historically been relatively limited for both card systems and interbank systems in most jurisdictions. Although there are a number of potential infrastructure providers, many payment systems have integrated the infrastructure into the payments operation,[65] or, where they are separate, have established a long-term relationship with a particular provider.[66] As such, instances of competitive tendering for infrastructure are rare and are typically limited to new payment system infrastructure (such as CEC in Belgium, Faster Payments in the UK or the New Payments Platform (NPP) in Australia). Where tenders for legacy systems infrastructure have been used, the incumbent has often been successful.[67]

---

[58] National card schemes include Cartes Bancaires (France), Girocard (Germany), Bancomat/PagoBancomat (Italy), Dankort (Denmark) and Carnet (Mexico). Some card systems such as RuPay (India) and UnionPay (China) are operated by the national banking associations under the control of the central bank.

[59] Nilson (2021a) estimate that Visa's global share was 40 per cent, Mastercard's was 24 per cent and UnionPay's was 32 per cent.

[60] Estimates suggest that the combined market share of Visa and Mastercard for general-purpose cards was 86 per cent in the USA in 2019, 99 per cent in Europe in 2020, and 98 per cent in Latin America (Nilson 2021b, c).

[61] Nilson (2021d) and Financial Express (2021).

[62] In three-party card systems, such as American Express, the card scheme directly attracts end-users (cardholders) and merchants to participate in their system.

[63] Independent sales organisations refer merchants to acquirers for card-acquiring services, but do not provide these services themselves.

[64] In 2020, the top merchant acquirers in the USA included banks (Chase and Bank of America) as well as other financial technology companies (FISERV, FIS and Global Payments). In Europe, the top merchant acquirers in 2020 also included banks (Barclays, JP Morgan and Credit Agricole) and financial technology companies (Worldpay, Worldline and Adyen). See Nilson (2021e, f).

[65] The card systems such as Visa and Mastercard use proprietary transactions processing networks (VisaNet or Visa Technology and Operations and Mastercard Banknet).

[66] In some cases, an infrastructure provider has developed bespoke standards and protocols (e.g. messaging standards) for that system, which limits the scope for entry by other systems.

[67] Such as NTT Data in Japan. See Lipis (2015).

Box 12.1	**Competition between real-time interbank and card payment systems**

Traditionally, the extent of substitution between retail interbank payment systems and card payment systems has been limited, given the different clearing times and security protocols,[68] and the different uses of each system. As noted above, interbank systems are traditionally used mainly for recurring or bulk consumer payments (such as to receive salaries or to pay for utility bills or a mortgage or one-off transfers of funds) and the card systems are traditionally used to buy goods and services from merchants (increasingly online). However, this traditional distinction between interbank and card systems may be changing as a result of the development of 'back-end' real-time, or instant, payment systems coupled with the emergence of new 'front-end' consumer-facing payment overlay services and applications.

At the 'back end', real-time payment systems allow for payments to be initiated and settled almost instantaneously on a 24/7 basis.[69] A growing number of countries have already introduced some form of real-time system,[70] or are in the process of developing or upgrading existing real-time systems.[71] An important design aspect of some new real-time payment systems – such as the NPP in Australia or the New Payments Architecture in the UK – is the vertical separation of the essential or central infrastructure services (such as clearing and settlement services) from overlay services which 'sit above' the central infrastructure and provide additional functionality to end-users.[72]

At the 'front end', there has been a strong focus on the development of customer-facing applications or overlays that can allow consumers to initiate or receive payments instantaneously using the real-time interbank system. Alongside banks and other PSPs, in jurisdictions that have introduced open banking policies, it is expected that a wide range of TPPs will be able to access the bank accounts of customers to offer payment initiation services to facilitate payments between consumers and merchants using the real-time payment system.[73] Request to pay is one example of an account overlay which allows a payee (such as a merchant, individual or other business) to request payment from a payer and, once confirmed, to 'pull' the funds from the payer's account to the payee almost immediately.[74]

---

[68] A particular difference is when a merchant is notified that the funds from the consumer have been cleared and transferred into their account, as this allows them to dispatch or release the goods and services. Card systems complete this process in milliseconds, while it can take much longer for traditional interbank systems (even if it seems immediate to the payer, it can take time for the funds to be available to the payee).

[69] There can be small but significant differences in the settlement times on these systems (some are real time while others are near-real time) which has implications for potential substitutability with cards. For example, a system that takes up to 30 seconds to make the funds available to the payee may not be seen as a substitute to cards (which can clear funds in milliseconds) for some consumer payments (e.g. using a contactless debit card to pass through a barrier at a busy underground or subway station, or when purchasing goods in a busy supermarket queue).

[70] FIS (2019) estimates that fifty-four countries have some form of real-time payment system in place, including India, the European Union euro countries, Singapore and China.

[71] Including the UK, the USA, Australia and Japan.

[72] In the UK, there is a distinction between market overlay services (which will use the services of the central infrastructure but are delivered by third parties) and account overlays (which are services that support end-users in initiating or receiving payments but do not directly use the central infrastructure). See PSR (2021b).

[73] This includes in Europe (as part of PSD 2), the UK and Australia.

[74] Request to pay initiatives have been introduced or considered in Europe, the UK, Australia and Malaysia.

In some Asian countries, payments using the real-time interbank system can be initiated through QR codes,[75] while, in a number of other countries, payments can be sent using a mobile phone number, specialist app or unique ID.[76] These developments avoid the need to log in to online banking apps or to enter long and complex bank account details, thus allowing funds to be transferred instantly. A key attribute of all of these customer-facing innovations is that, when used in combination with a real-time or instant payment system, they have the potential to be substitutes for the services currently provided by card payment systems.

Activities Subject to Regulation

While many retail payment systems are subject to central bank oversight, the extent of economic regulation of payment systems varies across jurisdictions and between interbank and card payment systems.[77] Some payment systems are characterised by economies of scale and network effects, which, as described in Chapter 2, can naturally lead to high levels of industry concentration and make it more efficient for there to be one or a small number of widely used 'open' payment systems (which are interoperable and allow for wide participation) than a larger number of smaller 'closed' systems.

As described above, in many jurisdictions retail interbank payment systems are owned by the central bank or a payment association that operates on a not-for-profit basis. Perhaps for this reason there has historically been limited economic regulatory oversight of prices and other non-price terms (e.g. terms of access) for such payment systems. However, from the late 1990s, concerns started to emerge about the unregulated nature of interbank payment systems, and, in some jurisdictions, this has led to regulation with the aim of promoting efficiency and competition.[78] A particular concern, which is familiar from the other industries discussed in Part III of this book, was that some retail payment systems provided an indispensable or essential input that other participants (such as smaller or challenger banks or non-bank PSPs) needed to access in order to be able to provide payment services to end-users in retail banking markets. In addition, there were concerns about the governance arrangements for interbank payment schemes, which in some jurisdictions were dominated by the largest banks and provided a limited role for smaller banks or new participants (such

---

[75] This includes China, Singapore, Thailand and India. Among other things, this allows street food vendors, small retailers or motorbike transport services to display a QR code which is scanned by the customer to allow for instant payment. See FIS (2019).

[76] A leading example is the United Payments Interface in India, which allows transfers to be made using a mobile phone and a unique UPI ID and PIN. Other examples include PayM in the UK, PayID in Australia and PayNow in Singapore.

[77] In addition, many participants in payment systems – such as banks and other deposit-taking institutions – are subject to conduct and consumer protection regulations by independent regulatory bodies such as the Office of the Comptroller of the Currency and the Consumer Financial Protection Bureau in the USA or the Financial Conduct Authority in the UK.

[78] As described below, this is most notably the case in Australia and the UK.

as challenger banks or financial technology companies (fintechs)) or for end-users of payment systems. In response, regulations have been introduced in some countries to ensure that the rules set by payment schemes for accessing the payment system are not unduly restrictive, and to address concerns about governance arrangements. In some jurisdictions, such as the EU and the USA, concerns have also been raised about the fragmentation of payment systems, and the limited interoperability between payment systems, such that network externalities are not being fully exploited.[79] This has sometimes led to policies that seek to ensure the adoption of common messaging standards for interbank systems (such as ISO 20022). Regulation has also been introduced to address the differential quality standards for direct participants of a payment system versus indirect participants, and the weak collective incentives that some payment schemes may have to innovate.[80]

Card payment schemes are subject to more intensive regulation than interbank systems, including price and non-price regulation in many parts of the world.[81] A growing number of jurisdictions have introduced restrictions on the level of interchange fee that can be levied for debit and credit card transactions.[82] Regulation of interchange fees followed directly from competition law investigations or payment system reviews in many countries,[83] which concluded that the members of four-party payment schemes (which at that time included the major banks) had collective incentives to set interchange fees at levels higher than cost and that these charges would be passed on to merchants and ultimately all retail consumers.[84]

The merits of regulating interchange fees have been extensively examined in academic studies using the two-sided markets framework discussed in Chapter 6.[85] These studies tend to focus on two issues. First, the relationship between the privately set and socially optimal interchange fee, and, in particular, whether 'non-zero' interchange fees can be socially optimal.[86] This includes examining the conditions under which the interchange

---

[79] See Directive (2007/64/EC – PSD 1) and Federal Reserve (2013).

[80] A particular issue in some jurisdictions has been the limited incentives for payment schemes (and the payment associations which own them) to develop faster or instant payment systems alongside the retail bulk payment systems. See Payment Strategy Forum (2017) and Federal Reserve (2013).

[81] Hayashi and Maniff (2021) report, in 2021, that some forty-two jurisdictions had taken action or initiated investigations into interchange fees or MSCs at that time.

[82] As described above, the interchange fee is a payment made from a merchant's acquirer to a cardholder's issuing bank each time a transaction is made. This fee is then recovered by the acquirer through the MSC they levy on merchants.

[83] See Wallis (1997), ACCC/RBA (2000), Cruickshank (2000), EC (2002, 2007b), OFT (2003, 2005), Autorité de la Concurrence (2011) and *United States v. Visa USA, Inc., 163 F. Supp. 2d 322* (S.D.N.Y. 2001). An early US antitrust case involving the collective setting of interchange fees in the Visa system was *National Bancard Corp. (NaBanco) v. Visa USA Inc. 13 596 F. Supp. 1231* (1984).

[84] The UK competition agency (OFT, 2003) described interchange fees as 'a tax on retail transactions that is paid by all consumers in shops that accept credit cards'. Tirole (2011) notes that, while interchange fee regulation was historically couched in terms of illegal price fixing arguments, this is an incorrect analogy, as an increase in interchange fees is not a price increase, but rather a reallocation of costs between two types of end-users (merchants and cardholders). This point was recognised in *National Bancard Corp. (NaBanco) v. Visa USA Inc. 13 596 F. Supp. 1231* (1984).

[85] See Rochet and Tirole (2002), Rochet (2003), Chakravorti (2003), Wright (2004), Evans and Schmalensee (2005) and Guthrie and Wright (2007).

[86] Baxter (1983), Chang and Evans (2000) and Schmalensee (2002) provide early contributions.

fee is 'neutral', meaning that the impacts of the interchange fee on consumer decisions, merchant profits and card issuer costs offset one another such that altering the interchange fee has no real effect and, therefore, does not need to be regulated.[87] For example, if increases in the interchange fee can be recovered through higher surcharges levied by merchants on cardholders, it can offset (neutralise) any reduction in cardholder fees that arises where card issuers use the higher interchange fee revenues to fund reductions in cardholder fees.[88] A second focus has been on the impacts of different interchange fee *structures* in getting 'both sides' of the two-sided market (i.e. merchants and cardholders) to participate, given network effects and various assumptions about underlying market conditions.[89] This shifted the focus away from the question of whether the *level* of the interchange fees is too high relative to applicable costs, to questions about the relative balance between consumer and merchant costs and benefits of a given interchange fee *structure*.[90]

In some jurisdictions, regulation has focused on the MSC, which is the charge levied by acquirers on merchants (and comprises the interchange fee, card scheme fees and the acquirer net revenue). This has involved the setting of a maximum MSC,[91] or the introduction of specific reporting requirements.[92] In the EU, merchants are provided with a breakdown of the MSC into the various components (known as unblending).

Regulation has also focused on specific 'business rules' introduced by card schemes, in particular, the 'no surcharging' rule, the 'no-steering' rule and the 'honour all cards' rule. Specifically, scheme rules that prohibit merchants from surcharging consumers to recover the costs of the MSC have been banned in some jurisdictions on the basis that it creates distortions by not revealing the true cost of alternative payment methods to consumers, and thus results in inefficiently high use of cards relative to other payment instruments.[93] The ban on surcharging is also seen to lead to higher prices for goods and services for all consumers (including those do not pay by card) as a result of interchange fees not being able to be directly recovered from card users only. Second, scheme rules that prevent merchants from steering consumers to use a particular payment method

---

[87] See Carlton and Frankel (1995) and Gans and King (2003b).

[88] For example, if the card issuer uses the higher interchange fees revenues to reduce cardholder fees by an amount equivalent to 50 cents per transaction, but at the same time the merchant imposes a surcharge of 50 cents per transaction to fund the higher interchange fees it has to pay (Rochet and Tirole, 2002). Gans and King (2003b) focus on the case where all customers who purchase goods and services 'at a credit card price' from a merchant offering credit card services use credit cards.

[89] Among these conditions: whether acquirers or issuers have market power; the benefits to merchants of card acceptance; the ability of merchants to surcharge; and the extent of consumer knowledge of card acceptance.

[90] Vickers (2005) considers the structure within the context of the maturity of the system, while Rochet and Tirole (2011) focus on the extent to which different structures facilitate merchants (and cardholders) internalising the externalities they impose on one another. Wright (2012) argues that fee structures can be systematically biased against merchants, resulting in excessive usage of cards to the detriment of cash customers.

[91] For example, in Argentina, MSCs for credit cards cannot exceed 3 per cent and merchant acquirers must charge the same merchant discount rate to all merchants in the same industry category.

[92] In Mexico, the maximum MSC applied to each line of business has to be reported to the regulator, along with other fees and commissions. This is then published.

[93] See discussions of this in Frankel (1998) and Rochet and Tirole (2002).

(cash or debit card or cheque) have also been prohibited in some jurisdictions on the basis that this limits the ability of merchants to steer consumers away from high-cost payment cards (premium cards) towards cheaper payment methods. This rule also limits the ability of merchants to avoid the higher costs of some payment cards, and requires them to pass on these higher costs to all consumers through higher prices. Finally, the 'honour all cards' rule obliges merchants to accept all cards issued under the same card scheme (e.g. a merchant is required to accept debit cards if they accept credit cards from the same scheme). Notwithstanding theoretical expositions suggesting that the 'honour all cards' rule can improve welfare in some settings,[94] they have been banned or subject to challenge in some jurisdictions on the basis that they are a form of anti-competitive tying.[95] Specifically, the rules are seen to inefficiently tie merchants into accepting high-cost products with low-cost products.[96] A final area of regulation of card systems in some jurisdictions has involved the functional separation of scheme operation from processing activities. As in other regulated sectors, this requirement is intended to address concerns that schemes that offer processing services might favour their own processing services over those of competitors and thus distort competition.[97]

12.2.2 Form and Scope of Regulation

The form and scope of economic regulation of payment systems differ significantly across jurisdictions. In some countries, no specific economic regulation is applied, while, in other jurisdictions, sector-specific regulators have been created to regulate and oversee the operation of the systems. The type and scope of regulation also differ between inter bank and card payment systems.

Regulation of Interbank Payment Systems
As described above, interbank payment systems are operated by a central bank or as not for-profit entities in many jurisdictions and there is typically no external regulation of the prices charged for accessing the payment system. Moreover, in many jurisdictions, the rules and regulations about access to, and operation of, the systems are determined by payment associations that operate as not-for-profits and often comprise scheme members. However, where specific economic regulation of interbank payment systems is applied, it has focused on issues of governance, access, competition for infrastructure, cross-border harmonisation of rules, and payment system development and innovation.

Governance rules have sought to ensure that decision making about the operation and development of interbank systems is not controlled by one set of stakeholders (such

---

[94] Rochet and Tirole (2008) examine the 'honour all cards' rule and find that, when merchants are homogeneous, it always improves welfare.

[95] Merchants and trade associations filed various lawsuits in the USA in the mid-1990s against the scheme rule that, if they accepted credit cards, they were also required to accept debit cards, in what is known as the Wal-Mart case. A 2003 settlement involved the payment of $3 billion damages and the removal of the rule. See *In re: Visa Check/MasterMoney Antitrust Litigation, 192 F.R.D. 68* (E.D.N.Y. 2000).

[96] For example, in the USA, the rules required merchants to accept Visa and Mastercard debit cards (which at the time were often more than ten times as expensive as other debit cards), if they also accepted Visa and Mastercard credit cards.

[97] See EBA (2016).

as the largest banks) and that there is a role for smaller participants (including indirect participants) and end-users in the decision making. In some jurisdictions, this has led to requirements for the boards of interbank payment systems to be more independent and representative of a wider group of users (including smaller banks and non-PSPs) and to the establishment of formal processes for end-user consultation.[98]

Rules about access to interbank payment systems have also been introduced in some jurisdictions to address concerns that it is difficult for smaller banks, or non-PSPs, to become either direct participants of a payment system or indirect participants. These regulations have sought to establish clear criteria by which PSPs can be eligible to become direct members, as well as rules for when a direct PSP can terminate an indirect access relationship with another PSP (to address concerns that they may be seeking to limit innovation or foreclose competitors access to payment systems). In some jurisdictions, the regulator can determine an access regime for a payment system, set standards for that system, and arbitrate in disputes relating to access terms.[99] Regulation also sometimes involves requirements for competitive tendering for interbank payment system infrastructure. This has been a particular focus in the UK, where the regulator has established rules that require interbank payments infrastructure to be competitively tendered in order to promote competition for the market.[100]

In the EU, regulation has focused on the creation of a Single European Payments Area and on the promotion of more innovative payment services. This has included rules related to: licensing (including 'passporting' to allow PSPs to operate throughout the EU); the authorisation and supervision of payment institutions; and harmonising the use of payment services.[101]

A final area of regulatory focus in interbank payment systems concerns innovation and payment system development. In some jurisdictions, this has involved facilitating greater participation and access to payment systems by different types of entities such as new categories of PSPs (i.e. non-banks) and other TPPs. In other jurisdictions, central banks and regulators have been actively involved in guiding and overseeing the strategic development of new real-time payment systems. In the USA, the Federal Reserve advocated for the development of a real-time payment system, and more recently developed its own real-time payment system. In Australia and the UK, the regulators have overseen the design of: overlay services and functionality; governance arrangements; access and participation rules; and the approach to pricing.[102]

Regulation of Card Payment Systems

As discussed above, interchange fees (and associated MSCs) can affect the incentives of card issuers (and their customers) to use a particular card system,[103] and the incentives

---

[98] For example, in the UK.

[99] For example, in Australia. Similarly, in the UK, the regulator has an ability to determine access rules in some circumstances.

[100] See PSR (2016).

[101] This includes rules about: payment execution time and time value dating; the liability of PSPs and payment service users; and the security requirements for initiation and processing of electronic payments

[102] See RBA (2019) and PSR (2021b).

[103] The EC (2013a) argued that the high interchange fees of Visa and Mastercard explained why the cheaper national card schemes in EU Member States continue to disappear, as they would need to offer issuing banks interchange fees at least the same as those prevailing in the market.

for merchants to accept cards from that system. The question of whether and how inter change fees are regulated is therefore of central importance. There is considerable diver sity in how interchange fees are regulated in practice. In some jurisdictions, four-part card systems (or elements of those card systems, such as specific cards within a system are not subject to any regulation of interchange fees.[104] In contrast, *ex ante* regulation c interchange fees (typically in the form of caps or a ceiling) is applied in a growing numbe of jurisdictions.[105]

Three main approaches to determining the interchange fee 'cap' are seen in practice One approach involves the cap simply being set by a central bank or other public bod sometimes following negotiations or voluntary commitments by scheme operators.[1] Another approach uses a 'cost-based' methodology to determine the cap.[107] The max mum interchange fee is set based on estimates of reasonable (incremental) costs incurre by a card issuer with respect to the transaction.[108] The basic idea is that the cap is set at level that reimburses card issuers for the incremental costs that they cannot recover from cardholders without increasing card user fees.[109] A third approach, adopted in Europe, based around the so-called 'merchant indifference test' or 'tourist test'.[110] The idea her is that the interchange fee should be capped at a level such that a merchant is indi ferent to whether a tourist pays for goods and services with cash or a card (i.e. there no possibility of repeat purchase, and so the decision to accept the card does not brin any longer-term benefit to the merchant).[111] In other words, the cost of accepting a car payment should not be set at a level higher than the benefits the merchant derives fro avoiding a cash payment.[112]

[104] For example, commercial cards are not subject to interchange fee caps in the EU, while credit cards are not subject to regulation in the USA, notwithstanding the fact that debit cards are regulated.
[105] In some countries, regulation of interchange fees is determined *ex post* through the application of competition law. For example, in the USA, credit card interchange fees have in the past been subject to a number of legal challenges by merchants. For example, *In re Payment Card Interchange Fee and Merchant Discount Antitrust Litigation* (2006).
[106] A 2006 agreement between the Bank of Mexico and the Mexican Bankers Association agreed to reduce interchange fees. See Hayashi and Maniff (2021).
[107] This is used in Australia and the USA (for debit cards).
[108] In Australia, the cost-based benchmark is calculated as the aggregate value of eligible costs of the nominated scheme participants for the previous year, divided by the aggregate value of credit (or debit) card transactions for the same and expressed as a percentage. Eligible costs include issuers' authorisation and processing costs, fraud-related costs, and the cost of funding the interest-free period. In the USA, the debit card interchange fee standard is based on estimates of the reasonable and proportional costs incurred by the issuer with respect to the transaction. See RBA (2002, 2005) and Federal Reserve (2021).
[109] Prager, Manuszak, Kiser and Borzekowski (2009).
[110] See Farrell (2006) and Rochet and Tirole (2011).
[111] Rochet and Tirole (2011) show that an interchange fee that satisfies the tourist test can in certain conditions (such as when banks are perfectly competitive) be the socially optimal interchange fee.
[112] While a card payment involves the levying of an interchange fee which raises the merchant's costs, thi could be offset by other savings (in the form of avoided costs) to the merchant *vis-à-vis* cash, such as faster processing times at the checkout, lower fraud risk and reduced cash handling costs. Tirole (2011) argues that the tourist test may be a conservative estimate of the desirable interchange fee, as it does not factor in any profits earned by the issuing bank (over and above the variable costs and what is passed back to cardholders), and also does not reflect the negative social externalities of other forms of payment (such as tax evasion for cash, or cash subsidisation). EC (2015b) sets out a methodology for measuring a merchant's costs of processing payments in cash and card for the purposes of applying the merchant indifference test in Europe.

There is debate about the relative merits of the 'cost-based' and 'tourist test' approaches to setting interchange fee caps. Some argue that the cost-based approach is arbitrary, raises difficult measurement issues and lacks theoretical justification.[113] However, others point out that the 'tourist test', while theoretically attractive, requires detailed information about the transactional costs and benefits of cards *vis-à-vis* cash acceptance to merchants, and that these costs and benefits are likely to differ significantly across merchants and transaction types.[114] Separate from the debate about the appropriate methodology for calculating interchange fee caps is the question of how the caps are applied to card transactions, given that there is no single interchange fee.[115] In some jurisdictions, a weighted average interchange fee approach is used, which allows the scheme and its members to choose the specific interchange fees for different types of transactions so long as, overall, the weighted average benchmark is satisfied.[116] In other jurisdictions, specific interchange fee caps apply to types of cards and transactions. For example, in the EU, domestic and intra-EEA (European Economic Area) consumer debit and prepaid card transactions are subject to the same interchange fee cap of 0.2 per cent of the transaction value. However, commercial cards are not currently subject to any interchange fee caps.

There is an important interaction between interchange fee regulation and merchant surcharging both in theory (e.g. the neutrality result discussed above)[117] and in practice, as the incentives for merchants to surcharge (and the level of surcharge) depend on the MSCs they face (the major component of which is the interchange fee).[118] There are different approaches to surcharging in jurisdictions where interchange fees are regulated. In some jurisdictions (such as Australia, the UK and the EU), notwithstanding the introduction of interchange fee caps, surcharging was initially allowed provided it was in accordance with relevant consumer laws. This led to concerns about 'excessive surcharging',[119] and

---

[113] Tirole (2011) criticises this approach, noting that the focus on issuer costs as the benchmark 'bears little relationship with the theoretically correct level', which focuses on the acquirer/merchant side rather than on the issuer side. See also Prager, Manuszak, Kiser and Borzekowski (2009).

[114] Prager, Manuszak, Kiser and Borzekowski (2009) also note that, in practice, the costs and benefits to a merchant would be determined by the merchant discount (or MSC), which comprises acquirer mark-up, scheme fees and other costs in addition to the interchange fee.

[115] Interchange fees can vary by merchant category, merchant size, type of payment instrument (PIN debit/ signature debit/credit, premium/basic, etc.). Interchange fees also vary for cross-border and domestic transactions, and for 'card present' and 'card not present' transactions.

[116] In some countries, such as Australia, there is also a maximum cap on the rates for specific types of transactions (e.g. individual rates for credit card transactions cannot exceed 0.8 per cent of a transaction).

[117] Bourguignon, Gomes and Tirole (2019) argue that 'when surcharging is allowed, capping interchange fees (or, equivalently, merchant fees) is unambiguously detrimental to welfare'.

[118] For this reason, it is argued that interchange fee regulations and surcharging rules should not be designed separately. See Bourguignon, Gomes and Tirole (2019) and EC (2013a), which notes that '[a]s the cost of a card payment for merchants is to a large extent determined by the [multilateral interchange fee], any regulation of the [multilateral interchange fee] should logically be accompanied by a revision of surcharging rules'.

[119] For example, the UK Government (2018) estimated that retailers levied surcharges higher than it costs them to process a payment, and that surcharging is estimated to have cost consumers £166 million in 2015. Similarly, in Australia, the RBA (2016) reported that surcharge levels on some transactions were found to be well in excess of merchants' likely acceptance costs (e.g. $8 per airline booking).

new rules have since been introduced which prohibit merchants from levying surcharge higher than the direct costs of the transaction,[120] or from surcharging at all for cards sub ject to interchange fee caps.[121] In the USA, merchants are permitted to apply a 'checkou fee' (or surcharge) for credit card transactions using Visa or Mastercard,[122] but are no permitted to surcharge for debit card transactions (which are subject to interchange fe caps).

A final area of regulation of card payment systems in some jurisdictions concern business rules established by schemes. In Australia and the EU, merchants are not subjec to the 'honour all cards' rule, and therefore do not have to accept all cards issued by th same card scheme.[123] In the USA, merchants are no longer required to accept differen types of card product following a legal settlement (e.g. they do not have to accept cred cards if they also accept debit cards of the same brand), but are required to accept al cards within a product type (e.g. if they accept standard credit cards from one scheme they must also accept premium credit cards from that scheme). Rules which prevent mer chants from steering consumers to use a particular payment method (so-called no-steer ing rules) have also been prohibited in Australia and the EU. In contrast, in the USA no-steering rules are permitted and have been found not to violate US antitrust law b the Supreme Court.[124]

12.3 THE SCOPE AND EFFECTS OF RESTRUCTURING POLICIES

12.3.1 The Scope of Restructuring Policies in Payment Systems

The scope of restructuring differs substantially across payment system types (interban versus card systems) and jurisdictions. In some jurisdictions, no restructuring policie have been introduced, while, in others, restructuring policies have been similar to othe sectors described in this book.

---

[120] In Australia, new rules introduced in 2016 required that surcharges must not be more than the amount that it costs a merchant to accept a particular type of card for a given transaction (which can be calculated from statements supplied by their bank or payments provider).

[121] Since implementation of Directive (2015/2366 – PSD 2) in January 2018, merchants in the EU are no longer allowed to surcharge on use of cards that are subject to the interchange fee caps. Surcharging can still be allowed for non-regulated cards (such as commercial cards or cards issued by three-party schemes). However, Member States retain the ability to impose a full ban on surcharging on all cards. In the UK, surcharging was prohibited for all debit card, credit card or electronic payment services (e.g. PayPal, mobile phone apps) from January 2018.

[122] This is pursuant to settlement agreements between Visa, Mastercard, several larger issuer banks and merchants. Only four states (Kansas, Connecticut, Colorado and Massachusetts) do not allow surcharging.

[123] Although they do have to accept all issuer brands under a particular category of card (e.g. all Visa debi cards) provided those cards are subject to the interchange fee caps.

[124] The legality of such rules was challenged in a lawsuit brought by the US Department of Justice and several states, but were ultimately found not to violate US antitrust. Among other findings, the Supreme Court found that 'there is nothing inherently anticompetitive about the provisions. They actually stem negative externalities in the credit-card market and promote inter-brand competition' and that 'evidence of a price increase on one side of a two-sided transaction platform cannot, by itself, demonstrate an anticompetitive exercise of market power'. See *Ohio et al. v. American Express Co. et a No. 16–1454* (2018).

Interbank Payment Systems

Policies directed at promoting efficiency and greater competition in interbank payments began to be introduced in the late 1990s. In Australia, a specialist Payment Systems Board (PSB) was established in 1998 with a remit (among other things) to promote the efficiency of payment systems and competition in payment services.[125] While its involvement in the day-to-day operation of retail interbank systems has been 'relatively hands-off',[126] it has sought to guide the strategic direction of interbank systems. A 2012 review identified fundamental impediments to innovation in interbank payment systems,[127] and found existing governance arrangements in the sector flawed and in need of reform.[128] It also identified a need for the development of a real-time payment system with additional functionality. Since then, the PSB has been involved in overseeing the industry development of this system (the NPP). This has included setting out recommendations regarding the functionality of, and access to, the new payment system.

In the UK, questions about the governance of interbank payment systems, and the fact they were controlled by the same few large banks that dominated the supply of banking services, were raised in the early 2000s.[129] Specifically, there were concerns that the governance arrangements (control by the major banks) might be limiting the ability of new entrants (such as new banks or non-bank financial technology companies) to access payment systems,[130] and reducing incentives to develop a new (near-)real-time payment system.[131] There were also concerns that end-user interests were not adequately being taken into consideration.[132] This ultimately led to the establishment of a new economic regulator for payment systems (the Payment Systems Regulator (PSR)) in 2014.[133] The PSR was created to be a competition-focused, utility-style regulator for retail payment systems with objectives

---

[125] This includes the relationships amongst different payment systems and the nature of the competitive forces within any given payment system; see RBA (2004). The creation of the Payment Systems Board (PSB) was preceded by an influential study (Wallis, 1997) that identified the scope for improving the efficiency of retail payment systems.

[126] Productivity Commission (2018). The PSB has noted that it uses its powers sparingly and that there is a presumption in favour of co-regulation (see discussion in Chapter 8 of this general approach).

[127] These included coordination problems, which made it difficult for industry players to agree to implement innovations that require a collective effort to succeed, and existing commercial arrangements, which made it difficult to build a business case for some innovations because new business arising from such innovations might attract business away from existing profitable business streams (RBA, 2012).

[128] Two problems in particular were identified: that insufficient regard was being paid to public interest objectives because, under the existing arrangements, decision making rested with commercial entities; and that coordination problems had tended to hamper cooperation between industry players.

[129] Cruickshank (2000).

[130] See OFT (2003).

[131] The slow progress in development of a Faster Payments system led to the creation of a Payment Systems Taskforce chaired by the competition authority which had a wide and diverse membership comprising both bank representatives and consumer representatives. See OFT (2007).

[132] A particular episode which highlighted the governance problems was the controversial decision of the Payments Council (which was responsible for self-regulation of the industry) to abolish cheques in 2009. This decision was subsequently reversed.

[133] The PSR is separate from but part of the Financial Conduct Authority. Proposals for such a regulator were first made in 2000 in the Cruickshank report (Cruickshank, 2000), which recommended an independent 'Payment Systems Commission (PayCom)'.

to promote competition, innovation and service-user interests.[134] Since its introduction, th
PSR's policy focus has been on: widening access to interbank payment systems and ensurin
that access criteria are 'proportionate, objective and non-discriminatory'; reforming goverr
ance arrangements to ensure greater independence from the major banks; promoting th
contestability of tenders for payments infrastructure; and overseeing the development of
new payment system (known as the New Payments Architecture). Interbank system opera
tors are also now required to consider service-user interests and make transparent decision

In EU Member States, the scheme rules for access to and operation of retail interbank sys
tems are largely determined by the payment association which operates the scheme in tha
Member State or by the European Payments Council.[135] There is no dedicated economic regu
lator of interbank payment systems at the EU level or in any EU Member State. However, tw
EU Directives have sought to restructure aspects of the payments industry and align rule
with the aim of the development of a Single European Payments Area. The first Paymer
Services Directive (PSD 1) implemented in 2009 sought to harmonise the rules for cred
transfers, direct debits, card payments and mobile and online payments, and introduced
new category of PSP which was a 'non-bank'.[136] The second Payment Services Directive (PS
2) became effective in 2018 and includes new rules which, among other things, are intende
to: enhance consumers' rights in certain areas;[137] strengthen requirements around paymen
security and consumer authorisation; and, perhaps most critically, introduce various prov
sions that allow TPPs to gain access to customer accounts held by a PSP (sometimes know
as 'open banking).[138] Subject to customers providing consent, TPPs will be able to acce
their accounts to offer innovative payment information services and to initiate paymen
on behalf of their customers. Critically, a customer's bank is required to treat any reque
from an authorised TPP in the same way as it would treat such a request directly from th
customer (i.e. they are not allowed to discriminate). There are two specific types of TPP'
'Payment initiation service providers' (PISPs) will be able to initiate payments on behalf of
customer from the customer's account with a bank. 'Account information service provider
(AISPs) bring together the information from the user's various bank or payment account
allowing them to see this information in one place. These changes are expected to pro
vide consumers and merchants with more control of their information, and, as discussed i
Box 12.1, potentially enhance competition between interbank and card systems.[139]

---

[134] The UK government sought to distinguish the PSR from the Financial Conduct Authority noting that:
'[T]he Payment Systems Regulator will adopt a utility-style approach, distinctive from the FCA's existir
remit (which spans consumer protection, the integrity of the UK financial system, and the promotion o
effective competition in the interests of consumers in the markets).' See HM Treasury (2013a, b).

[135] The European Payments Council is a not-for-profit entity comprising PSPs or associations of PSPs. It i
not part of the European Union institutional framework.

[136] Directive (2007/64/EC – PSD 1).

[137] This includes reducing the liability for non-authorised payments and introducing an unconditional ('n
questions asked') refund right for direct debits in euros. See Directive (2015/2366 – PSD 2).

[138] Open banking enables personal customers and small and medium-sized businesses to share their curre
account information with TPPs through open banking APIs. Similar open banking provisions were
introduced in the UK following a market study by the Competition Agency in 2016.

[139] Specifically, PISPs could 'push' cleared funds to merchants to pay for goods and services directly from
their bank accounts using the interbank infrastructure, and therefore offer an alternative to paying by
debit or credit card and the use of card systems infrastructure.

In the USA, rules for both bulk low-value payment systems (FedACH and EPN) are set by the scheme operator, Nacha, which operates as a not-for-profit and is constituted by a large number of members (which includes financial institutions and regional payments association). Nacha is not a government agency, and its members shape and influence the governance and direction of the ACH network and the Nacha operating rules. Similarly, the rules for the privately developed real-time payment network (known as RTP) are set by a business committee, which comprises the owner banks and representative from non-member financial institutions. The Federal Reserve (and other federal banking agencies) supervise private payment systems for systemic risk purposes and transparency, but not as an economic regulator (e.g. in terms of pricing).[140] However, as noted above, the Federal Reserve has played a role in setting the strategic direction for payment systems over the years to identify 'gaps and opportunities' in the US payment systems.[141] In Canada, the major wholesale and retail payment systems are operated by Payments Canada, which is a 'public-purpose' organisation which exists to meet various statutory objectives.[142] Among the primary objectives of Payments Canada is to 'facilitate the development of new payment methods and technologies'.[143]

Scope of Restructuring of Card Payment Systems

Concerns about card payment systems, including the setting of interchange fees, first began to emerge in the mid-1980s in the USA,[144] and, during the 1990s, various laws were passed to regulate and control certain aspects of card systems' behaviour in different parts of the world.[145] A comprehensive set of regulations for card systems was introduced in Australia in 2003,[146] which, as described above, involved setting cost-based interchange fee caps (benchmarks) for debit and credit cards which have been progressively adapted and lowered over the years.[147] Rules were also introduced allowing merchants to surcharge. The catalyst for the reforms to the Australian payment system was the

---

[140] The authority of the Federal Reserve and other banking agencies in supervising can be quite broad. Retail payment systems are also subject to federal consumer protection regulations, anti-money-laundering requirements and various state licensing, safety and soundness, anti-money-laundering and consumer protection requirements.

[141] See Federal Reserve (2002, 2012, 2022).

[142] Payments Canada is the operating brand name of the Canadian Payments Association (CPA). Although the CPA does not have any owners, it is argued that the structure of voting, and the arrangements for the payment of membership dues, treats the members as if they were owners

[143] Section 5(1) of the Canadian Payments Act.

[144] The 1984 NaBanco case alleged that interchange fees constituted unlawful price fixing and had an anti-competitive effect; see *National Bancard Corp. (NaBanco) v. Visa USA Inc. 13 596 F. Supp. 1231* (1984).

[145] In Denmark, a 1990 Act set the MSC on debit card fees at zero, and capped the MSC on international credit cards; while, in Argentina, a 1999 law established norms that regulate various aspects related to the credit, debit and retail card systems. Finally, in Canada, a consent order by the Competition Bureau in the mid-1990s allowed the debit card scheme (Interac) to set its own interchange fee (which it set at zero). See Hayashi and Maniff (2021).

[146] ACCC/RBA (2000). Gans and King (2001b) present a critique.

[147] A common cost benchmark was adopted in 2006, while rates were lowered for debit cards in 2016. In 2021 the interchange cap was reduced from 15 cents to 10 cents for all prepaid cards and dual-network debit cards and to 6 cents for single-network debit cards. From 2016 these caps also apply to companion cards or co-branded cards, which are cards (such as American Express) that are issued by a separate institution such as a bank rather than the scheme itself.

publication of a joint study by the Australian Competition and Consumer Commissio
and the Reserve Bank of Australia in 2000, which concluded, among other things, tha
the existing structure of the payments market was 'socially inefficient', and likely to b
anti-competitive in its effects. A particular concern of the joint study was that credit car
transactions were often more attractive to users than debit card transactions, despite th
fact that the debit card payment system was substantially less expensive to operate.

Competition law investigations in several European countries in the 2000s also led t
the conclusion that the collective setting of interchange fees was anti-competitive, anc
in some cases, this led to settlements between the major card schemes and competitio
authorities to lower interchange fees.[148] At the same time as these investigations wer
being conducted in EU Member States, the European Commission began prosecuting Visi
and Mastercard for their approach to the setting of interchange fees for cross-border an
domestic transactions.[149] In 2015, a new Interchange Fee Regulation (IFR) was adopted a
the European level. The IFR involved the capping of interchange fees for consumer cred
and debit cards,[150] the prohibition of certain business rules and practices, and require
ments in relation to the transparency of merchant fees.[151] The IFR also included require
ments that card scheme management and processing activities be structurally separate
and operate independently in terms of accounting, organisation and decision-makin
processes, with the aim of promoting competition in the processing of card services. Th
second Payment Services Directive (PSD 2), which became effective in January 201
introduced a ban on merchant surcharging for cards subject to the interchange fee cap
contained in the IFR.[152] In 2019, Visa and Mastercard committed to cap inter-regiona
interchange fees for cards issued outside of the EEA.

In the USA, card systems have faced various competition law investigations by federa
and state authorities and private litigation.[153] While the question of whether interchang
fees should be subject to regulation was considered during the 2000s,[154] it was not unt
2011 that a new law required the Federal Reserve to cap the debit card interchange fee fo
large banks.[155] Regulation also required that card issuers provide merchants with the optio

[148] Investigations include in Austria (2003), Belgium (2006), France (2011), Germany (2014), Greece (2008),
Hungary (2008), Italy (2010), Latvia (2011), the Netherlands (2004 and 2014), Poland (2007), Spain
(2005), Switzerland (2005) and the UK (2005).
[149] A 2002 agreement with Visa involved reducing cross-border interchange fees to the costs that issuing
banks incur. A subsequent decision in 2007 found Mastercard's interchange fees to be anti-competitive
while in 2009 a case was opened against Visa.
[150] The interchange fee caps were set at 0.3 per cent of transaction value for consumer credit cards and
0.2 per cent for consumer debit cards. This was based on the merchant indifference test, or 'tourist test'
discussed above. See Regulation (2015/751).
[151] This included requirements to separate the MSC, interchange fees and scheme fees for a merchant (so-
called unblending).
[152] Directive (2015/2366 – PSD 2).
[153] In 1998, Visa and Mastercard were sued by the Department of Justice for alleged antitrust violations,
including rules that in effect prevented issuers from issuing cards on their competitors' networks. See
United States v. Visa USA, Inc. (2004).
[154] See, for example, GAO (2009).
[155] The Durbin Amendment to the Dodd–Frank Wall Street Reform and Consumer Protection Act of 2010.
The law is given effect through the Federal Reserve Bank's Regulation II (Debit Card Interchange Fees
and Routing), which capped the interchange fee at 21 cents plus 0.05 per cent of the transaction (and
an additional 1 cent to account for fraud protection costs). Card issuers with consolidated assets of less
than $10 billion are exempt from the Regulation.

to choose between two unaffiliated payment card payment systems to process transactions, to prevent network exclusivity, as well as a choice about how to direct the routing of a transaction. In 2021 a Notice of Proposed Regulation sought to amend the regulation, allowing merchants to choose between two unaffiliated processing providers for card-not-present transactions. As noted above, credit cards are not currently subject to interchange fee caps in the USA; however, there are suggestions that they may be in the future.[156]

Card systems are subject to various degrees of regulation and oversight in other parts of the world. In Canada, interchange fees for debit cards are set at zero under a consent order; while, in Latin America, the rates of interchange fees have been capped by the central banks in Argentina and Brazil (debit cards). In China, the central bank has set the maximum merchant charges since 2002, and in 2016 a new policy was introduced to cap interchange fees for debit and credit cards; while, in Malaysia, interchange fee caps have applied since 2014. In India, the merchant discount rate for debit cards has been capped since 2012; while, in Pakistan, the merchant discount rate for both credit and debit cards has been capped since 2020. In Africa, interchange fees are capped by the central banks in both Nigeria (2016) and South Africa (2014). Finally, some jurisdictions, such as Chile and New Zealand, are currently debating legislative proposals to cap interchange fees

2.3.2 The Effects of Restructuring Policies for Payment Systems

Effects of Restructuring of Interbank Payment Systems

Given that restructuring policies for interbank payment systems have only been introduced in a limited number of jurisdictions, it is difficult to draw general conclusions about the effects of such policies. In Australia, a co-regulatory approach has been adopted, and, as noted above, the regulator has typically taken a relatively hands-off approach to interbank systems. However, along with industry, the regulator has been involved in promoting the development of the NPP, which is a near-real-time payment system,[157] and which over time is expected to replace the existing bulk payment system. In addition, where concerns have been raised about aspects of the implementation of the NPP,[158] the regulator has issued recommendations to industry, including about NPP functionality and overlay services, access (including the required capital contribution for participation) and governance (including requirements to appoint an independent director and introduce a process for assessing access applications).[159]

In the UK, the main areas of regulatory focus for interbank systems has been on access (including, in particular, indirect access for small PSPs), governance (including ensuring service users are represented), competitive tendering for payments infrastructure, and the development of a new payment system (known as the New Payments Architecture).

---

[156] See Forbes (2021a) and Bashur (2021).

[157] The NPP is mutually owned by thirteen shareholders, including the main banks and the Reserve Bank.

[158] These include: the slow pace of development; that access rules may be too restrictive and could create a conflict of interest for the major banks (who may be reluctant to provide access to smaller players); and that transaction fees for using the NPP as well as any additional fees added by participants may need to be monitored (to avoid the situation that has arisen with card interchange fees). See Productivity Commission (2018) and RBA (2019).

[159] RBA (2019)

According to the regulator, these policies have resulted in a greater number of new direc[t] participants joining interbank systems (including, in some cases, non-bank PSPs), mor[e] providers of indirect access services and the emergence of new forms of access such a[s] by technical aggregators.[160] However, as in Australia, there have been concerns about th[e] slow pace of the industry-led development of the New Payments Architecture, includin[g] the approach to the competitive tendering for infrastructure.[161]

In the EU, a recent assessment concluded that, while the harmonisation of retail pay[-] ments legislation has led to improvements, the EU payments market remains fragmente[d] and a small number of global card systems and technology companies have captured th[e] intra-European retail payments market.[162] In response, in 2020, the European Commissio[n] published a retail payments strategy which, among other things, seeks to support the rol[l] out of instant payments across Europe, reinforce the interoperability of infrastructur[e] and further develop open banking. It also seeks to ensure direct access for non-bank PSP[s] to all payment systems and enable 'home-grown' pan-European payment solutions.[163]

Finally, in the USA, a longstanding concern has been the absence of a widely use[d] real-time payment system.[164] Following the Federal Reserve's consultation on paymen[t] systems improvement in 2013, various new private proposals have emerged for a rea[l] time payment system. In 2017, The Clearing House launched a private real-time paymen[t] network, which is privately owned and operated, and steadily growing volumes. In 201[9] the Federal Reserve announced plans to develop its own interbank real-time paymen[t] network (FedNOW) which would be operational in 2023. While some commentators ar[e] concerned that the Federal Reserve entering this space could crowd out further inves[t] ment by private real-time systems, others fear that, without FedNOW, private sector ope[r] ators could take advantage of scale economies and network effects to monopolise th[e] market and act anti-competitively.[165]

Effects of Restructuring of Card Payment Systems

Given the two-sided nature of card payment systems, any assessment of the effects o[f] regulation – particularly interchange fee caps – needs to focus on merchant impacts (i[n] terms of lower MSCs), cardholder impacts (in terms of any changes to cardholder fee[s] interest rates and rewards and other benefits) and final consumer impacts (in terms o[f] whether they benefit from lower MSCs being passed through into lower retail prices[.] In short, any assessment of regulation needs to focus on the overall equilibrium effect[s] having regard in particular to the two-sided nature of the market.[166]

---

[160] PSR (2019).

[161] PSR (2021b).

[162] EC (2020e).

[163] EC (2020e).

[164] In 2019, the Federal Reserve chair, Jerome Powell, noted that 'the United States is far behind other countries in terms of having real-time payments available to the general public' (Federal Reserve, 2019[)]

[165] See CRS (2019).

[166] For example, Gans (2018) notes that 'inducements offered to consumers for credit card use must be examined in light of all activity in the system and not simply the prices that are observed', and that policies to eliminate negative prices could prove detrimental to both consumers and merchants. However, Agarwal, Presbitero, Silva, and Wix (2023) find that sophisticated individuals profit more from credit cards rewards at the expense of naïve consumers.

The effects of the introduction of interchange fee regulation in Australia in 2003 has been examined in various studies. A 2008 review of the impacts of the reforms concluded that they had fulfilled their objectives, estimating a welfare gain of some hundreds of millions of dollars per annum,[167] including gains to consumers of $580 million.[168] However, while MSCs were reduced, this was accompanied by an increase in merchant surcharging. There was also evidence of an increase in cardholder fees and reduction in benefits, and that credit card interest rates also increased.[169] A subsequent 2016 review concluded that the reforms continued to operate in the public interest, noting significant reductions in merchant service fee costs (estimated at $15 billion relative to pre-reform levels), which, it was argued, would have fed through into lower prices for all consumers.[170] However, the review raised concerns that the current benchmark interchange fee levels were still too high, and that some merchants were applying excessive surcharges.[171] To address this, it lowered the interchange fee benchmarks, and introduced rules on 'permitted surcharging'. A 2018 government review of interchange fees as part of a wider study proposed that interchange fees be abandoned given the maturity of the card payment systems in Australia.[172] Among the benefits of a 'ban' on card interchange fees identified were that: MSCs could fall significantly,[173] and it would remove the need for merchant surcharging; it would increase transparency and efficiency (as cardholders would face the card issuing costs directly and have an incentive to respond to the cost of the card transaction); and it would reduce the costs of card payments by making card issuers focus less on rewards and other incentives used to subsidise card payments.[174] Finally, it would reduce the 'cross-subsidisation' from the prices all consumers pay for goods and services for benefits that are only received by cardholders. Notwithstanding this recommendation, a subsequent 2021 review by the regulator chose to maintain interchange fees, albeit at a lower level for debit cards.[175]

---

[167] RBA (2008). A number of studies dispute this conclusion; for example, Hayes (2007) concludes that the reforms have had no impact on consumer payment instrument choice and use.

[168] Chang, Evans and Garcia Schwartz (2005) challenge this estimate and find no evidence of observed reductions in retail prices or improvements in quality of service to final consumers.

[169] The RBA viewed these as beneficial in terms of increasing the effective price of card transactions. One of the conclusions of the review was the possibility of replacing formal interchange fee regulation and relying on industry undertakings. However, suitable undertakings were unable to be agreed. See RBA (2015).

[170] However, the RBA (2016) did not seek to quantify the savings in this review, noting that: 'It is impossible given the imprecision in any econometric model of consumer price inflation to measure exactly how these reductions in merchant service fees have flowed through into prices for consumers.'

[171] Bourguignon, Gomes and Tirole (2019) discuss more generally the issues of designing interchange fee rules and surcharging separately from one another as in Australia.

[172] Productivity Commission (2018). The question of the desirability of zero interchange fees was examined in earlier analysis. Vickers (2005) notes that: '[I]n the presence of network externalities – that is to say, network effects that have not been internalized – there is no presumption that the optimal interchange fee is zero. But since network externalities can in principle go either way, neither is there a general presumption as to the desirable direction of rebalancing, relative to an interchange fee of zero.' Chang and Evans (2000) argue that setting a zero interchange fee would most likely decrease social welfare, while a recent analysis by Ardizzi, Scalise and Sene (2021) finds that reducing interchange fees, towards the 'near-zero interchange fee' level, may exert unintended and negative effects on card usage.

[173] The Productivity Commission (2018) estimated that the interchange fee comprised around 70 per cent of the merchant service fee for credit cards and 45 per cent for debit cards.

[174] It was suggested that rewards make up to one-quarter of the overall costs of issuing credit cards.

[175] RBA (2021). Interchange fees for credit cards were maintained at the same level. It also proposed greater transparency on card scheme fees, and that card issuers continue to offer dual-network debit cards and various changes to ensure low-cost routing for merchants.

A 2020 review of the impacts of the EU interchange fee regulation by the European Commission concluded that 'major positive results have been achieved', including that MSCs declined, and that, over time, the lower MSCs would pass into lower consumer prices and bring annual consumer cost savings of between €864 million and €1930 million.[176] Although the study found no systematic increase in cardholder fees nor change in cardholder benefits, it was acknowledged that cardholder fees increased in half of the Member States covered by the analysis.[177] There was also evidence that acquirer margins had increased (by €1.2 billion per year), as had card scheme fees which are not covered by the interchange fee regulation.[178]

Separate analysis of the impacts of the IFR in the UK (the largest card market in Europe by a substantial margin) by the regulator concluded that the full reduction in the interchange fee was not passed through to all merchants, and that small and medium-sized merchants got little or no pass-through of the IFR savings on average.[179] This is consistent with analysis that suggests that interchange fees for uncapped commercial cards have increased, and that overall MSCs in Europe are higher than they were prior to the regulation.[180] Prior to the 2018 prohibition on surcharges for cards covered by the IFR, there were also concerns about high levels of merchant surcharging in some countries.[181] More broadly, the expectation that a pan-European payment system would emerge as a result of the IFR does not appear to have been fulfilled yet,[182] while the separation of scheme and processing entities (to promote switching to independent processors) has, to date, had limited market impact.[183]

In contrast to the findings of the European Commission about the savings to consumers from lower retail prices associated with interchange fee caps, various studies

---

[176] The EC (2020d) estimates that: 'Merchants have saved costs in the range of €1,200 million per year, of which a part will eventually be passed-through to consumers through lower retail prices or improved services.' Notwithstanding these estimates of consumer savings, in an earlier analysis, the EC (2013a) acknowledged that it was very difficult to measure the precise effect of interchange fee reductions on retail prices given all the possible factors in the economy that contribute to pricing. This earlier position is consistent with Evans and Mateus (2011), who found that the degree of competition in the retail and banking markets is critical to any assessment of pass-through, while Mariotto and Verdier (2016) identify a number of limitations to pass-through estimates of this kind, including that they are often based on qualitative evidence and consumer surveys.

[177] This is consistent with evidence put before the English High Court case involving Mastercard and major retailers, where it was submitted that four card issuers had reduced or removed their reward offerings in late 2015 and 2016 following the interchange fee cap. See *Asda Stores Ld & Ors v. Mastercard Incorporated & Ors* (2017).

[178] Ernst & Young and Copenhagen Economics (2020) estimated that total gross scheme fees across Europe increased by 40 per cent according to its analysis, while, in the UK, PSR (2021a) estimated that scheme fees doubled between 2014 and 2018.

[179] PSR (2021a).

[180] CMSPI (2021) find that average MSC in Europe in 2021 is two basis points above its level prior to regulation, as a result of increases in scheme fees and acquirer margins.

[181] Some merchants have responded to the surcharge ban introduced in 2018 by introducing a range of new charges under different names such as 'booking fees', 'transaction fees' and 'administration charges', or in some cases stopping the acceptance of credit cards, including government bodies such as HM Revenue & Customs in the UK.

[182] EC (2013a) set out the expectation that it would facilitate entry of new pan-European payment schemes. However, in its 2020 retail payment strategy, the EC (2020e) observed that new pan-European actors face a number of significant challenges.

[183] EC (2020d).

of the impacts of the Durbin Amendment – which capped debit interchange fees in the USA from 2011 – have concluded that there is no evidence it has led to lower retail prices.[184] Other studies have concluded that the impact of the regulation on reducing merchants' costs has been limited and unequal.[185] Contrary to expectations, analysis also suggests that debit card issuers have not necessarily lost interchange fee income under the regulation.[186] At the same time, many banks withdrew debit card customer rewards programmes,[187] and reduced the number of free checking [current] accounts.[188] However, one benefit of the regulation of debit cards identified is that the 'no exclusivity' and routing provisions introduced competition in debit processing, and gave merchants greater leverage with card networks.[189] As described above, credit card interchange fees are not currently subject to interchange fee caps, and some studies estimate that such fees can average around 2.25 per cent per transaction (compared to a cap of 0.3 per cent in the EU).[190] This has led to suggestions by some that interchange fee regulation could be extended to credit cards.

12.4 CONCLUSION

Payment systems have sometimes been described as the 'plumbing' of modern banking and financial systems, and how they are governed and operate can have major impacts on how consumers choose to pay for goods and services, the overall prices for such goods and services, as well as how individuals, households and small businesses manage liquidity constraints.[191]

Many retail interbank systems are either operated by a central bank or are not-for-profit entities, and there is typically no external price regulation applied to these systems.

---

[184] Wang, Schwartz and Mitchell (2014) find that: 'By regulating the interchange fee, the goal of the Durbin Amendment was to lower merchants' costs of accepting debit cards and to pass along the cost savings to consumers in terms of reduced retail prices. A few years after the regulation was in place, however, it is unclear how effectively the regulation has fulfilled its intention.' Stavins (2017) concludes that '[s]ince the enactment of the Durbin Amendment, ... no evidence exists so far to indicate that the reduction in costs to merchants due to lower merchant fees has led to any drop in retail prices to consumers', while Mukharlyamov and Sarin (2019) find little evidence of across-the-board consumer savings. Finally, Zywicki, Manne and Morris (2014, 2017, 2022) find no 'evidence that merchants have lowered prices for retail consumers; for many small-ticket items, in fact, prices have been driven up'.

[185] Haltom and Wang (2015) and earlier analysis by Hayashi (2013). There have also been concerns raised about a two-tiered interchange fee pricing structure emerging; see CRS (2017). CMSPI (2021) conclude that all of the potential savings of the regulation were eroded by 2019.

[186] CRS (2017). This may reflect the fact that, although the interchange fee is lower, the volume of transactions has grown.

[187] CRS (2019).

[188] Manuszak and Wozniak (2017) find that 'banks subject to the cap raised checking account prices by decreasing the availability of free accounts, raising monthly fees, and increasing minimum balance requirements, with different adjustment across account types'.

[189] CMSPI (2021).

[190] CMSPI (2021). The Productivity Commission (2018) reported that fees could be 3.25 per cent plus 10 cents per transaction.

[191] Klein (2019) discusses the link between income inequality and payment systems, noting that the failure to introduce a real-time payment system costs billions of dollars to working families, as it requires them to use slow payment systems such as high-cost check [cheque] cashers, and small dollar payday lenders and to experience bank overdraft fees. Felt, Hayashi, Stavins, and Welte (2021) find that payment card pricing and merchant cost pass-through have regressive distributional effects in Canada and the USA.

However, some countries have introduced economic regulatory policies to improve th
efficiency of interbank systems, and to ensure that the manner in which they are ope
ated does not affect competition in related downstream banking and financial market
Where applied, economic regulation of interbank payment systems has focused on: issue
of governance; access rules; competition for infrastructure; cross-border harmonisatio
of rules; and guiding payment system development and innovation (including the deve
opment of new real-time payment systems).[192] The specific policies to regulate interbar
payment systems in Australia and the UK (which have dedicated payments regulator
have generally been seen as successful in terms of reforming the governance arrange
ments and ensuring wider access to payment systems. However, in both countries – a
well as in the USA and the EU – there remain concerns about the pace at which th
industry is developing new real-time interbank payment systems. In the EU, there are als
concerns about market fragmentation and a lack of cross-border interoperability.

Card payment systems are subject to more traditional forms of economic regulatio
of prices and conduct in some parts of the world. This includes maximum interchang
fee caps, and regulations about permissible business rules (such as no-surcharging rule
no-steering rules and the 'honour all cards' rule). There are, however, substantial diffe:
ences in the scope of regulation applied to card systems in different parts of the world, suc
as whether both debit and credit cards are subject to interchange fee caps, and the metho
used to calculate these caps (e.g. cost-based or merchant indifference approaches). Th
effects of the introduction of these policies have been examined in studies in Australi
the EU and the USA. Studies by the regulators in Australia and the EU estimate that inte:
change fee regulations have led to significant gains to merchants and consumers throug
lower retail prices (although there have been concerns about excessive surcharges in som
countries). The impacts of the reforms on cardholders (in terms of higher fees and low
benefits) is mixed across the studies,[193] while some studies have found that acquirers an
the card schemes (who have been able to raise scheme fees) have benefited substantial
from the interchange fee caps. A study on the impacts of interchange fee regulation in th
UK concluded that small and medium-sized merchants got little or no pass-through of th
IFR savings on average, while studies of the Durbin Amendment in the USA have ofte
concluded that there is no evidence that it has led to lower retail prices.

Looking ahead, the role of economic regulation of payment systems is likely to expan
in various ways, especially as more payments become digital (with the decline of cash) an
with the rapid expansion of electronic commerce. Real-time interbank payment systen
coupled with open banking policies offer the potential to transform interbank payment
making them more competitive with card systems. However, they also raise new question
about the governance of these platforms and the rules of access, particularly for new an
non-traditional participants (such as TPPs). In Australia and the UK, the regulators hav

---

[192] Ovum (2017) note that: 'In almost all cases, however, the move to Instant Payments at domestic or
European level has been driven by regulators.'

[193] A 2008 review in Australia found evidence of an increase in cardholder fees and credit card interest
rates and a reduction in benefits, while the European Commission study found no systematic evidence
of an increase in cardholder fees nor change in cardholder benefits. See RBA (2008) and EC (2020d).

suggested that the prices for using new real-time payment systems should be subject to regulatory oversight. For card systems, a question arising in some jurisdictions is whether the systems have reached a level of maturity such that interchange fees should be set at, or close to, zero. Others advocate that economic regulation of card systems be expanded to cover a greater number of products (such as credit cards in the USA, or commercial cards in the EU) and to focus on scheme fees or the MSC (rather than just the interchange fee). More broadly, entry by new payment systems and platforms based on distributed ledger technology, including initiatives by large private technology platforms, are likely to raise ongoing questions about the appropriate regulatory framework.

DISCUSSION QUESTIONS

1. What is a payment system, and what are some of the factors that have motivated the introduction of regulation for payment systems in some countries?
2. Describe the main steps involved in the processing of payments.
3. Discuss some of the differences between interbank payment systems and card payment systems.
4. What are some of the ways in which the payments landscape is changing, and what are some of the implications of these changes on the need to regulate payment systems?
5. To what extent do interbank and card payment systems compete with one another, and how might this change in the future?
6. What activities in interbank and card payment systems are subject to regulation, and what typically is the form of that regulation?
7. What are the different ways in which interchange fees for card payment systems have been regulated, or set, in practice across jurisdictions?
8. Discuss how interbank payment systems are regulated in jurisdictions where restructuring policies have been introduced. What factors have motivated such policies?
9. Describe the factors that led to the introduction of interchange fee regulation for card systems in different parts of the world.
10. Do you agree with the following statement? 'The experience of the capping of interchange fees has brought substantial benefits to merchants, cardholders and consumers, including in terms of lower retail prices.' Discuss.

13

Digital Platforms Regulation

Most of the industries discussed in Part III of this book have been subject to some form of regulation or oversight for many years. In contrast, interest in digital platforms regulation barely existed a decade ago. However, as we will discover, while the digital sector differs in important ways from the other industries considered in this book, many of the issues and debates arising in developing digital regulation are similar to those we have already considered. For example: the merits of the separation of large digital platforms; how to protect against discriminatory practices; whether mandatory access should be given to essential inputs, such as data and payments information; and how to make such platforms contestable. Behind these specific issues is the concern that some digital platforms may simply be too powerful, which,[1] as discussed in the next chapter, mirrors the concern about robber barons and trusts in the early US railroads industry, which motivated the establishment of the first economic regulator.[2]

While there is undoubtedly much experience from other regulated sectors to be drawn upon when developing and implementing digital regulation, there are also important differences to be considered. Most obviously, digital platform regulation is not focused on a single activity or the supply of a specific service to consumers. Rather, it comprises a range of companies, activities and products, from internet search engines to social networks, collaborative economy platforms, content aggregators, digital payment systems and online marketplaces. Second, the speed and scale with which digitisation can transform areas of economic and social life means that, to be effective, regulation needs to adapt quickly and raises risks about the potential error costs of regulatory action versus inaction. In addition, the global size and ubiquity of the largest digital platforms means that regulation often has a transnational aspect to it. Third, the capital investments that

---

[1] In the Americas, Europe and Australasia, these concerns relate to the power of the 'GAFAM' platforms (Google, Amazon, Facebook, Apple and Microsoft) while in China concerns focus on the 'BATX' platforms (Baidu, Alibaba, Tencent and Xiaomi).

[2] Tirole (2020) refers to this as 'techlash'. This concern is captured in the words of two US lawmakers (Cicilline and Buck, 2021) when introducing new regulatory bills before the US Congress: 'Right now, unregulated tech monopolies have too much power over our economy. They are in a unique position to pick winners and losers, destroy small businesses, raise prices on consumers, and put folks out of work. ... Big Tech has abused its dominance in the marketplace to crush competitors, censor speech, and control how we see and understand the world.' However, Shapiro (2023) challenges the 'factual underpinnings and economic reasoning behind the Big Tech regulatory bills' and expresses concern that '[c]ongress seems to be drafting legislation based on preconceived views about the Big Tech companies rather than following the evidence in a balanced manner'.

characterise many digital platforms revolve around software, algorithms, data storage an artificial intelligence, which differ from traditional regulated sectors, where capital inves ments tend to be physical and locationally specific (the pipes, cables, wires and rails Fourth, while many regulated sectors are based on a uni-directional supply chain (ofte with a producer/generator selling a product which is then transported to a consumer), dig ital peer-to-peer platforms allow consumers to assume multiple roles as both a consume and a producer/seller of a service. Fifth, services provided on some digital platforms diffe from traditional products insofar as they are 'free' at the point of consumption and a subsidised by revenues generated from other activities/users of a platform. Finally, som of the issues influencing digital regulation extend beyond economics, and encompa wider concerns about control over political speech, privacy and personal rights to dat as well as social concerns about the use and transmission of harmful materials online.

Looking ahead, digital platform regulation will likely be an active area of developmen and application for economic regulation. While a need for some form of regulation of dig tal markets is now recognised in many jurisdictions, the actual approach to regulation is an early stage, with institutions and policies being developed as this book is written. The are also important interactions between digital platform regulation and other regulated sec tors considered in this book. Most obviously, the chosen approach to telecommunication regulation can have significant impacts on the digital sector, given estimates that over ha of all global data traffic on fixed and mobile telecommunications currently comes from si digital content providers.[3] At the same time, the approach to regulation of digital platform could have implications for the development of distributed energy platforms, payment sys tems, transport and mobility services and unmanned aircraft systems traffic managemen

13.1   PHYSICAL AND ECONOMIC CHARACTERISTICS OF DIGITAL PLATFORMS

Regulators and policy makers have at times adopted different definitions of a digit platform. Some refer to such platforms as 'applications' that serve multiple groups users, and provide value to each user group because of the presence of the others while others define them as a 'service' that facilitates interactions between differen but interdependent groups of users via the Internet.[5] As explained below, commo to most definitions of digital platforms is the economic concept of a two-sided multi-sided market.

13.1.1   Characteristics of Digital Platforms

In this section, we provide a broad overview of: the different types of digital platform the types of users of digital platforms; and the characteristics of the entities that own an operate digital platforms. This is followed in Section 13.1.2 by a discussion of the eco nomics of digital platforms: how they generate revenue and who pays for their service

---

[3] See Axon (2022) and Financial Times (2022).
[4] ACCC (2019).
[5] OECD (2019a).

One of the differentiating features of digital platform regulation is that it does not refer to a specific product, service or activity. Rather, it encompasses a wide range of 'products' supplied to various users (individuals, companies, government) in a range of market and social contexts.

At the most general level, there appear to be three common attributes of digital platforms.[6] First, all 'platforms' can be conceptualised as a method, technology or forum that facilitates an *interaction* between different groups of platform users. While the focus in this chapter is on digital platforms, examples of non-digital 'platforms' include: village markets, where many sellers of fresh produce come to transact with many buyers of fresh produce; shopping malls, where mall owners seek to match shops and customers; stock exchanges, where buyers or sellers of shares meet and trade; or traditional print magazine or newspaper publishers, who seek to attract readers and also advertisers. A second attribute of digital platforms is that this interaction often involves *matching* or connecting one group of platform users with another group of users.[7] This differs from what are sometimes referred to as 'single-sided' digital service providers where there is no direct interaction between user groups, and the customer relationship is entirely controlled by the single-sided provider.[8] Third, the interaction on the platform is digital, meaning that it involves the generation, collection, storage, processing, exchange and distribution of data in digital format using computer technology on the Internet. This also means that the reach of digital platforms, unlike non-digital platforms, is global, allowing users to interact with one another around the world. In economic terms, digital platforms are sometimes conceptualised as online 'intermediaries' or 'matchmakers' that facilitate connections between different user groups to transact, share information, connect or exchange something of value using the Internet.[9]

While the fundamental characteristic of all digital platforms is that they facilitate an interaction between two or more user groups,[10] there is much variation in the 'value' that is actually produced and consumed (in a broad sense) on digital platforms, as well as who operates digital platforms and the purposes for which they are used.

Types of Digital Platforms

One way to distinguish between digital platforms is to focus on the types of interactions they facilitate between different groups of users. Table 13.1 presents a general functional typology of digital platforms.

---

[6] See de Reuver, Sørensen and Basole (2018) and Hein, Schreieck, Riasanow, *et al.* (2020), who consider how digital platforms are conceptualised across different disciplines.

[7] OECD (2019a) notes that the nature of any 'interaction' between different groups in the digital space may be passive and involve no action or message on the part of one or more of the parties, such that the interaction occurs in one direction only. For example, a search engine user may not pay any attention or take any action in response to advertisements displayed at the top of a website.

[8] Evans and Schmalensee (2016) refer to the example of Netflix, which pays movie and TV studios for the rights to certain content and then allows this content to be streamed to subscribers. In this setting, Netflix is completely in control of its supplier and customer relationships, and there is no direct interaction between the movie and TV studios and Netflix subscribers.

[9] See OECD (2019a) and Hein, Schreieck, Riasanow, *et al.* (2020).

[10] Evans and Schmalensee (2016) observe that the fundamental product that multi-sided platforms such as digital platforms sell is providing one group of users convenient access to one or more other groups of users.

Table 13.1 Broad typology of digital platforms[a]

Platform type	Function of platform	Examples
Search platforms	Matches information queries from one set of users with information provided by other users on websites to provide a ranked set of links to content websites.	Google, Bing, Baidu, Yahoo!
Information and data repository platforms	Allows one set of users to access information (including videos, music and other content) that is uploaded and stored by other users in a digital repository or library.	YouTube, Spotify, Wikipedia, SSRN, Google Maps
Communication and messaging platforms	Allows one set of users to communicate (via text, video or voice message) with other users of the platform with whom they are connected in real time.	WhatsApp, Instagram, Snapchat, Twitter, Tencent QQ, WeChat, Facebook Messenger, Viber
Payment platforms	Matches payees and payers.	PayPal, Square, Apple Pay, Google Pay, WeChat
Community and social networking platforms	Allows one set of users to connect with and share and exchange information and content (including content generated by other users, such as media publishers) with another set of users.	Facebook, LinkedIn, Tumblr, Twitter, WeChat
Online shopping and marketplaces, app stores and trading platforms	Match multiple buyers and multiple sellers of a product and service, or, in non-commercial contexts, two groups that are looking for each other for social reasons.	Alibaba, Booking.com, Amazon Marketplace, Uber, eBay, Airbnb, peer-to-peer trading and lending platforms, Apple App Store, Google Play Store, Freelancer, Tinder, BlaBlaCar
Digital content, video sharing and news aggregator platforms	Allows one set of users to access news, information, videos and movies collected and produced by a range of different content producers (such as publishers and content creators).	Google News, Facebook News, Yahoo! News, TikTok

[a]This typology builds on various sources, including Meyer (2019), ACCC (2019) and OECD (2019a).

While the functional typology of digital platforms in Table 13.1 is not intended to be exhaustive, it allows us to make a number of general observations. First, large digital platform operators often operate across multiple platform types, and for this reason are sometimes referred to as 'platform constellations' or 'superplatforms'.[11] For example, Google operates a search platform (Google Search), information platforms (YouTube, Google Maps), a communication and messaging platform (Google Chat), a payment platform (Google Pay), an online shopping platform (Google Shopping) and a news aggregation platform (Google News).[12] Similarly, in China, WeChat provides multiple functions, including communications and messaging, payments, social media and shopping. Second, some types of platforms could fall within different functional categories depending on the value provided to different users. For example, a peer-to-peer platform could be classified as either a commercial trading platform (e.g. where it facilitates electricity trades, acts as a jobs board or involves peer-to-peer lending) or a community or not-for-profit platform (e.g. if it facilitates sharing community-owned assets (toys, garden equipment) or is used to organise meal sharing among neighbours). Third, digital platforms derive revenues in different ways.[13] Some digital platforms are 'free' to use for some users, but not others. For example, subscribers to a social networking platform such as Facebook do not directly pay the platform operator for the services they provide. Rather, as discussed below, the costs of providing the social networking services are recovered from those who advertise their services on the social media platform. In contrast, some digital platforms charge some users directly for the services they provide (such as Airbnb) or offer users a free service or a premium service (with additional functionality) for a fee (LinkedIn).

Two further points can be made about digital platforms. The first is that not all digital products and services provided on the Internet are supplied on a digital platform. For example, businesses that provide digital cloud storage services on the Internet (such as Dropbox) are not digital platforms, as they do not facilitate an interaction between different groups of users. Rather, they simply provide digital cloud storage services to a user. Second, while there are considerable differences in types and functionality of digital platforms, they all involve the collection of user data and the use of sophisticated computer algorithms that then classify, filter, process and sort that data to facilitate the interaction between the different groups of users. As we will see below, data and algorithms are

---

[11] The OECD (2019a) defines a superplatform as 'a walled garden that users enter through a single portal (an app or a website) and that contains many individual platforms' while a platform constellation is defined as 'platforms owned by a single company and that may be seamlessly interoperable, share data or have synergies with one another, but can all be accessed separately without having to go through a single portal'.

[12] Google previously provided a social media platform known as Google+.

[13] Caffarra (2019) and Caffarra and Scott Morton (2021) distinguish between four platform business models: advertising-funded digital platforms which offer free services to end-users (Google, Facebook, Bing, Twitter, Snapchat); transaction or matchmaking platforms that intermediate between two or more sides and take a cut when a deal is struck (e.g. Uber, Airbnb, Deliveroo); online marketplaces where sellers find customers and vice versa and where the platform operators derive revenues when a transaction is made (e.g. Amazon, eBay); and operating ecosystem platforms such as operating systems and app stores (e.g. iOS, Apple App Store, Android, Google Play Store, Microsoft Windows, AWS, Microsoft Azure, etc.). Similarly, Belleflamme and Peitz (2021) classify platforms into five categories based on how they create value (those that charge users of services, or monetise via other users) and capture value (leverage direct effects, leverage indirect effects, or capitalise on stand-alone services).

fundamental to the operation of digital platforms, and are central to how digital platforms compete with one another. They also underlie some of the rationales for regulation.

Digital Platform Users

As noted, a key characteristic of digital platforms is that they facilitate interaction between different user groups. This raises a question about who are the 'users' of such platforms, and more specifically whose interactions are being matched or facilitated. Given the substantial diversity of digital platforms, it is unsurprising that there is a wide range of 'users' of these platforms.

At the most general level, the users which interact on a digital platform can be classified into five types: advertisers, buyers, sellers, content consumers and content producers.[14] Each of these different user groups gains different value from using the platform. Most obviously, those who use digital platforms as buyers or sellers gain value through the platform's ability to match them and facilitate trade and exchange. Buyers and sellers in this context can include: providers of goods and services who use online marketplaces; app developers and users; employers and workers on freelance work platforms; drivers and riders of ride-sharing platforms; hosts and guests on accommodation platforms; and payers and payees on payment platforms. Advertisers gain value from a digital platform through the ability to use data that has been collected on user preferences and behaviour to better target consumers that might be interested in purchasing their products. Content consumers on a social media site gain value from the ability to connect and communicate with friends, family or like-minded people around the world, while consumers on information and depository platforms gain the ability to access vast amounts of information that they need quickly. Content producers gain value through the ability to share new content (videos, text or other media) to either close contacts (e.g. messaging platforms) or to broadcast content to a wide audience (e.g. video or music streaming platforms). While the specific value that a user obtains from a digital platform varies according to platform type, as discussed below, a key insight is that, in exchange for that value, all users provide a platform operator with either direct remuneration/payment or user data and attention that can then be monetised by the platform operator in other ways such as advertising.

Within the five broad 'user groups' identified above, there are a range of different categories of users, including individuals, small and large businesses, governments and not-for-profit entities. Depending on the platform, each of these users could fall into multiple user groups – for example, individuals, small and large businesses, governments or not-for-profit entities could all produce content to share on a social media platform, and at the same time consume content produced by other users on that platform. Moreover, a particular user (e.g. an individual) can simultaneously be part of different user groups. For example, an individual might use a digital shopping platform such as eBay or Airbnb to be both a buyer and a seller, and might be a content producer and content user on platforms like Facebook and YouTube.

---

[14] See OECD (2019a).
[15] See Wu (2019) and Calvano and Polo (2021). Prat and Valetti (2021) define an attention broker as having an ability to: (i) obtain information about the preferences of individual users; and (ii) target ads to individual users.

Digital Platform Operators

Digital platform operators vary in size and market presence and include some of the world's largest and most valuable companies (such as Alibaba, Alphabet (which owns Google), Amazon, Apple, Meta (which owns Facebook) and Tencent) as well as government, non-profit and other non-commercial or community-based digital platforms. However, not all digital platforms are large. In Europe, for example, it is estimated that there are over 10,000 digital platforms, the majority of which are small and medium-sized enterprises.[16]

Some digital platform operators have been incredibly successful and occupy strong market positions in the markets in which they operate. Globally, in April 2022, Google accounted for over 90 per cent of online searches, while Facebook's market share of social networking platforms is estimated at about 75 per cent.[17] Amazon's revenue from third-party sales on its marketplace was estimated at $300 billion in 2020 in the USA alone,[18] while Alibaba's e-commerce sales in China from its Singles' Day event was estimated at $74 billion in 2020.[19] However, while some platform operators have been incredibly successful, this is not universally the case, and many platform operators have failed.[20] Similarly, while the positions of some large platforms appear to be entrenched and durable, the market positions of other large digital platform operators appear to be more precarious given 'intra-platform' competition. For example, in many jurisdictions, there is intensive *intra*-platform competition between travel and accommodation booking platforms (Booking.com, Expedia and Airbnb), ride-sharing platforms (Uber, Lyft, Ola, Didi) and payment platforms (PayPal, Apple Pay, Google Pay). The market position of platform operators also varies by jurisdiction. For example, in China, Baidu has a 72 per cent share of the search engine market (compared to around 2 per cent for Google), while Weibo has a share of around 38 per cent of social media (compared to 2.3 per cent for Facebook).

Many digital platform operators also compete with traditional providers of goods and services. As discussed in Chapter 12, digital payment platform providers (such as PayPal and WeChat) compete with the major card and interbank payment systems (Visa, Mastercard and UnionPay), while online market places like Amazon and Alibaba compete with traditional 'bricks and mortar' retailers. However, in many sectors, digital platforms have been highly successful in 'disrupting' and in some cases displacing traditional supply arrangements. For instance, the number of listings on the accommodation platform Airbnb is now greater than the number on the top five hotel brands combined,[21] while in 2018 the ride-sharing platform Uber's network spanned 700 cities in sixty-three countries and involved 14 million trips. This rapid growth has had substantial impacts on local taxi networks in many countries. Other traditional supply activities that have been severely

---

[16] EC (2020g).
[17] StatCounter (2022).
[18] Forbes (2021b).
[19] CNBC (2020).
[20] Cusumano, Yoffie and Gawer (2020) looked at the fortunes of different digital platforms and identified forty-three success stories, but also identified 209 platform companies that were their direct competitors that either failed or disappeared as independent companies. Similarly, Evans and Schmalensee (2016) observe that most 'matchmaker start-ups splutter and die'.
[21] See Hein, Schreieck, Riasanow, *et al.* (2020).

affected by the emergence of digital platforms include travel agents, high-street reta'
shopping, video rental stores and printed newspapers and magazines.

An important part of the operation of digital platforms relates to the governanc
arrangements that set and enforce the rules that determine which users can access a plat
form and how they interact with one another. Some digital platforms centralise contro
in a single owner that defines, establishes and maintains the rules and governance mech'
anisms. Facebook, Google and the Apple App Store are prominent examples of digita
platforms that have centralised governance arrangements, meaning that they determin'
who gets access to the platform and on what terms. Other digital platforms operate eithe
as not-for-profit consortia where multiple stakeholders are involved in establishing th
governance arrangements, or in a decentralised way and are governed through peer-to'
peer communities where users have voting rights and collectively determine the rules fo
the operation of the digital platform.[22]

As already noted, the activities of digital platform operators can extend *horizontall'*
across multiple markets and *vertically* to include other related activities. Major plat
form operators such as Alibaba, Amazon, Apple, Baidu, Facebook, Google and Tencen'
are active across different digital markets, which, as discussed below, has given rise t'
competition concerns in some jurisdictions. Some digital platform operators are also ver
tically integrated and provide their own services on the platform, which may compet'
with services provided by other independent users on the platform. For example, Amazo'
is a direct retailer as well as operating the Amazon Marketplace, which third partie
use to sell retail goods.[23] Alibaba provides retail and wholesale marketplaces, but als'
offers fulfilment services (AliExpress shipping) and operates its own payments platfor'
(Alipay). Google and Apple operate app stores but also put their own apps on phones an'
tablets. In addition, some major platform operators – such as Amazon, Apple, Microso'
and Tencent – generate substantial revenues from other activities such as mobile phone:
video game sales, computer hardware and software, and logistics. Looking ahead, som'
large digital platform operators are expanding into a range of new areas such as crypto'
currency (Facebook),[24] driverless vehicles (Google) and space travel (Amazon).

Infrastructure Needed by Digital Platform Operators and Users

All digital platforms need certain inputs and access to specific physical infrastructure t'
allow them to facilitate the interactions between different user groups. At the most basi
level, digital platforms need access to the Internet (a global network of computers) an'
the World Wide Web (the system of connected content – pictures, video and sound
transmitted over the Internet and accessed by a browser). They also need access to: fixe'
and mobile communications networks; computer hardware and software to allow them t'
process queries quickly; specialist algorithms that can sort, classify and match differen'

---

[22] Hein, Schreieck, Riasanow, *et al.* (2020) refer to the example of Cloud Foundry as a consortia, and blockchain platforms such as district0x, which is a network of decentralised marketplaces and communities.

[23] Evans and Schmalensee (2016) refer to Amazon as having 'blended' single-sided and multi-sided businesses.

[24] Although, as discussed in Chapter 12, Meta (Facebook's owner) sold its interest in Diem in 2022.

user requests and information; and data storage capability to hold the data they collect.[25] While some of these inputs are developed and operated by digital platform operators (algorithms and data storage), other essential inputs, such as the access to physical communications infrastructure, are provided by telecommunications network providers, which are separate from the digital platform operators. It follows that the cost and service quality of the services provided by the telecommunications infrastructure operators are central to the operation and performance of digital platforms. In areas where telecommunications networks offer poor coverage or variable service quality, this can limit the ability of a digital platform to connect different users. As discussed in Chapter 11, given the substantial and growing use of fixed and mobile telecommunications networks by large digital platforms, there are calls by some for such digital platforms to contribute more funding to these network infrastructure assets on which they rely.[26]

Users of digital platforms also need access to certain equipment and infrastructure in order to use a digital platform. At the most basic level this includes access to some form of computer (either a desktop, tablet or mobile device), an operating system and various types of software. Users also need access to an Internet Service Provider (ISP), which allows them to use a fixed or mobile telecommunications network to send and receive data and utilise the World Wide Web and the Internet.

3.1.2 Digital Platform Value Chain

Digital platforms differ from the other industries considered in this book in that they do not provide value to end-users by producing, transporting or selling products or services within a single supply chain.[27] Rather, the 'inputs' used in a digital platform are the different user groups, and the value that digital platforms generate for users derives from their ability to facilitate access to, and manage the interactions between, different but interdependent groups of users.[28] In other words, digital platforms provide value to users by reducing information and transaction costs, and resolving frictions, which may have made it too difficult or costly for different user groups to coordinate and interact in the past.[29]

Multi-Sided Markets and Network Effects

In economic terms, digital platforms are a 'two-sided' or 'multi-sided' market, and the principal function of a platform operator is to try to get two or more user groups (or

---

[25] Evans and Schmalensee (2016) identify six technologies that have driven growth in multi-sided platforms: more powerful computer chips; the Internet; the World Wide Web; broadband communications; programming languages and operating systems; and the Cloud.

[26] See Axon (2022) and Frontier Economics (2022).

[27] Parker, Petropoulos and Van Alstyne (2021) refer to digital platforms as 'inverted' firms for the reason that: '[E]normous value is created outside the firm itself and the standard upstream–downstream factions blur. Users often create value for other users, as in the case of user generated content, and suppliers often create value for other suppliers, as in the case of shared developer files.'

[28] Hein, Schreieck, Riasanow, Setzke, *et al.* (2020) note that digital platform operators rely on other autonomous agents in a digital 'ecosystem' to co-create value. This includes 'complementors' whose products and services add value to the platforms. Complementors include those that actively contribute to the digital platform or another platform that is compatible with but not actively engaged in the digital platform.

[29] Evans and Schmalensee (2016) provide examples of frictions overcome through digital platforms.

sides) to participate in the platform ('on board') by appropriately charging each use group (side).[30] User groups are considered *interdependent* because the demand for use of the platform for one user group is conditioned by the demand for the use of the platform by other user groups. For example, the higher the number of users of a particular search engine, the greater the demand will be for advertisers to promote services on that search engine. Multi-sided platforms thus give rise to network effects, which, as we discussed in Chapter 2, means that the value of a platform to a user depends on the number of other users that are connected to, or utilise, that platform. Network effects can be direct or indirect, and can be positive or negative.[31]

Direct network effects arise when the value of the platform to a user changes depending on the number of other platform users that are part of the *same* group (i.e. the number of users on the 'same side of the platform').[32] Positive direct network effects arise when a platform is successful in attracting users of the same group, and where each additional user makes the platform more attractive for each existing user. For example, the more users that a social media or instant messaging platform can attract, the greater the size of the platform, and the larger the number of users that any single user can engage with. Similarly, the use of review and ratings systems on some online shopping platforms can assist other potential buyers.[34] Negative direct network effects arise whenever additional users of the same group reduce the value of that platform to that group, often because they cause greater competition for a scarce resource or result in congestion. For example, the more customers that use a ride-sharing platform in a city late on a Friday evening, the longer each customer will have to wait. Similarly, the greater the number of workers on a freelancer website, the more competition that each worker faces.

Indirect network effects arise when the value of the platform to users of one group changes depending on the number of users that are part of a *different* group (i.e. the number of users 'on the other side of the platform').[35] Positive indirect network effects arise when the addition of a new user of one type increases the value of the platform to other types of users. For example, the higher the number of hotels listed on an accommodation platform (one group), the greater the options for those who want to choose a hotel (a different group). Negative indirect network effects arise where the addition of another user of one type reduces the value of the platform to other user groups. For example, a search platform may list too many advertisements prominently on the first results page, which reduces the value of that platform to those entering search queries. Similarly, advertisers might use personal

---

[30] See foundational papers by Rochet and Tirole (2002, 2003, 2006), Evans (2003), Armstrong (2006) and Rysman (2009). Evans and Schmalensee (2016) and Belleflamme and Peitz (2021) provide accessible overviews of the economics of multi-sided platforms, while Jullien, Pavan and Rysman (2021) provide a recent survey.

[31] Katz and Shapiro (1985) provide an early analysis.

[32] Varian, Farrell and Shapiro (2004) refer to this as 'demand-side economies of scale' to reflect the fact that average revenue (demand) increases with scale.

[33] This is sometimes referred to as 'identity-based network effects' and reflects the fact that people join networks that allow them to connect with people they want to connect with. See Bundeskartellamt (2017).

[34] Belleflamme and Peitz (2021) discuss how platforms use rating and recommender systems to address the asymmetric information problem that platform users face.

[35] These are sometimes referred to as cross-platform network effects (OECD, 2019a) or cross-sided network effects (ACCC, 2019).

data to present highly targeted advertisements on a search or social media platform, which can raise privacy concerns for some consumers and reduce the value of that digital platform. A number of points follow from the network effects generated by digital platforms.

Market Tipping and 'Winner Takes All' or 'Winner Takes Most' Competition

The existence of strong network effects can in some instances lead to what is sometimes referred to as 'market tipping' or a 'winner takes all/most' dynamic for digital platforms, which, as discussed below, feature prominently in discussions about the need for regulation of such platforms. The underlying idea is that, if a digital platform has an initial lead in attracting users on both sides of the market, this can result in a positive feedback spiral allowing it to exploit economies of scale and scope and ultimately dominate that market.[36] While the success of a digital platform is determined by its ability to attract and maintain the right number of users on *different* sides of the platform, the key challenge of a digital platform is to work out how to 'get all sides on board' and to keep them on board.[37] This can give rise to a 'chicken and egg' problem: in order to attract (or keep) enough users on one side of the platform, there needs to be enough active users on the other side of the platform.[38] Digital platforms that can resolve this chicken and egg problem and attract a sufficient number of different user groups can exploit positive indirect network effects and experience 'explosive growth'.[39] Conversely, digital platforms that are only attractive to one group of users can become 'lopsided', which can lead to a 'death spiral', in turn making them even less attractive to the other group of users. For example, a ride-sharing platform might initially attract a large number of riders (customers), but these customers will quickly abandon the platform if it cannot also attract and maintain enough drivers to service their needs when they need a ride.

Incentivising Participation by Different Groups through Price Structures

While gaining and maintaining scale in terms of the number of users can be important to a platform's success, of equal importance is a platform's ability to *match* different user groups. In other words, it is not just about getting the right number of users; a platform operator also has to be able to facilitate meaningful interactions between user groups from which each user group derives value.[40] Digital platform operators also want to

---

[36] As more and more users join that platform, existing users effectively become 'locked in' because, if they switch to another platform, they will lose the ability to connect with other users. Arthur (1989) provides an early discussion of increasing returns to scale and the potential for lock-in in the context of technology markets, noting that a technology that by chance gains an early lead in adoption may eventually 'corner the market' of potential adopters, with the other technologies becoming locked out. However, see Evans and Schmalensee (2016), who note that this overlooks the role of indirect network effects.

[37] This is sometimes described as a coordination problem: they need to 'coordinate' the right groups of users to interact with one another.

[38] This was first identified by Caillaud and Jullien (2003). Evans and Schmalensee (2016) discuss this in terms of the need to gain a critical mass on both sides of the market.

[39] Evans and Schmalensee (2016).

[40] Evans and Schmalensee (2016) give the example of the restaurant booking digital platform OpenTable, which in its early days managed to attract some restaurants in many cities, but did not attract lots of restaurants in any one city. As such, consumers in any one city did not actually have much choice of restaurants, which limited its usefulness to them.

maximise the number (volume) of interactions between the different user groups. This places a focus not only on the ability to attract a critical mass of the right types of user groups,[41] but also on the quality of the algorithms used to 'match' different platform user groups.

It follows that digital platform operators need to think carefully about how to incentivise different user groups to join and stay on their platform. In practical terms, this means that digital platform operators need to focus carefully on how they *structure* the prices they set for the different sides of the market.[42] For example, if a hotel booking digital platform introduces a high rate of commission for customers who book a hotel on that platform, this will, other things being equal, reduce the demand by customers to use that platform, which in turn will make it a less attractive platform for hotels to list their accommodation. Put simply, when setting prices for different user groups digital platform operators must take account of the *interdependence* of the demands between user groups and consider the price elasticity of demand of the different user groups.[43]

In setting a price structure, digital platform operators also need to take account of the costs of serving different user groups and whether the costs of one user group should be subsidised by another user group. In some circumstances, a digital platform operator might adopt a 'tilted' pricing structure which involves charging a negligible or zero price to one group of users (which is below the costs of serving them) and recover all of its revenues from another set of users.[44] This practice is common for social network platforms, instant messaging platforms and search engines which do not directly charge end-users for executing search queries or connecting with friends using their platforms. These digital platforms cover their costs and generate most of their revenues from another group of users, namely advertisers. Some digital operators may even choose to reward one group of users through loyalty points or other benefits and to subsidise the costs of such rewards through above-cost charges levied on another group of users.[45] While it may seem irrational to charge one set of users a price *below* the costs they impose on the digital platform operator, it can be a profit-maximising strategy if it achieves the right balance of different types of user groups on the platform.[46] Put simply, a pricing structure that involves subsidising one side of the platform with revenues generated from another

---

[41] Evans and Schmalensee (2017/18) note that 'network effects result from getting the right customers, and not just more customers'.

[42] Cusumano, Yoffie and Gawer (2020) found that the primary reasons for the failure of platforms was mispricing (under- or overcharging) on one side of the market or oversubsidising platform participants. Evans and Schmalensee (2016) note that: 'Multisided platforms better get all these prices right. If they don't, they won't attain critical mass, won't make any money, and won't be in business long.' Belleflamme and Peitz (2021) note that network effects makes pricing significantly more complex because: (i) a given price can result in different demand levels; (ii) the price that a platform can set is conditioned by user expectations about other users' participation; and (iii) small differences in price can 'tip' the market, leading either to all potential users joining a platform or to none at all.

[43] See Rochet and Tirole (2003).

[44] Evans and Schmalensee (2016) refer to this as a 'subsidy' side and a 'money' side.

[45] Evans and Schmalensee (2016) note that a user group may be offered a subsidy if it controls whether an interaction with another groups takes place at all.

[46] Wright (2004) describes how it may also be an efficient price structure because it takes account of the surplus that one side creates for another user.

side may be needed to make it attractive for specific groups to use the platform and thus to achieve the balanced participation of different types.[47]

In addition to advertising revenue, some digital platforms generate revenues from direct charges levied on specific user groups. Sellers who use digital platforms like Alibaba, Amazon and Rakuten to market and sell products or services are charged a fee for doing so. These charges can take the form of a listing fee, subscription charge (monthly, annual) and a usage or per-transaction charge. Buyers can also be levied charges for using some digital platforms. For example, guests who use Airbnb can be charged a service fee, as are consumers of food delivery platforms like Deliveroo or Uber Eats. Similarly, employers who use freelance sites to find workers can be charged a transaction fee. Consumers that subscribe to some digital platforms (such as dating platforms) can also pay a monthly subscription fee.

Non-Price Terms of Participation and Platform Governance

Participation and use of a digital platform can also be affected by (non-price) terms and conditions. Digital platform operators have to develop governance systems which set out the rules of participation, and establish a method for monitoring compliance with those rules and enforcing them.[48] The rules and wider governance systems can be critical to the use of digital payment systems by some user types, and can reinforce the network effects. For example, consumers who use a digital platform marketplace to buy products need to be confident that they will receive a full refund if the goods they receive are not as described. In turn, this may require sellers on the online marketplace committing to providing a full refund if a consumer is not happy with a service.

To ensure that users abide by various 'rules' established by the platform operator, some digital platforms have introduced novel monitoring and enforcement mechanisms. For example, on many digital platforms it is common for one group of users (e.g. users of a ride-sharing service) to be able to rate and provide comments about the service they receive from another group of users on the platform (the drivers). Some digital platforms allow users to report poor behaviour or performance by other users, which can lead to the expulsion of those who contravene the 'platform rules' (e.g. drivers who are unsafe, or members of Twitter who post hate speech).

Strategies for Attracting Users and Keeping Them

Digital platform operators adopt various strategies over time to attract and serve different user types. One common approach is known as a 'two-step' strategy, which focuses on getting one user group on the platform first (such as drivers) and then seeking out the other user group (riders). Another strategy involves introducing differential access and usage charges for some user groups (such as an annual access charge but a low or

---

[47] Evans and Schmalensee (2016) observe that, while free and negative prices are often seen as a gimmick and a way of gaining size, they actually reflect the interdependence of demand between different user groups.

[48] Boudreau and Hagiu (2009) refer to platform operators as private regulators who use non-price instruments to regulate access to and interactions around the platforms.

negligible usage charge) or delaying charging one side of the market until it has built u
enough users on that side.[49]

Once they have attracted users to their platform, many digital operators need to ensur
that different user groups are continually being matched in better and more accurat
ways. For this reason, digital platforms, particularly the largest platforms, spend substan
tial resources on innovation and investment. This can include investments to improve th
operation and functionality of the platform (such as improving the predictive capabil
ity of an algorithm), or investments in the form of cross-platform acquisitions of othe
digital platform operators (e.g. Facebook's acquisition of WhatsApp; Google's acquisi
tion of YouTube). Large digital platforms have also spent substantial sums in acqui
ing complementors whose products and services add value to their platforms and ca
allow them to leverage their position into another market through a process known a
platform envelopment.[50] As discussed below, the question of whether these acquisition
by large digital platforms has stifled dynamic competition is a major concern in som
jurisdictions.[51]

13.1.3 Digital Platforms and Data

As we have discussed, digital platform operators often charge different prices to differer
user groups, and in some cases will charge some user groups a 'zero' price (such as use
of a search engine) or even provide incentives or benefits to some users to encourage us
of the platform. How, then, do these digital platforms make money? Broadly speakin
digital platforms generate revenues from: advertising fees; access (subscription) charge
usage charges; or a combination of all of these sources.

For larger digital platforms, such as Google and Facebook, that offer 'free' services 1
end-users, advertising is the major way in which revenues are generated.[52] These revenu
are both substantial and growing; for instance, when Facebook started in 2004, its adver
tising revenues were $382,000, while in 2020 its revenues were $84 billion, an increase o
about 22,000,000 per cent.[53] This tremendous growth reflects the fact that these platforr
have developed sophisticated ways of collecting, combining and analysing personal da

---

[49] Evans and Schmalensee (2016) describe these and other strategies in more detail.

[50] Eisenmann, Parker and Van Alstyne (2011) define an envelopment strategy as where one platform
provider bundles its own platform's functionality with that of a target market, and thus benefits from
leveraging the shared user relationships and common components. They give the example of Microsoft
bundling its Windows Media Player with its operating system, which over time led to the exit of Real
Player, which was up until that point the dominant media streaming platform.

[51] Gautier and Lamesch (2021) found that, in two years (2015–2017), the five leading firms, Google, Apple,
Facebook, Amazon and Microsoft (GAFAM), acquired 175 companies. Parker, Petropoulos and Van Alsty
(2021) estimate that between 1987 and 2020, these same firms merged or acquired 825 firms (Google 30
per cent, Microsoft 29 per cent, Apple 16 per cent, Amazon 13 per cent and Facebook 12 per cent).

[52] See ACCC (2019) and CMA (2020).

[53] These revenue numbers are taken from Evans and Schmalensee (2016) and Facebook (2021). According
to the CMA (2020), over a third of UK internet users' time online is spent on Google and Facebook sites
and they account for around 80 per cent of all digital advertising in 2019.

[54] Zuboff (2019) describes how data was originally considered to be a by-product ('the fumes'). However,
as Calvano and Polo (2021) observe, data is now seen as valuable 'oil' that powers predictions on digita
platforms.

from their large number of users.[54] This personal data is highly valuable to advertisers and allows them to select and present highly targeted and relevant advertisements to an individual consumer in a fraction of a second.[55] Two main types of advertisements are used by these platforms: sponsored search ads, which are shown prominently (often at the top of a page) in response to a specific search query; and display advertising, where text or video ads are displayed alongside the content a user is viewing. Advertisers are attracted to these large platforms because of their large user base and it is for this reason that platform operators have an incentive not to levy charges directly on consumers.[56] In effect, the search and social networking services are 'free' to consumers at point of use; however, consumers might be said to 'pay' for the services they receive from the digital platform by providing their attention and data, which can then be used by advertisers to target them with products and services.[57]

Data that digital platforms collect include: information volunteered by users (such as a social media profile, a 'like' or an online review); data captured from online behaviour (how much time is spent on a website, what they search for, what they like or who they follow); data that can be inferred from analytic and predictive exercises; and data about where and how users access the platform and other third-party sites (what device is used, browser type, etc.).[58] Data about a user's activities can be collected from the digital platform operator's own websites, or from a third-party website which is accessed using an operating system owned by the digital platform operator.[59] User behaviour can also be observed by 'third parties' such as ad networks who have hidden trackers embedded on webpages and can access users' browsing histories through a combination of cookies and other tracking technologies.[60] The specific data collected from an individual can include: personal identification data (name, address, IP address); payment data (about how they

---

[55] CMA (2020). Tirole (2020) observes that theoretically a zero price may even be too high given the high value of this data to platforms.

[56] The ACCC (2019) observes: 'All else being equal, an advertiser is likely to prefer a large platform over a small one, on the grounds that running campaigns on the former has lower average fixed costs.' The CMA (2020) notes: '[F]or a wide range of firms, from the largest conglomerate to the local cafe, digital advertising provides a highly effective method of delivering ads that are relevant to consumers, helping to drive brand awareness and sales.'

[57] However, as Furman, Coyle, Fletcher, *et al.* (2019) observe: 'Many consumers are typically not consciously participating in this exchange, or do not appreciate the value of the attention they are providing.'

[58] See OECD (2019a) and ACCC (2019).

[59] CMA (2020) found that Google collected a 'vast amount of user data from three main sources: its user-facing services (it provides over 50 such services, including search and Gmail); from mobile devices running Android, Google's operating system; and from the analytical technology they place on third-party sites and apps (known as tags)'; while 'Facebook gathers user data from the three main services it provides in the UK (Facebook, Instagram and WhatsApp) and from Facebook analytics technology placed on third-party sites (known as pixels)'. Similarly, ACCC (2019) notes the example of Google, which not only obtains data from its own sites, such as its search engine (Google Search), YouTube, Google Shopping, Gmail, and Google Maps, but also obtains data from third-party sites when a consumer uses a device with an Android operating system or a Chrome browser to access a third-party website. This allows it to offer advertisers data about sales of search and display inventory on its own websites and data about sales of search and display inventory on third-party websites.

[60] See Englehardt and Narayanan (2016), who found that all of the top five 'third parties' were owned by Google, and that Google, Facebook and Twitter were present as third-party entities on more than 10 per cent of sites.

paid and the payment details); information about what products and services are viewed and which are purchased and on what terms (price paid, etc.); data about the content watched, listened to or viewed online; browsing data and search queries used; personal opinion data (posts on social media, comments, likes, ratings, etc.); contacts data, including people that are followed online; location data; and information on the type of connection used to access the platform. Once collected, this data can be used to make inferences and predictions about an individual user's personal needs, opinions and preferences, their creditworthiness, what products and services they might consume and their willingness to pay for those products.[61] It is this ability to access, combine and analyse personal data from a disparate set of sources which allows some large digital platforms to offer advertisers an ability to present highly targeted and timely advertisements.[62]

Data is also used to continually develop and refine the algorithms which underpin these digital platforms, improving their ability to more effectively 'match' different user groups and provide other predictive services (such as search platforms).[63] The more data that the platform can collect and analyse, the better its predictive capabilities, and even a single search query helps to improve the overall search capabilities of the predictive algorithm.[64] It follows that digital platform providers that operate in multiple markets (superplatforms) are able to collect and combine more personal data about a specific user across platforms, which provides them with an even better ability to offer highly targeted, personalised and timely advertisements. For example, Meta (which owns Facebook) can access data on a user from Facebook, Instagram and WhatsApp, while Google has consumer data from its search engine, Gmail, Google Maps, YouTube and Google Shopping.[65]

13.2 SHOULD DIGITAL PLATFORMS BE REGULATED?

At first sight, the question of why and how to regulate digital platforms appears far removed from the other industries and sectors considered in this book. Regulating an interaction where value is created through two or more users on a platform (and where some users often do not directly pay for the service) seems quite different from regulating an activity which involves the one-way production or transportation of a product or service. Nevertheless, many of the reasons motivating the regulation of digital platforms are similar to those which apply in other markets.

---

[61] See OECD (2019a). See also Zuboff (2019).

[62] ACCC (2019) notes that the data has value because it can reveal a user's intent and preferences at a particular point in time. Similarly, Calvano and Polo (2021) note that: '[N]ew technologies allow advertisers to "target" audiences in a number of dimensions: demographics, physical location, time of the day, personal tastes, browsing history and so on. ... Targeting means that competition is scaled at the individual level.'

[63] As Calvano and Polo (2021) note: 'Search engines need to predict the relevance of URLs to a consumer query. Matchmakers need to predict the value of a match in order to find good prospects for their users (for instance, employees and employers, single men and single women and so on); content distributors, such as Spotify, need to predict their user tastes to keep them entertained; mapping services need to predict traffic conditions and so on. Data is the oil that powers these predictions.'

[64] See Zuboff (2019) and Ducci (2020). Varian (2021) gives the example on the 412 ways to spell Britney Spears observed by Google over a three-month period.

[65] See ACCC (2019) and CMA (2020).

Before considering these rationales, it is useful to recognise that the question of whether to regulate digital platforms has only really emerged in the past five years, and that the issue itself is still under debate in many jurisdictions. In part, this reflects the fact that almost everyone, including those who advocate for regulation, acknowledge that digital platforms have generally brought enormous benefits to consumers and other users by lowering transaction costs and resolving coordination problems. Social media and instant messaging platforms allow for friends and family around the world to connect and reconnect, reducing isolation and loneliness and allowing them to share ideas and views. News aggregator platforms allow users to access news and information from a range of different sources and countries, thus providing different perspectives on current events. Online marketplace and sharing platforms allow users to buy and sell products from a range of other users (including internationally) and have thus expanded choice and intensified competition among suppliers. Finally, internet search engines allow users to navigate their way around the World Wide Web and to find information in a fraction of a second about a seemingly limitless array of topics. In addition, many digital platforms, particularly the larger ones, have become better and faster over time, continually improving the experience for their users.

While these benefits are generally undisputed, there are concerns that some digital platforms with large user bases now hold such a strong and unassailable market position that some form of regulation is necessary.[66] Broadly speaking, the arguments for regulation fall into the different categories identified in Chapter 2.

13.2.1 Efficiency Rationales for Regulation of Digital Platforms

In Chapter 2, we noted that a common rationale for regulation of particular sectors or activities is that the cost and demand conditions approximate a natural monopoly, and as such there are economies of scale or scope associated with that activity. Although the nature of the physical investments in digital platforms differs from those made in public utility industries (which involve large and lumpy capital investments in durable and immobile assets (pipes, cables, wires or rails)), the cost structures are broadly similar and often involve significant fixed costs and small, or even zero, marginal costs.[67] The fixed costs of digital platforms can include investments in computer hardware and software development (including the costs of developing algorithms), maintaining adequate data storage facilities, and research and development expenditure.[68] Marginal costs largely

---

[66] Indeed, the operators of some of these large platforms themselves have acknowledged the need for some form of regulation (see Zuckerberg, 2020).

[67] Varian, Farrell and Shapiro (2004) note that: '[M]any information- and technology-related businesses have cost structures with large fixed costs and small, or even zero, marginal costs. They are, to use the textbook term, "natural monopolies"'. Tirole (2020) makes a similar observation, noting that: '[T]oday's tech companies exhibit natural-monopoly characteristics like those of the network industries of the 20th century. Hence the occasional suggestion to apply public utility regulation to the tech sector.' Similarly, Vogelsang (2021) notes that: '[D]emand-side economies and supply-side economies may come together, thereby potentially creating strong natural monopoly conditions. Google's search engine may be a case in point.'

[68] Varian (2021) claims that Google's R&D spend increased ten times over the past ten years from $2.8 billion to $26 billion.

involve the costs of processing, storing, replicating and transmitting data, including th
costs of using telecommunications networks and the managing of user relationships.[69] I
broad terms, this structure means that, once a digital platform has incurred its fixed cost
the marginal costs of processing an additional search query or transaction or connectin
an additional user can often be very low or close to zero.[70]

This cost structure of high fixed costs and low marginal costs can naturally lead t
increased concentration. In the context of digital platforms, this can allow a single ope
ator to rapidly expand its user base to serve millions or even billions of users, leading t
significantly lower average costs – what some have termed 'extreme' or 'hyper' retur
to scale at the global level.[71] For some digital platforms, such as search platforms whic
use predictive algorithms to match user queries to relevant content, this tendency towar
concentration can be reinforced by the accumulation of large-scale datasets, which allov
them to continuously refine their algorithms and return better responses for uncommo
or 'tail' search queries.[72] For these platforms, it could be argued that a single digital pla
form operator that can serve all demand might, from a static efficiency perspective, b
the most efficient industry structure. However, the extent to which economies of sca
will naturally lead to a situation where there is only one digital platform operator varie
across platform types, and can depend on factors such as: the extent to which platform
offer differentiated products; whether data is accumulated for the purposes of predictio
or matching; and the specific conditions of demand in a particular market.[73]

In addition to economies of scale, some digital platforms benefit from economies o
scope, which arise from complementarities in supplying multiple services on a give

[69] The marginal costs incurred depend on the type of digital platform and its users. The cost of processing
a request by each additional user of a search engine or connecting users on a social media platform,
ride-sharing or accommodation platform is negligible. There may, however, be some marginal costs
associated with on-boarding checks for new users who want to sell or advertise services on a platform
a new driver who wants to use a ride-sharing platform, and from managing customer relationships (e.g
problems experienced by different users).

[70] See Evans and Schmalensee (2016).

[71] See OECD (2019a) and Crémer, de Montjoye and Schweitzer (2019). Furman, Coyle, Fletcher, et al.
(2019) note that, unlike traditional markets, the efficiencies of economies of scale are not constrained b
location or transport costs, and thus economies of scale support concentration on a global scale.

[72] CMA (2020) records that: 'Google and Microsoft told us that a substantial proportion of queries that
they see are uncommon or new, which suggests that the ability to return appropriate results for such ta
queries is likely to be valuable to consumers, and to be an important factor in users' assessment of sear
quality.' Biglaiser, Calvano and Crémer (2019) discuss two ways in which data can generate a competiti
advantage: '[F]irst, data about the past behavior of specific users make it easier to provide these same
consumers with better service. If a user has been a client of a platform for some time, the platform kno
his or her tastes and can give more prominence to goods or services that he or she prefers. Second, the
platform can use the data stemming from other users to increase the quality of the service to each of it
users (in jargon: "Training the algorithms").' Varian (2021) notes that: 'Paradoxically, rare queries are
common! On any given day, 15% of the queries on Google have never been seen before by Google – a
proportion that has remained unchanged for years.'

[73] Ducci (2020) argues that the competitive advantage of online marketplaces like Amazon derives not
from economies of scale but from the combination of its large online marketplace with efficient storage
and delivery infrastructure. Similarly, the extent to which ride-sharing platforms benefit from economi
of scale depends on the size of demand, density of population, and availability of alternative methods c
transportation. In contrast, the significant scale economies for search platforms such as Google derive
from the limited product differentiation and its ability to use large-scale datasets, which is important fc
prediction and results in lower quality adjusted costs.

platform or from a platform operating in multiple markets. Economies of scope reflect the cost efficiencies that a digital platform operator achieves through combining technical expertise, customer and supplier management, and perhaps most critically user data across platforms they own and operate.[74] In particular, large multi-platform operators can pool and aggregate the data they collect across multiple platforms to improve their understanding of user behaviour and preferences, which in turn can be used to offer more targeted advertising.[75] For example, Facebook experiences economies of scope by allowing Instagram to use Facebook's advertising infrastructure;[76] Amazon's economies of scope arise through its ability to allow customers to find hundreds of millions of products on its websites in addition to a host of other services;[77] while Google's economies of scope can arise from the collection of data about user behaviour across its various platforms (Google Search, YouTube, Google Maps, Gmail and Google Shopping).[78]

While there appears to be a consensus that some digital platforms benefit from economies of scale and scope, whether these characteristics necessitate a regulatory response (and what that response should be) is subject to less agreement. As described in Chapter 2, the two main efficiency rationales for regulation in industries that display economies of scale and scope are to restrict or prevent entry (to reduce the potential inefficient duplication of costs and prevent 'cream-skimming') and to impose price regulation to ensure that firms set efficient prices that maximise economic welfare. Applying these rationales to large digital platforms, it is not obvious that there is a need for entry regulations for either of these reasons.

Regulation to Promote Entry and Dynamic Efficiency

In terms of entry regulation, most digital platforms operate in a competitive space where more than one digital platform operator can be sustained. For example, in many parts of the world, there are competing ride-sharing and accommodation platforms, instant messaging platforms, online marketplaces and other platforms that compete with one another. This suggests that the characteristics of these settings are not those where the economies of scale and scope naturally lead to a single provider.[79] For larger digital platforms, such as Facebook, Amazon or Google, where extreme economies of scale and scope might naturally lead to a single digital platform operator in a market, the main regulatory policy concern is therefore *not to restrict* entry and thus harness the efficiency benefits of a single provider by avoiding inefficient duplication or avoiding cream-skimming. Rather,

---

[74] See Furman, Coyle, Fletcher, *et al.* (2019).

[75] The Stigler Center (2019) notes: 'Firms can apply machine learning to extensive datasets to improve their products and expand their activities into new areas. Because machine learning yields better insights when it is trained on larger datasets, firms with access to large amounts of data can raise the quality of their services in ways that smaller firms cannot.' Parker, Petropoulos and Van Alstyne (2021) discuss data-driven economies of scope and how this allows platforms to expand horizontally and vertically. They also discuss how artificial intelligence and machine learning have led to the development of revolutionary techniques that treat data as a valuable asset.

[76] CMA (2020).

[77] OECD (2019a).

[78] ACCC (2019).

[79] It is perhaps for this reason that Hovenkamp (2021a) argues that 'few platforms are natural monopolies'.

the main rationale for regulation of these large digital platforms is to take measures that lower entry barriers for competing digital platforms, and thus *promote* or facilitate entry.

Implicit in this view is the assumption that there are substantial dynamic efficiency gains to be had from facilitating competition between digital platforms, and that regulation should not seek to entrench the market positions of these large providers by restricting entry. In fact, it should be doing the opposite: reducing barriers to make entry easier which can allow a competing platform to displace the position of the dominant operator. In other words, while it may be appropriate for there to be entry restrictions for activities like water transportation networks to reflect the fact that there is expected to be limited technological innovation and that introducing competition might only result in inefficient duplication and cream-skimming, the same logic does not hold for digital platforms. In these industries, the view is that there is substantial dynamic benefits to be had by entry from new providers that offer new technologies with different cost profiles who can compete with, and potentially displace, existing providers.

Regulation of Prices

In terms of price regulation, the economies of scale and scope of some digital platforms that have led to a single operator may, on the face of it, require some form of price regulation to ensure the digital platform operator sets efficient prices that maximise economic welfare. However, for the reasons discussed above, applying price regulation to achieve efficient prices in multi-sided markets is complicated by the fact that digital platforms set multiple 'prices' to different user groups. The price structures involve some users paying zero or a price less than the marginal cost they impose, while others pay substantially more than the marginal cost of serving them. As discussed in earlier chapters, this type of differential price structure can be efficient in that it allows the platform operator to set prices that get all sides to participate.[80] That said, in principle, some form of regulation of price *structures* (rather than price *levels*) might be needed if a single provider over-recovers across different sides of the market,[81] or where one set of users is cross-subsidising the other side of the market in an inefficient way.[82]

However, in practice, applying price regulation to digital platforms is likely to raise complex questions not only about the relative costs of servicing different user groups but also about the relative surplus (benefits) they obtain from using the platform. Consideration will also need to be given to how price regulation will change price structures, and whether it will lead to a rebalancing of charges (resulting perhaps in some previously free service becoming subscription) or impact on the service quality of other platforms users (e.g. will regulating advertising revenues reduce the amount of investment in research to improve

---

[80] See the discussion in Chapter 6. In this case, it arises if the operator can price-discriminate among different users and set prices for each group which reflect their willingness to pay. Similarly, Varian, Farrell and Shapiro (2004) argue that, under certain conditions, competition to acquire a price-discriminating monopoly can dissipate all rents. That is, if consumers receive heavy discounts in the competition phase, then the gain in surplus they receive may offset, to some degree, the losses incurred in the monopoly phase.

[81] For example, if the overall revenues (or price levels) earned by the operator are substantially greater than the costs incurred on the different sides (e.g. it is earning monopoly rents across users as a whole).

[82] See the discussion of the motivations for card interchange fee regulation in Chapter 12.

algorithms, which in turn reduces the quality that searchers receive). It is perhaps for this reason that some jurisdictions – such as Australia, Japan and the UK – have focused on negotiated agreements being reached between designated platform operators and their users (particularly content publishers such as newspapers) over the price terms they receive. However, as discussed in Chapter 12, price regulation of two-sided markets is not unknown and has been introduced for debit and credit card systems in a number of jurisdictions.

More generally, regulation of digital platforms on efficiency grounds will need to account for the fact that the strong economies of scale and scope exhibited by large digital platforms, even when they result in a single provider, can benefit consumers if lower average costs flow through into prices (or allow for zero prices or subsidies for some users).[83] Consumers can also potentially benefit from economies of scope and scale where platforms combine data and operations across multiple platforms to reduce costs and provide other benefits to the consumer.[84]

3.2.2 Network Effects as a Rationale for Regulation

While the presence of economies of scale and scope, which might lead naturally to a single dominant platform operator, provides one efficiency-based rationale for regulation of some larger digital platforms, a complementary rationale stems from the presence of strong network effects.[85] As described above, direct and indirect network effects are key characteristics of digital platforms, which can give rise to positive feedback loops: the more users a platform can attract on both sides of the market, the more attractive that platform will be to other users. Once a 'critical mass' of the right type of users is achieved, a positive feedback effect ensues. For example, the attractiveness of a social media platform is related to the number of other subscribers of that network that someone can connect with (direct network effect),[86] and this large user base also makes that platform more attractive to developers, content providers and advertisers (indirect network effect).[87] Over time, improvements to the amount of content, and other developments and enhancements, can further increase the attractiveness of the platform to users on all sides,

---

[83] Furman, Coyle, Fletcher, *et al.* (2019) observe that 'a large part of the reason for the emergence of one or a small number of dominant firms is that it is more efficient and thus better for consumers or businesses'. Similarly, Varian, Farrell and Shapiro (2004) also note that the concentrated industries which naturally emerge from supply-side economies of scale may not be as bad for consumers as is often thought and that price discipline still asserts itself through: competition to acquire monopoly; reductions in fixed costs (especially the costs of information technology (IT)), which lead to more entry; competition with previous technology of the operator; and pressure from complementors.

[84] The OECD (2019a) notes: 'When one company owns two or more online platforms and they interoperate, economies of scope may be created that can boost consumer welfare by increasing value and convenience. For example, when eBay owned the payments platform PayPal, eBay customers benefited from the integration and ease of use that PayPal offered.' Similarly, the Stigler Center (2019) notes that the combination of 'mapping software in a platform that already offers email, for example, allows that platform to offer a higher quality restaurant recommendation product'.

[85] Evans and Schmalensee (2017/18) note that indirect network effects could result in some categories of online platforms being natural monopolies with high barriers to entry.

[86] As the Stigler Center (2019) notes: 'No one wants to be on their own social media site.'

[87] See CMA (2020) and ACCC (2019). Bundeskartellamt (2017) observes that 'from the users' perspective, decisive criteria for the choice of a social network are its size and the possibility to find the persons they want to be in contact with on it (so-called "identity-based network effects")'.

creating a positive spiral.[88] In short, strong positive network effects can naturally lead t
market concentration, and in some cases to the market 'tipping' in favour of one domir
ant platform which then becomes entrenched.[89]

As discussed in Chapter 2, in traditional network industries, economic regulation
sometimes used to harness positive network externalities by restricting entry (allowing
single firm to internalise the benefits associated with a larger network using a commo
technology) or through price regulation where the prices charged for network use (or t
specific categories of user) are adjusted from the underlying cost to account for the ber
efits associated with network growth and a larger network.[90] However, these rationale
for entry and price regulation do not tend to feature in discussions about regulation c
some digital platforms which already display strong network effects.[91] Rather, the argu
ment for regulation is that the existence of such strong network effects can lead to use
effectively being 'locked in' to a particular platform. For example, users may not want t
leave a specific social media or instant messaging platform because they will lose all c
their contacts, which places the platform in a powerful position. The reason users becom
locked in to the dominant platform is not because of any contractual obligations or eve
high search costs – switching is often said to be only 'a click away' for most digital pla
forms – but because of the difficulties of coordinating the migration of contacts to a ne
competing platform.[92]

Network effects can benefit users by promoting intensive competition among platform
to first build a critical mass,[93] and, once established, yield (static) efficiency benefits b

[88] Varian, Farrell and Shapiro (2004) note more generally that 'if the market can get above this critical
mass, the positive feedback kicks in and the product zooms off to success'.

[89] See Stigler Center (2019). In contrast, Weyl and White (2014) argue that the conventional wisdom that
network effects can cause a dominant firm to become inefficiently entrenched is misleading if firms
adopt realistically sophisticated strategies.

[90] Here it is important to recall the distinction between network externalities and network effects, the form
being defined as a type of network effect that has not been internalised. As discussed in Chapter 2, the
argument for regulation here is that a single supplier is the most efficient structure if it can capture
(internalise) the efficiencies of a demand-side natural monopoly (and there are no diseconomies of scal
in production, and users do not have heterogeneous tastes).

[91] A notable exception is Weyl and White (2014), who argue that entry into platform markets can lead to
excessive fragmentation similar to what is seen in other industries with economies of scale, and as such
can be inefficient and harmful to welfare. While they do not advocate entry restrictions, they argue tha
policy should focus on 'aiding, rather than slowing, the winner-take-all process, thereby ensuring that
dominant firms can appropriate reasonable rewards for innovation and limiting the profits that can
be achieved through fragmenting the market'. Furman, Coyle, Fletcher, et al. (2019) also observe that
the reason we may see one dominant firm may be because it is more efficient to have one firm with
substantial scope of network benefits instead of many firms. Similarly, Hovenkamp (2021a) observes
that some commentators refer to digital platforms as natural monopolies and thus *should* be served by
a single firm, and that, under this reasoning, natural monopoly status may indicate a need for utility-
style regulation. More generally, Lee (2014) finds that multiple competing platforms can be socially
inefficient.

[92] Crémer, de Montjoye and Schweitzer (2019) note that: 'Indeed, even if the users would all be better off
if they migrated *en masse* to a new platform, they would not necessarily have an individual incentive t
move to the new platform – whether or not they chose to do so depends on their expectation that other
will follow.' Biglaiser, Crémer and Veiga (2022) find, somewhat paradoxically, that the incumbency
advantage can be smaller if there is only a single migration opportunity, for the reason that multiple
opportunities to migrate reduce the cost of foregoing an early opportunity.

[93] Varian, Farrell and Shapiro (2004) refer to the use of 'penetration pricing', where a platform offers bette
terms to early adopters of the platform. The Stigler Center (2019) notes that Uber and Lyft have spent
billions of dollars subsidising riders' fares in an attempt to build their user base in ride sharing and that
one 2016 estimate suggested that Uber customers covered only about 40 per cent of the cost of their rid

allowing users to internalise the benefits of being part of a large installed user base. However, such network effects can limit the incentives for other platforms to challenge the position of the dominant platform through entry or expansion because of a fear that they will not be able to attract enough users away from the platform.[94] An inability to challenge the dominant operator reduces dynamic efficiency and can harm users if the dominant operator is able to unilaterally, and without the threat of competition, reduce quality or set adverse price terms for specific users (e.g. levy excessive charges on advertisers who need access to the platform) or introduce other non-price terms which are harmful to users (e.g. impose specific terms about the access and use of user data).[95] Moreover, if a dominant platform with a large installed user base moves into another platform area, it can benefit from leveraging its brand and large existing user base into the new platform activity and thus reduce the challenges of having to establish a new user base and exploit network effects for that activity (e.g. it can resolve the chicken and egg problem noted above).[96]

However, when thinking about network effects and the lock-in effects they can create as a rationale for regulation, a number of factors need to be considered. First, the strength of network effects differs across digital platforms. Some network effects may be exhausted relatively quickly (such as for messaging apps) and others may be constrained by the heterogeneous preferences of different users (e.g. social media platforms can tailor to different demographics: older users (Facebook), younger users (Snapchat) and professional users (LinkedIn)). Second, some caution against the simple determinism that network effects automatically lead to a 'winner takes all' dynamic, noting that digital platforms cannot just show up and expect to grow because of network effects.[97] Third, as described above, network effects can work both ways: the same factors that can lead digital platforms to experience rapid and explosive growth can also lead to rapid and explosive decline (a death spiral).[98] Some argue that this ability for markets to 'tip' rapidly can potentially sharpen the 'competition *for* the market', and in so doing make prices more efficient without the need for regulation.[99] Fourth, in many platform areas, users have

---

[94] Shapiro and Varian (1999) observe more broadly that the switching costs associated with migration to an alternative network in the presence of network externalities work in a non-linear way and that: '[C]onvincing ten people connected in a network to switch to your incompatible network is more than ten times as hard as getting one customer to switch. But you need all ten, or most of them: no one will want to be the first to give up the network externalities and risk being stranded.'

[95] This was an issue in the context of the Bundeskartellamt (2017, 2019) privacy case against Facebook.

[96] Crémer, de Montjoye and Schweitzer (2019). Katz and Shapiro (1985) discuss the importance of brand reputation in shaping consumer expectations.

[97] Evans and Schmalensee (2016) note that they cannot think of a multi-sided platform market where the first mover won it all, and that more generally: 'Multisided platforms can't come galloping out of the gates .... They have to figure out how to get all sides on board in order to create any value at all.' Cennamo and Santalo (2013) also challenge the unconditional logic of the winner-takes-all approach in platforms. Similarly, Hovenkamp (2021a) argues that: '[N]otwithstanding overwhelming evidence to the contrary, the market for digital platforms is often said to be winner-take-all. But this is rarely true.'

[98] The OECD (2019a) observes: 'Each user that leaves a platform with positive network effects makes other users more likely to leave, too. This was the case with MySpace, for example, when Facebook displaced it as the leading social media platform, as well as for Yahoo!, when Google entered internet search advertising and upended it.'

[99] Weyl and White (2014). In addition, they argue that 'platform industries with dominant firms are, in an important sense, highly competitive: even if, at most points in time, they are consolidated around a single firm, there is a constantly looming threat of displacement by a new dominant firm'.

an ability to 'multi-home', which means that they can simultaneously be part of multipl_ digital platforms. For example, many people use multiple social media platforms, or kno_ that they have a choice among competing search engines. Similarly, businesses often us_ multiple digital platforms to display their ads. In principle, this reduces the scope for user_ to be 'locked in' to a single platform, and allows users to benefit from the use of multipl_ platforms. Fifth, some argue that network effects, no matter how strong, can never o_ their own create enduring lock-in and that potential competitor platforms can always us_ certain strategies to undercut the incumbent operator (for example, by using dynami_ subsidisation strategies to address user coordination problems and attract users to it_ platform which are recouped after they reach a critical mass).[100] Finally, any regulation t_ reduce entry barriers and promote entry needs to achieve a balance between the risks _ users being 'locked in' to a particular provider and the static efficiency benefits that com_ from being able to access a large user base on a common platform (i.e. internalising th_ network effect). For this reason, some argue that efforts to promote entry should focus o_ competition *for* the market, rather than competition *in* the market.

Ultimately, the efficiency rationales for the regulation of some digital platforms, in jur_ isdictions where this is being considered, rest on the combination of strong economies _ scale and scope, and network effects. These characteristics are seen to be complementar_ and self-reinforcing: increasing returns to scale (economies of scale and scope) on th_ supply side lead to lower average unit costs per user,[101] which allows larger platforms t_ increase quality and potentially lower prices, leading to a bigger user base. This larg_ user base will, in turn, make the platform even more attractive to more users, leading t_ positive demand-side scale feedback effects (direct and indirect network effects).[102] Whil_ these potential outcomes (lower prices, higher quality) might be considered beneficial t_ users and efficient in a static sense, there remain concerns about dynamic efficiency. I_ particular, there is a concern that these characteristics can lead to insurmountable barrier_ to entry and expansion, inhibiting new platforms, including those with superior technol_ ogy, from entering and challenging an incumbent platform.[103]

13.2.3 Regulation to Control Monopoly Power

As discussed in Chapter 2, an alternative rationale for regulation in some industries i_ that there is only a single supplier of a service, and therefore the operator may have a_ incentive, and the ability, to behave in ways that exploit its position of power. A dom_ inant or monopoly provider might, for example, set prices considerably above underly_ ing costs, degrade quality, or be insufficiently responsive to cost and other productio_

---

[100] See Weyl and White (2014).
[101] This includes high and increasing returns to data which allow platforms to improve their algorithms an_ products.
[102] OECD (2019a) notes: 'when some or all of these traits are present in combination, they can magnify eac_ other and lead to explosive growth'.
[103] The UK regulator (CMA, 2020) notes that: 'Both Google and Facebook grew by offering better products than their rivals. However, they are now protected by such strong incumbency advantages – including network effects, economies of scale and unmatchable access to user data – that potential rivals can no longer compete on equal terms.'

efficiencies.[104] As applied to digital platforms, this rationale for regulation is not focused on ensuring such platforms behave in ways that are efficient and maximise social welfare, but on whether the *conduct* of the platform operators harms users, either through charging prices which deviate unduly from the underlying costs of the activity, degrading quality or impeding innovation, etc.[105] This section sets out the concerns that have been raised about the market power of some digital platforms and motivated calls for some form of economic regulation.[106]

Regulation to Control Digital Platforms from Using Market Power in an Exploitative Way

One set of market power concerns stems directly from the dominant, and seemingly entrenched, positions of some leading digital platforms. Most obviously, dominant platforms in such a position might charge high and potentially exploitative prices to some user groups.[107] For example, competition authorities in the UK and Australia have recently drawn attention to the substantial advertising revenues that some digital platforms (notably Google and Facebook) are deriving from one set of users.[108] Dominant platforms can also use their position to charge prices below competitive levels to other user groups, such as providers of content.[109] As discussed earlier, this is a more complex scenario to support regulation as, in the context of multi-sided platforms, an optimal pricing structure might involve setting prices for some user types above cost, while subsidising another user type by setting prices at zero or below marginal cost.[110]

---

[104] The term 'dominance' is used here broadly to capture platforms with substantial or significant market power, and does not reflect any specific meaning that might be ascribed to it under some competition laws.

[105] Caffarra (2019) sets out various examples of exploitative conduct in digital platform markets including: exploitation in terms of who can access data without user consent or understanding; misinformation; conduct that distorts/restricts the information available to consumers when choosing between products; and other 'coercive' practices.

[106] In the USA, the Biden Administration (White House, 2021) has recently argued a need for a new approach to controlling platforms on the basis that: '[A] small number of dominant Internet platforms use their power to exclude market entrants, to extract monopoly profits, and to gather intimate personal information that they can exploit for their own advantage. Too many small businesses across the economy depend on those platforms and a few online marketplaces for their survival.'

[107] Tirole (2020) argues that the core question is whether platforms enjoy 'supranormal profits' or '*ex ante* rents', insofar as profits are not aligned with investment costs. However, he notes that any such assessment of supranormal returns will require data not only on current profits, but also on the losses it may have incurred during its 'shakeout period' before it became dominant, as well as the probability of emerging as the winner of the contest to become dominant.

[108] See CMA (2020) and ACCC (2019). Prat and Valletti (2021) claim that Google and Facebook command at least 60 per cent of the online advertising spend market in the USA (and over 80 per cent in the UK). They focus on the impacts of such concentration in advertising-funded digital platforms, noting that they can create an 'attention bottleneck'. Varian (2021) claims that in 2018 for every $1 of ad revenue earned on Google, 70.8 cents went to the content provider and 29.2 cents went to Google.

[109] The issue of whether news media organisations and other publishers are compensated fairly for their content is one which has arisen in Australia, France and the UK. More generally, on pricing below competitive levels for content, see Stigler Center (2019) and Stucke and Ezrachi (2017). Bourreau and Gaudin (2022) find that streaming platforms can increase profit by reducing the royalty rate it pays to content providers through the use of a recommendation system that is strategically biased in favour of the cheaper content.

[110] See Wright (2004) for a more general discussion of using prices to assess market power in two-sided markets. The Stigler Center (2019) suggests that, even when one set of users do not pay for a service, the focus should be on quality-adjusted prices which increase if the price stays constant (e.g. is free) but quality deteriorates.

Dominant or monopoly platforms can also potentially exploit their position in non-price ways, such as by reducing quality of service. Here, too, quality rationales for regulation need to be approached with care, as 'quality' can be multi-dimensional in the context of digital platforms. In particular, while users might experience high quality on some dimensions of service (e.g. in terms of speed and relevance of responses to search queries, an ability to access a large number of sellers and buyers or to connect and share content with friends and family around the world), this may nevertheless involve them having to agree to certain terms and conditions that are set by a dominant platform operator. For example, platforms might unilaterally impose conditions about the collection, use and sharing of user personal data,[111] or impose onerous conditions on sellers using an online marketplace or accommodation-sharing platform.[112] Where there are limited or no alternatives to the dominant platform, users may feel the terms they are offered are 'take it or leave it' or are 'unfair'.[113] Some argue that quality can also be degraded, and users harmed, if digital platforms use psychological techniques to manipulate users to spend more time on the platform, which, in turn, makes that platform more attractive to advertisers.[114]

Regulation to Control Digital Platforms from Using Market Power in an Exclusionary Way

In addition to exploiting users through higher prices and/or lower quality, a dominant platform could use its position in an exclusionary way by controlling who accesses the platform, and how they access it.[115] The ability to exclude certain users can be harmful because of a significant degree of dependence of both business users and end-users on the services provided by some large digital platforms, which can create a 'mandatory bottleneck' or 'gatekeeper' role for the platform. In these circumstances, a dominant platform could engage in exclusive dealing (e.g. require that sellers or advertisers not use

---

[111] The German Cartel Office has raised proceedings against Facebook for making conditional the requirement that user data can be combined across different platforms (such as WhatsApp and Instagram); see Bundeskartellamt (2019). More recently, WhatsApp has required users to sign up to new privacy terms or lose access. In some cases, users can opt out of such terms, but this can result in reduction in the quality or functionality that users can access.

[112] Such as 'most favoured nation' clauses.

[113] Stucke and Ezrachi (2017) refer to the US case against Amazon where the Authors Guild suggested that: 'Amazon often removed the online "buy" buttons for titles from publishers that did not agree to Amazon's contract terms. Others complained about Amazon's exclusive distribution agreements with authors.' The Stigler Center (2019) notes more generally that: 'Merchants or vendors can find themselves banned, demoted in search results, or required to bear higher costs without the ability to move to a competing platform because either there is none or because the customers single-home ... and cannot be reached elsewhere.' See also Khan (2017).

[114] The Stigler Center (2019) notes: '[S]ome platforms have deliberately incorporated features that feed human "reward" centers into their products to induce users to give more and more of their time – and data – to the platform. These tools are designed for scale – they become even more valuable the more traffic they carry and the more users they garner – and hence the competition among producers has been described as a competition for eyeballs.'

[115] The Stigler Center (2019) notes: 'Amazon and Facebook regularly make decisions over which app or vendor is able to sell or is denied access to their stores and customers. Platforms often have a financial incentive to steer customers to particularly profitable products and can use the power of defaults and ordering to accomplish that effectively.' Similarly, Crémer, de Montjoye and Schweitzer (2019) note that platforms engage in rule setting and market design which determines the way in which competition takes place.

rival platforms) or use 'most favoured nation' or parity clauses which restrict the ability of sellers to offer lower prices through rival supply channels. A dominant platform could also distort competition in related markets (e.g. a specific product market) by establishing rules that can lead to the exclusion of certain users from accessing the platform (e.g. foreclosure).[116]

Where a dominant platform operator is vertically integrated – such that it competes alongside other users on its own platform – there is the familiar risk of non-equivalence and the ability to favour their own products.[117] For example, a dominant platform may engage in 'self-preferencing' or 'own-content bias' where it gives preferential treatment to its own products or services when they compete with products and services provided by other entities using the platform.[118] The dominant operator can also use data obtained in operating the platform to favour its own subsidiary operation when competing against rivals who use the platform.[119]

The expansion of some of the larger digital platform operators (such as Alphabet, Meta, Amazon) across multiple platform areas to become 'superplatforms' has raised additional concerns about concentration, leveraging and foreclosure.[120] The specific concern is that multi-platform conglomerates that compete across several product and service markets can strategically cross-leverage their position in adjacent or downstream markets to block entry by more focused or emerging rivals by using their superior access to data to gain insights on, and respond to, competitive threats.[121] Once again, data obtained by operating across multiple areas can be used to further entrench the position of the operator in the market in

---

[116] Dzieza (2018) describes the various ways in which rival sellers have used Amazon's own rules to seek to get competitors suspended from Amazon Marketplace. This includes buying fake five-star reviews for their competitors, and defacing a rival's listing.

[117] Zhu (2019) gives the extreme example of how, after vertically integrating into video streaming through the acquisition of a company called Periscope, Twitter then cut off access to its platform to a rival service.

[118] Cornière and Taylor (2019) and Calvano and Polo (2021) discuss this in terms of 'intermediation bias' where a platform steers customers to its own products or uses its technology to 'direct' user interactions. In 2017, Google was fined €2.42 billion in Europe for favouring its price comparison site, while the Stigler Center (2019) refers to the claim in the European Commission case against Android that independent apps that competed with Google apps were disadvantaged as a result of Google apps automatically being part of a mandatory bundle. Farronato, Fradkin and MacKay (2023) find evidence that Amazon engages in self-preferencing on its marketplace and that the prominence 'given to Amazon brands is 30 percent to 60 percent of the prominence granted to sponsored products'.

[119] Khan (2017) claims that Amazon uses its online marketplace as a 'laboratory to spot new products to sell, test sales of potential new goods' and that it 'uses sales data from outside merchants to make purchasing decisions in order to undercut them on price'. Similarly, the US House of Representatives (2020) found that 'dominant platforms have misappropriated the data of third parties that rely on their platforms, effectively collecting information from customers only to weaponize it against them as rivals'.

[120] Prat and Valletti (2021) show how, where digital platforms are concentrated, they can exploit an 'attention bottleneck' which can work to the benefit of incumbent retail producers and the detriment of entrants, and ultimately consumers (who have less product choice and higher prices).

[121] CMA (2020) records various complaints that: 'Facebook is using its position in social media to leverage into adjacent markets, or that Google is using its position in general search to undermine competition in different forms of specialised search, including online travel agents and shopping comparison services.' The Stigler Center (2019) notes that Amazon gains an advantage when it wishes to launch a store brand because it can analyse the data from its rivals to develop an entry plan against those rivals. More broadly, it notes that such foreclosure strategies can include preventing disintermediation by a partner (such as a content provider) where that partner could potentially access the platform's customers and challenge its dominant position. Similarly, Zhu (2019) notes that: '[M]any platform owners imitate complementors and enter their product spaces with similar offerings. These moves position the platform owners as direct competitors to their complementors.'

which they are dominant.[122] Additionally, some argue that the combination of big data an sophisticated algorithms which underpin digital platforms can facilitate coordination an tacit collusion among users who sell products and services on platforms.[123]

Regulation to Control Digital Platforms from Harming the Long-Term Interests of Consumer
In addition to concerns about immediate or short-term harm to users from a monopoly o dominant platform exercising its market power in terms of higher prices or lower quality many calls for policy action have been motivated by concerns that the entrenched an expanding positions of some dominant platform operators might be harmful to innov ation and the long-term interests of consumers.[124] Simply put, dominant platform oper ators might use their incumbency advantage to create entry barriers and structure th market in such a way as to stop the development of emerging competitors with bette products or technology. In other words, while platforms may have competed intensivel with other platforms before they became dominant, once they reach a dominant positio they erect barriers to make the market less contestable and reduce the scope for competi tion *for* the market to occur which could displace them from their incumbency position.[125]

Various ways have been suggested through which dominant platforms might harr innovation and the long-term interests of consumers. One way is to engage in a long-ter strategy of predation, for example, by enduring years of losses or small profits so as t structure the market in a particular way and cement their position as a dominant digit platform.[126] Another way is by raising entry barriers through increasing switching cost and 'locking in' users; in other words, making it more difficult for consumers to coord inate a shift to another platform.[127] Users can also make significant investments in som digital platforms (by curating profiles, building contacts, uploading content), and the fac

---

[122] Khan (2017) argues that: 'Amazon gleans information from these competitors as a service provider that it may use to gain a further advantage over them as rivals – enabling it to further entrench its dominar position.'

[123] See Ezrachi and Stucke (2016), OECD (2019a) and Bundeskartellamt and Autorité de la Concurrence (2019). Calvano, Calzolari, Denicolò and Pastorello (2020) find that the algorithms consistently learn to charge supra-competitive prices, without communicating with one another; Assad, Clark, Ershov and Xu (2020) examine algorithmic pricing in the German gasoline market; while Werner (2021) finds that oligopoly markets can be more prone to collusion if algorithms make pricing decisions instead of humans. Assad, Calvano, Calzolari, *et al.* (2021) present a recent survey, while the CMA (2021a) considers various other ways in which algorithms might reduce competition and harm consumers. Den Boer, Meylahn and Schinkel (2022) set out various criteria that need to be satisfied for pricing algorithms to collude, including that the algorithm must allow for supra-competitive prices to be maintained when it competes against a class of 'reasonable' alternative pricing algorithms (i.e., when a firms do not use a similar or identical algorithm).

[124] This ultimately reduces future consumer welfare by reducing product quality and variety and innovation. See Stigler Center (2019) and Khan (2017).

[125] For this reason, Furman, Coyle, Fletcher, *et al.* (2019) conclude that: 'Competition for the market canno be counted on, by itself, to solve the problems associated with market tipping and "winner-takes-most"

[126] Khan (2017) argues that Amazon has engaged in a decade-long quest to become the dominant online retailer and provider of internet infrastructure, in part through what she defines as predatory pricing practices.

[127] The Stigler Center (2019) notes that high search and switching costs, including strategies to reduce multi-homing, can be used to lock in users and reduce the ability of entrants and competitors to attract customers. Calvano and Polo (2021) discuss how consumer beliefs about the future dominance of a platform can also be important in the context of switching.

that their data is tied to a particular platform can reduce their incentives to switch.[128] Some platforms engage in so-called platform envelopment strategies where they bundle a competitive service with a core service (such as an operating system) and thus leverage their market position in the core service to attract all the customers from the competitive service.

Concerns have also arisen about so-called 'entry for buy-out' or 'killer acquisitions',[129] whereby dominant platforms target and acquire innovative start-ups with the aim of gaining access to their innovation and pre-empting future competition.[130] A final long-term concern is that some large digital platforms have an incumbency advantage over entrants because they have exclusive access to big datasets which can be used to 'train' algorithms to make predictions and to profile users.[131] In effect, the argument here is that data can be an 'essential input' or a 'bottleneck' that others need access to in order to compete successfully.[132]

Factors that Could Mitigate the Market Power Rationales for Regulation of Digital Platforms
The strength of the market power rationales for regulation described above depend on a number of factors. First is the extent of competition *in* the market, which in turn is conditioned by the intensity of *intra*-platform competition (e.g. the number of competing ride-sharing services or accommodation booking sites) and the ability of the demand side of the market to act as an effective constraint on market power. Some argue that switching costs are actually low for many digital platforms,[133] and it is easy for users to 'multi-home' across more than one digital platform with similar functionality (e.g. be connected to, and use, multiple social media platforms simultaneously).[134] However, as

---

[128] OECD (2019a). However, Varian (2021) challenges the view that the lack of portability of user data introduces a switching cost, noting that users can already use various services (such as Google Takeout) to transfer their data.

[129] A buy-out involves developing the innovation acquired, while a killer acquisition involves discontinuing the innovation rather than developing it. Frequently cited examples include Google's acquisition of YouTube, Facebook's acquisitions of Instagram and WhatsApp, and Microsoft's acquisition of GitHub. Furman, Coyle, Fletcher, *et al.* (2019) record that, over the years between 2009 and 2019, Google, Apple, Facebook, Amazon and Microsoft made over 400 acquisitions globally, and none was blocked and very few have had conditions attached to approval.

[130] See Gautier and Lamesch (2021), Affeldt and Kesler (2021), Katz (2021), Motta and Peitz (2021) and Calvano and Polo (2021). More generally, see OECD (2020b) and Cunningham, Ederer and Ma (2021).

[131] See Calvano and Polo (2021), who note that this ability depends on: data substitutability (Is it essential for an entrant?); data complementarity (Does the incumbent benefit from combining diverse data to give it an advantage?); and data returns to scale (At which point will the dataset increase prediction accuracy?).

[132] The CMA (2020) notes that some large platforms may use data protection regulations to justify restricting access to valuable data for third parties, while retaining it for use within their ecosystems, thus 'consolidating their data advantage and entrenching their market power'.

[133] Calvano and Polo (2021) note that: 'Subscribing to a service, installing an app or signing up on a website does not require [one] to invest in new equipment or sink in time to learn new skills.' Similarly, Varian (2021) notes that '[s]witching costs could *conceivably* lead to a barrier to entry for certain products and services, but this is very much dependent on the products and services involved' and that 'there are no meaningful switching costs in the search industry'.

[134] Calvano and Polo (2021) find a widespread tendency for users to use several platforms simultaneously (multi-homing) in digital markets and this allows users to try new services without losing the benefits of large established networks, and that there is often no opportunity cost to trying out new platforms as it does not require the user to give up being part of another platform. They also draw attention to the distinction between those who multi-home in terms of 'signing up' to another platform and those who use an alternative platform (multi-homing in usage).

discussed below, whether these factors operate as effective constraints in practice ca
depend on the extent to which users 'invest' in a platform and their decision-makin
biases (e.g. use of defaults).[135] The extent of competition *in* the market can also deper
on the number of competitors in a specific functional area. For example, general-purpos
search engines are argued to compete with specialist search engines for travel, shoppin,
etc.,[136] while the appeal and use of social media networks can depend on purpose ar
demographics (professional, family and friends, younger demographics).

Second, even where there is limited competition *in* the market, competition *for* the ma
ket could act as a disciplining force on the ability and incentive of some dominant digit
platforms to exercise their market power in exploitative ways. Some argue that dominar
platforms are constrained by an industry characterised by rapid innovation such th,
entry and potential competition are always 'only a click away'.[137] In particular, entran
that take advantage of the positive feedback effects of indirect network effects can gro
rapidly to displace incumbent platforms.[138] Frequently cited examples of when compet
tion *for* the market has operated on an incumbent include Facebook displacing MySpa
as the leading social media platform, and Google displacing Yahoo! in search activitie
In addition, the dominance of a platform in one functional area could be constrained t
the expansion by large or dominant platforms operating in a neighbouring function
area, or by competition between 'superplatforms' whose activities overlap.[139] In this cor
text, some argue that regulatory assumptions about the effects of acquisitions by larg
digital platforms should be approached with caution (e.g. assuming that every acquisitic
is a 'killer acquisition').[140] The extent to which 'big data' can entrench the position of a

---

[135] The OECD (2020c) notes that some digital platforms require or encourage investments by users that,
once made, are not easily transferable to other platforms (e.g. setting up and personalising an account
profile, uploading content, including photos, videos, posts, or product information and offers, and
establishing a community of friends, followers or customers on a social media platform). Similarly,
Khan (2017) notes that: 'Although competition for online services may seem to be "just one click away"
research drawing on behavioral tendencies shows that the "switching cost" of changing web services
can, in fact, be quite high.'

[136] Varian (2021) notes that users may have a preferred general search engine and switch (perhaps
temporarily) to another one when they were not satisfied with the answers from their preferred engine.
Evans and Schmalensee (2017/18) note that: 'Google is still the leading platform for conducting
searches for free, but when it comes to product searches – which is where Google makes all its money
it faces serious competition from Amazon.'

[137] As the OECD (2019a) observes: 'Consequently, becoming a leading online platform – even in a
winner-take-all market – does not come with a guarantee that the leading position will be maintained
permanently or that it is invulnerable to competition.'

[138] Evans and Schmalensee (2017/18) refer to systematic research on online platforms which 'shows
considerable churn in leadership for online platforms over periods shorter than a decade'.

[139] Varian (2021) notes that Google, Apple, Facebook, Amazon and Microsoft all have core lines of busine
but 'compete vigorously against each other in a number of other areas'. Wu (2019) argues that platform
are in the business of attracting 'attention' or 'eyeballs' and then reselling that attention to advertisers
for cash, and that on this basis all platforms who resell attention should therefore be in the same mark
regardless of their 'functional definition' (e.g. search engine, social media site).

[140] Varian (2021) notes that many acquisitions are actually motivated by the desire to acquire talent;
these are known as *acqui-hires* and are common in Silicon Valley due to the competition for skilled
employees. Gautier and Lamesch (2021) find that most of the products acquired by Google, Amazon,
Facebook, Apple and Microsoft during 2015 to 2017 were shut down post-acquisition and integrated in
their ecosystems. They conclude that these acquisitions were a substitute for in-house R&D and not kill
acquisitions. In contrast, Affeldt and Kesler (2021) focus on acquisitions of apps by Google, Amazon,
Facebook, Apple and Microsoft and find that about half of the apps acquired are discontinued. These
tend to be smaller, less frequently updated and less privacy-intrusive than apps that are continued.

incumbent dominant platform and act as a barrier to entry can also depend on various contextual factors, and may be overstated. For example, it is argued that big data is not 'inimitable nor rare', that there are many alternative data sources, and a flourishing data marketplace that entrants can access.[141]

Third, regulation premised on a market power rationale needs to take account of the fact that the *effects* of specific conduct can vary by user. For example, some users might consider a dominant platform's collection of data about their behaviour and preferences to send them highly targeted and timely advertisements as beneficial, in terms of expanding the relevance and choice of ads received. However, others may consider such targeted advertisements to be a nuisance and a breach of privacy.[142] Similarly, the effects of so-called 'intermediation bias' (where a platform seeks to steer a user in a particular direction) on consumer surplus can also depend on whether it creates conflict or congruence between a platform's revenue and user utility.[143]

Finally, when considering market power rationales for regulation of digital platforms, policy makers need to be aware of two further factors. Firstly, that most studies – including those by competition agencies – conclude that consumers have, to date, benefited substantially from the services that are provided by many digital platforms, including those which are considered to be dominant and for which regulation is being contemplated or introduced.[144] Accordingly, the benefits of any proposed regulatory measures must be balanced against potential risks, including any unintended consequences on current consumer benefits. Secondly, there is question about whether the market power of some digital platforms is best addressed through *ex ante* regulation, through *ex post* competition law or through a combination of both. As discussed in Section 13.3.1, there are differing views on this.

3.2.4 Regulation to Control the Exploitation of Behavioural Biases

A separate rationale for regulation of digital platforms is that some users may be making poor decisions or acting in ways that are not in their best interests. Regulation here is premised on reducing the incentives and ability of platform operators to actively exploit consumer decision-making biases. Recent reviews of digital platforms explicitly refer to some of the insights from behavioural economics discussed in Chapter 7 when discussing a need for regulation.[145] These reviews have identified various 'default' or systematic

---

[141] Calvano and Polo (2021), Lambrecht and Tucker (2017) and Evans and Schmalensee (2017/18).

[142] Stigler Center (2019).

[143] See De Corniere and Taylor (2019).

[144] The OECD (2019a) notes: 'Certain online platforms ... have brought powerful benefits to consumers, businesses and governments.' Furman, Coyle, Fletcher, *et al.* (2019) note that: 'The digital economy has benefited consumers by creating entirely new categories of products and services. Many of these products and services are high-quality with low prices, in many cases a monetary price of zero.' While the ACCC (2019) states that: 'Many of the services offered by digital platforms provide significant benefits to both consumers and business; as demonstrated by their widespread and frequent use.' Finally, in the USA, the Stigler Center (2019) reports that: 'Digital markets and platforms have already delivered great benefits to consumers, and the global concerns that have surfaced relating to actual or potential consumer harms may require action to ensure that the benefits are not undermined.'

[145] CMA (2020), Stigler Center (2019) and ACCC (2019).

behaviours that consumers display when using digital platforms,[146] particularly searc
and social media platforms, which may lead them not to seek out or use alternative plat
forms. In the presence of such decision-making biases, while competition may, in princi
ple, only be a 'click away', in practice, consumers may effectively 'lock themselves in' t
a default platform. This, it is argued, has obvious implications for the extent of demand
side pressure that consumers place on dominant incumbent platforms, and on the abilit
of potential competing platforms to challenge the incumbent.

While such systematic biases often reflect underlying consumer decision-making pro
cesses and contextual factors, they can also be shaped and influenced by the platform
in various ways. First, platforms can set themselves up as the default provider on certai
devices (such as phones or tablets) so consumers do not make a conscious choice of pro
vider and simply use the default presented to them. For example, Google is the defaul
search engine for almost all mobile devices in the UK.[147] Second, platforms can estab
lish various default settings that consumers must adopt to access a platform quickly (o
at all) or if they want to attain full functionality.[148] For example, users of social medi
platforms might face various default settings about what personal data is collected fror
them and how it is used. While some platforms give consumers an ability to opt out c
default privacy settings and data policies, numerous studies have shown that this ca
be time-consuming and complicated, and can exacerbate existing consumer biases (e.g
impatience).[149] Third, platforms can use recommender system algorithms to present con
sumers with personalised recommendations (e.g. what products they might like based o
past search or purchases, what songs or videos they might like to stream, etc.), whic
means that the choices that consumers face are framed in ways which encourage them t
select the recommendations of the platform.[150]

In some settings, such default strategies might be beneficial to some consumers b
working with the grain of how they make decisions and lowering the cognitive effort asso
ciated with using a digital platform (e.g. consumers might choose to automatically accep
a route on a map platform which is suggested as the fastest route). However, some digita
platforms may seek to more actively influence or exploit consumer decision-making biase
by framing choices in ways that make certain information salient,[151] exploit consumer
status quo biases, or use aggressive persuasion strategies.[152] The ability to actively explo

---

[146] The Stigler Center (2019) notes: '*Homo economicus* is hardly influenced by defaults – to a rational agen
scrolling down or unchecking a box is trivial – but real people are influenced.'

[147] CMA (2020). De Corniere and Taylor (2019) refer to claims that Google paid $300 million for the right t
be the default search engine in Mozilla Firefox and $1 billion for similar rights across Apple's suite of
products.

[148] CMA (2020) found that: 'Some platforms operate a take-it-or-leave-it model, where they do not
give their users the ability to control their data. This is particularly prevalent across most social
media platforms, including Facebook and Instagram, whose users are unable to turn off personalised
advertising while continuing to use the service.'

[149] Abrardi, Cambini and Hoernig (2021) link this to time inconsistency in that users neglect future privacy
costs when consenting to their data being collected.

[150] See Bourreau and Gaudin (2022) and Calvano and Polo (2021).

[151] The Stigler Center (2019) notes that some platforms can have total control over demand due to their
ability to control the framing of consumer choices.

[152] Stigler Center (2019).

and shape user decision making is aided by the extensive and real-time nature of the data that some large digital platforms have on consumer behaviour. Extensive real-time data about such behaviour can be analysed using machine learning techniques in ways which some argue allow some digital platforms to understand and manipulate individual preferences at a large scale.[153] In short, digital platforms can be in a position to develop a very sophisticated understanding of consumer behaviour, which it can use to its advantage.

While some digital platforms may have the *ability* to work with, or actively exploit, consumer decision-making biases, a separate question is whether they have an *incentive* to do so. For digital platforms that charge users directly and use differential prices, there may be incentives to frame choices in ways which lead one group of users to consume the services of another group of users where they obtain the greatest margin.[154] For vertically integrated digital platforms, the incentives can be to generate more sales of specific products by steering users towards a specific product or service.[155]

For digital platforms which are 'free' to consumers, the incentives to exploit or manipulate consumer biases are less immediately obvious but can arise because of the high markups that such platforms earn from advertising revenues. In other words, the incentives may be to make consumers spend as much time on the platform as possible; to grab their attention as long as they can. This can yield two benefits to the operator. First, the more time a user spends on a platform, the more data that the platform operator collects and the better the understanding it will have about that consumer's tastes and preferences, which in turn allows them to sell more targeted ads to that consumer. Second, the more time that a consumer spends on a platform, the greater the amount of time that advertisers have to attract the user towards their products. Some argue that this creates incentives for some digital platforms to present addictive content, which is of lower quality (generates outrage rather than promotes thought), and therefore is ultimately harmful to consumers.[156]

Digital platforms that attempt to actively exploit consumer decision-making biases can also produce adverse distributional outcomes. For example, some research suggests that so-called 'dark patterns' – user interfaces that manipulate users into taking actions that do not accord with their preferences or expectations, or make it difficult for them to express their actual preferences – mostly impact poor and uneducated consumers.[157]

---

[153] The Stigler Center (2019) notes that 'digital businesses can learn by using high-dimensional, large datasets to explore every nook and cranny of consumers' many behavioral shortcomings and biases in real time' and that '[a] platform can analyze a user's data in real time to determine when she is in an emotional "hot state" and offer a good that the user would not purchase when her self-control was higher'.

[154] For example, an accommodation platform might seek to steer consumers towards those hotels or properties which will pay them the highest commission for every booking.

[155] De Corniere and Taylor (2019) refer to a statement in *Forbes* magazine that: 'Eighty-five percent of Amazon customers select the recommended Amazon product when voice shopping.'

[156] The Stigler Center (2019) notes that 'advertising-supported digital businesses can use consumer biases to hold people's attention in ways that ultimately harm them' and that '[t]he platform is essentially degrading the quality of the content offered in a way that present-biased human beings find engaging'. However, it also notes that: '[T]his content is not chosen by human curators at the platform. Rather, the algorithm learns what content people will click on, and what content will cause them to stay on the platform longer, through many millions of small experiments.' See also Ichihashi and Kim (2022).

[157] Luguri and Strahilevitz (2021) and OECD (2022). However, Zac, Huang, von Moltke, Decker and Ezrachi (2023) find evidence that individuals across all groups are vulnerable to dark patterns, with only weak evidence that user vulnerability is materially affected by income, education or age.

In sum, the rationale for regulation based on exploitation of consumer decision-makin[g] biases is related to, but separate from, the rationale for regulation to address concern[s] about market power discussed above. While digital platforms with market power ma[y] have a greater ability to use aggressive exploitation and persuasion strategies to main[-] tain their position, the practices are not limited solely to these large or dominant digit[al] platforms. As such, greater competition between digital platforms will not of itself be ab[le] to address the incentives of digital platforms to exploit behavioural biases.[158] Here, th[e] policy choice is therefore not between *ex ante* economic regulation and *ex post* compet[i-] tion law, as it is with market power, but rather between *ex ante* regulation and consum[er] protection laws. As discussed in Chapter 7, in other regulated sectors it is not uncomm[on] for consumer protection aspects to have become part of wider economic regulation.

13.2.5 Other Rationales for Regulation of Digital Platforms

Debates about the need for, and nature of, regulation of digital platforms often exten[d] beyond the traditional rationales set out above to capture wider economic and soci[al] considerations. One general concern is that there is simply a lack of transparency [or] understanding about how some of these large digital platforms operate.[159] This opaci[ty] makes it difficult to understand for example: how charges are determined for differe[nt] users (e.g. the mark-ups that apply to advertisers);[160] how certain results are matched wi[th] one another (e.g. how an algorithm determines which search results appear on the fir[st] page or which products to recommend);[161] and whether an integrated platform operator [is] self-preferencing or favouring its own related operations.[162]

Another concern motivating the regulation of digital platforms relates to data prote[c-] tion and privacy. In a nutshell, the concern is that digital platforms collect too much pe[r-] sonal data, which reduces the privacy of individuals and can lead them to be constant[ly] surveilled.[163] Some digital platforms have in the past overridden users' privacy settings,[164]

---

[158] Stigler Center (2019). This picks up on a more general theme about industry-wide exploitation discusse[d] in Chapter 7.

[159] The CMA (2020) notes that one consequence of this reliance on 'black box' decision making is that market participants find it difficult to understand or challenge how decisions are made and to exercise choice effectively.

[160] Furman, Coyle, Fletcher, *et al.* (2019) observe that the lack of transparency in the market suggests that there is at least scope for advertisers and publishers to be getting an unfair deal. Similarly, the Stigler Center (2019) notes: 'One of the characteristics of the digital advertising environment is its opacity: major platforms are able to leave bidders and publishers in the dark with respect to the true success, costs, and profits from placement of advertising.' The CMA (2020) found that platforms have considerable discretion over a wide variety of parameters that affect the prices advertisers pay, includi[ng] how relevance is assessed and the level of reserve prices.

[161] The CMA (2020) recorded concerns by several newspapers about the impact of algorithms employed b[y] Google and Facebook on traffic to their sites: 'unexpected changes to the Google Search and Facebook News Feed algorithms that have resulted in dramatic reductions in traffic to certain newspapers overnight.'

[162] The CMA (2020) concludes that: '[R]eliance on opaque algorithms poses a fundamental challenge to traditional notions of how markets work. Since they are unable to scrutinise the basis on which decisions are made, platforms' users are often required to accept outcomes on trust.'

[163] Zuboff (2019). A particular concern is that some digital platforms require consumers to agree to terms that are unclear or difficult for them to understand, and are subject to constant change.

[164] For example, the UK's House of Commons (2019) has suggested that 'Facebook was in the past willing [to] override its users' privacy settings in order to transfer data to some app developers'.

combined data from different sources,[165] or shared personal data in ways that do not accord with the consent consumers have provided.[166] While data protection laws such as the EU's General Data Protection Regulation can, in principle, address some of the issues about user privacy, there are concerns that such rules may not be effective and may actually be used to the benefit of digital platforms and to stifle competition.[167]

A third concern motivating regulation is that the position of some digital platforms as news intermediaries is having detrimental impacts on media plurality and diversity, eroding the funding for investigative and local journalism, and leading to the spread of misinformation, conspiracy theories and 'fake news', which has wider social and political implications.[168] A related concern is that some digital platforms have insufficient incentives to control harmful content online, and that some platforms may actually view controversial content as a way to attract users and encourage them to spend more time on a platform. This brings up a further argument for regulation, already noted above, which is that some digital platforms, which are funded by advertising revenue, may have strong incentives to make users 'addicted' to their platform, with detrimental effects on individual well-being.[169] A final more general concern motivating the call for regulation of some large digital platforms is that they are now just 'too big and powerful' and that such excessive concentration of economic and political power provides them with an undue ability to shape and influence events.[170] As described below, this has led to calls

---

[165] See Bundeskartellamt (2019).

[166] Prominent examples include the LinkedIn data-sharing case and the Facebook and Cambridge Analytica scandal in 2018. The Stigler Center (2019) notes: 'most consumers have little idea what is being collected about them and re-sold'. The CMA (2020) notes that: 'Google and Facebook increasingly appear to be acting in a quasi-regulatory capacity in relation to data protection considerations, setting the rules around data sharing not just within their own ecosystems, but for other market participants.'

[167] The CMA (2020) notes that: 'Our concern is that such platforms have an incentive to interpret data protection regulation in a way that entrenches their own competitive advantage.' More generally, Campbell, Goldfarb and Tucker (2015) find that consent-based privacy regulations can disproportionately benefit firms that offer a larger scope of services insofar as they impose costs on all firms, but it is small firms and new firms that are most adversely affected. Abrardi, Cambini and Hoernig (2021) find that privacy laws that give platforms flexibility to determine consent forms, such as in the EU, can be worse for users than no consent mechanism. Baye and Sappington (2020) find that the welfare effects on consumers and merchants of privacy regulations, and opt-in or opt-out privacy policies, in an online market depend on the degree of consumer sophistication, and that sophisticated consumers benefit when data is shared with third parties. In a similar vein, Liu, Sockin and Xiong (2021) find that existing data protection rules may not provide sufficient protection to vulnerable consumers because of nuanced data-sharing externalities.

[168] The Stigler Center (2019) notes that Google and Facebook are the largest media companies in history and have unprecedented influence on news production, distribution and consumption, and are also rapidly changing the incentives, behaviour and norms of all players in the news media ecosystem. More generally, they note that digital technology has become: '[A] tool used by state and private powers to manipulate and propagate disinformation and hate. It has also disrupted the business model of original news creators, disintermediated them from their consumers and created a new news ecosystem.' See also ACCC (2019).

[169] Allcott, Braghieri, Eichmeyer and Gentzkow (2020) discuss the impacts of well-being for deactivating Facebook for four weeks. Turner and Lefevre (2017) link Instagram use to eating disorders. Alter (2017) discusses addictive technology. The Stigler Center (2019) concludes that: 'Since most societies regulate addictive products – drugs, alcohol, tobacco, and gambling – to protect the consumers, it is time we discuss how to regulate DPs [digital platforms] with the same goal in mind.'

[170] See Khan (2017) and Cicilline and Buck (2021). However, Varian (2021) argues that there have been several instances of similarly large firms and industries over time but that 'changes in technology and management missteps dramatically altered their fortunes'. Baye and Prince (2020) explore different dimensions of this 'bigness' argument.

that regulation should focus on the structural separation of some large platforms, such as Amazon, Facebook and Google.

13.3   APPROACH TO REGULATION OF DIGITAL PLATFORMS

In contrast to most of the industries described in this book, where there is typically long-established approach to regulation, the approach to regulating large digital platforms is still under development in many parts of the world. As this book is prepared, there are six bills before the US Congress dealing with different aspects of regulation; the Digital Markets Act and Digital Services Act have been going through the legislative process in the EU; and the UK is also looking to introduce new legislation for digital markets. As such the discussion in this section should be treated with caution, as it is likely that some regulatory policies described below may be amended, while others may be dropped entirely.

The discussion is organised under four headings. Section 13.3.1 considers whether large digital platforms should be subject to *ex ante* regulation or *ex post* competition law, while Section 13.3.2 discusses the potential scope of any *ex ante* regulatory measures. Section 13.3.3 describes the new types of institutions that are being developed to implement regulation. Finally, Section 13.3.4 discusses some of the policies that are being considered or in some cases actively implemented, to address concerns about some digital platforms.

13.3.1   *Ex Ante* or *Ex Post* Approaches to Controlling Digital Platform Market Power

In Chapter 3 we discussed two possible methods for controlling and influencing the conduct of firms with market power. We noted that standard forms of economic regulation anticipate the potential adverse effects of particular conduct by firms with market power and seek to limit the ability of firms to engage in that conduct, and cause harm, before it occurs (i.e. *ex ante*). An alternative approach does not impose any *ex ante* restrictions on price or conduct, but subjects firms with market power to the threat of *ex post* intervention if their conduct is assessed as inconsistent with desirable policy objectives. This typically includes subjecting firms to general competition (or antitrust) laws which apply across all sectors of the economy.

In the context of digital platforms, many recent reviews have considered whether existing competition law provisions are capable of addressing the unique issues arising for some digital platforms. Some advocate changes to competition law to address the potential harms associated with some large digital platforms rather than introducing *ex ante* economic regulation.[171] However, others argue that competition law alone

---

[171] Crémer, de Montjoye and Schweitzer (2019), for example, note that: '[I]n this very fast moving and diversified market, we believe that regulation organising the whole sector – akin to the type of regulation used for traditional utilities – is inappropriate. Rather, we must adapt the tools of competition policy to this new environment.' Similarly, Hovenkamp (2021a) argues that: 'Few platforms are natural monopolies. If the market contains room for competition among multiple incumbent firms, regulation is usually a poor alternative.' And, as such: '[T]he less intrusive and more individualized approach of the antitrust laws is better for consumers, input suppliers, and most other affected interest groups than broad-brush regulation. It will be less likely to reduce product or service quality, limit innovation, or reduce output.'

inadequate and that some digital platforms should be treated as if they are utilities and subject to additional *ex ante* regulation by a specialist regulatory body.[172] Among the arguments for why competition law alone may be insufficient to constrain market power is that digital platforms (of all sizes) can have 'intermediation power' (i.e. they can become an unavoidable trading partner for those users of that platform), while larger digital platforms where consumers primarily single-home have 'bottleneck power' which allows them to act as 'gatekeepers' between business users and their prospective customers.[173]

More generally, there is a view that markets dominated by large digital platforms will not 'self-correct' because the combination of economies of scale and scope, networks effects and low marginal costs makes entry barriers just too high for potential competitors.[174] In other words, similar to the other core network service providers described in this book, it is argued that large digital platforms occupy an entrenched position that affords them enduring market power and makes others in the supply chain dependent on access to these platforms.[175]

However, it is widely acknowledged, including by those who advocate for the introduction of *ex ante* regulation, that there are limitations of economic regulation particularly in fast-moving contexts.[176] Accordingly, many of the regulatory proposals discussed below do not focus on controlling the market power of platforms through setting prices or access terms on an enduring basis (as for traditional public utilities),[177] but rather focus on addressing specific conduct, or other impediments, that may raise entry barriers and restrict the potential for the incumbent digital platform to be challenged in the future.[178]

---

[172] See Khan (2017) and Rahman (2018). In the USA, the Stigler Center (2019) concluded that 'we believe the establishment of a sectoral regulator should be seriously considered'. Wheeler, Verveer and Kimmelman (2020) also advocate for a new specialist regulator in the USA. In the UK, the CMA (2020) notes: '[W]e believe that there is a compelling case for the development of a pro-competition ex ante regulatory regime, to oversee the activities of online platforms funded by digital advertising.'

[173] See Furman, Coyle, Fletcher, *et al.* (2019), Stigler Center (2019) and EC (2020g).

[174] Stigler Center (2019).

[175] Several commentators refer to access to some digital platforms as indispensable and an essential facility.

[176] See Rogerson and Shelanski (2020) and Tardiff (2021). Furman, Coyle, Fletcher, *et al.* (2019) note that regulators can be subject to behavioural biases and be captured by the companies they are regulating. Similarly, Hovenkamp (2021a) notes that: 'Regulation also entrenches existing technologies and, in doing so, bolsters existing incumbents and that "regulation usually is not the best answer". Cusumano, Gawer and Yoffie (2021) argue that 'a combination of self-regulation and credible threats of government regulation may yield the best results'.

[177] Tirole (2020) observes that rate of return and incentive regulation will be hard to apply in the tech sector for a number of reasons: first, because such firms are not followed by the regulator over their life cycle, it is difficult to measure the 'investment cost' (i.e. like the regulated asset base or rate base for public utilities) on which a 'reasonable rate of return' could be earned; second, any 'investment cost' (or rate base) would need to factor in an (unobserved) probability of success; and third, because, unlike traditional network industries, tech giants are global firms, and they may need to be overseen by a supranational regulator (or require high levels of international coordination).

[178] Furman, Coyle, Fletcher, *et al.* (2019) distinguish their proposed approach from the regulation of traditional utilities in that they advocate that the purpose of regulation is to 'provide every chance for competition to succeed in digital markets, tackling the factors that lead to winner-takes-most outcomes and to that position becoming entrenched'.

13.3.2 Scope of Economic Regulation

In jurisdictions where some form of *ex ante* regulation of digital platforms is being cor
templated, an initial question is this: Which platforms should be subject to regulatior
should it be all digital platforms or only selected platforms?

In the UK, regulation will apply to platforms, including those funded by digital adver
tising, which hold strategic market status (SMS), which has been defined as having 'sut
stantial and entrenched market power in at least one activity, providing it with a strateg
position'.[179] SMS will apply to the whole corporate entity, even when it has such a positio
in only one activity, and designation will apply for a period of five years. In determinin
which entities should be designated, it has been suggested that a test similar to the signif
cant market power test in the telecommunications industry be adopted (see Chapter 11),[
and that SMS be based on a finding of both substantial *and* entrenched market pow
(i.e. the platform's position must be established and unlikely to change in the foreseeab
future).[181] In Japan, new regulations introduced in 2021 will apply to 'specified digit.
platform providers' (at the moment this includes Amazon, Rakuten, Yahoo, Apple ar
Google). The regulations focus on improving transparency and fairness in trading c
digital platforms, and will require specified digital platforms to disclose terms and cor
ditions.[182] In Germany, amendments to German competition law which became effectiv
in January 2021 now allow the competition authority (the Bundeskartellamt) to plac
certain restrictions on platforms designated as having 'paramount cross-market signif
cance'.[183] Such an assessment will be determined for a period of five years and based o
whether the platform is dominant on one or several markets; its access to resources ar
financial strength; vertical integration and activities in other connected markets; and ho
important its services are in providing access to third parties in supply or sales markets a
well as its related influence on the business activities of third parties.[184] China also issue
guidelines in February 2021 which build on the existing anti-monopoly law and clari
how it will be applied to digital platforms. The scope of the Chinese guidelines is broa
and covers not only large digital platforms, but also smaller platform operators and bus
ness operators who utilise platforms.

In the EU, the Digital Markets Act introduces a new *ex ante* regulatory regime that w
apply to certain 'core platform services'[185] supplied by so-called 'gatekeepers'. A platfor

---

[179] UK Government (2021). Furman, Coyle, Fletcher, *et al.* (2019) had previously defined SMS as a positior
of 'enduring market power over a strategic bottleneck market'.

[180] Furman, Coyle, Fletcher, *et al.* (2019).

[181] It is suggested that designation could be based on factors such as: a firm's revenue; the characteristics
the activity (e.g. are there likely to be significant network effects, economies of scale and scope, and/o
high fixed entry costs); and whether a sectoral regulator is best placed to address the issue of concern.

[182] METI (2021).

[183] Franck and Peitz (2021) provide a critical review. Franck and Peitz (2023) describe the role of market
definition in the designation of Alphabet, Meta and Amazon under this law.

[184] Bundestag (2021); see also Bundeskartellamt (2021).

[185] Core platform services include: online intermediation services, online search engines, operating
systems, online social networking, video-sharing platform services, number-independent interpersona
communication services, cloud computing services, virtual assistants, web browsers and online
advertising services, including advertising intermediation services. See EU Regulation 2022/1925.

operator that supplies core platform services will be designated as a gatekeeper if it: (i) has a significant impact on the EU internal market; (ii) provides a core platform service which is an important gateway for business users to reach end-users; and (iii) enjoys an entrenched and durable position in its operations, or it is foreseeable that it will enjoy such a position in the near future.[186] Gatekeepers can also be designated through a market investigation process. Gatekeeper status is subject to a rebuttable presumption (i.e. the platform must show this is not the case) where a provider of a core platform service meets three cumulative requirements.[187] Emerging gatekeepers can also be designated where they do not yet have an entrenched and durable position, but it is foreseeable that they will enjoy such a position in the near future. Further, it is noted that a gatekeeper may not necessarily be a dominant player, and its practices may not be captured by existing competition law if there is no demonstrable effect on competition within clearly defined relevant markets. Designation as a gatekeeper will be reviewed at least every three years. Importantly, designation as a gatekeeper applies to a specific *service* and not to a provider; as such, a social media platform might be designated as a gatekeeper for that core platform service but not as a gatekeeper for other services it provides. While these rules are intended to apply only to selected large digital platforms, existing EU rules require a baseline of transparency and fairness from all providers for online intermediation services (including online search engines) where goods and services are sold to end-users.[188]

In the USA, recent studies have proposed a mix of potential regulations, some of which would apply only to those platforms that have 'bottleneck power',[189] while others would apply to all platforms (e.g. restrictions on practices that enhance behavioural mistakes).[190] While the US Congress is still debating the scope of future regulation, the bills being debated refer to such provisions applying to 'covered platforms', which are defined as online platforms which in the previous twelve months had: at least 50 million US-based monthly active users (or 100,000 US-based business users); net annual sales, or a market capitalisation, greater than $600 billion; or are a critical

---

[186] See EU Regulation 2022/1925.

[187] These are that: (a) based on certain financial and geographic metrics, that it has a significant impact in the internal market (the undertaking to which it belongs achieves an annual EEA turnover equal to or above EUR 7.5 billion in the last three financial years, or where the average market capitalisation or the equivalent fair market value of the undertaking to which it belongs amounted to at least EUR 75 billion in the last financial year, and it provides a core platform service in at least three EU Member States); (b) based on the number of active end users it serves, it is an important gateway for business to reach end-users (it has more than 45 million monthly active end-users established or located in the EU and more than 10,000 yearly active business users in the EU); and (c) based on the end-user thresholds in (b) being met for the last three financial years, it enjoys an entrenched and durable position. Even where these conditions are not satisfied, a platform can be designated as a gatekeeper in certain circumstances.

[188] See EU Regulation 2019/1150. Among other things, online intermediation service providers are required to be transparent about the grounds for restricting business users from offering the same goods and services to consumers under different conditions, when the goods and services are not provided through the intermediation service provider's platform; disclose the process used to rank contentious search results; and be transparent about any advantage given to its own goods and services over those of other business users.

[189] Bottleneck power has been defined as: 'a situation where consumers primarily single-home and rely upon a single service provider (a "bottleneck"), which makes obtaining access to those consumers for the relevant activity by other service providers prohibitively costly'. See Stigler Center (2019).

[190] See Stigler Center (2019) and US House of Representatives (2020).

trading partner for the sale or provision of any product or service offered on or directly related to the online platform. Responsibility for designation of 'covered platforms' will fall to the Federal Trade Commission or the Department of Justice and will apply for a period of ten years.[191]

13.3.3 Who Should Regulate Digital Platforms?

In Chapter 8 we described different regulatory institutions and oversight arrangements including the division of power and responsibilities between independent sectoral regulators and competition agencies. The question of which entities should regulate digital platforms – particularly whether it should be a sector-specific regulator, as in other industries, or a competition agency – is still under consideration in many jurisdictions. In Germany, the existing competition authority will be responsible for enacting the new rules introduced in the Competition Act. In the UK and Australia, a new 'Digital Markets Unit' or 'Branch' will be established within the competition regulator.[192] In Japan, a Headquarters for Digital Markets Competition has been established in the Prime Minister's Office and enforcement of new regulations will involve collaboration between the Japan Fair Trade Commission and the Ministry of Economy, Trade and Industry.[193]

In the EU, responsibility for applying the Digital Markets Act will be centralised in the European Commission and as a result some argue it will become similar to the US Federal Trade Commission in that it will exercise concurrent antitrust and regulatory powers.[194] The European Commission believes that such a centralisation at the EU level is necessary because gatekeepers typically operate across borders, often at a global scale, and also often deploy their business models globally. However, some argue that, if the Commission is to perform a regulatory function, it should be sufficiently independent from regulated platforms and also from political power.[195]

In the USA, there have been various calls for a new, separate regulator, a Digital Authority or Digital Platform Agency – styled perhaps on the Federal Communications Commission – to be created to regulate digital platforms.[196] However, the position is not yet settled, and the existing bills before Congress seem to focus on certain powers being assigned to the existing antitrust agencies such as the Federal Trade Commission or the Department of Justice.

---

[191] The Stigler Center (2019) suggested that the determination of who has bottleneck power should be made by a new Digital Authority and that the definition should be updated regularly or on an as-needed basis.

[192] However, while the UK's Digital Markets Unit is expected to have new powers under specific legislation, the ACCC's Digital Markets Branch works within the existing competition and regulatory framework.

[193] METI (2021).

[194] CERRE (2021).

[195] CERRE (2021) observes that 'this independence requirement may be in tension with the geo-political role that the Commission is increasingly eager to play'. See also Ibáñez Colomo (2021).

[196] The Stigler Center (2019) discusses the potential role for a 'Digital Authority' whose task would include overseeing any remedies introduced by an antitrust authority, and developing future regulations. It should also have the ability to determine which firms have 'bottleneck power'. Rogerson and Shelanski (2020) and Wheeler, Verveer and Kimmelman (2020) discuss alternative proposals, while Tardiff (2021) cautions against an *ex ante* regime, drawing on the experience of telecoms.

3.3.4 Specific Policies that Have Been Introduced or Proposed for Digital Platforms

The regulation of digital platforms is an area where policy is still being debated in most jurisdictions, and, as such, the specific proposed regulatory policies described below are not yet set in stone. Specific regulatory policies being considered are also being influenced by a broader political agenda; in particular, both the USA and the EU are seeking to develop the technology sector in those jurisdictions in response to concerns about the future dominance of China in that space.

Broadly speaking, proposals to regulate digital platforms are based around two changes. First, most jurisdictions are seeking to change or 'update' the way in which competition law is applied to digital platforms. While we do not consider these proposals in detail below, in brief, they include: shifting the burden of proof to the merging parties, in part, to address concerns about 'killer acquisitions';[197] changing the substantive test for blocking a merger;[198] greater use of interim measures to prevent damage to competition while a competition law investigation is ongoing; and adjusting appeals standards.

A second set of changes focus on the introduction of additional *ex ante* policies to regulate the activities and conduct of some digital platforms. While specific policies vary across jurisdictions, there is a high degree of commonality in the proposals, which include: the possibility of structural separation; regulations to require greater interoperability; non-discrimination and fairness regulations; and regulations relating to the use, combination and sharing of data. While some of these regulations could potentially apply to most digital platforms (irrespective of size or business model), others will apply only to certain large digital platforms that operate certain business models.[199] In the discussion below, the term 'designated' platforms will refer to platforms that would be classified as subject to specific regulations (such as 'gatekeepers' in the EU or 'covered platforms' in the US context).

Separation Policies

One suggested focus of regulation is to require the structural separation of designated platforms or to introduce line of business restrictions in order to address conflicts of interest.[200] This could include separating dominant platforms horizontally (so that a dominant platform would compete with a newly created provider) or vertically (where a dominant platform would no longer be able to operate in related markets, or would have to be operationally separated).[201]

Some advocate such policies on the basis that such structural regulatory policies have been used in the past in the telecommunications and railroads sectors (see discussions in

---

[197] The US House of Representatives (2020) recommends shifting presumptions for future acquisitions by the dominant platforms such that any acquisition by a dominant platform would be presumed anticompetitive. This presumption is given effect in the Bill in support of the US Platform Competition and Opportunity Act of 2021.

[198] The UK Government (2021) proposes that mergers could be blocked even if the probability of a substantial lessening of competition arising is lower than 50 per cent.

[199] Caffarra and Scott Morton (2021) emphasise the importance of tailoring regulations to specific business models.

[200] The US House of Representatives (2020) notes that structural separation would prohibit a dominant intermediary from operating in markets where it competes with firms dependent on its infrastructure, while line of business restrictions, meanwhile, generally limit the markets in which a dominant firm can engage. See also Khan (2019).

[201] See discussion in Chapter 6 on horizontal and vertical separation policies more generally.

Chapters 6 and 11) and that behavioural remedies have proven to be ineffective in digit markets.[202] However, others draw on the experience of applying such structural separatic in other sectors to argue that separation policies can be costly and difficult to implemen can impede rather than facilitate innovation, may not achieve the desired objectives ar should only be considered as a 'last resort'.[203] It is also argued that, if the economic facto that are leading to concentration or dominance by a single provider are 'natural' (stror economies of scale, scope and network effects) and consumers tend to single-home, the such separation might not be beneficial to welfare, and in any event the market may b expected to keep 'tipping' towards a single provider even after it is restructured.[204]

In the USA, regulatory proposals currently being debated would make it unlawful for covered platform to simultaneously own another line of business when that dual owne ship creates a conflict of interest (such as where an online marketplace such as Amazc also sells products on that platform).[205] Covered platforms that violate these rules cou be forced to divest lines of business. In the EU, the Digital Markets Act allows for th Commission to impose structural remedies where there is systematic non-compliance wi one or several of the obligations under the Act, and where a gatekeeper has maintaine extended or strengthened its gatekeeper position.[206] Similarly, in the UK, the competitic regulator has argued that the digital regulator should be able to implement ownersh separation or operational separation.[207] In China, recent changes allow the State Counc to force the divestiture of assets (including intellectual property, technology or data) fc digital platforms that have been found to have excluded or restricted competition.[208]

A related structural policy proposal involves empowering a regulator to 'unwin consummated mergers that have caused higher prices or lessened competition.[209] Th includes horizontal mergers between a digital platform and a potential competitor, or ve tical mergers such as between a platform and a business that provides a complementai service (e.g. develops tools to set ad prices).[210]

---

[202] See Khan (2019), US House of Representatives (2020), Van Loo (2020) and Kwoka and Valletti (2021).
[203] The Stigler Center (2019), for example, notes that structural remedies could be costly to consumers in various ways. Hovenkamp (2021a) notes: 'In many cases, breaking up large firms that benefit from extensive economies of scale and scope will injure consumers and most input suppliers, including the employees who supply labor.' See also Phillips (2019), Gilbert (2021) and Usman (2022) on past break-ups in the USA, including AT&T. Bourreau and Perrot (2020) advocate that separation should be a last resort. Lemley (2021) argues that separation to break up data monopolies may actually be bad for privacy, as it likely to involve more personal data in the hands of more companies. Dippon and Hoelle (2022) estimate that if laws requiring structural separation, common carrier obligations and line of business restrictions are introduced in the USA this could 'impose $319 billion in costs on Google, App Facebook, Amazon, and Microsoft' which would be passed through to consumers and business users.
[204] As Tirole (2020) observes: 'breaking a social network into two or three social networks might not raise consumer welfare. Either consumers will be split into separate communities, preventing them from reaping the benefits of network externalities; or separated from their friends, they will re-join on one c the broken-up sites, creating the monopoly again.'
[205] See the *Bill proposing The Ending Platforms Monopolies Act* (2021).
[206] See EU Regulation 2022/1925. In the original draft proposal, the Commission allowed for the possibili of legal, functional or structural separation, including the divestiture of a business, or parts of it, wher there had been systematic non-compliance with one or several obligations. See EC (2020g).
[207] CMA (2020).
[208] ANJIE (2020). Press reports claim that that Alibaba will be required to create a separate platform for Alipay, which is China's largest payment app.
[209] A notable example is the 2021 attempt by the US Federal Trade Commission to 'unwind' the Facebook and Instagram merger. Generally, see Kwoka and Valletti (2021).
[210] See Stigler Center (2019).

Non-Discrimination Policies

Many jurisdictions are considering rules to ensure designated platforms do not discriminate among different platform users and offer equivalent price and non-price terms of access.[211] These include policies to promote competition *on* a platform by ensuring that users are treated fairly and competition is not distorted such that there is a 'level playing field' among different users of a platform. These policies also focus on discriminatory practices that have the effect of foreclosing entry and limiting competition *for* the platform market, such as where a digital platform discriminates in ways that impede the ability of a rival to become a potential competitor of the designated platform. For example, a designated platform could use discriminatory incentives to induce single-homing by certain users (e.g. loyalty payments to keep one side of the market on board) or limit the ability of its users to multi-home by making it difficult and costly to access and port their data.[212] Non-discrimination rules also seek to restrict the ability of vertically integrated designated platform operators from engaging in self-preferencing or favouring their own content or products on the platform to the disadvantage of competitors.

In Germany, the competition authority is now empowered to prohibit certain types of conduct by platforms designated as having paramount significance for competition across markets, including self-preferencing or impeding access to data needed by third-party entrants. Similarly, in China, operators with a dominant position cannot discriminate by applying different standards, rules and algorithms in ways which restrict market competition. In the EU, gatekeepers will be required to apply fair and non-discriminatory conditions in ranking services and products, and will be prohibited from treating more favourably products offered by itself or an associated undertaking. Gatekeepers will also not be able to use any aggregated or non-aggregated data, which may include anonymised and personal data, that is not publicly available to offer similar services to those of business users on their platform. In the USA, a bill currently being debated would make unlawful certain discriminatory practices by covered platforms, including conduct which: advantages the covered platform operator's own products, services or lines of business; excludes or disadvantages the products, services or lines of business of another business user; or discriminates among similarly situated business users.[213]

Interoperability

Another set of regulatory policies focus on fostering greater interoperability between platforms and aim to address the fact that, when a market tips in favour of a single platform, its users can become 'closed off' from potentially competing platforms that could challenge the designated platform's position.[214] These regulations could include imposing requirements that designated platforms be built according to, or adopt, open standards that will allow users to be able to share and communicate across platforms. For example, a designated social media platform might be required to be interoperable with other social media platforms such that a user can share and see content from multiple platforms at the same time.

[211] The US House of Representatives (2020) draws a direct comparison to non-discrimination rules used for US railroads which are discussed in Chapter 14.
[212] Stigler Center (2019).
[213] See the *Bill in support of the American Innovation and Choice Online Act* (2021).
[214] See Kades and Scott Morton (2021).

In Germany, designated platforms with paramount significance can now poten
tially be prohibited from conduct which disallows or impedes the interoperability o
products or services.[215] The EU's Digital Markets Act requires designated gatekeepe
platforms: to allow third-party software applications or software app stores to b
interoperable with the operating system; not to restrict technically the ability o
end-users to switch between or subscribe to different software applications usin
the gatekeeper's operating system; and to allow providers of services and provider
of hardware free-of-charge access to, and interoperability with, the same operatin
system, hardware or software as used by the gatekeeper when providing services.[21]
In the USA, proposals will require covered platforms to maintain a set of transpar
ent, third-party-accessible interfaces (including application programming interfaces
to facilitate and maintain interoperability with a competing business or a potentia
competing business.[217]

Limits on Bundling

Regulatory policies also seek to limit the ability of designated digital platforms to com
bine or 'bundle' certain services. A designated online marketplace operator might not b
able to combine the use of the platform with requirements to use its logistics services, no
will it be able to require that business users utilise its identification services. In Germany
platforms with paramount significance can now be prohibited from automatically com
bining the use of one product with another, or pre-installing its services on products an
devices.[218] In China, operators with dominant positions can be prevented from bundlin
different goods through pop-up windows or mandatory steps that cannot be rejected b
the counterparty.

In the EU, gatekeepers will not be able to use their position to require dependent busi
ness users to include any identification services provided by the gatekeeper where othe
identification services are available to such business users. Regulation is also propose
to limit the ability of designated platforms that also provide devices and equipment – fo
example, a phone, tablet or other 'smart' equipment such as a fridge – to automaticall
pre-load onto that equipment or to make itself the default app (e.g. the use of a particula
search engine as the default on a tablet). Gatekeepers will also have to allow end-user
to uninstall any pre-installed software without affecting the functioning of the device o
the operating system.

Fairness and Creating a 'Level Playing Field'

Another set of regulatory policies focus on addressing the bargaining power imbalance
between the digital platform operators and those who use digital platforms (such a
businesses selling products, content providers or end-users). The focus here is on 'fai
ness' and on reducing the scope for designated digital platforms to exploit consume

---

[215] Bundestag (2021).
[216] See EU Regulation 2022/1925.
[217] See *Bill in support of Augmenting Compatibility and Competition by Enabling Service Switching Act* (2021).
[218] Bundestag (2021).

and businesses who are dependent on the platforms.[219] For businesses which use digital platforms to sell goods and services, these regulations might involve requirements that a designated platform does not place restrictions on the price and conditions that they can offer services on other alternative intermediation channels, as well as requirements that users are not mandatorily required to use or sign up to certain services provided by the designated operator.[220] For content providers, such as publishers, there is a focus on the designated platform being required to negotiate with publishers, newspapers and media companies to achieve a more appropriate share of the rents for the content they provide.[221] Advertisers and publishers may also have a right to find out information about the conditions of the advertising services offered by the designated platform, including the price paid for publishing a given ad.[222] For consumers, regulations could focus on ensuring fair ranking of search results and terms, and when use of a service can be suspended.

In Germany, designated platforms with paramount significance can now be prohibited from treating their own products more favourably than those of competitors, taking measures which interfere with business users' activities, limiting or hindering market access, or directly or indirectly impeding competitors in markets where the platform could rapidly expand its activities.[223] In China, dominant platforms can no longer compel users to accept other goods through the threat or imposition of traffic restrictions, search downgrades or technical barriers. In Japan, the focus is on specified digital platform providers and platform users voluntarily and proactively establishing a mutual understanding in terms of fair-trading relationships with minimal involvement by the government.[224] There are also proposals for new regulatory obligations that require transparency in digital advertising markets.[225]

In the EU, specific obligations will be imposed on gatekeepers to increase contestability and address unfair behaviour. In the UK, the proposal is for a wider code of conduct to be introduced between designated platforms and their users which would contain legally binding principles relating to fair trading, open choices and trust and transparency, and would be monitored and enforced by a Digital Markets Unit.[226] In Australia, a binding code has been introduced requiring designated digital platforms to negotiate payment for news content from publishers.[227]

---

[219] The US House of Representatives (2020) advocated for 'prohibitions on abuses of superior bargaining power, proscribing dominant platforms from engaging in contracting practices that derive from their dominant market position, and requirement of due process protections for individuals and businesses dependent on the dominant platforms'.

[220] In the EU, gatekeepers should not impose general conditions, including pricing conditions, that would be unfair or lead to unjustified differentiation when they provide software app stores. See EU Regulation 2022/1925.

[221] ACCC (2019), Stigler Center (2019) and US House of Representatives (2020).

[222] See EU Regulation 2022/1925.

[223] Bundestag (2021).

[224] METI (2021).

[225] Digital Market Competition Council (2020).

[226] The UK Government (2021) proposes three sets of principles: fair trading (fair terms and conditions, no undue discrimination, etc.); open choices (not unduly influence competitive process, bundle or tie, take reasonable steps to support interoperability, no undue restriction on ability of users to use competing providers, etc.); and trust and transparency (clear relevant information to users, fair warning of changes, ensure choices and defaults are presented in a way that facilitates informed and effective consumer choice, ensure decisions are taken in users' best interests). Furman, Coyle, Fletcher, *et al.* (2019) set out some examples of principles that might be contained in the code.

[227] Australian Government (2021).

Regulation of Data Sharing and Combination

Another key policy focus is on regulations relating to data combination, sharing and porability. One set of regulations seek to restrict the ability of designated platforms to combir data they collect on user behaviour across different platforms. In the EU, for exampl gatekeepers are restricted in their ability to combine data they source from core platforr services with personal data they obtain from other sources or with personal data obtaine from third-party services.[228] In order to promote contestability of core platform service end-users should be able to opt in to such data combination practices and be offered a le personalised alternative. In Germany, platforms of paramount significance can no long demand the transfer of data or rights not necessary to the service offered, nor make offe contingent on the transfer of data.

Other data regulations could require designated platforms to share data with (currer and potential) rivals in order to 'level the playing field'.[229] In some ways, these propo als are similar to access regimes that exist in other regulated sectors, and will involv designated digital platform operators opening up access to potential competitors to th privately held data they have accumulated on specific users. The purpose of these po icies is to address concerns described in Section 13.1.3 above that the substantial da holdings of some large digital platforms entrench their position and reduce the scope f competition *for* the market. In the EU, a gatekeeper is obliged to provide access (on fai reasonable and non-discriminatory terms) to ranking, query, click and view data gene ated by consumers using its online search engine services to any third-party online sear engine that makes such a request.

Another set of regulatory proposals focus on personal data portability and mobilit These policies aim to give consumers greater access to, and control of, the personal da that designated digital platforms hold about them (such as purchase history, profile ar content). Data portability policies will allow users to move their data from one platform another in a common format, and thus should reduce the barriers to consumer switchir and make it more attractive for new entrants to challenge incumbent platforms.[230] Da mobility policies allow consumers to move their data but also to authorise that this da can be accessed by a third-party business potentially on a continuous rather than discre basis.[231] The expectation is that third parties that access this personal data can then u it in ways to get more tailored advice or recommendations, or to better compare goo and services.[232] Competition thus focuses on the analysis of data rather than simply i collection.[233]

---

[228] This follows investigations in Europe and in Germany about how Facebook combines data from different sources. See EC (2017) and Bundeskartellamt (2019).

[229] This was advocated by the Stigler Center (2019), Furman, Coyle, Fletcher, *et al.* (2019) and Crémer, de Montjoye and Schweitzer (2019).

[230] The US House of Representatives (2020) notes that it can provide consumers and businesses with tools to easily port or rebuild their social graph, profile or other relevant data on a competing platform.

[231] Furman, Coyle, Fletcher, *et al.* (2019) distinguish between data 'mobility' and data 'portability'. The former involves just moving data from one provider to another, while the latter allows data to be move but also shared with a third party at a customer's request.

[232] This builds on the idea of open banking in the UK and the second EU Payments Services Directive (PSI 2); see discussion in Chapter 12.

[233] Parker, Petropoulos and Van Alstyne (2021) discuss how this might work in general terms.

In the USA, proposals currently being debated will require that covered platforms maintain a set of transparent, third-party-accessible interfaces that can enable the secure transfer of data to a user, or, with the user's consent, transfer of data to a business user in a structured, commonly used and machine-readable format.[234] In the EU, gatekeepers are required to provide effective portability of data generated through the activity of a business user or end-user and provide tools for end-users to facilitate the exercise of data portability, including by the provision of continuous and real-time access.[235] In addition, gatekeepers must on request provide business users, or third parties authorised by a business user, free of charge, with effective, high-quality, continuous and real-time access and use of aggregated or non-aggregated data, relating to those business users and the end-users engaging with the products or services provided by those business users.

Regulation of Algorithms and Databases

In the USA, the EU, China and the UK, regulations are also being considered that will provide greater transparency about how algorithms and databases are used in practice.[236] These rules could give a regulator the ability to demand access to databases and algorithms to conduct investigations and to monitor compliance with regulatory obligations. In the USA, a bill is being considered which would prohibit the discriminatory use of personal information by online platforms in any algorithmic process, in part to address concerns about manipulative dark patterns, and would require transparency in the use of algorithmic processes and content moderation.[237] In China, operators with a dominant position can be prohibited from discriminating by offering differential transaction prices or trading conditions based on algorithms or big data and based on the user's ability to pay, usage habits or preferences.

Other Proposed Regulations

Various other regulations have been proposed, some of which could be applied more widely to all digital platforms and not just to designated platforms. These include: regulations that mandate certain privacy protections to ensure that user data is not misused or over-collected; requirements to periodically report data to a regulator on the use of the digital platform;[238] prohibitions on certain practices which exploit biases in consumer decision making (such as dark patterns); open standards requirements that can allow users to control who can access their digital identities and data; and other policies to promote greater interoperability across platforms and services and facilitate the development of new products (e.g. micropayments).[239]

---

[234] See *Bill in support of Augmenting Compatibility and Competition by Enabling Service Switching Act* (2021) and *Bill in support of Algorithmic Justice and Online Platform Transparency Act* (2021), which also would provide a right to data portability.

[235] Changes to German competition law also require platforms with paramount significance not to disallow or impede the portability of data.

[236] China State Administration for Market Regulation (2021) and UK Government (2021).

[237] A *Bill in support of Algorithmic Justice and Online Platform Transparency Act* (2021).

[238] The Stigler Center (2019) notes that such information could include: information on types and volume of searches undertaken; search queries and subsequent purchase behaviour on online marketplaces; information about ads displayed on social media sites; and which apps are downloaded from an app store.

[239] See Stigler Center (2019).

Given the fast-moving context, in most jurisdictions, it is accepted that a mechanism i needed to allow for new regulations to be introduced in the future as the industry evolves In the EU, current proposals envisage that new regulations could follow a market investi gation that examines the potential impact of new core platform services and practices. I the UK, it is proposed that the Digital Markets Unit be given broad discretion to introduc other pro-competitive interventions that can 'overcome network effects and barriers t entry/expansion through mandating interoperability, third-party access to data or certai separation measures.[240]

13.4 CONCLUSION

Unlike the other industries discussed in this book, the regulation of digital platform does not relate to the regulation of a particular supply chain, product, service or busines model. Rather, regulation is focused on a specific type of intermediation activity, whic in broad terms can be defined as facilitating the online interaction between differen user groups. As described above, this interaction can take many forms: connecting buy ers and sellers in an online marketplace; matching workers and employers; exchangin information, views and content in a social network; or using a search engine to matc specific queries with information. Digital platforms differ not only in terms of size bu also in terms of how they provide value to different user groups and the types of user they attract. However, all digital platforms seek to provide value to users by reducin information and transaction costs and resolving frictions.

Two key economic attributes characterise digital platforms. The first is direct and indi rect network effects, which mean that the value of a platform to a user depends o the number and type of other users that are connected to, or utilise, that platform. Th second attribute is the ability of digital platform operators to collect various bits o data about users, including personal information. By matching or facilitating interaction between users, digital platform operators gain access to information about the behaviou preferences and situational context of business and personal users. While this data i continually fed back to improve the algorithms that drive the matching and predictiv capabilities of digital platforms, it can also be highly valuable. Indeed, two of the riche companies in the world – Google and Facebook – are sustained through an ability to se to advertisers the insights from the data they collect from their users which advertiser can then use to send highly targeted ads. To improve their functionality and their abilit to access data, some digital platform operators have rapidly expanded through a serie of acquisitions of nascent competitors and complementors to become 'superplatforms meaning that they now operate across multiple markets, often at the global level.

The rationale for the regulation of some large digital platforms is, in part, premise on the fact that they can have the characteristics of natural monopoly and can rapidl expand to the point where they display 'extreme' or 'hyper' returns to scale and scop Unlike in other sectors, regulatory policy here is motivated not by an attempt to con trol prices of the incumbent provider or restrict entry, but rather to reduce these natur

[240] UK Government (2021).

barriers to entry with the aim of facilitating greater contestability and competition *for* the market. Regulation is also premised on the fact that the strong network effects that can characterise some large digital platforms can lead to a market 'tipping' in favour of one provider. Here, too, and unlike in other sectors, regulation is focused not on harnessing or internalising positive externalities, but rather on addressing the risks that network effects can lead to users becoming locked in to a single provider, which acts as a substantial barrier to new entry. Finally, in many jurisdictions, regulation is premised on a need to control the dominant and seemingly entrenched market power of some leading digital platforms which can allow them to exploit users or to exclude actual or potential competitors.

While the fundamental economic rationales for digital platform regulation are similar across jurisdictions (and in many ways to the other industries discussed in this book), there are considerable differences in the proposed approaches to regulating digital platforms. This is perhaps unsurprising, as the issue is highly politically charged and one that involves more than just economics, touching on political concerns (bias and elections), social issues (online harms, privacy, addiction and exploitation) and geopolitical factors (the USA, Europe, Japan and China are all seeking to expand their presence in digital markets). Some jurisdictions are focused on updating existing competition laws to address digital platforms, while others are looking to introduce complementary forms of economic regulation. Among other things, the regulations could include: potential structural separation or line of business prohibitions; non-discrimination and interoperability requirements; regulations which require designated operators to treat users fairly and maintain a level playing field; and various regulations relating to data collection, use, sharing and portability. Jurisdictions are looking to implement these policies in different ways: some will make the rules mandatory while others will rely on a co-regulatory approach; some regulations will apply to all platforms while other regulations will apply only to 'designated platforms'; and some regulations will apply only to specific business models or core services while other regulations will apply to an entire entity or across the market. As I write, there is active debate about both the specific content of proposed regulations in the USA and the EU and whether they could harm or benefit consumers.[241] The experience of other areas of modern economic regulation suggests that the choices made on each of these dimensions will be critical for the implementation and effectiveness of the regulations.

DISCUSSION QUESTIONS

1. What is the fundamental characteristic of a digital platform, and what are some examples of the different types of digital platforms?
2. Discuss the economic implications of the multi-sided nature of digital platforms, and how platforms provide value to different user groups.

---

[241] See Hovenkamp (2021b) and Cennamo and Sokol (2021) on US proposals; and Caffarra and Scott Morton (2021), Budzinski and Mendelsohn (2021), Ibáñez Colomo (2021) and CERRE (2021) for assessments and critiques of the EU regulatory framework.

3. What are some of the ways in which digital platform operators can incentivise different user groups to use their platforms?

4. What types of data can be collected by digital platforms, and how can it be used and 'monetised' by digital platform operators?

5. Do you agree with the following statement? 'The substantial economies of scale and scope, and the presence of network effects, justify the regulation of some digital platforms to promote economic efficiency.' Discuss.

6. In what ways could large dominant digital platforms take advantage of their market position? What are possible constraints on that market power?

7. How might digital platforms exploit consumer biases? Will policies that promote greater competition between digital platforms address this concern?

8. What are some of the arguments for and against the introduction of *ex ante* economic regulation of digital platforms rather than a reliance on *ex post* competition law?

9. A range of regulatory policies have been proposed or introduced for digital platforms, including: separation policies; non-discrimination requirements; interoperability obligations; limits on bundling; and the regulation of data sharing and combination. Briefly discuss each of these policies and the 'problem' that each intended to address.

14

Rail Regulation

Railways are a critical form of passenger and freight transportation in many parts of the world. In 2016, passengers travelled over four trillion kilometres using railways, while some 7 per cent of global freight was transported on rail.[1] Railways have been central to economic development over the past two centuries and played a major part in the first industrial revolution in Europe and the second industrial revolution, particularly in the USA, in the late 1800s. The continued development of suburban and metro railways has also been central to the processes of urbanisation in many countries. Railways continue to play an important role in economic development, particularly in Asia, where countries such as China have rapidly expanded both their high-speed railways and metro systems over the past decade.

Railways occupy a unique place in economic regulation. The first Railway Regulation Act was passed in 1840 in Britain to regulate private railways. The first economic regulator, the Interstate Commerce Commission, was established in the USA in 1887 to regulate this sector,[2] and the rise of the railways 'barons' in the late 1880s ultimately led to the creation of US Antitrust law. Important concepts and developments in regulatory theory discussed in earlier chapters, such as the efficient component pricing rule (ECPR),[3] and destructive or 'ruinous' competition, all drew inspiration from the railway industry. It is also a sector where the ideas of regulatory economists have sometimes been influential in bringing about practical change.[4] Railways also offer useful insights into how regulation has adapted over time to changes in industry structure. As we will see, railways have at some points in time experienced intense competition from other forms of transport (road and air), while at other points in time they have occupied positions of monopoly in transport activities. There is also substantial diversity in how railroads are owned, operated and regulated across jurisdictions, ranging from full government control to policies based around horizontal or vertical separation. Questions about whether railways activities

---

[1] IEA (2019b).

[2] Clark (1891) describes the various temporary commissions established in the 1850s to 'arbitrate and settle disputes between parties', and later the establishment of permanent boards of arbitration and supervision such as the Massachusetts Commission in 1869.

[3] Baumol (1995) presents an exposition of the ECPR in terms of 'the railwayman's problem'.

[4] Pittman (2020a) discusses the influence of Alfred Kahn and George Stigler on the deregulation of the US railroads in the 1970s and 1980s.

should be combined under common ownership and operation have been debated for ove
a century and a half,[5] and the policies pursued at different times and in different countrie
reflect both economic and political considerations.[6]

Railways face direct competition from other 'modes' of transport (known as 'inter
modal' competition) such as road transport (cars, buses and trucks), and from airplane
for longer-distance journeys.[7] Unlike most of the industries discussed in this book (energy
water, communications), railways are not ubiquitous, with around 90 per cent of all ra
passenger travel concentrated in Europe, Russia, India and China.[8] Some railways, such a
those in North America and Australia, have evolved to primarily provide freight service
with limited passenger services. There are also considerable differences across countrie
in the condition of railroads; while countries like Japan and China have modern high
speed railroads that connect major cities, in many African countries the rail network i
similar to that which existed 100 years ago and is based around connecting an interic
mine to a trading hub, with limited international interconnections.[9] As we shall see, thes
differences have important implications for the regulation of railways.

14.1 PHYSICAL AND ECONOMIC CHARACTERISTICS OF RAILWAYS

14.1.1 Characteristics of the Product

Railways provide two broad types of services: passenger services and freight services.
Passenger rail is a type of mobility service alongside other motorised transport mode
such as cars, buses and two- and three-wheeled vehicles.[11] Passenger rail services dif
fer in terms of speed and coverage. High-speed rail services (greater than 250 km/h
connect major urban centres, while conventional (or mainline) rail services are use
for medium- to long-distance journeys between regional centres and to connect urba
centres with surrounding suburbs. Urban rail, including light rail services and metr
rail services, provide high-frequency services in densely populated cities. Freight ser
vices involve the surface transportation of goods, including natural resources and othe
products (cars), and compete with other surface transportation modes such as heav
and medium trucks and light commercial vehicles. Users of freight rail services a

---

[5] See Lardner (1850), Adams (1878) and Cooley (1884).
[6] There is often a political reluctance to have full competition in all railway activities given the impacts it
could have on route coverage and user pricing. Policies can also reflect wider political goals, such as the
interconnection of different markets (as in the Single European Railway Area) and the development of
certain strategically important export sectors.
[7] Ivaldi and Pouyet (2018) estimate that the elasticity of demand for railway transport in France is
relatively high, in part because of the competitive constraints imposed from other transport modes.
[8] IEA (2019b).
[9] Some countries such as Niger, Chad and the Central African Republic have no rail networks at all. Lowe
(2014) observes that in 2009 only 80 per cent of African networks were operational and that most are
non-electrified and rely on manual signalling systems. He also notes that: 'Even when lines are running,
transit time can be horrifically long – e.g. the 3,000km trip from Kolwez[i], DRC [Democratic Republic of
the Congo] to Durban [South Africa] takes 38 days, an effective speed of 4km/hr.' See also World Bank
(2010).
[10] According to Montero and Finger (2020), the first example of railway services involved using 'rail' track
to guide wheeled vehicles in coal mines in Germany and the UK in the early sixteenth century.
[11] Other forms of mobility such as cycling and walking are generally not seen as substitutes.

referred to as 'shippers'. Railway services cannot be stored, which means that poor scheduling and management that result in an under-utilised rail track, or trains that are only partially full, lead to losses for both track and train operators and service providers and users.

From the end-user perspective, rail services can be both a substitute for, and a complement to, other motorised transport or mobility services. For some journeys, rail services are substitutes for cars, buses or trucks. However, they are often not full substitutes, as they do not allow for point-to-point travel from origin to desired destination. Rather, passengers and freight board and alight trains at fixed points (railway stations), which are generally not the final destination. To get to a final destination, passengers and freight railway users must often use complementary forms of mobility. For example, passengers might alight at a station and then catch a bus, taxi or use a car to get to their final destination. Similarly, freight users generally use other forms of transport (such as a truck or light commercial vehicle) to get cargo to and from a railway station.

Globally, rail accounts for around 8 per cent of all motorised passenger activity, but the extent to which rail services are substitutes for other modes of transport varies by jurisdiction and service type. Conventional and high-speed rail accounts for around 15 per cent of all non-urban transport activity, which is a lower share than each of cars, aviation and buses. High-speed rail services offer frequent services but currently exist in only fourteen countries.[12] Conventional passenger railways services are heavily utilised in jurisdictions with extensive rail networks. India, China, Japan, Russia and Europe collectively account for 90 per cent of all passenger rail activity.[13] Notwithstanding sustained growth over the past century, urban rail services only account for around 2 per cent of urban transport activity worldwide, with the most popular forms of transport being cars (43 per cent), two- and three-wheeled vehicles (28 per cent) and buses (27 per cent).[14]

Freight rail services tend to be concentrated in jurisdictions with substantial natural resources (minerals, coal, agricultural products) such as in North America, China, Russia, India and Australia. This type of freight can be heavy and difficult to transport by air or road and often involves long distances between a specific origin (such as a mine) and a destination (such as a port).[15] Globally, around 28 per cent of surface freight is transported on rail, with road transport (heavy, medium and light trucks and commercial vehicles) accounting for the remainder.[16]

Demand for rail services has increased over the past two decades in almost all jurisdictions. Globally, passenger rail service activity grew by an estimated 70 per cent since 2000, with particularly strong growth in India and China. High-speed and conventional rail services grew at an annual rate of 4 per cent per annum, driven in particular by

[12] IEA (2019b) notes that the Tokyo and Nagoya line has a frequency of more than fifteen trains per hour at peak times, while the Train à Grande Vitesse (TGV) corridor between Paris and Lyon offers eight or nine trains per hour during peak times.

[13] IEA (2019b). In the USA, passenger traffic tends to be concentrated in certain areas, such as the northeast corridor which links Boston to Washington DC via Philadelphia and New York.

[14] IEA (2019b).

[15] Montero and Finger (2020).

[16] See IEA (2019b), although the share varies significantly across countries, from 75 per cent in Russia, 39 per cent in China and around 30 per cent in North America and India.

growth for conventional rail in India and high-speed rail in China. Demand for urban ra
services also increased dramatically following the development of new metro systems i
China and Asia.[17] Freight rail services also grew steadily at the global level since 200(
with the highest growth rates in China and Russia.[18]

Notwithstanding that demand for passenger and freight services has risen over th
past two decades, overall rail capacity (measured by the length of tracks that can b
used by passenger and freight rail services) in many jurisdictions has remained constan
Conventional rail and freight rail tracks (which account for around 94 per cent of trac
capacity) experienced limited growth, while rail track used for urban and high-spee
rail tracks have expanded capacity, particularly in Asia. This combination of growin
passenger and freight demand and constant rail track capacity has meant that passeng
rail track *utilisation* (passengers per kilometres travelled divided by track kilometre
increased by 75 per cent at the global level since 2000, while freight track utilisatio
increased by around 45 per cent at the global level over the same time period.

14.1.2 Railway Systems

Railways involve the carriage of passengers or freight in specialised vehicles on fixed ra
tracks between a point of origin and a destination. Railways thus comprise the rail infra
structure needed to facilitate the carriage of passengers or freight (such as tracks, signal
depots, stations) and the services provided by train operators which use that infrastruc
ture to transport passengers or freight. An indicative illustration of a railway system
presented in Figure 14.1.

The split between rail infrastructure costs and train operating costs varies across juri
dictions and can depend on the relative use of freight versus passenger services. In th
UK, some 40 per cent of total industry expenditure relates to rail network infrastructur
with the remaining 60 per cent incurred by train operators. In the EU, the split betwee
infrastructure and train operator costs is roughly 30 per cent and 70 per cent.[19]

This section focuses on three important components of railways: rail infrastructur
train operations; and stations. As discussed below, while in Europe these activities a
vertically separated from one another, in jurisdictions such as the USA and Japan, it
often the case that rail infrastructure and train operations are integrated.

Rail Infrastructure

Railway infrastructure comprises railway track, structures such as bridges and tunnel
train signalling, communications systems equipment, power supply in electrified se
tions and terminal infrastructure. Rail infrastructure tends to be physically fixed ar
location-specific and cannot be moved easily from a location. While all railway system
require broadly similar types of infrastructure (tracks, signals, communication systems), th
specific characteristics of rail infrastructure deployed differ for high-speed, convention

---

[17] Of the forty-three cities with new metro systems introduced in the past decade, thirty-two were in Asia.
[18] IEA (2019b).
[19] ORR (2020b) and Steer Davies Gleave (2015).

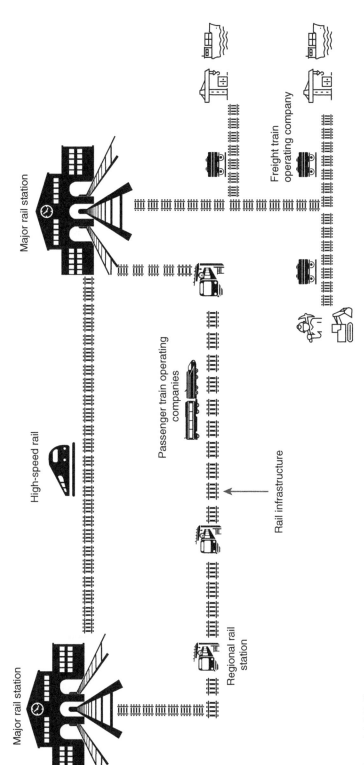

Figure 14.1 Railway system

and urban railways. High-speed railways can require different rail tracks to those used for conventional railways, while light railways typically require different rail tracks to those used for metro services.[20] Newer forms of rail travel, such as Maglev and Hyperloop, need even more specialised forms of infrastructure. The infrastructure needed will also depend on whether a system is electrified or not and the voltage used. Urban and high-speed rail services are fully electrified, as is around three-quarters of conventional passenger rail services and half of all freight services around the world.[21] The remaining services are provided on systems using diesel-powered trains.

Historically, the infrastructure needed to provide railway services involved the laying of dedicated rail lines to connect industrial sites or mines, or between major urban centres, such as the Liverpool to Manchester line, which opened in 1830. Although dedicated point-to-point railway lines still exist for some freight transport,[22] over time, railway 'networks' emerged that connected multiple isolated railway lines through the use of standardised and interoperable infrastructure.

Rail infrastructure interoperability depends on factors such as: whether a common track gauge is used;[23] the types of rails used; the use of a standardised 'railway time' for scheduling and management;[24] whether the line is electrified or not; and the ability of the rail track to accommodate vehicles of certain weight and length. The extent to which railway infrastructure is interoperable has important implications for capacity utilisation and the commercial viability of a railway network, and the costs faced by different users of that infrastructure. In some jurisdictions, high-speed and conventional rail infrastructure is sufficiently interoperable that they form a common rail network, while in others separate infrastructure is used to provide conventional and high-speed services. It is often the case that infrastructure used to provide urban rail services (such as metro systems) cannot be used to provide conventional and high-speed rail services, meaning that the urban and conventional rail systems operate as distinct networks. The extent to which freight services and passenger services utilise the same rail infrastructure also varies: freight services generally cannot use high-speed or urban railway infrastructure, but can use conventional rail infrastructure. However, given the differences in speed of freight and passenger services, it is often the case that freight services use different paths, or utilise rail infrastructure at night, when there is limited passenger traffic. Given that railway systems can cross national boundaries, there can also be an international dimension to interoperability. In Europe, for example, policy has been directed at enhancing infrastructure interoperability to facilitate the Single European Railway Area.

---

[20] Historically, rail tracks were made from wood but are now made from iron.

[21] IEA (2019b).

[22] Such as those connecting mines directly to ports. Examples include the Mount Newman railway in Australia, and the Sishen–Saldanha railway in South Africa. Point-to-point services also exist for certain passenger services, such as high-speed airport rail links.

[23] Montero and Finger (2020) describe how historically each railway line would define a time of operation using a different reference, which led to accidents.

[24] Track gauge refers to the width of the inner sides of rails on a railway track. Montero and Finger (2020) describe how historically the use of different gauges (broad or narrow) limited the development of railway systems, while the narrow gauge is now the international standard, although different gauges are still used in Russia and India (where four different gauges are in operation).

Rail infrastructure management involves managing, operating and maintaining rail infrastructure in a way which maintains safety and optimises use. Among other things, this involves: managing the track control and safety systems and power systems; maintaining the track lines and other equipment (signals); timetabling and coordination; managing short-term congestion and unexpected events; and setting appropriate speeds on different lines and for different forms of traffic. Rail infrastructure managers are also responsible for maintenance and development activities, such as capacity enhancements or expansions.

An important function of rail infrastructure managers is to allocate 'track slots' between different users, including freight services and passenger services, in an efficient and non-discriminatory way. Efficient track capacity allocation can increase utilisation and the financial viability of infrastructure, and can also affect how rail competes with other forms of transport. For example, allocating high-speed rail capacity can involve balancing the need for fast trains to be sufficiently separated from slower trains, while also ensuring that the high-speed services can travel at speeds which make them competitive with other forms of transport such as road and air. In order to allocate capacity among different types of passenger traffic (inter-city, regional and local services) and freight services, infrastructure managers adopt a priority order. In Europe, India and Japan, passenger services generally have priority, while freight services have priority in South Africa and North America.[25] Scheduled traffic generally has priority over charter traffic and 'one-off' services. Where train services cross jurisdictional borders, infrastructure managers are also responsible for international timetable coordination and harmonisation of the train paths for international passenger and freight rail traffic.

Rail infrastructure owners and managers derive income from the sale of track slots to passenger and freight train operating companies (see below) through what are known as track access charges. Given the high fixed costs associated with investments in long-term rail infrastructure (such as track, bridges and tunnels), and the costs associated with operating and maintaining the network to ensure safety, it is often the case that the track access charges are not sufficient to cover such costs and a government subsidy is required to make up the shortfall.

The ownership of railway infrastructure has changed over time. In the UK, Europe and the USA, the earliest railway lines were developed by private companies to connect major urban centres and countries in the mid- to late 1800s.[26] Intense competition between private railroads led to mergers and consolidation in countries such as the USA and the UK, resulting in a small number of powerful railroad companies occupying monopoly positions in certain regions and routes. By the time of the Second World War, railways in many industrialised countries faced increased competition from road and aviation, undermining the monopoly position and leading to a sharp decline in traffic and revenue. This initially led to railways being nationalised in most countries, a notable exception

---

[25] Montero and Finger (2020).

[26] Montero and Finger (2020) note that the first transcontinental railroad in the USA was developed in 1869; the Orient Express from Paris to Constantinople was inaugurated in 1883; and the Trans-Siberian line connecting Moscow to Vladivostok was completed in 1904. The European Alps were crossed for the first time in 1882.

being the USA.[27] The current situation is one where rail infrastructure is state-owned i
many jurisdictions (outside of North America), even though they may operate as legall
or functionally separate entities.[28]

In some jurisdictions, private companies are appointed to manage infrastructure und
a concession arrangement. The use of concession arrangements has a long history i
railways, dating back to the mid-1800s in Spain, India, Turkey and China,[29] and is still
common feature of railways in Africa, Australia, Latin America and parts of Europe, wit
the period of the concessions ranging from ten to ninety-nine years.[30] Given the need t
coordinate movements across a network, railway infrastructure managers tend to opera
as monopolies in specific regions or countries (such as SNCF Réseau in France, DB Netz i
Germany, Network Rail in the UK), although it can sometimes be the case that the own
of railway infrastructure is appointed for specific lines.[31]

Train Services

Passenger and freight train services are provided to end-users by train operating com
panies who operate trains that connect carriages or wagons on railway tracks. Trai
operating companies need rolling stock, sales networks and train crews to provide trai
services. The term 'rolling stock' refers to locomotives and motorised power vehicles, ar
unpowered rail carriages, wagons or other vehicles.

Originally powered by horsepower and steam power, most trains are now powered b
electricity or diesel, and in some cases magnetic power.[32] Rolling stock tends to be speci
ically designed for the rail infrastructure it uses, such that freight trains cannot use high
speed tracks, metro trains cannot use conventional rail tracks and electric trains cann
travel on lines that are not electrified or use a different voltage. Rolling stock must als
be compatible with other railway infrastructure, such as train station platform length ar
height, and freight loading facilities. As such, unlike other transport vehicles – such a
cars, planes, trucks or ships, which can be easily used or redeployed to other roads, ai
space or waters – the ability for roiling stock to be traded or to operate on different typ
of railway infrastructure can be more limited.[33]

---

[27] Montero and Finger (2020) note that, while Prussia nationalised its railways in the late 1800s and Japa
in 1906, most nationalisations occurred in or after the 1930s, including the creation of SNCF (Société
Nationale des Chemins de fer Français) in France in 1938, RENFE (Red Nacional de los Ferrocarriles
Españoles) in Spain in 1941, and British Rail in 1948. Later examples included the state monopolies in
China (1949) and Indian Railways in 1951. Based on a historical analysis of British railways, Lewis and
Offer (2022) conclude that: '[R]ailways are mostly in the public sector, for most of the time, and for goc
reasons. ... Entrepreneurial flair created the railways but tends to undermine their routine operation, as
in our three episodes, the mania of the 1840s, the tramways of the 1890s and privatization since 1993.'

[28] In an interesting study, Caves and Christensen (1980) compared the performance of two railways in
Canada (one privately owned and one publicly owned) over the post-war period and found no evidence
of inferior performance by the government-owned railroad. They conclude that any tendency towards
inefficiency resulting from public ownership was overcome by the benefits of competition between the
two railroads.

[29] Montero and Finger (2020).

[30] Laurino, Ramella and Beria (2015) and African Development Bank (2015).

[31] Finger and Messulam (2015) present examples such as the Eurotunnel, and the Perpignan–Figueras
tunnel concession.

[32] According to IRG (2020) around 55 per cent of routes in Europe are electrified.

[33] Where it does happen, this can sometimes involve changes to the rail infrastructure; for example,
non-Eurostar services that use the Eurotunnel.

Train services are provided under three types of supply structures. The first is where the train operating company is vertically integrated, such that a single railway operator owns and operates both the infrastructure and the rolling stock that uses the tracks to provide services to end-users. Up until the 1990s, this was the main structure observed in many countries, and is still the main structure in the USA (where it is estimated that around 600 freight railroads own both the infrastructure and trains that use those tracks), Canada, Russia and Japan (where passenger operators are all vertically integrated with one another).

A second structure is where rail infrastructure is separated from train operations, and where a train operating company has rights to operate a particular part of the rail network, such as to provide services on specific rail lines within a region or area under a concession or franchise agreement.[34] Concession or franchise contracts can be directly awarded to a train operating company, or be subject to a competitive tender. In the EU, competitive tenders for long-distance or regional services are used in eleven countries, which allows for 'competition *for* the market' from international private companies, public rail companies from other countries, or smaller regional operators. Under the terms of a concession agreement, train operating companies commit to certain performance and service levels in terms of frequency of services, pricing, punctuality, cleanliness and consumer satisfaction, etc. For passenger services, these contracts can vary in length from two to fifteen years and be concluded at a national, regional or local level. In the Netherlands, for example, a single company (Nederlandse Spoorwegen) operates the majority of passenger services in the country under a concession arrangement; while in Germany, there are estimated to be around 300 contracts in place between regional and local authorities and train operating companies. Concession contracts have also been used for freight services in Australia and Latin America for periods extending up to ninety-nine years.

The third structure through which train operating companies provide services is known as 'open access' or 'third-party access' and involves train operating companies bidding for 'slots' to operate services on certain routes for a specified time. Open access is the common way in which freight services gain access to rail infrastructure in many parts of the world such as Australia and Europe. For passenger services, 'open-access operators' work independently of, and often compete with, franchise operators. Examples of open-access operators that provide competing long-distance services in Europe include Italo in Italy, FlixTrain in Germany and various operators in Sweden. However, as discussed below, notwithstanding policies to promote open access in some jurisdictions, such as Europe, there are only limited examples of where such competition has emerged for passenger services.[35]

Train operating companies that provide passenger services are state-owned in many jurisdictions. In Europe, around 90 per cent of the inter-city passenger market is provided

---

[34] There is a question about the optimal size of franchises. Nash, Smith, Crozet, *et al.* (2019) note that, while there is reason to expect that there are some economies of scale in franchises, they can become too large. They also note that this is strong economies of density, such that splitting the services on a particular route between operators will raise costs.

[35] Examples include Austria, the Czech Republic, Germany, Italy, Sweden and Great Britain.

by state-owned companies.[36] In the USA, medium- and long-distance passenger services are provided by Amtrak, which is owned by the federal government but operates on for-profit basis; while in Canada, nationwide passenger rail services are provided by VIA Rail, which is also government-owned. Many of the passenger services provided by Amtrak and VIA Rail use rail infrastructure that is privately owned by freight operators.[37] Notable exceptions to state ownership are Japan, where privately owned operators provide the vast majority of passenger services, and the UK, where passenger services are franchised to private operators (see Box 14.1 later).[38] There are also limited examples of private operators of high-speed rail services (such as in Italy, Germany and Sweden), and of suburban or metro services (e.g. in Melbourne, Australia, and Boston, USA). A number of these 'private' operators are actually owned by foreign governments or by foreign state-owned railway companies.[39]

Ownership of freight operators varies across jurisdictions. In much of Europe and Japan freight operators are state-owned, for example, in France (SNCF Logistics), Germany (DB Schenker) and Japan (JR Freight). In the USA, Australia and Canada, freight operators are privately owned; while in Russia, private operators can act as carriers (provide wagons and railcars) but must use the locomotives of the state-owned Russian Railways.[40]

Train operating companies derive income from the sale of passenger and freight services to end-users. For passenger services, the income derived from a specific line is sometimes insufficient to make a profit, and a government subsidy is sometimes given to provide the service at reasonable frequency if the service is considered important. Freight services are generally not subsidised.[42] The main costs incurred by train operating companies include: rolling stock depreciation or leasing costs; operating and maintenance costs; fuel costs; staff costs; and sales and commercial costs.[43] While some train operating costs vary with traffic and number of services, others, such as those associated with rolling stock, are fixed.[44] In the Netherlands, Germany, Italy, Switzerland and Japan train operating companies typically own their rolling stock.[45] In other jurisdictions, train operating companies lease rolling stock from private companies (known as a rolling stock leasing company (ROSCO)). This is the case for freight services in the USA, Australia and parts of Africa, and for passenger services in the UK and Sweden.[46] An important

---

[36] OECD (2013).

[37] This is estimated to be above 90 per cent in Canada, while in the USA Amtrak owns some infrastructure in the northeast but uses freight-owned infrastructure in other parts of the country.

[38] Griek (2016). There are estimated to be over 200 railway companies in Japan, including private railways light rails and monorails. See also Drew and Ludewig (2011).

[39] For example, the Deutsche Bahn subsidiary Arriva operates around 13 per cent of the Danish rail network and 21 per cent of the UK network. Similarly, Keolis, which is part of a consortium for the Melbourne Metro system and the MBTA in Boston, is part-owned by SNCF in France.

[40] African Development Bank (2015).

[41] In Britain, franchised train operators received around £3.3 billion in government support in 2018–2019.

[42] However, in Britain, they do receive some support for inter-modal traffic from ports, in recognition of the role of rail in reducing congestion on roads.

[43] See ORR (2020b) for a breakdown of costs for Britain.

[44] According to Finger and Messulam (2015) rolling stock can last for thirty to forty years on average and represents around on average 20–30 per cent of a train operating company's fixed costs.

[45] Williams Rail Review (2019).

[46] In Sweden, they can be leased from regional authorities. See Dillon, Jan and Keogh (2015) for the UK experience.

operational cost incurred by train operating companies are the track access charges levied for use of rail infrastructure.[47] As discussed below, both the level and structure of these charges can have important implications for the frequency and type of services that are provided (i.e. type of trains used and how often they use a line).

In the future, autonomous trains will likely play a bigger role in railways. Driverless trains are already used for closed and secure services, such as metro lines, and are being tested for freight services, light rail services and conventional rail services.[48] However, the use of autonomous trains on open and unsecured lines, such as for inter-city passenger services or freight, raises novel operational coordination and social acceptance challenges that are not dissimilar to those faced by unmanned aircraft and driverless cars.

Railway Stations

Railway stations provide infrastructure and services that facilitate the loading and unloading of passengers and freight. For passengers, this includes the station facilities and associated customer service facilities (such as booking offices), while freight rail stations include facilities for loading and unloading of cargo. There are different types of passenger railway station (high-speed rail, inter-city, commuter and metro) and freight rail station (bulk, roll-on/roll-off, break-bulk, inter-modal (e.g. containers)).

Larger passenger railway stations seek to facilitate the easy transfer of passengers between different services (e.g. connect high-speed and conventional services with metro services). Even where passenger and freight services share the same rail infrastructure (i.e. they share conventional rail tracks), passenger and freight railway stations are typically not co-located. This reflects the fact that the end-users that they service have different needs: passenger stations need to be located close to populated areas, while freight services need to be located close to sources of natural resources, manufacturing sites or ports. In addition, the service and facilities offered can differ between passenger and freight stations. Larger passenger stations often feature retail services, restaurants and hotels, while freight stations often need specialist loading and unloading equipment, warehousing and distribution facilities. Railway terminals (which lie at the end of a railway line) often have separate yard facilities which facilitate shunting (which involves the assembly or reassembly of rolling stock into trains).

Station infrastructure management involves managing, operating and maintaining stations in a way which ensures safety, optimises use and meets end-user needs (e.g. in terms of retail facilities or freight loading/unloading facilities). Railway stations are managed in four ways. First, station management can be fully vertically integrated with rail infrastructure and rail services, such as is often seen for freight train stations and for passenger services in Japan. Second, stations can be managed by the rail infrastructure provider, such as occurs in the Netherlands. A third possibility is that stations can be managed by train operating companies that service that station; for example, in the

---

[47] Finger and Messulam (2015) estimate that these can be up to 20–25 per cent of total costs incurred by operators of long-distance passenger services in some countries. Such costs tend to be fixed within the medium to long term.

[48] For example, as part of the EU's 'Shift2Rail' initiative. See IEA (2019b).

UK, the management of some stations is leased to individual train operators, while i
France stations have been managed by the train operating division of SNCF. Finally, i
some countries a fully separate entity manages stations, such as occurs in Sweden an
Germany, where stations are managed by a separate government-owned business.

   Station owners and managers derive income from the sale of 'slots' to train operatin
companies through what is known as station access charges, and from associated activ
ities, such as the rental income from leasing space at stations to retailers and hotel
In addition, in Japan and other parts of Asia, station owners can derive a significar
proportion of income from integrated rail and property development at the stations o
along the lines. The principal costs of station management include property maintenanc
maintaining information and system displays, security, facilities and cleaning.[49]

14.2 APPROACH TO RAILWAYS REGULATION

14.2.1 Activities Subject to Regulation in the Supply Chain

There is considerable diversity in how railways are structured and regulated around th
world. Railways can be vertically integrated or separated, publicly or privately owne
open to competition or not, and supported through various subsidies. In part, this dive
sity reflects differences in the extent of competition that railways face with other tran.
port modes in a particular jurisdiction. However, it also reflects wider political, soci
and environmental factors, such as a desire to create a single interconnected rail ne
work (as in Europe), maintain services to isolated or politically important regions, pr
mote strategically important export sectors, and reduce emissions. The role of the priva
vis-à-vis the public sector in owning or operating rail infrastructure or services also h
an important impact on how railways are regulated. While almost all countries featu
some public involvement, the exact form of involvement ranges from railways being pa
of a ministry and governed by specific industrial or railways laws, to railway operato
being publicly owned corporations with separate boards that pursue commercial obje
tives at arm's length from the government but are subject to oversight by an econom
regulator.

Competitive Activities in the Supply Chain
The railway systems built in the nineteenth and early twentieth centuries were often cha
acterised by competition between numerous railways operating specific lines. Howeve
in the post-war period, this structure in many countries (with the exception of the US/
moved to one of monopoly provision where railways were operated by a single pul
licly owned entity. This structure still exists in some jurisdictions. For example, India
Railways owns and operates all of India's rail infrastructure, determines what services
provide, and owns and manages activities such as the design and manufacture of rolli
stock.[50] Similarly, China Rail is a state-owned entity that operates the rail and statio

---

[49] Finger and Messulam (2015).
[50] Gangwar and Raghuram (2017).

infrastructure and also provides all passenger and freight activities through twenty-one subsidiary companies.[51]

As described in Section 14.3 below, starting in the 1980s, many jurisdictions introduced policies to restructure the railways sector with the aim of introducing competition in the rail supply chain. However, the way in which competition has been introduced into railways differs across jurisdictions. Three different forms of competition can be observed in practice: competition *for* the market (franchises); competition *in* the market (on-rail competition); and direct competition between fully vertically integrated railways (sometimes referred to as horizontal competition).

Competition *for* the market involves passenger and freight train operators competing to be awarded a concession or franchise for a set period.[52] Competitive tendering for passenger services is common in some, but not all, European countries (notably Sweden, Germany and the UK), where they tend to operate at the regional level and be for periods of up to ten years. Competition for the market also exists for freight services in some jurisdictions and tends to be for longer periods.[53] While concession arrangements aim to introduce competition through the bidding process (see Chapter 3), in some circumstances there can also be competition between train operators even after the contract is awarded. For example, overlapping franchises (where one or more operators can provide services on the same track) or parallel franchises (where more than one operator provides services between an origin and destination using different lines)[54] can give passengers and shippers a choice between different franchised train operating companies or which specific route to use between a particular origin and destination. In addition, in some jurisdictions, and particularly for freight services, concession rights are not exclusive, meaning that other train operators can potentially gain access to rail infrastructure within a concession area.

A second form of competition in vertically separated structures is known as 'on-rail' or open-access competition. Broadly, this is competition *in* the market and involves authorised train operating companies competing head-to-head with one another on certain routes. 'On-rail' competition exists for *freight* services in many countries, but can take different forms depending on the rights of access that competing freight providers have to rail infrastructure. In some jurisdictions, competing train operators have a legal right to access rail infrastructure, but this is limited to access to specific routes at defined times.[55] In other jurisdictions, there can be a general right of access for competing freight providers to rail infrastructure, as is the case in the UK, Europe and for some railways in Australia. For example, in the UK, freight operators compete under open-access arrangements. 'On-rail' competition for *passenger* services involves indirect competition between different *types* of

---

[51] Cui, Pittman and Zhao (2021).
[52] These arrangements can take various forms, including: management contracts (operator is paid a fixed management fee and bears no risk); gross contracts (operator bears risks related to costs, but not revenues); and net cost contracts (operator bears both revenue and cost risks).
[53] Laurino, Ramella and Beria (2015).
[54] For example, passengers travelling between London and Oxford can travel via two lines operated by different companies.
[55] World Bank (2017c).

railway services (e.g. high-speed inter-city services and conventional services might com pete to connect a specific origin and destination),[56] as well as direct competition between train operators of the same type for specific routes. Direct on-rail passenger competition particularly for long-distance services, can be observed in Austria, the Czech Republic Germany, Italy, Poland, Sweden and the UK.[57] However, the extent of direct on-rail passenger competition is still very limited overall. In the UK, notwithstanding an expectation in the 1990s that this form of competition would develop, there are only two examples of on-rail competition representing less than 1 per cent of passenger miles.[58]

As described below, despite the limited success to date, there is still an expectation that direct on-rail competition for passenger services might develop in some parts of Europe, such as in France, Belgium and Spain. In part this expectation comes from comparison with other transport sectors with which rail competes where there is intense competition between service providers (e.g. different airlines, trucking companies or bus services) using a common infrastructure. However, the prospects for the development of intense and wide-scale direct 'on-rail' competition for passenger services are arguably limited by a number of factors. First, passenger services need high levels of utilisation to be commercially viable. For routes or services with low passenger volumes, introducing a competing service reduces the utilisation of a particular operator and may affect the commercial viability of servicing that route.[59] Second, it is often the case that passenger services are subsidised to some degree because the revenues derived from passenger ticket sales are insufficient to cover the costs of services. Introducing on-rail competition which focuses on price can further undermine the revenues obtained by train operating companies and lead to higher levels of public subsidy, which can be politically unattractive. Third, introducing 'on-rail' competition within a franchise or concession system can change the incentives for companies to compete *for* the market. In other words, because on-rail competition can reduce the revenue stream of a franchise operator, this could deter potential franchisees from bidding or induce them to submit 'lower' bids.

While the focus in the UK, Europe and Australia has been on facilitating competition in train services, in other jurisdictions, competition takes the form of direct competition between fully vertically integrated railways (sometimes referred to as horizontal competition).[60] This is the case for freight services in Canada and in Mexico, where in each country two large privately owned integrated freight railroads compete with one another to provide freight services to shippers. In the USA, numerous vertically integrated railroads compete for the business of shippers. There are currently seven large (Class I) railroads and hundreds of smaller Class II (regional) and Class III (local) railroads which often connect to the Class I railroads.[61] However, the number of competing

---

[56] For example, a high-speed train and a conventional train service might both be able to be used for a specific journey – such as Aachen to Berlin.

[57] EC (2016d).

[58] CMA (2016b).

[59] Using British data, Wheat, Smith and Rasmussen (2018) find that open-access operators are found to have comparable unit costs to franchised operators, which they attribute to lower input prices and an 'open-access business model' effect that outweigh any density disadvantages.

[60] See Pittman (2020b).

[61] The Surface Transportation Board categorises railroad carriers into the three classes according to annual revenue threshold. In 2019, Class I carriers' threshold was $504 million, while Class II was $40 million.

railroads available to shippers can vary across the country, and in some parts of the USA, shippers can depend on a single railroad operator.[62] For 'horizontal competition' between railroads to emerge – which is similar to the infrastructure- or facilities-based competition in telecommunications discussed in Chapter 11 – a number of conditions need to be in place. First, there need to be at least two or more railroads operating on parallel routes that connect different origins and destinations such that shippers have a choice (i.e. the same city pairs or common points). Second, the demand for services between the two points must be sufficiently great as to make it commercially viable for more than one railroad to operate the services.[63] Third, the prospects for laying down competing rail infrastructure can be conditioned by location and the land-use density; for example, in densely populated areas, it can be expensive to acquire the land to lay down the infrastructure.

While horizontal competition between competing integrated railroads can be successful for freight services, its potential for passenger services is seen as more limited.[64] Passengers tend to be time-sensitive and demand the most direct routes between an origin and destination. In contrast, demand for freight services is typically less time-sensitive and can utilise a mix of faster and slower routes to reach a particular destination. In addition, the infrastructure needed for freight services often does not need to satisfy the same speed and safety requirements and can involve lower maintenance costs, which means that, while it may be economical to operate two competing freight rail infrastructures, it would not be the case for passenger services. Notwithstanding these points, the experience of Japan, where passenger services are provided by six regional vertically integrated Japan Railways (JR) operators and a number of smaller typically private operators, suggests that some competitive tension can exist (see Box 14.1 later). Japan's railways are organised along geographical lines, but they are not regional monopolies and lines can overlap or interconnect in the same area, which can offer passengers a choice. For example, there are three competing routes between Tokyo and Yokohama, and between Osaka and Kobe. There can also be some competition in urban areas between suburban lines and JR lines.

Activities Subject to Price Regulation and Other Controls

The activities in the railways sector that are subject to regulation depend on the structure of industry adopted (e.g. whether it has been vertically separated or not) and the type and intensity of competition that exists. Depending on the jurisdiction, rail infrastructure charges (known as track access charges), station access charges and any fare or charges levied by train operating companies to end-users (shippers or passengers) can all potentially be subject to separate regulation.

---

[62] Pittman (2020a) notes that before the 1980s there were thirty-nine Class I railroads, which reduced to seventeen in the 1990s, and the current structure is one where the US freight rail system is effectively dominated by two giants in the west (Burlington Northern Santa Fe and Union Pacific) and two giants in the east (CSX and Norfolk Southern).

[63] Montero and Finger (2020) note that, in the USA, there is strong demand for rail to transport heavy bulk cargo such as coal and steel, while in Europe there is some competition from onshore maritime and inland waterways, which can be good substitutes for the transportation of heavy bulk cargo.

[64] See Montero and Finger (2020).

The rationale for price regulation of rail infrastructure operators is essentially that th
cost characteristics of these activities can approximate those of a natural monopoly.[65] Ra
infrastructure – such as tracks, bridges and tunnels – is generally immobile and physical
fixed in specific locations and can involve large investments in land. While there is som
debate about whether rail systems are characterised by significant economies of sca
beyond a particular point,[66] there do appear to be economies of density attached to ra
infrastructure such that each additional unit of traffic reduces the average unit cost (u
until the point where the capacity of the infrastructure is reached).[67] In other words, whi
there are not necessarily economies of scale from having a single large operator of rai
way infrastructure, there are economies of density attached to the effective utilisation
rail infrastructure.[68] An implication of this is that whether it is more efficient (i.e. resul
in lower average unit cost) to have a single railway infrastructure operator depends c
the level of demand on a specific route. As described above, where competing rail infr
structures do exist – such as for freight transport in parts of the USA and Canada – it
generally the case that traffic density is sufficient to make it commercially viable for mo
than one railroad to operate.[69] Regulation of infrastructure can also be premised on a nee
to protect 'captive' end-users where inter-modal and intra-modal competition is weak,
to facilitate entry and competition between competing train operators by requiring thir
party access to infrastructure on non-discriminatory terms. In the USA, where railroa
are vertically integrated, there is no general requirement placed on railroads to provi
access (trackage rights) to third parties. However, in jurisdictions where rail infrastructu
is separated from train operations, and open-access policies have been introduced – suc
as in the EU and for freight in Australia – the infrastructure manager has an effecti
monopoly on control of access to that infrastructure. This has led to the introduction
policies requiring rail infrastructure managers to provide access on non-discriminato

---

[65] See Directive 2001/14/EC which declares that 'a railway infrastructure is a natural monopoly'. See also
Montero and Finger (2020) and UNECE (2017). However, as Kahn (1971) observes, this designation is
challenged by the fact that the railroads in the USA in the last quarter of the nineteenth century were n
really natural monopolists.

[66] Such that long-run average costs decline as the size of the railway system operated by a single firm
increases. Griliches (1972) concluded that 'there is very little or almost no evidence of economies of
scale in the railroad industry (if one excludes the smallest roads from consideration)', and similarly
Savignat and Nash (1999) conclude that 'economies of scale are typically exhausted at a modest size
relative to that of many existing rail companies'. Pittman (2020b) estimates that a reasonable measure
of the economies of system size might be around 10,000 kilometres. In contrast, Mayo and Willig (2019
suggest that there are 'substantial economies of scale in the provision of some rail services, whether
along particular routes or for specific types of freight, which result from the heavy fixed costs associate
with rail infrastructure and operations'. Similarly, Ivaldi and Pouyet (2018) find evidence that the Frenc
railway industry 'as a whole exhibits increasing returns to scale, which is not compatible with the
presence of multiple firms'.

[67] See Harris (1977) and Caves, Christensen, Tretheway and Windle (1985). In an early study, Keeler (1974
found substantial unexploited economies of traffic density for most railroads, but constant long-run
returns to scale. Pittman (2020b) observes that, while there are economies of density, these too can be
exhausted after a point, and opines that all the US major freight railroads operate in regions of constan
returns to density.

[68] As Harris (1977) notes: 'A small firm with high traffic density may very well have lower average costs
than a large firm with low density.'

[69] The African Development Bank (2015) suggests that this approach might be replicable in Russia, China
and India, as they are large enough to sustain competing vertically integrated railways.

terms and conditions, and, as discussed below, placing limits on the track access charges (and other charges)[70] that can be levied on train operating companies.

Although not often stated, the rationale for regulation of station operation activities arises because, while train operators have an initial choice as to which rail infrastructure to provide services on, once they have signed up to provide services on that infrastructure,[71] station operators (particularly terminal station operators) effectively hold a monopoly position for allowing access to their stations. This gives rise to a risk of 'hold-up', which is exacerbated in many jurisdictions by the fact that there is a single monopoly station operator, and, as such, a train operator cannot choose to by-pass a station operator that is charging high access prices. In jurisdictions where station ownership and operation are separated from other activities, station managers are required to provide non-discriminatory access to station infrastructure and equal treatment of different train operators using that station.[72] The charges that station operators can levy on train operating companies (known as station access charges) are also often subject to *ex ante* regulation. Freight operators can also be subject to charges from station owners to recover the costs of operating freight terminals, marshalling yards, storage sidings and train formation facilities, some of which can be regulated.

Unlike rail infrastructure, train operating services are not considered to share the characteristics of a natural monopoly, and the operators of such services face competition from other forms of transport. However, historically, there have often been restrictions on entry and who can provide train operating services, and the charges levied by train operators (particularly for passenger services) have been subject to some form of price oversight or regulation, often for political and social reasons.[73] Price regulation of end-user passenger fares or shipper rates depends on the type of service (high-speed, conventional or urban), and whether there is intra-modal competition (between different train operators). For passenger services, it is the case in many parts of the world that fares are administered by a national, regional or local authority, or set, or subject to oversight, by a regulator.[74] Urban train fares are often set by administrative means by regional or local authorities. In some cases, a government department or regulator will set a maximum level of an individual fare (or a basket of fares), and an operator has freedom to price up to that level. In Japan, the transport ministry determines the maximum limit on fares, and operators have the freedom to set prices below those levels. In the UK, around half of all rail fares have been 'unregulated' since the time of privatisation, meaning that a train operator can

---

[70] Freight users can sometimes pay specific charges to reflect their use of the infrastructure – for example, coal spillage charges are set to recover the costs of coal spillage (e.g. clean-up costs and reduced asset lives) and are only levied on operators who transport coal.

[71] As described above, rolling stock is often tailored to specific rail infrastructure and often cannot easily be moved to alternative uses.

[72] Finger and Messulam (2015) observe that equal treatment includes information display, signage, connecting service management and other services.

[73] A tension that often arises is that a commercial train operator will have different incentives in choosing which lines to operate and how to price services than those which might be desired by a government (e.g. maintaining less profitable lines and keeping transport fares affordable).

[74] Administered fares are set by the government authority, whereas regulated fares are set by the operator subject to constraints by the relevant regulator or government authority.

determine the fare for those services.[75] Prices offered by entrant on-rail long-distance passenger service operators in Europe (such as in Austria, the Czech Republic, Italy and Sweden) are not regulated, and offering lower fares is an important way in which they compete with incumbents. However, these fares may be 'quasi-regulated', insofar as their ability to attract passengers through cheaper fares will be constrained by the level of the regulated fare on a route for the incumbent. The constraints imposed by inter-modal competition can also impact on whether end-user charges are regulated and the level at which they are set. Passenger fares in some countries such as Bulgaria, Slovakia, Poland, Portugal, Sweden and the UK are all influenced by the extent of inter-modal competition on a particular route.[76] Similarly, the fares for long-distance passenger services – such as the Eurostar in Europe or Shinkansen in Japan – can be constrained by the fares charged by airlines, ferries or buses. Freight transport charges are typically negotiated between train operating companies or railways and shippers and not usually subject to *ex ante* regulation, as they are typically constrained by intra-model competition between competing railroads or freight operating companies and inter-modal competition from road transport or waterway providers.

14.2.2 Form and Scope of Price Regulation

Two broad approaches to price setting for the use of rail infrastructure can be observed in practice. A first approach involves the *ex ante* setting, or approval, of prices by a regulator, which can be in the form of multi-year price caps, regulatory approvals of annual statements of access prices, or the setting of maximum prices. The second approach involves the negotiation of prices between parties in the first instance, with a regulator becoming involved only if agreement cannot be reached.

Two factors differentiate the approach to price regulation in railways as compared to the other public utility industries discussed in this book. First, as already noted, in many countries outside North America, rail infrastructure is in state ownership. This has two implications for price regulation. The first is that regulated charges may be set to serve multiple objectives, including cost recovery, but also other factors such as encouraging efficient network use, reducing congestion, ensuring certain geographic areas are served, and to account for various environmental externalities. State ownership can also mean that the ability of a regulator to incentivise efficient performance can be limited: operating more efficiently will not lead to commercial gain for the operator and there may be an implicit belief that any losses will be covered by the state.[77] Second, in many countries the railway sector receives substantial government subsidies in addition to any regulated revenue. Subsidies can be used to cover the cost of maintaining infrastructure, to fund the development of the network, or to recover the costs of fulfilling certain public

[75] Unregulated fares include first-class and advance purchase fares, but not standard ticket and weekly tickets. They also typically do not apply to London and major city commuter routes.
[76] EC (2016d).
[77] Nash, Crozet, Link, *et al.* (2018) query how effective incentives placed on infrastructure managers in the EU can be 'given that infrastructure managers are government owned and there are no shareholders to bear the costs'.

service obligations by train operating companies (e.g. providing services on unprofitable lines). In some jurisdictions, this means that regulated track access charges might be set to recover only the operational and maintenance costs, with the balance being recovered through subsidies. In other jurisdictions, regulated track access charges may seek to recover some proportion of infrastructure investment costs (including a return on capital) directly from train operating companies.[78]

Price Caps

In some jurisdictions, a regulator sets or approves an *ex ante* (up-front) maximum, or ceiling, on the average increase in prices (or revenues) related to a set of defined services.

In Britain, the rail regulator sets a forward-looking price control for a fixed period of five years, which includes a forecast revenue requirement such that the infrastructure manager (Network Rail) can recover its efficient costs and make any required investments in network infrastructure.[79] The price control is set after allowing for the level of government subsidy (estimated at around 70 per cent of its income) and includes incentives for Network Rail to outperform in terms of punctuality and delays.[80] However, as the infrastructure manager is a government-owned entity, it does not earn a return on a regulatory asset base (RAB), and the scope for the regulator to impose financial remedies for poor performance is limited.[81] Germany has also introduced a multi-year system of price cap regulation, where charges are set on a RPI-X (retail price index minus X) basis, with the X determined by industry-wide productivity growth.[82]

The approach to price regulation in other EU Member States does not necessarily involve a regulator setting forward-looking price caps for a fixed period to incentivise performance. Rather, the approach is based around a multi-annual contract where a rail infrastructure manager (which is publicly owned) is usually responsible for determining track access charges and setting them out in an annual network statement.[83] In preparing the network statement, the infrastructure manager must consult with applicants, and highlight where responses have led to changes in the statement. The regulator then typically reviews the network statement and can raise objections, including potentially disallowing costs which are not efficient.[84] The regulator can also hear any appeals made against proposed charges.

---

[78] Laurino, Ramella and Beria (2015) note that, in Germany, track access charges seek to recover a high proportion of railway infrastructure costs, while in Hungary, Russia and Australia, track charges recover a (generally small) part of the investment costs. In Sweden, the fixed costs of the infrastructure are covered by a subsidy, such that track access charges are set at marginal cost. See also Nash, Smith, Crozet, *et al.* (2019).

[79] A distinction is made in terms of the regulatory settlements for Network Rail as infrastructure owner and the system operation function, which has its own regulatory settlement.

[80] The regulator is looking to separate Network Rail's operations into different routes and to use internal benchmarking to assess the efficiency of costs.

[81] The regulator does, however, maintain an RAB for each geographical route, and also estimates a weighted average cost of capital (WACC) in part to show what the revenue requirements would be if it was financed in the private sector and to provide a benchmark internal rate of return.

[82] See BNETZA (2017) and Nash, Crozet, Link, *et al.* (2018).

[83] This is required under EU regulations.

[84] In order to facilitate the review, the infrastructure manager must provide data about the planned revenues, the volumes on which they are based and expected costs. A recent proposal for an increase in track access charges in France was disallowed because the costs were not considered to be efficient.

Under EU Directives, infrastructure managers are required to offer a 'minimum access package' and track access charges are based on the 'direct' costs of providing and operating the infrastructure – that is, the marginal costs which vary with volume (on a per kilometre basis).[85] As discussed in Section 14.4.2 below, any costs incurred above the direct cost such as fixed and common costs, can be recovered through a 'mark-up' which allows for the recovery of full costs including, in some cases, an appropriate return on capital. Mark-ups can vary according to the type of train operating service (long-distance, freight, conventional, regional) and market segments within those services (e.g. night service, charter, empty service). In setting the mark-ups, the infrastructure manager considers the competitive situation of the various market segments and the ability of the market segment to bear the charges.[87] In determining the level of required revenues to cover cost any government subsidies and other revenue are excluded. EU Directives also require that the infrastructure manager face incentives to improve efficiency. This can be achieved through: cost benchmarking (internationally or across different routes or franchises); disallowance of costs assessed as inefficient; or (as noted above) the introduction of multi-year price caps, as in Britain and Germany.[88] In addition to recovering direct costs, track access charges can also reflect other objectives and considerations. For example, surcharges can be used to reflect the scarcity of capacity and congestion and be applied to services (such as long-distance ones) which require priority access. Discounts can be used to promote greater utilisation of specific lines or promote new traffic growth (and thus shift traffic from road to rail), and noise-differentiated track access charges can be used to take account of the costs of the environmental impact of operating the train service. Surcharges and discounts to reflect environmental impacts can offset one another in revenue terms: higher mark-ups for noisier trains can be offset by discounts given to low-noise freight vehicles. In practice, the track access charges levied across EU Member States differ in how direct costs are both determined and estimated, which has implications for the size of mark-ups. The objectives pursued through the pricing policy have also differed: some countries have historically sought to incentivise efficient use of the network by keeping some charges low, while others have sought to ensure full cost recovery for the infrastructure operator.

---

[85] Directive 2012/34/EU. There can be differences in what is contained in this package across Member States, such as whether the costs of passenger platforms were included or not. For example, in Germany this minimum access package includes timetabling costs, operating costs, maintenance costs and depreciation of tracks, but not renewals. See Link (2018).

[86] Link (2018) raises the question of whether a return of capital is appropriate for 100 per cent state-owned companies.

[87] On average, around 88 per cent of revenues from track access charges is derived from passenger services in the EU. However, this varies significantly: in Spain, 99 per cent is collected from passenger services; while in Slovenia and Estonia, only 1 per cent is collected from passenger services. See IRG (2020).

[88] See Nash (2018).

[89] Under relevant Directives, environmental costs must not increase overall cost.

[90] Nash (2018) notes that, in Germany, expert judgement is used to determine if a cost is variable and the direct costs do not include renewals. In contrast, in France, renewals are included and based on engineering models, while maintenance costs are based on econometric models.

[91] Nash (2018) observes that, in Sweden and Britain, the emphasis has been on promoting efficient use of the network; while, in France and Germany, the emphasis has been on full cost recovery (after allowing for government subsidies). More broadly, Montero and Finger (2020) note that many countries have very low access charges, particularly for freight and suburban services, with higher charges for long-distance high-speed services and specific freight services.

In other jurisdictions, access charges or end-user prices are set by a government department or ministry. This might involve a ministry setting a maximum level of prices, as in Japan, where the maximum limit on passenger fares set by the transport ministry is determined based on a comparison, or benchmarking, of the costs of the different operators to determine efficient costs. In jurisdictions where competition *for* the market exists (e.g. concession or franchise contracts), the maximum level of track access charges or end-user prices can be set out in concession contracts, and can differ according to region and type of service.

Negotiated Approaches

In some jurisdictions, charges are not subject to *ex ante* regulation but are subject to negotiation between parties in the first instance. This is particularly the case in jurisdictions where rail infrastructure is predominantly used for freight transport, and there are limited or no government subsidies. In Australia, where some rail infrastructure managers are required to provide open access to rail infrastructure to train operating companies,[92] freight access charges are negotiated (in the first instance) between infrastructure managers and freight operating companies, but can be subject to arbitration by the regulator if agreement cannot be reached (see the discussion of the negotiate–arbitrate approach in Chapter 3).[93]

In Canada, freight charges are also determined through negotiation between vertically integrated railways and shippers in the first instance and there is no regulated maximum charge. If agreement cannot be reached, a shipper can apply for a final offer arbitration, which involves an arbitrator making a legally binding, confidential decision of which final offer is used to settle the dispute. The regulator can also sometimes require 'interswitching' on a railroad. This involves a railroad being required to carry a shipper's goods only to a particular interchange at a regulated 'interswitching' rate, after which the shipper is able to 'switch' to another preferred railroad that will carry the goods to a final destination.[94] Interswitching rates must be fair and reasonable and cover the full economic costs, including a rate of return.

In the USA, vertically integrated railroads compete to attract the freight business of shippers and this competition is an important way of controlling prices faced by shippers. Freight charges are privately negotiated, and in the absence of subsidies must be set to cover the full costs of the railway.[95] As rates are confidential, this can allow

---

[92] These include privately owned railways that have been 'declared' on the basis that: it is uneconomical for anyone to develop another facility; the facility is of national significance; the facility is important to the national economy; and access would not be contrary to the public interest. For example, the Pilbara Railway Declaration allowed third-party trains and rolling stock to move along the railways and use rail infrastructure, including railway tracks and structures, bridges, passing loops, signalling, and roads and other facilities which provide access to the railway line route.

[93] Charges can also sometimes be detailed in an access undertaking approved by the regulator; for example, the Australian Rail Track Corporation (ARTC) undertakings, which set out the terms of interstate access for nine major train operating companies.

[94] See CTA (2020).

[95] Pittman (2020a) refers to a study by the Surface Transportation Board which shows that Class I railroads approach and sometimes achieve 'revenue adequacy' (i.e. returns that are at or above their cost of capital).

railroads to engage in second- and third-degree price discrimination.[96] As described below, in some circumstances, the regulator (the Surface Transportation Board, STB) can challenge the reasonableness of rates, particularly where shippers are 'captive', in that they are served by a single railroad and do not have economic access to transportation alternatives.[97] In order for the regulator to intervene, a captive shipper must show that the rate it is offered is unreasonable, including that the rate offered is higher than the stand-alone cost (SAC) of a hypothetical railroad built to carry the shipper's traffic.[98] If the rate offered is higher than the estimated SAC (which allows for full cost and a return on capital invested), then the railroad will have to lower its rate (Box 11.0 discusses this approach in more detail). In contrast to the negotiated approach adopted for freight, where railroads are required to provide access to passenger services operated by the government-owned Amtrak, the access charge is set out in legislation and based on marginal cost.

14.3 THE SCOPE AND EFFECTS OF RESTRUCTURING POLICIES

14.3.1 The Scope of Restructuring Policies in the Railways Industry

In many parts of the world, railways have at times experienced the full spectrum of regulatory policies,[99] from being fully deregulated, and subject to the constraints imposed by competition between railroads and other forms of transport (road and air), to being nationalised, and fully controlled by a government department.[100] There remains substantial variation in the regulatory policies applied to the sector not only across jurisdictions but also for different types of railway services (passenger versus freight) within jurisdictions. This provides useful real-world insights as to the effectiveness of the different policies pursued.

Restructuring policies introduced over the past four decades for railways have involved changes to railway ownership or management, to organisational structures and to the approach to the regulation of access, entry and charging. However, the policies pursued have differed significantly between North America, Europe and elsewhere in the world. In particular, as discussed below, there have been important differences in the approach to separation and promoting competition.

---

[96] Pittman (2020b).

[97] Pittman (2020a) references estimates from the regulator which suggest that approximately 15 to 20 per cent of shipping volume is captive.

[98] The original full SAC test was based on the costs of a hypothetical and optimally efficient railroad, while the simplified SAC is based on a portion of the actual railroad, with whatever inefficiencies currently exist. See ICC (1986). Intervistas (2016) explain that: 'Complaining customers must develop detailed evidence to calculate both direct operating expenses (such as the cost of locomotives, crew, and railcars) and indirect operating expenses (such as maintenance of way) of a hypothetical railroad designed to serve its traffic.'

[99] Montero and Finger (2020) and Pittman (2020a) provide useful overviews.

[100] The railroad industry in the USA is described as having transitioned from one of the most heavily regulated settings in American industry prior to the 1970s to a market-oriented system. See Braeutigam (1993). For a historical overview of the development of US railways and regulation in the 1800s, see Clark (1891).

Scope of Restructuring in the USA

In the USA, the origins of economic regulation of railways date back to the establishment of the Interstate Commerce Commission (ICC) in the 1880s which, among other things, set maximum and minimum rates, prohibited discrimination and required that its approval be given for changes in rates and service terms and the abandonment of lines.[101] The railways then went through a period of nationalisation, followed by a return to private ownership. However, by the 1950s and 1960s, many railways were in decline. Various factors lay behind this decline. First, railroads faced more intense inter-modal competition. Widening car ownership and the expansion of bus and air travel reduced demand for passenger rail services, while freight services faced more intense competition from trucks on the Interstate highways and the development of inland waterway systems. Second, regulations which required the pre-approval of rates hampered the ability of the railroad operators to quickly respond to inter-modal competition. Regulations also required that railroads continue to provide passenger services on lines experiencing declining demand which were unprofitable.

In response, new restructuring policies were introduced in the 1970s and 1980s.[102] This included allowing railroads to pass on passenger services to the newly created government-owned Amtrak to operate,[103] removing requirements for freight rates to be pre-approved by the ICC, and allowing railways to abandon unprofitable lines and not service particular shippers. The approach sought to encourage intra-modal competition between vertically integrated railroads, as well as allowing railroads to compete more intensively with other modes of transport. These changes allowed railroads greater autonomy in choosing which lines to maintain and shippers to service, as well as greater flexibility in negotiating rates, including an ability to engage in some degree of differential pricing.[104] The aim was to allow railroads to achieve revenue adequacy by differential pricing. However, this ability was constrained, and a shipper still had an ability to challenge rates that it considered to be unreasonably high with the regulator, and the regulator could prescribe a maximum reasonable rate.[105]

Scope of Restructuring in Europe

In Europe, up until the late 1980s, almost all railways operated as government-owned vertically integrated monopolies operated under ministerial control. In many countries, this was perceived to have resulted in inefficient and loss-making operations, poor incentive properties that derived from the lack of hard budget constraints, and the running of uneconomic services in response to political demands.[106] Restructuring of railways

---

[101] Pittman (2020a) and STB (2019a).

[102] This includes the Regional Rail Reorganization Act (1973), the Railroad Revitalization and Regulatory Reform Act of 1976 and the Staggers Act (1980). Overviews are presented in Braeutigam (1993), National Academies of Sciences, Engineering and Medicine (2015) and Pittman (2020a).

[103] The Rail Passenger Service Act (1970).

[104] See STB (2019a). Mayo and Willig (2019) observe that it is also likely that individual contracts include heterogeneous non-price terms that respond to particular needs of the customers (e.g. assurances of deliveries' timeliness, reliability, etc.).

[105] This is known as a 'constrained market pricing' policy. Mayo and Sappington (2016) provide an overview of the approach.

[106] Abbott and Cohen (2017).

in Europe began with changes first introduced in Sweden in 1988, which involved th‹ separation of rail infrastructure from train operations.[107] Britain went one step furth‹ in the early 1990s by separating infrastructure from operations and also privatising th‹ provision of passenger train services (on a franchise basis) and the sale of freight trai‹ operations. Two new economic regulators were created to oversee the sector.[108] Howeve‹ as discussed in Box 14.1, the private ownership of rail infrastructure was abandoned fro‹ 2001, and several passenger franchises have since fallen back under state ownership an‹ operation.

In other Western European countries, restructuring also began in the early 1990s mot‹ vated by a desire to improve financial viability and increase the performance of th‹ sector (particularly against other transport modes) and facilitate the creation of a Sing‹ European Railway Area.[109] In the EU, high-level restructuring policies focused on the ve‹ tical separation of rail infrastructure and train services to facilitate competition in freigh‹ and passenger services.[110] Directives and Regulations (sometimes referred to as Railwa‹ Packages) issued by the European Commission have since sought to establish commc‹ rules across all EU Member States.

The First Railway Package (2001) introduced open access for the international ra‹ freight market and required the functional separation of infrastructure managers an‹ train operating companies, and that accounting separation be introduced for freight an‹ passenger train services. Rules for setting capacity allocation were established, and infra‹ structure managers were required to publish network statements that set out their infra‹ structure capacity, as well as their access arrangements and charges. It also required th‹ independent national regulators be established to monitor competition and ensure fa‹ access to infrastructure and services.[111] The Second Railway Package (2004) introduce‹ full open access for all freight traffic (national and international) from 2007, and create‹ a European Railway Agency, a technical and safety regulator to align and harmoni‹ technical and safety regulations to aid the development of the Single European Railwa‹ Area. The Third Railway Package (2007) introduced changes in how subsidies are alle‹ cated,[112] and opened up access for international passenger services (including cabotag‹ the right to onload and offload passengers on the domestic parts of an internation‹

---

[107] The Swedish reforms were motivated by, among other things, financial difficulties and subsidies for unprofitable lines, and not specifically with a focus on deregulation and introducing competition. See Nilsson (2002) and Alexandersson (2010.

[108] The Office of the Rail Regulator (ORR) was the regulator for the monopoly infrastructure operated by Railtrack, while an Office of Passenger Rail Franchising (OPRAF) was responsible for awarding franchises, regulating fares levels and overseeing the franchise agreements.

[109] Finger and Messulam (2015) provide an excellent overview.

[110] Although, as noted above, the forms of competition have varied for freight and passenger services: competition *for* the market has featured prominently in passenger services, while it has been based on competition *in* the market for freight services.

[111] Regulators could remain part of the transport ministry but needed to be independent from any infrastructure manager, charging body, allocation body or applicant.

[112] Funding must now follow state aid rules, and can only be used for rail infrastructure or for public service obligation contracts.

journey) from 2010.[113] However, open-access rights could be limited where the introduction of an international service may have a detrimental impact on an existing local or regional service covered by a public service contract. A 2012 'recast' of the First Railway Package sought to address identified shortcomings in the regulatory framework. This included: a lack of competition; inadequate regulatory oversight, mainly due to a lack of independence and powers of economic regulators; and the low levels of investment in the European rail infrastructure.[114] This recast involved: enhanced transparency of rail access conditions in more detailed network statements; strengthening the independence of regulators; and clarifying rules for infrastructure funding and management. A Fourth Railway Package (2016) was introduced with the aim of completing the creation of the Single European Railway Area.[115] It includes requirements for competitive tendering for public service rail contracts from 2023,[116] and extends the right of open access to purely domestic passenger services by December 2020.[117] It also sets down new rules aimed at improving impartiality in the governance of railway infrastructure and preventing discrimination.

Scope of Restructuring Policies in Other Jurisdictions

Restructuring in Japan started at around the same time as in Sweden and involved the break-up and subsequent privatisation of Japanese National Railways (JNR) (see Box 14.1).[118] This was motivated by high levels of debt, the near-collapse of JNR in 1986 and the sharp decline of passenger traffic.[119] JNR was divided into six fully integrated passenger railway companies and one freight railway company. In Latin America, policies introduced in the 1990s also involved the horizontal separation of previously state-owned monopoly railways, but the approach adopted involved using competition for the market. Long-term passenger (including suburban and metro services) and freight concessions were introduced in Argentina, Brazil and Mexico for periods of up to fifty years based on the vertically integrated model.[120] These contracts are often managed by regulators who can impose penalties for non-compliance or poor performance. Concession contracts

---

[113] This includes two Directives and two Regulations: Directive 2007/58/EC, Directive 2007/59/EC, Regulation 1371/2007 and Regulation 1371/2007.

[114] Finger and Messulam (2015).

[115] Comprising a Technical Pillar (Directives 2016/797 and 2016/798 and Regulation 2016/796) and a Market Pillar (Directive 2016/2370 and Regulations 2016/2337 and 2016/2338).

[116] This means that contracts can no longer be directly assigned to an operator.

[117] Restrictions can ensure the continuity of certain services can be permitted beyond that date subject to objective economic analysis by regulators.

[118] Mizutani and Nakamura (2004) provide useful background.

[119] The long-term debt of JNR was estimated at 25 trillion yen in 1986; while the passenger modal share of rail fell from 51 per cent in 1960 to 22 per cent in 1987. See Drew and Ludewig (2011).

[120] The former state-owned companies were often horizontally separated prior to the awarding of concessions. These were often structured to ensure competition to serve key markets, but also allowed for access right to parts of other networks. See Campos (2001) and Perkins (2016). In Brazil, a series of reforms were proposed in 2012 (but ultimately abandoned) which would have involved the vertical separation of infrastructure operations and maintenance from transportation service provision. See Sampaio and Daychoum (2017).

have also been used in sixteen African countries since the early 1990s, with estimate that by 2010 around 70 per cent of the sub-Saharan African rail network (excluding Sout Africa) was operating under private control.[121] Concessions were granted to mainly for eign private and semi-public operators for periods up to thirty years, and often allowe the concessionaire the freedom to determine freight tariffs with no or weak regulator oversight.[122] Restructuring in Australia has focused on freight and involved the vertica separation of the inter-state rail infrastructure from train operations, and allowing third party access for freight services (including on privately owned infrastructure) on term that can be approved by a regulator.[123]

Restructuring in Russian railways began in the mid-1990s prompted by the need fo substantial investment, and has at various times envisaged competition in freight rail ways.[124] To date, this has involved the corporatisation of the railways (separating govern ment and corporate functions), the separation of some non-core activities, and allowin private owners to operate rolling stock (but not locomotives).[125] Finally, restructurin policies are under consideration in China,[126] with a particular focus on whether policie based around vertical separation or horizontal separation should be pursued.[127]

Box 14.1	**Two tales of rail privatisation: Britain and Japan**

The shift of railways from state ownership to private ownership in Japan and Britain pro vides useful comparative insights into how industry structure can impact on the success c privatisation policies. At first sight, the two countries share a number of similarities. Bot are densely populated, highly urbanised and industrialised islands with globally importar cities (Tokyo and London) and a high demand for mainly passenger rail services.

In Japan, the restructuring process started in 1987 with the break-up of the Japa National Railway into six regional vertically integrated passenger operators and a freigl operator. These entities were first held in state ownership under a holding company, wit four gradually privatised in the early 1990s.[128] The principal motivations for privatisatio were the high levels of debt, poor efficiency, low productivity and loss of inter-moda passenger share to road vehicles.[129] In Britain, the restructuring process also started i the early 1990s when British Rail was split up into 100 different companies that wer

---

[121] See Lowe (2014).
[122] See Bullock (2009) and African Development Bank (2015).
[123] The government-owned Australian Rail Track Corporation, which manages *inter*-state rail infrastructure, was established in 1998. Train services were initially provided by another separate government-owned entity (the National Rail Corporation), but have since been privatised. Policies differ for *intra*-state railway with some states pursuing policies based around integration, and others focused on vertical separation.
[124] See Pittman (2013a, 2013b).
[125] Pittman (2020b) and Drew and Ludewig (2011) provide useful overviews.
[126] Policies introduced in 2013 involved the creation of the China Railway Corporation (CRC) (a state-owned enterprise), which is responsible for eighteen railway bureaus. See Li, Lang, Yu, *et al.* (2019) for an overview of changes.
[127] Cui, Pittman and Zhao (2021) provide an overview of this debate. Pittman (2004, 2011) provide useful background.
[128] Two loss-making regional Japan Railways companies (JR Hokkaido and JR Shikoku) and the freight division (JR Freight) remain under state ownership. In addition to the six JR railways, there are sixteen major private railways and 128 mid-sized to small privately run regional railways and commuter railways. See Kurosaki (2018) and Mizutani and Nakamura (1997) for overviews.
[129] Mizutani and Nakamura (2004).

gradually privatised.[130] As in Japan, privatisation was motivated by a gradual loss of passenger and freight traffic to road, and a desire to reduce the debts of British Rail and address issues with under-investment and ageing infrastructure.[131] Broader political factors were also at play.[132] At the time of privatisation, there were expectations that costs and the level of government subsidy would be reduced through a combination of fierce competition *for* the market for franchises, which would be followed by the development of 'on-rail' competition *in* the market, with different train companies competing head-to-head on various lines.

While the motivation, timing and process of privatisation were broadly similar in Japan and Britain, a critical difference was how the railways were privatised. In Japan, the privatisation involved the sale of vertically *integrated* entities which owned and operated the rail infrastructure, maintenance facilities, rolling stock and stations.[133] In contrast, in Britain, a policy of *separation* was pursued, which involved the horizontal and vertical separation and subsequent privatisation of multiple entities, including: a single rail infrastructure manager (Railtrack); seven infrastructure management companies; six track renewal companies; two freight companies; three rolling stock leasing companies; and the competitive franchising of twenty-five passenger operators.[134] The view at the time was that open-access competition would be gradually introduced and that the separation of rail infrastructure from train operations was necessary to maximise competition and prevent a privately owned infrastructure manager from abusing its position.[135]

---

[130] For useful overviews of the background to privatisation, see Nash (1993) and Pollitt and Smith (2002).

[131] However, Welsby and Nichols (1999) observe that the reforms introduced in the early 1980s meant that, by the end of 1989, the subsidy to the passenger railway was approximately halved in real terms: InterCity was moving into profitability; the subsidy for the commuter services around London was falling sharply; and the heavy-haul freight business was generating large cash surpluses. This changed following 1989, when over the next four years passenger demand fell by 10 per cent and revenues fell only marginally less, resulting in British Rail requiring a subsidy of £2 billion in 1991/92.

[132] Welsby and Nichols (1999) note that, in spite of evidence that railways in Britain were operated much more cost-efficiently than their European counterparts, there was a strong belief in the Conservative government that some activities remained fundamentally inefficient and that railways would always be vulnerable to trades union power in ways that had been eliminated elsewhere in the economy.

[133] There continue to be some elements of state ownership of railways in Japan. For example, Japan Freight Railway Company, which was one of the seven original JNR companies, remains in state control. Similarly, high-speed Shinkansen lines are built and owned by the government, but are handed over to private companies to operate under long-term concessions.

[134] Nash (2016) records that: '[T]he logic was that competition would be introduced wherever feasible in the structure, not just for all freight and (largely through competitive tendering) passenger operations but also for the leasing of rolling stock and the maintenance and renewal of infrastructure.' See also Pollitt and Smith (2002). The number of franchises was based on the existing British Rail profit structure. The aim was to have frequent competition for franchises and to set franchises for short periods (seven years). Franchise operators also had no asset base at privatisation and effectively leased rolling stock and paid track access charges.

[135] Nash (1993) observes that the approach may also have been influenced by the experience of other European countries such as Sweden and the European First Railway Package (which required the accounting separation of infrastructure and operations). Prior to this approach being adopted, there was debate as to the best way to introduce private ownership into railways. Starkie (1984) favoured an approach based around state ownership of rail infrastructure but with private trains competing to use that shared track. Gritten (1988) favoured an approach similar to Japan, where a series of regional independent vertically integrated operators were privatised; while British Rail is said to have advocated that no separation should be introduced and that the entire British Rail system (infrastructure and train services) should become a privately owned monopoly (while there would be no intra-modal competition, there would be inter-modal competition).

The experience of privatisation in the two countries over the past three decades is vast[ly] different. Early assessments of the British privatisation and restructuring using data u[p] to 1999/2000 was largely positive, concluding that it had increased output, and brough[t] efficiency savings and benefits to consumers.[136] However, problems were emerging wi[th] this structure, and a series of events following the Hatfield accident in October 2000 le[d] to the infrastructure manager (Railtrack) being subsequently placed in administration (a[s] Network Rail) and ultimately 're-nationalised'.[137] A new policy was introduced in 202[ ] which placed all railways under the control of a single authority (Great British Railway[s]) that will be responsible for strategic and operational decisions, rolling stock and station[s,] network and service density, and long-term finance.[138] Although the system of franchisir[g] will be retained, there have been persistent problems identified with the private operatio[n] of the passenger franchise system, with limited evidence of private operators being able [to] reduce costs.[139] The expectation of private operators providing direct head-to-head on-ra[il] competition, as originally envisaged, has not, to date, been realised.[140]

In Japan, the experience of privatisation is generally regarded as a 'triumph' and there [is] no current discussion of returning the privately run railways to state ownership.[141] Publ[ic] subsidies are rare, and price increases have been at levels below the rate of inflation fo[r] almost three decades. There are also constant and aligned incentives for the railway ope[r]ators to invest in all activities (infrastructure, rolling stock, stations), which may not ari[se] in a vertically separated system where incentives may be misaligned, or where franchise[s] have only limited incentive to invest beyond the period of their tenure. Although railwa[ys] are organised on geographical lines, there is some competitive tension where lines overl[ap] or interconnect in the same area, which can offer passengers a choice, or where there a[re] competing routes between destinations (e.g. three routes between Tokyo and Yokoham[a]). The approach to setting maximum rates also introduces a form of indirect or yardsti[ck] competition between the different operators.[142]

---

[136] Pollitt and Smith (2002). However, as Smith and Nash (2014) caution 'whilst restructuring and privatisation may have contributed to the strong performance of the British system, the major causes o[f] it lie elsewhere'.

[137] Nash (2016) explains that, following the accident, it was discovered that Railtrack had no adequate record of the state of its assets, which led to severe speed limits being imposed until this could be checked and remedial action taken where necessary. The compensation it had to pay to train operators for the line restrictions coupled with cost overrun on the West Coast Main Line upgrade put Railtrack into financial crisis. It asked the government for a bail-out, but was refused.

[138] See Department for Transport (2021). Lewis and Offer (2022) pose the question of whether this is 'the last gasp of privatization dogma, or an honest attempt to re-integrate the railways'.

[139] Nash (2016) notes that several of the first round of franchises failed because of failures to reduce costs. Recent examples of where franchises have been brought back into public ownership include the East Coast Main Line 2018, the Northern Franchise in 2020 and the ScotRail franchise from 2022. Successive government-commissioned reviews have found problems with risk sharing under the franchise arrangements. Brown (2012) found that franchising is an important component of the privatised industry structure but advocated that franchisees should not be expected to take external macroeconomic, or exogenous, revenue risk. Williams and Shapps (2019) identify numerous problems with the franchises and advocate them being replaced with a concession model where a public sector body tends to retain the revenue risk rather than passing this on to the appointed operator.

[140] CMA (2016b).

[141] Kurosaki (2016) concludes that: '[T]he JNR reform has been successful thus far. This success can mainl[y] be attributed to privatisation and regional division, both of which solved the problems underlying JNR[ ] failure.' See also Financial Times (2019) and Mizutani and Nakamura (1997).

[142] See Mizutani (2019).

4.3.2 The Effects of Restructuring Policies in the Railways Industry

Effects of Restructuring in the USA

The effects of reforms introduced in the USA in the 1980s for freight services are widely considered to be a success and a 'triumph of deregulation': freight traffic volumes, service levels, labour productivity and investment all increased, while rates paid by shippers have generally decreased in real terms compared to the 1980s.[143] Studies also suggest that major Class I railroads actively compete with one another while remaining revenue-sufficient (able to earn returns that are at their cost of capital),[144] and that rail's share of freight transport increased from 29.7 per cent in 2000 to 34.2 per cent in 2018.[145]

Notwithstanding these undeniably positive effects, a number of concerns have recently been raised. These include that: successive mergers have resulted in a concentrated structure with effectively two regional duopolies; routes have been rationalised and rates increased; and many shippers have little bargaining power, while captive shippers are unable to effectively challenge rates under existing 'rate reasonableness' regulations.[146] It has been argued that the rate reasonableness standard is a difficult hurdle for complaining shippers to clear and that, as a result, the majority of cases are found for the railroad.[147] Attention has focused in particular on the use of the SAC methodology. While some advocate its continued use as a well-designed, economically sensible regulatory fall-back to protect captive shippers,[148] others argue that it is ill-suited, complex, cumbersome and expensive, and that it should be modified or applied only in certain cases.[149] Various options for rate reform have been proposed, including by a taskforce established by the regulator (STB).[150] In 2019, the STB established a new rate case procedure for

---

[143] For early assessments, see McFarland (1989), Braeutigam (1993) and Wilson (1997), and more recently Mayo and Sappington (2016) and Pittman (2020a).

[144] Christensen Associates (2010) find that industry-level mark-ups generally decreased since the early 1990s and 2010, and that since 2006 the sector had become revenue-sufficient. STB (2019a) also concludes that all railroads are financially healthy.

[145] EC (2020h). Road share fell from 44.7 per cent to 40.2 per cent over the same period.

[146] See Pittman (2020a) and STB (2019a), which found that: '[M]any shippers find railroads largely uninterested in their business; many shippers feel that they have little bargaining power with respect to the contracts they are offered; and while intermodal and intramodal competition for much traffic remains vibrant, many captive shippers have no realistic avenue for relief from what they view, as their ancestors did in 1887, as abusive practices by powerful, dominant railroads.'

[147] See National Academies of Sciences, Engineering, and Medicine (2015), STB (2019a) and Pittman (2020a).

[148] See Mayo and Willig (2019).

[149] The regulator's own Rate Reform Taskforce (STB, 2019a) found that each SAC case can cost a shipper up to $10 million to litigate, and expressed its concern: 'that SAC as it is currently practiced promotes a sense of false precision', while the National Academies of Sciences, Engineering, and Medicine (2015) refer to the weak conceptual basis for the test. Similarly, Pittman (2020a) refers to comments from the chair of the regulator that this can involve the absurd situation where 'the STB, its staff, and the dueling parties' are debating the cost of constructing 'imaginary restrooms needed for the imaginary crew for the imaginary railroad'.

[150] The STB (2019a) taskforce recommendations included: standardising SAC; imposing administratively determined rates for small disputes arbitration; adopting an approach where the reasonableness of rates is assessed based on the incumbent carrier's assets and operating expenses, rather than those of a hypothetical entrant; and providing different remedies for cases where the railroad was long-term revenue-adequate. The National Academies of Sciences, Engineering, and Medicine (2015) advocated wider changes, including ending the STB's direct role in maximum rate rulings and replacing it with an independent arbitration process similar to that in Canada and allowing reciprocal switching (interswitching) as a remedy for unreasonable rates.

smaller cases known as the Final Offer Rate Review (FORR) whereby the regulator wi[ll] choose between either a shipper's or a railroad's final offer through an expedited proces[s]. This is similar to the process used in Canada.[151]

While restructuring policies in the freight sector in the USA introduced since the 1970[s] and 1980s are generally considered to have been a success (subject to the points jus[t] noted), the situation is different for passenger services. Amtrak, the passenger train oper[-] ator, continues to pay freight railroad operators only a track access charge based on mar[-] ginal cost. The services suffer from poor levels of reliability (in part because of the nee[d] to share tracks with freight) and have been historically unable to cover variable costs o[f] most routes.[152] While this has often given rise to recurring questions about the long-ter[m] viability of passenger services, recent years have seen an increase in passenger ridershi[p] and the financial position of Amtrak improving to the point where some forecast that i[t] could soon be in a position to cover its operating costs.[153]

Effects of Restructuring in Europe

In Europe, the effects of restructuring policies vary significantly across jurisdiction[s], reflecting the varied approaches that have been adopted and the heavy reliance on pas[-] senger services.[154] Sweden is still considered to be among the most advanced in terms o[f] restructuring and has allowed for 'on-rail' competition since 2010.[155] Although entry ha[s] been limited, where such 'on-rail' competition exists, it has reduced prices.[156]

The British experience of restructuring is mixed.[157] As described in Box 14.1, ra[il] infrastructure was re-nationalised in 2001, in part, because of deteriorating infrastruc[-] ture and investment overruns, and now operates as a state-owned entity. There hav[e] also been increases in unit costs,[158] and persistent problems with the franchising sys[-] tem, which has led to calls for it to be restructured or abandoned.[159] At the sam[e] time, passenger and freight traffic has continually grown[160] and state subsidies reduce[d]

---

[151] STB (2019b). Prior to this, in 2016, the STB issued a Notice of Proposed Rulemaking to adopt revised reciprocal switching regulations that would allow a party to seek a reciprocal switching prescription that is either practicable and in the public interest or necessary to provide competitive rail service.

[152] Smith (2019) notes that only 43.2 per cent of services ran on time in 2018. Overall revenues remain heavily reliant on services in the northeast corridor of Boston, New York and Washington, DC, which accounts for around 38 per cent of all journeys.

[153] Rail share of passenger inter-modal transport has remained constant at 0.4 per cent since 2000 (EC, 2020h).

[154] Across Europe, around 81 per cent of network usage is for passenger services.

[155] Nilsson, Pyddoke, Hulten and Alexandersson (2013) provide background. Nash, Smith, Crozet, *et al.* (2019) note that this is facilitated in part by the fact that subsidies cover the fixed costs of the infrastructure so that track access charges may be based on marginal cost.

[156] Vigren (2017). Although Nash, Smith, Crozet, *et al.* (2019) suggest that this is a short-run equilibrium and suggest that few other routes offer such potential. For an earlier assessment of the impacts of reforms, see Nash, Nilsson and Link (2013).

[157] See McNulty (2011), Nash (2016), Williams and Shapps (2019) and Nash and Smith (2020).

[158] See McNulty (2011) and Nash, Smith, Crozet, *et al.* (2019).

[159] Williams and Shapps (2019) advocate it being replaced with a concession model where a public sector body tends to retain the revenue risk rather than passing this on to the appointed operator and bidders generally do not have to produce timetables or revenue projections.

[160] Although as Nash, Smith, Crozet, *et al.* (2019) observe, it should not be assumed that the impact of reforms on passenger services were the sole, or even the most important, determinant and that growth of cities, suburbanisation and road congestion may be other major causes.

Overall, passenger fare levels have increased to recover higher industry costs because of reduced subsidies. In addition, there are concerns about poor punctuality and complex and confusing ticketing arrangements.[161] Although some have advocated that 'on-rail' competition be extended, it is likely that the franchise system will be maintained, albeit after being restructured.[162] In Germany, where there was resistance to the full vertical separation of rail infrastructure, a holding company structure emerged.[163] Large numbers of passenger and freight operators, including private operators, have since entered the market, costs and subsidies have decreased, and fares have grown at levels lower than in Sweden and Britain.[164]

The effects of restructuring in other EU countries vary significantly but are generally seen to have resulted in a more fragmented structure. All countries have now separated – albeit in different ways – infrastructure from train operations and created independent regulators. At the EU level, passenger and freight traffic, as well as track access charges, have been moderately increasing.[165] Around 60 per cent of income now comes from charges levied directly on users, with subsidies accounting for about 30 per cent.[166] Rail's share of inter-modal transport has remained constant, but rail infrastructure is considered to be degrading because of limited maintenance and low levels of investment.[167] In terms of competition, new entrants had a 24 per cent share of the passenger market in 2018.[168] However, entry is concentrated in a few countries (the UK, Sweden, Poland, Germany and Italy), and in nine EU Member States the incumbent had a *de facto* monopoly in the provision of passenger services. Competition *in* the market ('on-rail' competition) exists on major lines in nine countries, provided by thirty-six operators, mainly for domestic long-distance services.[169] Where 'on-rail' competition has been introduced, there is some evidence that it has reduced prices and increased frequency of service.[170] Notwithstanding these developments, new commercial operators still face discrimination in obtaining access to rail infrastructure and service facilities, and incumbents may

---

[161] Haylen (2019). This is in part because of complex yield management systems which offer substantial discounts for off-peak tickets bought in advance, and considerably higher prices for peak periods.

[162] CMA (2016b). See UK Department for Transport (2020).

[163] In 2012, the European Commission brought an action against the Federal Republic of Germany in order to move further towards the separation model. Germany and France were also apparently resistant to changes in the Fourth Railway Package requiring the opening of domestic competition.

[164] Nash, Nilsson and Link (2013) noted that, at that time, some sixty freight operators competed with the incumbent, and, of the fifty-nine passenger operators, twenty-one were private. See also Nash, Smith, Crozet, *et al.* (2019).

[165] IRG (2020). However, Montero and Finger (2020) observe that competition has had a negative effect on some routes in terms of frequencies and termination of some services. This is because these routes no longer benefit from cross-subsidies from the more profitable routes.

[166] According to Steer Davies Gleave (2015), of the 60 per cent of revenue from user charges: 40 per cent comes from passengers, 20 per cent comes from freight, 30 per cent comes from subsidy, and the remaining 10 per cent comes from other income sources, such as property rents and retail.

[167] EC (2020h) finds that rail's share of inter-modal transport in 2018 is the same as in 1995 at 6.9 per cent. See also EC (2019b).

[168] This includes foreign incumbents, non-incumbents and former incumbents that are now privately owned. See IRG (2020) and EC (2021g).

[169] IRG (2020) estimates that twenty-three of the operators are state-owned.

[170] Montero and Finger (2020). However, as they note, such '[C]ompetition seems to be limited to a low number of routes in each country (sometimes just one) with the best infrastructure (high-speed), and the highest volume of passengers. Competitors tend to be limited to the incumbent and a newcomer.'

engage in anti-competitive behaviour or rely on cross-subsidies to keep competitors ou
of the market.[171]

In the freight market, 'on-rail' competition is now widespread across Europe and ne⋅
entrants had a 44 per cent share of the freight market in 2018.[172] While freight market
are less concentrated than passenger markets, some EU countries still exhibit hig
levels of concentration by conventional standards.[173] Recent assessments have con
cluded that freight services suffer from low quality and reliability.[174] There is also n
evidence that vertical separation and competition increased European railways inter
modal share of transport: rail share of freight fell from 14.1 per cent in 2000 to 12.
per cent in 2018.[175]

Effects of Restructuring Policies in Other Jurisdictions

The effects of railways restructuring in other countries varies greatly. As discussed i
Box 14.1, restructuring in Japan is generally considered to have been a success and 'ou⋅
standing'.[176] Passenger journeys and productivity have increased and rail has increased i
share of all transport activity, while the lack of a need to cross-subsidise freight has le
to reinvestment into high-speed passenger services.[177]

In Latin America, while the early experiences of restructuring policies based aroun
the use of concessions was largely negative, this has improved over time. In Argentin⋅
there were early problems with incomplete concession agreements, lower-than-expecte
freight levels and under-investment, which led to the contracts being renegotiated.⋅
Brazil and Mexico also show how the process for the initial allocation of concession con
tracts (auctions or bilateral negotiations) can be critical.[179] However, recent evaluatio⋅
suggest that the situation has improved in all three countries. The use of rail concessio⋅
in Brazil has led to investments in existing lines, and improvements in service qua⋅
ity, productivity and freight movements, but they have faced difficulty in encouragir
new investment to expand the network.[180] In Mexico, restructuring is generally seen ⋅
have been successful, with freight traffic growing at rates of around 4 per cent, pro
ductivity increasing and higher levels of investment.[181] Although prices increased, the⋅

---

[171] EC (2019b).
[172] This includes foreign incumbents (13 per cent) and non-incumbents (31 per cent). See IRG (2020). EC
(2021g) notes that new operators compete with national incumbents in all countries except Greece,
Ireland, Lithuania and Luxembourg, and that in half of them the market share of competitors was over
30 per cent.
[173] See IRG (2020).
[174] EC (2019b).
[175] EC (2020h), while road grew from 48.8 per cent to 51 per cent during the same period. See also Tomeš
(2017) and Pittman, Jandová, Król, et al. (2020), which conclude that there has been little success in
developing inter-modal competition for certain freight services in Europe, which they attribute to
capacity limitations in infrastructure.
[176] Kim and Huang (2021) and Kurosaki (2016).
[177] See IEA (2019b) and Kim and Huang (2021).
[178] Gómez-Ibáñez (2003).
[179] Campos (2001).
[180] Betarelli, Domingues and Hewings (2020), Sampaio and Daychoum (2017) and Dutra, Sampaio and
Gonçalves (2016).
[181] Villa and Sacristán-Roy (2013) and OECD (2020d).

were initially no shipper complaints, as this was accompanied by expanded services and increased quality; however, more recently, concerns have arisen about a 'regulatory gap' in defining a methodology to determine tariffs for captive shippers.

In Africa, the use of rail concessions has proven difficult in many countries.[182] In many countries, they have not performed as expected, giving rise to multiple restructurings and renegotiations, and in some cases outright cancellations and a return to public ownership.[183] There have also been problems associated with the underestimation of demand and service requirements, leading to low revenues, and the investments made have had limited impact on performance.[184] However, as Bullock (2009) observed at that time, the performance of railways that have not been concessioned in other countries also continued to deteriorate, and, in a number of cases, these declines will prove to be terminal. Overall, although there is substantial potential for railways to grow in Africa to service mining developments and large urban areas, several factors hold back the development of railways, including a policy focus on road, inadequate infrastructure, rolling stock and poor regulatory governance.[185]

14.4 REGULATORY POLICY ISSUES IN THE RAILWAYS INDUSTRY

This section discusses two regulatory policy issues in the railways industry: the effects on competition of horizontal and vertical separation in the industry, and the experience of applying Ramsey–Boiteux pricing.

14.4.1 Horizontal or Vertical Separation: Which Promotes Competition More Effectively?

Until the 1980s, there were two main ways in which the railway sector was structured around the world: either in the form of fully integrated private railways, subject to a tight and intrusive regulatory framework that set prices and determined routes (as in the USA), or as a state-owned integrated monopoly with no competition. For the reasons described above, both of these structures could be detrimental to operational performance and financial viability and limit the ability of railways to compete with other forms of transport. To address these problems, policy makers in many parts of the world have sought to rely on competition to improve performance and outcomes.

The specific policies pursued reflected different visions of competition and involved different forms of restructuring.[186] Broadly speaking, two approaches to promoting

---

[182] See African Development Bank (2015). An earlier 2009 assessment was more sanguine and concluded that the results at that time were encouraging and that most of the concessionaires have improved the railways' traffic levels and productivity and provided better service to users than the state did, albeit after a major investment by donors and international financing institutions. See Bullock (2009).

[183] For example, in Zambia, Mozambique and Tanzania; see African Development Bank (2015). The African Development Bank (2015) notes that 'concessionaires have suffered unpredictable and arbitrary changes, such as requirements to run unfunded passenger services, or imposed salary increases'.

[184] African Development Bank (2015) and Vilardell (2015).

[185] See Vilardell (2015).

[186] Pittman (2013a) and Besanko and Cui (2016) provide excellent overviews. Preston (2002) provides a general overview of the advantages and disadvantages of vertical integration.

competition can be observed. The first approach focuses on direct competition betwee[n] fully vertically integrated railway operators operating on parallel lines. This approach i[s] sometimes referred to as 'horizontal competition' or the 'American model' and involve[s] several fully integrated railway operators competing with one another. Given the reli[-]ance on competition, this approach often involves removing most price and coverag[e] regulations, but provides a means of regulatory redress for captive shippers.[187] A secon[d] approach, sometimes referred to as 'vertical competition', involves promoting competi[-]tion between providers of train services (on-rail or above-rail competition) that utilise common rail infrastructure (below the rails) and is sometimes referred to as the 'Europea[n] model'. To facilitate vertical competition, restructuring policies have involved the full o[r] partial vertical separation of the core railway infrastructure management from the ser[-]vices that use that infrastructure, as well as policies that allow for entry of train operatin[g] companies and ensure non-discriminatory access to rail infrastructure.[188]

Horizontal Competition between Competing Railroads

The horizontal competition approach is often premised on there being substantial (ver[-]tical) economies of scope in such activities such that an integrated railroad operato[r] that manages the infrastructure and also provides train services will do so at lower cos[t] than separate providers of rail infrastructure and train services.[189] It also ensures coor[-]dination in operational activities, which can be particularly important in railways, as failure to maintain or upgrade rail infrastructure (tracks and signals, etc.) can impact trai[n] safety and performance,[190] while poorly maintained rolling stock can damage tracks.[1] Integration can also align the incentives to invest in rail infrastructure, rolling stock an[d] other train services.[192]

   The main risk of this structure is that an integrated railroad operator may in some cir[-]cumstances be able to exploit any market power it has, particularly over captive custom[-]ers, which can give rise to a need for regulation. The scope for such exploitation, and th[e]

---

[187] In Latin America, where concession agreements have been used, this has involved competition for the market.

[188] Full separation involves the infrastructure manager not being able to own or operate train services, while partial separation involves the structural, functional or operational separation of the infrastructure activities and train operating activities within a single entity.

[189] See Ivaldi and McCullough (2008), Wills-Johnson (2008), Growitsch and Wetzel (2009) and Mayo and Willig (2019).

[190] High-speed services, in particular, require that infrastructure (track and signals, etc.) are maintained to high standard.

[191] Nash (2016) identifies problems of misaligned incentives in the vertically separated British system, where train operators paid marginal costs and thus had no incentive to reduce total costs of the system or reduce the damage done by services which resulted in track maintenance and renewals.

[192] This can be particularly important in railways because both rail infrastructure and rolling stock need to be designed to work with one another (the so-called 'wheel–rail interface'). As such, in a separated structure, a rail infrastructure manager might not want to invest in new infrastructure (tracks, etc.) to accommodate the needs of a specific train operating company if there is uncertainty about whether the train operating company will make the investment. Similarly, as Finger and Messulam (2015) observe: '[T]echnical configurations adopted by railway infrastructure managers (such as signaling systems, speed and acceleration rates calculated for a given route) are vital to railway operators, since they can render assets with substantial residual value obsolete virtually overnight, with no opportunities for selling them to other operators.'

need for regulatory oversight, is conditioned by: the extent of *intra*-modal competition between railroads operating on parallel routes; the extent of *inter*-modal competition with road, air and waterways; and 'source' competition.[193] Another potential risk of this approach is that it could result in too many small railroads competing for traffic, which means that any economies of scale – or system size – might not be fully exploited.[194]

Vertical Competition at Different Activities in the Supply Chain

The vertical competition approach involves the vertical separation of the core network activities from the competitive activities in the supply chain. The aim of this approach is to exploit any economies of scale (system size) for rail infrastructure (the core network activity) and at the same time to introduce competition in activities that do not have the characteristics of a natural monopoly, and where multiple competing train operating companies could reduce overall costs and improve performance.[195]

The principal risk of this approach is that it could fail to realise any economies of scope and can involve significant transaction costs.[196] Coordination failures and misaligned incentives between different entities (separate rail infrastructure operators and train operators) could also lead to lower levels of service quality in the short term.[197] In addition, the risk of 'hold-up', or the short duration of franchise contracts, can reduce incentives for parties to invest in relationship-specific investments. For example, train operators may be concerned about future hold-up by the infrastructure manager.[198] Moreover, because infrastructure managers do not deal directly with end-users, investment decisions may be made on political rather than commercial bases.[199] In partial separation models (where an integrated infrastructure operator also provides train services alongside competitive

---

[193] This is where raw materials (such as coal or steel) can be sourced from different locations and transported to a specific point such as a power station or factory. See Drew (2009) and also Pittman (2007).

[194] Brown (2013) describes how historically this was discussed in terms of 'ruinous' or 'destructive' competition that did not lead to the construction of economically efficient networks, and/or incessant and ruinous price wars between competing railways. As discussed above, more recent studies have often concluded that such economies of scale only exist up until a particular point. See Savignat and Nash (1999) and Chapin and Schmidt (1999).

[195] Mizutani and Uranishi (2013) and Mizutani, Smith, Nash and Uranishi (2015) find that the impact of vertical separation on costs depends on the intensity of use. Vertical separation can increase costs (relative to vertical integration) on intensely used railways and reduce them on lightly used railways.

[196] See Bitzan (2003). Pittman (2007) notes that: '[T]he literature advocating vertical restructuring in railways is remarkable for its lack of references to the literature on transactions costs, and for its only grudging acknowledgement of the fact that the breaking up of a provider of railway ... services may entail huge losses of economies of vertical operations.'

[197] Gómez-Ibáñez (2016) finds that coordination costs are likely to be high in the rail industry if 'the access provider and access user interface is technically complex, the network is close to capacity, the access users are heterogeneous, there is little reciprocity between providers and users, and the access grants are broad'. Similarly, Lewis and Offer (2022) argue that: 'Integrated railways solve agency problems internally by means of command and control.'

[198] See Van de Velde, Nash, Smith, *et al.* (2012) and Van de Velde (2015). Yvrande-Billon and Ménard (2005) argue that incentives to invest in relationship-specific investments could also be affected by regulatory framework, particularly short franchise contracts. In contrast, Affuso and Newbery (2002) do not find that a higher degree of vertical separation by means of short-duration franchise contracts hinders incentives towards investment; rather, they identify a pattern of investment which increases in response to competitive forces in the market.

[199] See Drew and Ludewig (2011).

entrants), there may be the familiar risks to competition of discriminatory price and non price terms being imposed by the integrated entity on its rivals in the competitive activit (see Chapter 6).

Comparing the Effects of the Two Approaches

The two approaches have been applied in different parts of the world and provide a opportunity to compare the impacts on indicators such as prices, investment, servi quality, new entry and route coverage.

Generally speaking, studies which have investigated the impacts of the horizontal con petition approach, where railways remain vertically integrated, have concluded that it ha been relatively successful. As noted above, competition between vertically integrated rai roads in the US freight sector are seen to have lowered rates, increased traffic and servi levels, and improved the inter-modal freight share of railways.[200] Similar policies, pursue in Brazil and Mexico, are also considered to have improved service quality, productivi and freight movements, and, in Mexico, to have attracted new private investment.[201] A the same time, there are concerns in these countries about the concentrated indust structure, and that a 'regulatory gap' exists such that captive shippers cannot effectivel challenge rates under existing regulations. The success of restructuring and privatisatic in Japan has also been attributed to maintaining vertical integration, which has allowe for greater informal communication and coordination between infrastructure manage ment and train operating services and reduced the exposure to misaligned incentives (s Box 14.1).[202] It has also been suggested that the Japanese restructuring has introduce greater competition between railways.

The experience of the vertical competition approach is mixed. In Europe, this ma reflect the fact that the approach has been implemented in different ways: some countri have implemented full vertical separation, while others have implemented more parti separation policies.[203] In Britain, where a policy of full vertical separation was pursue reviews have found that costs have increased and there are concerns about misaligne incentives between the infrastructure manager and train operating companies, poor ope ational coordination, and under-investment in rail infrastructure.[204] In Sweden, studi conclude that, while vertical separation raised costs, this was offset by the introdu tion of vertical competition, which lowered costs.[205] In other EU countries, studies hav concluded that there is no evidence that full vertical separation increases competitio

---

[200] See Mayo and Sappington (2016) and Pittman (2020a).

[201] Sampaio and Daychoum (2017), Betarelli, Domingues and Hewings (2020) and OECD (2020d).

[202] Nakamura, Sakai and Shoji (2018), Financial Times (2019) and Nakamura and Sakai (2020).

[203] A distinction is sometimes made between full separation (introduced in Denmark, Portugal, Spain, Sweden and the UK) and partial separation, where separate subsidiary entities under common ownersh by a holding company provide infrastructure management and provide train operating services (introduced in Austria, France, Germany, Greece, Italy and Poland).

[204] See Smith (2006), McNulty (2011) and Nash (2016). A particular issue was the complexity of the arrangements introduced at the time of separation, which relied heavily on formal contractual coordination between multiple parties, such as track access agreements, station access agreements, depot contracts and rolling stock leasing agreements, etc. Preston (2002) refers to there being over 20C contracts underpinning the infrastructure manager's activities.

[205] Jensen and Stelling (2007).

and that it may increase costs at higher traffic densities.[206] More generally, there is no evidence that vertical competition has increased modal shares of European railways,[207] improved productivity,[208] or led to lower prices or higher quality for consumers.[209] Studies of the impacts of allowing for 'on-track' competition between train operating companies present conflicting results.[210] While some studies have found that full vertical separation has involved only modest increases in transaction costs,[211] others conclude that it has created antagonistic interests between all the actors involved.[212]

Of particular relevance are the European Commission's own assessments of the success of the vertical competition policies it has pursued. A 2011 review identified benefits in the vertical separation policies introduced in Sweden and the Netherlands, and noted that the greatest benefits are likely to arise from the separation of freight operations rather than passenger operations. The review also concluded that the costs of full separation can be significant where it involves a complex contractual framework.[213] A more recent assessment by the European Commission concluded that rail is struggling to achieve its potential, that rail infrastructure is degrading, that new commercial operators still face discrimination in obtaining access to rail infrastructure, and that incumbents may engage in anti-competitive behaviour to keep competitors out of the market.[214] The European Commission's expectation is that the Fourth Railway Package, which involves opening up passenger competition, will address these limitations through effective enforcement, and will also ensure non-discriminatory access to infrastructure. Finally, in Australia, policies requiring that private railways give third-party access to other providers have also been fraught, and involved long and lengthy legal disputes.[215]

While a sharp distinction between vertical competition and horizontal separation approaches has been made, three points should be borne in mind. First, many jurisdictions combine elements of both approaches. In the USA, passenger train services are vertically separated from rail infrastructure, while, in Britain and many EU countries,

---

[206] Van de Velde, Nash, Smith, *et al.* (2012). However, they find that partial separation (such as the holding company model) reduces costs relative to an integrated structure. Smith, Benedetto and Nash (2018) analyse the impact of reforms on costs in seventeen European countries and conclude that vertical separation and strong regulation are both needed in order to bring beneficial impacts in the form of cost reductions.

[207] Tomeš (2017). Montero and Finger (2020) note that: 'Evidence is unclear on the impact complete vertical separation (companies under completely different ownership) has on competition and growth.' Drew and Nash (2011) find that vertical separation results in slower growth in rail freight traffic than vertical integration but faster growth in rail passenger traffic.

[208] Bougna and Crozet (2016).

[209] See Esposito, Doleschel, Kaloud, *et al.* (2017).

[210] Casullo (2016) finds that on-track competition may result in higher costs resulting from duplication of functions and increased coordination costs. In contrast, Desmaris (2016) concludes that on-rail competition in the Italian high-speed rail market has increased capacity, frequency and connections, and lowered prices.

[211] Andersson and Hultén (2016) and Merkert, Smith and Nash (2012).

[212] Finger and Messulam (2015) note that this antagonism pits 'infrastructure managers against train operating companies, train operating companies against each other, station managers against everybody else'.

[213] EC (2011b).

[214] EC (2019b). These problems may reflect the historically low levels of transposition of, and compliance with, the Railway Packages by certain EU Member States.

[215] Notably the decade-long dispute about access to rail lines in the Pilbara region of Western Australia (which produces 95 per cent of Australia's iron ore), which ended in the High Court of Australia.

freight and passenger operations are horizontally separated.[216] Second, the nature and scale of any economies of scope can differ depending on which activities are combined. For example, across almost all jurisdictions where the rail sector has been restructured (including the USA and Japan), freight train services are separated from passenger rail services, presumably on the assumption that there are limited economies of scope (benefits of integration) in combining the two activities.[217] Finally, there is a need for caution in attributing the performance of railway systems in different jurisdictions solely to the separation policies pursued. In Europe, for example, the restructuring process has been slow and has taken time to be fully implemented across all EU Member States. The performance of any restructured railway system will also depend on factors such as: whether the railways are used for predominantly freight or passenger services; the route topographies and densities; the age and condition of rail infrastructure and rolling stock; the competition from other transport modes; and whether competition is *for* the market (use of concessions or franchises) or *in* the market (on-rail competition). In addition, wider factors such as the extent of private ownership; the political goals pursued; the degree and intensity of regulatory oversight; and the relative autonomy of government will all affect the performance of railways.

14.4.2 Ramsey–Boiteux Pricing in Railways: Pricing for What the Market Will Bear

In Part II we noted that a key regulatory challenge in public utility industries with high fixed costs, which includes railways, is how to set prices that maximise total surplus subject to the constraint that the firm breaks even. One possibility discussed was Ramsey–Boiteux pricing, where a mark-up is applied above marginal cost for different customer groups, and where the mark-up is inversely proportional to the elasticity of demand for the product by each particular group. This approach results in prices that will be higher for consumer groups with less elastic demand, and lower for consumer groups with more elastic demand, despite the fact that the marginal cost of production is the same for both groups (see Chapter 4).

In railways, the suggestion that different users of railway services should face different prices, and that prices be set according to 'what the traffic will bear' pre-dates the publication of Ramsey's famous article (Ramsey, 1927). Writing in 1904, Acworth describes an approach where railway 'prices are based, not on cost to the producer, but on value to the consumer'.[218] This approach, which is conceptually similar to Ramsey–Boiteux pricing,

---

[216] Kurosaki (2018) describes various forms of vertical separation in Japan for new high-speed Shinkansen, urban lines and unprofitable railways.

[217] For example, the EC (2011b) concludes that the benefits of separating freight train services from rail infrastructure management are greater than separating passenger services from infrastructure. This is because of the heavy reliance of passenger services on public subsidies and the more limited opportunities for purely commercial operations for passenger services.

[218] Acworth (1904). The merits of charging differential prices to different customers in railways was also considered by Hadley (1885), who saw such an approach as justified where it allows for services to be expanded, noting that it involved 'difference(s) in rates not based upon any corresponding difference in cost' and that such differential pricing can be observed 'between classes of business, localities, or individuals'.

still an important charging principle for railways in the USA and Europe. However, a key difference is whether the mark-ups applied to different users to recover fixed costs are determined privately through negotiations or are subject to regulatory approval.

Approach to Mark-Ups in the USA

In the USA, charges for freight services are privately negotiated between railroad operators and shippers.[219] Railroad operators can set differential prices to allow them to collect adequate revenues to cover their high fixed costs. This means that railroads can price their services in inverse relation to demand elasticity (the price sensitivity of the traffic) and charge captive shippers higher mark-ups over costs than they charge non-captive shippers with competitive alternatives.[220] The logic of this approach is that, if a railroad is required to sell all services at a uniform mark-up above full costs, some traffic with a high elasticity of substitution, such as container shippers, could shift to other transport modes (road and waterways), resulting in a loss in revenue from that traffic for the railroad operator, which may make it unable to recoup its total costs. However, as noted above, the ability to charge differential prices to captive shippers (those with low price elasticity) is not unconstrained, and shippers can challenge rates set by 'market-dominant' carriers that are unreasonably high.[221] Giving railroads the flexibility to set prices in a way that recovers their fixed costs has the potential for 'Ramsey-like' price schedules to emerge organically which reflect value of service and volume considerations.[222] However, as noted in Section 14.3, recent reviews have highlighted concerns about the adequacy of protections to ensure that captive shippers are not exploited through differential pricing.[223] Shippers have suggested that a railroad's ability to differentially price traffic should be restricted once revenue adequacy is achieved,[224] and that benchmarking should be introduced to allow rates to be compared to one another.[225]

Approach to Mark-Ups in Europe

In the EU, railway infrastructure managers are permitted to charge mark-ups above marginal cost to improve their ability to recover fixed costs.[226] While mark-ups must be

---

[219] In contrast, railroads cannot negotiate the access charges levied for passenger services operated by the government-owned Amtrak, which are based on marginal cost.

[220] STB (2019a).

[221] Market dominance refers to an 'absence of effective competition from other rail carriers or modes of transportation for the transportation to which a rate applies'. As Pittman (2020a) notes, a consequence of this is that railroads do not have unlimited freedom and 'there would be ceilings set on the degree to which the shippers with the most inelastic demand for rail were forced to shoulder the burden of the fixed costs of the system'. See, generally, STB (2019a) for an overview of this policy.

[222] Mayo and Willig (2019).

[223] STB (2019a) note that: 'An alarming number of shipper interests said that the railroads were "demarketing" their shipments, offering take-it-or-leave-it deals that unreasonably squeezed them.'

[224] That is, when a railroad's rate of return on net investment equals or exceeds the industry cost of capital.

[225] The 2019 Rate Reform Taskforce (STB, 2019a) confirmed that a fundamental goal of rail regulation is to allow railroads to price differentially to achieve revenue adequacy, but suggested that certain remedies be tied to a finding of long-term revenue adequacy, and that a rate increase constraint be introduced that would identify a point beyond which further application of differential pricing would be unwarranted.

[226] The term used in the EU Regulation is direct costs, rather than marginal costs. However, as Nash, Crozet, Link, *et al.* (2018) note, direct costs are defined to reflect short-run marginal social cost.

non-discriminatory, they can be differentiated according to market segments. As such mark-ups can in principle vary according to the type of train service (passenger, freight, domestic or international) and segments within those services (e.g. urban, regional, night services, charter, different types of freight commodities, empty service). In determining mark-ups, an infrastructure manager can consider the competitive situation of the various market segments and the ability of the market segment to bear the charges.[227] However, mark-ups should not be set at levels which exceed 100 per cent of cost recovery or exclude market segments that would otherwise be able to pay the direct costs of the services, plus a rate of return.

In theory, the ability to set mark-ups according to 'what the market can bear' provides the potential for rail infrastructure charges (track access charges) to reflect Ramsey–Boiteux principles under the EU rules. However, in practice, there have been differences in how mark-ups are calculated and applied across EU Member States. In France and Belgium, freight services only pay the direct (marginal) costs, while passenger services pay a mark-up that is up to four times higher.[228] In Britain, mark-ups are applied to freight services according to their ability to pay, and to franchise operators of passenger services according to allocated fixed costs. In Sweden, the mark-ups are only applied for services which cross the bridge connecting Sweden and Denmark.[229] Germany moved to a form of Ramsey–Boiteux–based charging scheme from 2018, which has involved the infrastructure manager determining the direct price elasticity for different types of passenger and freight end-users.[230]

There are various reasons why differential mark-ups based on Ramsey–Boiteux principles have not been widely adopted in Europe to date. First, because of vertical separation, the mark-ups are applied by infrastructure managers to train operating companies and not to the ultimate end-users (such as passengers or freight shippers).[231] This means that infrastructure managers do not have access to the detailed demand information they need to allow them to set mark-ups for different market segments in a way that is inversely proportional to demand.[232] Second, because the majority of train services in Europe are passenger services, this can further complicate the ability of an infrastructure manager to apply efficient mark-ups.[233] Some jurisdictions may decide to apply low or no mark-ups for some routes (e.g. suburban routes) and to recover fixed costs through subsidies, or link

---

[227] Setting mark-ups according to what the market will bear while guaranteeing optimal competitiveness of the rail market segment is recognised in the Regulation. Link (2018) notes that, in Germany, the design and level of mark-ups have to guarantee the 'best possible' competitiveness of market segments.

[228] IRG (2020). Nash, Crozet, Link, *et al.* (2018) note that mark-ups for high-speed trains vary by route, and the mark-ups for the most profitable routes can be up to 1000 per cent.

[229] Nash, Crozet, Link, *et al.* (2018).

[230] Link (2018).

[231] As the World Bank (2017c) has noted: '[V]ertical separation may have made it more difficult to maximize infrastructure utilization and to recover infrastructure fixed costs. … Will potential economic benefits from competition in services outweigh the dilution of economic benefits from Ramsey price differentiation and the transaction costs of separation? This remains to be seen.'

[232] Nash, Crozet, Link, *et al.* (2018) note that this requires access to data on demand and costs, which the train operators regard as confidential.

[233] For example, infrastructure managers will likely not have information about individual passenger usage such as relative demand for service classes, travel times, different types of tickets, etc.

the level of mark-ups to subsidy payments.[234] Alternatively, a decision might be taken not to apply high mark-ups to passenger services on the basis that it will encourage entry and the development of on-track competition.[235] Third, there could be difficulties in differentiating track access charges in ways which are not considered discriminatory under EU law; for example, applying different mark-ups to freight trains carrying different types of cargo (general freight versus coal) on the basis that they have different demand elasticities. Finally, unlike in the USA, mark-ups often have to be approved by a regulator, which increasingly involves the use of 'market can bear' studies to estimate elasticities. This has sometimes led to disputes between the regulator and the infrastructure manager about the precise elasticity estimates used to derive the mark-ups for different market segments.[236]

14.5 CONCLUSION

Railways have been, and continue to be, central to the economic development of many countries. Regulatory policy towards railways ranges from a reliance on intense competition between competing privately owned integrated railroads, to 'on-rail' competition between competing train operators using a common rail infrastructure, to reliance on a single integrated state-owned monopoly. While there remain high levels of state ownership of railways in many parts of the world, policies introduced since the late 1980s have focused on restructuring the sector and introducing greater competition with the aim of improving efficiency and performance.

How railways are structured and the extent of competition that exists differ significantly across countries. In the predominantly freight-based railway systems of North America, the approach is based around horizontal competition between privately owned and operated vertically integrated railroads. In Europe, rail infrastructure is under state ownership, and has been vertically separated from train operations with the aim of creating competition 'on the rails'. Other countries, such as Japan, have pursued policies of privatisation based on vertically integrated railways; while, in Latin America and Africa, the main focus has been on competition *for* the market and the granting of rail concessions. These approaches reflect differences not only in the perceived economic characteristics of railways, such as the extent of economies of scale, scope and density, but also in political factors.

Differences in how railways are structured have significant implications for the regulation of the industry. In the USA, Canada and Latin America, there is a focus on the negotiation of freight charges directly between parties in the first instance, with a regulator only becoming involved if agreement cannot be reached. There is also no general requirement to provide third-party access to infrastructure. However, railroads can be

---

[234] Link (2018) observes that, in Germany, mark-ups for regional rail passenger transport are not based on an (empirically) estimated price elasticity but rather are set to ensure that the applicable track access charges increase with the same rate as regionalisation funds.

[235] See Nash, Smith, Crozet, *et al.* (2019).

[236] Disputes have arisen in Germany regarding the elasticities used for standard freight trains, and for regional and dangerous goods trains, and in the Netherlands regarding the elasticity for the freight versus passenger sectors. See Link (2018) and Railfreight (2018).

required to provide access to passenger services and the charges are set at marginal cos
In contrast, in Britain and Europe, track access charges levied on train operating compa
nies are set up-front or need to be approved by a regulator. This can involve multi-yea
price caps, regulatory approval of annual statements of access prices, or the setting o
maximum prices. There are also requirements placed on rail infrastructure managers t
provide access to train operators on non-discriminatory terms and conditions, which ar
overseen by independent economic regulators.

The effects of the restructuring policies introduced in the rail sector around the worl
over the past four decades depend on a combination of factors, such as the extent an
form of any public ownership, the structural model applied to the sector, including th
extent of horizontal or vertical separation, and the form of competition pursued fo
passenger and freight services. The restructuring policies introduced in the USA in th
1980s for freight services are widely considered to have been a success, although there ar
current debates about whether more regulation is needed to protect captive shippers, an
the US experience of passenger rail is far less positive. The privatisation and restructurin
of Japanese railways is also considered to have been successful. The experience of th
use of concession contracts as a means of introducing competition for the market differ
across jurisdictions. Recent evaluations of Brazil and Mexico are generally positive, whil
in African countries the results have been more mixed, with some concessions giving ris
to multiple restructurings and renegotiations, and in some cases outright cancellation:
In the EU, the experience of restructuring policies based around vertical separation is als
mixed. In freight transport, despite the fact that on-rail competition has developed, ra
has not increased its inter-modal share. Direct 'on-rail' competition for passenger service
is concentrated in only a few countries, and some new operators still face discriminatio
in obtaining access to rail infrastructure.

Looking ahead, the future of railways in many countries will be shaped by a combi
nation of policy and technological and demographic factors. Railways will likely fac
strong inter-modal competition in many jurisdictions from new forms of urban mobilit
(scooters, Ubers) and passenger transport (unmanned aerial vehicles, taxis and buses
However, relative to other forms of transport (particularly roads), railways offer sub
stantial benefits in terms of safety and environmental impact, accounting for around
per cent of energy use in the transport sector,[237] and in some places there is considerabl
scope for inter-modal cooperation such as through air–rail agreements which can expan
rail's share of the market.[238] Technological developments such as the emergence of ultra
high-speed railways (such as Maglev and Hyperloop), driverless trains and the wid
impacts of digitisation may allow for closer integration of rail and other transport mode
(such as mobility as a service (MaaS) platforms).[239] As has been the case for the last 15
years, regulators and policy makers will need to adapt policies in light of these change
to achieve an appropriate balance between competition and regulation.

---

[237] IEA (2019b) provides an assessment of the interaction between rail and the environment.
[238] See Chiambaretto and Decker (2012).
[239] MaaS relies on digital platforms that allow users to seamlessly integrate public transport routes,
timetables, information, ticketing and payment systems to develop door-to-door trips. Examples are
Qixxit and ioki, which have been developed by Deutsche Bahn.

DISCUSSION QUESTIONS

1. What are some of the important characteristics of demand and supply for railway services, and how do passenger and freight rail services differ from one another?
2. Discuss the three main forms of competition that exist in the railways industry. In what circumstances, and for which services, is each form of competition likely to be most effective?
3. What activities in the railways industry are typically subject to price regulation, and what is the typical form and scope of that regulation?
5. What are some of the main differences between the scope of the railways restructuring policies introduced in North America, Europe and other countries?
6. Discuss some of the important differences in the experiences of privatisation of the railways industry in Britain and Japan.
7. Do you agree with the following statement? 'The effects of restructuring policies introduced in the railways industry around the world have not lived up to expectations.' Discuss.
8. Discuss the arguments in favour of and against the horizontal competition approach and the vertical competition approach to railways restructuring. What have been the impacts of each approach on indicators such as prices, investment, service quality, new entry and route coverage?
9. What are the potential benefits and risks of allowing railroad operators to price according to what the market will bear? What has been the experience of applying this approach in practice?

15

Aviation Regulation

The story of modern economic regulation often begins with reference to the policies introduced to 'deregulate' the aviation industry in the USA in the late 1970s. For consumers, the changes which followed had a profound effect in terms of the choice of routes and destinations, quality of service and prices paid for air travel, and for these reasons the sector is often touted as a 'poster child' of deregulation. Aviation has also been an important testing ground for key regulatory theoretical concepts discussed in earlier chapters, such as contestable markets theory and 'destructive competition'.[1] Like railways, the aviation sector comprises a mix of state and private ownership, and a supply chain characterised by both monopoly activities (such as airspace management) and activities subject to intense intra-modal competition (such as air passenger services). The sector also competes, albeit to different degrees, with other transport modes such as rail, sea and road transport (ships, railways, cars, buses and trucks).

While the aviation industry shares some similarities with the other industries discussed in this book, there are a number of important differences. First, in most countries, the industry has always been vertically separated: a single entity rarely manages the airspace, airports and operates an airline. Second, the cross-border nature of services means there is a need for a high degree of inter-jurisdictional technical and operational coordination underpinned by international conventions and bilateral and multilateral air services agreements. Third, aviation infrastructure differs from that used in other sectors; there is no need to lay an extensive physical network of pipes, cables wires or rails. Finally, the aviation sector is particularly susceptible to exogenous demand and cost shocks (e.g. September 11th, SARS, spikes in oil prices and Covid-19), all of which can make the commercial environment more volatile.

Looking ahead, the aviation industry faces several changes and challenges. Important among these is the impact that decarbonisation and other environmental policies, and changes in consumer behaviour, will have on the sector. There are also likely to be changes to competition as a result of the further development of large global hub airports, and subsidised carriers from the Gulf states and China. Technologically, the potential

---

[1] Levine (1987) notes that it 'is a relatively rare "natural experiment" with which to evaluate the predictions of academics by observing the effects of an abrupt policy change, and because theoreticians and government authorities alike have used the industry as a prototype for other deregulations ... and that the study of airline deregulation has become almost a cottage industry for economists'.

widespread deployment of unmanned aircraft systems (UAS or drones) and the emergenc
of space-based air traffic management (ATM) has the potential to radically transform th
sector and raise fundamental questions about the appropriate regulatory frameworks.

15.1 PHYSICAL AND ECONOMIC CHARACTERISTICS OF AVIATION

15.1.1 Characteristics of the Product

The aviation industry provides two types of services to end-users: passenger service
and air cargo services. Passenger aviation services are a form of long-distance mobil
ity service that allows individuals to travel from a point of origin to a destination. I
2019, there were more than 4.5 billion passenger journeys globally, providing connec
tions between 22,000 different city pairs. Roughly 58 per cent of these flights wer
international, with the remainder domestic. The USA has the largest domestic marke
(accounting for 610 million journeys), but there has been rapid growth in the Chines
domestic market (550 million journeys). These two markets are well ahead of the nex
highest market, India (125 million journeys).[2] Long-haul passenger flights are generall
defined as flights which cover distances of more than 3500 kilometres (or longer tha
six hours) and often involve intercontinental journeys. Medium-haul flights cover dis
tances between 1500 and 3500 km (three to six hours) and connect major cities withi
a continent; while short-haul flights are up to 1500 km (up to three hours) and connec
regional cities and smaller urban centres. Journey length has implications for the aircra
that can be used, and the choices passengers face in terms of which airports can be use
and the intensity of competition on different routes.

Passenger journeys can be separated into two types. Point-to-point passenger journey
provide direct connections between a specific origin and destination.[3] Point-to-point ser
vices have the advantage of a direct connection and particularly appeal to time-sensitiv
consumers. However, the extent and frequency of point-to-point services offered depend
on the density of traffic on that route. 'Hub-and-spoke' services provide indirect connec
tions and involve passengers changing planes at a hub airport on their way to their destina
tion.[4] Indirect (hub-and-spoke) passenger services often involve longer journey times, bu
allow airlines to exploit network externalities and provide services to a greater number c
locations and improve the load factor on particular routes, which can lead to more frequen
and cheaper services. A hub-and-spoke aviation network can therefore connect thousand
of origins and destinations: from 'anywhere to everywhere'.[5] The extent to which passen
gers consider direct and indirect (via a hub) services to be substitutable depends on th

---

[2] IATA (2020a).
[3] Point-to-point services can also involve multiple stops *en route* to a particular destination, but do not
   require a passenger to change planes.
[4] Levine (1987) defines a hub-and-spoke system as one which concentrates 'most of an airline's operation
   at one or a very few "hub" cities, serving virtually every other city on the system nonstop from the hub
   and providing predominantly one-stop or connecting service through the hub between cities on the
   "spokes". See also Brueckner, Dyer and Spiller (1992).
[5] Cook and Goodwin (2008) note that 'passengers making hub connections benefit from closely timed
   flights, single check-in, more convenient gate and facility locations, and reduced risk of lost baggage'.

type of consumer (how time-sensitive they are), the purpose of the journey (business versus leisure) and the availability of the service (connecting some origins to some destinations can inevitably involve transiting through a hub). As discussed below in Section 15.4.1, various levels of cooperation between airlines now exist (such as code shares or alliances), which from the passengers' perspective allows them to travel on multiple airlines on the same itinerary (and check luggage to a final destination), to book a ticket with one airline but travel with another, and to receive various benefits (loyalty points, faster check-in, etc.).

Air cargo (or freight) services involve the carriage of goods by air domestically and internationally, and can involve a mix of standard, express and temperature-controlled services. Air cargo services compete with other forms of freight transportation such as road and rail (for small and medium journeys) and container shipping for longer inter-continental journeys. Air cargo services are seen as preferable to other forms of transport where speed is seen as important. Typical goods transported by air include highly perishable items (such as fruit and flowers), products that require reliable and express delivery (such as key industrial parts or time-sensitive legal documents) and high-value technological products.[6] Air cargo services are provided by combination passenger/cargo airlines (where the cargo is carried in the belly of the passenger aircraft between major passenger airports) or by all-cargo airlines, which use specialised cargo airplanes and are often integrated with other transport modes (road) offering a door-to-door service.[7] Air cargo airlines utilise the slots at major passenger airports or provide services from 'cargo hubs' often based in secondary airports.[8] In 2017, the volume of freight transported by air was only around 0.5 per cent; however, the total value of that freight was $6.4 trillion, representing around 35 per cent of world trade by value.[9] Around 43 per cent of freight tonnage kilometres involved transport to/from Asia-Pacific, with transport to/from North America 35 per cent and to/from Europe accounting for 33 per cent.[10] This reflects the rapid industrialisation of China and its use of air freight to both export commodities and import key components. Looking ahead, the growth in e-commerce, and its requirements for rapid delivery, is anticipated to increase the use of air cargo services, as will the development of UAS, which can provide package deliveries door-to-door.

Finally, it should be noted that airspace within a given jurisdiction is used not only for commercial passenger and freight services but also by general aviation and military users. General aviation users can include balloon operators, gliders and light aircraft operators who may fly mainly on weekends in uncontrolled airspace (areas not subject to air traffic surveillance or management). Some areas of airspace are segregated exclusively for military use, and therefore cannot be used by other airspace users. The military reserves the airspace temporarily and then releases it for civil use when it is not required (a process known as flexible use of airspace).

---

[6] See Button (2008).
[7] Examples include Federal Express (Fedex), United Parcel Service (UPS) and Cargolux.
[8] For example, the FedEx 'superhub' in Memphis, USA. This can allow them to build dedicated facilities, avoid airport curfews, operate twenty-four hours a day and reduce conflicts with passenger arrivals and departure times.
[9] ICAO (2021).
[10] IATA (2020a).

15.1.2 Aviation Supply Chain

Like other forms of transport, the aviation supply chain involves the carriage of pas
sengers or cargo in aircraft between a point of origin and a destination. The tradition
structure for commercial manned aviation comprises three elements: the airspace, whic
is utilised by aircraft to facilitate the carriage of passengers and cargo between differer
locations; airports, which are located in specific fixed locations and allow passenger
cargo to access aircraft; and the services provided by airlines, which involve the carriag
of passengers and cargo and provide services to end-users. Figure 15.1 presents an indi
ative illustration of a traditional aviation supply chain.

Airspace Navigation Services
Airspace around the world is divided into Flight Information Regions (FIRs), which a
defined as areas in which a flight information service and alerting service are available
FIRs vary in size and can cover neighbouring airspace over an ocean. Small countri
tend to have one FIR and larger countries usually divide their airspace into several FIRs.
FIRs are managed by the controlling authorities appointed in a particular region wh
are responsible for ensuring that ATM services are provided to all civilian aircraft flyir
within a FIR.[13] FIRs can also be split into upper (*en route*) and lower sections, and in
different classifications (or classes of airspace) which determine the different rules
flying within that airspace.

Airspace can also be 'controlled' or 'uncontrolled'. As the name suggests, all aircra
flying in controlled airspace must follow structured routes and comply with air traff
control instructions.[14] Air navigation service providers (ANSPs) oversee controlled ai
space and constantly monitor the separation of aircraft in order to keep them safe as th
head towards their destinations.[15] Only one ANSP operates per airspace sector, whic
means that they have a geographical monopoly for that service in that area. In Europ
there are around forty active ANSPs across the continent,[16] while there is only a sing
ANSP in each of Australia, Canada and the USA.

The air traffic control service provided by ANSPs in controlled airspace depends
the phase of a flight.[17] *En route* air traffic control services are provided in airspace whe
aircraft are cruising or level flying as well as when flights are in ascending or descen
ing phases after taking off or before landing. Terminal or approach control services a

[11] According to ICAO, a flight information service is a service provided for the purpose of giving advice
and information useful for the safe and efficient conduct of flights.
[12] For example, UK airspace currently comprises three FIRs: London FIR (which covers England and Wale
Scottish FIR (which covers Scotland and Northern Ireland); and Shanwick Oceanic (which covers a
region of airspace totalling 700,000 square miles over the North East Atlantic).
[13] In many countries, the controlling authority is the Civil Aviation body.
[14] In uncontrolled airspace, where there are no air traffic services provided, an aircraft must navigate
independently using visual flight rules (VFR) and a 'see and avoid' approach to other aircraft.
[15] Those flying in uncontrolled airspace are not required to follow air traffic control instructions, but may
choose to voluntarily do so (where they are available).
[16] Buyle, Onghena, Dewulf and Kupfer (2017).
[17] There are broadly five types of air navigation services provided to aircraft: core ATM services;
communication, navigation and surveillance (CNS) services; meteorological services for air navigation
(MET); search and rescue services (SAR); and aeronautical information services (AIS).

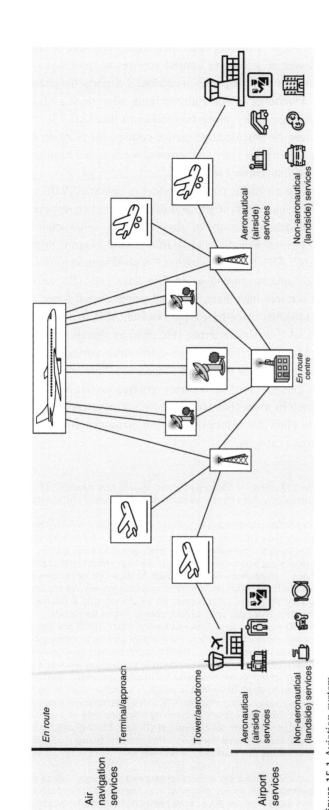

Figure 15.1 Aviation system

provided for arriving or departing controlled flights between *en route* and tower/aero
drome control. Tower or aerodrome control services are provided for aerodrome traffi
and involve the separation of airplanes at or around airports, the phase directly associate
with take-offs and landings. In many jurisdictions, all of these air traffic control service
are provided by a single entity, albeit from different locations.[18] However, in some juris
dictions, the services are provided by separate entities: for example, in the UK a majorit
private company provides *en route* and terminal services, but some airports provide thei
own tower or aerodrome control services.

In order to provide air traffic control services to aircraft, ANSPs use different aircra
surveillance technologies, each of which utilises different equipment and infrastructure
This infrastructure includes a range of physical assets, information technology (IT) an
communication systems, including: air traffic control centres, primary and secondar
surveillance radars,[19] ADS-B ground stations,[20] multilateration (or MLAT) stations,[21] VHF
HF communication towers, ground-based data links and ATM software. While, histor
ically, air traffic services have been provided using ground-based infrastructure, ther
is a policy shift towards 'space-based' (or satellite) ATM in some jurisdictions, such a
Europe and the USA.[22] In simple terms, this involves signals being broadcast from air
craft and received by a constellation of low-Earth-orbit satellites, which then re-transm
the signals to other aircraft or to ground-based users.[23] Space-based systems are seen a
a complement to ground-based surveillance systems insofar as they offer the ability t
provide surveillance in areas that are currently not covered,[24] and improve air–groun
communication to allow for reduced separation, improved safety and greater efficienc
in the use of airspace capacity.[25]

---

[18] For example, in the USA, there are 520 airport towers located near airports, 147 terminal control centre
in various states and twenty-five *en route* (or air route traffic) control centres spread across the country
(FAA, 2020b).

[19] Primary surveillance radars transmit an electromagnetic wave that is reflected by the target aircraft.
Secondary surveillance radars (SSR) involve the transmission of a radar signal from a ground-based
antenna to a piece of equipment installed on an aircraft known as a transponder. Many radars are
grouped together in clusters, which ensures multiple coverage and protects against redundancy.

[20] 'Automatic Dependent Surveillance – Broadcast' (ADS-B) allows aircraft to broadcast their position,
velocity, airspeed, identity and other operational information periodically at a high rate from an on-
board system to ground stations or other aircraft. On the ground, ADS-B Out transmissions are received
by ADS-B ground antennas or other receivers equipped to receive the signals.

[21] Multilateration (MLAT) is another surveillance technology that receives and processes the 'replies' sent
from aircraft fitted with certain transponders. These replies are sent in response to interrogations sent
by an SSR or from a multilateration station. Multilateration has very rapid update rates – up to every
second – which allows for an aircraft's movements to be displayed as 'smooth' on a radar screen.

[22] In Europe, the vision is for navigation to become based solely on satellites (with the exception of
contingency operations) by 2030. In the USA, a switch to a satellite-enabled navigation system is a key
element of the Federal Aviation Administration's NextGen modernisation programme.

[23] An example of a space-based ADS-B service currently being deployed on a commercial basis is offered
by Aireon (a joint initiative between NAV Canada, NATS (UK), ENAV (Italy), the Irish Aviation Authority
Naviair (Denmark) and Iridium Communications). This service is available to ADS-B-equipped aircraft
and currently operates using fifty satellites and provides a service covering Canada and the North
Atlantic traffic.

[24] For example, in vast and remote areas without existing radar coverage, such as over the North Atlantic,
with the aim of ensuring planes do not 'disappear' over remote and oceanic airspace.

[25] The Federal Aviation Administration (FAA, 2020c) notes that satellite-based navigation is more precise
than traditional ground-based navigation aids and allows for the creation of optimum routes anywhere
in the National Airspace System.

Most ANSPs around the world are fully state-owned or state-controlled, including in the USA, Australia and most EU Member States. A notable exception is NAV Canada, which was fully privatised in 1996 and operates as a not-for-profit entity.[26] Partial privatisations of ANSPs were introduced in the UK in 2001,[27] Italy in 2016 and for France and Switzerland.

Airport Services

Airport operators provide a mix of aeronautical and non-aeronautical services to different customers, and for this reason airports are sometimes described as a two-sided market or platform insofar as they bring together passengers and airlines, which gives rise to direct and indirect network effects.[28]

Aeronautical services are principally provided to airlines and include: maintenance and operation of runways, taxiways and aprons; allocating airport slots (or gates) and providing aerobridges; refuelling services; hangar and maintenance facilities; and ground handling services. They also include various terminal services, such as check-in and boarding facilities. The costs of these services are recovered through airport charges. Non-aeronautical services are provided to passengers and include the leasing of space to retail and hospitality services within an airport terminal, the operation of car parks and the leasing of land to hotels and business parks. Aeronautical and non-aeronautical services are seen as complementary to one another, which can affect the decisions made by an airport operator. Aeronautical and non-aeronautical services can be provided by a single integrated airport operator, or provided by separate entities (for example, ground handling facilities are sometimes provided by a third party, as are car parking services).

Airports can vary considerably in the services they offer and the passenger catchments that they serve. Major (or primary) airports are located close to urban centres and are highly integrated with other transport modes, such as rail (including high-speed, intercity and urban services), bus and car rental services. They can accommodate almost all types of passenger and cargo aircraft and comprise numerous terminals, which can feature extensive retail services, restaurants, hotels and business park services. Major cities – such as New York, London, Tokyo, Paris – are often served by a number of major airports. In contrast, smaller (secondary) airports are typically located in regional areas and typically cannot accommodate all types of aircraft. They generally have limited terminal facilities and inter-modal interconnections and provide basic services to airlines and passengers. The growth of low-cost carriers (LCCs) has seen an increasing use of secondary airports by some airlines. These airports tend to be located in more remote locations than primary airports.

Airport infrastructure capacity is determined by physical factors (such as the number of available gates and movements that can be safely accommodated on a runway)

---

[26] NAV Canada is a not-for-profit organisation that comprises the major airlines, private aircraft owners, the pilots' union and the air traffic employees.

[27] The UK government retains a 49 per cent share, 42 per cent is held by a consortium of airlines, 5 per cent by the ANSP staff, and 4 per cent by the operator of London Heathrow Airport.

[28] See Ivaldi, Sokullu and Toru (2012), Gillen and Mantin (2013), Malavolti (2016) and Starkie (2021). For an alternative view, see Fröhlich (2010) and Button (2017b).

and other factors (such as night-time curfews which restrict flights between certain hours), and demand by airlines to use airport infrastructure can vary significantly. Where demand to use airport infrastructure exceeds supply, this can give rise to capacity constraints, which in the absence of controls can lead to systemic delay. Capacity-constrained airports are known as 'coordinated airports'.[30] Access to coordinated airports involves the allocation of 'slots' to airlines, which permits access to airport infrastructure (such as runway, terminal, apron and gate facilities) on particular day during a specified time period.[31] The ability to access slots at coordinated airports at key times is an important determinant of airline profitability and airline competition, particularly between incumbent and new entrant airlines.[32] There is currently a single set of international standards for the management of airport slots whereby slots are allocated based on historical use (sometimes called 'grandfathering').[33] An airline is automatically entitled to continue using the same slot in the next scheduling period provided it has used that slot at least 80 per cent of the time in a previous period (the 'use-it-or-lose-it' rule). In some jurisdictions, such as the USA and UK, secondary trading of slots is allowed following negotiation between different airlines.[34] Although there has long been interest in the merits of alternative slot allocation processes – such as auctions,[35] peak or congestion pricing, or computational allocation[36] – to date no alternatives have been introduced.[37] However, the issue is receiving renewed policy interest particularly for 'super-congested' airports with expectations of growth in air travel.[38]

[29] Airports are generally designated into three levels according to the degree of congestion. Level 1 airports have sufficient capacity to meet demand; Level 2 airports can have congestion for some periods of the day, week or season, which can be resolved by voluntary cooperation between airlines and an appointed facilitator (who facilitates the planned operations of airlines using or planning to use the airport); Level 3 airports have demand that significantly exceeds the airport's capacity and, without controls, would have unacceptable systemic delays.

[30] They are called 'coordinated airports' because a coordinator is appointed to allocate slots to airlines and other aircraft operators. IATA (2020b) estimates that there were 204 slot-coordinated airports in the world which affected 1.5 billion passengers or 43 per cent of global air travel.

[31] Czerny, Forsyth, Gillen and Niemeier (2008) provide a useful overview of airport slot issues.

[32] Jones, Viehoff and Marks (1993) present an early analysis of problems entrants faced gaining access to London Heathrow slots.

[33] Once unchanged historical slots have been allocated, the coordinator will establish a slot pool including any newly created slots. There are also rules for allocation of slots to new entrant airlines. See ACI, IATA and Worldwide Airport Coordinators Group (2020) which sets out slot allocation principles.

[34] Bichler, Cramton, Gritzmann and Ockenfels (2021) quote reports that American Airlines paid $60 million for a pair of London Heathrow slots from SAS in 2015, and Oman Air paid $75 million for a London Heathrow pair from Air France.

[35] See Rassenti, Smith and Bulfin (1982), Jones, Viehoff and Marks (1993), Sentance (2003), Button (2008), Brueckner (2009), Basso and Zhang (2010) and Sheng, Li, Xiao and Fu (2015).

[36] See Pellegrini, Bolić, Castelli and Pesenti (2017) and Ribeiro, Jacquillat, Antunes, et al. (2018).

[37] In 2008, the US FAA issued proposed regulations to conduct auctions at three airports in the New York area (LaGuardia, JFK and Newark). However, this was challenged in the courts and ultimately abandoned. More recently, the European Commission has required that forty-eight Lufthansa slots at Frankfurt and Munich airports be assigned via auction; see Bichler, Cramton, Gritzmann and Ockenfels (2021). Generally, see Button (2020).

[38] The CMA (2018b) notes that the current system results in rigid slot holdings, especially at congested airports, which compound, the underlying capacity constraints, and that airlines find it difficult to obtain additional slots to expand existing and launch new services. IATA (2020b) defines 'super-congested' airports to include Amsterdam Schiphol, London Heathrow and Hong Kong International.

Many airports around the world operate as fully or partially state-owned entities or corporations, including almost all commercial airports in the USA.[39] However, it has been estimated that around a half of the world's *major* airports have some form of private participation.[40] Major UK airports were fully privatised in 1987, which was followed in the 1990s and 2000s by the main airports in Argentina, Australia, Japan, Italy, New Zealand and Portugal. In some jurisdictions, airports are partially privatised,[41] or are operated by private organisations under a private–public partnership or long-term concession arrangement.[42] It is important to note that, even when airports operate under state ownership, some activities – such as ground handling services, airport security and shuttle bus operations – can be outsourced to private operators.

Air Passenger and Cargo Transport Services

Passenger and cargo services are provided to end-users by airlines which operate aircraft that utilise airspace to fly between airports. Airlines need aircraft, sales networks and crew to provide aviation services to end-users, and the main costs incurred include those associated with aircraft ownership/leasing, maintenance costs, fuel costs, landing and air navigation charges, and labour costs.

The types of aircraft operated depend on the services provided (full cargo services or passenger services)[43] and the distance travelled (long-haul or short/medium-haul). The manufacture of commercial aircraft is dominated by two companies, Boeing and Airbus, which collectively have a share of over 90 per cent of the market.[44] The cost of purchasing an aircraft depends on its range and capability.[45] Many airlines do not own all the aircraft they operate; rather, they lease aircraft to allow greater flexibility in responding to market demand and to maintain the age of their fleet.[46] There are two broad types of leasing arrangement. Wet leases involve the lease of an aircraft and at least one crew member, and are typically provided on a short-term basis. The aircraft owner (the lessor) typically has operational responsibility for maintaining the aircraft and paying the insurance in a wet lease. Dry leases involve the lease of an aircraft without a crew for periods of up to

---

[39] ACI (2017) estimates that 86 per cent of the world's airports are state-owned. In the USA, GAO (2014) reports that nearly all the 3300 airports were state-owned (either by city, state, county or public authority (such as a Port Authority)). In 2021, only two US airports operated under private long-term leases. See CRS (2021).

[40] This includes full ownership, listed companies, concession agreements or long-term leases and management contracts. ACI (2017) reports that around 41 per cent of the world's major airports have some form of private sector participation, and that in continental Europe 25 per cent of airports are owned by mixed public–private shareholders. In the USA, GAO (2014) notes that nearly 450 airports have some form of private sector participation in their management or ownership.

[41] Examples in Europe include Paris, Frankfurt and Vienna. There is also private participation in some Chinese airports (such as Beijing, Shanghai, Guangzhou and Shenzhen) which are publicly listed. Hong and Yoo (2000) describe the motivations for privatisation and the different forms it can take.

[42] See examples in IATA (2018).

[43] The EC (2019d) notes that, in 2017, cargo represented around 3 per cent of all flights in Europe.

[44] Reported in Forbes (2020).

[45] A new Airbus A380 cost around US$440 million in 2018; an Airbus A320 cost around US$100 million; while a five-year-old A320 costs around US$46 million. See Airbus (2018).

[46] Boeing (2021) estimates that in 2020 around 46 per cent of aircraft were leased. However, the extent of leasing varies by airline. For example, Ryanair (Europe's largest airline) owns the majority of its aircraft fleet.

ten years. The airline (the lessee) typically exercises operational control under a dry lease and is responsible for maintenance and insurance.

An important determinant of airline profitability is the ability to achieve high levels of capacity utilisation (known as a load factor).[47] Modern airlines employ sophisticated yield management practices which allow them to determine how many seats on each flight should be sold at specific fares (and with particular conditions attached) at different times before the flight (including up to a few hours before a flight departs) based on the expected demand for that flight.[48] Yield management – effectively a form of price discrimination – is a response to the cost and demand conditions airlines face, in particular: uncertain demand coupled with short-term capacity constraints and substantial differences in the consumer valuation of specific flight attributes (including timing and other fare conditions), which is reflected in the prices that they are willing to pay.[49] While such price dispersion can sometimes be considered unfair by some consumers insofar as it results in a situation where passengers sitting next to each other on the same flight and class could have paid drastically different prices,[50] it is argued that it is an efficient way for airlines to cover their fixed costs, which in turn can allow for access to a greater number of origins and destinations.[51]

Two other important features of airline operations have emerged over the past four decades. The first, already noted above, relates to route planning and the shift made by some airlines that provide point-to-point services to the 'hub-and-spoke' model. While the hub-and-spoke system allows an airline to service a larger number of destinations with fewer individual flights, both lowering costs and increasing their attractiveness to passengers,[52] some airlines (particularly LCCs) do not operate such a system, but rather provide point-to-point shuttle services between cities.[53] The second, and related, development is the emergence of various forms of cooperation between airlines, which can take the form of interlining or code-share agreements, or through participation in an airline alliance. As discussed in Section 15.4.1, while such cooperation agreements can bring benefits to airlines and passengers by exploiting network externalities and reducing costs on some overlapping routes, they can give rise to competition concerns.

---

[47] The load factor for a single passenger flight is calculated by dividing the number of passengers by the number of seats. In 2019, the global passenger load factor was 82.5 per cent while the cargo load factor was 46.7 per cent. See IATA (2020a).

[48] Fares can be differentiated by: how far in advance they are purchased (three days, seven days, fourteen days); whether they are refundable; whether booking changes can be made; whether they involve a minimum or maximum stay; and the sales channel through which they are purchased.

[49] There is an extensive literature on price dispersion in the airline industry; see Gale and Holmes (1993), Dana (1999) and Stavins (2001).

[50] In an early analysis, Borenstein and Rose (1994) estimated that the difference in fares between two passengers on a route is 36 per cent of the airline's average ticket price. Sengupta and Wiggins (2014) found that online tickets were 11 per cent lower than offline tickets.

[51] Kahn (2005). In the early days of US airline deregulation, there was debate about how price discrimination interacts with the intensity of competition. See Borenstein and Rose (1994), Dana (1998) Stavins (2001) and Gerardi and Shapiro (2009).

[52] As Button (2002) notes, five destinations require only four routes with one hub and four spoke cities, but ten routes are required if the same destinations are connected with a point-to-point system. This reduces the need for the number of aircraft an airline needs to operate.

[53] For example, Southwest Airlines in the USA and Ryanair in Europe.

The ownership of airlines has changed over time. While airlines have always been privately owned and operated in the USA, in many other countries the major national flag carrier was state-owned up until the 1980s.[54] The process of privatisation of major flag carriers in Europe began with the sale of British Airways in 1987, which was followed by Lufthansa, Air France and KLM in the 1990s and Iberia in the early 2000s.[55] In the Pacific region, Japan Airlines was privatised in 1987, Air Canada in 1989, LAN Chile in 1994 and Qantas in 1995. However, the national flag carrier remains under full or partial state ownership in many countries, including India, New Zealand and Russia, and most countries in Asia, Africa and Eastern Europe. In recent years, concerns have been raised, particularly in the USA and Europe, about whether state ownership and subsidisation of the three major Gulf airlines (Emirates, Qatar Airways and Etihad) is distorting competition among international airlines and creating an unfair playing field.[56]

National flag carriers have sometimes competed head-to-head with full-scale large privately owned airlines such as Virgin Atlantic in the UK, All Nippon Airways in Japan and Jet Airways in India. In addition, as described below, an important change following restructuring policies introduced in many countries since the 1980s has been the emergence of LCCs, which are typically privately owned.[57] LCCs can be distinguished from traditional airlines in that they tend to: focus on short-haul routes; seek to maximise on-board capacity by short turn-around times; offer point-to-point services, sometimes from secondary airports; operate a single fleet type; seek to lower costs by minimising on-board services; and sell directly to passengers and not through travel agents. While some LCCs have lasted only a short time, others have been highly successful. In 2019, Ryanair carried the most international passengers, while Southwest Airlines carried the largest number of domestic passengers.[58]

5.1.3 Unmanned Aircraft Systems (UAS)

Initially developed for military purposes in the 1960s, UAS[59] – commonly known as drones – are evolving at a fast pace, and in many parts of the world the predicted growth in the volume of UAS operations across both controlled and uncontrolled airspace suggests that these could soon be on a scale comparable to, if not greater than, that of present-day manned air traffic. UAS will likely utilise airspace in different ways to manned aircraft, with many flying at lower altitudes, and operating in areas which

---

[54] Other examples of major airlines that were majority privately owned for much of their existence include Swissair, Cathay Pacific in Hong Kong and Korean Air (privatised in 1969).

[55] Some governments retain a stake in the airlines; for example, the French and Dutch states each retain a 14 per cent share of Air France–KLM.

[56] In 2019, Emirates was the largest international passenger airline (in terms of scheduled revenue passenger kilometres), Qatar Airways was the third largest and Etihad was the sixteenth. See IATA (2020a). Tiroual (2017) discusses the North American perspective; Lykotrafiti (2020) discusses the European policy response.

[57] In the early days of restructuring, it was common to observe national flag carriers establish their own type of LCCs to compete (such as GO Fly (British Airways), Iberia Express (Iberia) and Air India Express).

[58] IATA (2020a)

[59] ICAO (2019b) defines a UAS as 'an aircraft and its associated elements which are operated with no pilot on board'.

hitherto have not been used for aircraft. Commercial UAS in particular are expecte
to make extensive use of low-altitude controlled airspace in densely populated urba
areas. Some UAS are also expected to operate at higher altitudes (above 600 feet o
180 metres).[60]

There are a number of important differences between UAS and manned aircraft oper
ations.[61] First, there is expected to be considerable diversity in the types of UAS an
UAS operators, the airspace they use, and the purpose and frequency of use.[62] UAS i
the future could be used at a large scale for cargo and parcel transport (e.g. packag
deliveries) and potentially for passenger transport in the form of automated air vehicle
including driverless personal air vehicles and taxis.[63] Second, many UAS will general
not require access to shared airport services and infrastructure in the same way tha
traditional manned aircraft currently do. Rather, many are expected to take off and lan
vertically and to do so from private premises. Third, the management of UAS in share
airspace will also differ. As discussed in Section 15.4.2 below, although UAS traffic man
agement (UTM) concepts are still under development in many countries, they are gener
ally based on a decentralised structure that relies on participants *cooperating* with on
another to digitally share information in a way that provides an ability to plan mission
and to manage airspace in real time.[64]

15.2 APPROACH TO AVIATION REGULATION

15.2.1 Activities Subject to Regulation in the Aviation Supply Chain

Chapter 14 illustrated the considerable diversity in how railways are structured and reg
ulated around the world. The aviation sector is almost the polar opposite, and there
considerable similarity in how the sector is structured and regulated in many parts o
the world. Indeed, the aviation sector in most parts of the world has traditionally bee
vertically separated, meaning that separate entities provide air navigation services (ANS
airport services and operate airlines.[65]

Competitive Activities in the Supply Chain
As described in Section 15.3 below, from the late 1970s, many countries restructured th
approach to regulating the aviation sector. While restructuring was initially focused o

---

[60] Facebook, Google and others are looking at the use of high-altitude unmanned aircraft to provide a 4G
network in remote areas around the world.

[61] The discussion in this section is focused on the commercial or recreational use of UAS, and not the
use of UAS by the military. Although military use of UAS is increasingly prominent, it is subject to a
different form of air traffic management than commercial/recreational UAS use.

[62] A recreational UAS operator may use airspace infrequently, in uncongested remote areas. Conversely, a
operator of a fleet of commercial unmanned aerial vehicles (UAVs) – such as UAVs used to make packag
deliveries or to provide air taxi services – may be in operation constantly in congested urban areas.
These differences in UAS operations have obvious implications for the types of traffic management.

[63] Such as those being developed by Volocopter and Vahana, among others.

[64] Decker and Chiambaretto (2022) present an overview of the UTM concepts in the USA and Europe.

[65] Although, in some countries, these activities may be fully or partially state-owned, this is often at
different levels of government (e.g. airlines might be federally owned, while airports may be owned by
state, regional or municipal authorities).

airlines, in some jurisdictions, this has since led to greater competition in other activities, such as airports.

Prior to the 1980s, it was common in many parts of the world for airlines either to be directly owned by government or, where they operated in private hands, to be subject to strict economic regulation. This was sometimes based on the argument that airlines had characteristics of natural monopoly and exhibited economies of scale, particularly for smaller carriers.[66] Regulation included government oversight and control of factors such as: fares; permissible routes; schedules; and the entry of new competitor airlines. In many countries, there was either a single monopoly airline allowed to operate, or a distinction between airlines that could provide domestic versus international flights.[67] As these regulatory policies were gradually withdrawn, this led to new entry by privately owned airlines, some of which competed head-to-head on existing routes with previously state-owned carriers (flag carriers), while others sought to develop new routes (such as LCCs). There are now estimated to be around 300 airlines in operation around the world, and there are generally no restrictions on entry of airlines or the routes they choose to serve (subject to satisfying licensing criteria and international treaties).[68] The service offerings of airlines are determined independently and through competitive market forces, and airlines have an ability to shift activities from airports/routes as business conditions change.[69] Fare levels are determined through competition, although some coordination between airlines on international fares remained up until 2017.[70] In general terms, the withdrawal of economic regulation for airlines reflects the fact that the industry structure in many countries has transitioned from one based around an airline monopoly/duopoly to one based around competition between multiple airlines. Competition between airlines is now generally considered sufficient to ensure that prices on different routes are reasonable and reflect underlying costs, routes get serviced for which there is consumer demand, and a certain level of quality is maintained.[71]

---

[66] White (1978) presents a spirited critique of economies of scale at the firm level. Caves, Christensen and Tretheway (1984) find evidence of substantial economies of density, meaning that unit costs decline within a given network and therefore within city-pair markets. Biggar (1999) reviews other studies which find that average costs in a given city-pair market decrease up to a minimum level of traffic. However, beyond a certain level of traffic in a city-pair market, the airline industry exhibits constant returns to scale.

[67] Up until the late 1970s, Pan American was the principal international air carrier for the USA, while domestic services were provided by four airlines (American Airlines, Eastern Air Lines, Transcontinental and Western Air, and United Airlines). In the UK, up until the establishment of British Airways in 1972, the two major UK airlines were British Overseas Airways Corporation, which provided long-haul services, and British European Airways, which provided shorter European and domestic routes.

[68] Strict international rules are placed on the airworthiness of aircraft and airline operators by international bodies, and airlines which do not satisfy certain minimum safety standards (or which operate aircraft that are no longer certified) can be barred from using particular airspace in a jurisdiction.

[69] In some countries, certain essential routes can be subsidised, such as in the USA under the Essential Air Service programme where routes servicing around 110 communities receive funding.

[70] This involved YY fares, which were introduced in 1945 as a result of terms in bilateral air service agreements (ASAs) where governments relied on IATA to submit coordinated international fares and rates for approval. According to IATA (2017), the use of YY fares declined dramatically as a result of deregulation and intense competition between airlines. However, there remain international standards about fare construction, mileage principles and currency standards.

[71] However, in some places, like Australia, concerns have arisen about anti-competitive behaviour between airlines, such as capacity dumping, predatory pricing or hoarding of airport slots. See ACCC (2020).

Historically, competition between major airports located in close proximity to one another (such as in London) was seen as detrimental, and for this reason specific routes were allocated to different airports and restrictions on airport expansion and development were introduced.[72] The introduction of greater airline competition gave airlines greater flexibility as to which routes to serve and airports to use while also spurring entry by airlines pursuing different business models (LCCs).[73] This has led to greater airport competition at the international level (between global hubs and for cargo services) and at the national and regional levels.[74] In choosing routes, airlines can now exercise greater choice as to which airports they fly to and how they utilise a particular airport (frequency of service and the available seat capacity), which is said to give them some countervailing buyer power.[75] Passengers also have greater choice as to where to fly from/to, including greater use of secondary (non-major) airports and choices between various hub airports with which to make connecting journeys.[76] Taken together, the potential ability of both airlines and passengers – the two sides of the market – to switch to alternative airports can, in principle, constrain the market power of major airports and limit their ability to set excessive airport charges or otherwise restrict capacity.[77] Airport market power in some jurisdictions can also be constrained by other transport modes, such as high-speed rail links.[78]

The development of airport competition, particularly in Europe, has in some countries led to the withdrawal of regulation.[79] For example, in the UK, only two airports out of twelve major airports are considered to have substantial market power and are subject to up-front (*ex ante*) economic regulation.[80] In contrast, in other countries, such as the USA, the scope for airport competition is sometimes assessed as limited by factors such as limited options for passengers in specific metropolitan areas, low levels of competition for transfer passengers, and that airports serve different catchments areas for long-haul flights.[81] More generally, as described below, the extent to which airport competition

---

[72] For example, in the UK, a 1984 report (CAA, 1984) recommended a reallocation of routes between airports to encourage airline competition.

[73] Additionally, as Starkie (2012) observes, the increasing use of the Internet has reduced the costs of entry for airlines into local markets.

[74] ICAO (2013b). The OECD/ITF (2010) refer to various forms of airport competition: international or national hub competition (Paris CDG versus Amsterdam Schiphol versus London Heathrow); hub and secondary hub competition (Heathrow versus Manchester); and major airport and secondary airports (Vienna versus Bratislava; London Gatwick versus London Luton).

[75] Starkie (2012) observes that European LCCs have established multiple bases across Europe, making it easier for them to redeploy capacity among airports. Thelle and la Couer Sonne (2018) find that point-to-point carriers are more likely to switch airports than hub carriers in Europe, and that the airports most affected are smaller airports. In contrast, Wiltshire (2018) identifies various switching costs and notes that there is limited evidence of route switching among airlines, particularly at larger European airports.

[76] Thelle and la Couer Sonne (2018) report that almost two-thirds of European citizens are within two hours' drive of at least two airports, and that around half of local departing passengers on intra-European routes have a choice of more than one reasonably attractive substitute. Wiltshire (2018), however, notes that such passenger choice can be restricted by type of journey (business versus leisure).

[77] This assumes that proximate airports are under separate ownership, which is not always the case.

[78] For example, the Eurostar services between London and Paris, Brussels and Amsterdam. Generally, see Chiambaretto and Decker (2012), Kouwenhoven (2009) and Mandel (1999).

[79] An excellent overview is presented in Forsyth, Gillen, Muller and Niemeier (2016). See also ICAO (2013b).

[80] London Heathrow and London Gatwick (with the latter being subject to a cap on the maximum level of airport charges).

[81] See RAND (2020). However, arguably competition exists in some cities where the airports are separately owned and operated – e.g. between San Francisco and Oakland Airports.

constrains market power depends on locational, operational and policy factors, and many major airports around the world remain subject to economic regulatory oversight. However, even where airport charges are regulated, competition can still be present for other activities provided at airports. For example, there can be competition for the provision of ground handling services, or competition for provision of other non-aeronautical services, such as airport car parking or warehousing services provided to cargo shippers.

Finally, notwithstanding the fact that the provision of air navigation services (ANS) is considered to be a monopoly activity in almost all parts of the world, some argue that there is potential for a competition *for* the market approach to be adopted. This might involve the appointment of a concession operator for a specific period of time, or in a specific sector of a country.[82] Some countries have already adopted competitive tendering for airport (but not *en route*) air traffic control services,[83] while there is also the potential for some non-core ANS (such as meteorological services) to be provided by competitive entities.[84] As discussed in Section 15.4.2 below, a key element of the concepts for traffic management services for UAS are based around different UAS traffic management providers competing with one another.

Activities Subject to Price Regulation and Other Controls

Activities in the aviation sector that are generally subject to some form of price, and other regulatory, controls are the provision of ANS and the provision of certain services of major airports. While, as described above, in many jurisdictions there are no longer restrictions on entry of airlines or the routes they serve (subject to satisfying licensing criteria and international treaties), and the prices and service offerings are determined through competitive market forces, airlines can still be subject to sector-specific rules, notably in relation to consumer protection.[85] This can include requirements in terms of the presentation of airline prices and surcharges,[86] and the need to provide compensation to delayed passengers.

The rationale for price regulation of ANS stems from the fact that either the activity is perceived to be a natural monopoly and/or the providers are designated as a statutory monopoly in a particular jurisdiction.[87] Accordingly, for some routes, airlines do not have a choice of which ANSP provides them with services (i.e. they are captive) and are subject to the prices and services offered.[88] The provision of ANS involves large sunk investments in infrastructure (radars, ground stations, receivers, IT hardware and software,

---

[82] See Arblaster (2018) and Adler, Hanany and Proost (2018).

[83] Arblaster and Zhang (2020) record that Spain, the UK, Germany, Sweden and Norway have all used competitive tendering for airport air traffic control services.

[84] Compair (2017) notes that meteorological services are outsourced in twenty-two European countries.

[85] In June 2020, the Australian regulator began to monitor prices, costs and profits relating to the supply of domestic air passenger transport services for a period of three years. This was in response to concerns about anti-competitive conduct in the sector. See ACCC (2020).

[86] As discussed in Chapter 7, action against 'drip pricing' in airlines has been taken in Australia, the UK and Europe.

[87] Article 28(a) of the international treaty known as the Chicago Convention entrusts each state with responsibility to provide air navigation services above its land and territories. In addition, Article 6 explicitly forbids all international scheduled services operating over or into the territory of a state except with the special permission of that state.

[88] In some regions, such as Europe, airlines can by-pass a specific national airspace to avoid the charges being levied by the ANSP in that country. However, this can involve a trade-off between the lower air navigation services (ANS) charges and the additional costs in terms of time, fuel, etc. See Delgado (2015)

communications infrastructure), and as such can be subject to economies of scale, suc that one provider is more efficient than multiple providers.[89] However, the minimum efficient scale at which such economies of scale is achieved is unclear.[90] In some jurisdic tions, notably Europe, there have long been concerns about fragmentation and inefficien duplication of infrastructure,[91] and policy initiatives have focused on the consolidation o smaller ANSPs.[92] There is also a related question of whether there are economies of scop in combining the provision of different types of ANS. Historically, the view has been tha the economies of scope are extensive and that there can be benefits to internal sharing o information.[93] However, recent studies find limited evidence of cost efficiencies in com bining *en route* and terminal services,[94] and refer to examples of where tower air traff services are provided by separate entities to *en route* services.[95] Other studies argue tha non-core ANS (such as meteorological services, search-and-rescue services) do not hav natural monopoly characteristics and should be separated from core ANS.[96]

The second activity often subject to economic regulation is the services of majo airports. Historically, major airports were considered to be natural monopolies on th basis that they involve large sunk investments in generally immobile and physical fixed assets,[97] and that it would be inefficient to have multiple airports servicing a give amount of demand.[98] Some airports also have local monopoly power given the diffi culties in constructing another airport in close proximity (e.g. planning restrictions). However, estimates of where economies of scale (decreasing average costs) for airpor are exhausted are wide-ranging (from 3.5 million passengers to 90 million passengers), which has implications for this rationale for regulation.

As described above, in some jurisdictions, airports are no longer seen as necessari locational or natural monopolies,[101] and the rationale for economic regulation of certa airports has shifted towards one based on limiting the ability and incentive of certa

[89] See ICAO (2013a), Button and McDougall (2006) and Button and Neiva (2013).

[90] Buyle, Dewulf, Kupfer, *et al.* (2020) provide a useful overview of studies on economies of scale. Estimates of the extent of any economies of scale can depend on factors such as the number of flights handled, the size of the controlled space (in kilometres), the number of sectors served and whether bot en route and terminal services are combined.

[91] Buyle, Onghena, Dewulf, and Kupfer (2017) estimate that there are around forty active ANSPs in Europ and that the airspace controlled varies from 20,400 km² for Slovenia to 2,190,000 km² for Spain. The total number of controlled flights in 2014 varied from only 84,222 in Luxembourg to 2.8 million in France. See also Compair (2017), which finds that European airspaces are relatively small and hence de not enjoy real economies of scale.

[92] The focus has mainly been on *en route* air navigation services. Policy initiatives have included the development of functional airspace blocks for *en route* services, which restructure airspace according t traffic flows rather than national boundaries, with the aim of achieving economies of scale through th integration of services) or even mergers between national ANSPs. See European Parliament (2021).

[93] Button and McDougall (2006).

[94] Buyle, Dewulf, Kupfer, *et al.* (2020) and Compair (2017).

[95] Compair (2017) provides examples from the UK, Spain and Germany.

[96] Compair (2017).

[97] This includes 'airside' infrastructure (such as gates, taxiways and aprons, runways) and 'landside' infrastructure (such as terminals and gates, transport infrastructure, car parking).

[98] See IATA (2007) and ICAO (2013b).

[99] Button and McDougall (2006) and OECD/ITF (2010).

[100] See Salazar de la Cruz (1999), Jeong (2005) and OECD/ITF (2010).

[101] Forsyth, Gillen, Muller and Niemeier (2016).

airports that have substantial market power to use that power to the detriment of users.[102] This shift can be seen most clearly in the UK, which has moved from all large airports being considered as effectively natural monopolies (and designated on the basis of metrics such as annual turnover, or number of passenger movements) to one where there are periodic and detailed assessments of the extent of competition that individual airports face, and whether they hold a position of market power.[103] Market power assessments have also been conducted in the Netherlands (Amsterdam Schiphol) and Ireland (Dublin).[104] Similar approaches are adopted in other jurisdictions, such as Australia, where major airports are subject to a monitoring regime which applies to both aeronautical services and car parking services.[105]

However, in many countries, major airports are still subject to formal economic regulation.[106] As described below, EU regulations apply to airport charges, slot allocation and ground handling services, and additional price and quality regulations are applied by EU Member State regulators. In the USA, where most large and medium-sized airports are state-owned,[107] airlines and airports often negotiate and enter into use-and-lease agreements which set out the rate setting methodology and how the airport will be used by airlines.[108] These are private agreements between airlines and airports, and can include agreements on how airports spend the revenues obtained.[109] However, federal regulations apply to ensure that rates for aeronautical services are fair and reasonable, and the federal regulator – the Federal Aviation Administration (FAA) – can adjudicate rates and charges disputes. Particular regulations apply to airports in receipt of statutory grants (known as grant assurances) which can, among other things, require assurance on how revenues are collected and spent, how charges are levied on airlines, and require fair and reasonable terms with no unjust discrimination.[110]

---

[102] The extent to which airport competition constrains market power and the implications that this has for regulation are contested. Bilotkach and Bush (2020) and Thelle and la Couer Sonne (2018) find evidence of competition between airports, and suggest that regulation should therefore be adapted to address this fact. In contrast, Wiltshire (2018) finds limited evidence of secondary airports being able to compete effectively with larger neighbours, which he argues implies an ongoing need for regulation of primary airports across Europe.

[103] The market power assessment involves three stages: (i) determining whether the airport has substantial market power; (ii) considering whether competition law is sufficient to constrain the behaviour of the operator; and (iii) evaluating whether the benefits of regulation outweigh the costs. Even where an airport is assessed as holding market power, this does not necessarily mean that price regulation is imposed. Rather, the regulatory approach applied to some airports is to monitor the airport, or to rely on *ex post* competition law, to address any exploitation of market power as and when it arises.

[104] See NMa (2010).

[105] In Australia, price regulation was withdrawn in 2002, and since then there have been periodic reviews of whether airport operators exercise their market power over passengers and airlines through unduly high charges and poor service quality.

[106] Martimort, Pommey and Pouyet (2021) present a formal analysis of the optimal regulatory scheme, which is a price cap that encompasses both aeronautical and commercial services and is complemented with a subsidy scheme to address the airport's incentives to under-invest in infrastructure.

[107] Ownership by cities, counties or independent authorities.

[108] An excellent overview is presented in National Academies of Sciences, Engineering, and Medicine (2010).

[109] There is no requirement for such agreements and, where they are not put in place, an airport can unilaterally set out the conditions and terms under which airline tenants can use their airport. See National Academies of Sciences, Engineering, and Medicine (2010).

[110] FAA (2013), RAND (2020) and CRS (2021).

15.2.2 Form and Scope of Price Regulation

As we have described, the provision of ANS and the services of major airports can be subject to price regulation even in countries where they are state-owned or state-operated. Two factors differentiate the approach to price regulation in the aviation sector as compared to other sectors. First, unlike the other sectors examined in this book, charges that ANSPs and airport operators can levy are shaped and constrained by international policies and regulations such as those established in treaties or International Civil Aviation Organization (ICAO) charging policies.[111] Second, ANSPs and airport operators remain in state ownership in many jurisdictions, which has implications for how charges are determined and whether they are set or approved by a transport ministry rather than a specialist economic regulator as in other industries.

International Access and Charging Principles

The origins of access and charging principles for ANS and airport services can be traced back to the 1944 Chicago Convention, which established overarching principles such as that charges should be non-discriminatory and should be based on costs of services provided.[112] The Convention also created a framework for countries to exchange traffic rights to access their airspace (known as the 'freedoms of the air') with one another.[113] These principles are supplemented by policies and recommendations of ICAO.

In relation to charging, the policies recommend that air navigation charges and airport charges be based on the full cost of providing the services, including a return on capital, depreciation, and operating and maintenance costs (airport charges should take account of contributions from non-aeronautical revenues). In addition, ANSPs and airport operators are permitted to generate revenues that exceed all operating costs and provide for a reasonable return in order to fund necessary capital improvements. Air navigation charges should involve a single charge per flight for the use of the airspace, which is calculated based on the distance flown and the aircraft weight, while it is recommended that airport landing charges also be based on a weight formula. ICAO principles also state that air navigation charges and airport charges must not discriminate between foreign versus home state users.

While ICAO establishes global standards and recommendations, it is not a global aviation regulator, and countries have the right to establish their own approaches to price regulation. In some jurisdictions, such as the EU, economic regulation is also shaped by multilateral policies (such as the Single European Sky policy), which require EU Member States to implement a common charging scheme.

---

[111] ICAO (2009).

[112] Article 15 of the Convention on International Civil Aviation (also known as the Chicago Convention), signed on 7 December 1944.

[113] 'Freedoms of the air' provide different rights to granting a country's airlines the privilege to enter and land in another country's airspace. Important among these is the fifth freedom, which allows an airline to carry passengers from one's own country to a second country, and from that country to a third country (and so on). The sixth freedom is the right to carry passengers or cargo from a second country to a third country by stopping in one's own country, while the seventh freedom is the right to carry passengers or cargo between two foreign countries without any continuing service to one's own country.

Regulation of Air Navigation Service Charges

There are two main ways in which the costs of providing ANS are recovered: through charges levied on airlines; or through taxes imposed on passengers and cargo shippers. In the UK, the EU, Australia and Canada, charges are levied by ANSPs on airlines. Although, in principle, countries can use price caps or rate of return regulation for ANS,[114] there are only limited examples of where formal price caps are applied.

In the UK, an economic regulator sets a forward-looking price control for the (partially) private ANSP for a fixed period of five years for providing air traffic services to airlines, as well as quality requirements and other performance standards.[115] In South Africa, an independent body (known as the Regulating Committee) approves the charges for ANS using a five-year price cap that limits the increase in a basket of revenue weighted tariffs of the regulated charges.[116]

In New Zealand, where the ANSP is state-owned, there is no formal regulator or restrictions on pricing, although there is the threat of regulation.[117] In Canada, where the ANSP is a private not-for-profit entity, the charging principles are set out in legislation, and NAV Canada is required to consult with stakeholders about any proposed changes, incorporate any suggested changes and then lodge the changes with the Canadian Transportation Agency. Airlines can lodge appeals against such changes with the Canadian Transportation Agency if they consider them to be inconsistent with the legislation.

In EU Member States, ANS charges are set or approved by a national supervisory authority (NSA; which can be part of a ministry), a reflection of the fact that most ANSPs are state-owned. NSAs are required to draw up performance plans for specific reference periods (for a minimum of three years and maximum of five years). Performance plans are based on the business plans of ANSPs and include, among other things, details of how risks are shared between ANSPs and airspace users. Draft performance plans must be approved by the European Commission. EU Regulations also establish a common charging scheme for *en route* and terminal charges, which requires that charges be subject to consultation with airspace users' representatives on the cost bases and on the allocation of costs among different services.[118] A similar approach is adopted in Australia, where the ANSP (which is also state-owned) calculates charges on the basis of cost recovery plus a return on assets and must submit a pricing notification to the regulator, which can object to any increase in charges.

In the USA, the FAA Air Traffic Organization (ATO) is the sole provider of ANS. Its activities are funded through a combination of excise taxes (levied on passengers, cargo users and aviation fuel), which are deposited in the Airport and Airway Trust Fund

---

[114] See ICAO (2013a).
[115] The most recent price control set three separate price caps: for *en route* services, oceanic services and London approach.
[116] ATNS (2021) and ICAO (2008).
[117] Arblaster and Zhang (2021).
[118] EC (2013b).

(AATF),[119] with residual funding provided by the US Treasury.[120] The FAA also levie
charges for providing ANS to aircraft that fly in US-controlled airspace but do not tak
off or land in the USA (known as overflight fees). These charges are set to recover the fu
costs of providing such services and are calculated based on a historical year's cost an
air traffic activity.[121]

Regulation of Airport Charges

Price regulation and oversight of the charges levied for the use of major airports ca
take a range of forms, ranging from the *ex ante* regulation of control of revenues/prices
the application of light-touch price monitoring regimes, to a reliance on negotiation
between airports and airlines within a regulated framework. An important regulatory
choice is the extent to which aeronautical and non-aeronautical revenues are combine
when calculating charges that airlines must pay (see Box 15.1 on the dual-till versu
single-till debate).

In the EU, airports which handle more than five million passengers per year and/or a
the largest airport in a Member State are subject to the Airport Charging Directive, whic
requires that charges are non-discriminatory and transparently calculated, and that ai
lines and airports consult with one another. It also requires that a supervisory body h
established to settle disputes over charges. However, the Directive does not specify rule
about which airports must be price regulated, or how prices should be set or regulate
This decision is left to EU Member States and a range of approaches are adopted. Pric
cap regulation was applied at sixteen major European airports (or airport groups) in 201
including only one UK airport (London Heathrow), which is subject to a five-year pric
cap.[122] Rate of return regulation was applied at ten airports (or airport groups) in Europ
A form of 'light-handed regulation' – which involves airports and airlines reaching
voluntary agreement – is applied at major German airports, while no price regulatio
is applied to some other airports, such as Prague and Helsinki and certain UK airpor
(London Stansted, Edinburgh, Glasgow, Manchester).

In the USA, airport charges are either negotiated between airports (which, as note
above, are mostly state-owned) and airport users, or set unilaterally by an airport aft
consultation with airlines. Agreements can range from less than five years to longer tha
ten years.[123] The regulator (the FAA) will hear disputes to ensure rates are fair and re
sonable. Airports are not able to generate profits, but are required to maintain reserves
manage annual variability in revenue generation, major capital needs and emergencies.

---

[119] See FAA (2020b). GAO (2006b, 2007) provide further background.

[120] The AATF was established in 1970 to fund the development of a nationwide airport and airway system
The Trust Fund provides funding for: the Airport Improvement Program (AIP), improvements to the ai
traffic control system, and FAA operations such as ANS. Around 97 per cent of funding in 2020 came
from the AATF. See FAA (2020b).

[121] For example, the charges for 2017 onwards were based 2013 data. The overflight fee rate is calculated
by dividing its total ATO costs by the total flight miles. See FAA (2016).

[122] European Commission (2019). London Gatwick's airport charges are not subject to a price cap, but it
does have a licence, allowing the Civil Aviation Authority (CAA) to step in to protect users, for instanc
if there are reductions in service quality that are against the passengers' interests.

[123] See Starostina and Wu (2018).

[124] RAND (2020).

Federal regulations contain guidance on airport rates and charges, which sets out five principles for airports to follow, including that airline rates, fees and charges should: reflect local market conditions, be fair and reasonable, not unjustly discriminate, make the airport as financially self-sustainable as possible, and that revenue generated must only be used for statutorily allowable purposes.[125] While federal regulations do not stipulate a single approach to fee setting, it requires that any methodology must be applied in a non-discriminatory manner. Fees can be set according to a 'residual' or 'compensatory' rate setting methodology, a combination of the two, or according to another rate setting methodology.[126] Under 'residual agreements', airlines carry more risk and agree to cover any shortfall in the operating costs of the airport that cannot be met by non-aeronautical revenues or concession agreement revenues.[127] In exchange for airlines carrying more risk, the airport agrees to use any excess non-aeronautical revenues it generates to reduce airport charges.[128] In contrast, a 'compensatory agreement' involves the airport retaining all non-aeronautical revenue but being fully exposed to any cost shortfalls.[129] Under this approach, airlines face less risk and are only charged for the airport services they use, but do not benefit from reduced airport charges resulting from non-aeronautical revenues being applied to reduce charges. In practice, airports often adopt a hybrid approach that combines the residual and compensatory approaches, where airlines agree to be exposed to *some* airport costs in exchange for a share of some non-aeronautical revenues being applied to reduce airport charges (effectively a revenue sharing approach).[130] No rate setting methodology dominates, and a 2017 survey found that, of thirty large hub airports, eight used a residual approach, fifteen used a compensatory approach and seven used a hybrid approach.[131] In addition to the revenues generated from airport charges and non-aeronautical activities, airports in the USA can also obtain non-operating funds, including federal government grants, under the Airport Improvement Programme (AIP) grant programme,[132] and Passenger Facility Charges (PFCs).[133]

[125] FAA (2013).

[126] An early overview of these approaches is presented in the Congressional Budget Office (1984) study.

[127] National Academies of Sciences, Engineering, and Medicine (2010), FAA (2013), Wu (2015) and RAND (2020). Residual agreements can only be used where both parties agree (e.g. they cannot be unilaterally imposed by an airport).

[128] As in other jurisdictions, parking revenues and ground transportation (shuttle services, taxis and ride hailing services) are often the largest source of non-aeronautical revenues.

[129] Where an airport unilaterally sets charges, these must be set using a compensatory approach.

[130] National Academies of Sciences, Engineering, and Medicine (2010). Wu (2017) and Starostina and Wu (2018) describe different forms of hybrid approach which can involve different methods of sharing cost and revenue risk for airfield activities (runways, taxiways, aprons), terminal activities (restaurants and shops) and landside activities (parking garages, hotels, cargo terminals, business parks).

[131] Wu (2017).

[132] Funding for the AIP grants are drawn from the AATF (described above), which is generated by passenger and cargo user fees and taxes and fuel taxes. Funds are allocated by the FAA according to various national priorities and objectives. In practice, this means that airports responsible for the most passenger and cargo traffic (which generate the most revenues to the AATF) subsidise smaller airports. RAND (2020) estimates that large and medium-sized hub airports receive only a quarter of AIP funds, but are responsible for 90 per cent of enplanements.

[133] PFCs are subject to approval by the FAA and are imposed on departing passengers to fund eligible projects. The PFC is capped at $4.50 per segment. Eligible projects tend to involve landside projects which increase airline competition. According to RAND (2020) all medium-sized and large US airports charge a PFC.

Elsewhere in the world, a wide range of approaches to regulating airport charges and fees are adopted. In Australia and New Zealand, where there is a mix of private and public airport ownership, no formal price regulation is applied to major airports, which are instead subject to a monitoring regime for aeronautical services (including monitoring of car parking charges in Australia).[134] This monitoring includes reviews of quality indicators. In South Africa, major airports are operated by a single partially privatised company, which is required to gain approval for changes to regulated tariffs (known as permissions) from a semi-independent statutory body. Permissions are based on a CPI-X (consumer price index minus X) price cap approach and are valid for five years.[135] In Japan and Korea, charges are set by airport administrators and require approval by the relevant ministry. Airport administrators are not required to consult with users or publish the methods used for determining landing fees, although some do so.

Box 15.1

Dual-till and single-till approaches to airport charges

Airport operators generate revenues from providing a mix of aeronautical and non-aeronautical services. Aeronautical services (sometimes called airside services) are provided to airlines and allow for the necessary and safe operation of flights.[136] Non-aeronautical services (sometimes called landside services) are provided to passengers and businesses and include facilities necessary for the processing of passengers, cargo, freight and ground transportation vehicles.[137] Where airport charges are determined on the basis of both aeronautical and non-aeronautical activities of an airport, this is known as the single-till (or single-cash-register) approach. In contrast, under a dual-till approach, the aeronautical and non-aeronautical activities are treated as distinct, and airport charges are only set to recover the attributable costs of aeronautical activities. The choice between a single-till or dual-till approach is important, as the revenues generated from non-aeronautical activities for major airports are often greater than those generated from aeronautical activities.

Airlines prefer a single-till approach, as revenues from non-aeronautical activities are used to offset costs, resulting in lower airport charges. In their view, such an approach is justified because it is airlines that attract passengers to airports, which then generate the non-aeronautical revenues (e.g. retail) they provide for airports.[138] As it covers all revenues, a single-till approach is seen to control the market power of airports and creates equal incentives to invest in aeronautical and non-aeronautical infrastructure. It also avoids the challenges of allocating costs between aeronautical and non-aeronautical activities. In contrast, airports often prefer a dual-till approach, as this does not place any regulatory restrictions on

---

[134] This applies to four airports in Australia (Brisbane, Melbourne, Perth and Sydney) and three airports in New Zealand (Auckland, Wellington and Christchurch) and requires each airport to prepare and submit regulatory accounts which are broken down into aeronautical and non-aeronautical activities. In New Zealand, airports may set their own prices but must consult with substantial customers, such as airlines on charges and any major capital expenditure plans. See ACCC (2021c).

[135] See Regulating Committee (2015). The X factor is determined by applying the 'building blocks' methodology.

[136] Maintaining and operating runways, taxiways and aprons; providing aerobridges; refuelling services; hangar and maintenance facilities; and ground handling services.

[137] This can include include the leasing of space to retail and hospitality services within an airport terminal, the operation of car parks, and the leasing of land to hotels and business parks.

[138] IATA (2007).

the revenues that can be generated from their commercial activities.[139] It is argued that this approach creates incentives to improve the provision of non-aeronautical services (e.g. expand retail and hotel facilities), which, in turn, can improve the attractiveness of an airport to passengers and airlines and enhance airline competition. The approach is also seen to send the right economic signals to airlines about the actual costs they impose, and to provide the correct incentives for investment.[140]

In academic work, the debate has sometimes been framed in terms of whether the revenues from core monopoly activities (the aeronautical activities) should be combined with (or unbundled from) the non-core, contestable activities (non-aeronautical activities).[141] Some studies have found that the single-till approach can approximate a Ramsey–Boiteux price structure, and, because it results in lower airport charges, reduces airport market power and double marginalisation.[142] Others argue that a single-till approach is appropriate because it reflects the fact that airports are two-sided platforms and takes account of the externalities that exist between non-aeronautical and aeronautical services.[143] On the other hand, some studies have concluded that the single-till approach can result in charges that are too low, leading to excess congestion at major airports, and in these circumstances a dual-till price approach is more efficient, as it ensures that airport charges are not set at too low a level.[144] An important factor in determining the efficiency of each approach is the extent to which an airport can cover its fixed costs through aeronautical charges alone: if it cannot cover its fixed costs, then a single-till approach can improve efficiency; but if (efficient) aeronautical charges are sufficient to cover fixed costs, and the airport is congested, the dual-till approach is preferred.[145]

The relative merits of the single-till and dual-till approaches have been considered by regulators in many parts of the world,[146] and both single and dual tills are used in practice. In 2014, a single-till approach was used in 46 per cent of countries, a dual-till approach in 37 per cent of countries, with the remainder using a hybrid approach.[147] A dual-till or hybrid approach is now used for many European airports, in Latin American countries and in Australia and New Zealand.[148] In contrast, a single-till approach is used for major airports in Ireland, the UK, the Middle East and Africa. It is further estimated that around 44 per cent of privatised airports use a single-till approach, with 26 per cent using a dual-till approach, and the remainder a hybrid approach.[149]

---

[139] ACI (2017) reports that non-aeronautical revenue per passenger for dual-till airports was higher than for single-till airports (US$8.57 versus US$7.61).

[140] See ACI (2018).

[141] See Beesley (1999) and Starkie (2001).

[142] See Czerny (2006).

[143] Malavolti (2016).

[144] See Yang and Zhang (2011), who find that, if airport congestion is not a significant problem, single-till price cap regulation is preferred, but that, if congestion is present, then dual-till regulation can outperform single-till regulation. Czerny, Guiomard and Zhang (2016) argue that the problem of overcongestion in the single-till approach can be alleviated, at least partly, by the control and management of airport slots.

[145] See Yang and Zhang (2011) and Czerny, Guiomard and Zhang (2016).

[146] See Irish Commission for Aviation Regulation (2010) and Productivity Commission (2002). Also compare CAA (2000) and Competition Commission (2002), which take opposing views on the benefits of each approach.

[147] ICAO (2014). ICAO (2013c) defines a hybrid approach as one where the cost basis is established using a combination of the single-till and the dual-till approaches – e.g. landing costs could be recovered on the basis of the single-till approach, while terminal costs on the basis of the dual-till approach.

[148] EC (2019c) and ICAO (2014).

[149] ACI (2017).

15.3 THE SCOPE AND EFFECTS OF RESTRUCTURING POLICIES

15.3.1 The Scope of Restructuring Policies in Aviation

The aviation sector is often considered the poster child of 'deregulation' and regulatory restructuring. However, as described above, the sector as a whole is in no wa fully deregulated: ANSPs are generally state-owned; many major airports are also state owned, or subject to some form of price regulation or monitoring; and, while airlir services are competitive, some essential routes can receive government support, merge and alliances are closely scrutinised, and there are persistent concerns about low levels competition on some routes. Moreover, unlike the other industries discussed in this boo regulation is heavily shaped at the international level through treaties and policies an recommendations of bodies such as ICAO.

Restructuring of Airline Markets

Economic regulation in the USA began with the introduction of policies for the carria of cargo (airmail) in the 1920s, which led to regulatory oversight first by the Intersta Commerce Commission (ICC) and then the Civil Aeronautics Board (CAB) in the 1930s. Between the 1930s and the late 1970s, the CAB strictly controlled the routes that airlin could fly and the entry and expansion of airlines to prevent 'destructive' or 'excessiv competition'.[151] This strict regulatory approach influenced the development of the airli network into one similar to railways based on point-to-point journeys.[152] As a cons quence, many routes were serviced by a single airline (monopoly) or at best two airlin (duopoly), which meant that the CAB also had a role in setting minimum, maximum ar actual airfares.[153] Regulated fares were set to ensure that airlines covered costs and earn a reasonable rate of return, while the fare structures involved the cross-subsidisation certain routes (higher fares for long-distance and lower short-haul fares). As costs we automatically reflected in fares, this led to limited incentives to control costs, which turn was used as the basis to justify higher fares.[154] This resulted in fares that were abo efficient cost levels for many markets. Because fares were fixed, airlines competed service and non-price aspects, which resulted in higher flight frequencies (as a resu of airlines overscheduling flights) but low load factors, and raised the average costs p passenger mile.[155] Airlines also competed on various in-flight quality dimensions such

---

[150] Scheduled commercial passenger services began following the Air Mail Act (1925) and included Pan American Airways, Western Air Express and the Ford Air Transport Service. By the mid-1930s additional operators included United, American, Eastern and Transcontinental Western Air (TWA).

[151] Button (1989) observes that the low density of passenger traffic on most routes meant that they were essentially joint product, natural monopolies that could only be sustained by combining mail and passenger rights, and competition was thus seen as destructive and could lead to cream-skimming, which led to a preference for one carrier per route.

[152] There were also limitations on which airlines could fly internationally under bilateral air service agreements. Only two airlines offered such services: Pan Am and TWA.

[153] See Caves (1962).

[154] As Kahn (1988) observes, this led to costs rising to the level of the regulated price. Borenstein and Ros (2014) note that it was not until the early 1970s that a formal cost-based structure was used to assess the reasonableness of fares.

[155] Douglas and Miller (1974). Bailey (1985) notes that regulation resulted in excessive service competitio See also Kahn (1988) and Borenstein and Rose (2014).

food and drink and entertainment.[156] Regulation of cargo services was asymmetric, with tight controls imposed on permissible routes and rates for cargo carriers above a certain size, while smaller providers were not subject to regulation.

By the mid-1970s, the rationale for, and effects of, the federal regulation of airlines in the USA started to be closely scrutinised by both economists and politicians.[157] A particular focus was the significant gap between the fares for *inter*-state flights as compared to similar *intra*-state flights,[158] and that many planes flew with low load factors (i.e. were half-empty). In addition, notwithstanding the fact that prices were regulated, many airlines rarely earned their target rate of return.[159] This ultimately led to the Airline Deregulation Act 1978, which gradually phased out restrictions on entry and routes and the regulation of fares, and ultimately made the CAB itself redundant.[160] Rather than rely on regulation, the explicit aim of the Airline Deregulation Act 1978 was to rely on actual and potential competitive forces to provide efficiency, innovation and low prices, reduce concentration, and encourage the entry and the expansion of airlines into additional routes.[161] In short, airlines were now generally free to choose the routes they serviced, the fares they charged and the quality of service they offered passengers.[162] While these changes focused on the domestic market, from the early 1990s, the USA also sought to conclude deeper 'Open Skies Agreements' with other countries, which allowed for greater reciprocal access to their respective markets.[163] Such agreements also allowed foreign carriers to form alliances with US carriers and thus obtain antitrust immunity.

In Europe, up until the 1980s, all countries operated a state-owned national airline (which provided domestic, intercontinental and international services),[164] and the state also operated the major airports and controlled the airspace. Each country applied their own regulations, and intercontinental travel between European countries was strictly managed through a series of bilateral agreements. These agreements typically controlled

---

[156] Kahn (1988).

[157] Borenstein and Rose (2014) claim that the changes can be attributed to Hearings held by Senator Ted Kennedy on the costs and inconsistencies of CAB regulation in 1975, and the appointments of economists such as Alfred Kahn and Elizabeth Bailey to the CAB Board. Wider factors include stagnant growth and the impact of the OPEC oil price shock on prices. Button (2015) provides illuminating background.

[158] Borenstein and Rose (2014) note that among the factors was the contrast between the prices charged for *inter*-state flights (levied by the CAB) and fares set for *intra*-state flights in states like California, Texas and Florida. Levine (1965) first highlighted this based on the fares between Los Angeles and San Francisco.

[159] GAO (1990).

[160] One year prior to the Airline Deregulation Act 1978, the All-Cargo Deregulation Statute 1977 removed the CAB's control over entry into and exit from the all-cargo market, while 1979 amendments to the Federal Aviation Act removed government control over rates and routes.

[161] See Airline Deregulation Act 1978, Section 3. Bailey (1985) notes that the CAB adopted a policy of forbearance in implementing the Act, with the burden of proof being placed on those who would retain regulation. However, this did involve the monitoring of the market and the collection of data.

[162] Some routes remain subsidised under the Essential Air Service programme, and there were still some restrictions on fares.

[163] Such agreements seek to remove restrictions on fares, capacity, frequency and aircraft type for airlines that are designated in countries which are signatories to such an agreement. The first Open Skies Agreement was the USA–Netherlands Agreement in 1992. This was followed by agreements between the USA and Denmark, Sweden, Finland, Belgium, Luxembourg and Austria (1995), Germany (1996), Italy (1998) and France (2001). The EU–USA Open Skies Agreement was only introduced in 2007.

[164] In some countries, separate airlines provided domestic and international services.

entry and capacity, and often involved rules that only permitted one airline from eac[h] country to operate on that route (known as single designation). Fares were set by agree[e]ment between state-owned airlines under the oversight of the International Air Transpor[t] Association (IATA), and fares could be blocked by the governments of either state con[n]ected by the route. Beginning in the 1980s, these regulatory policies were graduall[y] withdrawn and the airline market opened to greater competition. In the UK, the change[s] began in the mid-1980s and culminated in the privatisation of British Airways in 1987,[165] which was followed by the privatisations of other major European airlines in the 1990[s] (Lufthansa, Air France). At the EU level, two Aviation Liberalisation Packages introduce[d] in 1987 and 1990 gradually sought to open up the sector and promote competition by[y] removing single designation provisions and allowing multiple airlines to service par[r]ticular routes; removing capacity restrictions; and allowing airlines to fly between tw[o] foreign countries when the flight is originating or terminating in its home country.[166] Th[e] Packages also removed restrictions in some Member States that required national fla[g] carriers be given a 50 per cent share of the market, and the ability of Member States t[o] block proposals for low fares. The packages introduced a 'double disapproval' procedur[e] where an airline fare was permitted unless both Member States disapproved it. Thes[e] changes led to the entry of new airlines (such as Ryanair and other LCCs) and the expan[n]sion of existing competitor airlines on key routes. A third package of reforms introduce[d] in 1992 went even further and granted airlines full access to all routes between Membe[r] States and the right to offer services between airports in two other Member States. [It] also allowed airlines to set their own fares and set out the circumstances in which cer[r]tain lifeline routes could be subsidised by national or local authorities.[167] Separately, th[e] European Commission issued guidelines on the use of subsidies (known as State Aid) fo[r] start-up airlines on new routes.[168]

Airline restructuring policies have also been introduced in many other parts of th[e] world.[169] Major airlines in Australia, Chile, Canada and Japan were all privatised i[n] the 1980s and 1990s. The New Zealand and Canadian domestic aviation markets wer[e] deregulated in 1983 and 1987, respectively, while in Australia the so-called 'two airlin[e] policy' was removed in 1990 while entry into international routes was permitted fro[m] 1992. Chile also pursued policies to open market access and remove restriction on fare[s] and sought airline service agreements with other countries in the late 1980s. The Chines[e] aviation sector underwent a restructuring in the 1980s which led to competition amon[g] regional airlines and the deregulation of airfares in 1997. This led to a price war amon[g] twenty airlines and fares were re-regulated in 1998.[170] However, further policy change[s] have since been introduced, including the removal of restrictions on domestic airfare[s] (such as minimum prices) and the entry of new airlines (although the domestic marke[t]

---

[165] Yarrow (1995) provides useful background.
[166] This is the Fifth Freedom of the Air; see earlier footnote 113.
[167] In 2008 these regulations were recast into the single Air Services Regulation (Regulation 1008/2008/EC[)].
[168] Under the guidelines, start-up aid can be provided to airlines for opening new routes from airports wit[h] up to three million passengers a year for a maximum of three years. See EC (2014).
[169] See ITF (2019) for an overview.
[170] See Lei and O'Connell (2011).

remains exclusive to Chinese carriers).[171] India's airline sector has gradually been opened to competition, with new private carriers entering and offering international services.[172] Japan's domestic airline market was gradually deregulated from 1985, but full deregulation was only achieved in 2000.[173]

In addition to domestic restructuring, many countries have sought to develop or expand regional international air service agreements with their major trading partners to provide for greater airline access to international markets and remove restrictions on frequency, routing and fares (such as the ability of one country to disallow fares).[174] Important among these are the USA and Canada Open Skies Agreement (1995),[175] the Trans-Tasman Single Aviation Market (2002) between Australia and New Zealand, and an agreement among ten countries in the Association of Southeast Asian Nations (ASEAN) which seeks to create a single aviation market in that region.[176] In Africa, despite the large distances between major cities, the airline market is small and the fleet ageing.[177] There are limited economies of density and scope and there can be considerable political involvement.[178] Various attempts at liberalisation have been made, including an agreement on the liberalisation of access to air transport markets in Africa which became binding in in 2002,[179] and more recently in 2018 efforts to create a Single African Air Transport Market which would cover 80 per cent of the market.[180]

Restructuring of Airports

While there has been considerable restructuring of airline services, there has been much less restructuring in airport activities. In the USA, most airports remain under state ownership and control but subject to regulatory oversight by the FAA. Although an Airport Privatisation Pilot Program was introduced in 1996, there has only been limited success with efforts at privatisations to date.[181] The most recent FAA Authorization Act introduced in 2018 renamed this initiative as the Airport Investment Partnership Program and now allows any US airport (including major hubs) to be long-term leased to a private operator.[182] In relation to airport slots, the FAA can impose mandatory slot coordination or engage in schedule facilitation with carriers at certain airports. Currently, three airports

---

[171] Reuters (2018) and Deville (2019). However, the removal of price restrictions was generally seen as benefiting airlines rather than consumers, as it allows them to set higher prices.

[172] ITF (2019).

[173] Yamaguchi (2013).

[174] These are sometimes called 'Open Skies Agreements' and differ from earlier bilateral agreements, which often restricted or specified the capacity, frequency and routes that designated carriers from each country were allowed to serve. Such agreements have often been facilitated by the fact that the US antitrust authorities will only allow an airline alliance if the carriers are from countries where an Open Skies Agreement is in place. See ITF (2019).

[175] This was expanded in 2006 to further reduce restrictions, including in relation to cargo.

[176] Tan (2010).

[177] Button, Martini and Scotti (2017) provide a useful overview.

[178] Button, Porta and Scotti (2022).

[179] This is known as the Yamoussoukro Decision. See Schlumberger (2010) and Njoya (2016).

[180] Button, Porta and Scotti (2022).

[181] The original programme was for five airports, which was expanded to ten airports in 2012. However, only one large hub can participate in the programme. See FAA (2013).

[182] FAA (2021). See also CRS (2021).

are subject to mandatory slot coordination,[183] while four airports are involved in schedu
facilitation.[184]

In contrast, airport privatisation in Europe started in the UK in 1987 and has sinc
been introduced in other European countries, where some major airports are either ful
or partially privately owned (such as Brussels, Copenhagen, Frankfurt, Paris and Vienn
or operated under long-term concession or lease agreements (Lisbon and Rome). In th
UK, a 2009 competition authority decision required the private owner of the UK's majo
airports to sell three of its major airports (two in London and one in Scotland) wit
the express aim of introducing greater airport competition.[185] While EU Member State
retain responsibility for how airports are regulated, since the mid-1990s, the Europea
Commission has issued high-level rules relating to airport charges, ground handlir
services and slot allocation. The 2009 Airports Charging Directive[186] (which appli
to all EU airports handling more than five million passengers per year and the larg
est airport in each Member State) requires that airport charges be non-discriminator
transparently calculated and consulted on, and that a supervisory body be establishe
in each Member State to settle disputes over charges. An earlier EU Directive introduce
competition for the majority of ground handling services at larger EU airports, with th
aim of providing airlines more choice in who provides baggage handling, ramp har
dling, fuelling and freight services.[187] Rules and guidance also apply to airport (take-o
and landing) slot allocation in EU Member States, which sets out criteria for when a
airport can be designated as a 'coordinated airport'. This requires that an independe
coordinator introduce rules relating to slot use (establishing 'grandfather rights' and th
80/20 or use-it-or-lose rule) and the secondary trading of airport slots.[188] Guidelin
have also been issued on the use of subsidies or investment aid (state aid) for airpor
which: set out rules for agreements between airlines and airports; permit state aid
fund infrastructure for a genuine transport need; and allow operational aid for region
airports under certain conditions.[189]

Restructuring policies involving the privatisation of airports have also been pursued
the Asia-Pacific region and Latin America and have generally involved competition f
the market and the use of concession arrangements (e.g. in Chile and Mexico), or bei
listed on a stock exchange (China, Japan, Malaysia).[190] In addition, the restructuring

---

[183] John F. Kennedy and LaGuardia Airports in New York and Ronald Reagan Washington National Airpo
[184] Chicago O'Hare International Airport (ORD), Los Angeles International Airport (LAX), Newark Liberty
International Airport (EWR) and San Francisco International Airport (SFO).
[185] British Airports Authority (BAA) was required to sell London Gatwick, London Stansted and Edinburg
airports. The airports served 65 million passengers in total in 2008. Littlechild (2018b) argues that this
acknowledged that it was a 'mistake' to create a single privatised company.
[186] EU Directive 2009/12/EC.
[187] An EU Member State cannot limit the number of suppliers to less than two suppliers, one of which has
to be independent of the airport or the dominant airline at that airport. See Directive 96/67/EC.
[188] See Regulation 2407/92/EEC. This Regulation has been amended several times to ensure that non-
utilisation of slots in times of unusually low demand does not mean airlines lose their entitlement,
including in response to the September 11 terrorist attacks, to the global financial crisis and to SARS i
2003 and Covid-19 in 2020–2021.
[189] See EC (2014).
[190] ACI (2017). China has the highest number of airports listed on a stock exchange.

the domestic and international airline sectors has led to increasing airport competition at the international level (between global hubs), and at the national and regional levels, including a greater use of secondary (non-major) airports in a number of countries.

Restructuring of Air Navigation Services

There has been more limited restructuring in ANS provision around the world. The most notable restructuring of airspace navigation service providers was the full privatisation of the Canadian ANSP in 1996 (which now operates as a not-for-profit entity) and the partial privatisation of the ANSP in the UK in 2001. In the USA, the FAA, which operates the National Airspace System, underwent a transition from a largely manual system in the mid-1960s to a semi-automated system, and is currently undergoing another transition to a Next Generation Air Transportation System (NextGen). NextGen will rely on satellite and digital technologies to manage aircraft in real time and requires investments in ground systems and avionics installed on aircraft.[191] The FAA receives its funding and authority through federal legislation.[192] The most recent FAA Authorization Act from 2018 lasts for five years and introduced changes to increase the safety and pace of UAS integration, and to expedite the financing and development of airport capital projects.

In the EU, the ownership and regulation of airspace navigation services remains within the competency of EU Member States. However, since the early 2000s, EU policies have sought to address concerns about fragmentation, duplication and poor performance in terms of delays and costs. The Single European Sky policy introduced in 2004 and expanded in 2009 requires, among other things, that each Member State establish an NSA that is independent of ANSPs, and that a network manager at the EU level be established to coordinate activities at the network level.[193] The policy seeks to promote the creation of 'functional airspace blocks'm which are airspace blocks based on operational requirements rather than national borders. It also sets out common rules and principles relating to charging schemes, and introduces requirements for Member States (or those which cooperate in functional airspace blocks) to establish performance targets and plans on the key areas of safety, the environment, capacity and cost efficiency.

5.3.2 The Effects of Restructuring Policies in Aviation

Effects of Airline Restructuring

The effects of the 1978 Airline Deregulation Act in the USA have been studied intensively for the last forty years,[194] with many studies declaring it a success from the consumer

---

[191] This includes the: Data Communications (Data Comm) tower service (which provides digital text-like messages instead of voice communications); Performance Based Navigation (PBN) take-off and landing procedures, which are more precise and efficient; and ADS-B.

[192] Although there was a proposal to privatise air traffic control by President Trump in 2017, this policy was ultimately not adopted.

[193] See EU Regulation 549/2004 and EU Regulation 1108/2009/EC. For background to this package, see Decker, Dumez, Jeunemaître, et al. (2003).

[194] See Bailey (1985), Bailey, Graham and Kaplan (1985), Levine (1987), Kahn (1988), Goetz and Vowles (2009) and Borenstein and Rose (2014). Also, see the references in Button (2015).

perspective.[195] Among the initial effects of the deregulation were: substantial decreases i
average fares;[196] increased passenger traffic and higher load factors;[197] the introductio
of differentiated fare and service offerings (including loyalty programmes);[198] significar
entry on routes; expansion of incumbents into new routes; the emergence of new low
cost operators with different business models;[199] and the shift in the airline network con
figuration from one based largely on direct point-to-point journeys to a hub-and-spok
system where passengers make indirect connections.[200] Airline markets generally becam
progressively more competitive during the 1990s and 2000s, leading to even lower aver
age fares,[201] and increased passenger traffic. However, persistent concerns exist about th
emergence of 'fortress hubs' (where a single airline contains a high proportion of acces
to that market) and that some smaller markets (the spokes) are only served by one o
two airlines.[202] Greater exposure to competition and cyclical financial conditions led to
number of failures (particularly among new airlines),[203] mergers and acquisitions,[204] an
a number of major legacy airlines going out of business or filing for bankruptcy.[205] Thes
changes have at times led to calls for the re-introduction of regulation.[206]

   In terms of competition, industry concentration has changed over time as the resu
of waves of entry and exit,[207] and recent estimates suggest that the top six US airline

---

[195] Borenstein and Rose (2014) conclude that: 'Airline deregulation has likely benefited consumers with
lower average prices, more extensive and frequent service, and continued technological progress in bot
aircraft and ticketing.' However, they also note that: 'For many airlines, it has been a costly experiment
though a few have prospered in the unregulated environment.' See also National Academies of Sciences
Engineering, and Medicine (1991, 1999), Kahn (2005), GAO (2006a) and Morrison and Winston (2008).
Levine (2006) examines the changes in the context of the interest group theory of regulation.

[196] See Bailey (1985), Morrison and Winston (1990) and Kahn's foreword in Barrett (2009). GAO (2006a)
estimated that median fare had declined almost 40 per cent between 1980 and 2005. Borenstein and
Rose (2014) estimate that average fares in 2011 were 26 per cent below the pre-deregulation standard
industry fare. However, they also note the need to compare fares pre- and post-deregulation to an
appropriate counterfactual.

[197] Borenstein and Rose (2014) suggest that average domestic load factors, which were below 50 per cent
prior to deregulation, rose to over 60 per cent in the mid-1980s and were 83 per cent in 2011.

[198] Bailey (1985) notes that the practice of mixing high-fare and low-fare passengers on a single flight,
which increases load factors, was not foreseen prior to regulation.

[199] GAO (1990) notes that, between 1978 and 1984, the number of certified airlines tripled from forty-
four to 114, and that routes served by two or more airlines increased by 55 per cent. Entrants included
Southwest Airlines and America West.

[200] Borenstein and Rose (2014) note that this change fundamentally altered the economics of airline
operations by providing cost, demand and competitive advantages.

[201] GAO (2006a). However, the National Academies of Sciences, Engineering, and Medicine (1991) shows
that fares for shorter distances or less travelled markets did not reduce by as much, with some fares
increasing. Similarly, Borenstein and Rose (2014) note that the gains from lower prices have not been
distributed evenly among customers, and that a third of economy-fare passengers in 2011 paid a fare
higher than the pre-deregulation rate for that route. RAND (2020) also find evidence of substantial
volatility in fares on different routes.

[202] National Academies of Sciences, Engineering, and Medicine (1999) and RAND (2020).

[203] Borenstein and Rose (2014) record that forty-eight carriers exited between 1984 and 1987.

[204] Mergers and acquisitions include TWA and American (2001); US Airways and America West (2005);
Delta and Northwest (2008); and the acquisition by United of Continental (2010).

[205] Notable examples of major legacy carriers exiting include Pan Am and TWA. Other major carriers that
have filed for bankruptcy protection include Delta, Northwest, Continental, United and US Airways.
Borenstein and Rose (2014) estimate that US airlines have lost billions of dollars during demand
downturns that occurred in the 1980s, 1990s, 2001–2005 and post-2008.

[206] See the discussion in Kahn (2005).

[207] Borenstein and Rose (2014) note that the lowest national average concentration (measured by the
Herfindahl–Hirschman index (HHI)) was 0.41 in 1986, after which it then rose until the late 1990s, before
declining again. In 2008–2011 it was estimated that concentration levels for all routes averaged about 0.4

account for around 89 per cent of seats offered.[208] Concerns about unfair competition, such as predatory pricing or loyalty programmes acting as barriers to entry, have also been raised at various times. Greater fare dispersion, largely associated with competition and sophisticated yield management policies, is seen to have been beneficial overall.[209] However, some passengers have been dissatisfied with the extreme price differentiation and the high spread between the highest and lowest tickets.[210] One important change flowing from airline deregulation is in terms of service quality.[211] While some aspects of service quality are seen to have improved (such as route offerings, choice, connections, frequency, etc.), other aspects such as in-flight amenities and service, crowded planes (as a result of higher load factors and narrower seats) and longer journey times (as a result of congestion and delays) are seen as having reduced the quality experienced by many passengers.[212] For some, this is a sign of the 'success' of deregulation in lowering prices and attracting more passengers and traffic,[213] while others argue that the real problem lies elsewhere in the aviation supply chain (airports and airspace) not keeping pace.[214]

The effects of restructuring policies for air services in Europe have been more gradual than in the USA.[215] The three EU Aviation Liberalisation Packages were fully implemented in 1997, creating a European single aviation market that allowed full access for airlines to each other's markets and to choose their own routes (freedom to operate). Many major airlines have since been fully or partially privatised,[216] fare levels are no longer subject to direct regulatory control or veto by Member States,[217] and strict rules restricting state subsidies to airlines have been introduced. All of this has led to a pan-European aviation market.[218] As in the USA, there has been substantial entry by new airlines and LCCs, and expansion by some existing legacy providers into the LCC market.[219] In the period since the restructuring policies were introduced, there have been substantial increases in passenger volumes and routes served. The number of daily flights has increased from

[208] EC (2019d). RAND (2020) estimate that, in 2018, the four largest airlines accounted for 73 per cent of air seat miles. In addition, Azar, Schmalz and Tecu (2018) find that, once common ownership is considered, increases in market concentration far exceed those indicated by the conventional measure of market concentration. They also estimate that airline ticket prices are 3–7 per cent higher due to common ownership.

[209] GAO (2006a). Smith, Leimkuhler and Darrow (1992) estimate the benefit of such yield management policies to airlines at that time to be around $500 million annually.

[210] National Academies of Sciences, Engineering, and Medicine (1999). Borenstein and Rose (2014) refer to the 'the often-bewildering array of fares available (and prices actually paid by different passengers) on any given airline-route'. See also Kahn (2001, 2005).

[211] See, for example, Department of Transportation (2016).

[212] See Kahn (2005).

[213] See Kahn (1988). As Breyer (2011) observes: 'So we sit in crowded planes, munch potato chips, flare up when the loudspeaker announces yet another flight delay. But how many now will vote to go back to the "good old days" of paying high, regulated prices for better service? Even among business travelers, who wants to pay "full fare for the briefcase"?'

[214] Kahn (2001) and Borenstein and Rose (2014).

[215] Dobruszkes (2009), Barrett (2009) and Burghouwt and de Wit (2015) provide useful overviews of the impacts at those points in time.

[216] In 1992, forty-two carriers in Europe had at least 50 per cent government ownership, which had decreased to twenty-five carriers by 2016 (EC, 2019d).

[217] Although there are still rules in place about how fares are presented to consumers – e.g. in terms of breakdown of charges, and transparent presentation of any optional charges.

[218] Thelle and la Couer Sonne (2018) conclude that: 'liberalisation and extension of the European aviation market stands out as one of the clearest success stories of the single European market'.

[219] Airlines such as British Airways, Lufthansa and Iberia all created LCC subsidiaries.

fewer than 10,000 in 1992 to around 26,000 in 2018, while the number of routes offered increased from under 2700 in 1992 to more than 8400 in 2017.[220] Routes served by LCCs have increased dramatically, while the number of flights operated by traditional legacy operators have generally declined to concentrate on key routes. By 2017, LCCs offered around 30 per cent more seats than traditional legacy operators, and Ryanair and easyJet had the highest market shares in Europe. LCCs have also established a large number of operational bases across Europe,[221] often at under-utilised secondary airports or former military airports, from which they offer point-to-point services. In contrast, many former legacy carriers have rationalised their routes around hub-and-spoke systems using the major airports in each country.[222] Similar to the USA, there have been a number of major mergers (such as KLM and Air France, British Airways and Iberia) and exits from the sector.[223] However, overall concentration levels in Europe are lower than in the USA,[224] and the instances of just a single carrier offering seat capacity on a particular route was 2 per cent in 2017 (down from 34 per cent in 1995).[225]

In terms of changes in passenger fares, the picture in Europe is mixed. Some data suggests that average fares have increased on some routes in the period since 1992.[226] However, such a comparison is potentially misleading, as it does not account for the fact that the fare structures used by most airlines (and particularly LCCs) today have been 'unbundled' and no longer include many elements that would have featured in the base fare in 1992 (e.g. baggage charges, seat allocation, priority boarding, etc.). Other comparisons of average fares on selected routes show a trend of decreasing fares, and there is also evidence of significant reductions in airline yields per passenger.[227] Similarly, a 2015 comparison of low-cost airline fares in the USA and the EU found that many were lower (per mile) in the EU than in the USA.[228] A recurring issue concerns how fares are presented to consumers, and in particular how airlines break down taxes and charges on websites, which can cause confusion and limit effective price comparability for passengers (see Chapter 7). In terms of service quality, restructuring has provided consumers with greater choice of destinations and increased airline responsiveness to passenger demand in terms of adding and removing routes.[229] As in the USA, the restructuring has

[220] EC (2019d).
[221] The ability to develop an operational base stems directly from the fact that airlines no longer need to only have a base in the country of their principal place of business. EC (2019d) records that there were 228 operational bases in 2017.
[222] Such as British Airways at London Heathrow; Air France at Paris CDG; Lufthansa at Frankfurt and Munich; and KLM at Amsterdam Schiphol.
[223] These exits include low-cost airlines such as Air Berlin and WOW, as well as smaller national carriers such as Swissair and Sabena.
[224] The top six airlines accounting for about 42 per cent of seats offered in 2017.
[225] This includes seats being offered under agreements or alliances or other forms of capacity sharing.
[226] EC (2019d).
[227] EC (2019d) examines eight routes and finds evidence of a reduction. ITF (2019) finds evidence of substantial real yield decreases from 21 cents in 1990 to 9 cents in 2013 However, they caution against automatically equating these reductions as full benefits to consumers in terms of lower fares.
[228] Button (2015).
[229] EC (2019d). Fulton (2021) estimates that 600 new air routes were added in Europe in 2021 (with 65 per cent being planned by LCCs). However, the number of routes where LCCs directly compete with one another is more limited. In 2017, it was estimated that the largest LCC Ryanair competed with other LCCs on just under 20 per cent of routes, while it competed with the second largest LCC easyJet on just seventy-four routes (or 7.5 per cent of flights). See Dunn (2017).

brought about changes to in-flight service quality, which in the eyes of some passengers has deteriorated.[230] Notwithstanding these views, a number of assessments conclude that, overall, EU consumers have benefited from the restructuring.[231]

Airline restructuring policies, including privatisation, introduced in Australia,[232] Canada, Chile, Japan, Korea, Mexico and New Zealand over the past three decades are largely considered to have resulted in more consumer choice, the entry of LCCs and the opening up of international markets through air service agreements.[233] In China and India, where some restructuring has been introduced, there are seen to be significant potential gains from further opening up the market and the introduction of LCCs, which could intensify competition, lower fares and attract millions of passengers away from the rail network. In Africa, progress with liberalising access to air transport markets has been slow.[234] Notwithstanding this, there has been new entry in some jurisdictions, and some studies suggest that, in those jurisdictions where restructuring has occurred, service quality has increased (in terms of departure frequency). However, fares have not necessarily been reduced.[235] Here, too, there is substantial scope for further airline liberalisation policies to improve trade, mobility and economic exchanges within Africa, which is currently constrained by poor road and rail infrastructure.[236] Participation by African airlines in global alliances could also be beneficial in increasing passenger flows and improving regional integration.[237]

Effects of Airport Restructuring

The effects of airport restructuring policies vary by jurisdiction.[238] As described above, there has been limited restructuring of airports in the USA, and a recent assessment concluded that the current system is a patchwork of federally authorised funding systems, which requires airports to gain approval from a combination of federal regulators, local governments, state governments and airlines before investing in airport infrastructure.[239] It also found that lack of investment in terminals has led to overcrowding, while low investment in control towers has contributed to delays. Perhaps most critically, it found that many airports and routes lack a healthy level of competition. Changes may be ahead though, and the US Congress recently considered whether airport privatisation could increase capacity and reduce the reliance of airports on federal funding.[240]

---

[230] EC (2019d) record that thirty-three of the seventy-eight citizens who replied to its consultation indicated a deterioration in service offerings.

[231] ITF (2019) note that: 'It is safe to conclude that the consumer has benefitted from EU liberalisation with the number of routes and frequencies increasing substantially since the early 1990s ... there is more choice for the consumer at the route level as well as lower fares, in particular from 2000 onwards.' See also EC (2019d).

[232] Although, in Australia, recent concerns about the intensity of airline competition and the provision of services to regional areas has led to the introduction of a monitoring regime. See ACCC (2021c).

[233] ITF (2019).

[234] Njoya (2016) concludes that, compared to the experience of Europe, it would seem to be a failure, which is attributed to four factors: fragmentation, dependence on the former colonial powers, institutional weaknesses, and poor cooperation.

[235] See Abate (2016) for a useful overview.

[236] ITF (2019) and Ismaila, Warnock-Smith and Hubbard (2014). See also Chapter 14.

[237] See Button, Porta and Scotti (2022).

[238] A useful overview of the effects at that time is presented in Forsyth, Gillen, Muller and Niemeier (2016).

[239] RAND (2020).

[240] CRS (2021).

Assessments of airport restructuring policies introduced in the UK, particularly those intended to promote greater airport competition and withdraw formal *ex ante* price regulation from most major airports, have evolved over time and are generally positive.[241] Passenger demand has grown, service quality to passengers and airlines has increased, there has been increased competition to attract additional airlines and routes, and the level of airport charges negotiated between the airports and airlines have sometimes been lower.[242]

In Europe, the number of airports that have been fully or partially privatised has increased over the past decade,[243] and airport competition has become more widespread.[244] However, competition remains limited for large capacity-constrained airports which have significant market power, and are subject to *ex ante* price regulation. A 2019 assessment of the EU Airport Charging Directive found that the type of economic regulation applied varies greatly across Member States, resulting in diverse charging approaches and a lack of transparency.[245] It also found that the process for setting airport charges might indirectly impose barriers to entry for airlines wishing to launch new or expand existing services at an airport, where an airline with significant buyer power at an airport uses its position to influence airport charges and investments. The review also found differences in the independence, and the powers and duties, of the supervisory authorities established in each Member State, which could affect their ability to address misuse of market power. Reviews of the Ground Handling and Slot Allocation Directive found increased competition and reduced prices for ground handling services,[246] but that airport slot allocation could be improved to provide greater access to entrants, allow for greater slot trading, and enhance the independence of the independent slot coordinator.[247]

Elsewhere in the world, a large number of studies have examined whether privatised airports perform better than state-owned airports. The evidence appears to be mixed and depends on factors such as the extent of private involvement, the size of the airport and whether the airport is a hub or not.[248] In terms of the approach to regulating airports, the shift away from formal economic regulation towards a monitoring approach for major airports in Australia and New Zealand is still generally considered as appropriate and fit for purpose.[249] Although, in Australia, it has been recommended that regulatory oversight be enhanced to better detect the exercise of market power.[250]

---

[241] Littlechild (2018b) notes that the evolution of regulation of UK airports 'has not been a straightforward or painless process' but that the introduction of competition and 'lighter-handed regulation has led to more efficient, innovative, flexible and customer-sensitive airports'.

[242] See CMA (2016c).

[243] EC (2019c) finds that the number of airports that are fully public decreased from 77 per cent in 2010 to 53.2 per cent in 2016.

[244] EC (2019c) notes, however, that this conclusion is debated, with some studies finding evidence of increased airport competition, and others seeing it as exceptional. See also Wiltshire (2018).

[245] EC (2019c).

[246] Airport Research Center (2009).

[247] EC (2011b).

[248] See Graham (2011, 2020) and Button (2020).

[249] Productivity Commission (2019). However, see ACCC (2018b).

[250] Productivity Commission (2019).

Effects of Restructuring of Air Navigation Service Provision

As noted above, there has been limited restructuring of ANS provision. While some studies conclude that less government control does not result in relatively more efficient ANSPs,[251] the one example of a full privatisation of an ANSP (NAV Canada) is considered to have resulted in increased efficiency and productivity (reduced flight delays), a faster pace of modernisation and a reduction in user fees.[252] In the USA, the potential restructuring and privatisation of ANS provision was considered by the Trump Administration, in part because of concerns about the slow implementation of NextGen. The FAA's transition plans have been assessed as lacking specificity and detail, and there are also concerns about programme delays, cost oversight and the benefits being lower than expected.[253]

Reviews of European airspace restructuring policies (the Single European Sky) have found that European airspace still remains fragmented, costly and inefficient, particularly when compared to the USA.[254] There are also problems with the independence of NSAs from ANSPs, the slow development of functional airspace blocks and the lack of public procurement for monopoly support services.[255] To address these issues, the European Commission has proposed additional measures known as the Single European Sky 2+.

Effects of Restructuring Policies on Safety and the Environment

While the above discussion focused on the effects of restructuring policies on factors such as competition, entry, service quality and prices, it has not considered the impacts that the changes have had on safety and the environment. Broadly speaking, there is no evidence of safety deteriorating in jurisdictions where restructuring policies have been introduced,[256] and indeed some argue that overall safety may have increased as more people fly rather than rely on road transport, which is relatively more unsafe, for intermediate distances.[257] At the international level, safety is said to have improved because international air service agreements have involved a harmonisation of safety standards across jurisdictions.

In contrast, the impact of restructuring policies on the environment is generally recognised to have been detrimental.[258] Market opening policies have led to substantial growth in air traffic (particularly LCCs, which may have attracted demand from lower-polluting rail) and indirect routings (via hub-and-spoke networks), which involve longer journeys and more environmental impact. These changes have resulted in various environmental externalities, such as increased aircraft noise, reduced local air quality and higher

---

[251] See Button and Neiva (2014).

[252] Floyd, Park and Sharma (2017) attribute this to the corporate structure adopted and the broad stakeholder representation model, which ensures that the interests of all stakeholders are heard.

[253] See National Research Council (2015) and US Department of Transport (2018, 2021).

[254] Eurocontrol (2019).

[255] EC (2013b).

[256] Borenstein and Rose (2014). Papatheodorou, Polychroniadis and Kapturski (2016) provide a useful summery of the evidence on the relationship between airline deregulation and safety.

[257] ITF (2019).

[258] Aviation emissions are said to be two to four times as harmful to the climate as surface emissions. Aviation accounted for about 3.8 per cent of total CO_2 emissions and about 13.9 per cent of the CO_2 emissions from all transport sources; see EC (2021h).

emissions of carbon dioxide and other pollutants, all of which can have a significan
climate effect.[259]

15.4 REGULATORY POLICY ISSUES IN THE AVIATION INDUSTRY

This section discusses two current regulatory policy issues in the aviation industry: th
effects of introducing airline competition and how they have changed over time; and th
approach to the regulation of UAS.

15.4.1 Airline Competition: Destructive, Contestable or Cooperative?

An important question that has influenced the different approaches to airline regulatio
over the past half-century is this: What are the potential impacts of allowing for greate
competition between airlines?

As described above, the dominant view that influenced regulatory policy until the lat
1970s was that intense airline competition is unsustainable and could, in fact, be destruc
tive.[260] On this reasoning, there was a need for regulation to control entry, to determin
routes to ensure smaller communities remain served, and to set prices that ensured tha
airlines could cover their costs, subsidise low-volume routes and avoid price wars tha
might encourage airlines to cut costs in ways that could impact safety or service quality.
In addition, it was assumed that, in the absence of price and entry regulation, the secto
would experience highly volatile earnings and potential bankruptcies, which, in turn, wou
require higher levels of state subsidy. Such earnings volatility would reflect the fact tha
airlines have high fixed costs and low marginal costs and face highly cyclical demand.[26]

Is Airline Competition Sustainable?

Although not articulated at the time, some have since argued that the reason why airlin
competition may be unsustainable is because there is an 'empty core'.[263] In a nutshel
this theory suggests that, because airlines need to recover their fixed costs (planes, fue
terminal and airport slot charges), once they have scheduled a flight, they will seek
generate revenues by competing to attract customers through price reductions, which,
competition is intense, will drive prices down to the level of short-run marginal cost.[264]

---

[259] ITF (2019). Non-CO_2 emissions include nitrogen oxides, water vapour, and sulfate and soot particles at
high altitudes (EASA, 2020).

[260] In the USA, this view was said to be influenced by what was perceived to be destructive competition in
railroads. See Kahn (1971, 2005) and National Academies of Sciences, Engineering, and Medicine (199

[261] Kahn (1971) considers in detail the relationship between destructive competition and quality of service

[262] In effect, airlines were characterised as natural monopolies.

[263] See Telser (1978) and Smith (1995). Sjostrom (1993) defines an empty core as arising: '[W]henever
capacity, defined here as the output associated with minimum short-run average avoidable cost, in the
industry exceeds the quantity demanded at the price equal to that minimum average cost. Competitive
equilibrium in such an industry requires that at least one firm shut down in the short run, with the
resultant price above minimum average cost. However, a group of buyers can join together with that
idle seller to upset the competitive equilibrium. The implication is simple: whenever there is short-run
excess capacity, there is unlikely to be a competitive equilibrium.'

[264] On the application of core theory to airlines, see Telser (1994) and Button (1996, 2003, 2015).

other words, once a flight is scheduled, an airline wants to fill as many seats as possible. However, because airlines continually undercut each other to fill seats, some airlines will be unable to recover their fixed costs, leading, over time, to bankruptcy and exit. This exit makes the market more concentrated, which will push up airfares (potentially to the monopoly level if there is only one airline serving a particular route), which, in turn, will attract new entry, and the cycle will continue. In short, it is argued that the competitive equilibrium will be volatile and unsustainable.[265]

As described above, the introduction of airline competition in many jurisdictions has led to reductions in prices (and periodic price wars), high-profile mergers, major bankruptcies and the exit of airlines. Does this mean that competition is destructive, or that there is an empty core?[266] Some argue that it does not. Rather, it is argued to reflect the inherent characteristics of the industry (e.g. high fixed costs, fluctuating demand and fuel costs, slow supply adjustment, infrastructure bottlenecks) and as such we should not be surprised to see drastic and rapid changes in profits.[267] For some, the fact that some airlines have entered and failed, or that some legacy airlines have gone bankrupt, simply reflects the high levels of dynamic experimentation in pricing, competitive strategies and business models (e.g. entry by LCCs) that deregulation unleashed and which characterises competition.[268] In other words, as might be expected in such a dynamic and competitive context, some airlines adapted and survived and others did not.[269] However, others are less convinced and argue that, while fluctuations in demand and changing input costs are factors contributing to significant swings in airline profitability, it is also indicative of the scheduled competitive airline market being characterised by an empty core problem.[270]

Are Airline Markets Contestable?

An alternative view, which is said to have influenced the move towards airline deregulation in the USA in the late 1970s, is that there is no need for regulation of prices or entry restrictions because airline markets are 'contestable'.[271] In particular, it was argued that airline markets are characterised by relatively easy entry and exit (an ability to shift or transfer planes onto specific routes) and capital is fixed but not sunk (so-called 'capital

---

[265] For this reason, it is argued that some form of cooperation or coordination among suppliers in other transport sectors such as liner shipping should be exempt from competition law provisions.

[266] Abate and Chrisitidis (2020) note that the question is receiving increasing attention in a global context because the expansion of the Gulf Carriers, long-haul low-cost flights and dominant global airline alliances.

[267] Borenstein and Rose (2014) find little empirical support for an empty core theory. See also Abate and Christidis (2020).

[268] Kahn (2005) notes that airline deregulation resulted in appalling financial losses to incumbents, but notes that: 'However painful to the incumbents, that is the nature and virtue of the competitive process that deregulation unleashed.'

[269] Kahn (1988) observes that the ultimate fear of destructive competition, which was that the industry would be unable to finance needed expansions of capacity leading to a deterioration in service, was not realised.

[270] See Button (2017a).

[271] Although the theory of contestable markets was only emerging at the time of airline deregulation, Kahn (2000) noted that 'an important part of the rationale of deregulation was the contestability of airline markets' and the threat of potential as well as actual competition to prevent exploitation of consumers.

on wings').[272] For the reasons discussed in Chapter 3, given these characteristics, th mere *threat* of entry by other airlines (so-called 'hit-and-run' entry) could, it was argued be sufficient to constrain prices to the average cost levels, and the imposition of entr restrictions will be undesirable because it removes the threat of these shadow entrants.[2]

While this *threat* of entry was seen by some as a constraint on airline markets in th early days of deregulation,[274] empirical studies of deregulation have found little support fc the predictions of contestability theory.[275] These studies conclude that *actual* competition i more important than potential competition,[276] that the entry of new competitor airlines o specific routes was not as 'ultra-free' as predicted,[277] and that the threat of entry had onl a limited impact on price levels.[278] However, other studies conclude that, while the airlin industry is not perfectly contestable, it may be imperfectly contestable,[279] and that regula tion of some aspects of incumbent airlines' behaviour (e.g. control over reservation or yiel management systems) could reduce barriers to entry and make them more contestable.[280]

Airline Alliances and Cooperation Arrangements

While restructuring policies have led to more intense competition between airlines, the have somewhat paradoxically, also given rise to greater levels of cooperation betwee airlines. Prior to the 1980s, most airlines used to sell tickets for carrying passengers o their own flight on the routes they serviced. Following deregulation, various forms c cooperation arrangements were established, originally between smaller regional airline (which operated on the shorter 'spoke' routes and acted as feeders to the major hubs) an larger airlines which provided long-haul services.

Over time, the level of airline cooperation has deepened to involve other aspects c an airline business, including agreements on routes, capacity, pricing and frequenc of services. As such, competition takes place not just between individual airlines bu also between alliances, and it is estimated that around half of global passenger traffi now flies on airlines that belong to one of three global airline alliances.[281] The effect c such cooperation arrangements or alliances is that airlines may compete with each othe on some routes, while they cooperate and jointly sell their services on other routes.[2]

---

[272] See Brock (1983). However, see the reconsideration of the assessment of airlines as 'capital on wings' b Baumol and Willig (1986).

[273] See Baumol (1982a).

[274] Kahn (2000) notes the importance of the threat of potential as well as actual competition to prevent exploitation of consumers.

[275] Borenstein (1989) submits that: 'It has by now been well established that airline pricing does not closel reflect the contestability ideal.' Baumol and Willig (1986) themselves subsequently noted that other forms of transportation (trucks, barges and buses) may be more highly contestable than air transport.

[276] Morrison (2001) quantifies the benefits of actual competition and potential competition.

[277] See Gilbert (1989) and Baumol and Willig (1986).

[278] See Graham, Kaplan and Sibley (1983), Borenstein (1989), Hurdle, Johnson, Joskow, *et al.* (1989), Abramowitz and Brown (1993) and Borenstein and Rose (2014).

[279] Goolsbee and Syverson (2008) find evidence that the mere threat of competing with Southwest in the USA was enough to induce substantial fare reductions from major incumbent carriers.

[280] Morrison and Winston (1987) argue that contestability is not an all-or-nothing proposition. While Kah (1987) observes that contestability theory does not afford sufficient protection to consumers over all city points or routes.

[281] Bilotkach (2019). However, as Morandi, Malighetti, Paleari and Redondi (2015) observe, only around only 25 per cent of LCCs are involved in code-sharing agreements.

[282] Borenstein and Rose (2014).

Common forms of cooperation arrangements in practice include: interlining (where one airline agrees to accept the tickets of another airline for the whole or a part of a passenger's trip); code-share agreements (where an airline agrees to include partner airline flights as part of their network, which enables them to sell tickets for new routes without having to operate any additional aircraft); airline alliances (where a group of airlines agree to coordinate on aspects such as fares, scheduling and capacity and to deliver additional benefits to passengers on a reciprocal basis, such as frequent flyer mileage points, priority boarding, etc.); and full joint ventures which involve high levels of coordination on pricing and schedules and can involve cost and revenue sharing.

Airlines cooperate with one another for various reasons. First, partnering with other airlines can expand their network presence, allowing them to offer passengers better services (e.g. loyalty programmes), seamless connections (improved scheduling) and increase the frequency of flights to more destinations using partner airlines. Second, cooperation can reduce costs and enhance efficiency,[283] and allow airlines to better manage seat capacity by optimising their route structures.[284] Third, international cooperation can allow airlines to substantially expand their reach and service offerings without adding additional flights and can also boost demand by feeding traffic between domestic and international routes.[285] International cooperation can also overcome various barriers which limit the ability of foreign airlines to establish themselves in other countries and provide domestic services.

Airline cooperation arrangements have been found to bring benefits to passengers by expanding destinations, lowering prices and increasing frequency of service.[286] However, where they involve cooperation between airlines that operate on parallel or overlapping routes,[287] they can reduce competition, leading to higher prices and/or less capacity being made available on specific routes.[288] For this reason, cooperation agreements are often

---

[283] Bilotkach (2019) argues that fixed cost savings can arise from joint use of airport facilities and coordinated marketing, while variable cost synergies can arise because of increased load factors arising from economies of traffic density.

[284] Morandi, Malighetti, Paleari and Redondi (2015) argue that cooperation allows airlines to rationalise their network structure and exploit economies of scale, density and scope.

[285] Oum, Park and Zhang (1996).

[286] See Brueckner and Whalen (2000), Morrish and Hamilton (2002), Brueckner (2003) and Bilotkach and Hüschelrath (2011). Bilotkach (2019) notes the general consensus is that antitrust immunity (i.e. the right of the partner airlines jointly to set the fares within their joint network) decreases airfares for interline passengers, but these have become smaller over time. Brueckner and Singer (2019) also find that fares are lower for interline trips involving alliances. Similarly, Ivaldi, Petrova and Urdanoz (2022) find that alliances are associated with both lower prices and lower price dispersion, as a result of a decrease in the fluctuation of their reservation costs.

[287] A distinction is made between *parallel* alliances (involving a partnership between two airlines that operate on the same routes) and *complementary* alliances (where two airlines link up their existing networks to build a new complementary network to provide improved services for connecting passengers). Park (1997) finds that parallel alliances can reduce welfare, while complementary alliances can increase welfare.

[288] Bilotkach and Hüschelrath (2011) note that airline alliances can be used to facilitate collusive behaviour and/or restrict entry through the implementation of foreclosure strategies. Bilotkach and Hüschelrath (2013) find evidence consistent with airlines operating under antitrust immunity refusing to accept connecting passengers from outside carriers at respective hub airports. Brueckner and Singer (2019) find that cooperation on routes where alliance partners overlap leads to higher economy fares, but that this anti-competitive effect is more than offset by gains to connecting passengers, making alliances beneficial on balance. Similarly, Bilotkach (2019) notes that consumers can potentially benefit from alliances even on the overlapping parts of the joint network if there are economies of density such that the higher volumes result in lower average cost.

subject to competition law scrutiny and approval.[289] In practice, to gain approval, airlir
alliances often must agree not to include various overlapping routes in the arrangeme:
(so-called 'carve outs'),[290] not to coordinate on tariffs or restrict the frequencies and cap
acities offered on specific routes, or to divest of slots at specific airports.[291]

15.4.2 Regulation of Unmanned Aircraft Systems

An emerging issue, given the forecasts of rapid and substantial growth of UAS, is ho
to effectively manage UAS operations, particularly in shared and segregated airspac
For a range of reasons, the general consensus is that conventional ATM systems will n
be able to 'scale up' to accommodate UAS operations,[292] and that a new form of traff
management is needed to accommodate the expected volume of UAS traffic and tl
diverse nature of UAS operations.[293] Accordingly, many jurisdictions are developing ne
UAS traffic management systems known as UAS traffic management (UTM).[294] Althoug
UTM concepts are still evolving, a common element is that these will rely on a more di
tributed, competitive and automated traffic management system than the current systen
used for manned ATM, which are centralised, monopolistic and human-centric.[295] Th
has obvious implications for regulation.

There are three main ways in which UTM is expected to differ from ATM. First, it
expected that traffic management and navigation services will be provided by UTM se
vice providers (UTMSPs) to UAS operators through a competitive industry structure rath
than the monopolistic structure that applies for ATM at the moment. UAS operators w
therefore have a choice as to which UTMSP provides it with core navigation service
and will also have a choice about different providers of supplementary services (such .
weather services). Second, UTM will involve the digital sharing of flight information in
way that each user will have the same situational awareness of the airspace. This mea:
that the services provided by competing UTMSPs will overlap with one another in a giv∈

---

[289] Bilotkach and Hüschelrath (2011) provide a useful overview of the approaches adopted in the USA
and the EU. A recent example is the 2021 US Department of Justice challenge to the domestic alliance
between American Airlines and JetBlue.

[290] Where specific city pairs are not included in the arrangement (such as Washington DC–Frankfurt).

[291] For example, slot divestures at London Heathrow airport was a condition for approval of the 'oneworl
Alliance'. See, generally, Bilotkach and Hüschelrath (2011).

[292] In the USA, the FAA (2020a) has noted that, because the number of daily operations could reach into t
millions, this would stretch the National Airspace System beyond its current requirements. In Europe,
ATM systems are also considered to be reaching their limits. See SESAR (2018) and Vidović, Mihetec,
Wang and Štimac (2019).

[293] Jiang, Geller, Ni and Collura (2016) and ITF (2021). ICAO (2020) notes that: 'Whilst segregated airspace
has been an initial solution to accommodate a safe operating environment it does not enable future
integration of manned and unmanned aviation, nor does it enable high density UAS operations.' There
is also a perception that conventional ATM might not be well suited to UAS safety and management
issues, particularly when it involves integrating UAS in urban areas where they are able to fly near
people and buildings.

[294] The long-term aspiration of the International Civil Aviation Organization (ICAO, 2019a) is that current
distinctions between specific airspace systems (such as ATM or UTM) and vehicles (manned, unmanne
or autonomous) will become redundant, and, as a result, policy will converge to allow for the flexible
accommodation of all types of operation at all altitudes.

[295] ICAO (2019a).

airspace, and that, to ensure safety and interoperability, UTMSPs must *cooperate* with one another and share information in a way that provides an ability to plan missions and to manage airspace in real time. This differs from the more integrated and centralised nature of ATM, where data and information is generally collected by a single central entity (an ANSP). In other words, for unmanned aircraft, interoperability will be achieved through individual entities exchanging data and information using common standards and protocols at different stages of a mission (pre-flight, during mission, post-flight). Third, while UTM is based around a more distributed (or federated)[296] architecture than conventional ATM, all UTM concepts still envisage a role for a centralised function, such as a flight notice board or a flight information management system (FIMS), to provide what might be called central UTM services. These are services that can be accessed by a range of private and public participants to gain information about any flight restrictions and constraints. In Europe, the EU's U-Space concept envisages that a designated common information service (CIS) provider would operate the centralised information gateway in designated U-Space areas. Similarly, the UTM concept being developed in the USA includes a FIMS, which will be operated at the centre by the FAA.

There are two UTM-related activities where some form of economic regulation may be required in the future.[297] The first is the provision of central UTM services, where regulation might be premised on the fact that there are likely to be significant fixed costs associated with the investments needed to provide the central UTM services.[298] This could give rise to economies of scale and scope at certain levels of demand, or economies of density such that it may be efficient for a single provider to service a particular geographical area. Regulation of this activity might also be premised on the fact that, in most UTM architectures, a single entity will be responsible for providing central UTM services within a particular geographical area. As such, regulation may be merited to ensure that it does not exploit that position of monopoly power.

In Europe, central UTM service providers (known as CIS providers) will be subject to restrictions on entry (there will only be one designated CIS provider per designated U-Space airspace),[299] but will not be subject to price regulation, notwithstanding the fact that some CIS services could be provided by a single entity on an exclusive basis.[300] While European policy does not preclude the possibility that CIS providers could be privately owned and operated, there are also vertical separation requirements such that a CIS provider cannot be vertically integrated with a UTM service provider in the airspace for which it has been designated or provide any UTM services itself in that airspace (i.e. a CIS provider cannot act as a UTMSP in that designated airspace).

---

[296] The term 'federated' is defined as: 'a group of systems and networks operating in a standard and connected environment'. See FAA (2020a).

[297] Decker and Chiambaretto (2022) expand on these points.

[298] These include the costs of investments in communications equipment, IT hardware and software.

[299] Although there can be more than one U-Space in a given Member State.

[300] The draft Regulation included a requirement that the prices charged for the CIS service shall be set by a competent authority, and that regulated prices be cost-based and allow an appropriate risk–return trade-off. However, no regulatory oversight of the prices charged by CIS providers is required under the final Regulation.

In the USA, the FAA will develop and manage a single FIMS, but does not expect to have an active operational role in UTM. Rather, the FAA sees its role in UTM as limited to setting the 'rules of the road' and only becoming involved in unusual ('off-nominal' events.[301] While there has only been limited consideration of how the costs of UTM development and operation will be recovered (in part, because many future costs are unknown), a recent report suggests that current funding levels for UAS integration efforts could erode resources for activities related to manned aviation (which, as noted above, are funded by excise taxes and fees on airline tickets, aviation fuel and cargo shipments paid by manned aircraft).[302] Various options are being considered to cover the costs of the FAA's UAS activities, including the possible introduction of user fees.

Although UTMSPs are expected to compete with one another to offer services to UAS operators (i.e.: they will compete for subscribers), there may also be a need for regulation of the terms and conditions that are struck between different competing UTMSPs for sharing data. In particular, where UTMSPs sets access terms and conditions for sharing data non-cooperatively, there is a risk that, in some circumstances, a UTMSP will set prices at inefficiently high levels in order to exploit its (termination) monopoly position over its subscriber base. Alternatively, where interconnection terms and conditions are set cooperatively, there are the risks of all UTMSPs collectively coordinating on the setting of prices and other terms. The general issue of two-way access pricing was discussed in Chapter 6, while in Chapter 11 we saw that, in the telecommunications industry, similar issues have led to price regulation in some jurisdictions. There may also be a need for regulated access principles and conditions to ensure that the price and non-price terms and conditions collectively imposed by UTMSPs, or by UTMSPs with significant market power, do not discriminate or hinder access to and utilisation of airspace. Ensuring 'fair' access to airspace is a key feature of the EU's UTM concept, which focuses on a need to develop a regulatory framework that provides fair access to all airspace users,[303] while in the USA the UTM concept is also based around 'equity of access' to airspace.[304]

15.5 CONCLUSION

Air passenger and cargo transportation services have been transformed over the past four decades from a highly regulated activity to one where routes, fares and service quality attributes are determined by intense competition between airlines in many parts of the world. Major airlines in many countries have been privatised, and the sector has also seen significant entry by new types of providers (LCCs) and the emergence of global airline alliances. Overall, the effects of the airline 'deregulation' policies are generally considered to have been a 'success' from a consumer perspective and to have yielded benefits in terms of lower fares and greater choice of destinations. While some aspects of service quality have improved (such as route offerings, choice, connections, frequency, etc.), other aspects (such

---

[301] FAA (2020a).
[302] GAO (2019).
[303] EASA (2020).
[304] FAA, (2020).

as in-flight amenities and longer delays) are seen as having reduced the quality experienced by some passengers. The airline industry has also experienced high-profile bankruptcies and exits, and a constant need to adapt to the significant fluctuations in demand associated with external events, such as wars, terrorist attacks and pandemics.

While price and entry regulation of airlines has largely been withdrawn, other activities in the aviation supply chain remain subject to greater regulatory oversight and control. Indeed, many airports around the world, including almost all airports in the USA, remain in majority state ownership. However, the number of fully or partially private airports in Europe, Australia and South Africa has increased over the past decade, while in the Asia-Pacific region and Latin America some countries have introduced competition for the market in the form of airport concession agreements. Although formal price regulation for some airports has been withdrawn in some countries (such as the UK), many airports with significant market power remain subject to price regulation in the form of price caps or rate of return regulation. Light-handed approaches to regulation, including monitoring, are also applied at some major airports in Germany, Australia and New Zealand. Irrespective of the approach to the regulation of airport charges, an important policy question is the extent to which such charges should reflect both aeronautical and non-aeronautical revenues and costs. One knock-on effect of airline deregulation has been major changes in the configuration and use of airports, including the development of hub-and-spoke networks and the greater use of secondary airports by LCCs. In some jurisdictions, such as the UK and Europe, this has led to greater levels of airport competition. Limited restructuring of airports in the USA has given rise to concerns that a lack of investment in terminals and control towers may have contributed to delays and overcrowding, and that many airports and routes lack a healthy level of competition.

Almost all ANSPs around the world are fully state-owned, with the notable exceptions of Canada and the UK. The privatisation of the ANSP in Canada is generally considered to have been beneficial, while the effects of the modernisation policies for ANS in the USA and Europe are largely seen as being incomplete and in need of reform. In the USA, the costs of providing ANS are recovered through excise taxes levied on passengers, cargo users and aviation fuel. In contrast, in the UK, the EU, Australia and Canada, charges are levied by the ANSP directly on airlines. In a small number of countries (notably the UK and South Africa), ANSPs are subject to *ex ante* price controls, while in other countries, such as EU Member States, Australia and Canada, ANS charges need to be approved by a supervisory or regulatory body.

The future regulation of the aviation sector will be influenced by various factors. First and foremost, the sector will need to recover from the impacts that the Covid-19 pandemic had on the revenues of airlines (which has led to increased concentration in some jurisdictions and concerns about reduced competition) and airports (many of which partially closed but still had to cover their fixed costs).[305] Second, the sector is facing significant

---

[305] ICAO (2021) estimates that passenger traffic fell by 60 per cent between 2019 and 2020, resulting in losses of $371 billion in that year alone. OECD (2020e) notes that the Covid-19 crisis has precipitated a new suite of loans, loan guarantees, wage subsidies and equity injections in the aviation sector, raising concerns about competition and the efficient use of public resources.

technological changes, including the expected rapid expansion of UAS and the shift from ground-based to space-based navigation. These changes will have direct impacts on how airspace is managed, and airports are utilised, which in turn will impact the ongoing rationale for economic regulation of these activities. Third, there are increasing concerns about excessive state subsidies for some airlines (particularly for Middle Eastern carriers) distorting airline competition, which have led to calls for more protectionist and less open policies towards international airline movements. Finally, wider societal expectations and policies will require the sector to confront the growing volume and share of harmful environmental emissions that are associated with aviation, and which have followed the policies of deregulation. The challenge here is to make air travel sustainable by mitigating the effect of air travel on global emissions while at the same time not unduly distorting competition between different carriers.

DISCUSSION QUESTIONS

1. What are some of the important characteristics of demand and supply for aviation services, and how do passenger and cargo aviation services differ from one another?
2. Describe the main attributes of, and the types of services provided by, the three elements in the traditional aviation supply chain.
3. Discuss some of the differences between unmanned and manned aircraft operations and the possible implications of these differences for economic regulation.
4. What activities in the aviation industry are typically subject to price regulation or oversight, and what is typically the form and scope of that regulation?
5. What are some of the main differences between the scope of the aviation industry restructuring policies introduced in the USA, Europe and other countries?
6. Discuss the differences between the 'single-till' and 'dual-till' approaches to airport charging. What are the arguments for and against each approach?
7. Do you agree with the following statement? 'The experience of restructuring of the aviation sector shows the substantial benefits of pursuing "deregulation" policies'. Discuss.
8. Discuss some of the benefits and risks of cooperation agreements between airlines.
9. Do you agree with this statement? 'There is no need for regulation of prices or entry regulation in airline markets because such markets are "contestable".'

16

Water and Wastewater Regulation

While the services provided by all the industries discussed in this book are, to different degrees, 'essential' to modern economies and societies, the services provided by the water and wastewater industry are arguably the most essential, given the intimate connection between these services and human health and survival.[1] For this reason, access to clean, safe and affordable water, and to safely managed sanitation services, are recognised by the United Nations as human rights. However, there remains a significant gap between developed and developing countries in terms of access to both water and sanitation services, and the quality of these supplies. The World Health Organization (WHO) estimates that in 2022 around a quarter of the world's population (2 billion people) do not have access to safe water, while 46 per cent (3.5 billion people) do not have access to safe sanitation services.[2] Indeed, more people worldwide have access to a mobile phone than to a toilet.

There are a number of characteristics of the water and wastewater industry which distinguish it from the industries considered in previous chapters. State ownership and operation of assets in the water and wastewater industry remain prevalent, even in countries that have been pioneers in the restructuring of other sectors, such as the USA, Australia and many countries in Europe. In part, this may reflect the view that competition in the industry creates too great a risk; if operators sacrifice quality for profits, the outcomes will be too serious.[3] However, it may also reflect the fact that the water and wastewater industry has generally been seen as a natural monopoly industry *par excellence*,[4] where the potential benefits of direct competition between different suppliers is limited.

---

[1] The preamble to the European Union's Water Framework Directive (2000/160 EC) makes this point explicit: 'Water is not a commercial product like any other but, rather, a heritage which must be protected, defended and treated as such.' More generally, water is often referred to as illustrating the 'paradox of value' (or the diamond–water paradox) attributed to Adam Smith. Simply put, this states that although diamonds obtain a considerably higher price on the market than water, water is the more useful of the two commodities; one can live without diamonds, but not without water.

[2] WHO (2022a, b).

[3] Concerns about water quality and safety – such as a desire to restrict the potential for cholera outbreaks – are said to have motivated the nationalisation of water systems in some countries. For this reason, in addition to being subject to economic regulation or public ownership, water and wastewater operators are subject to strict quality standards, typically imposed by other regulatory agencies or government departments, relating to the safety and quality of drinking water and the environment (in regard to both the abstraction of water and the treatment of effluent and disposal of waste).

[4] See Littlechild (1988). Contrast Noll (2002), who argues that this view has not been the subject of extensive empirical testing, and may not be accurate for all aspects of urban water systems in all locations.

Given the different application of economic regulation in the water and wastewater industry, the chapter brings to the fore some of the theoretical issues we discussed in Parts I and II of this book, including the fundamental question about the long-term benefits of privatisation *vis-à-vis* state ownership. Given the high levels of vertical integration in the industry around the world, this chapter also provides insight into whether and how, such monopoly firms have been regulated, and how the views and perspectives of consumers have featured in the decision-making process. The chapter also discusses the experience of applying the 'competition *for* the market' approach for water concession contracts, and what has happened in the limited instances where 'competition *in* the market' has been introduced for specific activities (such as non-household retail activities or the treatment of sewage). Finally, the chapter explores how regulators have attempted to satisfy multiple policy objectives in practice such as: affordability and widespread access; water conservation; and a need for water systems to be resilient to the uncertainties of climate change. This includes examining the trade-offs attached to regulatory choices about the price levels and price structures for water and wastewater services.

16.1 PHYSICAL AND ECONOMIC CHARACTERISTICS OF WATER AND WASTEWATER

16.1.1 Characteristics of the Product

Although water (H_2O) is the product of the combination of hydrogen and oxygen, it is rare for water in its liquid form in nature to be pure and contain only these two chemical elements. Almost all sources of raw water are contaminated to some degree with different compounds and organisms,[5] and raw (i.e. untreated) water, abstracted from different sources and locations, can differ significantly in terms of quality. However, given the different uses to which water is put, it is not necessarily the case that all water needs to be of the same quality.

An important distinction exists between potable and non-potable water, the former being water that humans can safely use as drinking water. Non-potable water can, depending on its quality, be used for a range of other purposes, such as in agricultural and industrial processes. Reclaimed or recycled water – which is wastewater treated to remove certain impurities and solids – is used primarily for non-potable purposes.[6] However, if reclaimed water is treated to a sufficiently high level, it can potentially be used as a form of potable water (i.e. for human consumption),[7] and has been considered as a possible way to deal with water shortages and droughts.[8] Water is also an important input into the

---

[5] 'Raw water' is water that has not been subject to filtering, disinfecting or any other treatment process.
[6] These uses include irrigation, public and private landscaping (such as public parks, artificial lakes or golf courses), dust control, certain production processes (such as concrete mixing, in paper mills or in cooling processes for power plants), street sweeping, sewer cleaning and vehicle washing.
[7] See National Research Council (2012) and Tortajada and van Rensburg (2020).
[8] In the USA, recycled wastewater is already used for drinking purposes in some counties, such as Orange County, California. It is also used in Singapore.

production of electricity in many jurisdictions, not only as an input to the generation of hydroelectric power but also to cool power plants.[9]

The demand for wastewater services tends to be highly correlated with the demand for water, as much water, once used, becomes wastewater and is then collected and transported by a wastewater system.[10] The characteristics of wastewater (or sewage) also tend to be heterogeneous, reflecting the fact that it originates from different sources. As described below, wastewater is collected in a wastewater or sewerage system (the name given to the infrastructure which transports sewage) through drains, manholes, storm overflows and sanitary/household sewers. The 'raw' sewage is then transported through the wastewater system to either a sewage treatment plant, or to be directly discharged into the environment. Two general classifications of wastewater are 'foul' (or domestic) sewage, which originates from waste generated in bathrooms and kitchens in households and businesses, and trade effluent, which is the liquid waste from industrial processes discharged into a wastewater system. Trade effluent can bring to the wastewater system various deposits, including: chemicals by industrial users; non-ambient water released by power plants; and various pesticides, animal waste and fertilisers from agricultural users. In addition, a wastewater system typically collects and disposes of storm water.

There are very limited substitution possibilities for consumers of water and wastewater services.[11] Globally, the three main sources of demand for water are agriculture (69 per cent), industry (including power generation, 19 per cent) and households (12 per cent).[12] However, there are important differences in water demand across countries. In developed countries, industry (particularly electricity generation) is the greatest water user, followed by agriculture and households.[13] Water demand varies by season, day of the week and time of day, and can be impacted by unusual changes in the weather.[14] There is a wide variation in the demand for water during a given day, with the bulk of demand for household water generally being between 6 a.m. and 10 a.m. in the morning and from 4 p.m. to 8 p.m. in the evening, when the level of household activity tends to be highest.[15]

---

[9] Just under half of water abstraction in the USA and Europe is used in electricity production, particularly the cooling of power plants.

[10] As Noll (2002) puts it: '[V]irtually all uses of water do not consume water, but instead diminish its quality for subsequent use ... as a result, waste water is the inevitable result of water usage.' In Europe, only 20 per cent of water from the public water supply is actually consumed, and the remaining 80 per cent is returned to the environment primarily as treated wastewater. There is also variation among different uses, with almost all water used for electricity generation being returned to a water body, while much of the water used for agriculture is consumed and not returned to a water body. See EEA (2009).

[11] There are, of course, differences in the ways in which such services can be provided, such as via bottled water, recycled water or water vendors (as a substitute for piped potable water), or the use of septic tanks and trucks for wastewater collection (as opposed to a piped wastewater distribution network).

[12] UN-Water (2019). In addition, estimates of the use of water in the public supply (mains) system differ. In England and Wales, households use around half the water that is put into the public supply.

[13] In the USA, in 2015: 47 per cent of water was used for power, industrial and mining; 40 per cent for aquaculture, irrigation and livestock; 12 per cent for public water supply; and only 1 per cent for domestic. See USGS (2015).

[14] For example, demand for water for some agricultural and domestic purposes (such as garden watering) is negatively correlated with the level of precipitation.

[15] Water use by households was estimated in one US study as involving the following activities: toilet use (26.7 per cent); clothes washing (21.7 per cent); showers (16.8 per cent); faucets and taps (15.7 per cent); leaks (13.7 per cent); and other uses (5.3 per cent). See EPA (2013b).

The summer months are the period of peak demand, but are also the time of year whe the available supply of water is most limited. In jurisdictions where the demand for wat in summer cannot be met with existing reserves, rationing policies are applied to curta demand.[16]

Finally, water comes from various sources of supply (described below), which tend to b very widely dispersed among different geographical areas. In some areas, such as whe a large river basin is located, there will be an abundance of natural water, while in oth areas there may be no access to natural water resources.[17] In addition, in many parts the world, it is difficult to draw water from neighbouring regions (i.e. there is limite interconnection in water supply services), meaning that issues of scarcity of water ter to be highly localised. Issues of supply-side externalities are obviously important in th water supply chain. For example, water abstracted from a river or a lake at one locatio limits the amount of water that can be abstracted at other locations downstream fro that point. Similarly, the deposit of wastewater from factories or other industrial process (such as cooling electricity generators) into river systems at one point can impact on th quality of water that can be abstracted by other users further downstream.

16.1.2 Water and Wastewater Supply Chain

There are a number of activities associated with the supply of water and wastewater se vices. In the *water* supply chain, these activities include abstraction (or extraction) of ra water, storage, the transfer of bulk water, water treatment, water distribution throug mains and reticulation pipes, and retailing activities for household and non-househo customers. In the *wastewater* supply chain, the activities include sewage collection, sew erage distribution (including reticulation and transfer), treatment of sewage, the dispos of sewage and sludge, and retailing activities. Figure 16.1 and (later) Figure 16.2 set o these activities in schematic form.

In terms of the costs of these different activities, in England and Wales, the abstractio of water resources accounts for about 7 per cent of total expenditure, water treatment a distribution accounts for 41 per cent, sewage collection and treatment accounts for 40 p cent, sludge treatment and disposal accounts for 5 per cent and retail activities accou for the remaining 7 per cent.

Water Abstraction
There are two main sources of water supply.[18] The first source, groundwater, is found 'aquifers', which are bodies of water-bearing underground permeable rock or other mat rial (such as silt or clay). The second main source of water is surface water, which is wat drawn from rivers, lakes and reservoirs. In the USA and Europe, around 75 per cent

---

[16] In Australia, for example, policies have been introduced at times in relation to the use of water in hosepipes for watering gardens, and for car-washing purposes.
[17] According to some estimates, around two-thirds of the world's population (four billion people) face severe water scarcity during at least one month of the year. See UN-Water (2019).
[18] Other possible sources of water are recycled wastewater, water that is generated through a desalination process, and collected rain water.

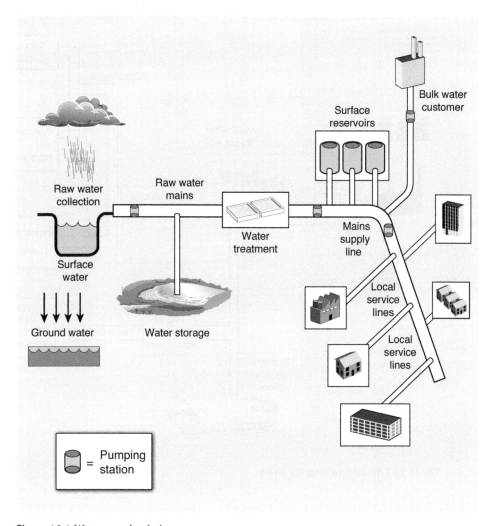

Figure 16.1 Water supply chain

all water used comes from surface water sources, with the remaining 25 per cent coming from groundwater sources.[19]

Corresponding to the different sources of water, there are two different processes for 'abstracting' or 'extracting' water.[20] The abstraction process for groundwater sources typically involves the drilling of a well into an aquifer, and then the use of a pumping mechanism to abstract water from the bottom of the well to the surface. For surface water, the abstraction process can involve the use of a pipe, or other water channel, that allows water to be extracted from a river, lake or reservoir. Among the entities that abstract water using these processes are operators of public (or mains) water systems, as

[19] USGS (2015) and EEA (2021).
[20] The terms 'extraction' and 'abstraction' tend to be used synonymously in different parts of the world to refer to this process.

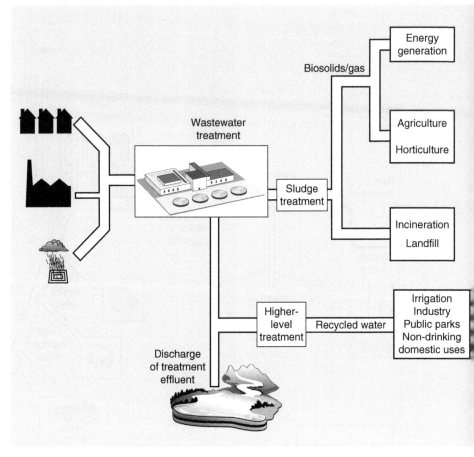

Figure 16.2 Wastewater supply chain

well as farmers and other industrial users. To control the overall volume of abstraction, a permit or licence is often required to abstract water from a source beyond a certai threshold.

Water Treatment

Once water has been abstracted, in many cases, such as for potable water supplies, is necessary to treat the water to remove various contaminants and pollutants (such as bacteria and viruses). Treatment plants are typically located close to where water abstracted. The level of treatment applied depends on the use to which the water wil be put, as well as the source of the water. Generally, water abstracted from groundwa ter sources requires less treatment than water from other sources, as there is a natura filtration process which occurs when the water is extracted, and the water itself tend to contain less contaminants than surface water, having been stored underground in a aquifer. In some cases, a disinfectant such as chlorine is added to water from groundwater sources to destroy any bacteria before it is supplied to final customers. Water abstracte from surface water systems, which generally contains more contaminants, is subject t a number of different treatment processes, including a process of coagulation (which removes dirt and other particles in the water), sedimentation and filtration, as well as the use of chlorine to act as a disinfectant. Once treated, water system operators use various forms of storage, such as closed tanks or reservoirs, to hold reserves of treated water to meet periods of peak demand.

Water Distribution

The distribution, or conveyance, of potable water to end-users occurs through a series of distribution pipelines. This includes a system of large-diameter pipelines (known as water mains), which are used to transport water under pressure over long distances, as well as smaller-diameter pipes (sometimes known as service lines or the reticulation system), which are used to distribute water from the mains pipelines to a customer's premises.[21] Water pipes can be made of various materials, including cast iron, ductile iron, steel, fibre cement, concrete, copper and, increasingly, different forms of plastic, are generally buried underground, and are of different sizes depending on the flow that is needed on the water system.[22]

Unlike the transportation of gas or electricity, water is heavy and therefore expensive to transport over long distances. The transportation of water is assisted through the use of gravity where possible, but it also typically requires some form of pumping to maintain the pressure in the pipe and move water around the distribution network. The age of the pipeline infrastructure can vary significantly, and it is not unusual for (refurbished) pipes installed up to 100 years ago to still be in operation. A major issue in the distribution of water are losses associated with leakage or broken water pipes, which can be affected by factors such as the material used in the pipe, the age of the pipe, and the conditions of the soil in which it is laid.[23]

In some jurisdictions, the distribution pipeline operator is responsible for the transportation of water only up until the boundary between the distribution network and the customer's property line. After that point, the service pipe which takes water to the customer's premises is deemed to be owned by the customer and is no longer the responsibility of the water operator. In many parts of the world, including in developed countries, such as Australia and the USA, the coverage of a water distribution system is not universal, and some users are not connected to a public (mains) water system and need to store and collect water from other sources.[24]

The distribution costs associated with the transportation of water and wastewater represent a high proportion of the final end-user prices, and it has been estimated that

---

[21] The available capacity of the infrastructure required to distribute water is determined by factors such as public health and safety considerations and, in some jurisdictions, fire protection.

[22] In the USA, mains pipelines generally range between 6 inches and 24 inches (approximately 15–60 cm) in diameter, while residential service lines range from 5/8 inch to 1 inch (approximately 16–25 mm) in diameter. See Denig-Chakroff (2008).

[23] Leakage rates are in the range of 10–20 per cent for OECD (Organisation for Economic Cooperation and Development) countries, but in developing countries frequently exceed 40 per cent and sometimes can be up to 70 per cent.

[24] In the USA, an estimated 10 per cent of the population do not get access to drinking water from public water systems. In Australia, around 6 per cent of the population are not connected to a public water supply.

some two-thirds of the costs associated with the supply of water can be attributed to this distribution function.[25] This contrasts with other industries, such as electricity an gas, where the costs associated with transportation tend to be a small component of th overall costs of supply. The high level of costs associated with water (and wastewate distribution reflects a number of factors: that water is heavy to transport, and cannot compressed (like, for example, gas); that there are high costs associated with investme in, and maintenance of, the pipelines; and that large amounts of electricity are consume pumping the water through the pipes.

Retail Activities

The final stage in the water supply process are the retail activities, which involve mete ing, billing and other customer-related activities. There are differences across jurisdi tions in terms of how customers are charged for water use. In some countries, custome (particularly households) are not charged based on the water they consume (i.e. they a unmetered) but on the basis of a fixed charge that reflects the value of the property whe the water is delivered.

Collection and Transportation of Wastewater

Wastewater services comprise the collection, transportation, treatment and disposal wastewater (see Figure 16.2). The first stage in that process involves the deposit of 'ra sewage or wastewater – either in the form of domestic sewage or trade effluent – into th wastewater (or sewerage) system through household sewers, drains, manholes or oth collection points.[26] Raw sewage is then transported through a series of pipelines to a trea ment plant or, in some cases, to a discharge point. Many of the points noted above abo the characteristics of the water distribution network apply equally to the transportati of wastewater, including a need to prevent leakages and sewer flooding.

Treatment of Wastewater

The treatment of wastewater delivered to a treatment works depends upon the natu of the sewage and how, and where, it will be disposed of. In general terms, the trea ment process involves the removal of any solids (sludge) from the wastewater, and th treatment of effluent (i.e. the liquid part of the wastewater) to levels sufficient to allo it to be discharged back into the environment. The number of treatment stages appli therefore depends on relevant environmental standards.[27] The required level of treatme

---

[25] See Wallsten and Kosec (2008).

[26] There is also the storm water collection process, which is typically also undertaken by the wastewater operator. This activity involves the collection of storm water run-off, which is then either directly disposed of, or is recycled back into a surface water system (i.e. rivers).

[27] Generally, there are four stages of treatment for wastewater: preliminary treatment (which involves the screening and removal of grit, oil and grease); primary treatment (placing sewage in large sedimentati tanks for a period, which allows the solids to separate and form a 'sludge' on the bottom of the tank, the liquid element (settled sewage) then being progressed to the next stage of treatment); secondary treatment (further biological treatment of the settled sewage to remove the residual organic pollutants) and tertiary treatment (which involves the use of sand or gravel filters, mechanical filtration, ponds or wetlands to further purify the water). This final stage is applied where there is a demand for high-quali effluent, such as when the water will be discharged into bathing areas or areas where shellfish grow.

varies across jurisdictions. In Ireland, Japan, Portugal, Slovakia and Canada, the majority of urban wastewater is treated to a secondary level only; while in Austria, Denmark, Germany, Sweden and the Netherlands, the majority of wastewater is treated to a tertiary level. In some jurisdictions, additional charges are levied on certain types of industrial customers for the treatment of trade effluent, and these charges can differ according to the quantity and composition of the effluent. In these circumstances, the possibility sometimes exists for these customers to reduce such charges by pretreating the waste before discharging it into the wastewater system or, in some cases, by undertaking the treatment themselves on-site.

Disposal

The last stage in the wastewater process involves the disposal of the sludge and the discharge of the effluent back into the environment. There are various ways in which sludge can be disposed of, including being incinerated, sold as fertiliser for agricultural purposes or, in some cases, deposited as landfill.[28] In recent years, there has been increased appreciation of the rich biological properties of treated sludge, and it is now used in some places as a source of fuel (for biogas, or as a fossil fuel in electricity production), for land reclamation purposes, and for various agricultural purposes. Effluent is released into various water systems, such as streams, rivers, lakes and the sea. In addition, as noted above, some treated effluent can be reclaimed or recycled, and supplied again through the water system for largely non-potable purposes.

6.1.3 Economies of Scale and Scope in the Water and Wastewater Supply Chain

When considering the water and wastewater supply process, two additional observations should be made. The first concerns the number and size of the water systems and companies that exist across different jurisdictions, and the second relates to the extent of vertical integration in the industry.

Number of Water and Wastewater Systems

There is significant variation in the number and size of water and wastewater systems, and water system operators, across different jurisdictions. In the USA, it is estimated that there are over 155,000 public water supply *systems* across the country, of which around 52,000 are community systems.[29] However, a large number of these systems serve only small populations, with an estimated 8 per cent of the water supply systems serving 82 per cent of the population.[30] The number of wastewater systems in the USA is also estimated to be around 50,000.[31] Similarly, in European countries, such as Austria, the Czech Republic,

---

[28] Up until the 1990s, it was not uncommon for sludge to be dumped at sea.

[29] That is a public water system that supplies water to the same population year-round and serves at least twenty-five people in their primary residence.

[30] See CDC (2021). However, it is important to note the distinction between a water *system* and a water *utility*. In some cases, a single utility company operator might own and operate a number of water systems of different sizes.

[31] See Marques (2010). Other estimates suggest that there are 16,000 publicly owned wastewater treatment systems in the USA.

Denmark, Finland, France, Germany, Greece, Norway, Romania, Spain and Switzerland, it has been estimated that there are over 1000 water utilities.[32] Again, in these cases, there may be a large number of small water company operators which serve local municipalities, and a small number of very large water companies that serve major urban areas. By contrast with jurisdictions that have a large number of water operators, England and Wales currently have eleven combined water and wastewater operators, nine water-only operators and six local water companies. In Scotland and Northern Ireland, there is only one water and wastewater company,[33] while in the Netherlands there are ten water-only companies and twenty-one regional water authorities responsible for treating wastewater.

Economies of Scale

The question of whether or not there are economies of scale in the water and wastewater industry has been studied extensively in different jurisdictions.[34] Some studies conclude that economies of scale exist in both water supply and wastewater supply.[35] However, other studies have concluded that there may be diseconomies of scale for the whole supply process,[36] or in relation to particular activities within that process (such as water production),[37] or that scale economies may exist for non-residential water supply but not for residential water supply.[38] In short, surveys of work on economies of scale have found no consensus on whether or not economies of scale exist in the industry.[39] Nevertheless, a clear conclusion to emerge from the empirical studies is that small water companies may benefit from economies of scale if they were to expand, while large water companies may have diseconomies of scale at the level of output at which they produce.[40] Taken together, these findings suggest that there is a critical level of output after which any scale economies will be exhausted.[41] This has led some to advocate policies that encourage mergers or joint operations, of small water companies or an 'aggregation' of their activities.

[32] In France, there are 35,000 water supply and sanitation suppliers; while, in Germany, there are over 6000 water utilities, of which the share of private companies is 40 per cent. See OECD (2020a).

[33] Although, as discussed below, in Scotland there are a number of retail suppliers of water to non-household customers. However, these retail companies do not own the water infrastructure, which is publicly owned.

[34] Carvalho, Marques and Berg (2012), Saal, Arocena, Maziotis and Triebs (2013) and Abbott and Cohen (2009) present useful surveys of this work. Specific country studies include: Knapp (1978) for Britain; Renzetti (1999) for Canada; Shih, Harrington, Pizer and Gillingham (2006) on US community water systems; Guerrini, Romano and Campedelli (2013) for Italy; Worthington and Higgs (2014) for Australia; Lavee and Bahar (2017) for Israel; and Molinos-Senante and Maziotis (2021) for Chile.

[35] The World Bank (2017b) argues that: 'There is ample empirical evidence in the literature on the existence of economies of scale in the WSS [water supply and sanitation] industry, at least up to a certain level.'

[36] See Ford and Warford (1969) and, more recently, Saal, Parker and Weyman-Jones (2007).

[37] See Fox and Hofler (1986). Mercadier, Cont and Ferro (2016) find economies for production and customer density only.

[38] See Kim and Clark (1988).

[39] See Carvalho, Marques and Berg (2012) and Abbott and Cohen (2009).

[40] See Carvalho, Marques and Berg (2012), Abbott and Cohen (2009) and Saal, Arocena, Maziotis and Triebs (2013), who conclude that economies of scale exist up to a certain level, but diseconomies arise if a company increases beyond this level.

[41] Various studies have suggested that the critical level of connections may lie between 100,000 and 1,000,000 connections. See, for example, Abbott and Cohen (2009).

[42] See World Bank (2017b) and OECD (2004). Rubin (2009) discusses the challenges associated with regulating smaller water utilities in the USA.

However, others have found that consolidating water utility companies does not necessarily decrease unit costs or improve performance, and thus that purported economies of scale are not always realised.[43]

Economies of Scope and Vertical Integration

Across the world, different levels of integration of activities in the water and wastewater industry can be observed. Full vertical integration is a feature of the industry in Chile, Austria, the Czech Republic, Denmark, England and Wales, Finland, France, Italy, Northern Ireland, Norway, Sweden and Switzerland.[44] Partial integration of some activities – typically the wholesale activities are separated from other activities in the chain – can be observed in Belgium, Portugal and Scotland. A mixed structure of integration and separation can be observed in other jurisdictions. In the USA, the level of integration differs across water systems and states; however, the majority of water utilities are vertically integrated.[45] Similarly, in Australia, some operators are fully integrated, while other operators are separated.[46] Finally, in some jurisdictions, notably parts of Germany, Switzerland and Italy, water services are sometimes supplied alongside other utility services such as urban waste, gas and electricity.

Numerous studies have focused on the question of whether or not there exist economies of scope in the water and wastewater industry. Here, too, the empirical evidence is mixed.[47] Some studies find scope economies arise when complementary activities in the water supply chain are integrated within a single organisation (particularly water abstraction and distribution),[48] while some have concluded that scope economies exist for smaller water supply companies but not for larger ones.[49] Conversely, other studies find no evidence of scope economies and, accordingly, imply that cost savings may be reaped from vertical separation of production and distribution activities (except for small companies).[50]

The empirical evidence is also mixed on whether scope economies arise from combining water and wastewater activities. Some studies find support for scope economies in these circumstances (especially for small companies),[51] while others find no such evidence, or suggest diseconomies of scope in combining the different activities.[52]

---

[43] Klien and Michaud (2019) look at the consolidation of 400 utilities in Central and Eastern Europe. They attribute the finding that economies of scale were not being realised to the one-off cost increase from consolidation which was not offset by post-consolidation performance.

[44] See Carvalho, Marques and Berg (2012).

[45] See Beecher and Kalmbach (2013).

[46] See Abbott, Cohen and Wang (2012) and Pollitt and Steer (2012).

[47] See Abbott and Cohen (2009) and Saal, Arocena, Maziotis and Triebs (2013) for surveys of this work.

[48] See García and Thomas (2001), Saal, Arocena, Maziotis and Triebs (2013) and Worthington and Higgs (2014).

[49] See Hayes (1987).

[50] See García, Moreaux and Reynaud (2007) and Molinos-Senante and Maziotis (2021). Estache and Iimi (2011) look at the bundling of treatment plant construction and distribution network installation in procurement contracts in the developing world, and conclude that there are significant diseconomies of scope between these activities and therefore no rationale for the bundling of these activities in procurement contracts in the water and wastewater industry.

[51] See Abbott and Cohen (2009).

[52] See Saal and Parker (2000), Stone and Webster Consultants (2004) and Saal, Arocena, Maziotis and Triebs (2013).

16.1.4 Trading Arrangements for Bulk Water

The development of wholesale market-based trading arrangements in the water industr▮ has, to date, been limited when compared to other public utility industries such as gas ar▮ electricity. Among other things, this may reflect the fact that: the abstraction and supp▮ of water tends to be highly localised; historically, there has been only limited interco▮ nection between different water systems; and, as discussed above, many of the activiti▮ in the water supply chain are typically vertically integrated within a single firm.[53]

There are, however, examples of wholesale trading arrangements being used for bu▮ raw (i.e. untreated) water and bulk treated water. Typically, these arrangements invol▮ transfers between neighbouring water companies. For example, in England and Wale▮ trading and transfer schemes are used for the transfer of raw water on specific lon▮ distance flows. In Germany, inter-regional wholesale suppliers sometimes sell potab▮ water to smaller local distribution companies under medium- to long-term contracts▮ Bulk water trading arrangements also feature, to differing degrees, in the water industri▮ in Australia, France and parts of the USA.[55] Arrangements involving the sharing ar▮ transportation of water across neighbouring properties are also a feature of the wat▮ sector in China, Oman, India and Pakistan. In many cases, these trading arrangements a▮ a response to conditions of severe water shortages or drought. In addition, in jurisdictio▮ where the coverage of the public supply (mains) network is limited – such as in ma▮ transitional and developing countries – competition can exist between private water ve▮ dors to supply water to households and businesses.

Another form of trading arrangement that can be observed in a small number of jur▮ dictions is trading in the 'rights', permits or licences to abstract water as part of form▮ water markets. As described in Section 16.4.2, formal water markets are a feature ▮ arrangements in parts of the USA (California and Colorado), Chile and Australia.

16.2 APPROACH TO WATER AND WASTEWATER REGULATION

16.2.1 Activities in the Supply Chain Subject to Regulation

Competitive and Potentially Competitive Activities in the Supply Chain
Although the prospects for direct competition in the water industry have, historical▮ been assessed as limited, there are examples of direct competition emerging, or bei▮ debated, in some activities in the water and wastewater supply process. This includes f▮ abstraction, transportation, treatment and retailing.

The abstraction of water does not typically have the attributes of a natural monopo▮ insofar as the potential exists for different operators to abstract water from locally sit▮ ated supply sources (i.e. competing reservoirs) in a given area or region, and then compe▮

---

[53] It may also reflect issues associated with accountability for water quality.
[54] See Stern (2012).
[55] Beecher and Kalmbach (2013) estimate that, in the USA, approximately 8760 water systems (around 18▮ per cent of the total) rely primarily on purchased water, and that wholesale sales for the largest surface water systems account for around a quarter of revenues.

to sell water to a distribution company (similar to gas production in some countries).[56] As already noted, wholesale transfers of bulk water, and trading in abstraction rights, are a feature of water industries in some jurisdictions, while, in many transitional and developing countries, there is competition between water vendors for the supply of raw water. However, historically, there has been a reluctance to allow for greater competition in water abstraction. This reluctance can be attributed to: concerns that competition may encourage the exploitation of water resources beyond sustainable levels;[57] the fact that water from different sources is not homogeneous, which can create quality and accountability issues if water is supplied into a pipeline from various operators; and issues associated with the potential 'unwinding' of cross-subsidies, which could lead to substantial increases in customer bills in some areas. In addition, environmental and ecological concerns can arise when large volumes of water are removed from a local catchment area.

In some jurisdictions, the activities of bulk water abstraction (for a whole region) and wholesale sales have been separated from distribution and retail activities.[58] The separation between wholesale and other 'downstream' activities has sometimes been predicated on a desire to encourage multiple suppliers of water. However, more commonly, it has been used to facilitate the joint ownership of wholesale water supply companies by a number of smaller regional water supply companies that directly supply retail customers.[59] An exception is in England and Wales, where, since 2017, new entrants are able to introduce water into an incumbent's distribution network without a requirement also to serve retail customers. The expectation is that this could allow for the development of a wholesale water market over time.

As in other public utility industries, one method for introducing competition where the prospects for direct infrastructure competition are limited is to allow for common carriage, or third-party access, to the distribution or transportation network. Under these arrangements, a user might be responsible for the procurement, treatment and retail supply of water to a final customer, but rely on the distribution network of the existing incumbent supplier in an area to transport the water from its source to a point of delivery. Common carriage for water supply has featured in some USA states,[60] England and Wales,[61] and some states in Australia (where common carriage for sewage is also potentially possible).[62] Another form

---

[56] See Noll (2002), who notes that in a given area one operator may abstract water from a surface source (such as a river) while another operator might abstract water from a groundwater source (such as an aquifer). However, there are potentially some scale economies associated with the development of large reservoirs.

[57] Noll (2002) defines 'sustainability' in the context of water as when the 'sum of all current uses (including protecting ecosystems that depend on the resource) does not exceed the rate at which the water system is refreshed'. In this respect, water should be regarded as a renewable resource to the extent that natural rainfall and water flows replenish water that is taken from the water system.

[58] Including parts of Australia, New Zealand and Portugal.

[59] See Abbott and Cohen (2011).

[60] The possibility of 'water wheeling' exists in some USA states under very specific circumstances. However, there is generally not an 'open-access' regime for distribution networks. See Beecher and Rubin (2000).

[61] Common carriage arrangements were put in place in England and Wales in 2003 for certain non-household customers. These were replaced by Wholesale Authorisations in 2017, which allow new upstream entrants to use an incumbent's water network without having also to be a retailer.

[62] See Gray and Gardner (2008).

of competition in distribution is where a new operator is given the right to supply water and/or wastewater services in the incumbent company's area for specific types of customer (known as 'inset appointments').[63]

In relation to treatment activities, for both water and wastewater, these again do not typically have the attributes of a natural monopoly (i.e. there are limited economies of scale) and, in principle, competition between different treatment operators could occur. For example, an entrant separate from the incumbent water operator could be charged with the treatment of water and sewage under an outsourcing contract or concession, even where the rest of the activities in the supply chain remain integrated.[64] Competition for the treatment of wastewater has been considered in some jurisdictions as a way to increase innovation in treatment methods. This includes the possibility of so-called 'sewer mining' – where a new entrant gains access to raw sewage prior to treatment and then treats it in a separate facility often to a higher level of treatment – which provides the possibility of sewage being treated to such a level that it could be released back into the environment as recycled water.[65] Notwithstanding these possibilities, in most jurisdictions, direct competition for water and wastewater treatment services has not developed to any large extent to date.

Finally, competition in retail activities for all non-household consumers has been introduced in Britain. Retail entrants can purchase wholesale water supplies for delivery to the premises of the relevant non-household customer (effectively bundling the service of commodity, treatment and transportation from the incumbent undertaking). In Scotland, retail competition for non-household customers was introduced in 2008 while in England and Wales it was introduced in 2017. Although there were proposals to extend retail competition in England and Wales to household customers, this appears to have been put on hold. More generally, there is debate about whether the benefits of retail competition (on its own) are of sufficient magnitude to outweigh the transaction costs associated with such a policy, given the small value added of retailing activities to the final price of water.

Activities in the Supply Chain Subject to Regulation

Water distribution and wastewater transportation – operating the local networks of pipes and sewers – are generally viewed as having the attributes of a natural monopoly activity. The costs associated with the water distribution system are principally capital in nature which are largely sunk, and the assets themselves are immobile and have limited alternative uses. The characteristics of wastewater transportation are similar, insofar as the costs

---

[63] These were introduced in England and Wales in 1990 as 'inset appointments', and are now known as 'new appointments and variations'.

[64] The potential for competition in the treatment of sewage was identified by Vickers and Yarrow (1988).

[65] For the description of one such proposal in Sydney, Australia, see ACCC (2007) and Gray and Gardner (2008). In England and Wales, since 2014, it has been possible for entrants to provide certain upstream sewerage activities including, for example, the removal and disposal of sludge. London Economics (2016) discusses other areas of potential competition in upstream sewage and sludge markets.

[66] Noll (2002) observes that a plausible alternative to piped distribution exists in some communities where water is distributed by vendors who sell it from tank trunks or large bottles. However, this form of distribution is considerably more expensive than that of piped water.

are largely sunk, the assets are immobile and have limited alternative uses. In addition, the potential for direct competition between pipeline operators from particular sources of raw water (equivalent, say, to the pipeline-to-pipeline competition in the gas industry, where multiple pipelines serve a single citygate) has typically been assessed as both uneconomic and inefficient.[67]

As described above, competition in the water and wastewater supply chain is largely non-existent in most jurisdictions and there are high levels of vertical integration in the supply chain. This means that in many jurisdictions water and wastewater companies operate as geographical monopolies (i.e. there are no deregulated activities, as there are in other public utility industries). Regulation is therefore applied to all activities in the water and wastewater supply chain in the form of either control through state ownership, or some kind of economic regulation or other government oversight of retail prices and quality.[68]

6.2.2 Form and Scope of Price Regulation

From the preceding discussion, it is clear that the form of economic regulation of the water and wastewater industry varies across jurisdictions. Indeed, the high levels of state ownership in many countries means that there is often no separate *economic* regulator of the industry. Rather, the principal 'regulators' of the water and wastewater industry in many jurisdictions are those that perform functions related to the quality of service and environmental protection. In most European countries, including France, Germany, Spain and the Netherlands, an industry-specific economic regulator has not been established for the water and wastewater industry. In the USA, responsibility for regulation of the industry is divided among various bodies at the federal, state and municipal level,[69] and not all states in the USA have an economic regulator for water and wastewater services.[70] The majority of states that do have an economic regulator only regulate privately owned water operators above a particular size. However, in some states, the Public Utility Commission (PUC) also regulates municipal providers, cooperative providers and not-for-profits.

In jurisdictions where water operators are state-owned and state-operated, the prices and tariffs for water and wastewater services are often determined administratively.

---

[67] This does not, however, preclude the possibility for direct competition to build a pipe to service particular large customers.

[68] An exception to this general point is that, in some jurisdictions, such as the USA, some smaller water and wastewater operators are not subject to formal state regulation by a Public Utility Commission.

[69] Other bodies include the federal Environmental Protection Authority (EPA), which is responsible for setting standards in relation to human health and environmental sustainability, and local or municipal (county) administrations, which are responsible for applying these standards to ensure that water and wastewater is of a suitable quality.

[70] Beecher (2018) notes that, in five states (Georgia, Michigan, Minnesota, North Dakota and South Dakota) and Washington DC, the PUCs do not have authority over the water industry. Moreover, it has been estimated that only about 20 per cent of all public water systems in the USA are regulated (recall that there are a large number of water systems in the USA); this includes around 8000 water utilities and 1000 wastewater companies (including combined companies). See Denig-Chakroff (2008) and Beecher (2009).

However, economic regulators also exist in some jurisdictions where the operators a[?] under state ownership.[71] In jurisdictions where price controls are applied, the two princ[?] pal forms of price regulation – rate of return and price and revenue caps – discussed i[?] Chapter 5 can be observed.

Rate of Return

Rate of return is a popular form of regulation in the water and wastewater industr[?] Marques (2010) estimated that up to 60 per cent of countries in which economic regula[?] tion was applied used rate of return regulation at that time.[72]

In the USA, the process for the determination of tariffs in the water and wastewat[?] industry is framed by the well-established principles and approaches adopted in the oth[?] public utility industries. This typically means that state PUCs ensure that rates are 'ju[?] and reasonable', and that the rates provide sufficient revenues to cover reasonable ope[?] ating costs and to provide the utility with an opportunity to earn a reasonable return c[?] its investment. As described in Chapter 5, a rate base is established on which the ope[?] ator can earn a fair return, costs must be prudently incurred, and all new investmen[?] must be deemed to be 'used and useful'. While there are no mandatory requirements f[?] water utilities to maintain regulatory accounts, which can serve as an important inp[?] into the rate setting process, a system of accounts has been developed by the Nation[?] Association of Regulatory Utility Commissioners (NARUC) and is widely applied (eve[?] by non-regulated water systems).[73] Some states allow water companies to pass throug[?] certain capital investment costs into rates between rate reviews (known as distributic[?] system improvement charges), while other states have introduced so-called 'fair valu[?] legislation, which values assets above their book value in certain circumstances.[74] As pa[?] of the regulatory process, some state PUCs allow for representation of water/wastewat[?] customers by independent customer representative bodies known as ratepayer advocate[?] As discussed in Chapter 5, some US states have introduced decoupling policies, whi[?] disassociate revenues from underlying sales in order to incentivise the firm to promo[?] greater conservation of water.[75]

Price and Revenue Caps

The price cap approach is also used in the water and wastewater industry. This applicatio[?] of price caps to the water and wastewater industry was pioneered in England and Wale[?] but is now applied in a number of other jurisdictions.[76]

At the time the price cap approach was first applied in England and Wales, there w[?] some concern that it might not be appropriate for the water and wastewater indust[?] These concerns related to the significant capital investments that were required in t[?]

---

[71] Like Australia, Scotland and some states in the USA.
[72] This included not only many states in the USA and some provinces of Canada, but also the Philippines[?] Indonesia, Mozambique, Niger, Kenya, Uruguay, Portugal, the Slovak Republic and Romania
[73] See Beecher (2011).
[74] See Zhang, González Rivas, Grant and Warner (2021).
[75] Crew and Kahlon (2014) and Teodoro and Zhang (2017) discuss the approach in California.
[76] According to Marques (2010), this included at the time: Armenia, Zambia, Jamaica, Panama, Italy, and some states in Australia. In addition, Ireland and Denmark also apply price and revenue caps.

industry at the time of privatisation and the long lifespan of the capital assets (which might encourage opportunistic behaviour by the regulator once the investments were sunk). There was also a concern that, unlike the other utility industries, the prospects for competition were limited, meaning price caps would have to be applied on a permanent basis. In particular, it was noted that, if the RPI-X (retail price index minus X) approach applied permanently, and the level of X was reset each period on the basis of past performance, this would introduce some of the disincentive properties associated with rate of return regulation (i.e. the 'ratchet effect' – see Chapters 5 and 8).[77]

Accordingly, a number of adaptations to the RPI-X approach were proposed to make it suitable for implementation on a permanent basis.[78] The first RPI + K price controls were introduced in England and Wales in 1989,[79] and prices were set on the basis of a modified tariff basket which comprised five components.[80]

Since that time, various changes have been introduced to the price cap arrangements applied in the water industry in different parts of the world. First, some price controls separate wholesale revenue activities and retail activities. In England and Wales, for example, wholesale revenue controls are based on a building block approach based on the regulated asset base (known as the regulatory capital value (RCV)), while retail revenue controls are based on the total cost to serve plus a net margin on costs to cover a return and an allowance for tax. Second, the approach in some jurisdictions has shifted away from companies providing 'inputs' to a price control process to a focus on 'outcomes'. As described in Chapter 5, this approach requires firms to consult extensively with stakeholders and consumers to identify desirable outcomes, which it then incorporates into a business plan or price submission. The business plan or price submission is then approved by the regulator. This 'outcomes-based' approach has been adopted in England and Wales, in Italy and in the Australian state of Victoria.[81] Third, in England and Wales and in Denmark, the price control is now based around the setting of a single allowance for the expected efficient *total expenditure* (Totex) for the business, rather than separate allowances for capital expenditure and operating expenditure. Fourth, some regulators have introduced a form of menu-type regulation, which allow companies to submit 'realistic business plans' to provide a better information base on which the revenue allowance can be established.[82] As discussed in Chapter 4, this approach can potentially address the information asymmetry between regulators and companies.

---

[77] See Littlechild (1988).

[78] See Littlechild (1986, 1988). These included the use of an industry yardstick as the basis for the revision of the X factor, and mechanisms whereby, if an individual firm outperformed the industry, it would retain any profits, while, if it underperformed relative to the industry, it would suffer losses of profit.

[79] A K factor was used rather than an X factor, which comprised both an efficiency component (X) as well as another component, known as a Q factor, to reflect higher costs associated with investments to satisfy higher water quality standards. The formula was therefore RPI – X + Q.

[80] The services included in the first tariff basket were measured and unmeasured water, measured and unmeasured sewerage, and trade effluent. The K values ranged from 3 to 7.

[81] In Victoria, the approach is known as 'PREMO': Performance, Risk, Engagement, Management, Outcomes. Bardelli and Biancardi (2018) present a summary of the Italian approach.

[82] Variants of the menu approach have been adopted in England and Wales (known as the Capital Expenditure Scheme, CIS), in the Australian state of Victoria (where the level return on equity varies according to the level of ambition shown in a price submission) and in Italy.

Yardstick and Comparative Competition

The yardstick, or benchmarking, approach to informing price controls, discussed in Chapter 4 and 5, has been an important part of regulating water and wastewater companies in England and Wales,[83] Ireland, Denmark and other countries.[84] In simple terms, this approach compares the performance of individual water companies to that of other water companies and, in particular, to the most efficient supplier.[85] To implement such an approach, it is necessary to have a sufficient number of suppliers and, for this reason, a special merger regime has at times applied in some jurisdictions that restricts mergers in the industry so as to preserve the prospects for comparative competition.[86] The approach has become more sophisticated over time and utilises econometric models, and other linear programming procedures (such as data envelopment analysis (DEA)), to estimate and compare the efficiency of companies in the industry and, on this basis, to determine the expected productivity gains in the next regulatory period.[87] A variation of this approach has been adopted in Chile and Peru. In these jurisdictions, tariffs are set by reference to a model of a hypothetical 'efficient company'. In setting tariffs in this way, it is assumed that the activities of the hypothetical company will be efficient in satisfying the projected demand.[88]

Sunshine Regulation

Regulators in a number of other jurisdictions undertake benchmarking exercises in the water and wastewater industry. However, the results of this analysis are not used for the purposes of setting prices, but rather as a means of public reporting on the comparative performance of different operators. This approach, sometimes referred to as 'sunshine regulation', is intended to 'name and shame' operators who are performing poorly in the hope that this will lead to improved performance. Variants of this approach have at times been used in Brazil, Germany, the Netherlands and Zambia.[89] A study reviewing the impact of sunshine regulation in the water industry in the Netherlands concluded that it was associated with improved productivity in the industry, some of which had been passed through to consumers in lower prices.[90]

Regulation of Quality

As already indicated, issues of quality are of particular importance in the water and wastewater industry because of the close connection with human health and life. Accordingly, in many jurisdictions, there are separate health and environmental regulations and

---

[83] Dassler, Parker and Saal (2006) observe that it is applications in this industry which come closest to Shleifer's benchmarking model described in Chapter 4. Byatt (2013) describes its early implementation.

[84] Ferreira da Cruz, Carvalho and Marques (2013) also discuss the use of the approach in Chile, Colombia and some states in Australia.

[85] Danish Water Regulatory Authority (2022) provides an overview of their approach. See Marques (2010) and Berg (2010) for an overview of variants of the approach as applied in the water and wastewater industry.

[86] The UK competition authorities have in the past blocked mergers solely on this basis.

[87] See Danish Water Regulatory Authority (2022), Dassler, Parker and Saal (2006) and Thanassoulis (2000a b). Worthington (2014) provides a survey of studies of efficiency.

[88] See Marques (2010).

[89] See OECD (2004), Marques (2010) and Ferreira da Cruz, Carvalho and Marques (2013).

[90] See De Witte and Saal (2010).

standards that apply to these industries. However, because the dominant industry structure for the supply of water and wastewater services in many jurisdictions is that of a vertically integrated provider that has a monopoly in a specific geographic area (i.e. implying that there is no real choice for consumers), issues of quality of service are also commonly addressed by economic regulators (in those jurisdictions where such bodies have been established). This is particularly the case where water and wastewater operators are privately owned and therefore may have incentives to degrade quality in order to increase profits.

One set of quality of service indicators typically focus on reducing water losses and controlling leakage, and companies can face specific performance targets for which they are rewarded for achieving (or penalised for not). In Italy, for example, quality of service regulation focuses on water losses, water interruption, water quality, sewerage system adequacy, sludge disposal and wastewater quality. In some jurisdictions, companies can also be incentivised to introduce measures to promote demand-side management and water conservation.

Another set of service standards focuses on customer service, and, in some cases, customer quality indicators have been incorporated into the price setting process. In England and Wales, two measures known as C-MeX (customer measure of experience) and D-MeX (developer services measure of experience) reward or penalise companies according to their level of service relative to other companies.[91] In the Australian state of Victoria, companies must identify the specific services they will provide to a required standard, the appropriate service level, and the payment or rebate amount for not achieving those standards as part of its consumer engagement.[92] In the USA, PUCs do not typically establish minimum standards for levels of service to customers or reliability standards; however, they may impose various service quality standards relating to pressure and aesthetics (colour, taste and odour).[93]

Rate Structures

As we discuss in Section 16.4.3, an important issue in the water and wastewater industry in many jurisdictions – regardless of their structure or ownership – relates to the pricing of water and wastewater services. In jurisdictions where water usage is metered, water tariffs are typically based on a two-part tariff structure comprising a fixed charge (which does not vary with usage) and a variable component (which does vary with usage). The recovery of a greater proportion of costs through the fixed component of the tariff can provide greater revenue stability for a water supply firm but reduces the incentives for consumers to control their marginal usage of the service (i.e. to engage in demand management practices).

In the USA, different rate structures are applied for water services across states.[94] In many states, there are generally two components of the tariff: a fixed component, such

---

[91] These measures replaced the service incentive mechanism in 2020. C-MeX and D-MeX are designed to be relative performance commitments whereby a company's performance is compared to other companies rather than against an absolute performance level.

[92] The regulator can also mandate certain standards.

[93] See Marques (2010) and Beecher (2009).

[94] See Beecher and Kalmbach (2013) and Rubin (2010).

as a meter or customer charge, and a variable charge that is calculated according to the amount of water used. Historically, the structure of tariffs in many states was based on declining block rates (i.e. price per unit decreased with greater consumption). However there has been a trend towards rate structures based on uniform usage rates, where the same rate is charged for units consumed (sometimes differentiated by customer class such as residential customers or commercial customers).[95] In addition, as discussed below some jurisdictions are applying increasing block rate tariff structures (i.e. price per unit increases with greater consumption) to encourage water conservation, while other states have introduced seasonal rates.

In jurisdictions where price caps are used, water companies set their own price structures within the allowed revenue allowance. In some jurisdictions, such price structures can be subject to regulatory approval or need to be consistent with certain charging principles or rules. In England and Wales, for example, the regulator has established a set of charging scheme rules, which require, among other things, that the prices for water and wastewater services reflect the long-run costs of providing those services.[96] Tariff structures typically comprise a fixed component and a variable component, even in circumstances where a meter does not exist. In this latter case, the variable component determined according to the characteristics of the property consuming the water, such as its rateable value.

16.3 THE SCOPE AND EFFECTS OF RESTRUCTURING POLICIES

16.3.1 The Scope of Restructuring Policies in the Water and Wastewater Industry

As already noted, the extent of restructuring in the water and wastewater industry over the past four decades has been limited in many jurisdictions. Policies have typically focused on water quality and water resources management, rather than on introducing competition, as has occurred in the other industries discussed in this book.

In general terms, three 'models' for water and wastewater industries can be observed in different parts of the world.[97] The first model, the 'English model', involves the private ownership and operation of the assets associated with water and wastewater supply. An independent economic regulator supervises the private operators, and may apply various forms of benchmarking or yardstick competition to encourage performance improvements.[98] In a second model, termed the 'French model', the assets are publicly owned but the management and operation of the assets is undertaken by private entities under medium- to long-term concession contracts. The contracts are typically awarded according to a tendering or bidding process. In effect, this involves 'competition for the market' as described in Chapter 3, and is the most common form of private sector participation water and wastewater management. Although this approach involves a form of 'regulation by contract', in some jurisdictions, regulatory agencies have been created to supervise

---

[95] See Rubin (2010).
[96] See Ofwat (2020).
[97] See Marques (2010).
[98] Marques (2010) notes that Chile, Sweden and the Czech Republic have sought to follow this model.

the quality of supplier outputs and to deal with any unforeseen circumstances. The third model, termed the 'public operator model', involves state ownership and operation of the assets, and is the predominant structure for the water and wastewater industry in a global context. In many jurisdictions where there is state ownership and operation, there is seen to be no need for a separate economic regulator of the industry. However, in some jurisdictions, such as Scotland, Ireland, Australia and some US states, regulatory agencies have some role overseeing the activities of the publicly owned and operated suppliers.

Scope of Restructuring in Britain

The most comprehensive restructuring policies in the water and wastewater industry have been applied in England and Wales, and the origins and stages of this process are well documented.[99] Privatisation of the ten regional authorities occurred in 1989 and, at the same time, the current framework for independent regulation was established.[100] Alongside a new economic regulator (Ofwat), a National Rivers Authority (NRA, now the Environment Agency) and a Drinking Water Inspectorate (DWI) were also created.[101] A statutorily independent body (the Consumer Council for Water) has since been established to represent consumer interests and provides advocacy into the price control process.

Five changes to the regulatory framework in England and Wales since privatisation are worth commenting on. First, since 2014, the water regulator has been under a legal requirement to ensure the long-term resilience of the privatised water supply and wastewater industries. This, in turn, obligates the water companies to anticipate, and plan for, potential future hazards and extreme events (such as those associated with climate change) that might lead to service disruptions or environmental damage. Second, the regulatory approach now requires each company to prepare a business plan which sets out various 'outcomes' for the company in the next five-year period and the costs associated with achieving those outcomes. This business plan is then approved by the regulator.[102] A third change has been greater customer involvement in the regulatory process. In preparing their business plan, each water company must undertake extensive local engagement and establish customer challenge panels charged with ensuring that the overall package is acceptable to consumers.[103] Aligned with this change is a recent focus on companies' understanding of the public value of their activities and reflecting this in their business

---

[99] See Vickers and Yarrow (1988) and Ofwat and Defra (2006).

[100] The original privatisation plans were published in 1986 but were badly received and were put on hold. Reform did not occur until the passing of the Water Act 1989. Gómez-Ibáñez (2003) argues that the government 'saw privatisation as a way to meet the new EC standards without raising public debt and taxes'.

[101] The Water Industry Act 1991 and the Water Act 2014 are also important pieces of legislation in terms of defining the roles and responsibilities of the various regulatory authorities.

[102] The UK government has set out two high-level priorities for the regulator in reviewing business plans: (1) to secure long-term resilience, particularly given the substantial risks from drought in some regions; and (2) to protect customers, largely through balancing resilience with affordability. See Defra (2017).

[103] In developing its 2020–2025 business plan, one company – Thames Water, which is responsible for London's water and wastewater supply – gathered insights from nearly a million customers. This focus on customer engagement has given rise to questions about the extent to which customers can effectively engage in the process, and possible tensions between different customer interests and those of the regulator. See Decker (2018) and CCWater (2020).

plans.[104] A fourth change involves the introduction of policies to encourage a water o
wastewater company to competitively tender for services in relation to the delivery o
certain large infrastructure projects (so-called direct procurement).[105] The expectation i
that this will encourage greater innovation and lower whole-life costs of the investment
Critically, the third-party infrastructure provider can be subject to economic regulation
including a determination of an allowed revenue, which, once the project is operational
is expected to be reset during periodic reviews. A final change introduced in 2017 wa
the full opening of the business market to retail competition, which provides 1.2 millio
business customers with retail choice about their supplier. While plans to extend suc
retail competition to domestic/household customers in England were introduced in 201
these have not yet been taken forward, and in 2019 the government stated that it would
learn lessons from competition in the business market first.

In Scotland, where the industry remains under state ownership, retail competition fo
non-household customers was introduced in 2008. This followed a restructuring of th
industry which saw the non-household retail supply activities of Scottish Water bein
(operationally) separated from other activities and placed within a separate entity. A cus
tomer forum has also been established that is charged with negotiating a business pla
with Scottish Water and, if an agreement is reached, the regulator has indicated that
'would be minded' to adopt that agreement.

Restructuring Policies in the EU

In the European Union, there is no requirement on Member States to establish an inde
pendent regulator in the water and wastewater industry as there is in relation to the othe
regulated industries. Similarly, while major restructuring of the energy, transport and tele
communications industries has occurred through various relatively detailed EU Directive
and Regulations, the EU Directives that apply to the water and wastewater industries ar
generally less specific about the design and implementation of economic regulation in th
industry.[106] The principal piece of legislation that addresses matters of economic regula
tion is the Water Framework Directive (2000/60/EC). The Directive requires all EU Membe
States to ensure that the costs of water supply (including environmental and resourc
costs) are recovered from customers, and that charges are cost-reflective according t
the different water uses (such as industry, household and agriculture). The Directive wa
introduced to address concerns that rates for water services did not reflect underlyin
costs and, in particular, were set at too low a level to encourage the efficient use of wate
or regard for the wider impacts of water usage on the environment.

---

[104] Cave and Wright (2021) refer to Ofwat as a pathbreaker in requiring firms to define their broader
purposes and show that they are pursuing them. They set out three areas where public value was
reflected in business plans: environmental benefits, distributional fairness and consumer–citizen
participation in decision making.

[105] An example is the Thames Tideway Tunnel, which is a 25 km super-sewer in London. It is being
developed by a consortium and is expected to cost over £4 billion.

[106] Directives that apply to the industry include the following: Nitrates Directive; Habitats Directive;
Freshwater Fish Directive; Shellfish Waters Directive; Dangerous Substances Directive; Groundwater
Directive; Urban Wastewater Treatment Directive; Drinking Water Directive; Bathing Water Directive;
Surface Water Abstraction Directive; and the Water Framework Directive.

The approach to water regulation differs significantly across EU Member States. Some countries have established independent economic regulators. In Bulgaria, for example, tariffs are proposed in five-year business plans that must be approved by an independent water regulator. In Denmark, new rules were introduced in 2009 which subject around 300 water companies to economic regulation. This regulator (a division of the competition agency) sets a revenue cap and sets efficiency targets based on a benchmarking exercise and using the Totex approach. In Italy, the economic regulation of the water sector was extended in 2011, and a combined independent energy and water regulator now oversees the sector. The national regulator sets industry-wide tariff rules, while municipal authorities remain responsible for approving tariffs and planning and investment. The regulator has also introduced a standard template for concession arrangements between water operators and municipalities.[107] In 2014, the remit of the Irish energy regulator was extended to cover the water industry. The regulator benchmarks the costs and performance of, and approves the revenue and charges for, Irish Water, a state-owned entity which is the monopoly provider of water and wastewater services.

As discussed below, in some European countries such as France and Spain, concession contracts are used in the water industry where private companies compete to operate in different municipalities. The concession contract usually defines the water tariffs for the period of application. In other European countries, such as Estonia, Finland, Germany, the Netherlands and Slovakia, the water sector largely operates under direct or delegated public management, meaning that a state-owned entity is responsible for service provision. Tariff setting can be governed by national laws which require that certain costs be recovered in charges by, or can be set by, or require the approval of, local municipalities.

Restructuring Policies in the USA

The extent of restructuring of the water and wastewater industry in the USA has been considerably more limited than in other public utility industries. This reflects a number of factors, including the high levels of vertical integration in the industry, the predominance of state and municipal ownership, and a perception of potentially high levels of public resistance to such restructuring policies. The use of private–public partnerships is relatively limited, with only 1.4 per cent of Americans receiving water from a public–private partnership (PPP) in 2021.[108] In most states, the rates and other investment decisions for *state-owned* water companies are generally overseen by locally elected officials. As outlined above, in most states, PUCs oversee and approve the rates for *private* water companies (and some public ones). As the water industry is highly fragmented in some states, this can mean that the regulator oversees hundreds of companies. In Arizona, for example, the state PUC regulates around 350 water companies, twenty wastewater companies and twenty combined companies. Finally, in some states, such as California and Texas, there has been increasing focus on water conservation. There is also a focus on reform to water rights and trading, given prolonged periods of drought in some states (such as California).

---

[107] See Bardelli and Biancardi (2018).
[108] See Hanna and McDonald (2021).

Restructuring Policies in Other Jurisdictions

While the most comprehensive restructuring policies for the water and wastewater indus try have been introduced in England and Wales, policies directed at introducing compet tion for some 'upstream' activities in the water supply process (such as at the abstraction or bulk water level) have been introduced in a small number of jurisdictions. Once agai Chile was an early pioneer of restructuring, introducing new policies in the early 1980 This included a Water Code that effectively created private water use rights nationwie and had implications for who could access and use water. As described in Section 16.4 below, the ability to transfer water rights facilitated the development of water market While these policies increased private sector participation in the allocation and manage ment of water and wastewater supply, there were concerns that they restricted access water, and in 2022 changes to the Water Code were introduced which reclassified wat as a national asset for public use and placed a time limit on water rights of thirty years.

In Australia, the rural and urban water sectors have undergone significant change ov the past two decades, including through the introduction of water trading for rural areas, ar the separation of bulk water activities from retail activities in cities such as Sydney ar Melbourne.[110] Policies have also been introduced to facilitate upstream water marke and trading (see Section 16.4.2). Although most water and wastewater companies a fully vertically integrated state-owned entities, economic regulators oversee the settir of retail prices. As in England and Wales, in some states, there has been a shift in foc towards 'outcomes', and requirements for greater customer engagement in the develo ment of business plans.[111]

Finally, as described in Section 16.4.1 below, public–private concession arrangemer have been extensively used in the water and wastewater industry in many countries East Asia (including China), in Latin American and in Europe (France). This restructurir has involved the introduction of periodic 'competitions *for* the market' for the supply water and wastewater services in specific geographic regions.

16.3.2 The Effects of Restructuring Policies in the Water and Wastewater Industry

Effects of Restructuring Policies in Britain

As described above, the most comprehensive restructuring of the water and wastewat industry has occurred in England and Wales. In the immediate period after the priv tisation and restructuring of the industry, assessments were mixed.[112] Now, some thr

---

[109] However, controversially, the changes do not affect the rights to water already acquired for perpetual u:
[110] See Byrnes (2013) for a discussion of the changes introduced to the Australian urban water sector.
[111] In the state of Victoria, companies can earn additional return on equity if they can demonstrate good customer engagement. The regulator in the state of South Australia has also introduced similar change
[112] For example, Armstrong, Cowan and Vickers (1994) concluded that the price regulation and the quality and environmental standard setting processes were more open, and that the achievement of overall environmental and quality goals may have been brought forward by the privatisation process. However, they also found that the prospects for competition were limited, that regulation of the sector was detailed and expensive, and that, because investments were being made by the private sector (which required private rates of return on capital), this might lead to prices being higher in the long ru than if investments had been undertaken by the public sector. Finally, they perceived the creation of separate environmental and economic regulators to be potentially inefficient, and questioned whether workable system of yardstick competition could be developed.

decades on, the overall assessment of impacts remains inconclusive and there continues to be active political debate about whether the water industry should be 're-nationalised'. In terms of prices, estimates suggest that bills in 2015 had risen by 40 per cent in real terms since privatisation,[113] with most of the change occurring in the first years after privatisation. However, some studies have found that average household bills for water and wastewater services in England and Wales are not 'out of line' with those in similar jurisdictions where operators remain under state ownership.[114] While prices in England and Wales have risen since privatisation, the level of investment in the water and wastewater industry over this period has also been substantial. The total investment by water companies in the period 1989–2015 has been estimated at around £126 billion.[115] These substantial investments in the industry are generally accepted to have led to improvements in quality and environmental standards.[116]

In terms of performance, there is evidence of improvements in productivity and efficiency in the industry since the 1990s and, in particular, that regulation may have been associated with improvements in efficiency.[117] However, while the evidence suggests that the industry as a whole has become more efficient, significant differences have been found between the performance of individual companies.[118] In addition, it has been suggested that the incremental efficiency gains have diminished over time, leading the regulator to adopt increasingly complex and elaborate techniques to assess potential efficiency gains, which has increased regulatory complexity and raised costs.[119] However, the recent introduction of the Totex approach, separate price controls for wholesale and retail activities, and a shift in focus towards 'outcomes' are seen to have improved comparability across companies.[120]

Despite the introduction of pro-competitive policies, such as inset appointments and common carriage, there appears to be consensus among the regulator, water companies and potential entrants that the experience of introducing competition for water and wastewater activities in England and Wales has so far been generally unsatisfactory.[121] New initiatives focused on promoting competition include changes to the 'new appointments and variations' regime (where an entrant can be appointed as supplier for a specific customer or geographic area) and the introduction of direct appointments for major infrastructure projects. These are both forms of 'competition *for* the market'. As noted above, the possibility of 'competition *in* the market' was introduced in 2017 for business (non-household) retail customers. Here, too, assessments by the regulator have repeatedly identified a number of market frictions that are preventing the development of competition, including: poor-quality data; cumbersome wholesaler–retailer interactions;

---

[113] See NAO (2015).
[114] See Ofwat (2008a) and GWI (2018).
[115] See NAO (2015).
[116] See NAO (2015) and Ofwat and Defra (2006).
[117] See NAO (2015) and also Abbott and Cohen (2009) and studies listed therein. Ballance (2006) suggests that operating expenditure efficiency improved significantly in the decade post-privatisation.
[118] See Cave and Wright (2010).
[119] See Gibson, McKean and Piffaut (2012) and Ballance (2006).
[120] NAO (2015).
[121] See Ofwat (2008b), Yarrow, Appleyard, Decker and Keyworth (2008), Cave (2009) and Byatt (2013). Some of these difficulties were foreshadowed in Cowan (1997).

and inadequate wholesaler performance. In 2021, there were nineteen retailers operating in the market. However, it was estimated that only 43 per cent of business customers were aware that they had retail choice, and incumbents continued to account for the largest market share, with entrants gaining around 1 per cent of supply points per year.[122] Finally, the regulatory framework applied since privatisation is perceived as having created weak incentives for innovation.[123] To address this, the regulator has introduced an innovation fund and a series of innovation competitions where parties (including regulated water companies) can compete for funding.

The experience of retail competition for non-household customers, introduced in Scotland in 2008, is also mixed.[124] As at the end of 2021, there were nineteen providers serving 160,000 premises. However, despite this entry, the non-household retail market continues to be dominated by the now-separate retail division of incumbent Scottish Water, with only around 5 per cent of customers being served by an entrant.[125] Notwithstanding this low level of penetration, the regulator has estimated that competition has brought several benefits, including lower prices, more tailored services, reduced water consumption (by around 20 per cent) and a shift towards more cost-reflective wholesale and retail tariffs.[126]

Effects of Restructuring Policies Elsewhere

The impacts of restructuring policies introduced in other parts of the world – including in Europe and the USA – have generally been subject to less intense scrutiny than in the other industries discussed in this book. In part, this reflects the more limited nature of restructuring policies introduced, and also the fact that many operators remain in state ownership.

In Chile, a pioneer of restructuring in the water industry in the late 1980s, there have been various changes to the policies over the past two decades. While some assessments have described the effects of the policies as a 'success story',[127] there has been ongoing concern about the private ownership of water rights, which, in the context of a decade-long drought, has been seen to limit community access to water and to exacerbate inequalities.

In Australia, the evidence on the impacts of policies directed at facilitating water trading indicates both positive and negative economic and social impacts.[128] As described in Section 16.4.2 below, water markets in the Murray–Darling region are seen to have

---

[122] Ofwat (2021a).

[123] See Cave (2009) and Cave and Wright (2010).

[124] At the time it was introduced, there were concerns that, in static terms, the benefits associated with restructuring would be limited given the size of the non-household retail market. See Yarrow, Appleyard, Decker and Keyworth (2008).

[125] According to Business Stream, it served 152,916 customers in 2021, out of the 160,000 potential customers. However, the share of volumes served by entrants is estimated to be greater than the share of customers.

[126] See WICS (2021).

[127] Marques (2010) refers to the performance relative to other Latin American countries in terms of the high levels of coverage of the network, the high levels of quality of service and the regulatory model introduced.

[128] Frontier Economics (2007) discusses these impacts.

brought benefits to individual users and communities, and wider benefits to the Australian economy.[129] However, a 2021 review found a need for reform of the governance arrangements, including the creation of an agency to oversee trading activities.[130] Restructuring policies in the urban water industry, including the separation of bulk water activities from retail activities in cities such as Sydney and Melbourne, have also been assessed as resulting in a more efficient and productive industry.[131]

Finally, as discussed in Section 16.4.1 below, the experience of the use of concession contracts and the 'competition *for* the market' approach in the water and wastewater industry is generally perceived to have achieved mixed effects on prices and efficiency across different jurisdictions. However, some studies find that coverage can increase, as can water quality.[132]

16.4 REGULATORY POLICY ISSUES IN THE WATER AND WASTEWATER INDUSTRY

This section discusses three important regulatory policy issues in the water and wastewater industry: the scope and impacts of private participation in the water industry; the use of formal water markets as a mechanism for discovering the value of water and efficiently allocating it across users; and issues associated with water pricing, including a need to balance affordability and access, resilience and water conservation objectives.

16.4.1 The Experience of Private Participation in the Water Industry

Given the high levels of state ownership of water and wastewater assets across the world, a much-studied issue has been the costs and benefits associated with privatisation of the industry and whether it improves performance.

In general, those in favour of private sector participation point to potential efficiency improvements, and the removal of political influences, on the operation of the sector. Conversely, those who oppose private sector participation argue that it is not compatible with the characteristics of the sector (such as the large externalities in supply and the limited scope for competition).[133] In countries such as the USA – where only 12.7 per cent of the population is served by a privately owned entity (including through a PPP) – two reasons have been identified for the dominance of state ownership: limited public appetite for private sector involvement; and concerns that private sector participation will lead to higher prices and lower performance.[134]

Overall, the available evidence on private sector participation is inconclusive. Some studies show that publicly owned water utilities perform better than private water utilities, others find the opposite, and some find there is insufficient evidence to form a secure

---

[129] See ACCC (2021b) and Productivity Commission (2021). NWC (2010) estimated benefits of $220 million in 2008–2009.

[130] ACCC (2021b).

[131] See Byrnes (2013) and Productivity Commission (2011, 2021).

[132] Porcher and Saussier (2018).

[133] See Wallsten and Kosec (2008).

[134] According to Hanna and McDonald (2021), most of the communities served by private entities were small rural communities and small private facilities such as trailer parks.

assessment.[135] For example, an analysis of the relative performance of community wat
systems in the USA over a six-year period found no evidence to support critics of priva
ownership, nor any comprehensive evidence that private ownership was inherently sup
rior.[136] However, other surveys of private participation in the USA and European countri
have generally found that private providers are generally associated with higher prices,[
and, in the USA, less affordability for low-income families.[138] Where it has been trie
privatisation in developing countries has been assessed as of limited success, achievir
neither the scale nor benefits anticipated.[139]

The English Experiment

In this context, the 'English experiment' with privatisation is instructive, given the con
prehensive nature of private sector participation. At the time of privatisation in 198
some commentators were sceptical of the net beneficial impacts of privatisation on ec
nomic welfare, noting that stronger incentives for operating cost efficiencies, and f
reductions in investment costs, might be achieved through compulsory franchising.[140] /
noted above, while water companies have made significant investments in water systen
since privatisation, real average household prices have increased and the overall profi
ability of the industry has increased significantly.[141] In terms of productivity, the eviden
is mixed over time. While there was relatively high annual productivity rates (above 2 p
cent) in the immediate post-privatisation period up until the 2000s, this was followed l
much lower, and in some cases negative, annual growth rates.[142]

One important development in the English model – not anticipated at the time
privatisation – has been the high level of overall gearing (leverage) of the industry. Tl
companies were privatised without debt and with the expectation that they would borro
to fund the substantial capital investment needed. However, since that time, the compani

---

[135] See Carvalho, Marques and Berg (2012) and the references therein.
[136] See Wallsten and Kosec (2005), who conclude: 'Privately-owned systems, on average, comply with drinking water regulations just as well as – and in some cases better than – publicly-owned systems. Consumers do not appear to pay more for water, on average, when served by private systems and may pay a bit less.' Similarly, Beecher and Kalmbach (2013) conclude that rates for non-private systems in the USA which are regulated were generally lower than both the rates charged by unregulated non-private systems and regulated private systems.
[137] See Bel (2020) and Warner (2021). In contrast, Romano, Masserini and Guerrini (2015) find evidence that, on average, in Italy, private water operators do not levy higher prices than do public operators.
[138] See Zhang, González Rivas, Grant and Warner (2021), who examine 500 community water systems in the USA. Critically, they find prices are higher in states where PUCs have adopted specific policies which are seen as favourable to private providers. These include allowing the pass-through of capital improvement costs through distribution system improvement charges or valuing a water system asset above the book value.
[139] See Budds and McGranahan (2003), Mugabi, Kayaga and Njiru (2007) and Estache and Grifell-Tatjé (2013).
[140] See Vickers and Yarrow (1988). See also Byatt (2013), who notes that the initial privatisation of the water companies in England and Wales was unpopular.
[141] Cave and Wright (2021) record that, on average, firms have made returns in excess of their allowed co of capital since privatisation, which is the result of cost savings on some projects, increases in efficien and financial engineering.
[142] Frontier Economics (2017). Saal, Parker and Weyman-Jones (2007) found that the productivity growth rates between 1995 and 2000 (i.e. six to ten years after privatisation) were lower than they had been before privatisation. See also Saal and Parker (2000, 2001).

have borrowed extensively, with some companies having a debt-to-equity (gearing) ratio of 80 per cent. As discussed in Box 16.1, these changes have given rise to a number of regulatory concerns, particularly: about the sustainability of such highly geared financial structures; how they may impact on the incentives of the firms to be innovative; whether they expose customers to greater risk in the event that the company fails; and whether consumers have fully benefited from this riskier type of financial structure.

Three decades on, the merits of privatisation of the English water industry continues to be fiercely debated. While the industry contends that it has delivered 'huge benefits for consumers and the environment',[143] others describe water privatisation as an 'organised rip-off'.[144] Helm (2020) concludes that the performance of the industry has not been 'unambiguously better than that which the public sector might have delivered', noting that 'the current model is unlikely to prove fit for purpose in the future'.

Box 16.1	The cost of capital and the capital structure of water companies in England and Wales

In Chapter 5 we saw that determining an appropriate cost of capital is a central (and often controversial) element of the price regulation process under all forms of price regulation and directly impacts on the revenues that the regulated firm is allowed to recover. An important part of estimating the cost of capital involves taking account of the capital structure of the firm: that is, the relative proportions of debt and equity used to finance the firm's activities, which is reflected in a gearing (or leverage) ratio. In the English and Welsh water industry, there has been some debate over the past decade about whether and how the regulator should account for the high levels of debt relative to equity that are used to finance private water firms. This issue has arisen because of the fact that the average ratio of debt to equity (i.e. gearing or leverage) in the water industry has gone from close to zero at privatisation to around 70 per cent in 2020 (with two companies having gearing levels above 80 per cent).[145] This is sometimes referred to colloquially as the 'dash for debt' or 'flight from equity'.[146]

It is often argued that the regulator should, in theory at least, not be concerned by high levels of gearing, as the average cost of capital should be invariant to the capital structure chosen by the firm. This follows from the well-known work of Modigliani and Miller (1958, 1963), which found that, under certain strong assumptions,[147] any benefit a company obtains from switching to higher levels of gearing in terms of cheaper debt payments is precisely offset by increases in the cost of equity.[148] The relevant insight of this theorem is

---

[143] Water UK (2019).

[144] Financial Times (2017).

[145] Ofwat (2020, 2021b). The average gearing for water-only companies was 71.8 per cent at 31 March 2020, while the gearing for water and wastewater companies was 69.8 per cent. Bortolotti, Cambini, Rondi and Spiegel (2011) examine the phenomenon for other European regulated utilities.

[146] See Helm (2003, 2009). Severn Trent Water and National Grid (2012) record that, in the water industry, borrowing has increased from zero at privatisation to around £35 billion at that time.

[147] Among the most important of these assumptions are that: taxes are neutral and apply equally to all sources of income; there are no bankruptcy costs; and financial markets are perfect.

[148] As the pool of risks is now concentrated over a smaller equity base. See Modigliani and Miller (1958).

that the market value of a firm is *independent* of its capital structure and is determined by its assets, not how those assets are financed, and it follows that the choice between debt and equity financing has no impact on the average cost or availability of capital.[149] However if the restrictive assumptions of the Modigliani–Miller theorem are relaxed, particularly if interest payments on debt are treated as expenses for corporation tax purposes, but no such allowance exists for dividends and capital gains, it may no longer be the case that cost savings associated with increased gearing are completely offset by the increase in the cost of equity.[150] An implication of this is that capital structures *can* impact on the weighted average cost of capital (WACC), although the empirical evidence on this issue is mixed.[151]

The high levels of gearing of water companies in England and Wales has given rise to a recurring question about whether there is a need to regulate the capital structure.[152] The essence of the concern is that high levels of gearing may not be sustainable, and that, if the cost of debt increases, firms would be forced to refinance their activities and may not be able to attract adequate finance to undertake new investments, to the detriment of consumers.[153] While the capital structures have not, to date, been formally regulated,[154] the regulator has focused on the need for companies to be financially resilient.[155]

The high levels of gearing of water companies have also prompted two more specific issues for the water regulator (Ofwat). The first issue is whether the WACC should be estimated based on the *actual* gearing ratios of each company or, alternatively, using a single industry-wide notional gearing ratio. Consistent with other regulated sectors in Britain, the approach to date has been to use a *notional* industry-wide gearing ratio which reflect what it considers necessary to allow the water firms to finance their activities and to invest efficiently. The rationale for using a notional approach is two-fold: first, that companies and investors (not regulators) should be left to determine the appropriate capital structure to finance their activities; and, second, that the approach encourages firms to choose an efficient mix of debt and equity when financing their activities.[156] However, some argue

---

[149] See Myers (2001) for a general survey of the work on capital structure.

[150] See Modigliani and Miller (1963).

[151] Myers (2001) concludes that financing clearly does matter because of taxes, differences in information and agency costs. Wright, Mason, Satchell, *et al.* (2006), using data on regulated businesses in Britain, conclude that, contrary to the Modigliani–Miller (MM) theorem, there is a *negative* relationship between gearing and the cost of equity capital; that is, higher levels of gearing are associated with *lower* costs of equity capital. Similarly, Wright and Mason (2020) argue that: '[R]egulators have for some time now recognised that the MM theory does not actually hold – that the financial structure of a regulated firm matters for value of that firm; and that the gearing of the firm affects its WACC.' In contrast, other work supports the Modigliani–Miller theorem in finding that any tax benefits associated with gearing are largely offset by increases in risk, which raise the cost of debt and equity. See NERA (2002) and Competition Commission (2000).

[152] Jenkinson (2006) examines whether capital structures should be regulated or not.

[153] See Mason and Wright (2021), who discuss this in the context of a mismatch between the private and social costs of financial distress (an externality). See also CCWater (2011), Severn Trent Water and National Grid (2012) and Cox (2013).

[154] A licence-based gearing 'cap' has to some degree been applied in the UK aviation sector.

[155] Ofwat (2021b).

[156] See Mason and Wright (2021), who argue that 'there are (at least) two problems with this stance'; first, the capital structure decisions are not left entirely to the management of regulated firms, and there are various conditions in place which may constrain managerial choices, and even if the *level* of gearing is not a concern, the *treatment* of gearing is.

that this stance creates incentives for companies to 'gear up' above the notional gearing level set by the regulator in an attempt to obtain a benefit as a result of the actual cost of debt being lower than that assumed by the regulator when setting the WACC.[157] The second issue is whether any financial gains associated with the highly geared structure should be shared with customers or not. As part of its 2019 price review, the regulator introduced a mechanism which required highly geared water companies (above 70 per cent) to share the benefits of higher gearing with customers. The rationale for this so-called 'gearing outperformance sharing mechanism' (GOSM) was two-fold. First, equity investors were benefiting from the higher equity returns that are associated with their increased risk, but were not passing on these benefits to customers. Second, by adopting high levels of gearing, companies reduce their financial resilience and transfer some risk to customers (and potentially taxpayers) in the event that a company fails. Whereas the GOSM was rejected on appeal for four companies, it still applies to other water companies.[158]

Private–Public Partnerships and Water Concessions

As described in Section 16.4.1, another form of private participation in the water industry is through concession contracts as part of a private–public partnership.[159] This is the most common form of private sector participation in water and wastewater supply, and is applied in East Asia and the Pacific, Latin America and the Caribbean, and some parts of Europe.[160] According to the World Bank (2022), there have been over 1160 PPPs in the water and sewerage sector over the past three decades across sixty-six countries. The use of PPPs in the water sector has been particularly prominent in China, accounting for around 49 per cent of all agreements between 1994 and 2013.[161]

While the widespread use of concession agreements suggests that they are effective, there is a general perception, particularly in the developing world, that the concession model has achieved mixed results in the water and wastewater industry. Projects that have been cancelled, or are under distress, account for around 17 per cent of the total investments in the water industry over the period 1990 to 2021.[162] In addition, most

---

[157] See CCWater (2011) and PWC (2013). Contrast NERA (2002), who note that this generally assumes that the actual cost of equity remains invariant to the level of gearing.

[158] See CMA (2021b). Among the reasons for rejecting the GOSM was that it would be ineffective either as a benefit-sharing mechanism or as a tool to improve financial resilience. The CMA also noted that the regulator had not adequately evidenced the existence of the benefits from high gearing that it said would be available to share (raising the more general Modigliani–Miller theorem).

[159] Lima, Brochado and Marques (2021) argue that: 'Water company privatisation in the United Kingdom has helped to strengthen PPP projects' dissemination across the water sector as a business model.'

[160] The term 'concession contract' is used in a general way here, and it is recognised that there are various forms that such contracts can take in practice involving different allocations of risk, revenue and obligations being assumed by the private entity. At one extreme, contracts might involve only subcontracting of the management activities (such as billing, maintenance and certain construction activities) to the private firm, with the firm assuming no responsibility for pricing or investment or interacting with customers. At the other extreme, a longer-term concession contract might involve the private firm taking on all the risks associated with the operation of the water and wastewater network over a long period, including interacting with customers, setting pricing and undertaking any necessary investments.

[161] Jensen (2017) notes that PPPs in China are monitored by local government officials under simple contracts.

[162] World Bank (2022). See also John, Mahalingam, Deep and Thillairajan (2015).

surveys of the use of PPPs in the water industry have generally found that they hav
resulted in either no change, or an increase, in price and no real impact on efficiency.
However, PPPs have been associated with improvements in water quality, and in broad
ening access and coverage of the water or wastewater network.[164]

In France, where concession contracts have applied to the water and wastewater indus
try for over a century, the effect of the arrangements has varied over time.[165] Prior to th
early 1990s, it was relatively rare for concession contracts to be open and transparen
giving the incumbent concessionaire an advantage at the expiration of the concessio
and resulting in the same operator being awarded multiple concession contracts ar
facing limited 'competition *for* the market' from new entrants. Since 1993, howeve
water concession contracts have been subject to open tendering procedures, and son
assessments have found that this has resulted in a change in the industry, including low
prices and higher levels of participation in tenders.[166] The issue of only a small numb
of competing bidders participating in tender contests is a general one that arises in
number of jurisdictions, and is seen to limit the benefits associated with a system bas
on competition for the market.[167]

A well-documented failure of concession arrangements in the water and wastewat
industry occurred in Buenos Aires in Argentina. The concession contract (the world
largest of its type) was awarded in 1993, but was cancelled by the government in 200
During this period, coverage of the water and wastewater network did not increase a
required under the agreement,[168] and the average bill for a residential customer increase
by more than 80 per cent in real terms, which, according to some accounts, resulted
the concessionaire becoming one of the most profitable water operators in the world.
Public-private arrangements in the water and wastewater industry have also been intr
duced in other parts of Latin America (including in Bolivia, Brazil, Chile, Colombi

---

[163] See Porcher and Saussier (2018).

[164] See Porcher and Saussier (2018). However, Thillairajan, Mahalingam and Deep (2013) find that, in
the developing world, private sector participation does not on its own have a significant impact on
improvements in access and quality.

[165] There are three general types of management arrangements that apply in France. *Gérance* is a
management arrangement where the private contractor provides services and operates and maintains
the water and sewerage facilities and collects charges on behalf of the municipal authority. In contrast
an *affermage* arrangement is a form of leasing contract where the municipality is responsible for any
investments, but the private contractor bills and collects revenues directly from customers (and where
the price that can be charged is usually part of the competitive tender). A further type of arrangement
is a form of build–operate–transfer (BOT) arrangement, where the private contractor bills customers
directly and is also responsible for any investments. See Allouche and Finger (2002).

[166] The OECD (2004) notes that, in 80–90 per cent of tenders, the existing operator still wins the contract,
but that an average of 2.4 bids is received. Marques (2010) describes the various laws introduced in the
1990s which improved the tendering process, and the transparency of the concession process.

[167] See Estache and Iimi (2011).

[168] However, some accounts emphasise that, during the period of the contract, there was increased
investment and that more than 2 million people gained access to the water service and 1.2 million
people gained access to the sewage networks. This increased access, in turn, improved health outcome
and child mortality for water-related diseases. See Galiani (2022).

[169] See Casarin, Delfino and Delfino (2007) and Galiani (2022). Various factors are seen to have contribute
to the problems encountered, including: several contract renegotiations (which made significant
tariff changes, relaxed the conditions that applied to the operator, and cancelled fines imposed on the
operator for delaying investment); a weak and inexpert regulator (which allowed the concessionaire to
act opportunistically); and predatory state behaviour.

Mexico and Uruguay). However, a considerable number of these arrangements involving concessions have been suspended, or have failed, because of either a failure to attract sufficient (or any) bidders,[170] political interference, or public opposition to substantial tariff hikes once the concession contract was awarded.[171] The frequent renegotiation of concession contracts in Latin American countries has, in some cases, been linked to corruption.[172]

Another high-profile example of a failed water concession agreement occurred in Mali, one of the poorest countries in the world. In the early 2000s, a French consortium was appointed under a twenty-year contract to provide water and sanitation services, overseen by a newly created regulator for the urban water sector. The contract was cancelled within five years, with the failure of the arrangement attributed to factors such as unclear contracts and political interference. Estache and Grifell-Tatjé (2013) suggest that an important factor was the lack of transparency about the potential distribution of gains from the private sector involvement. They found that, although a large number of consumers (particularly in urban areas) benefited through greater access and lower real prices, these gains were not as great as expected and, in addition, poor rural consumers actually suffered.

In Asia, there have also been a number of terminated or suspended contracts, including some large ones. This includes the court-sanctioned cancellation of a twenty–year contract for private water supply in Jakarta (the world's second largest metropolitan area) in 2017. Among the arguments for the cancellation was that the companies deliberately underserviced lower-income consumers to prioritise higher-revenue service to wealthier consumers. However, as Jensen (2017) observes, these arguments do not necessarily reflect a rejection of the PPP model, and in some Asian countries there have been cycles of supportive and restrictive public policy for PPPs. This may, in turn, reflect public perceptions of PPPs, with the public often sceptical of private involvement in the water industry.

An ongoing area of debate is whether external regulatory oversight of public–private contracts can improve their chance of success and reduce the scope for renegotiations. Some argue that such oversight can bring various benefits by: providing a mechanism to address conflicts conveniently; ensuring appropriate handling of complaints by users and customers; protecting the public interest in any renegotiations; and allowing for better, simpler and more transparent contracts.[173] One study found that the existence of a regulatory agency at the time a concession was awarded dramatically reduced the occurrence of subsequent renegotiations.[174] However, the mere existence of an independent regulator may not be a panacea, as the examples of Argentina and Mali above illustrate. The effectiveness of a regulator can depend

---

[170] Foster (2005) notes that the number of bidders for these contracts was fairly limited (with half of the contracts examined attracting only one bidder), and in many contests the bidders have tended to include only a small number of mainly French (but also Spanish and English) companies.

[171] OECD (2009) lists at that time six cancelled contracts in Argentina, two in Bolivia, one in Brazil, one in Chile, three in Colombia and four in Mexico.

[172] See Guasch and Straub (2009).

[173] See Marques (2017, 2018).

[174] See Guasch, Laffont and Straub (2008). This study also concludes that the use of price caps (which are applied to 75 per cent of Latin American concession contracts) led to more renegotiations, and that consideration should be given to the use of a rate of return approach (or a hybrid approach).

on various factors, such as their institutional capacity and expertise, and their ability to control and uphold the terms of a contract while balancing the need to ensure the wider public interest is met.[175]

The Trend towards Re-municipalisation or 'Reverse Privatisation'

Over the past decade there has been increasing interest in what is described as the trend towards re-municipalisation (or reverse privatisation) of the water and wastewater industry in some parts of the world, particularly in Latin America and Europe. According to some accounts, over thirty-seven countries have now re-municipalised water services in 235 cities.[176]

In the USA, around seventy-two municipalities have returned their water operators to public ownership over the past two decades.[177] Although ideological and political opposition to private participation in the water industry has featured to some extent, this shift in ownership has generally been attributed primarily to 'pragmatic' concerns about cost and quality in managing such private contracts.[178]

Elsewhere in the world, the trend towards re-municipalisation has also been driven by cost concerns, as well as by other factors, including concerns in some countries that corruption may have led to higher prices.[179] Political and ideological opposition has generally featured more prominently in the debates about ownership in countries outside the USA, often involving protests and online petitions for change.[180] Some commentators argue that calls for re-municipalisation may be misplaced, and that state ownership does not of itself address concerns about affordability and investment. Rather, the debate needs to focus less on ownership and more on regulation and measures to ensure water affordability.[181]

16.4.2 Using Water Markets to Discover the 'Value' of Water

One stage in the water supply process where some form of market has developed in some jurisdictions is in the 'upstream' activities associated with the abstraction and wholesale supply of raw and potable water to large users and to retail customers. As discussed in Section 12.1.4, this includes the physical trading or transfer of raw water between operators, as well as the trading of rights or licences to abstract water among different potential users. An important benefit of allowing for wholesale water trading is that can place a 'value' on water, and allow for the allocation of water to those who value

---

[175] Jensen and Wu (2017) use the example of a water and sanitation concession contract in Manila to illustrate potential tensions that a regulator faces in its roles in upholding and enforcing the contract, on the one hand, and defending the public interest, on the other.

[176] Kishimoto, Lobina and Petitjean (2015).

[177] Hanna and McDonald (2021). Warner (2021) notes that this is not necessarily a growing trend when considered over a longer time horizon.

[178] See Hanna and McDonald (2021).

[179] Hall, Lobina and Terhorst (2013) examine the cases of Paris and Grenoble. See also Bel (2020).

[180] See the re-municipalisation movements in: Colombia, Germany, Italy, Uruguay, Bulgaria and Spain. Protests about water industry privatisation have occurred in Latin America (Bolivia, Chile), Africa (Mali, Niger, South Africa and Tanzania) and India.

[181] See Zhang, González Rivas, Grant and Warner (2021) and Bel (2020).

most highly.[182] Ensuring that water is allocated to users who need or value it most is seen as increasingly important, given expectations of greater water scarcity and droughts in many parts of the world as a result of climate change.

In most jurisdictions, the current situation is that the value of the rights or licences to abstract water are set administratively, and are typically based on the management or regulatory costs associated with managing withdrawals. As such, these abstraction rights do not reflect the economic 'value' of water.[183] This results in a situation where the 'cost' of abstraction does not reflect the relative scarcity of water at the different points at which it is being abstracted, and can contribute to a situation where water is being over-abstracted in some catchments (because it is undervalued), raising issues about long-term sustainability.

Formal water markets have been introduced in some jurisdictions to address this issue. Such markets exist in some states in the USA, Australia and Chile.[184] In Chile, a system of water rights was established in 1981, and trading has historically involved trading between farmers in some areas, but has also included trading with urban water companies.[185] In Australia, the introduction of a national water market and the development of trading arrangements for water rights is more comprehensive in scale, and is focused on trading both in small unconnected water markets, as well as in large trading areas such as the Murray–Darling Basin.[186] Participants in trading include users, such as irrigators, farmers, rural and urban water utilities and industry, as well as intermediaries, such as water brokers. In California, the arrangements are organised by the government, and involve the development of 'water banks', whereby the 'bank' purchases a certain amount of water in specific areas at an administratively set price and then sells it on to agricultural users and, in some cases, urban water companies which need additional water.

In addition to these 'formal' established water markets, there are, of course, various 'informal' ways in which water is traded or shared among different abstractors around the world, notably farmers and other agricultural users.

The Experience of Formal Water Markets

In the small number of jurisdictions where formal water markets have been introduced, there is some evidence of benefits associated with the reallocation of raw water from low-value to high-value users. In Australia, assessments have generally identified significant benefits for individual users and communities associated with the ability to trade water between low-value and high-value users, particularly for the dairy industry and horticultural businesses, which would not have been able to survive with their seasonal

---

[182] See Yarrow, Appleyard, Decker and Keyworth (2008). For example, it has been estimated that around 80 per cent of water abstractions in OECD countries are for agricultural purposes, but that agricultural users typically place a lower marginal value on water than other potential users. See Hughes, Chinowsky and Strzepek (2010).

[183] See Beecher (2011) and Yarrow, Appleyard, Decker and Keyworth (2008).

[184] An excellent overview of water 'markets' is presented in Wheeler (2021). See also Easter and Huang (2014).

[185] See Simpson and Ringskog (1997) and Bauer (1997).

[186] Which covers four states and the Australian Capital Territory. The possibility to trade water licences in Australia has also existed since the early 1980s in some areas.

allocations.[187] New participants have entered the market, including water companies, env ronmental water holders and investors. There also appears to have been a growth in trad ing over time, and most irrigators have used the water market at some point.[188] Howeve there are differences in the 'southern' and 'northern' parts of the markets, with aroun 80 per cent of trading occurring in the southern market.[189] In addition, various problem have been identified, including the ability to monitor the trading of unregulated water,[1 concerns about the behaviour of unregulated water 'brokers', and the 'flow-on' impacts irrigators selling rights out of the system to other irrigators and farmers. A number deficiencies with the trading arrangements have also been identified, including a lac of rules governing the conduct of market participants, poor-quality information, an concerns that there is insufficient oversight of possible market manipulation and insid trading behaviour.[191] The impacts on the environment are also mixed. While the marke are seen to have brought some environmental benefits by allowing for the recovery water in over-allocated areas, there are concerns that increased volumes of trade hav had some negative environmental impacts (such as erosion and unseasonal high flov during the delivery of water traded downstream).[192] Early assessments have also identifie some social costs including: the ostracisation of farmers for trading in permanent right increased water charges for in-region users as a result of trades occurring out of th region; and reductions in populations and spending in communities that export water.[1

In Chile, where water trading has existed since the early 1980s, a comprehensi assessment of the markets by the World Bank in 1997 concluded that trading had resulte in efficiency gains as well as environmental gains, as farmers who sold rights sometim used the proceeds to invest in water-saving irrigation equipment.[194] However, anoth study, also published in 1997, found that the experience of water trading in Chile w uneven and, in particular, that water markets were fairly inactive due to transaction cos and other obstacles, and that active markets were the exception rather than the rule, ev in desert areas in the north of Chile.[195] Since then water markets have been general assessed as having matured, with increases in transaction frequency, including a partic larly high frequency of transactions during relatively dry years.[196] Hearne (2018) fou that water markets in key river basins in north and central Chile have allowed mines expand by acquiring water rights from farmers. The security of transferable water righ has also allowed for the development of permanent fruit crops that have been sold on t international market. The prices in the water markets appear to be highly variable, a depend on the bargaining ability of buyers and sellers. Most transactions are for relative

---

[187] See Frontier Economics (2007), NWC (2010) and Productivity Commission (2021).
[188] Grafton and Wheeler (2018).
[189] Wheeler and Garrick (2020) and Productivity Commission (2021).
[190] See Grafton and Wheeler (2018). Unregulated water is surface water that cannot be controlled and is captured by downstream irrigators in private dams or off-river storage.
[191] See ACCC (2021b).
[192] Productivity Commission (2021).
[193] Frontier Economics (2007).
[194] Simpson and Ringskog (1997). However, they note that problems have arisen in respect of consumptiv and non-consumptive uses of water. See also Rios and Quiroz (1995).
[195] See Bauer (1997).
[196] See Hearne (2018) and Donoso, Barria, Chadwick and Rivera (2021).

small amounts of water and transaction costs have not been prohibitive. In areas where mining and agricultural users have competed for scarce water, this has led to increased prices.[197] While water markets have resulted in significant gains in trade for both buyers and sellers, not all farmers participate in the market, and there continue to be issues about the political acceptability of such markets.[198] This includes concerns that intense competition for water rights between mining, agricultural and human users may have led to the over-exploitation of water resources in certain areas, such as the Copiapó Basin.[199] There has also been public concern, and an investigation by the competition authority, about the acquisition and control of substantial holdings of water rights by hydroelectric companies, particularly in the Patagonia region. A referendum held in September 2022 sought to amend the constitution to change the status of water rights as private property and to introduce changes to the tradability of water rights (capped at thirty years) and allow regulators to suspend rights that are not being used or if supplies are at risk.

In the USA, there has also been a mixed experience of water trading in the different states in which it has been implemented. In Colorado, the water trading arrangements have, at different points in time, been assessed as fair (although cumbersome) and to have resulted in a significant transfer of water resources from low-value uses, such as agriculture, to higher-value uses, such as industrial and urban customers.[200] More recent assessments have found that, while there is active participation in the market, there are important variations in the transaction costs faced by different types of users, with some studies identifying scale economies and higher transaction costs for water-scarce regions, senior water rights and higher-conflict legal outcomes.[201] In California, the experience of government-organised trading through 'water banks' has been seen as less efficient, and resulted in the government over-purchasing water.[202] The overall level of water trading is also low (at around 4 per cent of agricultural and urban use).[203] However, there is renewed interest in water trading and banking, and in 2020 a new financial product (the Nasdaq Veles California Water Index) was created to track the price of water rights leases and sales transactions across the five largest and most actively traded regions in California.

Can Formal Water Markets Work?

An overarching conclusion that can be drawn from the experience of jurisdictions where formal water markets have been introduced is that the efficacy and performance of the markets depends greatly on the design of the 'rights' and the institutional framework in which such trading takes place.[204] Two aspects are of particular importance to the 'success' of water markets: the size of transaction costs, and the governance and oversight arrangements.

[197] Donoso, Barria, Chadwick and Rivera (2021).
[198] Donoso, Barria, Chadwick and Rivera (2021).
[199] Bitran, Rivera and Villena (2014).
[200] See Counsell and Evans (2005).
[201] See Womble and Hanemann (2020). In addition, Leonard, Costello and Libecap (2019) find that the development of water markets in the USA is 'constrained by political and legal barriers at the local, state, and federal levels that increase the costs of transacting'.
[202] See OECD (2004). See also Anderson and Snyder (1997).
[203] See Ayres, Hanak, Gray, et al. (2021).
[204] Wheeler, Loch, Crase, et al. (2017) argue that the three key institutional factors for water markets are: (1) enabling institutions; (2) facilitating gains from trade; and (3) monitoring and enforcement. Wheeler (2021) uses this framework to assess the readiness of different regions around the world to introduce water markets.

Studies have identified various forms of physical and institutional transaction cost that can reduce the incentives for parties to participate in water markets and can result in mismatches between buyers and sellers.[205] Indeed, studies have estimated that transaction costs can range from 3 to 70 per cent in some water markets.[206] On governance, various surveys have concluded that strong governance and oversight are critical to the performance of water markets. This is because water rights holders need to be confident that water property rights are fair and well defined, that operational rules are being followed and that appropriate measurements and data are being collected.[207] Even in countries such as Chile and Australia with well-established formal markets, there have been ongoing concerns about governance and oversight.[208] Wheeler (2021) argues that the widespread introduction of formal water markets is not possible for many countries, in part, because they do not have strong independent water institutions and impartial governance.

16.4.3 Balancing Affordability, Resilience and Conservation in Setting Water Prices

Regardless of the structure or ownership of suppliers, the question of how to price water and wastewater services remains a challenging question confronting regulators in practice. This encompasses issues of the overall price *level* as well as the price *structure* for water services.[209] While water demand is often argued to be relatively price inelastic (given the close connection to human survival), some studies have shown that the demand for water is responsive to price, reflecting the fact that many uses of water are not purely for subsistence.[210] There is also some evidence that the level, and structure, of water tariffs can impact consumption to some degree.[211]

Balancing Multiple Objectives in Setting Water Price Levels
In many countries, water prices are often set at levels that reflect social and political objectives, particularly concerns about affordability. This has generally resulted in relatively low prices for water, which in some places is below the cost of supply.[212] Some argue that this approach to water pricing is consistent with the nature of water as a basic human right, and that water prices should not be set to recover the costs of water services

[205] See Meran, Siehlow and Von Hirschhausen (2021).
[206] See Garrick, Whitten and Coggan (2013).
[207] Wheeler and Garrick (2020) argue that the need for strong property rights and water governance institutions means that formal water markets are unsuitable for economies lacking regulatory capacity.
[208] Grafton and Wheeler (2018) argue that, in Australia, the abolishment of the National Water Commission in 2014 is seen as having left a governance gap. The ACCC (2021b) recommended that a new independent, basin-wide water markets agency be established.
[209] While there is a considerable literature on water price levels and structures, there is very limited work on wastewater pricing. This reflects the fact that such services tend not to be metered and the costs are often recovered through rates or bundled with water services. An exception is Beecher and Gould (2018) who examine the differences between water and wastewater services and the implications that these differences have for pricing and tariff structures.
[210] An early analysis by Noll (2002) presents estimates of elasticity in the range of 0.3 to 0.7, while Reynaud and Romano (2018) refer to meta-analysis estimated mean and median price elasticities equal to 0.365 and 0.291.
[211] See Beecher and Kalmbach (2013).
[212] Mercadier and Brenner (2020) note that, in Argentina, the level and structure of tariffs reflect the national administration's preferences about service cost allocation among stakeholders. This has resulted in revenue below operative expenditure, which has made it difficult for companies to remain financially sustainable.

but to reflect the importance of water services to humans and other societal values.[213] However, while affordability and access are undeniably relevant considerations in setting water prices, it is widely acknowledged that water pricing needs also to reflect a range of considerations, including economic efficiency, ensuring the financial sustainability of water providers and environmental factors.[214] In addition, the need to ensure water systems are resilient to climate change in the future suggests that price levels might need to increase to allow suppliers to recover their costs, and to ensure that water users receive the right signals about the impacts of their consumption patterns on water conservation.

It follows that an important challenge in many countries is balancing these considerations when setting water prices.[215] In Europe, the USA and Australia, policy has gradually moved towards so-called 'full cost' pricing for water services.[216] Although this is interpreted differently across the jurisdictions, in general terms, it seeks to ensure that the overall level of prices charged to consumers is sufficient to ensure the full recovery of the costs associated with providing water services, and that any government transfers or subsidies are made transparent.[217] In the EU, the principle of cost recovery includes the direct costs of water services, as well as environmental and resource costs.[218] The move towards full cost pricing is seen as particularly important for government- or municipal-owned water and wastewater operators, where the level of prices charged for water and wastewater services can sometimes be viewed as a form of taxation rather than as a means to recover the costs associated with supplying the services, with the result that prices can be lower than the full costs associated with supplying the services.

In addition, in many jurisdictions, there is growing recognition of the need for the price of water services to take account of the environmental costs associated with water usage, and to encourage consumers to manage their demand and conserve water. Against this background, there have been calls for the price of water and wastewater services to rise to more accurately reflect the costs of the service and to send signals to consumers that encourage more efficient usage of these services.[219]

Water Price Structures: Access and Affordability, Financial Sustainability and Conservation

While movements towards 'full cost pricing' for water and wastewater services focus on price *levels*, when designing specific water tariff *structures*, utilities and regulators also

---

[213] See Neto and Camkin (2020).

[214] OECD (2010).

[215] The trade-offs between different objectives are considered in Pinto and Marques (2015), Massarutto (2020) and Marques and Miranda (2020).

[216] Rogers, Bhatia and Huber (1999) define full costs as comprising the supply costs (operating expenditure plus capital expenditure) plus the economic costs (including opportunity costs and economic externalities) plus environmental externalities.

[217] The EPA (2013a) in the USA uses the following definition: 'Full cost pricing is usually interpreted to mean factoring all costs – past and future, operations, maintenance and capital costs – into prices.' In Australia, 'cost-reflective' pricing is defined as prices that reflect the full efficient cost of service provision. See Productivity Commission (2021).

[218] Article 9 of the EU Water Framework Directive (2000/160/EC). However, derogations from this principle are possible, for example, in less-favoured areas or to provide basic services at an affordable price.

[219] As Beecher (2011) observes: 'Water utilities may find themselves in the unenviable position of advancing economic efficiency by imposing higher rates that recover costs and send appropriate signals to customers about the value of water services.' At the same time, there is likely to be an ongoing tension between the objectives of keeping water affordable and using water more efficiently.

often seek to balance a number of factors, including: cost recovery, affordability, the pro
motion of efficiency, equity considerations, sustainability and resilience, and politica
acceptability. As described in Section 16.2.2, in jurisdictions where water usage is metered
water tariffs are typically based on a two-part tariff structure comprising a fixed charge
(which does not vary with usage) and a variable component (which does vary with usage).[220]

Three types of tariff structure are typically observed for urban residential water use:
uniform tariff (which involves a fixed charge *plus* a per unit price that is *constant* acros
all levels of consumption); a decreasing block tariff (involving a fixed charge *plus* a per
unit price that *decreases* with higher usage, measured in blocks of consumption); an
an increasing block tariff (involving a fixed charge *plus* a per unit price that *increase*
with higher usage, again measured in blocks of consumption). To the extent to which the
marginal costs of supplying an additional unit of water decreases as the volume of wate
purchased increases, a declining block tariff structure is consistent with an efficient pric
ing structure, as discussed in Chapter 4.[221] However, the use of increasing block tariffs
often favoured as a means to ensure that there is widespread access to water services an
increasingly, as a way of incentivising greater conservation of water.[222]

In Asia and many developing economies, water tariffs are based on an increasir
block tariff structure where the first block, sometimes known as the subsistence bloc
is set below cost (often at zero or very low prices) to make water affordable to very poo
households,[223] and tariffs increase for each block above this level. The rationale for th
structure is that it allows poor households to access a basic level of water service b
forcing rich households (which are assumed to use more water) to cross-subsidise poo
households.[224]

In other jurisdictions, such as developed OECD countries, increasing block tariff stru
tures are being used as a way of encouraging users to conserve water.[225] In some US state
there have been changes to how the variable usage charges are applied, and a movemen
towards increasing block rate tariff structures over time. This shift has, in part, bee
motivated by concerns that the low water tariffs which can result from decreasing bloc
tariffs do not accurately reflect the true 'value of water', and therefore do not encoura:
consumers to conserve it.[226] In addition, some water companies have introduced season

---

[220] Pinto and Marques (2015) and Massarutto (2020) describe the attributes of different tariff structures.
[221] This proposition depends, of course, on what is captured in the measurement of 'costs' and, in particul
whether they reflect the 'full costs' of water supply, including all the environmental and social costs
associated with water production and consumption.
[222] The OECD (2010) records that decreasing block tariffs are now only used in a few OECD countries.
[223] See Boland and Whittington (2000), OECD (2011c) and Meran, Siehlow and Von Hirschhausen (2021).
Oliveira (2008) discusses the use of increasing block tariffs in Brazil, and Whittington (2003) discusses
their use in South Asia.
[224] However, the OECD (2011c) concludes that increasing block tariffs can be regressive in countries
where the water network is incomplete, and the poor do not benefit from the consumption subsidy.
Whittington (2003) finds that the use of increasing block tariffs in South Asia: does not generate
sufficient revenues to ensure that utilities can recover their financial costs; does not send the correct
economic signals to households; and does not help the majority of the poor households. See also
Whittington, Nauges, Fuente and Wu (2015) and Nauges and Whittington (2017).
[225] See Rubin (2010) and Beecher (2011).
[226] Beecher, Mann, Hegazy and Stanford (1994) provide an excellent overview of the arguments for and
against conservation pricing.

rates, 'excess-use' rates or other forms of 'customer-specific' rates, which are based on an increasing block tariff structure.[227] Empirically, there is some evidence to suggest that customers are responsive to such signals, and that shifting to an increasing block rate structure can reduce average and peak-demand water consumption.[228]

Two design issues arise with the use of increasing block tariffs in the water industry.[229] The first concerns affordability and, in particular, the need for consumption blocks to be designed to take account of factors such as household size, the existence of metering equipment, and the ability of different types of consumers actually to conserve water. In particular, if the first consumption block does not take account of household size, then larger households (which may often be poorer households) may be pushed to pay a higher average price for water.[230] To avoid this, it has been suggested that consumption blocks be tailored to reflect underlying differences in the ability of different groups to pay, and the ability of different groups to conserve water.[231] A second issue with increasing block tariffs is that, by encouraging consumers to conserve water, such tariffs can reduce water sales, which, in the short term, can potentially lead to greater revenue volatility and decreased sales revenue for water utilities. Over time, water utilities may have to increase prices to allow the utility to fully recover their costs.[232] In some states, such as California, this has led to the introduction of revenue adjustment mechanisms that seek to decouple water sales from revenues in order to remove the disincentives for utilities to introduce tariff structures such as increasing block rates.[233]

16.5 CONCLUSION

The water and wastewater industry differs in some important respects from the other industries discussed in this book. The close association between the 'products' supplied and human health, and the considerable externalities associated with supply, mean that issues associated with quality are of particular importance in the industry. Relative to

---

[227] See Rubin (2010) and Beecher (2011).

[228] See, for example, the references in EPA (2009).

[229] In addition, Neto and Camkin (2020) argue that using price structures to change behaviour can be regressive, and that a more appropriate approach is to control 'volumes' by imposing water restrictions as a more equitable way of sharing the burden of water conservation.

[230] See Dahan and Nisan (2007) and Rubin (2010).

[231] See EPA (2009). In California, customer block and tier levels have been set by utilities according to specific regional or customer consumption patterns, and the regulator will examine the impact that the increasing block tariff structure will have on low-income customers. See Rubin (2010) and CPUC (2008).

[232] Revenue volatility can arise because a greater proportion of cost recovery is assigned to the variable usage charge, with a corresponding lower level of revenue coming from the fixed charge component. This makes revenues more dependent on sales volumes. The potential effects of volatility are seen to be greater for small water systems. Beecher, Mann, Hegazy and Stanford (1994) present an early discussion of this potential effect. In addition, Beecher and Chesnutt (2012) point out that reduced sales can also result in excess capacity and stranded assets for water utilities.

[233] Crew and Kahlon (2014) refer to the approach as 'guaranteed return regulation (GRR)' and note that the experience of its use in California is mixed: it did not promote efficiency and provided limited revenue guarantees to water companies. On the general arguments for and against decoupling, and the link to conservation initiatives in the electric industry, see Brennan (2010). Costello (2006) discusses the arguments for and against decoupling in the context of the gas industry, but which are of more general relevance.

other public utility industries, there are also high levels of state ownership and vertical integration, and the prospects for introducing direct competition in the various activities in the supply chain have generally been assessed as limited.

These characteristics of the water and wastewater industry have had significant implications for the regulation of the industry. In a number of jurisdictions, including in some states of the USA and in a number of EU Member States, no separate economic agency regulates the industry. In jurisdictions where restructuring policies have been introduced, considerable diversity can be observed. Indeed, apart from a few isolated examples, policies directed at the vertical separation or 'unbundling' of different activities in the supply chain have not been actively pursued as they have been in other industries. Nor have policies focused on direct competition between providers ('competition *in* the market') been widely introduced, with the notable exception of non-household competition in Britain. Instead, the principal focus has been on the development of various forms of indirect competition, including franchising or 'competition *for* the market', and yardstick or comparative competition. Where pursued, the effects of restructuring policies directed at promoting indirect forms of competition have been mixed. The use of concession contracts is the most common form of private sector participation in the water industry around the world, and, while such arrangements have a long history in some jurisdictions (such as France), the experience in other jurisdictions, particularly developing countries, is variable, and there have been some high-profile failures.

In many parts of the world, there are a number of future challenges facing the water and wastewater industry. Most important among these is increasing the coverage and quality of the water supply and sanitation networks, especially in developing countries. Issues related to sustainability, resilience and the environment (in particular, concern about future water scarcity, given changes in the climate and population growth) also loom large in the industry. Regulators and policy makers in different jurisdictions are considering various ways of addressing these challenges, including: through abstraction rights trading, and markets that establish a value for water; introducing new mechanisms for the direct procurement of large infrastructure projects using competitive tenders; and through the design of tariffs that encourage water conservation.

DISCUSSION QUESTIONS

1. What are some of the distinctive features of the water industry that distinguish from the other public utility industries described in this book (like energy, transport and telecommunications services)?
2. Why have public policies sometimes advocated for the merger or consolidation of water companies? Are these policies supported by the evidence?
3. What are the different forms of regulation that have been applied to the water industry around the world?
4. The most comprehensive restructuring of the water industry has been in England and Wales. What are the key elements of that restructuring, how has regulatory policy evolved over time, and what is the evidence on whether or not the 'English experiment' has been effective?

5. In what activities and areas have policies directed at competition in the water industry been introduced? Have they been effective in fostering a competitive market?

6. Do you agree with the following statement? 'Private participation in water supply should not be allowed, as it increases prices, reduces quality and limits access to water.' Please provide reasons.

7. Should a regulator of a private water company be concerned about capital structure where there is a high level of debt relative to equity (i.e. a high gearing)? Explain your reasons.

8. Would introducing an economic regulator that monitors and oversees a public–private concession agreement increase the chances of that agreement performing effectively?

9. What are some of potential benefits and drawbacks of the introduction of formal water markets? Are they likely to work in all countries?

17

Conclusions

We have covered considerable ground in the preceding pages. Given the breadth of issues and industries reviewed, it is not possible to present an overarching conclusion about how modern economic regulation *does* or *should* operate. However, it is possible to draw out some general themes or insights about modern economic regulation.

17.1 RATIONALES FOR, AND ALTERNATIVES TO, REGULATION

Understanding the rationales for regulation of an industry, or the activities within an industry, is critical to the design of regulatory policy, and to the assessment of the relative benefits and costs associated with alternative regulatory policies and strategies. It is also necessary to assess whether regulation is achieving its desired aims, or whether it has become disproportionately complex and cumbersome relative to the specific problem(s) it is intended to address, or has led to unforeseen adverse consequences. The need to understand *why* we regulate certain industries is of particular importance as competition develops, and competitive pressures start to perform the function that price and conduct regulation is intended (in part) to emulate.

However, as we have seen, there are elements of controversy surrounding the rationales for economic regulation. For example, while a conventional rationale for regulation is to achieve optimal or efficient outcomes in industries with natural monopoly characteristics, it is widely recognised that this aspiration is complicated in practice by issues such as asymmetric information, imperfect regulation and the limited tools at the disposal of a regulator to achieve such aims. It is also complicated by the need for regulators to take into account social considerations, such as fairness and affordability, which can affect their ability to establish efficient pricing structures. Further, as we saw in Chapter 2, there are other accounts for regulation that do not rely on the conventional natural monopoly rationale. These alternative accounts each imply different strategies for controlling and influencing the behaviour of firms. For example, if regulation is conceived of as a mechanism for administering a long-term regulatory contract between consumers and producers of certain services, this has implications for regulation, and implies a focus on the reasonableness of any agreed settlement, rather than on the efficiency of such a settlement.

A separate question involves how the objectives of regulation (however conceived) are best met. Chapter 3 considered the possibilities for achieving particular policy objectives through strategies other than traditional *ex ante* price, conduct and entry regulation.

635

As we have seen throughout the book, many of these alternatives to traditional *ex ant* regulation are actively used around the world, including the use of competition *for* th market (in the form of concessions or franchises), negotiated settlement-type approaches policies directed at the 'deregulation' of certain activities in the supply chain and, at th other end of the spectrum, state ownership. However, as we have also seen, each of thes alternatives to traditional regulation can raise its own challenges. For example, conces sion contracts have sometimes been plagued by difficulties relating to the competitive ness of the bidding process, contract design and frequent renegotiation of the contrac once awarded. These problems appear to have been particularly pronounced in develop ing countries, which has had implications for development and access to basic service (water and sanitation, transport and energy). Similarly, while policies to restructure publi utility industries, and introduce competition in some activities, have been implemente in many jurisdictions over the past four decades, the development of competitive activ ities has often proven challenging in practice, leading some to conclude that regulatin for competition is a more difficult task than the regulation of monopoly. Negotiated set tlement-type approaches, which offer much potential as an alternative to the traditiona regulatory process, can also face challenges, particularly in ensuring that all views ar adequately represented in the process. Finally, while state ownership of the public util ities is still prevalent across many jurisdictions, this form of control is increasingly bein supplemented by price and conduct regulation applied by an independent regulator authority. In sum, while many of the alternatives to standard price, conduct and entr regulation exist, they can raise their own challenges, and their suitability as an alterna tive to traditional regulation can depend on how these challenges are addressed.

17.2 LINKING REGULATORY THEORY AND PRACTICE

While this book has highlighted the interaction between theoretical principles and regu latory practice where possible (particularly through the use of boxes in Part III whic illustrate specific areas of interaction), readers may, at times, have sensed a degree of di connect between the principles of regulation developed in the analytical work describe in Part II of this book and the real-world regulatory settings described in Part III. In par this is inevitable. Many of the high-level principles of regulation have been develope using abstract analytical frameworks, which employ unrealistic assumptions to make th analysis tractable and the conclusions generalisable. In practice, regulators often hav limited tools at their disposal, can face difficult information conditions, and are gener ally subject to political constraints. We saw, for example, how many models for pricin of core network activities assume perfect information, or an ability for the regulator make transfer payments when, in practice, there is generally a substantial informatio asymmetry between regulators and the firms they regulate, and regulators typically d not have powers to make transfer payments.

It would, nevertheless, be inaccurate to conclude that the 'theory' of regulatio described in Part II of this book is of marginal relevance to the 'practice' of regulatio described in Part III. At a minimum, analytical models, and the principles they establis are important for clarifying various key concepts (such as different cost categories, an the notion of economic efficiency) and for allowing practitioners to identify relevant trade-offs between the likely effects of different types of regulatory strategies. We saw, for example, that rate of return regulation and price cap regulation can be conceived of as different forms of long-term contract, each of which can have different impacts on the behaviour of firms in the context of asymmetric information, and therefore different impacts on economic welfare. Similarly, in terms of pricing policies, we saw how different pricing approaches can create trade-offs between the attainment of economic efficiency and the other objectives of a government. Thus, Ramsey–Boiteux pricing, which has long been seen as the most efficient method for setting prices in the public utility industries, insofar as it minimises the distortions to allocative efficiency while allowing firms to cover all of their costs, has not been widely adopted in practice, in part, because of distributive concerns. While the merits of this outcome are open to debate, the policy maker or regulator has been presented with a clear trade-off on which to base their decision.

While regulatory theory has been important in terms of clarifying concepts and highlighting trade-offs, some parts of this work have also been highly influential in the development of specific regulatory policies and strategies. For example, as discussed in Chapter 5, the early work on the impact of the regulatory lag in rate of return regulation showed how the presence of a 'lag' could create incentives for regulated firms in terms of cost reduction. This insight was influential in the design of later fixed-period price control arrangements. Similarly, work on 'mechanism design', particularly in the 1980s and 1990s, has arguably been influential in terms of conceiving of the modern regulatory task as involving a trade-off between incentives and rent extraction, and in the design of policies that seek to address the information advantage that regulated firms hold. Likewise, theoretical developments in relation to 'two-way' access pricing principles discussed in Chapter 6 have featured in regulatory debates and proceedings across a number of jurisdictions; in particular, whether regulation is necessary in settings where networks compete for subscribers (i.e. competitive bottlenecks), and when considering the implications of adopting a 'bill and keep' approach to reciprocal access pricing. Similarly, theoretical work on multi-sided markets and network externalities has directly influenced regulation of the payments industry, and features prominently in discussions on the need for, and approach to, regulation of digital platforms. As we saw in Chapter 7, the work of researchers in behavioural economics is also having an important impact on regulatory practice in some jurisdictions.

Given the essential nature of the products and services discussed in this book, economic regulation will remain an active, and often controversial, area of public policy and academic inquiry. Fortunately, in confronting its task, the modern economic regulator can draw on an ever-expanding body of theory and insights about the impacts that different regulatory policies and strategies have had in practice.

Cases and Legislation

EUROPE

European Cases

Case C-280/08: *Deutsche Telekom AG v. Commission of the European Communities* (2010), ECR 2010 I-09555

Case C-424/07: *European Commission v. Federal Republic of Germany* (2009), ECR 2009 I-11431

Case C-202/07P: *France Télécom v. Commission* (2009), ECR 2009 I-02369

Case T-271/03: *Deutsche Telekom v. Commission* (2008), ECR 2008 II-477

Case C-18/88: *Régie des télégraphes et des téléphones v. GB-Inno-BM SA* (1991), ECR I-05941

Cases 6/73 and 7/73: *Commercial Solvents* (1974), ECR 223

EC Regulations and Directives

Regulation of the European Parliament and of the Council of 14 September 2022 on Contestable and Fair Markets in the Digital Sector and Amending Directives (EU) 2019/1937 and (EU) 2020/1828 (Digital Markets Act) (Regulation 2022/1925)

Regulation of the European Parliament and of the Council of 20 June 2019 on Promoting Fairness and Transparency for Business Users of Online Intermediation Services (Regulation 2019/1150)

Directive of the European Parliament and of the Council of 5 June 2019 on Common Rules for the Internal Market for Electricity and Amending Directive 2012/27/EU (Directive 2019/944)

Regulation of the European Parliament and of the Council of 5 June 2019 on the Internal Market for Electricity (Regulation 2019/943)

Directive of the European Parliament and of the Council of 11 December 2018 Establishing the European Electronic Communications Code (Directive 2018/1972)

Regulation of the European Parliament and of the Council of 11 December 2018 Establishing the Body of European Regulators for Electronic Communications (BEREC) and the Agency for Support for BEREC (BEREC Office), Amending Regulation (EU) 2015/2120 and Repealing Regulation (EC) No. 1211/2009 (Regulation (EU) 2018/1971)

Regulation of the European Parliament and of the Council of 25 October 2017 Concerning Measures to Safeguard the Security of Gas Supply and Repealing Regulation (EU) No. 994/2010 (Regulation 2017/1938)

Regulation No. 2017/460 of 16 March 2017 Establishing a Network Code on Harmonised Transmission Tariff Structures for Gas (Regulation (EU) 2017/460)

Regulation of 16 March 2017 Establishing a Network Code on Capacity Allocation Mechanisms in Gas Transmission Systems and Repealing Regulation (EU) No. 984/2013 (Regulation 2017/459)

Directive of the European Parliament and of the Council of 14 December 2016 Amending Directive 2012/34/EU as Regards the Opening of the Market for Domestic Passenger Transport Services by Rail and the Governance of the Railway Infrastructure (Directive 2016/2370)

Regulation of the European Parliament and of the Council of 14 December 2016 Amending Regulation (EC) No. 1370/2007 Concerning the Opening of the Market for Domestic Passenger Transport Services by Rail (Regulation 2016/2338)

Regulation of the European Parliament and of the Council of 14 December 2016 Repealing Regulation (EEC) No. 1192/69 of the Council on Common Rules for the Normalisation of the Accounts of Railway Undertakings (Regulation 2016/2337)

Directive of the European Parliament and of the Council of 11 May 2016 on Railway Safety (Directive 2016/798)

Directive of the European Parliament and of the Council of 11 May 2016 on the Interoperability of the Rail System within the European Union (Directive 2016/797)

Regulation of the European Parliament and of the Council of 11 May 2016 on the European Union Agency for Railways and Repealing Regulation (EC) No. 881/2004 (Regulation 2016/796)

Directive of the European Parliament and of the Council of 25 November 2015 on Payment Services in the Internal Market (Directive 2015/2366 – PSD 2)

Regulation of the European Parliament and of the Council of 25 November 2015 Laying Down Measures Concerning Open Internet Access (Regulation 2015/2120)

Regulation of the European Parliament and of the Council of 29 April 2015 on Interchange Fee for Card-Based Payment Transactions (Regulation 2015/751)

Regulation of the European Parliament and of the Council of 30 April 2015 Establishing a Network Code on Interoperability and Data Exchange Rules (Regulation 2015/703)

Regulation of the European Parliament and of the Council of 26 March 2014 Establishing a Network Code on Gas Balancing of Transmission Networks (Regulation 312/2014)

Regulation of the European Parliament and of the Council of 14 October 2013 Establishing a Network Code on Capacity Allocation Mechanism on Gas Transmission Systems (Regulation 984/2013)

Directive 2012/34/EU of the European Parliament and of the Council of 21 November 2012 Establishing a Single European Railway Area (Directive 2012/34/EU)

Regulation of the European Parliament and of the Council of 13 June 2012 on Roaming on Public Mobile Communications Networks within the Union (Regulation 531/2012)

Regulation (EU) No. 994/2010 of the European Parliament and of the Council of 20 October 2010 Concerning Measures to Safeguard Security of Gas Supply (Regulation 994/2010)

Directive of the European Parliament and of the Council of 25 November 2009 Amending Directives 2002/21/EC on a Common Regulatory Framework for Electronic Communication Networks and Services, 2002/19/EC on Access to, and Interconnection of, Electronic Communications Networks and Associated Facilities, and 2002/20/EC on the Authorisation of Electronic Communications Networks and Services (Directive 2009/140/EC)

Regulation of the European Parliament and of the Council of 21 October 2009 Amending Regulation (EC) No. 216/2008 in the Field of Aerodromes, Air Traffic Management and Air Navigation Services and Repealing Directive 2006/23/EC (Regulation 1108/2009)

Regulation (EC) No. 715/2009 of the European Parliament and of the Council of 13 July 2009 on Conditions for Access to the Natural Gas Transmission Networks (Regulation EC 715/2009)

Directive of the European Parliament and of the Council of 13 July 2009 Concerning Common Rules for the Internal Market in Natural Gas (Directive 2009/73/EC)

Directive of the European Parliament and of the Council of 12 July 2009 Concerning Common Rules for the Internal Market in Electricity (Directive 2009/72/EC)

Directive of the European Parliament and of the Council of 11 March 2009 on Airport Charges (Directive 2009/12/EC)

Regulation of the European Parliament and of the Council of 24 September 2008 on Common Rules for the Operation of Air Services in the Community (Recast) (Regulation 1008/2008)

Directive of the European Parliament and of the Council of 13 November 2007 on Payment Services in the Internal Market (Directive 2007/64/EC – PSD 1)

Regulation of the European Parliament and of the Council of 23 October 2007 on Rail Passengers' Rights and Obligations (Regulation (EC) 1371/2007)

Directive of the European Parliament and of the Council of 23 October 2007 on the Certification of Train Drivers Operating Locomotives and Trains on the Railway System in the Community (Directive 2007/59/EC)

Directive of the European Parliament and of the Council of 23 October 2007 Amending Council Directive 91/440/EEC on the Development of the Community's Railways (Directive 2007/58/EC)

Directive of 26 April 2004 Concerning Measures to Safeguard Security of Natural Gas Supply (Directive 2004/67/EC)

Regulation of the European Parliament and of the Council of 10 March 2004 Laying Down the Framework for the Creation of the Single European Sky (the Framework Regulation) (Regulation 549/2004)

Directive of the European Parliament and of the Council of 26 June 2003 Concerning Common Rules for the Internal Market in Natural Gas (Directive 2003/55/EC)

Directive of the European Parliament and of the Council of 26 June 2003 Concerning Common Rules for the Internal Market in Electricity (Directive 2003/54/EC)

Directive of the European Parliament and of the Council of 7 March 2002 on Universal Service and Users' Rights Relating to Electronic Communications Networks and Services ('Universal Service Directive') (Directive 2002/22/EC)

Directive of the European Parliament and of the Council of 7 March 2002 on a Common Regulatory Framework for Electronic Communications Networks and Services ('Framework Directive') (Directive 2002/21/EC)

Directive of the European Parliament and of the Council of 7 March 2002 on the Authorisation of Electronic Communications Networks and Services ('Authorisation Directive') (Directive 2002/20/EC)

Directive of the European Parliament and of the Council of 7 March 2002 on Access to, and Interconnection of, Electronic Communications Networks and Associated Facilities ('Access Directive') (Directive 2002/19/EC)

Directive of the European Parliament and of the Council of 26 February 2001 on the Allocation of Railway Infrastructure Capacity and the Levying of Charges for the Use of Railway Infrastructure and Safety Certification (Directive 2001/14/EC)

Regulation of the European Parliament and of the Council of 18 December 2000 on Unbundled Access to the Local Loop (EC/2887/2000)

Directive of the European Parliament and of the Council of 23 October 2000 Establishing a Framework for Community Action in the Field of Water Policy (Directive 2000/60/EC)

Commission Directive of 23 June 1999 Amending Directive 90/388/EEC in Order to Ensure that Telecommunications Networks and Cable TV Networks Owned by a Single Operator Are Separate Legal Entities (Directive 1999/64/EC)

Directive of the European Parliament and of the Council of 22 June 1998 Concerning Common
  Rules for the Internal Market in Natural Gas (Directive 98/30/EC)
Notice on the Application of the Competition Rules to Access Agreements in the
  Telecommunications Sector (98/C 265/02)
Directive of the European Parliament and of the Council of 30 June 1997 on Interconnection in
  Telecommunications with Regard to Ensuring Universal Service and Interoperability through
  Application of the Principles of Open Network Provision (ONP) (Directive 97/33/EC)
Directive of the European Parliament and of the Council of 19 December 1996 Concerning
  Common Rules for the Internal Market in Electricity (Directive 96/92/EC)
Directive of 15 October 1996 on Access to the Groundhandling Market at Community Airports
  (Directive 96/67/EC)
Directive of 13 March 1996 Amending Directive 90/388/EEC with Regard to the
  Implementation of Full Competition in Telecommunications Markets (Directive 96/19/EC)
Directive of 18 October 1995 Amending Directive 90/388/EEC with Regard to the Abolition
  of the Restrictions on the Use of Cable Television Networks for the Provision of Already
  Liberalised Telecommunications Services (Directive 95/51/EC)
Regulation of 23 July 1992 on Licensing of Air Carriers (Regulation No. 2407/92)
Commission Directive of 28 June 1990 on Competition in the Markets for Telecommunications
  Services (Directive 90/388/EEC)
Green Paper of 30 June 1987, Towards a Dynamic European Economy: Green Paper on the
  Development of the Common Market for Telecommunications Services and Equipment
  (COM (87) 290 final)

EU Legislation

Treaty on the Functioning of the European Union (Consolidated Version 2012), OJ C326/01
Single European Act 1987

UK

UK Cases

Asda Stores Ld & Ors v. Mastercard Incorporated & Ors (2017), EWHC 93 (Comm) (30 January
  2017)
Albion Water Limited v. Water Services Regulation Authority (2004). Competition Appeal
  Tribunal. Case No. 1046/2/4/04

UK Legislation

Water Act 2014
Water Industry Act 1991
Water Act 1989

USA

Federal Cases

Ohio et al. v. American Express Co. et al., No. 16–1454 (2018)
In re Payment Card Interchange Fee and Merchant Discount Antitrust Litigation, 2006 WL
  2038650 (E.D.N.Y. 2006)

United States v. Visa U.S.A., Inc., 344 F.3d 229 (2d Cir. 2003), aff'g, 163 F. Supp. 2d. 322 (S.D.N.Y. 2001) and cert. denied, 543 U.S. 811 (2004)

Verizon Communications, Inc. v. Law Offices of Curtis V. Trinko LLP, 540 US 398 (2004)

Verizon Communications, Inc. v. FCC, 122 S. Ct. 1646, 1655 (2002)

United States v. Visa USA, Inc., 163 F. Supp. 2d 322 (S.D.N.Y. 2001)

AT&T Corp. et al. v. Iowa Utilities Board et al., 525 US 366, 371, 119 S. Ct. 721 (1999)

Duquesne Light Co. v. Barasch, 488 U.S. 299, 310 (1989)

National Bancard Corp. (NaBanco) v. Visa U.S.A. Inc., 13 596 F. Supp. at 1231 (1984)

United States v. AT&T, 552 F. Supp. 131 (D.D.C. 1982)

Phillips Petroleum Co. v. Wisconsin, 347 US 672 [1954]

FPC v. Hope Natural Gas Co., 320 US 591 (1944)

Bluefield Water Works and Improvement Co. v. Public Service Commission of West Virginia, 262 US 679 (1923)

State of Missouri ex. rel. Southwestern Bell Telephone Co. v. Public Service Commission of Missouri, et al., 262 U.S. 276 (1923)

United States v. Terminal Road Association, 224 US 383 [1912]

Smyth v. Ames, 169 US 466 (1898)

US Legislation

Bill proposing The Ending Platforms Monopolies Act (2021)

Bill in support of the American Innovation and Choice Online Act (2021)

Bill in support of Augmenting Compatibility and Competition by Enabling Service Switching Act (2021)

Bill in support of Augmenting Compatibility and Competition by Enabling Service Switching Act (2021)

Bill in support of Algorithmic Justice and Online Platform Transparency Act which also would provide a right to Data Portability (2021)

Water Conservation Act 2009 – California

Energy Policy Act 2005

Telecommunications Act 1996

Public Utilities Regulatory Policies Act (PURPA) 1978

Airline Deregulation Act 1978

All-Cargo Deregulation Statute 1977

Administrative Procedures Act (APA) 1946

Federal Power Act 1935

Federal Communications Act 1934

Federal Water Power Act 1920

Sherman Act 1890

AUSTRALIA, CANADA, GERMANY AND NEW ZEALAND

Australian Cases

Australian Competition and Consumer Commission v. Telstra Corporation Limited (2010), FCA 790 (28 July 2010)

Australian Legislation

Competition and Consumer Act 2010

News Media and Digital Platforms Mandatory Bargaining Code Act (2021)

Canadian Legislation

Canadian Payments Act 1985

German Legislation

Gesetz zur Änderung des Gesetzes gegen Wettbewerbsbeschränkungen für ein fokussiertes, proaktives und digitales Wettbewerbsrecht 4.0 und anderer Bestimmungen (GWB-Digitalisierungsgesetz). 18 January 2021

New Zealand Cases

Clear Communications Ltd v. Telecom Corporation of New Zealand Ltd (1993), 5 TCLR 413

New Zealand Legislation

Telecommunications Act 2001
Commerce Act 1986

References

AAPSS, 1914. 'State Regulation of the Public Utilities.' *Annals of the American Academy of Political and Social Science* 53(spec. issue 1):1–346.

Abada, I. and O. Massol, 2011. 'Security of Supply and Retail Competition in the European Gas Market: Some Model Based Insights.' *Energy Policy* 39:4077–4088

Abate, M., 2016. 'Economic Effects of Air Transport Market Liberalization in Africa.' *Transportation Research, Part A: Policy and Practice* 92, 326–337

Abate, M. and P. Christidis, 2020. 'The Impact of Air Transport Market Liberalization: Evidence from EU's External Aviation Policy.' *Economics of Transportation* 22:100164

Abbott, M. and B. Cohen, 2009. 'Productivity and Efficiency in the Water Industry.' *Utilities Policy* 17:233–244

——2011. 'Competition in Urban Water and Sewage: The Case of Sydney, Australia.' *Urban Policy and Research* 29:167–181

——2017. 'Vertical Integration, Separation in the Rail Industry: A Survey of Empirical Studies on Efficiency.' *European Journal of Transport and Infrastructure Research* 17(2):207–224

Abbott, M., B. Cohen and W. C. Wang, 2012. 'The Performance of the Urban Water and Wastewater Sectors in Australia.' *Utilities Policy* 20:52–63

Abel, J. R., 2000. 'The Performance of the State Telecommunications Industry under Price Cap Regulation: An Assessment of the Empirical Evidence.' National Regulatory Research Institute, Working Paper NRRI 00-14. September

Abel, J. R. and M. E. Clements, 2001. 'Entry under Asymmetric Regulation.' *Review of Industrial Organization* 19:227–242

Abito, J. M., J. S. Han, J.-F. Houde and A. A. van Benthem, 2021. 'Agency Frictions and Procurement: New Evidence from U.S. Electricity Restructuring.' Working Paper. 2 September

Abramowitz, A. D. and S. M. Brown, 1993. 'Market Share and Price Determination in the Contemporary Airline Industry.' *Review of Industrial Organization* 8(4):419–433

Abrardi, L. and C. Cambini, 2019. 'Ultra-Fast Broadband Investment and Adoption: A Survey.' *Telecommunications Policy* 43(3):183–198

Abrardi, L., C. Cambini and S. Hoernig, 2021. 'I Don't Care about Cookies! Platform Data Disclosure and Time-Inconsistent Users.' Working Paper. 16 March

Abrardi, L., C. Carlo and R. Laura, 2018. 'The Impact of Regulation on Utilities' Investments: A Survey and New Evidence from the Energy Industry.' *De Economist* 166(1):41–62

ACCC, 2005. 'Optus's Undertaking with Respect to the Supply of Its Domestic GSM Terminating Access (DGTA) Service.' December

——2007. 'Access Dispute between Services Sydney Pty Ltd and Sydney Water Corporation.' Arbitration Report. 19 July

——2009a. 'Domestic Mobile Terminating Access Service Pricing Principles Determination and Indicative Prices for the Period 1 January 2009 to 31 December 2011.' March

——2009b. 'Pricing Principles and Indicative Prices for LCS, WLR, PSTN, OTA, ULLS, LSS: 1 August 2009 to 31 December 2010.' December

——2012a. 'Infrastructure: Why, When and How to Regulate.' Speech by Rod Sims at SMART Facility, 23 February

——2012b. 'Benchmarking Opex and Capex in Energy Networks.' Working Paper No. 6. May

——2013. 'Submission to Productivity Commission Review of the National Access Regime Issue Paper.' February

——2016. 'Inquiry into the East Coast Gas Market.' April

——2018a. 'Retail Electricity Pricing Inquiry – Final Report.' June

——2018b. 'Productivity Commission Inquiry into the Economic Regulation of Airports ACCC Submission in Response to the Issues Paper.' September

——2019. 'Digital Platforms Inquiry.' Final Report. June

——2020. 'Airline Competition in Australia.' September

——2021a. 'State of the Energy Market 2021.' Final Report

——2021b. 'Murray–Darling Basin Water Markets Inquiry.' Final Report. March

——2021c. 'Airport Monitoring Report 2019–20.' March

ACCC/RBA, 2000. 'Debit and Credit Card Schemes in Australia: A Study of Interchange Fees and Access.' Reserve Bank of Australia, Sydney. October

ACER, 2020. 'The Internal Gas Market in Europe: The Role of Transmission Tariffs.' 6 April

——2021. 'ACER's Preliminary Assessment of Europe's High Energy Prices and the Current Wholesale Electricity Market Design.' November

ACER/CEER, 2014. 'Annual Report on the Results of Monitoring the Internal Electricity and Natural Gas Markets in 2013.' October

——2021a. 'Annual Report on the Results of Monitoring the Internal Electricity and Natural Gas Markets in 2020. Energy Retail Markets and Consumer Protection Volume.' November

——2021b. 'Annual Report on the Results of Monitoring the Internal Electricity and Natural Gas Markets in 2020. Gas Wholesale Markets Volume.' July

ACI, 2017. 'Airport Ownership, Economic Regulation and Financial Performance.' Policy Brief

——2018. 'Behind the Regulatory Till Debate.' Report

ACI, IATA and Worldwide Airport Coordinators Group, 2020. 'Worldwide Airport Slot Guidelines (WASG).' 1 April

Acton, J. P and I. Vogelsang, 1989. 'Introduction to Symposium on Price Cap Regulation.' *RAND Journal of Economics* 20:369–372

Acworth, W. M, 1904. *The Elements of Railway Economics*. Oxford: Clarendon Press

Adams, C. F., 1878. *Railroads: Their Origin and Problems*. New York: G.P. Putnam's Sons

Adelowo. J and M. Bohland, 2023. 'Redesigning Automated Market Power Mitigation in Electricity Markets' Ifo Working Papers 387/2022

Adib, P., E. Schubert and S. Oren, 2008. 'Resource Adequacy: Alternative Perspectives and Divergent Paths.' In F. P. Sioshansi (ed.), *Competitive Electricity Markets: Design, Implementation and Performance*. Amsterdam: Elsevier

Adler, N., E. Hanany and S. Proost, 2018. 'Introducing Competition through Auctions in the Air Traffic Control Market.' *Perspective* 6:7

AEMC, 2008. 'Review of the Effectiveness of Competition in Electricity and Gas Retail Markets in Victoria.' 29 February

——2013. 'Review of Competition in the Retail Electricity and Natural Gas Markets in New South Wales.' Draft Report. 23 May

——2016a. 'Retail Competition Review.' Final Report, 30 June

——2016b. 'East Coast Wholesale Gas Markets and Pipeline Frameworks Review.' 23 May

——2022. 'Review into Extending the Regulatory Frameworks to Hydrogen and Renewable Gases.' Draft Report. 31 March

AER, 2021. 'State of the Energy Market 2021.' Australian Government

Affeldt, P. and R. Kesler, 2021. 'Big Tech Acquisitions – towards Empirical Evidence.' *Journal of European Competition Law and Practice* 12(6):471–478

Affuso, L. and D. M. Newbery, 2002. 'The Impact of Structural and Contractual Arrangements on a Vertically Separated Railway.' *Economic and Social Review* 33(1):83–92

AFP, 2015. 'Payments Cost Benchmarking Survey.' Report of Survey Results

African Development Bank, 2015. 'Rail Infrastructure in Africa Financing Policy Options.' Report. Côte d'Ivoire

——2021. 'Electricity Regulation Index (ERI) for Africa.' Report. Côte d'Ivoire

Agarwal, S., S. Chomsisengphet, N. Mahoney and J. Stroebel, 2015. 'Regulating Consumer Financial Products: Evidence from Credit Cards.' *Quarterly Journal of Economics* 130(1):111–164

Agarwal, S, A Presbitero, A.F. Silva, and C Wix, 2023. 'Who Pays For Your Rewards? Redistribution in the Credit Card Market,' Federal Reserve Discussion Paper Series 2023-007.

Aggarwal, S. 2018. 'America's Utility of the Future Forms Around Performance Based Regulation.' Energy Innovation, Policy and Technology Blog. 7 May

Aghion, P., N. Bloom, R. Blundell, R. Griffith and P. Howitt, 2005. 'Competition and Innovation: An Inverted-U Relationship.' *Quarterly Journal of Economics* 2:701–728

Ai, C., S. Martinez and D. E. M. Sappington, 2004. 'Incentive Regulation and Telecommunications Service Quality.' *Journal of Regulatory Economics* 26:263–285

Ai, C. and D. E. M. Sappington, 2002. 'The Impact of State Incentive Regulation on the US Telecommunications Industry.' *Journal of Regulatory Economics* 22:133–160

——2005. 'Reviewing the Impact of Incentive Regulation on U.S. Telephone Service Quality.' *Utilities Policy* 13(3):201–210

Airbus, 2018. 'Airbus Average 2018 Average List Prices.' Airbus Media Relations

Airport Research Center, 2009. 'Study on the Impact of Directive 96/67/EC on Ground Handling Services 1996–2007.' Final Report for European Commission. February

Ajayi, V. and T. Weyman-Jones, 2021. 'State-Level Electricity Generation Efficiency: Do Restructuring and Regulatory Institutions Matter in the US?' *Energy Economics* 104:105650

Ajodhia, V., T. Kristiansen, K. Petrov and G. C. Scarsi, 2006. 'Total Cost Efficiency Analysis for Regulatory Purposes: Statement of the Problem and Two European Case Studies.' *Competition and Regulation in Network Industries* 1(2):263–286

Akerlof, G. A. and R. J. Shiller, 2015. *Phishing for Phools*. Princeton, NJ: Princeton University Press

Alabama Public Service Commission, 2013. 'Telephone Tips'

Alesina, A. and G. Tabellini, 2007. 'Bureaucrats or Politicians? Part I: A Single Policy Task.' *American Economic Review* 97:169–179

Alexander, D. L. and R. M. Feinberg, 2004. 'Entry in Local Telecommunication Markets.' *Review of Industrial Organization* 25:107–127

Alexandersson, G. 2010. 'The Accidental Deregulation. Essays on Reforms in the Swedish, Bus and Railway Industries 1979–2009.' Doctoral Thesis. Stockholm School of Economics

Alexiadis, P. and C. M. da Silva Pereira Neto, 2019. 'Competing Architectures for Regulatory and Competition Law Governance.' Robert Schuman Centre for Advanced Studies Research Paper

Allcott, H., L. Braghieri, S. Eichmeyer and M. Gentzkow, 2020. 'The Welfare Effects of Social Media.' *American Economic Review* 110(3):629–676

Allouche, J. and M. Finger, 2002. *Water Privatisation: Transnational Corporations and the Re-regulation of the Global Water Industry*. London: Taylor & Francis

Al-Najjar, N., S. Baliga and D. Besanko, 2008. 'Market Forces Meet Behavioral Biases: Cost Misallocation and Irrational Pricing.' *RAND Journal of Economics* 39(1):214–237

Al-Sunaidy, A. and R. Green, 2006. 'Electricity Deregulation in OECD (Organisation for Economic Cooperation and Development) Countries.' *Energy* 31:769–787

Alter, A., 2017. *Irresistible: The Rise of Addictive Technology and the Business of Keeping Us Hooked.* New York: Penguin

Alvarez, P. and B. Steele, 2017. 'Price-Cap Electric Ratemaking: Does It Merit Consideration?' *Electricity Journal* 30(8):1–7

Analysys Mason, 2022. 'The Impact of Tech Companies' Network Investment on the Economics of Broadband ISPs.' A Report for Incompas

Anciaes, P., P. Metcalfe, C. Heywood and R. Sheldon, 2019. 'The Impact of Fare Complexity on Rail Demand.' *Transportation Research, Part A: Policy and Practice* 120:224–238

Anderson, R. D., A. Hollander, J. Monteiro and W. T. Stanbury, 1998. 'Competition Policy and Regulatory Reform in Canada, 1986–1997.' *Review of Industrial Organization* 13:177–20

Anderson, T. L. and P. Snyder, 1997. *Water Markets.* Washington, DC: CATO Institute

Andersson, M. and S. Hultén, 2016. 'Transaction and Transition Costs during the Deregulation of the Swedish Railway Market.' *Research in Transportation Economics* 59:349–357

Ando, A. W. and K. L. Palmer, 1998. 'Getting on the Map: The Political Economy of State-Level Electricity Restructuring.' Resources for the Future Discussion Paper 98–19-REV

Andor, M. A. and K. M. Fels, 2018. 'Behavioral Economics and Energy Conservation – A Systematic Review of Non-Price Interventions and Their Causal Effects.' *Ecological Economics* 148:178–210

Andrés, L. A., J. L. Guasch, T. Haven and V. Foster, 2008. *The Impact of Private Sector Participation in Infrastructure: Lights, Shadows, and the Road Ahead.* Washington, DC: World Bank

ANJIE, 2020. 'Anti-Monopoly Guidelines for the Platform Economy Industries.' Note

Arano, K. G. and B. F. Blair, 2008. 'An Ex-Post Welfare Analysis of Natural Gas Regulation in the Industrial Sector.' *Energy Economics* 30:789–806

Arblaster, M., 2014. 'The Design of Light-Handed Regulation of Airports: Lessons from Experience in Australia and New Zealand.' *Journal of Air Transport Management* 38:27–35

——2016. 'Negotiate–Arbitrate Regulation of Airport Services: Twenty Years of Experience in Australia.' *Journal of Air Transport Management* 51:27–38

——2018. *Air Traffic Management: Economics, Regulation and Governance.* Amsterdam: Elsevier

Arblaster, M. and C. Zhang, 2020. 'Liberalisation of Airport Air Traffic Control: A Case Study of Spain.' *Transport Policy* 91:38–47

——2021. 'Independent or Self-Regulation: An Assessment of Economic Oversight of Air Traffic Management in Australia and New Zealand.' *Utilities Policy* 68:101155

Arcos-Vargas, A., F. Núñez and J. A. Ballesteros, 2017. 'Quality, Remuneration and Regulatory Framework: Some Evidence on the European Electricity Distribution.' *Journal of Regulatory Economics* 51(1):98–118

Ardizzi, G., D. Scalise and G. Sene, 2021. 'Interchange Fee Regulation and Card Payments: A Cross-Country Analysis.' Banca d'Italia Occasional Paper No. 628

Arkes, H. R. and C. Blumer, 1985. 'The Psychology of Sunk Cost.' *Organizational Behavior and Human Decision Processes* 35(1):124–140

Armstrong, M., 1996a. 'Multi-Product Nonlinear Pricing.' *Econometrica* 64:51–75

——1996b. 'Network Interconnection.' Discussion Paper No. 9625. University of Southampton Department of Economics

——1997. 'Competition in Telecommunications.' *Oxford Review of Economic Policy* 13:64–82

——1998. 'Network Interconnection in Telecommunications.' *Economic Journal* 108:545–564

——2000. 'Optimal Multi-Object Auctions.' *Review of Economic Studies* 67(3):455–481

——2002. 'The Theory of Access Pricing and Interconnection.' In M. E. Cave, S. K. Majumdar and I. Vogelsang (eds.), *Handbook of Telecommunications Economics*, Volume 1. Amsterdam: Elsevier

——2006. 'Competition in Two-Sided Markets.' *RAND Journal of Economics* 37:668–691

——2015. 'Search and Ripoff Externalities.' *Review of Industrial Organization* 47(3):273

Armstrong, M., S. Cowan and J. Vickers, 1994. *Regulatory Reform: Economic Analysis and British Experience.* Cambridge, MA: MIT Press

Armstrong, M., C. Doyle and J. Vickers, 1996. 'The Access Pricing Problem: A Synthesis.' *Journal of Industrial Economics* 44:131–150

Armstrong, M. and S. Huck, 2010. 'Behavioral Economics as Applied to Firms: A Primer (CESifo Working Paper No. 2937).' *SSRN Electronic Journal* 1553645

Armstrong, M. and D. E. M. Sappington, 2004. 'Toward a Synthesis of Models of Regulatory Policy Design with Limited Information.' *Journal of Regulatory Economics* 26:5–21

——2006. 'Regulation, Competition, and Liberalization.' *Journal of Economic Literature* 44:325–366

——2007. 'Recent Developments in the Theory of Regulation.' In M. Armstrong and R. Porter (eds.), *Handbook of Industrial Organization*, Volume 3. Amsterdam: Elsevier

Armstrong, M. and J. Vickers, 2012. 'Consumer protection and contingent charges'. *Journal of Economic Literature*, 50(2), 477–493

Armstrong, M., J. Vickers and J. Zhou, 2009. 'Prominence and Consumer Search.' *RAND Journal of Economics* 40(2):209–233

Armstrong, M. and J. Wright, 2009. 'Mobile Call Termination.' *Economic Journal* 119:270–307

Armstrong, M. and J. Zhou, 2011. 'Paying for Prominence.' *Economic Journal* 121(556):368–395

Arnbak, J., B. Mitchell, W. Neu, *et al.*, 1994. 'Network Interconnection in the Domain of ONP.' Final Report, November

Arrow, K., 1962. 'Economic Welfare and the Allocation of Resources for Invention.' In *The Rate and Direction of Inventive Activity: Economic and Social Factors.* Princeton, NJ: Princeton University Press, pp. 609–626

Arthur, W. B., 1989. 'Competing Technologies, Increasing Returns, and Lock-In by Historical Events.' *Economic Journal* 99(394):116

Ascari, S., 2011. 'An American Model for the EU Gas Market?' Florence School of Regulation

Asia Financial, 2021. 'China's Massive Telecom and Gigabit Internet Plans Going Well.' 20 March

Assad, S., E. Calvano, G. Calzolari, *et al.*, 2021. 'Autonomous Algorithmic Collusion: Economic Research and Policy Implications.' *Oxford Review of Economic Policy* 37(3):459–478

Assad, S., R. Clark, D. Ershov and L. Xu, 2020. 'Algorithmic Pricing and Competition: Empirical Evidence from the German Retail Gasoline Market (CESifo Working Paper No. 8521).' *SSRN Electronic Journal* 3682021

ATNS, 2021. 'ATNS Corporate Plan 2021/22–2023/24.' Air Traffic and Navigation Services, Johannesburg. 23 February

Auer, R., J. Frost, L. Gambacorta, *et al.*, 2022. 'Central Bank Digital Currencies: Motives, Economic Implications and the Research Frontier.' *Annual Review of Economics* 14:697–721

Ault, R. W. and R. B. Ekelund, 1987. 'The Problem of Unnecessary Originality in Economics.' *Southern Economic Journal* 53:650–661

——2005. 'Telecommunication Reforms in Developing Countries.' *Communications & Strategies* (Special Issue), November, pp. 31–53

Auriol, E., C. Crampes and A. Estache, 2021. *Regulating Public Services: Bridging the Gap between Theory and Practice.* Cambridge: Cambridge University Press

Auriol, E., A. Estache and L. Wren-Lewis, 2018. 'Can Supranational Infrastructure Regulation Compensate for National Institutional Weaknesses?' *Revue Économique* 69(6):913–936

Australian Government, 2021. 'News Media and Digital Platforms Mandatory Bargaining Code Ac

Autoridade da Concorrência, 2009. 'Detailed Analysis of the Liquid Fuel and Bottled Gas Sectors in Portugal.' March

Autorité de la Concurrence, 2011. 'The Autorité de la Concurrence Has Obtained a Substantial Reduction in the Two Main Fees Associated with Payments and Withdrawals from the Groupement des Cartes Bancaires (CB Bank Cards Group).' Press Release. 7 July

Avdasheva, S. and Y. Orlova, 2020. 'Effects of Long-Term Tariff Regulation on Investments under Low Credibility of Rules: Rate-of-Return and Price Cap in Russian Electricity Grid *Energy Policy* 138:111276

Avenali, A., G. Matteucci and P. Reverberi, 2010. 'Dynamic Access Pricing and Investment in Alternative Infrastructures.' *International Journal of Industrial Organization* 28:167–175

Averch, H. and L. L. Johnson, 1962. 'Behavior of the Firm under Regulatory Constraint.' *American Economic Review* 52:1052–1069

Avilés, J. M., 2020. 'A Tale of Two Reforms: Telecommunications Reforms in Mexico.' *Telecommunications Policy* 44(7):101942

Axon, 2022. 'Europe's Internet Ecosystem: Socio-Economic Benefits of a Fairer Balance between Tech Giants and Telecom Operators.' A Report for ETNO. May

Ayres, A., E. Hanak, B. Gray, *et al.*, 2021. 'Improving California's Water Market.' Report. Septembe

Azar, J., M. C. Schmalz and I. Tecu, 2018. 'Anticompetitive Effects of Common Ownership.' *Journal of Finance* 73(4):1513–1565

Bacache, M., M. Bourreau and G. Gaudin, 2014. 'Dynamic Entry and Investment in New Infrastructures: Empirical Evidence from the Fixed Broadband Industry.' *Review of Industrial Organization* 44(2):179–209

Bachmeier, L. J. and J. M. Griffin, 2006. 'Testing for Market Integration: Crude Oil, Coal, and Natural Gas.' *Energy Journal* 27:55–71

Bagnoli, L., Bertomeu-Sanchez, S., Estache, A. and Vagliasindi, M., 2023. 'Does the ownership of utilities matter for social outcomes? A survey of the evidence for developing countrie *Journal of Economic Policy Reform*, 26(1), pp.24–43.

Bailey, E. E. 1981. 'Contestability and the Design of Regulatory and Antitrust Policy.' *America Economic Review* 71:178–183

——1985. 'Airline Deregulation in the United States: The Benefits Provided and the Lessons Learned.' *International Journal of Transport Economics* 12(2):119–144

Bailey, E. E. and R. D. Coleman, 1971. 'The Effect of Lagged Regulation in an Averch–Johnson Model.' *Bell Journal of Economics and Management Science* 2:278–292

Bailey, E. E., D. R. Graham and D. P. Kaplan, 1985. *Deregulating the Airlines.* Cambridge, MA: MIT Press

Bailey, E. E. and J. C. Panzar, 1981. 'The Contestability of Airline Markets during the Transitio to Deregulation.' *Law and Contemporary Problems* 44:125–145

Baldick, R., J. Bushnell, B. F. Hobbs and F. A. Wolak, 2011. 'Optimal Charging Arrangements f Energy Transmission: Final Report.' Report Prepared for the Office of Gas and Electricity Markets. 1 May

Baldick, R., S. S. Oren, E. S. Schubert and K. Anderson, 2021. 'ERCOT: Success (So Far) and Lessons Learned.' In J.-M. Glachant, P. L. Joskow and M. G. Pollitt (eds.), *Handbook on Electricity Markets.* Cheltenham: Edward Elgar

Baldwin, R., M. Cave and M. Lodge, 2012. *Understanding Regulation: Theory, Strategy, and Practice*, 2nd ed. New York: Oxford University Press

Ballance, A., 2006. 'The Regulation of Capex in Water.' *Utilities Policy* 14:234–239

Balza, L., R. Jimenez and J. Mercado, 2013. 'Privatization, Institutional Reform, and Performance in the Latin American Electricity Sector.' IDB Technical Note TN-599. Inter-American Development Bank, Washington, DC

Banerjee, A., 2003. 'Does Incentive Regulation "Cause" Degradation of Retail Telephone Service Quality?' *Information Economics and Policy* 15:243–269

Bank of Canada, 2022. 'Archetypes for a CBDC.' Staff Analytical Note 2022-14. October

Bank of England, 2020. 'Central Bank Digital Currency Opportunities, Challenges and Design.' Discussion Paper. March

Bankes, N. 2019. 'Negotiated Settlements and Just and Reasonable Rates.' ABlawg (University of Calgary, Faculty of Law Blog), 9 January

Baranes, E. and S. J. Savage, 2018. 'Access Prices, Unbundling and Product Variety in European Internet Markets.' *Applied Economics* 50(60):6576–6587

Bardelli, L. and A. Biancardi, 2018. 'Italian Water Regulation: A Changing Scene.' Oxera Agenda. August

Barker, A., 2018. 'Improving Online Disclosures with Behavioural Insights.' OECD Digital Economy Paper. April

Barnes, A. 2018. 'Competitive European Gas Markets Are Reality.' Interview with Euractiv

Baron, D. P., 1988. 'Regulation and Legislative Choice.' *RAND Journal of Economics* 19:467–477

——1989. 'Design of Regulatory Mechanisms and Institutions.' In R. Schmalensee and R. Willig (eds.), *Handbook of Industrial Organization*, Volume 2. Amsterdam: North-Holland

Baron, D. P. and D. Besanko, 1984a. 'Regulation, Asymmetric Information, and Auditing.' *RAND Journal of Economics* 15:447–470

——1984b. 'Regulation and Information in a Continuing Relationship.' *Information Economics and Policy* 1:267–302

——1987. 'Commitment and Fairness in a Dynamic Regulatory Relationship.' *Review of Economic Studies* 54:413–436

Baron, D. P. and R. B. Myerson, 1982. 'Regulating a Monopolist with Unknown Costs.' *Econometrica* 50:911–930

Barrett, S., 2009. *Deregulation and the Airline Business in Europe*. London: Routledge

Bashur, B., 2021. 'The Durbin Amendment Is a Disaster for Banks – Don't Expand It to Credit Cards.' The Hill. 10 October

Basso, L. J. and A. Zhang, 2010. 'Pricing vs. Slot Policies when Airport Profits Matter.' *Transportation Research, Part B: Methodological* 44(3):381–391

Bauer, C. J., 1997. 'Bringing Water Markets Down to Earth: The Political Economy of Water Rights in Chile, 1976–95.' *World Development* 25:639–656

Baumol, W. J., 1967. 'Reasonable Rules for Rate Regulation: Plausible Policies for an Imperfect World.' In A. Phillips and O. E. Williamson (eds.), *Prices*. Philadelphia: University of Pennsylvania Press, pp. 108–123

——1977. 'On the Proper Tests for Natural Monopoly in a Multi-Product Industry.' *American Economic Review* 67:809–822

——1982a. 'Contestable Markets: An Uprising in the Theory of Industrial Structure.' *American Economic Review* 72:1–15

——1982b. 'Productivity-Incentive Clauses and Rate Adjustment for Inflation.' *Public Utilities Fortnightly* July, p. 110

——1983. 'Some Subtle Issues in Railroad Deregulation.' *International Journal of Transport Economics* 10:341–355

——1986. *Superfairness: Applications and Theory*. Cambridge, MA: MIT Press

——1995. 'Modified Regulation of Telecommunications and the Public Interest Standard.' In M. Bishop, J. Kay and C. Mayer (eds.), *The Regulatory Challenge*. Oxford: Oxford University Press, pp. 254–282

Baumol, W. J. and D. F. Bradford, 1970. 'Optimal Departures from Marginal Cost Pricing.' *American Economic Review* 60:265–283

Baumol, W. J. and A. K. Klevorick, 1970. 'Input Choices and Rate of Return Regulation: An Overview of the Discussion.' *Bell Journal of Economics and Management Science* 1: 162–190

Baumol, W. J., J. A. Ordover and R. D. Willig, 1997. 'Parity Pricing and Its Critics: A Necessary Condition for Efficiency in the Provision of Bottleneck Services to Competitors.' *Yale Journal on Regulation* 14:145–162

Baumol, W. J., J. C. Panzar and R. D. Willig, 1982. *Contestable Markets and the Theory of Industry Structure*. New York: Harcourt Brace Jovanovich

Baumol, W. J. and J. G. Sidak, 1994a. 'The Pricing of Inputs Sold to Competitors.' *Yale Journal on Regulation* 11:172–202

——1994b. *Toward Competition in Local Telephony*. Cambridge, MA: MIT Press

——1995. 'The Pricing of Inputs Sold to Competitors: Rejoinder and Epilogue.' *Yale Journal on Regulation* 12:177–186

Baumol, W. J. and R. D. Willig, 1986. 'Contestability: Developments Since the Book.' *Oxford Economic Papers* 38:9–36

Baxter, W. F., 1983. 'Bank Interchange of Transactional Paper: Legal and Economic Perspectives.' *Journal of Law and Economics* 26(3):541–588

Baye, M. R. and J. Prince, 2020. 'The Economics of Digital Platforms: A Guide for Regulators.' The Global Antitrust Institute Report on the Digital Economy

Baye, M. R. and D. E. M. Sappington, 2020. 'Revealing Transactions Data to Third Parties: Implications of Privacy Regimes for Welfare in Online Markets.' *Journal of Economics and Management Strategy* 29(2):260–275

BBC, 2016. 'Energy Deal "Tease and Squeeze" Tactics.' 9 September. See www.bbc.co.uk/news/business-37318534

Beard, T. R., D. L. Kaserman and J. W. Mayo, 2001. 'Regulation, Vertical Integration and Sabotage.' *Journal of Industrial Economics* 49:319–333

Beard, T. R., J. T. Macher and C. Vickers, 2016. 'This Time Is Different(?): Telecommunications Unbundling and Lessons for Railroad Regulation.' *Review of Industrial Organization* 49(2):289–310

Beato, P. and C. Fuente, 2000. 'Liberalisation of the Gas Sector in Latin America: The Experience of Three Countries.' Inter-American Development Bank, Working Paper. June

Bech, M., Y. Shimizu and P. Wong, 2017. 'The Quest for Speed in Payments.' *BIS Quarterly Review*, March

Becker, G. S., 1983. 'A Theory of Competition Among Pressure Groups for Political Influence.' *Quarterly Journal of Economics* 98:371–400

——2002. 'Interview with Gary Becker.' Ed. D. Clement, Federal Reserve Bank of Minneapolis. 1 June

Beecher, J. A., 2009. 'Consumer Expenditure on Utilities 2007.' IPU Research Note. Michigan State University. April

——2011. 'Primer on Water Pricing.' IPU Primer. November

——2018. 'Potential for Economic Regulation of Michigan's Water Sector.' Policy Brief for the Incoming 2019 Gubernatorial Administration. Michigan State University Extension Center. 7 November

Beecher, J. A. and T. W. Chesnutt, 2012. 'Declining Water Sales and Utility Revenues: A Framework for Understanding and Adapting.' A White Paper for National Water Rates Summit. 29–30 August

Beecher, J. and T. Gould, 2018. 'Pricing Wastewater to Save Water: Are Theory and Practice Transferable?' *Utilities Policy* 52:81–87

Beecher, J. A. and J. A. Kalmbach, 2013. 'Structure, Regulation, and Pricing of Water in the USA: A Study of the Great Lakes Region.' *Utilities Policy* 24:32–47

Beecher, J. A., P. C. Mann, Y. Hegazy and J. D. Stanford, 1994. 'Revenue Effects of Water Conservation and Conservation Pricing: Issues and Practices.' NRRI Research Report. September

Beecher, J. A. and S. J. Rubin, 2000. *Deregulation! Impacts on the Water Industry*. Denver: AWWA Research Foundation

Beesley, M. E. 1999. 'Airport Regulation.' In M. E. Beesley (ed.), *Regulating Utilities: A New Era?* London: Institute of Economic Affairs

Beesley, M. E. and S. C. Littlechild, 1989. 'The Regulation of Privatized Monopolies in the UK.' *RAND Journal of Economics* 20:454–472

Behavioural Insights Team, 2015. 'Response to Energy Market Investigation: Supplemental Notice of Possible Remedies.' 9 November

——2019. 'Testing Comprehension of the Reference Price.' Final Report

BEIS, 2022. 'Economic Regulation Policy Paper.' January

Bel, G., 2020. 'Public versus Private Water Delivery, Remunicipalization and Water Tariffs.' *Utilities Policy* 62:100982

Bell, K., R. Green, I. Kockar, G. Ault and J. McDonald, 2011. 'Academic Review of Transmission Charging Arrangements.' A Report Produced for the Gas and Electricity Markets Authority. 3 May

Belleflamme, P. and Peitz, M., 2015. *Industrial Organization: Markets and Strategies*. Cambridge: Cambridge University Press

——2021. *The Economics of Platforms*. Cambridge: Cambridge University Press

Bensch, G., 2019. 'The Effects of Market-Based Reforms on Access to Electricity in Developing Countries: A Systematic Review.' *Journal of Development Effectiveness* 11(2):165–188

Bentley, A. F., 1908. *The Process of Government: A Study of Social Pressures*. Chicago: University of Chicago Press

BEREC, 2014. 'BEREC Guidance on the Regulatory Accounting Approach to the Economic Replicability Test (i.e. Ex-Ante/Sector Specific Margin Squeeze Tests).' 5 December

——2020. 'BEREC Strategy 2021–2025.' 5 March

——2021a. 'Termination Rates at European Level.' January

——2021b. 'BEREC Report Regulatory Accounting in Practice 2021.' 9 December

——2021c. 'BEREC Annual Reports for 2020.' 10 June

——2022. 'BEREC Preliminary Assessment of the Underlying Assumptions of Payments from Large CAPs to ISPs.' October

Berg, S., 2010. *Water Utility Benchmarking*. London: IWA Publishing

Berg, S. V. and J. Tschirhart, 1988. *Natural Monopoly Regulation: Principles and Practice*. Cambridge: Cambridge University Press

——1995. 'Contributions of Neoclassical Economics to Public Utility Analysis.' *Land Economics* 71:310–330

Berger, U., 2005. 'Bill-and-Keep vs. Cost-Based Access Pricing Revisited.' *Economics Letters* 86:107–112

Bernier, L., M. Florio and P. Bance (eds.), 2020. *The Routledge Handbook of State-Owned Enterprises*. London: Routledge

Bernoulli, D., 1738. 'Exposition of a New Theory on the Measurement of Risk' (1967 translation) *Econometrica* 22:23–36

Bernstein, M. H., 1955. *Regulating Business by Independent Commission*. Westport, CT: Greenwood

Bertoméu-Sánchez, S., D. Camos and A. Estache, 2018. 'Do Economic Regulatory Agencies Matter to Private-Sector Involvement in Water Utilities in Developing Countries?' *Utilities Policy* 50:153–163

Bertram, G. and D. Twaddle, 2005. 'Price-Cost Margins and Profit Rates in New Zealand Electricity Distribution Networks Since 1994: The Cost of Light Handed Regulation.' *Journal of Regulatory Economics* 27:281–307

Besanko, D. and S. Cui, 2016. 'Railway Restructuring and Organizational Choice: Network Quality and Welfare Impacts.' *Journal of Regulatory Economics* 50(2):164–206

——2019. 'Regulated versus Negotiated Access Pricing in Vertically Separated Railway Systems' *Journal of Regulatory Economics* 55(1):1–32

Betarelli, A. A., E. P. Domingues and G. J. D. Hewings, 2020. 'Transport Policy, Rail Freight Sector and Market Structure: The Economic Effects in Brazil.' *Transportation Research, Part A: Policy and Practice* 135:1–23

Bettman, J. R., M. F. Luce and J. W. Payne, 1998. 'Constructive Consumer Choice Processes.' *Journal of Consumer Research* 25(3):187–217

Bichler, M., P. Cramton, P. Gritzmann and A. Ockenfels, 2021. 'It Is Time to Auction Slots at Congested Airports.' OX, CEPR Policy Portal. 10 January

Biggar, D., 1999. 'Airline Mergers and Alliances.' Background Note. OECD Policy Roundtables

——2004. 'Incentive Regulation and the Building Block Model.' Unpublished Working Paper. 28 May

——2009. 'Is Protecting Sunk Investments by Consumers a Key Rationale for Natural Monopoly Regulation?' *Review of Network Economics* 8:1–25

Biggar, D. and A. Heimler, 2021. 'Is Protecting Sunk Investments an Economic Rationale for Antitrust Law?' *Journal of Antitrust Enforcement* 9(2):203–243

Biglaiser, G., E. Calvano and J. Crémer, 2019. 'Incumbency Advantage and Its Value.' *Journal of Economics and Management Strategy* 28(1):41–48

Biglaiser, G., J. Crémer and A. Veiga, 2022. 'Should I Stay or Should I Go? Migrating Away from an Incumbent Platform.' *RAND Journal of Economics* 53(3):453–483

Bilotkach, V., 2019. 'Airline Partnerships, Antitrust Immunity, and Joint Ventures: What We Know and What I Think We Would Like to Know.' *Review of Industrial Organization* 54(1):37–60

Bilotkach, V. and H. Bush, 2020. 'Airport Competition from Airports' Perspective: Evidence from a Survey of European Airports.' *Competition and Regulation in Network Industries* 21(3):275–296

Bilotkach, V. and K. Hüschelrath, 2011. 'Antitrust Immunity for Airline Alliances.' *Journal of Competition Law and Economics* 7(2):335–380

——2013. 'Airline Alliances, Antitrust Immunity and Market Foreclosure.' *Review of Economics and Statistics* 95(4):1368–1385

BIS Red Book, 2021. 'Payments Processed by Selected Payment Systems: Value of Transactions' See https://stats.bis.org/statx/srs/table/PS3

Bishop, M., J. Kay and C. Mayer, 1994. *Privatisation and Economic Performance*. Oxford: Oxford University Press

Bitran, E., P. Rivera and M. J. Villena, 2014. 'Water Management Problems in the Copiapó Basin, Chile: Markets, Severe Scarcity and the Regulator.' *Water Policy* 16(5):844–863

Bitzan, J. D., 2003. 'Railroad Costs and Competition: The Implications of Introducing Competition to Railroad Networks.' *Journal of Transport Economics and Policy* 37(2):201–225

Bjørner, T. B., J. V. Hansen and A. F. Jakobsen, 2021. 'Price Cap Regulation and Water Quality.' *Journal of Regulatory Economics* 60(2–3):95–116

Black, D., G. Harman and B. Moselle, 2009. 'The Case for *Ex Post* Regulation of Energy Networks.' A Report for Ofgem. 7 October

Blagrave, P. and D. Furceri, 2021. 'The Macroeconomic Effects of Electricity-Sector Privatization.' *Energy Economics* 100:105245

Blank, L., D. L. Kaserman and J. W. Mayo, 1998. 'Dominant Firm Pricing with Competitive Entry and Regulation: The Case of IntraLATA Toll.' *Journal of Regulatory Economics* 14:35–53

Bluhm, P. and S. Lichtenberg, 2011. 'Fundamentals of Telecommunications Regulation: Markets, Jurisdiction, and Challenges.' NRRI Research Paper. January

BNETZA 2017. 'Beschluss in dem Verwaltungsverfahren aufgrund der Mitteilung der DB Netz AG, BuGG vertreten durch den Vorstand, Betroffene zu 1., und der DB RegioNetz Infrastruktur GmbH, BuGG vertreten durch die Geschäftsführung.' Beschlusskammer 10 ['Resolution in the Administrative Procedure Based on the Notification from DB Netz AG, BuGG Represented by the Board of Directors, Affected 1, and DB RegioNetz Infrastructure GmbH, BuGG Represented by the Management.' Ruling Chamber 10] BK 10-17-0001_E. 28 June

Bobbio, E., S. Brandkamp, S. Chan, P. C. Cramton, D. Malec and L. Yu, 2022. 'Resilient Electricity Requires Consumer Engagement.' ECONtribute Discussion Paper No. 184

Boeing, 2021. 'Current Aircraft Finance Market Outlook.' Report

Bohn, R. E., M. C. Caramanis and F. C. Schweppe, 1984. 'Optimal Pricing in Electrical Networks Over Space and Time.' *RAND Journal of Economics* 15:360–376

Boisvert, R. N., P. A. Cappers and B. Neenan, 2002. 'The Benefits of Customer Participation in Wholesale Electricity Markets.' *Electricity Journal* 15(3):41–51

Boiteux, M., 1949. 'La Tarification des Demandes en Pointe: Application de la Théorie de la Vente au Coût Marginal.' *Revue Générale de l'Électricité* 58:321–340

——1956. 'Sur la Gestion des Monopoles Publics Astreints a l'Équilibre Budgétaire.' *Econometrica* 24: 22–40 [translated 1971. 'On the Management of Public Monopolies Subject to Budgetary Constraints.' *Journal of Economic Theory* 3:219–240]

Boland, J. J. and D. Whittington, 2000. 'The Political Economy of Increasing Block Tariffs in Developing Countries.' Unpublished Working Paper

Bonbright, J. C., 1961. *Principles of Public Utility Rates*. New York: Columbia University Press

Bonbright, J. C., A. L. Danielsen and D. R. Kamerschen, 1988. *Principles of Public Utility Rates*. Arlington, VA: Public Utilities Reports. Inc.

Bordalo, P., K. Coffman, N. Gennaioli and A. Shleifer, 2016. 'Stereotypes.' *Quarterly Journal of Economics* 131(4):1753–1794

Borenstein, S., 1988. 'On the Efficiency of Competitive Markets for Operating Licenses.' *Quarterly Journal of Economics* 103(2):357

——1989. 'Hubs and High Fares: Dominance and Market Power in the U.S. Airline Industry.' *RAND Journal of Economics* 20(3):344

——2000. 'Understanding Competitive Pricing and Market Power in Wholesale Electricity Markets.' *Electricity Journal* 13(6):49–57

——2002. 'The Trouble with Electricity Markets: Understanding California's Restructuring Disaster.' *Journal of Economic Perspectives* 16:191–211

Borenstein, S. and J. Bushnell, 2015. 'The US Electricity Industry after 20 Years of Restructuring.' *Annual Review of Economics* 7(1):437–463

Borenstein, S., J. B. Bushnell and F. A. Wolak, 2000. 'Diagnosing Market Power in California's Restructured Wholesale Electricity Market.' National Bureau of Economic Research. Working Paper 7868. September

——2002. 'Measuring Market Inefficiencies in California's Restructured Wholesale Electricity Market.' *American Economic Review* 92:1376–1405

Borenstein, S. and N. L. Rose, 1994. 'Competition and Price Dispersion in the US Airline Industry.' *Journal of Political Economy* 102(4):653–683

——2014. 'How Airline Markets Work ... or Do They? Regulatory Reform in the Airline Industry.' In N. L. Rose (ed.), *Economic Regulation and Its Reform: What Have We Learned?* Chicago: University of Chicago Press

Borrmann, J. and G. Brunekreeft, 2020. 'The Timing of Monopoly Investment under Cost-Based and Price-Based Regulation.' *Utilities Policy* 66:101102

Bortolotti, B., C. Cambini, L. Rondi and Y. Spiegel, 2011. 'Capital Structure and Regulation: Do Ownership and Regulatory Independence Matter?' *Journal of Economics and Management Strategy* 20(2):517–564

Bortolotti, B., M. Fantini and D. Siniscalco, 1998. 'Regulation and Privatization: The Case of Electricity.' Department of Economics, University of Turin, Working Paper

Bortolotti, B. and E. Perotti, 2007. 'From Government to Regulatory Governance: Privatization and the Residual Role of the State.' *World Bank Research Observer* 22:53–66

Bös, D., 1991. *Privatization: A Theoretical Treatment.* Oxford: Oxford University Press

Bouckaert, J., T. van Dijk and F. Verboven, 2010. 'Access Regulation, Competition and Broadband Penetration: An International Study.' *Telecommunications Policy* 34:661–671

Boudreau, K. J. and A. Hagiu, 2009. 'Platform Rules: Multi-Sided Platforms as Regulators.' In A Gawer (ed.), *Platforms, Markets and Innovation.* Cheltenham: Edward Elgar, pp. 163–191

Bougna, E. and Y. Crozet, 2016. 'Towards a Liberalised European Rail Transport: Analysing and Modelling the Impact of Competition on Productive Efficiency.' *Research in Transportation Economics* 59:358–367

Bourguignon, H., R. Gomes and J. Tirole, 2019. 'Shrouded Transaction Costs: Must-Take Cards, Discounts and Surcharges.' *International Journal of Industrial Organization* 63:99–144

Bourreau, M., C. Cambini and P. Doğan, 2012. 'Access Pricing, Competition, and Incentives to Migrate from "Old" to "New" Technology.' *International Journal of Industrial Organization* 30(6):713–723

Bourreau, M., C. Cambini and S. Hoernig, 2018. 'Cooperative Investment, Access, and Uncertainty.' *International Journal of Industrial Organization* 56:78–106

Bourreau, M., C. Cambini, S. Hoernig and I. Vogelsang, 2021. 'Co-investment, Uncertainty, and Opportunism: Ex-Ante and Ex-Post Remedies.' *Information Economics and Policy* 56:100913

Bourreau, M. and P. Doğan, 2004. 'Service-Based vs. Facility-Based Competition in Local Access Networks.' *Information Economics and Policy* 16:287–306

——2005. 'Unbundling the Local Loop.' *European Economic Review* 49:173–199

——2006. '"Build-or-Buy" Strategies in the Local Loop.' *American Economic Review* 96(2):72–7

Bourreau, M., P. Doğan and M. Manant, 2010. 'A Critical Review of the "Ladder of Investment" Approach.' *Telecommunications Policy* 34:683–696

Bourreau, M. and J. Drouard, 2014. 'Progressive Entry and the Incentives to Invest in Alternative Infrastructures.' *Journal of Regulatory Economics* 45(3):329–351

Bourreau, M. and G. Gaudin, 2022. 'Streaming Platform and Strategic Recommendation Bias.' *Journal of Economics and Management Strategy* 31(1):25–47

Bourreau, M., L. Grzybowski and M. Hasbi, 2019. 'Unbundling the Incumbent and Deployment of High-Speed Internet: Evidence from France.' *International Journal of Industrial Organization* 67:102526

Bourreau, M., F. Kourandi and T. Valletti, 2015. 'Net Neutrality with Competing Internet Platforms.' *Journal of Industrial Economics* 63(1):30–73

Bourreau, M. and R. Lestage, 2019. 'Net Neutrality and Asymmetric Platform Competition.' *Journal of Regulatory Economics* 55(2):140–171

Bourreau, M. and A. Perrot, 2020. 'Digital Platforms: Regulate Before It's Too Late.' *Notes du Conseil d'Analyse Économique* 60(6):1–12

Bovera, F., M. Delfanti, E. Fumagalli, L. Lo Schiavo and R. Vailati, 2021. 'Regulating Electricity Distribution Networks under Technological and Demand Uncertainty.' *Energy Policy* 149:111989

Boyd, W., 2018. 'Just Price, Public Utility, and the Long History of Economic Regulation in America.' *Yale Journal on Regulation* 35:59

Bradley, I. and C. Price, 1988. 'The Economic Regulation of Private Industries by Price Constraints.' *Journal of Industrial Economics* 37:99–106

Braeutigam, R. R., 1979. 'Optimal Pricing with Intermodal Competition.' *American Economic Review* 69:38–49

——1980. 'An Analysis of Fully Distributed Cost Pricing in Regulated Industries.' *Bell Journal of Economics* 11:182–196

——1989. 'Optimal Policies for Natural Monopolies.' In R. Schmalensee and R. Willig (eds.), *Handbook of Industrial Organization*, Volume 2. Amsterdam: North-Holland

——1993. 'Consequences of Regulatory Reform in the American Railroad Industry.' *Southern Economic Journal* 59(3):468–480

Braeutigam, R. R. and J. C. Panzar, 1989. 'Diversification Incentives under "Price-Based" and "Cost-Based" Regulation.' *RAND Journal of Economics* 20(3):373–391

——1993. 'Effects of the Change from Rate-of-Return to Price Cap Regulation.' *American Economic Review*. 83:191–198

Brandão, A., J. Pinho, J. Resende, P. Sarmento and I. Soares, 2016. 'Welfare Effects of Unbundling under Different Regulatory Regimes in Natural Gas Markets.' *Portuguese Economic Journal* 15(2):99–127

Brattle Group, 2018. 'International Experiences in Retail Electricity Markets.' Report for the ACCC. June

Bremberger, F., C. Cambini, K. Gugler and L. Rondi, 2016. 'Dividend Policy in Regulated Network Industries: Evidence from the EU.' *Economic Inquiry* 54(1):408–432

Brennan, T. J., 2010. 'Decoupling in Electric Utilities.' *Journal of Regulatory Economics* 38:49–69

——2013. 'Energy Efficient Policy Puzzles.' *Energy Journal* 34:1–24

——2016. 'Behavioral Economics and Energy-Efficiency Regulation.' *Network* 59(June):1–8

Brennan, T. J. and J. Boyd, 1997. 'Stranded Costs, Takings, and the Law and Economics of Implicit Contracts.' *Journal of Regulatory Economics* 11(1):41–54

Brennan, T. J. and M. Crew, 2016. 'Price Cap Regulation and Declining Demand.' In M. A. Crew and T. J. Brennan (eds.), *The Future of the Postal Sector in a Digital World*. New York: Springer

Breyer, S., 1982. *Regulation and Its Reform*. Cambridge, MA: Harvard University Press

——2011. 'Airline Deregulation, Revisited.' Bloomberg Business Week. 20 January

Briglauer, W., 2014. 'The Impact of Regulation and Competition on the Adoption of Fiber-Based Broadband Services: Recent Evidence from the European Union Member States.' *Journal of Regulatory Economics* 46(1):51–79

Briglauer, W., C. Cambini, T. Fetzer and K. Hüschelrath, 2017. 'The European Electronic Communications Code: A Critical Appraisal with a Focus on Incentivizing Investment in Next Generation Broadband Networks.' *Telecommunications Policy* 41(10):948–961

Briglauer, W., C. Cambini and M. Grajek, 2018. 'Speeding Up the Internet: Regulation and Investment in the European Fiber Optic Infrastructure.' *International Journal of Industrial Organization* 61:613–652

Briglauer, W., S. Frübing and I. Vogelsang, 2014. 'The Impact of Alternative Public Policies on the Deployment of New Communications Infrastructure – A Survey.' ZEW Discussion Papers 15-003

Briglauer, W. and M. Grajek, 2021. 'Effectiveness and Efficiency of State Aid for New Broadband Networks: Evidence from OECD Member States.' ESMT Working Paper

Briglauer, W. and I. Vogelsang, 2011. 'The Need for a New Approach to Regulating Fixed Networks.' *Telecommunications Policy* 35:102–114

Brito, J. D., M. Cave, R. W. Crandall, *et al.*, 2010. 'Net Neutrality Regulation: The Economic Evidence.' Submission to FCC. April

Brito, D., P. Pereira and J. Vareda, 2011. 'An Assessment of the Equality of Access and No-Regulation Approaches to Next Generation Networks.' *Telecommunications Policy* 35:818–826

——2012. 'Incentives to Invest and to Give Access to Non-Regulated New Technologies.' *Information Economics and Policy* 24(3–4):197–211

Brock, W. A., 1983. 'Contestable Markets and the Theory of Industry Structure: A Review Article.' *Journal of Political Economy* 91:1055–1066

——2002. 'Historical Overview.' In M. E. Cave, S. K. Majumdar and I. Vogelsang (eds.), *Handbook of Telecommunications Economics*, Volume 1. Amsterdam: Elsevier

Brock, G. W. and M. L. Katz, 1997. 'Regulation to Promote Competition: A First Look at the FCC's Implementation of the Local Competition Provisions of the Telecommunications Act of 1996.' *Information Economics and Policy* 9:103–117

Brown, A. C., J. Stern, B. Tenenbaum and D. Gencer, 2006. *Handbook for Evaluating Infrastructure Regulatory Systems*. Washington, DC: World Bank

Brown, D. P., A. Eckert and H. Eckert, 2017. 'Electricity Markets in Transition: Market Distortions Associated with Retail Price Controls.' *Electricity Journal* 30(5):32–37

Brown, D.P, Eckert A. and B. Shaffer, 2023. 'Evaluating the Impact of Divestitures on Competition: Evidence from Alberta's Wholesale Electricity Market' University of Alberta Department of Economics Working Paper No. 2023-02.

Brown, D. P. and D. E. M. Sappington, 2021. 'Market Structure, Risk Preferences, and Forward Contracting Incentives.' University of Alberta, Working Paper

——2022a. 'Vertical Integration and Capacity Investment in the Electricity Sector.' *Journal of Economics and Management Strategy* 31(1):193–226

——2022b. 'The Impact of Wholesale Price Caps on Forward Contracting.' University of Alberta Working Paper No. 2022-12. October

Brown, J. H., 2013. 'The "Railroad Problem" and the Interstate Commerce Act.' *Review of Industrial Organization* 43(1–2):7–19

Brown, R. 2012. *The Brown Review of the Rail Franchising Programme*. London: Stationery Office

Brown, S. J. and D. S. Sibley, 1986. *The Theory of Public Utility Pricing*. Cambridge: Cambridge University Press

Brown, S. P. A. and M. K. Yücel, 2008. 'What Drives Natural Gas Prices?' *Energy Journal* 29:43–58

Brueckner, J. K., 2003. 'International Airfares in the Age of Alliances: The Effects of Codesharing and Antitrust Immunity.' *Review of Economics and Statistics* 85(1):105–118

——2009. 'Price vs. Quantity-Based Approaches to Airport Congestion Management.' *Journal of Public Economics* 93(5–6):681–690

Brueckner, J. K., N. J. Dyer and P. T. Spiller, 1992. 'Fare Determination in Airline Hub-and-Spoke Networks.' *RAND Journal of Economics* 23(3):309–333

Brueckner, J. K. and E. Singer, 2019. 'Pricing by International Airline Alliances: A Retrospective Study.' *Economics of Transportation* 20:100139

Brueckner, J. K. and W. T. Whalen, 2000. 'The Price Effects of International Airline Alliances.' *Journal of Law and Economics* 43(2):503–546

Brunekreeft, G., 2005. 'Regulatory Issues in Merchant Transmission Investment.' *Utilities Policy* 13:175–186

Brunekreeft, G., K. Neuhoff and D. Newbery, 2005. 'Electricity Transmission: An Overview of the Current Debate.' *Utilities Policy* 13:73–93

Brunekreeft, G. and M. Rammerstorfer, 2021. 'OPEX-Risk as a Source of CAPEX-Bias in Monopoly Regulation.' *Competition and Regulation in Network Industries* 22(1):20–34

Bryan, G., D. Karlan and S. Nelson, 2010. 'Commitment Devices.' *Annual Review of Economics* 2(1):671–698

BT, 2020. 'Accounting Methodology Document: Long Run Incremental Cost Model: Relationships & Parameters.' 31 July

Buafua, P. M., 2015. 'Efficiency of Urban Water Supply in Sub-Saharan Africa: Do Organization and Regulation Matter?' *Utilities Policy* 37:13–22

Buchanan, J. M., 1965. 'An Economic Theory of Clubs.' *Economica* 32:1–14

Budds, J. and G. McGranahan, 2003. 'Are the Debates on Water Privatization Missing the Point? Experiences from Africa, Asia and Latin America.' *Environment and Urbanization* 15:87–113

Budzinski, O. and J. Mendelsohn, 2021. 'Regulating Big Tech: From Competition Policy to Sector Regulation?' Ilmenau Economics Discussion Papers No. 154

Bullock, R., 2009. 'Off Track: Sub-Saharan African Railways.' Africa Infrastructure Country Diagnostic Background Paper, 17. World Bank

Bundeskartellamt, 2017. 'Background Information on the Facebook Proceeding.' 19 December

——2019. 'Facebook, Exploitative Business Terms Pursuant to Section 19(1)GWB for Inadequate Data Processing.' Case Summary. B6-22/16. 6 February

——2021. 'Amendment of the German Act against Restraints of Competition.' Press Release. 19 January

Bundeskartellamt and Autorité de la Concurrence, 2019. 'Algorithms and Competition.' November

Bundestag, 2021. 'Gesetz zur Änderung des Gesetzes gegen Wettbewerbsbeschränkungen für ein fokussiertes, proaktives und digitales Wettbewerbsrecht 4.0 und anderer Bestimmungen (GWB-Digitalisierungsgesetz).' Bundesgesetzblatt ['Law Amending the Law against Restraints of Competition for a Focused, Proactive and Digital Competition Law 4.0 and Other Provisions (GWB-Digitization Act).' Federal Law Gazette]. 18 January

Burghouwt, G. and J. G. de Wit, 2015. 'In the Wake of Liberalisation: Long-Term Developments in the EU Air Transport Market.' *Transport Policy* 43:104–113

Burton, M. L., D. L. Kaserman and J. W. Mayo, 2009. 'Common Costs and Cross-Subsidies: Misestimation versus Misallocation.' *Contemporary Economic Policy* 27:193–199

Bushnell, J., 2021. 'To Fix the Power Market, First Fix the Natural Gas Market.' Energy Institute Blog. Haas School of Business, UC Berkeley. 1 March

Bushnell, J., E. T. Mansur and K. Novan, 2017. 'Review of the Economics Literature on US Electricity Restructuring.' Working Paper

Bushnell, J. and K. Novan, 2018. 'Setting with the Sun: The Impacts of Renewable Energy on Wholesale Power Markets.' National Bureau of Economic Research, No. W24980

Bushnell, J. B. and S. Stoft, 1996. 'Transmission and Generation Investment in a Competitive Electric Power Industry.' PWP Working Paper, PWP-030. January

Button, K., 1989. 'The Deregulation of U.S. Interstate Aviation: An Assessment of Causes and Consequences (Part 1).' *Transport Reviews* 9(2):99–118

——1996. 'Liberalising European Aviation: Is There an Empty Core Problem?' *Journal of Transport Economics and Policy* 30(3):275–291

——2002. 'Airline Network Economics.' In D. Jenkins (ed.), *Handbook of Airline Economics*, 2nd ed. New York: McGraw-Hill, pp. 27–33

——2003. 'Does the Theory of the "Core" Explain Why Airlines Fail to Cover Their Long-Run Costs of Capital?' *Journal of Air Transport Management* 9(1):5–14

——2008. 'The Impacts of Globalisation on International Air Transport Activity.' Global Forum on Transport and Environment in a Globalising World, Guadalajara, Mexico. OECD/ITF

——2015. 'A Book, the Application, and the Outcomes: How Right Was Alfred Kahn in *The Economics of Regulation* about the Effects of the Deregulation of the US Domestic Airline Market?' *History of Political Economy* 47(1):1–39

——2017a. 'Market Instability.' In M. Finger and K. Button (eds.), *Air Transport Liberalization*. Cheltenham: Edward Elgar

——2017b. 'The Other Side of an Airport's Two-Sided Market: Issues in Planning and Pricing Airport Surface Access.' *European Journal of Transport and Infrastructure Research* 17(4):442–456

——2020. 'Studying the Empirical Implications of the Liberalization of Airport Markets.' *Competition and Regulation in Network Industries* 21(3):223–243

Button, K., G. Martini and D. Scotti (eds.), 2017. *The Economics and Political Economy of African Air Transport*. London: Routledge

Button, K. and G. McDougall, 2006. 'Institutional and Structure Changes in Air Navigation Service-Providing Organizations.' *Journal of Air Transport Management* 12(5):236–252

Button, K. and R. Neiva, 2013. 'Single European Sky and the Functional Airspace Blocks: Will They Improve Economic Efficiency?' *Journal of Air Transport Management* 33:73

——2014. 'Economic Efficiency of European Air Traffic Control Systems.' *Journal of Transport Economics and Policy* 48(1):65–80

Button, K., F. Porta and D. Scotti, 2022. 'The Role of Strategic Airline Alliances in Africa.' *Journal of Transport Economics and Policy* 56(2):272–294

Buyle, S., W. Dewulf, F. Kupfer, *et al.*, 2020. 'Does ANSP Size and Scope Matter in the European ANS Market? A Multi-Product Stochastic Frontier Approach.' *Journal of Air Transport Management* 83:101754

Buyle, S., E. Onghena, W. Dewulf and F. Kupfer, 2017. 'The European Air Navigation Services Industry: A Market Analysis.' In Proceedings of 21st ATRS World Conference, Antwerp, Belgium, 5–8 July, pp. 1–15

Byatt, I., 2013. 'The Regulation of Water Services in the UK.' *Utilities Policy* 24:3–10

Byrnes, J., 2013. 'A Short Institutional and Regulatory History of the Australian Urban Water Sector.' *Utilities Policy* 24:11–19

CAA, 1984. 'Airline Competition Policy.' Paper 500, London

——2000. 'The "Single Till" and the "Dual Till" Approach to the Price Regulation of Airports.' Consultation Paper

Caffarra, C., 2019. '"Follow the Money" – Mapping Issues with Digital Platforms into Actionable Theories of Harm.' Concurrences. No. 91579. 29 August

Caffarra, C. and F. Scott Morton, 2021. 'The European Commission Digital Markets Act: A Translation.' VoxEU, CEPR Policy Portal. 5 January

Caillaud, B., R. Guesnerie, P. Rey and J. Tirole, 1987. 'Government Intervention in Production and Incentives Theory: A Review of Recent Contributions.' MIT Working Paper MIT-EL-87-019WP. December

Caillaud, B. and B. Jullien, 2003. 'Chicken & Egg: Competition among Intermediation Service Providers.' *RAND Journal of Economics* 34(2), 309–328

Cairns, R. D. and D. Mahabir, 1988. 'Contestability: A Revisionist View.' *Economica* 55(218):269–276

California Public Utilities Commission (CPUC), 2018. 'Order Instituting Rulemaking to Consider New Approaches to Disconnections and Reconnections to Improve Energy Access and Contain Costs.' 12 July

Calvano, E., G. Calzolari, V. Denicolò and S. Pastorello, 2020. 'Artificial Intelligence, Algorithmic Pricing, and Collusion.' *American Economic Review* 110(10):3267–3297

Calvano, E. and M. Polo, 2021. 'Market Power, Competition and Innovation in Digital Markets: A Survey.' *Information Economics and Policy* 54:100853

Cambini, C., R. Congiu and G. Soroush, 2020. 'Regulation, Innovation, and Systems Integration: Evidence from the EU.' *Energies* 13(7):1670

Cambini, C. and Y. Jiang, 2009. 'Broadband Investment and Regulation: A Literature Review.' *Telecommunications Policy* 33:559–574

Cambini, C. and L. Rondi, 2010. 'Incentive Regulation and Investment: Evidence from European Energy Utilities.' *Journal of Regulatory Economics* 38(1):1–26

——2017. 'Independent Agencies, Political Interference, and Firm Investment: Evidence from the European Union.' *Economic Inquiry* 55(1):281–304

Cambini, C. and T. M. Valletti, 2003. 'Network Competition with Price Discrimination: "Bill-and-Keep" Is Not So Bad after All.' *Economics Letters* 81:205–213

Camerer, C. F., 2008. 'Neuroeconomics: Opening the Gray Box.' *Neuron* 60(3):416–419

Camerer, C., G. Loewenstein and D. Prelec, 2005. 'Neuroeconomics: How Neuroscience Can Inform Economics.' *Journal of Economic Literature* 43(1):9–64

Campbell, J., A. Goldfarb and C. Tucker, 2015. 'Privacy Regulation and Market Structure.' *Journal of Economics and Management Strategy* 24(1):47–73

Campos, J., 2001. 'Lessons from Railway Reforms in Brazil and Mexico.' *Transport Policy* 8(2):85–95

Canzian, G., G. Mazzarella, S. Verzillo, F. Verboven and L. Ronchail, 2021. 'Evaluating the Impact of Price Caps – Evidence from the European Roam-Like-At-Home Regulation.' Working Paper

Cappers, P. A., A. J. Satchwell, M. Dupuy and C. Linvill, 2020. 'The Distribution of US Electric Utility Revenue Decoupling Rate Impacts from 2005 to 2017.' *Electricity Journal* 33(10):106858

Carlton, D. W. and A. S. Frankel, 1995. 'The Antitrust Economics of Credit Card Networks.' *Antitrust Law Journal* 63:643–668

Carlton, D. W. and J. M. Perloff, 2000. *Modern Industrial Organization*, 3rd ed. Reading, MA: Addison-Wesley

Carnicer, R. and I. Gomes, 2021. 'Will Argentina Become a Relevant Gas Exporter?' OIES Paper No. 167

Carter, M. and J. Wright, 1994. 'Symbiotic Production: The Case of Telecommunication Pricing.' *Review of Industrial Organization* 9:365–378

——1999. 'Interconnection in Network Industries.' *Review of Industrial Organization* 14:1–25

Carter, S., 2001. 'Breaking the Consumption Habit: Ratemaking for Efficient Resource Decisions.' *Electricity Journal* 14(10):66–74

Carvalho, P., R. C. Marques and S. Berg, 2012. 'A Meta-Regression Analysis of Benchmarking Studies on Water Utilities Market Structure.' *Utilities Policy* 21:40–49

Casarin, A. A., 2014. 'Regulated Price Reforms and Unregulated Substitutes: The Case of Residential Piped Gas in Argentina.' *Journal of Regulatory Economics* 45(1):34–56

Casarin, A. A., J. A. Delfino and M. E. Delfino, 2007. 'Failures in Water Reform: Lessons from the Buenos Aires's Concession.' *Utilities Policy* 15:234–247

Castelnovo, P., C. F. Del Bo and M. Florio, 2019. 'Quality of Institutions and Productivity of State-Invested Enterprises: International Evidence from Major Telecom Companies.' *European Journal of Political Economy* 58:102–117

Casullo, L., 2016. 'The Efficiency Impact of Open Access Competition in Rail Markets: The Case of Domestic Passenger Services in Europe.' OECD International Transport Forum. Discussion Paper No. 2016-07

Casullo, L., A. Durand and F. Cavassini. 2019. 'The 2018 Indicators on the Governance of Secto Regulators – Part of the Product Market Regulation (PMR) Survey.' OECD Working Paper No. 1564

CAT, 2006. 'Albion Water Limited v. Water Services Regulation Authority.' Case No. 1046/2/4/0

Cave, M., 2006a. 'Encouraging Infrastructure Competition via the Ladder of Investment.' *Telecommunications Policy* 30:223–237

——2006b. 'Six Degrees of Separation: Operational Separation as a Remedy in European Telecommunications Regulation.' *Communications & Strategies* 64:89–103

——2009. 'Independent Review of Competition and Innovation in Water Markets.' Final Report. April

——2010. 'Snakes and Ladders: Unbundling in a Next Generation World.' *Telecommunications Policy* 34:80–85

——2014. 'The Ladder of Investment in Europe, in Retrospect and Prospect.' *Telecommunication Policy* 38(8–9):674–683

Cave, M., C. Genakos and T. Valletti, 2019. 'The European Framework for Regulating Telecommunications: A 25-Year Appraisal.' *Review of Industrial Organization* 55(1):47–€

Cave, M. E., S. K. Majumdar and I. Vogelsang (eds.), 2002. *Handbook of Telecommunications Economics*, Volume 1. Amsterdam: Elsevier

Cave, M. E. and I. Vogelsang, 2003. 'How Access Pricing and Entry Interact.' *Telecommunications Policy* 27:717–727

Cave, M. E. and J. Wright, 2010. 'A Strategy for Introducing Competition in the Water Sector.' *Utilities Policy* 18:116–119

——2021. 'How Can the Concept of Public Value Influence UK Utility Regulation?' *Utilities Policy* 72:101280

Caves, D. W. and L. R. Christensen, 1980. 'The Relative Efficiency of Public and Private Firms in a Competitive Environment: The Case of Canadian Railroads.' *Journal of Political Economy* 88(5):958–976

Caves, D. W., L. R. Christensen and M. W. Tretheway, 1984. 'Economies of Density versus Economies of Scale: Why Trunk and Local Service Airline Costs Differ.' *RAND Journal o Economics* 15(4):471

Caves, D. W., L. R. Christensen, M. W. Tretheway and R. J. Windle, 1985. 'Network Effects and the Measurement of Returns to Scale and Density for US Railroads.' In A. Daughety (ed.) *Analytical Studies in Transport Economics*. Cambridge: Cambridge University Press, pp. 97–120

Caves, R. E., 1962. *Air Transport and Its Regulators*. Cambridge, MA: Harvard University Pres

CCWater, 2011. 'Financeability and Financing the Asset Base.' Response to an Ofwat Discussio Paper. June

——2020. 'Engaging Water Customers for Better Consumer and Business Outcomes.' April

CDC, 2021. 'Public Water Systems.' 30 March

CEER, 2011. 'CEER Vision for a European Gas Target Model: Conclusions Paper.' C11-GWG-82-03. 1 December

——2017. 'CEER Report on Barriers for Gas Storage Product Development.' 28 April

——2019. 'Pan-European Cost-Efficiency Benchmark for Gas Transmission System Operators.' 17 July

——2020. 'CEER–BEUC 2030 Vision for Energy Consumers.' Report

——2021. 'CEER Report on Innovative Business Models and Consumer Protection Challenges.' C20-CRM-DS-03-03. 20 September

Cennamo, C. and J. Santalo, 2013. 'Platform Competition: Strategic Trade-Offs in Platform Markets: Platform Competition.' *Strategic Management Journal* 34(11):1331–1350

Cennamo, C. and D. D. Sokol, 2021. 'Can the EU Regulate Platforms without Stifling Innovation?' *Harvard Business Review*. Digital Article

CEPA, 2018. 'Review of the RIIO framework and RIIO-1 Performance.' Report for Ofgem. March

CER, 2022. 'CER's Economic Regulation of Pipelines.' Online Report

CERRE, 2021. 'The European Proposal for a Digital Markets Act: A First Assessment.' January

——2022. 'Retail Energy Markets under Stress – Lessons Learnt for the Future of Market Design.' Issue Paper. July

CFPB, 2015. 'The Consumer Credit Card Market.' Market Report

——2017. 'Data Point; Frequent Overdrafters.' August

——2019. 'Director Kraninger's Speech at CFPB Symposium on Behavioral Economics.' 19 September

Chadwick, E. 1859. 'Results of Different Principles of Legislation and Administration in Europe: Of Competition for the Field, as Compared with Competition within the Field, of Service.' *Journal of the Statistical Society of London* 22:381–420

Chakravorti, S., 2003. 'Theory of Credit Card Networks: A Survey of the Literature.' *Review of Network Economics* 2(2):50–68

Chakravorty, S., 2015. 'A Study of the Negotiated-Settlement Practice in Regulation: Some Evidence from Florida.' *Utilities Policy* 32:12–18

Chambers, D. and C. O'Reilly, 2022. 'The Economic Theory of Regulation and Inequality.' *Public Choice* 193:63–78

Chambouleyron, A., 2014. 'Mitigating Expropriation Risk through Vertical Separation of Public Utilities: The Case of Argentina.' *Utilities Policy* 30:41–52

Chang, H. H. and D. S. Evans, 2000. 'The Competitive Effects of the Collective Setting of Interchange Fees by Payment Card Systems.' *Antitrust Bulletin* 45(3):641–677

Chang, H., D. S. Evans and D. D. Garcia Schwartz, 2005. 'The Effect of Regulatory Intervention in Two-Sided Markets: An Assessment of Interchange-Fee Capping in Australia.' *Review of Network Economics* 4(4):328–358

Chao, H., 2015. 'Two-Stage Auction and Subscription Pricing for Awarding Monopoly Franchises.' *Journal of Regulatory Economics* 47(3):219–238

Chao, H.-P., S. Oren and R. Wilson, 2005. 'Restructured Electricity Markets: Reevaluation of Vertical Integration and Unbundling.' Unpublished Working Paper

Chao, H.-P. and S. Peck, 1996. 'A Market Mechanism for Electric Power Transmission.' *Journal of Regulatory Economics* 10:25–59

Chao, H. and R. Wilson, 2020. 'Coordination of Electricity Transmission and Generation Investments.' *Energy Economics* 86:104623

Chapin, A. and S. Schmidt, 1999. 'Do Mergers Improve Efficiency? Evidence from Deregulated Rail Freight.' *Journal of Transport Economics and Policy* 33(2):147–162

Charalampopoulos, G., D. Katsianis and D. Varoutas, 2020. 'Investigating the Intertwining Impact of Wholesale Access Pricing and the Commitment to Net Neutrality Principle on European Next-Generation Access Networks Private Investment Plans: An Options-Game

Application for Capturing Market Players' Competitive Interactions.' *Telecommunications Policy* 44(3):101940

Che, Y.-K., 1995. 'Revolving Doors and the Optimal Tolerance for Agency Collusion.' *RAND Journal of Economics* 26:378–397

Cheng, H. K., S. Bandyopadhyay and H. Guo, 2011. 'The Debate on Net Neutrality: A Policy Perspective.' *Information Systems Research* 22:60–82

Chennells, L., 1997. 'The Windfall Tax.' *Fiscal Studies* 18:279–291

Chernev, A., U. Böckenholt and J. Goodman, 2015. 'Choice Overload: A Conceptual Review and Meta-Analysis.' *Journal of Consumer Psychology* 25(2):333–358

Chiambaretto, P. and C. Decker, 2012. 'Air–Rail Intermodal Agreements: Balancing the Competition and Environmental Effects.' *Journal of Air Transport Management* 23:36–40

China State Administration for Market Regulation, 2021. 'Regulations on the Administration of Internet Information Service Algorithms Recommendation.' (Translation) 31 December

Chioveanu, I. and J. Zhou, 2013. 'Price Competition with Consumer Confusion.' *Management Science* 59(11):2450–2469

Chiu, J. and T. V. Koeppl, 2022. 'PayTech and the D(ata) N(etwork) A(ctivities) of BigTech Platforms'. Bank of Canada, Staff Working Paper 2022-35

Choi, J.-P., D.-S. Jeon and B.-C. Kim, 2018. 'Net Neutrality, Network Capacity, and Innovation at the Edges: Net Neutrality, Network Capacity, and Innovation.' *Journal of Industrial Economics* 66(1):172–204

Choi, J.-P. and B.-C. Kim, 2010. 'Net Neutrality and Investment Incentives.' *RAND Journal of Economics* 41:446–471

Chong, E., S. Saussier and B. S. Silverman, 2015. 'Water Under the Bridge: Determinants of Franchise Renewal in Water Provision.' *Journal of Law, Economics, & Organization* 31(suppl.1): i3–i39

Christensen Associates, 2010. 'An Update to the Study of Competition in the U.S. Freight Railroad Industry.' Final Report. January

Chu, L. Y. and D. E. Sappington, 2013. 'Motivating Energy Suppliers to Promote Energy Conservation.' *Journal of Regulatory Economics* 43(3):229–247

Cicala, S., 2015. 'When Does Regulation Distort Costs? Lessons from Fuel Procurement in US Electricity Generation.' *American Economic Review* 105(1):411–444

——2022. 'Imperfect Markets versus Imperfect Regulation in US Electricity Generation.' *American Economic Review* 112(2):409–441

Cicchetti, C. J., J. A. Dubin and C. M. Long, 2004. *The California Electricity Crisis: What, Why and What's Next*. Boston, MA: Kluwer Academic

Cicilline D. N. and K. Buck, 2021. 'House Lawmakers Release Anti-Monopoly Agenda for "A Stronger Online Economy: Opportunity, Innovation, Choice".' Press Release

Clark, F. C., 1891. 'State Railroad Commissions, and How They May Be Made Effective.' *Publications of the American Economic Association* 6(6):11–110

Clark, J. M., 1911. 'Rates for Public Utilities.' *American Economic Review* 1:473–487

Cleary, K. and K. Palmer, 2020. 'US Electricity Markets.' Resources for the Future

CMA, 2016a. 'Energy Market Investigation.' Final Report

——2016b. 'Competition in Passenger Rail Services in Great Britain.' A Policy Document. 8 March

——2016c. 'BAA Airports: Evaluation of the Competition Commission's 2009 Market Investigation Remedies.' 16 May

——2018a. 'Tackling the Loyalty Penalty.' 19 December

——2018b. 'Advice for the Department for Transport on Competition Impacts of Airport Slot Allocation.' December

——2020. 'Online Platforms and Digital Advertising.' Final Report. 1 July

——2021a. 'Algorithms: How They Can Reduce Competition and Harm Consumers.' Report

——2021b. 'Anglian Water Services Limited, Bristol Water plc, Northumbrian Water Limited and Yorkshire Water Services Limited Price Determinations.' 17 March

CMSPI, 2021. 'Despite Regulation, Global Card Fees Continue to Grow and Threaten Merchants.' *Insights Magazine*. July

CNBC, 2020. 'Alibaba, JD Set New Records to Rack Up Record $115 Billion of Sales on Singles Day as Regulations Loom' 12 November

Coase, R. H., 1946. 'The Marginal Cost Controversy.' *Economica* 13:169–182

——1959. 'The Federal Communications Commission.' *Journal of Law and Economics* 2:1–40

——1960. 'The Problem of Social Cost.' *Journal of Law and Economics* 3:1–44

——1970. 'The Theory of Public Utility Pricing and Its Application.' *Bell Journal of Economics* 1:113–128

Commission de Régulation de l'Énergie, 2016. Activity Report

Comnes, G. A., S. Stoft, N. Greene and L. J. Hill, 1995. 'Revenue Caps: Implications for DSM.' In 'Performance-Based Ratemaking for Electric Utilities: Review of Plans and Analysis of Economic and Resource-Planning Issues.' Lawrence Berkeley Laboratory, Report LBL-37577. November

Compair, 2017. 'Competition for Air Traffic Management.' Report on Economic Analysis

Competition Commission, 2000. 'Mid Kent Water plc: A Report on the References under Sections 12 and 14 of the Water Industry Act 1991'

——2002. 'BAA plc: A Report on the Economic Regulation of the London Airports Companies (Heathrow Airport Ltd, Gatwick Airport Ltd and Stansted Airport Ltd).' Final Report

——2003. 'Vodafone, O2, Orange and T-Mobile: Reports on References under Section 13 of the Telecommunications Act 1984 on the Charges Made by Vodafone, O2, Orange and T-Mobile for Terminating Calls from Fixed and Mobile Networks'

Congressional Budget Office, 1984. 'Financing U.S. Airports in the 1980's.' A CBO Study. April

Cook, G. and J. Goodwin, 2008. 'Airline Networks: A Comparison of Hub-and-Spoke and Point-to-Point Systems.' *Journal of Aviation/Aerospace Education & Research* 17(2):art. 1

Cooley, T. M., 1884. 'Popular and Legal Views of Traffic Pooling.' *Railway Review* 24:211–213

Cornière, A. and G. Taylor, 2019. 'A Model of Biased Intermediation.' *RAND Journal of Economics* 50(4):854–882

Costello, K., 2006. 'Revenue Decoupling for Natural Gas Utilities.' NRRI Briefing Paper No. 06. April

——2010. 'The Natural Gas Industry at a Glance.' NRRI Working Paper 10-14. October

——2019. 'Design Considerations for Multiyear Public Utility Rate Plans.' *Utilities Policy* 59:100923

Costello, K. W. and D. J. Duann, 1996. 'Turning Up the Heat in the Natural Gas Industry.' *Regulation* 1:52–59

Counsell, K. G. and L. T. Evans, 2005. 'Essays on Water Allocation in New Zealand: The Way Forward.' Unpublished Paper. October

Cowan, S., 1997. 'Competition in the Water Industry.' *Oxford Review of Economic Policy* 13:83–92

——2002. 'Price Cap Regulation.' *Swedish Economic Policy Review* 9:167–188

Cox, J., 2013. 'Observations on the Regulation of the Water Sector.' Speech to Royal Academy of Engineering on 5 March 2012

CPUC, 2008. 'Progress and Achievements towards Water Conservation Goals.' June

Crain, W. M. and R. B. Ekelund, Jr., 1976. 'Chadwick and Demsetz on Competition and Regulation.' *Journal of Law and Economics* 19:149–162

Cramton, P., E. Filiz-Ozbay, E. Y. Ozbay and P. Sujarittanonta, 2012. 'Fear of Losing in a Clock Auction.' *Review of Economic Design* 16:119–134

Cramton, P., E. Kwerel, G. Rosston and A. Skrzypacz, 2011. 'Using Spectrum Auctions to Enhance Competition in Wireless Services.' *Journal of Law and Economics* 54(suppl.4):S167–S188

Cramton, P. and S. Stoft, 2005. 'A Capacity Market that Makes Sense.' *Electricity Journal* 18:43–54

Crandall, R. W., 2002. 'An Assessment of the Competitive Local Exchange Carriers Five Years After the Passage of the Telecommunications Act.' Unpublished Working Paper. January

Crandall, R. W., A. T. Ingraham and H. J. Singer, 2004. 'Do Unbundling Policies Discourage CLEC Facilities-Based Investment?' *B.E. Journal of Economic Analysis & Policy* 4(1):1–25

Crandall, R. W. and J. G. Sidak, 2007. 'Is Mandatory Unbundling the Key to Increasing Broadband Penetration in Mexico? A Survey of International Evidence.' Unpublished Working Paper

Crandall, R. W., J. G. Sidak and H. J. Singer, 2002. 'The Empirical Case against Asymmetric Regulation of Broadband Internet Access.' *Berkeley Technology Law Journal* 17:953–987

Crandall R. W. and L. Waverman, 1995. *Talk Is Cheap: The Promise of Regulatory Reform in North American Telecommunications.* Washington, DC: Brookings Institution

Cremer, H. and J. J. Laffont, 2002. 'Competition in Gas Markets.' *European Economic Review* 46:928–935

Crémer, J., Y.-A. de Montjoye and H. Schweitzer, 2019. 'Competition Policy for the Digital Era.' Final Report for the European Commission

Crew, M. A., C. S. Fernando and P. R. Kleindorfer, 1995. 'The Theory of Peak-Load Pricing: A Survey.' *Journal of Regulatory Economics* 8:215–248

Crew, M. A. and R. S. Kahlon, 2014. 'Guaranteed Return Regulation: A Case Study of Regulation of Water in California.' *Journal of Regulatory Economics* 46(1):112–121

Crew, M. A. and P. R. Kleindorfer, 1996. 'Incentive Regulation in the UK and the USA: Some Lessons.' *Journal of Regulatory Economics* 9:211–225

——2012. 'Regulatory Economics and the *Journal of Regulatory Economics*: A 30-Year Retrospective.' *Journal of Regulatory Economics* 41:1–18

Crocker, K. J. and S. E. Masten, 1996. 'Regulation and Administered Contracts Revisited: Lessons from Transaction-Cost Economics for Public Utility Regulation.' *Journal of Regulatory Economics* 9:5–39

Crowe, C. and E. E. Meade, 2007. 'The Evolution of Central Bank Governance Around the World.' *Journal of Economic Perspectives* 21:69–90

Crowley, N. and M. Meitzen, 2021. 'Measuring the Price Impact of Price-Cap Regulation Among Canadian Electricity Distribution Utilities.' *Utilities Policy* 72:101275

CRS, 2017. 'Regulation of Debit Interchange Fees.' 16 May

——2019. 'U.S. Payment System Policy Issues: Faster Payments and Innovation.' 23 September

——2021. 'Airport Privatization: Issues and Options for Congress.' Updated 11 March

Cruickshank, D. 2000. 'Competition in UK Banking. A Report to the Chancellor of the Exchequer.' March

Cruz, C. O. and R. C. Marques, 2013. 'Exogenous Determinants for Renegotiating Public Infrastructure Concessions: Evidence from Portugal.' *Journal of Construction Engineering and Management* 139(9):1082–1090

CTA, 2020. 'Determination No. R-2020-194: Determination by the Canadian Transportation Agency (Agency) of the 2021 regulated interswitching rates pursuant to Part III, Division IV of the Canada Transportation Act, SC 1996, c 10 (CTA).' Case number 20–00715. 30 November

Cui, S., R. Pittman and J. Zhao, 2021. 'Restructuring the Chinese Freight Railway: Two Scenarios.' *Asia and the Global Economy* 1(1):100002

Cui, S. and D. E. Sappington, 2021. 'Access Pricing in Network Industries with Mixed Oligopoly.' *Journal of Regulatory Economics* 59(3):193–225

Cullmann, A. and M. Nieswand, 2016. 'Regulation and Investment Incentives in Electricity Distribution: An Empirical Assessment.' *Energy Economics* 57:192–203

Cunningham, C., F. Ederer and S. Ma, 2021. 'Killer Acquisitions.' *Journal of Political Economy* 129(3):649–702

Cusumano, M. A., A. Gawer and D. B. Yoffie, 2021. Can Self-Regulation Save Digital Platforms? *Industrial and Corporate Change* 30(5):1259–1285

Cusumano, M. A., D. B. Yoffie and A. Gawer, 2020. 'The Future of Platforms.' MIT Sloan Management Review. Spring

Czerny, A. I., 2006. 'Price-Cap Regulation of Airports: Single-Till versus Dual-Till.' *Journal of Regulatory Economics* 30(1):85–97

Czerny, A. I., P. Forsyth, D. Gillen and H.-M. Niemeier, 2008. *Airport Slots: International Experiences and Options for Reform.* London: Routledge

Czerny, A. I., C. Guiomard and A. Zhang, 2016. 'Single-Till versus Dual-Till Regulation of Airports: Where Do Academics and Regulators (Dis)Agree?' *Journal of Transport Economics and Policy* 50(4):350–368

Dahan, M. and U. Nisan, 2007. 'Unintended Consequences of Increasing Block Tariffs Pricing Policy in Urban Water.' *Water Resources Research* 43:1–10

Dal Bó, E., 2006. 'Regulatory Capture: A Review.' *Oxford Review of Economic Policy* 22:203–225

Dana, J. D., 1998. 'Advance-Purchase Discounts and Price Discrimination in Competitive Markets.' *Journal of Political Economy* 106(2):395–422

——1999. 'Using Yield Management to Shift Demand when the Peak Time Is Unknown.' *RAND Journal of Economics* 30(3):456

Danish Water Regulatory Authority, 2022. 'Benchmarking'

Dassler, T., D. Parker and D. S. Saal, 2006. 'Methods and Trends of Performance Benchmarking in UK Utility Regulation.' *Utilities Policy* 14:166–174

Davies, R. J. and K. T. Hevert, 2020. 'Stay-Out Adjustments and Multi-Year Regulatory Rate Plans.' *Quarterly Review of Economics and Finance* 76:105–114

Davis, E. G., 1973. 'A Dynamic Model of the Regulated Firm with a Price Adjustment Mechanism.' *Bell Journal of Economics and Management Science* 4:270–282

Davis, W., 2011. 'From Futility to Utility – Recent Developments in Fixed Line Access Pricing.' *Telecommunications Journal of Australia* 61:1–16

de Bijl, P. W. and M. Peitz, 2005. 'Local Loop Unbundling in Europe: Experience, Prospects and Policy Challenges.' *Communications & Strategies* 57:33–57

DECC, 2011. 'Ofgem Review Final Report.' July

Decker, C., 2007. 'Bridging the Gap between Economic Principle and Regulatory Convention: The Case of Ramsey Pricing.' Unpublished Working Paper. June

——2013. 'Consumer Involvement in Regulatory Decision-Making.' Paper Prepared for Australian Competition and Consumer Commission Conference, 26 July

——2016. 'Regulating Networks in Decline.' *Journal of Regulatory Economics* 49(3):344–370

——2017. 'Concepts of the Consumer in Competition, Regulatory, and Consumer Protection Policies.' *Journal of Competition Law and Economics* 13(1):151–184

——2018. 'Utility and Regulatory Decision-Making under Conditions of Uncertainty: Balancing Resilience and Affordability.' *Utilities Policy* 51:51–60

——2021. 'Protecting Consumers in Digitized and Multi-Source Energy Systems.' *Energy Sources, Part B: Economics, Planning, and Policy* 16(11–12):1127–1142

Decker, C. and P. Chiambaretto, 2022. 'Economic Policy Choices and Trade-Offs for Unmanned Aircraft Systems Traffic Management (UTM): Insights from Europe and the United States.' *Transportation Research, Part A: Policy and Practice* 157:40–58

Decker, C., H. Dumez, A. Jeunemaître, *et al.*, 2003. 'The Implementation Rules of Economic Regulation within the Framework of the Implementation of the Single European Sky.' Report for European Commission

Decker, C. and H. Gray, 2012. 'Public Utilities: Competition Litigation versus Regulatory Arbitration.' *Global Competition Litigation Review* 3(1):26–34

Decker, C. and T. Keyworth, 2002. 'Competition Law and Commodity Markets: The Case of Wholesale Electricity.' *Economic Affairs* 22(4):32–39

De Corniere, A. and G. Taylor, 2019. 'A Model of Biased Intermediation.' *RAND Journal of Economics* 50(4):854–882

Defra, 2017. 'The Government's Strategic Priorities and Objectives for Ofwat.' March

DeGraba, P., 2003. 'Efficient Intercarrier Compensation for Competing Networks when Customers Share the Value of a Call.' *Journal of Economics & Management Strategy* 12:207–230

De Jong, A., J.-M. Glachant, M. Hafner, N. Ahner and S. Tagliapietra, 2012. 'A New EU Gas Security of Supply Architecture?' *European Energy Journal* 2:32–40

Delfino, J. and A. Casarin, 2003. 'The Reform of the Utilities Sector in Argentina.' In C. Ugaz (ed.), *Utility Privatization and Regulation*. Cheltenham: Edward Elgar

Delgado, L., 2015. 'European Route Choice Determinants: Examining Fuel and Route Charge Trade-Offs.' In *Proceedings of the 11th USA/Europe Air Traffic Management Research and Development Seminar, ATM 2015*

DellaVigna, S., 2009. 'Psychology and Economics: Evidence from the Field.' *Journal of Economic Literature* 47(2):315–372

DellaVigna, S. and U. Malmendier, 2004. 'Contract Design and Self-Control: Theory and Evidence.' *Quarterly Journal of Economics* 119(2):353–402

——2006. 'Paying Not to Go to the Gym.' *American Economic Review* 96(3):694–719

Delta-EE, 2022. 'Exploring Alternative Regulation of Energy Networks and Systems.' Final Report for Citizens Advice. May

De Meio Reggiani, M. C., M. Vazquez, M. Hallack and N. B. Brignole, 2019. 'The Role of Governmental Commitment on Regulated Utilities.' *Energy Economics* 84:104518

de Meza, D. and D. Reyniers, 2012. 'Every Shroud Has a Silver Lining: The Visible Benefits of Hidden Surcharges.' *Economics Letters* 116(2):151–153

Demsetz, H. 1968. 'Why Regulate Utilities?' *Journal of Law and Economics* 11:55–65

——1971. 'On the Regulation of Industry: A Reply.' *Journal of Political Economy* 79:356–363

den Boer, A. V., J. M. Meylahn and M. P. Schinkel, 2022. 'Artificial Collusion: Examining Supracompetitive Pricing by Q-Learning Algorithms.' Tinbergen Institute, Discussion Paper 067/VII

Denig-Chakroff, D., 2008. 'The Water Industry at a Glance.' NRRI Working Paper. April

Department of Business, Energy and Industrial Strategy (UK), 2022. 'Economic Regulation Policy Paper.' January

Department of Energy (USA), 2017. 'Staff Report to the Secretary on Electricity Markets and Reliability.' August

Department of Industry (UK), 1982. *The Future of Telecommunications in Britain*. Cmnd 8610. London: HMSO

Department for Transport (UK), 2021. 'Great British Railways: The Williams–Shapps Plan for Rail.' CP423. May

Department of Transportation (USA), 2016. 'Enhancing Airline Passenger Protections III.' Office of the Secretary, Final Rule. 3 November

de Reuver, M., C. Sørensen and R. C. Basole, 2018. 'The Digital Platform: A Research Agenda.' *Journal of Information Technology* 33(2):124–135

de Rus, G. and M. P. Socorro, 2014. 'Access Pricing, Infrastructure Investment and Intermodal Competition.' *Transportation Research, Part E: Logistics and Transportation Review* 70:374–387

Desmaris, C., 2016. 'High Speed Rail Competition in Italy: A Major Railway Reform with a "Win–Win Game"?' International Transport Forum Discussion Papers. OECD

Dessein, W., 2003. 'Network Competition in Nonlinear Pricing.' *RAND Journal of Economics* 34:593–611

Deville, J. 2019. 'A Portrait of the Chinese Airline Industry in 2019 (Part 1/2): A Historical Perspective.' The Chinese Aerospace Blog

De Witte, K. and D. S. Saal, 2010. 'Is a Little Sunshine All We Need? On the Impact of Sunshine Regulation on Profits, Productivity and Prices in the Dutch Drinking Water Sector.' *Journal of Regulatory Economics* 37:219–242

Dhar, R. and N. Novemsky, 2008. 'Beyond Rationality: The Content of Preferences.' *Journal of Consumer Psychology* 18(3):175–178

Diamond, P. A. and J. A. Mirrlees, 1971. 'Optimal Taxation and Public Production I: Production Efficiency.' *American Economic Review* 61:8–27

Digital Market Competition Council, 2020. 'Interim Report on the Evaluation of Competition in the Digital Advertising Market.' Report

Dillon, M., A. Jan and N. Keogh, 2015. 'Rolling Stock Companies (Roscos): Experience from Great Britain.' In *Rail Economics, Policy and Regulation in Europe*. Cheltenham: Edward Elgar

Dimasi, J. 2015. 'Rethinking Utility Regulation in Australia.' Monash Business Policy Forum. December

Di Pillio, F., L. Cricelli, M. Gastaldi and N. Levialdi, 2010. 'Asymmetry in Mobile Access Charges: Is It an Effective Regulatory Measure?' *Netnomics* 11:291–314

Dippon, C.M and M.D. Hoelle, 2022. 'The Economic Costs of Structural Separation, Line of Business Restrictions, and Common Carrier Regulation of Online Platforms and Marketplaces: A Quantitative Evaluation' Unpublished Working Paper.

Distaso, W., P. Lupi and F. M. Manenti, 2009. 'Static and Dynamic Efficiency in the European Telecommunications Market: The Role of Regulation on the Incentives to Invest and the Ladder of Investment.' In I. Lee (ed.), *Handbook of Research on Telecommunications Planning and Management for Business*. Hershey, PA: IGI Global

Dixit, A. K. and R. S. Pindyck, 1994. *Investment under Uncertainty*. Princeton, NJ: Princeton University Press

Doane, M. J. and D. F. Spulber, 1994. 'Open Access and the Evolution of the US Spot Market for Natural Gas.' *Journal of Law and Economics* 37:477–517

Dobbs, I. M., 2004. 'Intertemporal Price Cap Regulation under Uncertainty.' *Economic Journal* 114:421–440

Dobruszkes, F., 2009. 'Does Liberalisation of Air Transport Imply Increasing Competition? Lessons from the European Case.' *Transport Policy* 16(1):29–39

Donoso, G., P. Barria, C. Chadwick and D. Rivera, 2021. 'Assessment of Water Markets in Chile.' In *Water Markets*. Cheltenham: Edward Elgar, pp. 191–206

Doucet, J. and S. Littlechild, 2006. 'Negotiated Settlements: The Development of Legal and Economic Thinking.' *Utilities Policy* 14:266–277

——2009. 'Negotiated Settlements and the National Energy Board in Canada.' *Energy Policy* 37:4633–4644

Douglas, G. W. and J. C. Miller, 1974. 'Quality Competition, Industry Equilibrium, and Efficiency in the Price-Constrained Airline Market.' *American Economic Review* 64(4):657–669

Drew, J., 2009. 'The Benefits for Rail Freight Customers of Vertical Separation and Open Access.' *Transport Reviews* 29(2):223–237

Drew J. and J. Ludewig, 2011. *Reforming Railways – Learning from Experience*. Hamburg: Eurailpress

Drew, J. and C. A. Nash, 2011. 'Vertical Separation of Railway Infrastructure – Does It Always Make Sense?' Institute for Transport Studies, University of Leeds, Working Paper 594

D'Souza, J., W. Megginson and R. Nash, 2001. 'Determinants of Performance Improvements in Privatized Firms: The Role of Restructuring and Corporate Governance.' Unpublished Working Paper

DTe, 2002. 'Yardstick Competition. Regional Electricity Network Companies, Second Regulatory Period.' Information and Consultation Document. Deeptech Equity NL, 20 November

Ducci, F., 2020. *Natural Monopolies in Digital Platform Markets*. Cambridge: Cambridge University Press

Dunn, G., 2017. 'Where Do Europe's Major LCCs Compete Directly?' FlightGlobal. 18 April

Dunne, N., 2015. *Competition Law and Economic Regulation: Making and Managing Markets*. Cambridge: Cambridge University Press

Dupuit, J., 1844. 'De la Mesure de l'Utilité des Travaux Publics.' *Annales des Ponts et Chaussée* [reprinted 1995 in *Revue Française d'Économie* 10(2):55–94; translated 1952 by R. H. Barback as 'On the Measurement of the Utility of Public Works.' *International Economic Papers* 2:83–110]

Dutra, J., P. Sampaio and E. Gonçalves, 2016. 'Twenty Years of Infrastructure Concessions in Brazil.' *Network Industries Quarterly* 18(1):3–6

Dzieza, J., 2018. 'Prime and Punishment. Dirty Dealing in the $175 Billion Amazon Marketplace.' *The Verge*. 19 December

EASA, 2020. 'Updated Analysis of the Non-CO_2 Climate Impacts of Aviation and Potential Policy Measures Pursuant to EU Emissions Trading System Directive Article 30(4).' SWD (2020) 277 Final

Easter, K. W. and Q. Huang, 2014. 'Water Markets: How Do We Expand Their Use?' In *Water Markets for the 21st Century*. Dordrecht: Springer, pp. 1–9

EBA, 2016. 'EBA FINAL Draft Regulatory Technical Standards on Separation of Payment Card Schemes and Processing Entities under Article 7(6) of Regulation (EU) 2015/751.' 2 July

Eberhard, A., 2007. 'Infrastructure Regulation in Developing Countries: An Exploration of Hybrid and Transitional Models.' PPIAF Working Paper No. 4

EC, 1987. 'Towards a Dynamic European Economy: Green Paper on the Development of the Common Market for Telecommunications Services and Equipment.' COM (87) 290 Final. 30 June

——1998. 'Commission Recommendation on Interconnection in a Liberalised Telecommunications Market: Part 1 – Interconnection Pricing.' L 73/42. 12 March

——2002. 'Case No. COMP/29.373 – Visa International – Multilateral Interchange Fee.' 24 July

——2003. 'Commission Calls for Equal Treatment for Cable Networks in the Provision of Telecommunications Services in France.' IP/03/520. 9 April

——2007a. 'Telecoms: Commission to Take Germany to Court Over Its "Regulatory Holiday" Law.' European Commission Press Release. IP/07/889

——2007b. 'Case No. COMP/34.579 Mastercard.' 19 December

——2007c. 'DG Competition Report on Energy Sector Inquiry.' SEC (2006) 1724. 10 January

——2009. 'Commission Recommendation on the Regulatory Treatment of Fixed and Mobile Termination Rates in the EU: Implications for Industry, Competition and Consumers.' Commission Staff Working Document. SEC (2009) 599. 7 May

——2010. 'Commission Recommendation on Regulated Access to Next Generation Access Networks.' L251/35. 20 September

——2011a. 'A Quality Framework for Services of General Interest in Europe.' COM (2011) 900. 20 December

——2011b. 'Proposal for a Regulation on Common Rules for the Allocation of Slots at European Union Airports.' COM (2011) 827 Final

——2012. 'Unconventional Gas: Potential Energy Market Impacts in the European Union.' JRC Scientific and Policy Reports

——2013a. 'Proposal for a Regulation of the European Parliament and of the Council on Interchange Fees for Card-Based Payment Transactions: Impact Assessment.' Commission Staff Working Document. SWD (2013) 288 Final

——2013b. 'Commission Staff Working to Accompany the Legislative Proposals to Update the Regulations on Single European Sky – SES2+.' SWD (2013) 206 Final

——2014. 'Guidelines on State Aid to Airports and Airlines.' 2014/C99/03

——2015a. 'Delivering a New Deal for Energy Consumers.' COM (2015) 339

——2015b. 'Survey on Merchants' Costs of Processing Cash and Card Payments: Final Results.' March. Publications Office

——2016a. 'Behavioural Insights Applied to Policy: European Report 2016.' EUR 27726 EN

——2016b. 'New Electricity Market Design: A Fair Deal for Consumers.' Press Release

——2016c. 'Proposal for a Directive of the European Parliament and of the Council Establishing the European Electronic Communications Code.' COM (2016) 590 Final/2

——2016d. 'Study on the Prices and Quality of Rail Passenger Services.' Final Report. April

——2017. 'Commission Fines Facebook €110 Million for Providing Misleading Information about WhatsApp Takeover.' Press Release. 18 May

——2018. 'Guidelines on Market Analysis and the Assessment of Significant Market Power under the EU Regulatory Framework for Electronic Communications Networks and Services.' 2018/C159/01

——2019a. 'Report from the Commission to the European Parliament and the Council on the Implementation of the Open Internet Access Provisions of Regulation (EU) 2015/2120.' COM (2019) 203 Final

——2019b. 'Transport in the European Union Current Trends and Issues'

——2019c. 'Commission Staff Working Document Evaluation of the Directive 2009/12/EC of the European Parliament and of the Council of 11 March 2009 on Airport Charges.' SWD (2019) 289 Final

——2019d. 'Commission Staff Working Document Evaluation of the Regulation (EC) No. 1008/2008 on Common Rules for the Operation of Air Services in the Community.' SWD (2019) 295 Final

——2020a. 'The Role of Gas DSOs and Distribution Networks in the Context of the Energy Transition.' Asset Study

——2020b. 'Commission Recommendation of 18.12.2020 on Relevant Product and Service Markets within the Electronic Communications Sector Susceptible to Ex Ante Regulation in Accordance with Directive (EU) 2018/1972 of the European Parliament and of the Council of 11 December 2018 Establishing the European Electronic Communications Code.' SWD (2020) 337 Final

——2020c. 'Commission Delegated Regulation (EU) 2021/654 of 18 December 2020 Supplementing Directive (EU) 2018/1972 of the European Parliament and of the Council by Setting a Single Maximum Union-wide Mobile Voice Termination Rate and a Single Maximum Union-wide Fixed Voice Termination Rate.' 24 April. L 137/1

——2020d. 'Report on the Application of Regulation (EU) 2015/751 on Interchange Fees for Cardbased Payment Transactions.' Commission Staff Working Document. SWD (2020) 118

——2020e. 'A Retail Payments Strategy for the EU.' COM (2020) 592

——2020f. 'The Retail Payments Strategy at a Glance.' September

——2020g. Regulation of the European Parliament and of the Council on Contestable and Fair Markets in the Digital Sector (Digital Markets Act). COM (2020) 842

——2020h. 'EU Transport in Figures.' Statistical Pocketbook. September

——2021a. 'Proposal for a Regulation of the European Parliament and of the Council on the Internal Markets for Renewable and Natural Gases and for Hydrogen.' COM (2021) 804 Final

——2021b. 'Proposal for a Directive of the European Parliament and of the Council on Common Rules for the Internal Markets in Renewable and Natural Gases and in Hydrogen.' COM (2021) 803 Final

——2021c. 'State of the Energy Union 2021 – Contributing to the European Green Deal and the Union's Recovery.' COM (2021) 950 Final

——2021d. 'Quarterly Report on European Electricity Markets.' Volume 13, Quarter 4

——2021e. 'Broadband Coverage in Europe 2020: Mapping Progress towards the Coverage Objectives of the Digital Agenda.' Final Report

——2021f. 'Digital Economy and Society Index (DESI) 2021 Thematic Chapters.' Report

——2021g. 'The Impact of Separation between Infrastructure Management and Transport Operations on the EU Railway Sector.' Note. May

——2021h. 'Reducing Emissions from Aviation: Revision of the EU ETS Directive Concerning Aviation.' Press Statement

——2022. 'Security of Supply and Affordable Energy Prices: Options for Immediate Measures and Preparing for Next Winter.' COM (2022) 138 Final. 23 March

ECB, 2022. 'The Economics of Central Bank Digital Currency.' European Central Bank, Working Paper Series, No. 2713. August

Economides, N., 1998. 'The Incentive for Non-Price Discrimination by an Input Monopolist.' *International Journal of Industrial Organization* 16:271–284

——2003. 'The Tragic Inefficiency of the M-ECPR.' In A. L. Shampine (ed.), *Down to the Wire: Studies in the Diffusion and Regulation of Telecommunications Technologies*. Hauppauge NY: Nova Science

——2010. 'Why Imposing New Tolls on Third-Party Content and Application Threatens Innovation and Will Not Improve Broadband Providers' Investment.' NYU Law and Economics Research Paper Series, Working Paper No. 10-32. July

Economides, N., K. Seim and V. B. Viard, 2008. 'Quantifying the Benefits of Entry into Local Phone Service.' *RAND Journal of Economics* 39:699–730

Economides, N. and J. Tåg, 2012. 'Network Neutrality in the Internet: A Two-Sided Market Analysis.' *Information Economics and Policy* 24:91–104

Economides, N. and L. J. White, 1995. 'Access and Interconnection Pricing: How Efficient Is the "Efficient Component Pricing Rule"?' *Antitrust Bulletin* 15:557–579

EC Portugal, 2009. 'Case PT/2008/0851: Wholesale Broadband Access.' 5 May

Edwards, G. and L. Waverman, 2006. 'The Effects of Public Ownership and Regulatory Independence on Regulatory Outcomes.' *Journal of Regulatory Economics* 29:23–67

EEA, 2009. 'Water Resources across Europe – Confronting Water Scarcity and Drought.' EEA Report. No. 2/2009

——2021. 'Water Use in Europe – Quantity and Quality Face Big Challenges.' 11 May

EIA, 2007. 'An Analysis of Price Volatility in Natural Gas Markets.' Office of Oil and Gas. August

——2013. 'Technically Recoverable Shale Oil and Shale Gas Resources: An Assessment of 137 Shale Formations in 41 Countries Outside the USA.' June

——2018. 'Electricity Residential Retail Choice Participation Has Declined Since 2014 Peak.' Today in Energy. 8 November

——2020. 'U.S. Homes and Businesses Receive Natural Gas Mostly from Local Distribution Companies.' Today in Energy. 31 July

——2021a. 'Factors Affecting Electricity Prices.' 3 November

——2021b. 'Battery Storage in the United States: An Update on Market Trends.' August

——2021c. 'Electricity Monthly Update.' October

——2021d. 'Sales and Direct Use of Electricity to Ultimate Customers.' Table 2.2

——2022a. 'Annual Energy Outlook 2022: Low Oil and Gas Supply.' March

——2022b. 'Natural Gas Consumption by End Use.' 28 February

——2022c. 'Natural Gas Annual 2021'

——2022d. 'Three Countries Provided Almost 70% of Liquefied Natural Gas Received in Europe in 2021.' Today in Energy. 22 February

Eisenmann, T., G. Parker and M. Van Alstyne, 2011. 'Platform Envelopment.' *Strategic Management Journal* 32(12):1270–1285

Ekelund, R. B., 1968. 'Jules Dupuit and the Early Theory of Marginal Cost Pricing.' *Journal of Political Economy* 76:462–471

Eliaz, K. and R. Spiegler, 2006. 'Contracting with Diversely Naive Agents.' *Review of Economic Studies* 73(3):689–714

——2008. 'Consumer Optimism and Price Discrimination.' *Theoretical Economics* 3(4):459–497

Elkins, J., 2010. 'Natural Gas in the UK: An Industry in Search of a Policy?' Oxford Institute for Energy Studies, Working Paper NG 40. February

Ellison, G., 2006. 'Bounded Rationality in Industrial Organization.' *Econometric Society Monographs* 42:142

Ellison, G. and S. F. Ellison, 2009. 'Search, Obfuscation, and Price Elasticities on the Internet.' *Econometrica* 77(2):427–452

Ellison, G. and A. Wolitzky, 2012. 'A Search Cost Model of Obfuscation.' *RAND Journal of Economics* 43(3):417–441

Ely, R. T., 1937. *Outlines of Economics.* New York: Macmillan

Engel, C. and K. Heine, 2017. 'The Dark Side of Price Cap Regulation: A Laboratory Experiment.' *Public Choice* 173(1–2):217–240

Englehardt, S. and A. Narayanan, 2016. 'Online Tracking: A 1-Million-Site Measurement and Analysis.' In Proceedings of the 2016 ACM SIGSAC Conference on Computer and Communications Security, Vienna, Austria, ACM, pp. 1388–1401

Ennis, S., 2019. 'Independent Sector Regulators – Background Note.' OECD Working Party No. 2 on Competition and Regulation. 2 December

EPA, 2009. 'Water and Wastewater Pricing – An Informational Overview.' 832-F-03-027

——2013a. 'Pricing Structures.' Sustainable Infrastructure

——2013b. 'Water Use Today.' Water Sense

ERG, 2005. 'Broadband Market Competition Report.' ERG (05) 23

——2006. 'Revised ERG Common Position on the Approach to Appropriate Remedies in the ECNS Regulatory Framework.' ERG (06) 33. May

——2009. 'Report on Next Generation Access – Economic Analysis and Regulatory Principles.' ERG (09) 17. June

Ernst & Young and Copenhagen Economics, 2020. 'Study on the Application of the Interchange Fee Regulation.' Final Report for the European Commission

Eskesen, A., 2021a. 'A Contract Design Perspective on Balancing the Goals of Utility Regulation.' *Utilities Policy* 69:101161

Eskesen, A., 2021b. 'Essays on Utility Regulation: Evaluating Negotiation-Based Approaches in the Context of Danish Utility Regulation.' Copenhagen Business School. PhD Series No. 16.2021

Esposito, G., J. Doleschel, T. Kaloud, M. Mariotti and J. Urban-Kozłowska, 2017. 'The European Railway Sectors: Understanding and Assessing Change.' Università degli Studi di Milano, Working Paper

Estache, A., 1997. 'Designing Regulatory Institutions for Infrastructure – Lessons from Argentina.' World Bank Note No. 114. May

——2020. 'Infrastructure Privatization: When Ideology Meets Evidence.' ECARES Working Paper

Estache, A. and E. Grifell-Tatjé, 2013. 'How (Un)Even Was the Distribution of the Impacts of Mali's Water Privatisation across Stakeholders?' *Journal of Development Studies* 49(4):483–499

Estache, A. and A. Iimi, 2011. '(Un)bundling Infrastructure Procurement: Evidence from Water Supply and Sewage Projects.' *Utilities Policy* 19:104–114

Estache, A. and C. Philippe, 2016. 'What If the TTIP Changed the Regulation of Public Services? Lessons for Europe from Developing Countries.' *Reflets et Perspectives de la Vie Économique* LV(3):59–73

Estache, A. and L. Wren-Lewis, 2009. 'Toward a Theory of Regulation for Developing Countries Following Jean-Jacques Laffont's Lead.' *Journal of Economic Literature.* 47:729–770

Esteban, S. and E. Miyagawa, 2006. 'Temptation, Self-Control, and Competitive Nonlinear Pricing.' *Economics Letters* 90(3):348–355

Estrin, S., J. Hanousek, E. Kočenda and J. Svejnar, 2009. 'The Effects of Privatization and Ownership in Transition Economies.' *Journal of Economic Literature* 47(3):699–728

Estrin, S. and A. Pelletier, 2018. 'Privatization in Developing Countries: What Are the Lessons of Recent Experience?' *World Bank Research Observer* 33(1):65–102

Eto, J., S. Stoft and T. Belden, 1997. 'The Theory and Practice of Decoupling Utility Revenues from Sales.' *Utilities Policy* 6:43–55

EU 5G Observatory, 2022. 'Spectrum Release Timeline'

Eurocontrol, 2019. 'U.S.–Europe Continental Comparison of and Cost-Efficiency Trends.' March

European Parliament, 2011. 'Impacts of Shale Gas and Shale Oil Extraction on the Environment and Human Health.' Study IP/A/ENVI/ST/2011-07. June

——2021. 'Air Transport: Single European Sky.' Fact Sheets on the European Union

Evans, D. S., 2003. 'Some Empirical Aspects of Multi-Sided Platform Industries.' *Review of Network Economics* 2(3):191–209

Evans, D. S. and A. M. Mateus, 2011. 'How Changes in Payment Card Interchange Fees Affect Consumers Fees and Merchant Prices: An Economic Analysis with Applications to the European Union.' *SSRN Electronic Journal* 1878735

Evans, D. S. and R. Schmalensee, 2005. *Paying with Plastic: The Digital Revolution in Buying and Borrowing.* Cambridge, MA: MIT Press

——2016. *Matchmakers: The New Economics of Multisided Platforms.* Boston, MA: Harvard Business Review Press

——2017/18. 'Debunking the "Network Effects" Bogeyman.' *Regulation* 40(4):36–39

Evans, J., P. Levine, N. Rickman and F. Trillas, 2011. 'Delegation to Independent Regulators and the Ratchet Effect.' University of Surrey Discussion Paper in Economics DP 09/11. July

Evans, L. T., A. Grimes, B. Wilkinson and D. Teece, 1996. 'Economic Reform in New Zealand 1984–95: The Pursuit of Efficiency.' *Journal of Economic Literature* 34:1856–1902

Evans, L. T. and G. A. Guthrie, 2005. 'Risk, Price Regulation, and Irreversible Investment.' *International Journal of Industrial Organization* 23:109–128

Ezrachi, A. and M. E. Stucke, 2016. *Virtual Competition: The Promise and Perils of the Algorithm-Driven Economy.* Cambridge, MA: Harvard University Press

FAA, 2013. 'Fact Sheet – What Is the Airport Privatization Pilot Program.' 27 September

——2016. 'Update of Overflight Fee Rates.' Docket No. FAA-2015-3597; Amdt. No. 187-36

——2020a. 'Unmanned Aircraft System (UAS) Traffic Management (UTM). Concept of Operations.' V2.0. March

——2020b. 'Airport and Airway Trust Fund (AATF).' Fact Sheet. April

——2020c. 'Air Traffic by the Numbers.' August

——2021. 'Fact Sheet – Airport Investment Partnership Program (AIPP) – Formerly Airport Privatization Pilot Program.' 8 March

Façanha, L. O. and M. Resende, 2004. 'Price Cap Regulation, Incentives and Quality: The Case of Brazilian Telecommunications.' *International Journal of Production Economics* 92:133–144

Facebook, 2021. 'Facebook Reports Fourth Quarter and Full Year 2020 Results.' Press Release. 27 January

Farrell, J., 2006. 'Efficiency and Competition between Payment Instruments.' *Review of Network Economics* 5(1):26–44

Farrell, J. and P. Klemperer, 2007. 'Coordination and Lock-In: Competition with Switching Costs and Network Effects.' In M. Armstrong and R. Porter (eds.), *Handbook of Industrial Organization*, Volume 3. Amsterdam: Elsevier, pp. 1967–2072

Farronato C., A. Fradkin and A MacKay, 2023. 'Self-Preferencing at Amazon: Evidence from Search Rankings' NBER Working Paper No. 30894.

Faruqui, A., 2013. 'Surviving Sub-One-Percent Growth.' *Electricity Policy* June, pp. 1–11

——2015a. 'The Global Movement toward Cost-Reflective Tariffs.' EUCI Residential Demand Charges Summit. Denver, Colorado. 14 May

——2015b. 'The Movement towards Deploying Demand Charges for Residential Customers.' NARUC 127th Annual Meeting. 8 November

Faruqui, A., W. Davis, J. Duh and C. Warner, 2016. 'Curating the Future of Rate Design for Residential Customers.' *Electricity Daily* July, pp. 1–25

Faulhaber, G. R., 1975. 'Cross-Subsidization: Pricing in Public Enterprises.' *American Economic Review* 65:966–977

——2005a. 'Bottlenecks and Bandwagons: Access Policy in the New Telecommunications.' In S. K. Majumdar, I. Vogelsang and M. E. Cave (eds.), *Handbook of Telecommunications Economics*, Volume 2. Amsterdam: Elsevier

——2005b. 'Cross-Subsidy Analysis with More than Two Services.' *Journal of Competition Law and Economics* 1:441–448

——2015. 'What Hath the FCC Wrought.' *Regulation* 38:50

Faure-Grimaud, A. and D. Martimort, 2003. 'Regulatory Inertia.' *RAND Journal of Economics* 34:413–437

FCA, 2013. 'Applying Behavioural Economics at the Financial Conduct Authority.' Occasional Paper No. 1. April

——2016. 'Credit Card Market Study Final Findings Report.' MS14/6

——2018. 'The Semblance of Success in Nudging Consumers to Pay Down Credit Card Debt.' Occasional Paper 45

FCC, 1996. 'Implementation of the Local Competition Provisions in the Telecommunications Act of 1996: First Report and Order.' CC Docket No. 96-98. FCC 96-325. 8 August

——2003a. 'Review of the Commission's Rules Regarding the Pricing of Unbundled Network Elements and the Resale of Service by Incumbent Local Exchange Carriers.' Notice of Proposed Rulemaking. 15 September

——2003b. 'Review of the Section 251 Unbundling Obligations of Incumbent Local Exchange Carriers.' Report and Order and Further NOPR. 21 August

——2010a. 'Preserving the Open Internet Broadband Industry Practices.' Report and Order. 23 December

——2010b. 'Consumer and Governmental Affairs Bureau White Paper on Bill Shock.' 13 October

——2011. 'In the Matter of Establishing Just and Reasonable Rates for Local Exchange Carriers.' WC Docket No. 07-135

——2012. 'In the Matter of Petition for Declaratory Ruling to Clarify 47 U.S.C. § 572 in the Context of Transactions between Competitive Local Exchange Carriers and Cable Operators Conditional Petition for Forbearance from Section 652 of the Communications Act for Transactions between Competitive Local Exchange Carriers and Cable Operators.' WC Docket No. 11-118

——2015. 'In the Matter of Protecting and Promoting the Open Internet.' Docket No. 14-28

——2017a. 'In the Matter of Business Data Services in an Internet Protocol Environment Technology Transitions Special Access for Price Cap Local Exchange Carriers AT&T Corporation Petition for Rulemaking to Reform Regulation of Incumbent Local Exchange Carrier Rates for Interstate Special Access Services.' WC Docket No. 16-143

——2017b. 'In the Matter of Restoring Internet Freedom.' WC Docket No. 17-108

——2018. 'Eighth Measuring Broadband America Fixed Broadband.' Report

——2020a. '2021 Budget in Brief.' February

——2020b. 'In the Matter of Modernizing Unbundling and Resale Requirements in an Era of Next-Generation Networks and Services.' WC Docket No. 19-308

——2020c. 'In the Matter of Communications Marketplace.' Report. GN Docket No. 20-60

Federal Reserve, 2002. 'The Future of Retail Payments Systems: Industry Interviews and Analysis.' Staff Study. December

——2012. 'Collaborating to Improve the U.S. Payments System.' 22 October

——2013. 'Payment System Improvement – Public Consultation Paper.' 10 September

——2019. 'Transcript of Chair Powell's Press Conference.' 31 July

——2021. 'Regulation II (Debit Card Interchange Fees and Routing).' FAW. 12 May

——2022. 'An Update on the Federal Reserve's Efforts to Modernize the Payment System'. Speech. 4 October

Fehr, E. and K. M. Schmidt, 1999. 'A Theory of Fairness, Competition, and Cooperation.' *Quarterly Journal of Economics* 114(3):817–868

Feldstein, M. S., 1972. 'Equity and Efficiency in Public Sector Pricing: The Optimal Two-Part Tariff.' *Quarterly Journal of Economics* 86(2):175–187

Felt, M. H., F. Hayashi, J. Stavins and A. Welte, 2021. 'Distributional Effects of Payment Card Pricing and Merchant Cost Pass-Through in Canada and the United States.' No. 2021-8. Bank of Canada

FERC, 1996a. 'Order No. 888: Final Rule.' 24 April

——1996b 'Alternatives to Traditional Cost-of-Service Ratemaking for Natural Gas Pipelines; Regulation of Negotiated Transportation Services of Natural Gas Pipelines.' 74 FERC 61,076, Order Granting Clarification, 74 FERC 61,194

——1999. 'Certification of New Interstate Natural Gas Pipeline Facilities.' Docket No. PL 99-3-00. 15 September

——2000. 'Regulation of Short-Term Natural Gas Transportation Services, and Regulation of Interstate Natural Gas Transportation Services.' Order No. 637. Issued 9 February

——2007. 'Market-Based Rates for Wholesale Sales of Electric Energy, Capacity and Ancillary Services by Public Utilities.' Order No. 697. Issued 21 June

——2008. 'Market-Based Rates for Wholesale Sales of Electric Energy, Capacity and Ancillary Services by Public Utilities.' Order No, 697-A. Issued 12 April

——2011. 'Order Issuing Certificate, Requiring New Open Season, and Amending Tariff.' Issued 19 May

——2018. 'Interstate and Intrastate Natural Gas Pipelines; Rate Changes Relating to Federal Income Tax Rate.' Docket No. RM18-11-000

——2020. 'Energy Primer: A Handbook of Energy Market Basics.' April

Ferreira da Cruz, N. F., P. Carvalho and R. C. Marques, 2013. 'Disentangling the Cost Efficiency of Jointly Provided Water and Wastewater Services.' *Utilities Policy* 24:70–77

Fershtman, C. and A. Fishman, 1994. 'The "Perverse" Effects of Wage and Price Controls in Search Markets.' *European Economic Review* 38(5):1099–1112

Fesler, J. W., 1940. 'The Independence of State Utility Commissions I.' *Journal of Politics* 2(4):367–390

Financial Express, 2021. 'RuPay's Market Share by Volumes Is 34%.' 23 March

Financial Times, 2017. 'Water Privatisation Looks Little More than an Organised Rip-Off.' 10 September

——2019. 'Rail Privatisation: The UK Looks for Secrets of Japan's Success.' 28 January

——2022. 'Letter: Europe's Telecoms Market Risks Falling Behind Rivals.' 21 February

Finger, M. and P. Messulam, 2015. 'Rail Economics and Regulation.' In *Rail Economics, Policy and Regulation in Europe.* Cheltenham: Edward Elgar, pp. 1–21

Finsinger, J. and I. Vogelsang, 1985. 'Strategic Management Behaviour Under Reward Structures in a Planned Economy.' *Quarterly Journal of Economics* 100:263–269

FIS, 2019. 'Flavors of Fast.' Report

Fischhoff, B., 1975. 'Hindsight ≠ Foresight: The Effect of Outcome Knowledge on Judgment under Uncertainty.' *Journal of Experimental Psychology: Human Perception and Performance* 1(3):288–299

Fletcher, A., 2016. 'The Role of Demand-Side Remedies in Driving Effective Competition.' A Review for *Which?*

Florio, M., 2013. *Network Industries and Social Welfare: The Experiment that Reshuffled European Utilities.* Oxford: Oxford University Press

——2014. 'Energy Reforms and Consumer Prices in the EU Over Twenty Years.' *Economics of Energy & Environmental Policy* 3(1):37–52

Floyd, P., T. M. Park and P. Sharma, 2017. 'Canada's Experience with ATC Privatization.' *Air & Space Law* 30:23

Forbes, 2020. 'How Airbus Has Grown Over the Years to Dethrone Boeing As the Largest Commercial Aircraft Maker.' 6 January

——2021a. 'Extending the Durbin Amendment to the Credit-Card Market Will Harm Consumers.' 12 July

——2021b. 'Amazon's Third-Party Marketplace Is Its Cash Cow, Not AWS.' 5 February

Ford, G. S. and L. J. Spiwak, 2016. 'Lessons Learned from the U.S. Unbundling Experience.' *Federal Communications Law Journal* 68(1):95–138

Ford, J. L. and J. J. Warford, 1969. 'Cost Functions for the Water Industry.' *Journal of Industrial Economics* 18:53–63

Forsyth, P., 2004. 'Replacing Regulation: Airport Price Monitoring in Australia.' In P. Forsyth, D. W. Gillen, A. Knorr, *et al.* (eds.), *The Economic Regulation of Airports: Recent Developments in Australasia, North America and Europe.* Aldershot: Ashgate

Forsyth, P., D. Gillen, J. Muller and H. M. Niemeier (eds.), 2016. *Airport Competition: The European Experience*. London: Routledge

Foster, V., 2005. 'Ten Years of Water Service Reform in Latin America: Toward an Anglo-French Model.' World Bank Water Supply and Sanitation Sector Discussion Paper No. 3. January

Foster, V. and A. Rana, 2020. *Rethinking Power Sector Reform in the Developing World*. Washington, DC: World Bank

Foster, V., S. Witte, S. G. Banerjee and A. Moreno, 2017. *Charting the Diffusion of Power Sector Reforms across the Developing World*. Washington, DC: World Bank

Fox, W. F. and R. A. Hofler, 1986. 'Using Homothetic Composed Error Frontiers to Measure Water Utility Efficiency.' *Southern Economic Journal* 53:461–477

Franck, J. U. and M. Peitz, 2021. 'Digital Platforms and the New 19a Tool in the German Competition Act.' *Journal of European Competition Law and Practice* 12(7):513–528

——2023. 'Market Definition and Three 19a Designations under German Antitrust Law: Alphabet, Meta, and Amazon' CPI Antitrust Chronicle, January 2023

Frankel, A. S., 1998. 'Monopoly and Competition in the Supply and Exchange of Money.' *Antitrust Law Journal* 66:313

Frederick, S., G. Loewenstein and T. O'Donoghue, 2002. 'Time Discounting and Time Preference: A Critical Review.' *Journal of Economic Literature* 40(2):351–401

Frederiks, E. R., K. Stenner and E. V. Hobman, 2015. 'Household Energy Use: Applying Behavioural Economics to Understand Consumer Decision-Making and Behaviour.' *Renewable and Sustainable Energy Reviews* 41:1385–1394

Frey, B. S. and W. W. Pommerehne, 1993. 'On the Fairness of Pricing – An Empirical Survey among the General Population.' *Journal of Economic Behavior & Organization* 20(3):295–307

Friederiszick, H., M. Grajek and L.-H. Röller, 2008. 'Analyzing the Relationship between Regulation and Investment in the Telecom Sector.' EMST Working Paper. March

Friedlaender, A. F., 1969. *The Dilemma of Freight Transport Regulation*. Washington, DC: Brookings Institution

Friedman, J. W., 1971. 'A Non-Cooperative Equilibrium for Supergames.' *Review of Economic Studies* 38(1):1–12

Fröhlich, K., 2010. 'Airports as Two-Sided Markets? A Critical Contribution.' University of Applied Sciences, Bremen

Frontier Economics, 2007. 'The Economic and Social Impacts of Water Trading.' Report for the National Water Commission. September

——2017. 'Productivity Improvement in the Water and Sewerage Industry in England since Privatisation.' Final Report for Water UK. 29 September

——2022. 'Estimating OTT-Traffic Related Costs on European Telecommunications Networks.' A Report for Deutsche Telekom, Orange, Telefonica and Vodafone. 7 April

FTC, 2012. 'A Conference on the Economics of Drip Pricing.' 21 May

Fulton, D., 2021. 'Network Experimentation: Why New Airline Routes in Europe Are Hitting an All-Time High.' OAG Aviation. 13 May

Fulwood, M., 2019. 'Opportunities for Gas in Sub-Saharan Africa.' *OIES Energy Insight* 44(January):1–24

Furman, J., D. Coyle, A. Fletcher, D. McAukey and P. Marsden, 2019. 'Unlocking Digital Competition.' Report of the Digital Competition Expert Panel. March

Furnham, A. and H. C. Boo, 2011. 'A Literature Review of the Anchoring Effect.' *Journal of Socio-Economics* 40(1):35–42

Gabaix, X. and D. Laibson, 2006. 'Shrouded Attributes, Consumer Myopia, and Information Suppression in Competitive Markets.' *Quarterly Journal of Economics* 121(2):505–540

Gabel, D. and M. Kennet, 1991. 'Estimating the Cost Structure of the Local Telephone Exchange Network.' National Regulatory Research Institute

Gal, D. and D. D. Rucker, 2018. 'The Loss of Loss Aversion: Will It Loom Larger than Its Gain?' *Journal of Consumer Psychology* 28(3):497–516

Galal, A., 1996. 'Chile: Regulatory Specificity, Credibility of Commitment and Distributional Demands.' In B. Levy and P. T. Spiller (eds.), *Regulations, Institutions, and Commitment: Comparative Studies of Telecommunications*. Cambridge: Cambridge University Press

Galal, A., L. Jones, P. Tandon and I. Vogelsang, 1994. *Welfare Consequences of Selling Public Enterprises: An Empirical Analysis*. Oxford: Oxford University Press

Galal, A. and B. Nauriyal, 1994. 'Regulation of Telecom in Developing Countries: Outcomes, Incentives & Commitment.' World Bank Working Paper 9513

Gale, I. L. and T. J. Holmes, 1993. 'Advance-Purchase Discounts and Monopoly Allocation of Capacity.' *American Economic Review* 83(1):135–146

Galiani, S., 2022. 'Public Sector Participation in the Water Sector: Opportunities and Pitfalls.' In *Oxford Research Encyclopedia of Global Public Health*. Oxford: Oxford University Press

Gamp, T. and D. Krähmer, 2017. 'Deceptive Products and Competition in Search Markets.' Working Paper

Gangwar, R. and G. Raghuram, 2017. 'Implications of Vertical Unbundling on Indian Railways: Lessons from German Railway Reform.' *Transportation Research Procedia* 25, 4529–4543

Gans, J. S., 2018. 'Are We Too Negative on Negative Fees for Payment Cardholders?' Rotman School of Management. Working Paper, 3162627

Gans, J. S. and M. L. Katz, 2016. 'Weak versus Strong Net Neutrality: Correction and Clarification.' *Journal of Regulatory Economics* 50(1):99–110

Gans, J. S. and S. P. King, 2001a. 'Using 'Bill and Keep' Interconnect Arrangements to Soften Network Competition.' *Economics Letters* 71:413–420

——2001b. 'The Role of Interchange Fees in Credit Card Associations: Competitive Analysis and Regulatory Issues.' *Australian Business Law Review* 29(2):94–123

——2003a. 'Access Holidays for Network Infrastructure Investment.' *Agenda* 10:163–178

——2003b. 'The Neutrality of Interchange Fees in Payment Systems.' *Topics in Economic Analysis & Policy* 3 (1):1069

——2004a. 'Comparing Alternative Approaches to Calculating Long-Run Incremental Cost.' Unpublished Working Paper. June

——2004b. 'Access Holidays and the Timing of Infrastructure Investment.' *Economic Record* 80:89–100

Gans, J. S., S. P. King and J. Wright, 2005. 'Wireless Communications.' In S. K. Majumdar, I. Vogelsang and M. E. Cave (eds.), *Handbook of Telecommunications Economics*, Volume 2. Amsterdam: Elsevier

Gans, J. S. and P. L. Williams, 1999. 'Access Regulation and the Timing of Infrastructure Investment.' *Economic Record* 75:127–137

GAO, 1990. 'Fares and Service at Major Airports.' GAO/WED-99-102. 11 July

——2006a. 'Reregulating the Airline Industry Would Likely Reverse Consumer Benefits and Not Save Airline Pensions.' June

——2006b. 'Observations on Potential FAA Funding Options.' September

——2007. 'Assigning Air Traffic Control Costs to Users: Elements of FAA's Methodology Are Generally Consistent with Standards but Certain Assumptions and Methods Need Additional Support.' October

——2008. 'Electricity Restructuring.' Report to the Committee on Homeland Security and Governmental Affairs. September

——2009. 'Credit Cards: Rising Interchange Fees Have Increased Costs for Merchants, but Options for Reducing Fees Pose Challenges.' Report to Congressional Addressees. November

——2014. 'Airport Privatization: Limited Interest despite FAA's Pilot Program.' November

——2019. 'Unmanned Aircraft Systems. FAA Should Improve Drone-Related Cost Information and Consider Options to Recover Costs.' December

García, J. A. and J. D. Reitzes, 2007. 'International Perspectives on Electricity Market Monitoring and Market Power Mitigation.' *Review of Network Economics* 6:372–399

García, S., M. Moreaux and A. Reynaud, 2007. 'Measuring Economies of Vertical Integration in Network Industries: An Application to the Water Sector.' *International Journal of Industrial Organization* 25:791–820

García, S. and A. Thomas, 2001. 'The Structure of Municipal Water Supply Costs: Application t a Panel of French Local Communities.' *Journal of Productivity Analysis* 16:5–29

Garrick, D., S. M. Whitten and A. Coggan, 2013. 'Understanding the Evolution and Performanc of Water Markets and Allocation Policy: A Transaction Costs Analysis Framework.' *Ecological Economics* 88:195–205

Garrone, P. and M. Zaccagnino, 2015. 'Seeking the Links between Competition and Telecommunications Investments.' *Telecommunications Policy* 39(5):388–405

Gassner, K. and N. Pushak, 2014. '30 years of British Utility Regulation: Developing Country Experience and Outlook.' *Utilities Policy* 31:44–51

Gautier, A. and J. Lamesch, 2021. 'Mergers in the Digital Economy.' *Information Economics and Policy* 54:100890

Gayle, P. G. and D. L. Weisman, 2007. 'Are Input Prices Irrelevant for the Make-or-Buy Decisions?' *Journal of Regulatory Economics* 32:195–207

Genakos, C. and T. Valletti, 2007. 'Regulating the Mobile Phone Industry: Beware the "Waterbed" Effect.' *CentrePiece* Article CEPCP238. Centre for Economic Performance, LSE October

——2011a. 'Seesaw in the Air: Interconnection Regulation and the Structure of Mobile Tariffs.' *Information Economics and Policy* 23:159–170

——2011b. 'Testing the "Waterbed" Effect in Mobile Telephony.' *Journal of the European Economic Association* 9:1114–1142

——2015. 'Evaluating a Decade of Mobile Termination Rate Regulation.' *Economic Journal* 125(586):F31–F48

Genakos, C., T. Valletti and F. Verboven, 2018. 'Evaluating Market Consolidation in Mobile Communications.' *Economic Policy* 33(93):45–100

Geradin, D., 2000. 'Institutional Aspects of EU Regulatory Reforms in the Telecommunications Sector: An Analysis of the Role of National Regulatory Authorities.' *Journal of Network Industries* 1:5–32

Gerardi, K. S. and A. H. Shapiro, 2009. 'Does Competition Reduce Price Dispersion? New Evidence from the Airline Industry.' *Journal of Political Economy* 117(1):1–37

Gibson, C., C. McKean and H. Piffaut, 2012. 'Regulation of Water and Wastewater.' In R. Van den Bergh and A. M. Pacces (eds.), *Regulation and Economics: Encyclopedia of Law and Economics*, 2nd ed. Cheltenham: Edward Elgar

Gigerenzer, G., 1991. 'How to Make Cognitive Illusions Disappear: Beyond "Heuristics and Biases".' *European Review of Social Psychology* 2(1):83–115

——2018. 'The Bias Bias in Behavioral Economics.' *Review of Behavioral Economics* 5(3–4):303–336

Gilbert, R. J., 1989. 'The Role of Potential Competition in Industrial Organization.' *Journal of Economic Perspectives* 3:107–127

——2021. 'Separation: A Cure for Abuse of Platform Dominance?' *Information Economics and Policy* 54:100876

Gilbert, R. J. and D. M. Newbery, 1994. 'The Dynamic Efficiency of Regulatory Constitutions.' *RAND Journal of Economics* 25:538–554

Gillan, J. and D. Malfara, 2012. 'The Transition to an All-IP Network: A Primer on the Architectural Components of IP Interconnection.' NRRI Research Paper 12-05. May

Gillen, D. and B. Mantin, 2013. 'Transportation Infrastructure Management One- and Two-Sided Market Approaches.' *Journal of Transport Economics and Policy* 47(2):207–227

Giulietti, M. and C. Waddams Price, 2005. 'Incentive Regulation and Efficient Pricing.' *Annals of Public and Cooperative Economics* 76:121–149

Glachant, J.-M., P. L. Joskow and M. G. Pollitt, 2021. 'Introduction.' In J.-M. Glachant, P. L. Joskow and M. G. Pollitt (eds.), *Handbook on Electricity Markets*. Cheltenham: Edward Elgar

Glachant, J.-M. and F. Lévêque, 2009. *Electricity Reform in Europe*. Cheltenham: Edward Elgar

Glass, V., M. Kolesar, T. Tardiff and B. Williamson, 2022. 'Provider of Last Resort in Emerging Electricity Markets: Lessons from Telecommunications Deregulation.' *Electricity Journal*, 35(1):107064

Glimcher, P. W., C. F. Camerer, E. Fehr and R. A. Poldrack, 2009. 'Introduction: A Brief History of Neuroeconomics.' In P. W. Glimcher, C. F. Camerer, E. Fehr and R. A. Poldrack (eds.), *Neuroeconomics: Decision Making and the Brain*. London: Academic Press, pp. 1–12

Goetz, A. R. and T. M. Vowles, 2009. 'The Good, the Bad, and the Ugly: 30 Years of US Airline Deregulation.' *Journal of Transport Geography* 17(4):251–263

Goldberg, V. P., 1976. 'Regulation and Administered Contracts.' *Bell Journal of Economics* 7:426–448

Goldfarb, A., T.-H. Ho, W. Amaldoss, *et al.*, 2012. 'Behavioral Models of Managerial Decision-Making.' *Marketing Letters* 23(2):405–421

Goldfarb, A. and M. Xiao, 2011. 'Who Thinks about the Competition? Managerial Ability and Strategic Entry in US Local Telephone Markets.' *American Economic Review* 101(7):3130–3161

——2016. 'Transitory Shocks, Limited Attention, and a Firm's Decision to Exit.' Working Paper

Goldfarb, A. and B. Yang, 2009. 'Are All Managers Created Equal?' *Journal of Marketing Research* 46(5):612–622

Goldman, M. B., H. E. Leland and D. S. Sibley, 1984. 'Optimal Nonuniform Prices.' *Review of Economic Studies* 51:305–319

Gómez-Ibáñez, J. A., 2003. *Regulating Infrastructure: Monopoly, Contracts and Discretion*. Cambridge, MA: Harvard University Press

——2016. 'Open Access to Infrastructure Networks: The Experience of Railroads.' *Review of Industrial Organization* 49(2):311–345

Goodman, J. B., 1992. *Monetary Sovereignty: The Politics of Central Banking in Western Europe*. Ithaca, NY: Cornell University Press

Goolsbee, A. and C. Syverson, 2008. 'How Do Incumbents Respond to the Threat of Entry? Evidence from the Major Airlines.' *Quarterly Journal of Economics* 123(4):1611–1633

Gormley, W., 1981. 'Statewide Remedies for Public Underrepresentation in Regulatory Proceedings.' *Public Administration Review* 41:454–462

Grafton, R. Q. and S. A. Wheeler, 2018. 'Economics of Water Recovery in the Murray–Darling Basin, Australia.' *Annual Review of Resource Economics* 10(1):487–510

Graham, A., 2011. 'The Objectives and Outcomes of Airport Privatisation.' *Research in Transportation Business and Management* 1(1):3–14

——2020. 'Airport Privatisation: A Successful Journey?' *Journal of Air Transport Management* 89:101930

Graham, D. R., D. P. Kaplan and D. S. Sibley, 1983. 'Efficiency and Competition in the Airline Industry.' *Bell Journal of Economics* 14(1):118–138

Granderson, G., 2000. 'Regulation, Open-Access Transportation, and Productive Efficiency.' *Review of Industrial Organization* 16:251–266

Gray, D., 2011. 'Review of Ofwat and Consumer Representation in the Water Sector.' Report for Defra and the Welsh Minister

Gray, H. M., 1940. 'The Passing of the Public Utility Concept.' *Journal of Land and Public Utility Economics* 16:8–20

Gray, J. and A. Gardner, 2008. 'Exploiting the Unspeakable: Third Party Access to Sewage and Public Sector Sewerage Infrastructure.' In T. Patrick (ed.), *Troubled Waters*. Canberra: ANU Press

Green, R. J., 1997. 'Electricity Transmission Pricing: An International Comparison.' *Utilities Policy* 6:177–184

——2008. 'Electricity Wholesale Markets: Designs Now and in a Low-Carbon Future.' *Energy Journal* 29(spec. issue 2):95–124

——2021. 'Shifting Supply as Well as Demand: The New Economics of Electricity with High Renewables.' In J.-M. Glachant, P. L. Joskow and M. G. Pollitt (eds.), *Handbook on Electricity Markets*. Cheltenham: Edward Elgar

Green, R. J. and D. M. Newbery, 1992. 'Competition in the British Electricity Spot Market.' *Journal of Political Economy* 100:929–953

Greenstein, S., M. Peitz and T. Valletti, 2016. 'Net Neutrality: A Fast Lane to Understanding the Trade-Offs.' *Journal of Economic Perspectives* 30(2):127–150

Griek, L. 2016. 'The Railway Market in Japan.' EU–Japan Centre for Industrial Cooperation. September

Griffin, D., W. Liu and U. Khan, 2005. 'A New Look at Constructed Choice Processes.' *Marketing Letters* 16(3–4):321–333

Griffin, J. M. and S. L. Puller, 2005. *Electricity Deregulation: Choices and Challenges*. Chicago: University of Chicago Press

Griffith, R. and J. Van Reenen, 2021. *Product Market Competition, Creative Destruction and Innovation*. London: Centre for Economic Performance, LSE

Griliches, Z., 1972. 'Cost Allocation in Railroad Regulation.' *Bell Journal of Economics and Management Science* 3(1):26–41

Gritten, A. 1988. 'Reviving the Railways: A Victorian Future?' CPS Policy Study No. 97. June

Grossman, S. J. and O. D. Hart, 1986. 'The Costs and Benefits of Ownership: A Theory of Vertical and Lateral Integration.' *Journal of Political Economy* 94:691–719

Grout, P. A. and A. Jenkins, 2001. 'Regulatory Opportunism and Asset Valuation: Evidence from the US Supreme Court and UK Regulation.' CMPO Working Paper Series No. 01/38. August

Growitsch, C., T. Jamasb and M. Pollitt, 2009. 'Quality of Service, Efficiency and Scale in Network Industries: An Analysis of European Electricity Distribution.' *Applied Economics* 41:2555–2570

Growitsch, C., J. S. Marcus and C. Wernick, 2010. 'The Effects of Lower Termination Rates (MTRs) on Retail Price and Demand.' *Communications & Strategies* 80: 119–140

Growitsch, C. and M. Stronzik, 2014. 'Ownership Unbundling of Natural Gas Transmission Networks: Empirical Evidence.' *Journal of Regulatory Economics* 46(2):207–225

Growitsch, C. and H. Wetzel, 2009. 'Testing for Economies of Scope in European Railways: An Efficiency Analysis.' *Journal of Transport Economics and Policy* 43(1):1–24

Grubb, M. D., 2009. 'Selling to Overconfident Consumers.' *American Economic Review* 99(5):1770–1807

——2015a. 'Consumer Inattention and Bill-Shock Regulation.' *Review of Economic Studies* 82(1):219–257

——2015b. 'Behavioral Consumers in Industrial Organization: An Overview.' *Review of Industrial Organization* 47(3):247–258

——2015c. 'Overconfident Consumers in the Marketplace.' *Journal of Economic Perspectives* 29(4):9–36

Grubb, M. D. and M. Osborne, 2015. 'Cellular Service Demand: Biased Beliefs, Learning, and Bill Shock.' *American Economic Review* 105(1):234–271

Gruber, H. and P. Koutroumpis, 2013. 'Competition Enhancing Regulation and Diffusion of Innovation: The Case of Broadband Networks.' *Journal of Regulatory Economics* 43(2):168–195

GSMA, 2019. 'State of the Mobile Money Industry in Sub-Saharan Africa 2018.' Report

Guasch, J. L., J. J. Laffont and S. Straub, 2008. 'Renegotiation of Concession Contracts in Latin America: Evidence from the Water and Transport Sectors.' *International Journal of Industrial Organization* 26:421–442

Guasch, J. L. and S. Straub, 2009. 'Corruption and Concession Renegotiations. Evidence from the Water and Transport Sectors in Latin America.' *Utilities Policy* 17:185–190

Guerrini, A., G. Romano and B. Campedelli, 2013. 'Economies of Scale, Scope, and Density in the Italian Water Sector: A Two-Stage Data Envelopment Analysis Approach.' *Water Resources Management* 27(13):4559–4578

Gurung, A. and R. Martínez-Espiñeira, 2019. 'Determinants of the Water Rate Structure Choice by Canadian Municipalities.' *Utilities Policy* 58:89–101

Guthrie, G., 2006. 'Regulating Infrastructure: The Impact on Risk and Investment.' *Journal of Economic Literature* 44:925–972

——2020. 'Regulation, Welfare, and the Risk of Asset Stranding.' *Quarterly Review of Economics and Finance* 78:273–287

Guthrie, G. and J. Wright, 2007. 'Competing Payment Schemes.' *Journal of Industrial Economics* 55(1):37–67

Gutiérrez, G. and T. Philippon, 2019. 'The Failure of Free Entry.' National Bureau of Economic Research, Working Paper No. 26001

GWI, 2018. 'International Comparisons of Water Sector Performance.' Report

Hadley, A., 1885. *Railroad Transportation: Its History and Its Laws.* New York: Putnam

Hahn, J. H., 2004. 'Network Competition and Interconnection with Heterogeneous Subscribers.' *International Journal of Industrial Organization* 22:611–631

Hahn, R., R. Metcalfe and F. Rundhammer, 2020. 'Promoting Customer Engagement: A New Trend in Utility Regulation.' *Regulation and Governance* 14(1):121–149

Hakvoort, R. and V. Ajodhia, 2006. 'Design Framework for Electricity Quality Regulation.' In 29th IAEE International Conference, Potsdam, Germany

Hall, D., E. Lobina and P. Terhorst, 2013. 'Re-municipalisation in the Early Twenty-First Century: Water in France and Energy in Germany.' *International Review of Applied Economics* 27(2):193–214

Haltom, R. C. and Z. Wang, 2015. 'Did the Durbin Amendment Reduce Merchant Costs? Evidence from Survey Results.' Richmond Fed Economic Brief. December

Haney, A. B. and M. G. Pollitt, 2009. 'Efficiency Analysis of Energy Networks: An International Survey of Regulators.' *Energy Policy* 37:5814–5830

——2012. 'International Benchmarking of Electricity Transmission by Regulators: Theory and Practice.' EPRG Working Paper 1226

Hanna, T. M. and D. A. McDonald, 2021. 'From Pragmatic to Politicized? The Future of Water Remunicipalization in the United States.' *Utilities Policy* 72:101276

Haring, J., 1984 'Implication of Asymmetric Regulation for Competition Policy Analysis.' FCC OPP Working Paper Series. December

Harper, I., P. Anderson, S. McCluskey and M. O'Bryan, 2015. 'Competition Policy Review: Final Report.' Treasury, Commonwealth of Australia, Canberra

Harris, R. G., 1977. 'Economies of Traffic Density in the Rail Freight Industry.' *Bell Journal of Economics* 8(2):556–564

Harris, R. G. and C. J. Kraft, 1997. 'Meddling Through: Regulating Local Telephone Competition in the USA.' *Journal of Economic Perspectives* 11:93–112

Harstad, B., 2020. 'Technology and Time Inconsistency.' *Journal of Political Economy* 128(7):2653–2689

Harstad, R. M. and M. A. Crew, 1999. 'Franchise Bidding without Holdups: Utility Regulation with Efficient Pricing and Choice of Provider.' *Journal of Regulatory Economics* 15:141–163

Hart, O., 2017. 'Incomplete Contracts and Control.' *American Economic Review* 107(7):1731–1752

Hart, O. and J. Tirole, 1990. 'Vertical Integration and Market Foreclosure.' *Brookings Papers on Economic Activity* 21(Microeconomics):205–286

Hartley, P. R., K. B. Medlock, III and O. Jankovska, 2019. 'Electricity Reform and Retail Pricing in Texas.' *Energy Economics* 80:1–11

Hartman, R. S., M. J. Doane and C.-K. Woo, 1991. 'Consumer Rationality and the Status Quo.' *Quarterly Journal of Economics* 106(1):141–162

Hatfield, D. N., B. M. Mitchell and P. Srinagesh, 2005. 'Emerging Network Technologies.' In S. K. Majumdar, I. Vogelsang and M. E. Cave (eds.), *Handbook of Telecommunications Economics*, Volume 2. Amsterdam: Elsevier

Hauge, J. A., M. A. Jamison and J. E. Prieger, 2012. 'Oust the Louse: Does Political Pressure Discipline Regulators?' *Journal of Industrial Economics* 60(2):299–332

Hauge, J. and D. E. M. Sappington, 2010. 'Pricing in Network Industries.' In R. Baldwin, M. Cave, and M. Lodge (eds.), *The Oxford Handbook of Regulation*. Oxford: Oxford University Press

Hausman, J. A., 1997. 'Valuing the Effect of Regulation on New Services in Telecommunications.' *Brookings Papers on Economic Activity* 28(Microeconomics):1–38

——2000a. 'The Effect of Sunk Costs in Telecommunications Regulation.' In J. Alleman and E. Noam (eds.), *The New Investment Theory of Real Options and Its Implication for Telecommunications Economics*. Boston, MA: Kluwer Academic

——2000b. 'Regulated Costs and Prices in Telecommunications.' In G. Madden and S. Savage (eds.), *The International Handbook of Telecommunications Economics*, Volume II. Cheltenham: Edward Elgar

Hausman, J. A. and J. G. Sidak, 1999. 'A Consumer Welfare Approach to the Mandatory Unbundling of Telecommunications Networks.' *Yale Law Journal* 109:417–505

——2005. 'Did Mandatory Unbundling Achieve Its Purpose? Empirical Evidence from Five Countries.' *Journal of Competition Law and Economics* 1:173–245

——2007. 'Telecommunications Regulation: Current Approaches with the End in Sight.' Unpublished Working Paper. October

——2014. 'Telecommunications Regulation: Current Approaches with the End in Sight.' In N. L. Rose (ed.), *Economic Regulation and Its Reform: What Have We Learned?* Chicago: University of Chicago Press

Hausman, J. A. and T. J. Tardiff, 1995. 'Efficient Local Exchange Competition.' *Antitrust Bulletin* 40:529–556

Hausman, J. A. and W. E. Taylor, 2012. 'Telecommunications Deregulation.' *American Economic Review* 102:386–390

——2013. 'Telecommunication in the US: From Regulation to Competition (Almost).' *Review of Industrial Organization* 42(2):203–230

Hausman, J. and J. Wright, 2006. 'Two Sided Markets with Substitution: Mobile Termination.' Report

Hayashi, F., 2013. 'The New Debit Card Regulations: Effects on Merchants, Consumers, and Payments System Efficiency.' *Economic Review, Federal Reserve Bank of Kansas City* 98(Q1):89–118

Hayashi, F. and J. L. Maniff, 2021. 'Public Authority Involvement in Payment Card Markets: Various Countries.' August 2021 Update. Payments System Research Department, Federal Reserve Bank of Kansas City

Hayek, F. 1944. *The Road to Serfdom.* London: Routledge

——1968. *Der Wettbewerb als Entdeckungsverfahren.* Kiel Lectures 56. Kiel: University of Kiel

Hayes, K., 1987. 'Cost Structure of the Water Utility Industry.' *Applied Economics* 19:417–425

Hayes R., 2007. 'An Econometric Analysis of the Impact of the RBA's Credit Card Reforms.' Submission to the Reserve Bank of Australia's Payments Systems Board's 2007–08 Review of Payment System Reforms. 27 August'

Haylen, A., 2019. 'Rail Fares, Ticketing and Prospects for Reform.' House of Commons Briefing Paper. 24 April

Haynes, M. and S. Thompson, 2014. 'Hit and Run or Sit and Wait? Contestability Revisited in a Price-Comparison Site-Mediated Market.' *International Journal of the Economics of Business* 21(2):165–190

Hazlett, T. W., 2000. 'Economic and Political Consequences of the 1996 Telecommunications Act.' *Regulation* 23:36–45

——2005. 'Cable Television.' In S. K. Majumdar, I. Vogelsang and M. E. Cave (eds.), *Handbook of Telecommunications Economics*, Volume 2. Amsterdam: Elsevier

Hearne, R. R., 2018. 'Water Markets.' In G. Donoso (ed.), *Water Policy in Chile.* Cham: Springer, pp. 117–127

Heather, P., 2020. 'European Traded Gas Hubs: The Supremacy of TTF.' OIES Paper. May

Heidhues, P., J. Johnen and B. Kőszegi, 2021. 'Browsing versus Studying: A Pro-Market Case for Regulation.' *Review of Economic Studies* 88(2):708–729

Heidhues, P., J. Johnen and M. Rauber, 2020. 'Economic Research on Loyalty Price Discrimination.' Report Prepared for the Competition and Markets Authority. 7 October

Heidhues, P. and B. Kőszegi, 2004. 'The Impact of Consumer Loss Aversion on Pricing.' WZB, Markets and Political Economy Working Paper No. SP II 2004-17

——2008. 'Competition and Price Variation when Consumers Are Loss Averse.' *American Economic Review* 98(4):1245–1268

——2015. 'On the Welfare Costs of Naiveté in the US Credit-Card Market.' *Review of Industrial Organization* 47(3):341–354

——2017. 'Naïveté-Based Discrimination.' *Quarterly Journal of Economics* 132(2):1019–1054

——2018. 'Behavioral Industrial Organization.' In B. D. Bernheim, S. DellaVigna and D. Laibson (eds.), *Handbook of Behavioral Economics: Applications and Foundations 1.* Amsterdam: North-Holland, pp. 517–612

Heidhues, P., B. Kőszegi and T. Murooka, 2016. 'Exploitative Innovation.' *American Economic Journal: Microeconomics* 8(1):1–23

——2017. 'Inferior Products and Profitable Deception.' *Review of Economic Studies* 84(1):323–356

Heims, E. and M. Lodge, 2018. 'Customer Engagement in UK Water Regulation: Towards a Collaborative Regulatory State?' *Policy and Politics* 46(1):81–100

Hein, A., M. Schreieck, T. Riasanow, *et al.*, 2020. 'Digital Platform Ecosystems.' *Electronic Markets* 30(1):87–98

Helm, D., 2003. 'Whither Water Regulation?' Unpublished Discussion Paper

——2007. *The New Energy Paradigm*. Oxford: Oxford University Press

——2009. 'Infrastructure Investment: The Cost of Capital, and Regulation: An Assessment.' *Oxford Review of Economic Policy* 25:307–326

——2013. 'British Infrastructure Policy and the Gradual Return of the State.' *Oxford Review of Economic Policy* 29(2):287–306

——2017. 'Cost of Energy Review.' Department of Business, Energy and Industrial Strategy

——2020. 'Thirty Years after Water Privatization – Is the English Model the Envy of the World?' *Oxford Review of Economic Policy* 36(1):69–85

Helm, D. and T. Jenkinson, 1997. 'The Assessment: Introducing Competition into Regulated Industries.' *Oxford Review of Economic Policy* 13:1–14

Helm, D. and G. Yarrow, 1988. 'The Assessment: The Regulation of Utilities.' *Oxford Review of Economic Policy* 4:1–31

Hermalin, B. E. and M. L. Katz, 2007. 'The Economics of Product-Line Restrictions with an Application to the Network Neutrality Debate.' *Information Economics and Policy* 19(2):215–248

Herweg, F. and K. Mierendorff, 2013. 'Uncertain Demand, Consumer Loss Aversion, and Flat-Rate Tariffs'. *Journal of the European Economic Association* 11(2):399–432

Herweg, F. and K. M. Schmidt, 2015. 'Loss Aversion and Inefficient Renegotiation.' *Review of Economic Studies* 82(1):297–332

Herweg, N., S. Wurster and K. Dümig, 2018. 'The European Natural Gas Market Reforms Revisited: Differentiating between Regulatory Output and Outcome.' *Social Sciences* 7(4):57

Hesseling, D. and M. Sari, 2006. 'The Introduction of Quality Regulation for Electricity Distribution in The Netherlands.' In U. Hammer and M. M. Roggenkamp (eds.), *European Energy Law Report III*. Antwerp: Intersentia, pp. 127–145

Hicks, J. R., 1935. 'Annual Survey of Economic Theory: The Theory of Monopoly.' *Econometric* 3:1–20

Hilmer, F., 1993. *National Competition Policy*. Canberra: Australian Government Publishing Service

HM Treasury, 2013a. 'Opening Up UK Payments.' March

——2013b. 'Opening Up UK Payments: Response to Consultation.' October

Hoch, S. J. and G. F. Loewenstein, 1991. 'Time-Inconsistent Preferences and Consumer Self-Control.' *Journal of Consumer Research* 17(4):492–507

Hoernig, S., 2014a. 'Competition between Multiple Asymmetric Networks: Theory and Applications.' *International Journal of Industrial Organization* 32:57–69

——2014b. 'The Strength of the Waterbed Effect Depends on Tariff Type.' *Economics Letters* 125(2):291–294

Hoernig, S., S. Jay, W. Neu, *et al.*, 2011. 'Wholesale Pricing, NGA Take-up and Competition.' A Report for ECTA, WIK-Consult

Höffler, F., 2006. 'Monopoly Prices versus Ramsey–Boiteux Prices: Are They "Similar" and Do It Matter?' *Journal of Industry, Competition and Trade* 6:27–43

Hogan, W. W., 1992. 'Contract Networks for Electric Power Transmission.' *Journal of Regulatory Economics* 4:211–242

——1999. 'Transmission Congestion: The Nodal–Zonal Debate Revisited.' Unpublished Working Paper. 27 February

——2000. 'Flowgate Rights and Wrongs.' Unpublished Working Paper. 20 August

——2002. 'Electricity Market Restructuring: Reform of Reforms.' *Journal of Regulatory Economics* 21:103–132

——2005. 'On an "Energy Only" Electricity Market Design for Resource Adequacy.' Unpublished Working Paper. September

——2021. 'Strengths and Weaknesses of the PJM Market Model.' In J.-M. Glachant, P. L. Joskow and M. G. Pollitt (eds.), *Handbook on Electricity Markets.* Cheltenham: Edward Elgar

Hogan, W. W., M. Lindovska, J. Mann and S. L. Pope, 2018. 'Embracing Merchant Transmission Investment.' Working Paper. 15 October

Hogan, W. W., J. Rosellón and I. Vogelsang, 2010. 'Toward a Combined Merchant–Regulatory Mechanism for Electricity Transmission Expansion.' *Journal of Regulatory Economics* 38:113–143

Holburn, G. L. F. and P. Spiller, 2002. 'Interest Group Representation in Administrative Institutions: The Impact of Consumer Advocates and Elected Commissioners on Regulatory Policy in the USA.' Unpublished Working Paper. October

Hollas, D. R., 1994. 'Downstream Gas Pricing in an Era of Upstream Deregulation.' *Journal of Regulatory Economics* 6:227–245

Hong, S. K. and K. E. Yoo, 2000. 'A Study on Airport Privatization in Korea: Policy and Legal Aspects of Corporatization and Localization over Airport Management.' *Journal of Air Law and Commerce* 66(1):3–19

Honoré, A., 2004. 'Argentina: 2004 Gas Crisis.' Oxford Institute for Energy Studies, Working Paper NG 7. November

Hopkinson, J., 1892. 'The Cost of Electricity Supply.' *Transactions of the Junior Engineering Society* 3:33–46

Hortaçsu, A., F. Luco, S. L. Puller and D. Zhu, 2019. 'Does Strategic Ability Affect Efficiency? Evidence from Electricity Markets.' *American Economic Review* 109(12):4302–4342

Hortaçsu, A. and S. L. Puller, 2008. 'Understanding Strategic Bidding in Multi-Unit Auctions: A Case Study of the Texas Electricity Spot Market.' *RAND Journal of Economics* 39(1):86–114

Hotelling, H., 1938. 'The General Welfare in Relation to Problems of Taxation and of Railway and Utility Rates.' *Econometrica* 6:242–269

House of Commons, 2018. 'Pre-Legislative Scrutiny of the Draft Domestic Gas and Electricity (Tariff Cap) Bill.' Fourth Report of Session 2017–19. Report HC 517. 13 February

——2019. 'Disinformation and "Fake News".' Final Report. February

House of Lords, 2007. *Economic Regulators.* London: Stationery Office

Hovenkamp, H., 2021a. 'Antitrust and Platform Monopoly.' *Yale Law Journal* 130:1952

——2021b. 'Congress' Antitrust War on China and American Consumers.' ProMarket. 25 June

Howell, B., 2011. 'Strategic Interaction under Asymmetric Regulation: The Case of New Zealand.' In Y. Dwivedi (ed.), *Adoption, Usage and Global Impact of Broadband Technologies: Diffusion, Practice and Policy.* Hershey, PA: IGI Global

Howell, B., R. Meade and S. O'Connor, 2010. 'Structural Separation versus Vertical Integration: Lessons for Telecommunications from Electricity Reforms.' *Telecommunications Policy* 34(7):392–403

Howell, B. and B. Sadowski, 2018. 'Anatomy of a Public–Private Partnership: Hold-Up and Regulatory Commitment in Ultrafast Broadband.' *Telecommunications Policy* 42(7):552–565

Hsee, C. K. and J. Zhang, 2004. 'Distinction Bias: Misprediction and Mischoice Due to Joint Evaluation.' *Journal of Personality and Social Psychology* 86(5):680–695

Hsu, M., 1997. 'An Introduction to the Pricing of Electric Power Transmission.' *Utilities Policy* 6:257–270

Hughes, G., P. Chinowsky and K. Strzepek, 2010. 'The Costs of Adaptation to Climate Change for Water Infrastructure in OECD Countries.' *Utilities Policy* 18:142–153

Hughes, P., 2011. 'Europe's Evolving Gas Market: Future Direction and Implications for Asia.' Unpublished Working Paper. February

Hurdle, G. J., R. L. Johnson, A. S. Joskow, G. J. Werden and M. A. Williams, 1989. 'Concentration, Potential Entry, and Performance in the Airline Industry.' *Journal of Industrial Economics* 38(2):119–139

Hurkens, S. and Á. L. López, 2021. 'Mobile Termination Rates and Retail Regimes in Europe and the US: A Unified Theory of CPP and RPP.' *Information Economics and Policy* 56:100915

IATA, 2007. 'The Case for Independent Economic Regulation of Airports and Air Navigation Service Providers.' IATA Economics Briefing No. 6

——2017. 'YY Fares Retire after Seven Successful Decades.' Press Release. 6 July

——2018. 'Balanced Concessions for the Airport Industry.' IATA Guidance Booklet. December

——2020a. 'WATS+ World Air Transport Statistics 2020.' November

——2020b. 'Worldwide Airport Slots Fact Sheets.' November

Ibáñez Colomo, P., 2021. 'The Draft Digital Markets Act: A Legal and Institutional Analysis.' *Journal of European Competition Law and Practice* 12(7):561–575

ICAO, 2008. 'Case Study: South Africa.' 5 December

——2009. 'ICAO's Policies on Charges for Airports and Air Navigation Services.' Doc 9082. Eighth Edition

——2013a. 'Manual on Air Navigation Services Economics.' Fifth Edition

——2013b. 'Airport Competition.' ATConf/6-WP/90

——2013c. 'Airport Economics Manual.' Doc 9562. Third Edition

——2014. 'State of Airport Economics.' Report

——2019a. 'UAS Traffic Management.' Assembly, 40th Session, Working Paper A40-WP/209. 1 August

——2019b. 'Unmanned Aircraft Systems Traffic Management (UTM) – A Common Framework with Core Principles for Global Harmonization.' Second Edition

——2020. 'Unmanned Aircraft Systems Traffic Management (UTM) – A Common Framework with Core Principles for Global Harmonization.' Third Edition

——2021. 'Effects of Novel Coronavirus (COVID-19) on Civil Aviation: Economic Impact Analysis.' 29 June

ICC, 1985. 'Coal Rate Guidelines Nationwide.' Ex Parte No. 347 (Sub-No. 1). 3 August

——1986. 'Rate Guidelines – Non-Coal Proceedings.' EP 347 (Sub-No. 2). 21 May

Ichihashi, S. and B. C. Kim, 2022. 'Addictive Platforms.' Bank of Canada, Working Paper No. 2022-16

IEA, 2000. 'Regulatory Reform: European Gas.' Paris

——2008. 'Natural Gas Market Review.' Paris

——2009. 'Canada: 2009 Review.' Paris

——2012. 'Australia: 2012 Review.' Paris

——2019a. 'World Energy Outlook.' Paris

——2019b. 'The Future of Rail: Opportunities for Energy and the Environment.' Paris

——2020a. 'Electricity Market Report.' Paris

——2020b. 'Outlook for Biogas and Biomethane: Prospects for Organic Growth.' World Energy Outlook Special Report

——2021a. 'Net Zero by 2050: A Roadmap for the Global Energy Sector.' October

——2021b. 'Despite Short-Term Pain, the EU's Liberalised Gas Markets Have Brought Long-Term Financial Gains.' Commentary

——2021c. 'Decisive Action by Governments Is Critical to Unlock Growth for Low-Carbon Hydrogen.' Press Release. 4 October

——2021d. 'Electricity Information: Overview.' Paris. See www.iea.org/reports/ electricity-information-overview

Iossa, E., P. Rey and M. Waterson, 2022. 'Organising Competition for the Market.' *Journal of the European Economic Association* 20(2):822–868

Imam, M. I., T. Jamasb and M. Llorca, 2019. 'Sector Reforms and Institutional Corruption: Evidence from Electricity Industry in Sub-Saharan Africa.' *Energy Policy* 129:532–545

IMF, 2020. 'Fiscal Monitor: Policies to Support People during the COVID-19 Pandemic.' Washington, April

Inderst, R. and M. Peitz, 2014. 'Investment under Uncertainty and Regulation of New Access Networks.' *Information Economics and Policy* 26:28–41

Intervistas, 2016. 'An Examination of the STB's Approach to Freight Rail Rate Regulation and Options for Simplification.' Report for Surface Transportation Board. Project FY14-STB-157

IRENA, 2019a. 'Smart Charging for Electric Vehicles.' Innovation Landscape Brief

——2019b. 'Future Role of Distribution System Operators.' Innovation Landscape Brief

——2019c. 'Utility-Scale Batteries.' Innovation Landscape Brief

IRG, 2020. 'Eighth Annual Market Monitoring Working Document.' May

Irish Commission for Aviation Regulation, 2010. 'Defining the Regulatory Till.' Commission Paper 4/2010. 30 November

Irons, B. and C. Hepburn, 2007. 'Regret Theory and the Tyranny of Choice.' *Economic Record* 83(261):191–203

Ismaila, D. A., D. Warnock-Smith and N. Hubbard, 2014. 'The Impact of Air Service Agreement Liberalisation: The Case of Nigeria.' *Journal of Air Transport Management* 37:69–75

Isoni, A., G. Loomes and R. Sugden, 2011. 'The Willingness to Pay – Willingness to Accept Gap, the "Endowment Effect," Subject Misconceptions, and Experimental Procedures for Eliciting Valuations: Comment.' *American Economic Review* 101(2):991–1011

ITF, 2019. 'Liberalisation of Air Transport.' Research Report

——2021. 'Ready for Take-Off? Integrating Drones into the Transport System.' Research Report

ITU, 2013. 'Definition of Next Generation Network.' Study Group 13

——2020. *Global ICT Regulatory Outlook 2020.* Geneva: ITU Publications

——2021a. *The Impact of Policies, Regulation, and Institutions on ICT Sector Performance.* Geneva: ITU Publications

——2021b. *Measuring Digital Development: Facts and Figures 2021.* Geneva: ITU Publications

——2021c. 'Key ICT Indicators for Developed and Developing Countries, the World and Special Regions (Totals and Penetration Rates)'

——2022a. 'Spectrum Pricing and Trading.' Digital Regulation Platform

——2022b. 'Key ICT Indicators for Developed and Developing Countries, the World and Special Regions (Totals and Penetration Rates)'

Ivaldi, M. and G. McCullough, 2008. 'Subadditivity Tests for Network Separation with an Application to U.S. Railroads.' *Review of Network Economics* 7(1):159–171

Ivaldi, M., M. Petrova and M. Urdanoz, 2022. 'Airline Cooperation Effects on Airfare Distribution: An Auction-Model-Based Approach.' *Transport Policy* 115:239–250

Ivaldi, M. and J. Pouyet, 2018. 'Eliciting the Regulation of an Economic System: The Case of the French Rail Industry.' *Transport Policy* 62:21–30

Ivaldi, M., S. Sokullu and T. Toru, 2012. 'Are Airports Two-Sided Platforms?: A Methodological Approach.' In J. Peoples (ed.), *Pricing Behavior and Non-Price Characteristics in the Airline Industry*. Bingley, UK: Emerald, pp. 213–232

Iyengar, S. S. and E. Kamenica, 2010. 'Choice Proliferation, Simplicity Seeking, and Asset Allocation.' *Journal of Public Economics* 94(7–8):530–539

Iyengar, S. S. and M. R. Lepper, 2000. 'When Choice Is Demotivating: Can One Desire Too Much of a Good Thing?' *Journal of Personality and Social Psychology* 79(6):995–1006

Jamasb, T., R. Nepal and G. R. Timilsina, 2017. 'A Quarter Century Effort Yet to Come of Age: A Survey of Electricity Sector Reform in Developing Countries.' *Energy Journal* 38(3):195–234

Jamasb, T. and M. Pollitt, 2005. 'Electricity Market Reform in the European Union: Review of Progress toward Liberalization and Integration.' *Energy Journal* 26:11–41

Jamasb, T., M. Pollitt and T. Triebs, 2008. 'Productivity and Efficiency of US Gas Transmission Companies: A European Regulatory Perspective.' *Energy Policy* 36:3398–3412

Jamison, M. A., 2005. 'Leadership and the Independent Regulator.' World Bank, Policy Research Working Paper 3620. June

——2007. 'Regulation: Price Cap and Revenue Cap.' In B. L. Capehart (ed.), *Encyclopedia of Energy Engineering and Technology*, Volume 3. Boca Raton, FL: CRC Press, pp. 1245–125

Jarrell, G. A., 1978. 'The Demand for State Regulation of the Electric Utility Industry.' *Journal of Law and Economics* 21:269–295

Jeanjean, F., 2022. 'Co-investment in the sharing of Telecommunications Infrastructures' Unpublished Working Paper. April 2022.

Jehiel, P. and B. Moldovanu, 2003. 'An Economic Perspective on Auctions.' *Economic Policy* 18(36):269–308

Jenkins, C., 2011. 'RIIO Economics: Examining the Economics Underlying Ofgem's New Regulatory Framework.' Paper Presented at the Centre for Competition and Regulatory Policy Winter Workshop

Jenkins, J. D. and I. J. Pérez-Arriaga, 2017. 'Improved Regulatory Approaches for the Remuneration of Electricity Distribution Utilities with High Penetrations of Distributed Energy Resources.' *Energy Journal* 38(3):63–91

Jenkinson, T., 2006. 'Regulation and the Cost of Capital.' In M. Crew and D. Parker (eds.), *International Handbook on Economic Regulation*. Cheltenham: Edward Elgar

Jenkins-Smith, H. C., 1987. 'An Industry in Turmoil: The Remaking of the Natural Gas Industry' *Natural Resources Journal* 27:773–780

Jensen, A. and P. Stelling, 2007. 'Economic Impacts of Swedish Railway Deregulation: A Longitudinal Study.' *Transportation Research, Part E: Logistics and Transportation Review* 43(5):516–534

Jensen, O., 2017. 'Public–Private Partnerships for Water in Asia: A Review of Two Decades of Experience.' *International Journal of Water Resources Development* 33(1):4–30

Jensen, O. and X. Wu, 2017. 'The Hybrid Model for Economic Regulation of Water Utilities: Mission Impossible?' *Utilities Policy* 48:122–131

Jeon, D.-S. and S. Hurkens, 2008. 'A Retail Benchmarking Approach to Efficient Two-Way Access Pricing: No Termination-Based Price Discrimination.' *RAND Journal of Economics* 39:822–849

Jeon, D.-S., J. J. Laffont and J. Tirole, 2004. 'On the "Receiver-Pays" Principle.' *RAND Journal of Economics* 35:85–110

Jeong, J., 2005. 'An Investigation of Operating Cost of Airports: Focus on the Effects of Output Scale.' Doctoral Dissertation, University of British Columbia

Jiang, T., J. Geller, D. Ni and J. Collura, 2016. 'Unmanned Aircraft System Traffic Management: Concept of Operation and System Architecture.' *International Journal of Transportation Science and Technology* 5(3):123–135

John, P., A. Mahalingam, A. Deep and A. Thillairajan, 2015. 'Impact of Private Sector Participation on Access and Quality of Services: Systematic Review of Evidence from the Electricity, Telecommunications and Water Supply Sectors.' *Journal of Development Effectiveness* 7(1):64–89

Johnen, J., 2019. 'Automatic-Renewal Contracts with Heterogeneous Consumer Inertia.' *Journal of Economics and Management Strategy* 28(4):765–786

——2020. 'Dynamic Competition in Deceptive Markets.' *RAND Journal of Economics* 51(2):375–401

Johnen, J. and R. Somogyi, 2021. 'Deceptive Features on Platforms.' Working Paper

Jones, I., I. Viehoff and P. Marks, 1993. 'The Economics of Airport Slots.' *Fiscal Studies* 14(4):37–57

Jordan, W. A., 1972. 'Producer Protection: Prior Market Structure and the Effects of Government Regulation.' *Journal of Law and Economics* 15:151–176

Jorde, T. M., J. G. Sidak and D. J. Teece, 2000. 'Innovation, Investment and Unbundling.' *Yale Journal on Regulation* 17:2–36

Joseph, G., S. Ayling, P. Miquel-Florensa, H. Bejarano and A. Quevedo Cardona, 2022. 'Behavioral Insights in Infrastructure Sectors: A Survey.' Documento de Trabajo RedNIE No. 119

Joskow, P. L., 1972. 'The Determination of the Allowed Rate of Return in a Formal Regulatory Hearing.' *Bell Journal of Economics and Management Science* 3:632–644

——1973. 'Pricing Decisions of Regulated Firms: A Behavioral Approach.' *Bell Journal of Economics and Management Science* 4:118–140

——1974. 'Inflation and Environmental Concern: Structural Change in the Process of Public Utility Price Regulation.' *Journal of Law and Economics* 17:291–327

——1985. 'Vertical Integration and Long-Term Contracts: The Case of Coal-Burning Electric Generating Plants.' *Journal of Law, Economics, & Organization* 1:33–80

——1987. 'Contract Duration and Relationship-Specific Investments: Empirical Evidence from Coal Markets.' *American Economic Review* 77:168–185

——1988. 'Asset Specificity and the Structure of Vertical Relationships: Empirical Evidence.' *Journal of Law, Economics, & Organization* 4:95–117

——1989. 'Regulatory Failure, Regulatory Reform, and Structural Change in the Electrical Power Industry.' *Brookings Papers on Economic Activity* 20(Microeconomics):125–208

——1991. 'The Role of Transaction Cost Economics in Antitrust and Public Utility Regulatory Policies.' *Journal of Law, Economics, & Organization* 7:53–83

——2006. 'Markets for Power in the USA: An Interim Assessment.' *Energy Journal* 27:1–36

——2007a. 'Regulation of Natural Monopolies.' In A. M Polinsky and S. Shavell (eds.), *Handbook of Law and Economics*, Volume 2. Amsterdam: Elsevier

——2007b. 'Incentive Regulation in Theory and Practice: Electricity Distribution and Transmission Networks.' Unpublished Working Paper. August

——2008a. 'Lessons Learned from Electricity Market Liberalization.' *Energy Journal* 29(spec. issue 2):9–42

——2008b. 'Capacity Payments in Imperfect Electricity Markets: Need and Design.' *Utilities Policy* 16:159–170

——2008c. 'Vertical Integration.' In C. Menard and M. M. Shirley (eds.), *Handbook of New Institutional Economics*. Berlin: Springer

——2009. 'Challenges for Creating a Comprehensive National Electricity Policy.' EUI Working
Paper RSCAS 2009/01

——2010. 'Market Imperfections versus Regulatory Imperfections.' Unpublished Working Paper.
June

Joskow, P. L. and E. Kahn, 2002. 'A Quantitative Analysis of Pricing Behavior in California's
Wholesale Electricity Market during Summer 2000: The Final Word.' *Quarterly Journal of
the IAEE's Energy Economics Education Foundation* 23: 4

Joskow, P. L. and T. O. Léautier, 2021. 'Optimal Wholesale Pricing and Investment in
Generation: The Basics.' In J.-M. Glachant, P. L. Joskow and M. G. Pollitt (eds.), *Handbook
on Electricity Markets.* Cheltenham: Edward Elgar

Joskow, P. L. and R. C. Noll, 1981. 'Regulation in Theory and Practice: An Overview.' In G.
Fromm (ed.), *Studies in Public Regulation.* Cambridge, MA: MIT Press

Joskow, P. L. and N. L. Rose, 1989. 'The Effects of Economic Regulation.' In R. Schmalensee
and R. Willig (eds.), *Handbook of Industrial Organization,* Volume 2. Amsterdam:
North-Holland

Joskow, P. L. and R. Schmalensee, 1983. *Markets for Power: An Analysis of Electric Utility
Deregulation.* Cambridge, MA: MIT Press

——1986. 'Incentive Regulation for Electric Utilities.' *Yale Journal on Regulation* 4:1–49

Joskow, P. L. and J. Tirole, 2000. 'Transmission Rights and Market Power in Electric Power
Networks.' *RAND Journal of Economics* 31:450–487

——2005. 'Merchant Transmission Investment.' *Journal of Industrial Economics* 53:233–264

——2006. 'Retail Electricity Competition.' *RAND Journal of Economics* 37:799–815

——2007. 'Reliability and Competitive Electricity Markets.' *RAND Journal of Economics*
38:60–84

Joskow, P. L. and C. D. Wolfram, 2012. 'Dynamic Pricing of Electricity.' *American Economic
Review* 102:381–385

Jullien, B. and M. Bouvard, 2022. 'Fair Cost Sharing: Big Tech vs Telcos.' TSE Working Paper.
October

Jullien, B., A. Pavan and M. Rysman, 2021. 'Two-Sided Markets, Pricing, and Network Effects.'
In K. Ho, A. Hortaçsu and A. Lizzeri (eds.), *Handbook of Industrial Organization,* Volume
4. Amsterdam: Elsevier, pp. 485–592

Jullien, B. and W. Sand-Zantman, 2021. 'The Economics of Platforms: A Theory Guide for
Competition Policy.' *Information Economics and Policy* 54:100880

Kades, M. and F. Scott Morton, 2021. 'Interoperability as a Competition Remedy for Digital
Networks.' Washington Center for Equitable Growth, Working Paper Series

Kaestner, R. and B. Kahn, 1990. 'The Effects of Regulation and Competition on the Price of
AT&T Intrastate Telephone Service.' *Journal of Regulatory Economics* 2:363–377

Kahn, A. E., 1971. *The Economics of Regulation: Principles and Institutions.* Cambridge, MA:
MIT Press

——1981. 'Comment on Joskow and Noll.' In G. Fromm (ed.), *Studies in Public Regulation.*
Cambridge, MA: MIT Press

——1987. 'Deregulatory Schizophrenia.' *California Law Review* 75:1059–1068

——1988. 'Surprises of Airline Deregulation.' *American Economic Review* 78(2):316–322

——1998. 'Letting Go: Deregulating the Process of Deregulation, or: Temptation of the
Kleptocrats and the Political Economy of Regulatory Disingenuousness.' MSU Public
Utilities Papers

——2000. 'Submission to US Committee on Commerce on United Airlines/US Airways Merger.'
Wednesday 21 June

——2001. *Whom the Gods Would Destroy, or How Not to Deregulate.* Washington, DC: AEI Press

——2002. 'The Deregulatory Tar Baby: The Precarious Balance between Regulation and Deregulation, 1997-2000 and Henceforward.' *Journal of Regulatory Economics* 21:35-56

——2005. 'Reforming the FCC and Its Mission: Lessons from the Airline Experience.' *Journal on Telecommunications and High Technology Law* 4:43-58

——2007. 'Network Neutrality.' AEI–Brookings Joint Center for Regulatory Studies, Working Paper. March

Kahn, A. E., T. J. Tardiff and D. L. Weisman, 1999. 'The Telecommunications Act at Three Years: An Economic Evaluation of Its Implementation by the Federal Communications Commission.' *Information Economics and Policy* 11:319-365

Kahn, A. E. and W. E. Taylor, 1994. 'The Pricing of Inputs Sold to Competitors: A Comment.' *Yale Journal on Regulation* 11:226-240

Kahneman, D., 1973. *Attention and Effort.* Prentice-Hall Series in Experimental Psychology. Englewood Cliffs, NJ: Prentice-Hall

Kahneman, D., J. L. Knetsch and R. H. Thaler, 1986a. 'Fairness as a Constraint on Profit Seeking: Entitlements in the Market.' *American Economic Review* 76(4):728-741

——1986b. 'Fairness and the Assumptions of Economics.' *Journal of Business* 59(4/2):S285-S300

Kahneman, D. and A. Tversky, 1979. 'Prospect Theory: An Analysis of Decision under Risk.' *Econometrica* 47(2):263-292

——1984. 'Choices, Values, and Frames.' *American Psychologist* 39(4):341-350

——1996. 'On the Reality of Cognitive Illusions.' *Psychological Review*, 103(3):582-591

Kamerschen, D. R. and D. C. Keenan, 1983. 'Caveats on Applying Ramsey Pricing.' In A. L. Danielsen and D. R. Kamerschen (eds.), *Current Issues in Public Utility Economics.* Lexington, MA: D. C. Heath

Kang, L. and J. Zarnikau, 2009. 'Did the Expiration of Retail Price Caps Affect Prices in the Restructured Electricity Market?' *Energy Policy* 37:1713-1717

Kasberger, B., 2020. 'When Can Auctions Maximize Post-Auction Welfare?' *SSRN Electronic Journal* 3519866

Katz, M. L., 2021. 'Big Tech Mergers: Innovation, Competition for the Market, and the Acquisition of Emerging Competitors.' *Information Economics and Policy* 54:100883

Katz, M. L. and C. Shapiro, 1985. 'Network Externalities, Competition, and Compatibility.' *American Economic Review* 75(3):424-440

Kaufmann, L., 2019. 'The Past and Future of the X Factor in Performance-Based Regulation.' *Electricity Journal* 32(3):44-48

Keeler, T. E., 1974. 'Railroad Costs, Returns to Scale, and Excess Capacity.' *Review of Economics and Statistics* 56(2):201

Kellogg, R. and M. Reguant, 2021. 'Energy and Environmental Markets, Industrial Organization, and Regulation.' In K. Ho, A. Hortaçsu and A. Lizzeri (eds.), *Handbook of Industrial Organization*, Volume 5. Amsterdam: Elsevier, pp. 615-742

Kent Fellows, G., 2011. 'Negotiated Settlements with a Cost of Service Backstop: The Consequences for Depreciation.' *Energy Policy* 39:1505-1513

——2012. 'Negotiated Settlements: Long-Term Profits and Costs.' SPP Research Papers, University of Calgary. May

Kessides, I. N., 2012. 'The Impacts of Electricity Sector Reforms in Developing Countries.' *Electricity Journal* 25:79-88

Khan, L. M., 2017. 'Amazon's Antitrust Paradox.' *Yale Law Journal* 126:710

——2019. 'The Separation of Platforms and Commerce.' *Columbia Law Review* 119(4):973-1098

Kharpal, A. 2020. 'Big Tech's Calls for More Regulation Offers a Chance for Them to Increase Their Power.' CNBC. 28 January

Kim, C. J. and M. C. Huang, 2021. The Privatization of Japan Railways and Japan Post: Why, How, and Now. In *Reforming State-Owned Enterprises in Asia*. ADB Institute Series on Development Economics. Singapore: Springer Singapore, pp. 133–155

Kim, H. Y. and R. M. Clark, 1988. 'Economies of Scale and Scope in Water Supply.' *Regional Science and Urban Economics* 18:479–502

Kirsch, F. and C. Von Hirschhausen, 2008. 'Regulation of NGN: Structural Separation, Access Regulation, or No Regulation at All?' *Communications & Strategies* 69:63–83

Kishimoto S., E. Lobina and O. Petitjean, 2015. 'Our Public Water Future: The Global Experience with Remunicipalisation.' April

Kiss, A., 2014. 'Salience and Switching.' Working Paper

Klein, A., 2019. 'The Fastest Way to Address Income Inequality? Implement a Real Time Payment System.' Report. Brookings Institution. 2 January

Klein, B., 2007. 'The Economic Lessons of Fisher Body–General Motors.' *International Journal of Economics of Business* 14(1):1–36

Klein, B., R. G. Crawford and A. A. Alchian, 1978. 'Vertical Integration, Appropriable Rents, and the Competitive Contracting Process.' *Journal of Law and Economics* 21(2):297–32

Klemperer, P., 2002a. 'What Really Matters in Auction Design.' *Journal of Economic Perspective* 16:169–189

——2002b. 'How (Not) to Run Auctions: The European 3G Telecom Auctions.' *European Economic Review* 46:829–845

——2004. *Auctions: Theory and Practice*. Princeton, NJ: Princeton University Press

Klevorick, A. K., 1973. 'The Behavior of a Firm Subject to Stochastic Regulatory Review.' *Bell Journal of Economics and Management Science* 4:57–88

Klien, M. and D. Michaud, 2019. 'Water Utility Consolidation: Are Economies of Scale Realized?' *Utilities Policy* 61:100972

Knapp, M. R. J., 1978. 'Economies of Scale in Sewage Purification and Disposal.' *Journal of Industrial Economics* 27:163–183

Knieps, G., 2017. 'Internet of Things, Future Networks, and the Economics of Virtual Networks. *Competition and Regulation in Network Industries* 18(3–4):240–255

——2022. 'Internet of Things and the challenges for crossborder network slicing in 5G-based smart networks' Working Paper. June 2022.

Knittel, C. R., 2006. 'The Adoption of State Electricity Regulation: The Role of Interest Groups. *Journal of Industrial Economics* 54:201–222

Kőszegi, B., 2010. 'Utility from Anticipation and Personal Equilibrium.' *Economic Theory* 44(3):415–444

Kőszegi, B. and M. Rabin, 2006. 'A Model of Reference-Dependent Preferences.' *Quarterly Journal of Economics* 121(4):1133–1165

Kotovskaia, A. and N. Meier, 2022. 'Big Tech Cryptocurrencies – European Regulatory Solution in Sight.' Leibniz Institute for Financial Research SAFE, SAFE Policy Letter No. 97

Kouwenhoven, M., 2009. 'The Role of Accessibility in Passengers' Choice of Airports.' OECD Discussion Paper No. 2008-14. Paris

Krämer, J. and M. Peitz, 2018. 'A Fresh Look at Zero-Rating.' *Telecommunications Policy* 42(7):501–513

Krämer, J. and I. Vogelsang, 2016. 'Co-Investments and Tacit Collusion in Regulated Network Industries: Experimental Evidence.' *Review of Network Economics* 15(1):35–61

Krämer, J. and L. Wiewiorra, 2012. 'Network Neutrality and Congestion Sensitive Content Providers: Implications for Content Variety, Broadband Investment, and Regulation.' *Information Systems Research* 23(4):1303–1321

Krämer, J., L. Wiewiorra and C. Weinhardt, 2013. 'Net Neutrality: A Progress Report.' *Telecommunications Policy* 37(9):794–813

Kristiansen, T., 2004. 'Markets for Financial Transmission Rights.' *Energy Studies Review* 13:25–74

Kridel, D. J., D. E. M. Sappington and D. L. Weisman, 1996. 'The Effects of Incentive Regulation in the Telecommunications Industry: A Survey.' *Journal of Regulatory Economics* 9:269–306

Krieger, S., 1995. 'Problems for Captive Ratepayers in Nonunanimous Settlements of Public Utility Rate Cases.' *Yale Journal of Regulation* 257:259–342

Küfeoglu, S., M. Pollitt and K. Anaya, 2018. 'Electric Power Distribution in the World: Today and Tomorrow.' EPRG Working Paper 1826

Kurosaki, F., 2016. 'Reform of the Japanese National Railways (JNR).' *Network Industries Quarterly* 18(4):8–11

——2018. 'A Study of Vertical Separation in Japanese Passenger Railways.' *Case Studies on Transport Policy* 6(3):391–399

Kwoka, J. E., 1993. 'The Effects of Divestiture, Privatization, and Competition on Productivity in US and UK Telecommunications.' *Review of Industrial Organization* 8:49–61

Kwoka, J. and T. Valletti, 2021. 'Unscrambling the Eggs: Breaking Up Consummated Mergers and Dominant Firms.' *Industrial and Corporate Change* 30(5):1286–1306

Kydland, F. E. and E. C. Prescott, 1977. 'Rules Rather than Discretion: The Inconsistency of Optimal Plans.' *Journal of Political Economy* 85:473–492

Laffont, J. J., 1994. 'The New Economics of Regulation Ten Years After.' *Econometrica* 62:507–537

——1999. 'Translating Principles into Practice in Regulation Theory.' CEER Working Paper No. 1. March

——2005. *Regulation and Development.* Cambridge: Cambridge University Press

Laffont, J. J. and D. Martimort, 1999. 'Separation of Regulators against Collusive Behaviour.' *RAND Journal of Economics* 30:232–262

Laffont, J. J., P. Rey and J. Tirole, 1998a. 'Network Competition: I. Overview and Nondiscriminatory Pricing.' *RAND Journal of Economics* 29:1–37

——1998b. 'Network Competition: II. Price Discrimination.' *RAND Journal of Economics* 29:38–56

Laffont, J. J. and J. Tirole, 1986. 'Using Cost Observation to Regulate Firms.' *Journal of Political Economy* 94:614–641

——1987. 'Auctioning Incentive Contracts.' *Journal of Political Economy* 95:921–937

——1988. 'The Dynamics of Incentive Contracts.' *Econometrica* 56:1153–1175

——1991. 'The Politics of Government Decision Making: A Theory of Regulatory Capture.' *Quarterly Journal of Economics* 106:1089–1127

——1993. *A Theory of Incentives in Procurement and Regulation.* Cambridge, MA: MIT Press

——1994. 'Access Pricing and Competition.' *European Economic Review* 38:1673–1710

——2000. *Competition in Telecommunications.* Cambridge, MA: MIT Press

Lafontaine, F. and M. Slade, 2007. 'Vertical Integration and Firm Boundaries: The Evidence.' *Journal of Economic Literature* 45(3):629–685

Laibson, D., 1997. 'Golden Eggs and Hyperbolic Discounting.' *Quarterly Journal of Economics* 112(2):443–478

Lambrecht, A. and C. E. Tucker, 2017. 'Can Big Data Protect a Firm from Competition?' *SSRN Electronic Journal* 2705530

Lardner, D., 1850. *Railway Economy; A Treatise on the New Art of Transport, Its Management, Prospects, and Relations.* New York: Harper & Brothers

Laurino, A., F. Ramella and P. Beria, 2015. 'The Economic Regulation of Railway Networks: A Worldwide Survey.' *Transportation Research, Part A: Policy and Practice* 77:202–212

Lavee, D. and S. Bahar, 2017. 'Examining the Economies of Scale of Water and Sewage Utilities in the Urban Sector: The Case of Israel.' *Water Policy* 19(2):257–270

LECG, 2007. 'Access Regulation and Infrastructure Investment in the Telecommunications Sector: An Empirical Investigation.' Report for ETNO. September

Le Coq, C. and S. Schwenen, 2021. 'Strengths and Weaknesses of the Nordic Market Model.' In J.-M. Glachant, P. L. Joskow and M. G. Pollitt (eds.), *Handbook on Electricity Markets.* Cheltenham: Edward Elgar

Lee, R. S., 2014. 'Competing Platforms.' *Journal of Economics and Management Strategy* 23(3):507–526

Lee, R. S. and T. Wu, 2009. 'Subsidizing Creativity through Network Design: Zero-Pricing and Net Neutrality.' *Journal of Economic Perspectives* 23:61–76

Lehman, D. E. and D. Weisman, 2000. *The Telecommunications Act of 1996: The 'Costs' of Managed Competition.* Norwell, MA: Kluwer Academic

Lei, Z. and J. F. O'Connell, 2011. 'The Evolving Landscape of Chinese Aviation Policies and Impact of a Deregulating Environment on Chinese Carriers.' *Journal of Transport Geography* 19(4):829–839

Leibenstein, H., 1966. 'Allocative Efficiency vs. "X-Efficiency".' *American Economic Review* 56:392–415

Lemley, M. A., 2021. 'The Contradictions of Platform Regulation.' *SSRN Electronic Journal* 3778909

Leonard, B., C. Costello and G. D. Libecap, 2019. 'Expanding Water Markets in the Western United States: Barriers and Lessons from Other Natural Resource Markets.' *Review of Environmental Economics and Policy* 13(1):43–61

Leung, T. C., K. P. Ping and K. K. Tsui, 2019. 'What Can Deregulators Deregulate? The Case of Electricity.' *Journal of Regulatory Economics* 56(1):1–32

Levine, M. E., 1965. 'Is Regulation Necessary? California Air Transportation and National Regulatory Policy.' *Yale Law Journal* 74(8):1416

——1987. 'Airline Competition in Deregulated Markets: Theory, Firm Strategy, and Public Policy.' *Yale Journal on Regulation* 4:393–494

——2006. 'Why Weren't the Airlines Reregulated.' *Yale Journal on Regulation* 23:269–297

Levy, B. and P. T. Spiller, 1994. 'The Institutional Foundation of Regulatory Commitment: A Comparative Analysis of Telecommunications Regulation.' *Journal of Law, Economics, & Organization* 10:201–246

Lewis, O. and A. Offer, 2022. 'Railways as Patient Capital.' *Oxford Review of Economic Policy* 38(2):260–277

Lewis, T. R. and D. E. M. Sappington, 1988. 'Regulating a Monopolist with Unknown Demand.' *American Economic Review* 78:986–998

Li, S., M. Lang, X. Yu, *et al.*, 2019. 'A Sustainable Transport Competitiveness Analysis of the China Railway Express in the Context of the Belt and Road Initiative.' *Sustainability* 11(10):2896

Li, W. and L. C. Xu, 2004. 'The Impact of Privatization and Competition in the Telecommunications Sector around the World.' *Journal of Law and Economics* 47(2):395–430

Lichtenberg, S., 2011. 'Embracing the Future: Four Key Trends in Telecommunications.' NRRI Research Paper 11-19. November

——2015. 'Examining the Role of State Regulators as Telecommunications Oversight Is Reduced.' NRRI Report No. 15-07

Liebowitz, S. J. and S. E. Margolis, 1994. 'Network Externality: An Uncommon Tragedy.' *Journal of Economic Perspectives* 8:133–150

Lim, C. S. and A. Yurukoglu, 2018. 'Dynamic Natural Monopoly Regulation: Time Inconsistency, Moral Hazard, and Political Environments.' *Journal of Political Economy* 126(1):263–312

Lima, S., A. Brochado and R. C. Marques, 2021. 'Public–Private Partnerships in the Water Sector: A Review.' *Utilities Policy* 69:101182

Link, H., 2018. 'Track Access Charges: Reconciling Conflicting Objectives: Germany.' CERRE Report. Brussels

Lipis, 2015. 'Payment System Ownership and Access Models.' Report for PSR. December

Lipsey, R. G. and K. Lancaster, 1956. 'The General Theory of Second Best.' *Review of Economic Studies* 24:11–32

Liston, C., 1993. 'Price Cap versus Rate-of-Return Regulation.' *Journal of Regulatory Economics* 5:25–48

Littlechild, S. C., 1983. *Regulation of British Telecoms Profitability*. London: HMSO

——1986. *Economic Regulation of Privatised Water Authorities*. London: HMSO

——1988. 'Economic Regulation of Privatised Water Authorities and Some Further Reflections.' *Oxford Review of Economic Policy* 4:40–68

——2002. 'Regulators, Competition and Transitional Price Controls: A Critique of Price Restraints in Electricity Supply and Mobile Telephones.' Institute of Economic Affairs, London

——2003. 'Wholesale Spot Price Pass-Through.' *Journal of Regulatory Economics* 23:61–91

——2006a. 'Beyond Regulation.' University of Cambridge, Electricity Policy Research Group, Working Paper 0516

——2006b. 'Stipulations, the Consumer Advocate and Utility Regulation in Florida.' University of Cambridge, Electricity Policy Research Group, Working Paper 0615. May

——2006c. 'Competition and Contracts in the Nordic Residential Electricity Markets.' *Utilities Policy* 14:135–147

——2008a. 'Some Alternative Approaches to Utility Regulation.' *Economic Affairs* 28(3):32–37

——2008b. 'Regulation, Over-Regulation and Deregulation.' CRI Occasional Lecture 22. November

——2009a. 'Stipulated Settlements, the Consumer Advocate and Utility Regulation in Florida.' *Journal of Regulatory Economics* 35:96–109

——2009b. 'Consumer Involvement, Ex Post Regulation and Customer Appeal Mechanisms.' Unpublished Working Paper. 29 November

——2009c. 'Retail Competition in Electricity Markets – Expectations, Outcomes and Economics.' *Energy Policy* 37:759–763

——2012a. 'Regulation and Customer Engagement.' *Economics of Energy & Environmental Policy* 1:53–67

——2012b. 'The Process of Negotiating Settlements at FERC.' *Energy Policy* 50:174–191

——2015. 'The CMA Energy Market Investigation, the Well-Functioning Market, Ofgem, Government and Behavioural Economics.' *European Competition Journal* 11(2–3):574–636

——2018a. 'Regulation and the Nature of Competition.' *Journal of Air Transport Management* 67:211–223

——2018b. 'Economic Regulation of Privatised Airports: Some Lessons from UK Experience.' *Transportation Research, Part A: Policy and Practice* 114:100–114

——2020. 'Submission to the CMA on Ofwat Determinations.' 24 May

——2021a. 'Incentive-Based Regulation: An Historical Perspective and a Suggestion for the Future.' Regulatory Policy Workshop. 5 November

——2021b. 'The Evolution of Competitive Retail Electricity Markets.' In J.-M. Glachant, P. L. Joskow and M. G. Pollitt (eds.), *Handbook on Electricity Markets*. Cheltenham: Edward Elgar

——2021c. 'The Challenge of Removing a Mistaken Price Cap.' *Economic Affairs* 41(3):391–415

Littlechild, S. and N. Cornwall, 2009. 'Potential Scope for User Participation in the GB Energy Regulatory Framework, with Particular Reference to the Next Transmission Price Control Review.' Report to Ofgem. 28 March

Liu, J., M. Sockin and W. Xiong, 2021. 'Data Privacy and Consumer Vulnerability.' Princeton University, Working Paper. November

Liu, Y., Z. Jiang and B. Guo, 2022. 'Assessing China's Provincial Electricity Spot Market Pilot Operations: Lessons from Guangdong Province.' *Energy Policy* 164:112917

Lodge, M. and J. Stern, 2014. 'British Utility Regulation: Consolidation, Existential Angst, or Fiasco?' *Utilities Policy* 31:146–151

Loeb, M. and W. A. Magat, 1979. 'A Decentralized Model for Utility Regulation.' *Journal of Law and Economics* 22:399–404

Loewenstein, G., T. O'Donoghue and M. Rabin, 2003. 'Projection Bias in Predicting Future Utility.' *Quarterly Journal of Economics* 118(4):1209–1248

London Economics, 2010. 'Competition in Upstream Sewage and Sludge Markets.' Report for Ofwat

Lo Prete, C., W. W. Hogan, B. Liu and J. Wang, 2019. 'Cross-Product Manipulation in Electricity Markets, Microstructure Models and Asymmetric Information.' *Energy Journal* 40(5):221–246

Lowe, M., 2014. 'Rail Revival in Africa? The Impact of Privatization.' In Joint RES–SPR Conference on Macroeconomic Challenges Facing Low-Income Countries: New Perspectives

Lowry, E. D. 1973. 'Justification for Regulation: The Case for Natural Monopoly.' *Public Utilities Fortnightly* 28:1–7

Lowry, M. N., M. Makos, J. Deason and L. Schwartz, 2017. 'State Performance-Based Regulation Using Multiyear Rate Plans for U.S. Electric Utilities.' Lawrence Berkeley National Laboratory, Report LBNL-2001039

Luguri, J. and L. J. Strahilevitz, 2021. 'Shining a Light on Dark Patterns.' *Journal of Legal Analysis* 13(1):43–109

Lunn, P., 2014. 'Regulatory Policy and Behavioural Economics.' OECD

Lykotrafiti, A., 2020. 'What Does Europe Do about Fair Competition in International Air Transport? A Critique of Recent Actions.' *Common Market Law Review* 57(3):831–860

Lyon, T. P., 1996. 'A Model of Sliding-Scale Regulation.' *Journal of Regulatory Economics* 9:227–247

Macey, J. R., 1992. 'Organizational Design and Political Control of Administrative Agencies.' *Journal of Law, Economics, & Organization* 8:93–110

Majumdar, S. K., I. Vogelsang and M. E. Cave (eds.), 2005. *Handbook of Telecommunications Economics*, Volume 2. Amsterdam: Elsevier

Makholm, J. D., 2006. 'The Theory of Relationship-Specific Investments, Long-Term Contracts and Gas Pipeline Development in the USA.' Unpublished Working Paper

——2007. 'Seeking Competition and Supply Security in Natural Gas: The US Experience and European Challenge.' CESSA Conference Paper. 31 May

——2015. 'Regulation of Natural Gas in the United States, Canada, and Europe: Prospects for a Low Carbon Fuel.' *Review of Environmental Economics and Policy* 9(1):107–127

——2016. 'The REVolution Yields to a More Familiar Path: New York's Reforming the Energy Vision (REV).' *Electricity Journal* 29(9):48–55

——2018a. 'The Rise and Decline of the X Factor in Performance-Based Electricity Regulation.' *Electricity Journal* 31(9):38–43

——2018b. 'Natural Gas and Greenhouse Gases – What's the Connection?' *Natural Gas and Electricity* 35(3):25–28

——2020a. 'The Once and Future Argentine Energy Sectors.' *Natural Gas and Electricity* 36(12):28–32

——2020b. 'The Mysterious US Natural Gas Market.' *Climate and Energy* 37(4):21–27

——2021a. 'Decarbonization and the Future of Gas Distributors.' *Climate and Energy* 37(6):15–19

——2021b. 'The Texas Energy Debacle and the Economists.' *Climate and Energy* 37(10):19–25

Malavolti, E., 2016. 'Single Till or Dual Till at Airports: A Two-Sided Market Analysis.' *Transportation Research Procedia* 14:3696–3703

Malmendier, U. and G. Tate, 2008. 'Who Makes Acquisitions? CEO Overconfidence and the Market's Reaction.' *Journal of Financial Economics* 89(1):20–43

Mande Buafua, P., 2015. 'Efficiency of Urban Water Supply in Sub-Saharan Africa: Do Organization and Regulation Matter?' *Utilities Policy* 37:13–22

Mandel, B., 1999. 'Measuring Competition: Approaches for (De-)Regulated Markets.' In W. Pfähler, H.-M. Niemeier and O. Mayer (eds.), *Airports and Air Traffic: Regulation, Privatisation and Competition*. Frankfurt am Main: Peter Lang, pp. 71–92

Mandy, D. M., 2002. 'TELRIC Pricing with Vintage Capital.' *Journal of Regulatory Economics* 22:215–249

Mandy, D. M. and W. W. Sharkey, 2003. 'Dynamic Pricing and Investment from Static Proxy Models.' FCC OSP Working Paper Series 40. September

Mankiw, N. G. and M. D. Whinston, 1986. 'Free Entry and Social Inefficiency.' *RAND Journal of Economics* 17(1):48–58

Manove, M. and A. J. Padilla, 1999. 'Banking (Conservatively) with Optimists.' *RAND Journal of Economics* 30(2):324

Manuszak, M. and K. Wozniak, 2017. 'The Impact of Price Controls in Two-Sided Markets: Evidence from US Debit Card Interchange Fee Regulation.' Discussion Series 2017-074. Board of Governors of the Federal Reserve System, Washington

Marcus, J. S. and D. Elixmann, 2008. 'Regulatory Approaches to NGNs: An International Comparison.' *Communications & Strategies* 69:19–40

Mariotto, C. and M. Verdier, 2016. 'The Role of Merchants' Pass-Through in Payment Platform Markets.' *SSRN Electronic Journal* 2535558

Marques, R. C., 2010. *Regulation of Water and Wastewater Services*. London: IWA Publishing

——2017. 'Why Not Regulate PPPs?' *Utilities Policy* 48:141–146

——2018. 'Regulation by Contract: Overseeing PPPs.' *Utilities Policy* 50:211–214

Marques, R. C. and J. Miranda, 2020. 'Sustainable Tariffs for Water and Wastewater Services.' *Utilities Policy* 64:101054

Martimort, D., 1999. 'The Life Cycle of Regulatory Agencies: Dynamic Capture and Transaction Costs.' *Review of Economic Studies* 66:929–947

Martimort, D., G. Pommey and J. Pouyet, 2021. 'How to Regulate Airports?' Working Paper. HAL Archives. hal-03328394

Martimort, D., J. Pouyet and C. Staropoli, 2020. 'Use and Abuse of Regulated Prices in Electricity Markets: "How to Regulate Regulated Prices?"' *Journal of Economics and Management Strategy* 29(3):605–634

Mason, R. and S. Wright, 2021. 'A Report on Financial Resilience, Gearing and Price Controls.' Prepared for Ofwat. 3 December

Massarutto, A., 2020. 'Servant of Too Many Masters: Residential Water Pricing and the Challenge of Sustainability.' *Utilities Policy* 63:101018

Mathios, A. D. and R. P. Rogers, 1989. 'The Impact of Alternative Forms of State Regulation of AT&T on Direct-Dial, Long-Distance Telephone Rates.' *RAND Journal of Economics* 20:437–453

Mautino, L., P. Dudley, J. Prettyman and F. Heagney, 2013. 'Estimating Long-Run Incremental Costs in the Postal Sector: A UK Perspective.' In M. A. Crew and P. R. Kleindorfer (eds.), *Reforming the Postal Sector in the Face of Electronic Competition*. Cheltenham: Edward Elgar

Mayo, J. W., 2011. 'The Evolution of Regulation: 20th Century Lessons and 21st Century Opportunities.' Unpublished Manuscript

Mayo, J. W. and D. E. M. Sappington, 2016. 'Regulation in a "Deregulated" Industry: Railroads in the Post-Staggers Era.' *Review of Industrial Organization* 49(2):203–227

Mayo, J. W. and R. D. Willig, 2019. 'Economic Foundations for 21st Century Freight Rail Rate Regulation.' In J. T. Macher and J. W. Mayo (eds.), *U.S. Freight Rail Economics and Policy: Are We on the Right Track?* London: Routledge, pp. 32–57

McCarthy, C., 2004. 'Why Independent Regulators?' In M. Frison-Roche (ed.), *Droit et Économie de la Regulation*. Paris: Presses de Sciences Po

McDermott, K. A. and R. C. Hemphill, 2017. 'Next-Generation PBR.' *Electricity Journal* 30(1):1–7

McFadden, D., 1999. 'Rationality for Economists?' *Journal of Risk and Uncertainty* 19(1–3):73–105

McFarland, H., 1989. 'The Effects of United States Railroad Deregulation on Shippers, Labor, and Capital.' *Journal of Regulatory Economics* 1(3):259–270

McGowan, F., 2018. 'The Roaming Regulation and the Case for Applying Behavioural Industrial Organisation to EU Competition Policy.' ESRI Working Paper No. 598

McNulty, R. 2011. 'Realising the Potential of GB Rail. Report of the Rail Value for Money Study' May

Megginson, W. L., 2017. 'Privatization, State Capitalism, and State Ownership of Business in the 21st Century.' *Foundations and Trends in Finance* 11(1–2):1–153

Megginson, W. L. and J. M. Netter, 2001. 'From State to Market: A Survey of Empirical Studies of Privatization.' *Journal of Economic Literature* 39:321–389

Meitzen, M. E., P. E. Schoech and D. L. Weisman, 2017. 'The Alphabet of PBR in Electric Power: Why X Does Not Tell the Whole Story.' *Electricity Journal* 30(8):30–37

Melaina, M. W., O. Antonia and M. Penev, 2013. 'Blending Hydrogen into Natural Gas Pipeline Networks: A Review of Key Issues.' Technical Report. National Renewable Energy Laboratory

Meran, G., M. Siehlow and C. Von Hirschhausen, 2021. 'Water Tariffs.' In *The Economics of Water: Rules and Institutions*. Cham: Springer International, pp. 123–184

Mercadier, A. C. and F. S. Brenner, 2020. 'Tariff (Un)Sustainability in Contexts of Price (In) Stability: The Case of the Buenos Aires Water and Sanitation Concession.' *Utilities Policy* 63:101005

Mercadier, A. C., W. A. Cont and G. Ferro, 2016. 'Economies of Scale in Peru's Water and Sanitation Sector.' *Journal of Productivity Analysis* 45(2):215–228

Merkert, R., A. S. J. Smith and C. A. Nash, 2012. 'The Measurement of Transaction Costs – Evidence from European Railways.' *Journal of Transport Economics and Policy* 46(3):349–365

Mervis, C. B. and E. Rosch, 1981. 'Categorization of Natural Objects.' *Annual Review of Psychology* 32(1):89–115

METI, 2021. 'Cabinet Decision on the Bill for the Act on Improving Transparency and Fairness of Digital Platforms.' Press Release. 18 February

Meyer, R., 2012a. 'Economies of Scope in Electricity Supply and the Costs of Vertical Separation for Different Unbundling Scenarios.' *Journal of Regulatory Economics* 42:95–114

——2012b. 'Vertical Economies and the Costs of Separating Electricity Supply – A Review of Theoretical and Empirical Literature.' *Energy Journal* 33:161–185

——2019. 'Digital Strategy: Digital Platform Map.' TIAS School for Business and Society. 2 August

Meyer, R. A., 1975. 'Publicly Owned versus Privately Owned Utilities: A Policy Choice.' *Review of Economics and Statistics* 57:391–399

Michelfelder, R. A., P. Ahern and D. D'Ascendis, 2019. 'Decoupling Impact and Public Utility Conservation Investment.' *Energy Policy* 130:311–319

Milgrom, P., 2004. *Putting Auction Theory to Work.* Cambridge: Cambridge University Press

Miravete, E. J. and I. Palacios-Huerta, 2014. 'Consumer Inertia, Choice Dependence, and Learning from Experience in a Repeated Decision Problem.' *Review of Economics and Statistics* 96(3):524–537

Mitchell, B. M., 1989. 'Incremental Capital Costs of Telephone Access and Local Use.' RAND Corporation. Prepared for Incremental Cost Taskforce

Mitchell, B. M. and I. Vogelsang, 1991. *Telecommunications Pricing: Theory and Practice.* Cambridge: Cambridge University Press

Mizuno, K. and I. Yoshino, 2015. 'Overusing a Bypass under Cost-Based Access Regulation: Underinvestment with Spillovers.' *Journal of Regulatory Economics* 47(1):29–57

Mizutani, F., 2019. 'Going Places: Rail Transport in Japan.' Discussion Paper No. 2019-3. Kobe University, Graduate School of Business Administration

Mizutani, F. and K. Nakamura, 1997. 'Privatization of the Japan National Railway: Overview of Performance Changes.' *International Journal of Transport Economics* 24(1):75–99

——2004. 'The Japanese Experience with Railway Restructuring.' In T. Ito and A. O. Krueger (eds.), *Governance, Regulation and Privatization in the Asia-Pacific Region.* Chicago: University of Chicago Press, pp. 305–342

Mizutani, F., A. Smith, C. Nash and S. Uranishi, 2015. 'Comparing the Costs of Vertical Separation, Integration, and Intermediate Organisational Structures in European and East Asian Railways.' *Journal of Transport Economics and Policy* 49(3):496–515

Mizutani, F. and S. Uranishi, 2013. 'Does Vertical Separation Reduce Cost? An Empirical Analysis of the Rail Industry in European and East Asian OECD Countries.' *Journal of Regulatory Economics* 43(1):31–59

Modigliani, F. and M. H. Miller, 1958. 'The Cost of Capital, Corporation Finance and the Theory of Investment.' *American Economic Review* 48:261–297

——1963. 'Corporate Income Taxes and the Cost of Capital: A Correction.' *American Economic Review* 53:433–443

Mohamad, N., 2014. 'Telecommunications Reform and Efficiency Performance: Do Good Institutions Matter?' *Telecommunications Policy* 38(1):49–65

Molinos-Senante, M. and A. Maziotis, 2021. 'Productivity Growth, Economies of Scale and Scope in the Water and Sewerage Industry: The Chilean Case.' *PLOS ONE* 16(5):e0251874

Monopolies and Mergers Commission, 1982. 'Contraceptive Sheaths.' A Report on the Supply in the UK of Contraceptive Sheaths. Cmnd 8689

Montero, J. and M. Finger, 2020. 'Railway Regulation: A Comparative Analysis of a Diverging Reality.' In M. Finger and J. Montero (eds.), *Handbook on Railway Regulation.* Cheltenham: Edward Elgar

Moore, G. E., 1965. 'Cramming More Components onto Integrated Circuits.' *Electronics* 38:1–4

Morandi, V., P. Malighetti, S. Paleari and R. Redondi, 2015. 'Codesharing Agreements by Low-Cost Carriers: An Explorative Analysis.' *Journal of Air Transport Management* 42:184–191

Morey, M. J. and L. D. Kirsch, 2016. 'Retail Choice in Electricity: What Have We Learned in 20 Years?' Report for Electric Markets Research Foundation

Morgan, T., 1978. 'Toward a Revised Strategy for Ratemaking.' *University of Illinois Law Forum* 1978:21–78

Morrish, S. C. and R. T. Hamilton, 2002. 'Airline Alliances – Who Benefits?' *Journal of Air Transport Management* 8:401–407

Morrison, S. A., 2001. 'Actual, Adjacent, and Potential Competition Estimating the Full Effect of Southwest Airlines.' *Journal of Transport Economics and Policy* 35(2):239–256

Morrison, S. A. and C. Winston, 1987. 'Empirical Implications and Tests of the Contestability Hypothesis.' *Journal of Law and Economics* 30(1):53–66

——1990. 'The Dynamics of Airline Pricing and Competition.' *American Economic Review* 80(2):389–393

——2008. 'The Effect of FAA Expenditures on Air Travel Delays.' *Journal of Urban Economics* 63(2):669–678

Mosca, M., 2008. 'On the Origins of the Concept of Natural Monopoly: Economies of Scale and Competition.' *European Journal of the History of Economic Thought* 15:317–353

Moselle, B., D. Black, M. White and H. Piffaut, 2012. 'Regulation of the Natural Gas Industry.' In R. Van den Bergh and A. M. Pacces (eds.), *Regulation and Economics: Encyclopedia of Law and Economics*, 2nd ed. Cheltenham: Edward Elgar

Motta, M., 2004. *Competition Policy: Theory and Practice*. Cambridge: Cambridge University Press

Motta, M. and M. Peitz, 2021. 'Big Tech Mergers.' *Information Economics and Policy* 54:100868

Mountain, B., 2014. 'Independent Regulation of Government-Owned Monopolies: An Oxymoron? The Case of Electricity Distribution in Australia.' *Utilities Policy* 31:188–196

Mugabi, J., S. Kayaga and C. Njiru, 2007. 'Strategic Planning for Water Utilities in Developing Countries.' *Utilities Policy* 15:1–8

Mukharlyamov, V. and N. Sarin, 2019. 'The Impact of the Durbin Amendment on Banks, Merchants, and Consumers.' University of Pennsylvania, Carey Law School. Research Paper 2046

Mullainathan, S. and R. H. Thaler, 2000. 'Behavioral Economics.' NBER Working Paper 7948

Muris, T. J., 2002. 'The Interface of Competition and Consumer Protection.' 31 October

Murooka, T., 2015. 'Deception under Competitive Intermediation.' Working Paper

Murooka, T. and M. A. Schwarz, 2018. 'The Timing of Choice-Enhancing Policies.' *Journal of Public Economics* 157:27–40

Myers, S. C., 2001. 'Capital Structure.' *Journal of Economic Perspectives* 15:81–102

Myerson, R. B., 1981. 'Optimal Auction Design.' *Mathematics of Operations Research* 6(1):58–7

Nakamura, E. and H. Sakai, 2020. 'Does Vertical Integration Facilitate Coordination between Infrastructure Management and Train Operating Units in the Rail Sector? Implications for Japanese Railways.' *Utilities Policy* 66:101099

Nakamura, E., H. Sakai and K. Shoji, 2018. 'Managerial Transfers to Reduce Transaction Costs among Affiliated Firms: Case Study of Japanese Railway Holding Companies.' *Utilities Policy* 53:102–110

NAO, 1996. 'The Work of the Directors General of Telecommunications, Gas Supply, Water Services and Electricity Supply.' HC 645. Session 1995–96

——2002. 'Pipes and Wires.' Report by the Comptroller and Auditor General. HC 723. 10 April

——2008. 'Protecting Consumers? Removing Retail Price Controls.' HC 342 Session 2008

——2010. 'Review of UK's Competition Landscape.' Review by the Comptroller and Auditor General. 22 March

——2015. 'The Economic Regulation of the Water Sector.' Report by the Comptroller and Auditor General. HC 487. 14 October

——2020. 'Electricity Networks.' Report by the Comptroller and Auditor General. HC42. 30 January

Nardotto, M., T. Valletti and F. Verboven, 2015. 'Unbundling the Incumbent: Evidence from UK Broadband.' *Journal of the European Economic Association* 13(2):330-362

NARUC, 2003. 'Rate Case and Audit Manual.' Prepared for NARUC Staff Subcommittee on Accounting and Finance. Summer

Nash, C., 1993. 'Rail Privatisation in Britain.' *Journal of Transport Economics and Policy* 27(3):317-322

——2016. 'European Rail Policy – British Experience.' *Network Industries Quarterly* 18(4):3-7

——2018. 'Track Access Charges: Reconciling Conflicting Objectives: Project Report.' CERRE Report, Brussels. 9 May

Nash, C., Y. Crozet, H. Link, J. E. Nilsson and A. Smith, 2018. 'Track Access Charges: Reconciling Conflicting Objectives.' CERRE Report, Brussels

Nash, C., J. E. Nilsson and H. Link, 2013. 'Comparing Three Models for Introduction of Competition into Railways.' *Journal of Transport Economics and Policy* 47(2):191-206

Nash, C. and A. S. J. Smith, 2020. 'Developments in Rail Regulation in Britain.' In M. Finger and J. Montero (eds.), *Handbook on Railway Regulation*. Cheltenham: Edward Elgar

Nash, C., A. Smith, Y. Crozet, H. Link and J. E. Nilsson, 2019. 'How to Liberalise Rail Passenger Services? Lessons from European Experience.' *Transport Policy* 79:11-20

National Academies of Sciences, Engineering, and Medicine, 1991. 'Winds of Change: Domestic Air Transport Since Deregulation.' Special Report 230. Washington, DC

——1999. 'Entry and Competition in the U.S. Airline Industry: Issues and Opportunities.' Washington, DC

——2010. *Airport/Airline Agreements Practices and Characteristics*. Washington, DC: National Academies Press

——2015. 'Modernizing Freight Rail Regulation.' Report

National Grid, 2021. 'Breaking Down Your Bill'

National Research Council, 2012. *Water Reuse: Potential for Expanding the Nation's Water Supply through Reuse of Municipal Wastewater*. Washington, DC: National Academies Press

——2015. '*Transformation in the Air: A Review of the FAA's Certification Research Plan.*' Washington, DC: National Academies Press

Natural Gas, 2012. 'Industry and Market Structure.' NaturalGas.Org

Nauges, C. and D. Whittington, 2017. 'Evaluating the Performance of Alternative Municipal Water Tariff Designs: Quantifying the Tradeoffs between Equity, Economic Efficiency, and Cost Recovery.' *World Development* 91:125-143

NBN, 2021. 'NBN Co Special Access Undertaking Given to the ACCC in Accordance with Part XIC of the Competition and Consumer Act 2010 (Cth). Varied up to and including 1 April 2021'

NEB, 2002. 'Guidelines for Negotiated Settlements of Traffic, Tolls and Tariffs (Guidelines).' 12 June

Nepal, R. and T. Jamasb, 2015. 'Caught between Theory and Practice: Government, Market, and Regulatory Failure in Electricity Sector Reforms.' *Economic Analysis and Policy* 46:16-24

NERA, 2002. 'UK Water Cost of Capital and Gearing: What Is the Relationship?' Unpublished Report. October

Neto, S. and J. Camkin, 2020. 'What Rights and Whose Responsibilities in Water? Revisiting the Purpose and Reassessing the Value of Water Services Tariffs.' *Utilities Policy* 63:101016

Newbery, D. M., 1999. *Privatization, Restructuring, and Regulation of Network Utilities.* Cambridge, MA: MIT Press

——2002. 'Issues and Options for Restructuring Electricity Supply Industries.' Cambridge DAE, Working Paper WP 0210

——2003. 'Rate-of-Return Regulation versus Price Regulation for Public Utilities.' In P. Newman (ed.), *The New Palgrave Dictionary of Economics and the Law.* London: Palgrave Macmillan

——2011. 'High Level Principles for Guiding GB Transmission Charging and Some of the Practical Problems of Transition to an Enduring Regime.' Report for the Gas and Electricity Markets Authority. 22 April

——2021. 'Strengths and Weaknesses of the British Market Model.' In J.-M. Glachant, P. L. Joskow and M. G. Pollitt (eds.), *Handbook on Electricity Markets.* Cheltenham: Edward Elgar

Newbery, D. M. and M. G. Pollitt, 1997. 'The Restructuring and Privatisation of Britain's CEGB – Was It Worth It?' *Journal of Industrial Economics* 45:269–303

New Zealand Commerce Commission, 2022. 'Why Regulate?' See https://comcom.govt.nz/regulated-industries/our-role-in-regulated-industries/why-regulate

New Zealand Government, 2019. 'Electricity Price Review.' Final Report. 21 May

——2021. 'NZ Gas Infrastructure Future: Findings Report.' 13 August

Nicolson, M., G. Huebner and D. Shipworth, 2017. 'Are Consumers Willing to Switch to Smart Time of Use Electricity Tariffs? The Importance of Loss-Aversion and Electric Vehicle Ownership.' *Energy Research and Social Science* 23:82–96

Nilson, 2019. 'Consumer Payment Systems in the U.S.: Purchase Transactions in 2018.' Nilson Report. Issue 1166. December

——2021a. 'Global Network Cards: Purchase Transactions in 2020.' Nilson Report. Issue 1199. June

——2021b. 'Europe's Global Network Cards.' Nilson Report. Issue 1200. June

——2021c. 'Latin-America's Global General Purpose Cards.' Nilson Report. Issue 1194. March

——2021d. 'Asia-Pacific Global Network Cards.' Nilson Report. Issue 1201. July

——2021e. 'Top U.S Merchant Acquirers.' Nilson Report. Issue 1193. March

——2021f. 'Europe's Top Merchant Acquirers.' Nilson Report. Issue 1197. May

Nilsson, J.-E., 2002. 'Restructuring Sweden's Railways: The Unintentional Deregulation.' *Swedish Economic Policy Review* 9(2):229–254

Nilsson, J.-E., R. Pyddoke, S. Hulten and G. Alexandersson, 2013. 'The Liberalisation of Railway Passenger Transport in Sweden.' *Journal of Transport Economics and Policy* 47(2):307–312

Niskanen, W. A., 1971. *Bureaucracy and Representative Government.* New Brunswick: Transaction Publishers

Njoya, E. T., 2016. 'Africa's Single Aviation Market: The Progress so Far.' *Journal of Transport Geography* 50:4–11

NMa, 2010. 'Onderzoek Economische Machtspositie Schiphol en Wenselijkheid Regulering [Investigation of Economic Dominance at Schiphol and Desirability of Regulation].' 15 November

Noam, E. M., 1993. 'Assessing the Impacts of Divestiture and Deregulation in Telecommunications.' *Southern Economic Journal* 59:438–449

——2002. 'Interconnection Practices.' In M. E. Cave, S. K. Majumdar and I. Vogelsang (eds.), *Handbook of Telecommunications Economics*, Volume 1. Amsterdam: Elsevier

——2010. 'Regulation 3.0 for Telecom 3.0.' *Telecommunications Policy* 34:4–10

Noll, R. G., 1989. 'Economic Perspectives on the Politics of Regulation.' In R. Schmalensee and R. Willig (eds.), *Handbook of Industrial Organization*, Volume 2. Amsterdam: North-Holland

——2002. 'The Economics of Urban Water Systems.' In M. Shirley (ed.), *Thirsting for Efficiency: The Economics and Politics of Urban Water System Reform*. Washington, DC: Pergamon

Norad, 2020. 'Study on the Potential of Increased Use of LPG for Cooking in Developing Countries.' September

Nordgren, L. F., F. van Harreveld and J. van der Pligt, 2009. 'The Restraint Bias: How the Illusion of Self-Restraint Promotes Impulsive Behavior.' *Psychological Science* 20(12):1523–1528

North, D. C. 1990. *Institutions, Institutional Change, and Economic Performance*. Cambridge: Cambridge University Press

NWC, 2010. 'The Impacts of Water Trading in the Southern Murray–Darling Basin: An Economic and Social Assessment.' Australian Government National Water Commission. June

NYPSC, 2016. 'Proceeding on Motion of the Commission in Regard to Reforming the Energy Vision (CASE 14-M-0101): Order Adopting a Ratemaking and Utility Revenue Model Framework.' Report, New York

OECD, 2002. 'Regulatory Policies in OECD Countries: From Interventionism to Regulatory Governance.' Paris

——2004. 'Competition and Regulation in the Water Sector.' Competition Committee Report. August

——2007. 'Convergence and Next Generation Networks.' Ministerial Background Report

——2009. 'Private Sector Participation in Water Infrastructure: OECD Checklist for Public Action.' Paris

——2010. 'Towards Global Carbon Pricing: Direct and Indirect Linking of Carbon Markets.' Environment Working Paper No. 20. August

——2011a. 'Fibre Access – Network Developments in the OECD Area.' 16 June

——2011b. 'OECD Communications Outlook 2011'

——2011c. 'Water: Meeting the Reform Challenge.' Working Party on Biodiversity, Water and Ecosystems. 21 December

——2013. 'Recent Developments in Rail Transportation Services.' OECD Policy Roundtables, DAF/COMP(2013)24. 13 December

——2016a. 'Structural Separation in Regulated Industries.' Report on Implementing the OECD Recommendation No. 104

——2016b. 'Protecting Consumers through Behavioural Insights: Regulating the Communications Market in Colombia'

——2016c. 'Governance of Regulators' Practices: Accountability, Transparency and Co-ordination'

——2016d. 'Being an Independent Regulator'

——2017a. 'Behavioural Insights and Public Policy: Lessons from Around the World'

——2017b. 'Tackling Environmental Problems with the Help of Behavioural Insights'

——2017c. 'The Size and Sectoral Distribution of State-Owned Enterprises'

——2017d. 'Creating a Culture of Independence'

——2019a. 'An Introduction to Online Platforms and Their Role in the Digital Transformation'

——2019b. 'The Road to 5G Networks.' OECD Digital Economy Papers. July

——2020a. 'Financing Water Supply, Sanitation and Flood Protection: Challenges in EU Member States and Policy Options.' OECD Studies on Water

——2020b. 'Start-Ups, Killer Acquisitions and Merger Control'

——2020c. 'Digital Economy Outlook 2020'

——2020d. 'Regulatory Governance of the Rail Sector in Mexico'

——2020e. 'COVID-19 and the Aviation Industry: Impact and Policy Responses'

——2021a. 'OECD Broadband Statistics: OECD Fixed and Mobile Broadband Subscriptions, by Technology.' June

——2021b. 'OECD Broadband Statistics: OECD Historical Fixed Broadband Subscriptions per 100 Inhabitants.' June

——2021c. 'OECD Broadband Statistics: Mobile Termination Rates (MTRs) in the OECD Area.' June

——2021d. 'Behavioural Insights and Regulatory Governance'

——2022. 'Dark Commercial Patterns.' Digital Economy Paper No. 336. October

OECD/ITF, 2010. 'Airport Regulation Investment & Development of Aviation'

Ofcom, 2004a. 'Wholesale Mobile Voice Call Termination: Statement.' June

——2004b. 'Partial Private Circuits Charge Control: Final Statement.' September

——2005. 'Provision of Technical Platform Services: A Consultation on Proposed Guidance as to How Ofcom May Interpret the Meaning of "Fair, Reasonable and Non-Discriminatory". 2 November

——2009. 'Determination to Resolve Disputes between Each of Cable & Wireless, THUS, Global Crossing, Verizon, Virgin Media and COLT and BT Regarding BT's Charges for Partial Private Circuits.' 14 October

——2010. 'Using Experiments in Consumer Research.' Research Document. 1 March

——2012. 'Disputes between Each of Sky, TalkTalk, Virgin Media, Cable & Wireless and Verizon and BT Regarding BT's Charges for Ethernet Services.' 20 December

——2013. 'Cost Orientation Review.' 5 June

——2020a. 'Wholesale Fixed Telecoms Market Review 2021–26: Further Consultation on Certain Proposed Remedies.' 6 November

——2020b. 'Making Communications Markets Work Well for Customers: A Framework for Assessing Fairness in Broadband, Mobile, Home Phone and Pay TV.' 23 January

——2020c. 'Mobile Strategy: Terms of Reference.' 11 May

——2021a. 'The Communications Market 2021.' 22 July

——2021b. 'Promoting Competition and Investment in Fibre Networks: Wholesale Fixed Telecoms Market Review 2021–26.' 18 March

——2021c. 'Wholesale Voice Markets Review 2021–26 Statement.' 20 March

——2021d. 'Net Neutrality Review: Call for Evidence.' 7 September

Ofgem, 2000. 'The Structure of Electricity Distribution Charges: Initial Consultation Paper.' December

——2002. 'Competition in Gas and Electricity Supply – Separating Fact from Fiction.' Fact Sheet

——2007. 'Domestic Retail Report – June 2007.' Ref 160/07. July

——2010. 'Project Discovery: Options for Delivering Secure and Sustainable Energy Supplies.' Consultation. 3 February

——2011a. 'Do Energy Bills Respond Faster to Rising Costs than Falling Costs?' Discussion Paper. 21 March

——2011b. 'What Can Behavioural Economics Say about GB Energy Consumers?' Discussion Paper. 21 March

——2012. 'Updated Household Energy Bills Explained.' Factsheet 97. May

——2016. 'Quick Guide to the CATO Regime.' November

——2019. 'Consumer Vulnerability Strategy.' October

——2020. 'RIIO-2 Final Determinations – Impact Assessment Annex.' 8 December

——2021. 'Call for Evidence: Transmission Network Use of System Charges.' OFG 1161

——2022. 'Check if the Energy Price Cap Affects You'

OFT, 2003. 'Mastercard Interchange Fees: Preliminary Conclusions.' February

——2005. 'OFT Issues Statement of Objections on Visa Agreement.' Press Release. 19 October

——2007. 'Final Report of the Payment Systems Task Force.' OFT 901. February

——2010. 'What Does Behavioural Economics Mean for Competition Policy?' OFT 1224. March

——2011a. 'Consumer Behavioural Biases in Competition: A Survey.' May

——2011b. 'Off-Grid Energy Market Study.' October

——2013. 'UK Payment Systems: How Regulation of UK Payment Systems Could Enhance Competition and Innovation.' OFT 1498. July

Oftel, 1997. 'Network Charges from 1997.' Consultation Document. July

Ofwat, 2007. 'Outcomes of Ofwat's Internal Review of Market Competition in the Water Sector.' April

——2008a. 'International Comparison of Water and Sewerage Service: 2008 Report'

——2008b. 'Ofwat's Review of Competition in the Water and Sewerage Industries: Part II'

——2011. 'Involving Customers in Price Setting – Ofwat's Customer Engagement Policy Statement.' August

——2020. 'Charges Scheme Rules Effective from 1 April 2020.' 27 March

——2021a. 'State of the Market 2020–21.' December

——2021b. 'Financial Resilience in the Water Sector: A Discussion Paper.' December

Ofwat and Defra, 2006. 'The Development of the Water Industry in England and Wales'

Ogus, A. I., 1994. *Regulation: Legal Form and Economic Theory*. Oxford: Hart

Oldale, A. and A. J. Padilla, 2004. 'From State Monopoly to the "Investment Ladder": Competition Policy and the NRF.' In *The Pros and Cons of Antitrust in Deregulated Markets*. Stockholm: Swedish Competition Authority

Oliveira, A. R., 2008. 'Private Provision of Water Service in Brazil: Impacts on Access and Affordability.' Unpublished Working Paper. 30 May

Oliver, M. E., 2019. 'Pricing Flexibility under Rate-of-Return Regulation: Effects on Network Infrastructure Investment.' *Economic Modelling* 78:150–161

Olsen, O. J., T. A. Johnsen and P. Lewis, 2006. 'A Mixed Nordic Experience: Implementing Competitive Retail Electricity Markets for Household Customers.' *Electricity Journal* 19:37–44

Olson, M., 1965. *The Logic of Collective Action: Public Goods and the Theory of Groups*. Cambridge, MA: Harvard University Press

O'Neill, R., 2005. 'Natural Gas Pipelines.' In D. Moss (ed.), *Network Access, Regulation and Antitrust*. London: Routledge

Oren, S. S., 2000. 'Transmission Pricing and Congestion Management: Efficiency, Simplicity and Open Access.' Unpublished Working Paper

Oren, S. S., P. T. Spiller, P. Varaiya and F. Wu, 1995. 'Nodal Prices and Transmission Rights: A Critical Appraisal.' *Electricity Journal* 8(3):24–35

ORR, 2010. 'High Level Review of Track Access Charges and Options for CP5.' Report Prepared by CEPA. June

——2018. 'Performance Incentives for Network Rail: A Perspective from Behavioural Economics.' Report for ORR by Nick Charter

——2019. 'Delay Repay Claims Companies – Market Review.' Report for ORR by Europe Economics

——2020a. 'Regulation and Incentivisation of the Rail Infrastructure Manager in a Changing Industry.' Report for ORR by Steer

——2020b. 'UK Rail Industry Financial Information 2018–19.' 26 February

Ottow, A. T., 2014. 'Erosion or Innovation?' *Journal of Antitrust Enforcement* 2(1):25–43

Oum, T. H., J. H. Park and A. Zhang, 1996. 'The Effects of Airline Codesharing Agreements on Firm Conduct and International Air Fares.' *Journal of Transport Economics and Policy* 30(2):187–202

Ovington, T., R. Smith, J. Santamaría and L. Stammati, 2017. 'The Impact of Intra-Platform Competition on Broadband Penetration.' *Telecommunications Policy* 41(3):185–196

Ovum, 2017. 'Instant Payments and the Post-PSD2 Landscape.' 14 June

Owen, A. and J. Barrett, 2020. 'Reducing Inequality Resulting from UK Low-Carbon Policy.' *Climate Policy* 20(10):1193–1208

Panzar, J. C., 1976. 'A Neoclassical Approach to Peak-Load Pricing.' *Bell Journal of Economics* 7:521–530

Panzar, J. C. and R. D. Willig 1977. 'Free Entry and the Sustainability of Natural Monopoly.' *Bell Journal of Economics* 8:1–22

Papatheodorou, A., K. Polychroniadis and T. Kapturski, 2016. 'Airline Liberalization and Implications for Safety: A Theoretical and Empirical Conundrum.' In *Liberalization in Aviation*. London: Routledge, pp. 151–160

Park, J.-H., 1997. 'The Effects of Airline Alliances on Markets and Economic Welfare.' *Transportation Research, Part E: Logistics and Transportation Review* 33(3): 181–195

Parker, D., 2021. 'Privatization of State-Owned Enterprises.' In *Oxford Research Encyclopedia of Business and Management*. Oxford: Oxford University Press

Parker, G., G. Petropoulos and M. Van Alstyne, 2021 'Platform Mergers and Antitrust.' Bruegel Working Paper 01/2021

Patterson, R., 2011. 'Regulation of Telecommunications: The Lessons Learned over the Last 25 Years and Their Application in a Broadband World.' Paper Delivered at Competition Law and Policy Institute of New Zealand

Payment Strategy Forum, 2017. 'NPA Design and Transition Blueprint.' December

Peci, A., M. L. D'Assunção, M. M. Holperin and C. F. de Souza, 2017. 'Regulation inside Government: The Challenges of Regulating a Government-Owned Utility.' *Utilities Policy* 49:61–70

Peitz, M., 2005. 'Asymmetric Access Price Regulation in Telecommunications Markets.' *European Economic Review* 49:341–358

Peitz, M. and F. Schuett, 2016. 'Net Neutrality and Inflation of Traffic.' *International Journal of Industrial Organization* 46:16–62

Peles, Y. C. and J. L. Stein, 1976. 'The Effect of Rate of Return Regulation Is Highly Sensitive to the Nature of the Uncertainty.' *American Economic Review* 66:278–289

Pellegrini, P., T. Bolić, L. Castelli and R. Pesenti, 2017. 'SOSTA: An Effective Model for the Simultaneous Optimisation of Airport Slot Allocation.' *Transportation Research, Part E: Logistics and Transportation Review* 99:34–53

Peltzman, S., 1971. 'Pricing in Public and Private Enterprises: Electric Utilities in the USA.' *Journal of Law and Economics* 14:109–147

——1976. 'Toward a More General Theory of Regulation.' *Journal of Law and Economics* 19:211–240

——1989. 'The Economic Theory of Regulation after a Decade of Deregulation.' *Brookings Paper on Economic Activity* 20(Microeconomics):1–59

——1993. 'George Stigler's Contribution to the Economic Analysis of Regulation.' *Journal of Political Economy* 101:818–832

——2021. 'Stigler's Theory of Economic Regulation After Fifty Years' (University of Chicago Coase–Sandor Institute for Law & Economics Research Paper No. 925). *SSRN Electronic Journal* 3785342

Pérez-Arriaga, I. J. and A. Bharatkumar, 2014. 'A Framework for Redesigning Distribution Network Use of System Charges Under High Penetration of Distributed Energy Resources: New Principles for New Problems.' CEEPR Working Paper No. 2014-006

Pérez-Arriaga, I. J., J. D. Jenkins and C. Batlle, 2017. 'A Regulatory Framework for an Evolving Electricity Sector: Highlights of the MIT Utility of the Future Study.' *Economics of Energy & Environmental Policy* 6(1):71–92

Pérez-Arriaga, I. J., L. Olmos and M. Rivier, 2013. 'Transmission Pricing.' In J. Rosellón and T. Kristiansen (eds.), *Financial Transmission Rights: Analysis, Experiences and Prospects.* London: Springer, pp. 49–76

Pérez-Arriaga, I. J., F. J. Rubio, J. F. Puerta, J. Arceluz and J. Marín, 1995. Marginal Pricing of Transmission Services: An Analysis of Cost Recovery. *IEEE Transactions on Power Systems* 10(1):546–553

Perkins, S., 2016. 'Regulation, Competition and Performance of Mexico's Freight Railways.' *Network Industries Quarterly* 18(4):21–26

Phillips, C. F., 1993. *The Regulation of Public Utilities: Theory and Practice.* Arlington, VA: Public Utilities Reports

Phillips, N. J., 2019. 'We Need to Talk: Toward a Serious Conversation about Breakups.' FTC Speech. 30 April

Piccione, M. and R. Spiegler, 2012. 'Price Competition Under Limited Comparability.' *Quarterly Journal of Economics* 127(1):97–135

Pierce, R. J., 1994. 'The State of the Transition to Competitive Markets in Natural Gas and Electricity.' *Energy Law Journal* 15:323–350

Pigou, A. C., 1932. *The Economics of Welfare.* London: Macmillan

Pindyck, R. S., 2007. 'Mandatory Unbundling and Irreversible Investment in Telecom Networks.' *Review of Network Economics* 6:274–298

Pinto, F. S. and R. C. Marques, 2015. 'Tariff Structures for Water and Sanitation Urban Households: A Primer.' *Water Policy* 17(6):1108–1126

Piper, K., 2020. 'What Kenya Can Teach Its Neighbors – and the US – about Improving the Lives of the "Unbanked".' *Vox.* 11 September

Pittman, R., 2004. 'Chinese Railway Reform and Competition: Lessons from the Experience in Other Countries.' *Journal of Transport Economics and Policy* 38(2):309–332

——2007. 'Make or Buy on the Russian Railway? Coase, Williamson, and Tsar Nicholas II.' *Economic Change and Restructuring* 40(3):207–221

——2010. 'Against the Stand-Alone-Cost Test in US Freight Rail Regulation.' *Journal of Regulatory Economics* 38:313–326

——2011. 'Risk-Averse Restructuring of Freight Railways in China.' *Utilities Policy* 19:152–160

——2013a. 'Blame the Switchman? Russian Railways Restructuring after Ten Years.' In M. Alexeev and S. Weber (eds.), *The Oxford Handbook of the Russian Economy.* Oxford University Press

——2013b. 'The Freight Railways of the Former Soviet Union, Twenty Years on: Reforms Lose Steam.' *Research in Transportation Business and Management* 6:99–115

——2020a. 'Railways and Railways Regulation in the United States: Surely You Don't Want Jones Back?' In M. Finger and J. Montero (eds.), *Handbook on Railway Regulation.* Cheltenham: Edward Elgar

——2020b. 'On the Economics of Restructuring World Railways, with a Focus on Russia.' *Man and the Economy* 7(2):20200014

Pittman, R., M. Jandová, M. Król, L. Nekrasenko and T. Paleta, 2020. 'The Effectiveness of EC Policies to Move Freight from Road to Rail: Evidence from CEE Grain Markets.' *Research in Transportation Business and Management* 37:100482

Plott, C. R. and K. Zeiler, 2005. 'The Willingness to Pay–Willingness to Accept Gap, the "Endowment Effect," Subject Misconceptions, and Experimental Procedures for Eliciting Valuations.' *American Economic Review* 95(3):530–545

Pollitt, M. G., 2004. 'Electricity Reform in Chile: Lessons for Developing Countries.' *Journal of Network Industries* 5:221–262

——2007. 'Liberalisation and Regulation in Electricity Systems: How Can We Get the Balance Right?' EPRG Working Paper No. 0724. October

——2008. 'The Future of Electricity (and Gas) Regulation in a Low-Carbon Policy World.' *Energy Journal* 29(spec. issue 2):63–94

——2009. 'Electricity Liberalisation in the European Union: A Progress Report.' EPRG Working Paper No. 0929. December

——2012. 'The Role of Policy in Energy Transitions: Lessons from the Energy Liberalisation Era.' *Energy Policy* 50:128–137

——2018. 'Electricity Network Charging in the Presence of Distributed Energy Resources.' *Economics of Energy & Environmental Policy* 7(1):89–104

——2021. 'The Future Design of the Electricity Market.' In J.-M. Glachant, P. L. Joskow and M. G. Pollitt (eds.), *Handbook on Electricity Markets.* Cheltenham: Edward Elgar

Pollitt, M. G. and I. Shaorshadze, 2013. 'The Role of Behavioural Economics in Energy and Climate Policy.' In *Handbook on Energy and Climate Change.* Cheltenham: Edward Elgar, pp. 523–546

Pollitt, M. G. and A. S. J. Smith, 2002. 'The Restructuring and Privatisation of British Rail: Was It Really That Bad?' *Fiscal Studies* 23(4):463–502

Pollitt, M. G. and S. J. Steer, 2012. 'Economies of Scale and Scope in Network Industries: Lessons for the UK Water and Sewerage Sectors.' *Utilities Policy* 21:17–31

Porcher, S. and S. Saussier, 2018. 'Public versus Private Management in Water Public Services. Taking Stock, Looking Ahead.' Sorbonne Business School Discussion Paper. EPPP DP No. 2018-1

Posner, R. A., 1971. 'Taxation by Regulation.' *Bell Journal of Economics and Management Science* 2:22–50

——1974. 'Theories of Economic Regulation.' *Bell Journal of Economics and Management Science* 5:335–358

Postcomm, 2006. 'The Postal Market – 2010 and Beyond: Key Questions for Stakeholders.' August

Pownall, T., I. Soutar and C. Mitchell, 2021. 'Re-Designing GB's Electricity Market Design: A Conceptual Framework which Recognises the Value of Distributed Energy Resources.' *Energies* 14(4):1124

Prager, R. A., 1990. 'Firm Behaviour in Franchise Monopoly Markets.' *RAND Journal of Economics* 21:211–225

Prager, R. A., M. D. Manuszak, E. K. Kiser and R. Borzekowski, 2009. 'Interchange Fees and Payment Card Networks: Economics, Industry Developments, and Policy Issues.' Report No. 2009-23. Board of Governors of the Federal Reserve System

Prat, A. and T. M. Valletti, 2021. 'Attention Oligopoly.' *American Economic Journal: Microeconomics* 14(3):530–557

Preston, J., 2002. 'The Transaction Cost Economics of Railways.' *Trasporti Europei* 20/21:6–15

Priest, G. L., 1993. 'The Origins of Utility Regulation and the "Theories of Regulation" Debate.' *Journal of Law and Economics* 36:289–323

Productivity Commission, 2002. 'Price Regulation of Airport Services.' Report No. 19

——2004. 'Inquiry into the National Third Party Access Regime for Natural Gas.' Final Report
——2007. 'Behavioural Economics and Public Policy.' Roundtable Proceedings. 1–9 August
——2011. 'Australia's Urban Water Sector.' Inquiry Report No. 55
——2015. 'Examining Barriers to More Efficient Gas Markets.' Australian Government
——2018. 'Competition in the Australian Financial System.' Report No. 89. Canberra
——2019. 'Economic Regulation of Airports.' Report No. 92. Canberra
——2021. 'National Water Reform 2020.' Inquiry Report No. 96
Prosser, T., 1997. *Law and the Regulators*. Oxford: Oxford University Press
Prosser, T. and L. Butler, 2018. 'Rail Franchises, Competition and Public Service.' *Modern Law Review* 81(1):23–50
PSR, 2016. 'Market Review into the Ownership and Competitiveness of Infrastructure Provision.' Final Report. 28 July
——2019. 'Access and Governance Report on Payment Systems: Update on Progress.' June
——2021a. 'Market Review into the Supply of Card-Acquiring Services.' Final Report
——2021b. 'Delivery and Regulation of the New Payments Architecture.' Consultation Paper. February
Public Utilities Commission of Ohio, 2013. 'About the Commission'
PWC, 2013. 'Cost of Capital for PR14: Methodological Considerations.' Report for Ofwat. July
Rábago, K. R. and R. Valova, 2018. 'Revisiting Bonbright's Principles of Public Utility Rates in a DER World.' *Electricity Journal* 31(8):9–13
Rabin, M., 1993. 'Incorporating Fairness into Game Theory and Economics.' *American Economic Review* 83(5):1281–1302
——1998. 'Psychology and Economics.' *Journal of Economic Literature* 36(1):11–46
Radić, M., D. Ravasi and K. Munir, 2021. 'Privatization: Implications of a Shift from State to Private Ownership.' *Journal of Management* 47(6):1596–1629
Rahman, K. S., 2018. 'Regulating Informational Infrastructure: Internet Platforms as the New Public Utilities.' *Georgetown Law and Technology Review* 2:2
Railfreight, 2018. 'Rail Freight Operators Not Happy with Dutch New Track Access Charges.' Press Release. 4 September
Ramsey, F. P., 1927. 'A Contribution to the Theory of Taxation.' *Economic Journal* 37(145):47–61
RAND, 2020. 'US Airport Infrastructure Funding and Financing.' Report
Rashad, M., 2022. 'Explainer: Should Europe Use More Long Term LNG Contracts?' Reuters. 7 February
Rassenti, S. J., V. L. Smith and R. L. Bulfin, 1982. 'A Combinatorial Auction Mechanism for Airport Time Slot Allocation.' *Bell Journal of Economics* 13(2):402–417
RBA, 2002. 'Reform of Credit Card Schemes in Australia IV. Final Reforms and Regulation Impact Statement.' August
——2004. 'Payments System Board.' Annual Report
——2005. 'Common Benchmark for the Setting of Credit Card Interchange Fees.' November
——2008. 'Reform of Australia's Payments System: Conclusions of the 2007/08 Review'
——2012. 'Strategic Review of Innovation in the Payments System: Conclusions.' June
——2015. 'Review of Card Payments Regulation: Issues Paper.' March
——2016. 'Review of Card Payments Regulation: Conclusions Paper.' May
——2019. 'NPP Functionality and Access Consultation: Conclusions Paper.' June
——2021. 'Review of Retail Payments Regulation: Conclusions Paper.' October
Regulating Committee, 2015. 'Permission for Airports Company South Africa to Levy Airport Charges.' Notice 473

Reichl, J., A. Kollmann, R. Tichler and F. Schneider, 2008. 'The Importance of Incorporating Reliability of Supply Criteria in a Regulatory System of Electricity Distribution: An Empirical Analysis for Austria.' *Energy Policy* 36(10):3862–3871

Renda, A., 2010. 'Competition–Regulation Interface in Telecommunications: What's Left of the Essential Facility Doctrine.' *Telecommunications Policy* 34:23–35

——2012. 'Telecommunications Regulation.' In R. Van den Bergh and A. M. Pacces (eds.), *Regulation and Economics: Encyclopedia of Law and Economics*, 2nd ed. Cheltenham: Edward Elgar

Renou-Maissant, P., 2012. 'Toward the Integration of European Natural Gas Markets: A Time-Varying Approach.' *Energy Policy* 51:779–790

Renzetti, S., 1999. 'Municipal Water Supply and Sewage Treatment: Costs, Prices and Distortions.' *Canadian Journal of Economics* 32:688–704

Resende, M., 1999. 'Productivity Growth and Regulation in US Local Telephony.' *Information Economics and Policy* 11:23–44

Reuters, 2018. 'Chinese Airlines Soar on Fare Price Liberalization.' 8 January

Rey, P. and D. Salant, 2019. 'Allocating Essential Inputs.' Report No. 17-820. Toulouse School of Economics (TSE)

Reynaud, A. and G. Romano, 2018. 'Advances in the Economic Analysis of Residential Water Use: An Introduction.' *Water* 10(9):1162

Ribeiro, N. A., A. Jacquillat, A. P. Antunes, A. R. Odoni and J. P. Pita, 2018. 'An Optimization Approach for Airport Slot Allocation under IATA Guidelines.' *Transportation Research, Part B: Methodological* 112:132–156

Riley, A., 2012. 'Commission v. Gazprom: The Antitrust Clash of the Decade?' CEPS Policy Brief No. 285. 31 October

Riordan, M. H., 1984. 'On Delegating Price Authority to a Regulated Firm.' *RAND Journal of Economics* 15:108–115

——1998. 'Anticompetitive Vertical Integration by a Dominant Firm.' *American Economic Review* 88:1232–1248

Riordan, M. H. and D. E. M. Sappington, 1987. 'Awarding Monopoly Franchises.' *American Economic Review* 77:375–387

Rios, M. A. and J. A. Quiroz, 1995. 'The Market of Water Rights in Chile: Major Issues.' *Cuadernos de Economía* 32:317–345

Roberts, D., 2019. 'Fracking May Be a Bigger Climate Problem than We Thought.' *Vox.* 29 August

Roberts, S., 2018. 'Making "No One Left Behind" Meaningful in our Future Energy System.' In *Price Control for Everyone*. London: Citizens Advice, pp. 12–15

Robinson, G. O. and D. L. Weisman, 2008. 'Designing Competition Policy for Telecommunications.' *Review of Network Economics* 7:509–546

Robson, W. A., 1951. *Justice and Administrative Law*. London: Stevens & Sons

Rochet, J.-C., 2003. 'The Theory of Interchange Fees: A Synthesis of Recent Contributions.' *Review of Network Economics* 2(2):97–124

Rochet, J.-C. and J. Tirole, 2002. 'Cooperation among Competitors: Some Economics of Payment Card Associations.' *RAND Journal of Economics* 33(4):549

——2003. 'Platform Competition in Two-Sided Markets.' *Journal of the European Economic Association* 1:990–1029

——2006. 'Two-Sided Markets: A Progress Report.' *RAND Journal of Economics* 37(3):645–667

——2008. 'Tying in Two-Sided Markets and the Honor All Cards Rule.' *International Journal of Industrial Organization* 26(6):1333–1347

——2011. 'Must-Take Cards: Merchant Discounts and Avoided Costs.' *Journal of the European Economic Association* 9(3):462–495

Rodríguez Pardina, M. and J. Schiro, 2018. 'Taking Stock of Economic Regulation of Power Utilities in the Developing World: A Literature Review.' World Bank, Washington, DC

Roese, N. J. and K. D. Vohs, 2012. 'Hindsight Bias.' *Perspectives on Psychological Science* 7(5):411–426

Rogers, P., R. Bhatia and A. Huber, 1999. *Water as a Social and Economic Good: How to Put the Principle into Practice*. Stockholm: Swedish International Development Authority

Rogerson, W. P. and H. Shelanski, 2020. 'Antitrust Enforcement, Regulation, and Digital Platforms.' *University of Pennsylvania Law Review* 168(7):1911–1940

Rogoff, K., 1985. 'The Optimal Degree of Commitment to an Intermediate Monetary Target.' *Quarterly Journal of Economics* 100:1169–1189

Rohlfs, J., 1974. 'A Theory of Interdependent Demand for a Communications Service.' *Bell Journal of Economics and Management Science* 5:16–37

——1979. 'Economically Efficient Bell System Prices.' Bell Laboratories Discussion Paper. No. 138

——2005. 'Bandwagon Effects in Telecommunications.' In S. K. Majumdar, I. Vogelsang and M. E. Cave (eds.), *Handbook of Telecommunications Economics*, Volume 2. Amsterdam: Elsevier

Rohlfs, J., C. Jackson and T. Kelley, 1991. 'Estimate of the Loss to the United States Caused by the FCC's Delay in Licensing Cellular Telecommunications.' National Economic Research Associates, Washington, DC

Roll, R., 1986. 'The Hubris Hypothesis of Corporate Takeovers.' *Journal of Business* 59(2):197

Romano, G., L. Masserini and A. Guerrini, 2015. 'Does Water Utilities' Ownership Matter in Water Pricing Policy? An Analysis of Endogenous and Environmental Determinants of Water Tariffs in Italy.' *Water Policy* 17(5):918–931

Roques, F., 2021. 'The Evolution of the European Model for Electricity Markets.' In J.-M. Glachant, P. L. Joskow and M. G. Pollitt (eds.), *Handbook on Electricity Markets*. Cheltenham: Edward Elgar

Rosato, A., 2016. 'Selling Substitute Goods to Loss-Averse Consumers: Limited Availability, Bargains, and Rip-Offs.' *RAND Journal of Economics* 47(3):709–733

Rose, K., 2004. 'The State of Retail Electricity Markets in the U.S.' *Electricity Journal* 17(1):26–36

Rossi, M. A, 2021. 'The Performance of Privatised Utilities: Evidence from Latin America.' Universidad de San Andres, Working Paper

Roycroft, T. and M. Garcia-Murrilo, 2000. 'Trouble Reports as an Indicator of Service Quality: The Influence of Competition, Technology, and Regulation.' *Telecommunications Policy* 24:947–967

Rubin, S. J., 2009. 'How Should We Regulate Small Water Utilities?' NRRI Research Paper 09-16. November

——2010. 'What Does Water Really Cost? Rate Design Principles for an Era of Supply Shortages, Infrastructure Upgrades, and Enhanced Water Conservation.' NRRI Research Paper 10-10. July

Rubinstein, A., 1993. 'On Price Recognition and Computational Complexity in a Monopolistic Model.' *Journal of Political Economy* 101(3):473–484

Ruiz Diaz, G., 2017. 'The Contractual and Administrative Regulation of Public–Private Partnership.' *Utilities Policy* 48:109–121

Rysman, M., 2009. 'The Economics of Two-Sided Markets.' *Journal of Economic Perspectives* 23(3):125–143

Saal, D. S., P. Arocena, A. Maziotis and T. Triebs, 2013. 'Scale and Scope Economies and the Efficient Vertical and Horizontal Configuration of the Water Industry: A Survey of the Literature.' *Review of Network Economics* 12(1):93–129

Saal, D. S. and D. Parker, 2000. 'The Impact of Privatization and Regulation on the Water and Sewerage Industry in England and Wales: A Translog Cost Function Model.' *Managerial and Decision Economics* 21:253–268

——2001. 'Productivity and Price Performance in the Privatized Water and Sewerage Companies of England and Wales.' *Journal of Regulatory Economics* 20:61–90

Saal, D. S., D. Parker and T. Weyman-Jones, 2007. 'Determining the Contribution of Technical Change and Scale Change to Productivity Growth in Privatized English and Welsh Water and Sewerage Industry: 1985–2000.' *Journal of Productivity Analysis* 28:127–139

Salant, D. J., 1995. 'Behind the Revolving Door: A New View of Public Utility Regulation.' *RAND Journal of Economics* 26:362–377

——2014. *A Primer on Auction Design, Management, and Strategy*. Cambridge, MA: MIT Press

Salant, D. J. and G. A. Woroch, 1992. 'Trigger Price Regulation.' *RAND Journal of Economics* 23:29–51

Salazar de la Cruz,F. 1999. 'A DEA Approach to the Airport Production Function.' *International Journal of Transport Economics* 26(2):255–270

Salies, E. and C. Waddams Price, 2004. 'Charges, Costs and Market Power: The Deregulated UK Electricity Retail Market.' *Energy Journal* 25:19–35

Salinger, M. A., 1998. 'Regulating Prices to Equal Forward-Looking Costs: Cost-Based Prices o Price-Based Costs?' *Journal of Regulatory Economics* 14:149–163

Salop, S. C. and D. T. Scheffman, 1983. 'Raising Rivals' Costs.' *American Economic Review* 73:267–271

Sampaio, P. R. P. and M. T. Daychoum, 2017. 'Two Decades of Rail Regulatory Reform in Brazil (1996–2016).' *Utilities Policy* 49:93–103

Samuelson, P. A., 1938. 'A Note on the Pure Theory of Consumer's Behaviour.' *Economica* 5(17):61–71

——1948. 'Consumption Theory in Terms of Revealed Preference.' *Economica* 15(60):243–253

Samuelson, W. and R. Zeckhauser, 1988. 'Status Quo Bias in Decision Making.' *Journal of Risk and Uncertainty* 1(1):7–59

Sanin, M. E., F. Trillas, A. Mejdalani, D. Lopez-Sato and M. Hallack, 2019. 'Using Behavioural Economics in the Design of Energy Policies.' IDB Technical Note 1840. December

Sappington, D. E. M., 1983. 'Optimal Regulation of a Multi-Product Monopoly with Unknown Technological Capabilities.' *Bell Journal of Economics* 14:453–463

——1994. 'Designing Incentive Regulation.' *Review of Industrial Organization* 9:245–272

——2002. 'Price Regulation.' In M. E. Cave, S. K. Majumdar and I. Vogelsang (eds.), *Handbook Telecommunications Economics*, Volume 1. Amsterdam: Elsevier

——2003. 'The Effects of Incentive Regulation on Retail Telephone Service Quality in the Unite States.' *Review of Network Economics* 2 (4):355–375

——2005a. 'Regulating Service Quality: A Survey.' *Journal of Regulatory Economics* 27:123–15

——2005b. 'On the Irrelevance of Input Prices for Make-or-Buy Decisions.' *American Economic Review* 95:1631–1638

Sappington, D. E. M., J. P. Pfeifenberger, P. Hanser and G. N. Basheda, 2001. 'The State of Performance-Based Regulation in the U.S. Electric Utility Industry.' *Electricity Journal* 14(8):71–79

Sappington, D. E. M. and D. S. Sibley, 1988. 'Regulating without Cost Information: The Incremental Surplus Subsidy Scheme.' *International Economic Review* 29:297–306

——1992. 'Strategic Nonlinear Pricing under Price-Cap Regulation.' *RAND Journal of Economi* 23:1–19

Sappington, D. E. M. and J. E. Stiglitz, 1987. 'Privatization, Information and Incentives.' *Journ of Policy Analysis and Management* 6:567–582

Sappington, D. E. M. and D. L. Weisman, 2010. 'Price Cap Regulation: What Have We Learned from 25 Years of Experience in the Telecommunications Industry?' *Journal of Regulatory Economics* 38:227–257

——2012. 'Regulating Regulators in Transitionally Competitive Markets.' *Journal of Regulatory Economics* 41:19–40

——2016a. 'The Disparate Adoption of Price Cap Regulation in the U.S. Telecommunications and Electricity Sectors.' *Journal of Regulatory Economics* 49(2):250–264

——2016b. 'The Price Cap Regulation Paradox in the Electricity Sector.' *Electricity Journal* 29(3):1–5

——2021. 'Designing Performance-Based Regulation to Enhance Industry Performance and Consumer Welfare.' *Electricity Journal* 34(2):106902

Sarr, B., 2015. 'Does Independent Regulation of Public Utilities in Developing Countries Improve Efficiency?' *Electricity Journal* 28(6):72–81

Savage, L. J. 1954. *Foundations of Statistics.* New York: Wiley

Savignat, M. G. and C. Nash, 1999. 'The Case for Rail Reform in Europe – Evidence from Studies of Production Characteristics of the Rail Industry.' *International Journal of Transport Economics* 26(2):201–217

Sawkins, J. W., 1996. 'Balancing Multiple Interests in Regulation: An Event Study of the English and Welsh Water Industry.' *Journal of Regulatory Economics* 9:249–268

——2001. 'The Development of Competition in the English and Welsh Water and Sewerage Industry.' *Fiscal Studies* 22:189–215

Schankerman, M., 1996. 'Symmetric Regulation for Competitive Telecommunications.' *Information Economics and Policy* 8:3–23

Schenk, D. H., 2011. 'Exploiting the Salience Bias in Designing Taxes.' *Yale Journal on Regulation* 28:253

Scherer, F. M., 1980. *Industrial Market Structure and Economic Performance*, 2nd ed. Chicago: Rand McNally

Schittekatte, T., D. S. Mallapragada, P. L. Joskow and R. Schmalensee, 2022. 'Electricity Retail Rate Design in a Decarbonized Economy: An Analysis of Time-of-Use and Critical Peak Pricing.' National Bureau of Economic Research. Report No. w30560

Schlumberger, C. E, 2010. '*Open Skies for Africa Implementing the Yamoussoukro Decision.*' World Bank,

Schmalensee, R., 1979. *The Control of Natural Monopolies.* Lexington, MA: Lexington Books

——2002. 'Payment Systems and Interchange Fees.' *Journal of Industrial Economics* 50(2):103–122

Schmidthaler, M., J. Cohen, J. Reichl and S. Schmidinger, 2015. 'The Effects of Network Regulation on Electricity Supply Security: A European Analysis.' *Journal of Regulatory Economics* 48(3):285–316

Schumpeter, J. A., 1943. *Capitalism, Socialism and Democracy.* New York: Harper & Row

——1954. *History of Economic Analysis.* London: Routledge

Schwartz, M., 1986. 'The Nature and Scope of Contestability Theory.' *Oxford Economic Papers* 38:37–57

Schwartz, M. and R. J. Reynolds, 1983. 'Contestable Markets: An Uprising in the Theory of Industrial Structure: Comment.' *American Economic Review* 73:488–490

Schwartzstein, J., 2014. 'Selective Attention and Learning.' *Journal of the European Economic Association* 12(6):1423–1452

Schweppe, F. C., M. C. Caramanis, R. D. Tabors and R. E. Bohn, 1988. *Spot Pricing of Electricity.* Boston, MA: Kluwer Academic

Scitovsky, T., 1950. 'Ignorance as a Source of Oligopoly Power.' *American Economic Review* 40(2):48–53

Segendorf, B., H. Eklööf, P. Gustafsson, A. Landelius and S. Cicović, 2019. 'What Is Libra?' Sveriges Riksbank. Economic Commentaries. 29 October

Sengupta, A. and S. N. Wiggins, 2014. 'Airline Pricing, Price Dispersion, and Ticket Characteristics On and Off the Internet.' *American Economic Journal: Economic Policy* 6(1):272–307

Sentance, A., 2003. 'Airport Slot Auctions: Desirable or Feasible?' *Utilities Policy* 11:53

Serdarević, G., M. Hunt, T. Ovington and C. Kenny, 2016. 'Evidence for a Ladder of Investment in Central and Eastern European Countries.' *Telecommunications Policy* 40(6):515–531

Serra, P., 2022. 'Chile's Electricity Markets: Four Decades on from Their Original Design.' *Energy Strategy Reviews* 39:100798

SESAR, 2018. 'European ATM Master Plan: Roadmap for the Safe Integration of Drones into All Classes of Airspace.' Eurocontrol

Severn Trent Water and National Grid, 2012. 'Changing Course through Sustainable Financing: Options to Encourage Equity Financing in the Water and Energy Sectors.' September

Shaffer, S., 1983. 'Demand-Side Determinants of Natural Monopoly.' *Atlantic Economic Journal* 11:71–73

Shapiro, C., 1995. 'Aftermarkets and Consumer Welfare: Making Sense of Kodak.' *Antitrust Law Journal* 63:483

——2011. 'Competition and Innovation: Did Arrow Hit the Bull's Eye?' In *The Rate and Direction of Inventive Activity Revisited*. Chicago: University of Chicago Press, pp. 361–404

——2023. 'Regulating Big Tech: Factual Foundations and Policy Goals'. Network Law Review. 1. February 2023.

Shapiro, C. and H. R. Varian, 1999. *Information Rules: A Strategic Guide to the Network Economy*. Boston, MA: Harvard Business School Press

Sharkey, W. W., 1979. 'A Decentralized Method for Utility Regulation: A Comment.' *Journal of Law and Economics* 22:405–407

——1982. *The Theory of Natural Monopoly*. Cambridge: Cambridge University Press

——2002. 'Representation of Technology and Production.' In M. E. Cave, S. K. Majumdar and I. Vogelsang (eds.), *Handbook of Telecommunications Economics*, Volume 1. Amsterdam: Elsevier

Sharot, T., 2011. 'The Optimism Bias.' *Current Biology* 21(23):R941–945

Sheng, D., Z.-C. Li, Y. Xiao and X. Fu, 2015. 'Slot Auction in an Airport Network with Demand Uncertainty.' *Transportation Research, Part E: Logistics and Transportation Review* 82:79–100

Shepherd, W. G., 1984. '"Contestability" vs. Competition.' *American Economic Review* 74:572–587

Sheshinski, E., 1976. 'Price, Quality and Quantity Regulation in Monopoly Situations.' *Economica* 43:127–137

Shih, J.-S., W. Harrington, W. A. Pizer and K. Gillingham, 2006. 'Economies of Scale in Community Water Systems.' *Journal of the American Water Works Association* 98(9):100–108

Shleifer, A., 1985. 'A Theory of Yardstick Competition.' *RAND Journal of Economics* 16:319–327

——1998. 'State versus Private Ownership.' *Journal of Economic Perspectives* 12:133–150

——2011. 'Efficient Regulation.' In D. P. Kessler (ed.), *Regulation versus Litigation: Perspectives from Economics and Law*. Chicago: University of Chicago Press

Shleifer, A. and R. W. Vishny, 1994. 'Politicians and Firms.' *Quarterly Journal of Economics* 109(4):995–1025

Shughart, W. F. and D. W. Thomas, 2019. 'Interest Groups and Regulatory Capture.' In R. D. Congleton, B. Grofman and S. Voigt (eds.), *The Oxford Handbook of Public Choice*, Volume 1. Oxford: Oxford University Press, pp. 584–603

Sibley, D. S., M. J. Doane, M. A. Williams and S. Tsai, 2004. 'Pricing Access to a Monopoly Input.' *Journal of Public Economic Theory* 6:541–555

Sibley, D. S. and D. L. Weisman, 1998. 'Raising Rivals' Costs: The Entry of an Upstream Monopolist into Downstream Markets.' *Information Economics and Policy* 10:451–470

Sickles, R. C. and M. L. Streitwieser, 1998. 'An Analysis of Technology, Productivity, and Regulatory Distortion in the Interstate Natural Gas Transmission Industry: 1977–1985.' *Journal of Applied Econometrics* 13:377–395

Sidak, J. G., 2012. 'How Does the Experience of US Telecommunications Regulation Inform the Forced Sharing of Intellectual Property Rights Under Global Competition Law?' Unpublished Working Paper

Sidak, J. G. and D. F. Spulber, 1998. *Deregulatory Takings and the Regulatory Contract: The Competitive Transformation of Network Industries in the USA.* Cambridge: Cambridge University Press

Sidak, J. G. and D. J. Teece, 2010. 'Innovation, Spillovers and the "Dirt Road" Fallacy: The Intellectual Bankruptcy of Banning Optional Transactions for Enhanced Delivery over the Internet.' *Journal of Competition Law and Economics* 6:521–594

Simon, H. A., 1955. 'A Behavioral Model of Rational Choice.' *Quarterly Journal of Economics* 69(1):99–118

——1956. 'Rational Choice and the Structure of the Environment.' *Psychological Review* 63(2):129–138

——1957. *Models of Man: Social and Rational.* New York: Wiley

——1979. 'Rational Decision Making in Business Organizations.' *American Economic Review* 69(4):493–513

Simpson, L. and K. Ringskog, 1997. *Water Markets in the Americas.* Washington, DC: World Bank

Simshauser, P., 2016. 'Distribution Network Prices and Solar PV: Resolving Rate Instability and Wealth Transfers through Demand Tariffs.' *Energy Economics* 54:108–122

——2021. 'Lessons from Australia's National Electricity Market 1998–2018: Strengths and Weaknesses of the Reform Experience.' In J.-M. Glachant, P. L. Joskow and M. G. Pollitt (eds.), *Handbook on Electricity Markets.* Cheltenham: Edward Elgar

Simshauser, P. and A. Akimov, 2019. 'Regulated Electricity Networks, Investment Mistakes in Retrospect and Stranded Assets under Uncertainty.' *Energy Economics* 81:117–133

Simshauser, P. Nelson. T and J. Gilmore, 2023. 'The sunshine state: implications from mass rooftop solar PV take-up rates in Queensland' EPRG Working Paper 2219

Sioshansi, F. P., 2008. *Competitive Electricity Markets: Design, Implementation, Performance.* Amsterdam: Elsevier

——2021. 'New Technologies on the Demand Side.' In J.-M. Glachant, P. L. Joskow and M. G. Pollitt (eds.), *Handbook on Electricity Markets.* Cheltenham: Edward Elgar

Sirin, S. M. and I. Erten, 2022. 'Price Spikes, Temporary Price Caps, and Welfare Effects of Regulatory Interventions on Wholesale Electricity Markets.' *Energy Policy* 163:112816

Sjostrom, W., 1993. 'Antitrust Immunity for Shipping Conferences: An Empty Core Approach.' *Antitrust Bulletin* 38(2):419–423

Smith, A., 1776. *The Wealth of Nations.* Reprinted 1991 Everyman's Library Classic edition with introduction by W. Letwin. London: J. M. Dent

Smith, A. S. J., 2006. 'Are Britain's Railways Costing Too Much? Perspectives Based on TFP Comparisons with British Rail 1963–2002.' *Journal of Transport Economics and Policy* 40(1):1–44

Smith, A. S. J., V. Benedetto and C. Nash, 2018. 'The Impact of Economic Regulation on the Efficiency of European Railway Systems.' *Journal of Transport Economics and Policy* 52(2):113–136

Smith, A. S. J. and C. Nash, 2014. 'Rail Efficiency: Cost Research and Its Implications for Policy.' OECD International Transport Forum. Discussion Paper 2014-22. Paris

Smith, B. C., J. F. Leimkuhler and R. M. Darrow, 1992. 'Yield Management at American Airlines.' *Interfaces* 22(1):8–31

Smith, K., 2019. 'Rethinking Amtrak.' *International Railway Journal*. 23 September

Smith, T. K., 1995. 'Why Air Travel Doesn't Work ....' *Fortune Magazine*, 3 April

Smith, W., 1997a. 'Utility Regulators – Roles and Responsibilities.' World Bank Note No. 128. Octobe

——1997b. 'Utility Regulators – Decision Making Structures, Resources, and Start-Up Strategy.' World Bank Note No. 129. October

——1997c. 'Utility Regulators – The Independence Debate.' World Bank Note No. 127. October

Snow, M. S., 2002. 'Competition as a Discovery Procedure' (translation of F. A. Hayek). *Quarterly Journal of Austrian Economics* 5:9–23

Sollisch, J., 2016. 'The Cure for Decision Fatigue.' *Wall Street Journal*, 10 June

Soman, D. and J. T. Gourville, 2001. 'Transaction Decoupling: How Price Bundling Affects the Decision to Consume.' *Journal of Marketing Research* 38(1):30–44

Spence, A. M., 1975. 'Monopoly, Quality, and Regulation.' *Bell Journal of Economics* 6:417–42!

——1983. 'Contestable Markets and the Theory of Industry Structure: A Review Article.' *Journa of Economic Literature* 21:981–990

Spengler, J. J., 1950. 'Vertical Integration and Antitrust Policy.' *Journal of Political Economy* 50:347–352

Spiegel-Feld, D. and B. Mandel, 2015. 'Reforming Electricity Regulation in New York State: Lessons from the United Kingdom.' Roundtable Report. Guarini Center, NYU Law

Spiegler, R., 2006a. 'Competition over Agents with Boundedly Rational Expectations.' *Theoretical Economics* 1:207–231

——2006b. 'The Market for Quacks.' *Review of Economic Studies* 73(4):1113–1131

——2011. *Bounded Rationality and Industrial Organization.* Oxford: Oxford University Press

——2012. 'Monopoly Pricing when Consumers Are Antagonized by Unexpected Price Increases: A "Cover Version" of the Heidhues–Kőszegi–Rabin Model.' *Economic Theory* 51(3):695–711

——2014. 'Competitive Framing.' *American Economic Journal: Microeconomics* 6(3):35–58

——2015. 'On the Equilibrium Effects of Nudging.' *Journal of Legal Studies* 44(2):389–416

Spiller, P. T., 1990. 'Politicians, Interest Groups, and Regulators: A Multiple-Principals Agency Theory of Regulation, or "Let Them Be Bribed".' *Journal of Law and Economics* 33:65–1C

——2013.'Transaction Cost Regulation.' *Journal of Economic Behavior & Organization* 89:232–24

Spiller, P. T. and M. Tommasi, 2008. 'The Institutions of Regulation: An Application to Public Utilities.' In C. Menard and M. M. Shirley (eds.), *Handbook of New Institutional Economics.* Berlin: Springer

Spiller, P. T. and S. Urbiztondo, 1994. 'Political Appointees vs. Career Civil Servants: A Multip Principals Theory of Political Bureaucracies.' *European Journal of Political Economy* 10:465–497

Spiller, P. T. and I. Vogelsang, 1994. 'Regulation, Institutions, and Commitment in the British Telecommunications Sector.' World Bank, Policy Research Working Paper 1241. January

Spulber, D. F. and D. Besanko, 1992. 'Delegation, Commitment, and the Regulatory Mandate.' *Journal of Law, Economics, & Organization* 8:126–154

Spulber, D. F. and C. S. Yoo, 2005. 'Network Regulation: The Many Faces of Access.' *Journal o Competition Law and Economics* 1:635–678

Stalon, C. G. and R. H. Lock, 1990. 'State–Federal Relations in the Economic Regulation of Energy.' *Yale Journal on Regulation* 7:427–497

Stango, V. and J. Zinman, 2020. 'We Are All Behavioral, More or Less: A Taxonomy of Consumer Decision Making.' NBER Working Paper No. 28138. November

Starkie, D., 1984. 'BR – Privatisation without Tears.' *Economic Affairs* 5(1):16–19

——2001. 'Reforming UK Airport Regulation.' *Journal of Transport Economics and Policy* 35(1):119–135

——2012. 'European Airports and Airlines: Evolving Relationships and the Regulatory Implications.' *Journal of Air Transport Management* 21:40–49

——2021.'Two-Sided Airport Markets Reprised.' *Journal of Transport Economics and Policy* 55(1):1–15

Starostina T. and D. Wu, 2018. 'ACI-NA 2017–18 Business Term Survey.' Airport/Airline Business Working Group

StatCounter, 2022. 'Search Engine Market Share Worldwide.' April

Stavins, J., 2001. 'Price Discrimination in the Airline Market: The Effect of Market Concentration.' *Review of Economics and Statistics* 83(1):200–202

——2017. 'How Do Consumers Make Their Payment Choices?' No. 17-1. Federal Reserve Bank of Boston

STB, 2019a. 'Rate Reform Task Force.' Report to the Surface Transportation Board. 25 April

——2019b. 'Expanding Access to Rate Relief.' Final Offer Rate Review. Docket No. EP 665 (Sub-No. 2)

Steer Davies Gleave, 2015. 'Study on the Cost and Contribution of the Rail Sector.' Report for European Commission. September

Steiner, P. O., 1957. 'Peak Loads and Efficient Pricing.' *Quarterly Journal of Economics* 71:585–610

Steinhurst, W., 2011. 'The Electric Industry at a Glance.' NRRI Working Paper 11-04. January

Stern, J. P, 2004. 'UK Gas Security: Time to Get Serious.' *Energy Policy* 32:1967–1979

——2007. 'Is There a Rationale for the Continuing Link to Oil Product Price in Continental European Long-Term Gas Contracts?' Oxford Institute for Energy Studies. Working Paper NG 19. April

——2018. '"Huge Progress" in EU Gas Markets but Supply Still an Issue.' Interview with Euractiv

Stern, J. 2012. 'Developing Upstream Competition in the England and Wales Water Supply Industry: A New Approach.' *Utilities Policy* 21:1–16

——2017. 'Competition, Economic Regulation and Affordability in Infrastructure Industries: An Economic History 1840–1980.' CCRP Working Paper Series No. 30

Stern, J. and S. Holder, 1999. 'Regulatory Governance: Criteria for Assessing the Performance of Regulatory Systems: An Application to Infrastructure Industries in the Developing Countries of Asia.' *Utilities Policy* 8(1):33–50

Stern, J. P and K. Yafimava, 2017. 'The EU Competition Investigation of Gazprom's Sales in Central and Eastern Europe: A Detailed Analysis of the Commitments and the Way Forward.' Oxford Institute for Energy Studies. OIES Paper NG 121. July

Stigler, G. J., 1971. 'The Theory of Economic Regulation.' *Bell Journal of Economics and Management Science* 2:3–21

——1976. 'The Xistence of X-Efficiency.' *American Economic Review* 66:213–216

——1980. 'Economics of Ethics?' The Tanner Lectures on Human Values. April

Stigler, G. J. and C. Friedland, 1962. 'What Can Regulators Regulate? The Case of Electricity.' *Journal of Law and Economics* 5:1–16

Stigler Center, 2019. 'Stigler Committee on Digital Platforms.' Final Report. September

Stiglitz, J. E., 1987. 'Technological Change, Sunk Costs and Competition.' *Brookings Papers on Economic Activity* 18(Microeconomics):883–947

Stoft, S., 2002. *Power System Economics: Designing Markets for Electricity*. Hoboken, NJ: Wiley Interscience

Stone and Webster Consultants, 2004. 'Investigation into Evidence for Economies of Scale in the Water and Sewerage Industry in England and Wales.' Report. January

Strbac, G., 2008. 'Demand Side Management: Benefits and Challenges.' *Energy Policy* 36:4419–4426

Strbac, G., M. Aunedi, I. Konstantelos, *et al.*, 2017. 'Opportunities for Energy Storage: Assessing Whole-System Economic Benefits of Energy Storage in Future Electricity Systems.' *IEEE Power and Energy Magazine* 15(5):32–41

Strotz, R. H., 1955. 'Myopia and Inconsistency in Dynamic Utility Maximization.' *Review of Economic Studies* 23(3):165–180

Stucke, M. E. and A. Ezrachi, 2017. 'Looking Up in the Data-Driven Economy.' University of Tennessee Legal Studies Research Paper 333

Su, X., 2015. 'Have Customers Benefited from Electricity Retail Competition?' *Journal of Regulatory Economics* 47(2):146–182

Sunstein, C. R., 2017. 'Nudges that Fail.' *Behavioural Public Policy* 1(1):4–25

Sustainability First, 2020. 'Developing and Embedding a Sustainable Licence to Operate and a Purposeful Business Approach.' September

Swadley, A. and M. Yücel, 2011. 'Did Residential Electricity Rates Fall after Retail Competition? A Dynamic Panel Analysis.' *Energy Policy* 39:7702–7711

Sweeting, A., 2007. 'Market Power in the England and Wales Wholesale Electricity Market 1995–2000.' *Economic Journal* 117:654–685

Tan, A. K.-J., 2010. 'The ASEAN Multilateral Agreement on Air Services: En Route to Open Skies?' *Journal of Air Transport Management* 16(6):289–294

Tardiff, T. J., 2002. 'Pricing Unbundled Network Elements and the FCC's TELRIC Rule: Economic Modelling Issues.' *Review of Network Economics* 1:132–146

——2015. 'Prices Based on Current Cost or Historical Cost: How Different Are They?' *Journal of Regulatory Economics* 47(2):201–217

——2021. 'Ex Ante Regulation of Digital Platforms?: Cautionary Tales from Telecommunications.' *CPI Antitrust Chronicle.* January

Tardiff, T. J. and D. L. Weisman, 2018. 'Mandatory Upstream Inputs and Upward Pricing Pressure: Implications for Competition Policy.' In J. Langenfeld and E. Galeano (eds.), *Research in Law and Economics.* Bingley, UK: Emerald, pp. 401–421

Taylor, M., 2010. 'Access Regulation versus Infrastructure Investment: Important Lessons from Australia.' In A. Gentzoglanis and A. Henten (eds.), *Regulation and the Evolution of the Global Telecommunications Industry.* Cheltenham: Edward Elgar

Taylor, W. E. and L. D. Taylor, 1993. 'Post-Divestiture Long-Distance Competition in the USA.' *American Economic Review* 83:185–190

Teece, D. J., 1980. 'Economies of Scope and the Scope of the Enterprise.' *Journal of Economic Behavior & Organization* 1:223–247

Telser, L. G., 1969. 'On the Regulation of Industry: A Note.' *Journal of Political Economy* 77:937–952

——1978. *Economic Theory and the Core.* Chicago: University of Chicago Press

——1994. 'The Usefulness of Core Theory in Economics.' *Journal of Economic Perspectives* 8(2):151–164

Teodoro, M. and Y. Zhang, 2017. 'Privatization as Political Decoupling: Water Conservation and the 2014–2017 California Drought.' Texas A&M University, Working Paper

Ter-Martirosyan, A., 2003. 'The Effects of Incentive Regulation on Quality of Service in Electricity Markets.' George Washington University, Working Paper. March

Ter-Martirosyan, A. and J. Kwoka, 2010. 'Incentive Regulation, Service Quality, and Standards in U.S. Electricity Distribution.' *Journal of Regulatory Economics* 38(3):258–273

Thaler, R., 1980. 'Toward a Positive Theory of Consumer Choice.' *Journal of Economic Behavior & Organization* 1(1):39–60

——1985. 'Mental Accounting and Consumer Choice.' *Marketing Science* 4(3):199–214

——1988. 'Anomalies: The Ultimatum Game.' *Journal of Economic Perspectives* 2(4):195-206

——2018. 'Nudge, Not Sludge.' *Science* 361(6401):431

Thaler, R. H. and H. M. Shefrin, 1981. 'An Economic Theory of Self-Control.' *Journal of Political Economy* 89(2):392-406

Thaler, R. H. and C. R. Sunstein, 2008. *Nudge: Improving Decisions about Health, Wealth, and Happiness*. New Haven, CT: Yale University Press

Thanassoulis, E., 2000a. 'DEA and Its Use in the Regulation of Water Companies.' *European Journal of Operational Research* 127:1-13

——2000b. 'The Use of Data Envelopment Analysis in the Regulation of UK Water Utilities: Water Distribution.' *European Journal of Operational Research* 126:436-453

Thatcher, M., 1998. 'Regulating the Regulators: The Regulatory Regime for the British Privatised Utilities.' *Parliamentary Affairs* 51(2):209-222

Thelle, M. H. and M. la Couer Sonne, 2018. 'Airport Competition in Europe.' *Journal of Air Transport Management* 67:232-240

Thillairajan, A., A. Mahalingam and A. Deep, 2013. 'Impact of Private-Sector Involvement on Access and Quality of Service in Electricity, Telecom, and Water Supply Sectors.' Social Science Research Unit, Institute of Education, University of London

Timera, 2020. 'US Gas Driving TTF & LNG Prices: 4 Charts.' 29 June

Tirole, J., 1994. 'The Internal Organization of Government.' *Oxford Economic Papers* 46(1): 1-29

——2011. 'Payment Card Regulation and the Use of Economic Analysis in Antitrust.' *Competition Policy International* 7(1):136-158

——2017. *Economics for the Common Good*. Princeton, NJ: Princeton University Press

——2020. 'Competition and the Industrial Challenge for the Digital Age.' Paper for IFS Deaton Review on Inequalities in the Twenty-First Century

Tiroual, R., 2017. 'Competition and Subsidies in Air Transport Liberalization – The UAE-North American Dispute.' *Journal of Air Law and Commerce* 82(2):345-395

Tomeš, Z., 2017. 'Do European Reforms Increase Modal Shares of Railways?' *Transport Policy* 60:143-151

Tortajada, C. and P. van Rensburg, 2020. 'Drink More Recycled Wastewater.' *Nature* 577(7788): 26-28

Train, K. E., 1991. *Optimal Regulation*. Cambridge, MA: MIT Press

Train, K. E., D. L. McFadden and A. A. Goett, 1987. 'Consumer Attitudes and Voluntary Rate Schedules for Public Utilities.' *Review of Economics and Statistics* 69(3):383

Trillas, F., 2010. 'Independent Regulators: Theory, Evidence and Reform Proposals.' IESE Working Paper WP-860. May

——2016. 'Behavioral Regulatory Agencies.' Universitat Autònoma de Barcelona. Departament d'Economia Aplicada. Working Paper No. 6

——2020. 'Innovative Behavioral Regulatory Agencies as Second Generation Commitment Devices.' *Journal of Economic Policy Reform* 23(1):83-99

Trillas, F. and M. A. Montoya, 2013. 'Independent Regulators: Theory, Evidence and Reform Proposals.' *info* 15(3):39-53

Trillas, F. and R. Xifré, 2016. 'Institutional Reforms to Integrate Regulation and Competition Policy: Economic Analysis, International Perspectives, and the Case of the CNMC in Spain.' *Utilities Policy* 40:75-87

Turner, P. G. and C. E. Lefevre, 2017. 'Instagram Use Is Linked to Increased Symptoms of Orthorexia Nervosa.' *Eating and Weight Disorders – Studies on Anorexia, Bulimia and Obesity* 22(2):277-284

Tversky, A. and D. Kahneman, 1971. 'Belief in the Law of Small Numbers.' *Psychological Bulletin* 76(2):105

——1973a. 'Judgement under Uncertainty: Heuristics and Biases.' Prepared for Office of Naval Research Advanced Research Projects Agency. August

——1973b. 'Availability: A Heuristic for Judging Frequency and Probability.' *Cognitive Psychology* 5(2):207–232

——1977. 'On the Elicitation of Preferences: Descriptive and Prescriptive Considerations.' In D. E. Bell, R. L. Keeney and H. Raiffa (eds.), *Conflicting Objectives in Decisions*. IIASA International Series on Applied Systems Analysis. Chichester: Wiley, pp. 209–222

——1981. 'The Framing of Decisions and the Psychology of Choice.' *Science* 211(4481):453–458

——1983. 'Extensional versus Intuitive Reasoning: The Conjunction Fallacy in Probability Judgment.' *Psychological Review* 90(4):293

——1986. 'Rational Choice and the Framing of Decisions.' *Journal of Business* 59(4/2):S251–S278

Tversky, A. and E. Shafir, 1992. 'Choice under Conflict: The Dynamics of Deferred Decision.' *Psychological Science* 3(6):358–361

Tversky, A. and I. Simonson, 1993. 'Context-Dependent Preferences.' *Management Science* 39(10):1179–1189

Twomey, P., R. Green, K. Neuhoff and D. Newbery, 2005. 'A Review of the Monitoring of Market Power: The Possible Roles of TSOs in Monitoring for Market Power Issues in Congested Transmission Systems.' Faculty of Economics, University of Cambridge, Working Paper in Economics 0504

Tye, W. B. and J. A. García, 2007. 'Who Pays, Who Benefits and Adequate Investment in Natural Gas Infrastructure.' *Energy Law Journal* 28:2–40

UK Department for Transport, 2017. 'An Exploration of Potential Behavioural Biases in Project Delivery in the Department for Transport.' Report Prepared by Behavioural Insights Team July

——2020. 'Rail Franchising Reaches the Terminus as a New Railway Takes Shape.' News Story. 21 September

UK Government, 2018. 'Card Surcharge Ban Means No More Nasty Surprises for Shoppers.' Press Release. 13 January

——2021. 'A New Pro-Competition Regime for Digital Markets.' CP 489. July

UKRN, 2020. 'Cost of Capital Annual Update Report.' Information Paper

UN, 2020. 'For a Livable Climate: Net-Zero Commitments Must Be Backed by Credible Action.' Net Zero Coalition, United Nations

UNECE, 2017. 'Railway Reform in the ECE region.' Final Report. Geneva

Ünver, M. B., 2015. 'Is a Fine-Tuning Approach Sufficient for EU NGA Policy? A Global Review around the Long-Lasting Debate.' *Telecommunications Policy* 39(11):957–979

UN-Water, 2019. 'Leaving No One Behind: Facts and Figures.' The United Nations World Water Development Report

USAID, 2013. 'The Causes and Impacts of Power Sector Circular Debt in Pakistan.' March

US Department of Transport, 2018. 'FAA Needs to Strengthen Its Management Controls over the Use and Oversight of NextGen Developmental Funding.' Report No. AV2018030

——2021. 'NextGen Benefits Have Not Kept Pace with Initial Projections, but Opportunities Remain to Improve Future Modernization Efforts.' Report No. AV2021023

USGS, 2015. 'Estimated Use of Water in the United States in 2015.' Circular 1441

Usher, A., E. Reshidi, F. Rivadeneyra and S. Hendry, 2021. 'The Positive Case for a CBDC.' Bank of Canada. Report No. 2021-11

US House of Representatives, 2020. 'Investigation of Competition in Digital Markets. Majority Staff Report and Recommendations.' Subcommittee on Antitrust, Commercial and Administrative Law

Usman, M., 2022. 'Breaking Up Big Tech: Lessons from AT&T.' *University of Pennsylvania Law Review* 170:523–548

Valletti, T. M., 2003. 'The Theory of Access Pricing and Its Linkage with Investment Incentives.' *Telecommunications Policy* 27:659–675

Valletti, T. M. and C. Cambini, 2005. 'Investments and Network Competition.' *RAND Journal of Economics* 36:446–467

Valletti, T. M. and G. Houpis, 2005. 'Mobile Termination: What Is the "Right" Charge?' *Journal of Regulatory Economics* 28:235–258

Van de Velde, D., 2015. 'European Railway Reform: Unbundling and the Need for Coordination.' In *Rail Economics, Policy and Regulation in Europe.* Cheltenham: Edward Elgar

Van de Velde, D., C. Nash, A. Smith, *et al.*, 2012. 'Economic Effects of Vertical Separation in the Railway Sector.' Report for Community of European Railway and Infrastructure Companies

Van de Walle, S., 2009. 'When Is a Service an Essential Public Service?' *Annals of Public and Cooperative Economics* 80(4):521–545

Van Loo, R. 2020. 'In Defense of Breakups: Administering "Radical" Remedy.' *Cornell Law Review* 105(7):1955–2022

Van Schewick, B., 2006. 'Towards an Economic Framework for Network Neutrality Regulation.' *Journal on Telecommunications and High Technology Law* 5:329

Varian, H. R., 1980. 'A Model of Sales.' *American Economic Review* 70(4):651–659

——2021. 'Seven Deadly Sins of Tech?' *Information Economics and Policy* 54:100893

Varian, H. R., J. Farrell and C. Shapiro, 2004. *The Economics of Information Technology: An Introduction.* Cambridge: Cambridge University Press

Vickers, J., 1995. 'Concepts of Competition.' *Oxford Economic Papers* 47:1–23

——1997. 'Regulation, Competition, and the Structure of Prices.' *Oxford Review of Economic Policy* 13:15–26

——2005. 'Public Policy and the Invisible Price: Competition Law, Regulation and the Interchange Fee.' *Competition Law Journal* 4:5

——2010. 'Competition Policy and Property Rights.' *Economic Journal* 120:375–392

Vickers, J. and G. Yarrow, 1988. *Privatization: An Economic Analysis.* Cambridge, MA: MIT Press

Vickrey, W., 1971. 'Responsive Pricing of Public Utility Services.' *Bell Journal of Economics* 2:337–346

Vidović, A., T. Mihetec, B. Wang and I. Štimac, 2019. 'Operations of Drones in Controlled Airspace in Europe.' *International Journal for Traffic and Transport Engineering* 9(1):38–52

Vigren, A., 2017. 'Competition in Swedish Passenger Railway: Entry in an Open Access Market and Its Effect on Prices.' *Economics of Transportation* 11–12:49–59

Vilardell, J. M., 2015. 'Railway Concession in Africa: Lessons Learnt.' ADB Transport Forum

Villa, J. C. and E. Sacristán-Roy, 2013. 'Privatization of Mexican Railroads: Fifteen Years Later.' *Research in Transportation Business and Management* 6:45–50

Viscusi, W. and T. Gayer, 2015. 'Behavioral Public Choice: The Behavioral Paradox of Government Policy.' *Harvard Journal of Law & Public Policy* 38(3):973–1008

Vogel, S. K., 1996. *Freer Markets, More Rules.* Ithaca, NY: Cornell University Press

Vogelsang, I., 2002. 'Incentive Regulation and Competition in Public Utility Markets: A 20-Year Perspective.' *Journal of Regulatory Economics* 22:5–27

——2003.– 'Price Regulation of Access to Telecommunications Networks.' *Journal of Economic Literature* 41:830–862

——2006. 'Network Utilities in the USA: Sector Reforms without Privatization.' In M. Köthen-Bürger, H.-W. Sinn and J. Whalley (eds.), *Privatization Experiences in the European Union.* Cambridge, MA: MIT Press

——2012. 'Incentive Regulation, Investments and Technological Change.' In G. R. Faulhaber, G. Madden and J. Petchey (eds.), *Regulation and the Performance of Communication and Information Networks*. Cheltenham: Edward Elgar

——2014a. 'Regulating in the Face of Declining Demand.' Presentation at ACCC/AER Regulatory Conference

——2014b. 'Current Academic Thinking about How Best to Implement TSLRIC in Pricing Telecommunications Network Services and the Implications for Pricing UCLL in New Zealand.' Report for the Commerce Commission. 25 November

——2017. 'Regulatory Inertia versus ICT Dynamics: The Case of Product Innovations.' *Telecommunications Policy* 41(10):978–990

——2019. 'Has Europe Missed the Endgame of Telecommunications Policy?' *Telecommunications Policy* 43(1):1–10

——2021. *The Economics and Regulation of Network Industries: Telecommunications and Beyond*. Cambridge: Cambridge University Press

Vogelsang, I. and J. Finsinger, 1979. 'A Regulatory Adjustment Process for Optimal Pricing by Multi-Product Monopoly Firms.' *Bell Journal of Economics* 10:157–171

Von Hirschhausen, C., 2006. 'Infrastructure Investments and Resource Adequacy in the Restructured US Natural Gas Market – Is Supply Security at Risk?' CEEPR Working Paper No. 06-018. December

——2008. 'Infrastructure, Regulation, Investment and Security of Supply: A Case Study of the Restructured US Natural Gas Market.' *Utilities Policy* 16:1–10

Von Neumann, J. and O. Morgenstern, 1944. *Theory of Games and Economic Behavior*. Princeton, NJ: Princeton University Press

Waddams Price, C., 2005. 'The Effect of Liberalizing UK Retail Energy Markets on Consumers.' *Oxford Review of Economic Policy* 21:128–144

Waddams Price, C., B. Brigham and L. Fitzgerald, 2002. 'Service Quality in Regulated Monopolies.' CCR Working Paper CCR 02-04

Waidelich, P., T. Haug and L. Wieshammer, 2022. 'German Efficiency Gone Wrong: Unintended Incentives Arising from the Gas TSOs' Benchmarking.' *Energy Policy* 160:112595

Wallis, 1997. 'Financial System Inquiry Committee (Wallis Committee) 1997.' Final Report, AGPS, Canberra

Wallsten, S., 2001. 'An Econometric Analysis of Telecom Competition, Privatization, and Regulation in Africa and Latin America.' *Journal of Industrial Economics* 49(1):1–19

——2002. 'Does Sequencing Matter? Regulation and Privatization in Telecommunications Reforms.' World Bank, Policy Research Working Paper No. 2817. February

Wallsten, S. and K. Kosec, 2005. 'Public or Private Drinking Water? The Effects of Ownership and Benchmark Competition on US Water System Regulatory Compliance and Household Water Expenditures.' AEI–Brookings Center for Regulatory Studies, Working Paper

——2008. 'The Effects of Ownership and Benchmark Competition: An Empirical Analysis of US Water Systems.' *International Journal of Industrial Organization* 26:186–205

Wang, Z., 2004. 'Settling Utility Rate Cases: An Alternative Ratemaking Procedure.' *Journal of Regulatory Economics* 26:141–163

Wang, Z., S. Schwartz and N. Mitchell, 2014. The Impact of the Durbin Amendment on Merchants: A Survey Study. *Federal Reserve Bank of Richmond – Economic Quarterly* 100(3):183–208

Warner, M. E., 2021. 'Key Issues in Water Privatization and Remunicipalization.' *Utilities Policy* 73:101300

Wassum, M. and F. De Francesco, 2020. 'Explaining Regulatory Autonomy in EU Network Sectors: Varieties of Utility Regulation?' *Governance* 33(1):41–60

Water UK, 2019. '30 Years of Cleaner, Safer, Better Water.' Report

Weinstein, N. D., 1980. 'Unrealistic Optimism about Future Life Events.' *Journal of Personality and Social Psychology* 39(5):806

Weisman, D. L., 1993. 'Superior Regulatory Regimes in Theory and Practice.' *Journal of Regulatory Economics* 5:355-366

——2000. 'The (In)Efficiency of the "Efficient Firm" Cost Standard.' *Antitrust Bulletin* 45:195-211

——2002. 'Is There "Hope" for Price Cap Regulation?' *Information Economics and Policy* 14:349-370

——2005. 'Price Regulation and Quality.' *Information Economics and Policy* 17(2):165-174

——2014. 'Safe Harbor Input Prices and Market Exclusion.' *Journal of Regulatory Economics* 46(2):226-236

——2017. 'Are Electric Utilities Aboard the "Train to Ithaca"?' *Electricity Journal* 30:6-9

——2019a. 'Why the Efficiency Gains from PBR May Turn on Hope.' *Electricity Journal* 32(1):13-17

——2019b. 'The Power of Regulatory Regimes Reexamined.' *Journal of Regulatory Economics* 56 (2-3):125-148

——2021. 'The (In)Efficiency of the Retail-Minus Rule.' *Utilities Policy* 70:101220

Weisman, D. L. and R. B. Kulick, 2010. 'Price Discrimination, Two-Sided Markets and Net Neutrality Regulation.' *Tulane Journal of Technology & Intellectual Property* 13:82-101

Weiss, L. W., 1975. 'Antitrust in the Electric Power Industry.' In A. Phillips (ed.), *Promoting Competition in Regulated Markets*. Washington, DC: Brookings Institution

Weitzman, M. L., 1978. 'Optimal Rewards for Economic Regulation.' *American Economic Review* 68:683-691

Welsby, J. and A. Nichols, 1999. 'The Privatisation of Britain's Railways: An Inside View.' *Journal of Transport Economics and Policy* 33(1):55-76

Werner, T., 2021. 'Algorithmic and Human Collusion.' DICE Discussion Paper No. 372

Weyl, E. G. and A. White, 2014. 'Let the Right "One" Win: Policy Lessons from the New Economics of Platforms.' *Competition Policy International* 10(2):29-51

Wheat, P., A. S. J. Smith and T. Rasmussen, 2018. 'Can Competition For and In the Market Co-exist in Terms of Delivering Cost Efficient Services? Evidence from Open Access Train Operators and Their Franchised Counterparts in Britain.' *Transportation Research, Part A: Policy and Practice* 113:114-124

Wheeler, G., 2020. 'Bounded Rationality.' In *The Stanford Encyclopedia of Philosophy* (Fall 2020 Edition)

Wheeler, S. A. (ed.), 2021. *Water Markets: A Global Assessment*. Cheltenham: Edward Elgar

Wheeler, S. A. and D. E. Garrick, 2020. 'A Tale of Two Water Markets in Australia: Lessons for Understanding Participation in Formal Water Markets.' *Oxford Review of Economic Policy* 36(1):132-153

Wheeler, S. A., A. Loch, L. Crase, M. Young and R. Q. Grafton, 2017. 'Developing a Water Market Readiness Assessment Framework.' *Journal of Hydrology* 552:807-820

Wheeler, T., P. Verveer and G. Kimmelman, 2020. 'New Digital Realities; New Oversight Solutions in the U.S.' The Shorenstein Center on Media, Politics and Public Policy, Harvard. Report

White, L. J., 1978. 'Economies of Scale and the Question of "Natural Monopoly" in the Airline Industry.' *Journal of Air Law and Commerce* 44(3):545-573

White House, 2021. 'Executive Order on Promoting Competition in the American Economy.' 9 July

Whittington, D., 2003. 'Municipal Water Pricing and Tariff Design: A Reform Agenda for South Asia.' *Water Policy* 5:61-76

Whittington, D., C. Nauges, D. Fuente and X. Wu, 2015. 'A Diagnostic Tool for Estimating the Incidence of Subsidies Delivered by Water Utilities in Low- and Medium-Income Countries, with Illustrative Simulations'. *Utilities Policy* 34:70–81

WHO, 2022a. 'Drinking-Water: Key Facts.' 21 March

——2022b. 'Sanitation: Key Facts.' 21 March

WICS, 2021. 'Establishing a Market Health Check for the Non-Household Retail Market.' 13 December

WIK, 2011. 'Cost Benchmarking in Energy Regulation in European Countries.' Study for the Australian Energy Regulator. 14 December

——2016. 'Review of the Significant Market Power (SMP) Guidelines.' Report for European Commission

——2019. 'Prospective Competition and Deregulation: An Analysis of European Approaches to Regulating Full Fibre.' Report for BT. 28 February

Willems, B., M. Pollitt, N-H von der Fehr and C. Banet, 2022. 'The European Wholesale electricity market: from crisis to net zero;' Report of Centre on regulation in Europe (CERRE).

Williams, J. H. and R. Ghanadan, 2006. 'Electricity Reform in Developing and Transition Countries: A Reappraisal.' *Energy* 31:815–844

Williams, K. and G. Shapps, 2021. 'Great British Railways: The Williams–Shapps Plan for Rail'. CP 423. May

Williams Rail Review, 2019. 'Current Railway Models: Great Britain and Overseas.' Evidence Paper. March

Williamson, B., D. Black and J. Wilby, 2011. 'Costing Methodology and the Transition to Next Generation Access.' Report for ETNO. March

Williamson, O. E., 1971. 'The Vertical Integration of Production: Market Failure Considerations.' *American Economic Review* 61:112–113

——1975. *Markets and Hierarchies: Analysis and Antitrust Implications.* New York: Free Press

——1976. 'Franchise Bidding for Natural Monopolies in General and with Respect to CATV.' *Bell Journal of Economics* 7:73–104

——1983. 'Credible Commitments: Using Hostages to Support Exchange.' *American Economic Review* 73:519–540

——1985. *The Economic Institutions of Capitalism.* New York: Free Press

Willig, R. D., 1978. 'Pareto-Superior Nonlinear Outlay Schedules.' *Bell Journal of Economics* 9(1):56–69

——1979. 'The Theory of Network Access Pricing.' In H. M. Trebing (ed.), *Issues in Public Utility Regulation: Proceedings of the Institute of Public Utilities Tenth Annual Conference.* MSU Public Utilities Papers. East Lansing, MI: Michigan State University

Wills-Johnson, N., 2008. 'Separability and Subadditivity in Australian Railways.' *Economic Record* 84(264):95–108

Wilson, W. W., 1997. 'Cost Savings and Productivity in the Railroad Industry.' *Journal of Regulatory Economics* 11(1):21–40

Wiltshire, J., 2018. 'Airport Competition: Reality or Myth?' *Journal of Air Transport Management* 67:241–248

Winsor, T., 2010. 'Effective Regulatory Institutions: The Regulator's Role in the Policy Process, Including Issues of Regulatory Independence.' OECD Discussion Paper No. 2010-2021

Winston, C., 1993. 'Economic Deregulation: Days of Reckoning for Microeconomists.' *Journal Economic Literature* 31:1263–1289

Wolak, F. A., 2021. 'Wholesale Electricity Market Design.' In J.-M. Glachant, P. L. Joskow and M. G. Pollitt (eds.), *Handbook on Electricity Markets.* Cheltenham: Edward Elgar

Wolak, F. A., J. Bushnell and B. F. Hobbs, 2007. 'Final Opinion on "Long-Term Resource Adequacy under MRTU"'. Market Surveillance Committee of the California ISO. 5 November

Wolfram, C. D., 1999. 'Measuring Duopoly Power in the British Electricity Spot Market.' *American Economic Review* 89:805–826

Womble, P. and W. M. Hanemann, 2020. 'Water Markets, Water Courts, and Transaction Costs in Colorado.' *Water Resources Research* 56(4):2019WR025507

World Bank, 1995. 'Bureaucrats in Business.' World Bank Policy Research Report. October

——2000. 'The Single Buyer Model.' Note No. 225. December

——2001. 'Power and Gas Regulation – Issues and International Experience.' April

——2010. '*Africa's Infrastructure: A Time for Transformation.*' Eds. V. Foster and C. Briceño-Garmendia. Washington, DC: International Bank for Reconstruction and Development/World Bank.

——2017a. 'Increasing the Use of Liquefied Petroleum Gas in Cooking in Developing Countries'

——2017b. 'Joining Forces for Better Services?: When, Why, and How Water and Sanitation Utilities Can Benefit from Working Together.' Washington, DC

——2017c. 'Railway Reform: Toolkit for Improving Rail Sector Performance'

——2018. *The Global Findex Database 2017: Measuring Financial Inclusion and the Fintech Revolution.* Washington, DC: World Bank

——2021. 'Subsidizing Bottled Gas: Approaches and Effects on Household Use.' June

——2022. 'Private Participation in Infrastructure (PPI): Water and Sewerage'

Woroch, G. A., 2002. 'Local Network Competition.' In M. E. Cave, S. K. Majumdar and I. Vogelsang (eds.), *Handbook of Telecommunications Economics*, Volume 1. Amsterdam: Elsevier

Worthington, A. C., 2014. 'A Review of Frontier Approaches to Efficiency and Productivity Measurement in Urban Water Utilities.' *Urban Water Journal* 11(1):55–73

Worthington, A. C. and H. Higgs, 2014. 'Economies of Scale and Scope in Australian Urban Water Utilities.' *Utilities Policy* 31:52–62

Wren-Lewis, L., 2013. 'Commitment in Utility Regulation: A Model of Reputation and Policy Applications.' *Journal of Economic Behavior & Organization* 89:210–223

——2014. 'Utility Regulation in Africa: How Relevant Is the British Model?' *Utilities Policy* 31:203–205

Wright, J., 2004. 'One-Sided Logic in Two-Sided Markets.' *Review of Network Economics* 3(1):44–64

——2012. 'Why Payment Card Fees Are Biased against Retailers.' *RAND Journal of Economics* 43(4):761–780

Wright, S. and R. Mason, 2020. 'Comments Prepared for Ofwat on the CMA's Provisional Findings: Anglian Water Services Limited, Bristol Water plc, Northumbrian Water Limited and Yorkshire Water Services Limited Price Determinations: Cost of Capital Considerations.' Final Report. 26 October

Wright, S., R. Mason, S. Satchell, K. Hori and M. Baskaya, 2006. 'Report on the Cost of Capital.' Report for Ofgem. 1 September

Wu, D. 2015. 'Classifying Airline Rates and Charges Methodologies.' Report

——2017. 'Airport Finance 101.' 14 March

Wu, T., 2003. 'Network Neutrality, Broadband Discrimination.' *Journal on Telecommunications and High Technology Law* 2:141–179

——2019. 'Blind Spot: The Attention Economy and the Law.' *Antitrust Law Journal* 82:771

Wu. T. and C. Yoo, 2007. 'Keeping the Internet Neutral? Tim Wu and Christopher Yoo Debate.' *Federal Communications Law Journal* 59:575–592

Xu, J., M. Hallack and M. Vazquez, 2017. 'Applying a Third Party Access Model for China's Gas Pipeline Network: An Independent Pipeline Operator and Congestion Rent Transfer.' *Journal of Regulatory Economics* 51(1):72–97

Yafimava, K, 2013. 'The EU Third Package for Gas and the Gas Target Model: Major Contentious Issues Inside and Outside the EU.' OIES Report NG 75. April

Yamaguchi, K., 2013. 'Evolution of Metropolitan Airports in Japan: Air Development in Tokyo and Osaka.' ITF Discussion Paper 2013/03

Yandle, B., 1983. 'Bootleggers and Baptists – the Education of a Regulatory Economist.' *Regulation: AEI Journal on Government and Society* 7(3):12–16

——2021. 'George J. Stigler's Theory of Economic Regulation, Bootleggers, Baptists and the Rebirth of the Public Interest Imperative.' *Public Choice* 193:23–34

Yang, H. and A. Zhang, 2011. 'Price-Cap Regulation of Congested Airports.' *Journal of Regulatory Economics* 39(3):293–312

Yang, Y. and A. Faruqui, 2019. 'Reducing Electricity Prices and Establishing Electricity Markets in China: Dos and Don'ts.' *Electricity Journal* 32(8):106633

Yariv, L. and D. Laibson, 2004. 'Safety in Markets: An Impossibility Theorem for Dutch Books.' Society for Economic Dynamics, Meeting Papers No. 867

Yarrow, G. K., 1995. 'Airline Deregulation and Privatisation in the UK.' *Keizai Bunseki [Economic Analysis]* 143:49–83

——2000. 'New Gas Trading Arrangements.' Beesley Lecture on Regulation Series X. 31 October

Yarrow, G. K., T. Appleyard, C. Decker and T. Keyworth, 2008. 'Competition in the Provision of Water Services.' Regulatory Policy Institute, Working Paper. April

Yarrow, G. K., C. Decker and T. Keyworth, 2008. 'Report on the Impact of Maintaining Price Regulation.' Report to the Australian Energy Market Commission. January

Yoo, C. S., 2017. 'An Unsung Success Story: A Forty-Year Retrospective on U.S. Communications Policy.' *Telecommunications Policy* 41(10):891–903

——2018. 'Common Carriage's Domain.' *Yale Journal on Regulation* 35(3)991–1026

Yvrande-Billon, A., 2006. 'The Attribution Process of Delegation Contracts in the French Urban Public Transport Sector: Why Competitive Tendering Is a Myth?' *Annals of Public and Cooperative Economics* 77:453–478

Yvrande-Billon, A. and C. Ménard, 2005. 'Institutional Constraints and Organizational Changes: The Case of the British Rail Reform.' *Journal of Economic Behavior and Organization* 56(4):675–699

Zac A, Y.C Huang, A. von Moltke, C. Decker and A. Ezrachi, 2023. 'Dark Patterns and Online Consumer Vulnerability'. Oxford Univ. CCLP Working Paper.

Zajac, E. E., 1978. *Fairness or Efficiency: An Introduction to Public Utility Pricing*. Cambridge, MA: Ballinger

Zhang, D., T. Wang, X. Shi and J. Liu, 2018. 'Is Hub-Based Pricing a Better Choice than Oil Indexation for Natural Gas? Evidence from a Multiple Bubble Test.' *Energy Economics* 76:495–503

Zhang X., M. González Rivas, M. Grant and M. E. Warner, 2021. 'Water Pricing and Affordability in the US: Public vs Private Ownership.' Cornell Working Paper, posted to SocArXiv, June

Zhu, F., 2019. 'Friends or Foes? Examining Platform Owners' Entry into Complementors' Spaces.' *Journal of Economics and Management Strategy* 28(1):23–28

Zolnierek, J., J. Eisner and E. Burton, 2001. 'An Empirical Examination of Entry Patterns in Local Telephone Markets.' *Journal of Regulatory Economics* 19:143–159

Zuboff, S., 2019. *The Age of Surveillance Capitalism: The Fight for a Human Future at the New Frontier of Power.* London: Profile Books

Zuckerberg, M., 2020. 'Big Tech Needs More Regulation.' *Financial Times.* 16 February

Zupan, M. A., 1989. 'Cable Franchise Renewals: Do Incumbent Firms Behave Opportunistically?' *RAND Journal of Economics* 20:473–482

Zywicki, T. J., G. A. Manne and J. Morris, 2014. 'Price Controls on Payment Card Interchange Fees: The US Experience (George Mason Law & Economics Research Paper No. 14-18).' *SSRN Electronic Journal* 2446080

——2017. 'Unreasonable and Disproportionate: How the Durbin Amendment Harms Poorer Americans and Small Businesses.' Working Paper

——2022. 'The Effects of Price Controls on Payment-Card Interchange Fees: A Review and Update.' ICLE White Paper 2022-03-04

Index

5G networks, 368
ACCC (Australian Competition and Consumer
    Commission), 249
access holidays, 179, 406
access in regulated industries, 151–156
    access pricing issue, 152–153
    access terms determination, 151
    multiple objectives pursued through access pricing
        policies, 153–154
access pricing and investment, 178–182, *See also*
        one-way access pricing, two-way access pricing
    access pricing approaches, 180–182
    Australia, 167, 178
    by-pass and the 'make-or-buy' decision, 180–181
    dynamic access pricing, 182
    Germany, 170
    incentives for investment, 180–182
    incentives to invest in new infrastructure, 181
    infrastructure competition, 153, 180–181, 182
    ladder of investment approach, 182
    timing of infrastructure investment, 179–180
accounting separation
    margin squeeze, 188
    vertical integration and separation, 188
ACER/CEER, 36, 302, 334, 339, 350
adjacent monopolies
    Germany, 170
    two-way access pricing, 169–170, 172
administered pricing, price regulation, 145–146
Administrative Procedures Act 1946 (APA), 110, 246
affordability of essential services
    contextual change of economic regulation, 5
    public utilities household expenditure, 1–2
affordability, rationale for regulation, 35–39
African Development Bank Group, 250–251
agencies, regulatory. *See* independent regulation/
        agencies
air traffic management (ATM), 67, 586–588
airline alliances and cooperation arrangements, 584–586
airline markets
    Association of Southeast Asian Nations (ASEAN), 573
    Australia, 572, 573
    China, 572
    Europe, 571
    France, 557

New Zealand, 573
    restructuring policies, 570–573
    Single African Air Transport Market, 573
    USA, 570–571
airline restructuring effects, restructuring policies,
        aviation industry, 575–579
airport charges
    Australia, 66, 250, 568, 589
    dual-till approach, 568–569
    European Union, 566
    Germany, 589
    light-handed approach, 66, 566, 589
    market power, 560–561, 562, 568–569, 580
    New Zealand, 66, 250, 589
    price regulation, 566
    single-till approach, 568–569
    USA, 566
airport services, 553–555
    competition for the market, 574, 589
    Government Accountability Office (GAO), 555,
        575–577
    price regulation, 562–563
    two-sided markets, 553
airports restructuring policies, 573–575, 579–580
    Asia-Pacific region,
    Europe, 574
    privatisation, 573–575
    USA, 573
airspace navigation services
    Australia, 565
    Canada, 550, 553, 565, 575, 581, 589
    competition for the market, 561
    European Union, 565, 575
    France, 553
    price regulation, 550–553, 561, 564, 565–566
    privatisation, 575, 581
    privatisation, France, 553
    privatisation, UK, 553
    restructuring policies, 575, 581
    UK, 565
    USA, 565
A–J (Averch–Johnson) effect, rate of return regulation,
        117–119
algorithms regulation, digital platforms regulation,
        499

allocation of capacity, telecommunications networks and services, 370–372
allocative efficiency, 16
 fixed costs, 18
 hidden information, 91–93
 marginal cost pricing, 17–18
 monopoly, 17
 price regulation, 17–19
 Ramsey–Boiteux pricing, 19
alternative explanations for regulation, 28–34
 economic theories of regulation, 29–33
 interest group theories of regulation, 29–33
 other potential explanations for the existence of regulation, 34
 regulation as a form of administration of a long-term contract, 33–34
alternatives to regulation, 635–636
ancillary electricity services, electricity markets and exchanges, 283
ANS. See airspace navigation services
antitrust law. See competition law
APA (Administrative Procedures Act 1946), 110, 246
Argentina, restructuring policies, gas industry, 343, 347
ASEAN (Association of Southeast Asian Nations), airline markets, 573
Asia-Pacific region, airports restructuring policies, 574
asset 'rate base', rate case process, 111
Association of Southeast Asian Nations (ASEAN), airline markets, 573
asymmetric information, 90–95, See also full information, hidden information, imperfect information
 demand information asymmetries, 94
 dynamic regulation, 96–98
 hidden action, 93–94
 hidden information, 91–93
 incentive mechanism, 98–100
 regulatory commitment, 97–98
 transfer payments, 96–98
 yardstick competition, 100
ATM (air traffic management), 67, 586–588
Australia
 access pricing and investment, 167, 178
 airline markets, 572, 573
 airport charges, 66, 250, 568, 589
 airspace navigation services, 565
 behavioural economics, 218, 223
 competition, card payment systems, 432
 digital platforms regulation, 492
 division of powers and responsibilities, government levels/regulators, 258
 electricity generation, 274
 evolution of independent regulatory agencies, 249–250
 fracking, 356
 gas transmission and distribution networks, 323, 326
 independent regulation/agencies, 249, 253, 258
 legal cases, 643
 legislation, 643
 light-handed approach, 66, 250, 589
 liquefied natural gas (LNG), 330
 natural gas supply chain, 322
 negotiated approaches, railways regulation, 523
 negotiated settlements, 63

 ownership structures, 53
 payment systems, 420, 423, 431, 440, 441, 443
 price cap regulation, 288, 334
 price regulation, 61
 privatisation, telecommunications industry, 395
 railways industry, 511–512
 restructuring policies, aviation industry, 572–573, 579, 580
 restructuring policies, electricity industry, 303–304
 restructuring policies, gas industry, 343, 347
 restructuring policies, payment systems, 445, 447, 450
 restructuring policies, telecommunications industry, 395
 restructuring policies, water and wastewater industry, 614, 616
 retail price controls, electricity regulation, 295
 retail price regulation, 219
 retailing of gas, 327
 service providers, telecommunications, 369
 terminology, 7
 two-way access pricing, 178
 unbundling policies, telecommunications regulation, 395
 vertical separation, 186
 water and wastewater industry, 597
 water markets, 625, 628
 wholesale gas spot markets, 328, 329
Australian Competition and Consumer Commission (ACCC), 249
average cost pricing, 77–79
average revenue approach, price cap regulation, 130
Averch–Johnson (A–J) effect, rate of return regulation, 117–119
aviation industry, 547–590, See also restructuring policies, aviation industry
 airport charges, 566
 airport services, 553–555, 562–563
 airspace navigation services, 550–553, 561, 564
 cargo services, 549, 555–557
 characteristics of the product, 548–549
 China, 549
 drones, 557–558
 Flight Information Regions (FIRs), 550
 India, 548, 557, 572
 load factor, 556
 national flag carriers, 557
 ownership of airlines, 557
 ownership of airlines, Canada, 557
 passenger services, 548–549, 555–557
 privatisation, 557, 571
 privatisation, France, 571
 privatisation, UK, 571
 supply chain, 550–557
 unmanned aircraft systems (UAS), 557–558
aviation regulation, 375
 airline alliances and cooperation arrangements, 584–586
 airline competition, 582–583
 airport charges, 566
 airport services, 553–555, 562–563
 airspace navigation services, 550–553, 561, 564, 565–566
 competition, 582–586
 competitive activities, supply chain, 561
 contestability theory, 583–584

future, 589
international access and charging principles, 564
policy issues, 582–588
price regulation, 561–562
scope economies, 561
supply chain, 561
unmanned aircraft systems (UAS), 586–588
voided cost pricing, telecommunications regulation, 384–385
voided-cost resale provision, telecommunications regulation, 384–385

aron and Myerson model, 93
regulatory commitment, 97, 238
versus Laffont and Tirole model, 93–94
askets
price cap regulation, 124, 131
tariff basket approach (weighted average price cap), 131
behavioural biases, 197, 201, 203, 483–486
digital platforms, 225, 483–486
energy sector, 218–221
payment systems, 224–225
telecommunications industry, 221
water sector, 223
behavioural economics, 197–228
application of behavioural economics in practice, 218–226
assumptions about consumer behaviour, 198–200
Australia, 218, 223
behavioural industrial organisation and regulation, 204–218
consumer behaviour, 198–204
contextual change of economic regulation, 5
core insights, 198–204
digital platforms, 225
energy sector, 218–221
Netherlands, 221
payment systems, 224–225
telecommunications industry, 221–222
transport industry, 223
water sector, 223
behavioural industrial organisation and regulation, 204–218
competition, 205–211
consumer mistakes or biases, 214
distributional issues, 216
framing and the incentives to educate or obfuscate, 208–210
implications for firms, 212–213
implications for regulation, 214–218
implications for the rationale for regulation, 214–216
integrating non-standard consumers, 205–206
loss- and risk-averse consumers, 211
non-standard consumers, 205–208, 214, 215, 216–218
price structures, 215
pricing decisions with non-standard consumers, 207–208
regulatory initiatives to address non-standard behaviour, 216–218
risk-averse consumers, 211
behavioural obligations, horizontal integration and separation, 190

benchmarking
price regulation, 144–145
retail benchmarking, two-way access pricing, 177
biases
behavioural biases, 197, 201, 203, 483–486
behavioural biases, digital platforms, 225
behavioural biases, energy sector, 218–221
behavioural biases, payment systems, 224–225
behavioural biases, telecommunications industry, 221–222
behavioural biases, water sector, 223
consumer biases, 39, 197, 199, 200, 210–213, 226–228
bilateral transactions, trading arrangement for wholesale electricity, 281
bill and keep, price control, telecommunications regulation, 386–388
blockchain, payment systems, 426–428
bottom-up long-run incremental cost (BU-LRIC), 381
building block approach
ex ante revenue requirement, 126–128
financial capital maintenance (FCM), 127–128
operating expenses (OPEX), 127
regulatory asset base (RAB), 127–128
BU-LRIC (bottom-up long-run incremental cost), 381
bundling limits. See unbundling policies
China, 496
digital platforms regulation, 496
Germany, 496
business separation, vertical integration and separation, 188
by-pass
efficient component pricing rule (ECPR), 158–161
make-or-buy decision, 180–181

cable modem services, 368
cable networks
Europe, 375–377
telecommunications regulation, 375–377
USA, 375–377
calling party network pays (CPNP) principle, mobile networks, 377
Canada
airspace navigation services, 550, 553, 565, 575, 581, 589
aviation industry, ownership structures, 557
competitive activities, supply chain, 330, 516
division of powers and responsibilities, government levels/regulators, 258
gas extraction and production, 323
legislation, 643
liquefied petroleum gas (LPG), 348
mark-ups approach, railways industry, 543
mobile networks, 377
negotiated approaches, railways regulation, 145, 523
net neutrality, 412
next-generation networks (NGNs), 407
payment systems, 443, 445
price cap regulation, 288, 335
price regulation, 518
privatisation, airspace navigation services, 575, 581
railways industry, 511–512, 518
rate of return regulation, 337
regulatory decisions, 263

Canada (*cont.*)
    regulatory responsibility, 254, 258–259
    restructuring policies, aviation industry, 572–573, 579
    restructuring policies, electricity industry, 297, 309
    restructuring policies, gas industry, 343, 344, 357
    restructuring policies, railways industry, 531
    train services, 511–512
    two-way access pricing, 178
    water and wastewater industry, 598
    wholesale gas spot markets, 328
capacity allocation, telecommunications networks and
    services, 370–372
capacity markets, electricity, 283
capital asset pricing model (CAPM), cost of capital, 114
capital cost. *See* cost of capital
capital investments
    core network activities, 95–96
    cost of capital, rate case process, 111–115
    rate case process, 111–115
capital structure, water and wastewater industry,
    618–619
CAPM (capital asset pricing model), cost of capital, 114
carbon dioxide (CO$_2$) emissions. *See* decarbonisation
    policies, greenhouse gas emission
CARD (Credit Card Accountability Responsibility and
    Disclosure) Act, 224
card payment systems, 424–426, 428
    Chile, 445
    regulation, 437–440
    restructuring policies, 443–445, 446–449
CATO (Competitively Appointed Transmission Owner)
    regime, 285
centralised electricity supply system, 270, 273–275
Chile
    airport privatisation, 574
    card payment systems, 445
    competition, 297
    liquefied natural gas (LNG), 347
    market power, 306
    net neutrality, 412
    ownership of airlines, 557
    private-public partnerships and water concessions,
        622
    privatisation, 296
    privatisation, aviation industry, 574
    privatisation, telecommunications industry, 395
    restructuring policies, aviation industry, 572, 579
    restructuring policies, electricity industry, 299, 303
    restructuring policies, gas industry, 343
    restructuring policies, telecommunications industry,
        395
    restructuring policies, water and wastewater industry,
        614, 616
    rule-based approach, 242
    vertical integration, 601
    water markets, 625–627, 628
    wholesale electricity markets, 280, 281
    yardstick competition, 608
China
    airline markets, 572
    aviation industry, 549
    bundling limits, 496
    data services, 499
    decarbonisation policies, 311
    digital platforms, 459, 490, 493, 494, 495, 497

digital platforms regulation, 501
electricity regulation, 245
level playing field, 497
liquefied natural gas (LNG), 330
next-generation networks (NGNs), 407
non-discrimination policies, 495
payment systems, 424, 429, 445, 457
price regulation, 332
private-public partnerships and water concessions,
    621
rail services, 505
railways industry, 503–504, 505–506, 510, 514
restructuring policies, aviation industry, 574, 579
restructuring policies, electricity industry, 297, 299
restructuring policies, railways industry, 528
shale gas, 318, 323
state support, 49
water and wastewater industry, 602, 614, 621
wholesale electricity markets, 297
circuit switching, telecommunications, 365
CMA (Competition and Markets Authority), 217, 530,
    620
CO$_2$ (carbon dioxide) emissions. *See* decarbonisation
    policies, greenhouse gas emission
Colombia, restructuring policies, gas industry, 343
commitment, regulatory. *See* regulatory commitment
common costs, multi-product firms, 84–85
competition, 151–198, *See also* markets
    access in regulated industries, 151–156
    access pricing and investment, 178–182
    aviation regulation, 582–586
    behavioural industrial organisation and regulation,
        205–211
    Chile, 297
    deregulation policies, 56–63
    destructive competition, 19, 547, 582, 583
    digital platforms regulation, 474–476
    effective competition, 61
    electricity regulation, 305–311
    electricity supply chain, 284–286
    entry restrictions, removing, 57–60
    established competition, 61
    fixed line networks, telecommunications, 372–375
    franchise competition, 43–46
    horizontal competition, railways industry, 536–540
    horizontal competition, railways regulation, 516–517
    horizontal integration and separation, 189–191
    horizontal separation versus vertical separation,
        railways industry, 535–536
    introducing competition, 57–60
    market power, 146–147
    multiple competing suppliers, 194
    multi-sided markets, 191–194, 461
    network effects, 474–476
    one-way access pricing, 154–172
    on-rail competition, railways regulation, 515–516
    open-access competition, railways regulation,
        515–516
    pre-competitive market stage, 61
    pre-entry stage, 61
    price regulation, 144–145, 146–147
    railways industry, 503–504, 516–517, 535–540
    reliance on competition, 56–63
    restructuring policies, electricity industry, 305–311
    retail competition, water and wastewater industry, 6

retail electricity supply, 308–311
retail gas competition, 331
telecommunications regulation, 401–404
two-way access pricing, 169–178
vertical competition, railways industry, 537–540
vertical integration and separation, 183–189
vertical integration with competition in some
    activities, 73–75
vertical separation versus horizontal separation,
    railways industry, 535–536
vertical separation with competition in some
    activities, 72
vertically integrated railways, 516–517
wholesale electricity markets, 305–306
yardstick competition, 144–145
Competition and Markets Authority (CMA), 217, 530,
    620
competition authorities/regulators, division of powers
    and responsibilities, 256–257
competition between real-time interbank and card
    payment systems, 430, 431
competition for subscribers, two-way access pricing,
    171–176
competition for the market, 43–46
  airport services, 574, 589
  airspace navigation services, 561
  contracts, 44–46
  data services, 498
  digital platforms regulation, 500
  electricity regulation, 285
  network effects, 26, 475–476
  payment systems regulation, 415
  price regulation, 145
  railways industry, 511, 528, 544
  railways regulation, 515, 528
  restructuring policies, railways industry, 526, 535
  water and wastewater regulation, 592, 610, 615, 617,
    632
competition in the market
  digital platforms regulation, 481–483
  network effects, 475–476
  railways regulation, 515, 528
  restructuring policies, electricity industry, 301
  restructuring policies, railways industry, 526
  restructuring policies, telecommunications industry,
    378
  restructuring policies, water and wastewater industry,
    615, 632
  telecommunications networks and services, 249
  vertical integration and separation, 183
  water and wastewater regulation, 592
competition law
  European Union, 257
  ex post (after the fact) competition law, 54–56
  Federal Communications Commission (FCC), 257
  Federal Energy Regulatory Commission (FERC), 257
  limitations, 55
  margin squeeze, 378
  New Zealand example, 55
  public utilities, 54–56
  Surface Transportation Board (STB), 257
  telecommunications regulation, 377–378
competitive activities
  aviation supply chain, 561
  gas supply chain, Canada, 330

natural gas supply chain, 330–332
payment systems, 429–433
railways supply chain, 514–517
railways supply chain, Canada, 516
restructuring policies, water and wastewater industry,
    615, 616, 617
water and wastewater regulation, 602–604
competitive bottlenecks, telecommunications regulation,
    377–378
Competitively Appointed Transmission Owner (CATO)
    regime, 285
consumer and producer interests, independent
    regulation/agencies, 240
consumer behaviour
  behavioural economics, 198–204
  consumer biases, 39–41, 198–204
consumer biases, 39, 197, 199, 200, 210–213, 226–228
consumer inertia, France, 219
consumer mistakes or biases, behavioural industrial
    organisation and regulation, 214
consumers' characteristics, rationales for regulation,
    39–41
contestability theory, 46–48
  aviation regulation, 583–584
  telecommunications regulation, 385–386
  threat of entry, 46–48
contestable markets theory. See contestability theory
context specificity
  independent regulation/agencies, 242
  opportunistic behaviour, 242
contextual changes of economic regulation, 3–6
  affordability of essential services, 5
  behavioural economics research, 5
  digitalisation, 4
  environmental and sustainability policies, 4
contracts
  competition for the market, 44–46
  franchise competition, 44–46
  long-term contracts for wholesale gas supply,
    329–330
  long-term contracts: regulation as a form of
    administration of a long-term contract, 33–34
  opportunistic behaviour, 240
  price regulation, 145–146
  private contracting approach, 65–66
  regulation as a form of administration of a long-term
    contract, 33–34
  regulatory commitment, 240
  versus negotiated settlements, 65
cooperative determination of access prices, two-way
    access pricing, 173–175
core network activities
  capital investments, 95–96
  fixed costs, 76–77
  marginal cost pricing, 76
  principles of regulation, 71–75
  versus competitive activities, 56, 68
core network services
  declining demand, 147–149
  price regulation, 147–149
co-regulation, industries/regulators, 259–261
  industry codes, 259–261
correspondence with public utility industries, 16
cost concepts, cost-based access charges,
    163–165

cost efficiency
  efficiency rationales for regulation, 12–15
  monopoly power, 22–23
  natural monopoly, 16
  principles, 104–105
cost of capital
  capital asset pricing model (CAPM), 114
  dividend growth model, 115
  rate case process, 111–115
  regulated asset base (RAB), 112
  weighted average cost of capital (WACC), 113–114, 115
cost-based access charges
  cost concepts, 163–165
  indirect costs, measuring and estimating, 165
  one-way access pricing, 162–168
cost-based allocation, multi-product firms, 84–85
costs of supply
  electricity supply system, 270
  natural gas, 320–322
CPNP (calling party network pays) principle, mobile
    networks, 377
cream-skimming, 16
Credit Card Accountability Responsibility and Disclosure
    (CARD) Act, 224

data combination, digital platforms regulation, 498–499
data portability, digital platforms regulation, 498–499
data protection and privacy, digital platforms regulation,
    486
data services
  China, 499
  competition for the market, 498
  telecommunications, 368
data sharing
  digital platforms regulation, 498–499
  Germany, 498
data, digital platforms, 466–468
databases regulation, digital platforms regulation, 499
decarbonisation policies. See also greenhouse gas
    emission
  China, 311
  electricity regulation, 311–314
  France, 312, 318
  Germany, 312
  impact on regulation, 313–314
decarbonised gas markets, 356–357
decentralised electricity supply system, 270, 273–275
decentralised gas markets, 356–357
decentralised provision of services, 67
declining demand, price regulation, 147–149
default tariffs
  energy sector, 219
  restructuring policies, electricity industry, 303
  retail competition, electricity industry, 194, 295,
    309–311
  retail competition, gas industry, 194, 339
delegation risks, independent regulation/agencies,
    243–245
demand information asymmetries, 94
deregulation policies, 56–63
  entry restrictions, removing, 57–60
  introducing competition, 57–60
  price regulation, removing, 60–63
  reliance on competition, 56–63
descriptions of economic regulation, 3

destructive competition, 19, 547, 582, 583
developing and transitional economies
  evolution of independent regulatory agencies,
    250–251
  privatisation, 250–251
  restructuring policies, electricity industry, 299,
    303–304
  restructuring policies, railways industry, 527–528,
    534–535
  restructuring policies, telecommunications industry,
    395, 400–401
Diem transactions, payment systems, 427–428
digital platforms
  attraction/retention strategies, users, 465–466
  behavioural biases, 225, 483–486
  behavioural economics, 225
  characteristics, 454–469
  China, 459, 490, 493, 494, 495, 497
  data, 466–468
  economic attributes, 500
  governance arrangements, 460
  horizontal and vertical integration, 460
  incentivising participation, 463–465
  infrastructure, 460–461
  market tipping, 463
  multi-sided markets, 461
  network effects, 462–463
  non-price terms of participation, 465
  operators, 459–460
  participation, incentivising, 463–465
  participation, non-price terms of, 465
  physical and economic characteristics, 454–478
  price structures, 463–465
  types of digital platforms, 455–465
  users, 458
  users attraction/retention strategies, 465–466
  value chain, 461–466
  vertical and horizontal integration, 460
  winner takes all/most, 463
digital platforms regulation, 453–456
  algorithms regulation, 499
  approach to regulation, 488–500, 501
  Australia, 492
  bundling limits, 496
  China, 490, 501
  competition, 474–476
  competition for the market, 500
  data combination, 498–499
  data portability, 498–499
  data protection and privacy, 486
  data sharing, 498–499
  databases regulation, 499
  discriminatory practices, 495
  dynamic efficiency, 471–472
  economic regulation, 490–492
  efficiency rationales for regulation, 469–473
  entry promotion, 471–472
  European Union, 490, 492
  evolution of regulations, 500
  fairness, 496–497
  Germany, 490, 492
  interoperability, 495–496, 499–500
  level playing field, 496–497
  market power, 476, 478–480, 481–483, 488–490
  monopoly power, 476–483

natural monopoly, 500
network effects, 473–476, 500
network effects as a rationale for regulation, 473–476
news intermediaries, 487
non-discrimination policies, 495
policies that have been introduced or proposed for digital platforms, 493–500
price regulation, 472–473
privacy protections, 499–500
rationales for regulation, 468–488
scale economies, 469–472
scope economies, 470, 473
scope of economic regulation, 490–492
separation policies, 493–494
strategic market status (SMS), 490
transparency/opacity, 486
UK, 490, 492
USA, 491, 492
who should regulate digital platforms?, 492
igital Subscriber Line (DSL)
    data services, 368
    telecommunications, 364
igital wallets, 428–429
igitalisation, contextual change of economic regulation, 4
iscriminatory practices, digital platforms regulation, 495
iscriminatory pricing
    optimal linear pricing, 79
    versus uniform pricing, 75
stributed ledger technology, payment systems, 426–428
stributed stand-alone cost (DSAC) test, price control, telecommunications regulation, 385–386
stribution. See electricity distribution, electricity transmission and distribution networks, gas distribution, gas transmission and distribution networks
stributional issues, behavioural industrial organisation and regulation, 216
vidend growth model, cost of capital, 115
vision of powers and responsibilities, 254–259
    competition authorities/regulators, 256–257
    government levels/regulators, 257–259
    government ministries/regulators, 254–256
ones, 557–558
SAC (distributed stand-alone cost) test, price control, telecommunications regulation, 385–386
SL. See Digital Subscriber Line
namic access pricing, access pricing and investment, 182
namic efficiency, digital platforms regulation, 471–472
namic regulation
    asymmetric information, 96–98
    imperfect information, 98–100
    transfer payments, 96–100

rnings sharing mechanisms, price regulation, 142–143
onomic attributes, digital platforms, 500
onomic theories of regulation, 29–33
onomies of scale. See scale economies
onomies of scope. See scope economies
PR. See efficient component pricing rule
ective competition, 61

efficiency rationales for regulation, 12–21
    cost efficiency, 12–15
    digital platforms regulation, 469–473
    natural monopoly, 12–14, 15–16, 19–21
efficient access prices
    efficient component pricing rule (ECPR), 160–161
    generalised efficient component pricing rule (GECPR), 160
efficient component pricing rule (ECPR)
    arguments for and against, 161–162
    by-pass, 158–161
    efficient access prices, 160–161
    margin rule, 158, 160, 162
    margin squeeze, 384
    margin squeeze tests, 384, 387
    National Regulatory Authority (NRA), 384
    one-way access pricing, 157–162
    telecommunications regulation, 384–385
electricity distribution, 278–279, See also electricity transmission and distribution networks
    distribution network use of system charges, 294
    France, 278
electricity generation, 270–275
    Australia, 274
    Germany, 273
electricity markets and exchanges, 282–284
    ancillary electricity services, 283
    capacity markets, 283
    electricity-trading exchanges, 284
    financial transmission rights (FTRs), 283, 291–294
    France, 283
    regional markets, 283, 284
electricity pool, trading arrangement for wholesale electricity, 280
electricity production
    gas-fired electricity production, 355
    greenhouse gas emission, 269
electricity regulation, 267–320, See also restructuring policies, electricity industry
    adaptation of regulation, 268
    attributes of electricity, 268–269
    characteristics of electricity, 268–269
    China, 245
    competition, 305–311
    competition for the market, 285
    competition, retail electricity supply, 308–311
    customer types, 269
    decarbonisation policies, 311–314
    demand for electricity, 269
    electricity storage, 287
    electricity supply system, 270–288
    greenhouse gas emission, 269
    market power, 285, 299
    missing money problem, 306
    policy issues, 305–315
    price control, 286–288, 295
    price regulation, 287–294
    restructuring policies, 295–304
    retail electricity supply, competition, 308–311
    retail price controls, 295
    supply chain, competitive activities, 284–286
    system operation, 276, 287
    trading arrangements for wholesale electricity, 280–284
    wholesale electricity markets, 305–306

electricity storage, 275–276
  electricity regulation, 287
electricity supply chain, competition, 284–286
electricity supply system, 270–288, *See also* trading
    arrangements for wholesale electricity
  centralised electricity system, 270, 273–275
  costs of supply, 270
  decentralised electricity system, 270, 273–275
  electricity distribution, 278–279
  electricity storage, 275–276
  electricity transmission, 276–277
  electricity transmission and distribution networks,
    288–294
  energy inputs, 270–273
  generation of electricity, 270–275
  retail supply, 279
  virtual power plants (VPP), 274, 275
electricity transmission and distribution networks,
    276–277
  efficiency, 277
  France, 276
  Germany, 276, 278
  locational marginal pricing (LMP), 291
  nodal pricing, 291
  price cap regulation, 288–289
  price regulation, 288–294
  rate of return regulation, 289–290
  rate structures regulation, 291
  system operation, 276, 287
  transmission network pricing, 291–294
electricity trading exchanges, 284
energy inputs, electricity supply system, 270–273
energy sector
  behavioural biases, 218–221
  behavioural economics, 218–221
  default tariffs, 219
English experiment
  privatisation, 618–619
  water and wastewater industry, 618–619
entry promotion, digital platforms regulation,
    471–472
entry regulation, productive efficiency, 19–21
entry restrictions, removing, 57–60
entry threat, contestability theory, 46–48
environmental and sustainability policies. *See also*
    decarbonisation policies, greenhouse gas emission
  contextual change of economic regulation, 4
  gas regulation, 356–357
  hydrogen networks, 355–357
Europe
  airline markets, 571
  airports, restructuring policies, 574
  cable networks regulation, telecommunications,
    375–377
  mark-ups approach, railways industry, 541–543
  restructuring policies, aviation industry, 577–579
  restructuring policies, electricity industry, 298,
    301–303
  restructuring policies, gas industry, 341–343, 345–347
  restructuring policies, railways industry, 525–527,
    532–534
  restructuring policies, telecommunications industry,
    393–394, 397–399
  security of gas supply, 350–352
European Union

airport charges, 566
airspace navigation services, 565, 575
  competition law, 257
  digital platforms regulation, 490, 492
  division of powers and responsibilities, government
    levels/regulators, 259
  EC Regulations and Directives, 639–642
  evolution of independent regulatory agencies,
    248–249
  legal cases, 639
  legislation, 642
  market power, 375, 394
  National Regulatory Authority (NRA), 248, 259, 384,
    403
  Open Internet Regulation, 412
  price cap regulation, railways regulation, 521–522
  restructuring policies, water and wastewater industry,
    612–613
  telecommunications regulation, 375, 394
evolution of independent regulatory agencies, 251
  Australia, 249–250
  developing and transitional economies, 250–251
  European Union, 248–249
  New Zealand, 249–250
  UK, 247–248
  USA, 245–247
evolution of regulations, digital platforms regulation,
    500
ex ante or *ex post* approaches to controlling digital
    platform market power, 488–489
ex ante revenue requirement
  building block approach, 126–128
  price cap regulation, 126–129
ex post (after the fact) competition law, public utilities,
    54–56
externalities as a rationale for regulation, 24

fairness
  digital platforms regulation, 496–497
  interpretations, 37–38
  rationale for regulation, 35–39
FCC (Federal Communications Commission), competition
    law, 257
FDC (fully distributed costs), multi-product firms, 84–8▮
Federal Communications Commission (FCC), competitio▮
    law, 257
Federal Energy Regulatory Commission (FERC), 245
  competition law, 257
  restructuring policies, electricity industry, 297
feed-in tariffs (FITs), trading arrangement for wholesal▮
    electricity, 282
FERC. *See* Federal Energy Regulatory Commission
fibre to the premises/cabinet (FTTP/C), data services, 3▮
fibre-optic cable infrastructure, telecommunications, 3▮
financial capital maintenance (FCM), building block
    approach, 127–128
financial hedging markets, trading arrangements for
    wholesale gas, 329
financial transmission rights (FTRs), 283, 291–294
FIRs (Flight Information Regions), aviation industry,
    550
first-best pricing, 18, 75, 81, *See also* marginal cost
    pricing
FITs (feed-in-tariffs), trading arrangement for wholesal▮
    electricity, 282

fixed costs
    allocative efficiency, 18
    core network activities, 76–77
    marginal cost pricing, 76–77
    multi-product firms, 84–85
    pricing principles, 76–77
fixed line networks
    competition, 372–375
    France, 375
    Germany, 375
    National Regulatory Authority (NRA), 375
    telecommunications regulation, 372–375
fixed revenue cap, price cap regulation, 130
fixed-to-mobile (FTM) interconnections, one-to-many
        access pricing, 170–171
flexibility, independent regulation/agencies, 242
Flight Information Regions (FIRs), aviation industry, 550
four-party card system, 424–426
fracking, 318, 323, 355, See also shale gas
    Australia, 356
    France, 318
    Germany, 318
    greenhouse gas emission, 355
France
    airline markets, 557
    airspace navigation services, 553
    consumer inertia, 219
    decarbonisation policies, 312, 318
    electricity distribution, 278
    electricity markets and exchanges, 283
    electricity transmission and distribution networks, 276
    fixed line networks, 375
    fracking, 318
    gas distribution, 326
    gas extraction and production, 323
    investment incentives, 354
    liquefied natural gas (LNG), 348
    mark-ups approach, railways industry, 542
    price regulation, 605
    private–public partnerships and water concessions,
        622, 632
    privatisation, aviation industry, 571
    railway stations, 513
    railways infrastructure, 510
    railways supply chain, 516
    regulatory decisions, 263
    restructuring policies, aviation industry, 571, 577
    restructuring policies, electricity industry, 301
    restructuring policies, water and wastewater industry,
        613, 614
    retail price controls, 295
    telecommunications networks and services, 369
    train services, 512
    vertical integration, 601
    water and wastewater industry, 599, 602
franchise competition, 43–46
    contracts, 44–46
FTM (fixed-to-mobile) interconnections, one-to-many
        access pricing, 170–171
FTRs (financial transmission rights), 283, 291–294
FTTP/C (fibre to the premises/cabinet), data services, 368
full information. See also asymmetric information,
        See also hidden information, imperfect information
    pricing principles under, 75–83
fully distributed costs (FDC), multi-product firms, 84–85

GAO. See Government Accountability Office
gas distribution, 326, See also gas transmission and
        distribution networks
    France, 326
    Germany, 326
gas extraction and production, 322–323
    Canada, 323
    France, 323
    Germany, 323
    non-conventional gas extraction, 355
gas industry. See restructuring policies, gas industry
gas markets, 356–357
gas networks, 319–320
gas physical and economic characteristics, 318
    characteristics of the product, 318–320
    costs of supply, 320–322
    fracking, 318, 323, 355
    gas distribution, 326
    gas extraction and production, 322–323
    gas networks, 319–320
    gas storage, 326
    gas transmission, 323–325
    natural gas supply chain, 320–333
    non-conventional gas sources, 323
    production and supply, 319–320
    retailing of gas, 327
    transportation, 318–320
gas regulation, 317–363
    activities subject to regulation in the supply chain,
        330–334
    competitive activities in the supply chain, 330–332
    decarbonised gas markets, 356–357
    decentralised gas markets, 356–357
    environmental and sustainability policies, 355–357
    policy issues, 350–357
    price regulation, 332–334
    prices and investment: restructuring impact,
        352–355
    retail gas competition, 331
    security of gas supply, 350–352
gas storage, 326
    price regulation, 333–334, 338–339
gas transmission and distribution networks, 323–325,
        See also trading arrangements for wholesale gas
    Australia, 323, 326
    capacity allocation, 325
    pipeline pressure maintenance, 324
    price regulation, 332–333, 334–338
    rate of return regulation, 335–337
    rate structures regulation, 337–338
gas transmission, distribution, storage and retail supply,
        price regulation, 332–334
gas-fired electricity production, 355
generalised efficient component pricing rule (GECPR),
        160
Germany
    access pricing and investment, 170
    adjacent monopolies, 170
    airport charges, 589
    bundling limits, 496
    competition, retail electricity markets, 309
    data sharing, 498
    decarbonisation policies, 312
    digital platforms regulation, 490, 492
    electricity generation, 273

Germany (*cont.*)
  electricity transmission and distribution networks,
    276, 278
  fixed line networks, 375
  fracking, 318
  gas distribution, 326
  gas extraction and production, 323
  industry-specific regulators, 254
  interoperability, 496
  legislation, 644
  level playing field, 497
  light-handed approach, 589
  mark-ups approach, railways industry, 542
  multi-sectoral regulators, 254
  next-generation networks (NGNs), 407
  non-discrimination policies, 495
  payment systems, 420
  price cap regulation, 332, 521–522
  price regulation, 332, 605
  railway stations, 513
  railways infrastructure, 510
  rate of return regulation, 137
  restructuring policies, electricity industry, 301–302
  restructuring policies, railways industry, 532–534
  restructuring policies, telecommunications industry,
    407
  restructuring policies, water and wastewater industry,
    613
  retail electricity supply, 309
  retail price controls, 295
  scope of economic regulation, 490
  service providers, telecommunications, 369
  sunshine regulation, 608
  supply chain, competitive activities, 515–516
  telecommunications regulation, 369
  total expenditure (Totex) approach, 606
  trading arrangements for bulk water, 602
  trading arrangements for wholesale electricity, 282
  train services, 511–513
  vertical integration, 601
  water and wastewater industry, 598, 599
  wholesale electricity markets, 282
  wholesale gas spot markets, 328
  yardstick competition, 145
global price caps, one-way access pricing, 166
Government Accountability Office (GAO)
  airport services, 555, 575–577
  who regulates the regulators?, 264
government levels/regulators, division of powers and
    responsibilities, 257–259
government ministries/regulators, division of powers
    and responsibilities, 254–256
government price guarantees, trading arrangement for
    wholesale electricity, 282
greenhouse gas emission. *See also* decarbonisation
    policies, environmental and sustainability policies
  electricity production, 269
  fracking, 355

hedging markets, wholesale gas, 329
hidden action, asymmetric information, 93–94
hidden information, 91–93, *See also* asymmetric
    information, full information, imperfect information
  allocative efficiency, 91–93
  Loeb-Magat incentive arrangement, 91–93

hold-up, 22
  sunk asset expropriation, 235–237
  vertical integration and separation, 184–185
horizontal competition
  railways industry, 536–540
  railways regulation, 516–517
horizontal integration and separation, 189–191
  behavioural obligations, 190
  competition, 189–191
  forms of horizontal separation, 190–191
household expenditure, public utilities, 1–2
hybrid caps, price cap regulation, 131
hybrid fibre coaxial (HFC) infrastructure,
    telecommunications, 365
hydrogen networks, environmental and sustainability
    policies, 355–357

ICC (Interstate Commerce Commission), 245–247
imperfect information, 90–95, *See also* asymmetric
    information, full information, hidden information
  dynamic regulation, 98–100
  transfer payments, 98–100
incentive mechanism, asymmetric information,
    98–100
incentives and performance under different ownership
    structures, 49–51
incentives for investment, access pricing, 180–182
incentives to invest in new infrastructure, 181
incentivising investment in next-generation networks
    (NGNs), 405–407
incentivising participation in digital platforms, 463–465
incremental cost, price setting, 48
incremental surplus subsidy scheme, transfer payments,
    96–97
independent power producers (IPPs), 282, 285
independent regulation/agencies. *See also* evolution of
    independent regulatory agencies, who regulates the
    regulators?
  Australia, 249, 253, 258
  consumer and producer interests, 240
  context specificity, 242
  delegation risks, 243–245
  design of regulatory agencies, 252–259
  division of powers and responsibilities, 254–259
  establishment of independent regulators, 251
  flexibility, 242
  important characteristic, 234
  industry-specific regulators, 252–254
  intertemporal pricing, 111, 237–238
  legal framework, 241–242
  multi-sectoral regulators, 252–254
  objectives of the regulator, 240
  opportunistic behaviour, 238–242
  organisational structures, 252–254
  oversight of regulators, 261–265
  rationale for economic regulatory agencies,
    233–245
  reconciling factors motivating the establishment of
    independent regulators, 251
  regulatory commitment, 97–98, 234–245
  risks associated with the creation of independent
    regulators, 243–245
  scope of their power, 252–259
  specialisation, 243
  state-owned utilities, 53–54

sunk asset expropriation, 235–237
time-inconsistency problem, 234–237
ndia
aviation industry, 548, 557, 572
liquefied petroleum gas (LPG), 348
net neutrality, 412
next-generation networks (NGNs), 407
payment systems, 424, 430, 445
railways industry, 505–506, 510, 514
railways regulation, 504
restructuring policies, aviation industry, 579, 602
restructuring policies, electricity industry, 297
retail electricity supply, 297
spectrum licences, telecommunications networks and
    services, 371
state support, 49
ndirect costs
cost-based access charges, 165
measuring and estimating, 165
ndustry codes, co-regulation, industries/regulators,
    259–261
ndustry structures, 71–75
vertical integration with competition in some
    activities, 73–75
vertical separation with competition in some
    activities, 72
vertically integrated monopoly, 72
ndustry-specific regulators, 252–254
Germany, 254
nformation. See asymmetric information, full
    information, hidden information, imperfect
    information
nfrastructure based competition, next-generation
    networks (NGNs), 404
nfrastructure competition
access pricing and investment, 153, 180–181, 182
next-generation networks (NGNs), 404
payment systems regulation, 415
telecommunications regulation, 373, 398
vertical integration, 71
water and wastewater regulation, 603
set appointments, water and wastewater regulation,
    603, 615
nstitutions of regulation. See independent regulation/
    agencies
nterbank payment systems, 418, 422–423, 428
regulation, 436–437
restructuring policies, 441–443, 445–446
nterest group theories of regulation, 29–33
nternational access and charging principles, airspace
    navigation services, 564
nteroperability, digital platforms regulation, 495–496,
    499–500
nterstate Commerce Commission (ICC), 245–247
ntertemporal pricing
independent regulation/agencies, 111, 237–238
ratchet effect, 237–238
nvestment incentives. See also access pricing and
    investment, capital investments
France, 354
new infrastructure, 181
next-generation networks (NGNs), 405–407
restructuring impact on gas industry prices and
    investment, 352–355
Ps (independent power producers), 282, 285
ly, total expenditure (Totex) approach, 606

Jakarta, private–public partnerships and water
    concessions, 623
Japan
privatisation, railways industry, 528–529
restructuring policies, aviation industry, 579
restructuring policies, railways industry, 527,
    528–529
joint costs, 83, 85
judicial review, who regulates the regulators?, 246, 247,
    261

ladder of investment approach
access pricing and investment, 182
next-generation networks (NGNs),
    404–405
Laffont and Tirole model, 138
regulatory commitment, 98
versus Baron and Myerson model, 93–94
lag period, rate of return regulation, 120
Latin America, private–public partnerships and water
    concessions, 622
legacy networks, telecommunications, 363
transition from legacy copper networks to NGN,
    404–407
legal and ownership separation, vertical integration and
    separation, 189
legal cases
Australia, 643
European Union, 639
New Zealand, 644
UK, 642
USA, 642–643
legal framework
independent regulation/agencies, 241–242
opportunistic behaviour, 241–242
legislation
Australia, 643
Canada, 643
European Union, 642
Germany, 644
New Zealand, 644
UK, 642
USA, 643
level playing field
China, 497
digital platforms regulation, 496–497
Germany, 497
light-handed approach
airport charges, 66, 566, 589
Australia, 66, 250, 589
Germany, 589
New Zealand, 55, 66, 250, 589
non-standard consumers, 216
telecommunications regulation, 374
linear pricing. See also non-linear pricing
optimal linear pricing, 79
versus non-linear pricing, 75
liquefied natural gas (LNG), 317, See also natural gas
    supply chain
Australia, 330
Chile, 347
China, 330
France, 348
restructuring policies, gas industry, 347
storage, 339
wholesale trading, 330

liquefied petroleum gas (LPG)
  Canada, 348
  India, 348
  supply and regulation, 348–349
LMP (locational marginal pricing), electricity
  transmission and distribution networks, 291
LNG. *See* liquefied natural gas
locational marginal pricing (LMP), electricity
  transmission and distribution networks, 291
Loeb–Magat incentive arrangement, hidden information,
  91–93
long-run incremental costs (LRIC)
  bottom-up long-run incremental cost (BU-LRIC), 381
  revenue requirement determination, 128–129
  telecommunications regulation, 381–384
  total element long-run incremental cost (TELRIC), 381,
    382, 383–384
  total service long-run incremental cost (TSLRIC), 381,
    382, 383–384
  variants, 381, 382, 383–384
long-run marginal cost pricing (LRMC), 95–96
long-term contracts
  regulation as a form of administration of a long-term
    contract, 33–34
  wholesale gas supply, 329–330
LPG (liquefied petroleum gas), supply and regulation,
  348–349
LRIC. *See* long-run incremental costs
LRMC (long-run marginal cost pricing), 95–96

make-or-buy decision
  by-pass and the make-or-buy decision, 180–181
  telecommunications regulation, 372
mandatory and voluntary separation, vertical integration
  and separation, 189
margin rule, efficient component pricing rule (ECPR),
  158, 160, 162
margin squeeze
  accounting separation, 188
  competition law, 378
  efficient component pricing rule (ECPR), 384
  price cap regulation, 125, 166
  restructuring policies, telecommunications industry,
    390
  telecommunications regulation, 378
  vertical separation, 185
margin squeeze tests, efficient component pricing rule
  (ECPR), 384, 387
marginal cost pricing. *See also* first-best pricing
  allocative efficiency, 17–18
  average cost pricing, 78
  core network activities, 76
  fixed costs, 76–77
  long-run marginal cost pricing (LRMC), 95–96
  multi-product firms, 83–90
  non-linear pricing, 80, 83
  productive efficiency, 19
  short-run marginal cost (SRMC) pricing, 95–96
  starting principle for price regulation, 75–76
market demand, 12
  natural monopoly, 13
market power
  airport charges, 560–561, 562, 568–569, 580
  Chile, 306
  competition, 146–147

digital platforms regulation, 476, 478–480, 481–483,
  488–490
electricity regulation, 285, 299
European Union, 375, 394
ex ante or *ex post* approaches to controlling digital
  platform market power, 488–489
market power mitigation, 481–483
multiple competing suppliers, regulation, 194
Netherlands, 562
non-standard consumers, 210
price regulation, 60–62
rationales for regulation, 481–483
removing price regulation, 60–62
restructuring policies, gas industry, 341
telecommunications regulation, 373, 375, 394
two-way access pricing, 176
USA, 299
wholesale electricity markets, 305–306
market tipping
  digital platforms, 463
  network effects, 463
markets. *See also* airline markets, competition, electricit
    markets and exchanges, multi-sided markets,
    trading arrangements for wholesale electricity,
    trading arrangements for wholesale gas
  competition for the market, 44–46
  contestability theory, 46–48, 385–386, 583–584
  gas markets, 356–357
  water markets, 602, 624–628
  wholesale market-based trading arrangements, water
    and wastewater industry, 602
mark-ups
  constant mark-ups to recover fixed and common
    costs, multi-product firms, 84–85
  equi-proportionate mark-ups (EPMU), multi-product
    firms, 84–85
mark-ups approach, railways industry
  Canada, 543
  Europe, 541–543
  France, 542
  Germany, 542
  USA, 541
merchant investments, electricity supply chain, 285
merchant service charge (MSC), 424
Mexico, restructuring policies, gas industry, 343
missing money problem, electricity industry, 306
mobile networks
  calling party network pays (CPNP) principle, 377
  Canada, 377
  telecommunications regulation, 377
mobile virtual network operators (MVNOs),
    telecommunications networks and services, 370
modern economic regulation, 3–6
monetary policy, time-inconsistency problem, 234–235
monitoring public utilities, 66
monopoly. *See also* natural monopoly
  adjacent monopolies, two-way access pricing,
    169–170, 172
  allocative efficiency, 17
  termination monopoly problem, 172
  two-way access pricing, 172
  vertically integrated monopoly, 72
monopoly power
  cost efficiency, 22–23
  digital platforms regulation, 476–483

market power mitigation, 481–483
regulation to control digital platforms from harming
     the long-term interests of consumers, 480–481
regulation to control monopoly power, 21–24,
     476–483
two-sided markets, 477
X-inefficiency, 22
MSC (merchant service charge), 424
multimedia and broadcasting services, 369
multi-period context, pricing in a, 95–100
multiple competing suppliers, regulation, 194
   market power, 194
multiple objectives pursued through access pricing
     policies, 153–154
multi-product firms, 83–90
   common costs, 84–85
   constant mark-ups to recover fixed and common
       costs, 84–85
   cost-based allocation, 84–85
   equi-proportionate mark-ups (EPMU), 84–85
   fixed costs, 84–85
   fully distributed costs (FDC), 84–85
   marginal cost pricing, 83–90
   non-linear pricing, 89
   peak-load pricing, 87–89
   pricing principles, 83–90
   Ramsey–Boiteux pricing, 85–87
multi-sectoral regulators, 252–254
   Germany, 254
multi-sided markets
   competition, 191–194, 461
   digital platforms, 461
   platform operators, 191–194
   price structures, 192
MVNOs (mobile virtual network operators),
     telecommunications networks and services, 370

NAO. See National Audit Office
National Association of Regulatory Utility
     Commissioners (NARUC), 264
   rate of return regulation, 290, 606
National Audit Office (NAO), 55, 247, 614–615
   who regulates the regulators?, 264
National Regulatory Authority (NRA)
   efficient component pricing rule (ECPR), 384
   European Union, 248, 259, 384, 403
   fixed line networks, 375
   next-generation networks (NGNs), 404, 406
   price regulation, 61
   restructuring policies, telecommunications industry,
       394
   telecommunications regulation, 375, 378, 394
natural gas supply chain, 320–333, See also liquefied
     natural gas
   Australia, 322
   competitive activities, 330–332
natural monopoly
   cost efficiency, 16
   digital platforms regulation, 500
   efficiency rationales for regulation, 12–14, 15–16,
       19–21
   entry regulation to achieve productive efficiency,
       19–21
   market demand, 13
   terminology, 7

negotiated approaches, railways regulation, 523–524
   Canada, 145, 523
negotiated settlements, 63–65, See also price regulation
   advantages, 63
   Australia, 63
   disadvantages, 64
   negotiate–arbitrate approach, 65
   North American gas industry, 335–337
   rate of return regulation, 120
   USA, 335–337
   variants, 65
   versus private contracting approach, 65
negotiation, 63–65
   access prices, one-way access pricing, 167–168
   price regulation, 145–146
net neutrality
   Canada, 412
   Chile, 412
   economic trade-offs, 409–411
   India, 412
   over-the-top (OTT) applications, 408
   regulatory response, 411–412
   telecommunications regulation, 407–412
   two-sided markets, 408
   two sides of the net neutrality debate, 408–409
   USA, 411
Netherlands
   behavioural economics, 221
   market power, 562
   price regulation, 122
   railway stations, 513
   restructuring policies, aviation industry, 571
   restructuring policies, water and wastewater industry,
       613
   sunshine regulation, 608
   total expenditure (Totex) approach, 606
   wastewater treatment, 598, 599
   wholesale gas spot markets, 328
   yardstick competition, 145
network decline, price regulation, 147–149
network effects
   competition, 474–476
   competition for the market, 26, 475–476
   digital platforms, 462–463
   digital platforms regulation, 473–476, 500
   direct network effects, 462
   indirect network effects, 462
   market tipping, 463
   scale economies, 25–26, 27
   two-sided markets, 25
   winner takes all/most, 463
network effects as a rationale for regulation, 25–28
   digital platforms regulation, 473–476
   network effects, 25–27
   network externalities, 27–28
new appointments and variations, water and wastewater
     regulation, 603, 615
New Zealand
   airline markets, 573
   airport charges, 66, 250, 589
   evolution of independent regulatory agencies,
       249–250
   legal cases, 644
   legislation, 644
   light-handed approach, 55, 66, 250, 589

New Zealand (*cont.*)
  restructuring policies, electricity industry,
    303–304
  restructuring policies, gas industry, 343
  restructuring policies, telecommunications industry,
    395
news intermediaries, digital platforms regulation, 487
next-generation networks (NGNs)
  Canada, 407
  China, 407
  Germany, 407
  incentivising investment in NGNs, 405–407
  India, 407
  infrastructure-based competition, 404
  infrastructure competition, 404
  ladder of investment approach, 404–405
  National Regulatory Authority (NRA), 404, 406
  telecommunications networks and services, 363,
    404–407
  unbundling policies, 363, 375, 404–405
nodal pricing, electricity transmission and distribution
  networks, 291
non-conventional gas extraction, 355
non-conventional gas sources, 323
non-cooperative access price determination, two-way
  access pricing, 173
non-discrimination policies
  China, 495
  digital platforms regulation, 495
  Germany, 495
non-linear pricing. *See also* linear pricing
  marginal cost pricing, 80, 83
  multi-product firms, 89
  optimal non-linear pricing, 80–83
  two-part tariffs, uniform, 80–83
  versus linear pricing, 75
non-price regulation
  Public Utility Commissions (PUCs), 389
  service level agreement (SLA), 388
  telecommunications regulation, 388–389
non-standard consumers
  behavioural industrial organisation and regulation,
    205–208, 214, 215, 216–218
  integrating non-standard consumers, 205–206
  light-handed approach, 216
  market power, 210
  pricing decisions with non-standard consumers,
    207–208
NRA. *See* National Regulatory Authority

objectives of the regulator, 240
one-to-many access pricing
  fixed-to-mobile (FTM) interconnections, 170–171
  two-way access pricing, 170–171
one-way access pricing, 154–172
  competition, 154–172
  cost-based access charges, 162–168
  efficient component pricing rule (ECPR), 157–162
  fair and reasonable access requirements, 168
  generalised efficient component pricing rule (GECPR),
    160
  global price caps, 166
  negotiation of access prices, 167–168
  non-discriminatory access requirements, 167
  open-access requirements, 167
  Ramsey–Boiteux pricing, 156–157

static efficiency, 156
  vertical integration, 156
  vertical separation, 154–155
on-rail competition, railways regulation, 515–516
opacity/transparency, digital platforms regulation, 486
Open Internet Regulation, European Union, 412
open-access competition, railways regulation, 515–516
operating expenses (OPEX)
  building block approach, 127
  rate of return regulation, 110
opportunistic behaviour. *See also* regulatory
    commitment
  context specificity, 242
  contracts, 240
  independent regulation/agencies, 238–242
  legal framework, 241–242
  objectives of the regulator, 240
  price regulation, 239
  voluntary solutions, 238–239
optimal linear pricing, discriminatory pricing versus
    uniform pricing, 79
optimal non-linear pricing, uniform two-part tariffs,
    80–83
organisational structures, independent regulation/
    agencies, 252–254
OTT. *See* over-the-top applications
oversight of regulators. *See* who regulates the
    regulators?
over-the-top (OTT) applications
  net neutrality, 408
  telecommunications, 367, 386–388, 403
ownership structures. *See also* privately owned utilities,
    public utilities, state-owned utilities
  incentives and performance under different structures
    49–51
  performance investigations, 51–53
  principal–agent model, 49–51

packet switching, telecommunications, 366–367
payment interface providers (PIPs), 427
payment systems. *See also* restructuring policies,
    payment systems, transfer payments
  Australia, 420, 423, 431, 440, 441, 443
  behavioural biases, 224–225
  behavioural economics, 224–225
  blockchain, 426–428
  Canada, 443, 445
  card payment systems, 424–426, 428
  cash payments and non-cash payments, 417
  characteristics of the product, 416–418
  China, 424, 429, 445, 457
  competition between real-time interbank and card
    payment systems, 430, 431
  competitive activities, 429–433
  Credit Card Accountability Responsibility and
    Disclosure (CARD) Act, 224
  Diem transactions, 427–428
  digital wallets, 428–429
  distributed ledger technology, 426–428
  emerging payment systems, 426–429
  end-users of payment systems, 419
  expansion by card and interbank payment systems,
    428
  four-party card system, 424–426
  Germany, 420
  India, 424, 430, 445

interbank payment systems, 418, 422–423, 428
inter-payment system competition, 429–433
intra-payment system competition, 429–433
merchant service charge (MSC), 424
non-cash payments and cash payments, 417
participants, 418–420
payment interface providers (PIPs), 427
payment schemes, 419
payment service providers (PSPs), 419, 421–422, 429, 437
payment system infrastructure providers, 420
payment system operators, 420
processing of payments, 420–422
retail payment systems, 416–417
three-party card system, 424
two-sided markets, 379, 426, 434, 472
wholesale payment systems, 416–417
ayment systems regulation, 415–451
  activities subject to regulation, 433–436
  card payment systems, 437–440
  competition for the market, 415
  form and scope of regulation, 436–440
  infrastructure competition, 415
  interbank payment systems, 436–437
eak-load pricing, 77
  multi-product firms, 87–89
eering, price control, telecommunications regulation, 386–388
erformance and incentives under different ownership structures, 49–51
erformance investigations
  ownership structures, 51–53
  privately owned utilities, 51–53
  state-owned utilities, 51–53
hysical hedging markets, trading arrangements for wholesale gas, 329
IPs (payment interface providers), 427
atform operators, multi-sided markets, 191–194
olicy issues
  aviation regulation, 582–588
  electricity regulation, 305–315
  gas regulation, 350–357
  railways regulation, 535–543
  telecommunications regulation, 401–413
  water and wastewater industry, 617–631
ower purchase agreement (PPA), trading arrangement for wholesale electricity, 281
re-competitive market stage, competition, 61
re-entry stage, competition, 61
ice and revenue caps
  RPI-K approach, 607
  RPI-X approach, 607
  water and wastewater regulation, 606–607
ice cap regulation, 121–141, See also price regulation
  advantages and disadvantages, 132–135
  Australia, 288, 334
  average revenue approach, 130
  baskets, 124
  Canada, 288, 335
  determining the value of X, 125–126
  developments, 136–138
  duration of the price cap, 123–124
  electricity transmission and distribution networks, 288–289
  ex ante revenue requirement, 126–129
  fixed revenue cap, 130

gas transmission and distribution networks, 334–335
general price cap approach, 122–126
Germany, 332, 521–522
hybrid caps, 131
margin squeeze, 125, 166
origins, 121–122
products scope, 124–125
railways regulation, 521–523
regulatory lag, 123
revenue requirement determination, 126–129
RPI-K approach, 607
RPI-X approach, 122–123, 125–126, 133, 607
tariff basket approach (weighted average price cap), 131
telecommunications regulation, 381
total expenditure (totex) approach, 136–138
total factor productivity (TFP) approaches, 289
versus rate of return regulation, 116, 133, 138–141
weighted average price cap (tariff basket approach), 131
price control, electricity regulation, 286–288, 295
price control, telecommunications regulation, 380–388
  avoided-cost resale provision, 384–385
  bill and keep, 386–388
  contestability theory, 385–386
  distributed stand-alone cost (DSAC) test, 385–386
  efficient component pricing rule (ECPR), 384–385
  long-run incremental costs (LRIC), 381–384
  peering, 386–388
  price cap regulation, 381
  price-cost tests, 385–386
  rate of return regulation, 381
  retail-minus price setting, 384–385
price discrimination. See discriminatory pricing
price regulation, 109–150, See also negotiated settlements, price cap regulation, pricing principles
  administered pricing, 145–146
  airport charges, 566
  airport services, 562–563
  airspace navigation services, 550–553, 561, 564, 565–566
  allocative efficiency, 17–19
  Australia, 61
  aviation regulation, 561–562
  benchmarking, 144–145
  Canada, 518
  China, 332
  competition, 144–145, 146–147
  competition for the market, 145
  contracts, 145–146
  core network services, 147–149
  declining demand, 147–149
  digital platforms, 472–473
  earnings sharing mechanisms, 142–143
  electricity regulation, 287–294
  electricity transmission and distribution networks, 288–294
  form and scope of water and wastewater regulation, 605–610
  forms of price regulation, 239, 287–294
  France, 605
  gas regulation, 332–334
  gas storage, 333–334, 338–339
  gas transmission and distribution networks, 334–338
  gas transmission, distribution, storage and retail supply, 332–334

price regulation (*cont.*)
  Germany, 332, 605
  hybrid approaches, 141–143
  market power, 60–62
  National Regulatory Authority (NRA), 61
  negotiation, 145–146
  Netherlands, 122
  network decline, 147–149
  opportunistic behaviour, 239
  price and revenue caps, 606–607
  railways regulation, 517–524
  rate of return regulation, 109–120, 335–337, 606
  rate structures regulation, 291, 337–338, 609–610
  removing price regulation, 60–63
  retail price controls, electricity regulation, 295
  retailing of gas, 334, 339
  revenue sharing mechanisms, 143
  sunshine regulation, 608
  transmission network pricing, electricity, 291–294
  two-sided markets, 193
  water and wastewater regulation, 605–610
  yardstick and comparative competition, 608
  yardstick competition, 144–145
price setting
  incremental cost, 48
  stand-alone cost (SAC), 48
  water and wastewater industry, 628–631
price structures
  behavioural industrial organisation and regulation,
    215
  digital platforms, 463–465
  multi-sided markets, 192
  water and wastewater industry, 629–631
price-cost tests, telecommunications regulation,
  385–386
pricing decisions with non-standard consumers,
  207–208
pricing principles. *See also* marginal cost pricing, price
  regulation
  average cost pricing, 77–79
  constant mark-ups to recover fixed and common
    costs, 84–85
  discriminatory pricing versus uniform pricing, 75
  first-best pricing, 18, 75, 81
  fixed costs, 76–77
  linear pricing versus non-linear pricing, 75
  multi-product firms, 83–90
  non-linear pricing, 75, 80–83, 89
  optimal linear pricing, 79
  peak-load pricing, 77, 87–89
  Ramsey–Boiteux pricing, 77, 85–87
  under full information, 75–83
  uniform pricing versus discriminatory pricing, 75
principal–agent model, ownership structures, 49–51
privacy protections, digital platforms regulation,
  499–500
private contracting approach, 65–66
  versus negotiated settlements, 65
private participation, water and wastewater industry,
  617–624
privately owned utilities. *See also* ownership structures,
  public utilities, state-owned utilities
  performance investigations, 51–53
private–public partnerships and water concessions
  Chile, 622
  China, 621

  France, 622, 632
  Jakarta, 623
  Latin America, 622
  reverse privatisation, 624
  water and wastewater industry, 621–624
privatisation
  airports restructuring policies, 573–575
  airspace navigation services, 575, 581
  aviation industry, 557, 571
  aviation industry, Chile, 574
  Canada, airspace navigation services, 575, 581
  Chile, 296
  Chile, aviation industry, 574
  Chile, telecommunications industry, 395
  developing and transitional economies, 250–251
  effects, 51–53, 401
  English experiment, 618–619
  France, airspace navigation services, 553
  Japan, railways industry, 528–529
  restructuring policies, electricity industry, 295–296
  restructuring policies, water and wastewater industry,
    614–616
  reverse privatisation, 5, 624
  telecommunications industry, 393, 395, 401
  UK, airspace navigation services, 553, 575
  UK, gas industry, 341, 345
  UK, railways industry, 528–529
  UK, telecommunications industry, 393
  USA, airspace navigation services, 581
  water and wastewater industry, 611–612
producer and consumer interests, independent
  regulation/agencies, 240
productive efficiency, 16
  entry regulation, 19–21
  marginal cost pricing, 19
public utilities. *See also* ownership structures, privately
  owned utilities, state-owned utilities
  competition law, 54–56
  ex post (after the fact) competition law, 54–56
  household expenditure, 1–2
Public Utility Commissions (PUCs)
  gas price regulation, 333–334, 341
  non-price regulation, 389
  origins, 245–247
  responsibilities, 258
  retail price regulation, 339
Public Utility Regulatory Policies Act 1978 (PURPA), 28●
PUCs. *See* Public Utility Commissions
PURPA (Public Utility Regulatory Policies Act 1978), 28●

quality principles, 102–104
quality regulation, water and wastewater regulation,
  608–609

RAB. *See* regulatory asset base
radio waves/base stations, telecommunications,
  365
railways industry, 503–544, *See also* restructuring
  policies, railways industry
  Australia, 511–512
  autonomous trains, 513
  Canada, 511–512, 518
  characteristics of the product, 504–506
  China, 503–504, 505–506, 510, 514
  competition, 503–504, 516–517, 535–540
  competition for the market, 511, 528, 544

freight services, 504–506
horizontal competition, 536–540
India, 505–506, 510, 514
infrastructure, 506–510
infrastructure interoperability, 508
infrastructure management, 509, 510
infrastructure ownership, 509
infrastructure, France, 510
infrastructure, railway stations, 513–514
Netherlands, 513
passenger services, 504–506
physical and economic characteristics, 504–514
privatisation, 528–529
rail services, China, 505
railway stations, 513–514
railway stations, France, 513
railway stations, Germany, 513
railway systems, 506–514
Ramsey–Boiteux pricing, 540–543
scope economies, 13, 536, 537, 539
state-owned companies, 511
supply structures, train services, 511
train operating companies, 512
train services, 510–513
train services, Canada, 511
train services, France, 512
train services, Germany, 511–513
vertical competition, 537–540
railways regulation, 514–524
Australia, negotiated approaches, 523
Canada, negotiated approaches, 523
competition for the market, 515, 528
competitive activities in the supply chain, 514–517
European Union, price cap regulation, 521–522
horizontal competition, 516–517
horizontal separation versus vertical separation, 535–536
India, 504
infrastructure price regulation, 518–519
negotiated approaches, 523–524
on-rail competition, 515–516
open-access competition, 515–516
policy issues, 535–543
price cap regulation, 521–523
price regulation, 517–524
supply chain, 514–520
train operating services, 519
UK, price cap regulation, 521
USA, negotiated approaches, 523
vertical separation versus horizontal separation, 535–536
vertically integrated railways, 516–517
railways supply chain
competitive activities, 514–517
France, 516
Ramsey–Boiteux pricing
allocative efficiency, 19
multi-product firms, 85–87
one-way access pricing, 156–157
pricing principles, 77, 85–87
railways industry, 540–543
rate of return regulation, 115
single-product firms, 79, 83
ratchet effect, intertemporal pricing, 237–238
rate base, 109–110
rate case process

asset 'rate base', 111
capital investments, 111–115
cost of capital, 111–115
determination of rates or prices, 115–116
rate of return regulation, 110–116
revenue requirement determination, 111–115
Takings Clause, 111
rate of return regulation, 109–120, 335–337, 606
advantages and disadvantages, 116–119
Averch–Johnson (A–J) effect, 117–119
Canada, 337
developments, 119–120
electricity transmission and distribution networks, 289–290
gas transmission and distribution networks, 335–337
Germany, 137
lag period, 120
negotiated settlements, 120
operating expenses (OPEX), 110
Ramsey–Boiteux pricing, 115
rate case process, 110–116
regulatory lag, 117, 118, 121, 290, 637
telecommunications regulation, 381
versus price cap regulation, 116, 133, 138–141
water and wastewater regulation, 606
rate structures regulation
electricity transmission and distribution networks, 291
gas transmission and distribution networks, 337–338
water and wastewater regulation, 609–610
rate structures, desirable attributes, 100–107
rationales for regulation, 635–636
affordability, 35–39
alternatives to regulation, 635–636
consumers' characteristics, 39–41
cost efficiency, 12–15
digital platforms, 468–488
efficiency rationales for regulation, 12–21
externalities, 24
fairness, 35–39
implications of the different rationales, 41–42
independent regulation/agencies, 233–245
market power, 481–483
monopoly power, 481–483
natural monopoly, 12–14, 15–16, 19–21
network effects, 25–28
scope economies, 13–14, 470
reasons for regulation, 1–3, 11–12
efficiency rationales, 12–21
reciprocal agreement and 'bill and keep', two-way access pricing, 175–176, 178
regional markets, electricity, 283, 284
regulators, regulation of. See who regulates the regulators?
regulatory agencies. See independent regulation/agencies
regulatory asset base (RAB)
building block approach, 127–128
cost of capital, 112
regulatory commitment. See also opportunistic behaviour
asymmetric information, 97–98
Baron and Myerson model, 97, 238
contracts, 240
independent regulation/agencies, 234–245
Laffont and Tirole model, 98
regulatory decisions, Canada, 263

regulatory holidays, 179, 406
regulatory lag, 99
  price cap regulation, 123
  rate of return regulation, 117, 118, 121, 290, 637
regulatory responsibility, Canada, 254, 258–259
regulatory theory and practice, linking, 636–637
re-municipalisation, water and wastewater industry,
  624
restructuring policies, aviation industry, 570–582
  airline markets, 570–573
  airports, 573–575, 579–580
  airspace navigation services, 575, 581
  Australia, 572–573, 579, 580
  Canada, 572–573, 579
  Chile, 572, 579
  China, 574, 579
  environment, 581
  Europe, 577–579
  France, 571, 577
  India, 579, 602
  Japan, 579
  Netherlands, 571
  safety, 581
  scope, 570–575
  USA, 575–577
restructuring policies, electricity industry, 295–304
  Australia, 303–304
  Canada, 297, 309
  Chile, 299, 303
  China, 297, 299
  competition, 305–311
  default tariffs, 303
  developing and transitional economies, 299, 303–304
  effects in the electricity industry, 299–304
  Europe, 298, 301–303
  France, 301
  Germany, 301–302
  India, 297
  New Zealand, 303–304
  privatisation, 295–296
  standard restructuring model, 295–297
  unbundling policies, 296, 298
  USA, 297, 299–301
restructuring policies, gas industry, 340
  Argentina, 343, 347
  Australia, 343, 347
  Canada, 343, 344, 357
  Chile, 343
  Colombia, 343
  Europe, 341–343, 345–347
  liquefied natural gas (LNG), 347
  market power, 341
  Mexico, 343
  New Zealand, 343
  prices and investment: restructuring impact, 352–355
  security of gas supply, 350–352
  UK, 341–343, 345–347
  unbundling policies, 342, 357
  USA, 340–341, 343–345
restructuring policies, payment systems, 440–451
  Australia, 445, 447, 450
  card payment systems, 443–445, 446–449
  interbank payment systems, 441–443, 445–446
  scope of policies, 440–445

restructuring policies, railways industry, 524–535
  Canada, 531
  China, 528
  competition for the market, 526, 535
  developing and transitional economies, 527–528,
    534–535
  Europe, 525–527, 532–534
  Germany, 532–534
  Japan, 527, 528–529
  Russia, 528
  scope, 524
  UK, 528–529, 532–534
  USA, 525, 531–532
restructuring policies, telecommunications industry,
  389–401
  Australia, 395
  Chile, 395
  developing and transitional economies, 395, 400–401
  Europe, 393–394, 397–399
  Germany, 407
  margin squeeze, 390
  National Regulatory Authority (NRA), 394
  New Zealand, 395
  stages of regulation, 389–391
  UK, 393–394, 397–399
  unbundling policies, 390, 391
  USA, 392–393, 395–397
restructuring policies, water and wastewater industry,
  610–617
  Australia, 614, 616
  Chile, 614, 616
  competitive activities, 615, 616, 617
  European Union, 612–613
  France, 613, 614
  Germany, 613
  models, 610
  Netherlands, 613
  privatisation, 614–616
  retail competition, 616
  UK, 611–612, 614–616
  USA, 613
retail activities, water and wastewater industry, 598, 616
retail benchmarking, two-way access pricing, 177
retail competition
  electricity industry, default tariffs, 194, 295, 303,
    309–311
  gas industry, default tariffs, 194, 339
  restructuring policies, water and wastewater industry,
    616
retail electricity supply
  competition, 308–311
  Germany, 309
  India, 297
retail payment systems, 416–417
retail price controls, electricity regulation
  Australia, 295
  France, 295
  Germany, 295
retail price regulation
  Australia, 219
  Public Utility Commissions (PUCs), 339
retail supply, electricity supply system, 279
retailing of gas, 327
  Australia, 327

competition, 331
price regulation, 334, 339
retail-minus price setting, telecommunications
regulation, 384–385
revenue requirement determination
ex ante revenue requirement, 126–129
long-run incremental costs (LRIC), 128–129
price cap regulation, 126–129
rate case process, 111–115
revenue sharing mechanisms, price regulation, 143
reverse privatisation, 5
private–public partnerships and water concessions,
624
water and wastewater industry, 624
risks associated with the creation of independent
regulators, 243–245
RPI-K approach, price cap regulation, 607
RPI-X approach, price cap regulation, 122–123,
125–126, 133, 607
Russia, restructuring policies, railways industry, 528

SAC. *See* stand-alone cost
scale economies, 12–16
digital platforms regulation, 469–472
network effects, 25–26, 27
subadditivity, 15
water and wastewater industry, 599–601
scope economies
aviation regulation, 561
digital platforms regulation, 470, 473
railways industry, 13, 536, 537, 539
rationales for regulation, 13–14, 470
vertical integration, 601
vertical integration and separation, 183
water and wastewater industry, 601
scope of economic regulation
digital platforms regulation, 490–492
Germany, 490
security of gas supply
Europe, 350–352
gas regulation, 350–352
restructured competitive gas industry, 350–352
UK, 350–352
self-supply, trading arrangement for wholesale
electricity, 280
separation policies, digital platforms regulation, 493–494
service level agreement (SLA), non-price regulation,
388
service providers, telecommunications networks and
services, 369–370
Australia, 369
service quality regulation, water and wastewater
regulation, 608–609
shale gas. *See also* fracking
China, 318, 323
USA, 318
short-run marginal cost (SRMC) pricing, 95–96
significance of economic regulation, 1–2
single-product firms, Ramsey-Boiteux pricing, 79, 83
single-buyer model, trading arrangement for wholesale
electricity, 281
SLA (service level agreement), non-price regulation, 388
SMS (strategic market status), digital platforms
regulation, 490
specialisation, independent regulation/agencies, 243

spectrum licences, telecommunications networks and
services, 370–372
India, 371
USA, 371
SRMC (short-run marginal cost) pricing, 95–96
stand-alone cost (SAC)
price control, telecommunications regulation, 385–386
price setting, 48
state-owned companies, railways industry, 511
state-owned utilities, 48–54, *See also* ownership
structures, privately owned utilities, public utilities
benefits of state ownership *vis-à-vis* private
ownership, 49
independent regulation, 53–54
performance investigations, 51–53
static efficiency, one-way access pricing, 156
STB (Surface Transportation Board), competition law,
257
stepping stone hypothesis. *See* ladder of investment
approach
storage. *See also* electricity storage, gas storage
liquefied natural gas (LNG), 339
strategic market status (SMS), digital platforms
regulation, 490
subadditivity, 14–16
scale economies, 15
sunk asset expropriation, time-inconsistency problem,
235–237
sunshine regulation
Germany, 608
Netherlands, 608
water and wastewater regulation, 608
Surface Transportation Board (STB), competition law,
257
sustainability. *See* environmental and sustainability
policies
switching technologies, telecommunications, 365–367
system operation, electricity regulation, 276, 287

Takings Clause, rate case process, 111
tariff basket approach (weighted average price cap), price
cap regulation, 131
telecommunications industry. *See also* restructuring
policies, telecommunications industry
behavioural biases, 221–222
behavioural economics, 221–222
telecommunications networks and services, 359–372
5G networks, 368
allocation of capacity, 370–372
cable modem services, 368
capacity allocation, 370–372
characteristics of the product, 360–361
circuit switching, 365
data services, 368
Digital Subscriber Line (DSL), 364, 368
fibre to the premises/cabinet (FTTP/C), 368
fibre-optic cable infrastructure, 364
fixed line telecommunications network architecture,
361–363
France, 369
hybrid fibre coaxial (HFC) infrastructure, 365
legacy networks, 363
mobile virtual network operators (MVNOs), 370
multimedia and broadcasting services, 369
next-generation networks (NGNs), 363, 404–407

telecommunications networks and services (*cont.*)
  over-the-top (OTT) applications, 367, 386–388, 403
  packet switching, 366–367
  radio waves/base stations, 365
  service providers, 369–370
  services, 367–369
  spectrum licences, 370–372
  supply structure for telecommunications services,
    363–370
  switching technologies, 365–367
  transmission infrastructure, 363–365
  Voice over IP (VoIP), 367, 368
telecommunications regulation, 359–413
  avoided cost pricing, 384–385
  cable networks, 375–377
  competition, 401–404
  competition law, 377–378
  competitive bottlenecks, 377–378
  European Union, 375, 394
  fixed line networks, 372–375
  Germany, 369
  infrastructure competition, 373, 398
  light-handed approach, 374
  make-or-buy decision, 372
  margin squeeze, 378
  market power, 373, 375, 394
  mobile networks, 377
  National Regulatory Authority (NRA), 375, 378, 394
  net neutrality, 407–412
  next-generation networks (NGNs), 404–407
  non-price regulation, 388–389
  policy issues, 401–413
  price control, 380–388
  retail-minus price setting, 384–385
  transition from legacy copper networks to NGN,
    404–407
  two-sided markets, 379
  unbundling policies, 372, 376, 384, 393, 395
  waterbed effect, 178, 377–378
TELRIC (total element long-run incremental cost), 381,
    382, 383–384
termination monopoly problem, two-way access pricing,
    172
terminology, 7
Tesla Virtual Power Plant project, 274
TFP (total factor productivity) approaches, price cap
    regulation, 289
threat of entry, contestability theory, 46–48
three party card system, 424
time-inconsistency problem
  independent regulation/agencies, 234–237
  monetary policy, 234–235
  sunk asset expropriation, 235–237
timing of infrastructure investment, 179–180
total element long-run incremental cost (TELRIC), 381,
    382, 383–384
total expenditure (Totex) approach
  Germany, 606
  Italy, 606
  Netherlands, 606
  price cap regulation, 136–138
  UK, 606
total factor productivity (TFP) approaches, price cap
    regulation, 289

total service long-run incremental cost (TSLRIC), 381,
    382, 383–384
Totex. *See* total expenditure approach
trading 'hubs', wholesale gas spot markets, 327–329
trading arrangements for bulk water, 602
  Germany, 602
trading arrangements for wholesale electricity, 280–284.
    See also electricity supply system
  bilateral transactions, 281
  competition, wholesale electricity markets, 305–306
  electricity markets and exchanges, 282–284
  electricity pool, 280
  feed-in tariffs (FITs), 282
  Germany, 282
  government price guarantees, 282
  power purchase agreement (PPA), 281
  Public Utility Regulatory Policies Act 1978 (PURPA),
    280
  self-supply, 280
  single-buyer model, 281
  wholesale electricity markets, competition, 305–306
  wholesale market-based trading arrangements, 602
trading arrangements for wholesale gas, 327–330
  financial hedging markets, 329
  liquefied natural gas (LNG) wholesale trading, 330
  long term contracts for wholesale gas supply, 329–33?
  physical hedging markets, 329
  restructuring policies, 327
  trading 'hubs', 327–329
  wholesale gas spot markets, 327–329
train services. *See* railways industry
transfer payments
  asymmetric information, 96–98
  core network activities, 77
  dynamic regulation, 96–100
  hidden action, 93
  hidden information, 93
  imperfect information, 98–100
  incremental surplus subsidy scheme, 96–97
transition from legacy copper networks to NGN,
    telecommunications regulation, 404–407
transitional economies. *See* developing and transitional
    economies
transmission, electricity/gas. *See* electricity transmissio?
    and distribution networks, gas transmission and
    distribution networks
transparency/opacity, digital platforms regulation, 486
transport industry, behavioural economics, 223
TSLRIC. *See* total service long-run incremental cost
two-part tariffs, uniform
  non-linear pricing, 80–83
  optimal non-linear pricing, 80–83
two-sided markets
  airport services, 553
  monopoly power, 477
  net neutrality, 408
  network effects, 25
  payment systems, 379, 426, 434, 472
  price regulation, 193
  telecommunications regulation, 379
two-way access pricing, 169–178
  adjacent monopolies, 169–170, 172
  Australia, 178
  Canada, 178
  competition, 169–178

competition for subscribers, 171–176
cooperative determination of access prices, 173–175
efficient two-way access prices, 176–178
implications for regulation, 178
market power, 176
non-cooperative access price determination, 173
one-to-many access pricing, 170–171
reciprocal agreement and 'bill and keep', 175–176, 178
retail benchmarking, 177
termination monopoly problem, 172

UAS. *See* unmanned aircraft systems
UK
    airspace navigation services, 565
    digital platforms regulation, 490, 492
    evolution of independent regulatory agencies, 247–248
    legal cases, 642
    legislation, 642
    price cap regulation, railways regulation, 521
    privatisation, airspace navigation services, 575
    privatisation, aviation industry, 571
    privatisation, gas industry, 341, 345
    privatisation, railways industry, 528–529
    privatisation, telecommunications industry, 393
    restructuring policies, gas industry, 341–343, 345–347
    restructuring policies, railways industry, 528–529, 532–534
    restructuring policies, telecommunications industry, 393–394, 397–399
    restructuring policies, water and wastewater industry, 611–612, 614–616
    security of gas supply, 350–352
    total expenditure (Totex) approach, 606
    unbundling policies, telecommunications regulation, 393, 398–399
unbundling policies, 16
    Australia, telecommunications regulation, 395
    next-generation networks (NGNs), 363, 375, 404–405
    restructuring policies, electricity industry, 296, 298
    restructuring policies, gas industry, 342, 356
    restructuring policies, telecommunications industry, 390, 391
    telecommunications regulation, 372, 376, 384, 393, 395
    UK, telecommunications regulation, 393, 398–399
    USA, telecommunications regulation, 384, 392–393, 397
    water and wastewater regulation, 632
uniform pricing, versus discriminatory pricing, 75
uniform two-part tariffs
    non-linear pricing, 80–83
    optimal non-linear pricing, 80–83
unmanned aircraft system traffic management (UTM), 67, 586–588
unmanned aircraft systems (UAS), 557–558
    aviation regulation, 586–588
USA
    airline markets, 570–571
    airport charges, 566
    airports, restructuring policies, 573
    airspace navigation services, 565
    cable networks regulation, telecommunications, 375–377

digital platforms regulation, 491, 492
division of powers and responsibilities, government levels/regulators, 258
evolution of independent regulatory agencies, 245–247
Federal Energy Regulatory Commission (FERC), 245, 257, 297
federal legal cases, 642–643
legislation, 643
market power, 299
mark-ups approach, railways industry, 541
negotiated approaches, railways regulation, 523
negotiated settlements, gas industry, 335–337
net neutrality regulations, 411
privatisation, airspace navigation services, 581
restructuring policies, aviation industry, 575–577
restructuring policies, electricity industry, 297, 299–301
restructuring policies, gas industry, 340–341, 343–345
restructuring policies, railways industry, 525, 531–532
restructuring policies, telecommunications industry, 392–393, 395–397
restructuring policies, water and wastewater industry, 613
shale gas, 318
spectrum licences, telecommunications networks and services, 371
unbundling policies, telecommunications regulation, 384, 392–393, 397
water markets, 627
use-of-system charges, 294
UTM (unmanned aircraft system traffic management), 67, 586–588

value chain, digital platforms, 461–466
vertical competition, railways industry, 537–540
vertical integration
    Chile, 601
    France, 601
    Germany, 601
    infrastructure competition, 71
    scope economies, 601
    water and wastewater industry, 601
vertical integration and separation, 183–189
    accounting separation, 188
    business separation, 188
    competition, 183–189
    forms of vertical separation, 187–189
    hold-up, 184–185
    legal and ownership separation, 189
    mandatory and voluntary separation, 189
    potential benefits of vertical integration, 183–185
    potential benefits of vertical separation, 185–187
    scope economies, 183
    vertical integration with competition in some activities, industry structure, 73–75
    vertical integration, one-way access pricing, 156
    vertical separation with competition in some activities, industry structure, 72
    vertical separation, one-way access pricing, 154–155
    vertically integrated monopoly, industry structure, 72
    voluntary and mandatory separation, 189
vertical separation
    Australia, 186
    margin squeeze, 185

virtual power plants (VPP), electricity supply system, 274, 275
Voice over IP (VoIP), telecommunications, 367, 368
voluntary and mandatory separation, vertical integration and separation, 189
VPP (virtual power plants), electricity supply system, 274, 275

WACC. *See* weighted average cost of capital
water and wastewater industry, 591–632, *See also* restructuring policies, water and wastewater industry
  Australia, 597
  behavioural biases, 223
  behavioural economics, 223
  Canada, 598
  capital structure, 618–619
  characteristics, 591–592
  characteristics of the product, 592–602
  China, 602, 614, 621
  collection and transportation of wastewater, 598
  demand for water, 593
  disposal, 599
  English experiment, 618–619
  France, 599, 602, 622
  Germany, 598, 599
  Jakarta, 623
  Latin America, 622
  Netherlands, 598, 599
  policy issues, 617–631
  potable versus non-potable water, 592
  price levels, 628–629
  price setting, 628–631
  price structures, 629–631
  private participation, 617–624
  private–public partnerships and water concessions, 621–624
  privatisation, 611–612
  re-municipalisation, 624
  retail activities, 598
  reverse privatisation, 624
  scale economies, 599–601
  scope economies, 601
  sources, 594
  supply chain, 594–599
  trading arrangements for bulk water, 602
  transportation of wastewater, 598
  value of water, 624–628
  vertical integration, 601
  wastewater characteristics, 593
  wastewater treatment, 598
  water abstraction, 594–596, 602–603
  water distribution, 597–598
  water markets, 602, 624–628
  water treatment, 596
  wholesale market-based trading arrangements, 602
water and wastewater regulation, 602–610
  competition for the market, 592, 610, 615, 617, 632
  competitive activities, 602–604
  infrastructure competition, 603
  inset appointments, 603, 615
  new appointments and variations, 603, 615
  price and revenue caps, 606–607

  price regulation, 605–610
  quality regulation, 608–609
  rate of return regulation, 606
  rate structures regulation, 609–610
  service quality regulation, 608–609
  sunshine regulation, 608
  supply chain, 602–605
  unbundling policies, 632
  water abstraction, 602–603
  yardstick and comparative competition, 608
water markets, 624–628
  Australia, 625, 628
  Chile, 625–627, 628
  USA, 627
waterbed effect, telecommunications regulation, 178, 377–378
weighted average cost of capital (WACC)
  cost of capital, 113–114, 115
  vanilla WACC, 115
weighted average price cap (tariff basket approach), price cap regulation, 131
who regulates the regulators?, 261–265
  appeals of process or substance, 261–262
  general courts, 262–263
  general oversight and accountability, 263–264
  Government Accountability Office (GAO), 264
  judicial review, 246, 247, 261
  National Association of Regulatory Utility Commissioners (NARUC), 264
  National Audit Office (NAO), 264
  political or executive oversight, 264
  review of specific regulatory decisions, 261–263
  rights of appeal, 261–263
  specialist tribunals, 262–263
  standing to appeal decisions, 263
wholesale electricity markets
  Chile, 280, 281
  China, 297
  Germany, 282
  market power, 305–306
wholesale gas spot markets
  Australia, 328, 329
  Canada, 328
  Germany, 328
  Netherlands, 328
wholesale payment systems, 416–417
wholesale trading arrangements. *See* trading arrangements for wholesale electricity, trading arrangements for wholesale gas
winner takes all/most
  digital platforms, 463
  network effects, 463

X-inefficiency, monopoly power, 22

yardstick and comparative competition
  price regulation, 608
  water and wastewater regulation, 608
yardstick competition
  asymmetric information, 100
  Chile, 608
  Germany, 145
  Netherlands, 145
  price regulation, 144–145